In the name of Allah,
the Beneficent, the Merciful

The Meaning of

The Glorious Qur'an

[Arabic/English]

Translation & Explanatory Notes by
Muhammad M. Pickthall

Revised and Edited by
Arafat K. El-Ashi, Ph.D.

amana publications

First Edition
©1427 AH / 2006 AC
amana publications
10710 Tucker Street
Beltsville, Maryland 20705-2223 USA
Tel: (301) 595-5777 • Fax: (301) 595-5888
e-mail: amana@igprinting.com
Website: www.amana-publications.com

Library of Congress Cataloging-in-Publication Data

Koran. English & Arabic.
 The meaning of the glorious Qur'an / translation & explanatory notes by
Muhammad M. Pickthall ; revised and edited by Arafat K. El-Ashi.-- 1st ed.
    p. cm.
Includes index.
ISBN 1-59008-034-3
I. Pickthall, Marmaduke William, 1875-1936. II. 'Ashshi, 'Arafat Kamil.
III. Title.

BP109.K4913 2005
297.1'22521--dc22

                                            2005008356

Printed in India

Published by amana publications
10710 Tucker Street,
Beltsville, Maryland 20705-2223, USA
Tel. (301) 595-5999 Fax (301) 595-5888

Web: www.amana-publications.com
E-mail: amana@igprinting.com

CONTENTS

Editor's Preface

...eral attempts have been made to convey the meaning of the Holy Qur'an ...the English-speaking world. I believe that Pickthall's translation was the first attempt to do so by an Englishman who is also a Muslim. In it, he tried to present "the meaning of the Qur'an—and perhaps some of its stylistic and linguistic charm—in English."

At last we now have Pickthall's translation both in English and Arabic which required a lot of revision and typesetting effort from both editor and publisher. May Allah (SWT) make this edition useful to readers and may it contribute in bringing them closer to the message of this last Testament.

The preparation of this new Arabic/English edition of The Divine Book has involved much time, resources and advice from astute brothers, and I wish to thank each one of them for their time and effort. My thanks also to Amana Publications for their production services; typesetting and proofreading the Arabic/English text; designing the cover and printing the Book.

May Allah (SWT) reward abundantly all those who put in their effort towards this noble endeavor and may He accept this humble service for His Book. Ameen.

Dr. Arafat El-Ashi
Toronto, Canada
Ramadan 1426 AH / October 2005 AC

Translator's Foreword

The aim of this work is to present to English readers what Muslims hold to be the meaning of the words and the nature of the Qur'an in a concise and accurate manner. It may be reasonably claimed that no religion's holy text(s) can be presented fairly by one who does not believe in its inspiration and message. That is why this English translation—the first by an Englishman who is also a Muslim—is so important. Other translations include commentary that is offensive to Muslims, and almost all employ a style of language that Muslims do not consider either adequate or worthy.

It is the belief of the traditional shaykhs and the present writer that the Qur'an cannot be translated. Although I have sought to present an almost-literal and appropriate rendering worthy of the Arabic original, I cannot reproduce its inimitable symphony, the very sounds of which move men to tears and ecstasy. This present volume represents only an attempt to present the meaning and some of the charm of the Qur'an in English. It can never take the place of the original Arabic Qur'an, nor is it meant to do so.

The work has been scrutinized word by word and thoroughly revised in Egypt with the help of a native Arabic speaker who has studied the Qur'an and is very familiar with the English language. When difficulties arose, the translator had recourse to perhaps the greatest living authority on the subject. Every effort has been made to avoid unwarrantable renderings. On the one or two occasions where there is a departure from the traditional interpretation, the traditional rendering will be found in a footnote.

The translator's thanks are due to Lord Lloyd for an introduction of great use in Egypt; to Dr. F. Krenkow for supplying him with old meanings of Arabic words that are not found in dictionaries; to Muḥammad Aḥmad al Ghamrawī Bey of Cairo College of Medicine for his invaluable and patient help with the revision of the manuscript, a work which occupied three months; to Shaykh Muṣṭafā al Marāghī, former Rector of al Azhar University, for his advice and guidance in the revision; and to His Excellency Fū'ād Bey Sālim al Hijāzī, by whose efforts such revision was made possible.

The *mushaf* (copy of the Qur'an) used throughout is a lithograph copy of the one written by al Ḥājj Muḥammad Shakarzādeh at the command of Sulṭān Maḥmūd of Turkey in 1246 AH. In the introduction and notes to individual surahs, Ibn Hishām (Bulāq ed. 1295 AH) has been followed, with occasional reference to the much later, much abbreviated, but more critical *Life of the Prophet* by Ibn Khaldūn (published as an appendix to his *Tārīkh*, Bulāq ed.). Other *sīrahs*, like that of Abū al Fidā, which is of a later date and uncritical, have been read but not followed. The commentators al Baydāwī and Zamakhsharī must be mentioned, while for reference during the work of revision, the brief commentary of *al Jalālayn* was kept at hand. Wāḥidī's *Asbāb al Nuzūl* has been largely consulted, and for the authenticity of the Traditions, the translator has relied upon Bukhārī.

Part I
At Makkah

MUHAMMAD, son of ʿAbd Allāh, son of ʿAbd al Muṭṭalib, of the tribe of Quraysh, was born in Makkah fifty-three years before the Hijrah. As his father died before he was born, the young Muhammad was raised under the protection of his grandfather ʿAbd al Muṭṭalib and, after this man's death, by his uncle Abū Ṭālib. As a young boy, he travelled with his uncle in the merchants' caravan to Syria and, some years later, made the same journey in the service of a wealthy widow named Khadījah. So faithfully did he transact her business and so excellent was the report of his behavior that she received from her old servant who had accompanied him, that she soon proposed to and then married her young agent. The marriage proved to be a very happy one, though she was fifteen years older than he was. Throughout the twenty-six years of their life together, Muhammad was devoted to her. Even after her death, when he married other women, he always mentioned her name with the greatest love and reverence. This marriage gave him rank among the Makkan notables, while his conduct earned for him the surname *al Amīn,* the "trustworthy."

The Makkans claimed descent from Abraham through Ishmael, and tradition stated that their temple (the Kaʿbah) had been built by Abraham for the worship of the One God. It was still called the House of Allah, even though by the Prophet's time it housed the chief objects of the local pagan cult: several idols known as the "daughters of Allah" and regarded as intercessors. The few who were disgusted with the prevailing idolatry, which had prevailed for centuries, longed for the religion of Abraham and tried to discover its original teachings. Such seekers of the truth were known as Ḥunafāʾ (sing. Ḥanīf), a word that had originally meant "those who turn away" (from the existing idol-worship) but later on came to have the sense of "upright" or "by nature upright," because such persons held the way of truth to be right conduct. The Ḥunafāʾ did not form a community: they were the agnostics of their day, each seeking truth by the light of his own inner consciousness.

Muhammad became one of these people. It was his practice to retire for one month (Ramaḍān, the "month of heat") every year to a cave in the desert for meditation. His place of retreat was Ḥirāʾ, a desert hill located close to Makkah. It was there one night toward the end of his retreat that the first revelation came to him when he was forty years old. He was asleep or in a trance when he heard a voice say: "Read!" He replied: "I cannot read." The voice again said: "Read!" and he again replied: "I cannot read." A third time, the voice commanded: "Read!" He said: "What can I read?" The voice said:

> "Read: In the name of your Lord who creates,
>
> Creates man from a clot.
>
> Read: And your Lord is the Most Bounteous
>
> Who teaches by the pen,
>
> Teaches man that which he knew not."[1]

When he awoke, the words remained "as if inscribed upon his heart." He went out of the cave and heard the same awe-inspiring voice say: "O Muhammad! You are Allah's Messenger, and I am Gabriel." Then he raised his eyes and saw the angel, in the likeness of a man, standing in the sky above the horizon. Again the awesome voice said: "O Muhammad! You are Allah's Messenger, and I am Gabriel." Muhammad (God's grace and peace be with him) stood quite still, turning his face away from the brightness of the vision. But wherever he turned his face, the angel was always standing there, confronting him. He remained thus a long while, until the angel vanished, and then returned in great distress to his wife Khadījah. She did her best to reassure him, saying that his conduct had been such that Allah would not let a harmful spirit come to him and that she hoped that he would become the prophet of his people. She took him to her cousin Waraqa ibn Nawfal, a very old man "who knew the Scriptures of Jews and Christians." This man declared his belief that the heavenly messenger who had come to Moses had now come to Muhammad and that he had been chosen to serve as the prophet of his people.

To understand why the Prophet felt extreme distress after this, it must be remembered that the Ḥunafā' sought true religion in the natural world and distrusted any communication with those spirits about which men "avid of the Unseen,"[2] sorcerers, soothsayers, and even poets boasted in those days. Moreover, he was a man of humble and devout intelligence, a lover of quiet and solitude. The very thought of being chosen to face mankind alone with such a message at first appalled him. His recognition of the divine nature of the call caused a change in his whole mental outlook that was enough to disturb his sensitive and honest mind and caused him to forsake his quiet and honored way

---

[1]Surah 96:1-5.
[2]Surah 81:24

of life. The early biographers tell how Khadījah "tried the spirit" that came to him and proved it to be good, and how, when the revelations continued and his conviction in them grew, he at length accepted the tremendous task and was filled with an enthusiasm of obedience that justifies his proudest title: "The Slave of Allah."

The words that were revealed to him are held sacred by all Muslims and are never confounded with those uttered when no physical change was apparent in him. The former make up the Qur'an, while the latter form the Hadith or the Sunnah of the Prophet. Since the angel on Mt. Ḥirā' commanded him to "Read!" and insisted on his "reading," even though the Prophet was illiterate, the sacred book is known as al Qur'an, "The Reading,"[3] the Reading of the man who did not know how to read.

During the first three years of his mission, the Prophet preached only to his family and intimate friends. The people of Makkah as a whole regarded him as having become a little mad. His first convert was Khadījah, the second was his first cousin 'Alī (whom he had adopted), and the third was his servant Zayd (a former slave). His old friend Abū Bakr was among the early converts, along with some of his slaves and dependents.

At the end of the third year, the Prophet received the command to "arise and warn."[4] He now began to preach in public, pointing out the wretched folly of idolatry in face of the tremendous laws of day and night, of life and death, of growth and decay, all of which manifest the power of Allah and attest to His sovereignty. When he began to speak against their gods, the Quraysh became actively hostile and began to persecute his poorer disciples and to mock and insult him. The one consideration that prevented them from killing him was their fear of the Prophet's clan's right to blood-vengeance in the event of his murder. Strong in his inspiration, the Prophet continued to warn, plead, and threaten while the Quraysh did what they could to ridicule his teaching and spread dejection among his followers. The converts of the first four years were mostly humble folk who could not defend themselves. So cruel was the persecution they endured that the Prophet advised all who could possibly do so to emigrate to Abyssinia, a Christian country.[5]

---

[3]Or "the Lecture," as it is translated in those verses in which it is analogous to "Scripture."
[4]Surah 74:2.
[5]See Surah 19, introductory note.

Despite the persecution and emigration, the number of Muslims grew. The Quraysh were seriously alarmed. The idol worship at the Ka'bah, the holy place to which all inhabitants of Arabia made pilgrimage and of which they were the guardian, was among their most important vested interests. During the pilgrimage season, they posted men on all the roads to warn the tribes against "the madman" preaching in their midst. They tried to persuade the Prophet to compromise by offering to accept his religion if he would modify it to make room for their gods as intercessors with Allah. When this failed, they said that he could be their king if he would give up attacking idolatry. When their efforts at negotiation failed, they went to his uncle Abū Ṭālib and said that they would give him the best of their young men in place of Muhammad and, moreover, give him all that he desired, if only he would let them kill Muhammad. Abū Ṭālib refused.

The exasperation of the idolaters was increased by the conversion of 'Umar,[6] one of their stalwarts. They grew more and more embittered, till things came to such a pass that they decided to ostracize the Prophet's whole clan, regardless of whether or not they believed in his message. Their chief men drew up a document to the effect that none of them or their dependents would have any dealings, business or otherwise, with the Prophet's clan. They all signed this document and deposited it in the Ka'bah. For the next three years, the Prophet and his people were enclosed in their stronghold, which was located in one of the gorges leading to Makkah. Only at the time of pilgrimage could he go out and preach or did any of his kinsfolk dare go into the city.

Finally, some of the more sensitive members of the Quraysh grew weary of this boycott against their old friends and neighbors. They managed to have the document brought out of the Ka'bah for reconsideration. It was then discovered that all of the writing had been destroyed by white ants, except for the words *Bismika Allāhuma* ("In Your name, O God"). When the elders saw this miracle, they lifted the ban and allowed the Prophet to resume his former way of life in the city. However, as the opposition to his preaching had grown rigid, he had little success among the Makkans. In addition, his attempt to preach in the city of Ṭā'if also ended in failure. Judged by the narrow worldly standards, his mission was until then a failure.

---

[6]See Surah 20, introductory note.

But then he met a small group of men who listened to him and believed. They came from Yathrib, a city more than two hundred miles away, which has since become famous as al Madinah, "the City" *par excellence*. Among Yathrib's inhabitants were Jewish tribes whose learned rabbis had often spoken to the Arab pagans of a soon-to-come prophet who, along with the Jews, would destroy them as the tribes of 'Ād and Thamūd had been destroyed for their idolatry. After this group of men listened to Muhammad, they recognized him as the prophet described by the Jewish rabbis. On their return to Yathrib, they told others what they had seen and heard. As a result, when the next season of pilgrimage arrived, a deputation came from Yathrib in order to meet the Prophet. Its members swore allegiance to him in the first pact of al 'Aqabah. They returned to Yathrib with a Muslim teacher in their company, and soon "there was not a house in Yathrib wherein there was not a mention of the Messenger of Allah."

In the following year at the time of pilgrimage, seventy-three Muslims from Yathrib came to Makkah to swear allegiance to the Prophet and invite him to their city. At al 'Aqabah, they swore to defend him as they would their own wives and children. It was then that the Hijrah, or the Flight to Yathrib, was decided.

Soon those Muslims began to sell their property and leave Makkah unobtrusively. The Quraysh eventually learned what was going on and, although they hated having Muhammad in their midst, they were even more afraid of what he might do if he was beyond their reach. They decided that it would be better to kill him as soon as possible. When his chief protector, Abū Ṭālib, was removed by death, they saw their chance, even though they would still have to reckon with the vengeance of his clan. To avoid this, they cast lots and chose one member from every clan to participate in the attack on the Prophet. These men then pledged themselves to strike the Prophet at exactly the same time, so that his blood would be on the entire Quraysh tribe. It was at this time (asserts Ibn Khaldūn, and it is the only satisfactory explanation of what happened afterwards) that the Prophet received the first revelation ordering him to make war upon his persecutors "until persecution is no more and religion is for Allah only."[7]

---

[7]Surah 8:39.

The last of the able Muslims in Makkah were Abū Bakr, 'Alī, and the Prophet. Abū Bakr, who was a wealthy man, had bought two riding camels and retained a guide in readiness for the Prophet's departure, which would take place when God ordered it.

On the appointed night, the murderers gathered in front of the Prophet's house. The Prophet gave his cloak to 'Alī and asked him to lie down on the bed so that if anyone looked in, they would think that it was the Prophet lying there. The mur-derers had decided to attack the Prophet whenever he came out of his house. Knowing that they would not injure 'Alī, the Prophet left the house unseen by his opponents. It is said that blindness fell upon the would-be mur-derers: he put dust on their heads as he passed by without them being aware of his departure. After picking up Abū Bakr at the latter's house, the two men went to a cave in the nearby mountains and stayed there until the immediate danger was past. Abū Bakr's son, daughter, and his herdsman brought them food and news after nightfall. The Makkans sent out search parties, one of which came quite near to their hiding place. Seeing that Abū Bakr was sad, the Prophet told him: "Grieve not! Allah is with us."[8] When the coast was clear, Abū Bakr told the guide to bring the riding camels to the cave one night so that they could begin the long ride to Yathrib.

After travelling for many days by unfrequented paths, the fugitives reached a suburb of Yathrib. The people of the city had been going there every morning for weeks in anticipation of the Prophet's arrival. They would give up their watch only when it became so hot that they had to seek shelter. It was at just such a time that the two travellers arrived. The man who spread the news was a Jew, who called out to the Muslims in derisive tones that the men for whom they were waiting had arrived at last. Such was the Hijrah, the Flight from Makkah to Yathrib, which marks the beginning of the Muslim era. The thirteen years of humiliation, persecution, apparent failure, unfulfilled prophecies were now over. The ten years of success, the fullest period that has ever crowned one man's endeavor, would now begin.

The Hijrah marks a clear division in the story of the Prophet's mission, which is evident in the Qur'an. Up until this time, he had only been a preacher. From now on, he would be the ruler of a state, admittedly at first a very small one,

---

[8]Surah 9:40.

but one that would grow during the next ten years into the empire of Arabia. The kind of guidance that he and his people needed after the Hijrah was different from that which they had received in Makkah. Therefore, the surahs revealed during this period differ from those revealed earlier. Whereas the Makkan surahs give guidance to the individual soul and to the Prophet in his capacity as a warner, the Madinah surahs give guidance to a growing social and political community and to the Prophet as example, lawgiver, and reformer.

For classification purposes, the Makkan surahs are sub-divided into four groups: very early, early, middle, and late. Though the historical data and traditions are insufficient for a strict chronological grouping, the very early surahs were, roughly speaking, revealed before the persecution began; the early surahs were revealed between the beginning of the persecution and 'Umar's conversion; the middle surahs were revealed between 'Umar's conversion and the destruction of the deed of ostracism; and the late surahs were revealed between the end of the ostracism and the Hijrah.

Part II
At al Madinah

In the first year of his reign at Yathrib, the Prophet and the Jews negotiated a solemn treaty by which the latter were given full rights of citizenship and religious liberty in exchange for their support of the new state. However, their idea of a prophet was an individual who would give them dominion over others, not one who would make those who followed the same message (i.e., Arab Muslims) their brothers and equals. When they discovered that they could not use the Prophet for their own purposes, they tried to weaken his faith in his mission and to seduce his followers. They received secret support for these efforts from some   professing Muslims who thought that the presence of the Prophet in their city would weaken or even end their influence and therefore resented his presence. In the Madinah surahs, these Jews and Hypocrites are mentioned with great frequency.

Until this time, the *qiblah* (the place toward which Mus-lims face when praying) had been Jerusalem. The Jews, be-lieving that this implied a pro-Judaism bias on the part of the Prophet, began to say that he needed to be instructed by them. To clear up this misunderstanding, it was revealed to the Prophet that the Muslims should turn their faces toward Makkah and the Ka'bah when praying.[9] The whole first part of the second surah deals with this Jewish controversy.

Now that he was a ruler, the Prophet's first concern was to establish public worship and to lay down his state's constitution. He did not forget, however, that the Quraysh had sworn to oppose his religion or that he had been ordered by God to fight against his persecutors until they were completely defeated. One year after his arrival in Yathrib, he sent out small expeditions, led by himself or someone else, in order to see what was going on and to persuade other local tribes not to side with the Quraysh.

These are generally represented as warlike but, considering their weakness and the fact that there was no actual fighting (although they were prepared to fight), they can hardly have been that. It is noteworthy that these expeditions were composed only of Muslims who had originally come from Makkah. The

---

[9]Surah 2:144-150.

natives of Yathrib did not participate, for the reason that (if we accept Ibn Khaldūn's theory) the command to fight had been revealed to the Prophet at Makkah after the men from Yathrib men sworn their oath of allegiance at al 'Aqabah, and in their absence. They had undertaken to protect the Prophet from attack, not to fight with him in actual campaigns. Blood was shed and booty taken—against the Prophet's express orders—in only one of those early expeditions. One purpose of those expeditions may have been to prepare the Makkan Muslims for actual warfare. For thirteen years they had been strict pacifists and it is clear from several Qur'anic passages that many, including perhaps even the Prophet, hated the idea of fighting even in self-defense and had to accept it gradually.[10]

In the second year of the Hijrah, a caravan belonging to Makkan merchants was returning from Syria by the usual route, which happened to be located not far from Yathrib. Its leader, Abū Sufyān, learned of the Prophet's plan to capture the caravan as he approached the territory of Yathrib. At once he sent a camel-rider to Makkah. Upon his arrival, the exhausted rider shouted frantically from the valley to the Quraysh to ride as fast as they could to protect their wealth and honor. A force of one thousand warriors was soon on its way to Yathrib—apparently less concerned with saving the caravan than with punishing the raiders, since the Prophet might have taken the caravan before their departure.

Did the Prophet ever intend to raid the caravan? According to Ibn Hishām's account of the Tābūk expedition, on that one occasion the Prophet did not hide his real objective. The caravan was the pretext for the campaign of Badr, and the real objective was the Makkan army. He had received the command to fight his persecutors, had been promised victory, and was ready to fight against all odds (as was the case with the battle of Badr). The Muslims, until then not very eager for war and also ill-equipped, would have despaired if they had known at the outset that they would face a well-armed force three times their number.

The Qurayshī army advanced more than half-way to Yathrib before the Prophet set out. The two armies, in addition to the caravan, were all heading for the water located at Badr. Abū Sufyān, the caravan leader, heard from one of his scouts that the Muslims were near the water and so turned back to the

---

[10]i.e., Surah 2:216.

coastal plain. The Muslims met the Quraysh by the water. Before the battle, the Prophet was prepared to increase the odds against him. He told the Anṣār (natives of Yathrib) that they could return to their homes unreproached, since their oath did not include participating in actual warfare. The Anṣār, however, were hurt by the very thought that they would even consider leaving the Prophet when he was in danger.

Despite the clear difference in numbers in favor of the Quraysh, Muslims emerged victorious.[11] This victory gave the Prophet new prestige among the Arab tribes, but it also resulted in a blood feud, in addition to the religious conflict, between the Quraysh and the Prophet. The Qur'anic passages that refer to the battle of Badr warn of much greater struggles to come.

In fact, the very next year saw an army of three thousand Makkan warriors on their way to Yathrib to destroy it. The Prophet's first idea was to defend the city. This plan received the strong support of 'Abd Allāh ibn 'Ubayy, leader of "the Hypocrites" (or lukewarm Muslims). However, the veterans of Badr believed that God would help them against any odds and thought they would shame themselves if they remained behind walls. The Prophet, approving of their faith and zeal, agreed and set out with one thousand men toward the enemy encampment at Mt. Uhud. 'Abd Allāh ibn 'Ubayy opposed this change in plan, for he claimed that the Prophet would really fight in such disadvantageous circumstances and did not want to take part in a demonstration of power. He therefore withdrew with his men and decreased the size of the Muslim army by one-third.

Despite the heavy odds, the battle at Mt. Uhud would have been an even greater Muslim victory than that at Badr if the band of fifty Muslim archers, whom the Prophet set to guard a pass against the enemy cavalry, had not deserted their posts upon seeing their comrades victorious, fearing that they might miss out on the resulting spoils. The Qurayshī cavalry rode through the gap, fell on the exultant Muslims, and wounded the Prophet. The cry arose that the Prophet had been killed. However, someone recognized him and shouted that he was still living, which caused the demoralized Mus-lims to rally. They gathered around the Prophet and began to retreat, leaving many fallen warriors on the hillside.[12]

---

[11]See also Surah 8, introductory note.
[12]See also Surah 3, introductory note.

On the following day, the Prophet again sallied forth with what remained of his army so that the Quraysh would hear that he was in the field and perhaps be deterred from attacking the city. The stratagem succeeded, thanks to a friendly bedouin who, after meeting and talking with the Muslims, encountered the Quraysh. Upon being questioned by Abū Sufyān, he said that Muhammad was in the field, stronger than ever, and thirsting for revenge. Based on this information, Abū Sufyān decided to quickly return to Makkah.

This setback lowered the Muslims' prestige with the Arab tribes and also with the Jews of Yathrib. Tribes that had inclined towards the Muslims before now inclined towards the Quraysh. The Prophet's followers were attacked and murdered when they went abroad in little companies. Khubayb, an envoy of the Prophet, was captured by a desert tribe and sold to the Quraysh, who then tortured him to death before the people of Makkah. The Jews, despite their treaty with the Prophet, became almost open in their hostility and told the Quraysh that their pagan religion was superior to Islam.[13] The Prophet was obliged to take punitive action against some of them. The Banī Naḍīr tribe was besieged in its strong forts, eventually subdued, and then forced to emigrate. The Hypocrites had sympathized with the Jews and encouraged them secretly.[14]

In the fifth year of the Hijrah, the idolaters made a great effort to destroy Islam in an event called the War of the Clans or War of the Trench. The Quraysh gathered all of its clans and allied its army with that of the Ghatafān, a great desert tribe. This alliance, ten thousand warriors strong, then marched on Yathrib, by now known as al Madinah. The Prophet ordered (supposedly upon the advice of Salmān the Persian) and participated in the digging of a deep trench around the city. The enemy army did not know what to do when faced with such a novelty; they had never seen such a defense before. As their cavalry, which formed their strength, did not know how, or was unable, to breach it, they camped in sight of it and daily showered their arrows on its defenders.

While the Muslims awaited the assault, news came that Banī Qurayẓah, a Jewish tribe of Yathrib that had till then been loyal, had gone over to the enemy. The case seemed desperate. However, the delay caused by the trench had dampened the enemy's enthusiasm, and an individual who was secretly a Muslim was able to sow distrust between the Quraysh and their Jewish allies.

[13]Surah 4:51.
[14]Surah 59.

This caused both sides to hesitate. During their hesitation, a bitter wind from the sea reached them. It engulfed them for three days and nights and was so strong that no tent could be kept standing, no fire lit, or no water boiled. Seeing that the tribesmen were in utter misery, one night the leader of the Qurayshī army decided that the torment could be borne no longer and gave the order to retire.[15] When the Ghatafān awoke the next morning and saw that the Quraysh had departed, they gathered their supplies and retreated.

Upon his return from the trench, the Prophet ordered war against the treacherous Banī Qurayẓah who, conscious of their guilt, had already taken to their towers of refuge. After a siege of nearly a month, they surrendered unconditionally and begged to be judged by a member of the Arab tribe to which they were affiliated. The Prophet granted their request and carried out the sentence of the judge: the execution of the men and the enslavement of the women and children.

Early in the sixth year of the Hijrah, the Prophet led a campaign against the Banī Mustaliq tribe, as it had been preparing to attack the Muslims. During the return from this camping, 'Ā'ishah, the Prophet's young wife, was left behind unnoticed. A young soldier found her and brought her back to the Muslim camp. This incident gave rise to the scandal denounced in Surah 24.[16] In addition, 'Abd Allāh ibn 'Ubayy, the "Hypo-crite" chief, planned to exploit the situation. He is reported to have said: "When we return to the city the mightier will soon expel the weaker,"[17] upon witnessing a quarrel between the Muhājirīn (immigrants from Makkah) and the Anṣār (natives of Yathrib).

In the same year, the Prophet had a vision in which he saw himself entering the holy precincts of Makkah unopposed and made the intention to perform the pilgrimage.[18] Along with a number of Muslims from Yathrib (which we shall hereafter call al Madinah), he called upon those Arabs who were sympathetic to his cause, whose numbers had increased since the miraculous (as it was considered) discomfiture of the clans, to accompany him. Most of them did not respond.[19] This did not deter him, however, and he set out for Makkah with fourteen hundred men attired as pilgrims and driving the flocks for the

---

[15] See also Surah 33, introductory note.
[16] Surah 24:11 ff.
[17] Surah 63:8.
[18] Surah 48:27.
[19] Surah 48:11 ff.

customary offerings. As they approached the holy valley, they were met by a friend from the city who warned the Prophet that the Quraysh had put on their leopardskins (a badge of valor), had sworn to prevent him from entering the sanctuary, and that their cavalry was on the road in front of him. After hearing this, the Prophet ordered a detour through mountain gorges. When his exhausted troops finally reached al Ḥudaybīyah, a site located within the valley of Makkah, they set up camp and rested.

The Prophet now sought to open negotiations. He sent a messenger to the enemy camp to inform the Quraysh that he and his men wanted to enter Makkah only as pilgrims. This man was maltreated, his camel was hamstrung, and he had to return before he could deliver his message. The Quraysh then sent a man to convey their message in a very threatening and arrogant tone. Another of their messengers was too familiar and had to be reminded sternly of the respect due to the Prophet. When this second messenger returned to Makkah, he said: "I have seen Caesar and Chosroes in their pomp, but never have I seen a man so honored by his comrades as is Muhammad."

The Prophet decided to send another messenger whom the Quraysh would be forced to treat with respect. Eventually, he chose to send 'Uthmān, who had ties of kinship with the powerful 'Umayyad family. While the Muslims were awaiting his return, they received the false news that he had been murdered. This turn of events caused the Prophet, who was sitting under a tree at al Ḥudaybīyah, to bind his followers to an oath that they would all stand or fall together.[20] After a while, however, it became known that 'Uthmān had not been murdered. A group of Makkan warriors that tried to harm the Muslims in their camp was captured before any harm was done, and the men were forgiven and released after they promised the Prophet that they would renounce their previous hostility.[21]

This incident marked the beginning of serious negotiations, for the Quraysh now sent proper envoys. The resulting agreement, known as the truce of al Ḥudabīyah, enshrined a cessation of hostilities for a period of ten years. The Prophet was to return to al Madinah without visiting the Ka'bah with the understanding that he and his comrades would be able to perform the pilgrimage the following year. At that time, the Quraysh would evacuate Makkah for three days so that his pilgrimage could be made properly. The Prophet promised to

[20]Surah 48:10.
[21]Surah 48:24.

return all members of the Quraysh who sought to join the Muslims, even though the Quraysh did not have to assume a corresponding obligation. It was also accepted by both sides that any tribe or clan that wished to participate in the treaty as allies of the Prophet or of the Quraysh could do so.

There was dismay among the Muslims when they learned of the terms. They asked one another: "Where is the victory that we were promised?" In response, Surah al Fath (Victory) was revealed while the troops were returning to al Madinah.[22] What these men did not know was that this truce would prove to be the greatest victory achieved by the Muslims up to that time, for armed hostilities, which had been a barrier between them and the non-Muslims, had prevented both parties from meeting and talking with each other. Now that this barrier had been removed, the new religion spread more rapidly. In the two years that elapsed between the signing of the truce and the fall of Makkah, more people embraced Islam than had done so since the beginning of the Prophet's mission. The Prophet had travelled to al Ḥudaybīyah with 1400 men. Two years later, when the Makkans broke the truce, he marched against them with an army of ten thousand.

In the seventh year of the Hijrah, the Prophet led a campaign against the Jewish stronghold of Khaybar, which was located in northern Arabia and had become a focal point for his enemies. The forts of Khaybar were reduced one by one, and their Jewish inhabitants were turned into tenants of the Muslims until all Jews were expelled from Arabia during the caliphate of 'Umar. On the day when the last fort surrendered, Ja'far, son of Abū Ṭālib and the Prophet's cousin, arrived from Abyssinia with the Muslims whom the Prophet had advised to leave Makkah fifteen years earlier.

After the Muslims' victory at Khaybar, a Jewess prepared a meal of poisoned meat for the Prophet. He tasted, but did not swallow, a small piece of it and then told his comrades that it was poisoned. One Muslim, who had already swallowed some of it, died instantly. The Prophet, even though he had only tasted it, contracted the illness that eventually caused his death. When the guilty woman was brought before him, she said that she had done it to avenge the humiliation of her people. The Prophet forgave her.

During this same year, the Prophet's vision was fulfilled; he visited the holy place at Makkah unopposed. In accordance with the terms of the truce, the non-

---

[22]Surah 48.

Muslims evacuated the city and watched the Muslim pilgrimage from the s urrounding heights. At the end of the stipulated three days, the chiefs of the Quraysh sent word to the Prophet to remind him that they had fulfilled their part of the treaty and that it was now time for him to leave Makkah. He withdrew, and the idolaters reoccupied the city.

In the eighth year of the Hijrah, hearing that the Byzantine emperor was gathering a force in Syria to send against the Muslims, the Prophet dispatched three thousand men under the command of his freedman Zayd. The campaign was not successful, but the reckless valor of the Muslims—three thousand of them did not hesitate to take the battle field against one hundred thousand enemy troops—left an impression on the Syrians. When all of the three leaders appointed by the Prophet had been killed, the survivors obeyed Khālid ibn al Walīd, whose strategy and courage preserved the Muslim army and got it back to al Madinah.

Also in this year, the Quraysh broke the truce by attacking a tribe allied to the Prophet and massacring its members even in the sanctuary at Makkah. After this breach, the Quraysh sent Abū Sufyān to al Madinah to ask for the existing treaty to be renewed and prolonged before the Prophet learned what had happened to his allies. His mission ended in failure, however, for a survivor was able to reach the Prophet and inform him of the massacre.

The Prophet now summoned all of the Muslims who could bear arms and marched on Makkah. The Quraysh were overwhelmed and, after putting up a show of defense in front of the town, were routed without bloodshed. The Prophet, upon entering Makkah as a conqueror, proclaimed a general amnesty for all but a few known criminals, most of whom were eventually forgiven. In their relief and surprise, the whole population of Makkah hastened to swear allegiance to him. The Prophet then destroyed all of the idols housed in the Ka'bah, saying: "Truth has come; falsehood has vanished,"[23] and the Muslim call to prayer rang out over Makkah.

But not all tribes were so eager to embrace Islam. In that same year, an angry gathering of pagan tribes tried to regain control of the Ka'bah. The Prophet, who led twelve thousand men against them, met this new enemy at Ḥunayn. When the Muslims advanced into a deep ravine, they were ambushed and almost put to flight. With difficulty, they managed to rally to the Prophet and

---

[23]Surah 17:81.

his bodyguard of faithful comrades who stood firm. But the victory, when it came, was complete and the booty enormous, for many of the hostile tribes had brought with them all of their possessions. The tribe of Thaqīf, which had participated in this campaign, soon saw its own city of Ṭā'if besieged and reduced to submission.

After all of this, the Prophet appointed a governor for Makkah and returned to al Madinah to the boundless joy of the Anṣār, who had feared that he might forsake them and return to his native city.

In the ninth year of the Hijrah, hearing that a new army was being assembled in Syria, the Prophet called upon the Muslims to support him in a great campaign. Many excused themselves on the grounds that the distances involved were great, that it was the hot season, that it was harvest time, and that the enemy had a great deal of prestige. Others just refused to go without offering any excuse. Both groups were denounced in the Qur'an.[24] The campaign ended peacefully, for the Muslims advanced to Tābūk, on the borders of Syria, and discovered that the enemy had not yet gathered.

Although Makkah had been conquered and its people were now Muslims, the official order of the pilgrimage had not been changed: the pagan Arabs performed it as usual, and the Muslims performed it in the way ordained by God. Only after the pilgrims' caravan left al Madinah in the ninth year of the Hijrah, by which time Islam was dominant in northern Arabia, was the Declaration of Disavowal revealed.[25] The Prophet sent a copy of it by messenger to Abū Bakr, leader of the pilgrimage, with the instructions that 'Alī was to read it to the multitudes at Makkah. In essence, it stated that after that year only Muslims and certain non-Muslims (those who had never broken their treaties with the Muslims or actively sided against them) would be allowed to make the pilgrimage. These treaties would be honored until their expiration date, after which these non-Muslims would be treated like all of the other non-Muslims. This proclamation marks the end of idol worship in Arabia.

The ninth year of the Hijrah, the Year of Deputations, saw delegations from all over Arabia coming to al Madinah to swear allegiance to the Prophet and to hear the Qur'an.[26] The Prophet had become, in fact, the emperor of Arabia, but his way of life remained as simple as before.

---

[24]Surah 9:117-118.
[25]Surah 9:28.
[26]Surah 49.

During the last ten years of his life, the Prophet led twenty-seven campaigns, nine of which saw heavy fighting. He planned, but let other people lead, a further thirty-eight expeditions. He personally controlled each detail of the organization, judged each case, and was accessible to each suppliant. He destroyed idolatry in Arabia, raised women from the status of chattel to human beings with complete legal equality vis-à-vis men, and ended the drunkenness and immorality that had until his time disgraced the Arabs. His followers fell in love with faith, sincerity, and honest dealing. Previously ignorant tribes who had been content with their ignorance were transformed into tribes with a great thirst for knowledge. And, for the first time in history, the ideal of universal human brotherhood was a fact and a principle of common law. The Prophet's support and guide in all of this work was the Qur'an.

In the tenth year of the Hijrah, the Prophet performed the pilgrimage to Makkah for the last time. This has become known as the Farewell Pilgrimage. From Mount 'Arafat, he preached to an enormous throng of pilgrims, reminded them of the duties enjoined upon them by God, and that one day they would meet and be judged by their Lord on the basis of what they had done here on Earth. At the end of the discourse, he asked: "Have I conveyed the message?" And from that great multitude of people, who a few months or years before had all been conscienceless idolaters, the shout went up: "O Allah! Yes!" The Prophet said: "O Allah! You are a witness!"

It was during this Farewell Pilgrimage that Surah al Naṣr (Succour), which he received as an announcement of his approaching death, was revealed. Soon after his return to al Madinah he fell ill, an event that caused dismay throughout Arabia and anguish to the people of al Madinah, Makkah, and Ṭā'if. In the early dawn on his last day of earthly life, he came out of his room beside the mosque at al Madinah and joined the public prayer, which Abū Bakr had been leading since his illness. This event caused a great relief among the people, who took this as an indication that he was well again.

When later in the day the rumor spread that he had died, 'Umar declared it a crime to think that the Prophet could die and threatened to punish severely anyone who said such a thing. Abū Bakr, upon entering the mosque and seeing what 'Umar was doing, went to 'Ā'ishah's (his daughter's) chamber to see the Prophet. Ascertaining that the Prophet really was dead, he kissed the Prophet's forehead, returned to the mosque, and tried to whisper the information to 'Umar, who was still threatening the people. Finally, because 'Umar refused to listen to him, Abū Bakr called out to the people. Recognizing his voice, they left 'Umar and turned their attention to Abū Bakr who, after praising God, said: "O people! As for him who used to worship Muhammad, Muhammad is dead. But as for him who used to worship Allah, Allah is alive and does not die." He then recited the following verse:

> And Muhammad is but a Messenger, messengers the like of whom have passed away before him. Will it be that, when he dies or is slain, you will turn back on your heels? He who turns back does no hurt to Allah and Allah will reward the thankful.[27]

"And," says the narrator, an eye-witness, "it was as if the people had not known that such a verse had been revealed until Abū Bakr recited it." Another witness tells how 'Umar used to say: "As soon as I heard Abū Bakr recite that verse, my feet were cut from beneath me and I fell to the ground, for I knew that Allah's Messenger was dead. May Allah bless and keep him!"

All the surahs of the Qur'an had been recorded in writing before the Prophet's death, and many Muslims had committed the whole Qur'an to memory. But the written surahs were dispersed among the people. This soon became a problem, for within two years of the Prophet's death, many of those who had memorized the entire Qur'an were killed during a battle. It was therefore decided to collect the written portions and prepare a complete and undeniably authentic written copy of the Qur'an. This was done under the instruction of Abū Bakr, the first caliph. A master copy of the Qur'an was kept in the custody of Ḥafṣah, one of the Prophet's wives.

With the passage of time, people in different places started to differ on the Qur'an's contents. To end such disputes once and for all, Caliph 'Uthmān formed a committee composed of the Prophet's Companions and those who had memorized either all or part of the Qur'an. All existing copies were collected during the reign of 'Uthmān, and an authoritative version based on Abū Bakr's collection and the testimony of those who could recite the entire Qur'an from memory was compiled. This is the Qur'an that exists today, which is regarded as traditional and as being arranged according to the Prophet's own instructions. The caliph 'Uthmān and his helpers, all Companions of the Prophet and the most devout students of the revelation, saw that this task was completed. The Qur'an has thus been very carefully preserved.

---

[27]Surah 3:144.

The arrangement is not easy to understand. Revelations of various dates and on different subjects are found together; verses revealed in al Madinah are found in Makkan surahs; some Madinan surahs that were revealed quite late are found in the front of the Qur'an while the very early Makkan surahs come at the end. This arrangement is not haphazard, however, as some have hastily supposed. Closer study reveals a sequence and significance, for instance, with regard to placing the very early Makkan surahs at the end. The inspiration of the Prophet progressed from the internal to the external, whereas most people find their way through the external to the internal.

Another disconcerting peculiarity proceeds from one of the beauties of the original and is unavoidable without abolishing the division of the verses, which is of great importance for reference. In Arabic, verses are divided according to the rhythm of the language. When a certain sound marking the rhythm recurs, there is a strong pause and the verse ends naturally, although the sentence may go on to the next verse or to several subsequent verses. This is the spirit of the Arabic language. Unfortunately, attempts to reproduce such rhythm in English have the opposite effect. Here only the division is preserved, the verses being divided as in the Qur'an, and numbered.

The Opening

Al Fātiḥah, "The Opening," or *Fātiḥat al Kitāb*, "The Opening of the Scripture" or *Umm al Qur'ān*, "The Essence of the Qur'an," as it is variously named, has been called the Lord's Prayer of the Muslims. It is an essential part of all Muslim public and private worship. Although the date of its revelation is uncertain, the fact that it has formed, even from the very earliest times, a part of Muslim worship, that there is no record or remembrance of its introduction or of public prayer without it, makes it clear that it was revealed before the fourth year of the Prophet's mission (the tenth year before the hijrah). This can be stated with confidence, because we know for certain that by that time regular congregational prayers were being offered by the little group of Muslims in Makkah. In that year, as a result of insults and attacks[28] by the idolaters, the Prophet arranged for the services, which had till then been held out of doors, to take place in a private house.

This surah is also called *Sab'an min al Mathānī*, "Seven of the Oft-repeated" ("verses" being understood), a phrase found in Sūrah 15:87 which is taken as referring to this sūrah.[29]

---

[28]Ibn Hishām *Sīrah* (Cairo Edition), 1:88
[29]See Noldeke, *Geschichte des Qorans*, Zweite Auflage, bearbeitet von Fr. Schwally, 1:110.

TRANSLATOR'S NOTE: I have retained the word Allah throughout, because there is no corresponding word in English. The word Allah (the stress is on the last syllable) has neither feminine nor plural, and has never been applied to anything other than the unimaginable Supreme Being. I use the word "God" only where the corresponding word *ilah* is found in the Arabic.

The words in brackets are interpolated to explain the meaning.

بِسْمِ اللهِ الرَّحْمٰنِ الرَّحِيمِ

الْحَمْدُ لِلّٰهِ رَبِّ الْعَالَمِينَ ۞ الرَّحْمٰنِ

الرَّحِيمِ ۞ مَالِكِ يَوْمِ الدِّينِ ۞

إِيَّاكَ نَعْبُدُ وَإِيَّاكَ نَسْتَعِينُ ۞

اهْدِنَا الصِّرَاطَ الْمُسْتَقِيمَ ۞ صِرَاطَ الَّذِينَ

أَنْعَمْتَ عَلَيْهِمْ غَيْرِ الْمَغْضُوبِ عَلَيْهِمْ وَلَا الضَّالِّينَ ۞

The Opening

Revealed at Makkah

1. In the name of Allah, the Beneficent, the Merciful

2. Praise be to Allah, Lord of the Worlds,

3. The Beneficent, the Merciful.

4. Sovereign of the Day of Judgment,

5. You (alone) we worship; You (alone) we ask for help.

6. Guide us to the straight path:

7. The path of those whom You have favored; Not of those who earn Your anger nor of those who go astray.

The Cow

Al Baqarah (The Cow) derives its name from the story of the yellow heifer (2: 67-71). As is the case with many other surahs, the title is taken from a word or an incident that surprised the listeners. Despite suggestions to the contrary, it seems probable that the entire surah was revealed during the first four years after the hijrah, and that by far the greater portion of it was revealed during the first eighteen months of the Prophet's reign at al Madinah—that is to say, before the battle of Badr.[30]

Shortly before the coming of Islam, the Jewish tribes of Yathrib (the pre-Islamic name of al Madinah) had lost their paramount position to the pagan Arab tribes of Aws and Khazraj and had affiliated themselves with one or the other. They still maintained, however, a sort of intellectual ascendancy over the Arabs because of their possession of the Scripture and their skills in the occult sciences. The pagan Arabs used to consult the Jewish rabbis on occasions and paid heed to what they said.

Before the coming of Islam,[31] these rabbis had often told their neighbors that a Prophet was about to come and that when he came, they (the Jews) would destroy the pagan Arabs as the ancient tribes of 'Ād and Thamūd had been destroyed.[32] So plainly did they describe the coming prophet that pilgrims from Yathrib recognized Muhammad, when he addressed them in Makkah, as the prophet described to them by the Jews. The Jews believed that the prophet would give them dominion over others, not that he would make them the brothers of every pagan Arab who accepted Islam. When they found that they could not use Muhammad for their own purposes, they opposed him and tried to destroy his credibility by asking him theological questions and speaking to him as men who possessed superior wisdom. What they failed to understand was that from the Prophet's standpoint, theology is childish nonsense, the very opposite of religion, and its enemy. For the Prophet, religion, was not a matter of conjecture and speech but of fact and conduct.

Ibn Isḥāq[33] states definitely that verses 1-141 deal with these rabbis and those new Muslims who were half-hearted and inclined to listen to them. There follows the order to change the *qiblah* (the place toward which the Muslims turn their face in prayer) from Jerusalem to the Ka'bah at Makkah, which was built by Abraham. This was ordered by Allah to clear up a misunderstanding by the Jews that the Prophet was groping his way toward their religion and so needed their guidance and instruction.

All through this surah, as throughout the entire Qur'an, one is warned that true religion is not the mere profession of a creed, but that it is righteous conduct. There is the repeated announcement that the religion of Abraham, to which Judaism and Christianity (which springs from Judaism) trace their origin, is the only true religion, and that it consists in the surrender of man's will and purpose to the will and purpose of the Lord of Creation, as manifested in His creation and revealed through successive prophets sent to guide mankind. The one test of sincerity in that religion is conduct, and right conduct is the standard to be followed by all who claim to belong to that religion.

---

[30]See Noldeke, *Geschichte des Qorans*, Zweite Auflage, bearbeitet von Fr. Schwally, 1:173.
[31]Islam means "surrender"—man's surrender to God's will and purpose.
[32]Ibn Hishām (Cairo Ed.), 1:180.
[33]Ibn Hishām, *Sīrah* (Cairo Ed.), pp. 189 seq.

When this surah was revealed at al Madinah, the Prophet's own tribe, the pagan Quraysh, were preparing to attack the Muslims. Cruel persecution was the lot of Muslims who had stayed in Makkah or who had journeyed there, and Muslims were prevented from performing the pilgrimage. The possible necessity of fighting had been foreseen in the terms of the oath taken at al 'Aqabah by the Muslims of Yathrib before the Migration to defend the Prophet as they would their own wives and children. Although the first command to fight was revealed before the Prophet's departure from Makkah, the Muslims did not actually fight until the battle of Badr. Many were reluctant to fight, due to their previous observance of strict nonviolence. It was difficult for them to accept the idea of fighting even in self-defense, as can be seen from several verses.

This surah also contains rules for fasting and the pilgrimage, inheritance, alms-giving, divorce and contracts, and verses that discourage usury, strong drink, and gambling. It concludes by stating the universal character of Islam, the religion of Allah's sovereignty, and with a prayer for the forgiveness of shortcomings. It might be described as a condensation of the Qur'an, for it mentions all of its essential points, which are then elaborated elsewhere. This accounts for the precedence given to it in the arrangement of the Qur'an.

For the most part, this surah was revealed during 1-2 AH. Certain verses dealing with legislative matters are considered to have been revealed at a later date.

The Cow

Revealed at Madinah

*In the name of Allah,
the Beneficent, the Merciful*

1. **A**lif. Lām. Mīm.[34]

2. This is the Scripture whereof there is no doubt, a guidance unto those who ward off (evil).

3. Who believe in the unseen, and establish prayer, and spend of that We have bestowed upon them;

4. And who believe in that which is revealed unto you (Muhammad) and that which was revealed before you, and are certain of the Hereafter.

5. These are on guidance from their Lord, and these are the successful ones.

6. As for the disbelievers, whether you warn them or you warn them not it is all one for them; they believe not.

7. Allah has sealed their hearts and their hearing, and on their eyes there is a covering and theirs will be an awful doom.

8. And of mankind are some who say: We believe in Allah and the Last Day, when they believe not.

9. They try to deceive Allah and those who believe, and they deceive none save themselves; but they perceive not.

10. In their hearts is a disease, so Allah increased their disease. And a painful doom is theirs because they lie.

---

[34]Three letters of the Arabic alphabet: many surahs begin thus with letters of the alphabet. Opinions differ as to their significance, the prevalent view being that they indicate some mystic words. Some have opined that they are merely the initials of the scribe. They are always included in the text and recited as part of it.

11. And when it is said unto them: Make not mischief in the land, they say: We are reformers only.

12. They are indeed the mischief mongers. But they perceive not.

13. And when it is said unto them: Believe as the people[35] believe, they say: Shall we believe as the foolish believe? Surely they are the fools. But they know not.

14. And when they fall in with those who believe, they say: We believe; but when they go apart to their devils they declare: Lo! we are with you; surely we did but mock.

15. Allah (Himself) mocks them, leaving them to wander blindly on in their contumacy.

16. These are they who purchase error at the price of guidance, so their commerce did not prosper, neither were they guided.

17. Their likeness is as the likeness of one who kindles fire, and when it sheds its light around him Allah takes away their light and leaves them in darkness, where they cannot see,

18. Deaf, dumb and blind; so they return not

19. Or like a rainstorm from the sky, wherein is darkness, thunder and the flash of lightning. They thrust their fingers in their ears by reason of the thunder-claps, for fear of death. And Allah encompasses the disbelievers (in His might).

20. The lightning almost snatches away their sight from them. As often as it flashes forth for them they walk therein, and when it darkens against them they stand still. And if Allah willed, He could destroy their hearing and their sight. Indeed Allah is Able to do all things.

وَإِذَا قِيلَ لَهُمْ لَا تُفْسِدُوا فِي الْأَرْضِ قَالُوا ١١ إِنَّمَا نَحْنُ مُصْلِحُونَ

أَلَا إِنَّهُمْ هُمُ الْمُفْسِدُونَ وَلَٰكِن لَّا يَشْعُرُونَ ١٢

وَإِذَا قِيلَ لَهُمْ ءَامِنُوا كَمَا ءَامَنَ النَّاسُ قَالُوا ١٣ أَنُؤْمِنُ كَمَا ءَامَنَ السُّفَهَاءُ أَلَا إِنَّهُمْ هُمُ السُّفَهَاءُ وَلَٰكِن لَّا يَعْلَمُونَ

وَإِذَا لَقُوا الَّذِينَ ءَامَنُوا قَالُوا ءَامَنَّا وَإِذَا ١٤ خَلَوْا إِلَىٰ شَيَٰطِينِهِمْ قَالُوا إِنَّا مَعَكُمْ إِنَّمَا نَحْنُ مُسْتَهْزِءُونَ

اللَّهُ يَسْتَهْزِئُ بِهِمْ وَيَمُدُّهُمْ فِي طُغْيَٰنِهِمْ يَعْمَهُونَ ١٥

أُولَٰئِكَ الَّذِينَ اشْتَرَوُا الضَّلَٰلَةَ بِالْهُدَىٰ ١٦ فَمَا رَبِحَت تِّجَٰرَتُهُمْ وَمَا كَانُوا مُهْتَدِينَ

مَثَلُهُمْ كَمَثَلِ الَّذِي اسْتَوْقَدَ نَارًا فَلَمَّا أَضَاءَتْ ١٧ مَا حَوْلَهُ ذَهَبَ اللَّهُ بِنُورِهِمْ وَتَرَكَهُمْ فِي ظُلُمَٰتٍ لَّا يُبْصِرُونَ

صُمٌّ بُكْمٌ عُمْيٌ فَهُمْ لَا يَرْجِعُونَ ١٨

أَوْ كَصَيِّبٍ مِّنَ السَّمَاءِ فِيهِ ظُلُمَٰتٌ وَرَعْدٌ وَبَرْقٌ ١٩ يَجْعَلُونَ أَصَٰبِعَهُمْ فِي ءَاذَانِهِم مِّنَ الصَّوَٰعِقِ حَذَرَ الْمَوْتِ وَاللَّهُ مُحِيطٌ بِالْكَٰفِرِينَ

يَكَادُ الْبَرْقُ يَخْطَفُ أَبْصَٰرَهُمْ كُلَّمَا أَضَاءَ لَهُم ٢٠ مَّشَوْا فِيهِ وَإِذَا أَظْلَمَ عَلَيْهِمْ قَامُوا وَلَوْ شَاءَ اللَّهُ لَذَهَبَ بِسَمْعِهِمْ وَأَبْصَٰرِهِمْ إِنَّ اللَّهَ عَلَىٰ كُلِّ شَيْءٍ قَدِيرٌ

---

[35] i.e., the people of al Madinah, most of whom were Muslims. Verses 8-19 refer to the "Hypocrites," or the lukewarm Muslims of al Madinah whose leader was ‘Abd Allāh ibn Ubayy. They pretended that they wanted to make peace between the Muslims and the Jewish rabbis, while in reality they sought to inflame the controversy.

21. O mankind! worship your Lord, Who has created you and those before you, so that you may ward off (evil).

22. Who has appointed the earth a resting-place for you, and the sky a canopy; and causes water to pour down from the sky, thereby producing fruits as food for you. So do not set up rivals to Allah when you know (better).

23. And if you are in doubt concerning that which We revealed unto Our slave[36] (Muhammad), then produce a surah like it, and call your witnesses apart from Allah if you are truthful.

24. And if you do it not—and you can never do it—then guard yourselves against the fire whose fuel is men and stones, prepared for disbelievers.

25. And give glad tidings (O Muhammad) unto those who believe and do good works; that theirs are Gardens underneath which rivers flow; as often as they are provided with food of the fruit thereof, they say: This is what was given us before[37]; and it is given to them in resemblance. There for them are pure spouses; therein forever they abide.

26. Lo! Allah disdains not to coin the similitude even of a gnat or what is above it. Those who believe know that it is the truth from their Lord; but those who disbelieve say: What does Allah wish (to teach) by such a similitude? He misleads many thereby, and He guides many thereby; and He misleads thereby only miscreants;

27. Those who break the covenant of Allah after ratifying it and sever that which Allah ordered to be joined, and (who) make mischief in the earth: Those are they who are the losers.

---

[36]To be the slave of Allah is a Muslim's proudest boast, as bondage to Him frees one from all other servitudes. In the Qur'an, a believer is often called God's "slave" or "bondman," a stronger and more accurate expression than the more common translation of "servant." The word "slave," however, might be offensive to Westerners as it has negative connotations. I could not find an English equivalent to 'abd (derived from 'abada [to worship]). The noun 'abd is not just a "slave in bondage" but rather refers to the humble worshipper of Allah, i.e., an obedient believer and a title of honor. The closest term to it is "slave." The Editor.

[37]The joys of Paradise will recall, in a rapturous degree, the joys the righteous tasted during their life on earth.

28. How disbelieve you in Allah when you were dead and He gave life to you! then he will give you death, then life again, and then unto Him you will be returned.

29. He it is Who created for you all that is in the earth. Then turned He to the heaven, and fashioned it as seven heavens. And He is Knower of all things.

30. And when your Lord said unto the angels: Lo! I am about to place a viceroy in the earth, they said: Will You place therein one who will do harm therein and will shed blood, while we, we hymn Your praise and sanctify You? He said: Surely I know that which you know not.

31. And He taught Adam all the names,[38] then showed them to the angels, saying: Inform me of the names of these, if you are truthful.

32. They said: Be glorified! We have no knowledge saving that which You have taught us. Lo! You, only You, are the Knower, the Wise.

33. He said: O Adam! inform them of their names, and when he had informed them of their names, He said: Did I not tell you that I know the secret of the heavens and the earth? And I know that which you disclose and that which you used to hide.

34. And when We said unto the angels: Prostrate yourselves before Adam, they fell prostrate, all save Iblīs. He demurred through pride, and so became a disbeliever.

35. And We said: O Adam! dwell you and your wife in the Garden, and eat you[39] freely (of the fruits) thereof where you will; but come not near this tree lest you become of the wrong-doers.

---

[38]Some, especially Sufis, hold "the names" to be the attributes of Allah, while others maintain that they are the names of animals and plants.
[39]Here the command is in the dual, as addressed to Adam and his wife.

36. But the Devil caused them to deflect therefrom and expelled them from the (happy) state in which they were; and We said: Fall down,[40] one of you a foe unto the other! There shall be for you on earth a habitation and a provision for a time.

37. Then Adam received from his Lord words (of revelation), and He relented toward him. Indeed! He is the Relenting, the Merciful.

38. We said: Go down, all of you, from hence; so when there comes unto you from Me a guidance; whoso follows My guidance, there shall no fear come upon them neither shall they grieve.

39. But those who disbelieve, and deny our revelations, such are rightful owners of the Fire. They will abide therein forever.

40. O Children of Israel! Remember My favor wherewith I favored you, and fulfill your (part of the) covenant, I shall fulfill My (part of the) covenant and fear Me.

41. And believe in that which I revealed, confirming that which you possess already (of the Scripture), and be not first to disbelieve therein, and part not with My revelations for a trifling price, and keep your duty unto Me.

42. Confound not truth with falsehood, nor knowingly conceal the truth.

43. And establish prayer, pay the poor-due,[41] and bow your heads with those who bow (in prayer).

44. Do you enjoin righteousness upon mankind while you yourselves forget (to practice it)? And you are readers of the Scripture! Have you then no sense?

45. And seek help in patience and prayer; for truly it is hard save for the humble-minded,

46. Who know that they will have to meet their Lord, and that unto Him they are returning.

---

[40]Here the command is in the plural, as addressed to the three: Adam, Eve, and the Devil (Satan).
[41]Zakah: A tax at a fixed rate in proportion in worth of property, collected from the well-to-do Muslims and distributed among the poor Muslims, and the rest of the eight categories (cf. 9:60).

47. O Children of Israel! Remember My favor wherewith I favored you and how I preferred you to (all) the worlds.

48. And guard yourselves against a day when no soul will in anything avail another, nor will intercession be accepted from it, nor will compensation be received from it, neither will they be helped.

49. And (remember) when We did deliver you from Pharaoh's folk, who were afflicting you with dreadful torment, slaying your sons and sparing your women: That was a tremendous trial from your Lord.

50. And when We brought you through the sea and rescued you, and drowned the folk of Pharaoh in your sight.

51. And when We did appoint for Moses forty nights (of solitude), and then you chose the calf, when he had gone from you, and you were wrongdoers.

52. Then, even after that, We pardoned you in order that you might give thanks.

53. And when We gave unto Moses the Scripture and the Criterion (of right and wrong), that you might be led rightfully.

54. And when Moses said unto his people: O my people! You have wronged yourselves by your choosing of the calf (for worship) so turn in penitence to your Creator, and kill (the guilty) among yourselves. That will be best for you with your Creator and He will relent toward you. Lo! He is the Relenting, the Merciful.

55. And when you said: O Moses! We will not believe in you till we see Allah plainly; and even while you gazed the lightning seized you.

56. Then We revived you after your death, that you might give thanks.

 يَـٰبَنِىٓ إِسْرَٰٓءِيلَ ٱذْكُرُوا۟ نِعْمَتِىَ ٱلَّتِىٓ أَنْعَمْتُ عَلَيْكُمْ وَأَنِّى فَضَّلْتُكُمْ عَلَى ٱلْعَـٰلَمِينَ ﴿٤٧﴾

وَٱتَّقُوا۟ يَوْمًا لَّا تَجْزِى نَفْسٌ عَن نَّفْسٍ شَيْـًٔا وَلَا يُقْبَلُ مِنْهَا شَفَـٰعَةٌ وَلَا يُؤْخَذُ مِنْهَا عَدْلٌ وَلَا هُمْ يُنصَرُونَ ﴿٤٨﴾

وَإِذْ نَجَّيْنَـٰكُم مِّنْ ءَالِ فِرْعَوْنَ يَسُومُونَكُمْ سُوٓءَ ٱلْعَذَابِ يُذَبِّحُونَ أَبْنَآءَكُمْ وَيَسْتَحْيُونَ نِسَآءَكُمْ وَفِى ذَٰلِكُم بَلَآءٌ مِّن رَّبِّكُمْ عَظِيمٌ ﴿٤٩﴾

وَإِذْ فَرَقْنَا بِكُمُ ٱلْبَحْرَ فَأَنجَيْنَـٰكُمْ وَأَغْرَقْنَآ ءَالَ فِرْعَوْنَ وَأَنتُمْ تَنظُرُونَ ﴿٥٠﴾

وَإِذْ وَٰعَدْنَا مُوسَىٰٓ أَرْبَعِينَ لَيْلَةً ثُمَّ ٱتَّخَذْتُمُ ٱلْعِجْلَ مِنۢ بَعْدِهِۦ وَأَنتُمْ ظَـٰلِمُونَ ﴿٥١﴾

ثُمَّ عَفَوْنَا عَنكُم مِّنۢ بَعْدِ ذَٰلِكَ لَعَلَّكُمْ تَشْكُرُونَ ﴿٥٢﴾

وَإِذْ ءَاتَيْنَا مُوسَى ٱلْكِتَـٰبَ وَٱلْفُرْقَانَ لَعَلَّكُمْ تَهْتَدُونَ ﴿٥٣﴾

وَإِذْ قَالَ مُوسَىٰ لِقَوْمِهِۦ يَـٰقَوْمِ إِنَّكُمْ ظَلَمْتُمْ أَنفُسَكُم بِٱتِّخَاذِكُمُ ٱلْعِجْلَ فَتُوبُوٓا۟ إِلَىٰ بَارِئِكُمْ فَٱقْتُلُوٓا۟ أَنفُسَكُمْ ذَٰلِكُمْ خَيْرٌ لَّكُمْ عِندَ بَارِئِكُمْ فَتَابَ عَلَيْكُمْ إِنَّهُۥ هُوَ ٱلتَّوَّابُ ٱلرَّحِيمُ ﴿٥٤﴾

وَإِذْ قُلْتُمْ يَـٰمُوسَىٰ لَن نُّؤْمِنَ لَكَ حَتَّىٰ نَرَى ٱللَّهَ جَهْرَةً فَأَخَذَتْكُمُ ٱلصَّـٰعِقَةُ وَأَنتُمْ تَنظُرُونَ ﴿٥٥﴾

ثُمَّ بَعَثْنَـٰكُم مِّنۢ بَعْدِ مَوْتِكُمْ لَعَلَّكُمْ تَشْكُرُونَ ﴿٥٦﴾

57. And We caused the white cloud to overshadow you and sent down on you honey and quails, (saying): Eat of the good things wherewith We have provided you They wronged us not, but they did wrong themselves.

58. And when We said: Go into this township and eat freely of that which is therein, and enter the gate prostrate, and say: "Repentance."[42] We will forgive you your sins and increase (reward) for the right-doers.

59. But those who did wrong changed the word which had been told them for another word, and We sent down upon the evildoers wrath from Heaven for their evildoing.

60. And when Moses asked for water for his people, We said: Smite with your staff the rock. And there gushed out therefrom twelve springs (so that) each tribe knew their drinking place. Eat and drink of that which Allah has provided, and do not act corruptly, making mischief in the earth.

61. And when you said: O Moses! We will not endure one kind of food; so pray unto your Lord for us that he bring forth for us of that which the earth grows of its herbs and its cucumbers and its corn and its lentils and its onions. He said: Would you exchange that which is higher for that which is lower? Go down to any city, thus you shall get that which you demand. And humiliation and wretchedness were stamped upon them and they were visited with wrath from Allah.That was because they disbelieved in Allah's revelations and slew the prophets wrongfully. That was for their disobedience and transgression.

٥٧ وَظَلَّلْنَا عَلَيْكُمُ الْغَمَامَ وَأَنزَلْنَا عَلَيْكُمُ الْمَنَّ وَالسَّلْوَىٰ كُلُوا مِن طَيِّبَاتِ مَا رَزَقْنَاكُمْ وَمَا ظَلَمُونَا وَلَٰكِن كَانُوٓا أَنفُسَهُمْ يَظْلِمُونَ

٥٨ وَإِذْ قُلْنَا ادْخُلُوا هَٰذِهِ الْقَرْيَةَ فَكُلُوا مِنْهَا حَيْثُ شِئْتُمْ رَغَدًا وَادْخُلُوا الْبَابَ سُجَّدًا وَقُولُوا حِطَّةٌ نَّغْفِرْ لَكُمْ خَطَايَاكُمْ وَسَنَزِيدُ الْمُحْسِنِينَ

٥٩ فَبَدَّلَ الَّذِينَ ظَلَمُوا قَوْلًا غَيْرَ الَّذِى قِيلَ لَهُمْ فَأَنزَلْنَا عَلَى الَّذِينَ ظَلَمُوا رِجْزًا مِّنَ السَّمَاءِ بِمَا كَانُوا يَفْسُقُونَ

٦٠ وَإِذِ اسْتَسْقَىٰ مُوسَىٰ لِقَوْمِهِ فَقُلْنَا اضْرِب بِّعَصَاكَ الْحَجَرَ فَانفَجَرَتْ مِنْهُ اثْنَتَا عَشْرَةَ عَيْنًا قَدْ عَلِمَ كُلُّ أُنَاسٍ مَّشْرَبَهُمْ كُلُوا وَاشْرَبُوا مِن رِّزْقِ اللَّهِ وَلَا تَعْثَوْا فِى الْأَرْضِ مُفْسِدِينَ

٦١ وَإِذْ قُلْتُمْ يَٰمُوسَىٰ لَن نَّصْبِرَ عَلَىٰ طَعَامٍ وَاحِدٍ فَادْعُ لَنَا رَبَّكَ يُخْرِجْ لَنَا مِمَّا تُنبِتُ الْأَرْضُ مِنۢ بَقْلِهَا وَقِثَّآئِهَا وَفُومِهَا وَعَدَسِهَا وَبَصَلِهَا قَالَ أَتَسْتَبْدِلُونَ الَّذِى هُوَ أَدْنَىٰ بِالَّذِى هُوَ خَيْرٌ اهْبِطُوا مِصْرًا فَإِنَّ لَكُم مَّا سَأَلْتُمْ وَضُرِبَتْ عَلَيْهِمُ الذِّلَّةُ وَالْمَسْكَنَةُ وَبَآءُو بِغَضَبٍ مِّنَ اللَّهِ ذَٰلِكَ بِأَنَّهُمْ كَانُوا يَكْفُرُونَ بِآيَاتِ اللَّهِ وَيَقْتُلُونَ النَّبِيِّنَ بِغَيْرِ الْحَقِّ ذَٰلِكَ بِمَا عَصَوا وَّكَانُوا يَعْتَدُونَ

---

[42]According to the tradition of the Prophet, *ḥiṭṭatun* is a word implying submission to Allah and repentance. The evil-doers changed it for a word of rebellion - i.e., they were disobedient.

62. Lo! those who believe (in that which is revealed unto you, Muhammad), and those who are Jews, and Christians, and Sabaeans, whoever believes in Allah and the Last Day and does right, surely their reward is with their Lord, and there shall no fear come upon them neither shall they grieve.

٦٢ إِنَّ الَّذِينَ ءَامَنُوا وَالَّذِينَ هَادُوا وَالنَّصَارَى وَالصَّابِـِينَ مَنْ ءَامَنَ بِاللَّهِ وَالْيَوْمِ الْأَخِرِ وَعَمِلَ صَلِحًا فَلَهُمْ أَجْرُهُمْ عِندَ رَبِّهِمْ وَلَا خَوْفٌ عَلَيْهِمْ وَلَا هُمْ يَحْزَنُونَ

63. And (remember, O children of Israel) when We made a covenant with you and caused the Mount to tower above you, (saying): Hold fast that which We have given you, and remember that which is therein, that you may ward off (evil).

٦٣ وَإِذْ أَخَذْنَا مِيثَاقَكُمْ وَرَفَعْنَا فَوْقَكُمُ الطُّورَ خُذُوا مَا ءَاتَيْنَاكُم بِقُوَّةٍ وَاذْكُرُوا مَا فِيهِ لَعَلَّكُمْ تَتَّقُونَ

64. Then, even after that, you turned away, and if it had not been for the grace of Allah upon you and His mercy you had been among the losers.

٦٤ ثُمَّ تَوَلَّيْتُم مِّنْ بَعْدِ ذَلِكَ فَلَوْلَا فَضْلُ اللَّهِ عَلَيْكُمْ وَرَحْمَتُهُ لَكُنتُم مِّنَ الْخَسِرِينَ

65. And you know of those of you who broke the Sabbath, how We said unto them: Be you apes, despised and hated!

٦٥ وَلَقَدْ عَلِمْتُمُ الَّذِينَ اعْتَدَوْا مِنكُمْ فِي السَّبْتِ فَقُلْنَا لَهُمْ كُونُوا قِرَدَةً خَاسِئِينَ

66. And We made it an example to their own and to succeeding generations, and an admonition to the God fearing.

٦٦ فَجَعَلْنَاهَا نَكَالًا لِّمَا بَيْنَ يَدَيْهَا وَمَا خَلْفَهَا وَمَوْعِظَةً لِّلْمُتَّقِينَ

67. And when Moses said unto his people: Lo! Allah commands you that you sacrifice a cow, they said: Do you make game of us? He answered: Allah forbid that I should be among the foolish!

٦٧ وَإِذْ قَالَ مُوسَى لِقَوْمِهِ إِنَّ اللَّهَ يَأْمُرُكُمْ أَن تَذْبَحُوا بَقَرَةً قَالُوا أَتَتَّخِذُنَا هُزُوًا قَالَ أَعُوذُ بِاللَّهِ أَنْ أَكُونَ مِنَ الْجَهِلِينَ

68. They said: Pray for us unto your Lord that He make clear to us what (cow) she is. (Moses) answered: Lo! He says, Surely she is a cow neither old nor immature; (she is) between the two conditions; so do that which you are commanded.

٦٨ قَالُوا ادْعُ لَنَا رَبَّكَ يُبَيِّن لَّنَا مَا هِيَ قَالَ إِنَّهُ يَقُولُ إِنَّهَا بَقَرَةٌ لَّا فَارِضٌ وَلَا بِكْرٌ عَوَانٌ بَيْنَ ذَلِكَ فَافْعَلُوا مَا تُؤْمَرُونَ

69. They said: Pray for us unto your Lord that He make clear to us of what color she is. (Moses) answered: Lo! He says: Surely she is a yellow cow. Bright is her color, gladdening beholders.

٦٩ قَالُوا ادْعُ لَنَا رَبَّكَ يُبَيِّن لَّنَا مَا لَوْنُهَا قَالَ إِنَّهُ يَقُولُ إِنَّهَا بَقَرَةٌ صَفْرَاءُ فَاقِعٌ لَّوْنُهَا تَسُرُّ النَّاظِرِينَ

70. They said: Pray for us unto your Lord that He make clear to us what (cow) she is. Lo! cows are much alike to us; and lo! if Allah wills, we may be led rightfully.

٧٠ قَالُوا ادْعُ لَنَا رَبَّكَ يُبَيِّن لَّنَا مَا هِيَ إِنَّ الْبَقَرَ تَشَبَهَ عَلَيْنَا وَإِنَّا إِن شَاءَ اللَّهُ لَمُهْتَدُونَ

71. (Moses) answered: Lo! He says: Surely she is a cow unyoked; she ploughs not the soil nor waters the tilth; whole and without mark. They said: Now you bring the truth. So they sacrificed her, though almost they did not.

72. And (remember) when you slew a man and disagreed concerning it and Allah brought forth that which you were hiding.

73. And We said: Smite him with some of it. Thus Allah brings the dead to life and shows you His portents so that you may understand.

74. Then, even after that, your hearts were hardened and became as rocks, or worse than rocks, for hardness. For indeed there are rocks from out which rivers gush, and in-deed there are some which split asunder so that water flows from them. And indeed there are some which fall down for the fear of Allah. Allah is not unaware of what you do.

75. Have you any hope that they will be true to you when a party of them used to listen to the Word of Allah, then used to change it, after they had understood it knowingly?

76. And when they fall in with those who believe, they say: We believe. But when they go apart one with another they say: Do you tell them of that which Allah has disclosed to you so that they may contend with you before your Lord concerning it? Have you then no sense?

77. Are they then unaware that Allah knows that which they keep hidden and that which they proclaim?

78. Among them are unlettered folk who know not the scripture except from hearsay. They but guess.

79. Therefore woe be unto those who write the Scripture with their hands and then say, "This is from Allah," that they may purchase a small gain there-with. Woe unto them for what their hands have written, and woe unto them for what they earn thereby.

٧١ قَالَ إِنَّهُ يَقُولُ إِنَّهَا بَقَرَةٌ لَّا ذَلُولٌ تُثِيرُ الْأَرْضَ وَلَا تَسْقِي الْحَرْثَ مُسَلَّمَةٌ لَّا شِيَةَ فِيهَا قَالُوا الْآنَ جِئْتَ بِالْحَقِّ فَذَبَحُوهَا وَمَا كَادُوا يَفْعَلُونَ

٧٢ وَإِذْ قَتَلْتُمْ نَفْسًا فَادَّارَأْتُمْ فِيهَا وَاللَّهُ مُخْرِجٌ مَّا كُنْتُمْ تَكْتُمُونَ

٧٣ فَقُلْنَا اضْرِبُوهُ بِبَعْضِهَا كَذَلِكَ يُحْيِ اللَّهُ الْمَوْتَى وَيُرِيكُمْ آيَاتِهِ لَعَلَّكُمْ تَعْقِلُونَ

٧٤ ثُمَّ قَسَتْ قُلُوبُكُمْ مِّنْ بَعْدِ ذَلِكَ فَهِيَ كَالْحِجَارَةِ أَوْ أَشَدُّ قَسْوَةً وَإِنَّ مِنَ الْحِجَارَةِ لَمَا يَتَفَجَّرُ مِنْهُ الْأَنْهَارُ وَإِنَّ مِنْهَا لَمَا يَشَّقَّقُ فَيَخْرُجُ مِنْهُ الْمَاءُ وَإِنَّ مِنْهَا لَمَا يَهْبِطُ مِنْ خَشْيَةِ اللَّهِ وَمَا اللَّهُ بِغَافِلٍ عَمَّا تَعْمَلُونَ

٧٥ أَفَتَطْمَعُونَ أَنْ يُؤْمِنُوا لَكُمْ وَقَدْ كَانَ فَرِيقٌ مِّنْهُمْ يَسْمَعُونَ كَلَامَ اللَّهِ ثُمَّ يُحَرِّفُونَهُ مِنْ بَعْدِ مَا عَقَلُوهُ وَهُمْ يَعْلَمُونَ

٧٦ وَإِذَا لَقُوا الَّذِينَ آمَنُوا قَالُوا آمَنَّا وَإِذَا خَلَا بَعْضُهُمْ إِلَى بَعْضٍ قَالُوا أَتُحَدِّثُونَهُمْ بِمَا فَتَحَ اللَّهُ عَلَيْكُمْ لِيُحَاجُّوكُمْ بِهِ عِنْدَ رَبِّكُمْ أَفَلَا تَعْقِلُونَ

٧٧ أَوَلَا يَعْلَمُونَ أَنَّ اللَّهَ يَعْلَمُ مَا يُسِرُّونَ وَمَا يُعْلِنُونَ

٧٨ وَمِنْهُمْ أُمِّيُّونَ لَا يَعْلَمُونَ الْكِتَابَ إِلَّا أَمَانِيَّ وَإِنْ هُمْ إِلَّا يَظُنُّونَ

٧٩ فَوَيْلٌ لِّلَّذِينَ يَكْتُبُونَ الْكِتَابَ بِأَيْدِيهِمْ ثُمَّ يَقُولُونَ هَذَا مِنْ عِنْدِ اللَّهِ لِيَشْتَرُوا بِهِ ثَمَنًا قَلِيلًا فَوَيْلٌ لَّهُمْ مِّمَّا كَتَبَتْ أَيْدِيهِمْ وَوَيْلٌ لَّهُمْ مِّمَّا يَكْسِبُونَ

80. And they say: Hell fire will not touch us save for a certain number of days. Say: Have you received a covenant from Allah—truly Allah will not break His covenant—or do you tell concerning Allah that which you know not?

81. Nay, but whoever has done evil and his sin surrounds him; such are rightful owners of the Fire; they will abide therein forever.

82. And those who believe and do good works: such are rightful owners of Paradise. They will abide therein forever.

83. And (remember) when We made a covenant with the Children of Israel, (saying):Worship none save Allah (only), and be good to parents and to kindred and to orphans and the needy, and speak kindly to mankind; and establish prayer and pay the poor due. Then, after that, you slid back, save a few of you, being averse.

84. And when We made with you a covenant (saying): Shed not the blood of your people nor turn (a party of) your people out of your dwellings. Then you ratified (Our covenant) and you were witnesses (thereto).[43]

85. Yet you it is who slay each other and drive out a party of your people from their homes, supporting one another against them by sin and transgression[44]— and if they came to you as captives you would ransom them whereas their expulsion was itself unlawful for you— Believe you in part of the Scripture and disbelieve you in part thereof? And what is the reward of those who do so save ignominy in the life of the world, and on the Day of Resurrection they will be consigned to the most grievous doom. For Allah is not unaware of what you do.

---

[43]Verse 83 is generally taken as referring to the Biblical covenant, and verse 84 as referring to the solemn treaty which the Jews of al Madinah made with the Prophet in the year 1 A.H.

[44]The reference is to the wars between the Arab tribes of al Madinah, in which the Jews used to take part as allies of one tribe or another.

86. Such are those who buy the life of the world at the price of the Hereafter: Their punishment will not be lightened, neither will they have support.

87. And surely We gave unto Moses the Scripture and We caused a train of messengers to follow after him, and We gave unto Jesus son of Mary clear proofs (of Allah's sovereignty), and We supported him with the holy Spirit.[45] Is it ever so, that, when there comes unto you a messenger (from Allah) with that which you yourselves desire not, you grow arrogant, so some you disbelieve and some you slay?

88. And they say: Our hearts are hardened. Nay, but Allah has cursed them for their unbelief. Little is that which they believe.

89. And when there came unto them a Scripture from Allah, confirming that in their possession though before that they were asking for a signal triumph over those who disbelieved and when there came unto them that which they knew (to be the Truth) they disbelieved therein. The curse of Allah is on disbelievers.

90. Evil is that for which they sold their souls: that they should disbelieve in that which Allah has revealed, grudging that Allah should reveal of His bounty unto whom He will of His bondmen.[46] They have incurred anger upon anger. For disbelievers is a shameful doom.

91. And when it is said unto them: Believe in that which Allah has revealed, they say: We believe in that which was revealed unto us. And they disbelieve in that which comes after it, though it is the truth confirming that which they possess. Say (unto them, O Muhammad): Why then slew you the Prophets of Allah before, if you are (indeed) believers?

92. And Moses came unto you with clear proofs (of Allah's sovereignty) yet while he was away you chose the calf (for worship) and you were wrongdoers.

---

[45]"The holy Spirit" is a term for the angel of Revelation, Gabriel.
[46]See v. 23, footnote.

93. And when We made with you a covenant and caused the Mount to tower above you, (saying): Hold fast by that which We have given you, and hear (Our Word), they said: We hear and we rebel. And (worship of) the calf was made to sink into their hearts because of their rejection (of the Covenant). Say (unto them): Evil is that which your belief enjoins on you, if you are believers.

94. Say (unto them): If the abode of the Hereafter in the providence of Allah is indeed for you alone and not for others of mankind (as you pretend), then long for death if you are truthful.

95. But they will never long for it, because of that which their own hands have sent before them. And Allah is Aware of evildoers.

96. And you will find them greediest of mankind for any life and (greedier) than the idolaters. (Each) one of them would like to be allowed to live a thousand years. And to live (that long) would by no means remove him from the doom. And Allah is Seer of what they do.

97. Say (O Muhammad, to mankind): Who is an enemy to Gabriel! For he it is who has revealed (this Scripture) to your heart by Allah's leave, confirming that which was (revealed) before it, and a guidance and glad tidings to believers;

98. Who is an enemy to Allah, and His angels and His Messengers, and Gabriel and Michael! Then, lo! Allah (Himself) is an enemy to disbelievers.

99. Surely We have revealed unto you clear tokens, and only miscreants will disbelieve in them.

100. Is it ever so that when they make a covenant a party of them set it aside? The truth is, most of them believe not.

101. And when there comes unto them a messenger from Allah, confirming that which they possess, a party of those who have received the Scripture fling the Scripture of Allah behind their backs as if they knew not,

١٠١ وَلَمَّا جَآءَهُمْ رَسُولٌ مِّنْ عِنْدِ اللَّهِ مُصَدِّقٌ لِّمَا مَعَهُمْ نَبَذَ فَرِيقٌ مِّنَ الَّذِينَ أُوتُوا الْكِتَابَ كِتَابَ اللَّهِ وَرَآءَ ظُهُورِهِمْ كَأَنَّهُمْ لَا يَعْلَمُونَ

102. And they followed that which the devils falsely related against the kingdom of Solomon. Solomon disbelieved not; but the devils disbelieved, teaching mankind magic and that which was revealed to the two angels in Babel, Hārūt and Mārūt. Nor did they (the two angels) teach it to anyone till they had said: We are only a temptation, therefore disbelieve not (in the guidance of Allah). And from these two (angels) people learn that by which they cause division between man and wife; but they injure thereby no one save by Allah's leave. And they learn that which harms them and profits them not. And surely they do know that he who traffics therein will have no (happy) portion in the Hereafter; and surely evil is the price for which they sold their souls, if they but knew.[47]

١٠٢ وَاتَّبَعُوا مَا تَتْلُوا الشَّيَاطِينُ عَلَى مُلْكِ سُلَيْمَانَ وَمَا كَفَرَ سُلَيْمَانُ وَلَكِنَّ الشَّيَاطِينَ كَفَرُوا يُعَلِّمُونَ النَّاسَ السِّحْرَ وَمَا أُنْزِلَ عَلَى الْمَلَكَيْنِ بِبَابِلَ هَارُوتَ وَمَارُوتَ وَمَا يُعَلِّمَانِ مِنْ أَحَدٍ حَتَّى يَقُولَا إِنَّمَا نَحْنُ فِتْنَةٌ فَلَا تَكْفُرْ فَيَتَعَلَّمُونَ مِنْهُمَا مَا يُفَرِّقُونَ بِهِ بَيْنَ الْمَرْءِ وَزَوْجِهِ وَمَا هُمْ بِضَارِّينَ بِهِ مِنْ أَحَدٍ إِلَّا بِإِذْنِ اللَّهِ وَيَتَعَلَّمُونَ مَا يَضُرُّهُمْ وَلَا يَنْفَعُهُمْ وَلَقَدْ عَلِمُوا لَمَنِ اشْتَرَاهُ مَالَهُ فِي الْآخِرَةِ مِنْ خَلَاقٍ وَلَبِئْسَ مَا شَرَوْا بِهِ أَنْفُسَهُمْ لَوْ كَانُوا يَعْلَمُونَ

103. And if they had believed and kept from evil, a recompense from Allah would be better, if they only knew.

١٠٣ وَلَوْ أَنَّهُمْ آمَنُوا وَاتَّقَوْا لَمَثُوبَةٌ مِّنْ عِنْدِ اللَّهِ خَيْرٌ لَوْ كَانُوا يَعْلَمُونَ

104. O you who believe, say not (unto the Prophet): "Listen to us" but say "Look upon us,"[48] and be you attentive listeners. For disbelievers is a painful doom.

١٠٤ يَا أَيُّهَا الَّذِينَ آمَنُوا لَا تَقُولُوا رَاعِنَا وَقُولُوا انْظُرْنَا وَاسْمَعُوا وَلِلْكَافِرِينَ عَذَابٌ أَلِيمٌ

105. Neither those who disbelieve among the People of the Scripture[49] nor the idolaters love that there should be sent down unto you any good thing from your Lord. But Allah chooses for His mercy whom He will, and Allah is of infinite bounty.

١٠٥ مَا يَوَدُّ الَّذِينَ كَفَرُوا مِنْ أَهْلِ الْكِتَابِ وَلَا الْمُشْرِكِينَ أَنْ يُنَزَّلَ عَلَيْكُمْ مِنْ خَيْرٍ مِنْ رَبِّكُمْ وَاللَّهُ يَخْتَصُّ بِرَحْمَتِهِ مَنْ يَشَاءُ وَاللَّهُ ذُو الْفَضْلِ الْعَظِيمِ

106. Such of Our revelations as We abrogate or cause to be forgotten, we bring (in place) one better or the like. Do not you know that Allah is Able to do all things?

١٠٦ مَا نَنْسَخْ مِنْ آيَةٍ أَوْ نُنْسِهَا نَأْتِ بِخَيْرٍ مِنْهَا أَوْ مِثْلِهَا أَلَمْ تَعْلَمْ أَنَّ اللَّهَ عَلَى كُلِّ شَيْءٍ قَدِيرٌ

---

[47]The reference is to the occult science practised by the Jews, the origin of which was ascribed to Solomon.
[48]The first word which the Muslims used to attract the Prophet's attention respectfully, *rā'inā*, the Jews could change into an insult by a slight mispronunciation.
[49]i.e., Jews and Christians.

107. Do not you know that it is Allah unto Whom belongs the sovereignty of the heavens and the earth; and you have not, apart from Allah, any friend or helper?

108. Or would you question your Messenger as Moses was questioned before? He who chooses disbelief instead of faith, surely he has gone astray from a plain road.

109. Many of the People of the Scripture long to make you disbelievers after your belief, through envy on their own account, after the truth has become manifest unto them. So forgive and be indulgent (toward them) until Allah gives command. Lo! Allah is Able to do all things.

110. And establish prayer, and pay the poor due[50]; and whatever of good you send before (you) for your souls, you will find it with Allah. Lo! Allah is Seer of what you do.

111. And they say: None will enter Paradise unless he be a Jew or a Christian. These are their own wishes. Say: Bring your proof (of what you state) if you are truthful.

112. Nay, but whoever surrenders his purpose to Allah while doing good, his reward is with his Lord; and there shall no fear come upon them neither shall they grieve.

113. And Jews say Christians follow nothing (true), and Christians say Jews follow nothing (true); though both are readers of the Scripture. Even thus spoke those who know not. Allah will judge between them on the Day of Resurrection concerning that wherein they differed.

---

[50]Zakah in Arabic. See note 41.

114. And who does greater wrong than he who forbids the approach to mosques of Allah lest His name should be mentioned therein, and strives for their ruin? As for such, it was never meant that they should enter them except in fear. Theirs in the world is ignominy and theirs in the Hereafter is an awful doom.

115. Unto Allah belong the East and the West, so wherever you turn, there is Allah's countenance. Lo! Allah is All Embracing, All Knowing.

116. And they say: Allah has taken unto Himself a Son. Be He glorified! Nay, but whatsoever is in the heavens and the earth is His. All are subservient unto Him.

117. The Originator of the heavens and the earth! When He decrees a thing, He says unto it only: Be! and it is.

118. And those who have no knowledge say: Why does not Allah speak unto us, or some sign come unto us? Even thus, as they now speak, spoke those (who were) before them. Their hearts are all alike. We have made clear the revelations for people who are sure.

119. Lo! We have sent you (O Muhammad) with the truth, a bringer of glad tidings and a warner. And you will not be asked about the owners of hellfire.

120. And Jews will not be pleased with you, nor will Christians, till you follow their creed. Say: Lo! the guidance of Allah (Himself) is the Guidance. And if you should follow their desires after the knowledge which has come unto you, then would you have from Allah no protecting friend nor helper.

121. Those unto whom We have given the Scripture, who read it with the right reading, those believe in it. And who disbelieves in it, those are they who are losers.

١١٤ وَمَنْ أَظْلَمُ مِمَّن مَّنَعَ مَسَاجِدَ ٱللَّهِ أَن يُذْكَرَ فِيهَا ٱسْمُهُ وَسَعَىٰ فِى خَرَابِهَآ أُوْلَـٰٓئِكَ مَا كَانَ لَهُمْ أَن يَدْخُلُوهَآ إِلَّا خَآئِفِينَ لَهُمْ فِى ٱلدُّنْيَا خِزْىٌ وَلَهُمْ فِى ٱلْأَخِرَةِ عَذَابٌ عَظِيمٌ

١١٥ وَلِلَّهِ ٱلْمَشْرِقُ وَٱلْمَغْرِبُ فَأَيْنَمَا تُوَلُّوا فَثَمَّ وَجْهُ ٱللَّهِ إِنَّ ٱللَّهَ وَٰسِعٌ عَلِيمٌ

١١٦ وَقَالُوا ٱتَّخَذَ ٱللَّهُ وَلَدًا سُبْحَـٰنَهُۥ بَل لَّهُۥ مَا فِى ٱلسَّمَٰوَٰتِ وَٱلْأَرْضِ كُلٌّ لَّهُۥ قَٰنِتُونَ

١١٧ بَدِيعُ ٱلسَّمَٰوَٰتِ وَٱلْأَرْضِ وَإِذَا قَضَىٰٓ أَمْرًا فَإِنَّمَا يَقُولُ لَهُۥ كُن فَيَكُونُ

١١٨ وَقَالَ ٱلَّذِينَ لَا يَعْلَمُونَ لَوْلَا يُكَلِّمُنَا ٱللَّهُ أَوْ تَأْتِينَآ ءَايَةٌ كَذَٰلِكَ قَالَ ٱلَّذِينَ مِن قَبْلِهِم مِّثْلَ قَوْلِهِمْ تَشَٰبَهَتْ قُلُوبُهُمْ قَدْ بَيَّنَّا ٱلْأَيَٰتِ لِقَوْمٍ يُوقِنُونَ

١١٩ إِنَّآ أَرْسَلْنَٰكَ بِٱلْحَقِّ بَشِيرًا وَنَذِيرًا وَلَا تُسْـَٔلُ عَنْ أَصْحَٰبِ ٱلْجَحِيمِ

١٢٠ وَلَن تَرْضَىٰ عَنكَ ٱلْيَهُودُ وَلَا ٱلنَّصَٰرَىٰ حَتَّىٰ تَتَّبِعَ مِلَّتَهُمْ قُلْ إِنَّ هُدَى ٱللَّهِ هُوَ ٱلْهُدَىٰ وَلَئِنِ ٱتَّبَعْتَ أَهْوَآءَهُم بَعْدَ ٱلَّذِى جَآءَكَ مِنَ ٱلْعِلْمِ مَا لَكَ مِنَ ٱللَّهِ مِن وَلِىٍّ وَلَا نَصِيرٍ

١٢١ ٱلَّذِينَ ءَاتَيْنَٰهُمُ ٱلْكِتَٰبَ يَتْلُونَهُۥ حَقَّ تِلَاوَتِهِۦٓ أُوْلَـٰٓئِكَ يُؤْمِنُونَ بِهِۦ وَمَن يَكْفُرْ بِهِۦ فَأُوْلَـٰٓئِكَ هُمُ ٱلْخَٰسِرُونَ

122. O Children of Israel! Remember My favor wherewith I favored you and how I preferred you to (all) the worlds.

123. And guard (yourselves) against a day when no soul will in anything avail another, nor will compensation be accepted from it, nor will intercession be of use to it; nor will they be helped.

124. And (remember) when his Lord tried Abraham with some words, and he fulfilled them, He said: Lo! I have appointed you a leader for mankind. (Abraham) said: And of my offspring (will there be leaders)? He said: My covenant includes not wrongdoers.

125. And when We made the House (at Makkah) a resort for mankind and a sanctuary, (saying): Take as your place of worship the place where Abraham stood (to pray). And We imposed a duty upon Abraham and Ishmael, (saying): Purify My house for those who go around and those who meditate therein and those who bow down and prostrate themselves (in worship).

126. And when Abraham prayed: My Lord! Make this a region of security and bestow upon its people fruits, such of them as believe in Allah and the Last Day, He answered: As for him who disbelieves, I shall leave him in contentment for a while, then I shall compel him to the doom of fire, a hapless journey's end!

127. And when Abraham and Ishmael were raising the foundations of the House, (praying): Our Lord! Accept from us (this duty). Lo! You, only You, are the Hearer, the Knower.

128. Our Lord! And make us submissive unto You and of our seed a nation submissive unto You, and show us our rites, and relent toward us. Lo! You, only You, are the Relenting, the Merciful.

١٢٢ يَـٰبَنِىٓ إِسْرَٰٓءِيلَ ٱذْكُرُوا۟ نِعْمَتِىَ ٱلَّتِىٓ أَنْعَمْتُ عَلَيْكُمْ وَأَنِّى فَضَّلْتُكُمْ عَلَى ٱلْعَٰلَمِينَ

١٢٣ وَٱتَّقُوا۟ يَوْمًا لَّا تَجْزِى نَفْسٌ عَن نَّفْسٍ شَيْـًٔا وَلَا يُقْبَلُ مِنْهَا عَدْلٌ وَلَا تَنفَعُهَا شَفَٰعَةٌ وَلَا هُمْ يُنصَرُونَ

١٢٤ ۞ وَإِذِ ٱبْتَلَىٰٓ إِبْرَٰهِـۧمَ رَبُّهُۥ بِكَلِمَٰتٍ فَأَتَمَّهُنَّ قَالَ إِنِّى جَاعِلُكَ لِلنَّاسِ إِمَامًا قَالَ وَمِن ذُرِّيَّتِى قَالَ لَا يَنَالُ عَهْدِى ٱلظَّٰلِمِينَ

١٢٥ وَإِذْ جَعَلْنَا ٱلْبَيْتَ مَثَابَةً لِّلنَّاسِ وَأَمْنًا وَٱتَّخِذُوا۟ مِن مَّقَامِ إِبْرَٰهِـۧمَ مُصَلًّى وَعَهِدْنَآ إِلَىٰٓ إِبْرَٰهِـۧمَ وَإِسْمَٰعِيلَ أَن طَهِّرَا بَيْتِىَ لِلطَّآئِفِينَ وَٱلْعَٰكِفِينَ وَٱلرُّكَّعِ ٱلسُّجُودِ

١٢٦ وَإِذْ قَالَ إِبْرَٰهِـۧمُ رَبِّ ٱجْعَلْ هَٰذَا بَلَدًا ءَامِنًا وَٱرْزُقْ أَهْلَهُۥ مِنَ ٱلثَّمَرَٰتِ مَنْ ءَامَنَ مِنْهُم بِٱللَّهِ وَٱلْيَوْمِ ٱلْءَاخِرِ قَالَ وَمَن كَفَرَ فَأُمَتِّعُهُۥ قَلِيلًا ثُمَّ أَضْطَرُّهُۥٓ إِلَىٰ عَذَابِ ٱلنَّارِ وَبِئْسَ ٱلْمَصِيرُ

١٢٧ وَإِذْ يَرْفَعُ إِبْرَٰهِـۧمُ ٱلْقَوَاعِدَ مِنَ ٱلْبَيْتِ وَإِسْمَٰعِيلُ رَبَّنَا تَقَبَّلْ مِنَّآ إِنَّكَ أَنتَ ٱلسَّمِيعُ ٱلْعَلِيمُ

١٢٨ رَبَّنَا وَٱجْعَلْنَا مُسْلِمَيْنِ لَكَ وَمِن ذُرِّيَّتِنَآ أُمَّةً مُّسْلِمَةً لَّكَ وَأَرِنَا مَنَاسِكَنَا وَتُبْ عَلَيْنَآ إِنَّكَ أَنتَ ٱلتَّوَّابُ ٱلرَّحِيمُ

129. Our Lord! And raise up in their midst a Messenger from among them who shall recite unto them Your revelations, and shall instruct them in the Scripture and in wisdom and shall make them pure. Lo! You, only You, are the Mighty, the Wise.

130. And who forsakes the religion of Abraham save him who befools himself? Surely We chose him in the world, and lo! in the Hereafter he is among the righteous ones.

131. When his Lord said unto him: Surrender! he said: I have surrendered to the Lord of the Worlds.

132. The same did Abraham enjoin upon his sons, and also Jacob, (saying): O my sons! Lo! Allah has chosen for you the (true) religion; therefore die not save as men who have surrendered (unto Him).

133. Or were you witnesses when death came to Jacob, when he said unto his sons: What will you worship after me? They said: We shall worship your God, the God of your fathers, Abraham, Ishmael and Isaac, One God, and unto Him we have surrendered.

134. Those are a people who have passed away. Theirs is that which they earned, and yours is that which you earn. And you will not be asked of what they used to do.

135. And they say: Be Jews or Christians, then you will be rightly guided. Say (unto them, O Muhammad): Nay, but (we follow) the religion of Abraham, the upright, and he was not of the idolaters.

136. Say: We believe in Allah and that which is revealed unto Us and that which was revealed unto Abraham, and Ishmael, and Isaac, and Jacob. and the tribes, and that which Moses and Jesus received, and that which the Prophets received from their Lord. We make no distinction between any of them, and unto Him we have surrendered.

١٢٩ رَبَّنَا وَابۡعَثۡ فِيهِمۡ رَسُولًا مِّنۡهُمۡ يَتۡلُوا عَلَيۡهِمۡ ءَايَٰتِكَ وَيُعَلِّمُهُمُ الۡكِتَٰبَ وَالۡحِكۡمَةَ وَيُزَكِّيهِمۡ إِنَّكَ أَنتَ الۡعَزِيزُ الۡحَكِيمُ

١٣٠ وَمَن يَرۡغَبُ عَن مِّلَّةِ إِبۡرَٰهِۦمَ إِلَّا مَن سَفِهَ نَفۡسَهُ وَلَقَدِ اصۡطَفَيۡنَٰهُ فِي الدُّنۡيَا وَإِنَّهُ فِي الۡءَاخِرَةِ لَمِنَ الصَّٰلِحِينَ

١٣١ إِذۡ قَالَ لَهُ رَبُّهُ أَسۡلِمۡ قَالَ أَسۡلَمۡتُ لِرَبِّ الۡعَٰلَمِينَ

١٣٢ وَوَصَّىٰ بِهَا إِبۡرَٰهِۦمُ بَنِيهِ وَيَعۡقُوبُ يَٰبَنِيَّ إِنَّ اللَّهَ اصۡطَفَىٰ لَكُمُ الدِّينَ فَلَا تَمُوتُنَّ إِلَّا وَأَنتُم مُّسۡلِمُونَ

١٣٣ أَمۡ كُنتُمۡ شُهَدَاءَ إِذۡ حَضَرَ يَعۡقُوبَ الۡمَوۡتُ إِذۡ قَالَ لِبَنِيهِ مَا تَعۡبُدُونَ مِنۢ بَعۡدِي قَالُوا نَعۡبُدُ إِلَٰهَكَ وَإِلَٰهَ ءَابَائِكَ إِبۡرَٰهِۦمَ وَإِسۡمَٰعِيلَ وَإِسۡحَٰقَ إِلَٰهًا وَٰحِدًا وَنَحۡنُ لَهُ مُسۡلِمُونَ

١٣٤ تِلۡكَ أُمَّةٌ قَدۡ خَلَتۡ لَهَا مَا كَسَبَتۡ وَلَكُم مَّا كَسَبۡتُمۡ وَلَا تُسۡئَلُونَ عَمَّا كَانُوا يَعۡمَلُونَ

١٣٥ وَقَالُوا كُونُوا هُودًا أَوۡ نَصَٰرَىٰ تَهۡتَدُوا قُلۡ بَلۡ مِلَّةَ إِبۡرَٰهِۦمَ حَنِيفًا وَمَا كَانَ مِنَ الۡمُشۡرِكِينَ

١٣٦ قُولُوا ءَامَنَّا بِاللَّهِ وَمَا أُنزِلَ إِلَيۡنَا وَمَا أُنزِلَ إِلَىٰ إِبۡرَٰهِۦمَ وَإِسۡمَٰعِيلَ وَإِسۡحَٰقَ وَيَعۡقُوبَ وَالۡأَسۡبَاطِ وَمَا أُوتِيَ مُوسَىٰ وَعِيسَىٰ وَمَا أُوتِيَ النَّبِيُّونَ مِن رَّبِّهِمۡ لَا نُفَرِّقُ بَيۡنَ أَحَدٍ مِّنۡهُمۡ وَنَحۡنُ لَهُ مُسۡلِمُونَ

137. And if they believe in the like of that which you believe, then are they rightly guided. But if they turn away, then are they in schism, and Allah will suffice you (for defense) against them. And He is the Hearer, the Knower.

138. Our religion takes its hue from Allah, and who can give a better hue than Allah. And We are His worshippers.

139. Say (unto the People of the Scripture): Dispute you with us concerning Allah when He is our Lord and your Lord? Ours are our works and yours your works. and We are sincere (in our faith) in Him.

140. Or say you that Abraham, and Ishmael, and Isaac, and Jacob, and the tribes were Jews or Christians? Say: Do you know best, or does Allah? And who is more unjust than he who hides a testimony which he has received from Allah? Allah is not unaware of what you do.

141. Those are a people who have passed away; theirs is that which they earned and yours is that which you earn. And you will not be asked of what they used to do.

142. The foolish among the people will say: What has turned them from the *qiblah*[51] which they formerly observed? Say: Unto Allah belong the East and the West. He guides whom He will unto a straight path.

143. Thus We have appointed you a middle nation, that you may be witnesses over mankind. and that the Messenger may be a witness over you. And We appointed the *qiblah* which you formerly observed only that We might know him who follows the Messenger, from him who turns on his heels. In truth it was a hard (test) save for those whom Allah guided. But it was not Allah's purpose that your faith should be in vain, for Allah is full of pity, Merciful toward mankind.

(١٣٧) فَإِنْ ءَامَنُوا بِمِثْلِ مَاۤ ءَامَنتُم بِهِۦ فَقَدِ اهْتَدَواۡ وَّإِن تَوَلَّوْاْ فَإِنَّمَا هُمْ فِى شِقَاقٍ فَسَيَكْفِيكَهُمُ اللّٰهُ وَهُوَ السَّمِيعُ الْعَلِيمُ

(١٣٨) صِبْغَةَ اللّٰهِ وَمَنْ أَحْسَنُ مِنَ اللّٰهِ صِبْغَةً وَنَحْنُ لَهُۥ عَبِدُونَ

(١٣٩) قُلْ أَتُحَآجُّونَنَا فِى اللّٰهِ وَهُوَ رَبُّنَا وَرَبُّكُمْ وَلَنَآ أَعْمَلُنَا وَلَكُمْ أَعْمَلُكُمْ وَنَحْنُ لَهُۥ مُخْلِصُونَ

(١٤٠) أَمْ تَقُولُونَ إِنَّ إِبْرَهِۦمَ وَإِسْمَعِيلَ وَإِسْحَقَ وَيَعْقُوبَ وَالْأَسْبَاطَ كَانُوا هُودًا أَوْ نَصَرَىٰ قُلْ ءَأَنتُمْ أَعْلَمُ أَمِ اللّٰهُ وَمَنْ أَظْلَمُ مِمَّن كَتَمَ شَهَدَةً عِندَهُۥ مِنَ اللّٰهِ وَمَا اللّٰهُ بِغَفِلٍ عَمَّا تَعْمَلُونَ

(١٤١) تِلْكَ أُمَّةٌ قَدْ خَلَتْ لَهَا مَا كَسَبَتْ وَلَكُم مَّا كَسَبْتُمْ وَلَا تُسْـَٔلُونَ عَمَّا كَانُوا يَعْمَلُونَ

(١٤٢) سَيَقُولُ السُّفَهَآءُ مِنَ النَّاسِ مَا وَلَّىٰهُمْ عَن قِبْلَتِهِمُ الَّتِى كَانُوا عَلَيْهَا قُل لِّلّٰهِ الْمَشْرِقُ وَالْمَغْرِبُ يَهْدِى مَن يَشَآءُ إِلَىٰ صِرَٰطٍ مُّسْتَقِيمٍ

(١٤٣) وَكَذَلِكَ جَعَلْنَكُمْ أُمَّةً وَسَطًا لِّتَكُونُواْ شُهَدَآءَ عَلَى النَّاسِ وَيَكُونَ الرَّسُولُ عَلَيْكُمْ شَهِيدًا وَمَا جَعَلْنَا الْقِبْلَةَ الَّتِى كُنتَ عَلَيْهَا إِلَّا لِنَعْلَمَ مَن يَتَّبِعُ الرَّسُولَ مِمَّن يَنقَلِبُ عَلَىٰ عَقِبَيْهِ وَإِن كَانَتْ لَكَبِيرَةً إِلَّا عَلَى الَّذِينَ هَدَى اللّٰهُ وَمَا كَانَ اللّٰهُ لِيُضِيعَ إِيمَنَكُمْ إِنَّ اللّٰهَ بِالنَّاسِ لَرَءُوفٌ رَّحِيمٌ

---

[51]i.e., the place towards which the face is turned at prayer. The first *qiblah* for the Muslims was Jerusalem, which gave rise to a misunderstanding on the part of the Jews of al Madinah, who wished to draw the Muslims into Judaism. This was the cause of the Prophet's anxiety mentioned in the next verse.

144. We have seen the turning of your face to heaven (for guidance, O Muhammad). And now surely We shall make you turn (in prayer) toward a *qiblah* that satisfies you. So turn your face toward the Sacred Mosque[52] (in Makkah), and you (O Muslims), wheresoever you may be, turn your faces (when you pray) toward it. Lo! those who have received the Scripture know that (this Revelation) is the Truth from their Lord. And Allah is not unaware of what they do.

145. And even if you bring unto those who have re-ceived the Scripture all kinds of portents, they would not follow your *qiblah*, nor can you be a follower of their *qib-lah*; nor are some of them followers of the *qiblah* of others. And if you should follow their desires after the knowledge which has come unto you, then surely were you of the evildoers.

146. Those unto whom We gave the Scripture recognize (this revelation) as they recognize their children. But lo! a party of them knowingly conceal the truth.

147. It is the Truth from your Lord (O Muhammad), so be not you of those who waver.

148. And each one has a goal toward which he turns; so vie with one another in good works. Wheresoever you may be, Allah will bring you all together. Lo! Allah is Able to do all things.

149. And whencesoever you come forth (for prayer, O Muhammad) turn your face toward the Sacred Mosque. Lo! it is the Truth from your Lord. And Allah is not unaware of what you do.

150. Whencesoever you come forth turn your face to-ward the Sacred Mosque; and wheresoever you may be (O Mus-lims) turn your faces toward it (when you pray) so that men may have no argument against you, save such of them as do injustice—Fear them not, but fear Me—so that I may complete My grace upon you, and that you may be guided.

١٤٤ قَدْ نَرَىٰ تَقَلُّبَ وَجْهِكَ فِى السَّمَاءِ فَلَنُوَلِّيَنَّكَ قِبْلَةً تَرْضَاهَا فَوَلِّ وَجْهَكَ شَطْرَ الْمَسْجِدِ الْحَرَامِ وَحَيْثُ مَا كُنتُمْ فَوَلُّوا وُجُوهَكُمْ شَطْرَهُ وَإِنَّ الَّذِينَ أُوتُوا الْكِتَابَ لَيَعْلَمُونَ أَنَّهُ الْحَقُّ مِن رَّبِّهِمْ وَمَا اللَّهُ بِغَافِلٍ عَمَّا يَعْمَلُونَ

١٤٥ وَلَئِنْ أَتَيْتَ الَّذِينَ أُوتُوا الْكِتَابَ بِكُلِّ ءَايَةٍ مَّا تَبِعُوا قِبْلَتَكَ وَمَا أَنتَ بِتَابِعٍ قِبْلَتَهُمْ وَمَا بَعْضُهُم بِتَابِعٍ قِبْلَةَ بَعْضٍ وَلَئِنِ اتَّبَعْتَ أَهْوَاءَهُم مِّنْ بَعْدِ مَا جَاءَكَ مِنَ الْعِلْمِ إِنَّكَ إِذًا لَّمِنَ الظَّالِمِينَ

١٤٦ الَّذِينَ ءَاتَيْنَاهُمُ الْكِتَابَ يَعْرِفُونَهُ كَمَا يَعْرِفُونَ أَبْنَاءَهُمْ وَإِنَّ فَرِيقًا مِّنْهُمْ لَيَكْتُمُونَ الْحَقَّ وَهُمْ يَعْلَمُونَ

١٤٧ الْحَقُّ مِن رَّبِّكَ فَلَا تَكُونَنَّ مِنَ الْمُمْتَرِينَ

١٤٨ وَلِكُلٍّ وِجْهَةٌ هُوَ مُوَلِّيهَا فَاسْتَبِقُوا الْخَيْرَاتِ أَيْنَ مَا تَكُونُوا يَأْتِ بِكُمُ اللَّهُ جَمِيعًا إِنَّ اللَّهَ عَلَىٰ كُلِّ شَيْءٍ قَدِيرٌ

١٤٩ وَمِنْ حَيْثُ خَرَجْتَ فَوَلِّ وَجْهَكَ شَطْرَ الْمَسْجِدِ الْحَرَامِ وَإِنَّهُ لَلْحَقُّ مِن رَّبِّكَ وَمَا اللَّهُ بِغَافِلٍ عَمَّا تَعْمَلُونَ

١٥٠ وَمِنْ حَيْثُ خَرَجْتَ فَوَلِّ وَجْهَكَ شَطْرَ الْمَسْجِدِ الْحَرَامِ وَحَيْثُ مَا كُنتُمْ فَوَلُّوا وُجُوهَكُمْ شَطْرَهُ لِئَلَّا يَكُونَ لِلنَّاسِ عَلَيْكُمْ حُجَّةٌ إِلَّا الَّذِينَ ظَلَمُوا مِنْهُمْ فَلَا تَخْشَوْهُمْ وَاخْشَوْنِي وَلِأُتِمَّ نِعْمَتِي عَلَيْكُمْ وَلَعَلَّكُمْ تَهْتَدُونَ

---

[52]The Ka'bah at Makkah.

151. Even as We have sent unto you a Messenger from among you, who recites unto you Our revelations and purifies you, and teaches you the Scripture and wisdom, and teaches you that which you knew not.[53]

١٥١﴿ كَمَا أَرْسَلْنَا فِيكُمْ رَسُولًا مِنكُمْ يَتْلُوا عَلَيْكُمْ ءَايَٰتِنَا وَيُزَكِّيكُمْ وَيُعَلِّمُكُمُ ٱلْكِتَٰبَ وَٱلْحِكْمَةَ وَيُعَلِّمُكُم مَّا لَمْ تَكُونُوا تَعْلَمُونَ

152. Therefore remember Me, I will remember you. Give thanks to Me, and reject not Me.

١٥٢﴿ فَٱذْكُرُونِىٓ أَذْكُرْكُمْ وَٱشْكُرُوا لِى وَلَا تَكْفُرُونِ

153. O you who believe! Seek help in steadfastness, and prayer. Lo! Allah is with the steadfast.

١٥٣﴿ يَٰٓأَيُّهَا ٱلَّذِينَ ءَامَنُوا ٱسْتَعِينُوا بِٱلصَّبْرِ وَٱلصَّلَوٰةِ إِنَّ ٱللَّهَ مَعَ ٱلصَّٰبِرِينَ

154. And call not those who are slain in the way of Allah "dead." Nay, they are living, only you perceive not.

١٥٤﴿ وَلَا تَقُولُوا لِمَن يُقْتَلُ فِى سَبِيلِ ٱللَّهِ أَمْوَٰتٌ بَلْ أَحْيَآءٌ وَلَٰكِن لَّا تَشْعُرُونَ

155. And surely We shall try you with something of fear and hunger, and loss of wealth and lives and crops; but give glad tidings to the steadfast,

١٥٥﴿ وَلَنَبْلُوَنَّكُم بِشَىْءٍ مِّنَ ٱلْخَوْفِ وَٱلْجُوعِ وَنَقْصٍ مِّنَ ٱلْأَمْوَٰلِ وَٱلْأَنفُسِ وَٱلثَّمَرَٰتِ وَبَشِّرِ ٱلصَّٰبِرِينَ

156. Who say, when a misfortune strikes them: Lo! we are Allah's and Lo! unto Him we are returning.

١٥٦﴿ ٱلَّذِينَ إِذَآ أَصَٰبَتْهُم مُّصِيبَةٌ قَالُوٓا إِنَّا لِلَّهِ وَإِنَّآ إِلَيْهِ رَٰجِعُونَ

157. Such are they on whom are blessings from their Lord, and mercy. And such are they who are rightly guided.

١٥٧﴿ أُولَٰٓئِكَ عَلَيْهِمْ صَلَوَٰتٌ مِّن رَّبِّهِمْ وَرَحْمَةٌ وَأُولَٰٓئِكَ هُمُ ٱلْمُهْتَدُونَ

158. Lo! (the hills) al Ṣafā and al Marwah are among the rites of Allah. It is therefore no sin for him who is on pilgrimage to the House (of Allah) or visits it, to go around them. And he who does good of his own accord (for him), Lo! Allah is Responsive, Aware.

١٥٨﴿ ۞ إِنَّ ٱلصَّفَا وَٱلْمَرْوَةَ مِن شَعَآئِرِ ٱللَّهِ فَمَنْ حَجَّ ٱلْبَيْتَ أَوِ ٱعْتَمَرَ فَلَا جُنَاحَ عَلَيْهِ أَن يَطَّوَّفَ بِهِمَا وَمَن تَطَوَّعَ خَيْرًا فَإِنَّ ٱللَّهَ شَاكِرٌ عَلِيمٌ

159. Those who hide the proofs and the guidance which We revealed, after We had made it clear in the Scripture: such are accursed of Allah and are accursed of those who have the power to curse.

١٥٩﴿ إِنَّ ٱلَّذِينَ يَكْتُمُونَ مَآ أَنزَلْنَا مِنَ ٱلْبَيِّنَٰتِ وَٱلْهُدَىٰ مِنۢ بَعْدِ مَا بَيَّنَّٰهُ لِلنَّاسِ فِى ٱلْكِتَٰبِ أُولَٰٓئِكَ يَلْعَنُهُمُ ٱللَّهُ وَيَلْعَنُهُمُ ٱللَّٰعِنُونَ

160. Except such of them as repent and amend and make manifest (the truth). These it is toward whom I relent. I am the Relenting, the Merciful.

١٦٠﴿ إِلَّا ٱلَّذِينَ تَابُوا وَأَصْلَحُوا وَبَيَّنُوا فَأُولَٰٓئِكَ أَتُوبُ عَلَيْهِمْ وَأَنَا ٱلتَّوَّابُ ٱلرَّحِيمُ

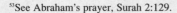

[53]See Abraham's prayer, Surah 2:129.

161. Lo! those who disbelieve, and die while they are disbelievers; on them is the curse of Allah and of angels and of men combined.

162. They ever dwell therein. The doom will not be lightened for them, neither will they be reprieved.

163. Your God is One God; there is no God save Him, the Beneficent, the Merciful.

164. Lo! in the creation of the heavens and the earth, and the difference of night and day, and the ships which run upon the sea with that which is of use to men, and the water which Allah sends down from the sky, thereby reviving the earth after its death, and dispersing all kinds of beasts therein, and (in) the ordinance of the winds, and the clouds obedient between heaven and earth: are signs (of Allah's sovereignty) for people who have sense.

165. Yet of mankind are some who take unto themselves (objects of worship which they set as) rivals to Allah, loving them with a love like (that which is the due) of Allah (only) —Those who believe are stauncher in their love for Allah—that those who do evil had but known, (on the day) when they behold the doom, that power belongs wholly to Allah, and that Allah is severe in punishment!

166. (On the day) when those who were followed disown those who followed (them), and they behold the doom, and all their aims collapse with them.

167. And those who were but followers will say: If a return were possible for us, we would disown them even as they have disowned us. Thus will Allah show them their own deeds as anguish for them, and they will not emerge from the Fire.

168. O mankind! Eat of that which is lawful and wholesome in the earth, and follow not the footsteps of the devil. Lo! he is an open enemy for you.

١٦١ إِنَّ الَّذِينَ كَفَرُوا وَمَاتُوا وَهُمْ كُفَّارٌ أُوْلَئِكَ عَلَيْهِمْ لَعْنَةُ اللَّهِ وَالْمَلَائِكَةِ وَالنَّاسِ أَجْمَعِينَ

١٦٢ خَالِدِينَ فِيهَا لَا يُخَفَّفُ عَنْهُمُ الْعَذَابُ وَلَا هُمْ يُنْظَرُونَ

١٦٣ وَإِلَهُكُمْ إِلَهٌ وَاحِدٌ لَا إِلَهَ إِلَّا هُوَ الرَّحْمَنُ الرَّحِيمُ

١٦٤ إِنَّ فِي خَلْقِ السَّمَاوَاتِ وَالْأَرْضِ وَاخْتِلَافِ اللَّيْلِ وَالنَّهَارِ وَالْفُلْكِ الَّتِي تَجْرِي فِي الْبَحْرِ بِمَا يَنْفَعُ النَّاسَ وَمَا أَنْزَلَ اللَّهُ مِنَ السَّمَاءِ مِنْ مَاءٍ فَأَحْيَا بِهِ الْأَرْضَ بَعْدَ مَوْتِهَا وَبَثَّ فِيهَا مِنْ كُلِّ دَابَّةٍ وَتَصْرِيفِ الرِّيَاحِ وَالسَّحَابِ الْمُسَخَّرِ بَيْنَ السَّمَاءِ وَالْأَرْضِ لَآيَاتٍ لِقَوْمٍ يَعْقِلُونَ

١٦٥ وَمِنَ النَّاسِ مَنْ يَتَّخِذُ مِنْ دُونِ اللَّهِ أَنْدَادًا يُحِبُّونَهُمْ كَحُبِّ اللَّهِ وَالَّذِينَ آمَنُوا أَشَدُّ حُبًّا لِلَّهِ وَلَوْ يَرَى الَّذِينَ ظَلَمُوا إِذْ يَرَوْنَ الْعَذَابَ أَنَّ الْقُوَّةَ لِلَّهِ جَمِيعًا وَأَنَّ اللَّهَ شَدِيدُ الْعَذَابِ

١٦٦ إِذْ تَبَرَّأَ الَّذِينَ اتُّبِعُوا مِنَ الَّذِينَ اتَّبَعُوا وَرَأَوُا الْعَذَابَ وَتَقَطَّعَتْ بِهِمُ الْأَسْبَابُ

١٦٧ وَقَالَ الَّذِينَ اتَّبَعُوا لَوْ أَنَّ لَنَا كَرَّةً فَنَتَبَرَّأَ مِنْهُمْ كَمَا تَبَرَّءُوا مِنَّا كَذَلِكَ يُرِيهِمُ اللَّهُ أَعْمَالَهُمْ حَسَرَاتٍ عَلَيْهِمْ وَمَا هُمْ بِخَارِجِينَ مِنَ النَّارِ

١٦٨ يَا أَيُّهَا النَّاسُ كُلُوا مِمَّا فِي الْأَرْضِ حَلَالًا طَيِّبًا وَلَا تَتَّبِعُوا خُطُوَاتِ الشَّيْطَانِ إِنَّهُ لَكُمْ عَدُوٌّ مُبِينٌ

169. He enjoins upon you only the evil and the foul, and that you should tell concerning Allah that which you know not.

170. And when it is said unto them: Follow that which Allah has revealed, they say: We follow that wherein we found our fathers. What! Even though their fathers were wholly unintelligent and had no guidance?

171. The likeness of those who disbelieve (in relation to the Messenger) is as the likeness of one who calls unto that which hears nothing except a shout and a cry. Deaf, dumb, blind, therefore they have no sense.

172. O you who believe! Eat of the good things wherewith We have provided you, and render thanks to Allah if it is (indeed) He whom you worship.

173. He has forbidden you only carrion, and blood, and swineflesh, and that which has been immolated to (the name of) any other than Allah. But he who is driven by necessity, neither craving nor transgressing, it is no sin for him. Lo! Allah is Forgiving, Merciful.

174. Lo! those who hide anything of the Scripture which Allah has revealed, and purchase a small gain therewith, they eat into their bellies nothing else than fire. And Allah will not speak to them on the Day of Resurrection, nor will He make them pure. Theirs will be a painful doom.

175. Those are they who purchase error at the price of gui-dance, and torment at the price of pardon. How constant are they in their strife to reach the Fire!

176. That is because Allah has revealed the Scripture with the truth. Lo! those who find (a cause of) disagreement in the Scripture are in open schism.

﴿١٦٩﴾ إِنَّمَا يَأْمُرُكُم بِالسُّوٓءِ وَالْفَحْشَآءِ وَأَن تَقُولُوا۟ عَلَى اللَّهِ مَا لَا تَعْلَمُونَ

﴿١٧٠﴾ وَإِذَا قِيلَ لَهُمُ اتَّبِعُوا۟ مَآ أَنزَلَ اللَّهُ قَالُوا۟ بَلْ نَتَّبِعُ مَآ أَلْفَيْنَا عَلَيْهِ ءَابَآءَنَآ أَوَلَوْ كَانَ ءَابَآؤُهُمْ لَا يَعْقِلُونَ شَيْـًٔا وَلَا يَهْتَدُونَ

﴿١٧١﴾ وَمَثَلُ الَّذِينَ كَفَرُوا۟ كَمَثَلِ الَّذِى يَنْعِقُ بِمَا لَا يَسْمَعُ إِلَّا دُعَآءً وَنِدَآءً صُمٌّۢ بُكْمٌ عُمْىٌ فَهُمْ لَا يَعْقِلُونَ

﴿١٧٢﴾ يَٰٓأَيُّهَا الَّذِينَ ءَامَنُوا۟ كُلُوا۟ مِن طَيِّبَٰتِ مَا رَزَقْنَٰكُمْ وَاشْكُرُوا۟ لِلَّهِ إِن كُنتُمْ إِيَّاهُ تَعْبُدُونَ

﴿١٧٣﴾ إِنَّمَا حَرَّمَ عَلَيْكُمُ الْمَيْتَةَ وَالدَّمَ وَلَحْمَ الْخِنزِيرِ وَمَآ أُهِلَّ بِهِۦ لِغَيْرِ اللَّهِ فَمَنِ اضْطُرَّ غَيْرَ بَاغٍ وَلَا عَادٍ فَلَآ إِثْمَ عَلَيْهِ إِنَّ اللَّهَ غَفُورٌ رَّحِيمٌ

﴿١٧٤﴾ إِنَّ الَّذِينَ يَكْتُمُونَ مَآ أَنزَلَ اللَّهُ مِنَ الْكِتَٰبِ وَيَشْتَرُونَ بِهِۦ ثَمَنًا قَلِيلًا أُو۟لَٰٓئِكَ مَا يَأْكُلُونَ فِى بُطُونِهِمْ إِلَّا النَّارَ وَلَا يُكَلِّمُهُمُ اللَّهُ يَوْمَ الْقِيَٰمَةِ وَلَا يُزَكِّيهِمْ وَلَهُمْ عَذَابٌ أَلِيمٌ

﴿١٧٥﴾ أُو۟لَٰٓئِكَ الَّذِينَ اشْتَرَوُا۟ الضَّلَٰلَةَ بِالْهُدَىٰ وَالْعَذَابَ بِالْمَغْفِرَةِ فَمَآ أَصْبَرَهُمْ عَلَى النَّارِ

﴿١٧٦﴾ ذَٰلِكَ بِأَنَّ اللَّهَ نَزَّلَ الْكِتَٰبَ بِالْحَقِّ وَإِنَّ الَّذِينَ اخْتَلَفُوا۟ فِى الْكِتَٰبِ لَفِى شِقَاقٍۭ بَعِيدٍ

177. It is not righteousness that you merely turn your faces to the East and the West; but righteous is he who believes in Allah and the Last Day and the angels and the Scripture and the Prophets; and gives wealth, for love of Him, to kinsfolk and to orphans and the needy and the wayfarer and to those who ask, and to set slaves free; and establishes prayer and pays the poor due.[54] And those who keep their treaty when they make one, and the patient in tribulation and adversity and time of stress. Such are they who are sincere. And such are the God fearing.

178. O you who believe! Retaliation is prescribed for you in the matter of the murdered ones; the freeman for the freeman, and the slave for the slave, and the female for the female. And for him who is forgiven somewhat by his (injured) brother, prosecution according to usage and payment unto him in kindness. This is an alleviation and a mercy from your Lord. He who transgresses after this will have a painful doom.

179. And there is life for you in retaliation, O men of understanding, that you may ward off (evil).

180. It is prescribed for you, when death approaches one of you, if he leave wealth, that he bequeath unto parents and near relatives in kindness. (This is) a duty for all those who ward off (evil).

181. And who changes (the will) after he has heard it—the sin thereof is only upon those who change it. For Allah is Hearer, Knower.

182. But he who fears from a testator some unjust or sinful clause, and makes peace between the parties, (it shall be) no sin for him. Lo! Allah is Forgiving, Merciful.

183. O you who believe! Fasting is prescribed for you, even as it was prescribed for those before you, that you may achieve piety;

وَلَٰكِنَّ ٱلۡبِرَّ مَنۡ ءَامَنَ بِٱللَّهِ وَٱلۡيَوۡمِ ٱلۡءَاخِرِ وَٱلۡمَلَٰٓئِكَةِ وَٱلۡكِتَٰبِ وَٱلنَّبِيِّۦنَ وَءَاتَى ٱلۡمَالَ عَلَىٰ حُبِّهِۦ ذَوِى ٱلۡقُرۡبَىٰ وَٱلۡيَتَٰمَىٰ وَٱلۡمَسَٰكِينَ وَٱبۡنَ ٱلسَّبِيلِ وَٱلسَّآئِلِينَ وَفِى ٱلرِّقَابِ وَأَقَامَ ٱلصَّلَوٰةَ وَءَاتَى ٱلزَّكَوٰةَ وَٱلۡمُوفُونَ بِعَهۡدِهِمۡ إِذَا عَٰهَدُواْ وَٱلصَّٰبِرِينَ فِى ٱلۡبَأۡسَآءِ وَٱلضَّرَّآءِ وَحِينَ ٱلۡبَأۡسِ أُوْلَٰٓئِكَ ٱلَّذِينَ صَدَقُواْ وَأُوْلَٰٓئِكَ هُمُ ٱلۡمُتَّقُونَ ﴿١٧٧﴾

يَٰٓأَيُّهَا ٱلَّذِينَ ءَامَنُواْ كُتِبَ عَلَيۡكُمُ ٱلۡقِصَاصُ فِى ٱلۡقَتۡلَى ٱلۡحُرُّ بِٱلۡحُرِّ وَٱلۡعَبۡدُ بِٱلۡعَبۡدِ وَٱلۡأُنثَىٰ بِٱلۡأُنثَىٰ فَمَنۡ عُفِىَ لَهُۥ مِنۡ أَخِيهِ شَىۡءٌ فَٱتِّبَاعٌۢ بِٱلۡمَعۡرُوفِ وَأَدَآءٌ إِلَيۡهِ بِإِحۡسَٰنٍ ذَٰلِكَ تَخۡفِيفٌ مِّن رَّبِّكُمۡ وَرَحۡمَةٌ فَمَنِ ٱعۡتَدَىٰ بَعۡدَ ذَٰلِكَ فَلَهُۥ عَذَابٌ أَلِيمٌ ﴿١٧٨﴾

وَلَكُمۡ فِى ٱلۡقِصَاصِ حَيَوٰةٌ يَٰٓأُوْلِى ٱلۡأَلۡبَٰبِ لَعَلَّكُمۡ تَتَّقُونَ ﴿١٧٩﴾

كُتِبَ عَلَيۡكُمۡ إِذَا حَضَرَ أَحَدَكُمُ ٱلۡمَوۡتُ إِن تَرَكَ خَيۡرًا ٱلۡوَصِيَّةُ لِلۡوَٰلِدَيۡنِ وَٱلۡأَقۡرَبِينَ بِٱلۡمَعۡرُوفِ حَقًّا عَلَى ٱلۡمُتَّقِينَ ﴿١٨٠﴾

فَمَنۢ بَدَّلَهُۥ بَعۡدَ مَا سَمِعَهُۥ فَإِنَّمَآ إِثۡمُهُۥ عَلَى ٱلَّذِينَ يُبَدِّلُونَهُۥٓ إِنَّ ٱللَّهَ سَمِيعٌ عَلِيمٌ ﴿١٨١﴾

فَمَنۡ خَافَ مِن مُّوصٍ جَنَفًا أَوۡ إِثۡمًا فَأَصۡلَحَ بَيۡنَهُمۡ فَلَآ إِثۡمَ عَلَيۡهِ إِنَّ ٱللَّهَ غَفُورٌ رَّحِيمٌ ﴿١٨٢﴾

يَٰٓأَيُّهَا ٱلَّذِينَ ءَامَنُواْ كُتِبَ عَلَيۡكُمُ ٱلصِّيَامُ كَمَا كُتِبَ عَلَى ٱلَّذِينَ مِن قَبۡلِكُمۡ لَعَلَّكُمۡ تَتَّقُونَ ﴿١٨٣﴾

---

[54] See verse 43, footnote.

184. (Fast) a certain number of days; and (for) him who is sick among you, or on a journey, (the same) number of other days; and for those who can afford it with hardship there is a ransom: the feeding of a man in need—But who does good of his own accord, it is better for him: and that you fast is better for you if you did but know—

185. The month of Ramadan in which was revealed the Qur'an, a guidance for mankind, and clear proofs of the guidance, and the Criterion (of right and wrong). And whoever of you is present, let him fast the month, and whoever of you is sick or on a journey, (let him fast the same) number of other days. Allah desires for you ease; He desires not hardship for you; and (He desires) that you should complete the period, and that you should magnify Allah for having guided you, and that peradventure you may be thankful.

186. And when My servants question you concerning Me, then surely I am nigh. I answer the prayer of the suppliant when he cries unto Me. So let them respond to Me and believe in Me, in order that they may be led rightfully.

187. It is made lawful for you to go unto your wives on the night of the fast. They are raiment for you and you are raiment for them. Allah is aware that you were deceiving yourselves[55] in this respect and He has turned in mercy toward you and relieved you. So hold intercourse with them and seek that which Allah has ordained for you, and eat and drink until the white thread becomes distinct to you from the black thread of the dawn. Then strictly observe the fast till nightfall and touch them not, while you are at your devotions in the mosques. These are the limits imposed by Allah, so approach them not. Thus Allah expounds His revelations to mankind that they may ward off (evil).

---

[55]Until this verse was revealed, the Muslims used to fast completely from the evening meal of one day till the evening meal of the next. If they fell asleep before they had taken their meal, they considered it their duty to abstain, with the result that men fainted and came near to death. Intercourse with their wives had been similarly restricted.

188. And eat not up your property among yourselves in vanity, nor seek by it to gain the hearing of the judges that you may knowingly devour a portion of the property of others wrongfully.

189. They ask you, (O Muhammad), of new moons. Say: They are fixed seasons for mankind and for the pilgrimage. It is not righteousness that you go to houses by the backs thereof (as do the idolaters at certain seasons), but the righteous man is he who wards off (evil). So go to houses by the gates thereof, and observe your duty to Allah, that you may be successful.

190. Fight in the way of Allah against those who fight against you, but begin not hostilities. Lo! Allah loves not aggressors.

191. And slay them wherever you find them, and drive them out of the places whence they drove you out, for persecution is worse than slaughter. And fight not with them at the Sacred Mosque until they first attack you there, but if they attack you (there) then slay them. Such is the reward of disbelievers.

192. But if they desist, then lo! Allah is Forgiving, Merciful.

193. And fight them until persecution is no more, and religion is for Allah. But if they desist, then let there be no hostility except against wrongdoers.

194. The forbidden month is for the forbidden month, and forbidden things in retaliation. And one who attacks you, attack him in like manner as he attacked you. And observe your duty to Allah, and know that Allah is with those who are pious.

195. Spend your wealth for the cause of Allah, and be not cast by your own hands to ruin; and do good. Lo! Allah loves the beneficent.

١٨٨ وَلَا تَأْكُلُوٓا أَمْوَٰلَكُم بَيْنَكُم بِٱلْبَٰطِلِ وَتُدْلُوا۟ بِهَآ إِلَى ٱلْحُكَّامِ لِتَأْكُلُوا۟ فَرِيقًا مِّنْ أَمْوَٰلِ ٱلنَّاسِ بِٱلْإِثْمِ وَأَنتُمْ تَعْلَمُونَ

١٨٩ ۞ يَسْـَٔلُونَكَ عَنِ ٱلْأَهِلَّةِ قُلْ هِىَ مَوَٰقِيتُ لِلنَّاسِ وَٱلْحَجِّ وَلَيْسَ ٱلْبِرُّ بِأَن تَأْتُوا۟ ٱلْبُيُوتَ مِن ظُهُورِهَا وَلَٰكِنَّ ٱلْبِرَّ مَنِ ٱتَّقَىٰ وَأْتُوا۟ ٱلْبُيُوتَ مِنْ أَبْوَٰبِهَا وَٱتَّقُوا۟ ٱللَّهَ لَعَلَّكُمْ تُفْلِحُونَ

١٩٠ وَقَٰتِلُوا۟ فِى سَبِيلِ ٱللَّهِ ٱلَّذِينَ يُقَٰتِلُونَكُمْ وَلَا تَعْتَدُوٓا۟ إِنَّ ٱللَّهَ لَا يُحِبُّ ٱلْمُعْتَدِينَ

١٩١ وَٱقْتُلُوهُمْ حَيْثُ ثَقِفْتُمُوهُمْ وَأَخْرِجُوهُم مِّنْ حَيْثُ أَخْرَجُوكُمْ وَٱلْفِتْنَةُ أَشَدُّ مِنَ ٱلْقَتْلِ وَلَا تُقَٰتِلُوهُمْ عِندَ ٱلْمَسْجِدِ ٱلْحَرَامِ حَتَّىٰ يُقَٰتِلُوكُمْ فِيهِ فَإِن قَٰتَلُوكُمْ فَٱقْتُلُوهُمْ كَذَٰلِكَ جَزَآءُ ٱلْكَٰفِرِينَ

١٩٢ فَإِنِ ٱنتَهَوْا۟ فَإِنَّ ٱللَّهَ غَفُورٌ رَّحِيمٌ

١٩٣ وَقَٰتِلُوهُمْ حَتَّىٰ لَا تَكُونَ فِتْنَةٌ وَيَكُونَ ٱلدِّينُ لِلَّهِ فَإِنِ ٱنتَهَوْا۟ فَلَا عُدْوَٰنَ إِلَّا عَلَى ٱلظَّٰلِمِينَ

١٩٤ ٱلشَّهْرُ ٱلْحَرَامُ بِٱلشَّهْرِ ٱلْحَرَامِ وَٱلْحُرُمَٰتُ قِصَاصٌ فَمَنِ ٱعْتَدَىٰ عَلَيْكُمْ فَٱعْتَدُوا۟ عَلَيْهِ بِمِثْلِ مَا ٱعْتَدَىٰ عَلَيْكُمْ وَٱتَّقُوا۟ ٱللَّهَ وَٱعْلَمُوٓا۟ أَنَّ ٱللَّهَ مَعَ ٱلْمُتَّقِينَ

١٩٥ وَأَنفِقُوا۟ فِى سَبِيلِ ٱللَّهِ وَلَا تُلْقُوا۟ بِأَيْدِيكُمْ إِلَى ٱلتَّهْلُكَةِ وَأَحْسِنُوٓا۟ إِنَّ ٱللَّهَ يُحِبُّ ٱلْمُحْسِنِينَ

196. Perform the pilgrimage and the visit (to Makkah) for Allah.[56] And if you are prevented, then send such gifts as can be obtained with ease, and shave not your heads until the gifts have reached their destination. And whoever among you is sick or has an ailment of the head must pay a ransom of fasting or almsgiving or offering. And if you are in safety, then whoever contents himself with the visit for the Pilgrimage (shall give) such gifts as can be had with ease. And whoever cannot find (such gifts), then a fast of three days while on the pilgrimage, and of seven when you have returned; that is, ten in all. That is for him whose folk are not present at the Sacred Mosque. Observe your duty to Allah, and know that Allah is severe in punishment.

197. The pilgrimage is (in) the well known months, and whoever is minded to perform the pilgrimage therein (let him remember that) there is (to be) no lewdness nor abuse nor angry conversation on the pilgrimage. And whatsoever good you do Allah knows it. So make provision for yourselves (hereafter); for the best provision is to ward off evil. Therefore keep your duty unto Me, O men of understanding.

198. It is no sin for you that you seek the bounty of your Lord (by trading). But, when you press on in the multitude from Arafat, remember Allah by the sacred monument. Remember Him as He has guided you, although before you were of those astray.

199. Then hasten onward from the place whence the multitude hastens onward, and ask forgiveness of Allah. Lo! Allah is Forgiving, Merciful.

200. And when you have completed your devotions, then remember Allah as you remember your fathers[57] or with a more lively remembrance. But of mankind is he who says: "Our Lord! Give unto us in the world," and he has no portion in the Hereafter.

---

[56]The visit, i.e., the 'Umrah or Lesser Pilgrimage; see also Surah 22:26-37 for more information on the Greater Pilgrimage.

[57]It was the custom of the pagan Arabs to praise their forefathers at the conclusion of the Pilgrimage.

201. And of them (also) is he who says: "Our Lord! Give unto us in the world that which is good and in the Here-after that which is good, and guard us from the doom of Fire."

202. For these there is in store a goodly portion out of that which they have earned. Allah is swift at reckoning.

203. Remember Allah through the appointed days. Then who hastens (his departure) by two days, it is no sin for him, and who delays, it is no sin for him; that is for him who has piety. Be careful of your duty to Allah, and know that unto Him you will be gathered.

204. And of mankind there is he whose conversation on the life of this world pleases you (Muhammad), and he calls Allah to witness as to that which is in his heart; yet he is the most rigid of opponents.

205. And when he turns away (from you) his effort in the land is to make mischief therein and to destroy the crops and the cattle; and Allah loves not mischief.

206. And when it is said unto him: Be careful of your duty to Allah, pride takes him to sin. Hell will settle his account, an evil resting place.

207. And of mankind is he who would sell himself, seeking the pleasure of Allah; and Allah has compassion on (His) bondmen.

208. O you who believe! Come, all of you, into submission (unto Him); and follow not the footsteps of the devil. Lo! he is an open enemy for you.

209. And if you slide back after the clear proofs have come unto you, then know that Allah is Mighty, Wise.

210. Wait they for nothing else than that Allah should come unto them in the shadows of the clouds with the angels? Then the case would be already judged. All cases go back to Allah (for judgment).

٢٠١ وَمِنْهُم مَّن يَقُولُ رَبَّنَآ ءَاتِنَا فِى ٱلدُّنْيَا حَسَنَةً وَفِى ٱلْأَخِرَةِ حَسَنَةً وَقِنَا عَذَابَ ٱلنَّارِ

٢٠٢ أُوْلَٰٓئِكَ لَهُمْ نَصِيبٌ مِّمَّا كَسَبُوا وَٱللَّهُ سَرِيعُ ٱلْحِسَابِ

٢٠٣ ۞ وَٱذْكُرُوا ٱللَّهَ فِىٓ أَيَّامٍ مَّعْدُودَٰتٍ فَمَن تَعَجَّلَ فِى يَوْمَيْنِ فَلَآ إِثْمَ عَلَيْهِ وَمَن تَأَخَّرَ فَلَآ إِثْمَ عَلَيْهِ لِمَنِ ٱتَّقَىٰ وَٱتَّقُوا ٱللَّهَ وَٱعْلَمُوٓا أَنَّكُمْ إِلَيْهِ تُحْشَرُونَ

٢٠٤ وَمِنَ ٱلنَّاسِ مَن يُعْجِبُكَ قَوْلُهُۥ فِى ٱلْحَيَوٰةِ ٱلدُّنْيَا وَيُشْهِدُ ٱللَّهَ عَلَىٰ مَا فِى قَلْبِهِۦ وَهُوَ أَلَدُّ ٱلْخِصَامِ

٢٠٥ وَإِذَا تَوَلَّىٰ سَعَىٰ فِى ٱلْأَرْضِ لِيُفْسِدَ فِيهَا وَيُهْلِكَ ٱلْحَرْثَ وَٱلنَّسْلَ وَٱللَّهُ لَا يُحِبُّ ٱلْفَسَادَ

٢٠٦ وَإِذَا قِيلَ لَهُ ٱتَّقِ ٱللَّهَ أَخَذَتْهُ ٱلْعِزَّةُ بِٱلْإِثْمِ فَحَسْبُهُۥ جَهَنَّمُ وَلَبِئْسَ ٱلْمِهَادُ

٢٠٧ وَمِنَ ٱلنَّاسِ مَن يَشْرِى نَفْسَهُ ٱبْتِغَآءَ مَرْضَاتِ ٱللَّهِ وَٱللَّهُ رَءُوفٌ بِٱلْعِبَادِ

٢٠٨ يَٰٓأَيُّهَا ٱلَّذِينَ ءَامَنُوا ٱدْخُلُوا فِى ٱلسِّلْمِ كَآفَّةً وَلَا تَتَّبِعُوا خُطُوَٰتِ ٱلشَّيْطَٰنِ إِنَّهُۥ لَكُمْ عَدُوٌّ مُّبِينٌ

٢٠٩ فَإِن زَلَلْتُم مِّنۢ بَعْدِ مَا جَآءَتْكُمُ ٱلْبَيِّنَٰتُ فَٱعْلَمُوٓا أَنَّ ٱللَّهَ عَزِيزٌ حَكِيمٌ

٢١٠ هَلْ يَنظُرُونَ إِلَّآ أَن يَأْتِيَهُمُ ٱللَّهُ فِى ظُلَلٍ مِّنَ ٱلْغَمَامِ وَٱلْمَلَٰٓئِكَةُ وَقُضِىَ ٱلْأَمْرُ وَإِلَى ٱللَّهِ تُرْجَعُ ٱلْأُمُورُ

211. Ask the Children of Israel how many a clear revelation We gave them! He who alters the grace of Allah after it has come unto him (for him), lo! Allah is severe in punishment.

سَلْ بَنِي إِسْرَآءِيلَ كَمْ ءَاتَيْنَهُم مِّنْ ءَايَةٍ بَيِّنَةٍ ۗ وَمَن يُبَدِّلْ نِعْمَةَ اللَّهِ مِنۢ بَعْدِ مَا جَآءَتْهُ فَإِنَّ اللَّهَ شَدِيدُ الْعِقَابِ ۝

212. Beautified is the life of the world for those who disbelieve; they make a jest of believers. But those who keep their duty to Allah will be above them on the Day of Resurrection. Allah gives without stint to whom He will.

زُيِّنَ لِلَّذِينَ كَفَرُوا الْحَيَوٰةُ الدُّنْيَا وَيَسْخَرُونَ مِنَ الَّذِينَ ءَامَنُوا ۘ وَالَّذِينَ اتَّقَوْا فَوْقَهُمْ يَوْمَ الْقِيَمَةِ ۗ وَاللَّهُ يَرْزُقُ مَن يَشَآءُ بِغَيْرِ حِسَابٍ ۝

213. Mankind were one community, and Allah sent (unto them) Prophets as bearers of good tidings and as warners, and revealed therewith the Scripture with the truth that it might judge between mankind concerning that wherein they differed. And only those unto whom (the Scripture) was given differed concerning it, after clear proofs had come unto them, through hatred one of another. And Allah by His will guided those who believe unto the truth of that concerning which they differed. Allah guides whom He will unto a straight path.

كَانَ النَّاسُ أُمَّةً وَاحِدَةً فَبَعَثَ اللَّهُ النَّبِيِّـنَ مُبَشِّرِينَ وَمُنذِرِينَ وَأَنزَلَ مَعَهُمُ الْكِتَبَ بِالْحَقِّ لِيَحْكُمَ بَيْنَ النَّاسِ فِيمَا اخْتَلَفُوا فِيهِ ۚ وَمَا اخْتَلَفَ فِيهِ إِلَّا الَّذِينَ أُوتُوهُ مِنۢ بَعْدِ مَا جَآءَتْهُمُ الْبَيِّنَتُ بَغْيًا بَيْنَهُمْ ۖ فَهَدَى اللَّهُ الَّذِينَ ءَامَنُوا لِمَا اخْتَلَفُوا فِيهِ مِنَ الْحَقِّ بِإِذْنِهِ ۗ وَاللَّهُ يَهْدِي مَن يَشَآءُ إِلَىٰ صِرَٰطٍ مُّسْتَقِيمٍ ۝

214. Or think you that you will enter Paradise while yet there has not come unto you the like of (that which came to) those who passed away before you? Affliction and adver-sity befell them, they were shaken as with earthquake, till the Messenger (of Allah) and those who believed along with him said: When comes Allah's help? Now surely Allah's help is near.

أَمْ حَسِبْتُمْ أَن تَدْخُلُوا الْجَنَّةَ وَلَمَّا يَأْتِكُم مَّثَلُ الَّذِينَ خَلَوْا مِن قَبْلِكُم ۖ مَّسَّتْهُمُ الْبَأْسَآءُ وَالضَّرَّآءُ وَزُلْزِلُوا حَتَّىٰ يَقُولَ الرَّسُولُ وَالَّذِينَ ءَامَنُوا مَعَهُ مَتَىٰ نَصْرُ اللَّهِ ۗ أَلَا إِنَّ نَصْرَ اللَّهِ قَرِيبٌ ۝

215. They ask you, (O Muhammad), what they shall spend. Say: That which you spend for good (must go) to parents and near kindred and orphans and the needy and the wayfarer. And whatsoever good you do, lo! Allah is Aware of it.

يَسْـَٔلُونَكَ مَاذَا يُنفِقُونَ ۖ قُلْ مَا أَنفَقْتُم مِّنْ خَيْرٍ فَلِلْوَٰلِدَيْنِ وَالْأَقْرَبِينَ وَالْيَتَمَىٰ وَالْمَسَكِينِ وَابْنِ السَّبِيلِ ۗ وَمَا تَفْعَلُوا مِنْ خَيْرٍ فَإِنَّ اللَّهَ بِهِ عَلِيمٌ ۝

216. Warfare is ordained for you, though it is hateful unto you; but it may happen that you hate a thing which is good for you, and it may happen that you love a thing which is bad for you. And Allah knows, but you know not.

217. They question you (O Muhammad) with regard to warfare in the sacred month. Say: Warfare therein is a great (transgression), but to turn (men) from the way of Allah, and to disbelieve in Him and in the Sacred Mosque, and to expel its people from it, is a greater sin with Allah; for persecution is worse than slaughter. And they will not cease from fighting against you till they have made you renegades from your religion, if they can. And who becomes a renegade and dies in his disbelief: such are they whose works have fallen both in the world and the Hereafter. And such are rightful owners of the Fire: they will abide therein forever.

218. Lo! those who believe, and those who emigrate (to escape the persecution) and strive in the way of Allah, these have hope of Allah's mercy. And Allah is Forgiving, Merciful.

219. They question you about strong drink and games of chance. Say: In both is great sin, and (some) utility for men; but the sin of them is greater than their usefulness. And they ask you what they ought to spend. Say: That which is superfluous. Thus Allah makes plain to you (the) revelations, that you may reflect

220. Upon the world and the Hereafter. And they question you concerning orphans. Say: To improve their lot is best. And if you mingle your affairs with theirs, then (they are) your brothers. And Allah knows him who spoils from him who improves. Had Allah willed He could have overburdened you. Indeed Allah is Mighty, Wise.

221. Wed not idolatresses till they believe; for lo! a believing bondwoman is better than an idolatress though she pleases you; and give not your daughters in marriage to idolaters till they believe, for lo! a believing slave is better than an idolater though he pleases you. These invite unto the Fire, and Allah invites unto the Garden, and unto forgiveness by His grace, and He expounds thus His revelations to mankind that they may remember.

222. They question you (O Muhammad) concerning menstruation. Say: It is harmful, so keep away from women at such time and go not in unto them till they are cleansed. And when they have purified themselves, then go in unto them as Allah has enjoined upon you. Truly Allah loves those who turn unto Him, and loves those who have a care for cleanness.

223. Your women are a tilth for you (to cultivate) so go to your tilth as you will, and send (good deeds) before you for your souls, and fear Allah, and know that you will (one day) meet Him. Give glad tidings to believers, (O Muhammad).

224. And make not Allah, by your oaths, a hindrance to your being right-eous and observing your duty unto Him and making peace among mankind. For Allah is Hearer, Knower.

225. Allah will not take you to task for that which is un-intentional in your oaths. But He will take you to task for that which your hearts have garnered. And Allah is Forgiving, Clement.

226. Those who forswear their wives may wait up to four months; then, if they change their mind, lo! Allah is Forgiv-ing, Merciful.

227. And if they decide upon divorce (let them remember that) Allah is Hearer, Knower.

٢٢١ وَلَا تَنكِحُوا الْمُشْرِكَاتِ حَتَّىٰ يُؤْمِنَّ وَلَأَمَةٌ مُؤْمِنَةٌ خَيْرٌ مِّن مُّشْرِكَةٍ وَلَوْ أَعْجَبَتْكُمْ وَلَا تُنكِحُوا الْمُشْرِكِينَ حَتَّىٰ يُؤْمِنُوا وَلَعَبْدٌ مُؤْمِنٌ خَيْرٌ مِّن مُّشْرِكٍ وَلَوْ أَعْجَبَكُمْ أُولَٰئِكَ يَدْعُونَ إِلَى النَّارِ وَاللَّهُ يَدْعُوا إِلَى الْجَنَّةِ وَالْمَغْفِرَةِ بِإِذْنِهِ وَيُبَيِّنُ آيَاتِهِ لِلنَّاسِ لَعَلَّهُمْ يَتَذَكَّرُونَ

٢٢٢ وَيَسْأَلُونَكَ عَنِ الْمَحِيضِ قُلْ هُوَ أَذًى فَاعْتَزِلُوا النِّسَاءَ فِي الْمَحِيضِ وَلَا تَقْرَبُوهُنَّ حَتَّىٰ يَطْهُرْنَ فَإِذَا تَطَهَّرْنَ فَأْتُوهُنَّ مِنْ حَيْثُ أَمَرَكُمُ اللَّهُ إِنَّ اللَّهَ يُحِبُّ التَّوَّابِينَ وَيُحِبُّ الْمُتَطَهِّرِينَ

٢٢٣ نِسَاؤُكُمْ حَرْثٌ لَّكُمْ فَأْتُوا حَرْثَكُمْ أَنَّىٰ شِئْتُمْ وَقَدِّمُوا لِأَنفُسِكُمْ وَاتَّقُوا اللَّهَ وَاعْلَمُوا أَنَّكُم مُّلَاقُوهُ وَبَشِّرِ الْمُؤْمِنِينَ

٢٢٤ وَلَا تَجْعَلُوا اللَّهَ عُرْضَةً لِّأَيْمَانِكُمْ أَن تَبَرُّوا وَتَتَّقُوا وَتُصْلِحُوا بَيْنَ النَّاسِ وَاللَّهُ سَمِيعٌ عَلِيمٌ

٢٢٥ لَّا يُؤَاخِذُكُمُ اللَّهُ بِاللَّغْوِ فِي أَيْمَانِكُمْ وَلَٰكِن يُؤَاخِذُكُم بِمَا كَسَبَتْ قُلُوبُكُمْ وَاللَّهُ غَفُورٌ حَلِيمٌ

٢٢٦ لِّلَّذِينَ يُؤْلُونَ مِن نِّسَائِهِمْ تَرَبُّصُ أَرْبَعَةِ أَشْهُرٍ فَإِن فَاءُوا فَإِنَّ اللَّهَ غَفُورٌ رَّحِيمٌ

٢٢٧ وَإِنْ عَزَمُوا الطَّلَاقَ فَإِنَّ اللَّهَ سَمِيعٌ عَلِيمٌ

228. Women who are divorced shall wait, keeping themselves apart, three (monthly) courses. And it is not lawful for them that they should conceal that which Allah has created in their wombs if they are believers in Allah and the Last Day. And their husbands would do better to take them back in that case if they desire a reconciliation. And they (women) have rights similar to those (of men) over them in kindness, and men are a degree above them. Allah is Mighty, Wise.

229. Divorce must be pronounced twice and then (a woman) must be retained in honor or released in kindness. And it is not lawful for you that you take from them anything of that which you have given them; except (in the case) when both arbiters fear that they may not be able to keep within the limits (imposed by) Allah. And if you fear that they may not be able to keep the limits of Allah, in that case it is no sin for either of them if the woman ransom herself. These are the limits (imposed by) Allah. Transgress them not. For who transgresses Allah's limits: such are wrongdoers.

230. And if he has divorced her (the third time), then she is not lawful unto him thereafter until she has wedded another husband. Then if he (the other husband) divorce her it is no sin for both of them that they come together again if they consider that they are able to observe the limits of Allah. These are the limits of Allah. He manifests them for people who have knowledge.

231. When you have divorced women, and they have reached their term, then retain them in kindness or release them in kindness. Retain them not to their hurt so that you transgress (the limits). He who does that has wronged his own soul. Make not the revelations of Allah a laughing stock (by your behavior), but remember Allah's grace upon you and that which He has revealed unto you of the Scripture and of wisdom, whereby He does exhort you. Observe your duty to Allah and know that Allah is Aware of all things.

٢٢٨ وَالْمُطَلَّقَاتُ يَتَرَبَّصْنَ بِأَنفُسِهِنَّ ثَلَاثَةَ قُرُوءٍ وَلَا يَحِلُّ لَهُنَّ أَن يَكْتُمْنَ مَا خَلَقَ اللَّهُ فِي أَرْحَامِهِنَّ إِن كُنَّ يُؤْمِنَّ بِاللَّهِ وَالْيَوْمِ الْآخِرِ وَبُعُولَتُهُنَّ أَحَقُّ بِرَدِّهِنَّ فِي ذَلِكَ إِنْ أَرَادُوا إِصْلَاحًا وَلَهُنَّ مِثْلُ الَّذِي عَلَيْهِنَّ بِالْمَعْرُوفِ وَلِلرِّجَالِ عَلَيْهِنَّ دَرَجَةٌ وَاللَّهُ عَزِيزٌ حَكِيمٌ

٢٢٩ الطَّلَاقُ مَرَّتَانِ فَإِمْسَاكٌ بِمَعْرُوفٍ أَوْ تَسْرِيحٌ بِإِحْسَانٍ وَلَا يَحِلُّ لَكُمْ أَن تَأْخُذُوا مِمَّا آتَيْتُمُوهُنَّ شَيْئًا إِلَّا أَن يَخَافَا أَلَّا يُقِيمَا حُدُودَ اللَّهِ فَإِنْ خِفْتُمْ أَلَّا يُقِيمَا حُدُودَ اللَّهِ فَلَا جُنَاحَ عَلَيْهِمَا فِيمَا افْتَدَتْ بِهِ تِلْكَ حُدُودُ اللَّهِ فَلَا تَعْتَدُوهَا وَمَن يَتَعَدَّ حُدُودَ اللَّهِ فَأُولَئِكَ هُمُ الظَّالِمُونَ

٢٣٠ فَإِن طَلَّقَهَا فَلَا تَحِلُّ لَهُ مِن بَعْدُ حَتَّى تَنكِحَ زَوْجًا غَيْرَهُ فَإِن طَلَّقَهَا فَلَا جُنَاحَ عَلَيْهِمَا أَن يَتَرَاجَعَا إِن ظَنَّا أَن يُقِيمَا حُدُودَ اللَّهِ وَتِلْكَ حُدُودُ اللَّهِ يُبَيِّنُهَا لِقَوْمٍ يَعْلَمُونَ

٢٣١ وَإِذَا طَلَّقْتُمُ النِّسَاءَ فَبَلَغْنَ أَجَلَهُنَّ فَأَمْسِكُوهُنَّ بِمَعْرُوفٍ أَوْ سَرِّحُوهُنَّ بِمَعْرُوفٍ وَلَا تُمْسِكُوهُنَّ ضِرَارًا لِّتَعْتَدُوا وَمَن يَفْعَلْ ذَلِكَ فَقَدْ ظَلَمَ نَفْسَهُ وَلَا تَتَّخِذُوا آيَاتِ اللَّهِ هُزُوًا وَاذْكُرُوا نِعْمَتَ اللَّهِ عَلَيْكُمْ وَمَا أَنزَلَ عَلَيْكُم مِّنَ الْكِتَابِ وَالْحِكْمَةِ يَعِظُكُم بِهِ وَاتَّقُوا اللَّهَ وَاعْلَمُوا أَنَّ اللَّهَ بِكُلِّ شَيْءٍ عَلِيمٌ

232. And when you have divorced women and they reach their term, place not difficulties in the way of their marrying their husbands if it is agreed between them in kindness. This is an admonition for him among you who believes in Allah and the Last Day. That is more virtuous for you, and cleaner. And Allah knows: while you know not.

233. Mothers shall suckle their children for two whole years; (that is) for those who wish to complete the suckling. The duty of feeding and clothing nursing mothers in a seemly manner is upon the father of the child. No soul should be charged beyond its capacity. A mother should not be made to suffer because of her child, nor should he to whom the child is born (be made to suffer) because of his child. And on the (father's) heir is incumbent the like of that (which was incumbent on the father). If they desire to wean the child by mutual consent and (after) consultation, it is no sin for them; and if you wish to give your children out to nurse, it is no sin for you, provided that you pay what is due from you in kindness. And observe your duty to Allah, and know that Allah is Seer of what you do.

234. Such of you as die and leave behind them wives, they (the wives) shall wait, keeping themselves apart, four months and ten days. And when they reach the term (prescribed for them) then there is no blame for you in anything that they may do with themselves in decency. And Allah is Informed of what you do.

235. There is no blame on you in that which you proclaim or hide in your minds concerning your pledge with women. Allah knows that you will remember them. But plight not your pledge with them except by uttering a recognized form of words. And do not consummate the marriage until (the term) prescribed is run. And know that Allah knows what is in your minds, so beware of Him; and know that Allah is Forgiving, Clement.

٢٣٢ ۞ وَإِذَا طَلَّقْتُمُ ٱلنِّسَآءَ فَبَلَغْنَ أَجَلَهُنَّ فَلَا تَعْضُلُوهُنَّ أَن يَنكِحْنَ أَزْوَٰجَهُنَّ إِذَا تَرَٰضَوْا۟ بَيْنَهُم بِٱلْمَعْرُوفِ ذَٰلِكَ يُوعَظُ بِهِۦ مَن كَانَ مِنكُمْ يُؤْمِنُ بِٱللَّهِ وَٱلْيَوْمِ ٱلْءَاخِرِ ذَٰلِكُمْ أَزْكَىٰ لَكُمْ وَأَطْهَرُ وَٱللَّهُ يَعْلَمُ وَأَنتُمْ لَا تَعْلَمُونَ

٢٣٣ وَٱلْوَٰلِدَٰتُ يُرْضِعْنَ أَوْلَٰدَهُنَّ حَوْلَيْنِ كَامِلَيْنِ لِمَنْ أَرَادَ أَن يُتِمَّ ٱلرَّضَاعَةَ وَعَلَى ٱلْمَوْلُودِ لَهُۥ رِزْقُهُنَّ وَكِسْوَتُهُنَّ بِٱلْمَعْرُوفِ لَا تُكَلَّفُ نَفْسٌ إِلَّا وُسْعَهَا لَا تُضَآرَّ وَٰلِدَةٌۢ بِوَلَدِهَا وَلَا مَوْلُودٌ لَّهُۥ بِوَلَدِهِۦ وَعَلَى ٱلْوَارِثِ مِثْلُ ذَٰلِكَ فَإِنْ أَرَادَا فِصَالًا عَن تَرَاضٍ مِّنْهُمَا وَتَشَاوُرٍ فَلَا جُنَاحَ عَلَيْهِمَا وَإِنْ أَرَدتُّمْ أَن تَسْتَرْضِعُوٓا۟ أَوْلَٰدَكُمْ فَلَا جُنَاحَ عَلَيْكُمْ إِذَا سَلَّمْتُم مَّآ ءَاتَيْتُم بِٱلْمَعْرُوفِ وَٱتَّقُوا۟ ٱللَّهَ وَٱعْلَمُوٓا۟ أَنَّ ٱللَّهَ بِمَا تَعْمَلُونَ بَصِيرٌ

٢٣٤ وَٱلَّذِينَ يُتَوَفَّوْنَ مِنكُمْ وَيَذَرُونَ أَزْوَٰجًا يَتَرَبَّصْنَ بِأَنفُسِهِنَّ أَرْبَعَةَ أَشْهُرٍ وَعَشْرًا فَإِذَا بَلَغْنَ أَجَلَهُنَّ فَلَا جُنَاحَ عَلَيْكُمْ فِيمَا فَعَلْنَ فِىٓ أَنفُسِهِنَّ بِٱلْمَعْرُوفِ وَٱللَّهُ بِمَا تَعْمَلُونَ خَبِيرٌ

٢٣٥ وَلَا جُنَاحَ عَلَيْكُمْ فِيمَا عَرَّضْتُم بِهِۦ مِنْ خِطْبَةِ ٱلنِّسَآءِ أَوْ أَكْنَنتُمْ فِىٓ أَنفُسِكُمْ عَلِمَ ٱللَّهُ أَنَّكُمْ سَتَذْكُرُونَهُنَّ وَلَٰكِن لَّا تُوَاعِدُوهُنَّ سِرًّا إِلَّآ أَن تَقُولُوا۟ قَوْلًا مَّعْرُوفًا وَلَا تَعْزِمُوا۟ عُقْدَةَ ٱلنِّكَاحِ حَتَّىٰ يَبْلُغَ ٱلْكِتَٰبُ أَجَلَهُۥ وَٱعْلَمُوٓا۟ أَنَّ ٱللَّهَ يَعْلَمُ مَا فِىٓ أَنفُسِكُمْ فَٱحْذَرُوهُ وَٱعْلَمُوٓا۟ أَنَّ ٱللَّهَ غَفُورٌ حَلِيمٌ

236. There is no blame on you if you divorce women while yet you have not touched them, nor appointed unto them a portion. Provide for them, the rich according to his means, and the straitened according to his means, a fair provision. (This is) a bounden duty for those who do good.

237. And if you divorce them before you have touched them and you have appointed unto them a portion, then (pay the) half of that which you appointed, unless they (the women) agree to forgo it, or he agrees to forgo it in whose hand is the marriage tie.[58] To forgo is nearer to piety; And forget not kindness among yourselves. Indeed Allah is Seer of what you do.

238. Be guardians of your prayers, and of the midmost prayer,[59] and stand up with devotion to Allah.

239. And if you go in fear, then (pray) standing or on horseback. And when you are again in safety, remember Allah, as He has taught you that which you knew not.

240. (In the case of) those of you who are about to die and leave behind them wives, they should bequeath unto their wives a provision for the year without turning them out, but if they go out (of their own accord) there is no blame on you in that which they do of themselves within their rights. Allah is Mighty, Wise.

241. For divorced women a provision in kindness: a duty for those who are pious.

242. Thus Allah expounds unto you His revelations so that you may understand.

---

[58]i.e., the bridegroom.
[59]Meaning, probably, the best amid all forms of prayer. Some authorities think the reference is to the 'aṣr (afternoon) prayer, which Muslims are most apt to forget.

243. Bethink you not (O Muhammad) of those of old, who went forth from their habitations in their thousands, fearing death,[60] then Allah said unto them: Die, and then He brought them back to life. Lo! Allah is a Lord of Kindness to mankind, but most of mankind give not thanks.

244. And fight in the way of Allah, and know that Allah is Hearer, Knower.

245. Who is it that will lend unto Allah a goodly loan,[61] so that He may give it increase manifold? Allah straitens and enlarges. Unto Him you will return.

246. Bethink you of the leaders of the Children of Israel after Moses, how they said unto a Prophet whom they had: Set up for us a king and we will fight in Allah's way. He said: Would you then refrain from fighting if fighting were prescribed for you? They said: Why should we not fight in Allah's way when we have been expelled from our dwellings and separated from our children? Yet, when fighting was prescribed for them, they turned away, all save a few of them. And Allah is Aware of evildoers.

247. Their Prophet said unto them: Lo! Allah has raised up Saul to be a king for you. They said: How can he have kingdom over us when we are more deserving of the kingdom than he is, since he has not been given wealth enough? He said: Lo! Allah has chosen him above you, and has increased him abundantly in wisdom and stature. Allah bestows His sovereignty on whom He will. Allah is All Embracing, All Knowing.

﴿٢٤٣﴾ اَلَمْ تَرَ اِلَى الَّذِيْنَ خَرَجُوْا مِنْ دِيَارِهِمْ وَهُمْ اُلُوْفٌ حَذَرَ الْمَوْتِ فَقَالَ لَهُمُ اللهُ مُوْتُوْا ثُمَّ اَحْيَاهُمْ ۖ اِنَّ اللهَ لَذُوْ فَضْلٍ عَلَى النَّاسِ وَلَكِنَّ اَكْثَرَ النَّاسِ لَا يَشْكُرُوْنَ

﴿٢٤٤﴾ وَقَاتِلُوْا فِيْ سَبِيْلِ اللهِ وَاعْلَمُوْا اَنَّ اللهَ سَمِيْعٌ عَلِيْمٌ

﴿٢٤٥﴾ مَنْ ذَا الَّذِيْ يُقْرِضُ اللهَ قَرْضًا حَسَنًا فَيُضَاعِفَهُ لَهٗٓ اَضْعَافًا كَثِيْرَةً ۚ وَاللهُ يَقْبِضُ وَيَبْصُطُ ۖ وَاِلَيْهِ تُرْجَعُوْنَ

﴿٢٤٦﴾ اَلَمْ تَرَ اِلَى الْمَلَاِ مِنْ بَنِيْٓ اِسْرَآءِيْلَ مِنْۢ بَعْدِ مُوْسٰى ۘ اِذْ قَالُوْا لِنَبِيٍّ لَّهُمُ ابْعَثْ لَنَا مَلِكًا نُّقَاتِلْ فِيْ سَبِيْلِ اللهِ ۖ قَالَ هَلْ عَسَيْتُمْ اِنْ كُتِبَ عَلَيْكُمُ الْقِتَالُ اَلَّا تُقَاتِلُوْا ۚ قَالُوْا وَمَا لَنَآ اَلَّا نُقَاتِلَ فِيْ سَبِيْلِ اللهِ وَقَدْ اُخْرِجْنَا مِنْ دِيَارِنَا وَاَبْنَآئِنَا ۖ فَلَمَّا كُتِبَ عَلَيْهِمُ الْقِتَالُ تَوَلَّوْا اِلَّا قَلِيْلًا مِّنْهُمْ ۗ وَاللهُ عَلِيْمٌۢ بِالظَّالِمِيْنَ

﴿٢٤٧﴾ وَقَالَ لَهُمْ نَبِيُّهُمْ اِنَّ اللهَ قَدْ بَعَثَ لَكُمْ طَالُوْتَ مَلِكًا ۚ قَالُوْٓا اَنّٰى يَكُوْنُ لَهُ الْمُلْكُ عَلَيْنَا وَنَحْنُ اَحَقُّ بِالْمُلْكِ مِنْهُ وَلَمْ يُؤْتَ سَعَةً مِّنَ الْمَالِ ۚ قَالَ اِنَّ اللهَ اصْطَفَاهُ عَلَيْكُمْ وَزَادَهٗ بَسْطَةً فِى الْعِلْمِ وَالْجِسْمِ ۖ وَاللهُ يُؤْتِيْ مُلْكَهٗ مَنْ يَّشَآءُ ۚ وَاللهُ وَاسِعٌ عَلِيْمٌ

---

[60]The reference is to the Exodus.
[61]A loan without interest—i.e., without thought of gain.

248. And their Prophet said unto them: Lo! the token of his kingdom is that there shall come unto you the casket wherein is peace of reassurance from your Lord, and a remnant of that which the house of Moses and the house of Aaron left be-hind, the angels bearing it. Lo! herein shall be a token for you if (in truth) you are believers.

249. And when Saul set out with the army, he said: Lo! Allah will try you by (the ordeal of) a river. Whosoever there-fore drinks thereof he is not of me, and whoever tastes it not he is of me, save him who takes (thereof) in the hollow of his hand. But they drank thereof, all save a few of them. And after he had crossed (the river), he and those who believed with him, they said: We have no power this day against Goliath and his hosts. But those who knew that they would meet Allah exclaimed: How many a little company has overcome a mighty host by Allah's leave! And Allah is with the steadfast.

250. And when they went into the field against Goliath and his hosts they said: Our Lord! Bestow on us endurance, make our foothold sure, and give us vic-tory against the disbelieving folk.

251. So they routed them by Allah's leave and David slew Goliath; and Allah gave him the kingdom and wis-dom, and taught him of that which He wills. And if Allah had not repelled some men by others the earth would have been corrupted. But Allah is a Lord of Kindness to all the worlds.

252. These are the revelations of Allah which We recite unto you (Muhammad) with truth, and Lo! you are of the number of (the) messengers;

﴿٢٤٨﴾ وَقَالَ لَهُمْ نَبِيُّهُمْ إِنَّ ءَايَةَ مُلْكِهِ أَن يَأْتِيَكُمُ التَّابُوتُ فِيهِ سَكِينَةٌ مِّن رَّبِّكُمْ وَبَقِيَّةٌ مِّمَّا تَرَكَ ءَالُ مُوسَىٰ وَءَالُ هَـٰرُونَ تَحْمِلُهُ الْمَلَـٰٓئِكَةُ إِنَّ فِي ذَٰلِكَ لَءَايَةً لَّكُمْ إِن كُنتُم مُّؤْمِنِينَ

﴿٢٤٩﴾ فَلَمَّا فَصَلَ طَالُوتُ بِالْجُنُودِ قَالَ إِنَّ اللَّهَ مُبْتَلِيكُم بِنَهَرٍ فَمَن شَرِبَ مِنْهُ فَلَيْسَ مِنِّي وَمَن لَّمْ يَطْعَمْهُ فَإِنَّهُ مِنِّيٓ إِلَّا مَنِ اغْتَرَفَ غُرْفَةً بِيَدِهِ فَشَرِبُوا مِنْهُ إِلَّا قَلِيلًا مِّنْهُمْ فَلَمَّا جَاوَزَهُ هُوَ وَالَّذِينَ ءَامَنُوا مَعَهُ قَالُوا لَا طَاقَةَ لَنَا الْيَوْمَ بِجَالُوتَ وَجُنُودِهِ قَالَ الَّذِينَ يَظُنُّونَ أَنَّهُم مُّلَـٰقُوا اللَّهِ كَم مِّن فِئَةٍ قَلِيلَةٍ غَلَبَتْ فِئَةً كَثِيرَةً بِإِذْنِ اللَّهِ وَاللَّهُ مَعَ الصَّابِرِينَ

﴿٢٥٠﴾ وَلَمَّا بَرَزُوا لِجَالُوتَ وَجُنُودِهِ قَالُوا رَبَّنَآ أَفْرِغْ عَلَيْنَا صَبْرًا وَثَبِّتْ أَقْدَامَنَا وَانصُرْنَا عَلَى الْقَوْمِ الْكَـٰفِرِينَ

﴿٢٥١﴾ فَهَزَمُوهُم بِإِذْنِ اللَّهِ وَقَتَلَ دَاوُدُ جَالُوتَ وَءَاتَىٰهُ اللَّهُ الْمُلْكَ وَالْحِكْمَةَ وَعَلَّمَهُ مِمَّا يَشَآءُ وَلَوْ لَا دَفْعُ اللَّهِ النَّاسَ بَعْضَهُم بِبَعْضٍ لَّفَسَدَتِ الْأَرْضُ وَلَـٰكِنَّ اللَّهَ ذُو فَضْلٍ عَلَى الْعَـٰلَمِينَ

﴿٢٥٢﴾ تِلْكَ ءَايَـٰتُ اللَّهِ نَتْلُوهَا عَلَيْكَ بِالْحَقِّ وَإِنَّكَ لَمِنَ الْمُرْسَلِينَ

253. Of those messengers, some of whom We have caused to excel others, and of whom there are some unto whom Allah spoke, while some of them He exalted (above others) in degree; and We gave Jesus son of Mary clear proofs (of Allah's sovereignty) and We supported him with the holy Spirit.[62] And if Allah had so willed it, those who followed after them would not have fought one with another after the clear proofs had come unto them. But they differed, some of them believing and some disbelieving. And if Allah had so willed it, they would not have fought one with another; but Allah does what He will.

254. O you who believe! Spend of that wherewith We have provided you ere a day come when there will be no trafficking, nor friendship, nor intercession. Disbelievers are the wrongdoers.

255. Allah! There is no God save Him, the Alive, the Eternal. Neither slumber nor sleep overtakes Him. Unto Him belongs whatever is in the heavens and whatever is in the earth. Who is he that intercedes with Him save by His leave? He knows that which is in front of them and that which is behind them, while they encompass nothing of His knowledge save what He will. His Chair includes the heavens and the earth, and He is never weary of preserving them. He is the Sublime, the Tremendous.

256. There is no compulsion in religion. The right direction is henceforth distinct from error. And he who rejects false deities and believes in Allah has grasped a firm hand- hold which will never break. Allah is Hearer, Knower.

257. Allah is the Protecting Friend of those who believe. He brings them out of darkness into light. As for those who disbelieve, their patrons are false deities. They bring them out of light into darkness. Such are rightful owners of the Fire. They will abide therein forever.

---

[62] i.e., the angel Gabriel.

258. Bethink you not of him who had an argument with Abraham about his Lord, because Allah had given him the kingdom; how, when Abraham said: My Lord is He who gives life and causes death, he answered: I give life and cause death. Abraham said: Lo! Allah causes the sun to rise in the East, so do you cause it to come up from the West. Thus was the disbeliever abashed. And Allah guides not wrongdoing folk.

259. Or (bethink you of) the like of him who, passing by a township which had fallen into utter ruin, exclaimed: How shall Allah give this township[63] life after its death? So Allah made him die a hundred years, then brought him back to life. He said: How long have you tarried? (The man) said: I have tarried a day or part of a day. (He) said: Nay, but you have tarried for a hundred years. Just look at your food and drink which have not rotted! Look at your ass! And, that We may make you a token unto mankind, look at the bones, how We adjust them and then cover them with flesh! And when (the matter) became clear unto him, he said: I know now that Allah is Able to do all things.

260. And when Abraham said (unto his Lord): My lord! Show me how You give life to the dead, He said: Do you not believe? Abraham said: Yea, but (I ask) in order that my heart may be at ease. (His Lord) said: Take four of the birds and cause them to incline unto you, then place a part of them on each hill, then call them, they will come to you in haste. And know that Allah is Mighty, Wise.

261. The likeness of those who spend their wealth in Allah's way is as the likeness of a grain which grows seven ears, in every ear a hundred grains. Allah gives increase manifold to whom He will. Allah is All Embracing, All Knowing.

---

[63]Most of the commentators agree that this refers to Jerusalem in ruins, while the following words tell of the vision of Ezekiel.

262. Those who spend their wealth for the cause of Allah and afterward make not reproach and injury to follow that which they have spent; their reward is with their Lord, and there shall be no fear come upon them, neither shall they grieve.

٢٦٢ ۞ ٱلَّذِينَ يُنفِقُونَ أَمْوَٰلَهُمْ فِى سَبِيلِ ٱللَّهِ ثُمَّ لَا يُتْبِعُونَ مَآ أَنفَقُوا۟ مَنًّا وَلَآ أَذًى لَّهُمْ أَجْرُهُمْ عِندَ رَبِّهِمْ وَلَا خَوْفٌ عَلَيْهِمْ وَلَا هُمْ يَحْزَنُونَ

263. A kind word with forgiveness is better than almsgiving followed by injury. Allah is Absolute, Clement.

٢٦٣ قَوْلٌ مَّعْرُوفٌ وَمَغْفِرَةٌ خَيْرٌ مِّن صَدَقَةٍ يَتْبَعُهَآ أَذًى وَٱللَّهُ غَنِىٌّ حَلِيمٌ

264. O you who believe! Render not vain your almsgiving by reproach and injury, like him who spends his wealth only to be seen of men and believes not in Allah and the Last Day. His likeness is as the likeness of a rock whereon is dust of earth; a rainstorm smites it, leaving it smooth and bare. They have no control of anything of that which they have gained. Allah guides not the disbelieving folk.

٢٦٤ يَٰٓأَيُّهَا ٱلَّذِينَ ءَامَنُوا۟ لَا تُبْطِلُوا۟ صَدَقَٰتِكُم بِٱلْمَنِّ وَٱلْأَذَىٰ كَٱلَّذِى يُنفِقُ مَالَهُ رِئَآءَ ٱلنَّاسِ وَلَا يُؤْمِنُ بِٱللَّهِ وَٱلْيَوْمِ ٱلْءَاخِرِ فَمَثَلُهُۥ كَمَثَلِ صَفْوَانٍ عَلَيْهِ تُرَابٌ فَأَصَابَهُۥ وَابِلٌ فَتَرَكَهُۥ صَلْدًا لَّا يَقْدِرُونَ عَلَىٰ شَىْءٍ مِّمَّا كَسَبُوا۟ وَٱللَّهُ لَا يَهْدِى ٱلْقَوْمَ ٱلْكَٰفِرِينَ

265. And the likeness of those who spend their wealth in search of Allah's pleasure, and for the strengthening of their souls, is as the likeness of a garden on a height. The rainstorm smites it and it brings forth its fruit twofold. And if the rainstorm smite it not, then dew. Allah is Seer of what you do.

٢٦٥ وَمَثَلُ ٱلَّذِينَ يُنفِقُونَ أَمْوَٰلَهُمُ ٱبْتِغَآءَ مَرْضَاتِ ٱللَّهِ وَتَثْبِيتًا مِّنْ أَنفُسِهِمْ كَمَثَلِ جَنَّةٍ بِرَبْوَةٍ أَصَابَهَا وَابِلٌ فَـَٔاتَتْ أُكُلَهَا ضِعْفَيْنِ فَإِن لَّمْ يُصِبْهَا وَابِلٌ فَطَلٌّ وَٱللَّهُ بِمَا تَعْمَلُونَ بَصِيرٌ

266. Would any of you like to have a garden of palm trees and vines, with rivers flowing underneath it, with all kinds of fruit for him therein; and old age has stricken him and he has feeble off-spring; and a fiery whirlwind strikes it and it is (all) consumed by fire. Thus Allah makes plain His revelations unto you, in order that you may give thought.

٢٦٦ أَيَوَدُّ أَحَدُكُمْ أَن تَكُونَ لَهُۥ جَنَّةٌ مِّن نَّخِيلٍ وَأَعْنَابٍ تَجْرِى مِن تَحْتِهَا ٱلْأَنْهَٰرُ لَهُۥ فِيهَا مِن كُلِّ ٱلثَّمَرَٰتِ وَأَصَابَهُ ٱلْكِبَرُ وَلَهُۥ ذُرِّيَّةٌ ضُعَفَآءُ فَأَصَابَهَآ إِعْصَارٌ فِيهِ نَارٌ فَٱحْتَرَقَتْ كَذَٰلِكَ يُبَيِّنُ ٱللَّهُ لَكُمُ ٱلْءَايَٰتِ لَعَلَّكُمْ تَتَفَكَّرُونَ

267. O you who believe! Spend of the good things which you have earned, and of that which we bring forth from the earth for you, and seek not the bad (with intent) to spend thereof (in charity) when you would not take it for yourselves save with disdain; and know that Allah is Absolute, Owner of Praise.

268. The devil promises you destitution and enjoins on you lewdness. But Allah promises you forgiveness from Himself with bounty. Allah is All Embracing, All Knowing.

269. He gives wisdom unto whom He will, and he unto whom wisdom is given, he truly has received abundant good But none remember except men of understanding.

270. Whatever alms you spend or vow you vow, Lo! Allah knows it. Wrongdoers have no helpers.

271. If you publish your almsgiving, it is well, but if you hide it and give it to the poor, it will be better for you, and will atone for some of your ill deeds. Allah is Informed of what you do.

272. The guiding of them is not your duty (O Muhammad), but Allah guides whom He will. And whatsoever good thing you spend, it·is for yourselves, when you spend not save in search of Allah's countenance; and whatsoever good thing you spend, it will be repaid to you in full, and you will not be wronged.

273. (Alms are) for the poor who are straitened for the cause of Allah, who cannot travel in the land (for trade). The unknowing person deems them wealthy due to their restraint. You shall know them by their mark: They do not beg of men with importunity. And whatsoever good thing you spend, lo! Allah knows it.

يَـٰٓأَيُّهَا ٱلَّذِينَ ءَامَنُوٓا۟ أَنفِقُوا۟ مِن طَيِّبَـٰتِ مَا كَسَبۡتُمۡ وَمِمَّآ أَخۡرَجۡنَا لَكُم مِّنَ ٱلۡأَرۡضِ وَلَا تَيَمَّمُوا۟ ٱلۡخَبِيثَ مِنۡهُ تُنفِقُونَ وَلَسۡتُم بِـَٔاخِذِيهِ إِلَّآ أَن تُغۡمِضُوا۟ فِيهِ وَٱعۡلَمُوٓا۟ أَنَّ ٱللَّهَ غَنِىٌّ حَمِيدٌ ﴿٢٦٧﴾ ٱلشَّيۡطَـٰنُ يَعِدُكُمُ ٱلۡفَقۡرَ وَيَأۡمُرُكُم بِٱلۡفَحۡشَآءِ وَٱللَّهُ يَعِدُكُم مَّغۡفِرَةً مِّنۡهُ وَفَضۡلًا وَٱللَّهُ وَٰسِعٌ عَلِيمٌ ﴿٢٦٨﴾ يُؤۡتِى ٱلۡحِكۡمَةَ مَن يَشَآءُ وَمَن يُؤۡتَ ٱلۡحِكۡمَةَ فَقَدۡ أُوتِىَ خَيۡرًا كَثِيرًا وَمَا يَذَّكَّرُ إِلَّآ أُو۟لُوا۟ ٱلۡأَلۡبَـٰبِ ﴿٢٦٩﴾ وَمَآ أَنفَقۡتُم مِّن نَّفَقَةٍ أَوۡ نَذَرۡتُم مِّن نَّذۡرٍ فَإِنَّ ٱللَّهَ يَعۡلَمُهُۥ وَمَا لِلظَّـٰلِمِينَ مِنۡ أَنصَارٍ ﴿٢٧٠﴾ إِن تُبۡدُوا۟ ٱلصَّدَقَـٰتِ فَنِعِمَّا هِىَ وَإِن تُخۡفُوهَا وَتُؤۡتُوهَا ٱلۡفُقَرَآءَ فَهُوَ خَيۡرٌ لَّكُمۡ وَيُكَفِّرُ عَنكُم مِّن سَيِّـَٔاتِكُمۡ وَٱللَّهُ بِمَا تَعۡمَلُونَ خَبِيرٌ ﴿٢٧١﴾ لَّيۡسَ عَلَيۡكَ هُدَىٰهُمۡ وَلَـٰكِنَّ ٱللَّهَ يَهۡدِى مَن يَشَآءُ وَمَا تُنفِقُوا۟ مِنۡ خَيۡرٍ فَلِأَنفُسِكُمۡ وَمَا تُنفِقُونَ إِلَّا ٱبۡتِغَآءَ وَجۡهِ ٱللَّهِ وَمَا تُنفِقُوا۟ مِنۡ خَيۡرٍ يُوَفَّ إِلَيۡكُمۡ وَأَنتُمۡ لَا تُظۡلَمُونَ ﴿٢٧٢﴾ لِلۡفُقَرَآءِ ٱلَّذِينَ أُحۡصِرُوا۟ فِى سَبِيلِ ٱللَّهِ لَا يَسۡتَطِيعُونَ ضَرۡبًا فِى ٱلۡأَرۡضِ يَحۡسَبُهُمُ ٱلۡجَاهِلُ أَغۡنِيَآءَ مِنَ ٱلتَّعَفُّفِ تَعۡرِفُهُم بِسِيمَـٰهُمۡ لَا يَسۡـَٔلُونَ ٱلنَّاسَ إِلۡحَافًا وَمَا تُنفِقُوا۟ مِنۡ خَيۡرٍ فَإِنَّ ٱللَّهَ بِهِۦ عَلِيمٌ ﴿٢٧٣﴾

274. Those who spend their wealth by night and day, in secret and openly, surely their reward is with their Lord, and there shall no fear come upon them neither shall they grieve.

275. Those who swallow usury cannot rise up save as he arises whom the Devil has prostrated by (his) touch. That is because they say: Trade is just like usury; whereas Allah permits trading and forbids usury. He unto whom an admonition from his Lord comes, and (he) refrains (in obedience thereto), he shall keep (the profits of) that which is past, and his affair (henceforth) is with Allah. As for him who returns (to usury)—Such are rightful owners of the Fire. They will abide therein forever.

276. Allah has blighted usury and made almsgiving fruitful. Allah loves not the impious and the guilty.

277. Lo! those who believe and do good works and establish prayer and pay the poor due, their reward is with their Lord and there shall no fear come upon them neither shall they grieve.

278. O you who believe! Observe your duty to Allah, and give up what remains (due to you) from usury, if you are (in truth) believers.

279. And if you do not, then be warned of war (against you) from Allah and His Messenger. And if you repent, then you have your principal (without interest). Wrong not, and you shall not be wronged,

280. And if the debtor is in straitened circumstances, then (let there be) postponement to (the time of) ease; and that you remit the debt as almsgiving would be better for you if you did but know.

281. And guard yourselves against a day in which you will be brought back to Allah. Then every soul will be paid in full that which it has earned, and they will not be wronged.

282. O you who believe! When you contract a debt for a fixed term, record it in writing. Let a scribe record it in writing between you in (terms of) equity. No scribe should refuse to write as Allah has taught him, so let him write, and let him who incurs the debt dictate, and let him observe his duty to Allah his Lord, and diminish nothing thereof. But if he who owes the debt is of low understanding, or weak, or unable himself to dictate, then let the guardian of his interests dictate in (terms of) equity. And call to witness, from among your men, two witnesses. And if two men be not (at hand) then a man and two women, of such as you approve as witnesses, so that if the one errs (through forgetfulness) the other will remind her. And the witnesses must not refuse when they are summoned. Be not averse to writing down (the contract) whether it be small or great, with (record of) the term thereof. That is more equitable in the sight of Allah and more sure for testimony, and the best way of avoiding doubt between you; save only in the case when it is actual merchandise which you transfer among yourselves from hand to hand. In that case it is no sin for you if you write it not. And have witnesses when you sell one to another, and let no harm be done to scribe or witness. If you do (harm to them) lo! it is a sin in you. Observe your duty to Allah. Allah is teaching you. And Allah is Knower of all things.

283. If you be on a journey and cannot find a scribe, then a pledge in hand (shall suffice). And if one of you entrusts another let him who is trusted deliver up that which is entrusted to him (according to the pact between them) and let him observe his duty to Allah, his Lord. Hide not testimony. He who hides it, surely his heart is sinful. Allah is Aware of what you do.

284. Unto Allah (belongs) whatsoever is in the heavens and whatsoever is in the earth; and whether you make known what is in your minds or hide it, Allah will bring you to account for it. He will forgive whom He will and He will punish whom He will. And Allah is Able to do all things.

285. The Messenger believes in that which has been revealed unto him from his Lord and (so do) the believers. Each one believes in Allah and His angels and His scriptures and His messengers—We make no distinction between any of His messengers—and they say: We hear, and we obey. (Grant us) Your forgiveness, our Lord. Unto You is the journeying.

286. Allah tasks not a soul beyond its scope. For it (is only) that which it has earned, and against it (only) that which it has deserved. Our Lord! Condemn us not if we forget, or miss the mark! Our Lord! Lay not on us such a burden as You did lay on those before us! Our Lord! Impose not on us that which we have not the strength to bear! Pardon us, absolve us and have mercy on us. You are our Protector; so grant us victory over the disbelieving folk.

۞ لِّلَّهِ مَا فِى ٱلسَّمَـٰوَٰتِ وَمَا فِى ٱلْأَرْضِ ۗ وَإِن تُبْدُوا۟ مَا فِىٓ أَنفُسِكُمْ أَوْ تُخْفُوهُ يُحَاسِبْكُم بِهِ ٱللَّهُ ۖ فَيَغْفِرُ لِمَن يَشَآءُ وَيُعَذِّبُ مَن يَشَآءُ ۗ وَٱللَّهُ عَلَىٰ كُلِّ شَىْءٍ قَدِيرٌ ﴿٢٨٤﴾

ءَامَنَ ٱلرَّسُولُ بِمَآ أُنزِلَ إِلَيْهِ مِن رَّبِّهِ وَٱلْمُؤْمِنُونَ ۚ كُلٌّ ءَامَنَ بِٱللَّهِ وَمَلَـٰٓئِكَتِهِ وَكُتُبِهِ وَرُسُلِهِ لَا نُفَرِّقُ بَيْنَ أَحَدٍ مِّن رُّسُلِهِ ۚ وَقَالُوا۟ سَمِعْنَا وَأَطَعْنَا ۖ غُفْرَانَكَ رَبَّنَا وَإِلَيْكَ ٱلْمَصِيرُ ﴿٢٨٥﴾

﴿٢٨٦﴾ لَا يُكَلِّفُ ٱللَّهُ نَفْسًا إِلَّا وُسْعَهَا ۚ لَهَا مَا كَسَبَتْ وَعَلَيْهَا مَا ٱكْتَسَبَتْ ۗ رَبَّنَا لَا تُؤَاخِذْنَآ إِن نَّسِينَآ أَوْ أَخْطَأْنَا ۚ رَبَّنَا وَلَا تَحْمِلْ عَلَيْنَآ إِصْرًا كَمَا حَمَلْتَهُۥ عَلَى ٱلَّذِينَ مِن قَبْلِنَا ۚ رَبَّنَا وَلَا تُحَمِّلْنَا مَا لَا طَاقَةَ لَنَا بِهِ ۖ وَٱعْفُ عَنَّا وَٱغْفِرْ لَنَا وَٱرْحَمْنَآ ۚ أَنتَ مَوْلَىٰنَا فَٱنصُرْنَا عَلَى ٱلْقَوْمِ ٱلْكَـٰفِرِينَ

The Family of 'Imrān

Āl 'Imrān takes its title from verse 32, where "the family of 'Imrān" occurs as a generic name for all Hebrew prophets from Moses to John the Baptist and Jesus.

If verses 1-34 were, as tradition states, revealed on the occasion of the deputation from the Christians of Najran, which took place in 10 A.H. ("the year of deputations," as it is called), then they are of much later date than the rest of the surah. But it seems possible that they were only recited by the Prophet on that occasion, having been revealed before.

By this time, the Jews had become bolder and more bitter in their opposition which, as Noldeke points out, cannot have been the case, after the signal victory of Badr, until after the Muslims suffered a reverse at Uhud. This battle is referred to in verses 120-188.

In 3A.H. the Makkans attacked al Madinah with an army of 3,000 men in order to avenge their defeat at Badr the previous year and to wipe out the Muslims. The Prophet, who at first had planned to defend al Madinah, decided, at the insistence of his Companions, to meet the enemy at Mt. Uhud and thus stationed his men carefully. He led an army of 1,000 men, a third of whom under 'Abd Allāh ibn 'Ubayy (the "Hypocrite" leader) deserted him before the battle and said afterwards that they had thought that there would be no fighting that day. The battle began well for the Muslims, but was changed to something near defeat by the disobedience of a band of fifty archers placed on a hill to defend the back of the Muslim army. Seeing the Muslims winning, they feared that they might lose their share of the spoils and so ran to join the others. Their action left an opening for the Makkan cavalry, and the idolaters managed to rally and inflict considerable loss upon the Muslims. The Prophet himself was wounded. A cry arose that the Prophet had been killed, and the Muslims were in despair until someone recognized the Prophet and cried out that he was still alive. The Muslims then rallied to his side and retired in some sort of order. The Qurayshī army also retired after the battle.

The wives of the Qurayshī leaders, who had been brought with the army to encourage the men by their presence and their chanting, mutilated the Muslim corpses and made necklaces and bracelets of severed ears and noses. Hind, the wife of Abu Sufyān, extracted the liver of the Prophet's uncle, Hamzah, and tried to eat it. When the Prophet saw what was happening, he was moved to vow reprisal. But he was relieved of his vow by a revelation that forbade Muslims to mutilate the corpses of the enemy.

On the following day, the Prophet took the field with those who had survived the earlier battle so that the Quraysh might hear that he was in the field and perhaps be deterred from attacking al Madinah in its weakened state. Many wounded men went out with him. Tradition tells how a friendly nomad met the Muslims and afterwards met the Qurayshī army. Questioned by Abū Sufyān, he said that the Prophet was seeking vengeance with an overwhelming force. This report caused Abū Sufyān to march back to Makkah.

The period of revelation is 3-4 A.H.

The Family of ʿImrān

Revealed at al Madinah

*In the name of Allah,
the Beneficent, the Merciful*

1. **A**lif. Lām. Mīm.[64]

2. Allah! There is no God save Him, the Alive, the Eternal.

3. He has revealed unto you (Muhammad) the Scripture with truth, confirming that which was (revealed) before it, even as He revealed the Torah and the Gospel

4. Aforetime, as a guidance to mankind; and has revealed the Criterion (of right and wrong). Lo! those who disbelieve the revelations of Allah, theirs will be a heavy doom. Allah is Mighty, Able to Requite (the wrong).

5. Lo! nothing in the earth or in the heavens is hidden from Allah.

6. He it is who fashions you in the wombs as pleases Him. There is no God save Him, the Almighty, the Wise.

7. He it is Who has revealed unto you (Muhammad) the Scripture wherein are clear revelations. They are the substance of the Book. and others (which are) allegorical. But those in whose hearts is doubt pursue, forsooth, that which is allegorical seeking (to cause) dissension by seeking to explain it their way. None knows its real meaning save Allah. And those who are of sound knowledge say: We believe therein; the whole is from our Lord; but only men of understanding really heed.

8. Our Lord! Cause not our hearts to stray after You have guided us, and bestow upon us mercy from Your Presence. Lo! You, only You are the Bestower.

---

[64]See Surah 2, v. 1, footnote.

9. Our Lord! it is You Who will gather mankind together to a Day of which there is no doubt. Lo! Allah fails not to keep the appointed time.

١٠. (On that day) neither the riches nor the progeny of those who disbelieve will anything avail them with Allah. those will be fuel for fire.

10. (On that day) neither the riches nor the progeny of those who disbelieve will anything avail them with Allah. those will be fuel for fire.

11. Like Pharaoh's folk and those who were before them, they disbelieved Our revelations and so Allah seized them for their sins. And Allah is severe in punishment.

12. Say (O Muhammad) unto those who disbelieve: You shall be overcome and gathered unto Hell, an evil resting ·place.

13. There was a token for you in two hosts which met:[65] one army fighting in the way of Allah, and another disbelieving, whom they saw as twice their number, clearly, with their very eyes. But Allah strengthens with His succor whom He will. In this is a lesson for those who have eyes.

14. Beautified for mankind is love of the joys (that come) from women and offspring, and stored up heaps of gold and silver, and horses branded (with their mark), and cattle and land. That is comfort of the life of the world. And Allah! With Him is a more excellent abode.

15. Say: Shall I inform you of something better than that? For those who keep from evil, with their Lord, are Gardens underneath which rivers flow wherein they will abide forever, and pure companions, and contentment from Allah. And Allah is Seer of His bondmen,

---

[65]This refers to the battle of Badr.

16. Those who say: Our Lord! Lo! we believe. So forgive us our sins and guard us from the punishment of Fire;

17. The steadfast, the truthful, the obedient, those who spend (and hoard not), and those who pray for pardon in the watches of the night.

18. Allah (Himself) is witness that there is no God save Him. And the angels and the men of learning (too are witness). Maintaining His creation in justice, there is no God save Him, the Almighty, the Wise.

19. Lo! religion with Allah (is) Islam (Submission to His Will). Those who (formerly) received the Scripture differed only after knowledge came unto them, through transgression among themselves. Who disbelieves the revelations of Allah (will find that) Lo! Allah is swift at reckoning.

20. And if they argue with you, (O Muhammad), say: I have surrendered my purpose to Allah and (so have) those who follow me. And say unto those who have received the Scripture and those who read not: Have you (too) surrendered? If they surrender, then truly they are rightly guided, and if they turn away, then it is your duty only to convey the message (unto them). And Allah is Seer of (His) bondmen.

21. Lo! those who disbelieve the revelations of Allah, and slay the Prophets wrongfully, and slay those of mankind who enjoin equity: promise them a painful doom.

22. Those are they whose works have failed in the world and the Hereafter; and they have no helpers.

23. Have you not seen how those who have received the Scripture invoke the Scripture of Allah (in their disputes) that it may judge between them; then a faction of them turn away, being opposed (to it)?

24. That is because they say: The Fire will not touch us save for a counted number of days. That which they used to invent has deceived them regarding their religion.

25. How (will it be with them) when We have brought them all together to a Day of which there is no doubt, when every soul will be paid in full what it has earned, and they will not be wronged.

26. Say: O Allah! Owner of Sovereignty! You give sovereignty unto whom You will, and You withdraw sovereignty from whom You will. You exalt whom You will and You abase whom You will. In Your hand is the good. Lo! You are Able to do all things.

27. You cause the night to pass into the day, and You cause the day to pass into the night. And You bring forth the living from the dead, and You bring forth the dead from the living. And You give sustenance to whom You choose, without stint.

28. Let not the believers take disbelievers for their friends in preference to believers. Who does that has no connection with Allah unless (it be) that you but guard yourselves against them, taking (as it were) security. Allah bids you beware (only) of Himself. Unto Allah is the journeying.

29. Say, (O Muhammad): Whether you hide that which is in your breasts or reveal it, Allah knows it. He knows that which is in the heavens and that which is in the earth, and Allah is Able to do all things.

30. On the day when every soul will find itself confronted with all that it has done of good and all that it has done of evil (every soul) will long that there might be a mighty space of distance between it and that (evil). Allah bids you beware of Him. And Allah is full of pity for (His) bondmen.

31. Say, (O Muhammad, to mankind): If you love Allah, then follow me; Allah will love you and forgive you your sins; for Allah is Forgiving, Merciful.

32. Say: Obey Allah and the Messenger. But if they turn away, Lo! Allah loves not the disbelievers (in His guidance).

٣٢ ۞ قُلْ أَطِيعُوا اللَّهَ وَالرَّسُولَ فَإِن تَوَلَّوْا فَإِنَّ اللَّهَ لَا يُحِبُّ الْكَافِرِينَ

33. Lo! Allah preferred Adam and Noah and the Family of Abraham and the Family of 'Imrān above the worlds.

٣٣ إِنَّ اللَّهَ اصْطَفَى آدَمَ وَنُوحًا وَءَالَ إِبْرَاهِيمَ وَءَالَ عِمْرَانَ عَلَى الْعَالَمِينَ

34. They were descendants one of another. And Allah is Hearer, Knower.

٣٤ ذُرِّيَّةً بَعْضُهَا مِنْ بَعْضٍ وَاللَّهُ سَمِيعٌ عَلِيمٌ

35. (Remember) when the wife of 'Imrān said: My Lord I have vowed unto You that which is in my belly as a consecrated (offering). So accept it from me. Lo! You, only You, are the Hearer, the Knower!

٣٥ إِذْ قَالَتِ امْرَأَتُ عِمْرَانَ رَبِّ إِنِّي نَذَرْتُ لَكَ مَا فِي بَطْنِي مُحَرَّرًا فَتَقَبَّلْ مِنِّي إِنَّكَ أَنتَ السَّمِيعُ الْعَلِيمُ

36. And when she was delivered she said: My Lord! O! I am delivered of a female—Allah knew best of what she was delivered and the male is not as the female; and Lo! I have named her Mary, and Lo! I crave Your protection for her and for her offspring from the outcast devil.

٣٦ فَلَمَّا وَضَعَتْهَا قَالَتْ رَبِّ إِنِّي وَضَعْتُهَا أُنثَى وَاللَّهُ أَعْلَمُ بِمَا وَضَعَتْ وَلَيْسَ الذَّكَرُ كَالْأُنثَى وَإِنِّي سَمَّيْتُهَا مَرْيَمَ وَإِنِّي أُعِيذُهَا بِكَ وَذُرِّيَّتَهَا مِنَ الشَّيْطَانِ الرَّجِيمِ

37. Thus her Lord accepted her with full acceptance and vouchsafed to her a goodly growth; and made Zachariah her guardian. Whenever Zachariah went into the sanctuary where she was, he found that she had food. He said: O Mary! Whence comes unto you this (food)? She answered: It is from Allah. Allah gives without stint to whom He will.

٣٧ فَتَقَبَّلَهَا رَبُّهَا بِقَبُولٍ حَسَنٍ وَأَنبَتَهَا نَبَاتًا حَسَنًا وَكَفَّلَهَا زَكَرِيَّا كُلَّمَا دَخَلَ عَلَيْهَا زَكَرِيَّا الْمِحْرَابَ وَجَدَ عِندَهَا رِزْقًا قَالَ يَا مَرْيَمُ أَنَّى لَكِ هَذَا قَالَتْ هُوَ مِنْ عِندِ اللَّهِ إِنَّ اللَّهَ يَرْزُقُ مَن يَشَاءُ بِغَيْرِ حِسَابٍ

38. Then Zachariah prayed unto his Lord and said: My Lord! Bestow upon me of Your bounty goodly offspring. Lo! You are the Hearer of supplication.

٣٨ هُنَالِكَ دَعَا زَكَرِيَّا رَبَّهُ قَالَ رَبِّ هَبْ لِي مِن لَّدُنكَ ذُرِّيَّةً طَيِّبَةً إِنَّكَ سَمِيعُ الدُّعَاءِ

39. And the angels called to him as he stood praying in the sanctuary: Allah gives you glad tidings of (a son whose name is) John (Yaḥyā), (who comes) to confirm a word from Allah, lordly, chaste, a Prophet of the righteous.

٣٩ فَنَادَتْهُ الْمَلَائِكَةُ وَهُوَ قَائِمٌ يُصَلِّي فِي الْمِحْرَابِ أَنَّ اللَّهَ يُبَشِّرُكَ بِيَحْيَى مُصَدِّقًا بِكَلِمَةٍ مِنَ اللَّهِ وَسَيِّدًا وَحَصُورًا وَنَبِيًّا مِنَ الصَّالِحِينَ

40. He said: My Lord! How can I have a son when age has overtaken me already and my wife is barren? (The angel) answered: So (it will be). Allah does what He will.

41. He said: My Lord! Appoint a token for me. (The angel) said: The token unto you (shall be) that you shall not speak unto mankind three days except by signs. Remember your Lord much, and praise (Him) in the early hours of night and morning.

42. And when the angels said: O Mary! Lo! Allah has chosen you and made you pure, and has preferred you above (all) the women of creation.

43. O Mary! Be obedient to your Lord, prostrate yourself and bow with those who bow (in worship).

44. This is of the tidings of the unseen. We reveal it unto you (Muhammad). You were not present with them when they threw their pens (to know) which of them should be the guardian of Mary, nor were you present with them when they quarreled (thereupon).

45. (And remember) when the angels said: O Mary! Allah gives you glad tidings of a word from Him, whose name is the Messiah, Jesus son of Mary illustrious in the world and the Hereafter, and one of those brought near (unto Allah).

46. He will speak unto mankind in his cradle and in his manhood, and he is of the righteous.

47. She said: My Lord! How can I have a child when no mortal has touched me? He said: So (it will be). Allah creates what He will. if He decrees a thing, He says unto it only: Be! and it is.

48. And He will teach him the Scripture and wisdom, and the Torah and the Gospel.

49. And will make him a messenger unto the children of Israel, (saying): Lo! I come unto you with a sign from your Lord. Lo! I fashion for you out of clay the likeness of a bird, and I breathe into it and it is a bird, by Allah's leave. I heal him who was born blind, and the leper, and I raise the dead, by Allah's leave. And I announce unto you what you eat and what you store up in your houses. Lo! herein surely is a portent for you, if you are believers.

50. And (I come) confirming that which was before me of the Torah, and to make lawful some of that which was forbidden unto you. I come unto you with a sign from your Lord, so keep your duty to Allah and obey me.

51. Lo! Allah is my Lord and your Lord, so worship Him. That is a straight path.

52. But when Jesus became conscious of their disbelief, he cried: Who will be my helpers in the cause of Allah? The disciples said: We will be Allah's helpers. We believe in Allah, and bear you witness that we have surrendered[66] (unto Him).

53. Our Lord! We believe in that which You have revealed and we follow him whom You have sent. Enroll us among those who witness (to the truth).

54. And they (the disbelievers) schemed, and Allah schemed (against them): and Allah is the best of schemers.

55. (And remember) when Allah said: O Jesus! Lo! I am gathering you and causing you to ascend unto Me, and am cleansing you of those who disbelieve and am setting those who follow you above those who disbelieve until the Day of Resurrection. Then unto Me you will (all) return, and I shall judge between you as to that wherein you used to differ.

56. As for those who disbelieve I shall chastise them with a heavy chastisement in the world and the Hereafter; and they will have no helpers.

﴿٤٩﴾ وَرَسُولًا إِلَىٰ بَنِىٓ إِسْرَٰٓءِيلَ أَنِّى قَدْ جِئْتُكُم بِـَٔايَةٍ مِّن رَّبِّكُمْ أَنِّىٓ أَخْلُقُ لَكُم مِّنَ ٱلطِّينِ كَهَيْـَٔةِ ٱلطَّيْرِ فَأَنفُخُ فِيهِ فَيَكُونُ طَيْرًۢا بِإِذْنِ ٱللَّهِ وَأُبْرِئُ ٱلْأَكْمَهَ وَٱلْأَبْرَصَ وَأُحْىِ ٱلْمَوْتَىٰ بِإِذْنِ ٱللَّهِ وَأُنَبِّئُكُم بِمَا تَأْكُلُونَ وَمَا تَدَّخِرُونَ فِى بُيُوتِكُمْ إِنَّ فِى ذَٰلِكَ لَـَٔايَةً لَّكُمْ إِن كُنتُم مُّؤْمِنِينَ

﴿٥٠﴾ وَمُصَدِّقًا لِّمَا بَيْنَ يَدَىَّ مِنَ ٱلتَّوْرَىٰةِ وَلِأُحِلَّ لَكُم بَعْضَ ٱلَّذِى حُرِّمَ عَلَيْكُمْ وَجِئْتُكُم بِـَٔايَةٍ مِّن رَّبِّكُمْ فَٱتَّقُوا۟ ٱللَّهَ وَأَطِيعُونِ

﴿٥١﴾ إِنَّ ٱللَّهَ رَبِّى وَرَبُّكُمْ فَٱعْبُدُوهُ هَٰذَا صِرَٰطٌ مُّسْتَقِيمٌ

﴿٥٢﴾ فَلَمَّآ أَحَسَّ عِيسَىٰ مِنْهُمُ ٱلْكُفْرَ قَالَ مَنْ أَنصَارِىٓ إِلَى ٱللَّهِ قَالَ ٱلْحَوَارِيُّونَ نَحْنُ أَنصَارُ ٱللَّهِ ءَامَنَّا بِٱللَّهِ وَٱشْهَدْ بِأَنَّا مُسْلِمُونَ

﴿٥٣﴾ رَبَّنَآ ءَامَنَّا بِمَآ أَنزَلْتَ وَٱتَّبَعْنَا ٱلرَّسُولَ فَٱكْتُبْنَا مَعَ ٱلشَّٰهِدِينَ

﴿٥٤﴾ وَمَكَرُوا۟ وَمَكَرَ ٱللَّهُ وَٱللَّهُ خَيْرُ ٱلْمَٰكِرِينَ

﴿٥٥﴾ إِذْ قَالَ ٱللَّهُ يَٰعِيسَىٰٓ إِنِّى مُتَوَفِّيكَ وَرَافِعُكَ إِلَىَّ وَمُطَهِّرُكَ مِنَ ٱلَّذِينَ كَفَرُوا۟ وَجَاعِلُ ٱلَّذِينَ ٱتَّبَعُوكَ فَوْقَ ٱلَّذِينَ كَفَرُوٓا۟ إِلَىٰ يَوْمِ ٱلْقِيَٰمَةِ ثُمَّ إِلَىَّ مَرْجِعُكُمْ فَأَحْكُمُ بَيْنَكُمْ فِيمَا كُنتُمْ فِيهِ تَخْتَلِفُونَ

﴿٥٦﴾ فَأَمَّا ٱلَّذِينَ كَفَرُوا۟ فَأُعَذِّبُهُمْ عَذَابًا شَدِيدًا فِى ٱلدُّنْيَا وَٱلْءَاخِرَةِ وَمَا لَهُم مِّن نَّٰصِرِينَ

66Or "are Muslims."

57. And as for those who believe and do good works, He will pay them their wages in full. And Allah loves not wrongdoers.

٥٧ وَأَمَّا الَّذِينَ ءَامَنُوا وَعَمِلُوا الصَّـٰلِحَـٰتِ فَيُوَفِّيهِمْ أُجُورَهُمْ وَاللَّهُ لَا يُحِبُّ الظَّـٰلِمِينَ

58. This (which) We recite unto you is part of the revelation and a wise reminder.

٥٨ ذَٰلِكَ نَتْلُوهُ عَلَيْكَ مِنَ الْآيَـٰتِ وَالذِّكْرِ الْحَكِيمِ

59. Lo! the likeness of Jesus with Allah is as the likeness of Adam. He created him of dust, then He said unto him: Be! and he is.

٥٩ إِنَّ مَثَلَ عِيسَىٰ عِندَ اللَّهِ كَمَثَلِ ءَادَمَ خَلَقَهُ مِن تُرَابٍ ثُمَّ قَالَ لَهُ كُن فَيَكُونُ

60. (This is) the truth from your Lord (O Muhammad), so be not you of those who waver.

٦٠ الْحَقُّ مِن رَّبِّكَ فَلَا تَكُن مِّنَ الْمُمْتَرِينَ

61. And who disputes with you concerning him, after the knowledge which has come unto you, say (unto him): Come! We will summon our children and your children, and our women and your women, and ourselves and yourselves, then we will pray humbly (to our Lord) and (solemnly) invoke the curse of Allah upon those who lie.

٦١ فَمَنْ حَاجَّكَ فِيهِ مِنْ بَعْدِ مَا جَاءَكَ مِنَ الْعِلْمِ فَقُلْ تَعَالَوْا نَدْعُ أَبْنَاءَنَا وَأَبْنَاءَكُمْ وَنِسَاءَنَا وَنِسَاءَكُمْ وَأَنفُسَنَا وَأَنفُسَكُمْ ثُمَّ نَبْتَهِلْ فَنَجْعَل لَّعْنَتَ اللَّهِ عَلَى الْكَـٰذِبِينَ

62. Lo! This surely is the true narrative. There is no God save Allah, and lo! Allah is the Mighty, the Wise.

٦٢ إِنَّ هَـٰذَا لَهُوَ الْقَصَصُ الْحَقُّ وَمَا مِنْ إِلَـٰهٍ إِلَّا اللَّهُ وَإِنَّ اللَّهَ لَهُوَ الْعَزِيزُ الْحَكِيمُ

63. And if they turn away, then Lo! Allah is Aware of (who are) the corrupters.

٦٣ فَإِن تَوَلَّوْا فَإِنَّ اللَّهَ عَلِيمٌ بِالْمُفْسِدِينَ

64. Say: O People of the Scripture![67] Come to an agreement between us and you: that we shall worship none but Allah, and that we shall ascribe no partners unto Him, and that none of us shall take others for lords beside Allah. And if they turn away, then say: Bear witness that we are they who have surrendered[68] (unto Him).

٦٤ قُلْ يَـٰأَهْلَ الْكِتَـٰبِ تَعَالَوْا إِلَىٰ كَلِمَةٍ سَوَاءٍ بَيْنَنَا وَبَيْنَكُمْ أَلَّا نَعْبُدَ إِلَّا اللَّهَ وَلَا نُشْرِكَ بِهِ شَيْئًا وَلَا يَتَّخِذَ بَعْضُنَا بَعْضًا أَرْبَابًا مِّن دُونِ اللَّهِ فَإِن تَوَلَّوْا فَقُولُوا اشْهَدُوا بِأَنَّا مُسْلِمُونَ

65. O People of the Scripture! Why will you argue about Abraham, when the Torah and the Gospel were not revealed till after him? Have you then no sense?

٦٥ يَـٰأَهْلَ الْكِتَـٰبِ لِمَ تُحَاجُّونَ فِي إِبْرَٰهِيمَ وَمَا أُنزِلَتِ التَّوْرَىٰةُ وَالْإِنجِيلُ إِلَّا مِن بَعْدِهِ أَفَلَا تَعْقِلُونَ

66. Lo! you are those who argue about matters of which you have some knowledge: Why then argue you concerning that whereof you have no knowledge? Allah knows. You know not.

٦٦ هَـٰأَنتُمْ هَـٰؤُلَاءِ حَاجَجْتُمْ فِيمَا لَكُم بِهِ عِلْمٌ فَلِمَ تُحَاجُّونَ فِيمَا لَيْسَ لَكُم بِهِ عِلْمٌ وَاللَّهُ يَعْلَمُ وَأَنتُمْ لَا تَعْلَمُونَ

---

[67] Jews and Christians.
[68] Arabic: Muslimūn (i.e., Muslims).

67. Abraham was not a Jew, nor yet a Christian; but he was an upright man who had surrendered (to Allah), and he was not of the idolaters.

68. Lo! those of mankind who have the best claim to Abraham are those who followed him, and this Prophet and those who believe (with him); and Allah is the Protecting Friend of the believers.

69. A party of the people of the Scripture long to make you go astray; and they make none to go astray except themselves, but they perceive not.

70. O People of the Scripture! Why disbelieve you in the revelations of Allah, when you (yourselves) bear witness (to the truth)?

71. O People of the Scripture! Why confound you truth with falsehood and knowingly conceal the truth?

72. And a party of the People of the Scripture say: Believe in that which has been revealed unto those who believe at the opening of the day and disbelieve at the end thereof, in order that they may return;[69]

73. And believe not save in one who follows your religion—Say (O Muhammad): Lo! the guidance is Allah's guidance—that any one is given the like of that which was given unto you or that they may argue with you in the presence of your Lord. Say (O Muhammad): Lo! the bounty is in Allah's hand. He bestows it on whom He will. Allah is All Embracing, All Knowing.

74. He selects for His mercy whom He will. Allah is of infinite bounty.

75. Among the People of the Scripture there is he who, if you trust him with a weight of treasure, will return it to you. And among them there is he who, if you trust him with a piece of gold, will not return it to you unless you keep standing over him. That is because they say: We have no duty to the Gentiles. They speak a lie concerning Allah knowingly.

٦٧ مَا كَانَ إِبْرَٰهِيمُ يَهُودِيًّا وَلَا نَصْرَانِيًّا وَلَٰكِن كَانَ حَنِيفًا مُّسْلِمًا وَمَا كَانَ مِنَ ٱلْمُشْرِكِينَ

٦٨ إِنَّ أَوْلَى ٱلنَّاسِ بِإِبْرَٰهِيمَ لَلَّذِينَ ٱتَّبَعُوهُ وَهَٰذَا ٱلنَّبِىُّ وَٱلَّذِينَ ءَامَنُوا وَٱللَّهُ وَلِىُّ ٱلْمُؤْمِنِينَ

٦٩ وَدَّت طَّآئِفَةٌ مِّنْ أَهْلِ ٱلْكِتَٰبِ لَوْ يُضِلُّونَكُمْ وَمَا يُضِلُّونَ إِلَّا أَنفُسَهُمْ وَمَا يَشْعُرُونَ

٧٠ يَٰأَهْلَ ٱلْكِتَٰبِ لِمَ تَكْفُرُونَ بِـَٔايَٰتِ ٱللَّهِ وَأَنتُمْ تَشْهَدُونَ

٧١ يَٰأَهْلَ ٱلْكِتَٰبِ لِمَ تَلْبِسُونَ ٱلْحَقَّ بِٱلْبَٰطِلِ وَتَكْتُمُونَ ٱلْحَقَّ وَأَنتُمْ تَعْلَمُونَ

٧٢ وَقَالَت طَّآئِفَةٌ مِّنْ أَهْلِ ٱلْكِتَٰبِ ءَامِنُوا بِٱلَّذِى أُنزِلَ عَلَى ٱلَّذِينَ ءَامَنُوا وَجْهَ ٱلنَّهَارِ وَٱكْفُرُوا ءَاخِرَهُ لَعَلَّهُمْ يَرْجِعُونَ

٧٣ وَلَا تُؤْمِنُوا إِلَّا لِمَن تَبِعَ دِينَكُمْ قُلْ إِنَّ ٱلْهُدَىٰ هُدَى ٱللَّهِ أَن يُؤْتَىٰ أَحَدٌ مِّثْلَ مَا أُوتِيتُمْ أَوْ يُحَآجُّوكُمْ عِندَ رَبِّكُمْ قُلْ إِنَّ ٱلْفَضْلَ بِيَدِ ٱللَّهِ يُؤْتِيهِ مَن يَشَآءُ وَٱللَّهُ وَٰسِعٌ عَلِيمٌ

٧٤ يَخْتَصُّ بِرَحْمَتِهِ مَن يَشَآءُ وَٱللَّهُ ذُو ٱلْفَضْلِ ٱلْعَظِيمِ

٧٥ وَمِنْ أَهْلِ ٱلْكِتَٰبِ مَنْ إِن تَأْمَنْهُ بِقِنطَارٍ يُؤَدِّهِ إِلَيْكَ وَمِنْهُم مَّنْ إِن تَأْمَنْهُ بِدِينَارٍ لَّا يُؤَدِّهِ إِلَيْكَ إِلَّا مَا دُمْتَ عَلَيْهِ قَآئِمًا ذَٰلِكَ بِأَنَّهُمْ قَالُوا لَيْسَ عَلَيْنَا فِى ٱلْأُمِّيِّنَ سَبِيلٌ وَيَقُولُونَ عَلَى ٱللَّهِ ٱلْكَذِبَ وَهُمْ يَعْلَمُونَ

---

[69]This refers to some Jews of al Madinah who feigned an interest in Islam in the hope of detaching some of the Muslims by their subtle arguments.

76. Nay, but (the chosen of Allah is) he who fulfills his pledge and wards off (evil); for lo! Allah loves those who ward off (evil).

77. Lo! those who purchase a small gain at the cost of Allah's covenant and their oaths, they have no portion in the Hereafter.[70] Allah will neither speak to them nor look upon them on the Day of Resurrection, nor will He make them grow. Theirs will be a painful doom.

78. And Lo! there is a party of them who distort the Scripture with their tongues, that you may think that what they say is from the Scripture, when it is not from the Scrip-ture. And they say: It is from Allah, when it is not from Allah; and they speak a lie concerning Allah knowingly.

79. It is not (possible) for any human being unto whom Allah had given the Scripture and wisdom and the prophet-hood that he should afterwards have said unto mankind: Be slaves of me instead of Allah; but: Be you faithful servants of the Lord by virtue of your constant teaching of the Scripture and of your constant study thereof.

80. And he commanded you not that you should take the angels and the Prophets for lords. Would he command you to disbelieve after you had surren-dered (to Allah)?

81. When Allah made (His) covenant with the Prophets, (He said): Behold that which I have given you of the Scrip-ture and knowledge. And afterward there will come unto you a Messenger, confirming that which you possess. You shall believe in him and you shall help him. He said: Do you agree, and will you take up My burden (which I lay upon you) in this (matter)? They answered: We agree. He said: Then bear you witness. I will be a witness with you.

﴿٧٦﴾ بَلَىٰ مَنْ أَوْفَىٰ بِعَهْدِهِ وَاتَّقَىٰ فَإِنَّ اللَّهَ يُحِبُّ الْمُتَّقِينَ

﴿٧٧﴾ إِنَّ الَّذِينَ يَشْتَرُونَ بِعَهْدِ اللَّهِ وَأَيْمَانِهِمْ ثَمَنًا قَلِيلًا أُولَٰئِكَ لَا خَلَاقَ لَهُمْ فِي الْآخِرَةِ وَلَا يُكَلِّمُهُمُ اللَّهُ وَلَا يَنظُرُ إِلَيْهِمْ يَوْمَ الْقِيَامَةِ وَلَا يُزَكِّيهِمْ وَلَهُمْ عَذَابٌ أَلِيمٌ

﴿٧٨﴾ وَإِنَّ مِنْهُمْ لَفَرِيقًا يَلْوُونَ أَلْسِنَتَهُم بِالْكِتَابِ لِتَحْسَبُوهُ مِنَ الْكِتَابِ وَمَا هُوَ مِنَ الْكِتَابِ وَيَقُولُونَ هُوَ مِنْ عِندِ اللَّهِ وَمَا هُوَ مِنْ عِندِ اللَّهِ وَيَقُولُونَ عَلَى اللَّهِ الْكَذِبَ وَهُمْ يَعْلَمُونَ

﴿٧٩﴾ مَا كَانَ لِبَشَرٍ أَن يُؤْتِيَهُ اللَّهُ الْكِتَابَ وَالْحُكْمَ وَالنُّبُوَّةَ ثُمَّ يَقُولَ لِلنَّاسِ كُونُوا عِبَادًا لِّي مِن دُونِ اللَّهِ وَلَٰكِن كُونُوا رَبَّانِيِّينَ بِمَا كُنتُمْ تُعَلِّمُونَ الْكِتَابَ وَبِمَا كُنتُمْ تَدْرُسُونَ

﴿٨٠﴾ وَلَا يَأْمُرَكُمْ أَن تَتَّخِذُوا الْمَلَائِكَةَ وَالنَّبِيِّينَ أَرْبَابًا أَيَأْمُرُكُم بِالْكُفْرِ بَعْدَ إِذْ أَنتُم مُّسْلِمُونَ

﴿٨١﴾ وَإِذْ أَخَذَ اللَّهُ مِيثَاقَ النَّبِيِّينَ لَمَا آتَيْتُكُم مِّن كِتَابٍ وَحِكْمَةٍ ثُمَّ جَاءَكُمْ رَسُولٌ مُّصَدِّقٌ لِّمَا مَعَكُمْ لَتُؤْمِنُنَّ بِهِ وَلَتَنصُرُنَّهُ قَالَ أَأَقْرَرْتُمْ وَأَخَذْتُمْ عَلَىٰ ذَٰلِكُمْ إِصْرِي قَالُوا أَقْرَرْنَا قَالَ فَاشْهَدُوا وَأَنَا مَعَكُم مِّنَ الشَّاهِدِينَ

---

[70]The Jews of al Madinah had made a solemn treaty with the Prophet in the year 1 A.H.

82. Then whoever after this shall turn away: they will be miscreants.

٨٢ فَمَن تَوَلَّىٰ بَعْدَ ذَٰلِكَ فَأُوْلَـٰئِكَ هُمُ الْفَـٰسِقُونَ

83. Seek they other than the religion of Allah, when unto Him submits whoever is in the heavens and the earth, willingly, or unwillingly, and unto Him they will be returned.

٨٣ أَفَغَيْرَ دِينِ اللَّهِ يَبْغُونَ وَلَهُ أَسْلَمَ مَن فِي السَّمَـٰوَاتِ وَالْأَرْضِ طَوْعًا وَكَرْهًا وَإِلَيْهِ يُرْجَعُونَ

84. Say (O Muhammad): We believe in Allah and that which is revealed unto us and that which was revealed unto Abraham and Ishmael and Isaac and Jacob and the tribes, and that which was vouchsafed unto Moses and Jesus and the Prophets from their Lord. We make no distinction between any of them, and unto Him we have surrendered.[71]

٨٤ قُلْ ءَامَنَّا بِاللَّهِ وَمَا أُنزِلَ عَلَيْنَا وَمَا أُنزِلَ عَلَىٰ إِبْرَٰهِيمَ وَإِسْمَـٰعِيلَ وَإِسْحَـٰقَ وَيَعْقُوبَ وَالْأَسْبَاطِ وَمَا أُوتِيَ مُوسَىٰ وَعِيسَىٰ وَالنَّبِيُّونَ مِن رَّبِّهِمْ لَا نُفَرِّقُ بَيْنَ أَحَدٍ مِّنْهُمْ وَنَحْنُ لَهُ مُسْلِمُونَ

85. And who seeks as religion other than Islam[72] it will not be accepted from him, and he will be one of the losers in the Hereafter.

٨٥ وَمَن يَبْتَغِ غَيْرَ الْإِسْلَـٰمِ دِينًا فَلَن يُقْبَلَ مِنْهُ وَهُوَ فِي الْآخِرَةِ مِنَ الْخَـٰسِرِينَ

86. How shall Allah guide a people who disbelieved after their belief and (after) they bore witness that the Messenger is true and after clear proofs (of Allah's sovereignty) had come unto them? And Allah guides not wrongdoing folk.

٨٦ كَيْفَ يَهْدِي اللَّهُ قَوْمًا كَفَرُوا بَعْدَ إِيمَـٰنِهِمْ وَشَهِدُوا أَنَّ الرَّسُولَ حَقٌّ وَجَاءَهُمُ الْبَيِّنَـٰتُ وَاللَّهُ لَا يَهْدِي الْقَوْمَ الظَّـٰلِمِينَ

87. As for such, their reward is that on them rests the curse of Allah and of angels and of men combined.

٨٧ أُوْلَـٰئِكَ جَزَآؤُهُمْ أَنَّ عَلَيْهِمْ لَعْنَةَ اللَّهِ وَالْمَلَـٰئِكَةِ وَالنَّاسِ أَجْمَعِينَ

88. There will they abide. Their doom will not be lightened, neither will they be reprieved;

٨٨ خَـٰلِدِينَ فِيهَا لَا يُخَفَّفُ عَنْهُمُ الْعَذَابُ وَلَا هُمْ يُنظَرُونَ

89. Save those who afterward repent and do right. Lo! Allah is Forgiving, Merciful.

٨٩ إِلَّا الَّذِينَ تَابُوا مِن بَعْدِ ذَٰلِكَ وَأَصْلَحُوا فَإِنَّ اللَّهَ غَفُورٌ رَّحِيمٌ

90. Lo! those who disbelieve after their (profession of) belief, and afterward grow violent in disbelief: their repentance will not be accepted. And such are those who are astray.

٩٠ إِنَّ الَّذِينَ كَفَرُوا بَعْدَ إِيمَـٰنِهِمْ ثُمَّ ازْدَادُوا كُفْرًا لَّن تُقْبَلَ تَوْبَتُهُمْ وَأُوْلَـٰئِكَ هُمُ الضَّآلُّونَ

---

[71]Almost identical with Surah 2:136.

[72]Islam (Arabic) means submission and surrender to Allah.

٩١ إِنَّ الَّذِينَ كَفَرُوا وَمَاتُوا وَهُمْ كُفَّارٌ فَلَن يُقْبَلَ مِنْ أَحَدِهِم مِّلْءُ الْأَرْضِ ذَهَبًا وَلَوِ افْتَدَىٰ بِهِ ۚ أُوْلَٰئِكَ لَهُمْ عَذَابٌ أَلِيمٌ وَمَا لَهُم مِّن نَّاصِرِينَ

91. Lo! those who disbelieve, and die in disbelief, the (whole) earth full of gold would not be accepted from such a one if it were offered as a ransom (for his soul). Theirs will be a painful doom and they will have no helpers.

٩٢ لَن تَنَالُوا الْبِرَّ حَتَّىٰ تُنفِقُوا مِمَّا تُحِبُّونَ ۚ وَمَا تُنفِقُوا مِن شَيْءٍ فَإِنَّ اللَّهَ بِهِ عَلِيمٌ

92. You will not attain unto piety until you spend of that which you love. And whatsoever you spend, Allah is aware thereof.

٩٣ كُلُّ الطَّعَامِ كَانَ حِلًّا لِّبَنِي إِسْرَائِيلَ إِلَّا مَا حَرَّمَ إِسْرَائِيلُ عَلَىٰ نَفْسِهِ مِن قَبْلِ أَن تُنَزَّلَ التَّوْرَاةُ ۚ قُلْ فَأْتُوا بِالتَّوْرَاةِ فَاتْلُوهَا إِن كُنتُمْ صَادِقِينَ

93. All food was lawful unto the children of Israel, save that which Israel forbade himself, (in days) before the Torah was revealed. Say: Produce the Torah and read it (unto us) if you are truthful.

٩٤ فَمَنِ افْتَرَىٰ عَلَى اللَّهِ الْكَذِبَ مِنۢ بَعْدِ ذَٰلِكَ فَأُوْلَٰئِكَ هُمُ الظَّالِمُونَ

94. And whoever shall invent a falsehood after that concerning Allah, such will be wrongdoers.

٩٥ قُلْ صَدَقَ اللَّهُ ۚ فَاتَّبِعُوا مِلَّةَ إِبْرَاهِيمَ حَنِيفًا وَمَا كَانَ مِنَ الْمُشْرِكِينَ

95. Say: Allah speaks truth. So follow the religion of Abra-ham, the upright. He was not of the idolaters.

٩٦ إِنَّ أَوَّلَ بَيْتٍ وُضِعَ لِلنَّاسِ لَلَّذِي بِبَكَّةَ مُبَارَكًا وَهُدًى لِّلْعَالَمِينَ

96. Lo! the first Sanctuary appointed for mankind was that at Bakkah (Makkah), a blessed place, a guidance to the worlds;

٩٧ فِيهِ ءَايَاتٌ بَيِّنَاتٌ مَّقَامُ إِبْرَاهِيمَ ۖ وَمَن دَخَلَهُ كَانَ ءَامِنًا ۗ وَلِلَّهِ عَلَى النَّاسِ حِجُّ الْبَيْتِ مَنِ اسْتَطَاعَ إِلَيْهِ سَبِيلًا ۚ وَمَن كَفَرَ فَإِنَّ اللَّهَ غَنِيٌّ عَنِ الْعَالَمِينَ

97. Where there are plain memorials (of Allah's guidance); the place where Abraham stood up to pray; and whoever enters it is safe. And pilgrimage to the House is a duty unto Allah for mankind, for him who can find a way there. As for him who disbelieves, (let him know that) Lo! Allah is Independent of (all) the worlds.

٩٨ قُلْ يَا أَهْلَ الْكِتَابِ لِمَ تَكْفُرُونَ بِآيَاتِ اللَّهِ وَاللَّهُ شَهِيدٌ عَلَىٰ مَا تَعْمَلُونَ

98. Say: O People of the Scripture! Why disbelieve you in the revelations of Allah, when Allah (Himself) is Witness of what you do?

٩٩ قُلْ يَا أَهْلَ الْكِتَابِ لِمَ تَصُدُّونَ عَن سَبِيلِ اللَّهِ مَنْ ءَامَنَ تَبْغُونَهَا عِوَجًا وَأَنتُمْ شُهَدَاءُ ۗ وَمَا اللَّهُ بِغَافِلٍ عَمَّا تَعْمَلُونَ

99. Say: O People of the Scripture! Why drive you back believers from the way of Allah, seeking to make it crooked, when you are witnesses (to Allah's guidance)? Allah is not unaware of what you do.

100. O you who believe! If you obey a party of those who have received the Scripture they will make you disbelievers after your belief.

101. How can you disbelieve, when Allah's revelations are recited unto you, and His Messenger is in your midst? He who holds fast to Allah, he indeed is guided unto a right path.

102. O you who believe! Observe your duty to Allah with right observance, and die not save as Muslims;

103. And hold fast, all of you together, to the bond of Allah, and do not be divided. And remember Allah's favor unto you: how you were enemies and He made friendship between your hearts so that you became as brothers by His grace; and (how) you were upon the brink of an abyss of fire, and He did save you from it. Thus Allah makes clear His revelations unto you, that you may be guided,

104. And let there emerge from you a group who invite to goodness, and enjoin right conduct and forbid indecency. Such are they who are successful.

105. And be you not as those who separated and disputed after the clear proofs had come unto them. For such there is an awful doom,

106. On the day when (some) faces will be whitened and (some) faces will be blackened; and as for those whose faces have been blackened, it will be said unto them: Disbelieved you after your (profession of) belief? Then taste the punishment for that you disbelieved.

يَـٰٓأَيُّهَا ٱلَّذِينَ ءَامَنُوٓا۟ إِن تُطِيعُوا۟ فَرِيقًا مِّنَ ٱلَّذِينَ أُوتُوا۟ ٱلْكِتَـٰبَ يَرُدُّوكُم بَعْدَ إِيمَـٰنِكُمْ كَـٰفِرِينَ ۝

وَكَيْفَ تَكْفُرُونَ وَأَنتُمْ تُتْلَىٰ عَلَيْكُمْ ءَايَـٰتُ ٱللَّهِ وَفِيكُمْ رَسُولُهُۥ وَمَن يَعْتَصِم بِٱللَّهِ فَقَدْ هُدِىَ إِلَىٰ صِرَٰطٍ مُّسْتَقِيمٍ ۝

يَـٰٓأَيُّهَا ٱلَّذِينَ ءَامَنُوا۟ ٱتَّقُوا۟ ٱللَّهَ حَقَّ تُقَاتِهِۦ وَلَا تَمُوتُنَّ إِلَّا وَأَنتُم مُّسْلِمُونَ ۝

وَٱعْتَصِمُوا۟ بِحَبْلِ ٱللَّهِ جَمِيعًا وَلَا تَفَرَّقُوا۟ وَٱذْكُرُوا۟ نِعْمَتَ ٱللَّهِ عَلَيْكُمْ إِذْ كُنتُمْ أَعْدَآءً فَأَلَّفَ بَيْنَ قُلُوبِكُمْ فَأَصْبَحْتُم بِنِعْمَتِهِۦٓ إِخْوَٰنًا وَكُنتُمْ عَلَىٰ شَفَا حُفْرَةٍ مِّنَ ٱلنَّارِ فَأَنقَذَكُم مِّنْهَا كَذَٰلِكَ يُبَيِّنُ ٱللَّهُ لَكُمْ ءَايَـٰتِهِۦ لَعَلَّكُمْ تَهْتَدُونَ ۝

وَلْتَكُن مِّنكُمْ أُمَّةٌ يَدْعُونَ إِلَى ٱلْخَيْرِ وَيَأْمُرُونَ بِٱلْمَعْرُوفِ وَيَنْهَوْنَ عَنِ ٱلْمُنكَرِ وَأُو۟لَـٰٓئِكَ هُمُ ٱلْمُفْلِحُونَ ۝

وَلَا تَكُونُوا۟ كَٱلَّذِينَ تَفَرَّقُوا۟ وَٱخْتَلَفُوا۟ مِنۢ بَعْدِ مَا جَآءَهُمُ ٱلْبَيِّنَـٰتُ وَأُو۟لَـٰٓئِكَ لَهُمْ عَذَابٌ عَظِيمٌ ۝

يَوْمَ تَبْيَضُّ وُجُوهٌ وَتَسْوَدُّ وُجُوهٌ فَأَمَّا ٱلَّذِينَ ٱسْوَدَّتْ وُجُوهُهُمْ أَكَفَرْتُم بَعْدَ إِيمَـٰنِكُمْ فَذُوقُوا۟ ٱلْعَذَابَ بِمَا كُنتُمْ تَكْفُرُونَ ۝

107. As for those whose faces have been whitened, Lo! in the mercy of Allah they dwell forever.

﴿١٠٧﴾ وَأَمَّا الَّذِينَ ابْيَضَّتْ وُجُوهُهُمْ فَفِي رَحْمَةِ اللّٰهِ هُمْ فِيهَا خَالِدُونَ

108. These are revelations of Allah. We recite them unto you in truth. Allah wills no injustice to (His) creatures.

﴿١٠٨﴾ تِلْكَ آيَاتُ اللّٰهِ نَتْلُوهَا عَلَيْكَ بِالْحَقِّ وَمَا اللّٰهُ يُرِيدُ ظُلْمًا لِلْعَالَمِينَ

109. Unto Allah belongs whatsoever is in the heavens and whatsoever is in the earth; and unto Allah all things are returned.

﴿١٠٩﴾ وَلِلّٰهِ مَا فِي السَّمَوَاتِ وَمَا فِي الْأَرْضِ وَإِلَى اللّٰهِ تُرْجَعُ الْأُمُورُ

110. You are the best community that has been raised up for mankind. You enjoin right conduct and forbid indecency; and you believe in Allah. And if the People of the Scripture had believed it had been better for them. Some of them are believers; but most of them are evil livers.

﴿١١٠﴾ كُنْتُمْ خَيْرَ أُمَّةٍ أُخْرِجَتْ لِلنَّاسِ تَأْمُرُونَ بِالْمَعْرُوفِ وَتَنْهَوْنَ عَنِ الْمُنْكَرِ وَتُؤْمِنُونَ بِاللّٰهِ وَلَوْ آمَنَ أَهْلُ الْكِتَابِ لَكَانَ خَيْرًا لَهُمْ مِنْهُمُ الْمُؤْمِنُونَ وَأَكْثَرُهُمُ الْفَاسِقُونَ

111. They will not harm you save a trifling hurt, and if they fight against you they will turn and flee. And afterward they will not be helped.

﴿١١١﴾ لَنْ يَضُرُّوكُمْ إِلَّا أَذًى وَإِنْ يُقَاتِلُوكُمْ يُوَلُّوكُمُ الْأَدْبَارَ ثُمَّ لَا يُنْصَرُونَ

112. Ignominy shall be their portion wheresoever they are found save (where they grasp) a rope from Allah and a rope from men.[73] They have incurred anger from their Lord, and wretchedness is laid upon them. That is because they used to disbelieve the revelations of Allah, and slew the Prophets wrongfully. That is because they were rebellious and used to transgress.

﴿١١٢﴾ ضُرِبَتْ عَلَيْهِمُ الذِّلَّةُ أَيْنَ مَا ثُقِفُوا إِلَّا بِحَبْلٍ مِنَ اللّٰهِ وَحَبْلٍ مِنَ النَّاسِ وَبَاءُوا بِغَضَبٍ مِنَ اللّٰهِ وَضُرِبَتْ عَلَيْهِمُ الْمَسْكَنَةُ ذَلِكَ بِأَنَّهُمْ كَانُوا يَكْفُرُونَ بِآيَاتِ اللّٰهِ وَيَقْتُلُونَ الْأَنْبِيَاءَ بِغَيْرِ حَقٍّ ذَلِكَ بِمَا عَصَوْا وَكَانُوا يَعْتَدُونَ

113. They are not all alike. Of the People of the Scripture there is a staunch community who recite the revelations of Allah in the night season, falling prostrate (before Him).

﴿١١٣﴾ لَيْسُوا سَوَاءً مِنْ أَهْلِ الْكِتَابِ أُمَّةٌ قَائِمَةٌ يَتْلُونَ آيَاتِ اللّٰهِ آنَاءَ اللَّيْلِ وَهُمْ يَسْجُدُونَ

114. They believe in Allah and the Last Day, and enjoin right conduct and forbid indecency, and vie one with another in good works. They are of the righteous.

﴿١١٤﴾ يُؤْمِنُونَ بِاللّٰهِ وَالْيَوْمِ الْآخِرِ وَيَأْمُرُونَ بِالْمَعْرُوفِ وَيَنْهَوْنَ عَنِ الْمُنْكَرِ وَيُسَارِعُونَ فِي الْخَيْرَاتِ وَأُولَئِكَ مِنَ الصَّالِحِينَ

115. And whatever good they do, they will not be denied the meed thereof. Allah is Aware of those who ward off (evil).

﴿١١٥﴾ وَمَا يَفْعَلُوا مِنْ خَيْرٍ فَلَنْ يُكْفَرُوهُ وَاللّٰهُ عَلِيمٌ بِالْمُتَّقِينَ

---

[73]i.e., when they keep the covenant which the Prophet had made with the Jews of al Madinah.

116. Lo! the riches and the progeny of those who disbelieve will not avail them anything against Allah; and such are rightful owners of the Fire. They will abide therein forever.

﴾١١٦﴿ إِنَّ الَّذِينَ كَفَرُوا لَن تُغْنِيَ عَنْهُمْ أَمْوَٰلُهُمْ وَلَا أَوْلَٰدُهُم مِّنَ اللَّهِ شَيْئًا وَأُو۟لَٰٓئِكَ أَصْحَٰبُ النَّارِ هُمْ فِيهَا خَٰلِدُونَ

117. The likeness of that which they spend in this life of the world is as the likeness of a biting, icy wind which smites the harvest of a people who have wronged themselves, and devastates it. Allah wronged them not, but they did wrong themselves.

﴾١١٧﴿ مَثَلُ مَا يُنفِقُونَ فِى هَٰذِهِ الْحَيَوٰةِ الدُّنْيَا كَمَثَلِ رِيحٍ فِيهَا صِرٌّ أَصَابَتْ حَرْثَ قَوْمٍ ظَلَمُوٓا أَنفُسَهُمْ فَأَهْلَكَتْهُ وَمَا ظَلَمَهُمُ اللَّهُ وَلَٰكِنْ أَنفُسَهُمْ يَظْلِمُونَ

118. O you who believe! Take not for intimates others than your own folk, who would spare no pains to ruin you; they love to hamper you. Hatred is revealed by (the utterance of) their mouths, but that which their breasts hide is greater. We have made plain for you the revelations if you will understand.

﴾١١٨﴿ يَٰٓأَيُّهَا الَّذِينَ ءَامَنُوا لَا تَتَّخِذُوا بِطَانَةً مِّن دُونِكُمْ لَا يَأْلُونَكُمْ خَبَالًا وَدُّوا مَا عَنِتُّمْ قَدْ بَدَتِ الْبَغْضَآءُ مِنْ أَفْوَٰهِهِمْ وَمَا تُخْفِى صُدُورُهُمْ أَكْبَرُ قَدْ بَيَّنَّا لَكُمُ الْءَايَٰتِ إِن كُنتُمْ تَعْقِلُونَ

119. Ah! you are those who love them though they love you not, and you believe in all the Scripture. When they fall in with you they say: We believe; but when they go apart they bite their fingertips at you, for rage. Say: Perish in your rage! Lo! Allah is Aware of what is hidden in (your) breasts.

﴾١١٩﴿ هَٰٓأَنتُمْ أُو۟لَآءِ تُحِبُّونَهُمْ وَلَا يُحِبُّونَكُمْ وَتُؤْمِنُونَ بِالْكِتَٰبِ كُلِّهِ وَإِذَا لَقُوكُمْ قَالُوٓا ءَامَنَّا وَإِذَا خَلَوْا عَضُّوا عَلَيْكُمُ الْأَنَامِلَ مِنَ الْغَيْظِ قُلْ مُوتُوا بِغَيْظِكُمْ إِنَّ اللَّهَ عَلِيمٌ بِذَاتِ الصُّدُورِ

120. If a lucky chance befall you, it is evil unto them, and if disaster strike you they rejoice thereat. But if you persevere and keep from evil their guile will never harm you. Lo! Allah is Surrounding what they do.

﴾١٢٠﴿ إِن تَمْسَسْكُمْ حَسَنَةٌ تَسُؤْهُمْ وَإِن تُصِبْكُمْ سَيِّئَةٌ يَفْرَحُوا بِهَا وَإِن تَصْبِرُوا وَتَتَّقُوا لَا يَضُرُّكُمْ كَيْدُهُمْ شَيْئًا إِنَّ اللَّهَ بِمَا يَعْمَلُونَ مُحِيطٌ

121. And remember (O Muhammad) when you set forth at daybreak from your housefolk to assign to the believers their positions for the battle, Allah was Hearer, Knower.[74]

﴾١٢١﴿ وَإِذْ غَدَوْتَ مِنْ أَهْلِكَ تُبَوِّئُ الْمُؤْمِنِينَ مَقَٰعِدَ لِلْقِتَالِ وَاللَّهُ سَمِيعٌ عَلِيمٌ

---

[74]The battle of Mount Uhud, located near al Madinah, which took place in 3 A.H. (see introduction to this surah).

122. When two parties of you almost fell away, and Allah was their Protecting Friend. In Allah do believers put their trust.

123. Allah had already given you the victory at Badr, when you were contemptible. So observe your duty to Allah in order that you may be thankful.

124. And when you did say unto the believers: Is it not sufficient for you that your Lord should support you with three thousand angels sent down (to your help)?

125. Nay, but if you persevere, and keep from evil, and (the enemy) attack you suddenly, your Lord will help you with five thousand angels sweeping on.

126. Allah ordained this only as a message of good cheer for you, and that thereby your hearts might be at rest—Victory comes only from Allah, the Mighty, the Wise—

127. That He may cut off a part of those who disbelieve, or overwhelm them so that they retire, frustrated.

128. It is no concern at all of you (Muhammad) whether He relent toward them or punish them; for they are evil-doers.

129. Unto Allah belongs whatsoever is in the heavens and whatsoever is in the earth. He forgives whom He will, and punishes whom He will. Allah is Forgiving, Merciful.

130. O you who believe! Devour not usury, doubling and quadrupling (the sum lent). Observe your duty to Allah, that you may be successful.

131. And ward off (from yourselves) the Fire prepared for disbelievers.

132. And obey Allah and the Messenger, that you may find mercy.

133. And vie one with another for forgiveness from your Lord, and for a Paradise as wide as are the heavens and the earth, prepared for those who ward off (evil);

134. Those who spend (of that which Allah has given them) in ease and in adversity, those who control their wrath and are forgiving toward mankind; Allah loves the good;

135. And those who, when they do an evil thing or wrong themselves, remember Allah and implore forgiveness for their sins—Who forgives sins save Allah only?—and do not insist on (the wrong) they did for they know.

136. The reward of such will be forgiveness from their Lord, and Gardens underneath which rivers flow, wherein they will abide forever, a bountiful reward for workers!

137. Systems have passed away before you. Do but travel in the land and see the nature of the consequence for those who did deny (the messengers).

138. This is a declaration for mankind, a guidance and an admonition unto those who ward off (evil).

139. Faint not nor grieve, for you will overcome them if you are (indeed) believers.

140. If you have received a blow, (disbelieving) people have received a blow the like thereof:[75] These are (only) the vicissitudes which We cause to follow one another for mankind, to the end that Allah may know those who believe and may choose witnesses[76] from among you; and Allah loves not wrongdoers.

141. And that Allah may prove those who believe, and may blight disbelievers.

142. Or deemed you that you would enter Paradise while yet Allah knows not those of you who really strive, nor knows those (of you) who are steadfast?

---

[75]At Badr.
[76]Or martyrs.

143. And surely you used to wish for death before you met it (in the field). Now you have seen it with your eyes!

144. Muhammad is but a Messenger, messengers (the like of whom) have passed away before him. Will it be that, when he dies or is slain, you will turn back on your heels? He who turns back does no hurt to Allah, and Allah will reward the thankful.

145. No soul can ever die except by Allah's leave and at a term appointed. Who desires the reward of the world, We bestow on him thereof; and who desires the reward of the Hereafter, We bestow on him thereof. We shall reward the thankful.[77]

146. And with how many a prophet have there been a number of devoted men who fought (beside him). They quailed not for anything that befell them in the way of Allah, nor did they weaken, nor were they brought low. Allah loves the steadfast.

147. Their cry was only that they said: Our Lord! Forgive us for our sins and wasted efforts, make our foothold sure, and give us victory over the disbelieving folk.

148. So Allah gave them the reward of the world and the good reward of the Hereafter. Allah loves those whose deeds are good.

149. O you who believe! If you obey those who disbelieve, they will make you turn back on your heels, and so you turn back as losers.

150. But Allah is your Protector, and He is the best of helpers.

---

[77]On the morning when the Prophet died, Abū Bakr came into the mosque at al Madinah. He found the people distracted and 'Umar ibn al Khaṭṭāb telling them that it was a sin to say that the Prophet was dead. Abū Bakr left in order to ascertain the truth, returned to the mosque and informed the people that: "As for him who worshiped Muhammad, Muhammad is dead, but as for him who worshiped Allah, Allah is alive and does not die." When he recited this verse: "it was as if the people had not known till then that such a verse had been revealed."

151. We shall cast terror into the hearts of those who disbelieve because they ascribe unto Allah partners, for which no warrant has been revealed. Their habitation is the Fire, and hapless is the abode of the wrongdoers.

152. Allah surely made good His promise unto you when you routed them by His leave, until (the moment) when your courage failed you, and you disagreed about the matter and you disobeyed, after He had shown you that for which you long.[78] Some of you desired the world, and some of you desired the Hereafter. Therefore He made you flee from them, that He might try you. Yet now He has forgiven you. Allah is a Lord of Kindness to believers.

153. When you escaped to the valley and paid no heed to anyone, while the Messenger, in your rear, was calling you (to fight). Therefor He rewarded you grief for (his) grief, that (He might teach) you not to sorrow either for that which you missed or for that which befell you. Allah is Informed of what you do.

154. Then, after grief, He sent down security for you. As slumber did overcome a party of you, while (the other) party, who were anxious on their own account, thought wrongly of Allah, the thought of ignorance. They said: Have we any part in the cause? Say (O Muhammad): The cause belongs wholly to Allah. They hide within themselves (a thought) which they reveal not unto you, saying: Had we had any part in the cause we should not have been slain here. Say: Even though you had been in your houses, those appointed to be slain would have gone forth to the places where they were to lie. (All this has been) in order that Allah might try what is in your breasts and prove what is in your hearts. Allah is Aware of what is hidden in the breasts (of men).

سَنُلْقِى فِى قُلُوبِ ٱلَّذِينَ كَفَرُوا ٱلرُّعْبَ ۝ بِمَآ أَشْرَكُوا بِٱللَّهِ مَا لَمْ يُنَزِّلْ بِهِۦ سُلْطَٰنًا وَمَأْوَىٰهُمُ ٱلنَّارُ وَبِئْسَ مَثْوَى ٱلظَّٰلِمِينَ ۝ وَلَقَدْ صَدَقَكُمُ ٱللَّهُ وَعْدَهُۥٓ إِذْ تَحُسُّونَهُم بِإِذْنِهِۦ ۖ حَتَّىٰٓ إِذَا فَشِلْتُمْ وَتَنَٰزَعْتُمْ فِى ٱلْأَمْرِ وَعَصَيْتُم مِّنۢ بَعْدِ مَآ أَرَىٰكُم مَّا تُحِبُّونَ ۚ مِنكُم مَّن يُرِيدُ ٱلدُّنْيَا وَمِنكُم مَّن يُرِيدُ ٱلْآخِرَةَ ۚ ثُمَّ صَرَفَكُمْ عَنْهُمْ لِيَبْتَلِيَكُمْ ۖ وَلَقَدْ عَفَا عَنكُمْ ۗ وَٱللَّهُ ذُو فَضْلٍ عَلَى ٱلْمُؤْمِنِينَ ۝ إِذْ تُصْعِدُونَ وَلَا تَلْوُۥنَ عَلَىٰٓ أَحَدٍ وَٱلرَّسُولُ يَدْعُوكُمْ فِىٓ أُخْرَىٰكُمْ فَأَثَٰبَكُمْ غَمًّۢا بِغَمٍّ لِّكَيْلَا تَحْزَنُوا عَلَىٰ مَا فَاتَكُمْ وَلَا مَآ أَصَٰبَكُمْ ۗ وَٱللَّهُ خَبِيرٌۢ بِمَا تَعْمَلُونَ ۝ ثُمَّ أَنزَلَ عَلَيْكُم مِّنۢ بَعْدِ ٱلْغَمِّ أَمَنَةً نُّعَاسًا يَغْشَىٰ طَآئِفَةً مِّنكُمْ ۖ وَطَآئِفَةٌ قَدْ أَهَمَّتْهُمْ أَنفُسُهُمْ يَظُنُّونَ بِٱللَّهِ غَيْرَ ٱلْحَقِّ ظَنَّ ٱلْجَٰهِلِيَّةِ ۖ يَقُولُونَ هَل لَّنَا مِنَ ٱلْأَمْرِ مِن شَىْءٍ ۗ قُلْ إِنَّ ٱلْأَمْرَ كُلَّهُۥ لِلَّهِ ۗ يُخْفُونَ فِىٓ أَنفُسِهِم مَّا لَا يُبْدُونَ لَكَ ۖ يَقُولُونَ لَوْ كَانَ لَنَا مِنَ ٱلْأَمْرِ شَىْءٌ مَّا قُتِلْنَا هَٰهُنَا ۗ قُل لَّوْ كُنتُمْ فِى بُيُوتِكُمْ لَبَرَزَ ٱلَّذِينَ كُتِبَ عَلَيْهِمُ ٱلْقَتْلُ إِلَىٰ مَضَاجِعِهِمْ ۖ وَلِيَبْتَلِىَ ٱللَّهُ مَا فِى صُدُورِكُمْ وَلِيُمَحِّصَ مَا فِى قُلُوبِكُمْ ۚ وَٱللَّهُ عَلِيمٌۢ بِذَاتِ ٱلصُّدُورِ

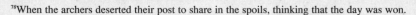

---

[78]When the archers deserted their post to share in the spoils, thinking that the day was won.

155. Lo! those of you who turned back on the day when the two hosts met, the Devil alone it was who caused them to backslide, because of some of that which they have earned. Now Allah has forgiven them. Lo! Allah is Forgiving. Clement.

156. O you who believe! Be not as those who disbelieved and said of their brethren who went abroad in the land or were fighting in the field: If they had been (here) with us they would not have died or been killed; that Allah may make it anguish in their hearts. Allah gives life and causes death; and Allah is Seer of what you do.

157. And what though you be slain in Allah's way or die therein? Surely pardon from Allah and mercy are better than all that they amass.

158. Should you die or be slain, surely unto Allah you are gathered?

159. It was by the mercy of Allah that you were lenient with them (O Muhammad), for if you had been stern and fierce of heart they would have dispersed from round about you. So pardon them and ask forgiveness for them and consult with them upon the conduct of affairs. And when you are resolved, then put your trust in Allah. Lo! Allah loves those who put their trust (in Him).

160. If Allah is your helper none can overcome you, and if He withdraws His help from you, who is there who can help you? In Allah let believers put their trust.

161. It is not for any Prophet to deceive (mankind). Who deceives will bring his deceit with him on the Day of Resurrection. Then every soul will be paid in full what it has earned; and they will not be wronged.

162. Is one who follows the pleasure of Allah as one who has earned condemnation from Allah, whose habitation is the Fire, a hapless journey's end?

163. There are degrees (of grace and reprobation) with Allah, and Allah is Seer of what you do.

164. Allah surely has shown grace to the believers by sending unto them a Messenger of their own who recites unto them His revelations, and causes them to grow, and teaches them the Scripture and wisdom; although before (he came to them) they were in flagrant error.[79]

165. And was it so, when a disaster smote you, though you had smitten (them with a disaster) twice (as great),[80] that you said: How is this? Say (unto them, O Muhammad): It is from yourselves. Lo! Allah is Able to do all things.

166. That which befell you, on the day when the two armies met, was by permission of Allah; that He might know the true believers;

167. And that He might know the hypocrites, unto whom it was said: Come, fight in the way of Allah, or defend yourselves. They answered: If we knew any fighting we would follow you. On that day they were nearer disbelief than faith. They utter with their mouths a thing which is not in their hearts. Allah is best aware of what they hide.

168. Those who, while they sat at home, said of their brothers (who were fighting for the cause of Allah): If they had been guided by us they would not have been slain. Say (unto them, O Muhammad): Then avert death from yourselves if you are truthful.

169. Think not of those, who are slain in the way of Allah, as dead. Nay, they are living. With their Lord they have provision.

---

[79]In fulfillment of the prayer of Abraham (Surah 2:129).
[80]At Badr.

170. Jubilant (are they) because of that which Allah has bestowed upon them of His bounty, rejoicing for the sake of those who have not joined them but are left behind: that there shall no fear come upon them neither shall they grieve.

171. They rejoice because of favor from Allah and kindness, and that Allah wastes not the wage of believers.

172. As for those who heard the call of Allah and His Messenger after the harm befell them (in the fight); for such of them as do right and ward off (evil), there is great reward.

173. Those unto whom men said: Lo! people have gathered against you, therefor fear them. (The threat of danger) but increased the faith of them and they cried: Allah is sufficient for us! Most Excellent is He in Whom we trust!

174. So they returned with grace and favor from Allah, and no harm touched them. They followed the good pleasure of Allah, and Allah is of infinite bounty.

175. It is only the Devil who would make his partisans fear (men). Fear them not; fear Me, if you are true believers.

176. Let not their conduct grieve you, who run easily to disbelief, for Lo! they injure Allah not at all. It is Allah's will to assign them no portion in the Hereafter, and theirs will be an awful doom.

177. Those who purchase disbelief at the price of faith harm Allah not at all, but theirs will be a painful doom.

178. And let not those who disbelieve imagine that the rein We give them bodes good unto their souls. We only give them rein that they may grow in sinfulness. And theirs will be a shameful doom.

١٧٠ فَرِحِينَ بِمَا آتَاهُمُ اللَّهُ مِن فَضْلِهِ وَيَسْتَبْشِرُونَ بِالَّذِينَ لَمْ يَلْحَقُوا بِهِم مِّنْ خَلْفِهِمْ أَلَّا خَوْفٌ عَلَيْهِمْ وَلَا هُمْ يَحْزَنُونَ

١٧١ يَسْتَبْشِرُونَ بِنِعْمَةٍ مِّنَ اللَّهِ وَفَضْلٍ وَأَنَّ اللَّهَ لَا يُضِيعُ أَجْرَ الْمُؤْمِنِينَ

١٧٢ الَّذِينَ اسْتَجَابُوا لِلَّهِ وَالرَّسُولِ مِن بَعْدِ مَا أَصَابَهُمُ الْقَرْحُ لِلَّذِينَ أَحْسَنُوا مِنْهُمْ وَاتَّقَوْا أَجْرٌ عَظِيمٌ

١٧٣ الَّذِينَ قَالَ لَهُمُ النَّاسُ إِنَّ النَّاسَ قَدْ جَمَعُوا لَكُمْ فَاخْشَوْهُمْ فَزَادَهُمْ إِيمَانًا وَقَالُوا حَسْبُنَا اللَّهُ وَنِعْمَ الْوَكِيلُ

١٧٤ فَانقَلَبُوا بِنِعْمَةٍ مِّنَ اللَّهِ وَفَضْلٍ لَّمْ يَمْسَسْهُمْ سُوءٌ وَاتَّبَعُوا رِضْوَانَ اللَّهِ وَاللَّهُ ذُو فَضْلٍ عَظِيمٍ

١٧٥ إِنَّمَا ذَٰلِكُمُ الشَّيْطَانُ يُخَوِّفُ أَوْلِيَاءَهُ فَلَا تَخَافُوهُمْ وَخَافُونِ إِن كُنتُم مُّؤْمِنِينَ

١٧٦ وَلَا يَحْزُنكَ الَّذِينَ يُسَارِعُونَ فِي الْكُفْرِ إِنَّهُمْ لَن يَضُرُّوا اللَّهَ شَيْئًا يُرِيدُ اللَّهُ أَلَّا يَجْعَلَ لَهُمْ حَظًّا فِي الْآخِرَةِ وَلَهُمْ عَذَابٌ عَظِيمٌ

١٧٧ إِنَّ الَّذِينَ اشْتَرَوُا الْكُفْرَ بِالْإِيمَانِ لَن يَضُرُّوا اللَّهَ شَيْئًا وَلَهُمْ عَذَابٌ أَلِيمٌ

١٧٨ وَلَا يَحْسَبَنَّ الَّذِينَ كَفَرُوا أَنَّمَا نُمْلِي لَهُمْ خَيْرٌ لِّأَنفُسِهِمْ إِنَّمَا نُمْلِي لَهُمْ لِيَزْدَادُوا إِثْمًا وَلَهُمْ عَذَابٌ مُّهِينٌ

179. It is not (the purpose) of Allah to leave you believers in your present state till He shall separate the wicked from the good. And it is not (the purpose of) Allah to let you know the unseen. But Allah chooses of His messengers whom He will (to receive knowledge thereof). So believe in Allah and His messengers. If you believe and ward off (evil), yours will be a vast reward.

180. And let not those who hoard up that which Allah has bestowed upon them of His bounty think that it is good for them. Nay, it is evil for them. That which they hoard will be their collar on the Day of Resurrection. Allah's is the heritage of the heavens and the earth, and Allah is Informed of what you do.

181. Surely Allah heard the saying of those who said: "Allah, forsooth, is poor, and we are rich!"[81] We shall record their saying with their slaying of the Prophets wrongfully and We shall say: Taste you the punishment of burning!

182. This is on account of that which your own hands have sent before (you to the judgment). Allah is no oppressor of (His) bondmen.

183. (The same are) those who say: Lo! Allah has charged us that we believe not in any messenger until he bring us an offering which fire (from heaven) shall devour. Say (unto them, O Muhammad): Messengers came unto you before me with miracles, and with that (very miracle) which you describe. Why then did you slay them? (Answer that) if you are truthful.

184. And if they deny you, even so did they deny messengers who were before you, who came with miracles and with the Psalms and with the Scripture giving light.

185. Every soul will taste of death. And you will be paid on the Day of Resurrection only that which you have fairly earned. Who is removed from the Fire and is made to enter Paradise, he indeed is triumphant. The life of this world is but comfort of illusion.

---

[81] A saying of some Jews of Al Madinah.

186. Assuredly you will be tried in your property and in your persons, and you will hear much wrong from those who were given the Scripture before you, and from the idolaters. But if you persevere and ward off (evil), then that is of the steadfast heart of things.

187. And (remember) when Allah laid a charge on those who had received the Scripture; (He said): You are to ex-pound it to mankind and not to hide it. But they flung it be-hind their backs and bought thereby a little gain. Surely evil is that which they have gained thereby.

188. Think not that those who exult in what they have given, and love to be praised for what they have not done— Think not, they are in safety from the doom. A painful doom is theirs.

189. Unto Allah belongs the Sovereignty of the heavens and the earth. Allah is Able to do all things.

190. Lo! in the creation of the heavens and the earth and (in) the difference of night and day are tokens (of His sovereignty) for men of understanding,

191. Such as remember Allah, standing, sitting, and reclining, and contemplate the creation of the heavens and the earth, (and say): Our Lord! You created not this in vain. Glory be to You! Preserve us from the doom of Fire.

192. Our Lord! Whom You cause to enter the Fire: him indeed You have confounded. For evildoers there will be no helpers.

193. Our Lord! Lo! we have heard a crier calling unto Faith: "Believe you in your Lord!" So we believed. Our Lord! Therefore forgive us our sins, and remit from us our evil deeds, and make us die the death of the righteous.

194. Our Lord! And give us that which You have promised to us by Your messengers. Confound us not upon the Day of Resurrection. Lo! You break not the appointed time.

195. And their Lord has heard them (and He said): Lo! I suffer not the work of any worker, male or female, to be lost. You proceed one from another.[82] So those who fled and were driven forth from their homes and suffered damage for My cause, and fought and were slain, surely I shall remit their evil deeds from them and surely I shall bring them into Gardens underneath which rivers flow. A reward from Allah. And with Allah is the fairest of rewards.

196. Let not the vicissitude (of the success) of those who disbelieve, in the land, deceive you (O Muhammad).

197. It is but a brief comfort. And afterward their habitation will be Hell, an ill abode.

198. But those who keep their duty to their Lord, for them are Gardens underneath which rivers flow, wherein they will be safe forever. A gift of welcome from their Lord. That which Allah has in store is better for the righteous.

199. And Lo! of the People of the Scripture there are some who believe in Allah and that which is revealed unto you and that which was revealed unto them, humbling themselves before Allah. They purchase not a trifling gain at the price of the revelations of Allah. Surely their reward is with their Lord, and Lo! Allah is swift to take account.

200. O you who believe! Endure, outdo all others in endurance, be ready, and firm and observe your duty to Allah, in order that you may succeed.

---

[82]This expression, which recurs in the Qur'an, is a reminder to men that women enjoy the same human status as they do.

Women

Al Nisā', "Women," deals largely with women's rights. The period of revelation is the months following the battle of Uhud, or, as Noldeke,[83] a careful critic, puts it, "between the end of the third year and the end of the fifth year" of the Prophet's reign at al Madinah. As the surah contains no reference to the siege of al Madinah ("The War of the Trench") by the allied tribes, which took place in the fifth year. I would place it between the end of the third year and the beginning of the fifth year.

Many Muslims were killed at the battle of Uhud, which explains the concern for orphans and widows in the opening verses. This is followed by a declaration of some rights for women that they had been deprived of by the pagan Arabs. The defection of some of the Jewish tribes, who had till then observed their treaty with the Prophet, to the pagan Arab side, their proclamation that the old Arab idolatry was preferable to Islam, and their active provision of aid and information to the Quraysh, forced the Muslims to declare war on them. This surah deals with the Hypocrites at some length, with the rebellious Jews, and also makes a reference to Christian beliefs (verses 171-172).

The period of revelation is the fourth year of the hijrah.

---

[83]Noldeke, *Geschichte des Qorans* (2nd ed.), 1:195.

Women

Revealed at Madinah

*In the name of Allah,
the Beneficent, the Merciful.*

1. mankind! Be careful of your duty to your Lord Who created you from a single soul and from it created its mate and from the two has spread abroad a multitude of men and women. Be careful of your duty toward Allah in Whom you claim (your rights) of one another, and toward the wombs (that bore you). Lo! Allah has been a Watcher over you.

2. Give unto orphans their wealth. Exchange not the good for the bad (in your management thereof) nor absorb their wealth into your own wealth. Lo! that would be a great sin.

3. And if you fear that you will not deal fairly with the orphans, marry of the women, who seem good to you, two or three or four; and if you fear that you cannot do justice (to so many) then one (only) or (the captives) that your right hands possess. Thus it is more likely that you will not do injustice.

4. And give unto the women (whom you marry) free gift of their marriage portions; but if they of their own accord remit unto you a part thereof, then you are welcome to absorb it (in your wealth).

5. Give not unto the foolish (what is in) your (keeping of their) wealth, which Allah has given you to maintain; but feed and clothe them from it, and speak kindly unto them.

6. Test orphans till they reach the marriageable age; then, if you find them of sound judgment, deliver over unto them their fortune; and devour it not squandering and in haste lest they should grow up. Who (of the guardians) is rich, let him abstain generously (from taking of the property of orphans); and who is poor let him take thereof in reason (for his guar-dianship). And when you deliver up their fortune unto them (the orphans), have (the transaction) witnessed in their presence. Allah suffices as a Reckoner.

7. Unto the men (of a family) belongs a share of that which parents and near kindred leave, and unto the women a share of that which parents and near kindred leave, whether it be little or much, a legal share.

8. And when kinsfolk and orphans and the needy are present at the division (of the heritage), bestow on them therefrom and speak kindly unto them.

9. And let those fear (in their behavior toward orphans) who if they left behind them weak offspring would be afraid for them. So let them mind their duty to Allah, and speak justly.

10. Lo! those who devour the wealth of orphans wrongfully, they do but swallow fire into their bellies, and they will be exposed to burning flame.

11. Allah charges you concerning (the provision for) your children: to the male the equivalent of the portion of two females, and if there be women more than two, then theirs is two-thirds of the inheritance, and if there be one (only) then the half. And to his[84] parents a sixth of the inheritance, if he has a son; and if he has no son and his parents are his heirs, then to his mother appertains the third; and if he has brothers then to his mother appertains the sixth, after any legacy he may have bequeathed, or debt (has been paid). Your parents or your children: You know not which of them is nearer unto you in usefulness. It is an injunction from Allah. Lo! Allah is Knower, Wise.

---

[84]The deceased.

12. And unto you belongs a half of that which your wives leave, if they have no child; but if they have a child then unto you the fourth of that which they leave, after any legacy they may have bequeathed, or debt (they may have contracted, has been paid). And unto them belongs the fourth of that which you leave if you have no child, but if you have a child then the eighth of that which you leave, after any legacy you may have bequeathed, or debt (you may have contracted, has been paid). And if a man or a woman has a distant heir (having left neither parent nor child), and he (or she) has a brother or a sister (only on the mother's side) then to each of the two (the brother and the sister) the sixth, and if they be more than two, then they shall be sharers in the third, after any legacy that may have been bequeathed or debt (contracted) not injuring (the heirs by willing away more than a third of the heritage) has been paid. A commandment from Allah. Allah is Knower, Indul-gent.

13. These are the limits (imposed by) Allah. Who obeys Allah and His Messenger, He will make him enter Gardens underneath which rivers flow, where such will dwell for-ever. That will be the great success.

14. And who disobeys Allah and His Messenger and transgresses His limits, He will make him enter Fire, where such will dwell forever; his will be a shameful doom.

15. As for those of your women who are guilty of lewdness, call to witness four of you against them. And if they testify (to the truth of the allegation) then confine them to the houses until death take them or (until) Allah appoint for them a way (through new legislation).[85]

16. And as for the two of you who are guilty thereof, punish them both. And if they repent and improve, then let them be. Lo! Allah is Relenting, Merciful.

---

[85]See Surah 24:2-10.

17. Forgiveness is only incumbent on Allah toward those who do evil in ignorance (and) then turn quickly (in repentance) to Allah. These are they toward whom Allah relents. Allah is ever Knower, Wise.

١٧ إِنَّمَا التَّوْبَةُ عَلَى اللَّهِ لِلَّذِينَ يَعْمَلُونَ السُّوءَ بِجَهَالَةٍ ثُمَّ يَتُوبُونَ مِن قَرِيبٍ فَأُوْلَئِكَ يَتُوبُ اللَّهُ عَلَيْهِمْ وَكَانَ اللَّهُ عَلِيمًا حَكِيمًا

18. Forgiveness is not for those who do ill deeds until, when death approaches one of them, he says: Lo! I repent now; nor yet for those who die while they are disbelievers. For such We have prepared a painful doom.

١٨ وَلَيْسَتِ التَّوْبَةُ لِلَّذِينَ يَعْمَلُونَ السَّيِّئَاتِ حَتَّى إِذَا حَضَرَ أَحَدَهُمُ الْمَوْتُ قَالَ إِنِّي تُبْتُ الْآنَ وَلَا الَّذِينَ يَمُوتُونَ وَهُمْ كُفَّارٌ أُوْلَئِكَ أَعْتَدْنَا لَهُمْ عَذَابًا أَلِيمًا

19. O you who believe! It is not lawful for you forcibly to inherit the women (of your deceased kinsmen), nor (that) you should put constraint upon them that you may take away a part of that which you have given them, unless they be guilty of flagrant lewdness. But consort with them in kindness, for if you hate them it may happen that you hate a thing wherein Allah has placed much good.

١٩ يَا أَيُّهَا الَّذِينَ آمَنُوا لَا يَحِلُّ لَكُمْ أَن تَرِثُوا النِّسَاءَ كَرْهًا وَلَا تَعْضُلُوهُنَّ لِتَذْهَبُوا بِبَعْضِ مَا آتَيْتُمُوهُنَّ إِلَّا أَن يَأْتِينَ بِفَاحِشَةٍ مُّبَيِّنَةٍ وَعَاشِرُوهُنَّ بِالْمَعْرُوفِ فَإِن كَرِهْتُمُوهُنَّ فَعَسَى أَن تَكْرَهُوا شَيْئًا وَيَجْعَلَ اللَّهُ فِيهِ خَيْرًا كَثِيرًا

20. And if you wish to exchange one wife for another and you have given unto one of them a sum of money (however great), take nothing from it. Would you take it by the way of calumny and open wrong?

٢٠ وَإِنْ أَرَدتُّمُ اسْتِبْدَالَ زَوْجٍ مَّكَانَ زَوْجٍ وَآتَيْتُمْ إِحْدَاهُنَّ قِنطَارًا فَلَا تَأْخُذُوا مِنْهُ شَيْئًا أَتَأْخُذُونَهُ بُهْتَانًا وَإِثْمًا مُّبِينًا

21. How can you take it (back) after one of you has gone in unto the other, and they have taken a strong pledge from you?

٢١ وَكَيْفَ تَأْخُذُونَهُ وَقَدْ أَفْضَى بَعْضُكُمْ إِلَى بَعْضٍ وَأَخَذْنَ مِنكُم مِّيثَاقًا غَلِيظًا

22. And marry not those women whom your fathers married, except what has already happened (of that nature) in the past. Lo! it was ever lewdness and abomination, and an evil way.

٢٢ وَلَا تَنكِحُوا مَا نَكَحَ آبَاؤُكُم مِّنَ النِّسَاءِ إِلَّا مَا قَدْ سَلَفَ إِنَّهُ كَانَ فَاحِشَةً وَمَقْتًا وَسَاءَ سَبِيلًا

23. Forbidden unto you are your mothers, your daughters, your sisters, your fathers' sisters, your mothers' sisters, your brothers' daughters, your sisters' daughters, your foster mothers, your foster sisters, your mothers-in-law, and your stepdaughters who are under your protection (born) of your women unto whom you have gone in—but if you have not gone in unto them, then it is no sin for you (to marry their daughters)—and the wives of your sons who (spring) from your own loins. And (it is forbidden unto you) that you should have two sisters together, except what has already happened (of that nature) in the past. Lo! Allah is ever For-giving, Merciful.

24. And all married women (are forbidden unto you save those (captives) whom your right hands possess. It is a decree of Allah for you. Lawful unto you are all beyond those mentioned, so that you seek them with your wealth in honest wedlock, not debauchery. And those of whom you seek content (by marrying them), give unto them their portions as an obligation. And there is no sin for you in what you do by mutual agreement after the obligation (has been done). Lo! Allah is ever Knower, Wise.

25. And who is not able to afford to marry free, believing women, let them marry from the believing maids whom your right hands possess. Allah knows best (concerning) your faith. You (proceed) one from another[86]; so wed them by permission of their folk, and give unto them their portions in kindness, they being honest, not debauched nor of loose conduct. And if when they are honorably married they commit lewdness they shall incur half of the punishment (prescribed) for free women (in that case). This is for him among you who fears to commit sin. But to have patience would be better for you. Allah is Forgiving, Merciful.

---

[86]This expression, which recurs in the Qur'an, is a reminder to men that women enjoy the same human status as they do.

26. Allah would explain to you and guide you by the examples of those who were before you, and would turn to you in mercy. Allah is Knower, Wise.

27. And Allah would turn to you in mercy; but those who follow vain desires would have you go tremendously astray.

28. Allah would make the burden light for you, for man was created weak.

29. O you who believe! Squander not your wealth among yourselves in vanity, except it be a trade by mutual consent, and kill not one another. Lo! Allah is ever Merciful unto you.

30. Who does that through aggression and injustice, We shall cast him into Fire, and that is ever easy for Allah.

31. If you avoid the great (things) which you are forbidden, We will remit from you your evil deeds and make you enter at a noble gate.

32. And covet not the thing in which Allah has made some of you excel others. Unto men a fortune from that which they have earned, and unto women a fortune from that which they have earned. (Envy not one another) but ask Allah of His bounty. Lo! Allah is ever Knower of all things.

33. And unto each We have appointed heirs of that which parents and near kindred leave; and as for those with whom your right hands have made a covenant, give them their due. Lo! Allah is ever Witness over all things.

34. Men are in charge of women, because Allah has made the one of them to excel the other, and because they spend of their property (for the support of women). So good women are the obedient, guarding in secret that which Allah has guarded. As for those from whom you fear rebellion, admonish them and banish them to beds apart, and scourge them. Then if they obey you, seek not a way against them. Lo! Allah is ever High Exalted, Great.

35. And if you fear a breech between the two (the man and wife), appoint an arbiter from his folk and an arbiter from her folk. If they desire amendment Allah will make them of one mind. Lo! Allah is ever Knower, Aware.

36. And worship Allah. Ascribe nothing as partner unto Him. (Show) kindness unto parents, unto near kindred, orphans, the needy, unto the neighbor who is of kin (unto you), the neighbor who is not of kin, and the fellow traveller, the wayfarer and (the slaves) whom your right hands possess. Lo! Allah loves not such as are proud and boastful,

37. Who hoard their wealth and enjoin avarice on others, and hide that which Allah has bestowed upon them of His bounty. For disbelievers We prepare a shameful doom;

38. And (also) those who spend their wealth in order to be seen of men, and believe not in Allah nor the Last Day. Who takes the Devil for a comrade, a bad comrade has he.

39. What have they (to fear) if they believe in Allah and the Last Day and spend (aright) of that which Allah has bestowed upon them, when Allah is ever Aware of them (and all they do)?

40. Lo! Allah wrongs not even of the weight of an ant; and if there is a good deed, He will double it and will give (the doer) from His presence an immense reward.

41. But how (will it be with them) when we bring of every people a witness, and We bring you (O Muhammad) a witness against these?

42. On that day those who disbelieved and disobeyed the Messenger will wish that they were level with the ground, and they can hide no fact from Allah.

43. O you who believe! Draw not near unto prayer when you are drunken, till you know that which you utter, nor when you are polluted, save when journeying upon the road, till you have bathed. And if you be ill, or on a journey, or one of you comes from the closet, or you have touched women, and you find not water, then go to high clean soil and rub your faces and your hands (with it). Lo! Allah is Benign, Forgiving.

44. Do you not see those unto whom a portion of the Scripture has been given, how they purchase error, and seek to make you (Muslims) err from the right way?

45. Allah knows best (who are) your enemies. Allah is sufficient as a Friend, and Allah is sufficient as a Helper.

46. Some of those who are Jews change words from their context and say: "We hear and disobey; hear you as one who hears not" and "Listen to us!" distorting with their tongues and slandering religion.[87] If they had said: "We hear and we obey; hear you, and look at us" it had been better for them, and more upright. But Allah has cursed them for their disbelief, so they believe not, save a few.

---

[87]Some of the Jews of al Madinah sought to annoy the Muslims by distorting words of the Scripture. *Rā'inā* (meaning "listen to us"), which the Muslims used to attract the Prophet's attention, was turned by means of a slight mispronunciation into a Hebrew word of insult (cf. 2:104, footnote).

47. O you unto whom the Scripture has been given! Believe in what We have revealed concerning that which you possess, before We destroy countenances so as to confound them, or curse them as We cursed the Sabbath breakers (of old time). The commandment of Allah is always executed.

48. Lo! Allah forgives not that a partner should be ascribed unto Him. He forgives (all) save that to whom He will. Who ascribes partners to Allah, he has indeed invented a tremendous sin.

49. Have you not seen those who praise themselves for purity? Nay, Allah purifies whom He will, and they will not be wronged even the hair upon a date stone.

50. See, how they invent lies about Allah! That of itself is flagrant sin.

51. Have you not seen those unto whom a portion of the Scripture has been given, how they believe in idols and false deities, and how they say of those (idolaters) who disbelieve: "These are more rightly guided than those who believe?"

52. Those are they whom Allah has cursed, and he whom Allah has cursed, you (O Muhammad) will find for him no helper.

53. Or have they even a share in the Sovereignty? Then in that case, they would not give mankind even the speck on a date stone.

54. Or are they jealous of mankind (i.e. Muhammad) because of that which Allah of His bounty has bestowed upon them? For We bestowed upon the house of Abraham (of old) the Scripture and Wisdom, and We bestowed on them a mighty kingdom.

55. And of them were (some) who believed Our revelation and of them were (some) who disbelieved Our revelation. Hell is sufficient for (their) burning.

﴿٤٧﴾ يَـٰٓأَيُّهَا ٱلَّذِينَ أُوتُوا۟ ٱلۡكِتَـٰبَ ءَامِنُوا۟ بِمَا نَزَّلۡنَا مُصَدِّقًا لِّمَا مَعَكُم مِّن قَبۡلِ أَن نَّطۡمِسَ وُجُوهًا فَنَرُدَّهَا عَلَىٰٓ أَدۡبَارِهَآ أَوۡ نَلۡعَنَهُمۡ كَمَا لَعَنَّآ أَصۡحَـٰبَ ٱلسَّبۡتِ وَكَانَ أَمۡرُ ٱللَّهِ مَفۡعُولًا

﴿٤٨﴾ إِنَّ ٱللَّهَ لَا يَغۡفِرُ أَن يُشۡرَكَ بِهِۦ وَيَغۡفِرُ مَا دُونَ ذَٰلِكَ لِمَن يَشَآءُ وَمَن يُشۡرِكۡ بِٱللَّهِ فَقَدِ ٱفۡتَرَىٰٓ إِثۡمًا عَظِيمًا

﴿٤٩﴾ أَلَمۡ تَرَ إِلَى ٱلَّذِينَ يُزَكُّونَ أَنفُسَهُم بَلِ ٱللَّهُ يُزَكِّي مَن يَشَآءُ وَلَا يُظۡلَمُونَ فَتِيلًا

﴿٥٠﴾ ٱنظُرۡ كَيۡفَ يَفۡتَرُونَ عَلَى ٱللَّهِ ٱلۡكَذِبَ وَكَفَىٰ بِهِۦٓ إِثۡمًا مُّبِينًا

﴿٥١﴾ أَلَمۡ تَرَ إِلَى ٱلَّذِينَ أُوتُوا۟ نَصِيبًا مِّنَ ٱلۡكِتَـٰبِ يُؤۡمِنُونَ بِٱلۡجِبۡتِ وَٱلطَّـٰغُوتِ وَيَقُولُونَ لِلَّذِينَ كَفَرُوا۟ هَـٰٓؤُلَآءِ أَهۡدَىٰ مِنَ ٱلَّذِينَ ءَامَنُوا۟ سَبِيلًا

﴿٥٢﴾ أُو۟لَـٰٓئِكَ ٱلَّذِينَ لَعَنَهُمُ ٱللَّهُ وَمَن يَلۡعَنِ ٱللَّهُ فَلَن تَجِدَ لَهُۥ نَصِيرًا

﴿٥٣﴾ أَمۡ لَهُمۡ نَصِيبٌ مِّنَ ٱلۡمُلۡكِ فَإِذًا لَّا يُؤۡتُونَ ٱلنَّاسَ نَقِيرًا

﴿٥٤﴾ أَمۡ يَحۡسُدُونَ ٱلنَّاسَ عَلَىٰ مَآ ءَاتَىٰهُمُ ٱللَّهُ مِن فَضۡلِهِۦ فَقَدۡ ءَاتَيۡنَآ ءَالَ إِبۡرَٰهِيمَ ٱلۡكِتَـٰبَ وَٱلۡحِكۡمَةَ وَءَاتَيۡنَـٰهُم مُّلۡكًا عَظِيمًا

﴿٥٥﴾ فَمِنۡهُم مَّنۡ ءَامَنَ بِهِۦ وَمِنۡهُم مَّن صَدَّ عَنۡهُ وَكَفَىٰ بِجَهَنَّمَ سَعِيرًا

56. Lo! those who disbelieve Our revelations, We shall expose them to the Fire. As often as their skins are consumed We shall exchange them for fresh skins that they may taste the torment. Lo! Allah is ever Mighty, Wise.

57. And as for those who believe and do good works, We shall make them enter Gardens underneath which rivers flow to dwell there forever; there for them are pure companions and We shall make them enter plenteous shade.

58. Lo! Allah commands you that you restore deposits to their owners, and, if you judge between mankind, that you judge justly. Lo! comely is this which Allah admonishes you. Lo! Allah is ever Hearer, Seer.

59. O you who believe! Obey Allah, and obey the Messenger and those of you who are in authority; and if you have a dispute concerning any matter, refer it to Allah and the Messenger if you are (in truth) believers in Allah and the Last Day. That is better and more seemly in the end.

60. Have you not seen those who pretend that they believe in that which is revealed unto you and that which was revealed before you, how they would go for judgment (in their disputes) to false deities when they have been ordered to abjure them? The Devil would mislead them far astray.

61. And when it is said unto them: Come unto that which Allah has revealed and unto the Messenger, you see the hypocrites turn from you with aversion.

62. How would it be if a misfortune smote them because of that which their own hands have sent before (them)? Then would they come unto you, swearing by Allah that they were seeking nothing but kindness and harmony.

٥٦ إِنَّ الَّذِينَ كَفَرُوا بِـَٔايَٰتِنَا سَوْفَ نُصْلِيهِمْ نَارًا كُلَّمَا نَضِجَتْ جُلُودُهُم بَدَّلْنَٰهُمْ جُلُودًا غَيْرَهَا لِيَذُوقُوا الْعَذَابَ إِنَّ اللَّهَ كَانَ عَزِيزًا حَكِيمًا

٥٧ وَالَّذِينَ ءَامَنُوا وَعَمِلُوا الصَّٰلِحَٰتِ سَنُدْخِلُهُمْ جَنَّٰتٍ تَجْرِى مِن تَحْتِهَا الْأَنْهَٰرُ خَٰلِدِينَ فِيهَا أَبَدًا لَّهُمْ فِيهَا أَزْوَٰجٌ مُّطَهَّرَةٌ وَنُدْخِلُهُمْ ظِلًّا ظَلِيلًا

٥٨ إِنَّ اللَّهَ يَأْمُرُكُمْ أَن تُؤَدُّوا الْأَمَٰنَٰتِ إِلَىٰ أَهْلِهَا وَإِذَا حَكَمْتُم بَيْنَ النَّاسِ أَن تَحْكُمُوا بِالْعَدْلِ إِنَّ اللَّهَ نِعِمَّا يَعِظُكُم بِهِ إِنَّ اللَّهَ كَانَ سَمِيعًا بَصِيرًا

٥٩ يَٰٓأَيُّهَا الَّذِينَ ءَامَنُوا أَطِيعُوا اللَّهَ وَأَطِيعُوا الرَّسُولَ وَأُولِى الْأَمْرِ مِنكُمْ فَإِن تَنَٰزَعْتُمْ فِى شَىْءٍ فَرُدُّوهُ إِلَى اللَّهِ وَالرَّسُولِ إِن كُنتُمْ تُؤْمِنُونَ بِاللَّهِ وَالْيَوْمِ الْءَاخِرِ ذَٰلِكَ خَيْرٌ وَأَحْسَنُ تَأْوِيلًا

٦٠ أَلَمْ تَرَ إِلَى الَّذِينَ يَزْعُمُونَ أَنَّهُمْ ءَامَنُوا بِمَا أُنزِلَ إِلَيْكَ وَمَا أُنزِلَ مِن قَبْلِكَ يُرِيدُونَ أَن يَتَحَاكَمُوا إِلَى الطَّٰغُوتِ وَقَدْ أُمِرُوا أَن يَكْفُرُوا بِهِ وَيُرِيدُ الشَّيْطَٰنُ أَن يُضِلَّهُمْ ضَلَٰلًا بَعِيدًا

٦١ وَإِذَا قِيلَ لَهُمْ تَعَالَوْا إِلَىٰ مَا أَنزَلَ اللَّهُ وَإِلَى الرَّسُولِ رَأَيْتَ الْمُنَٰفِقِينَ يَصُدُّونَ عَنكَ صُدُودًا

٦٢ فَكَيْفَ إِذَا أَصَٰبَتْهُم مُّصِيبَةٌ بِمَا قَدَّمَتْ أَيْدِيهِمْ ثُمَّ جَآءُوكَ يَحْلِفُونَ بِاللَّهِ إِنْ أَرَدْنَا إِلَّا إِحْسَٰنًا وَتَوْفِيقًا

63. Those are they, the secrets of whose hearts Allah knows. So oppose them, admonish them, and address them in plain terms about their souls.

64. We sent no messenger save that he should be obeyed by Allah's leave. And if, when they had wronged themselves, they had but come unto you and asked forgiveness of Allah and the Messenger asked forgiveness for them, they would have found Allah Forgiving, Merciful.

65. But nay, by your lord, they will not believe (in truth) until they make you judge of what is in dispute between them and find within themselves no dislike of that which you decide, and submit with full submission.

66. And if We had decreed for them: Lay down your lives or go forth from your dwellings, few of them would have done it, though if they did what they are exhorted to do it would be better for them, and more strengthening;

67. And then We should bestow upon them from Our presence an immense reward,

68. And should guide them unto a straight path.

69. Who obeys Allah and the Messenger, they are with those unto whom Allah has shown favor, of the Prophets and the saints and the martyrs and the righteous. The best of company are they!

70. Such is the bounty of Allah, and Allah suffices as Knower.

71. O you who believe! Take your precautions, then advance in groups, or advance all together.

72. Lo! among you there is he who loiters; and if disaster overtook you, he would say: Allah has been gracious unto me since I was not present with them.

۞ أُوْلَٰٓئِكَ ٱلَّذِينَ يَعْلَمُ ٱللَّهُ مَا فِى قُلُوبِهِمْ فَأَعْرِضْ عَنْهُمْ وَعِظْهُمْ وَقُل لَّهُمْ فِىٓ أَنفُسِهِمْ قَوْلًۢا بَلِيغًا ۞

۞ وَمَآ أَرْسَلْنَا مِن رَّسُولٍ إِلَّا لِيُطَاعَ بِإِذْنِ ٱللَّهِ وَلَوْ أَنَّهُمْ إِذ ظَّلَمُوٓاْ أَنفُسَهُمْ جَآءُوكَ فَٱسْتَغْفَرُواْ ٱللَّهَ وَٱسْتَغْفَرَ لَهُمُ ٱلرَّسُولُ لَوَجَدُواْ ٱللَّهَ تَوَّابًا رَّحِيمًا ۞

۞ فَلَا وَرَبِّكَ لَا يُؤْمِنُونَ حَتَّىٰ يُحَكِّمُوكَ فِيمَا شَجَرَ بَيْنَهُمْ ثُمَّ لَا يَجِدُواْ فِىٓ أَنفُسِهِمْ حَرَجًا مِّمَّا قَضَيْتَ وَيُسَلِّمُواْ تَسْلِيمًا ۞

۞ وَلَوْ أَنَّا كَتَبْنَا عَلَيْهِمْ أَنِ ٱقْتُلُوٓاْ أَنفُسَكُمْ أَوِ ٱخْرُجُواْ مِن دِيَٰرِكُم مَّا فَعَلُوهُ إِلَّا قَلِيلٌ مِّنْهُمْ وَلَوْ أَنَّهُمْ فَعَلُواْ مَا يُوعَظُونَ بِهِۦ لَكَانَ خَيْرًا لَّهُمْ وَأَشَدَّ تَثْبِيتًا ۞

۞ وَإِذًا لَّءَاتَيْنَٰهُم مِّن لَّدُنَّآ أَجْرًا عَظِيمًا ۞

۞ وَلَهَدَيْنَٰهُمْ صِرَٰطًا مُّسْتَقِيمًا ۞

۞ وَمَن يُطِعِ ٱللَّهَ وَٱلرَّسُولَ فَأُوْلَٰٓئِكَ مَعَ ٱلَّذِينَ أَنْعَمَ ٱللَّهُ عَلَيْهِم مِّنَ ٱلنَّبِيِّۦنَ وَٱلصِّدِّيقِينَ وَٱلشُّهَدَآءِ وَٱلصَّٰلِحِينَ وَحَسُنَ أُوْلَٰٓئِكَ رَفِيقًا ۞

۞ ذَٰلِكَ ٱلْفَضْلُ مِنَ ٱللَّهِ وَكَفَىٰ بِٱللَّهِ عَلِيمًا ۞

۞ يَٰٓأَيُّهَا ٱلَّذِينَ ءَامَنُواْ خُذُواْ حِذْرَكُمْ فَٱنفِرُواْ ثُبَاتٍ أَوِ ٱنفِرُواْ جَمِيعًا ۞

۞ وَإِنَّ مِنكُمْ لَمَن لَّيُبَطِّئَنَّ فَإِنْ أَصَٰبَتْكُم مُّصِيبَةٌ قَالَ قَدْ أَنْعَمَ ٱللَّهُ عَلَىَّ إِذْ لَمْ أَكُن مَّعَهُمْ شَهِيدًا

73. And if a bounty from Allah befell you, he would surely cry, as if there had been no love between you and him: Oh, would that I had been with them, then should I have achieved a great success!

74. Let those fight in the way of Allah who sell the life of this world for the other. Who fights in the way of Allah, be he slain or be he victorious, on him We shall bestow a vast reward.

75. How should you not fight for the cause of Allah and of the feeble among men and of the women and the children who are crying: Our Lord! Bring us forth from out this town[88] of which the people are oppressors! Oh, give us from Your presence some protecting friend! Oh, give us from Your presence some defender!

76. Those who believe do battle for the cause of Allah; and those who disbelieve do battle for the cause of idols. So fight the minions of the devil. Lo! the devil's strategy is ever weak.

77. Have you not seen those unto whom it was said: Withhold your hands, establish prayer and pay the poor due, but when fighting was prescribed for them, behold, a party of them fear mankind even as their fear of Allah or with greater fear, and say: Our Lord! Why have you ordained fighting for us? If only You would give us respite yet a while! Say (unto them, O Muhammad): The comfort of this world is scant; the Hereafter will be better for him who wards off (evil); and you will not be wronged the down upon a date stone.

---

[88]Makkah.

78. Wheresoever you may be, death will overtake you, even though you were in lofty towers. Yet if a happy thing befalls them they say: This is from Allah; and if an evil thing befalls them they say: This is of your doing (O Muhammad). Say (unto them): All is from Allah. What is amiss with these people that they come not nigh to understand a discourse?[89]

79. Whatever of good befalls you (O man) it is from Allah, and whatever of ill befalls you it is from yourself. We have sent you (Muhammad) as a Messenger unto mankind and Allah is sufficient as witness.

80. Who obeys the Messenger obeys Allah, and who turns away: We have not sent you as a warder over them.

81. And they say: (It is) obedience; but when they have gone forth from you, a party of them spend the night in planning other than what you say. Allah records what they plan by night. So ignore them and put your trust in Allah. Allah is sufficient as Trustee.

82. Will they not then ponder on the Qur'an? If it had been from other than Allah they would have found much incongruity in it.

83. And if any tidings, whether of safety or fear, come unto them, they noise it abroad, whereas if they had referred it to the Messenger and such of them as are in authority, those among them who are able to think out the matter would have known it. If it had not been for the grace of Allah and His mercy, you would have followed the Devil save a few (of you).

84. So fight (O Muhammad) in the way of Allah—You are not taxed (with the responsibility for anyone) except for yourself—and urge on the believers. Peradventure Allah will restrain the might of those who disbelieve. Allah is stronger in might and stronger in inflicting punishment.

---

[89]The reference is to the reverse that the Muslims suffered at Mount Uhud, which was caused by their own disobedience to the Prophet's orders.

85. Who intervenes in a good cause will have the reward thereof, and Who intervenes in an evil cause will bear the consequence thereof. Allah oversees all things.

86. When you are greeted with a greeting, greet you with a better than it or return it. Lo! Allah takes count of all things.

87. Allah! There is no God save Him. He will surely gather you all unto the Day of Resurrection whereof there is no doubt. Who is more true in statement than Allah?

88. What ails you that you are become two parties regarding the hypocrites,[90] when Allah cast them back (to disbelief) because of what they earned? Seek you to guide him whom Allah has sent astray? He whom Allah sends astray, for him you (O Muhammad) can not find a road.

89. They long that you should disbelieve even as they disbelieve, that you may be upon a level (with them). So choose not friends from them till they forsake their homes in the way of Allah; if they turn back (to enmity) then take them and kill them wherever you find them, and choose no friend nor helper from among them,

90. Except those who seek refuge with a people between whom and you there is a covenant, or (those who) come unto you because their hearts forbid them to make war on you or make war on their own folk. Had Allah willed He could have given them power over you so that assuredly they would have fought you. So, if they hold aloof from you and wage not war against you and offer you peace, Allah allows you no way against them.

91. You will find others who desire that they should have security from you, and security from their own folk. So often as they are returned to hostility they are plunged therein. If they keep not aloof from you nor offer you peace nor hold their hands, then take them and kill them wherever you find them. Against such We have given you clear warrant.

---

[90]According to tradition, this does not refer to the lukewarm Muslims of al Madinah but to a particular group of alleged Arab converts, who afterwards relapsed into idolatry. The Muslims had two opinions about this group.

92. It is not for a believer to kill a believer unless (it be) by mistake. He who has killed a believer by mistake must set free a believing slave, and pay the blood money to the family of the slain, unless they remit it as a charity. If he (the victim) be of a people hostile unto you, and he is a believer, then (the penance is) to set free a believing slave. And if he comes of a folk between whom and you there is a covenant, then the blood money must be paid unto his folk and (also) a believing slave must be set free. And Who has not the wherewithal must fast two consecutive months. A penance from Allah. Allah is Knower, Wise.

93. Who slays a believer of set purpose, his reward is Hell forever. Allah is wroth against him and He has cursed him and prepared for him an awful doom.

94. O you who believe! When you go forth (to fight) in the way of Allah, be careful to discriminate, and say not unto one who offers you peace: "You are not a believer;" seeking the chance profits of this life (so that you may despoil him). With Allah are plenteous spoils. Even thus (as he now is) were you before; but Allah has since then been gracious unto you. Therefore take care to discriminate. Allah is ever informed of what you do.

95. Those of the believers who sit still, other than those who have a (disabling) hurt, are not on an equality with those who strive in the way of Allah with their wealth and lives. Allah has conferred on those who strive with their wealth and lives a rank above the sedentary. Unto each Allah has promised good, but He has bestowed on those who strive a great reward above the sedentary;

96. Degrees of rank from Him, and forgiveness and mercy. Allah is ever Forgiving, Merciful.

٩٢ وَمَا كَانَ لِمُؤْمِنٍ أَن يَقْتُلَ مُؤْمِنًا إِلَّا خَطَأً وَمَن قَتَلَ مُؤْمِنًا خَطَأً فَتَحْرِيرُ رَقَبَةٍ مُّؤْمِنَةٍ وَدِيَةٌ مُّسَلَّمَةٌ إِلَىٰ أَهْلِهِ إِلَّا أَن يَصَّدَّقُوا فَإِن كَانَ مِن قَوْمٍ عَدُوٍّ لَّكُمْ وَهُوَ مُؤْمِنٌ فَتَحْرِيرُ رَقَبَةٍ مُّؤْمِنَةٍ وَإِن كَانَ مِن قَوْمٍ بَيْنَكُمْ وَبَيْنَهُم مِّيثَاقٌ فَدِيَةٌ مُّسَلَّمَةٌ إِلَىٰ أَهْلِهِ وَتَحْرِيرُ رَقَبَةٍ مُّؤْمِنَةٍ فَمَن لَّمْ يَجِدْ فَصِيَامُ شَهْرَيْنِ مُتَتَابِعَيْنِ تَوْبَةً مِّنَ اللَّهِ وَكَانَ اللَّهُ عَلِيمًا حَكِيمًا

٩٣ وَمَن يَقْتُلْ مُؤْمِنًا مُّتَعَمِّدًا فَجَزَآؤُهُ جَهَنَّمُ خَالِدًا فِيهَا وَغَضِبَ اللَّهُ عَلَيْهِ وَلَعَنَهُ وَأَعَدَّ لَهُ عَذَابًا عَظِيمًا

٩٤ يَٰأَيُّهَا الَّذِينَ ءَامَنُوا إِذَا ضَرَبْتُمْ فِي سَبِيلِ اللَّهِ فَتَبَيَّنُوا وَلَا تَقُولُوا لِمَنْ أَلْقَىٰ إِلَيْكُمُ السَّلَامَ لَسْتَ مُؤْمِنًا تَبْتَغُونَ عَرَضَ الْحَيَوٰةِ الدُّنْيَا فَعِندَ اللَّهِ مَغَانِمُ كَثِيرَةٌ كَذَٰلِكَ كُنتُم مِّن قَبْلُ فَمَنَّ اللَّهُ عَلَيْكُمْ فَتَبَيَّنُوا إِنَّ اللَّهَ كَانَ بِمَا تَعْمَلُونَ خَبِيرًا

٩٥ لَّا يَسْتَوِي الْقَاعِدُونَ مِنَ الْمُؤْمِنِينَ غَيْرُ أُولِي الضَّرَرِ وَالْمُجَاهِدُونَ فِي سَبِيلِ اللَّهِ بِأَمْوَالِهِمْ وَأَنفُسِهِمْ فَضَّلَ اللَّهُ الْمُجَاهِدِينَ بِأَمْوَالِهِمْ وَأَنفُسِهِمْ عَلَى الْقَاعِدِينَ دَرَجَةً وَكُلًّا وَعَدَ اللَّهُ الْحُسْنَىٰ وَفَضَّلَ اللَّهُ الْمُجَاهِدِينَ عَلَى الْقَاعِدِينَ أَجْرًا عَظِيمًا

٩٦ دَرَجَاتٍ مِّنْهُ وَمَغْفِرَةً وَرَحْمَةً وَكَانَ اللَّهُ غَفُورًا رَّحِيمًا

97. Lo! as for those whom the angels take (in death) while they wrong themselves, (the angels) will ask: In what were you engaged? They will say: We were oppressed in the land. (The angels) will say: Was not Allah's earth spacious that you could have migrated therein? As for such, their habitation will be Hell, an evil journey's end;

98. Except the feeble among men, women, and children, who are unable to devise a plan and are not shown a way.

99. As for such, it may be that Allah will pardon them. Allah is ever Clement, Forgiving.

100. Who migrates for the cause of Allah will find much refuge and abundance in the earth, and who forsakes his home, a fugitive unto Allah and His Messenger, and death overtakes him, his reward is then incumbent on Allah. Allah is ever Forgiving, Merciful.

101. And when you go forth in the land, it is no sin for you to curtail (your) prayer if you fear that those who disbelieve may persecute you. In truth the disbelievers are an open enemy to you.

102. And when you (O Muhammad) are among them and arrange (their) prayer for them, let only a party of them stand with you (to pray) and let them take their arms. Then when they have performed their prostrations let them fall to the rear and let another party come that has not prayed and let them pray with you, and let them take their precaution and their arms. Those who disbelieve long for you to neglect your arms and your baggage that they may attack you once for all. It is no sin for you to lay aside your arms, if rain impedes you or you are sick. But take your precaution. Lo! Allah prepares for the disbelievers a shameful punishment.

٩٧ إِنَّ الَّذِينَ تَوَفَّاهُمُ الْمَلَائِكَةُ ظَالِمِي أَنفُسِهِمْ قَالُوا فِيمَ كُنتُمْ قَالُوا كُنَّا مُسْتَضْعَفِينَ فِي الْأَرْضِ قَالُوا أَلَمْ تَكُنْ أَرْضُ اللَّهِ وَاسِعَةً فَتُهَاجِرُوا فِيهَا فَأُولَٰئِكَ مَأْوَاهُمْ جَهَنَّمُ وَسَاءَتْ مَصِيرًا

٩٨ إِلَّا الْمُسْتَضْعَفِينَ مِنَ الرِّجَالِ وَالنِّسَاءِ وَالْوِلْدَانِ لَا يَسْتَطِيعُونَ حِيلَةً وَلَا يَهْتَدُونَ سَبِيلًا

٩٩ فَأُولَٰئِكَ عَسَى اللَّهُ أَن يَعْفُوَ عَنْهُمْ وَكَانَ اللَّهُ عَفُوًّا غَفُورًا

١٠٠ وَمَن يُهَاجِرْ فِي سَبِيلِ اللَّهِ يَجِدْ فِي الْأَرْضِ مُرَاغَمًا كَثِيرًا وَسَعَةً وَمَن يَخْرُجْ مِن بَيْتِهِ مُهَاجِرًا إِلَى اللَّهِ وَرَسُولِهِ ثُمَّ يُدْرِكْهُ الْمَوْتُ فَقَدْ وَقَعَ أَجْرُهُ عَلَى اللَّهِ وَكَانَ اللَّهُ غَفُورًا رَّحِيمًا

١٠١ وَإِذَا ضَرَبْتُمْ فِي الْأَرْضِ فَلَيْسَ عَلَيْكُمْ جُنَاحٌ أَن تَقْصُرُوا مِنَ الصَّلَاةِ إِنْ خِفْتُمْ أَن يَفْتِنَكُمُ الَّذِينَ كَفَرُوا إِنَّ الْكَافِرِينَ كَانُوا لَكُمْ عَدُوًّا مُّبِينًا

١٠٢ وَإِذَا كُنتَ فِيهِمْ فَأَقَمْتَ لَهُمُ الصَّلَاةَ فَلْتَقُمْ طَائِفَةٌ مِّنْهُم مَّعَكَ وَلْيَأْخُذُوا أَسْلِحَتَهُمْ فَإِذَا سَجَدُوا فَلْيَكُونُوا مِن وَرَائِكُمْ وَلْتَأْتِ طَائِفَةٌ أُخْرَىٰ لَمْ يُصَلُّوا فَلْيُصَلُّوا مَعَكَ وَلْيَأْخُذُوا حِذْرَهُمْ وَأَسْلِحَتَهُمْ وَدَّ الَّذِينَ كَفَرُوا لَوْ تَغْفُلُونَ عَنْ أَسْلِحَتِكُمْ وَأَمْتِعَتِكُمْ فَيَمِيلُونَ عَلَيْكُم مَّيْلَةً وَاحِدَةً وَلَا جُنَاحَ عَلَيْكُمْ إِن كَانَ بِكُمْ أَذًى مِّن مَّطَرٍ أَوْ كُنتُم مَّرْضَىٰ أَن تَضَعُوا أَسْلِحَتَكُمْ وَخُذُوا حِذْرَكُمْ إِنَّ اللَّهَ أَعَدَّ لِلْكَافِرِينَ عَذَابًا مُّهِينًا

103. When you have performed prayer, remember Allah, standing, sitting and reclining. And when you are in safety, observe proper prayer. Prayer at fixed hours has been enjoined on the believers.

١٠٣ فَإِذَا قَضَيْتُمُ الصَّلَوٰةَ فَاذْكُرُوا اللّٰهَ قِيَامًا وَّقُعُودًا وَّعَلَىٰ جُنُوبِكُمْ فَإِذَا اطْمَأْنَنْتُمْ فَأَقِيمُوا الصَّلَوٰةَ إِنَّ الصَّلَوٰةَ كَانَتْ عَلَى الْمُؤْمِنِينَ كِتَابًا مَّوْقُوتًا

104. Relent not in pursuit of the enemy. If you are suffering, lo! they suffer even as you suffer and you hope from Allah that for which they cannot hope. Allah is ever Knower, Wise.

١٠٤ وَلَا تَهِنُوا فِي ابْتِغَاءِ الْقَوْمِ إِنْ تَكُونُوا تَأْلَمُونَ فَإِنَّهُمْ يَأْلَمُونَ كَمَا تَأْلَمُونَ وَتَرْجُونَ مِنَ اللّٰهِ مَا لَا يَرْجُونَ وَكَانَ اللّٰهُ عَلِيمًا حَكِيمًا

105. Lo! We reveal unto you the Book with the truth, that you may judge between mankind by that which Allah shows you. And be not you a pleader for the treacherous;

١٠٥ إِنَّا أَنْزَلْنَا إِلَيْكَ الْكِتَابَ بِالْحَقِّ لِتَحْكُمَ بَيْنَ النَّاسِ بِمَا أَرَاكَ اللّٰهُ وَلَا تَكُنْ لِّلْخَائِنِينَ خَصِيمًا

106. And seek forgiveness of Allah. Lo! Allah is ever Forgiving, Merciful.

١٠٦ وَاسْتَغْفِرِ اللّٰهَ إِنَّ اللّٰهَ كَانَ غَفُورًا رَّحِيمًا

107. And plead not on behalf of (people) who deceive themselves. Lo! Allah loves not one who is treacherous and sinful.

١٠٧ وَلَا تُجَادِلْ عَنِ الَّذِينَ يَخْتَانُونَ أَنْفُسَهُمْ إِنَّ اللّٰهَ لَا يُحِبُّ مَنْ كَانَ خَوَّانًا أَثِيمًا

108. They seek to hide from men and seek not to hide from Allah. He is with them when by night they hold discourse displeasing unto Him. Allah ever surrounds what they do.

١٠٨ يَسْتَخْفُونَ مِنَ النَّاسِ وَلَا يَسْتَخْفُونَ مِنَ اللّٰهِ وَهُوَ مَعَهُمْ إِذْ يُبَيِّتُونَ مَا لَا يَرْضَىٰ مِنَ الْقَوْلِ وَكَانَ اللّٰهُ بِمَا يَعْمَلُونَ مُحِيطًا

109. Lo! you are they who pleaded for them in the life of the world. But who will plead with Allah for them on the Day of Resurrection, or who will then be their defender?

١٠٩ هَا أَنْتُمْ هَٰؤُلَاءِ جَادَلْتُمْ عَنْهُمْ فِي الْحَيَوٰةِ الدُّنْيَا فَمَنْ يُجَادِلُ اللّٰهَ عَنْهُمْ يَوْمَ الْقِيَامَةِ أَمْ مَّنْ يَكُونُ عَلَيْهِمْ وَكِيلًا

110. Yet who does evil or wrongs his own soul, then seeks pardon of Allah, will find Allah Forgiving, Merciful.

١١٠ وَمَنْ يَعْمَلْ سُوءًا أَوْ يَظْلِمْ نَفْسَهُ ثُمَّ يَسْتَغْفِرِ اللّٰهَ يَجِدِ اللّٰهَ غَفُورًا رَّحِيمًا

111. Who commits sin commits it only against himself. Allah is ever Knower, Wise.

١١١ وَمَنْ يَكْسِبْ إِثْمًا فَإِنَّمَا يَكْسِبُهُ عَلَىٰ نَفْسِهِ وَكَانَ اللّٰهُ عَلِيمًا حَكِيمًا

112. And who commits a delinquency or crime, then throws (the blame) thereof upon the innocent, has burdened himself with falsehood and a flagrant crime.

﴿١١٢﴾ وَمَن يَكْسِبْ خَطِيئَةً أَوْ إِثْمًا ثُمَّ يَرْمِ بِهِ بَرِيًّا فَقَدِ احْتَمَلَ بُهْتَـٰنًا وَإِثْمًا مُّبِينًا

113. But for the grace of Allah upon you (Muhammad), and His mercy, a party of them had resolved to mislead you, but they will mislead only themselves and they will hurt you not at all. Allah revealed unto you the Book and wisdom, and taught you that which you knew not. The grace of Allah toward you has been infinite.

﴿١١٣﴾ وَلَوْلَا فَضْلُ اللَّهِ عَلَيْكَ وَرَحْمَتُهُ لَهَمَّت طَّآئِفَةٌ مِّنْهُمْ أَن يُضِلُّوكَ وَمَا يُضِلُّونَ إِلَّا أَنفُسَهُمْ وَمَا يَضُرُّونَكَ مِن شَيْءٍ وَأَنزَلَ اللَّهُ عَلَيْكَ الْكِتَـٰبَ وَالْحِكْمَةَ وَعَلَّمَكَ مَا لَمْ تَكُن تَعْلَمُ وَكَانَ فَضْلُ اللَّهِ عَلَيْكَ عَظِيمًا

114. There is no good in much of their secret conferences save (in) him who enjoins almsgiving and kindness and peace making among the people. Who does that, seeking the good pleasure of Allah, We shall bestow on him a vast reward.

﴿١١٤﴾ ۞ لَّا خَيْرَ فِى كَثِيرٍ مِّن نَّجْوَىٰهُمْ إِلَّا مَنْ أَمَرَ بِصَدَقَةٍ أَوْ مَعْرُوفٍ أَوْ إِصْلَـٰحِ بَيْنَ النَّاسِ وَمَن يَفْعَلْ ذَٰلِكَ ابْتِغَآءَ مَرْضَاتِ اللَّهِ فَسَوْفَ نُؤْتِيهِ أَجْرًا عَظِيمًا

115. And who opposes the Messenger after the guidance (of Allah) has been manifested unto him, and follows other than the believers' way, We appoint for him that unto which he himself has turned, and expose him unto Hell, an unfortunate journey's end!

﴿١١٥﴾ وَمَن يُشَاقِقِ الرَّسُولَ مِنۢ بَعْدِ مَا تَبَيَّنَ لَهُ الْهُدَىٰ وَيَتَّبِعْ غَيْرَ سَبِيلِ الْمُؤْمِنِينَ نُوَلِّهِ مَا تَوَلَّىٰ وَنُصْلِهِ جَهَنَّمَ وَسَآءَتْ مَصِيرًا

116. Lo! Allah pardons not that partners should be ascribed unto Him. He pardons all save that to whom He will. Who ascribes partners unto Allah has wandered far astray.

﴿١١٦﴾ إِنَّ اللَّهَ لَا يَغْفِرُ أَن يُشْرَكَ بِهِ وَيَغْفِرُ مَا دُونَ ذَٰلِكَ لِمَن يَشَآءُ وَمَن يُشْرِكْ بِاللَّهِ فَقَدْ ضَلَّ ضَلَـٰلًۢا بَعِيدًا

117. They invoke in His stead only females;[91] they pray to none else than a rebellious devil

﴿١١٧﴾ إِن يَدْعُونَ مِن دُونِهِ إِلَّآ إِنَـٰثًا وَإِن يَدْعُونَ إِلَّا شَيْطَـٰنًا مَّرِيدًا

118. Whom Allah cursed, and he said: Surely I will take of Your bondmen an appointed portion,

﴿١١٨﴾ لَّعَنَهُ اللَّهُ وَقَالَ لَأَتَّخِذَنَّ مِنْ عِبَادِكَ نَصِيبًا مَّفْرُوضًا

---

[91] The idols which the pagan Arabs worshiped were all female.

119. And surely I will lead them astray, and surely I will arouse desires in them, and surely I will command them and they will cut the cattle's ears, and surely I will command them and they will change Allah's creation. Who chooses the Devil for a patron instead of Allah is truly a loser and his loss is manifest.

120. He promises them and stirs up desires in them, and the Devil promises them only to beguile.

121. For such, their habitation will be Hell, and they will find no refuge from it.

122. But as for those who believe and do good works We shall bring them into gardens underneath which rivers flow, wherein they will abide forever. It is a promise from Allah in truth; and who can be more truthful than Allah in utterance?

123. It will not be in accordance with your desires, nor the desires of the People of the Scripture.[92] He who does wrong will have the recompense thereof, and will not find against Allah any protecting friend or helper.

124. And who does good works, whether of male or female, and he (or she) is a believer, such will enter Paradise and they will not be wronged the dint in a date stone.

125. Who is better in religion than he who surrenders his purpose to Allah while doing good (to men) and follows the tradition of Abraham, the upright? Allah (Himself) chose Abraham for friend.

126. Unto Allah belongs whatever is in the heavens and whatever is in the earth. Allah ever surrounds all things.

وَلَأُضِلَّنَّهُمْ وَلَأُمَنِّيَنَّهُمْ وَلَآمُرَنَّهُمْ فَلَيُبَتِّكُنَّ ءَاذَانَ ٱلْأَنْعَٰمِ وَلَآمُرَنَّهُمْ فَلَيُغَيِّرُنَّ خَلْقَ ٱللَّهِ وَمَن يَتَّخِذِ ٱلشَّيْطَٰنَ وَلِيًّا مِّن دُونِ ٱللَّهِ فَقَدْ خَسِرَ خُسْرَانًا مُّبِينًا ۝

يَعِدُهُمْ وَيُمَنِّيهِمْ وَمَا يَعِدُهُمُ ٱلشَّيْطَٰنُ إِلَّا غُرُورًا ۝

أُو۟لَٰٓئِكَ مَأْوَىٰهُمْ جَهَنَّمُ وَلَا يَجِدُونَ عَنْهَا مَحِيصًا ۝

وَٱلَّذِينَ ءَامَنُوا۟ وَعَمِلُوا۟ ٱلصَّٰلِحَٰتِ سَنُدْخِلُهُمْ جَنَّٰتٍ تَجْرِى مِن تَحْتِهَا ٱلْأَنْهَٰرُ خَٰلِدِينَ فِيهَآ أَبَدًا وَعْدَ ٱللَّهِ حَقًّا وَمَنْ أَصْدَقُ مِنَ ٱللَّهِ قِيلًا ۝

لَّيْسَ بِأَمَانِيِّكُمْ وَلَآ أَمَانِىِّ أَهْلِ ٱلْكِتَٰبِ مَن يَعْمَلْ سُوٓءًا يُجْزَ بِهِ وَلَا يَجِدْ لَهُۥ مِن دُونِ ٱللَّهِ وَلِيًّا وَلَا نَصِيرًا ۝

وَمَن يَعْمَلْ مِنَ ٱلصَّٰلِحَٰتِ مِن ذَكَرٍ أَوْ أُنثَىٰ وَهُوَ مُؤْمِنٌ فَأُو۟لَٰٓئِكَ يَدْخُلُونَ ٱلْجَنَّةَ وَلَا يُظْلَمُونَ نَقِيرًا ۝

وَمَنْ أَحْسَنُ دِينًا مِّمَّنْ أَسْلَمَ وَجْهَهُۥ لِلَّهِ وَهُوَ مُحْسِنٌ وَٱتَّبَعَ مِلَّةَ إِبْرَٰهِيمَ حَنِيفًا وَٱتَّخَذَ ٱللَّهُ إِبْرَٰهِيمَ خَلِيلًا ۝

وَلِلَّهِ مَا فِى ٱلسَّمَٰوَٰتِ وَمَا فِى ٱلْأَرْضِ وَكَانَ ٱللَّهُ بِكُلِّ شَىْءٍ مُّحِيطًا ۝

---

[92]Jews and Christians.

127. They consult you concerning women. Say: Allah gives to you decree concerning them, and the Scripture which has been recited unto you (gives decree), concerning female orphans unto whom you give not that which is ordained for them though you desire to marry them, and (concerning) the weak among children, and that you should deal justly with orphans. Whatever good you do, lo! Allah is ever Aware of it.

128. If a woman fears ill treatment from her husband, or desertion, it is no sin for them both if they make terms of peace between themselves. Peace is better. But greed has been made present in the minds (of men). If you do good and keep from evil, Lo! Allah is ever Informed of what you do.

129. You will not be able to deal equally between (your) wives, however much you wish (to do so): But turn not altogether away (from one), leaving her as in suspense. If you do good and keep from evil, lo! Allah is ever Forgiving, Merciful.

130. But if they separate, Allah will compensate each out of His abundance. Allah is ever All Embracing, All Knowing.

131. Unto Allah belongs whatsoever is in the heavens and whatsoever is in the earth. And We charged those who received the Scripture before you, and (We charge) you, that you keep your duty toward Allah. And if you disbelieve, lo! unto Allah belongs whatever is in the heavens and whatever is in the earth, and Allah is ever Absolute, Owner of Praise.

132. Unto Allah belongs whatever is in the heavens and whatever is in the earth. And Allah is sufficient as Defender.

133. If He will, He can remove you, O people, and produce others (in your stead). Allah is Able to do that.

134. Who desires the reward of the world, (let him know that) with Allah is the reward of the world and the Hereafter. Allah is ever Hearer, Seer.

135. O you who believe! Be you staunch in justice, witnesses for Allah, even though it be against yourselves or (your) parents or (your) kindred, whether (the case be of) a rich man or a poor man, for Allah is nearer unto both (than you are). So follow not passion lest you lapse (from truth) and if you lapse or fall away, then lo! Allah is ever Informed of what you do.

136. O you who believe! Believe in Allah and His Mes-senger and the Book which He has revealed unto His Mes-senger, and the Scripture which He formerly revealed. Who disbelieves in Allah, His angels, His scriptures, His messengers and the Last Day, he truly has wandered far astray.

137. Lo! those who believe, then dis believe and then (again) believe, then disbelieve, and then increase in disbelief, Allah will never pardon them, nor will He guide them unto a way.

138. Bear unto the hypocrites the tidings that for them there is a painful doom;

139. Those who choose disbelievers for their friends instead of believers! Do they look for power at their hands? Lo! all power appertains to Allah.

140. He has already revealed unto you in the Scripture that, when you hear the revelations of Allah rejected and derided, (you) sit not with them (who disbelieve and mock) until they engage in some other conversation. Lo! in that case (if you stayed) you would be like unto them. Lo! Allah will gather hypocrites and dis believers, all together, into Hell;

141. Those who wait upon occasion in regard to you and, if a victory comes unto you from Allah, say: Are we not with you? and if the disbelievers meet with a success say: Had we not the mastery of you, and did we not protect you from the believers? Allah will judge between you on the Day of Resurrection, and Allah will not give disbelievers any way (of success) against believers.

142. Lo! the hypocrites seek to deceive Allah, but it is Allah who deceives them. When they stand up to prayer they perform it languidly and to be seen of men, and are mindful of Allah but little;

143. Swaying between this (and that), (belonging) neither to these nor to those. He whom Allah causes to go astray, you (O Muhammad) will not find a way for him:

144. O you who believe! Choose not disbelievers for (your) bosom friends in place of believers. Would you give Allah a clear warrant against you?

145. Lo! the hypocrites (will be) in the lowest deep of the Fire, and you will find no helper for them;

146. Save those who repent and amend and hold fast to Allah and make their religion pure for Allah (only). Those are with the believers. And Allah will bestow on the believers an immense reward.

147. What concern has Allah for your punishment if you are thankful (for His mercies) and believe (in Him)? Allah was ever Responsive, Aware.

148. Allah loves not the utterance of harsh speech save by one who has been wronged. Allah is ever Hearer, Knower.

١٤١ اَلَّذِينَ يَتَرَبَّصُونَ بِكُمْ فَإِن كَانَ لَكُمْ فَتْحٌ مِّنَ اللَّهِ قَالُوٓاْ أَلَمْ نَكُن مَّعَكُمْ وَإِن كَانَ لِلْكَٰفِرِينَ نَصِيبٌ قَالُوٓاْ أَلَمْ نَسْتَحْوِذْ عَلَيْكُمْ وَنَمْنَعْكُم مِّنَ ٱلْمُؤْمِنِينَ فَٱللَّهُ يَحْكُمُ بَيْنَكُمْ يَوْمَ ٱلْقِيَٰمَةِ وَلَن يَجْعَلَ ٱللَّهُ لِلْكَٰفِرِينَ عَلَى ٱلْمُؤْمِنِينَ سَبِيلًا

١٤٢ إِنَّ ٱلْمُنَٰفِقِينَ يُخَٰدِعُونَ ٱللَّهَ وَهُوَ خَٰدِعُهُمْ وَإِذَا قَامُوٓاْ إِلَى ٱلصَّلَوٰةِ قَامُواْ كُسَالَىٰ يُرَآءُونَ ٱلنَّاسَ وَلَا يَذْكُرُونَ ٱللَّهَ إِلَّا قَلِيلًا

١٤٣ مُّذَبْذَبِينَ بَيْنَ ذَٰلِكَ لَآ إِلَىٰ هَٰٓؤُلَآءِ وَلَآ إِلَىٰ هَٰٓؤُلَآءِ وَمَن يُضْلِلِ ٱللَّهُ فَلَن تَجِدَ لَهُۥ سَبِيلًا

١٤٤ يَٰٓأَيُّهَا ٱلَّذِينَ ءَامَنُواْ لَا تَتَّخِذُواْ ٱلْكَٰفِرِينَ أَوْلِيَآءَ مِن دُونِ ٱلْمُؤْمِنِينَ أَتُرِيدُونَ أَن تَجْعَلُواْ لِلَّهِ عَلَيْكُمْ سُلْطَٰنًا مُّبِينًا

١٤٥ إِنَّ ٱلْمُنَٰفِقِينَ فِى ٱلدَّرْكِ ٱلْأَسْفَلِ مِنَ ٱلنَّارِ وَلَن تَجِدَ لَهُمْ نَصِيرًا

١٤٦ إِلَّا ٱلَّذِينَ تَابُواْ وَأَصْلَحُواْ وَٱعْتَصَمُواْ بِٱللَّهِ وَأَخْلَصُواْ دِينَهُمْ لِلَّهِ فَأُوْلَٰٓئِكَ مَعَ ٱلْمُؤْمِنِينَ وَسَوْفَ يُؤْتِ ٱللَّهُ ٱلْمُؤْمِنِينَ أَجْرًا عَظِيمًا

١٤٧ مَّا يَفْعَلُ ٱللَّهُ بِعَذَابِكُمْ إِن شَكَرْتُمْ وَءَامَنتُمْ وَكَانَ ٱللَّهُ شَاكِرًا عَلِيمًا

١٤٨ لَّا يُحِبُّ ٱللَّهُ ٱلْجَهْرَ بِٱلسُّوٓءِ مِنَ ٱلْقَوْلِ إِلَّا مَن ظُلِمَ وَكَانَ ٱللَّهُ سَمِيعًا عَلِيمًا

149. If you do good openly or keep it secret, or forgive evil, lo! Allah is Forgiving, Powerful.

﴿١٤٩﴾ إِن تُبْدُوا خَيْرًا أَوْ تُخْفُوهُ أَوْ تَعْفُوا عَن سُوَءٍ فَإِنَّ اللَّهَ كَانَ عَفُوًّا قَدِيرًا

150. Lo! those who disbelieve in Allah and His messengers, and seek to make distinction between Allah and His messengers, and say: We believe in some and disbelieve in others, and seek to choose a way in between;

﴿١٥٠﴾ إِنَّ الَّذِينَ يَكْفُرُونَ بِاللَّهِ وَرُسُلِهِ وَيُرِيدُونَ أَن يُفَرِّقُوا بَيْنَ اللَّهِ وَرُسُلِهِ وَيَقُولُونَ نُؤْمِنُ بِبَعْضٍ وَنَكْفُرُ بِبَعْضٍ وَيُرِيدُونَ أَن يَتَّخِذُوا بَيْنَ ذَلِكَ سَبِيلًا

151. Such are disbelievers in truth; and for disbelievers We prepare a shameful doom.

﴿١٥١﴾ أُوْلَئِكَ هُمُ الْكَافِرُونَ حَقًّا وَأَعْتَدْنَا لِلْكَافِرِينَ عَذَابًا مُّهِينًا

152. But those who believe in Allah and His messengers and make no distinction between any of them, unto them Allah will give their wages; and Allah was ever Forgiving, Merciful.

﴿١٥٢﴾ وَالَّذِينَ ءَامَنُوا بِاللَّهِ وَرُسُلِهِ وَلَمْ يُفَرِّقُوا بَيْنَ أَحَدٍ مِّنْهُمْ أُوْلَئِكَ سَوْفَ يُؤْتِيهِمْ أُجُورَهُمْ وَكَانَ اللَّهُ غَفُورًا رَّحِيمًا

153. The People of the Scripture ask of you that you should cause an (actual) Book to descend upon them from heaven. They asked a greater thing of Moses, for they said: Show us Allah plainly. The storm of lightning seized them for their wickedness. Then (even after that) they chose the calf (for worship) after clear proofs (of Allah's Sovereignty) had come unto them. And We forgave them that! And We bestowed on Moses evident authority.

﴿١٥٣﴾ يَسْأَلُكَ أَهْلُ الْكِتَابِ أَن تُنَزِّلَ عَلَيْهِمْ كِتَابًا مِّنَ السَّمَاءِ فَقَدْ سَأَلُوا مُوسَىٰ أَكْبَرَ مِن ذَلِكَ فَقَالُوا أَرِنَا اللَّهَ جَهْرَةً فَأَخَذَتْهُمُ الصَّاعِقَةُ بِظُلْمِهِمْ ثُمَّ اتَّخَذُوا الْعِجْلَ مِنْ بَعْدِ مَا جَاءَتْهُمُ الْبَيِّنَاتُ فَعَفَوْنَا عَن ذَلِكَ وَءَاتَيْنَا مُوسَىٰ سُلْطَانًا مُّبِينًا

154. And We caused the Mount to tower above them at (the taking of) their covenant: and We bade them: Enter the gate, prostrate! and we bade them: Transgress not on the Sabbath! and We took from them a firm covenant.

﴿١٥٤﴾ وَرَفَعْنَا فَوْقَهُمُ الطُّورَ بِمِيثَاقِهِمْ وَقُلْنَا لَهُمُ ادْخُلُوا الْبَابَ سُجَّدًا وَقُلْنَا لَهُمْ لَا تَعْدُوا فِي السَّبْتِ وَأَخَذْنَا مِنْهُم مِّيثَاقًا غَلِيظًا

155. Then because of their breaking of their covenant, and their disbelieving in the revelations of Allah, and their slaying of the Prophets wrongfully, and their saying: Our hearts are hardened.— Nay, but Allah has set a seal upon them for their disbelief, so that they believe not save a few—

﴿١٥٥﴾ فَبِمَا نَقْضِهِم مِّيثَاقَهُمْ وَكُفْرِهِم بِآيَاتِ اللَّهِ وَقَتْلِهِمُ الْأَنبِيَاءَ بِغَيْرِ حَقٍّ وَقَوْلِهِمْ قُلُوبُنَا غُلْفٌ بَلْ طَبَعَ اللَّهُ عَلَيْهَا بِكُفْرِهِمْ فَلَا يُؤْمِنُونَ إِلَّا قَلِيلًا

156. And because of their disbelief and of their speaking against Mary a tremendous calumny;

157. And because of their saying: We slew the Messiah, Jesus son of Mary, Allah's messenger—They slew him not nor crucified him, but it appeared so unto them; and lo! those who disagree concerning it are in doubt thereof; they have no knowledge thereof save pursuit of a conjecture; they slew him not for certain,

158. But Allah took him up unto Himself. Allah was ever Mighty, Wise.

159. There is not one of the People of the Scripture but will believe in him before his death, and on the Day of Resurrection he will be a witness against them—

160. Because of the wrongdoing of the Jews We forbade them good things which were (before) made lawful unto them, and because of their much hindering from Allah's way,

161. And of their taking usury when they were forbidden it, and of their devouring people's wealth by false pretenses. We have prepared for those of them who disbelieve a painful doom.

162. But those of them who are firm in knowledge and the believers believe in that which is revealed unto you, and that which was revealed before you, especially the diligent in prayer and those who pay the poor due, the believers in Allah and the Last Day. Upon these We shall bestow immense reward.

163. Lo! We have inspired you as We have inspired Noah and the prophets after him. We also inspired Abraham and Ishmael and Isaac and Jacob and the tribes, and Jesus and Job and Jonah and Aaron and Solomon, and We imparted unto David the Psalms;

١٥٦ وَبِكُفْرِهِمْ وَقَوْلِهِمْ عَلَىٰ مَرْيَمَ بُهْتَانًا عَظِيمًا

١٥٧ وَقَوْلِهِمْ إِنَّا قَتَلْنَا الْمَسِيحَ عِيسَى ابْنَ مَرْيَمَ رَسُولَ اللَّهِ وَمَا قَتَلُوهُ وَمَا صَلَبُوهُ وَلَٰكِن شُبِّهَ لَهُمْ وَإِنَّ الَّذِينَ اخْتَلَفُوا فِيهِ لَفِي شَكٍّ مِّنْهُ مَا لَهُم بِهِ مِنْ عِلْمٍ إِلَّا اتِّبَاعَ الظَّنِّ وَمَا قَتَلُوهُ يَقِينًا

١٥٨ بَل رَّفَعَهُ اللَّهُ إِلَيْهِ وَكَانَ اللَّهُ عَزِيزًا حَكِيمًا

١٥٩ وَإِن مِّنْ أَهْلِ الْكِتَابِ إِلَّا لَيُؤْمِنَنَّ بِهِ قَبْلَ مَوْتِهِ وَيَوْمَ الْقِيَامَةِ يَكُونُ عَلَيْهِمْ شَهِيدًا

١٦٠ فَبِظُلْمٍ مِّنَ الَّذِينَ هَادُوا حَرَّمْنَا عَلَيْهِمْ طَيِّبَاتٍ أُحِلَّتْ لَهُمْ وَبِصَدِّهِمْ عَن سَبِيلِ اللَّهِ كَثِيرًا

١٦١ وَأَخْذِهِمُ الرِّبَا وَقَدْ نُهُوا عَنْهُ وَأَكْلِهِمْ أَمْوَالَ النَّاسِ بِالْبَاطِلِ وَأَعْتَدْنَا لِلْكَافِرِينَ مِنْهُمْ عَذَابًا أَلِيمًا

١٦٢ لَّٰكِنِ الرَّاسِخُونَ فِي الْعِلْمِ مِنْهُمْ وَالْمُؤْمِنُونَ يُؤْمِنُونَ بِمَا أُنزِلَ إِلَيْكَ وَمَا أُنزِلَ مِن قَبْلِكَ وَالْمُقِيمِينَ الصَّلَاةَ وَالْمُؤْتُونَ الزَّكَاةَ وَالْمُؤْمِنُونَ بِاللَّهِ وَالْيَوْمِ الْآخِرِ أُولَٰئِكَ سَنُؤْتِيهِمْ أَجْرًا عَظِيمًا

١٦٣ إِنَّا أَوْحَيْنَا إِلَيْكَ كَمَا أَوْحَيْنَا إِلَىٰ نُوحٍ وَالنَّبِيِّينَ مِن بَعْدِهِ وَأَوْحَيْنَا إِلَىٰ إِبْرَاهِيمَ وَإِسْمَاعِيلَ وَإِسْحَاقَ وَيَعْقُوبَ وَالْأَسْبَاطِ وَعِيسَى وَأَيُّوبَ وَيُونُسَ وَهَارُونَ وَسُلَيْمَانَ وَآتَيْنَا دَاوُودَ زَبُورًا

164. And messengers We have mentioned unto you before and messengers We have not mentioned unto you; and Allah spoke directly unto Moses;

١٦٤ وَرُسُلًا قَدْ قَصَصْنَهُمْ عَلَيْكَ مِن قَبْلُ وَرُسُلًا لَّمْ نَقْصُصْهُمْ عَلَيْكَ وَكَلَّمَ اللَّهُ مُوسَىٰ تَكْلِيمًا

165. Messengers of good cheer and of warning, in order that mankind might have no argument against Allah after the messengers. Allah was ever Mighty, Wise.

١٦٥ رُّسُلًا مُّبَشِّرِينَ وَمُنذِرِينَ لِئَلَّا يَكُونَ لِلنَّاسِ عَلَى اللَّهِ حُجَّةٌ بَعْدَ الرُّسُلِ وَكَانَ اللَّهُ عَزِيزًا حَكِيمًا

166. But Allah (Himself) testifies concerning that which He has revealed unto you; in His knowledge has He revealed it; and the Angels also testify. And Allah is sufficient as witness.

١٦٦ لَّٰكِنِ اللَّهُ يَشْهَدُ بِمَا أَنزَلَ إِلَيْكَ أَنزَلَهُ بِعِلْمِهِ وَالْمَلَٰئِكَةُ يَشْهَدُونَ وَكَفَىٰ بِاللَّهِ شَهِيدًا

167. Lo! those who disbelieve and hinder (others) from the way of Allah, they verily have wandered far astray.

١٦٧ إِنَّ الَّذِينَ كَفَرُوا وَصَدُّوا عَن سَبِيلِ اللَّهِ قَدْ ضَلُّوا ضَلَٰلًا بَعِيدًا

168. Lo! those who disbelieve and deal in wrong, Allah will never forgive them, neither will He guide them unto a road,

١٦٨ إِنَّ الَّذِينَ كَفَرُوا وَظَلَمُوا لَمْ يَكُنِ اللَّهُ لِيَغْفِرَ لَهُمْ وَلَا لِيَهْدِيَهُمْ طَرِيقًا

169. Except the road of Hell, wherein they will abide forever. And that is ever easy for Allah.

١٦٩ إِلَّا طَرِيقَ جَهَنَّمَ خَٰلِدِينَ فِيهَا أَبَدًا وَكَانَ ذَٰلِكَ عَلَى اللَّهِ يَسِيرًا

170. O mankind! The Messenger has come unto you with the truth from your Lord. Therefor believe; (it is) better for you. But if you disbelieve, still, lo! unto Allah belongs whatever is in the heavens and the earth. Allah is ever Knower, Wise.

١٧٠ يَٰٓأَيُّهَا النَّاسُ قَدْ جَاءَكُمُ الرَّسُولُ بِالْحَقِّ مِن رَّبِّكُمْ فَـَٔامِنُوا خَيْرًا لَّكُمْ وَإِن تَكْفُرُوا فَإِنَّ لِلَّهِ مَا فِي السَّمَٰوَٰتِ وَالْأَرْضِ وَكَانَ اللَّهُ عَلِيمًا حَكِيمًا

171. O People of the Scripture! Do not exaggerate in your religion nor utter anything concerning Allah save the truth. The Messiah, Jesus son of Mary, was only a messenger of Allah, and His word which He conveyed unto Mary, and a spirit from Him. So believe in Allah and His messengers, and say not "Three". Cease! (it is) better for you! Allah is only One God. Far is it removed from His transcendent majesty that he should have a son. His is all that is in the heavens and all that is in the earth. And Allah is sufficient as Defender.

١٧١ يَٰٓأَهْلَ الْكِتَٰبِ لَا تَغْلُوا فِي دِينِكُمْ وَلَا تَقُولُوا عَلَى اللَّهِ إِلَّا الْحَقَّ إِنَّمَا الْمَسِيحُ عِيسَى ابْنُ مَرْيَمَ رَسُولُ اللَّهِ وَكَلِمَتُهُ أَلْقَٰهَا إِلَىٰ مَرْيَمَ وَرُوحٌ مِّنْهُ فَـَٔامِنُوا بِاللَّهِ وَرُسُلِهِ وَلَا تَقُولُوا ثَلَٰثَةٌ انتَهُوا خَيْرًا لَّكُمْ إِنَّمَا اللَّهُ إِلَٰهٌ وَٰحِدٌ سُبْحَٰنَهُ أَن يَكُونَ لَهُ وَلَدٌ لَّهُ مَا فِي السَّمَٰوَٰتِ وَمَا فِي الْأَرْضِ وَكَفَىٰ بِاللَّهِ وَكِيلًا

172. The Messiah will never scorn to be a slave unto Allah, nor will the favored angels. Who scorns His service and is proud, all such will He assemble unto Him;

173. Then, as for those who believed and did good works, unto them will He pay their wages in full, adding unto them of His bounty; and as for those who were scornful and proud, them will He punish with a painful doom. And they will not find for them, against Allah, any protecting friend or helper.

174. O mankind! Now has a proof from your Lord come unto you, and We have sent down unto you a clear light;

175. As for those who believe in Allah, and hold fast unto Him, them He will cause to enter into His mercy and grace, and will guide them unto Him by a straight road.

176. They ask you for a pronouncement. Say: Allah has pronounced for you concerning distant kindred. If a man die childless and he has a sister, hers is half the heritage, and he would have inherited from her had she died childless. And if there be two sisters, then theirs are two-thirds of the heritage, and if they be brothers, men and women, unto the male is the equivalent of the share of two females. Allah expounds unto you, so that you err not. Allah is Knower of all things.

لَّن يَسْتَنكِفَ ٱلْمَسِيحُ أَن يَكُونَ عَبْدًا لِّلَّهِ ﴿١٧٢﴾
وَلَا ٱلْمَلَـٰٓئِكَةُ ٱلْمُقَرَّبُونَ وَمَن يَسْتَنكِفْ عَنْ
عِبَادَتِهِ وَيَسْتَكْبِرْ فَسَيَحْشُرُهُمْ إِلَيْهِ جَمِيعًا

فَأَمَّا ٱلَّذِينَ ءَامَنُوا۟ وَعَمِلُوا۟ ٱلصَّـٰلِحَـٰتِ ﴿١٧٣﴾
فَيُوَفِّيهِمْ أُجُورَهُمْ وَيَزِيدُهُم مِّن فَضْلِهِۦ وَأَمَّا
ٱلَّذِينَ ٱسْتَنكَفُوا۟ وَٱسْتَكْبَرُوا۟ فَيُعَذِّبُهُمْ
عَذَابًا أَلِيمًا وَلَا يَجِدُونَ لَهُم مِّن دُونِ ٱللَّهِ
وَلِيًّا وَلَا نَصِيرًا

يَـٰٓأَيُّهَا ٱلنَّاسُ قَدْ جَآءَكُم بُرْهَـٰنٌ مِّن رَّبِّكُمْ ﴿١٧٤﴾
وَأَنزَلْنَآ إِلَيْكُمْ نُورًا مُّبِينًا

فَأَمَّا ٱلَّذِينَ ءَامَنُوا۟ بِٱللَّهِ وَٱعْتَصَمُوا۟ بِهِۦ ﴿١٧٥﴾
فَسَيُدْخِلُهُمْ فِى رَحْمَةٍ مِّنْهُ وَفَضْلٍ وَيَهْدِيهِمْ إِلَيْهِ
صِرَٰطًا مُّسْتَقِيمًا

يَسْتَفْتُونَكَ قُلِ ٱللَّهُ يُفْتِيكُمْ فِى ٱلْكَلَـٰلَةِ ﴿١٧٦﴾
إِنِ ٱمْرُؤٌا۟ هَلَكَ لَيْسَ لَهُۥ وَلَدٌ وَلَهُۥٓ أُخْتٌ فَلَهَا نِصْفُ
مَا تَرَكَ وَهُوَ يَرِثُهَآ إِن لَّمْ يَكُن لَّهَا وَلَدٌ فَإِن كَانَتَا
ٱثْنَتَيْنِ فَلَهُمَا ٱلثُّلُثَانِ مِمَّا تَرَكَ وَإِن كَانُوٓا۟ إِخْوَةً
رِّجَالًا وَنِسَآءً فَلِلذَّكَرِ مِثْلُ حَظِّ ٱلْأُنثَيَيْنِ يُبَيِّنُ
ٱللَّهُ لَكُمْ أَن تَضِلُّوا۟ وَٱللَّهُ بِكُلِّ شَىْءٍ عَلِيمٌۢ

The Table Spread

Al Mā'idah, "The Table Spread," derives its name from vv. 112 ff., where it is told how the disciples of Jesus asked that a table spread with food might be sent down from Heaven, and their prayer was granted, a passage in which some have seen an allusion to the Eucharist. Many authorities regard it as the last surah in order of revelation, and Rodwell has so placed it in his chronological arrangement; but the claim can only be established in the case of verse 3, which announces the completion of their religion for the Muslims, and the choice for them of Islam (the Surrender to Allah) as their religion. That verse is undoubtedly the latest of the whole Qur'an. It was revealed during the Prophet's last pilgrimage (the Farewell Pilgrimage," as it is called) to Makkah, and spoken by him in the course of his address to the assembled thousands at Arafat, when all Arabia had embraced Islam, only a little while before his death. It is possible that, as Noldeke supposes, two other verses near to it are of the same date, but the remainder of the revelations contained in this surah belong rather to the period between the fourth and seventh years of the Hijrah. Its subject is observance of religious duties. The followers of former prophets had failed through breaking their covenant, and so the Muslims are adjured to keep their covenant with God and all their obligations watchfully, because God's covenant is only with those who do right. There is more mention of the Christians here than in the former surahs, from which some writers infer that this surah must have been revealed at the time when the Prophet was at war with certain Christian tribes belonging to the Eastern Roman Empire. But there is no evidence for that either in Tradition or in the text itself.

The period of revelation is between the fifth and tenth years of the hijrah.

The Table Spread

Revealed at Madinah

*In the name of Allah,
the Beneficent, the Merciful*

1. **O** you who believe! Fulfill the covenants. The beast of cattle is made lawful unto you (for food) except that which is announced unto you (herein), game being unlawful when you are on pilgrimage. Lo! Allah ordains that which He wills.

2. O you who believe! Profane not Allah's monuments nor the Sacred Month nor the offerings nor the garlands, nor those repairing to the Sacred House,[93] seeking the grace and pleasure of Allah. But when you have left the sacred territory, then go hunting (if you will). And let not your hatred of a folk who (once) stopped your going to the Sacred Mosque seduce you to transgress; but help you one another unto righteousness and pious duty. Help not one another unto sin and transgression, but keep your duty to Allah. Lo! Allah is severe in punishment.

3. Forbidden unto you (for food) are carrion and blood and swine flesh, and that which has been dedicated unto any other than Allah, and the strangled, and the dead through beating, and the dead through falling from a height, and that which has been killed by (the goring of) horns, and the devoured of wild beasts, saving that which you make lawful (by the death stroke), and that which has been immolated unto idols. And (forbidden is it) that you swear by the divining arrows. This is an abomination. This day are those who disbelieve in despair of (ever harming) your religion; so fear them not, fear Me! This day have I perfected your religion for you and completed My favor unto you, and have chosen for you as religion al ISLAM.[94] Whoso is forced by hunger, not by will, to sin: (for him) lo! Allah is Forgiving, Merciful.

---

[93] i.e., the Ka'bah at Makkah.

[94] I.e., "The Surrender" to Allah. Thus solemnly the religion which the Pro-phet had established received its name.

٤. They ask you (O Muhammad) what is made lawful for them. Say: (all) good things are made lawful for you. And those beasts and birds of prey which you have trained as hounds are trained, you teach them that which Allah taught you; so eat of that which they catch for you and mention Allah's name upon it, and observe your duty to Allah. Lo! Allah is swift to take account.

5. This day are (all) good things made lawful for you. The food of those who have received the Scripture is lawful for you, and your food is lawful for them. And so are the virtuous women of the believers and the virtuous women of those who received the Scripture before you (lawful for you) when you give them their marriage portions and live with them in honor, not in fornication, nor taking them as secret concubines. Who denies the faith, his work is vain and he will be among the losers in the Hereafter.

6. O you who believe! When you rise up for prayer, wash your face, and your hands up to the elbows, and lightly rub your heads and (wash) your feet up to the ankles. And if you are unclean, purify yourselves. And if you are sick or on a journey, or one of you comes from the closet, or you have had contact with women, and you find not water, then go to clean, high ground and rub your faces and your hands with some of it. Allah would not place a burden on you, but He would purify you and would perfect His grace upon you, that you may give thanks.

7. Remember Allah's grace upon you and His covenant by which He bound you when you said: We hear and we obey; and keep your duty to Allah. Allah knows what is in the breasts (of men).

8. O you who believe! Be steadfast witnesses for Allah in equity, and let not hatred of any people seduce you that you deal not justly. Deal justly, that is nearer to piety. Observe your duty to Allah. Lo! Allah is Informed of what you do.

9. Allah has promised those who believe and do good works: Theirs will be forgiveness and immense reward.

10. And they who disbelieve and deny Our revelations, such are rightful owners of Hell.

11. O you who believe! Remember Allah's favor unto you, how a people were minded to stretch out their hands against you but He withheld their hands from you; and keep your duty to Allah. In Allah let believers put their trust.

12. Allah made a covenant of old with the Children of Israel and We raised among them twelve chieftains, and Allah said: Lo! I am with you. If you establish prayer and pay the poor due, and believe in My messengers and support them, and lend unto Allah a kindly loan,[95] surely I shall remit your sins, and surely I shall bring you into gardens underneath which rivers flow. Who among you disbelieves after this will go astray from a plain road.

13. And because of their breaking their covenant, We have cursed them and made hard their hearts. They change words from their context and forget a part of that whereof they were admonished. You will not cease to discover treachery from all save a few of them. But bear with them and pardon them. Lo! Allah loves the kindly.

---

[95] i.e., a loan without interest or thought of gain.

14. And with those who say: "Lo! we are Christians," We made a covenant, but they forgot a part of that whereof they were admonished. Therefore We have stirred up enmity and hatred among them till the Day of Resurrection, when Allah will inform them of their handiwork.

15. O people of the Scripture! Now has Our Messenger come unto you, expounding unto you much of that which you used to hide in the Scripture, and forgiving much. Now has come unto you light from Allah and a plain Book.

16. Whereby Allah guides him who seeks His good pleasure unto paths of peace. He brings them out of darkness unto light by His decree, and guides them unto a straight path.

17. They indeed have disbelieved who say: Lo! Allah is the Messiah, son of Mary. Say: Who then can do anything against Allah, if He had willed to destroy the Messiah son of Mary, and his mother and everyone on earth? Allah's is the Sovereignty of the heavens and the earth and all that is between them. He creates what He will. And Allah is Able to do all things.

18. The Jews and Christians say: We are children of Allah and His loved ones. Say; Why then does He chastise you for your sins? Nay, you are but mortals of His creating. He forgives whom He will, and chastises whom He will. Allah's is the Sovereignty of the heavens and the earth and all that is between them, and unto Him is the journeying.

19. O people of the Scripture! Now has Our Messenger come unto you to make things plain after an interval (of cessation) of the messengers, lest you should say: There came not unto us a messenger of cheer nor any warner. Now has a Messenger of cheer and a warner come unto you. Allah is Able to do all things.

20. And (remember) when Moses said unto his people: O my people! Remember Allah's favor unto you, how He placed among you Prophets, and He made you Kings, and gave you that (which) He gave not to any (other) of (His) creatures.

21. O my people! Go into the holy land which Allah has ordained for you. Turn not in flight, for surely you turn back as losers;

22. They said: O Moses! Lo! a giant people (dwell) therein, and lo! we go not in till they go forth from thence. When they go forth, then we will enter (not till then).

23. Then spoke two of those who feared (their Lord, men) unto whom Allah had been gracious: Enter in upon them by the gate, for if you enter by it, lo! you will be victorious. So put your trust (in Allah) if you are indeed believers.

24. They said: O Moses! We will never enter (the land) while they are in it. So go you and your Lord and fight! We will sit here.

25. He said: My Lord! I have control of none but myself and my brother, so distinguish between us and the wrongdoing folk.

26. (Their Lord) said: For this the land will surely be forbidden them for forty years that they will wander in the earth, bewildered. So grieve not over the wrongdoing folk.

27. But recite unto them with truth the tale of the two sons of Adam, how they offered each a sacrifice, and it was accepted from the one of them and it was not accepted from the other. (The one) said: I will surely kill you. (The other) answered: Allah accepts only from those who ward off (evil).

28. Even if you stretch out your hand against me to kill me, I shall not stretch out my hand against you to kill you, lo! I fear Allah, the Lord of the Worlds.

29. Lo! I would rather you should bear the punishment of the sin against me and your own sin and become one of the owners of the Fire. That is the reward of evildoers.

30. But (the other's) mind imposed on him the killing of his brother, so he slew him and became one of the losers.

31. Then Allah sent a raven scratching up the ground, to show him how to hide his brother's naked corpse. He said: Woe unto me! Am I not able to be as this raven and so hide my brother's naked corpse? And he became repentant.

32. For that cause We decreed for the Children of Israel that whoever kills a human being for other than murder or corruption in the earth, it shall be as if he had killed all mankind, and who saves the life of one, it shall be as if he had saved the life of all mankind. Our messengers came unto them of old with clear proofs (of Allah's sovereignty), but afterwards lo! many of them became prodigals in the earth.

33. The only reward of those who make war upon Allah and His Messenger and strive after corruption in the land will be that they will be killed or crucified, or have their hands and feet on alternate sides cut off, or will be expelled out of the land. Such will be their degradation in the world, and in the Hereafter theirs will be an awful doom;

34. Save those who repent before you overpower them. Then know that Allah is Forgiving, Merciful.

35. O you who believe! Be mindful of your duty to Allah, and seek the way of approach unto Him, and strive in His way in order that you may succeed.

36. As for those who disbelieve, lo! if all that is in the earth were theirs, and as much again therewith, to ransom them from the doom on the day of Resurrection, it would not be accepted from them. Theirs will be a painful doom.

37. They will wish to come forth from the Fire, but they will not come forth from it. Theirs will be a lasting doom.

38. As for the thief, both male and female, cut off their hands. It is the reward of their own deeds, an exemplary punishment from Allah. Allah is Mighty, Wise.

39. But who repents after his wrongdoing and amends, lo! Allah will relent toward him. Lo! Allah is Forgiving, Merciful.

40. Do you not know that unto Allah belongs the Sovereignty of the heavens and the earth? He punishes whom He will, and forgives whom He will. Allah is Able to do all things.

41. O Messenger! Let not them grieve you who vie one with another in the race to disbelief, of such as say with their mouths: "We believe," but their hearts believe not, and of the Jews: listeners for the sake of falsehood, listeners on behalf of other folk who come not unto you, changing words from their context and saying: If this be given unto you, receive it but if this be not given unto you, then beware! He whom Allah dooms unto sin, you (by your efforts) will avail him nothing against Allah. Those are they for whom the will of Allah is that He cleanse not their hearts. Theirs in the world will be ignominy, and in the Hereafter an awful doom;

42. Listeners for the sake of falsehood! Greedy for illicit gain! If then they have recourse unto you (Muhammad), judge between them or disclaim jurisdiction. If you disclaim jurisdiction, then they cannot harm you at all. But if you judge, judge between them with equity. Lo! Allah loves the equitable.

43. How come they unto you for judgment when they have the Torah, wherein Allah has delivered judgment (for them)? Yet even after that they turn away. Such (folk) are not believers.

44. Lo! We did reveal the Torah, wherein is guidance and a light, by which the Prophets who surrendered (unto Allah) judged the Jews, and the rabbis and the priests (judged) by such of Allah's Scripture as they were bidden to observe, and thereunto were they witnesses. So fear not mankind, but fear Me. And barter not My revelations for a little gain. Who judges not by that which Allah has revealed: such are disbelievers.

45. And We prescribed for them therein: a life for a life, an eye for an eye, a nose for a nose, an ear for an ear, a tooth for a tooth, and for wounds is retaliation. But who forgoes it (in the way of charity) it shall be expiation for him. Who judges not by that which Allah has revealed: such are wrongdoers.

46. And We caused Jesus son of Mary to follow in their footsteps, confirming that which was (revealed) before him, and We bestowed on him the Gospel wherein is guidance and a light, confirming that which was (revealed) before it in the Torah a guidance and an admonition unto those who ward off (evil).

﴿٤٢﴾ سَمَّاعُونَ لِلْكَذِبِ أَكَّالُونَ لِلسُّحْتِ فَإِن جَآءُوكَ فَاحْكُم بَيْنَهُمْ أَوْ أَعْرِضْ عَنْهُمْ وَإِن تُعْرِضْ عَنْهُمْ فَلَن يَضُرُّوكَ شَيْئًا وَإِنْ حَكَمْتَ فَاحْكُم بَيْنَهُم بِالْقِسْطِ إِنَّ اللَّهَ يُحِبُّ الْمُقْسِطِينَ

﴿٤٣﴾ وَكَيْفَ يُحَكِّمُونَكَ وَعِندَهُمُ التَّوْرَاةُ فِيهَا حُكْمُ اللَّهِ ثُمَّ يَتَوَلَّوْنَ مِنۢ بَعْدِ ذَلِكَ وَمَا أُوْلَئِكَ بِالْمُؤْمِنِينَ

﴿٤٤﴾ إِنَّا أَنزَلْنَا التَّوْرَاةَ فِيهَا هُدًى وَنُورٌ يَحْكُمُ بِهَا النَّبِيُّونَ الَّذِينَ أَسْلَمُوا لِلَّذِينَ هَادُوا وَالرَّبَّانِيُّونَ وَالْأَحْبَارُ بِمَا اسْتُحْفِظُوا مِن كِتَابِ اللَّهِ وَكَانُوا عَلَيْهِ شُهَدَآءَ فَلَا تَخْشَوُا النَّاسَ وَاخْشَوْنِ وَلَا تَشْتَرُوا بِآيَاتِي ثَمَنًا قَلِيلًا وَمَن لَّمْ يَحْكُم بِمَآ أَنزَلَ اللَّهُ فَأُوْلَئِكَ هُمُ الْكَافِرُونَ

﴿٤٥﴾ وَكَتَبْنَا عَلَيْهِمْ فِيهَا أَنَّ النَّفْسَ بِالنَّفْسِ وَالْعَيْنَ بِالْعَيْنِ وَالْأَنفَ بِالْأَنفِ وَالْأُذُنَ بِالْأُذُنِ وَالسِّنَّ بِالسِّنِّ وَالْجُرُوحَ قِصَاصٌ فَمَن تَصَدَّقَ بِهِ فَهُوَ كَفَّارَةٌ لَّهُ وَمَن لَّمْ يَحْكُم بِمَآ أَنزَلَ اللَّهُ فَأُوْلَئِكَ هُمُ الظَّالِمُونَ

﴿٤٦﴾ وَقَفَّيْنَا عَلَى آثَارِهِم بِعِيسَى ابْنِ مَرْيَمَ مُصَدِّقًا لِّمَا بَيْنَ يَدَيْهِ مِنَ التَّوْرَاةِ وَآتَيْنَاهُ الْإِنجِيلَ فِيهِ هُدًى وَنُورٌ وَمُصَدِّقًا لِّمَا بَيْنَ يَدَيْهِ مِنَ التَّوْرَاةِ وَهُدًى وَمَوْعِظَةً لِّلْمُتَّقِينَ

47. Let the People of the Gospel judge by that which Allah has revealed therein. Who judges not by that which Allah has revealed; such are evildoers.

48. And unto you have We revealed the Scripture with the truth, confirming whatever Scripture was before it, and a watcher over it. So judge between them by that which Allah has revealed, and follow not their desires away from the truth which has come unto you. For each We have appointed a divine law and a traced out way. Had Allah willed He could have made you one community. But that He may try you by that which He has given you (He has made you as you are). So vie one with another in good works. Unto Allah you will all return, and He will then inform you of that wherein you differ.

49. So judge between them by that which Allah has revealed, and follow not their desires, but beware of them lest they seduce you from some part of that which Allah has revealed unto you. And if they turn away, then know that Allah's will is to smite them for some sin of theirs. Lo! many of mankind are evildoers.

50. Is it a judgment of the time of (pagan) ignorance that they are seeking? Who is better than Allah for judgment to a people who have certainty (in their belief)?

51. O you who believe! Take not the Jews and Christians for bosom friends. They are friends one to another. He among you who takes them for bosom friends is (one) of them. Lo! Allah guides not wrongdoing folk.

52. And you see those in whose heart is a disease race toward them, saying: We fear lest a change of fortune befall us. And it may happen that Allah will vouchsafe (unto you) the victory, or a commandment from His presence. Then will they repent of their secret thoughts.

٤٧ وَلْيَحْكُمْ أَهْلُ الْإِنجِيلِ بِمَا أَنزَلَ اللَّهُ فِيهِ وَمَن لَّمْ يَحْكُم بِمَا أَنزَلَ اللَّهُ فَأُولَٰئِكَ هُمُ الْفَاسِقُونَ

٤٨ وَأَنزَلْنَا إِلَيْكَ الْكِتَابَ بِالْحَقِّ مُصَدِّقًا لِّمَا بَيْنَ يَدَيْهِ مِنَ الْكِتَابِ وَمُهَيْمِنًا عَلَيْهِ فَاحْكُم بَيْنَهُم بِمَا أَنزَلَ اللَّهُ وَلَا تَتَّبِعْ أَهْوَاءَهُمْ عَمَّا جَاءَكَ مِنَ الْحَقِّ لِكُلٍّ جَعَلْنَا مِنكُمْ شِرْعَةً وَمِنْهَاجًا وَلَوْ شَاءَ اللَّهُ لَجَعَلَكُمْ أُمَّةً وَاحِدَةً وَلَٰكِن لِّيَبْلُوَكُمْ فِي مَا آتَاكُمْ فَاسْتَبِقُوا الْخَيْرَاتِ إِلَى اللَّهِ مَرْجِعُكُمْ جَمِيعًا فَيُنَبِّئُكُم بِمَا كُنتُمْ فِيهِ تَخْتَلِفُونَ

٤٩ وَأَنِ احْكُم بَيْنَهُم بِمَا أَنزَلَ اللَّهُ وَلَا تَتَّبِعْ أَهْوَاءَهُمْ وَاحْذَرْهُمْ أَن يَفْتِنُوكَ عَن بَعْضِ مَا أَنزَلَ اللَّهُ إِلَيْكَ فَإِن تَوَلَّوْا فَاعْلَمْ أَنَّمَا يُرِيدُ اللَّهُ أَن يُصِيبَهُم بِبَعْضِ ذُنُوبِهِمْ وَإِنَّ كَثِيرًا مِّنَ النَّاسِ لَفَاسِقُونَ

٥٠ أَفَحُكْمَ الْجَاهِلِيَّةِ يَبْغُونَ وَمَنْ أَحْسَنُ مِنَ اللَّهِ حُكْمًا لِّقَوْمٍ يُوقِنُونَ

٥١ يَا أَيُّهَا الَّذِينَ آمَنُوا لَا تَتَّخِذُوا الْيَهُودَ وَالنَّصَارَىٰ أَوْلِيَاءَ بَعْضُهُمْ أَوْلِيَاءُ بَعْضٍ وَمَن يَتَوَلَّهُم مِّنكُمْ فَإِنَّهُ مِنْهُمْ إِنَّ اللَّهَ لَا يَهْدِي الْقَوْمَ الظَّالِمِينَ

٥٢ فَتَرَى الَّذِينَ فِي قُلُوبِهِم مَّرَضٌ يُسَارِعُونَ فِيهِمْ يَقُولُونَ نَخْشَىٰ أَن تُصِيبَنَا دَائِرَةٌ فَعَسَى اللَّهُ أَن يَأْتِيَ بِالْفَتْحِ أَوْ أَمْرٍ مِّنْ عِندِهِ فَيُصْبِحُوا عَلَىٰ مَا أَسَرُّوا فِي أَنفُسِهِمْ نَادِمِينَ

53. Then will the believers say (unto the people of the Scripture): Are these they who swore by Allah their most binding oaths that they were surely with you? Their works have failed, and they have become the losers.

54. O you who believe! Who of you becomes a renegade from his religion, (know that in his stead) Allah will bring a people whom He loves and who love Him, humble toward believers, stern toward disbelievers, striving in the way of Allah, and fearing not the blame of any blamer. Such is the grace of Allah which He gives unto whom He will. Allah is All Embracing, All Knowing.

55. Your friend can be only Allah; and His Messenger and those who believe, who establish prayer and pay the poor due, and bow down (in prayer).

56. And who takes Allah, His Messenger, and those who believe for friends, then surely the party of Allah are the victorious.

57. O you who believe! Choose not for friends such of those who received the Scripture before you, and of the disbelievers, as make a jest and sport of your religion. But keep your duty to Allah if you are true believers.

58. And when you call to prayer they take it for a jest and sport. That is because they are a folk who understand not.

59. Say: O, People of the Scripture! Do you blame us for anything else than that we believe in Allah and that which is revealed unto us and that which was formerly revealed, and because most of you are wrongdoers?

60. Shall I tell you of a worse (case) than theirs for retribution with Allah? Worse (is the case of him) whom Allah has cursed, him on whom His wrath has fallen! Worse is he of whose sort Allah has turned some to apes and swine, and who serves idols. Such are in worse plight and further astray from the plain road.

٦١ وَإِذَا جَاءُوكُمْ قَالُوا آمَنَّا وَقَد دَّخَلُوا بِالْكُفْرِ وَهُمْ قَدْ خَرَجُوا بِهِ وَاللَّهُ أَعْلَمُ بِمَا كَانُوا يَكْتُمُونَ

61. When they come unto you (Muslims), they say: We believe; but they came in unbelief and they went out in the same; and Allah knows best what they were hiding.

٦٢ وَتَرَى كَثِيرًا مِّنْهُمْ يُسَارِعُونَ فِي الْإِثْمِ وَالْعُدْوَانِ وَأَكْلِهِمُ السُّحْتَ لَبِئْسَ مَا كَانُوا يَعْمَلُونَ

62. And you see many of them vying one with another in sin and transgression and their devouring of illicit gain. Verily evil is what they do.

٦٣ لَوْلَا يَنْهَاهُمُ الرَّبَّانِيُّونَ وَالْأَحْبَارُ عَن قَوْلِهِمُ الْإِثْمَ وَأَكْلِهِمُ السُّحْتَ لَبِئْسَ مَا كَانُوا يَصْنَعُونَ

63. Why do not the rabbis and the priests forbid their evil speaking and their devouring of illicit gain? Verily evil is their handiwork.

٦٤ وَقَالَتِ الْيَهُودُ يَدُ اللَّهِ مَغْلُولَةٌ غُلَّتْ أَيْدِيهِمْ وَلُعِنُوا بِمَا قَالُوا بَلْ يَدَاهُ مَبْسُوطَتَانِ يُنفِقُ كَيْفَ يَشَاءُ وَلَيَزِيدَنَّ كَثِيرًا مِّنْهُم مَّا أُنزِلَ إِلَيْكَ مِن رَّبِّكَ طُغْيَانًا وَكُفْرًا وَأَلْقَيْنَا بَيْنَهُمُ الْعَدَاوَةَ وَالْبَغْضَاءَ إِلَى يَوْمِ الْقِيَامَةِ كُلَّمَا أَوْقَدُوا نَارًا لِّلْحَرْبِ أَطْفَأَهَا اللَّهُ وَيَسْعَوْنَ فِي الْأَرْضِ فَسَادًا وَاللَّهُ لَا يُحِبُّ الْمُفْسِدِينَ

64. Jews say: Allah's hand is fettered. Their hands are fettered and they are accursed for saying so. Nay, but both His hands are spread out wide in bounty. He bestows as He will. That which has been revealed unto you from your Lord is certain to increase the contumacy and disbelief of many of them, and We have cast among them enmity and hatred till the Day of Resurrection. As often as they light a fire for war, Allah extinguishes it. Their effort is for corruption on earth, and Allah loves not corrupters.

٦٥ وَلَوْ أَنَّ أَهْلَ الْكِتَابِ آمَنُوا وَاتَّقَوْا لَكَفَّرْنَا عَنْهُمْ سَيِّئَاتِهِمْ وَلَأَدْخَلْنَاهُمْ جَنَّاتِ النَّعِيمِ

65. If only the People of the Scripture would believe and ward off (evil), surely We should remit their sins from them and surely We should bring them into Gardens of Delight.

٦٦ وَلَوْ أَنَّهُمْ أَقَامُوا التَّوْرَاةَ وَالْإِنجِيلَ وَمَا أُنزِلَ إِلَيْهِم مِّن رَّبِّهِمْ لَأَكَلُوا مِن فَوْقِهِمْ وَمِن تَحْتِ أَرْجُلِهِم مِّنْهُمْ أُمَّةٌ مُّقْتَصِدَةٌ وَكَثِيرٌ مِّنْهُمْ سَاءَ مَا يَعْمَلُونَ

66. If they had observed the Torah and the Gospel and that which was revealed unto them from their Lord, they would surely have been nourished from above them and from beneath their feet. Among them there are people who are moderate, but many of them are of evil conduct.

٦٧ يَا أَيُّهَا الرَّسُولُ بَلِّغْ مَا أُنزِلَ إِلَيْكَ مِن رَّبِّكَ وَإِن لَّمْ تَفْعَلْ فَمَا بَلَّغْتَ رِسَالَتَهُ وَاللَّهُ يَعْصِمُكَ مِنَ النَّاسِ إِنَّ اللَّهَ لَا يَهْدِي الْقَوْمَ الْكَافِرِينَ

67. O Messenger! Make known that which has been revealed unto you from your Lord, for if you do it not, you will not have conveyed His message. Allah will protect you from mankind. Lo! Allah guides not the disbelieving folk.

68. Say: O People of the Scripture! You have nothing (of guidance) till you observe the Torah and the Gospel and that which was revealed unto you from your Lord. That which is revealed unto you (Muhammad) from your Lord is certain to increase the contumacy and disbelief of many of them. But grieve not for the disbelieving folk.

69. Lo! those who believe, and those who are Jews, and Sabaeans, and Christians—Whosoever believes in Allah and the Last Day and does right—there shall no fear come upon them neither shall they grieve.[96]

70. We made a covenant of old with the Children of Israel and We sent unto them messengers. As often as a messenger came unto them with that which their souls desired not (they became rebellious). Some (of them) they denied and some they slew.

71. They thought no harm would come of it, so they were willfully blind and deaf. And afterward Allah turned (in mercy) toward them. Now (even after that) are many of them willfully blind and deaf. Allah is Seer of what they do.

72. They surely disbelieve who say: Lo! Allah is the Mes-siah, son of Mary. The Messiah (himself) said: O Children of Israel, worship Allah, my Lord and your Lord. Lo! who ascribes partners unto Allah, for him Allah has forbidden Paradise. His abode is the Fire. For evil-doers there will be no helpers.

73. They surely disbelieve who say: Lo! Allah is the third of three; when there is no God save the One God. If they desist not from so saying, a painful doom will fall on those of them who disbelieve.

74. Will they not rather turn unto Allah and seek forgiveness of Him? For Allah is Forgiving, Merciful.

---

[96]Almost identical with Surah 2:62.

75. The Messiah son of Mary was no other than a messenger, messengers (the like of whom) had passed away before him. And his mother was a saintly woman. And they both used to eat (earthly) food. See how we make the revelations clear for them, and see how they are turned away!

76. Say: Worship you in place of Allah that which possesses for you neither hurt nor use? Allah it is Who is the Hearer, the Knower.

77. Say: O People of the Scripture! Stress not in your religion other than the truth, and follow not the vain desires of folk who erred of old and led many astray, and erred from a plain road.

78. Those of the children of Israel who went astray were cursed by the tongue of David, and of Jesus son of Mary. That was because they rebelled and used to transgress.

79. They restrained not one another from the wickedness they did. Verily evil was that they used to do!

80. You see many of them making friends with those who disbelieve. Surely ill for them is that which they themselves send on before them: that Allah will be wroth with them and in the doom they will abide.

81. If they believed in Allah and the Prophet and that which is revealed unto him, they would not choose them for their friends. But many of them are of evil conduct.

82. You will find the most vehement of mankind in hostility to those who believe (to be) the Jews and the idolaters. And you will find the nearest of them in affection to those who believe (to be) those who say: Lo! we are Christians. That is because there are among them priests and monks,[97] and because they are not proud.

---

[97]i.e., persons entirely devoted to the service of God, as were the Muslims.

83. When they listen to that which has been revealed unto the Messenger, you see their eyes overflow with tears because of their recognition of the Truth. They say: Our Lord, we believe. Inscribe us as among the witnesses.

84. How should we not believe in Allah and that which has come unto us of the Truth. And (how should we not) hope that our Lord will bring us in along with righteous folk?

85. Allah has rewarded them for that their saying—Gardens underneath which rivers flow, wherein they will abide forever. That is the reward of the good.

86. But those who disbelieve and deny Our revelations, they are owners of hell-fire.

87. O you who believe! Forbid not the good things which Allah has made lawful for you, and transgress not. Lo! Allah loves not transgressors.

88. Eat of that which Allah has bestowed on you as food lawful and good, and keep your duty to Allah in Whom you are believers.

89. Allah will not take you to task for that which is unintentional in your oaths, but He will take you to task for the oaths which you swear in earnest. The expiation thereof is the feeding of ten of the needy with the average of that with which you feed your own folk, or the clothing of them, or the liberation of a slave, and for him who finds not (the means to do so) then a three day fast. This is the expiation of your oaths when you have sworn; and keep your oaths. Thus Allah expounds unto you His revelations in order that you may give thanks.

90. O you who believe! Intoxicants and games of chance and idols and divining arrows are only an infamy of the Devil's handiwork. Leave it aside in order that you may succeed.

91. The Devil seeks only to cast among you enmity and hatred by means of intoxicants and games of chance, and to turn you from remembrance of Allah and from prayer. Will you then not desist?

92. Obey Allah and obey the Messenger, and beware! But if you turn away, then know that the duty of Our Messenger is only plain conveyance (of the message).

93. There shall be no sin (imputed) unto those who believe and do good works for what they may have eaten (in the past). So be mindful of your duty (to Allah), and do good works; and again: be mindful of your duty, and believe; and once again: be mindful of your duty, and do right. Allah loves the good.

94. O you who believe! Allah will surely try you somewhat (in the matter) of the game which you take with your hands and your spears, that Allah may know him who fears Him in secret. Who transgresses after this, for him there is a painful doom.

95. O you who believe! Kill no wild game while you are on the pilgrimage. Who of you kills it of set purpose he shall pay its forfeit in the equivalent of that which he has killed, of domestic animals, the judge to be two men among you known for justice; (the compensation) to be brought as an offering to the Ka'bah; or, for expiation, he shall feed poor persons, or the equivalent of which in fasting, that he may taste the evil consequences of his deed. Allah forgives whatever (of this kind) may have happened in the past, but who relapses, Allah will take retribution from him. Allah is Mighty, Able to Requite (the wrong).

96. To hunt and to eat the fish of the sea is made lawful for you, a provision for you and for seafarers; but to hunt on land is forbidden you so long as you are on the pilgrimage. Be mindful of your duty to Allah, unto Whom you will be gathered.

97. Allah has appointed the Ka'bah, the Sacred House, a standard for mankind, and the Sacred Month and the offerings and the garlands. That is so that you may know that Allah knows whatsoever is in the heavens and whatsoever is in the earth, and that Allah is Knower of all things.

98. Know that Allah is severe in punishment, but that Allah (also) is Forgiving, Merciful.

99. The duty of the Messenger is only to convey (the message). Allah knows what you proclaim and what you hide.

100. Say: The evil, and the good are not alike even though the plenty of the evil attract you. So be mindful of your duty to Allah, O men of understanding, that you may succeed.

101. O you who believe! Ask not of things which, if they were made known unto you, would trouble you; but if you ask of them when the Qur'an is being revealed, they will be made known unto you. Allah pardons this, for Allah is Forgiving, Clement.

102. A folk before you asked (for such disclosures) and then disbelieved there in.

103. Allah has not appointed anything in the nature of a *Baḥīrah* or a *Sā'ibah* or a *Waṣīlah* or a *Ḥāmi*,[98] but those who disbelieve invent a lie against Allah. Most of them have no sense.

104. And when it is said unto them: Come unto that which Allah has revealed and unto the Messenger, they say: Enough for us are the ways we found our fathers following. What! Even though their fathers had no knowledge whatsoever, and no guidance?

---

[98]Different classes of cattle liberated in honor of idols and reverenced by the pagan Arabs.

105. O you who believe! You have charge of your own souls. He who errs cannot injure you if you are rightly guided. Unto Allah you will all return; and then He will inform you of what you used to do.

106. O you who believe! Let there be witnesses between you when death draws nigh unto one of you, at the time of bequest—two witnesses, just men from among you, or two others from another tribe, in case you are campaigning in the land and the calamity of death befall you. You shall detain them both after the prayer, and, if you doubt, they shall be made to swear by Allah (saying): We will not take a bribe, even though it were (on behalf of) a near kinsman nor will we hide the testimony of Allah, for then indeed we should be of the sinful.

107. But then, if it is afterwards ascertained that both of them merit (the suspicion of) sin, let two others take their place of those nearly concerned, and let them swear by Allah, (saying): Surely our testimony is truer than their testimony and we have not transgressed (the bounds of duty), for then indeed we should be of the evil-doers.

108. Thus it is more likely that they will bear true witness or fear that after their oath the oath (of others) will be taken. So be mindful of your duty (to Allah) and hearken. Allah guides not the froward folk.

109. On the day when Allah gathers together the messengers, and says: What was your response (from mankind)? they say: We have no knowledge. Lo! You, only You are the Knower of Things Hidden.

110. When Allah says: O Jesus son of Mary! Remember My favor unto you and unto your mother; how I strengthened you with the holy Spirit, so that you spoke unto mankind in the cradle as in maturity; and how I taught you the Scripture and Wisdom and the Torah and the Gospel; and how you did shape of clay as it were the   likeness of a bird by My permission, and did blow upon it and it was a bird by My permission, and you did heal him who was born blind and the leper by My permission; and how you did raise the dead, by My permission; and how I restrained the Children of Israel from (harming) you when you came unto them with clear proofs, and those of them who disbelieved exclaimed: This is nothing else than mere magic;

111. And when I inspired the disciples, (saying): Believe in Me and in My Messenger, they said: We believe. Bear witness that we have surrendered[99] (unto Allah).

112. When the disciples said: O Jesus son of Mary! Is your Lord able to send down for us a table spread with food from heaven? He said: Observe your duty to Allah, if you are true believers.

113. (They said:) We wish to eat thereof, that we may satisfy our hearts and know that you have spoken truth to us, and that thereof we may be witnesses.

114. Jesus son of Mary said: O Allah, Lord of us! Send down for us a table spread with food from heaven, that it may be a feast for Us, for the first of us and for the last of us, and a sign from You. Give us sustenance, for You are the Best of Sustainers.

115. Allah said: Lo! I am sending it down for you. And who disbelieves of you afterward, him surely will I punish with a punishment with which I have not punished any of (My) creatures.

﴿١١٠﴾ إِذْ قَالَ اللّٰهُ يَـٰعِيسَى ابْنَ مَرْيَمَ اذْكُرْ نِعْمَتِى عَلَيْكَ وَعَلَىٰ وَالِدَتِكَ إِذْ أَيَّدتُّكَ بِرُوحِ الْقُدُسِ تُكَلِّمُ النَّاسَ فِى الْمَهْدِ وَكَهْلًا وَإِذْ عَلَّمْتُكَ الْكِتَـٰبَ وَالْحِكْمَةَ وَالتَّوْرَىٰةَ وَالْإِنجِيلَ وَإِذْ تَخْلُقُ مِنَ الطِّينِ كَهَيْـَٔةِ الطَّيْرِ بِإِذْنِى فَتَنفُخُ فِيهَا فَتَكُونُ طَيْرًا بِإِذْنِى وَتُبْرِئُ الْأَكْمَهَ وَالْأَبْرَصَ بِإِذْنِى وَإِذْ تُخْرِجُ الْمَوْتَىٰ بِإِذْنِى وَإِذْ كَفَفْتُ بَنِى إِسْرَٰٓءِيلَ عَنكَ إِذْ جِئْتَهُم بِالْبَيِّنَـٰتِ فَقَالَ الَّذِينَ كَفَرُوا مِنْهُمْ إِنْ هَـٰذَآ إِلَّا سِحْرٌ مُّبِينٌ

﴿١١١﴾ وَإِذْ أَوْحَيْتُ إِلَى الْحَوَارِيِّـۧنَ أَنْ ءَامِنُوا بِى وَبِرَسُولِى قَالُوٓا ءَامَنَّا وَاشْهَدْ بِأَنَّنَا مُسْلِمُونَ

﴿١١٢﴾ إِذْ قَالَ الْحَوَارِيُّونَ يَـٰعِيسَى ابْنَ مَرْيَمَ هَلْ يَسْتَطِيعُ رَبُّكَ أَن يُنَزِّلَ عَلَيْنَا مَآئِدَةً مِّنَ السَّمَآءِ قَالَ اتَّقُوا اللّٰهَ إِن كُنتُم مُّؤْمِنِينَ

﴿١١٣﴾ قَالُوا نُرِيدُ أَن نَّأْكُلَ مِنْهَا وَتَطْمَئِنَّ قُلُوبُنَا وَنَعْلَمَ أَن قَدْ صَدَقْتَنَا وَنَكُونَ عَلَيْهَا مِنَ الشَّـٰهِدِينَ

﴿١١٤﴾ قَالَ عِيسَى ابْنُ مَرْيَمَ اللّٰهُمَّ رَبَّنَآ أَنزِلْ عَلَيْنَا مَآئِدَةً مِّنَ السَّمَآءِ تَكُونُ لَنَا عِيدًا لِّأَوَّلِنَا وَءَاخِرِنَا وَءَايَةً مِّنكَ وَارْزُقْنَا وَأَنتَ خَيْرُ الرَّٰزِقِينَ

﴿١١٥﴾ قَالَ اللّٰهُ إِنِّى مُنَزِّلُهَا عَلَيْكُمْ فَمَن يَكْفُرْ بَعْدُ مِنكُمْ فَإِنِّى أُعَذِّبُهُ عَذَابًا لَّآ أُعَذِّبُهُ أَحَدًا مِّنَ الْعَٰلَمِينَ

---

[99] Or "are Muslims."

116. And when Allah says: O Jesus son of Mary! Did you say unto mankind: Take me and my mother for two gods beside Allah? he says: Be glorified! It was not mine to utter that to which I had no right. If I used to say it, then You knew it. You know what is in my mind, and I know not what is in Your mind. Lo! You, only You are the Knower of Things Hidden.

117. I spoke unto them only that which You commanded me, (saying): Worship Allah, my Lord and your Lord. I was a witness of them while I dwelt among them, and when You took me You were the Watcher over them. You are Witness over all things.

118. If You punish them, lo! they are Your slaves, and if You forgive them (lo! they are Your slaves). Lo! You, only You are the Mighty, the Wise.

119. Allah says: This is a day in which their truthfulness profits the truthful, for theirs are Gardens underneath which rivers flow, wherein they are secure forever, Allah taking pleasure in them and they in Him. That is the great triumph.

120. Unto Allah belongs the Sovereignty of the heavens and the earth and whatever is therein, and He is Able to do all things.

١١٦) وَإِذْ قَالَ اللَّهُ يَـٰعِيسَى ابْنَ مَرْيَمَ ءَأَنتَ قُلْتَ لِلنَّاسِ اتَّخِذُونِي وَأُمِّيَ إِلَـٰهَيْنِ مِن دُونِ اللَّهِ قَالَ سُبْحَـٰنَكَ مَا يَكُونُ لِي أَنْ أَقُولَ مَا لَيْسَ لِي بِحَقٍّ إِن كُنتُ قُلْتُهُ فَقَدْ عَلِمْتَهُ تَعْلَمُ مَا فِي نَفْسِي وَلَا أَعْلَمُ مَا فِي نَفْسِكَ إِنَّكَ أَنتَ عَلَّامُ الْغُيُوبِ

١١٧) مَا قُلْتُ لَهُمْ إِلَّا مَا أَمَرْتَنِي بِهِ أَنِ اعْبُدُوا اللَّهَ رَبِّي وَرَبَّكُمْ وَكُنتُ عَلَيْهِمْ شَهِيدًا مَّا دُمْتُ فِيهِمْ فَلَمَّا تَوَفَّيْتَنِي كُنتَ أَنتَ الرَّقِيبَ عَلَيْهِمْ وَأَنتَ عَلَى كُلِّ شَيْءٍ شَهِيدٌ

١١٨) إِن تُعَذِّبْهُمْ فَإِنَّهُمْ عِبَادُكَ وَإِن تَغْفِرْ لَهُمْ فَإِنَّكَ أَنتَ الْعَزِيزُ الْحَكِيمُ

١١٩) قَالَ اللَّهُ هَـٰذَا يَوْمُ يَنفَعُ الصَّادِقِينَ صِدْقُهُمْ لَهُمْ جَنَّاتٌ تَجْرِي مِن تَحْتِهَا الْأَنْهَارُ خَالِدِينَ فِيهَا أَبَدًا رَّضِيَ اللَّهُ عَنْهُمْ وَرَضُوا عَنْهُ ذَٰلِكَ الْفَوْزُ الْعَظِيمُ

١٢٠) لِلَّهِ مُلْكُ السَّمَـٰوَاتِ وَالْأَرْضِ وَمَا فِيهِنَّ وَهُوَ عَلَى كُلِّ شَيْءٍ قَدِيرٌ

Cattle

Al An'ām, "Cattle," takes its name from a word in v. 137, repeated in vv. 139-140, where cattle are mentioned in connection with superstitious practices condemned by Islam.

With the possible exception of nine verses, which some authorities—e.g. Ibn Salamah—ascribe to the Madinah period, the whole of this Surah belongs to the year before the Hijrah. It is related, on the authority of Ibn 'Abbās, that it was revealed in a single visitation. It is placed here on account of the subject, vindication of the Divine Unity, which fitly follows on the subjects of the previous Surahs. The note of certain triumph is remarkable in the circumstances of its revelation, when the Prophet, after thirteen years of effort, saw himself obliged to flee from Makkah and seek help from strangers.

A late Makkan Surah.

Cattle

Revealed at Makkah

*In the name of Allah,
the Beneficent, the Merciful*

1. Praise be to Allah, Who has created the heavens and the earth, and has appointed darkness and light. Yet those who disbelieve ascribe rivals unto their Lord.

2. He it is Who has created you from clay, and has decreed a term for you. A term is fixed with Him. Yet still you doubt!

3. He is Allah in the heavens and in the earth. He knows both your secret and your utterance, and He knows what you earn.

4. Never came there unto them a revelation of the revelations of Allah but they did turn away from it.

5. And they denied the truth when it came unto them. But there will come unto them the tidings of that which they used to deride.

6. See they not how many a generation We destroyed before them, whom We had established in the earth more firmly than We have established you, and We shed on them abundant showers from the sky, and made rivers flow beneath them. Yet We destroyed them for their sins, and created after them another generation.

7. Had we sent down unto you (Muhammad) (actual) writing upon parchment, so that they could feel it with their hands, those who disbelieve would have said: This is nothing else than mere magic.

8. They say: Why has not an angel been sent down unto him? If We sent down an angel, then the matter would be judged; no further time would be allowed them (for reflection).

9. Had We appointed an angel (Our messenger), We as-suredly had made him (as) a man (that he might speak to men); and (thus) obscured for them (the truth) they (now) obscure.

10. Messengers (of Allah) have been derided before you, but that whereat they scoffed surrounded such of them as did deride.

11. Say (unto the disbelievers): Travel in the land, and see the nature of the consequence for the rejecters!

12. Say: Unto whom belongs whatsoever is in the heavens and the earth? Say: Unto Allah. He has prescribed for Him-self mercy, that He may bring you all together to the Day of Resurrection whereof there is no doubt. Those who ruin their own souls will not believe.

13. Unto Him belongs whatsoever rests in the night and the day. He is the Hearer, the Knower.

14. Say: Shall I choose for a protecting friend other than Allah, the Originator of the heavens and the earth, who feeds and is never fed? Say: I am ordered to be the first to surrender (unto Him). And be not you (O Muhammad) of the idolaters.

15. Say: I fear, if I rebel against my Lord, the retribution of an Awful Day.

16. He from whom (such retribution) is averted on that day (Allah) has in truth had mercy on him. That will be the signal triumph.

17. If Allah touch you with affliction, there is none that can relieve therefrom save Him, and if He touch you with good fortune (there is none that can impair it); for He is Able to do all things.

18. He is the Omnipotent over His slaves, and He is the Wise, the Knower.

٩ وَلَوْ جَعَلْنَاهُ مَلَكًا لَّجَعَلْنَاهُ رَجُلًا وَلَلَبَسْنَا عَلَيْهِم مَّا يَلْبِسُونَ

١٠ وَلَقَدِ اسْتُهْزِئَ بِرُسُلٍ مِّن قَبْلِكَ فَحَاقَ بِالَّذِينَ سَخِرُوا مِنْهُم مَّا كَانُوا بِهِ يَسْتَهْزِئُونَ

١١ قُلْ سِيرُوا فِي الْأَرْضِ ثُمَّ انظُرُوا كَيْفَ كَانَ عَاقِبَةُ الْمُكَذِّبِينَ

١٢ قُل لِّمَن مَّا فِي السَّمَاوَاتِ وَالْأَرْضِ قُل لِّلَّهِ كَتَبَ عَلَىٰ نَفْسِهِ الرَّحْمَةَ لَيَجْمَعَنَّكُمْ إِلَىٰ يَوْمِ الْقِيَامَةِ لَا رَيْبَ فِيهِ الَّذِينَ خَسِرُوا أَنفُسَهُمْ فَهُمْ لَا يُؤْمِنُونَ

١٣ وَلَهُ مَا سَكَنَ فِي اللَّيْلِ وَالنَّهَارِ وَهُوَ السَّمِيعُ الْعَلِيمُ

١٤ قُلْ أَغَيْرَ اللَّهِ أَتَّخِذُ وَلِيًّا فَاطِرِ السَّمَاوَاتِ وَالْأَرْضِ وَهُوَ يُطْعِمُ وَلَا يُطْعَمُ قُلْ إِنِّي أُمِرْتُ أَنْ أَكُونَ أَوَّلَ مَنْ أَسْلَمَ وَلَا تَكُونَنَّ مِنَ الْمُشْرِكِينَ

١٥ قُلْ إِنِّي أَخَافُ إِنْ عَصَيْتُ رَبِّي عَذَابَ يَوْمٍ عَظِيمٍ

١٦ مَّن يُصْرَفْ عَنْهُ يَوْمَئِذٍ فَقَدْ رَحِمَهُ وَذَٰلِكَ الْفَوْزُ الْمُبِينُ

١٧ وَإِن يَمْسَسْكَ اللَّهُ بِضُرٍّ فَلَا كَاشِفَ لَهُ إِلَّا هُوَ وَإِن يَمْسَسْكَ بِخَيْرٍ فَهُوَ عَلَىٰ كُلِّ شَيْءٍ قَدِيرٌ

١٨ وَهُوَ الْقَاهِرُ فَوْقَ عِبَادِهِ وَهُوَ الْحَكِيمُ الْخَبِيرُ

19. Say (O Muhammad): What thing is of most weight in testimony? Say: Allah is witness between you and me. And this Qur'an has been inspired in me, that I may warn therewith you and whomsoever it may reach. Do you possibly bear witness that there are gods beside Allah? Say: I bear no such witness. Say: He is only One God. Lo! I am innocent of that which you associate (with Him).

20. Those unto whom We gave the Scripture recognize (this Revelation) as they recognize their sons. Those who ruin their own souls will not believe.

21. Who does greater wrong than he who invents a lie against Allah and denies His revelations? Lo! the wrong-doers will not be successful.

22. And on the Day We gather them together We shall say unto those who ascribed partners (unto Allah): Where are (now) those partners of your make-believe?

23. Then will they have no contention save that they will say: By Allah, our Lord, we never were idolaters.

24. See how they lie against them-selves, and (how) the thing which they devised has failed them!

25. Of them are some who listen unto you, but We have placed upon their hearts veils, lest they should understand, and in their ears a deafness. If they saw every token they would not believe therein; to the point that, when they come unto you to argue with you, disbelievers say: This is nothing but fables of the men of old.

26. And they forbid (men) from it and avoid it, and they ruin none save them-selves, though they perceive not.

27. If you could see when they are set before the Fire and say: Oh, would that we might return! Then would we not deny the revelations of our Lord but we would be of the believers!

28. Nay, but that has become clear unto them which before they used to hide. And if they were sent back they would return unto that which they are forbidden. Lo! they are liars.

29. And they say: There is nothing save our life of the world, and we shall not be raised (again).

30. If you could see when they are set before their Lord! He will say: Is not this real? They will say: Yea, verily, by our Lord! He will say: Taste now the retribution for that you used to disbelieve.

31. They indeed are losers who deny their meeting with Allah until, when the hour comes on them suddenly, they cry: Alas for us, that we neglected it! They bear upon their back their burdens. Ah, evil is that which they bear!

32. The life of the world is nothing but a pastime and a sport. Better by far is the abode of the Hereafter for those who keep their duty (to Allah). Have you then no sense?

33. We know well how their talk grieves you, though in truth they deny not you (Muhammad) but evildoers flout the revelations of Allah.

34. Messengers indeed have been denied before you, and they were patient under the denial and the persecution till Our succor reached them. There is none to alter the decisions of Allah. Already there has reached you (somewhat) of the tidings of the messengers (We sent before).

35. And if their aversion is grievous unto you, then, if you can, seek a way down into the earth or a ladder unto the sky that you may bring unto them a portent (to convince them all)!—If Allah willed, He could have brought them all together to the guidance—So be not you among the foolish ones.

﴿٢٨﴾ بَلْ بَدَا لَهُم مَّا كَانُوا يُخْفُونَ مِن قَبْلُ وَلَوْ رُدُّوا لَعَادُوا لِمَا نُهُوا عَنْهُ وَإِنَّهُمْ لَكَاذِبُونَ

﴿٢٩﴾ وَقَالُوا إِنْ هِيَ إِلَّا حَيَاتُنَا الدُّنْيَا وَمَا نَحْنُ بِمَبْعُوثِينَ

﴿٣٠﴾ وَلَوْ تَرَى إِذْ وُقِفُوا عَلَى رَبِّهِمْ قَالَ أَلَيْسَ هَٰذَا بِالْحَقِّ قَالُوا بَلَى وَرَبِّنَا قَالَ فَذُوقُوا الْعَذَابَ بِمَا كُنتُمْ تَكْفُرُونَ

﴿٣١﴾ قَدْ خَسِرَ الَّذِينَ كَذَّبُوا بِلِقَاءِ اللَّهِ حَتَّى إِذَا جَاءَتْهُمُ السَّاعَةُ بَغْتَةً قَالُوا يَا حَسْرَتَنَا عَلَى مَا فَرَّطْنَا فِيهَا وَهُمْ يَحْمِلُونَ أَوْزَارَهُمْ عَلَى ظُهُورِهِمْ أَلَا سَاءَ مَا يَزِرُونَ

﴿٣٢﴾ وَمَا الْحَيَاةُ الدُّنْيَا إِلَّا لَعِبٌ وَلَهْوٌ وَلَلدَّارُ الْآخِرَةُ خَيْرٌ لِّلَّذِينَ يَتَّقُونَ أَفَلَا تَعْقِلُونَ

﴿٣٣﴾ قَدْ نَعْلَمُ إِنَّهُ لَيَحْزُنُكَ الَّذِي يَقُولُونَ فَإِنَّهُمْ لَا يُكَذِّبُونَكَ وَلَٰكِنَّ الظَّالِمِينَ بِآيَاتِ اللَّهِ يَجْحَدُونَ

﴿٣٤﴾ وَلَقَدْ كُذِّبَتْ رُسُلٌ مِّن قَبْلِكَ فَصَبَرُوا عَلَى مَا كُذِّبُوا وَأُوذُوا حَتَّى أَتَاهُمْ نَصْرُنَا وَلَا مُبَدِّلَ لِكَلِمَاتِ اللَّهِ وَلَقَدْ جَاءَكَ مِن نَّبَإِ الْمُرْسَلِينَ

﴿٣٥﴾ وَإِن كَانَ كَبُرَ عَلَيْكَ إِعْرَاضُهُمْ فَإِنِ اسْتَطَعْتَ أَن تَبْتَغِيَ نَفَقًا فِي الْأَرْضِ أَوْ سُلَّمًا فِي السَّمَاءِ فَتَأْتِيَهُم بِآيَةٍ وَلَوْ شَاءَ اللَّهُ لَجَمَعَهُمْ عَلَى الْهُدَى فَلَا تَكُونَنَّ مِنَ الْجَاهِلِينَ

36. Only those can accept who hear. As for the dead, Allah will raise them up; then unto Him they will be returned.

إِنَّمَا يَسْتَجِيبُ الَّذِينَ يَسْمَعُونَ وَالْمَوْتَى يَبْعَثُهُمُ اللَّهُ ثُمَّ إِلَيْهِ يُرْجَعُونَ ٣٦

37. They say: Why has no portent been sent down upon him from his Lord? Say: Lo! Allah is Able to send down a portent. But most of them know not.

وَقَالُوا لَوْلَا نُزِّلَ عَلَيْهِ آيَةٌ مِّن رَّبِّهِ قُلْ إِنَّ اللَّهَ قَادِرٌ عَلَى أَن يُنَزِّلَ آيَةً وَلَكِنَّ أَكْثَرَهُمْ لَا يَعْلَمُونَ ٣٧

38. There is not an animal in the earth, nor a flying creature flying on two wings, but they are nations like unto you. We have neglected nothing in the Book (of Our decrees). Then unto their Lord they will be gathered.

وَمَا مِن دَابَّةٍ فِي الْأَرْضِ وَلَا طَائِرٍ يَطِيرُ بِجَنَاحَيْهِ إِلَّا أُمَمٌ أَمْثَالُكُم مَّا فَرَّطْنَا فِي الْكِتَابِ مِن شَيْءٍ ثُمَّ إِلَى رَبِّهِمْ يُحْشَرُونَ ٣٨

39. Those who deny our revelations are deaf and dumb in darkness. Whom Allah will He sends astray, and whom He will He places on a straight path.

وَالَّذِينَ كَذَّبُوا بِآيَاتِنَا صُمٌّ وَبُكْمٌ فِي الظُّلُمَاتِ مَن يَشَإِ اللَّهُ يُضْلِلْهُ وَمَن يَشَأْ يَجْعَلْهُ عَلَى صِرَاطٍ مُّسْتَقِيمٍ ٣٩

40. Say: Can you see yourselves, if the punishment of Allah come upon you or the Hour come upon you, calling upon other than Allah? Do you then call (for help) to any other than Allah? (Answer that) if you are truthful.

قُلْ أَرَأَيْتَكُمْ إِنْ أَتَاكُمْ عَذَابُ اللَّهِ أَوْ أَتَتْكُمُ السَّاعَةُ أَغَيْرَ اللَّهِ تَدْعُونَ إِن كُنتُمْ صَادِقِينَ ٤٠

41. Nay, but unto Him you call, and He removes that because of which you call unto Him, if He will, and you forget whatever partners you ascribed unto Him.

بَلْ إِيَّاهُ تَدْعُونَ فَيَكْشِفُ مَا تَدْعُونَ إِلَيْهِ إِن شَاءَ وَتَنسَوْنَ مَا تُشْرِكُونَ ٤١

42. We have sent already unto peoples that were before you, and We visited them with tribulation and adversity, in order that they might grow humble.

وَلَقَدْ أَرْسَلْنَا إِلَى أُمَمٍ مِّن قَبْلِكَ فَأَخَذْنَاهُم بِالْبَأْسَاءِ وَالضَّرَّاءِ لَعَلَّهُمْ يَتَضَرَّعُونَ ٤٢

43. If only, when our disaster came on them, they had been humble! But their hearts were hardened and the Devil made all that they used to do seem fair unto them!

فَلَوْلَا إِذْ جَاءَهُم بَأْسُنَا تَضَرَّعُوا وَلَكِن قَسَتْ قُلُوبُهُمْ وَزَيَّنَ لَهُمُ الشَّيْطَانُ مَا كَانُوا يَعْمَلُونَ ٤٣

44. Then, when they forgot that whereof they had been reminded, We opened unto them the gates of all things till, even as they were rejoicing in that which they were given, We seized them unawares, and lo! they were dumfounded.

فَلَمَّا نَسُوا مَا ذُكِّرُوا بِهِ فَتَحْنَا عَلَيْهِمْ أَبْوَابَ كُلِّ شَيْءٍ حَتَّى إِذَا فَرِحُوا بِمَا أُوتُوا أَخَذْنَاهُم بَغْتَةً فَإِذَا هُم مُّبْلِسُونَ ٤٤

45. So of the people who did wrong the last remnant was cut off. Praise be to Allah, Lord of the Worlds!

٤٥ فَقُطِعَ دَابِرُ الْقَوْمِ الَّذِينَ ظَلَمُوا وَالْحَمْدُ لِلّٰهِ رَبِّ الْعَالَمِينَ

46. Say: Have you imagined, if Allah should take away your hearing and your sight and seal your hearts, who is the God who could restore it to you save Allah? See how We display the revelations unto them? Yet still they turn away.

٤٦ قُلْ أَرَأَيْتُمْ إِنْ أَخَذَ اللّٰهُ سَمْعَكُمْ وَأَبْصَارَكُمْ وَخَتَمَ عَلَىٰ قُلُوبِكُمْ مَنْ إِلٰهٌ غَيْرُ اللّٰهِ يَأْتِيكُمْ بِهِ أُنْظُرْ كَيْفَ نُصَرِّفُ الْآيَاتِ ثُمَّ هُمْ يَصْدِفُونَ

47. Say: Can you see yourselves, if the punishment of Allah come upon you unawares or openly? Would any perish save wrongdoing folk?

٤٧ قُلْ أَرَأَيْتَكُمْ إِنْ أَتَاكُمْ عَذَابُ اللّٰهِ بَغْتَةً أَوْ جَهْرَةً هَلْ يُهْلَكُ إِلَّا الْقَوْمُ الظَّالِمُونَ

48. We send not the messengers save as bearers of good news and warners. Who believes and does right, there shall no fear come upon them neither shall they grieve.

٤٨ وَمَا نُرْسِلُ الْمُرْسَلِينَ إِلَّا مُبَشِّرِينَ وَمُنْذِرِينَ فَمَنْ آمَنَ وَأَصْلَحَ فَلَا خَوْفٌ عَلَيْهِمْ وَلَا هُمْ يَحْزَنُونَ

49. But as for those who deny Our revelations, torment will afflict them for that they used to disobey.

٤٩ وَالَّذِينَ كَذَّبُوا بِآيَاتِنَا يَمَسُّهُمُ الْعَذَابُ بِمَا كَانُوا يَفْسُقُونَ

50. Say (O Muhammad, to disbelievers): I say not unto you (that) I possess the treasures of Allah, nor that I have knowledge of the Unseen; and I say not unto you: Lo! I am an angel. I follow only that which is inspired in me. Say: Are the blind man and the seer equal? Will you not then take thought?

٥٠ قُلْ لَا أَقُولُ لَكُمْ عِنْدِي خَزَائِنُ اللّٰهِ وَلَا أَعْلَمُ الْغَيْبَ وَلَا أَقُولُ لَكُمْ إِنِّي مَلَكٌ إِنْ أَتَّبِعُ إِلَّا مَا يُوحَىٰ إِلَيَّ قُلْ هَلْ يَسْتَوِي الْأَعْمَىٰ وَالْبَصِيرُ أَفَلَا تَتَفَكَّرُونَ

51. Warn hereby those who fear (because they know) that they will be gathered unto their Lord, for whom there is no protecting friend nor intercessor beside Him, that they may ward off (evil).

٥١ وَأَنْذِرْ بِهِ الَّذِينَ يَخَافُونَ أَنْ يُحْشَرُوا إِلَىٰ رَبِّهِمْ لَيْسَ لَهُمْ مِنْ دُونِهِ وَلِيٌّ وَلَا شَفِيعٌ لَعَلَّهُمْ يَتَّقُونَ

52. Repel not those who call upon their Lord at morn and evening, seeking His countenance. You are not accountable for them in anything, nor are they accountable for you in anything, that you should repel them and be of the wrongdoers.

٥٢ وَلَا تَطْرُدِ الَّذِينَ يَدْعُونَ رَبَّهُمْ بِالْغَدَاةِ وَالْعَشِيِّ يُرِيدُونَ وَجْهَهُ مَا عَلَيْكَ مِنْ حِسَابِهِمْ مِنْ شَيْءٍ وَمَا مِنْ حِسَابِكَ عَلَيْهِمْ مِنْ شَيْءٍ فَتَطْرُدَهُمْ فَتَكُونَ مِنَ الظَّالِمِينَ

53. And even so do We try some of them by others, that they say: Are these they whom Allah favors among us? Is not Allah best aware of the thanksgivers?

54. And when those who believe in Our revelations come unto you, say: Peace be unto you! Your Lord has prescribed for Himself mercy, that whoso of you does evil through ignorance and repents afterwards thereof and does right, (for him) lo! Allah is Forgiving, Merciful.

55. Thus do We expound the revelations that the way of the criminals may be manifest.

56. Say: I am forbidden to worship those on whom you call instead of Allah. Say: I will not follow your desires, for then should I go astray and I should not be of the rightly guided.

57. Say: I am (relying) on clear proof from my Lord, while you deny Him. I have not that for which you are impatient. The decision is for Allah only. He tells the truth and He is the Best of Deciders.

58. Say: If I had that for which you are impatient, then would the case (ere this) have been decided between me and you. Allah is best aware of the wrongdoers.

59. And with Him are the keys of the invisible. None but He knows them. And He knows what is in the land and the sea. Not a leaf falls but He knows it, not a grain amid the darkness of the earth, nothing of wet or dry but (it is noted) in a clear record.

60. He it is Who gathers you at night and knows that which you commit by day. Then He raises you again to life therein, that the term appointed (for you) may be accomplished. And afterward unto Him is your return. Then He will proclaim unto you what you used to do.

٥٣ وَكَذَلِكَ فَتَنَّا بَعْضَهُم بِبَعْضٍ لِّيَقُولُوٓا أَهَٰؤُلَآءِ مَنَّ ٱللَّهُ عَلَيْهِم مِّنۢ بَيْنِنَآ أَلَيْسَ ٱللَّهُ بِأَعْلَمَ بِٱلشَّٰكِرِينَ

٥٤ وَإِذَا جَآءَكَ ٱلَّذِينَ يُؤْمِنُونَ بِـَٔايَٰتِنَا فَقُلْ سَلَٰمٌ عَلَيْكُمْ كَتَبَ رَبُّكُمْ عَلَىٰ نَفْسِهِ ٱلرَّحْمَةَ أَنَّهُۥ مَنْ عَمِلَ مِنكُمْ سُوٓءًۢا بِجَهَٰلَةٍ ثُمَّ تَابَ مِنۢ بَعْدِهِۦ وَأَصْلَحَ فَأَنَّهُۥ غَفُورٌ رَّحِيمٌ

٥٥ وَكَذَلِكَ نُفَصِّلُ ٱلْأَيَٰتِ وَلِتَسْتَبِينَ سَبِيلُ ٱلْمُجْرِمِينَ

٥٦ قُلْ إِنِّى نُهِيتُ أَنْ أَعْبُدَ ٱلَّذِينَ تَدْعُونَ مِن دُونِ ٱللَّهِ قُل لَّآ أَتَّبِعُ أَهْوَآءَكُمْ قَدْ ضَلَلْتُ إِذًا وَمَآ أَنَا۠ مِنَ ٱلْمُهْتَدِينَ

٥٧ قُلْ إِنِّى عَلَىٰ بَيِّنَةٍ مِّن رَّبِّى وَكَذَّبْتُم بِهِۦ مَا عِندِى مَا تَسْتَعْجِلُونَ بِهِۦٓ إِنِ ٱلْحُكْمُ إِلَّا لِلَّهِ يَقُصُّ ٱلْحَقَّ وَهُوَ خَيْرُ ٱلْفَٰصِلِينَ

٥٨ قُل لَّوْ أَنَّ عِندِى مَا تَسْتَعْجِلُونَ بِهِۦ لَقُضِىَ ٱلْأَمْرُ بَيْنِى وَبَيْنَكُمْ وَٱللَّهُ أَعْلَمُ بِٱلظَّٰلِمِينَ

٥٩ وَعِندَهُۥ مَفَاتِحُ ٱلْغَيْبِ لَا يَعْلَمُهَآ إِلَّا هُوَ وَيَعْلَمُ مَا فِى ٱلْبَرِّ وَٱلْبَحْرِ وَمَا تَسْقُطُ مِن وَرَقَةٍ إِلَّا يَعْلَمُهَا وَلَا حَبَّةٍ فِى ظُلُمَٰتِ ٱلْأَرْضِ وَلَا رَطْبٍ وَلَا يَابِسٍ إِلَّا فِى كِتَٰبٍ مُّبِينٍ

٦٠ وَهُوَ ٱلَّذِى يَتَوَفَّىٰكُم بِٱلَّيْلِ وَيَعْلَمُ مَا جَرَحْتُم بِٱلنَّهَارِ ثُمَّ يَبْعَثُكُمْ فِيهِ لِيُقْضَىٰٓ أَجَلٌ مُّسَمًّى ثُمَّ إِلَيْهِ مَرْجِعُكُمْ ثُمَّ يُنَبِّئُكُم بِمَا كُنتُمْ تَعْمَلُونَ

61. He is the Omnipotent over His slaves. He sends guardians over you until, when death comes unto one of you, Our messengers[100] take his life and they never fail in their duty.

62. Then are they restored unto Allah, their Lord, the Just. Surely His is the judgment. And He is the most swift of reckoners.

63. Say: Who delivers you from the darkness of the land and the sea? You call upon Him humbly and in secret, (saying): If He delivers us from this (fear) we truly will be of the thankful.

64. Say: Allah delivers you from this and from all afflictions. Yet you attribute partners unto Him.

65. Say: He is able to send punishment upon you from above you or from beneath your feet, or to bewilder you with dissension and make you taste the tyranny one of another. See how We display the revelations so that they may understand.

66. Your people (O Muhammad) have denied it, though it is the Truth. Say: I am not put in charge of you.

67. For every announcement there is a term, and you will come to know.

68. And when you see those who meddle with Our revelations, withdraw from them until they meddle with another topic. And if the Devil cause you to forget, sit not, after the remembrance, with the congregation of wrongdoers.

69. Those who ward off (evil) are not accountable for them in anything, but the Reminder (must be given them) that haply they (too) may ward off (evil).

---

[100] i.e., angels. The same word *rasūl* is used for angels and for prophets.

70. And forsake those who take their religion for a pastime and a jest, and whom the life of the world beguiles. Remind (mankind) hereby lest a soul be destroyed by what it earns. It has beside Allah no friend nor intercessor, and though it offer every compensation it will not be accepted from it. Those are they who perish by their own deserts. For them is drink of boiling water and a painful doom, because they disbelieved.

٧٠ وَذَرِ الَّذِينَ اتَّخَذُوا دِينَهُمْ لَعِبًا وَلَهْوًا وَغَرَّتْهُمُ الْحَيَوٰةُ الدُّنْيَا وَذَكِّرْ بِهِ أَن تُبْسَلَ نَفْسٌ بِمَا كَسَبَتْ لَيْسَ لَهَا مِن دُونِ اللَّهِ وَلِيٌّ وَلَا شَفِيعٌ وَإِن تَعْدِلْ كُلَّ عَدْلٍ لَّا يُؤْخَذْ مِنْهَا أُوْلَٰئِكَ الَّذِينَ أُبْسِلُوا بِمَا كَسَبُوا لَهُمْ شَرَابٌ مِّنْ حَمِيمٍ وَعَذَابٌ أَلِيمٌ بِمَا كَانُوا يَكْفُرُونَ

71. Say: Shall we cry, instead of unto Allah, unto that which neither profits us nor hurts us, and shall we turn back after Allah has guided us, like one bewildered whom the devils have infatuated in the earth, who has companions who invite him to the guidance (saying): Come unto us? Say: Lo! the guidance of Allah is indeed the Guidance, and we are ordered to surrender to the Lord of the Worlds,

٧١ قُلْ أَنَدْعُوا مِن دُونِ اللَّهِ مَا لَا يَنفَعُنَا وَلَا يَضُرُّنَا وَنُرَدُّ عَلَىٰ أَعْقَابِنَا بَعْدَ إِذْ هَدَىٰنَا اللَّهُ كَالَّذِي اسْتَهْوَتْهُ الشَّيَٰطِينُ فِي الْأَرْضِ حَيْرَانَ لَهُ أَصْحَٰبٌ يَدْعُونَهُ إِلَى الْهُدَى ائْتِنَا قُلْ إِنَّ هُدَى اللَّهِ هُوَ الْهُدَىٰ وَأُمِرْنَا لِنُسْلِمَ لِرَبِّ الْعَٰلَمِينَ

72. And to establish prayer and ward off (evil), and He it is unto Whom you will be gathered.

٧٢ وَأَنْ أَقِيمُوا الصَّلَوٰةَ وَاتَّقُوهُ وَهُوَ الَّذِي إِلَيْهِ تُحْشَرُونَ

73. He it is Who created the heavens and the earth in truth. On that day when He says: Be! it is. His word is the truth, and His will be the Sovereignty on the day when the trumpet is blown. Knower of the invisible and the visible, He is the Wise, the Aware.

٧٣ وَهُوَ الَّذِي خَلَقَ السَّمَٰوَٰتِ وَالْأَرْضَ بِالْحَقِّ وَيَوْمَ يَقُولُ كُن فَيَكُونُ قَوْلُهُ الْحَقُّ وَلَهُ الْمُلْكُ يَوْمَ يُنفَخُ فِي الصُّورِ عَٰلِمُ الْغَيْبِ وَالشَّهَٰدَةِ وَهُوَ الْحَكِيمُ الْخَبِيرُ

74. (Remember) when Abraham said unto his father Azar: Do you take idols for gods? Lo! I see you and your folk in error manifest.

٧٤ ۞ وَإِذْ قَالَ إِبْرَٰهِيمُ لِأَبِيهِ ءَازَرَ أَتَتَّخِذُ أَصْنَامًا ءَالِهَةً إِنِّي أَرَىٰكَ وَقَوْمَكَ فِي ضَلَٰلٍ مُّبِينٍ

75. Thus did We show Abraham the kingdom of the heavens and the earth that he mighty be of those possessing certainty:

٧٥ وَكَذَٰلِكَ نُرِي إِبْرَٰهِيمَ مَلَكُوتَ السَّمَٰوَٰتِ وَالْأَرْضِ وَلِيَكُونَ مِنَ الْمُوقِنِينَ

76. When the night grew dark upon him he beheld a planet. He said: This is my Lord. But when it set, he said: I love not things that set.

77. And when he saw the moon uprising, he exclaimed: This is my Lord. But when it set, he said: Unless my Lord guide me, I surely shall become one of the folk who are astray.

78. And when he saw the sun uprising, he cried: This is my Lord! This is greater! And when it set he exclaimed: O my people! Lo! I am free from all that you associate (with Him).

79. Lo! I have turned my face toward him Who created the heavens and the earth, as one by nature upright, and I am not of the idolaters.

80. His people argued with him. He said: Do you dispute with me concerning Allah when He has guided me? I fear not at all that which you set beside Him unless my Lord wills. My Lord includes all things in His knowledge: Will you not then remember?

81. How should I fear that which you set up beside Him, when you fear not to set up beside Allah that for which He has revealed unto you no warrant? Which of the two factions has more right to safety?, (Answer me that) if you have knowledge.

82. Those who believe and obscure not their belief by wrongdoing, theirs is safety; and they are rightly guided.

83. That is Our argument. We gave it unto Abraham against his folk. We raise unto degrees of wisdom whom We will. Lo! your Lord is Wise, Aware.

84. And We granted him Isaac and Jacob; each of them We guided; and Noah did We guide before; and of his seed (We guided) David and Solomon and Job and Joseph and Moses and Aaron. Thus do We reward the good.

85. And Zachariah and John and Jesus and Elias. Each one (of them) was of the righteous.

٨٥ وَزَكَرِيَّا وَيَحْيَىٰ وَعِيسَىٰ وَإِلْيَاسَ كُلٌّ مِّنَ الصَّٰلِحِينَ

86. And Ishmael and Elisha and Jonah and Lot. Each one of them did We prefer above the worlds,

٨٦ وَإِسْمَٰعِيلَ وَالْيَسَعَ وَيُونُسَ وَلُوطًا وَكُلًّا فَضَّلْنَا عَلَى الْعَٰلَمِينَ

87. With some of their forefathers and their offspring and their brothers; and We chose them and guided them unto a straight path:

٨٧ وَمِنْ ءَابَآئِهِمْ وَذُرِّيَّٰتِهِمْ وَإِخْوَٰنِهِمْ وَاجْتَبَيْنَٰهُمْ وَهَدَيْنَٰهُمْ إِلَىٰ صِرَٰطٍ مُّسْتَقِيمٍ

88. Such is the guidance of Allah wherewith He guides whom He will of His bondmen. But if they had set up (for worship) anything beside Him, (all) that they did would have been vain.

٨٨ ذَٰلِكَ هُدَى اللَّهِ يَهْدِى بِهِ مَن يَشَآءُ مِنْ عِبَادِهِ وَلَوْ أَشْرَكُوا لَحَبِطَ عَنْهُم مَّا كَانُوا يَعْمَلُونَ

89. Those are they unto whom We gave the Scripture and command and prophethood. But if these disbelieve therein, then indeed We shall entrust it to a people who will not be disbelievers therein.

٨٩ أُولَٰٓئِكَ الَّذِينَ ءَاتَيْنَٰهُمُ الْكِتَٰبَ وَالْحُكْمَ وَالنُّبُوَّةَ فَإِن يَكْفُرْ بِهَا هَٰٓؤُلَآءِ فَقَدْ وَكَّلْنَا بِهَا قَوْمًا لَّيْسُوا بِهَا بِكَٰفِرِينَ

90. Those are they whom Allah guides, so follow their gui-dance. Say (O Muhammad, unto mankind): I ask of you no fee for it. Lo! it is nothing but a Reminder to the worlds.

٩٠ أُولَٰٓئِكَ الَّذِينَ هَدَى اللَّهُ فَبِهُدَىٰهُمُ اقْتَدِهْ قُل لَّآ أَسْـَٔلُكُمْ عَلَيْهِ أَجْرًا إِنْ هُوَ إِلَّا ذِكْرَىٰ لِلْعَٰلَمِينَ

91. And they measure not the power of Allah its true measure when they say: Allah has nothing revealed unto a human being. Say: Who revealed the Book which Moses brought, a light and guidance for mankind, which you have put on parchments which you show, but you hide much (thereof), and by which you were taught that which you knew not yourselves nor (did) your fathers (know it)? Say: Allah. Then leave them to their play of caviling.

٩١ وَمَا قَدَرُوا اللَّهَ حَقَّ قَدْرِهِ إِذْ قَالُوا مَآ أَنزَلَ اللَّهُ عَلَىٰ بَشَرٍ مِّن شَيْءٍ قُلْ مَنْ أَنزَلَ الْكِتَٰبَ الَّذِى جَآءَ بِهِ مُوسَىٰ نُورًا وَهُدًى لِّلنَّاسِ تَجْعَلُونَهُ قَرَاطِيسَ تُبْدُونَهَا وَتُخْفُونَ كَثِيرًا وَعُلِّمْتُم مَّا لَمْ تَعْلَمُوا أَنتُمْ وَلَآ ءَابَآؤُكُمْ قُلِ اللَّهُ ثُمَّ ذَرْهُمْ فِى خَوْضِهِمْ يَلْعَبُونَ

92. And this is a blessed Book which We have revealed, confirming that which (was revealed) before it, that you may warn the Mother of Villages (Makkah) and those around it. Those who believe in the Hereafter believe herein, and they are careful of their prayer.

٩٢ وَهَٰذَا كِتَٰبٌ أَنزَلْنَٰهُ مُبَارَكٌ مُّصَدِّقُ الَّذِى بَيْنَ يَدَيْهِ وَلِتُنذِرَ أُمَّ الْقُرَىٰ وَمَنْ حَوْلَهَا وَالَّذِينَ يُؤْمِنُونَ بِالْءَاخِرَةِ يُؤْمِنُونَ بِهِ وَهُمْ عَلَىٰ صَلَاتِهِمْ يُحَافِظُونَ

93. Who is guilty of more wrong than he who forges a lie against Allah, or says: I am inspired, when he is not inspired in anything; and who says: I will reveal the like of that which Allah has revealed? If you could see, when the wrongdoers reach the pangs of death and the angels stretch their hands out, saying: Deliver up your souls. This day you are awarded doom of degradation for that you spoke concerning Allah other than the truth, and scorned His portents.

94. Now have you come unto Us solitary as We did create you at the first, and you have left behind you all that We bestowed upon you, and We behold not with you those your intercessors, of whom you claimed that they possessed a share in you. Now is the bond between you severed, and that which you presumed has failed you.

95. Lo! Allah (it is) who splits the grain of corn and the date-stone (for sprouting). He brings forth the living from the dead, and is the bringer forth of the dead from the living. Such is Allah. How then are you perverted?

96. He is the Cleaver of the Daybreak, and He has appointed the night for stillness, and the sun and the moon for reckoning. That is the measuring of the Mighty, the Wise..

97. And He it is Who has set for you the stars that you may guide your course by them amid the darkness of the land and the sea. We have detailed Our revelations for a people who have knowledge.

98. And He it is Who has produced you from a single being, and (has given you) a habitation and a repository. We have detailed Our revelations for a people who have understanding.

٩٣ وَمَنْ أَظْلَمُ مِمَّنِ افْتَرَى عَلَى اللّٰهِ كَذِبًا أَوْ قَالَ أُوحِيَ إِلَيَّ وَلَمْ يُوحَ إِلَيْهِ شَيْءٌ وَمَنْ قَالَ سَأُنْزِلُ مِثْلَ مَا أَنْزَلَ اللّٰهُ وَلَوْ تَرَى إِذِ الظَّالِمُونَ فِي غَمَرَاتِ الْمَوْتِ وَالْمَلَٰئِكَةُ بَاسِطُوٓا أَيْدِيهِمْ أَخْرِجُوٓا أَنْفُسَكُمُ الْيَوْمَ تُجْزَوْنَ عَذَابَ الْهُونِ بِمَا كُنْتُمْ تَقُولُونَ عَلَى اللّٰهِ غَيْرَ الْحَقِّ وَكُنْتُمْ عَنْ ءَايَٰتِهِ تَسْتَكْبِرُونَ

٩٤ وَلَقَدْ جِئْتُمُونَا فُرَادَىٰ كَمَا خَلَقْنَٰكُمْ أَوَّلَ مَرَّةٍ وَتَرَكْتُمْ مَّا خَوَّلْنَٰكُمْ وَرَآءَ ظُهُورِكُمْ وَمَا نَرَىٰ مَعَكُمْ شُفَعَآءَكُمُ الَّذِينَ زَعَمْتُمْ أَنَّهُمْ فِيكُمْ شُرَكَٰٓؤُا۟ لَقَد تَّقَطَّعَ بَيْنَكُمْ وَضَلَّ عَنكُم مَّا كُنتُمْ تَزْعُمُونَ

٩٥ ۞ إِنَّ اللّٰهَ فَالِقُ الْحَبِّ وَالنَّوَىٰ يُخْرِجُ الْحَيَّ مِنَ الْمَيِّتِ وَمُخْرِجُ الْمَيِّتِ مِنَ الْحَيِّ ذَٰلِكُمُ اللّٰهُ فَأَنَّىٰ تُؤْفَكُونَ

٩٦ فَالِقُ الْإِصْبَاحِ وَجَعَلَ الَّيْلَ سَكَنًا وَالشَّمْسَ وَالْقَمَرَ حُسْبَانًا ذَٰلِكَ تَقْدِيرُ الْعَزِيزِ الْعَلِيمِ

٩٧ وَهُوَ الَّذِي جَعَلَ لَكُمُ النُّجُومَ لِتَهْتَدُوا۟ بِهَا فِي ظُلُمَٰتِ الْبَرِّ وَالْبَحْرِ قَدْ فَصَّلْنَا الْآيَٰتِ لِقَوْمٍ يَعْلَمُونَ

٩٨ وَهُوَ الَّذِيٓ أَنشَأَكُم مِّن نَّفْسٍ وَٰحِدَةٍ فَمُسْتَقَرٌّ وَمُسْتَوْدَعٌ قَدْ فَصَّلْنَا الْآيَٰتِ لِقَوْمٍ يَفْقَهُونَ

99. He it is Who sends down water from the sky, and therewith We bring forth buds of every kind; We bring forth the green blade from which we bring forth the thick clustered grain; and from the date palm, from the pollen thereof, spring pendant bunches; and (We bring forth) gardens of grapes, and the olive and the pomegranate, alike and unlike. Look upon the fruit thereof, when they bear fruit, and upon its ripening. Lo! herein verily are portents for a people who believe.

100. Yet they ascribe as partners unto Him the jinn, although He did create them, and impute falsely, without knowledge, sons and daughters unto Him. Glorified be He and high exalted above (all) that they ascribe (unto Him).

101. The Originator of the heavens and the earth! How can He have a child, when there is for Him no consort, when He created all things and is Aware of all things?

102. Such is Allah, your Lord. There is no God save Him, the Creator of all things, so worship Him. And He takes care of all things.

103. Vision comprehends Him not, but He comprehends (all) vision. He is the Subtle, the Aware.

104. Proofs have come unto you from your Lord, so who sees, it is for his own good, and who is blind is blind to his own hurt. And I am not a keeper over you.

105. Thus do We display Our revelations that they may say (unto you, Muhammad): "You have studied," and that We may make (it) clear for people who have knowledge.

106. Follow that which is inspired in you from your Lord; there is no God save Him; and turn away from the idolaters.

107. Had Allah willed, they had not been idolatrous. We have not set you as a keeper over them, nor are you responsible for them.

108. Revile not those unto whom they pray beside Allah lest they wrongfully revile Allah through ignorance. Thus unto every nation have We made their deed seem fair. Then unto their Lord is their return, and He will tell them what they used to do.

109. And they swear a solemn oath by Allah that if there come unto them a portent they will believe therein. Say: Portents are with Allah and who can tell you that if they (the portents) came they would not believe?

110. We confound their hearts and their eyes. As they believed not therein at the first, We let them wander blindly on in their contumacy.

111. And though We should send down the angels unto them, and the dead should speak unto them, and We should gather against them all things in array, they would not believe unless Allah so willed. But, most of them are ignorant.

112. Thus have We appointed unto every prophet an adversary—devils of humankind and jinn who inspire in one another plausible discourse through guile. If your Lord willed, they would not do so; so leave them alone with their devising;

113. That the hearts of those who believe not in the Hereafter may incline thereto, and that they may take pleasure therein, and that they may earn what they are earning.

114. Shall I seek other than Allah for judge, when He it is who has revealed unto you (this) Scripture, fully explained? Those unto whom We gave the Scripture (in the past) know that it is revealed from your Lord in truth. So be not you (O Muhammad) of the waverers.

١٠٧ وَلَوْ شَاءَ اللّٰهُ مَاۤ أَشْرَكُوْاۗ وَمَا جَعَلْنَاكَ عَلَيْهِمْ حَفِيظًاۚ وَمَاۤ أَنْتَ عَلَيْهِمْ بِوَكِيلٍ

١٠٨ وَلَا تَسُبُّوا الَّذِيْنَ يَدْعُوْنَ مِنْ دُوْنِ اللّٰهِ فَيَسُبُّوا اللّٰهَ عَدْوًا بِغَيْرِ عِلْمٍۗ كَذٰلِكَ زَيَّنَّا لِكُلِّ أُمَّةٍ عَمَلَهُمْ ثُمَّ إِلٰى رَبِّهِمْ مَّرْجِعُهُمْ فَيُنَبِّئُهُمْ بِمَا كَانُوْا يَعْمَلُوْنَ

١٠٩ وَأَقْسَمُوْا بِاللّٰهِ جَهْدَ أَيْمَانِهِمْ لَئِنْ جَاءَتْهُمْ ءَايَةٌ لَّيُؤْمِنُنَّ بِهَاۚ قُلْ إِنَّمَا الْأَيٰتُ عِنْدَ اللّٰهِۖ وَمَا يُشْعِرُكُمْ أَنَّهَاۤ إِذَا جَاءَتْ لَا يُؤْمِنُوْنَ

١١٠ وَنُقَلِّبُ أَفْئِدَتَهُمْ وَأَبْصَارَهُمْ كَمَا لَمْ يُؤْمِنُوْا بِهٖۤ أَوَّلَ مَرَّةٍ وَّنَذَرُهُمْ فِيْ طُغْيَانِهِمْ يَعْمَهُوْنَ

١١١ وَلَوْ أَنَّنَا نَزَّلْنَاۤ إِلَيْهِمُ الْمَلٰٓئِكَةَ وَكَلَّمَهُمُ الْمَوْتٰى وَحَشَرْنَا عَلَيْهِمْ كُلَّ شَيْءٍ قُبُلًا مَّا كَانُوْا لِيُؤْمِنُوْۤا إِلَّاۤ أَنْ يَّشَاءَ اللّٰهُ وَلٰكِنَّ أَكْثَرَهُمْ يَجْهَلُوْنَ

١١٢ وَكَذٰلِكَ جَعَلْنَا لِكُلِّ نَبِيٍّ عَدُوًّا شَيٰطِيْنَ الْإِنْسِ وَالْجِنِّ يُوْحِيْ بَعْضُهُمْ إِلٰى بَعْضٍ زُخْرُفَ الْقَوْلِ غُرُوْرًاۚ وَلَوْ شَاءَ رَبُّكَ مَا فَعَلُوْهُ فَذَرْهُمْ وَمَا يَفْتَرُوْنَ

١١٣ وَلِتَصْغٰۤى إِلَيْهِ أَفْئِدَةُ الَّذِيْنَ لَا يُؤْمِنُوْنَ بِالْأٰخِرَةِ وَلِيَرْضَوْهُ وَلِيَقْتَرِفُوْا مَا هُمْ مُّقْتَرِفُوْنَ

١١٤ أَفَغَيْرَ اللّٰهِ أَبْتَغِيْ حَكَمًا وَّهُوَ الَّذِيْۤ أَنْزَلَ إِلَيْكُمُ الْكِتٰبَ مُفَصَّلًاۚ وَالَّذِيْنَ ءَاتَيْنٰهُمُ الْكِتٰبَ يَعْلَمُوْنَ أَنَّهٗ مُنَزَّلٌ مِّنْ رَّبِّكَ بِالْحَقِّ فَلَا تَكُوْنَنَّ مِنَ الْمُمْتَرِيْنَ

115. Perfected is the Word of your Lord in truth and justice. There is nothing that can change His words. He is the Hearer, the Knower.

116. If you obeyed most of those on earth they would mislead you far from Allah's way. They follow nothing but an opinion, and they do but guess.

117. Lo! your Lord, He knows best who errs from His way; and He knows best (who are) the rightly guided.

118. Eat of that over which the name of Allah has been mentioned, if you are believers in His revelations.

119. How should you not eat of that over which the name of Allah has been mentioned, when He has explained unto you that which is forbidden unto you, unless you are compelled thereto. But lo! many lead (others) astray by their own lusts through ignorance. Lo! your Lord, He is best aware of the transgressors.

120. Forsake the outwardness of sin and the inwardness thereof. Lo! those who garner sin will be awarded that which they have earned.

121. And eat not of that on which Allah's name has not been mentioned, for lo! it is abomination. Lo! the devils do inspire their minions to dispute with you. But if you obey them, you will be in truth idolaters.

122. Is he who was dead and We have raised him unto life, and set for him a light wherein he walks among men, as him whose similitude is in utter darkness whence he cannot emerge? Thus is their conduct made fair seeming for disbelievers.

123. And thus have We made in every city great ones of its criminals, that they should plot therein. They do but plot against themselves, though they perceive not.

124. And when a token comes unto them, they say: We will not believe till we are given that which Allah's messengers are given. Allah knows best with whom to place His message. Humiliation from Allah and heavy punishment will smite the criminals for their scheming.

125. And whomsoever it is Allah's will to guide, He expands his bosom unto Islam, and whomsoever it is His will to send astray, He makes his bosom close and narrow as if he were engaged in sheer ascent to the sky. Thus Allah lays ignominy upon those who believe not.

126. This is the path of your Lord, a straight path. We have detailed Our revelations for a people who take heed.

127. For them is the abode of peace with their Lord. He will be their Protecting Friend because of what they used to do.

128. On the day when He will gather them together (He will say): O you assembly of the jinn! Many of humankind did you seduce. And their adherents among humankind will say: Our Lord! We enjoyed one another, but now we have arrived at the appointed term which You appointed for us. He will say: Fire is your home. Abide therein forever, save him whom Allah wills (to deliver). Lo! your Lord is Wise, Aware.

129. Thus We let some of the wrong-doers have power over others because of what they are wont to earn.

١٢٣ وَكَذَلِكَ جَعَلْنَا فِي كُلِّ قَرْيَةٍ أَكَـٰبِرَ مُجْرِمِيهَا لِيَمْكُرُوا فِيهَا وَمَا يَمْكُرُونَ إِلَّا بِأَنْفُسِهِمْ وَمَا يَشْعُرُونَ

١٢٤ وَإِذَا جَاءَتْهُمْ ءَايَةٌ قَالُوا لَن نُّؤْمِنَ حَتَّىٰ نُؤْتَىٰ مِثْلَ مَا أُوتِيَ رُسُلُ اللَّهِ اللَّهُ أَعْلَمُ حَيْثُ يَجْعَلُ رِسَالَتَهُ سَيُصِيبُ الَّذِينَ أَجْرَمُوا صَغَارٌ عِندَ اللَّهِ وَعَذَابٌ شَدِيدٌ بِمَا كَانُوا يَمْكُرُونَ

١٢٥ فَمَن يُرِدِ اللَّهُ أَن يَهْدِيَهُ يَشْرَحْ صَدْرَهُ لِلْإِسْلَامِ وَمَن يُرِدْ أَن يُضِلَّهُ يَجْعَلْ صَدْرَهُ ضَيِّقًا حَرَجًا كَأَنَّمَا يَصَّعَّدُ فِي السَّمَاءِ كَذَلِكَ يَجْعَلُ اللَّهُ الرِّجْسَ عَلَى الَّذِينَ لَا يُؤْمِنُونَ

١٢٦ وَهَذَا صِرَاطُ رَبِّكَ مُسْتَقِيمًا قَدْ فَصَّلْنَا الْآيَاتِ لِقَوْمٍ يَذَّكَّرُونَ

١٢٧ لَهُمْ دَارُ السَّلَامِ عِندَ رَبِّهِمْ وَهُوَ وَلِيُّهُم بِمَا كَانُوا يَعْمَلُونَ

١٢٨ وَيَوْمَ يَحْشُرُهُمْ جَمِيعًا يَا مَعْشَرَ الْجِنِّ قَدِ اسْتَكْثَرْتُم مِّنَ الْإِنسِ وَقَالَ أَوْلِيَاؤُهُم مِّنَ الْإِنسِ رَبَّنَا اسْتَمْتَعَ بَعْضُنَا بِبَعْضٍ وَبَلَغْنَا أَجَلَنَا الَّذِي أَجَّلْتَ لَنَا قَالَ النَّارُ مَثْوَاكُمْ خَالِدِينَ فِيهَا إِلَّا مَا شَاءَ اللَّهُ إِنَّ رَبَّكَ حَكِيمٌ عَلِيمٌ

١٢٩ وَكَذَلِكَ نُوَلِّي بَعْضَ الظَّالِمِينَ بَعْضًا بِمَا كَانُوا يَكْسِبُونَ

130. O you assembly of the jinn and humankind! Came there not unto you messengers of your own who recounted unto you My tokens and warned you of the meeting of this your Day? They will say: We testify against ourselves. And the life of the world beguiled them. And they testify against themselves that they were disbelievers.

131. This is because your Lord destroys not the townships arbitrarily while their people are unconscious (of the wrong they do).

132. For all there will be ranks from what they did. Your Lord is not unaware of what they do.

133. Your Lord is the Absolute, the Lord of Mercy. If He will, He can remove you and can cause what He will to follow after you, even as He raised you from the seed of other folk.

134. Lo! that which you are promised will surely come to pass, and you cannot escape.

135. Say (O Muhammad): O my people! Work according to your power. Lo! I too am working. Thus you will come to know for which of us will be the happy sequel. Lo! the wrongdoers will not be successful.

136. They assign unto Allah of the crops and cattle which He created, a portion, and they say: "This is Allah's"— in their make believe—"and this is for (His) partners in regard to us." Thus that which (they assign) unto His partners in them reaches not Allah and that which (they assign) unto Allah goes to their (so called) partners. Evil is their ordinance.

137. Thus have their (so called) partners (of Allah) made the killing of their children to seem fair unto many of the idolaters, that they may ruin them and make their faith obscure for them. Had Allah willed (it otherwise), they had not done so. So leave them alone with their devices.

138. And they say: Such cattle and crops are forbidden. No one is to eat of them save whom We will—in their make believe—cattle whose backs are forbidden, cattle over which they mention not the name of Allah. (All that is) a lie against Him. He will repay them for that which they invent.

139. And they say: That which is in the bellies of such cattle is reserved for our males and is forbidden to our wives; but if it be born dead, then they (all) may be partakers thereof. He will reward them for their attribution (of such ordinances unto Him).[101] Lo, He is Wise, Aware.

140. They are losers who, out of folly, have slain their children without knowledge,[102] and have forbidden that which Allah bestowed upon them, inventing a lie against Allah. They indeed have gone astray and are not guided.

141. He it is Who produces gardens trellised and untrellised, and the date palm, and crops of divers flavor, and the olive and the pomegranate, like and unlike. Eat you of the fruit thereof when it fruits, and pay the due thereof upon the harvest day, and be not prodigal. Lo! Allah loves not the prodigals.

142. And of the cattle (He produces) some for burdens, some for food. Eat of that which Allah has bestowed upon you, and follow not the footsteps of the devil, for lo! he is an open foe to you.

143. Eight pairs: Of the sheep twain, and of the goats twain. Say: Has He forbidden the two males or the two females, or that which the wombs of the two females contain? Expound to me (the case) with knowledge, if you are truthful.[103]

---

[101]Verses 138 and 139 refer to customs of the pagan Arabs.
[102]The reference is to the burial alive of female children who were deemed superfluous, and the practice of human sacrifice to idols.
[103]This and the following verses relate to superstitons of the pagan Arabs with regard to cattle used for food.

144. And of the camels twain and of the oxen twain. Say: Has He forbidden the two males or the two females, or that which the wombs of the two females contain; or were you by to witness when Allah commanded you (all) this? Then who does greater wrong than he who devises a lie concerning Allah, that he may lead mankind astray without knowledge. Lo! Allah guides not wrong-doing folk.

145. Say: I find not in that which is revealed unto me anything prohibited to an eater that he eat thereof, except it be carrion, or blood poured forth, or swine flesh—for that verily is foul—or the abomination which was immolated to the name of other than Allah. But who is compelled (thereto), neither craving nor transgressing, (for him) lo! your Lord is Forgiving, Merciful.

146. Unto those who are Jews We forbade every animal with claws. And of the oxen and the sheep forbade We unto them the fat thereof save that upon the backs or the entrails, or that which is mixed with the bone. That We awarded them for their rebellion. And lo! We verily are Truthful.

147. So if they give the lie to you (Muhammad), say: Your Lord is a Lord of all embracing mercy, and His wrath will never be withdrawn from the wicked ones.

148. They who are idolaters will say: Had Allah willed, we had not ascribed (unto Him) partners neither had our fathers, nor had we forbidden anything. Thus did those who were before them give the lie (to Allah's messengers) till they tasted of the fear of Us. Say: Have you any knowledge that you can adduce for us? Lo! you follow nothing but a guess. Lo! You do but guess.

149. Say—For Allah's is the final argument—Had He willed He could indeed have guided all of you.

150. Say: Come, bring your witnesses who can bear witness that Allah forbade (all) this. And if they bear witness, do not you bear witness with them. Follow you not the whims of those who deny Our revelations, those who be-lieve not in the Hereafter and deem (others) equal with their Lord.

151. Say: Come, I will recite unto you that which your Lord has made a sacred duty for you: that you ascribe nothing as partner unto Him and that you do good to parents, and that you slay not your children because of penury—We provide for you and for them—and that you draw not nigh to lewd things whether open or concealed. And that you slay not the life which Allah has made sacred, save in the course of justice. This He has command-ed you, in order that you may discern.

152. And approach not the wealth of the orphan save with that which is better, till he reach maturity. Give full measure and full weight, in justice. We task not any soul beyond its scope. And if you give your word, do justice thereunto, even though it be (against) a kinsman; and fulfill the cove-nant of Allah. This He commands you that haply you may remember.

153. And (He commands you, saying): This is My straight path, so follow it. Follow not other ways, lest you be parted from His way: This has He ordained for you, that you may ward off (evil).

154. Again, We gave the Scripture unto Moses, complete for him who would do good, an explanation of all things, a guidance and a mercy, that they might believe in the meeting with their Lord.

قُلْ هَلُمَّ شُهَدَآءَكُمُ الَّذِينَ يَشْهَدُونَ أَنَّ اللَّهَ حَرَّمَ هَذَا فَإِن شَهِدُواْ فَلَا تَشْهَدْ مَعَهُمْ وَلَا تَتَّبِعْ أَهْوَآءَ الَّذِينَ كَذَّبُواْ بِآيَاتِنَا وَالَّذِينَ لَا يُؤْمِنُونَ بِالْآخِرَةِ وَهُم بِرَبِّهِمْ يَعْدِلُونَ ﴿١٥٠﴾

قُلْ تَعَالَوْاْ أَتْلُ مَا حَرَّمَ رَبُّكُمْ عَلَيْكُمْ أَلَّا تُشْرِكُواْ بِهِ شَيْئًا وَبِالْوَالِدَيْنِ إِحْسَانًا وَلَا تَقْتُلُواْ أَوْلَادَكُم مِّنْ إِمْلَاقٍ نَّحْنُ نَرْزُقُكُمْ وَإِيَّاهُمْ وَلَا تَقْرَبُواْ الْفَوَاحِشَ مَا ظَهَرَ مِنْهَا وَمَا بَطَنَ وَلَا تَقْتُلُواْ النَّفْسَ الَّتِي حَرَّمَ اللَّهُ إِلَّا بِالْحَقِّ ذَلِكُمْ وَصَّاكُم بِهِ لَعَلَّكُمْ تَعْقِلُونَ ﴿١٥١﴾

وَلَا تَقْرَبُواْ مَالَ الْيَتِيمِ إِلَّا بِالَّتِي هِيَ أَحْسَنُ حَتَّى يَبْلُغَ أَشُدَّهُ وَأَوْفُواْ الْكَيْلَ وَالْمِيزَانَ بِالْقِسْطِ لَا نُكَلِّفُ نَفْسًا إِلَّا وُسْعَهَا وَإِذَا قُلْتُمْ فَاعْدِلُواْ وَلَوْ كَانَ ذَا قُرْبَى وَبِعَهْدِ اللَّهِ أَوْفُواْ ذَلِكُمْ وَصَّاكُم بِهِ لَعَلَّكُمْ تَذَكَّرُونَ ﴿١٥٢﴾

وَأَنَّ هَذَا صِرَاطِي مُسْتَقِيمًا فَاتَّبِعُوهُ وَلَا تَتَّبِعُواْ السُّبُلَ فَتَفَرَّقَ بِكُمْ عَن سَبِيلِهِ ذَلِكُمْ وَصَّاكُم بِهِ لَعَلَّكُمْ تَتَّقُونَ ﴿١٥٣﴾

ثُمَّ ءَاتَيْنَا مُوسَى الْكِتَابَ تَمَامًا عَلَى الَّذِي أَحْسَنَ وَتَفْصِيلًا لِّكُلِّ شَيْءٍ وَهُدًى وَرَحْمَةً لَّعَلَّهُم بِلِقَآءِ رَبِّهِمْ يُؤْمِنُونَ ﴿١٥٤﴾

155. And this is a blessed Book which We have revealed. So follow it and ward off (evil), that you may find mercy.

156. Lest you should say: The Scripture was revealed only to two sects before us, and we, for our part, were unaware of what they study;

157. Or lest you should say: If the Scripture had been revealed unto us, we surely had been better guided than are they. Now has there come unto you a clear proof from your Lord, a guidance and a mercy; and who does greater wrong than he who denies the revelations of Allah, and turns away from them? We award unto those who turn away from Our revelations an evil doom because of their aversion.

158. Wait they, indeed, for nothing less than that the angels should come unto them, or your Lord should come, or there should come one of the portents from your Lord? In the day when some of the portents from your Lord come, its belief will not avail any soul which did not believe before, nor in its belief earned good (by works). Say: Wait you! Lo! We (too) are waiting.

159. Lo! as for those who sunder their religion and be-come schismatics, no concern at all have you with them. Their case will go to Allah, who then will tell them what they used to do.

160. Who brings a good deed will receive tenfold the like thereof, while who brings an ill deed will be awarded but the like thereof; and they will not be wronged.

161. Say: Lo! as for me, my Lord has guided me unto a straight path, a right religion, the religion of Abraham, the upright, who was no idolater.

162. Say: Lo! my prayer, my sacrifice, my living and my dying are for Allah, Lord of the Worlds.

163. He has no partner. This am I commanded, and I am the first Muslim.

164. Say: Shall I seek other than Allah for Lord, when He is Lord of all things? Each soul earns only on its own account, nor does any laden bear another's load. Then unto your Lord is your return and He will tell you that wherein you differed.

165. He it is who has placed you as viceroys of the earth and has exalted some of you in rank above others, that He may try you by (the test of) that which He has given you. Lo! your Lord is swift in prosecution, and lo! He is Forgiving, Merciful.

١٦٢ قُلْ إِنَّ صَلَاتِي وَنُسُكِي وَمَحْيَايَ وَمَمَاتِي لِلَّهِ رَبِّ الْعَالَمِينَ

١٦٣ لَا شَرِيكَ لَهُ وَبِذَلِكَ أُمِرْتُ وَأَنَا أَوَّلُ الْمُسْلِمِينَ

١٦٤ قُلْ أَغَيْرَ اللَّهِ أَبْغِي رَبًّا وَهُوَ رَبُّ كُلِّ شَيْءٍ وَلَا تَكْسِبُ كُلُّ نَفْسٍ إِلَّا عَلَيْهَا وَلَا تَزِرُ وَازِرَةٌ وِزْرَ أُخْرَى ثُمَّ إِلَى رَبِّكُمْ مَرْجِعُكُمْ فَيُنَبِّئُكُمْ بِمَا كُنْتُمْ فِيهِ تَخْتَلِفُونَ

١٦٥ وَهُوَ الَّذِي جَعَلَكُمْ خَلَائِفَ الْأَرْضِ وَرَفَعَ بَعْضَكُمْ فَوْقَ بَعْضٍ دَرَجَاتٍ لِيَبْلُوَكُمْ فِي مَا آتَاكُمْ إِنَّ رَبَّكَ سَرِيعُ الْعِقَابِ وَإِنَّهُ لَغَفُورٌ رَحِيمٌ

The Heights

Al A'rāf, "The Heights," takes its name from a word in verses 4 and 6, "And on the Heights are men who know them all by their marks." The best authorities assign the whole of it to about the same period as Surah 6, i.e., the Prophet's last year in Makkah, though some consider vv. 163-167 to have been revealed at Madinah. The subject may be said to be the opponents of God's will and purpose, from Satan onward, through the history of Divine Guidance.

A late Makkan Surah.

The Heights

Revealed at Makkah

*In the name of Allah,
the Beneficent, the Merciful.*

1. **A**lif. Lām Mīm. Ṣād.[104]

2. (It is) a Scripture that is revealed unto you (Muham-mad)—so let there be no heaviness in your heart therefrom—that you may warn thereby, and (it is) a Reminder unto believers.

3. (Saying): Follow that which is sent down unto you from your Lord, and follow no protecting friends beside Him. Little do you recollect!

4. How many a township have We destroyed! As a raid by night, or while they slept at noon, Our terror came unto them.

5. No plea had they, when Our terror came unto them, save that they said: Lo! we were wrongdoers.

6. Then surely We shall question those unto whom (Our message) has been sent, and surely We shall question the messengers.

7. Then surely We shall narrate unto them (the event) with knowledge, for surely We were not absent, (when it came to pass).

8. The weighing on that day is the true (weighing). As for those whose scale is heavy, they are the successful.

9. And as for those whose scale is light: those are they who lost their souls because they disbelieved Our revelations.

10. And We have given you (mankind) power in the earth, and appointed for you therein a livelihood. Little give you thanks!

11. And We created you, then fashioned you, then told the angels: Fall you prostrate before Adam! And they fell prostrate, all save Iblīs, who was not of those who made prostration.

[104]See Surah 2:1, footnote.

12. He said: What hindered you that you did not fall prostrate when I bade you? (Iblīs) said: I am better than him. You created me of fire while him You did create of mud.

١٢ قَالَ مَا مَنَعَكَ أَلَّا تَسْجُدَ إِذْ أَمَرْتُكَ قَالَ أَنَا خَيْرٌ مِّنْهُ خَلَقْتَنِي مِن نَّارٍ وَخَلَقْتَهُ مِن طِينٍ

13. He said: Then go down hence! It is not for you to show pride here, so go forth! Lo! you are of those degraded.

١٣ قَالَ فَاهْبِطْ مِنْهَا فَمَا يَكُونُ لَكَ أَن تَتَكَبَّرَ فِيهَا فَاخْرُجْ إِنَّكَ مِنَ الصَّاغِرِينَ

14. He said: Reprieve me till the day when they are raised (from the dead).

١٤ قَالَ أَنظِرْنِي إِلَىٰ يَوْمِ يُبْعَثُونَ

15. He said: Lo! you are of those reprieved.

١٥ قَالَ إِنَّكَ مِنَ الْمُنظَرِينَ

16. He said: Now, because You have sent me astray, surely I shall lurk in ambush for them on Your Right Path.

١٦ قَالَ فَبِمَا أَغْوَيْتَنِي لَأَقْعُدَنَّ لَهُمْ صِرَاطَكَ الْمُسْتَقِيمَ

17. Then I shall come upon them from before them and from behind them and from their right hands and from their left hands, and You will not find most of them thankful.

١٧ ثُمَّ لَآتِيَنَّهُم مِّن بَيْنِ أَيْدِيهِمْ وَمِنْ خَلْفِهِمْ وَعَنْ أَيْمَانِهِمْ وَعَن شَمَائِلِهِمْ وَلَا تَجِدُ أَكْثَرَهُمْ شَاكِرِينَ

18. He said: Go forth from hence, degraded, banished. As for such of them as follow you, surely I will fill Hell with all of you.

١٨ قَالَ اخْرُجْ مِنْهَا مَذْءُومًا مَّدْحُورًا لَّمَن تَبِعَكَ مِنْهُمْ لَأَمْلَأَنَّ جَهَنَّمَ مِنكُمْ أَجْمَعِينَ

19. And O Adam! Dwell you and your wife in the Garden and eat from whence you will, but come not near this tree lest you become wrongdoers.

١٩ وَيَا آدَمُ اسْكُنْ أَنتَ وَزَوْجُكَ الْجَنَّةَ فَكُلَا مِنْ حَيْثُ شِئْتُمَا وَلَا تَقْرَبَا هَٰذِهِ الشَّجَرَةَ فَتَكُونَا مِنَ الظَّالِمِينَ

20. Then the Devil whispered to them that he might manifest unto them that which was hidden from them of their shame, and he said: Your Lord forbade you from this tree only lest you should become angels or become of the immortals.

٢٠ فَوَسْوَسَ لَهُمَا الشَّيْطَانُ لِيُبْدِيَ لَهُمَا مَا وُورِيَ عَنْهُمَا مِن سَوْءَاتِهِمَا وَقَالَ مَا نَهَاكُمَا رَبُّكُمَا عَنْ هَٰذِهِ الشَّجَرَةِ إِلَّا أَن تَكُونَا مَلَكَيْنِ أَوْ تَكُونَا مِنَ الْخَالِدِينَ

21. And he swore unto them (saying): Lo! I am a sincere adviser unto you.

٢١ وَقَاسَمَهُمَا إِنِّي لَكُمَا لَمِنَ النَّاصِحِينَ

22. Thus did he lead them on with guile. And when they tasted of the tree their shame was manifest to them and they began to hide (by heaping) on themselves some of the leaves of the Garden. And their Lord called them, (saying): Did I not forbid you from that tree and tell you: Lo! the Devil is an open enemy to you?

٢٢ فَدَلَّٰهُمَا بِغُرُورٍ فَلَمَّا ذَاقَا الشَّجَرَةَ بَدَتْ لَهُمَا سَوْءَٰتُهُمَا وَطَفِقَا يَخْصِفَانِ عَلَيْهِمَا مِن وَرَقِ الْجَنَّةِ وَنَادَاهُمَا رَبُّهُمَا أَلَمْ أَنْهَكُمَا عَن تِلْكُمَا الشَّجَرَةِ وَأَقُل لَّكُمَا إِنَّ الشَّيْطَانَ لَكُمَا عَدُوٌّ مُّبِينٌ

23. They said: Our Lord! We have wronged ourselves. If You forgive us not and have not mercy on us, surely we are of the lost!

٢٣ قَالَا رَبَّنَا ظَلَمْنَا أَنفُسَنَا وَإِن لَّمْ تَغْفِرْ لَنَا وَتَرْحَمْنَا لَنَكُونَنَّ مِنَ الْخَاسِرِينَ

24. He said: Go down (from hence), one of you a foe unto the other. There will be for you on earth a habitation and a provision for a while.

٢٤ قَالَ اهْبِطُوا بَعْضُكُمْ لِبَعْضٍ عَدُوٌّ وَلَكُمْ فِي الْأَرْضِ مُسْتَقَرٌّ وَمَتَاعٌ إِلَىٰ حِينٍ

25. He said: There shall you live, and there shall you die, and thence shall you be brought forth.

٢٥ قَالَ فِيهَا تَحْيَوْنَ وَفِيهَا تَمُوتُونَ وَمِنْهَا تُخْرَجُونَ

26. O Children of Adam! We have revealed unto you raiment to conceal your shame, and splendid vesture, but the raiment of restraint from evil, that is best. This is of the revelations of Allah, that they may remember.

٢٦ يَٰبَنِي ءَادَمَ قَدْ أَنزَلْنَا عَلَيْكُمْ لِبَاسًا يُوَارِي سَوْءَٰتِكُمْ وَرِيشًا وَلِبَاسُ التَّقْوَىٰ ذَٰلِكَ خَيْرٌ ذَٰلِكَ مِنْ ءَايَٰتِ اللَّهِ لَعَلَّهُمْ يَذَّكَّرُونَ

27. O Children of Adam! Let not the Devil seduce you as he caused your (first) parents to go forth from the Garden and tore off from them their robe (of innocence) that he might manifest their shame to them. Lo! He sees you, he and his tribe, from where you see him not. Lo! We have made the devils protecting friends for those who believe not.

٢٧ يَٰبَنِي ءَادَمَ لَا يَفْتِنَنَّكُمُ الشَّيْطَانُ كَمَا أَخْرَجَ أَبَوَيْكُم مِّنَ الْجَنَّةِ يَنزِعُ عَنْهُمَا لِبَاسَهُمَا لِيُرِيَهُمَا سَوْءَٰتِهِمَا إِنَّهُ يَرَاكُمْ هُوَ وَقَبِيلُهُ مِنْ حَيْثُ لَا تَرَوْنَهُمْ إِنَّا جَعَلْنَا الشَّيَٰطِينَ أَوْلِيَاءَ لِلَّذِينَ لَا يُؤْمِنُونَ

28. And when they do some lewdness they say: We found our fathers doing it and Allah has enjoined it on us. Say: Allah, surely, enjoins not lewdness. Tell you concerning Allah that which you know not?

٢٨ وَإِذَا فَعَلُوا فَٰحِشَةً قَالُوا وَجَدْنَا عَلَيْهَا ءَابَاءَنَا وَاللَّهُ أَمَرَنَا بِهَا قُلْ إِنَّ اللَّهَ لَا يَأْمُرُ بِالْفَحْشَاءِ أَتَقُولُونَ عَلَى اللَّهِ مَا لَا تَعْلَمُونَ

29. Say: My Lord enjoins justice. And set your faces, upright (toward Him) at every mosque and call upon Him, making religion pure for Him (only). As He brought you into being, so return you (unto Him).

٢٩ قُلْ أَمَرَ رَبِّي بِالْقِسْطِ وَأَقِيمُوا وُجُوهَكُمْ عِنْدَ كُلِّ مَسْجِدٍ وَادْعُوهُ مُخْلِصِينَ لَهُ الدِّينَ كَمَا بَدَأَكُمْ تَعُودُونَ

30. A party has He led aright, while error has just held over (another) party, for lo! they choose the devils for protecting friends instead of Allah and deem that they are rightly guided.

٣٠ فَرِيقًا هَدَى وَفَرِيقًا حَقَّ عَلَيْهِمُ الضَّلَالَةُ إِنَّهُمُ اتَّخَذُوا الشَّيَاطِينَ أَوْلِيَاءَ مِنْ دُونِ اللَّهِ وَيَحْسَبُونَ أَنَّهُمْ مُهْتَدُونَ

31. O Children of Adam! Look to your adornment at every mosque, and eat and drink, but be not prodigal. Lo! He loves not the prodigals.

٣١ يَا بَنِي آدَمَ خُذُوا زِينَتَكُمْ عِنْدَ كُلِّ مَسْجِدٍ وَكُلُوا وَاشْرَبُوا وَلَا تُسْرِفُوا إِنَّهُ لَا يُحِبُّ الْمُسْرِفِينَ

32. Say: Who has forbidden the adornment of Allah which He has brought forth for His bondmen, and the good things of His providing? Say: such, on the Day of Resurrection, will be only for those who believed during the life of the world. Thus do We detail Our revelations for people who have knowledge.

٣٢ قُلْ مَنْ حَرَّمَ زِينَةَ اللَّهِ الَّتِي أَخْرَجَ لِعِبَادِهِ وَالطَّيِّبَاتِ مِنَ الرِّزْقِ قُلْ هِيَ لِلَّذِينَ آمَنُوا فِي الْحَيَاةِ الدُّنْيَا خَالِصَةً يَوْمَ الْقِيَامَةِ كَذَلِكَ نُفَصِّلُ الْآيَاتِ لِقَوْمٍ يَعْلَمُونَ

33. Say: My Lord forbids only indecencies, such of them as are apparent and such as are within, and sin and wrongful oppression, and that you associate with Allah that for which no warrant has been revealed, and that you tell concerning Allah that which you know not.

٣٣ قُلْ إِنَّمَا حَرَّمَ رَبِّيَ الْفَوَاحِشَ مَا ظَهَرَ مِنْهَا وَمَا بَطَنَ وَالْإِثْمَ وَالْبَغْيَ بِغَيْرِ الْحَقِّ وَأَنْ تُشْرِكُوا بِاللَّهِ مَا لَمْ يُنَزِّلْ بِهِ سُلْطَانًا وَأَنْ تَقُولُوا عَلَى اللَّهِ مَا لَا تَعْلَمُونَ

34. And every nation has its term, and when its term comes, they cannot put it off an hour nor yet advance (it).

٣٤ وَلِكُلِّ أُمَّةٍ أَجَلٌ فَإِذَا جَاءَ أَجَلُهُمْ لَا يَسْتَأْخِرُونَ سَاعَةً وَلَا يَسْتَقْدِمُونَ

35. O Children of Adam! If messengers of your own come unto you who narrate unto you My revelations, then whoever refrains from evil and amends, there shall no fear come upon them neither shall they grieve.

٣٥ يَا بَنِي آدَمَ إِمَّا يَأْتِيَنَّكُمْ رُسُلٌ مِنْكُمْ يَقُصُّونَ عَلَيْكُمْ آيَاتِي فَمَنِ اتَّقَى وَأَصْلَحَ فَلَا خَوْفٌ عَلَيْهِمْ وَلَا هُمْ يَحْزَنُونَ

36. But they who deny Our revelations and scorn them—such are rightful owners of the Fire; they will abide therein.

٣٦ وَالَّذِينَ كَذَّبُوا بِآيَاتِنَا وَاسْتَكْبَرُوا عَنْهَا أُولَٰئِكَ أَصْحَابُ النَّارِ هُمْ فِيهَا خَالِدُونَ

37. Who does greater wrong than he who invents a lie concerning Allah or denies His tokens. (For such) their appointed portion of the Book (of destiny) reaches them till, when Our messengers[105] come to gather them, they say: Where (now) is that to which you cried beside Allah? They say: They have strayed from us. And they testify against themselves that they were disbelievers.

38. He says: Enter into the Fire among nations of the jinn and humankind who passed away before you. Every time a nation enters, it curses its sister (nation) till, when they have all been made to follow one another there, the last of them says unto the first of them: Our Lord! These led us astray, so give them double torment of the Fire. He says: For each one there is double (torment), but you know not.

39. And the first of them says unto the last of them: You were no better than us, so taste the doom for what you used to earn.

40. Lo! those who deny Our revelations and scorn them, for them the gates of Heaven will not be opened nor will they enter the Garden until the camel goes through the needle's eye. Thus do We requite the criminals.

41. Theirs will be a bed of Hell, and over them coverings (of Hell). Thus do We requite wrongdoers.

42. But (as for) those who believe and do good works—We tax not any soul beyond its scope—Such are rightful owners of the Garden. They abide therein.

﴿٣٧﴾ فَمَنْ أَظْلَمُ مِمَّنِ افْتَرَى عَلَى اللّٰهِ كَذِبًا أَوْ كَذَّبَ بِآيَاتِهِ أُولَٰئِكَ يَنَالُهُمْ نَصِيبُهُمْ مِنَ الْكِتَابِ حَتَّى إِذَا جَاءَتْهُمْ رُسُلُنَا يَتَوَفَّوْنَهُمْ قَالُوا أَيْنَ مَا كُنْتُمْ تَدْعُونَ مِنْ دُونِ اللّٰهِ قَالُوا ضَلُّوا عَنَّا وَشَهِدُوا عَلَى أَنْفُسِهِمْ أَنَّهُمْ كَانُوا كَافِرِينَ

﴿٣٨﴾ قَالَ ادْخُلُوا فِي أُمَمٍ قَدْ خَلَتْ مِنْ قَبْلِكُمْ مِنَ الْجِنِّ وَالْإِنْسِ فِي النَّارِ كُلَّمَا دَخَلَتْ أُمَّةٌ لَعَنَتْ أُخْتَهَا حَتَّى إِذَا ادَّارَكُوا فِيهَا جَمِيعًا قَالَتْ أُخْرَاهُمْ لِأُولَاهُمْ رَبَّنَا هَٰؤُلَاءِ أَضَلُّونَا فَآتِهِمْ عَذَابًا ضِعْفًا مِنَ النَّارِ قَالَ لِكُلٍّ ضِعْفٌ وَلَٰكِنْ لَا تَعْلَمُونَ

﴿٣٩﴾ وَقَالَتْ أُولَاهُمْ لِأُخْرَاهُمْ فَمَا كَانَ لَكُمْ عَلَيْنَا مِنْ فَضْلٍ فَذُوقُوا الْعَذَابَ بِمَا كُنْتُمْ تَكْسِبُونَ

﴿٤٠﴾ إِنَّ الَّذِينَ كَذَّبُوا بِآيَاتِنَا وَاسْتَكْبَرُوا عَنْهَا لَا تُفَتَّحُ لَهُمْ أَبْوَابُ السَّمَاءِ وَلَا يَدْخُلُونَ الْجَنَّةَ حَتَّى يَلِجَ الْجَمَلُ فِي سَمِّ الْخِيَاطِ وَكَذَٰلِكَ نَجْزِي الْمُجْرِمِينَ

﴿٤١﴾ لَهُمْ مِنْ جَهَنَّمَ مِهَادٌ وَمِنْ فَوْقِهِمْ غَوَاشٍ وَكَذَٰلِكَ نَجْزِي الظَّالِمِينَ

﴿٤٢﴾ وَالَّذِينَ آمَنُوا وَعَمِلُوا الصَّالِحَاتِ لَا نُكَلِّفُ نَفْسًا إِلَّا وُسْعَهَا أُولَٰئِكَ أَصْحَابُ الْجَنَّةِ هُمْ فِيهَا خَالِدُونَ

---

[105]i.e., angels.

٤٣ وَنَزَعْنَا مَا فِي صُدُورِهِم مِّنْ غِلٍّ تَجْرِي مِن تَحْتِهِمُ الْأَنْهَارُ وَقَالُوا الْحَمْدُ لِلَّهِ الَّذِي هَدَانَا لِهَٰذَا وَمَا كُنَّا لِنَهْتَدِيَ لَوْلَا أَنْ هَدَانَا اللَّهُ لَقَدْ جَاءَتْ رُسُلُ رَبِّنَا بِالْحَقِّ وَنُودُوا أَن تِلْكُمُ الْجَنَّةُ أُورِثْتُمُوهَا بِمَا كُنتُمْ تَعْمَلُونَ

43. And We remove whatever rancor may be in their hearts. Rivers flow beneath them. And they say: Praise be to Allah, Who has guided us to this. We could not truly have been led aright if Allah had not guided us. Verily the messengers of our Lord did bring the Truth. And it is cried unto them: This is the Garden. You inherit it for what you used to do.

٤٤ وَنَادَىٰ أَصْحَابُ الْجَنَّةِ أَصْحَابَ النَّارِ أَن قَدْ وَجَدْنَا مَا وَعَدَنَا رَبُّنَا حَقًّا فَهَلْ وَجَدتُّم مَّا وَعَدَ رَبُّكُمْ حَقًّا قَالُوا نَعَمْ فَأَذَّنَ مُؤَذِّنٌ بَيْنَهُمْ أَن لَّعْنَةُ اللَّهِ عَلَى الظَّالِمِينَ

44. And the dwellers of the Garden cry unto the dwellers of the Fire: We have found that which our Lord promised us (to be) the Truth. Have you (too) found that which your Lord promised the Truth? They say: Yes, surely. And a crier in between them cries: The curse of Allah is on evildoers.

٤٥ الَّذِينَ يَصُدُّونَ عَن سَبِيلِ اللَّهِ وَيَبْغُونَهَا عِوَجًا وَهُم بِالْآخِرَةِ كَافِرُونَ

45. Who debar (men) from the path of Allah and would have it crooked, and who are disbelievers in the Last Day.

٤٦ وَبَيْنَهُمَا حِجَابٌ وَعَلَى الْأَعْرَافِ رِجَالٌ يَعْرِفُونَ كُلًّا بِسِيمَاهُمْ وَنَادَوْا أَصْحَابَ الْجَنَّةِ أَن سَلَامٌ عَلَيْكُمْ لَمْ يَدْخُلُوهَا وَهُمْ يَطْمَعُونَ

46. And between them is a veil. And on the Heights are men who know them all by their marks. And they call unto the dwellers of the Garden: Peace be unto you! They entered it not although they hoped (to enter).

٤٧ وَإِذَا صُرِفَتْ أَبْصَارُهُمْ تِلْقَاءَ أَصْحَابِ النَّارِ قَالُوا رَبَّنَا لَا تَجْعَلْنَا مَعَ الْقَوْمِ الظَّالِمِينَ

47. And when their eyes are turned toward the dwellers of the Fire, they say: Our Lord! Place us not with the wrong-doing folk.

٤٨ وَنَادَىٰ أَصْحَابُ الْأَعْرَافِ رِجَالًا يَعْرِفُونَهُم بِسِيمَاهُمْ قَالُوا مَا أَغْنَىٰ عَنكُمْ جَمْعُكُمْ وَمَا كُنتُمْ تَسْتَكْبِرُونَ

48. And the dwellers on the Heights call unto men whom they know by their marks, (saying): What did your multitude and that in which you took your pride avail you?

٤٩ أَهَٰؤُلَاءِ الَّذِينَ أَقْسَمْتُمْ لَا يَنَالُهُمُ اللَّهُ بِرَحْمَةٍ ادْخُلُوا الْجَنَّةَ لَا خَوْفٌ عَلَيْكُمْ وَلَا أَنتُمْ تَحْزَنُونَ

49. Are these they of whom you swore that Allah would not show them mercy? (Unto them it has been said): Enter the Garden. No fear shall come upon you nor is it you who will grieve.

٥٠ وَنَادَىٰ أَصْحَابُ النَّارِ أَصْحَابَ الْجَنَّةِ أَنْ أَفِيضُوا عَلَيْنَا مِنَ الْمَاءِ أَوْ مِمَّا رَزَقَكُمُ اللَّهُ قَالُوا إِنَّ اللَّهَ حَرَّمَهُمَا عَلَى الْكَافِرِينَ

50. And the dwellers of the Fire cry out unto the dwellers of the Garden; Pour on us some water or some of that wherewith Allah has provided you. They say: Lo! Allah has forbidden both to disbelievers,

51. Who took their religion for a sport and pastime, and whom the life of the world beguiled. So this day We have forgotten them even as they forgot the meeting of this Day and as they used to deny Our tokens.

52. Verily We have brought them a Scripture which We expound with knowledge, a guidance and a mercy for a people who believe.

53. Await they anything save the fulfillment thereof? On the day when the fulfillment thereof comes, those who were before forgetful thereof will say: The messengers of our Lord did bring the Truth! Have we any intercessors, that they may intercede for us? Or can we be returned (to life on earth), that we may act otherwise than we used to act? They have lost their souls, and that which they devised has failed them.

54. Lo! your Lord is Allah Who created the heavens and the earth in six Days, then He established Himself on the Throne. He covers the night with the day, which is in haste to follow it, and has made the sun and the moon and the stars subservient by His command. His verily is all creation and commandment. Blessed be Allah, the Lord of the Worlds!

55. O mankind!) Call upon your Lord humbly and in secret. Lo! He loves not aggressors.

56. Work not confusion in the earth after the fair ordering (thereof), and call on Him in fear and hope. Lo! the mercy of Allah is near unto the good.

57. And He it is Who sends the winds as tidings heralding His mercy, till, when they bear a cloud heavy (with rain), We lead it to a dead land, and then cause water to descend thereon, and thereby bring forth fruits of every kind. Thus bring We forth the dead. Perhaps you may remember.

﴿٥١﴾ اَلَّذِينَ اتَّخَذُوا دِينَهُمْ لَهْوًا وَلَعِبًا وَغَرَّتْهُمُ الْحَيَوةُ الدُّنْيَا فَالْيَوْمَ نَنْسَىٰهُمْ كَمَا نَسُوا لِقَاءَ يَوْمِهِمْ هَذَا وَمَا كَانُوا بِآيَاتِنَا يَجْحَدُونَ

﴿٥٢﴾ وَلَقَدْ جِئْنَاهُمْ بِكِتَابٍ فَصَّلْنَاهُ عَلَىٰ عِلْمٍ هُدًى وَرَحْمَةً لِقَوْمٍ يُؤْمِنُونَ

﴿٥٣﴾ هَلْ يَنْظُرُونَ إِلَّا تَأْوِيلَهُ يَوْمَ يَأْتِي تَأْوِيلُهُ يَقُولُ الَّذِينَ نَسُوهُ مِنْ قَبْلُ قَدْ جَاءَتْ رُسُلُ رَبِّنَا بِالْحَقِّ فَهَلْ لَنَا مِنْ شُفَعَاءَ فَيَشْفَعُوا لَنَا أَوْ نُرَدُّ فَنَعْمَلَ غَيْرَ الَّذِي كُنَّا نَعْمَلُ قَدْ خَسِرُوا أَنْفُسَهُمْ وَضَلَّ عَنْهُمْ مَا كَانُوا يَفْتَرُونَ

﴿٥٤﴾ إِنَّ رَبَّكُمُ اللَّهُ الَّذِي خَلَقَ السَّمَاوَاتِ وَالْأَرْضَ فِي سِتَّةِ أَيَّامٍ ثُمَّ اسْتَوَىٰ عَلَى الْعَرْشِ يُغْشِي اللَّيْلَ النَّهَارَ يَطْلُبُهُ حَثِيثًا وَالشَّمْسَ وَالْقَمَرَ وَالنُّجُومَ مُسَخَّرَاتٍ بِأَمْرِهِ أَلَا لَهُ الْخَلْقُ وَالْأَمْرُ تَبَارَكَ اللَّهُ رَبُّ الْعَالَمِينَ

﴿٥٥﴾ ادْعُوا رَبَّكُمْ تَضَرُّعًا وَخُفْيَةً إِنَّهُ لَا يُحِبُّ الْمُعْتَدِينَ

﴿٥٦﴾ وَلَا تُفْسِدُوا فِي الْأَرْضِ بَعْدَ إِصْلَاحِهَا وَادْعُوهُ خَوْفًا وَطَمَعًا إِنَّ رَحْمَتَ اللَّهِ قَرِيبٌ مِنَ الْمُحْسِنِينَ

﴿٥٧﴾ وَهُوَ الَّذِي يُرْسِلُ الرِّيَاحَ بُشْرًا بَيْنَ يَدَيْ رَحْمَتِهِ حَتَّىٰ إِذَا أَقَلَّتْ سَحَابًا ثِقَالًا سُقْنَاهُ لِبَلَدٍ مَيِّتٍ فَأَنْزَلْنَا بِهِ الْمَاءَ فَأَخْرَجْنَا بِهِ مِنْ كُلِّ الثَّمَرَاتِ كَذَلِكَ نُخْرِجُ الْمَوْتَىٰ لَعَلَّكُمْ تَذَكَّرُونَ

58. As for the good land, its vegetation comes forth by permission of its Lord; while as for that which is bad, only evil comes forth (from it). Thus do We recount the tokens for people who give thanks.

59. We sent Noah (of old) unto his people, and he said: O my people! Worship Allah. You have no other God save Him. Lo! I fear for you the retribution of an Awful Day.

60. The chieftains of his people said: Lo! we see you surely in plain error.

61. He said: O my people! There is no error in me, but I am a Messenger from the Lord of the Worlds.

62. I convey unto you the messages of my Lord and give good counsel unto you, and know from Allah that which you know not.

63. Marvel you that there should come unto you a Reminder from your Lord by means of a man among you, that he may warn you, and that you may keep from evil, and that haply you may find mercy.

64. But they denied him, so We saved him and those with him in the ship, and We drowned those who denied Our tokens Lo! they were blind folk.

65. And unto (the tribe of) 'Ād (We sent) their brother, Hūd.[106] He said: O my people! Worship Allah. You have no other God save Him. Will you not ward off (evil)?

66. The chieftains of his people, who were disbelieving, said: Lo! we surely see you in foolishness, and lo! we deem you of the liars.

67. He said: O my people; There is no foolishness in me, but I am a Messenger from the Lord of the Worlds.

68. I convey unto you the messages of my Lord and am for you a true adviser.

---

[106]An ancient Arab prophet.

69. Marvel you that there should come unto you a Reminder from your Lord by means of a man among you, that he may warn you? Remember how He made you vice-roys after Noah's folk, and gave you growth of stature. Remember (all) the bounties of your Lord, that haply you may be successful.

70. They said: Have you come unto us that we should worship Allah alone, and forsake what our fathers worshiped? Then bring upon us that wherewith you threaten us if you are of the truthful.

71. He said: Terror and wrath from your Lord have already fallen on you. Would you wrangle with me over names which you have named, you and your fathers, for which no warrant from Allah has been revealed? Then await (the consequence), Lo! I (also) am of those awaiting (it).

72. And We saved him and those with him by a mercy from Us, and We cut the root of those who denied Our revelations and were not believers.

73. And to (the tribe of) Thamūd (We sent) their brother Ṣāliḥ.[107] He said: O my people! Worship Allah. You have no other God save Him. A wonder from your Lord has come unto you. Lo! this is the she-camel of Allah, a token unto you; so let her feed in Allah's earth, and touch her not with hurt lest painful torment seize you.

74. And remember how He made you viceroys after 'Ād and gave you station in the earth. You choose castles in the plains and hew the mountains into dwellings. So remember (all) the bounties of Allah and do not evil, making mischief in the earth.

---

[107]An ancient Arab prophet.

75. The chieftains of his people, who were scornful, said unto those whom they despised, unto such of them as believed: Know you that Ṣāliḥ is one sent from his Lord? They said: Lo! in that wherewith he has been sent we are believers.

76. Those who were scornful said: Lo! in that which you believe we are disbelievers.

77. So they hamstrung the she-camel, and they flouted the commandment of their Lord, and they said: O Ṣāliḥ! Bring upon us what you threaten if you are indeed of those sent (from Allah).

78. So the earthquake seized them, and morning found them prostrate in their dwelling place.

79. And Ṣāliḥ turned on them and said: O my people! I delivered my Lord's message unto you and gave you good advice, but you love not good advisers.

80. And Lot (Remember) when he said unto his folk: Will you commit abomination such as no creature ever did before you?

81. Lo! you come with lust unto men instead of women. Nay, but you are wanton folk.

82. And the answer of his people was only that they said (one to another): Turn them out of your township.[108] They are folk, forsooth, who keep pure.

83. And We rescued him and his household, save his wife, who was of those who stayed behind.

84. And We rained a rain upon them. See now the nature of the consequence for evildoers!

85. And unto Madian (We sent) their brother, Shu'ayb.[109] He said: O my people! Worship Allah. You have no other God save Him. Lo! a clear proof has come unto you from your Lord; so give full measure and full weight and wrong not mankind in their goods, and work not confusion in the earth after the fair ordering thereof. That will be better for you, if you are believers.

---

[108]The Arabic word *qaryah* means originally a settled community, polity or civilization.
[109]Identified with Jethro.

86. Lurk not on every road to threaten (wayfarers), and to turn away from Allah's path him who believes in Him, and to seek to make it crooked. And remember, when you were but few, how He did multiply you. And see the nature of the consequence for the corrupters!

87. And if there is a party of you which believes in that wherewith I have been sent, and there is a party which believes not, then have patience until Allah judge between us. He is the best of all who deal in judgment.

88. The chieftains of his people, who were scornful, said: Surely we will drive you out, O Shu'ayb, and those who believe with you, from our township, unless you return to our religion. He said: Even though we hate it?

89. We should have invented a lie against Allah if we returned to your religion after Allah has rescued us from it. It is not for us to return to it unless Allah should (so) will. Our Lord comprehends all things in knowledge. In Allah do we put our trust. Our Lord! Decide with truth between us and our folk, for You are the best of those who make decision.

90. But the chieftains of his people, who were disbelieving, said: If you follow Shu'ayb, then truly you will be the losers.

91. So the earthquake seized them, and morning found them prostrate in their dwelling place.

92. Those who denied Shu'ayb became as though they had not dwelt there. Those who denied Shu'ayb, they were the losers.

93. So he turned from them and said: O my people! I delivered my Lord's messages unto you and gave you good advice; then how can I sorrow for a people that rejected (truth)?

٨٦ وَلَا تَقْعُدُوا بِكُلِّ صِرَاطٍ تُوعِدُونَ وَتَصُدُّونَ عَن سَبِيلِ اللَّهِ مَنْ ءَامَنَ بِهِ وَتَبْغُونَهَا عِوَجًا وَاذْكُرُوا إِذْ كُنتُمْ قَلِيلًا فَكَثَّرَكُمْ وَانظُرُوا كَيْفَ كَانَ عَٰقِبَةُ الْمُفْسِدِينَ

٨٧ وَإِن كَانَ طَائِفَةٌ مِّنكُمْ ءَامَنُوا بِالَّذِى أُرْسِلْتُ بِهِ وَطَائِفَةٌ لَّمْ يُؤْمِنُوا فَاصْبِرُوا حَتَّىٰ يَحْكُمَ اللَّهُ بَيْنَنَا وَهُوَ خَيْرُ الْحَٰكِمِينَ

٨٨ قَالَ الْمَلَأُ الَّذِينَ اسْتَكْبَرُوا مِن قَوْمِهِ لَنُخْرِجَنَّكَ يَٰشُعَيْبُ وَالَّذِينَ ءَامَنُوا مَعَكَ مِن قَرْيَتِنَا أَوْ لَتَعُودُنَّ فِى مِلَّتِنَا قَالَ أَوَلَوْ كُنَّا كَٰرِهِينَ

٨٩ قَدِ افْتَرَيْنَا عَلَى اللَّهِ كَذِبًا إِنْ عُدْنَا فِى مِلَّتِكُم بَعْدَ إِذْ نَجَّىٰنَا اللَّهُ مِنْهَا وَمَا يَكُونُ لَنَا أَن نَّعُودَ فِيهَا إِلَّا أَن يَشَاءَ اللَّهُ رَبُّنَا وَسِعَ رَبُّنَا كُلَّ شَىْءٍ عِلْمًا عَلَى اللَّهِ تَوَكَّلْنَا رَبَّنَا افْتَحْ بَيْنَنَا وَبَيْنَ قَوْمِنَا بِالْحَقِّ وَأَنتَ خَيْرُ الْفَٰتِحِينَ

٩٠ وَقَالَ الْمَلَأُ الَّذِينَ كَفَرُوا مِن قَوْمِهِ لَئِنِ اتَّبَعْتُمْ شُعَيْبًا إِنَّكُمْ إِذًا لَّخَٰسِرُونَ

٩١ فَأَخَذَتْهُمُ الرَّجْفَةُ فَأَصْبَحُوا فِى دَارِهِمْ جَٰثِمِينَ

٩٢ الَّذِينَ كَذَّبُوا شُعَيْبًا كَأَن لَّمْ يَغْنَوْا فِيهَا الَّذِينَ كَذَّبُوا شُعَيْبًا كَانُوا هُمُ الْخَٰسِرِينَ

٩٣ فَتَوَلَّىٰ عَنْهُمْ وَقَالَ يَٰقَوْمِ لَقَدْ أَبْلَغْتُكُمْ رِسَٰلَٰتِ رَبِّى وَنَصَحْتُ لَكُمْ فَكَيْفَ ءَاسَىٰ عَلَىٰ قَوْمٍ كَٰفِرِينَ

94. And We sent no prophet unto any township but We did afflict its folk with tribulation and adversity that they might grow humble.

95. Then changed We the evil plight for good till they grew affluent and said: Tribulation and distress did touch our fathers. Then We seized them unawares, when they perceived not.

96. And if the people of the townships had believed and kept from evil, surely We should have opened for them, blessings from Heaven and from the earth. But (unto every Messenger) they gave the lie, and so We seized them on account of what they used to earn.

97. Are the people of the townships then secure from the coming of Our wrath upon them as a night raid while they sleep?

98. Or are the people of the townships then secure from the coming of Our wrath upon them in the daytime while they play?

99. Are they then secure from Allah's scheme? None deems himself secure from Allah's scheme save folk doomed to ruin.

100. Is it not an indication to those who inherit the land after its people (who thus reaped the consequence of evil-doing) that, if We will, We can smite them for their sins and print upon their hearts so that they hear not?

101. Such were the townships. We relate some tidings of them unto you (Muhammad). Their messengers surely came unto them with clear proofs (of Allah's Sovereignty), but they could not believe because they had before denied. Thus does Allah print upon the hearts of disbelievers (that they hear not).

102. We found no (loyalty to any) covenant in most of them. Nay, most of them We found wrongdoers.

103. Then, after them, We sent Moses with our tokens unto Pharaoh and his chiefs, but they repelled them. Now, see the nature of the consequence for `the corrupters!

وَمَا أَرْسَلْنَا فِي قَرْيَةٍ مِّن نَّبِيٍّ إِلَّا أَخَذْنَا أَهْلَهَا بِالْبَأْسَاءِ وَالضَّرَّاءِ لَعَلَّهُمْ يَضَّرَّعُونَ ﴿٩٤﴾

ثُمَّ بَدَّلْنَا مَكَانَ السَّيِّئَةِ الْحَسَنَةَ حَتَّىٰ عَفَوْا وَقَالُوا قَدْ مَسَّ ءَابَاءَنَا الضَّرَّاءُ وَالسَّرَّاءُ فَأَخَذْنَٰهُم بَغْتَةً وَهُمْ لَا يَشْعُرُونَ ﴿٩٥﴾

وَلَوْ أَنَّ أَهْلَ الْقُرَىٰ ءَامَنُوا وَاتَّقَوْا لَفَتَحْنَا عَلَيْهِم بَرَكَاتٍ مِّنَ السَّمَاءِ وَالْأَرْضِ وَلَٰكِن كَذَّبُوا فَأَخَذْنَٰهُم بِمَا كَانُوا يَكْسِبُونَ ﴿٩٦﴾

أَفَأَمِنَ أَهْلُ الْقُرَىٰ أَن يَأْتِيَهُم بَأْسُنَا بَيَاتًا وَهُمْ نَائِمُونَ ﴿٩٧﴾ أَوَأَمِنَ أَهْلُ الْقُرَىٰ أَن يَأْتِيَهُم بَأْسُنَا ضُحًى وَهُمْ يَلْعَبُونَ ﴿٩٨﴾

أَفَأَمِنُوا مَكْرَ اللَّهِ فَلَا يَأْمَنُ مَكْرَ اللَّهِ إِلَّا الْقَوْمُ الْخَاسِرُونَ ﴿٩٩﴾

أَوَلَمْ يَهْدِ لِلَّذِينَ يَرِثُونَ الْأَرْضَ مِنْ بَعْدِ أَهْلِهَا أَن لَّوْ نَشَاءُ أَصَبْنَٰهُم بِذُنُوبِهِمْ وَنَطْبَعُ عَلَىٰ قُلُوبِهِمْ فَهُمْ لَا يَسْمَعُونَ ﴿١٠٠﴾

تِلْكَ الْقُرَىٰ نَقُصُّ عَلَيْكَ مِنْ أَنبَائِهَا وَلَقَدْ جَاءَتْهُمْ رُسُلُهُم بِالْبَيِّنَاتِ فَمَا كَانُوا لِيُؤْمِنُوا بِمَا كَذَّبُوا مِن قَبْلُ كَذَٰلِكَ يَطْبَعُ اللَّهُ عَلَىٰ قُلُوبِ الْكَافِرِينَ ﴿١٠١﴾

وَمَا وَجَدْنَا لِأَكْثَرِهِم مِّنْ عَهْدٍ وَإِن وَجَدْنَا أَكْثَرَهُمْ لَفَٰسِقِينَ ﴿١٠٢﴾

ثُمَّ بَعَثْنَا مِنْ بَعْدِهِم مُّوسَىٰ بِآيَاتِنَا إِلَىٰ فِرْعَوْنَ وَمَلَئِهِ فَظَلَمُوا بِهَا فَانظُرْ كَيْفَ كَانَ عَاقِبَةُ الْمُفْسِدِينَ ﴿١٠٣﴾

104. Moses said: O Pharaoh! Lo! I am a Messenger from the Lord of the Worlds,

105. Approved upon condition that I speak concerning Allah nothing but the truth. I come unto you (lords of Egypt) with a clear proof from your Lord. So let the Children of Israel go with me.

106. (Pharaoh) said: If you come with a token, then produce it, if you are of those who speak the truth.

107. Then he flung down his staff and lo! it was a serpent manifest;

108. And he drew forth his hand (from his bosom): and lo! it was white for the beholders.

109. The chiefs of Pharaoh's people said: Lo! this is some knowing wizard,

110. Who would expel you from your land. Now what do you advise?

111. They said (unto Pharaoh): Put him off (a while) as well as his brother and send into the cities summoners,

112. To bring each knowing wizard unto you.

113. And the wizards came to Pharaoh, asking: Will there be a reward for us if we are victors?

114. He answered: Yes, and surely you shall be of those brought near (to me).

115. They said: O Moses! Either throw (first) or let us be the first throwers?

116. He said: Throw! And when they threw they cast a spell upon the people's eyes, and overawed them, and produced a mighty spell.

117. And We inspired Moses (saying): Throw your staff! And lo! it swallowed up their lying show.

118. Thus was the Truth vindicated and that which they were doing was made vain.

وَقَالَ مُوسَىٰ يَـٰفِرْعَوْنُ إِنِّى رَسُولٌ مِّن رَّبِّ ﴿١٠٤﴾ الْعَٰلَمِينَ

حَقِيقٌ عَلَىٰٓ أَن لَّآ أَقُولَ عَلَى اللَّهِ إِلَّا الْحَقَّ قَدْ ﴿١٠٥﴾ جِئْتُكُم بِبَيِّنَةٍ مِّن رَّبِّكُمْ فَأَرْسِلْ مَعِىَ بَنِىٓ إِسْرَٰٓئِيلَ

قَالَ إِن كُنتَ جِئْتَ بِـَٔايَةٍ فَأْتِ بِهَآ إِن كُنتَ مِنَ ﴿١٠٦﴾ الصَّٰدِقِينَ

فَأَلْقَىٰ عَصَاهُ فَإِذَا هِىَ ثُعْبَانٌ مُّبِينٌ ﴿١٠٧﴾

وَنَزَعَ يَدَهُۥ فَإِذَا هِىَ بَيْضَآءُ لِلنَّٰظِرِينَ ﴿١٠٨﴾

قَالَ الْمَلَأُ مِن قَوْمِ فِرْعَوْنَ إِنَّ هَٰذَا لَسَٰحِرٌ ﴿١٠٩﴾ عَلِيمٌ

يُرِيدُ أَن يُخْرِجَكُم مِّنْ أَرْضِكُمْ فَمَاذَا تَأْمُرُونَ ﴿١١٠﴾

قَالُوٓا أَرْجِهْ وَأَخَاهُ وَأَرْسِلْ فِى الْمَدَآئِنِ حَٰشِرِينَ ﴿١١١﴾

يَأْتُوكَ بِكُلِّ سَٰحِرٍ عَلِيمٍ ﴿١١٢﴾

وَجَآءَ السَّحَرَةُ فِرْعَوْنَ قَالُوٓا إِنَّ لَنَا لَأَجْرًا ﴿١١٣﴾ إِن كُنَّا نَحْنُ الْغَٰلِبِينَ

قَالَ نَعَمْ وَإِنَّكُمْ لَمِنَ الْمُقَرَّبِينَ ﴿١١٤﴾

قَالُوا يَٰمُوسَىٰٓ إِمَّآ أَن تُلْقِىَ وَإِمَّآ أَن نَّكُونَ ﴿١١٥﴾ نَحْنُ الْمُلْقِينَ

قَالَ أَلْقُوا فَلَمَّآ أَلْقَوْا سَحَرُوٓا أَعْيُنَ ﴿١١٦﴾ النَّاسِ وَاسْتَرْهَبُوهُمْ وَجَآءُو بِسِحْرٍ عَظِيمٍ

وَأَوْحَيْنَآ إِلَىٰ مُوسَىٰٓ أَنْ أَلْقِ عَصَاكَ ﴿١١٧﴾ فَإِذَا هِىَ تَلْقَفُ مَا يَأْفِكُونَ

فَوَقَعَ الْحَقُّ وَبَطَلَ مَا كَانُوا يَعْمَلُونَ ﴿١١٨﴾

119. Thus were they there defeated and brought low.

120. And the wizards fell down prostrate,

121. Crying: We believe in the Lord of the Worlds,

122. The Lord of Moses and Aaron.

123. Pharaoh said: You believe in Him before I give you leave! Lo! this is a plot you have plotted in the city that you may drive its people hence. But you shall come to know!

124. Surely I shall have your hands and feet cut off upon alternate sides. Then I shall crucify you every one.

125. They said: Lo! we are about to return unto our Lord!

126. You take vengeance on us only forasmuch as we believed the tokens of our Lord when they came unto us. Our Lord! Vouchsafe unto us steadfastness and make us die as Muslims (unto You).

127. The chiefs of Pharaoh's people said: (O King), will you suffer Moses and his people to make mischief in the land, and flout you and your gods? He said: We will slay their sons and spare their women, for lo! we are in power over them.

128. And Moses said unto his people: Seek help in Allah and endure. Lo! the earth is Allah's. He gives it for an inheritance to whom He will. And lo! the sequel is for those who keep their duty (unto Him).

129. They said: We suffered hurt before you came unto us, and since you have come unto us. He said: it may be that your Lord is going to destroy your adversary and make you viceroys in the earth, that He may see how you behave.

١١٩ فَغُلِبُوا هُنَالِكَ وَانقَلَبُوا صَاغِرِينَ

١٢٠ وَأُلْقِيَ السَّحَرَةُ سَاجِدِينَ

١٢١ قَالُوٓا ءَامَنَّا بِرَبِّ الْعَالَمِينَ

١٢٢ رَبِّ مُوسَىٰ وَهَارُونَ

١٢٣ قَالَ فِرْعَوْنُ ءَامَنتُم بِهِۦ قَبْلَ أَنْ ءَاذَنَ لَكُمْ إِنَّ هَٰذَا لَمَكْرٌ مَّكَرْتُمُوهُ فِي الْمَدِينَةِ لِتُخْرِجُوا مِنْهَآ أَهْلَهَا فَسَوْفَ تَعْلَمُونَ

١٢٤ لَأُقَطِّعَنَّ أَيْدِيَكُمْ وَأَرْجُلَكُم مِّنْ خِلَٰفٍ ثُمَّ لَأُصَلِّبَنَّكُمْ أَجْمَعِينَ

١٢٥ قَالُوٓا إِنَّآ إِلَىٰ رَبِّنَا مُنقَلِبُونَ

١٢٦ وَمَا تَنقِمُ مِنَّآ إِلَّآ أَنْ ءَامَنَّا بِـَٔايَٰتِ رَبِّنَا لَمَّا جَآءَتْنَا رَبَّنَآ أَفْرِغْ عَلَيْنَا صَبْرًا وَتَوَفَّنَا مُسْلِمِينَ

١٢٧ وَقَالَ الْمَلَأُ مِن قَوْمِ فِرْعَوْنَ أَتَذَرُ مُوسَىٰ وَقَوْمَهُۥ لِيُفْسِدُوا فِي الْأَرْضِ وَيَذَرَكَ وَءَالِهَتَكَ قَالَ سَنُقَتِّلُ أَبْنَآءَهُمْ وَنَسْتَحْيِۦ نِسَآءَهُمْ وَإِنَّا فَوْقَهُمْ قَٰهِرُونَ

١٢٨ قَالَ مُوسَىٰ لِقَوْمِهِ اسْتَعِينُوا بِاللَّهِ وَاصْبِرُوٓا إِنَّ الْأَرْضَ لِلَّهِ يُورِثُهَا مَن يَشَآءُ مِنْ عِبَادِهِ وَالْعَٰقِبَةُ لِلْمُتَّقِينَ

١٢٩ قَالُوٓا أُوذِينَا مِن قَبْلِ أَن تَأْتِيَنَا وَمِنۢ بَعْدِ مَا جِئْتَنَا قَالَ عَسَىٰ رَبُّكُمْ أَن يُهْلِكَ عَدُوَّكُمْ وَيَسْتَخْلِفَكُمْ فِي الْأَرْضِ فَيَنظُرَ كَيْفَ تَعْمَلُونَ

130. And We straitened Pharaoh's folk with famine and the dearth of fruits, that peradventure they might heed.

۱۳۰ وَلَقَدْ أَخَذْنَا ءَالَ فِرْعَوْنَ بِالسِّنِينَ وَنَقْصٍ مِّنَ الثَّمَرَٰتِ لَعَلَّهُمْ يَذَّكَّرُونَ

131. But whenever good befell them, they said: This is ours; and whenever evil smote them they ascribed it to the evil auspices of Moses and those with him. Surely their evil auspice was only with Allah. But most of them knew not.

۱۳۱ فَإِذَا جَآءَتْهُمُ الْحَسَنَةُ قَالُوا لَنَا هَٰذِهِۦ وَإِن تُصِبْهُمْ سَيِّئَةٌ يَطَّيَّرُوا بِمُوسَىٰ وَمَن مَّعَهُۥٓ أَلَآ إِنَّمَا طَٰٓئِرُهُمْ عِندَ اللَّهِ وَلَٰكِنَّ أَكْثَرَهُمْ لَا يَعْلَمُونَ

132. And they said: Whatever portent you bring wherewith to bewitch us, we shall not put faith in you.

۱۳۲ وَقَالُوا مَهْمَا تَأْتِنَا بِهِۦ مِنْ ءَايَةٍ لِّتَسْحَرَنَا بِهَا فَمَا نَحْنُ لَكَ بِمُؤْمِنِينَ

133. So We sent them the flood and the locusts and the vermin and the frogs and the blood—a succession of clear signs. But they were arrogant and became criminals.

۱۳۳ فَأَرْسَلْنَا عَلَيْهِمُ الطُّوفَانَ وَالْجَرَادَ وَالْقُمَّلَ وَالضَّفَادِعَ وَالدَّمَ ءَايَٰتٍ مُّفَصَّلَٰتٍ فَاسْتَكْبَرُوا وَكَانُوا قَوْمًا مُّجْرِمِينَ

134. And when the terror fell on them they cried: O Moses! Pray for us unto your Lord, because He has a covenant with you. If you remove the terror from us we surely will trust you and will let the Children of Israel go with you.

۱۳۴ وَلَمَّا وَقَعَ عَلَيْهِمُ الرِّجْزُ قَالُوا يَٰمُوسَى ادْعُ لَنَا رَبَّكَ بِمَا عَهِدَ عِندَكَ لَئِن كَشَفْتَ عَنَّا الرِّجْزَ لَنُؤْمِنَنَّ لَكَ وَلَنُرْسِلَنَّ مَعَكَ بَنِىٓ إِسْرَٰٓءِيلَ

135. But when We did remove from them the terror for a term which they must reach, behold! they broke their cove-nant.

۱۳۵ فَلَمَّا كَشَفْنَا عَنْهُمُ الرِّجْزَ إِلَىٰٓ أَجَلٍ هُم بَٰلِغُوهُ إِذَا هُمْ يَنكُثُونَ

136. Therefore We took retribution from them; therefore We drowned them in the sea: because they denied Our revelations and were heedless of them.

۱۳۶ فَانتَقَمْنَا مِنْهُمْ فَأَغْرَقْنَٰهُمْ فِى الْيَمِّ بِأَنَّهُمْ كَذَّبُوا بِـَٔايَٰتِنَا وَكَانُوا عَنْهَا غَٰفِلِينَ

137. And We caused the folk who were despised to inherit the eastern parts of the land and the western parts thereof which We had blessed. And the fair word of your Lord was fulfilled for the Children of Israel because of their endurance; and We annihilated (all) that Pharaoh and his folk had done and that they had contrived.

۱۳۷ وَأَوْرَثْنَا الْقَوْمَ الَّذِينَ كَانُوا يُسْتَضْعَفُونَ مَشَٰرِقَ الْأَرْضِ وَمَغَٰرِبَهَا الَّتِى بَٰرَكْنَا فِيهَا وَتَمَّتْ كَلِمَتُ رَبِّكَ الْحُسْنَىٰ عَلَىٰ بَنِىٓ إِسْرَٰٓءِيلَ بِمَا صَبَرُوا وَدَمَّرْنَا مَا كَانَ يَصْنَعُ فِرْعَوْنُ وَقَوْمُهُۥ وَمَا كَانُوا يَعْرِشُونَ

138. And We brought the Children of Israel across the sea, and they came unto a people who were given up to idols which they had. They said: O Moses! Make for us a god even as they have gods. He said: Lo! you are a folk who know not.

۱۳۸ وَجَاوَزْنَا بِبَنِىٓ إِسْرَٰٓءِيلَ ٱلْبَحْرَ فَأَتَوْا۟ عَلَىٰ قَوْمٍ يَعْكُفُونَ عَلَىٰٓ أَصْنَامٍ لَّهُمْ قَالُوا۟ يَٰمُوسَى ٱجْعَل لَّنَآ إِلَٰهًا كَمَا لَهُمْ ءَالِهَةٌ قَالَ إِنَّكُمْ قَوْمٌ تَجْهَلُونَ

139. Lo! as for these, their way will be destroyed and all that they are doing is in vain.

۱۳۹ إِنَّ هَٰٓؤُلَآءِ مُتَبَّرٌ مَّا هُمْ فِيهِ وَبَٰطِلٌ مَّا كَانُوا۟ يَعْمَلُونَ

140. He said: Shall I seek for you a god other than Allah when He has favored you above (all) creatures?

۱٤۰ قَالَ أَغَيْرَ ٱللَّهِ أَبْغِيكُمْ إِلَٰهًا وَهُوَ فَضَّلَكُمْ عَلَى ٱلْعَٰلَمِينَ

141. And (remember) when We did deliver you from Pharaoh's folk who were afflicting you with dreadful torment, slaughtering your sons and sparing your women. That was a tremendous trial from your Lord.

۱٤۱ وَإِذْ أَنجَيْنَٰكُم مِّنْ ءَالِ فِرْعَوْنَ يَسُومُونَكُمْ سُوٓءَ ٱلْعَذَابِ يُقَتِّلُونَ أَبْنَآءَكُمْ وَيَسْتَحْيُونَ نِسَآءَكُمْ وَفِى ذَٰلِكُم بَلَآءٌ مِّن رَّبِّكُمْ عَظِيمٌ

142. And when We did appoint for Moses thirty nights (of solitude), and added to them ten, and he completed the whole time appointed by his Lord of forty nights; and Moses said unto his brother, Aaron: Take my place among the people. Do right, and follow not the way of mischief-makers.

۱٤۲ ۞ وَوَٰعَدْنَا مُوسَىٰ ثَلَٰثِينَ لَيْلَةً وَأَتْمَمْنَٰهَا بِعَشْرٍ فَتَمَّ مِيقَٰتُ رَبِّهِۦٓ أَرْبَعِينَ لَيْلَةً وَقَالَ مُوسَىٰ لِأَخِيهِ هَٰرُونَ ٱخْلُفْنِى فِى قَوْمِى وَأَصْلِحْ وَلَا تَتَّبِعْ سَبِيلَ ٱلْمُفْسِدِينَ

143. And when Moses came to Our appointed appointed time and his Lord had spoken unto him, he said: My Lord! Show me (Your self), that I may gaze upon You. He said: You will not see Me, but gaze upon the mountain! If it stand still in its place, then you will see Me. And when his Lord revealed (His) glory to the mountain He sent it crashing down. And Moses fell down senseless. And when he awoke he said: Glory unto You! I turn unto You repentant, and I am the first of (true) believers.

۱٤۳ وَلَمَّا جَآءَ مُوسَىٰ لِمِيقَٰتِنَا وَكَلَّمَهُۥ رَبُّهُۥ قَالَ رَبِّ أَرِنِىٓ أَنظُرْ إِلَيْكَ قَالَ لَن تَرَىٰنِى وَلَٰكِنِ ٱنظُرْ إِلَى ٱلْجَبَلِ فَإِنِ ٱسْتَقَرَّ مَكَانَهُۥ فَسَوْفَ تَرَىٰنِى فَلَمَّا تَجَلَّىٰ رَبُّهُۥ لِلْجَبَلِ جَعَلَهُۥ دَكًّا وَخَرَّ مُوسَىٰ صَعِقًا فَلَمَّآ أَفَاقَ قَالَ سُبْحَٰنَكَ تُبْتُ إِلَيْكَ وَأَنَا۠ أَوَّلُ ٱلْمُؤْمِنِينَ

144. He said: O Moses! I have preferred you above mankind by My messages and by My speaking (unto you). So hold that which I have given you, and be among the thankful.

۱٤٤ قَالَ يَٰمُوسَىٰٓ إِنِّى ٱصْطَفَيْتُكَ عَلَى ٱلنَّاسِ بِرِسَٰلَٰتِى وَبِكَلَٰمِى فَخُذْ مَآ ءَاتَيْتُكَ وَكُن مِّنَ ٱلشَّٰكِرِينَ

145. And We wrote for him, upon the tablets, the lesson to be drawn from all things and the explanation of all things, then (bade him): Hold it fast; and command your people (saying): Take the better (course made clear) therein. I shall show you the abode of evil-livers.

146. I shall turn away from My revelations those who magnify themselves wrongfully in the earth, and if they see each token they believe it not, and if they see the way of righteousness they choose it not for (their) way, and if they see the way of error they choose it for (their) way. That is because they deny Our revelations and are used to disregard them.

147. Those who deny Our revelations and the meeting of the Hereafter, their works are fruitless. Are they requited anything save what they used to do?

148. And the folk of Moses, after (he had left them), made of their ornaments, the image of a calf (for their worship), which gave a lowing sound. Did they not see that it spoke not unto them nor guided them to any way? They chose it, and became wrongdoers.

149. And when they feared the consequences thereof and saw that they had gone astray, they said: Unless our Lord have mercy on us and forgive us, we surely are of the lost.

150. And when Moses returned unto his people, angry and grieved, he said: Evil is that (course) which you took after I had left you. Would you hasten on the judgment of your Lord? And he cast down the tablets, and he seized his brother by the head, dragging him toward him. He said: Son of my mother! Lo! the folk did judge me weak and almost killed me. Oh, make not mine enemies to triumph over me and place me not among the evildoers!

151. He said: My Lord! Have mercy on me and on my brother; bring us into Your mercy, You are indeed the Most Merciful of all who show mercy.

﴿١٥١﴾ قَالَ رَبِّ اغْفِرْ لِى وَلِأَخِى وَأَدْخِلْنَا فِى رَحْمَتِكَ وَأَنْتَ أَرْحَمُ الرَّاحِمِينَ

152. Lo! those who chose the calf (for worship), terror from their Lord and humiliation will come upon them in the life of the world. Thus do We requite those who invent a lie.

﴿١٥٢﴾ إِنَّ الَّذِينَ اتَّخَذُوا الْعِجْلَ سَيَنَالُهُمْ غَضَبٌ مِّن رَّبِّهِمْ وَذِلَّةٌ فِى الْحَيَوٰةِ الدُّنْيَا وَكَذَلِكَ نَجْزِى الْمُفْتَرِينَ

153. But those who do ill deeds and afterward repent and believe—lo! for them, afterward, Allah is Forgiving, Merci-ful.

﴿١٥٣﴾ وَالَّذِينَ عَمِلُوا السَّيِّئَاتِ ثُمَّ تَابُوا مِنْ بَعْدِهَا وَءَامَنُوا إِنَّ رَبَّكَ مِنْ بَعْدِهَا لَغَفُورٌ رَّحِيمٌ

154. Then, when the anger of Moses abated, he took up the tablets, and in their inscription there was guidance and mercy for all those who fear their Lord.

﴿١٥٤﴾ وَلَمَّا سَكَتَ عَن مُّوسَى الْغَضَبُ أَخَذَ الْأَلْوَاحَ وَفِى نُسْخَتِهَا هُدًى وَرَحْمَةٌ لِّلَّذِينَ هُمْ لِرَبِّهِمْ يَرْهَبُونَ

155. And Moses chose of his people seventy men for Our appointed time and, when the trembling came on them, he said: My Lord! If you had willed You had destroyed them long before, and me with them. Will you destroy us for that which the foolish among us did? It is but Your trial (of us). You send whom You will astray and guide whom You will. You are our Protecting Friend, therefore forgive us and have mercy on us, You are the Best of all who show forgiveness.

﴿١٥٥﴾ وَاخْتَارَ مُوسَى قَوْمَهُ سَبْعِينَ رَجُلاً لِّمِيقَاتِنَا فَلَمَّا أَخَذَتْهُمُ الرَّجْفَةُ قَالَ رَبِّ لَوْ شِئْتَ أَهْلَكْتَهُم مِّن قَبْلُ وَإِيَّايَ أَتُهْلِكُنَا بِمَا فَعَلَ السُّفَهَاءُ مِنَّا إِنْ هِىَ إِلَّا فِتْنَتُكَ تُضِلُّ بِهَا مَن تَشَاءُ وَتَهْدِى مَن تَشَاءُ أَنتَ وَلِيُّنَا فَاغْفِرْ لَنَا وَارْحَمْنَا وَأَنتَ خَيْرُ الْغَافِرِينَ

156. And ordain for us in this world that which is good, and in the Hereafter (that which is good), Lo! we have turned unto You. He said: I smite with My punish-ment whom I will, and My mercy embraces all things, therefore I shall ordain It for those who ward off (evil) and pay the poor due, and those who believe Our revelations;

﴿١٥٦﴾ ۞ وَاكْتُبْ لَنَا فِى هَذِهِ الدُّنْيَا حَسَنَةً وَفِى الْآخِرَةِ إِنَّا هُدْنَا إِلَيْكَ قَالَ عَذَابِى أُصِيبُ بِهِ مَنْ أَشَاءُ وَرَحْمَتِى وَسِعَتْ كُلَّ شَىْءٍ فَسَأَكْتُبُهَا لِلَّذِينَ يَتَّقُونَ وَيُؤْتُونَ الزَّكَوٰةَ وَالَّذِينَ هُم بِآيَاتِنَا يُؤْمِنُونَ

157. Those who follow the Messenger, the unlettered Prophet, whom they will find described in the Torah and the Gospel (which are) with them. He will enjoin on them that which is right and forbid them that which is wrong. He will make lawful for them all good things and prohibit for them only the foul; and he will relieve them of their burden and the fetters that they used to wear. Then those who believe in him, honor him, help him, and follow the light which is sent down with him: they are the successful.

158. Say (Muhammad): O mankind! Lo! I am the Messenger of Allah to you all—(the Messenger of) Him unto whom belongs the Sovereignty of the heavens and the earth. There is no God save Him. He quickens and He gives death. So believe in Allah and His Messenger, the unlettered[110] Prophet, who believes in Allah and in His words and follow him that you may be led aright.

159. And of Moses' folk there is a community who lead with truth and establish justice therewith.

160. We divided them into twelve tribes, nations; and We inspired Moses, when his people asked him for water, saying: Smite with your staff the rock! And there gushed forth therefrom twelve springs, so that each tribe knew their drinking place. And we caused the white cloud to overshadow them and sent down for them honey and quails (saying): Eat of the good things wherewith We have provided you. They wronged Us not, but they were wont to wrong themselves.

161. And when it was said unto them: Dwell in this township and eat therefrom whence you will, and say "Repentance,"[111] and enter the gate prostrate; We shall forgive you your sins; We shall increase (reward) for the right-doers.

---

[110]I give the usual rendering. Some modern criticism, while not denying the comparative illiteracy of the Prophet, would prefer the rendering "who is not of those who read the Scriptures" or "Gentile."

[111]Surah 2:58, footnote.

162. But those of them who did wrong changed the word which had been told them for another saying, and We sent down upon them wrath from heaven for their wrongdoing.

163. Ask them (O Muhammad) of the township that was by the sea, how they did break the sabbath, how their big fish came unto them visibly upon their sabbath day and on a day when they did not keep sabbath came they not unto them. Thus did We try them for that they were evildoers.

164. And when a community among them said: Why preach you to a folk whom Allah is about to destroy and punish with an awful doom, they said: In order to be free from guilt before your Lord, and that they may ward off (evil).

165. And when they forgot that whereof they had been reminded, We rescued those who forbade wrong, and visited those who did wrong with dreadful punishment because they were evildoers.

166. So when they took pride in that which they had been forbidden, We said unto them: Be you apes despised and loathed!

167. And (remember) when your Lord proclaimed that He would raise against them till the Day of Resurrection those who would lay on them a cruel torment. Lo! surely your Lord is swift in prosecution and lo! verily He is Forgiving, Merciful.

168. And We have sundered them in the earth as (separate) nations. Some of them are righteous, and some far from that. And We have tried them with good things and evil things that haply they might return.

﴿١٦٢﴾ فَبَدَّلَ الَّذِينَ ظَلَمُوا مِنْهُمْ قَوْلًا غَيْرَ الَّذِى قِيلَ لَهُمْ فَأَرْسَلْنَا عَلَيْهِمْ رِجْزًا مِّنَ السَّمَاءِ بِمَا كَانُوا يَظْلِمُونَ

﴿١٦٣﴾ وَسْئَلْهُمْ عَنِ الْقَرْيَةِ الَّتِى كَانَتْ حَاضِرَةَ الْبَحْرِ إِذْ يَعْدُونَ فِى السَّبْتِ إِذْ تَأْتِيهِمْ حِيتَانُهُمْ يَوْمَ سَبْتِهِمْ شُرَّعًا وَيَوْمَ لَا يَسْبِتُونَ لَا تَأْتِيهِمْ كَذَلِكَ نَبْلُوهُمْ بِمَا كَانُوا يَفْسُقُونَ

﴿١٦٤﴾ وَإِذْ قَالَتْ أُمَّةٌ مِّنْهُمْ لِمَ تَعِظُونَ قَوْمًا اللَّهُ مُهْلِكُهُمْ أَوْ مُعَذِّبُهُمْ عَذَابًا شَدِيدًا قَالُوا مَعْذِرَةً إِلَى رَبِّكُمْ وَلَعَلَّهُمْ يَتَّقُونَ

﴿١٦٥﴾ فَلَمَّا نَسُوا مَا ذُكِّرُوا بِهِ أَنجَيْنَا الَّذِينَ يَنْهَوْنَ عَنِ السُّوءِ وَأَخَذْنَا الَّذِينَ ظَلَمُوا بِعَذَابٍ بَئِيسٍ بِمَا كَانُوا يَفْسُقُونَ

﴿١٦٦﴾ فَلَمَّا عَتَوْا عَن مَّا نُهُوا عَنْهُ قُلْنَا لَهُمْ كُونُوا قِرَدَةً خَاسِئِينَ

﴿١٦٧﴾ وَإِذْ تَأَذَّنَ رَبُّكَ لَيَبْعَثَنَّ عَلَيْهِمْ إِلَى يَوْمِ الْقِيَامَةِ مَن يَسُومُهُمْ سُوءَ الْعَذَابِ إِنَّ رَبَّكَ لَسَرِيعُ الْعِقَابِ وَإِنَّهُ لَغَفُورٌ رَّحِيمٌ

﴿١٦٨﴾ وَقَطَّعْنَاهُمْ فِى الْأَرْضِ أُمَمًا مِّنْهُمُ الصَّالِحُونَ وَمِنْهُمْ دُونَ ذَلِكَ وَبَلَوْنَاهُم بِالْحَسَنَاتِ وَالسَّيِّئَاتِ لَعَلَّهُمْ يَرْجِعُونَ

169. And a generation has succeeded them who inherited the Scriptures. They grasp the goods of this low life (as the price of evildoing) and say: It will be forgiven us. And if there came to them (again) the offer of the like, they would accept it (and would sin again). Has not the covenant of the Scripture been taken on their behalf that they should not speak anything concerning Allah save the truth? And they have studied that which is therein. And the abode of the Hereafter is better for those who ward off (evil). Have you then no sense?

170. And as for those who make (men) keep the Scripture, and establish prayer—lo! We squander not the wages of re-formers.

171. And when We shook the Mount above them as it were a covering, ahd they supposed that it was going to fall upon them (and We said): Hold fast that which We have given you, and remember that which is there-in, that you may ward off (evil).

172. And (remember) when your Lord brought forth from the Children of Adam, from their loins, their seed, and made them testify of themselves, (saying): Am I not your Lord? They said: Yea, surely. We testify. (That was) lest you should say on the Day of Resurrection: Lo! of this we were unaware;

173. Or lest you should say: (It is) only (that) our fathers ascribed partners to Allah of old and we were (their) seed after them. Will You destroy us on account of that which those who follow falsehood did?

174. Thus We detail Our revelations, that haply they may return.

175. Recite unto them the tale of him to whom We gave Our revelations, but he sloughed them off, so the Devil overtook him and he became of those who lead astray.

176. And had We willed We could have raised him by their means, but he clung to the earth and followed his own lust. Therefore his likeness is as the likeness of a dog; if you attack him he pants with his tongue out, and if you leave him he pants with his tongue out. Such is the likeness of the people who deny Our revelations. Narrate unto them the history (of the men of old), that they may take thought.

١٦٩ فَخَلَفَ مِنْ بَعْدِهِمْ خَلْفٌ وَرِثُوا الْكِتَابَ يَأْخُذُونَ عَرَضَ هَذَا الْأَدْنَى وَيَقُولُونَ سَيُغْفَرُ لَنَا وَإِنْ يَأْتِهِمْ عَرَضٌ مِثْلُهُ يَأْخُذُوهُ أَلَمْ يُؤْخَذْ عَلَيْهِمْ مِيثَاقُ الْكِتَابِ أَنْ لَا يَقُولُوا عَلَى اللَّهِ إِلَّا الْحَقَّ وَدَرَسُوا مَا فِيهِ وَالدَّارُ الْآخِرَةُ خَيْرٌ لِلَّذِينَ يَتَّقُونَ أَفَلَا تَعْقِلُونَ

١٧٠ وَالَّذِينَ يُمَسِّكُونَ بِالْكِتَابِ وَأَقَامُوا الصَّلَوَةَ إِنَّا لَا نُضِيعُ أَجْرَ الْمُصْلِحِينَ

١٧١ وَإِذْ نَتَقْنَا الْجَبَلَ فَوْقَهُمْ كَأَنَّهُ ظُلَّةٌ وَظَنُّوا أَنَّهُ وَاقِعٌ بِهِمْ خُذُوا مَا آتَيْنَاكُمْ بِقُوَّةٍ وَاذْكُرُوا مَا فِيهِ لَعَلَّكُمْ تَتَّقُونَ

١٧٢ وَإِذْ أَخَذَ رَبُّكَ مِنْ بَنِي آدَمَ مِنْ ظُهُورِهِمْ ذُرِّيَّتَهُمْ وَأَشْهَدَهُمْ عَلَى أَنْفُسِهِمْ أَلَسْتُ بِرَبِّكُمْ قَالُوا بَلَى شَهِدْنَا أَنْ تَقُولُوا يَوْمَ الْقِيَامَةِ إِنَّا كُنَّا عَنْ هَذَا غَافِلِينَ

١٧٣ أَوْ تَقُولُوا إِنَّمَا أَشْرَكَ آبَاؤُنَا مِنْ قَبْلُ وَكُنَّا ذُرِّيَّةً مِنْ بَعْدِهِمْ أَفَتُهْلِكُنَا بِمَا فَعَلَ الْمُبْطِلُونَ

١٧٤ وَكَذَلِكَ نُفَصِّلُ الْآيَاتِ وَلَعَلَّهُمْ يَرْجِعُونَ

١٧٥ وَاتْلُ عَلَيْهِمْ نَبَأَ الَّذِي آتَيْنَاهُ آيَاتِنَا فَانْسَلَخَ مِنْهَا فَأَتْبَعَهُ الشَّيْطَانُ فَكَانَ مِنَ الْغَاوِينَ

١٧٦ وَلَوْ شِئْنَا لَرَفَعْنَاهُ بِهَا وَلَكِنَّهُ أَخْلَدَ إِلَى الْأَرْضِ وَاتَّبَعَ هَوَاهُ فَمَثَلُهُ كَمَثَلِ الْكَلْبِ إِنْ تَحْمِلْ عَلَيْهِ يَلْهَثْ أَوْ تَتْرُكْهُ يَلْهَثْ ذَلِكَ مَثَلُ الْقَوْمِ الَّذِينَ كَذَّبُوا بِآيَاتِنَا فَاقْصُصِ الْقَصَصَ لَعَلَّهُمْ يَتَفَكَّرُونَ

177. Evil as an example are the folk who denied Our revelations, and were wont to wrong themselves.

178. He who Allah guides, he indeed is led aright, while he whom Allah sends astray they indeed are losers.

179. Already have We urged unto Hell many of the jinn and humankind, having hearts wherewith they understand not, and having eyes wherewith they see not, and having ears wherewith they hear not. These are as the cattle—nay, but they are worse! These are the neglectful.

180. Allah's are the fairest names. Invoke Him by them. And leave the company of those who blaspheme His names. They will be requited what they do.

181. And of those whom We created there is a nation who guide with the Truth and establish justice therewith.

182. And those who deny Our revelations—step by step We lead them on from whence they know not.

183. I give them rein (for) lo! My scheme is strong.

184. Have they not bethought them (that) there is no madness in their comrade? He is but a plain warner.

185. Have they not considered the dominion of the heavens and the earth, and what things Allah has created, and that it may be that their own term draws near? In what fact after this will they believe?

186. Those whom Allah sends astray, there is no guide for them. He leaves them to wander blindly on in their contumacy.

187. They ask you of the (destined) Hour, when will it come to port. Say: Knowledge thereof is with my Lord only. He alone will manifest it at its proper time. It is heavy in the heavens and the earth. It comes not to you save unawares. They question you as if you could be well informed thereof. Say: Knowledge thereof is with Allah only, but most of man-kind know not.

188. Say: For myself I have no power to benefit, nor power to hurt, save that which Allah wills. Had I knowledge of the Unseen, I should have abundance of wealth, and adversity would not touch me. I am but a warner, and a bearer of good tidings unto folk who believe.

189. He it is who did create you from a single soul, and therefrom did make his mate that he might take rest in her. And when he covered her she bore a light burden, and she passed (unnoticed) with it, but when it became heavy they cried unto Allah, their Lord, saying: If you give unto us aright we shall be of the thankful.

190. But when He gave unto them aright, they ascribed unto Him partners in respect of that which He had given them. High is He exalted above all that they associate (with Him).

191. Attribute they as partners to Allah those who created nothing, but are themselves created,

192. And cannot give them help, nor can they help themselves?

193. And if you call them to the Guidance, they follow you not. Whether you call them or are silent is all one to them.

194. Lo! those on whom you call beside Allah are slaves like unto you. Call on them now, and let them answer you, if you are truthful!

وَسْتُلُونَكَ عَنِ السَّاعَةِ أَيَّانَ مُرْسَىٰهَا قُلْ إِنَّمَا عِلْمُهَا عِندَ رَبِّى لَا يُجَلِّيهَا لِوَقْتِهَا إِلَّا هُوَ ثَقُلَتْ فِى السَّمَٰوَٰتِ وَالْأَرْضِ لَا تَأْتِيكُمْ إِلَّا بَغْتَةً يَسْتُلُونَكَ كَأَنَّكَ حَفِىٌّ عَنْهَا قُلْ إِنَّمَا عِلْمُهَا عِندَ اللَّهِ وَلَٰكِنَّ أَكْثَرَ النَّاسِ لَا يَعْلَمُونَ ۝

قُل لَّا أَمْلِكُ لِنَفْسِى نَفْعًا وَلَا ضَرًّا إِلَّا مَا شَاءَ اللَّهُ وَلَوْ كُنتُ أَعْلَمُ الْغَيْبَ لَاسْتَكْثَرْتُ مِنَ الْخَيْرِ وَمَا مَسَّنِىَ السُّوٓءُ إِنْ أَنَا۠ إِلَّا نَذِيرٌ وَبَشِيرٌ لِّقَوْمٍ يُؤْمِنُونَ ۝

هُوَ الَّذِى خَلَقَكُم مِّن نَّفْسٍ وَٰحِدَةٍ وَجَعَلَ مِنْهَا زَوْجَهَا لِيَسْكُنَ إِلَيْهَا فَلَمَّا تَغَشَّىٰهَا حَمَلَتْ حَمْلًا خَفِيفًا فَمَرَّتْ بِهِ فَلَمَّا أَثْقَلَت دَّعَوَا اللَّهَ رَبَّهُمَا لَئِنْ ءَاتَيْتَنَا صَٰلِحًا لَّنَكُونَنَّ مِنَ الشَّٰكِرِينَ ۝

فَلَمَّا ءَاتَىٰهُمَا صَٰلِحًا جَعَلَا لَهُ شُرَكَآءَ فِيمَا ءَاتَىٰهُمَا فَتَعَٰلَى اللَّهُ عَمَّا يُشْرِكُونَ ۝

أَيُشْرِكُونَ مَا لَا يَخْلُقُ شَيْئًا وَهُمْ يُخْلَقُونَ ۝

وَلَا يَسْتَطِيعُونَ لَهُمْ نَصْرًا وَلَا أَنفُسَهُمْ يَنصُرُونَ ۝

وَإِن تَدْعُوهُمْ إِلَى الْهُدَىٰ لَا يَتَّبِعُوكُمْ سَوَآءٌ عَلَيْكُمْ أَدَعَوْتُمُوهُمْ أَمْ أَنتُمْ صَٰمِتُونَ ۝

إِنَّ الَّذِينَ تَدْعُونَ مِن دُونِ اللَّهِ عِبَادٌ أَمْثَالُكُمْ فَادْعُوهُمْ فَلْيَسْتَجِيبُوا لَكُمْ إِن كُنتُمْ صَٰدِقِينَ ۝

195. Have they feet wherewith they walk, or have they hands wherewith they hold, or have they eyes wherewith they see, or have they ears wherewith they hear? Say: Call upon your (so called) partners (of Allah), and then contrive against me, spare me not!

196. Lo! my Protecting Friend is Allah who reveals the Scripture. He befriends the righteous.

197. They on whom you call beside Him have no power to help you, nor can they help themselves.

198. And if you (Muslims) call them to the Guidance they hear not; and you (Muhammad) see them looking toward you, but they see not.

199. Keep to forgiveness (O Muhammad), and enjoin kindness, and turn away from the ignorant.

200. And if a slander from the Devil wound you, then seek refuge in Allah. Lo! He is Hearer, Knower.

201. Lo! those who ward off (evil), when a glamour from the Devil troubles them, they do but remember (Allah's guidance) and behold them seers!

202. Their brothers plunge them further into error and cease not.

203. And when you bring not a verse for them they say: Why have you not chosen it? Say: I follow only that which is inspired in me from my Lord. This (Qur'an) is insight from your Lord, and a guidance and a mercy for a people that believe.

204. And when the Qur'an is recited, give ear to it and pay heed, that you may obtain mercy.

205. And do you [O Muhammad] remember your Lord within yourself humbly and with awe, below your breath, at morn and evening. And be you not of the neglectful.

206. Lo! those who are with your Lord are not too proud to do Him worship, but they glorify Him and to Him they prostrate.

The Spoils of War

Al Anfāl, "The Spoils," takes its name from the first verse, which proclaims that property acquired during war belongs "to Allah and His Messenger,"—that is to say, to the theocratic state, and is to be used for the common welfare. The date of the surah's revelation has been established, based on the nature of its contents, to be sometime between the battle of Badr and the division of the spoils—a space of one month during the year 2 AH. The concluding verses are of later date and lead up to the subject of the ninth surah.

A Makkan caravan was returning from Syria. Its leader, Abū Sufyān, feared an attack from al Madinah and therefore sent a rider to Makkah with a frantic appeal for help. This must have come too late if, considering the distances involved and the claim even by some Muslim writers, that the Prophet had always intended to attack the caravan. Ibn Isḥāq (Ibn Hishām), when dealing with the Tabūk expedition, says that the Prophet announced the destination, which was a departure from his usual practice of concealing the real objective.

Was not the real objective hidden in this first campaign? It is a fact that he advanced only when the army sent to protect the caravan, or rather—probably—to punish the Muslims for having threatened it, was approaching al Madinah. His little army of three hundred and thirteen ill-armed and roughly equipped men traversed the desert for three days, halting only when they were near the water of Badr. There, they learned that the Qurayshī army was approaching on the other side of the valley. Rain began to fall heavily on the Quraysh, and the resulting muddy ground made it impossible for them to advance any further. The Muslims took advantage of this situation and secured the water. At the same time, Abū Sufyān, whose caravan was also heading for the water of Badr, was warned of the Muslim advance by a scout and thus turned back to the coastal plain. Before the battle against what must have seemed to be overwhelming odds, the Prophet gave the Anṣār (the men of al Madinah whose oath of allegiance had not included participating in actual warfare) the chance of returning if they wished. The mere suggestion that they could possibly forsake him hurt them. On the other hand, several men of Quraysh, including the whole Zuhrī clan, returned to Makkah when they heard that the caravan was safe. They held no grudge against the Prophet and his followers, whom they regarded as men who had been wronged.

Still, the Qurayshī army outnumbered the Muslims by more than two to one and was much better mounted and equipped. Therefore its leaders expected an easy victory. When the Prophet saw them streaming down the sandhills, he cried: "O Allah! Here are the Quraysh with all their chivalry and pomp, who oppose You and deny Your messenger. O Allah! Your help which You have promised me! O Allah! Make them bow this day!"

Although the Muslims were successful in the single combat with which Arab battles opened, the real battle at first went hard against them. The Prophet stood and prayed under a shelter that had been constructed to screen him from the sun: "O Allah! If this little company is destroyed, there will be none left in the land to worship You." Then he fell into a trance and, when he spoke again, informed Abu Bakr, who was with him, that the promised help had come. Thereupon he went out to encourage his people. Taking up a handful of gravel, he ran towards the Quraysh and flung it at them, saying: "The faces are confounded!" The tide of battle now turned in favor of the Muslims. The Quraysh's leader and several of its greatest men were killed, many were taken prisoner, and their baggage and camels were captured by the Muslims.

It was indeed a day to be remembered in the early history of Islam, and there was great rejoicing in al Madinah. However, the Muslims are warned that this is only the beginning of their struggle against heavy odds. In fact, in the following year at Mt. Uhud (referred to in the third surah), the enemy took the field with an army of three thousand. In the year 5 AH, a ten-thousand-man strong allied army of the pagan clans besieged al Madinah in the "War of the Trench" (see Surah 33, "The Clans").

The date of revelation is primarily the year 2 AH. Some reliable Arabic authorities maintain that verses 30-40, or some of them, were revealed at Makkah just before the Hijrah.

SPOILS OF WAR

Revealed at al Madinah

In the name of Allah,
the Beneficent, the Merciful.

1. They ask you (O Muhammad) of the spoils of war. Say: The spoils of war belong to Allah and the Messenger, so keep your duty to Allah, and adjust the matter of your difference, and obey Allah and His Messenger, if you are (true) believers.

2. They only are the (true) believers whose hearts feel fear when Allah is mentioned, and when the revelations of Allah are recited unto them they increase their faith, and who trust in their Lord;

3. Who establish prayer and spend of that We have be-stowed on them.

4. Those are they who are in truth believers. For them are grades (of honor) with their Lord, and pardon, and a bountiful provision.

5. Even as your Lord caused you (Muhammad) to go forth from your home with the Truth, and lo! a party of the believers were averse (to it),

6. Disputing with you of the Truth after it had been made manifest, as if they were being driven to death visible.

7. And when Allah promised you one of the two bands[112] (of the enemy) that it should be yours, and you longed that other than the armed one might be yours. And Allah willed that He should cause the Truth to triumph by His words, and cut the root of the disbelievers;

8. That He might cause the Truth to triumph and bring vanity to nothing, however much the criminals might oppose;

---

[112]Either the army or the caravan.

9. When you sought help of your Lord and He answered you (saying): I will help you with a thousand of the angels, rank on rank.

10. Allah appointed it only as good tidings, and that your hearts thereby might be at rest. Victory comes only by the help of Allah. Lo! Allah is Mighty, Wise.

11. When he made the slumber fall upon you as a reassurance from Him and sent down water from the sky upon you, that thereby He might purify you, and remove from you the fear of the Devil, and make strong your hearts and firm (your) feet thereby.

12. When your Lord inspired the angels, (saying:) I am with you. So make those who believe stand firm. I will throw fear into the hearts of those who disbelieve. Then smite above the necks and smite of them each finger.

13. That is because they opposed Allah and His Messenger. Who opposes Allah and His Messenger, (for him) lo! Allah is severe in punishment.

14. That (is the award), so taste it, and (know) that for disbelievers is the torment of the Fire.

15. O you who believe! When you meet those who disbelieve in battle, turn not your backs to them.

16. Who on that day turns his back to them, unless maneuvering for battle or intent to join a company, he truly has incurred wrath from Allah, and his habitation will be Hell, a hapless journey's end.

17. You (Muslims) slew them not, but Allah slew them. And you (Muhammad) threw not when you did throw, but Allah threw, that He might test the believers by a fair test from Him. Lo! Allah is Hearer, Knower.

18. That (is the case); and (know) that Allah (it is) who makes weak the plan of disbelievers.

٩- إِذْ تَسْتَغِيثُونَ رَبَّكُمْ فَاسْتَجَابَ لَكُمْ أَنِّي مُمِدُّكُم بِأَلْفٍ مِّنَ الْمَلَائِكَةِ مُرْدِفِينَ

١٠- وَمَا جَعَلَهُ اللَّهُ إِلَّا بُشْرَىٰ وَلِتَطْمَئِنَّ بِهِ قُلُوبُكُمْ وَمَا النَّصْرُ إِلَّا مِنْ عِندِ اللَّهِ إِنَّ اللَّهَ عَزِيزٌ حَكِيمٌ

١١- إِذْ يُغَشِّيكُمُ النُّعَاسَ أَمَنَةً مِّنْهُ وَيُنَزِّلُ عَلَيْكُم مِّنَ السَّمَاءِ مَاءً لِّيُطَهِّرَكُم بِهِ وَيُذْهِبَ عَنكُمْ رِجْزَ الشَّيْطَانِ وَلِيَرْبِطَ عَلَىٰ قُلُوبِكُمْ وَيُثَبِّتَ بِهِ الْأَقْدَامَ

١٢- إِذْ يُوحِي رَبُّكَ إِلَى الْمَلَائِكَةِ أَنِّي مَعَكُمْ فَثَبِّتُوا الَّذِينَ آمَنُوا سَأُلْقِي فِي قُلُوبِ الَّذِينَ كَفَرُوا الرُّعْبَ فَاضْرِبُوا فَوْقَ الْأَعْنَاقِ وَاضْرِبُوا مِنْهُمْ كُلَّ بَنَانٍ

١٣- ذَٰلِكَ بِأَنَّهُمْ شَاقُّوا اللَّهَ وَرَسُولَهُ وَمَن يُشَاقِقِ اللَّهَ وَرَسُولَهُ فَإِنَّ اللَّهَ شَدِيدُ الْعِقَابِ

١٤- ذَٰلِكُمْ فَذُوقُوهُ وَأَنَّ لِلْكَافِرِينَ عَذَابَ النَّارِ

١٥- يَا أَيُّهَا الَّذِينَ آمَنُوا إِذَا لَقِيتُمُ الَّذِينَ كَفَرُوا زَحْفًا فَلَا تُوَلُّوهُمُ الْأَدْبَارَ

١٦- وَمَن يُوَلِّهِمْ يَوْمَئِذٍ دُبُرَهُ إِلَّا مُتَحَرِّفًا لِّقِتَالٍ أَوْ مُتَحَيِّزًا إِلَىٰ فِئَةٍ فَقَدْ بَاءَ بِغَضَبٍ مِّنَ اللَّهِ وَمَأْوَاهُ جَهَنَّمُ وَبِئْسَ الْمَصِيرُ

١٧- فَلَمْ تَقْتُلُوهُمْ وَلَٰكِنَّ اللَّهَ قَتَلَهُمْ وَمَا رَمَيْتَ إِذْ رَمَيْتَ وَلَٰكِنَّ اللَّهَ رَمَىٰ وَلِيُبْلِيَ الْمُؤْمِنِينَ مِنْهُ بَلَاءً حَسَنًا إِنَّ اللَّهَ سَمِيعٌ عَلِيمٌ

١٨- ذَٰلِكُمْ وَأَنَّ اللَّهَ مُوهِنُ كَيْدِ الْكَافِرِينَ

19. (O Quraysh!) If you sought a judgment, now has the judgment come unto you. And if you cease (from persecuting believers) it will be better for you, but if you return (to the attack) We also shall return. And your host will avail you not, however numerous it be, and (know) that Allah is with the believers (in His guidance).

20. O you who believe! Obey Allah and His Messenger, and turn not away from him when you hear (him speak).

21. Be not as those who say, We hear, and they hear not.

22. Lo! the worst of beasts in Allah's sight are the deaf, the dumb, who have no sense.

23. Had Allah Known of any good in them He would have made them hear, but had He made them hear they would have turned away, averse.

24. O you who believe; Answer Allah, and the Messenger when He calls you to that which quickens you, and know that Allah comes in between the man and his own heart, and that He it is unto Whom you will be gathered.

25. And guard yourselves against a chastisement which cannot fall exclusively on those of you who are wrong-doers, and know that Allah is severe in punishment.

26. And remember, when you were few and reckoned feeble in the land, and were in fear lest men should extirpate you, how He gave you refuge, and strengthened you with His help, and made provision of good things for you, that you might be thankful.

27. O you who believe! Betray not Allah and the Messen-ger, nor knowing-ly betray your trusts.

28. And know that your possessions and your children are a test, and that with Allah is immense reward.

29. O you who believe! If you keep your duty to Allah, He will make a criterion for you (to distinguish between right and wrong) and will rid you of your sins, and will forgive you. Allah is of infinite bounty.

30. And when those who disbelieve plot against you (O Muhammad) to keep you in bonds, or to kill you or to drive you forth; they plot, but Allah (also) plots; and Allah is the best of plotters.

31. And when Our revelations are recited unto them they say: We have heard. If we wish we can speak the like of this. Lo! this is nothing but fables of the men of old.

32. And when they said: O Allah! If this be indeed the truth from You, then rain down stones on us or bring on us some painful doom!

33. But Allah would not punish them while you were with them, nor will He punish them while they seek forgiveness.

34. What (plea) have they that Allah should not punish them, when they debar (His servants) from the Sacred Mosque, though they are not its fitting guardians. Its fitting guardians are those only who keep their duty to Allah. But most of them know not.

35. And their worship at the (holy) House is nothing but whistling and hand clapping. Therefore (it is said unto them): Taste of the doom because you disbelieve.

36. Lo! those who disbelieve spend their wealth in order that they may debar (men) from the way of Allah. They will spend it, then it will become an anguish for them, then they will be conquered. And those who disbelieve will be gathered unto Hell,

37. That Allah may separate the wicked from the good. The wicked will He place piece upon piece, and heap them all together, and consign them unto Hell. Such verily are the losers.

38. Tell those who disbelieve that if they cease (from persecution of believers) that which is past will be forgiven them; but if they return (thereto) then the example of the men of old has already gone (before them, for a warning).

39. And fight them until persecution is no more, and religion is all for Allah. But if they cease, then lo! Allah is Seer of what they do.

40. And if they turn away, then know that Allah is your Befriender—a transcendent Patron, a transcendent Helper!

41. And know that whatever you take as spoils of war, lo! a fifth thereof is for Allah, and for the Messenger[113] and for the kinsmen (who have need) and the orphans and the needy and the wayfarer; if you believe in Allah and that which We revealed unto Our slave on the Day of Discrimination, the day when the two armies met. And Allah is Able to do all things.

42. When you were on the near bank (of the valley) and they were on the farther bank, and the caravan was below you (on the coast plain). And had you tried to meet one another you surely would have failed to keep the trial, but (it happened as it did without the forethought of either of you) that Allah might conclude a thing that must be done; that he who perished (on that day) might perish by a clear proof (of His sovereignty) and he who survived might survive by a clear proof (of His sovereignty). Lo! Allah in truth is Hearer, Knower.

43. When Allah showed them unto you (O Muhammad) in your dream as few in number, and if He had shown them to you as many, you (Muslims) would have faltered and would have quarreled over the affair. But Allah saved (you). Lo! He knows what is in the breasts (of men).

---

[113]I.e., for the state, to be used for the common welfare.

44. And when He made you (Muslims), when you met (them), see them with your eyes as few, and lessened you in their eyes, (it was) that Allah might conclude a thing that must be done. Unto Allah all things are brought back.

45. O you who believe! When you meet an army, hold firm and remember Allah much, that you may be successful.

46. And obey Allah and His Messenger, and dispute not one with another lest you falter and your strength depart from you; but be steadfast! Lo! Allah is with the steadfast.

47. Be not as those who came forth from their dwellings boastfully and to be seen of men, and debar (men) from the way of Allah, while Allah is surrounding all they do.

48. And when the Devil made their deeds seem fair to them and said: No one of mankind can conquer you this day, for I am your protector. But when the armies came in sight of one another, he took flight, saying: Lo! I am clear of you. Lo! I see that which you see not. Lo! I fear Allah. And Allah is severe in punishment.

49. When the hypocrites and those in whose hearts is a disease said: Their religion has deluded these. Who puts his trust in Allah (will find that) lo! Allah is Mighty, Wise.

50. If you could see how the angels receive those who disbelieve, smiting their faces and their backs and (saying): Taste the punishment of burning!

51. This is for that which your own hands have sent before (to the Judgment), and (know) that Allah is not a tyrant to His slaves.

٤٤ وَإِذْ يُرِيكُمُوهُمْ إِذِ ٱلْتَقَيْتُمْ فِىٓ أَعْيُنِكُمْ قَلِيلًا وَيُقَلِّلُكُمْ فِىٓ أَعْيُنِهِمْ لِيَقْضِىَ ٱللَّهُ أَمْرًا كَانَ مَفْعُولًا وَإِلَى ٱللَّهِ تُرْجَعُ ٱلْأُمُورُ

٤٥ يَٰٓأَيُّهَا ٱلَّذِينَ ءَامَنُوٓا إِذَا لَقِيتُمْ فِئَةً فَٱثْبُتُوا وَٱذْكُرُوا ٱللَّهَ كَثِيرًا لَّعَلَّكُمْ تُفْلِحُونَ

٤٦ وَأَطِيعُوا ٱللَّهَ وَرَسُولَهُۥ وَلَا تَنَٰزَعُوا فَتَفْشَلُوا وَتَذْهَبَ رِيحُكُمْ وَٱصْبِرُوٓا إِنَّ ٱللَّهَ مَعَ ٱلصَّٰبِرِينَ

٤٧ وَلَا تَكُونُوا كَٱلَّذِينَ خَرَجُوا مِن دِيَٰرِهِم بَطَرًا وَرِئَآءَ ٱلنَّاسِ وَيَصُدُّونَ عَن سَبِيلِ ٱللَّهِ وَٱللَّهُ بِمَا يَعْمَلُونَ مُحِيطٌ

٤٨ وَإِذْ زَيَّنَ لَهُمُ ٱلشَّيْطَٰنُ أَعْمَٰلَهُمْ وَقَالَ لَا غَالِبَ لَكُمُ ٱلْيَوْمَ مِنَ ٱلنَّاسِ وَإِنِّى جَارٌ لَّكُمْ فَلَمَّا تَرَآءَتِ ٱلْفِئَتَانِ نَكَصَ عَلَىٰ عَقِبَيْهِ وَقَالَ إِنِّى بَرِىٓءٌ مِّنكُمْ إِنِّىٓ أَرَىٰ مَا لَا تَرَوْنَ إِنِّىٓ أَخَافُ ٱللَّهَ وَٱللَّهُ شَدِيدُ ٱلْعِقَابِ

٤٩ إِذْ يَقُولُ ٱلْمُنَٰفِقُونَ وَٱلَّذِينَ فِى قُلُوبِهِم مَّرَضٌ غَرَّ هَٰٓؤُلَآءِ دِينُهُمْ وَمَن يَتَوَكَّلْ عَلَى ٱللَّهِ فَإِنَّ ٱللَّهَ عَزِيزٌ حَكِيمٌ

٥٠ وَلَوْ تَرَىٰٓ إِذْ يَتَوَفَّى ٱلَّذِينَ كَفَرُوا ٱلْمَلَٰٓئِكَةُ يَضْرِبُونَ وُجُوهَهُمْ وَأَدْبَٰرَهُمْ وَذُوقُوا عَذَابَ ٱلْحَرِيقِ

٥١ ذَٰلِكَ بِمَا قَدَّمَتْ أَيْدِيكُمْ وَأَنَّ ٱللَّهَ لَيْسَ بِظَلَّٰمٍ لِّلْعَبِيدِ

52. (Their way is) as the way of Pharaoh's folk and those before them; they disbelieved the revelations of Allah, and Allah took them in their sins. Lo! Allah is Strong, severe in punishment.

53. That is because Allah never changes the grace He has bestowed on any people until they first change that which is in their hearts, and (that is) because Allah is Hearer, Knower.

54. (Their way is) as the way of Pharaoh's folk and those before them; they denied the revelations of their Lord, so We destroyed them in their sins. And We drowned the folk of Pharaoh. All were evildoers.

55. Lo! the worst of beasts in Allah's sight are the ungrateful who will not believe;

56. Those of them with whom you made a treaty, and, then at every opportunity they break their treaty, and they have no fear (of Allah).

57. If you come on them in the war, deal with them so as to strike fear in those who are behind them, that they may remember.

58. And if you fear treachery from any folk, then throw back to them (their treaty) fairly. Lo! Allah loves not the treacherous.

59. And let not those who disbelieve suppose that they can outstrip (Allah's purpose). Lo! they cannot escape.

60. Make ready for them all you can of (armed) force and of horses tethered, that thereby you may dismay the enemy of Allah and your enemy, and others beside them whom you know not. Allah knows them. Whatsoever you spend in the way of Allah it will be repaid to you in full, and you will not be wronged.

٥٢ كَدَأْبِ ءَالِ فِرْعَوْنَ وَالَّذِينَ مِن قَبْلِهِمْ كَفَرُوا بِـَٔايَـٰتِ اللَّهِ فَأَخَذَهُمُ اللَّهُ بِذُنُوبِهِمْ إِنَّ اللَّهَ قَوِيٌّ شَدِيدُ الْعِقَابِ

٥٣ ذَٰلِكَ بِأَنَّ اللَّهَ لَمْ يَكُ مُغَيِّرًا نِّعْمَةً أَنْعَمَهَا عَلَىٰ قَوْمٍ حَتَّىٰ يُغَيِّرُوا مَا بِأَنفُسِهِمْ وَأَنَّ اللَّهَ سَمِيعٌ عَلِيمٌ

٥٤ كَدَأْبِ ءَالِ فِرْعَوْنَ وَالَّذِينَ مِن قَبْلِهِمْ كَذَّبُوا بِـَٔايَـٰتِ رَبِّهِمْ فَأَهْلَكْنَهُم بِذُنُوبِهِمْ وَأَغْرَقْنَا ءَالَ فِرْعَوْنَ وَكُلٌّ كَانُوا ظَٰلِمِينَ

٥٥ إِنَّ شَرَّ الدَّوَابِّ عِندَ اللَّهِ الَّذِينَ كَفَرُوا فَهُمْ لَا يُؤْمِنُونَ

٥٦ الَّذِينَ عَٰهَدتَّ مِنْهُمْ ثُمَّ يَنقُضُونَ عَهْدَهُمْ فِي كُلِّ مَرَّةٍ وَهُمْ لَا يَتَّقُونَ

٥٧ فَإِمَّا تَثْقَفَنَّهُمْ فِي الْحَرْبِ فَشَرِّدْ بِهِم مَّنْ خَلْفَهُمْ لَعَلَّهُمْ يَذَّكَّرُونَ

٥٨ وَإِمَّا تَخَافَنَّ مِن قَوْمٍ خِيَانَةً فَانبِذْ إِلَيْهِمْ عَلَىٰ سَوَاءٍ إِنَّ اللَّهَ لَا يُحِبُّ الْخَائِنِينَ

٥٩ وَلَا يَحْسَبَنَّ الَّذِينَ كَفَرُوا سَبَقُوا إِنَّهُمْ لَا يُعْجِزُونَ

٦٠ وَأَعِدُّوا لَهُم مَّا اسْتَطَعْتُم مِّن قُوَّةٍ وَمِن رِّبَاطِ الْخَيْلِ تُرْهِبُونَ بِهِ عَدُوَّ اللَّهِ وَعَدُوَّكُمْ وَءَاخَرِينَ مِن دُونِهِمْ لَا تَعْلَمُونَهُمُ اللَّهُ يَعْلَمُهُمْ وَمَا تُنفِقُوا مِن شَيْءٍ فِي سَبِيلِ اللَّهِ يُوَفَّ إِلَيْكُمْ وَأَنتُمْ لَا تُظْلَمُونَ

61. And if they incline to peace, incline you also to it, and trust in Allah. Lo! He is the Hearer, the Knower.

62. And if they would deceive you, then lo! Allah is sufficient for you. He it is Who supports you with His help and with the believers,

63. And (as for the believers) has attuned their hearts. If you had spent all that is in the earth you could not have attuned their hearts, but Allah has attuned them. Lo! He is Mighty, Wise.

64. O Prophet! Allah is sufficient for you and those who follow you of the believers.

65. O Prophet! Exhort the believers to fight. If there be of you twenty steadfast they shall overcome two hundred, and if there be of you a hundred steadfast they shall overcome a thousand of those who disbelieve, because they (the disbelievers) are a folk without intelligence.

66. Now has Allah lightened your burden, for He knows that there is weakness in you. So if there be of you a steadfast hundred they shall overcome two hundred, and if there be of you a thousand (steadfast) they shall overcome two thousand by permission of Allah. Allah is with the steadfast.

67. It is not for any prophet to have captives until he has made slaughter in the land. You desire the lure of this world and Allah desires (for you) the Hereafter, and Allah is Mighty, Wise.

68. Had it not been for an ordinance of Allah which had gone before, an awful doom had come upon you on account of what you took.

69. Now eat of what you have won, as lawful and good, and keep your duty to Allah. Lo! Allah is Forgiving, Mer-ciful.[114]

٦١ ۞ وَإِن جَنَحُوا لِلسَّلْمِ فَاجْنَحْ لَهَا وَتَوَكَّلْ عَلَى اللّٰهِ إِنَّهُ هُوَ السَّمِيعُ الْعَلِيمُ

٦٢ وَإِن يُرِيدُوٓا أَن يَخْدَعُوكَ فَإِنَّ حَسْبَكَ اللّٰهُ هُوَ الَّذِىٓ أَيَّدَكَ بِنَصْرِهِۦ وَبِالْمُؤْمِنِينَ

٦٣ وَأَلَّفَ بَيْنَ قُلُوبِهِمْ لَوْ أَنفَقْتَ مَا فِى الْأَرْضِ جَمِيعًا مَّآ أَلَّفْتَ بَيْنَ قُلُوبِهِمْ وَلَٰكِنَّ اللّٰهَ أَلَّفَ بَيْنَهُمْ إِنَّهُۥ عَزِيزٌ حَكِيمٌ

٦٤ يَٰٓأَيُّهَا النَّبِىُّ حَسْبُكَ اللّٰهُ وَمَنِ اتَّبَعَكَ مِنَ الْمُؤْمِنِينَ

٦٥ يَٰٓأَيُّهَا النَّبِىُّ حَرِّضِ الْمُؤْمِنِينَ عَلَى الْقِتَالِ إِن يَكُن مِّنكُمْ عِشْرُونَ صَٰبِرُونَ يَغْلِبُوا مِائَتَيْنِ وَإِن يَكُن مِّنكُم مِّائَةٌ يَغْلِبُوٓا أَلْفًا مِّنَ الَّذِينَ كَفَرُوا بِأَنَّهُمْ قَوْمٌ لَّا يَفْقَهُونَ

٦٦ الْـَٰٔنَ خَفَّفَ اللّٰهُ عَنكُمْ وَعَلِمَ أَنَّ فِيكُمْ ضَعْفًا فَإِن يَكُن مِّنكُم مِّائَةٌ صَابِرَةٌ يَغْلِبُوا مِائَتَيْنِ وَإِن يَكُن مِّنكُمْ أَلْفٌ يَغْلِبُوٓا أَلْفَيْنِ بِإِذْنِ اللّٰهِ وَاللّٰهُ مَعَ الصَّٰبِرِينَ

٦٧ مَا كَانَ لِنَبِىٍّ أَن يَكُونَ لَهُۥٓ أَسْرَىٰ حَتَّىٰ يُثْخِنَ فِى الْأَرْضِ تُرِيدُونَ عَرَضَ الدُّنْيَا وَاللّٰهُ يُرِيدُ الْءَاخِرَةَ وَاللّٰهُ عَزِيزٌ حَكِيمٌ

٦٨ لَّوْلَا كِتَٰبٌ مِّنَ اللّٰهِ سَبَقَ لَمَسَّكُمْ فِيمَآ أَخَذْتُمْ عَذَابٌ عَظِيمٌ

٦٩ فَكُلُوا مِمَّا غَنِمْتُمْ حَلَٰلًا طَيِّبًا وَاتَّقُوا اللّٰهَ إِنَّ اللّٰهَ غَفُورٌ رَّحِيمٌ

---

[114]Verses 67-69 were revealed when the Prophet had decided to spare the prisoners taken at Badr and hold them to ransom, against the wish of 'Umar, who would have executed them for their past crimes. The Prophet took the verses as a reproof, and they are generally understood to mean that no quarter ought to have been given in that first battle.

70. O Prophet, Say unto those captives who are in your hands: If Allah knows any good in your hearts He will give you better than that which has been taken from you, and will forgive you. Lo! Allah is Forgiving, Merciful.

71. And if they would betray you, they betrayed Allah before, and He gave (you) power over them. Allah is Knower, Wise.

72. Lo! those who believed and left their homes and strove with their wealth and their lives for the cause of Allah, and those who took them in and helped them; these are protecting friends one of another. And those who believed but did not leave their homes, you have no duty to protect them till they leave their homes; but if they seek help from you in the matter of religion then it is your duty to help (them) except against a folk between whom and you there is a treaty. Allah is Seer of what you do.

73. And those who disbelieve are protectors one of another: If you do not do so, there will be mischief in the land, and great corruption.

74. Those who believed and left their homes and strove for the cause of Allah, and those who took them in and helped them these are the believers in truth. For them is pardon, and a bountiful provision.

75. And those who afterwards believed and left their homes and strove along with you, they are of you; and those who are akin are nearer one to another in the ordinance of Allah. Lo! Allah is Knower of all things.

٧٠ يَـٰٓأَيُّهَا ٱلنَّبِىُّ قُل لِّمَن فِىٓ أَيْدِيكُم مِّنَ ٱلْأَسْرَىٰٓ إِن يَعْلَمِ ٱللَّهُ فِى قُلُوبِكُمْ خَيْرًا يُؤْتِكُمْ خَيْرًا مِّمَّآ أُخِذَ مِنكُمْ وَيَغْفِرْ لَكُمْ وَٱللَّهُ غَفُورٌ رَّحِيمٌ

٧١ وَإِن يُرِيدُوا۟ خِيَانَتَكَ فَقَدْ خَانُوا۟ ٱللَّهَ مِن قَبْلُ فَأَمْكَنَ مِنْهُمْ وَٱللَّهُ عَلِيمٌ حَكِيمٌ

٧٢ إِنَّ ٱلَّذِينَ ءَامَنُوا۟ وَهَاجَرُوا۟ وَجَٰهَدُوا۟ بِأَمْوَٰلِهِمْ وَأَنفُسِهِمْ فِى سَبِيلِ ٱللَّهِ وَٱلَّذِينَ ءَاوَوا۟ وَّنَصَرُوٓا۟ أُو۟لَٰٓئِكَ بَعْضُهُمْ أَوْلِيَآءُ بَعْضٍ وَٱلَّذِينَ ءَامَنُوا۟ وَلَمْ يُهَاجِرُوا۟ مَا لَكُم مِّن وَلَٰيَتِهِم مِّن شَىْءٍ حَتَّىٰ يُهَاجِرُوا۟ وَإِنِ ٱسْتَنصَرُوكُمْ فِى ٱلدِّينِ فَعَلَيْكُمُ ٱلنَّصْرُ إِلَّا عَلَىٰ قَوْمٍ بَيْنَكُمْ وَبَيْنَهُم مِّيثَٰقٌ وَٱللَّهُ بِمَا تَعْمَلُونَ بَصِيرٌ

٧٣ وَٱلَّذِينَ كَفَرُوا۟ بَعْضُهُمْ أَوْلِيَآءُ بَعْضٍ إِلَّا تَفْعَلُوهُ تَكُن فِتْنَةٌ فِى ٱلْأَرْضِ وَفَسَادٌ كَبِيرٌ

٧٤ وَٱلَّذِينَ ءَامَنُوا۟ وَهَاجَرُوا۟ وَجَٰهَدُوا۟ فِى سَبِيلِ ٱللَّهِ وَٱلَّذِينَ ءَاوَوا۟ وَّنَصَرُوٓا۟ أُو۟لَٰٓئِكَ هُمُ ٱلْمُؤْمِنُونَ حَقًّا لَّهُم مَّغْفِرَةٌ وَرِزْقٌ كَرِيمٌ

٧٥ وَٱلَّذِينَ ءَامَنُوا۟ مِنۢ بَعْدُ وَهَاجَرُوا۟ وَجَٰهَدُوا۟ مَعَكُمْ فَأُو۟لَٰٓئِكَ مِنكُمْ وَأُو۟لُوا۟ ٱلْأَرْحَامِ بَعْضُهُمْ أَوْلَىٰ بِبَعْضٍ فِى كِتَٰبِ ٱللَّهِ إِنَّ ٱللَّهَ بِكُلِّ شَىْءٍ عَلِيمٌ

Repentance

Al Tawbah, "Repentance," takes its name from verse 104. It is often called *Barā'ah* (Disavowal), from the first word. It is the only surah that does not begin with the phrase *Bism Allāh al Raḥmān al Raḥīm* ("In the name of Allah, the Beneficent, the Merciful"). The usual reason given for this departure from the norm is that it contains stern statements directed at the idolaters (verses 1-12), the proclamation of disavowal from obligation toward the idolaters which were revealed after the pilgrims had started for Makkah in the year 9 AH. These were sent by special messenger to Abū Bakr, leader of the pilgrimage, to be announced by 'Alī to the multitudes at Makkah. It signified the end of idolatry in Arabia.

The Christian Byzantine Empire had begun to move against the growing Muslim power, and this surah mentions a greater war to come and contains instructions related to it. Verses 38-99 refer to the Tabūk campaign and especially to those Arab tribes who did not join the Muslim side. The "Hypocrites," as the half-hearted supporters of Islam were called, had long been a thorn in the side of the Muslims. Once, they had even formed a congregation and built a mosque of their own surreptitiously. On the Prophet's return from Tabūk, they invited him to visit their mosque. This is referred to in verses 107 ff.

The date of revelation is the year 9 AH.

Repentance

Revealed at al Madinah

1. **F**reedom from obligation (is proclaimed) from Allah and His Messenger toward those of the idolaters with whom you made a treaty:

2. Travel freely in the land four months, and know that you cannot escape Allah and that Allah will confound the disbelievers (in His guidance).

3. And a proclamation from Allah and His Messenger to all men on the day of the Greater Pilgrimage that Allah is free from obligation to the idolaters, and (so is) His Mes-senger. So, if you repent, it will be better for you; but if you are averse, then know that you cannot escape Allah. Give tidings (O Muhammad) of a painful doom to those who disbelieve.

4. Excepting those of the idolaters with whom you (Muslims) have a treaty, and who have since abated nothing of your right nor have supported anyone against you. (As for these), fulfill their treaty to them till their term. Lo! Allah loves those who keep their duty (unto Him).

5. Then, when the sacred months have passed, slay the idolaters wherever you find them, and take them (captive), and besiege them, and prepare for them each ambush. But if they repent and establish prayer and pay the poor due, then leave their way free. Lo! Allah is Forgiving, Merciful.

6. And if anyone of the idolaters seeks your protection (O Muhammad), then protect him so that he may hear the word of Allah; and afterward convey him to his place of safety. That is because they are a folk who know not.

7. How can there be a treaty with Allah and with His Mes-senger for the idolaters save those with whom you made a treaty at the Sacred Mosque? So long as they are true to you, be true to them. Lo! Allah loves those who keep their duty.

8. How (can there be any treaty for the others) when, if they have the upper hand of you, they regard not pact nor honor in respect of you? They satisfy you with their mouths the while their hearts refuse. And most of them are wrong-doers.

9. They have purchased with the revelations of Allah a little gain, so they debar (men) from His way. Lo! evil is that which they are wont to do.

10. And they observe toward a believer neither pact nor honor. These are they who are transgressors.

11. But if they repent and establish prayer and pay the poor due, then are they your brothers in religion. We detail Our revelations for a people who have knowledge.

12. And if they break their pledges after their treaty (has been made with you) and assail your religion, then fight the heads of disbelief Lo! they have no binding oaths in order that they may desist.

13. Will you not fight a folk who broke their solemn pledges, and purposed to drive out the Messenger and did attack you first? What! Fear you them? Now Allah has more right that you should fear Him, if you are believers.

14. Fight them! Allah will chastise them at your hands, and He will lay them low and give you victory over them, and He will heal the breasts of folk who are believers.

15. And He will remove the anger of their hearts. Allah relents toward whom He will. Allah is Knower, Wise.

٧ كَيْفَ يَكُونُ لِلْمُشْرِكِينَ عَهْدٌ عِندَ ٱللَّهِ وَعِندَ رَسُولِهِ إِلَّا ٱلَّذِينَ عَٰهَدتُّمْ عِندَ ٱلْمَسْجِدِ ٱلْحَرَامِ فَمَا ٱسْتَقَٰمُوا۟ لَكُمْ فَٱسْتَقِيمُوا۟ لَهُمْ إِنَّ ٱللَّهَ يُحِبُّ ٱلْمُتَّقِينَ

٨ كَيْفَ وَإِن يَظْهَرُوا۟ عَلَيْكُمْ لَا يَرْقُبُوا۟ فِيكُمْ إِلًّا وَلَا ذِمَّةً يُرْضُونَكُم بِأَفْوَٰهِهِمْ وَتَأْبَىٰ قُلُوبُهُمْ وَأَكْثَرُهُمْ فَٰسِقُونَ

٩ ٱشْتَرَوْا۟ بِـَٔايَٰتِ ٱللَّهِ ثَمَنًا قَلِيلًا فَصَدُّوا۟ عَن سَبِيلِهِ إِنَّهُمْ سَاءَ مَا كَانُوا۟ يَعْمَلُونَ

١٠ لَا يَرْقُبُونَ فِى مُؤْمِنٍ إِلًّا وَلَا ذِمَّةً وَأُو۟لَٰٓئِكَ هُمُ ٱلْمُعْتَدُونَ

١١ فَإِن تَابُوا۟ وَأَقَامُوا۟ ٱلصَّلَوٰةَ وَءَاتَوُا۟ ٱلزَّكَوٰةَ فَإِخْوَٰنُكُمْ فِى ٱلدِّينِ وَنُفَصِّلُ ٱلْءَايَٰتِ لِقَوْمٍ يَعْلَمُونَ

١٢ وَإِن نَّكَثُوٓا۟ أَيْمَٰنَهُم مِّنۢ بَعْدِ عَهْدِهِمْ وَطَعَنُوا۟ فِى دِينِكُمْ فَقَٰتِلُوٓا۟ أَئِمَّةَ ٱلْكُفْرِ إِنَّهُمْ لَآ أَيْمَٰنَ لَهُمْ لَعَلَّهُمْ يَنتَهُونَ

١٣ أَلَا تُقَٰتِلُونَ قَوْمًا نَّكَثُوٓا۟ أَيْمَٰنَهُمْ وَهَمُّوا۟ بِإِخْرَاجِ ٱلرَّسُولِ وَهُم بَدَءُوكُمْ أَوَّلَ مَرَّةٍ أَتَخْشَوْنَهُمْ فَٱللَّهُ أَحَقُّ أَن تَخْشَوْهُ إِن كُنتُم مُّؤْمِنِينَ

١٤ قَٰتِلُوهُمْ يُعَذِّبْهُمُ ٱللَّهُ بِأَيْدِيكُمْ وَيُخْزِهِمْ وَيَنصُرْكُمْ عَلَيْهِمْ وَيَشْفِ صُدُورَ قَوْمٍ مُّؤْمِنِينَ

١٥ وَيُذْهِبْ غَيْظَ قُلُوبِهِمْ وَيَتُوبُ ٱللَّهُ عَلَىٰ مَن يَشَاءُ وَٱللَّهُ عَلِيمٌ حَكِيمٌ

16. Or deemed you that you would be left (in peace) when Allah yet knows not those of you who strive, choosing none for friends and protectors save Allah and His Messenger and the believers? Allah is Informed of what you do.

١٦ أَمْ حَسِبْتُمْ أَن تُتْرَكُوا وَلَمَّا يَعْلَمِ اللَّهُ الَّذِينَ جَاهَدُوا مِنكُمْ وَلَمْ يَتَّخِذُوا مِن دُونِ اللَّهِ وَلَا رَسُولِهِ وَلَا الْمُؤْمِنِينَ وَلِيجَةً وَاللَّهُ خَبِيرٌ بِمَا تَعْمَلُونَ

17. It is not for the idolaters to tend Allah's sanctuaries, bearing witness against themselves of disbelief. As for such, their works are vain and in the Fire they will abide.

١٧ مَا كَانَ لِلْمُشْرِكِينَ أَن يَعْمُرُوا مَسَاجِدَ اللَّهِ شَاهِدِينَ عَلَى أَنفُسِهِم بِالْكُفْرِ أُوْلَئِكَ حَبِطَتْ أَعْمَالُهُمْ وَفِي النَّارِ هُمْ خَالِدُونَ

18. He only shall tend Allah's sanctuaries who believes in Allah and the Last Day and observes proper prayer and pays the poor due and fears none save Allah. For such (only) is it possible that they can be of the rightly guided.

١٨ إِنَّمَا يَعْمُرُ مَسَاجِدَ اللَّهِ مَنْ آمَنَ بِاللَّهِ وَالْيَوْمِ الْآخِرِ وَأَقَامَ الصَّلَوٰةَ وَآتَى الزَّكَوٰةَ وَلَمْ يَخْشَ إِلَّا اللَّهَ فَعَسَى أُوْلَئِكَ أَن يَكُونُوا مِنَ الْمُهْتَدِينَ

19. Count you the slaking of a pilgrim's thirst and tendance of the Sacred Mosque as (equal to the worth of him) who believes in Allah and the Last Day, and strives in the way of Allah? They are not equal in the sight of Allah. Allah guides not wrongdoing folk.

١٩ أَجَعَلْتُمْ سِقَايَةَ الْحَاجِّ وَعِمَارَةَ الْمَسْجِدِ الْحَرَامِ كَمَنْ آمَنَ بِاللَّهِ وَالْيَوْمِ الْآخِرِ وَجَاهَدَ فِي سَبِيلِ اللَّهِ لَا يَسْتَوُونَ عِندَ اللَّهِ وَاللَّهُ لَا يَهْدِي الْقَوْمَ الظَّالِمِينَ

20. Those who believe, and have left their homes and striven with their wealth and their lives in Allah's way are of much greater worth in Allah's sight. These are they who are triumphant.

٢٠ الَّذِينَ آمَنُوا وَهَاجَرُوا وَجَاهَدُوا فِي سَبِيلِ اللَّهِ بِأَمْوَالِهِمْ وَأَنفُسِهِمْ أَعْظَمُ دَرَجَةً عِندَ اللَّهِ وَأُوْلَئِكَ هُمُ الْفَائِزُونَ

21. Their Lord gives them good tidings of mercy from Him, and acceptance, and Gardens where enduring pleasure will be theirs;

٢١ يُبَشِّرُهُمْ رَبُّهُم بِرَحْمَةٍ مِّنْهُ وَرِضْوَانٍ وَجَنَّاتٍ لَّهُمْ فِيهَا نَعِيمٌ مُّقِيمٌ

22. There they will abide for ever. Lo! with Allah there is immense reward.

٢٢ خَالِدِينَ فِيهَا أَبَدًا إِنَّ اللَّهَ عِندَهُ أَجْرٌ عَظِيمٌ

23. O you who believe! Choose not your fathers nor your brothers for friends if they take pleasure in disbelief rather than faith. Whoever of you takes them for friends, such are wrongdoers.

٢٣ يَا أَيُّهَا الَّذِينَ آمَنُوا لَا تَتَّخِذُوا آبَاءَكُمْ وَإِخْوَانَكُمْ أَوْلِيَاءَ إِنِ اسْتَحَبُّوا الْكُفْرَ عَلَى الْإِيمَانِ وَمَن يَتَوَلَّهُم مِّنكُمْ فَأُوْلَئِكَ هُمُ الظَّالِمُونَ

24. Say: If your fathers, your sons, your brothers, your wives, your tribe, the wealth you have acquired, merchandise for which you fear that there will be no sale,[115] and dwellings you desire are dearer to you than Allah and His Messenger and striving in His way: then wait till Allah brings His command to pass. Allah guides not wrongdoing folk.

25. Allah has given you victory on many fields and on the day of Ḥunayn,[116] when you exulted in your multitude but it availed you nothing, and the earth, vast as it is, was straitened for you; then you turned back in flight;

26. Then Allah sent His peace of reassurance down upon His Messenger and upon the believers, and sent down hosts you could not see, and punished those who disbelieved. Such is the reward of disbelievers.

27. Then afterward Allah will relent toward whom He will; for Allah is Forgiving, Merciful.

28. O you who believe! The idolaters are truly unclean. So let them not come near the Sacred Mosque after this their year. If you fear poverty (from the loss of their merchandise) Allah shall preserve you of His bounty if He will. Lo! Allah is Knower, Wise.

29. Fight against such of those who have been given the Scripture as believe not in Allah nor the Last Day, and forbid not that which Allah has forbidden by His Messenger, and follow not the religion of truth, until they pay the tribute readily, being brought low.

---

[115]Some people raised the objection that if the idolaters were forbidden to make the pilgrimage, the trade of Makkah would decline.

[116]The Muslim army, ambushed at Ḥunayn, gained a great victory after being nearly routed.

30. And the Jews say: Ezra is the son of Allah, and the Christians say: The Messiah is the son of Allah. That is their saying with their mouths. They imitate the saying of those who disbelieved of old. Allah (himself) fights against them. How perverse are they!

31. They have taken as lords beside Allah their rabbis and their monks and the Messiah son of Mary, when they were bidden to worship only One God. There is no god save Him. Be He glorified from all that they ascribe as partner (unto Him)!

32. Fain would they put out the light of Allah with their mouths, but Allah disdains (everything) save that He shall perfect His light, however much the disbelievers are averse.

33. He it is who has sent His Messenger with the guidance and the Religion of Truth, that He may cause it to prevail over all religion, however much the idolaters may be averse.

34. O you, who believe! Lo! many of the (Jewish) rabbis and the (Christian) monks devour the wealth of mankind wantonly and debar (men) from the way of Allah. They who hoard up gold and silver and spend it not in the way of Allah, unto them give tidings (O Muhammad) of a painful doom.

35. On the day when it will (all) be heated in the fire of Hell, and their foreheads and their flanks and their backs will be branded therewith (and it will be said unto them): Here is that which you hoarded for yourselves. Now taste of what you used to hoard.

36. Lo! the number of the months with Allah is twelve months by Allah's ordinance on the day that He created the heavens and the earth. Four of them are sacred: that is the right religion. So wrong not yourselves in them. And wage war on all the idolaters as they are waging war on all of you. And know that Allah is with those who keep their duty (unto Him).

٣٠ وَقَالَتِ الْيَهُودُ عُزَيْرُۨ ابْنُ اللّٰهِ وَقَالَتِ النَّصَارَى الْمَسِيحُ ابْنُ اللّٰهِ ذَٰلِكَ قَوْلُهُم بِأَفْوَاهِهِمْ يُضَاهِـُٔونَ قَوْلَ الَّذِينَ كَفَرُوا مِن قَبْلُ قَاتَلَهُمُ اللّٰهُ أَنَّىٰ يُؤْفَكُونَ

٣١ اتَّخَذُوا أَحْبَارَهُمْ وَرُهْبَانَهُمْ أَرْبَابًا مِّن دُونِ اللّٰهِ وَالْمَسِيحَ ابْنَ مَرْيَمَ وَمَا أُمِرُوا إِلَّا لِيَعْبُدُوا إِلَٰهًا وَاحِدًا لَّا إِلَٰهَ إِلَّا هُوَ سُبْحَانَهُ عَمَّا يُشْرِكُونَ

٣٢ يُرِيدُونَ أَن يُطْفِـُٔوا نُورَ اللّٰهِ بِأَفْوَاهِهِمْ وَيَأْبَى اللّٰهُ إِلَّا أَن يُتِمَّ نُورَهُ وَلَوْ كَرِهَ الْكَافِرُونَ

٣٣ هُوَ الَّذِي أَرْسَلَ رَسُولَهُ بِالْهُدَىٰ وَدِينِ الْحَقِّ لِيُظْهِرَهُ عَلَى الدِّينِ كُلِّهِ وَلَوْ كَرِهَ الْمُشْرِكُونَ

٣٤ يَا أَيُّهَا الَّذِينَ آمَنُوا إِنَّ كَثِيرًا مِّنَ الْأَحْبَارِ وَالرُّهْبَانِ لَيَأْكُلُونَ أَمْوَالَ النَّاسِ بِالْبَاطِلِ وَيَصُدُّونَ عَن سَبِيلِ اللّٰهِ وَالَّذِينَ يَكْنِزُونَ الذَّهَبَ وَالْفِضَّةَ وَلَا يُنفِقُونَهَا فِي سَبِيلِ اللّٰهِ فَبَشِّرْهُم بِعَذَابٍ أَلِيمٍ

٣٥ يَوْمَ يُحْمَىٰ عَلَيْهَا فِي نَارِ جَهَنَّمَ فَتُكْوَىٰ بِهَا جِبَاهُهُمْ وَجُنُوبُهُمْ وَظُهُورُهُمْ هَٰذَا مَا كَنَزْتُمْ لِأَنفُسِكُمْ فَذُوقُوا مَا كُنتُمْ تَكْنِزُونَ

٣٦ إِنَّ عِدَّةَ الشُّهُورِ عِندَ اللّٰهِ اثْنَا عَشَرَ شَهْرًا فِي كِتَابِ اللّٰهِ يَوْمَ خَلَقَ السَّمَاوَاتِ وَالْأَرْضَ مِنْهَا أَرْبَعَةٌ حُرُمٌ ذَٰلِكَ الدِّينُ الْقَيِّمُ فَلَا تَظْلِمُوا فِيهِنَّ أَنفُسَكُمْ وَقَاتِلُوا الْمُشْرِكِينَ كَافَّةً كَمَا يُقَاتِلُونَكُمْ كَافَّةً وَاعْلَمُوا أَنَّ اللّٰهَ مَعَ الْمُتَّقِينَ

37. Postponement (of a sacred month)[117] is only an excess of disbelief whereby those who disbelieve are misled, they allow it one year and forbid it (another) year, that they may make up the number of the months which Allah has hallowed, so that they allow that which Allah has forbidden. The evil of their deeds is made fair-seeming unto them. Allah guides not the disbelieving folk.

38. O you who believe! What ails us that when it is said unto you: Go forth in the way of Allah, you are bowed down to the ground with heaviness. Take you pleasure in the life of the world rather than in the Hereafter? The comfort of the life of the world is but little in the Hereafter.

39. If you go not forth He will afflict you with a painful doom, and will choose instead of you a folk other than you. You cannot harm Him at all. Allah is Able to do all things.

40. If you help him not, still Allah helped him when those who disbelieve drove him forth, the second of two;[118] when they two were in the cave, when he said unto his comrade: Grieve not. Lo! Allah is with us. Then Allah caused His peace of reassurance to descend upon him and supported him with hosts you could not see, and made the word of those who disbelieved the lowermost, while Allah's word it was that became the uppermost. Allah is Mighty, Wise.

41. Go forth, light armed and heavy armed, and strive with your wealth and your lives in the way of Allah! That is best for you if you but knew.

42. Had it been a near adventure and an easy journey they had followed you, but the distance seemed too far for them.[119] Yet will they swear by Allah (saying): If we had been able we would surely have set out with you. They destroy their souls, and Allah knows that they truly are liars.

---

[117]The idolaters would postpone a sacred month in which war was forbidden when they wanted to make war, and make up for it by hallowing another month.

[118]The Prophet and Abū Bakr, during the flight from Makkah to al Madīnah.

[119]The reference is to the Tabūk expedition. Tabūk is located half-way between al Madīnah and Damascus.

43. Allah forgive you (O Muhammad)! Wherefore did you grant them leave ere those who told the truth were manifest to you and you did know the liars?

﴿٤٣﴾ عَفَا اللّٰهُ عَنْكَ لِمَ أَذِنْتَ لَهُمْ حَتّٰى يَتَبَيَّنَ لَكَ الَّذِيْنَ صَدَقُوْا وَتَعْلَمَ الْكٰذِبِيْنَ

44. Those who believe in Allah and the Last Day ask no leave of you lest they should strive with their wealth and their lives. Allah is Aware of those who keep their duty (unto Him).

﴿٤٤﴾ لَا يَسْتَأْذِنُكَ الَّذِيْنَ يُؤْمِنُوْنَ بِاللّٰهِ وَالْيَوْمِ الْاٰخِرِ اَنْ يُّجَاهِدُوْا بِاَمْوَالِهِمْ وَاَنْفُسِهِمْ وَاللّٰهُ عَلِيْمٌ بِالْمُتَّقِيْنَ

45. They alone ask leave of you who believe not in Allah and the Last Day, and whose hearts feel doubt, so in their doubt they waver.

﴿٤٥﴾ اِنَّمَا يَسْتَأْذِنُكَ الَّذِيْنَ لَا يُؤْمِنُوْنَ بِاللّٰهِ وَالْيَوْمِ الْاٰخِرِ وَارْتَابَتْ قُلُوْبُهُمْ فَهُمْ فِيْ رَيْبِهِمْ يَتَرَدَّدُوْنَ

46. And if they had wished to go forth they would assuredly have made ready some equipment, but Allah was averse to their being sent forth and held them back and (it was said unto them): Sit you with the sedentary!

﴿٤٦﴾ ۞ وَلَوْ اَرَادُوا الْخُرُوْجَ لَاَعَدُّوْا لَهٗ عُدَّةً وَّلٰكِنْ كَرِهَ اللّٰهُ انْبِعَاثَهُمْ فَثَبَّطَهُمْ وَقِيْلَ اقْعُدُوْا مَعَ الْقَاعِدِيْنَ

47. Had they gone forth among you they had added to you nothing save trouble and had hurried to and fro among you with mischief, seeking to cause sedition among you; and among you there are some who would have listened to them. Allah is Aware of evildoers.

﴿٤٧﴾ لَوْ خَرَجُوْا فِيْكُمْ مَّا زَادُوْكُمْ اِلَّا خَبَالًا وَّلَاَوْضَعُوْا خِلَالَكُمْ يَبْغُوْنَكُمُ الْفِتْنَةَ وَفِيْكُمْ سَمّٰعُوْنَ لَهُمْ وَاللّٰهُ عَلِيْمٌ بِالظّٰلِمِيْنَ

48. Aforetime they sought to cause sedition and raised difficulties for you till the Truth came and the decree of Allah was made manifest, though they were loth.

﴿٤٨﴾ لَقَدِ ابْتَغَوُا الْفِتْنَةَ مِنْ قَبْلُ وَقَلَّبُوْا لَكَ الْاُمُوْرَ حَتّٰى جَاءَ الْحَقُّ وَظَهَرَ اَمْرُ اللّٰهِ وَهُمْ كٰرِهُوْنَ

49. Of them is he who says: Grant me leave (to stay at home) and tempt me not.[120] Surely it is into temptation that they (thus) have fallen. Lo! Hell is all around the disbelievers.

﴿٤٩﴾ وَمِنْهُمْ مَّنْ يَّقُوْلُ ائْذَنْ لِّيْ وَلَا تَفْتِنِّيْ اَلَا فِي الْفِتْنَةِ سَقَطُوْا وَاِنَّ جَهَنَّمَ لَمُحِيْطَةٌ بِالْكٰفِرِيْنَ

50. If good befalls you (O Muhammad) it afflicts them, and if calamity befalls you, they say: We took precaution, and they turn away well pleased.

﴿٥٠﴾ اِنْ تُصِبْكَ حَسَنَةٌ تَسُؤْهُمْ وَاِنْ تُصِبْكَ مُصِيْبَةٌ يَّقُوْلُوْا قَدْ اَخَذْنَا اَمْرَنَا مِنْ قَبْلُ وَيَتَوَلَّوْا وَّهُمْ فَرِحُوْنَ

51. Say: Nothing befalls us save that which Allah has de-creed for us. He is our protecting Friend. In Allah let believers put their trust!

﴿٥١﴾ قُلْ لَّنْ يُّصِيْبَنَا اِلَّا مَا كَتَبَ اللّٰهُ لَنَا هُوَ مَوْلٰنَا وَعَلَى اللّٰهِ فَلْيَتَوَكَّلِ الْمُؤْمِنُوْنَ

---

[120]The temptation here referred to is generally explained as being the beauty of the women of Syria, the country against which the campaign was directed.

52. Say: Can you await for us anything save one of two good things (death or victory in Allah's way)? while we await for you that Allah will afflict you with a doom from Him or at our hands. Await then! Lo! we are awaiting with you.

٥٢ قُلْ هَلْ تَرَبَّصُونَ بِنَآ إِلَّا إِحْدَى الْحُسْنَيَيْنِ وَنَحْنُ نَتَرَبَّصُ بِكُمْ أَنْ يُّصِيبَكُمُ اللّٰهُ بِعَذَابٍ مِّنْ عِنْدِهٖ أَوْ بِأَيْدِيْنَا فَتَرَبَّصُوا إِنَّا مَعَكُمْ مُّتَرَبِّصُونَ

53. Say: Pay (your contribution), willingly or unwillingly, it will not be accepted from you. Lo! you were ever froward folk.

٥٣ قُلْ أَنْفِقُوا طَوْعًا أَوْ كَرْهًا لَّنْ يُّتَقَبَّلَ مِنْكُمْ إِنَّكُمْ كُنْتُمْ قَوْمًا فَاسِقِيْنَ

54. And nothing prevents that their contributions should be accepted from them save that they have disbelieved in Allah and in His Messenger, and they come not to prayer save as idlers, and pay not (their contribution) save hatingly.

٥٤ وَمَا مَنَعَهُمْ أَنْ تُقْبَلَ مِنْهُمْ نَفَقَاتُهُمْ إِلَّا أَنَّهُمْ كَفَرُوا بِاللّٰهِ وَبِرَسُوْلِهٖ وَلَا يَأْتُوْنَ الصَّلٰوةَ إِلَّا وَهُمْ كُسَالَى وَلَا يُنْفِقُوْنَ إِلَّا وَهُمْ كٰرِهُوْنَ

55. So let not their riches nor their children please you (O Muhammad). Allah thereby intends but to punish them in the life of the world and that their souls shall pass away while they are disbelievers.

٥٥ فَلَا تُعْجِبْكَ أَمْوَالُهُمْ وَلَا أَوْلَادُهُمْ إِنَّمَا يُرِيْدُ اللّٰهُ لِيُعَذِّبَهُمْ بِهَا فِي الْحَيٰوةِ الدُّنْيَا وَتَزْهَقَ أَنْفُسُهُمْ وَهُمْ كٰفِرُوْنَ

56. And they swear by Allah that they are in truth of you, when they are not of you, but they are folk who are horrified to death.

٥٦ وَيَحْلِفُوْنَ بِاللّٰهِ إِنَّهُمْ لَمِنْكُمْ وَمَا هُمْ مِّنْكُمْ وَلٰكِنَّهُمْ قَوْمٌ يَّفْرَقُوْنَ

57. Had they but found a refuge, or caverns, or a place to enter, they surely had resorted thereto swift as runaways.

٥٧ لَوْ يَجِدُوْنَ مَلْجَأً أَوْ مَغٰرٰتٍ أَوْ مُدَّخَلًا لَّوَلَّوْا إِلَيْهِ وَهُمْ يَجْمَحُوْنَ

58. And of them is he who defames you in the matter of the alms. If they are given thereof they are content, and if they are not given thereof, behold! they are enraged.

٥٨ وَمِنْهُمْ مَّنْ يَّلْمِزُكَ فِي الصَّدَقٰتِ فَإِنْ أُعْطُوا مِنْهَا رَضُوا وَإِنْ لَّمْ يُعْطَوْا مِنْهَآ إِذَا هُمْ يَسْخَطُوْنَ

59. (How much more seemly) had they been content with that which Allah and His Messenger had given them and had said: Allah suffices us. Allah will give us of His bounty, and (also) His Messenger. Unto Allah we are suppliants.

٥٩ وَلَوْ أَنَّهُمْ رَضُوا مَآ ءَاتٰهُمُ اللّٰهُ وَرَسُوْلُهٗ وَقَالُوا حَسْبُنَا اللّٰهُ سَيُؤْتِيْنَا اللّٰهُ مِنْ فَضْلِهٖ وَرَسُوْلُهٗ إِنَّآ إِلَى اللّٰهِ رٰغِبُوْنَ

60. The alms are only for the poor, the needy, those who collect them, those whose hearts are to be reconciled,[121] to free the captives and the debtors, for the cause of Allah, and (for) the wayfarers; a duty imposed by Allah. Allah is Knower, Wise.

61. And of them are those who vex the Prophet and say: He is only a hearer. Say: A hearer of good for you, who believes in Allah and is true to the believers, and a mercy for such of you as believe. Those who vex the Messenger of Allah, for them there is a painful doom.

62. They swear by Allah to you (Muslims) to please you, but Allah, with His Messenger, has more right that they should please Him if they are believers.

63. Know they not that who opposes Allah and His Messenger, his portion verily is Hell, to abide therein? That is the extreme abasement.

64. The hypocrites fear lest a surah should be revealed concerning them, proclaiming what is in their hearts. Say: Scoff (your fill)! Lo! Allah is disclosing what you fear.

65. And if you ask them (O Muhammad) they will say: We did but talk and jest. Say: was it at Allah and His revelations and His Messenger that you did scoff?

66. Make no excuse. You have disbelieved after your (confession of) belief. If We forgive a party of you, a party of you We shall punish because they have been criminals.

67. The hypocrites, both men and women, proceed one from another. They enjoin the wrong, and they forbid the right, and they withhold their hands (from spending for the cause of Allah). They forget Allah, so He has forgotten them. Lo! the hypocrites, they are the perverted ones.

---

[121]A special portion of the alms was allotted to the people of Makkah, the former enemies of Islam, who entered the fold of Islam en masse after the capture of the city and whose "hearts were to be reconciled."

68. Allah promises the hypocrites, both men and women, and the disbelievers fire of Hell for their abode. It will suffice them. Allah curses them, and theirs is lasting torment.

٦٨ وَعَدَ اللهُ الْمُنَافِقِينَ وَالْمُنَافِقَاتِ وَالْكُفَّارَ نَارَ جَهَنَّمَ خَالِدِينَ فِيهَا هِيَ حَسْبُهُمْ وَلَعَنَهُمُ اللهُ وَلَهُمْ عَذَابٌ مُقِيمٌ

69. Even as those before you were mightier than you in strength, and more affluent than you in wealth and children. They enjoyed their lot awhile, so you enjoy your lot awhile even as those before you did enjoy their lot awhile. And you prate even as they prated. Such are they whose works have perished in the world and the Hereafter. Such are they who are the losers.

٦٩ كَالَّذِينَ مِن قَبْلِكُمْ كَانُوا أَشَدَّ مِنكُمْ قُوَّةً وَأَكْثَرَ أَمْوَالًا وَأَوْلَادًا فَاسْتَمْتَعُوا بِخَلَاقِهِمْ فَاسْتَمْتَعْتُم بِخَلَاقِكُمْ كَمَا اسْتَمْتَعَ الَّذِينَ مِن قَبْلِكُم بِخَلَاقِهِمْ وَخُضْتُمْ كَالَّذِي خَاضُوا أُولَٰئِكَ حَبِطَتْ أَعْمَالُهُمْ فِي الدُّنْيَا وَالْآخِرَةِ وَأُولَٰئِكَ هُمُ الْخَاسِرُونَ

70. Has not the news of those before them reached them— the folk of Noah, ʿĀd, Thamūd, the folk of Abraham, the dwellers of Madian and the villages turned upside down (Lot's people)? Their messengers (from Allah) came unto them with proofs (of Allah's sovereignty). So Allah surely wronged them not, but they did wrong themselves.

٧٠ أَلَمْ يَأْتِهِمْ نَبَأُ الَّذِينَ مِن قَبْلِهِمْ قَوْمِ نُوحٍ وَعَادٍ وَثَمُودَ وَقَوْمِ إِبْرَاهِيمَ وَأَصْحَابِ مَدْيَنَ وَالْمُؤْتَفِكَاتِ أَتَتْهُمْ رُسُلُهُم بِالْبَيِّنَاتِ فَمَا كَانَ اللهُ لِيَظْلِمَهُمْ وَلَٰكِن كَانُوا أَنفُسَهُمْ يَظْلِمُونَ

71. And the believers, men and women, are protecting friends one of another; they enjoin the right and forbid the wrong, and they establish prayer, pay the poor-due, and obey Allah and His Messenger. As for these, Allah will have mercy on them. Lo! Allah is Mighty, Wise.

٧١ وَالْمُؤْمِنُونَ وَالْمُؤْمِنَاتُ بَعْضُهُمْ أَوْلِيَاءُ بَعْضٍ يَأْمُرُونَ بِالْمَعْرُوفِ وَيَنْهَوْنَ عَنِ الْمُنكَرِ وَيُقِيمُونَ الصَّلَاةَ وَيُؤْتُونَ الزَّكَاةَ وَيُطِيعُونَ اللهَ وَرَسُولَهُ أُولَٰئِكَ سَيَرْحَمُهُمُ اللهُ إِنَّ اللهَ عَزِيزٌ حَكِيمٌ

72. Allah promises to the believers, men and women, Gardens underneath which rivers flow, wherein they will abide—blessed dwellings in Gardens of Eden. And—greater (far)!—acceptance from Allah. That is the supreme triumph.

٧٢ وَعَدَ اللهُ الْمُؤْمِنِينَ وَالْمُؤْمِنَاتِ جَنَّاتٍ تَجْرِي مِن تَحْتِهَا الْأَنْهَارُ خَالِدِينَ فِيهَا وَمَسَاكِنَ طَيِّبَةً فِي جَنَّاتِ عَدْنٍ وَرِضْوَانٌ مِّنَ اللهِ أَكْبَرُ ذَٰلِكَ هُوَ الْفَوْزُ الْعَظِيمُ

٧٣ يَا أَيُّهَا النَّبِيُّ جَاهِدِ الْكُفَّارَ وَالْمُنَافِقِينَ وَاغْلُظْ عَلَيْهِمْ وَمَأْوَاهُمْ جَهَنَّمُ وَبِئْسَ الْمَصِيرُ

73. O Prophet! Strive against the disbelievers and the hypocrites! Be harsh with them. Their ultimate abode is Hell, an unfortunate journey's end.

٧٤ يَحْلِفُونَ بِاللَّهِ مَا قَالُوا وَلَقَدْ قَالُوا كَلِمَةَ الْكُفْرِ وَكَفَرُوا بَعْدَ إِسْلَامِهِمْ وَهَمُّوا بِمَا لَمْ يَنَالُوا وَمَا نَقَمُوا إِلَّا أَنْ أَغْنَاهُمُ اللَّهُ وَرَسُولُهُ مِنْ فَضْلِهِ فَإِنْ يَتُوبُوا يَكُ خَيْرًا لَهُمْ وَإِنْ يَتَوَلَّوْا يُعَذِّبْهُمُ اللَّهُ عَذَابًا أَلِيمًا فِي الدُّنْيَا وَالْآخِرَةِ وَمَا لَهُمْ فِي الْأَرْضِ مِنْ وَلِيٍّ وَلَا نَصِيرٍ

74. They swear by Allah that they said nothing (wrong), yet they did say the word of disbelief, and did disbelieve after their Surrender (to Allah). And they purposed that which they could not attain, and they sought revenge only that Allah and His Messenger had enriched them of His bounty. If they repent it will be better for them; and if they turn away, Allah will afflict them with a painful doom in the world and the Hereafter, and they have no protecting friend nor helper in the earth.

٧٥ وَمِنْهُمْ مَنْ عَاهَدَ اللَّهَ لَئِنْ آتَانَا مِنْ فَضْلِهِ لَنَصَّدَّقَنَّ وَلَنَكُونَنَّ مِنَ الصَّالِحِينَ

75. And of them is he who made a covenant with Allah (saying): If He give us of His bounty We will give alms and become of the righteous.

٧٦ فَلَمَّا آتَاهُمْ مِنْ فَضْلِهِ بَخِلُوا بِهِ وَتَوَلَّوْا وَهُمْ مُعْرِضُونَ

76. Yet when He gave them of His bounty, they hoarded it and turned away, averse;

٧٧ فَأَعْقَبَهُمْ نِفَاقًا فِي قُلُوبِهِمْ إِلَى يَوْمِ يَلْقَوْنَهُ بِمَا أَخْلَفُوا اللَّهَ مَا وَعَدُوهُ وَبِمَا كَانُوا يَكْذِبُونَ

77. So He has made the consequence (to be) hypocrisy in their hearts until the day when they shall meet Him, because they broke their word to Allah that they promised Him, and because they lied.

٧٨ أَلَمْ يَعْلَمُوا أَنَّ اللَّهَ يَعْلَمُ سِرَّهُمْ وَنَجْوَاهُمْ وَأَنَّ اللَّهَ عَلَّامُ الْغُيُوبِ

78. Know they not that Allah knows both their secret and the thought that they confide, and that Allah is the Knower of Things Hidden?

٧٩ الَّذِينَ يَلْمِزُونَ الْمُطَّوِّعِينَ مِنَ الْمُؤْمِنِينَ فِي الصَّدَقَاتِ وَالَّذِينَ لَا يَجِدُونَ إِلَّا جُهْدَهُمْ فَيَسْخَرُونَ مِنْهُمْ سَخِرَ اللَّهُ مِنْهُمْ وَلَهُمْ عَذَابٌ أَلِيمٌ

79. Those who point at such of the believers as give the alms willingly and such as can find nothing to give but their endeavors, and deride them. Allah (Himself) derides them. Theirs will be a painful doom.

٨٠ اسْتَغْفِرْ لَهُمْ أَوْ لَا تَسْتَغْفِرْ لَهُمْ إِنْ تَسْتَغْفِرْ لَهُمْ سَبْعِينَ مَرَّةً فَلَنْ يَغْفِرَ اللَّهُ لَهُمْ ذَلِكَ بِأَنَّهُمْ كَفَرُوا بِاللَّهِ وَرَسُولِهِ وَاللَّهُ لَا يَهْدِي الْقَوْمَ الْفَاسِقِينَ

80. Ask forgiveness for them (O Muhammad), or ask not forgiveness for them; though you ask forgiveness for them seventy times Allah will not forgive them. That is because they disbelieved in Allah and His Messenger, and Allah guides not wrongdoing folk.

81. Those who were left behind rejoiced at sitting still behind the Messenger of Allah, and were averse to striving with their wealth and their lives in Allah's way. And they said: Go not forth in the heat! Say: The heat of Hell is more intense, if they but understood.

٨١) فَرِحَ الْمُخَلَّفُونَ بِمَقْعَدِهِمْ خِلَفَ رَسُولِ اللهِ وَكَرِهُوا أَنْ يُجَهِدُوا بِأَمْوَلِهِمْ وَأَنْفُسِهِمْ فِي سَبِيلِ اللهِ وَقَالُوا لَا تَنْفِرُوا فِي الْحَرِّ قُلْ نَارُ جَهَنَّمَ أَشَدُّ حَرًّا لَوْ كَانُوا يَفْقَهُونَ

82. Then let them laugh a little: they will weep much, as the award of what they used to earn.

٨٢) فَلْيَضْحَكُوا قَلِيلًا وَلْيَبْكُوا كَثِيرًا جَزَاءً بِمَا كَانُوا يَكْسِبُونَ

83. If Allah bring you back (from the campaign) unto a party of them and they ask of you leave to go out (to fight), then say unto them: You shall never more go out with me nor fight with me against a foe. You were content with sitting still the first time. So sit still, with the useless.

٨٣) فَإِنْ رَجَعَكَ اللهُ إِلَى طَائِفَةٍ مِنْهُمْ فَاسْتَأْذَنُوكَ لِلْخُرُوجِ فَقُلْ لَنْ تَخْرُجُوا مَعِيَ أَبَدًا وَلَنْ تُقَتِلُوا مَعِيَ عَدُوًّا إِنَّكُمْ رَضِيتُمْ بِالْقُعُودِ أَوَّلَ مَرَّةٍ فَاقْعُدُوا مَعَ الْخَالِفِينَ

84. And never (O Muhammad) pray for one of them who dies, nor stand by his grave. Lo! they disbelieved in Allah and His Messenger, and they died while they were evil-doers.

٨٤) وَلَا تُصَلِّ عَلَى أَحَدٍ مِنْهُمْ مَاتَ أَبَدًا وَلَا تَقُمْ عَلَى قَبْرِهِ إِنَّهُمْ كَفَرُوا بِاللهِ وَرَسُولِهِ وَمَاتُوا وَهُمْ فَاسِقُونَ

85. Let not their wealth nor their children please you! Allah purposes only to punish them thereby in the world, and that their souls shall pass away while they are disbelievers.

٨٥) وَلَا تُعْجِبْكَ أَمْوَالُهُمْ وَأَوْلَادُهُمْ إِنَّمَا يُرِيدُ اللهُ أَنْ يُعَذِّبَهُمْ بِهَا فِي الدُّنْيَا وَتَزْهَقَ أَنْفُسُهُمْ وَهُمْ كَافِرُونَ

86. And when a surah (of the Qur'an) is revealed (which says): Believe in Allah and strive along with His Messenger, the men of wealth among them still ask leave of you and say: Leave us to be with those who sit (at home).

٨٦) وَإِذَا أُنْزِلَتْ سُورَةٌ أَنْ آمِنُوا بِاللهِ وَجَاهِدُوا مَعَ رَسُولِهِ اسْتَأْذَنَكَ أُولُوا الطَّوْلِ مِنْهُمْ وَقَالُوا ذَرْنَا نَكُنْ مَعَ الْقَاعِدِينَ

87. They are content that they should be with the useless and their hearts are sealed, so that they apprehend not.

٨٧) رَضُوا بِأَنْ يَكُونُوا مَعَ الْخَوَالِفِ وَطُبِعَ عَلَى قُلُوبِهِمْ فَهُمْ لَا يَفْقَهُونَ

88. But the Messenger and those who believe with him strive with their wealth and their lives. Such are they for whom are the good things. Such are they who are the successful.

٨٨ لَكِنِ الرَّسُولُ وَالَّذِينَ ءَامَنُوا مَعَهُ جَهَدُوا بِأَمْوَالِهِمْ وَأَنفُسِهِمْ وَأُولَٰئِكَ لَهُمُ الْخَيْرَٰتُ وَأُولَٰئِكَ هُمُ الْمُفْلِحُونَ

89. Allah has made ready for them Gardens underneath which rivers flow, wherein they will abide. That is the supreme triumph.

٨٩ أَعَدَّ اللَّهُ لَهُمْ جَنَّٰتٍ تَجْرِى مِن تَحْتِهَا الْأَنْهَٰرُ خَٰلِدِينَ فِيهَا ذَٰلِكَ الْفَوْزُ الْعَظِيمُ

90. And those among the wandering Arabs who had an excuse came in order that permission might be granted them. And those who lied to Allah and His Messenger sat at home. A painful doom will fall on those of them who disbelieve.

٩٠ وَجَاءَ الْمُعَذِّرُونَ مِنَ الْأَعْرَابِ لِيُؤْذَنَ لَهُمْ وَقَعَدَ الَّذِينَ كَذَبُوا اللَّهَ وَرَسُولَهُ سَيُصِيبُ الَّذِينَ كَفَرُوا مِنْهُمْ عَذَابٌ أَلِيمٌ

91. Not unto the weak nor unto the sick nor unto those who can find nothing to spend is any fault (to be imputed though they stay at home) if they are true to Allah and His Messenger. Not unto the good is there any way (of blame). Allah is Forgiving, Merciful.

٩١ لَيْسَ عَلَى الضُّعَفَاءِ وَلَا عَلَى الْمَرْضَى وَلَا عَلَى الَّذِينَ لَا يَجِدُونَ مَا يُنفِقُونَ حَرَجٌ إِذَا نَصَحُوا لِلَّهِ وَرَسُولِهِ مَا عَلَى الْمُحْسِنِينَ مِن سَبِيلٍ وَاللَّهُ غَفُورٌ رَّحِيمٌ

92. Nor unto those whom, when they came to you (asking) that you should mount them, you did tell: I cannot find whereon to mount you. They turned back with eyes flowing with tears, for sorrow that they could not find the means to spend.

٩٢ وَلَا عَلَى الَّذِينَ إِذَا مَا أَتَوْكَ لِتَحْمِلَهُمْ قُلْتَ لَا أَجِدُ مَا أَحْمِلُكُمْ عَلَيْهِ تَوَلَّوْا وَأَعْيُنُهُمْ تَفِيضُ مِنَ الدَّمْعِ حَزَنًا أَلَّا يَجِدُوا مَا يُنفِقُونَ

93. The way (of blame) is only against those who ask for leave of you (to stay at home) when they are rich. They are content to be with the useless. Allah has sealed their hearts so that they know not.

٩٣ إِنَّمَا السَّبِيلُ عَلَى الَّذِينَ يَسْتَـْٔذِنُونَكَ وَهُمْ أَغْنِيَاءُ رَضُوا بِأَن يَكُونُوا مَعَ الْخَوَالِفِ وَطَبَعَ اللَّهُ عَلَىٰ قُلُوبِهِمْ فَهُمْ لَا يَعْلَمُونَ

94. They will make excuse to you (Muslims) when you return unto them. Say: Make no excuse, for we shall not believe you. Allah has told us tidings of you. Allah and His Messenger will see your conduct, and then you will be brought back unto Him Who knows the invisible as well as the visible, and He will tell you what you used to do.

٩٤ يَعْتَذِرُونَ إِلَيْكُمْ إِذَا رَجَعْتُمْ إِلَيْهِمْ قُل لَّا تَعْتَذِرُوا لَن نُّؤْمِنَ لَكُمْ قَدْ نَبَّأَنَا اللَّهُ مِنْ أَخْبَارِكُمْ وَسَيَرَى اللَّهُ عَمَلَكُمْ وَرَسُولُهُ ثُمَّ تُرَدُّونَ إِلَىٰ عَٰلِمِ الْغَيْبِ وَالشَّهَٰدَةِ فَيُنَبِّئُكُم بِمَا كُنتُمْ تَعْمَلُونَ

95. They will swear by Allah unto you, when you return unto them, that you may let them be. Let them be, for lo! they are unclean, and their abode is Hell as the reward for what they used to earn.

96. They swear unto you, that you may accept them. Though you accept them, Allah verily accepts not wrong-doing folk.

97. The wandering Arabs are more hard in disbelief and hypocrisy, and more likely to be ignorant of the limits which Allah has revealed unto His Messenger. And Allah is Knower, Wise.

98. And of the wandering Arabs there is he who takes that which he expends (for the cause of Allah), as a loss, and awaits (evil) turns of fortune for you (that he may be rid of it). The evil turn of fortune will be theirs. Allah is Hearer, Knower.

99. And of the wandering Arabs there is he who believes in Allah and the Last Day, and takes that which he spends and also the prayers of the Messenger as acceptable offering in the sight of Allah. Lo! verily it is an acceptable offering for them. Allah will bring them into His mercy. Lo! Allah is Forgiving, Merciful.

100. And the first and the early ones to lead the way, of the Muhājirīn[122] and the Anṣār,[123] and those who followed them in goodness Allah is well pleased with them and they are well pleased with Him and He has made ready for them Gardens underneath which rivers flow, wherein they will abide for ever. That is the supreme triumph.

101. And among those around you of the wandering Arabs there are hypocrites, and among the townspeople of al Madinah (there are some who) persist in hypocrisy whom you (O Muhammad) know not. We know them, and We shall chastise them twice; then they will be relegated to a painful doom.

---

[122]The Muslim Makkans who fled with the Prophet to al Madinah.

[123]The Muslims of al Madinah who welcomed the fugitives from Makkah and helped the Prophet with their wealth and defended him with their lives.

102. And (there are) others who have acknowledged their faults. They mixed a righteous action with another that was bad. It may be that Allah will relent toward them. Lo! Allah is Relenting, Merciful.

103. Take alms of their wealth, wherewith you may purify them and may make them grow, and pray for them. Lo! your prayer is an assuagement for them. Allah is Hearer, Knower.

104. Know they not that Allah is He Who accepts repentance from His bondmen and takes the alms, and that Allah is He Who is the Relenting, the Merciful.

105. And say (unto them): Act! Allah will behold your actions, and (so will) His Messenger and the believers, and you will be brought back to the Knower of the invisible and the visible, and He will tell you what you used to do.

106. And (there are) others who await Allah's decree, whether He will punish them or will forgive them. Allah is Knower, Wise.

107. And as for those who chose a place of worship out of opposition and disbelief, and in order to cause dissent among the believers, and as an outpost for those who warred against Allah and His Messenger aforetime, they will surely swear: We purposed nothing save good. Allah bears witness that they verily are liars.

108. Never stand (to pray) there. A mosque which was founded upon piety (to Allah) from the first day is more worthy that you should stand (to pray) therein, wherein are men who love to purify themselves. Allah loves the purifiers.

109. Is he who founded his building upon piety to Allah and His good pleasure better; or he who founded his building on the brink of a crumbling, overhanging precipice so that it toppled with him into the fire of Hell? Allah guides not wrongdoing folk.

110. The building which they built will never cease to be a misgiving in their hearts unless their hearts be torn to pieces. Allah is Knower, Wise.

111. Lo! Allah has bought from the believers their lives and their wealth because the Garden will be theirs: they shall fight in the way of Allah and shall slay and be slain. It is a promise which is binding on Him in the Torah and the Gospel and the Qur'an. Who fulfills His covenant better than Allah? Rejoice then in your bargain that you have made, for that is the supreme triumph.

112. (Triumphant) are those who turn repentant (to Allah), those who worship (Him), those who praise (Him), those who fast, these who bow down, those who fall prostrate (in worship), those who enjoin the right and who forbid the wrong, and those who keep the limits (ordained) of Allah—So give glad tidings to believers!

113. It is not for the Prophet and those who believe to pray for the forgiveness of idolaters even though they may be near of kin (to them) after it has become clear that they are people of hellfire.

114. The prayer of Abraham for the forgiveness of his father was only because of a promise he had promised him, but when it had become clear unto him that he (his father) was an enemy to Allah he (Abraham) disowned him. Lo! Abraham was soft of heart, long suffering.

115. It was never Allah's (part) that he should send a folk astray after He had guided them until He had made clear unto them what they should avoid. Lo! Allah is Aware of all things.

116. Lo! Allah! Unto Him belongs the sovereignty of the heavens and the earth. He quickens and He gives death. And you have, instead of Allah, no protecting friend nor helper.

١١٠ لَا يَزَالُ بُنْيَانُهُمُ الَّذِي بَنَوْا رِيبَةً فِي قُلُوبِهِمْ إِلَّا أَن تَقَطَّعَ قُلُوبُهُمْ وَاللَّهُ عَلِيمٌ حَكِيمٌ

١١١ ۞ إِنَّ اللَّهَ اشْتَرَىٰ مِنَ الْمُؤْمِنِينَ أَنفُسَهُمْ وَأَمْوَالَهُم بِأَنَّ لَهُمُ الْجَنَّةَ يُقَاتِلُونَ فِي سَبِيلِ اللَّهِ فَيَقْتُلُونَ وَيُقْتَلُونَ وَعْدًا عَلَيْهِ حَقًّا فِي التَّوْرَاةِ وَالْإِنجِيلِ وَالْقُرْآنِ وَمَنْ أَوْفَىٰ بِعَهْدِهِ مِنَ اللَّهِ فَاسْتَبْشِرُوا بِبَيْعِكُمُ الَّذِي بَايَعْتُم بِهِ وَذَٰلِكَ هُوَ الْفَوْزُ الْعَظِيمُ

١١٢ التَّائِبُونَ الْعَابِدُونَ الْحَامِدُونَ السَّائِحُونَ الرَّاكِعُونَ السَّاجِدُونَ الْآمِرُونَ بِالْمَعْرُوفِ وَالنَّاهُونَ عَنِ الْمُنكَرِ وَالْحَافِظُونَ لِحُدُودِ اللَّهِ وَبَشِّرِ الْمُؤْمِنِينَ

١١٣ مَا كَانَ لِلنَّبِيِّ وَالَّذِينَ آمَنُوا أَن يَسْتَغْفِرُوا لِلْمُشْرِكِينَ وَلَوْ كَانُوا أُولِي قُرْبَىٰ مِن بَعْدِ مَا تَبَيَّنَ لَهُمْ أَنَّهُمْ أَصْحَابُ الْجَحِيمِ

١١٤ وَمَا كَانَ اسْتِغْفَارُ إِبْرَاهِيمَ لِأَبِيهِ إِلَّا عَن مَّوْعِدَةٍ وَعَدَهَا إِيَّاهُ فَلَمَّا تَبَيَّنَ لَهُ أَنَّهُ عَدُوٌّ لِّلَّهِ تَبَرَّأَ مِنْهُ إِنَّ إِبْرَاهِيمَ لَأَوَّاهٌ حَلِيمٌ

١١٥ وَمَا كَانَ اللَّهُ لِيُضِلَّ قَوْمًا بَعْدَ إِذْ هَدَاهُمْ حَتَّىٰ يُبَيِّنَ لَهُم مَّا يَتَّقُونَ إِنَّ اللَّهَ بِكُلِّ شَيْءٍ عَلِيمٌ

١١٦ إِنَّ اللَّهَ لَهُ مُلْكُ السَّمَاوَاتِ وَالْأَرْضِ يُحْيِي وَيُمِيتُ وَمَا لَكُم مِّن دُونِ اللَّهِ مِن وَلِيٍّ وَلَا نَصِيرٍ

117. Allah has turned in mercy to the Prophet, and to the Muhājirīn and the Anṣār[125] who followed him in the hour of hardship. After the hearts of a party of them had almost swerved aside, then turned He unto them in mercy. Lo! He is Full of Pity, Merciful for them.

118. And to the three also (did He turn in mercy) who were left behind: when the earth, vast as it is, was straitened for them, and their own souls were straitened for them till they bethought them that there is no refuge from Allah save toward Him. Then turned He unto them in mercy that they (too) might turn (repentant unto Him).[125] Lo! Allah! He is the Relenting, the Merciful.

119. O you who believe! Be careful of your duty to Allah, and be with the truthful.

120. It is not for the townsfolk of al Madinah and for those around them of the wandering Arabs to stay behind the Messenger of Allah and prefer their lives to his life. That is because neither thirst nor toil nor hunger afflicts them in the way of Allah, nor step they any step that angers the disbelievers, nor gain they from the enemy a gain, but a good deed is recorded for them therefor. Allah loses not the wages of the good.

121. Nor spend they any spending, small or great, nor do they cross a valley, but it is recorded for them, that Allah may repay them the best of what they used to do.

122. And the believers would not all go forth together. Of every group of them, a party only would go forth, that they may gain sound knowledge in religion, and that they may warn their folk when they return to them, so that they may beware.

---

[125]See verse 100, footnote.

[125]The reference is to three men of al Madinah who were ostracized for some misdeed but afterwards repented and were forgiven.

123. O you who believe! Fight those of the disbelievers who are near to you, and let them find harshness in you, and know that Allah is with those who keep their duty (unto Him).

﴿١٢٣﴾ يَـٰٓأَيُّهَا ٱلَّذِينَ ءَامَنُوٓا۟ قَـٰتِلُوا۟ ٱلَّذِينَ يَلُونَكُم مِّنَ ٱلْكُفَّارِ وَلْيَجِدُوا۟ فِيكُمْ غِلْظَةً وَٱعْلَمُوٓا۟ أَنَّ ٱللَّهَ مَعَ ٱلْمُتَّقِينَ

124. And whenever a surah (of the Qur'an) is revealed there are some of them who say: Which one of you has this increased in faith? As for those who believe, it has increased them in faith and they rejoice (therefor).

﴿١٢٤﴾ وَإِذَا مَآ أُنزِلَتْ سُورَةٌ فَمِنْهُم مَّن يَقُولُ أَيُّكُمْ زَادَتْهُ هَـٰذِهِۦٓ إِيمَـٰنًا فَأَمَّا ٱلَّذِينَ ءَامَنُوا۟ فَزَادَتْهُمْ إِيمَـٰنًا وَهُمْ يَسْتَبْشِرُونَ

125. But as for those in whose hearts is disease, it only adds wickedness to their wickedness, and they die while they are disbelievers.

﴿١٢٥﴾ وَأَمَّا ٱلَّذِينَ فِى قُلُوبِهِم مَّرَضٌ فَزَادَتْهُمْ رِجْسًا إِلَىٰ رِجْسِهِمْ وَمَاتُوا۟ وَهُمْ كَـٰفِرُونَ

126. See they not that they are tested once or twice in every year? Still they turn not in repentance, neither pay they heed.

﴿١٢٦﴾ أَوَلَا يَرَوْنَ أَنَّهُمْ يُفْتَنُونَ فِى كُلِّ عَامٍ مَّرَّةً أَوْ مَرَّتَيْنِ ثُمَّ لَا يَتُوبُونَ وَلَا هُمْ يَذَّكَّرُونَ

127. And whenever a surah (of the Qur'an) is revealed, they look one at another (as who should say): Does anybody see you? Then they turn away. Allah turns away their hearts because they are a folk who understand not.

﴿١٢٧﴾ وَإِذَا مَآ أُنزِلَتْ سُورَةٌ نَّظَرَ بَعْضُهُمْ إِلَىٰ بَعْضٍ هَلْ يَرَىٰكُم مِّنْ أَحَدٍ ثُمَّ ٱنصَرَفُوا۟ صَرَفَ ٱللَّهُ قُلُوبَهُم بِأَنَّهُمْ قَوْمٌ لَّا يَفْقَهُونَ

128. There has come unto you a messenger, (one) of yourselves, and it grieves him when you are overburdened with anything, he is full of concern for you, and to believers full of compassion and mercy.

﴿١٢٨﴾ لَقَدْ جَآءَكُمْ رَسُولٌ مِّنْ أَنفُسِكُمْ عَزِيزٌ عَلَيْهِ مَا عَنِتُّمْ حَرِيصٌ عَلَيْكُم بِٱلْمُؤْمِنِينَ رَءُوفٌ رَّحِيمٌ

129. Now, if they turn away (O Muhammad) say: Allah suffices me. There is no God save Him. In Him have I put my trust, and He is Lord of the Tremendous Throne.

﴿١٢٩﴾ فَإِن تَوَلَّوْا۟ فَقُلْ حَسْبِىَ ٱللَّهُ لَآ إِلَـٰهَ إِلَّا هُوَ عَلَيْهِ تَوَكَّلْتُ وَهُوَ رَبُّ ٱلْعَرْشِ ٱلْعَظِيمِ

Jonah

This surah derives its title from verse 98: "If only there had been a community (of those that were) destroyed of old that believed and profited by its belief as did the folk of Jonah!" As is the case with nearly all Makkan surahs, the date of revelation is uncertain due to of the dearth of historical allusion. All that can be said with certainty is that it belongs to the latest group of Makkan surahs and must therefore have been revealed at some time during the last four years before the Hijrah.

It is a late Makkan surah, with the exception of three verses revealed at al Madinah.

Jonah

Revealed at Makkah

*In the name of Allah,
the Beneficent, the Merciful.*

1. **A**lif. Lām. Rā'.[126] These are verses of the wise Scripture.

2. Is it a wonder for mankind that We have inspired a man among them, saying: Warn mankind and bring unto those who believe the good tidings that they have a true footing with their Lord? The disbelievers say: Lo! this is a mere wizard.

3. Lo! your Lord is Allah Who created the heavens and the earth in six days,[127] then He established Himself upon the Throne, directing all things. There is no intercessor (with Him) save after His permission. That is Allah, your Lord, so worship Him. Oh, will you not remember?

4. Unto Him is the return of all of you; it is a promise of Allah in truth. Lo! He produces creation, then reproduces it, that He may reward those who believe and do good works with equity; while, as for those who disbelieve, theirs will be a boiling drink and painful doom because they dis-believed.

5. He it is who appointed the sun a splendor and the moon a light, and measured for her stages, that you might know the number of the years, and the reckoning. Allah created not (all) that save in truth. He details the revelations for people who have knowledge.

6. Lo! in the difference of day and night and all that Allah has created in the heavens and the earth are portents, verily, for folk who ward off (evil).

---

[126]See Surah 2:1, footnote.
[127]See Surahs 22:47, 32:5, and 70:4.

٧ إِنَّ الَّذِينَ لَا يَرْجُونَ لِقَاءَنَا وَرَضُوا بِالْحَيَوٰةِ الدُّنْيَا وَاطْمَأَنُّوا بِهَا وَالَّذِينَ هُمْ عَنْ ءَايَاتِنَا غَافِلُونَ

7. Lo! those who expect not the meeting with Us but desire the life of the world and feel secure therein, and those who are neglectful of Our revelations,

٨ أُولَٰئِكَ مَأْوَاهُمُ النَّارُ بِمَا كَانُوا يَكْسِبُونَ

8. Their home will be the Fire because of what they used to earn.

٩ إِنَّ الَّذِينَ ءَامَنُوا وَعَمِلُوا الصَّالِحَاتِ يَهْدِيهِمْ رَبُّهُم بِإِيمَانِهِمْ تَجْرِي مِن تَحْتِهِمُ الْأَنْهَارُ فِي جَنَّاتِ النَّعِيمِ

9. Lo! those who believe and do good works, their Lord guides them by their faith. Rivers (will) flow beneath them in the Gardens of Delight;

١٠ دَعْوَاهُمْ فِيهَا سُبْحَانَكَ اللَّهُمَّ وَتَحِيَّتُهُمْ فِيهَا سَلَامٌ وَءَاخِرُ دَعْوَاهُمْ أَنِ الْحَمْدُ لِلَّهِ رَبِّ الْعَالَمِينَ

10. Their prayer therein will be: Glory be to You, O Allah! and their greeting therein will be: Peace. And the conclusion of their prayer will be: Praise be to Allah, Lord of the Worlds!

١١ ۞ وَلَوْ يُعَجِّلُ اللَّهُ لِلنَّاسِ الشَّرَّ اسْتِعْجَالَهُم بِالْخَيْرِ لَقُضِيَ إِلَيْهِمْ أَجَلُهُمْ فَنَذَرُ الَّذِينَ لَا يَرْجُونَ لِقَاءَنَا فِي طُغْيَانِهِمْ يَعْمَهُونَ

11. If Allah were to hasten on for men the ill (that they have earned) as they would hasten on the good, their respite would already have expired. But We suffer those who look not for the meeting with Us to wander blindly on in their contumacy.

١٢ وَإِذَا مَسَّ الْإِنسَانَ الضُّرُّ دَعَانَا لِجَنبِهِ أَوْ قَاعِدًا أَوْ قَائِمًا فَلَمَّا كَشَفْنَا عَنْهُ ضُرَّهُ مَرَّ كَأَن لَّمْ يَدْعُنَا إِلَىٰ ضُرٍّ مَّسَّهُ كَذَٰلِكَ زُيِّنَ لِلْمُسْرِفِينَ مَا كَانُوا يَعْمَلُونَ

12. And if misfortune touch a man he cries unto Us, (while reclining) on his side, or sitting or standing, but when We have relieved him of the misfortune he goes his way as though he had not cried unto Us because of a misfortune that afflicted him. Thus do the deeds of prodigals seem fair in their eyes.

١٣ وَلَقَدْ أَهْلَكْنَا الْقُرُونَ مِن قَبْلِكُمْ لَمَّا ظَلَمُوا وَجَاءَتْهُمْ رُسُلُهُم بِالْبَيِّنَاتِ وَمَا كَانُوا لِيُؤْمِنُوا كَذَٰلِكَ نَجْزِي الْقَوْمَ الْمُجْرِمِينَ

13. We destroyed the generations before you when they did wrong; and their messengers (from Allah) came unto them with clear proofs (of His Sovereignty) but they would not believe. Thus do We reward the guilty folk:

١٤ ثُمَّ جَعَلْنَاكُمْ خَلَائِفَ فِي الْأَرْضِ مِن بَعْدِهِمْ لِنَنظُرَ كَيْفَ تَعْمَلُونَ

14. Then We appointed you viceroys in the earth after them, that We might see how you behave.

١٥ وَإِذَا تُتْلَىٰ عَلَيْهِمْ ءَايَاتُنَا بَيِّنَاتٍ قَالَ الَّذِينَ لَا يَرْجُونَ لِقَاءَنَا ائْتِ بِقُرْءَانٍ غَيْرِ هَٰذَا أَوْ بَدِّلْهُ قُلْ مَا يَكُونُ لِي أَنْ أُبَدِّلَهُ مِن تِلْقَاءِ نَفْسِي إِنْ أَتَّبِعُ إِلَّا مَا يُوحَىٰ إِلَيَّ إِنِّي أَخَافُ إِنْ عَصَيْتُ رَبِّي عَذَابَ يَوْمٍ عَظِيمٍ

15. And when Our clear revelations are recited unto them they who look not for the meeting with Us say: Bring a Lecture 128 other than this, or change it. Say (O Muhammad): It is not for me to change it of my own accord. I only follow that which is inspired in me. Lo! if I disobey my Lord I fear the retribution of an awful Day.

---

128 Arabic: Qur'an.

16. Say: If Allah had so willed I should not have recited it to you nor would He have made it known to you, for I dwelt among you a whole lifetime before it (came to me). Have you then no sense?

17. Who does greater wrong than he who invents a lie concerning Allah and denies His revelations? Lo! criminals are never successful.

18. They worship beside Allah that which neither hurts them nor profits them, and they say: These are our intercessors with Allah. Say: Would you inform Allah of (something) that He knows not in the heavens or in the earth? Praised be He and high exalted above all that you associate (with Him)!

19. Mankind were but one community; then they differed; and had it not been for a word that had already gone forth from your Lord it had been judged between them in respect of that wherein they differ.

20. And they will say: If only a portent were sent down upon him from his Lord! Then say (O Muhammad): The Unseen belongs to Allah. So wait! Lo, I am waiting with you.

21. And when We cause mankind to taste of mercy after some adversity which had afflicted them, behold! they have some plot against Our revelations. Say: Allah is more swift in plotting. Lo! Our messengers write down that which you plot.

22. He it is Who makes you to go on the land and the sea till, when you are in the ships and they sail with them with a fair breeze and they are glad therein, a stormy wind reaches them and waves come unto them from every side and they deem that they are overwhelmed therein; (then) they cry unto Allah, making their faith pure for Him only: If You deliver us from this, we truly will be of the thankful.

١٦ قُلْ لَوْ شَاءَ اللّٰهُ مَا تَلَوْتُهُ عَلَيْكُمْ وَلَا أَدْرَاكُمْ بِهِ فَقَدْ لَبِثْتُ فِيكُمْ عُمُرًا مِّنْ قَبْلِهِ أَفَلَا تَعْقِلُونَ

١٧ فَمَنْ أَظْلَمُ مِمَّنِ افْتَرَىٰ عَلَى اللّٰهِ كَذِبًا أَوْ كَذَّبَ بِآيَاتِهِ إِنَّهُ لَا يُفْلِحُ الْمُجْرِمُونَ

١٨ وَيَعْبُدُونَ مِن دُونِ اللّٰهِ مَا لَا يَضُرُّهُمْ وَلَا يَنفَعُهُمْ وَيَقُولُونَ هَٰؤُلَاءِ شُفَعَاؤُنَا عِندَ اللّٰهِ قُلْ أَتُنَبِّئُونَ اللّٰهَ بِمَا لَا يَعْلَمُ فِي السَّمَاوَاتِ وَلَا فِي الْأَرْضِ سُبْحَانَهُ وَتَعَالَىٰ عَمَّا يُشْرِكُونَ

١٩ وَمَا كَانَ النَّاسُ إِلَّا أُمَّةً وَاحِدَةً فَاخْتَلَفُوا وَلَوْلَا كَلِمَةٌ سَبَقَتْ مِن رَّبِّكَ لَقُضِيَ بَيْنَهُمْ فِيمَا فِيهِ يَخْتَلِفُونَ

٢٠ وَيَقُولُونَ لَوْلَا أُنزِلَ عَلَيْهِ آيَةٌ مِّن رَّبِّهِ فَقُلْ إِنَّمَا الْغَيْبُ لِلّٰهِ فَانتَظِرُوا إِنِّي مَعَكُم مِّنَ الْمُنتَظِرِينَ

٢١ وَإِذَا أَذَقْنَا النَّاسَ رَحْمَةً مِّنْ بَعْدِ ضَرَّاءَ مَسَّتْهُمْ إِذَا لَهُم مَّكْرٌ فِي آيَاتِنَا قُلِ اللّٰهُ أَسْرَعُ مَكْرًا إِنَّ رُسُلَنَا يَكْتُبُونَ مَا تَمْكُرُونَ

٢٢ هُوَ الَّذِي يُسَيِّرُكُمْ فِي الْبَرِّ وَالْبَحْرِ حَتَّىٰ إِذَا كُنتُمْ فِي الْفُلْكِ وَجَرَيْنَ بِهِم بِرِيحٍ طَيِّبَةٍ وَفَرِحُوا بِهَا جَاءَتْهَا رِيحٌ عَاصِفٌ وَجَاءَهُمُ الْمَوْجُ مِن كُلِّ مَكَانٍ وَظَنُّوا أَنَّهُمْ أُحِيطَ بِهِمْ دَعَوُا اللّٰهَ مُخْلِصِينَ لَهُ الدِّينَ لَئِنْ أَنْجَيْتَنَا مِنْ هَٰذِهِ لَنَكُونَنَّ مِنَ الشَّاكِرِينَ

23. Yet when He has delivered them, behold! they rebel in the earth wrongfully. O mankind! Your rebellion is only against yourselves. (You have) enjoyment of the life of the world; then unto Us is your return and We shall proclaim unto you what you used to do.

٢٣ فَلَمَّا أَنْجَاهُمْ إِذَا هُمْ يَبْغُونَ فِي الْأَرْضِ بِغَيْرِ الْحَقِّ يَا أَيُّهَا النَّاسُ إِنَّمَا بَغْيُكُمْ عَلَى أَنْفُسِكُمْ مَتَاعَ الْحَيَوٰةِ الدُّنْيَا ثُمَّ إِلَيْنَا مَرْجِعُكُمْ فَنُنَبِّئُكُمْ بِمَا كُنْتُمْ تَعْمَلُونَ

24. The similitude of the life of the world is only as water which We send down from the sky, then the earth's growth of that which men and cattle eat mingles with it till, when the earth has taken on her ornaments and is embellished, and her people deem that they are masters of her, Our commandment comes to it by night or by day. Thus we make it as reaped corn as if it had not flourished yesterday. Thus do We expound the revelations for people who reflect.

٢٤ إِنَّمَا مَثَلُ الْحَيَوٰةِ الدُّنْيَا كَمَاءٍ أَنْزَلْنَاهُ مِنَ السَّمَاءِ فَاخْتَلَطَ بِهِ نَبَاتُ الْأَرْضِ مِمَّا يَأْكُلُ النَّاسُ وَالْأَنْعَامُ حَتَّى إِذَا أَخَذَتِ الْأَرْضُ زُخْرُفَهَا وَازَّيَّنَتْ وَظَنَّ أَهْلُهَا أَنَّهُمْ قَادِرُونَ عَلَيْهَا أَتَاهَا أَمْرُنَا لَيْلًا أَوْ نَهَارًا فَجَعَلْنَاهَا حَصِيدًا كَأَنْ لَمْ تَغْنَ بِالْأَمْسِ كَذَلِكَ نُفَصِّلُ الْآيَاتِ لِقَوْمٍ يَتَفَكَّرُونَ

25. And Allah summons to the abode of peace, and leads whom He will to a straight path.

٢٥ وَاللّٰهُ يَدْعُو إِلَى دَارِ السَّلَامِ وَيَهْدِي مَنْ يَشَاءُ إِلَى صِرَاطٍ مُسْتَقِيمٍ

26. For those who do good is the best (reward) and more (thereto). Neither dust nor ignominy comes near their faces. Such are rightful owners of the Garden; they will abide therein.

٢٦ لِلَّذِينَ أَحْسَنُوا الْحُسْنَى وَزِيَادَةٌ وَلَا يَرْهَقُ وُجُوهَهُمْ قَتَرٌ وَلَا ذِلَّةٌ أُولَئِكَ أَصْحَابُ الْجَنَّةِ هُمْ فِيهَا خَالِدُونَ

27. And those who earn ill deeds, (for them) requital of each ill deed is by the like thereof; and ignominy overtakes them. They have no protector from Allah. As if their faces had been covered with a cloak of darkest night. Such are rightful owners of the Fire; they will abide therein.

٢٧ وَالَّذِينَ كَسَبُوا السَّيِّئَاتِ جَزَاءُ سَيِّئَةٍ بِمِثْلِهَا وَتَرْهَقُهُمْ ذِلَّةٌ مَا لَهُمْ مِنَ اللّٰهِ مِنْ عَاصِمٍ كَأَنَّمَا أُغْشِيَتْ وُجُوهُهُمْ قِطَعًا مِنَ اللَّيْلِ مُظْلِمًا أُولَئِكَ أَصْحَابُ النَّارِ هُمْ فِيهَا خَالِدُونَ

28. On the day when We gather them all together, then We say unto those who ascribed partners (unto Us): Stand back, you and your (pretended) partners (of Allah)! And We separate them, the one from the other, and their (pretended) partners say: It was not us you worshiped.

٢٨ وَيَوْمَ نَحْشُرُهُمْ جَمِيعًا ثُمَّ نَقُولُ لِلَّذِينَ أَشْرَكُوا مَكَانَكُمْ أَنْتُمْ وَشُرَكَاؤُكُمْ فَزَيَّلْنَا بَيْنَهُمْ وَقَالَ شُرَكَاؤُهُمْ مَا كُنْتُمْ إِيَّانَا تَعْبُدُونَ

29. Allah suffices as a witness between us and you that we were unaware of your worship.

٢٩ فَكَفَى بِاللّٰهِ شَهِيدًا بَيْنَنَا وَبَيْنَكُمْ إِنْ كُنَّا عَنْ عِبَادَتِكُمْ لَغَافِلِينَ

30. There does every soul experience that which it did aforetime, and they are returned unto Allah, their rightful Lord, and that which they used to invent has failed them.

٣٠ هُنَالِكَ تَبْلُوا كُلُّ نَفْسٍ مَّا أَسْلَفَتْ وَرُدُّوا إِلَى اللّٰهِ مَوْلَاهُمُ الْحَقِّ وَضَلَّ عَنْهُمْ مَّا كَانُوا يَفْتَرُونَ

31. Say (unto them, O Muhammad): Who provides for you from the sky and the earth, or Who owns hearing and sight; and Who brings forth the living from the dead and brings forth the dead from the living; and Who directs the course? They will say: Allah. Then say: Will you not then keep your duty (unto Him)?

٣١ قُلْ مَنْ يَرْزُقُكُمْ مِّنَ السَّمَاءِ وَالْأَرْضِ أَمَّنْ يَمْلِكُ السَّمْعَ وَالْأَبْصَارَ وَمَنْ يُخْرِجُ الْحَيَّ مِنَ الْمَيِّتِ وَيُخْرِجُ الْمَيِّتَ مِنَ الْحَيِّ وَمَنْ يُدَبِّرُ الْأَمْرَ فَسَيَقُولُونَ اللّٰهُ فَقُلْ أَفَلَا تَتَّقُونَ

32. Such then is Allah, your rightful Lord. After the Truth what is there saving error? How then are you turned away!

٣٢ فَذَلِكُمُ اللّٰهُ رَبُّكُمُ الْحَقُّ فَمَاذَا بَعْدَ الْحَقِّ إِلَّا الضَّلَالُ فَأَنَّى تُصْرَفُونَ

33. Thus is the Word of your Lord justified concerning those who do wrong: that they believe not.

٣٣ كَذَلِكَ حَقَّتْ كَلِمَتُ رَبِّكَ عَلَى الَّذِينَ فَسَقُوا أَنَّهُمْ لَا يُؤْمِنُونَ

34. Say: Is there of your partners (whom you ascribe unto Allah) one that produces creation and then reproduces it? Say: Allah produces creation, then reproduces it. How then, are you misled!

٣٤ قُلْ هَلْ مِنْ شُرَكَائِكُمْ مَنْ يَبْدَؤُا الْخَلْقَ ثُمَّ يُعِيدُهُ قُلِ اللّٰهُ يَبْدَؤُا الْخَلْقَ ثُمَّ يُعِيدُهُ فَأَنَّى تُؤْفَكُونَ

35. Say: Is there of your partners (whom you ascribe unto Allah) one that leads to the Truth? Say: Allah leads to the Truth. Is He Who leads to the Truth more deserving that He should be followed, or he who finds not the way unless he (himself) be guided. What ails you? How judge you?

٣٥ قُلْ هَلْ مِنْ شُرَكَائِكُمْ مَنْ يَهْدِي إِلَى الْحَقِّ قُلِ اللّٰهُ يَهْدِي لِلْحَقِّ أَفَمَنْ يَهْدِي إِلَى الْحَقِّ أَحَقُّ أَنْ يُتَّبَعَ أَمَّنْ لَا يَهِدِّي إِلَّا أَنْ يُهْدَى فَمَا لَكُمْ كَيْفَ تَحْكُمُونَ

36. Most of them follow nothing but conjecture. Assuredly conjecture can by no means take the place of truth. Lo! Allah is Aware of what they do.

٣٦ وَمَا يَتَّبِعُ أَكْثَرُهُمْ إِلَّا ظَنًّا إِنَّ الظَّنَّ لَا يُغْنِي مِنَ الْحَقِّ شَيْئًا إِنَّ اللّٰهَ عَلِيمٌ بِمَا يَفْعَلُونَ

37. And this Qur'an is not such as could ever be invented in despite of Allah; but it is a confirmation of that which was before it and an exposition of that which is decreed for mankind. Therein is no doubt from the Lord of the Worlds.

٣٧ وَمَا كَانَ هَـٰذَا ٱلْقُرْءَانُ أَن يُفْتَرَىٰ مِن دُونِ ٱللَّهِ وَلَـٰكِن تَصْدِيقَ ٱلَّذِى بَيْنَ يَدَيْهِ وَتَفْصِيلَ ٱلْكِتَٰبِ لَا رَيْبَ فِيهِ مِن رَّبِّ ٱلْعَٰلَمِينَ

38. Or say they: He has invented it? Say: Then bring a surah (of the Qur'an) like unto it, and call (for help) on all you can besides Allah, if you are truthful.

٣٨ أَمْ يَقُولُونَ ٱفْتَرَىٰهُ قُلْ فَأْتُوا۟ بِسُورَةٍ مِّثْلِهِ وَٱدْعُوا۟ مَنِ ٱسْتَطَعْتُم مِّن دُونِ ٱللَّهِ إِن كُنتُمْ صَٰدِقِينَ

39. Nay, but they denied that, the knowledge whereof they could not compass, and whereof the interpretation (in events) has not yet come unto them. Even so did those before them deny. Then see what was the consequence for the wrongdoers!

٣٩ بَلْ كَذَّبُوا۟ بِمَا لَمْ يُحِيطُوا۟ بِعِلْمِهِ وَلَمَّا يَأْتِهِمْ تَأْوِيلُهُ كَذَٰلِكَ كَذَّبَ ٱلَّذِينَ مِن قَبْلِهِمْ فَٱنظُرْ كَيْفَ كَانَ عَٰقِبَةُ ٱلظَّٰلِمِينَ

40. And of them is he who believes therein, and of them is he who believes not therein, and your Lord is best aware of the corrupters.

٤٠ وَمِنْهُم مَّن يُؤْمِنُ بِهِ وَمِنْهُم مَّن لَّا يُؤْمِنُ بِهِ وَرَبُّكَ أَعْلَمُ بِٱلْمُفْسِدِينَ

41. And if they deny you, say: Unto me is my work, and unto you is your work. You are innocent of what I do, and I am innocent of what you do.

٤١ وَإِن كَذَّبُوكَ فَقُل لِّى عَمَلِى وَلَكُمْ عَمَلُكُمْ أَنتُم بَرِيٓـُٔونَ مِمَّآ أَعْمَلُ وَأَنَا۠ بَرِىٓءٌ مِّمَّا تَعْمَلُونَ

42. And of them are some who listen unto you. But can you make the deaf to hear even though they apprehend not?

٤٢ وَمِنْهُم مَّن يَسْتَمِعُونَ إِلَيْكَ أَفَأَنتَ تُسْمِعُ ٱلصُّمَّ وَلَوْ كَانُوا۟ لَا يَعْقِلُونَ

43. And of them is he who looks toward you. But can you guide the blind even though they see not?

٤٣ وَمِنْهُم مَّن يَنظُرُ إِلَيْكَ أَفَأَنتَ تَهْدِى ٱلْعُمْىَ وَلَوْ كَانُوا۟ لَا يُبْصِرُونَ

44. Lo! Allah wrongs not mankind in anything; but man-kind wrong themselves.

٤٤ إِنَّ ٱللَّهَ لَا يَظْلِمُ ٱلنَّاسَ شَيْـًٔا وَلَٰكِنَّ ٱلنَّاسَ أَنفُسَهُمْ يَظْلِمُونَ

45. And on the day when He shall gather them together, (when it will seem) as though they had tarried but an hour of the day, recognizing one another, those will verily have perished who denied the meeting with Allah and were not guided.

٤٥ وَيَوْمَ يَحْشُرُهُمْ كَأَن لَّمْ يَلْبَثُوٓا۟ إِلَّا سَاعَةً مِّنَ ٱلنَّهَارِ يَتَعَارَفُونَ بَيْنَهُمْ قَدْ خَسِرَ ٱلَّذِينَ كَذَّبُوا۟ بِلِقَآءِ ٱللَّهِ وَمَا كَانُوا۟ مُهْتَدِينَ

46. Whether We let you (O Muhammad) behold something of that which We promise them or (whether We) cause you to die, still unto Us is their return, and Allah, moreover, is Witness over what they do.

٤٦ وَإِمَّا نُرِيَنَّكَ بَعْضَ الَّذِي نَعِدُهُمْ أَوْ نَتَوَفَّيَنَّكَ فَإِلَيْنَا مَرْجِعُهُمْ ثُمَّ اللَّهُ شَهِيدٌ عَلَى مَا يَفْعَلُونَ

47. And for every nation there is a messenger. And when their messenger comes (on the Day of Judgment) it will be judged between them fairly, and they will not be wronged.

٤٧ وَلِكُلِّ أُمَّةٍ رَسُولٌ فَإِذَا جَاءَ رَسُولُهُمْ قُضِيَ بَيْنَهُمْ بِالْقِسْطِ وَهُمْ لَا يُظْلَمُونَ

48. And they say: When will this promise be fulfilled, if you are truthful?

٤٨ وَيَقُولُونَ مَتَى هَذَا الْوَعْدُ إِنْ كُنْتُمْ صَادِقِينَ

49. Say: I have no power to hurt or benefit myself, save that which Allah wills. For every nation there is an appointed time. When their time comes, then they cannot put it off an hour, nor hasten (it).

٤٩ قُلْ لَا أَمْلِكُ لِنَفْسِي ضَرًّا وَلَا نَفْعًا إِلَّا مَا شَاءَ اللَّهُ لِكُلِّ أُمَّةٍ أَجَلٌ إِذَا جَاءَ أَجَلُهُمْ فَلَا يَسْتَأْخِرُونَ سَاعَةً وَلَا يَسْتَقْدِمُونَ

50. Say: Have you thought: When His doom comes unto you as a raid by night, or in the (busy) day; what is there of it that the guilty ones desire to hasten?

٥٠ قُلْ أَرَأَيْتُمْ إِنْ أَتَاكُمْ عَذَابُهُ بَيَاتًا أَوْ نَهَارًا مَاذَا يَسْتَعْجِلُ مِنْهُ الْمُجْرِمُونَ

51. Is it (only) then, when it has befallen you, that you will believe? What! (Believe) now, when (until now) you have been hastening it on (through disbelief)?

٥١ أَثُمَّ إِذَا مَا وَقَعَ آمَنْتُمْ بِهِ آلْآنَ وَقَدْ كُنْتُمْ بِهِ تَسْتَعْجِلُونَ

52. Then will it be said unto those who dealt unjustly: Taste the torment of eternity. Are you requited anything save what you used to earn?

٥٢ ثُمَّ قِيلَ لِلَّذِينَ ظَلَمُوا ذُوقُوا عَذَابَ الْخُلْدِ هَلْ تُجْزَوْنَ إِلَّا بِمَا كُنْتُمْ تَكْسِبُونَ

53. And they ask you to inform them (saying): Is it true? Say: Yea, by my Lord, verily it is true, and you cannot escape.

٥٣ وَيَسْتَنْبِئُونَكَ أَحَقٌّ هُوَ قُلْ إِي وَرَبِّي إِنَّهُ لَحَقٌّ وَمَا أَنْتُمْ بِمُعْجِزِينَ

54. And if each soul that does wrong had all that is in the earth it would seek to ransom itself therewith; and they will feel remorse within them, when they see the doom. But it has been judged between them fairly and they are not wronged.

٥٤ وَلَوْ أَنَّ لِكُلِّ نَفْسٍ ظَلَمَتْ مَا فِي الْأَرْضِ لَافْتَدَتْ بِهِ وَأَسَرُّوا النَّدَامَةَ لَمَّا رَأَوُا الْعَذَابَ وَقُضِيَ بَيْنَهُمْ بِالْقِسْطِ وَهُمْ لَا يُظْلَمُونَ

55. Lo! verily all that is in the heavens and the earth is Allah's. Lo! verily Allah's promise is true. But most of them know not.

٥٥ أَلَا إِنَّ لِلَّهِ مَا فِي السَّمَوَاتِ وَالْأَرْضِ أَلَا إِنَّ وَعْدَ اللَّهِ حَقٌّ وَلَكِنَّ أَكْثَرَهُمْ لَا يَعْلَمُونَ

56. He quickens and gives death, and unto Him you will be returned.

٥٦ هُوَ يُحْيِي وَيُمِيتُ وَإِلَيْهِ تُرْجَعُونَ

57. O mankind! There has come unto you an exhortation from your Lord, a balm for that which is in the breasts, a guidance and a mercy for believers.

58. Say: In the bounty of Allah and in His mercy: therein let them rejoice. It is better than what they accumulate.

59. Say: Have you considered what provision Allah has sent down for you, how you have made of it lawful and unlawful? Say: Has Allah permitted you, or do you invent a lie concerning Allah?

60. And what think those who invent a lie concerning Allah (will be their plight) upon the Day of Resurrection? Lo! Allah truly is Bountiful toward mankind, but most of them give not thanks.

61. And you (Muhammad) are not occupied with any business and you recite not a lecture[129] from this (Scripture), and you (mankind) perform no act, but We are Witness of you when you are engaged therein. And not an atom's weight in the earth or in the sky escapes your Lord, nor what is less than that or greater than that, but it is (written) in a clear Book.

62. Lo! verily the friends of Allah are (those) on whom fear (comes) not, nor do they grieve.

63. Those who believe and keep their duty (to Allah),

64. Theirs are good tidings in the life of the world and in the Hereafter—There is no changing the Words of Allah—that is the Supreme Triumph.

65. And let not their speech grieve you (O Muhammad). Lo! power belongs wholly to Allah. He is the Hearer, the Knower.

---

[129] Arabic: Qur'an.

66. Lo! whosoever is in the heavens and whosoever is in the earth belongs to Allah. Those who follow anything instead of Allah follow not (His) partners. They follow only a conjecture. and they do but guess.

67. He it is who has appointed for you the night that you should rest therein and the day giving sight. Lo! herein verily are portents for a folk that heed.

68. They say: Allah has taken (unto Him) a son. Glorified be He! He has no needs! His is all that is in the heavens and all that is in the earth. You have no warrant for this. Tell you concerning Allah that which you know not?

69. Say: Verily those who invent a lie concerning Allah will not succeed.

70. This world's portion (will be theirs), then unto Us is their return. Then We make them taste a dreadful doom because they used to disbelieve.

71. Recite unto them the story of Noah, when he told his people: O my people! If my sojourn (here) and my reminding you by Allah's revelations are an offence unto you, in Allah have I put my trust, so decide upon your course of action, you and your partners. Let not your course of action be in doubt, for you. Then come forth against me, give me no respite.

72. But if you are averse I have asked of you no wage. My wage is the concern of Allah only, and I am commanded to be of those who surrender (unto Him).

73. But they denied him, so We saved him and those with him in the ship, and made them viceroys (in the earth), while We drowned those who denied Our revelations. See then the nature of the consequence for those who had been warned.

74. Then, after him, We sent messengers unto their folk, and they brought them clear proofs. But they were not ready to believe in that which they before denied. Thus print We on the hearts of the transgressors.

75. Then, after them, We sent Moses and Aaron unto Pharaoh and his chiefs with Our revelations, but they were arrogant and were a guilty folk.

76. And when the Truth from Our presence came unto them, they said: This is mere magic.

77. Moses said: Speak you (so) of the Truth when it has come unto you? Is this magic? Now magicians thrive not.

78. They said: Have you come unto us to pervert us from that (faith) in which we found our fathers, and that you two may be arrogant in the land? We will not believe you two.

79. And Pharaoh said: Bring every cunning wizard unto me.

80. And when the wizards came, Moses said unto them: Cast your cast!

81. And when they had cast, Moses said: That which you have brought is magic. Lo! Allah will make it vain. Lo! Allah reforms not the work of mischief makers.

82. And Allah will vindicate the Truth by His words, however much the criminals be averse.

83. But none believed in Moses, save some scions of his people, (and they were) in fear of Pharaoh and their chiefs, that they would persecute them. Lo! Pharaoh was truly a tyrant in the land, and lo! he truly was of the wanton.

84. And Moses said: O my people! If you have believed in Allah then put trust in Him, if you have indeed surrendered (unto Him)!

٧٤ ثُمَّ بَعَثْنَا مِنْ بَعْدِهِ رُسُلًا إِلَى قَوْمِهِمْ فَجَاءُوهُمْ بِالْبَيِّنَاتِ فَمَا كَانُوا لِيُؤْمِنُوا بِمَا كَذَّبُوا بِهِ مِنْ قَبْلُ كَذَلِكَ نَطْبَعُ عَلَى قُلُوبِ الْمُعْتَدِينَ

٧٥ ثُمَّ بَعَثْنَا مِنْ بَعْدِهِمْ مُوسَى وَهَارُونَ إِلَى فِرْعَوْنَ وَمَلَإِيهِ بِآيَاتِنَا فَاسْتَكْبَرُوا وَكَانُوا قَوْمًا مُّجْرِمِينَ

٧٦ فَلَمَّا جَاءَهُمُ الْحَقُّ مِنْ عِنْدِنَا قَالُوا إِنَّ هَذَا لَسِحْرٌ مُبِينٌ

٧٧ قَالَ مُوسَى أَتَقُولُونَ لِلْحَقِّ لَمَّا جَاءَكُمْ أَسِحْرٌ هَذَا وَلَا يُفْلِحُ السَّاحِرُونَ

٧٨ قَالُوا أَجِئْتَنَا لِتَلْفِتَنَا عَمَّا وَجَدْنَا عَلَيْهِ آبَاءَنَا وَتَكُونَ لَكُمَا الْكِبْرِيَاءُ فِي الْأَرْضِ وَمَا نَحْنُ لَكُمَا بِمُؤْمِنِينَ

٧٩ وَقَالَ فِرْعَوْنُ ائْتُونِي بِكُلِّ سَاحِرٍ عَلِيمٍ

٨٠ فَلَمَّا جَاءَ السَّحَرَةُ قَالَ لَهُمْ مُوسَى أَلْقُوا مَا أَنْتُمْ مُلْقُونَ

٨١ فَلَمَّا أَلْقَوْا قَالَ مُوسَى مَا جِئْتُمْ بِهِ السِّحْرُ إِنَّ اللَّهَ سَيُبْطِلُهُ إِنَّ اللَّهَ لَا يُصْلِحُ عَمَلَ الْمُفْسِدِينَ

٨٢ وَيُحِقُّ اللَّهُ الْحَقَّ بِكَلِمَاتِهِ وَلَوْ كَرِهَ الْمُجْرِمُونَ

٨٣ فَمَا آمَنَ لِمُوسَى إِلَّا ذُرِّيَّةٌ مِنْ قَوْمِهِ عَلَى خَوْفٍ مِنْ فِرْعَوْنَ وَمَلَإِهِمْ أَنْ يَفْتِنَهُمْ وَإِنَّ فِرْعَوْنَ لَعَالٍ فِي الْأَرْضِ وَإِنَّهُ لَمِنَ الْمُسْرِفِينَ

٨٤ وَقَالَ مُوسَى يَا قَوْمِ إِنْ كُنْتُمْ آمَنْتُمْ بِاللَّهِ فَعَلَيْهِ تَوَكَّلُوا إِنْ كُنْتُمْ مُسْلِمِينَ

85. They said: In Allah we put trust. Our Lord! Oh, make us not a lure for the wrongdoing folk;

86. And, of Your mercy, save us from the folk that disbelieve.

87. And We inspired Moses and his brother, (saying): Appoint houses for your people in Egypt and make your houses mosques, and establish prayer. And give good news to the believers.

88. And Moses said: Our Lord! Lo! You have given Phar-aoh and his chiefs splendor and riches in the life of the world, Our Lord! that they may lead men astray from Your way. Our Lord! Destroy their riches and harden their hearts so that they believe not till they see the painful doom.

89. He said: Your prayer is accepted. Do you both keep to the straight path, and follow not the road of those who have no knowledge.

90. And We brought the Children of Israel across the sea, and Pharaoh with his hosts pursued them in rebellion and transgression, till, when the (fate of) drowning overtook him, he exclaimed: I believe that there is no God save Him in whom the Children of Israel believe, and I am of those who surrender (unto Him).

91. What! Now! When hitherto you have rebelled and been of the wrong-doers?

92. But this day We save you in your body that you may be a portent for those after you. Lo! most of mankind are heedless of Our portents.

93 And We verify did allot unto the Children of Israel a fixed abode, and did provide them with good things; and they differed not until knowledge came unto them. Lo! your Lord will judge between them on the Day of Resurrection concerning that wherein they used to differ.

٨٥ فَقَالُوا عَلَى اللهِ تَوَكَّلْنَا رَبَّنَا لَا تَجْعَلْنَا فِتْنَةً لِّلْقَوْمِ الظَّالِمِينَ

٨٦ وَنَجِّنَا بِرَحْمَتِكَ مِنَ الْقَوْمِ الْكَافِرِينَ

٨٧ وَأَوْحَيْنَا إِلَى مُوسَى وَأَخِيهِ أَنْ تَبَوَّءَا لِقَوْمِكُمَا بِمِصْرَ بُيُوتًا وَاجْعَلُوا بُيُوتَكُمْ قِبْلَةً وَأَقِيمُوا الصَّلَاةَ وَبَشِّرِ الْمُؤْمِنِينَ

٨٨ وَقَالَ مُوسَى رَبَّنَا إِنَّكَ آتَيْتَ فِرْعَوْنَ وَمَلَأَهُ زِينَةً وَأَمْوَالًا فِي الْحَيَاةِ الدُّنْيَا رَبَّنَا لِيُضِلُّوا عَنْ سَبِيلِكَ رَبَّنَا اطْمِسْ عَلَى أَمْوَالِهِمْ وَاشْدُدْ عَلَى قُلُوبِهِمْ فَلَا يُؤْمِنُوا حَتَّى يَرَوُا الْعَذَابَ الْأَلِيمَ

٨٩ قَالَ قَدْ أُجِيبَتْ دَعْوَتُكُمَا فَاسْتَقِيمَا وَلَا تَتَّبِعَانِّ سَبِيلَ الَّذِينَ لَا يَعْلَمُونَ

٩٠ وَجَاوَزْنَا بِبَنِي إِسْرَائِيلَ الْبَحْرَ فَأَتْبَعَهُمْ فِرْعَوْنُ وَجُنُودُهُ بَغْيًا وَعَدْوًا حَتَّى إِذَا أَدْرَكَهُ الْغَرَقُ قَالَ آمَنْتُ أَنَّهُ لَا إِلَهَ إِلَّا الَّذِي آمَنَتْ بِهِ بَنُوا إِسْرَائِيلَ وَأَنَا مِنَ الْمُسْلِمِينَ

٩١ آلْآنَ وَقَدْ عَصَيْتَ قَبْلُ وَكُنْتَ مِنَ الْمُفْسِدِينَ

٩٢ فَالْيَوْمَ نُنَجِّيكَ بِبَدَنِكَ لِتَكُونَ لِمَنْ خَلْفَكَ آيَةً وَإِنَّ كَثِيرًا مِنَ النَّاسِ عَنْ آيَاتِنَا لَغَافِلُونَ

٩٣ وَلَقَدْ بَوَّأْنَا بَنِي إِسْرَائِيلَ مُبَوَّأَ صِدْقٍ وَرَزَقْنَاهُمْ مِنَ الطَّيِّبَاتِ فَمَا اخْتَلَفُوا حَتَّى جَاءَهُمُ الْعِلْمُ إِنَّ رَبَّكَ يَقْضِي بَيْنَهُمْ يَوْمَ الْقِيَامَةِ فِيمَا كَانُوا فِيهِ يَخْتَلِفُونَ

94. And if you (Muhammad) are in doubt concerning that which We reveal unto you, then question those who read the Scripture (that was) before you. Verily the Truth from your Lord has come unto you. So be not you of the waverers.

95. And be not you of those who deny the revelations of Allah, for then were you of the losers.

96. Lo! those for whom the word of your Lord (concerning sinners) has effect will not believe,

97. Though every token come unto them, till they see the painful doom.

98. If only there had been a community (of all those that were destroyed of old) that believed and profited by its belief as did the folk of Jonah. When they believed We drew off from them the torment of disgrace in the life of the world and gave them comfort for a while.

99. And if your Lord willed, all who are in the earth would have believed together. Would you (Muhammad) compel people until they are believers?

100. It is not for any soul to believe save by the permission of Allah. He has set uncleanness upon those who have no sense.

101. Say: Behold what is in the heavens and the earth! But revelations and warnings avail not folk who will not believe.

102. What expect they save the like of the days of those who passed away before them? Say: Expect then! I am with you among the expectant.

103. Then shall We save Our messengers and the believers, in like manner (as of old). It is incumbent upon Us to save believers.

104. Say (O Muhammad): O mankind! If you are in doubt of my religion, then (know that) I worship not those whom you worship instead of Allah, but I worship Allah who causes you to die, and I have been commanded to be of the believers.

105. And, (O Muhammad) set your purpose resolutely for religion, as a man by nature upright, and be not of those who ascribe partners (to Allah).

106. And cry not, beside Allah, unto that which cannot profit you nor hurt you, for if you did so then were you of the wrongdoers.

107. If Allah afflicts you with some hurt, there is none who can remove it save Him; and if He desires good for you, there is none who can repel His bounty. He strikes with it whom He will of His bondmen. He is the Forgiving, the Merciful.

108. Say: O mankind! Now has the Truth from your Lord come unto you. So whoever is guided, is guided only for (the good of) his soul, and whoever errs errs only against it. And I am not a warder over you.

109. And (O Muhammad) follow that which is inspired in you, and forbear until Allah give judgment. And He is the Best of Judges.

قُلْ يَا أَيُّهَا النَّاسُ إِنْ كُنْتُمْ فِى شَكٍّ مِنْ دِينِى ﴿١٠٤﴾ فَلَا أَعْبُدُ الَّذِينَ تَعْبُدُونَ مِنْ دُونِ اللَّهِ وَلَٰكِنْ أَعْبُدُ اللَّهَ الَّذِى يَتَوَفَّاكُمْ وَأُمِرْتُ أَنْ أَكُونَ مِنَ الْمُؤْمِنِينَ

وَأَنْ أَقِمْ وَجْهَكَ لِلدِّينِ حَنِيفًا وَلَا تَكُونَنَّ مِنَ الْمُشْرِكِينَ ﴿١٠٥﴾

وَلَا تَدْعُ مِنْ دُونِ اللَّهِ مَا لَا يَنْفَعُكَ وَلَا يَضُرُّكَ ﴿١٠٦﴾ فَإِنْ فَعَلْتَ فَإِنَّكَ إِذًا مِنَ الظَّالِمِينَ

وَإِنْ يَمْسَسْكَ اللَّهُ بِضُرٍّ فَلَا كَاشِفَ لَهُ ﴿١٠٧﴾ إِلَّا هُوَ وَإِنْ يُرِدْكَ بِخَيْرٍ فَلَا رَادَّ لِفَضْلِهِ يُصِيبُ بِهِ مَنْ يَشَاءُ مِنْ عِبَادِهِ وَهُوَ الْغَفُورُ الرَّحِيمُ

قُلْ يَا أَيُّهَا النَّاسُ قَدْ جَاءَكُمُ الْحَقُّ مِنْ ﴿١٠٨﴾ رَبِّكُمْ فَمَنِ اهْتَدَى فَإِنَّمَا يَهْتَدِى لِنَفْسِهِ وَمَنْ ضَلَّ فَإِنَّمَا يَضِلُّ عَلَيْهَا وَمَا أَنَا عَلَيْكُمْ بِوَكِيلٍ

وَاتَّبِعْ مَا يُوحَى إِلَيْكَ وَاصْبِرْ حَتَّى يَحْكُمَ اللَّهُ ﴿١٠٩﴾ وَهُوَ خَيْرُ الْحَاكِمِينَ

Hūd

This surah takes its name from verse 50, which begins the story of Hūd, of the tribe of 'Ād, one of the prophets of Arabia who is not mentioned in the Hebrew Scriptures. This surah also contains the stories of two other Arab prophets: Ṣāliḥ, of the tribe of Thamūd, and Shu'ayb of Madian (identified with Jethro). These accounts, along with those of Noah and Moses, are quoted as part of the history of divine revelation, the truth of which is here vindicated. The manner is that of a supplement to the tenth surah.

It is a late Makkan surah, except for verses 114 f., which were revealed at al Madinah.

Hūd

Revealed at Makkah

*In the name of Allah,
the Beneficent, the Merciful*

1. **A**lif. Lām. Rā'.[130] (This is) a Scripture the revelations whereof are perfected and then expounded. (It comes) from One Wise, Informed,

2. (Saying): Worship none but Allah. Lo! I am unto you from Him a warner and a bringer of good tidings.

3. And (bidding you): Ask pardon of your Lord and turn to Him repentant. He will cause you to enjoy a fair estate until a time appointed. He gives His bounty unto every bountiful one. But if you turn away, Lo! (then) I fear for you the retribution of an awful Day.

4. Unto Allah is your return, and He is able to do all things.

5. Lo! now they fold up their breasts that they may hide (their thoughts) from Him. At the very moment when they cover themselves with their clothing, Allah knows that which they keep hidden and that which they proclaim. Lo! He is Aware of what is in the breasts (of men).

6. And there is not a beast in the earth but the sustenance thereof depends on Allah. He knows its habitation and its repository. All is in a clear record.

7. And He it is Who created the heavens and the earth in six days[131] and His Throne was upon the water that He might try you, which of you is best in conduct. Yet if you (O Muhammad) say: Lo! you will be raised again after death! those who disbelieve will surely say: This is nothing but mere magic.

---

[130]See Surah 2:1, footnote.
[131]See Surahs 22:47, 32:5, and 70:4.

8. And if We delay for them the doom until a reckoned time, they will surely say: What withholds it? Verily on the day when it comes unto them, it cannot be averted from them, and that which they derided will surround them.

9. And if We cause man to taste some mercy from Us and afterward withdraw it from him, lo! he is despairing, thankless.

10. And if We cause him to taste grace after some misfortune that had befallen him, he says: The ills have gone from me. Lo! he is exultant, boastful;

11. Save those who persevere and do good works. Theirs will be forgiveness and a great reward.

12. A likely thing, that you would forsake anything of that which has been revealed unto you, and that your breast should be straitened for it, because they say: Why has not a treasure been sent down for him, or an angel come with him? You are but a warner, and Allah is in charge of all things.

13. Or they say: He has invented it. Say: Then bring ten surahs, the like thereof, invented, and call on everyone you can beside Allah, if you are truthful!

14. And if they answer not your prayer, then know that it is revealed only in the knowledge of Allah; and that there is no God save Him. Will you then be (of) those who surrender?[132]

15. Who desires the life of the world and its pomp, We shall repay them their deeds herein, and therein they will not be wronged.

16. Those are they for whom is nothing in the Hereafter save the Fire. (All) that they contrive here is vain and (all) that they are wont to do is fruitless.

[132] Arabic: Muslimīn.

17. Is he (to be counted equal with them) who relies on a clear proof from his Lord, and a witness from Him recites it, and before it was the Book of Moses, an example and a mercy? Such believe therein, and who disbelieves therein of the clans, the Fire is his appointed place. So be not you in doubt concerning it. Lo! it is the Truth from your Lord; but most of mankind believe not.

18. Who does greater wrong than he who invents a lie concerning Allah? Such will be brought before their Lord, and the witnesses will say: These are they who lied concerning their Lord. Now the curse of Allah is upon wrong-doers,

19. Who debar (men) from the way of Allah and would have it crooked, and who are disbelievers in the Hereafter.

20. Such will not escape in the earth, nor have they any protecting friends beside Allah. For them the torment will be double. They could not bear to hear, and they used not to see.

21. Such are they who have lost their souls, and that which they used to invent has failed them.

22. Assuredly in the Hereafter they will be the greatest losers.

23. Lo! those who believe and do good works and humble themselves before their Lord: such are rightful owners of the Garden; they will abide therein.

24. The similitude of the two parties is as the blind and the deaf and the seer and the hearer. Are they equal in similitude? Will you not then be admonished?

١٧ أَفَمَن كَانَ عَلَىٰ بَيِّنَةٍ مِّن رَّبِّهِۦ وَيَتْلُوهُ شَاهِدٌ مِّنْهُ وَمِن قَبْلِهِۦ كِتَٰبُ مُوسَىٰٓ إِمَامًا وَرَحْمَةً أُوْلَٰٓئِكَ يُؤْمِنُونَ بِهِۦ وَمَن يَكْفُرْ بِهِۦ مِنَ ٱلْأَحْزَابِ فَٱلنَّارُ مَوْعِدُهُۥ فَلَا تَكُ فِى مِرْيَةٍ مِّنْهُ إِنَّهُ ٱلْحَقُّ مِن رَّبِّكَ وَلَٰكِنَّ أَكْثَرَ ٱلنَّاسِ لَا يُؤْمِنُونَ

١٨ وَمَنْ أَظْلَمُ مِمَّنِ ٱفْتَرَىٰ عَلَى ٱللَّهِ كَذِبًا أُوْلَٰٓئِكَ يُعْرَضُونَ عَلَىٰ رَبِّهِمْ وَيَقُولُ ٱلْأَشْهَٰدُ هَٰٓؤُلَآءِ ٱلَّذِينَ كَذَبُوا۟ عَلَىٰ رَبِّهِمْ أَلَا لَعْنَةُ ٱللَّهِ عَلَى ٱلظَّٰلِمِينَ

١٩ ٱلَّذِينَ يَصُدُّونَ عَن سَبِيلِ ٱللَّهِ وَيَبْغُونَهَا عِوَجًا وَهُم بِٱلْآخِرَةِ هُمْ كَٰفِرُونَ

٢٠ أُوْلَٰٓئِكَ لَمْ يَكُونُوا۟ مُعْجِزِينَ فِى ٱلْأَرْضِ وَمَا كَانَ لَهُم مِّن دُونِ ٱللَّهِ مِنْ أَوْلِيَآءَ يُضَٰعَفُ لَهُمُ ٱلْعَذَابُ مَا كَانُوا۟ يَسْتَطِيعُونَ ٱلسَّمْعَ وَمَا كَانُوا۟ يُبْصِرُونَ

٢١ أُوْلَٰٓئِكَ ٱلَّذِينَ خَسِرُوٓا۟ أَنفُسَهُمْ وَضَلَّ عَنْهُم مَّا كَانُوا۟ يَفْتَرُونَ

٢٢ لَا جَرَمَ أَنَّهُمْ فِى ٱلْآخِرَةِ هُمُ ٱلْأَخْسَرُونَ

٢٣ إِنَّ ٱلَّذِينَ ءَامَنُوا۟ وَعَمِلُوا۟ ٱلصَّٰلِحَٰتِ وَأَخْبَتُوٓا۟ إِلَىٰ رَبِّهِمْ أُوْلَٰٓئِكَ أَصْحَٰبُ ٱلْجَنَّةِ هُمْ فِيهَا خَٰلِدُونَ

٢٤ مَثَلُ ٱلْفَرِيقَيْنِ كَٱلْأَعْمَىٰ وَٱلْأَصَمِّ وَٱلْبَصِيرِ وَٱلسَّمِيعِ هَلْ يَسْتَوِيَانِ مَثَلًا أَفَلَا تَذَكَّرُونَ

25. And We sent Noah unto his folk (and he said): I am a plain warner unto you.

26. That you worship none, save Allah. Lo! I fear for you the retribution of a painful Day.

27. The chieftains of his folk, who disbelieved, said: We see you but a mortal like us, and we see not that any follow you save the most abject among us, without reflection. We behold in you no merit above us—nay, we deem you liars.

28. He said: O my people! Bethink you, if I rely on a clear proof from my Lord and there has come unto me a mercy from His presence, and it has been made obscure to you, can we compel you to accept it when you are averse thereto?

29. And O my people! I ask of you no wealth therefor. My reward is the concern only of Allah, and I am not going to thrust away those who believe—Lo! they have to meet their Lord—but I see you a folk that are ignorant.

30. And, O my people! who would deliver me from Allah if I thrust them away? Will you not then reflect?

31. I say not unto you: "I have the treasures of Allah" nor "I have knowledge of the Unseen," nor say I: "Lo! I am an angel!" Nor say I unto those whom your eyes scorn that Allah will not give them good—Allah knows best what is in their hearts—Lo! then indeed I should be of the wrongdoers.

32. They said: O Noah! You have disputed with us and multiplied disputation with us; now bring upon us that with which you threaten us, if you are of the truthful.

٢٥ وَلَقَدْ أَرْسَلْنَا نُوحًا إِلَىٰ قَوْمِهِ إِنِّي لَكُمْ نَذِيرٌ مُبِينٌ

٢٦ أَن لَّا تَعْبُدُوا إِلَّا اللَّهَ إِنِّي أَخَافُ عَلَيْكُمْ عَذَابَ يَوْمٍ أَلِيمٍ

٢٧ فَقَالَ الْمَلَأُ الَّذِينَ كَفَرُوا مِن قَوْمِهِ مَا نَرَاكَ إِلَّا بَشَرًا مِّثْلَنَا وَمَا نَرَاكَ اتَّبَعَكَ إِلَّا الَّذِينَ هُمْ أَرَاذِلُنَا بَادِيَ الرَّأْيِ وَمَا نَرَىٰ لَكُمْ عَلَيْنَا مِن فَضْلٍ بَلْ نَظُنُّكُمْ كَاذِبِينَ

٢٨ قَالَ يَا قَوْمِ أَرَأَيْتُمْ إِن كُنتُ عَلَىٰ بَيِّنَةٍ مِّن رَّبِّي وَآتَانِي رَحْمَةً مِّنْ عِندِهِ فَعُمِّيَتْ عَلَيْكُمْ أَنُلْزِمُكُمُوهَا وَأَنتُمْ لَهَا كَارِهُونَ

٢٩ وَيَا قَوْمِ لَا أَسْأَلُكُمْ عَلَيْهِ مَالًا إِنْ أَجْرِيَ إِلَّا عَلَى اللَّهِ وَمَا أَنَا بِطَارِدِ الَّذِينَ آمَنُوا إِنَّهُم مُّلَاقُو رَبِّهِمْ وَلَٰكِنِّي أَرَاكُمْ قَوْمًا تَجْهَلُونَ

٣٠ وَيَا قَوْمِ مَن يَنصُرُنِي مِنَ اللَّهِ إِن طَرَدتُّهُمْ أَفَلَا تَذَكَّرُونَ

٣١ وَلَا أَقُولُ لَكُمْ عِندِي خَزَائِنُ اللَّهِ وَلَا أَعْلَمُ الْغَيْبَ وَلَا أَقُولُ إِنِّي مَلَكٌ وَلَا أَقُولُ لِلَّذِينَ تَزْدَرِي أَعْيُنُكُمْ لَن يُؤْتِيَهُمُ اللَّهُ خَيْرًا اللَّهُ أَعْلَمُ بِمَا فِي أَنفُسِهِمْ إِنِّي إِذًا لَّمِنَ الظَّالِمِينَ

٣٢ قَالُوا يَا نُوحُ قَدْ جَادَلْتَنَا فَأَكْثَرْتَ جِدَالَنَا فَأْتِنَا بِمَا تَعِدُنَا إِن كُنتَ مِنَ الصَّادِقِينَ

33. He said: Only Allah will bring it upon you if He will, and you can by no means escape.

٣٣ قَالَ إِنَّمَا يَأْتِيكُمْ بِهِ اللَّهُ إِنْ شَاءَ وَمَا أَنْتُمْ بِمُعْجِزِينَ

34. My counsel will not profit you if I were minded to advise you, if Allah's will is to keep you astray. He is your Lord and unto Him you will be brought back.

٣٤ وَلَا يَنْفَعُكُمْ نُصْحِي إِنْ أَرَدْتُ أَنْ أَنْصَحَ لَكُمْ إِنْ كَانَ اللَّهُ يُرِيدُ أَنْ يُغْوِيَكُمْ هُوَ رَبُّكُمْ وَإِلَيْهِ تُرْجَعُونَ

35. Or say they (again) He has invented it? Say: If I have invented it, upon me be my crimes, but I am innocent of (all) that you commit.

٣٥ أَمْ يَقُولُونَ افْتَرَاهُ قُلْ إِنِ افْتَرَيْتُهُ فَعَلَيَّ إِجْرَامِي وَأَنَا بَرِيءٌ مِمَّا تُجْرِمُونَ

36. And it was inspired in Noah, (saying): No one of your folk will believe save him who has believed already. Be not distressed because of what they do.

٣٦ وَأُوحِيَ إِلَى نُوحٍ أَنَّهُ لَنْ يُؤْمِنَ مِنْ قَوْمِكَ إِلَّا مَنْ قَدْ آمَنَ فَلَا تَبْتَئِسْ بِمَا كَانُوا يَفْعَلُونَ

37. Build the ship under Our Eyes and by Our inspiration, and speak not unto Me on behalf of those who do wrong. Lo! They will be drowned.

٣٧ وَاصْنَعِ الْفُلْكَ بِأَعْيُنِنَا وَوَحْيِنَا وَلَا تُخَاطِبْنِي فِي الَّذِينَ ظَلَمُوا إِنَّهُمْ مُغْرَقُونَ

38. And he was building the ship, and every time that chieftains of his people passed him, they made mock of him. He said: Though you make mock of us, yet we mock at you even as you mock;

٣٨ وَيَصْنَعُ الْفُلْكَ وَكُلَّمَا مَرَّ عَلَيْهِ مَلَأٌ مِّنْ قَوْمِهِ سَخِرُوا مِنْهُ قَالَ إِنْ تَسْخَرُوا مِنَّا فَإِنَّا نَسْخَرُ مِنْكُمْ كَمَا تَسْخَرُونَ

39. And you shall know to whom a punishment that will confound him comes, and upon whom a lasting doom will fall.

٣٩ فَسَوْفَ تَعْلَمُونَ مَنْ يَأْتِيهِ عَذَابٌ يُخْزِيهِ وَيَحِلُّ عَلَيْهِ عَذَابٌ مُقِيمٌ

40. (Thus it was) till, when Our commandment came to pass and the oven gushed forth (with water),[133] We said: Load therein two of every kind, a pair (the male and female), and your household, save him against whom the word has gone forth already, and those who believe. And but a few were they who believed with him.

٤٠ حَتَّى إِذَا جَاءَ أَمْرُنَا وَفَارَ التَّنُّورُ قُلْنَا احْمِلْ فِيهَا مِنْ كُلٍّ زَوْجَيْنِ اثْنَيْنِ وَأَهْلَكَ إِلَّا مَنْ سَبَقَ عَلَيْهِ الْقَوْلُ وَمَنْ آمَنَ وَمَا آمَنَ مَعَهُ إِلَّا قَلِيلٌ

41. And he said: Embark therein! In the name of Allah be its course and its mooring. Lo! my Lord is Forgiving, Merciful.

٤١ وَقَالَ ارْكَبُوا فِيهَا بِسْمِ اللَّهِ مَجْرَاهَا وَمُرْسَاهَا إِنَّ رَبِّي لَغَفُورٌ رَحِيمٌ

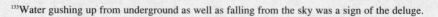

---

[133]Water gushing up from underground as well as falling from the sky was a sign of the deluge.

42. And it sailed with them amid waves like mountains, and Noah cried unto his son—and he was standing aloof—O my son! Come ride with us, and be not with the disbelievers.

٤٢) وَهِيَ تَجْرِي بِهِمْ فِي مَوْجٍ كَالْجِبَالِ وَنَادَى نُوحٌ ابْنَهُ وَكَانَ فِي مَعْزِلٍ يَبُنَيَّ ارْكَب مَّعَنَا وَلَا تَكُن مَّعَ الْكَافِرِينَ

43. He said: I shall betake me to some mountain that will save me from the water. (Noah) said: This day there is none that saves from the commandment of Allah save him on whom He has had mercy. And waves came in between them, so he was among the drowned.

٤٣) قَالَ سَآوِي إِلَى جَبَلٍ يَعْصِمُنِي مِنَ الْمَاءِ قَالَ لَا عَاصِمَ الْيَوْمَ مِنْ أَمْرِ اللَّهِ إِلَّا مَن رَّحِمَ وَحَالَ بَيْنَهُمَا الْمَوْجُ فَكَانَ مِنَ الْمُغْرَقِينَ

44. And it was said: O earth! Swallow your water and, O sky! be cleared of clouds! And the water was made to subside. And the commandment was fulfilled. And it (the ship) came to rest upon (the mount) al Jūdī and it was said: A far removal for wrongdoing folk!

٤٤) وَقِيلَ يَا أَرْضُ ابْلَعِي مَاءَكِ وَيَا سَمَاءُ أَقْلِعِي وَغِيضَ الْمَاءُ وَقُضِيَ الْأَمْرُ وَاسْتَوَتْ عَلَى الْجُودِيِّ وَقِيلَ بُعْدًا لِّلْقَوْمِ الظَّالِمِينَ

45. And Noah cried unto his Lord and said: My Lord! Lo! my son is of my household! Surely Your promise is the Truth and You are the Most Just of Judges.

٤٥) وَنَادَى نُوحٌ رَّبَّهُ فَقَالَ رَبِّ إِنَّ ابْنِي مِنْ أَهْلِي وَإِنَّ وَعْدَكَ الْحَقُّ وَأَنتَ أَحْكَمُ الْحَاكِمِينَ

46. He said: O Noah! Lo! he is not of your household; lo! he is of evil conduct, so ask not of Me that whereof you have no knowledge. I admonish you lest you be among the ignorant.

٤٦) قَالَ يَا نُوحُ إِنَّهُ لَيْسَ مِنْ أَهْلِكَ إِنَّهُ عَمَلٌ غَيْرُ صَالِحٍ فَلَا تَسْأَلْنِ مَا لَيْسَ لَكَ بِهِ عِلْمٌ إِنِّي أَعِظُكَ أَن تَكُونَ مِنَ الْجَاهِلِينَ

47. He said: My Lord! Lo! in You do I seek refuge (from the sin) that I should ask of You that whereof I have no knowledge. Unless You forgive me and have mercy on me I shall be among the losers.

٤٧) قَالَ رَبِّ إِنِّي أَعُوذُ بِكَ أَنْ أَسْأَلَكَ مَا لَيْسَ لِي بِهِ عِلْمٌ وَإِلَّا تَغْفِرْ لِي وَتَرْحَمْنِي أَكُن مِّنَ الْخَاسِرِينَ

48. It was said (unto him): O Noah! Go you down (from the mountain) with peace from Us and blessings upon you and some nations (that will spring) from those with you. (There will be other) nations unto whom We shall give enjoyment a long while and then a painful doom from Us will overtake them.

٤٨) قِيلَ يَا نُوحُ اهْبِطْ بِسَلَامٍ مِّنَّا وَبَرَكَاتٍ عَلَيْكَ وَعَلَى أُمَمٍ مِّمَّن مَّعَكَ وَأُمَمٌ سَنُمَتِّعُهُمْ ثُمَّ يَمَسُّهُم مِّنَّا عَذَابٌ أَلِيمٌ

49. This is of the tidings of the Unseen which We inspire in you (Muhammad). You yourself knew it not, nor did your folk (know it) before this. Then have patience. Lo! the sequel is for those who ward off (evil).

٤٩) تِلْكَ مِنْ أَنبَاءِ الْغَيْبِ نُوحِيهَا إِلَيْكَ مَا كُنتَ تَعْلَمُهَا أَنتَ وَلَا قَوْمُكَ مِن قَبْلِ هَذَا فَاصْبِرْ إِنَّ الْعَاقِبَةَ لِلْمُتَّقِينَ

50. And unto (the tribe of) 'Ād (We sent) their brother, Hūd. He said: O my people! Worship Allah! You have no other God save Him. Lo! you do but invent!

51. O my people! I ask of you no reward for it. Lo! my reward is the concern only of Him who made me. Have you then no sense?

52. And, O my people! Ask forgiveness of your Lord, then turn unto Him repentant; He will cause the sky to rain abundance on you and will add unto you strength to your strength. Turn not away, guilty!

53. They said: O Hūd! You have brought us no clear proof and we are not going to forsake our gods on your (mere) saying, and we are not believers in you.

54. We say nothing save that one of our gods has possessed you in an evil way. He said: I call Allah to witness, and do you (too) bear witness, that I am innocent of (all) that you ascribe as partners (to Allah)

55. Beside Him. So (try to) circumvent me, all of you, give me no respite.

56. Lo! I have put my trust in Allah, my Lord and your Lord. Not an animal but He does grasp it by the forelock! Lo! my Lord is on a straight path.

57. And if you turn away, still I have conveyed unto you that with which I was sent unto you, and my Lord will set in place of you a folk other than you. You cannot cause hurt to Him at all. Lo! my Lord is Guardian over all things.

58. And when Our commandment came to pass We saved Hūd and those who believed with him by a mercy from Us; We saved them from a harsh doom.

59. And such were 'Ād. They denied the revelations of their Lord and flouted His messengers and followed the command of every froward potentate.

60. And a curse was made to follow them in the world and on the Day of Resurrection. Lo! 'Ād disbelieved in their Lord. A far removal for 'Ād, the folk of Hūd!

61. And unto (the tribe of) Thamūd (We sent) their brother Ṣāliḥ. He said: O my people! Worship Allah, You have no other God save Him. He brought you forth from the earth and has made you husband it. So ask forgiveness of Him and turn unto Him repentant. Lo, my Lord is Nigh, Respon-sive.

62. They said: O Ṣāliḥ! You have been among us hitherto as that wherein our hope was placed. Do you ask us not to worship what our fathers worshiped? Lo! we surely are in grave doubt concerning that to which you call us.

63. He said: O my people! Bethink you: if I am (acting) on clear proof from my Lord and there has come unto me a mercy from Him, who will help me against Allah if I disobey Him? You would add to me nothing but perdition.

64. O my people! This is the she-camel of Allah, a token unto you, so suffer her to feed in Allah's earth, and touch her not with harm lest a near torment seize you.

65. But they hamstrung her, and then he said: Enjoy life in your dwelling place three days! This is a threat that will not be belied.

66. So, when Our commandment came to pass, We saved Ṣāliḥ and those who believed with him, by a mercy from Us, from the ignominy of that day. Lo, your Lord! He is the Strong, the Mighty.

67. And the (Awful) Cry overtook those who did wrong, so that morning found them prostrate in their dwellings,

٦٠ وَأُتْبِعُوا فِي هَٰذِهِ الدُّنْيَا لَعْنَةً وَيَوْمَ الْقِيَامَةِ أَلَا إِنَّ عَادًا كَفَرُوا رَبَّهُمْ أَلَا بُعْدًا لِعَادٍ قَوْمِ هُودٍ

٦١ ۞ وَإِلَىٰ ثَمُودَ أَخَاهُمْ صَالِحًا قَالَ يَا قَوْمِ اعْبُدُوا اللَّهَ مَا لَكُمْ مِنْ إِلَٰهٍ غَيْرُهُ هُوَ أَنْشَأَكُمْ مِنَ الْأَرْضِ وَاسْتَعْمَرَكُمْ فِيهَا فَاسْتَغْفِرُوهُ ثُمَّ تُوبُوا إِلَيْهِ إِنَّ رَبِّي قَرِيبٌ مُجِيبٌ

٦٢ قَالُوا يَا صَالِحُ قَدْ كُنْتَ فِينَا مَرْجُوًّا قَبْلَ هَٰذَا أَتَنْهَانَا أَنْ نَعْبُدَ مَا يَعْبُدُ آبَاؤُنَا وَإِنَّنَا لَفِي شَكٍّ مِمَّا تَدْعُونَا إِلَيْهِ مُرِيبٍ

٦٣ قَالَ يَا قَوْمِ أَرَأَيْتُمْ إِنْ كُنْتُ عَلَىٰ بَيِّنَةٍ مِنْ رَبِّي وَآتَانِي مِنْهُ رَحْمَةً فَمَنْ يَنْصُرُنِي مِنَ اللَّهِ إِنْ عَصَيْتُهُ فَمَا تَزِيدُونَنِي غَيْرَ تَخْسِيرٍ

٦٤ وَيَا قَوْمِ هَٰذِهِ نَاقَةُ اللَّهِ لَكُمْ آيَةً فَذَرُوهَا تَأْكُلْ فِي أَرْضِ اللَّهِ وَلَا تَمَسُّوهَا بِسُوءٍ فَيَأْخُذَكُمْ عَذَابٌ قَرِيبٌ

٦٥ فَعَقَرُوهَا فَقَالَ تَمَتَّعُوا فِي دَارِكُمْ ثَلَاثَةَ أَيَّامٍ ذَٰلِكَ وَعْدٌ غَيْرُ مَكْذُوبٍ

٦٦ فَلَمَّا جَاءَ أَمْرُنَا نَجَّيْنَا صَالِحًا وَالَّذِينَ آمَنُوا مَعَهُ بِرَحْمَةٍ مِنَّا وَمِنْ خِزْيِ يَوْمِئِذٍ إِنَّ رَبَّكَ هُوَ الْقَوِيُّ الْعَزِيزُ

٦٧ وَأَخَذَ الَّذِينَ ظَلَمُوا الصَّيْحَةُ فَأَصْبَحُوا فِي دِيَارِهِمْ جَاثِمِينَ

68. As though they had not dwelt there. Lo! Thamūd disbelieved in their Lord. A far removal for Thamūd!

69. And Our messengers came unto Abraham with good news. They said: Peace! He answered: Peace!, and delayed not to bring a roasted calf.

70. And when he saw their hands reached not to it, he mistrusted them and conceived a fear of them. They said: Fear not! Lo! we are sent unto the folk of Lot.

71. And his wife, standing by, laughed when We gave her good tidings (of the birth) of Isaac, and, after Isaac, of Jacob.

72. She said: Oh, woe is me! Shall I bear a child when I am an old woman, and this my husband is an old man? Lo! this is an astonishing thing!

73. They said: Do you wonder at the commandment of Allah? The mercy of Allah and His blessings be upon you, O people of the house! Lo! He is Owner of Praise, Owner of Glory!

74. And when the awe departed from Abraham, and the glad news reached him, he pleaded with Us on behalf of the folk of Lot.

75. Lo! Abraham was mild, imploring, penitent.

76. (It was said) O Abraham! Forsake this! Lo! your Lord's commandment has gone forth, and lo! there comes unto them a doom which cannot be repelled.

77. And when Our messengers came unto Lot, he was distressed and knew not how to protect them. He said: This is a distressful day.

٦٨ كَأَن لَّمْ يَغْنَوْا فِيهَآ أَلَآ إِنَّ ثَمُودَاْ كَفَرُوا۟ رَبَّهُمْ أَلَا بُعْدًا لِّثَمُودَ

٦٩ وَلَقَدْ جَآءَتْ رُسُلُنَآ إِبْرَٰهِيمَ بِالْبُشْرَىٰ قَالُوا۟ سَلَـٰمًا قَالَ سَلَـٰمٌ فَمَا لَبِثَ أَن جَآءَ بِعِجْلٍ حَنِيذٍ

٧٠ فَلَمَّا رَءَآ أَيْدِيَهُمْ لَا تَصِلُ إِلَيْهِ نَكِرَهُمْ وَأَوْجَسَ مِنْهُمْ خِيفَةً قَالُوا۟ لَا تَخَفْ إِنَّآ أُرْسِلْنَآ إِلَىٰ قَوْمِ لُوطٍ

٧١ وَٱمْرَأَتُهُۥ قَآئِمَةٌ فَضَحِكَتْ فَبَشَّرْنَٰهَا بِإِسْحَٰقَ وَمِن وَرَآءِ إِسْحَٰقَ يَعْقُوبَ

٧٢ قَالَتْ يَٰوَيْلَتَىٰٓ ءَأَلِدُ وَأَنَا۠ عَجُوزٌ وَهَٰذَا بَعْلِى شَيْخًا إِنَّ هَٰذَا لَشَىْءٌ عَجِيبٌ

٧٣ قَالُوا۟ أَتَعْجَبِينَ مِنْ أَمْرِ ٱللَّهِ رَحْمَتُ ٱللَّهِ وَبَرَكَٰتُهُۥ عَلَيْكُمْ أَهْلَ ٱلْبَيْتِ إِنَّهُۥ حَمِيدٌ مَّجِيدٌ

٧٤ فَلَمَّا ذَهَبَ عَنْ إِبْرَٰهِيمَ ٱلرَّوْعُ وَجَآءَتْهُ ٱلْبُشْرَىٰ يُجَٰدِلُنَا فِى قَوْمِ لُوطٍ

٧٥ إِنَّ إِبْرَٰهِيمَ لَحَلِيمٌ أَوَّٰهٌ مُّنِيبٌ

٧٦ يَٰٓإِبْرَٰهِيمُ أَعْرِضْ عَنْ هَٰذَآ إِنَّهُۥ قَدْ جَآءَ أَمْرُ رَبِّكَ وَإِنَّهُمْ ءَاتِيهِمْ عَذَابٌ غَيْرُ مَرْدُودٍ

٧٧ وَلَمَّا جَآءَتْ رُسُلُنَا لُوطًا سِىٓءَ بِهِمْ وَضَاقَ بِهِمْ ذَرْعًا وَقَالَ هَٰذَا يَوْمٌ عَصِيبٌ

78. And his people came unto him, running towards him—and before then they used to commit abominations—He said: O my people! Here are my daughters! They are purer for you. Beware of Allah, and degrade me not in (the person of) my guests. Is there not among you any upright man?

79. They said: Well you know that we have no right to your daughters, and well you know what we want.

80. He said: Would that I had strength to resist you or had some strong support (among you)!

81. (The messengers) said: O Lot! Lo! we are messengers of your Lord; they shall not reach you. So travel with your people in a part of the night, and let not one of you turn round—(all) save your wife. Lo! that which smites them will smite her (also). Lo! their appointed time is (for) the morning. Is not the morning nigh?

82. So when Our commandment came to pass We overthrew (that township) and rained upon it stones of clay, one after another,

83. Marked with fire in the providence of your Lord (for the destruction of the wicked). And they are never far from the wrongdoers.

84. And unto Madian (We sent) their brother Shu'ayb. He said: O my people! Worship Allah. You have no other God save Him! And give not short measure and short weight. Lo! I see you well to do, and lo! I fear for you the doom of a besetting Day.

85. O my people! Give full measure and full weight in justice, and wrong not people in respect of their goods. And do not evil in the earth, causing corruption.

86. That which Allah leaves with you is better for you if you are believers; and I am not a keeper over you.

87. They said: O Shu'ayb! Does your way of prayer command you that we should forsake that which our fathers (used to) worship, or that we (should leave off) doing what we will with our own property. Lo! you are the mild, the guide to right behavior!

88. He said: O my people! Bethink you: if I am (acting) on a clear proof from my Lord and He sustains me with fair sustenance from Him (how can I concede anything to you)? I desire not to do behind your backs that which I ask you not to do. I desire nothing save reform so far as I am able. My welfare is only in Allah. In Him I trust and unto Him I turn (repentant).

89. And, O my people! Let not the schism with me cause you to sin so that there befall you that which befell the folk of Noah and the folk of Hūd, and the folk of Ṣāliḥ; and the folk of Lot are not far off from you.

90. Ask pardon of your Lord and then turn unto Him (repentant). Lo! my Lord is Merciful, Loving.

91. They said: O Shu'ayb! We understand not much of that you tell, and lo! we do behold you weak among us. But for your family, we should have stoned you, for you are not strong against us.

92. He said: O my people! Is my family more to be honored by you than Allah? And you put Him behind you, neglected! Lo! my Lord surrounds what you do.

93. And, O my people! Act according to your power, lo, I (too) am acting. You will soon know on whom there comes a doom that will abase him, and who it is that lies. And watch! Lo! I am watcher with you.

بَقِيَّتُ اللّٰهِ خَيْرٌ لَّكُمْ إِنْ كُنْتُمْ مُّؤْمِنِيْنَ ۚ وَمَآ أَنَا عَلَيْكُمْ بِحَفِيْظٍ ۞

قَالُوْا يَا شُعَيْبُ أَصَلَوٰتُكَ تَأْمُرُكَ أَنْ نَّتْرُكَ مَا يَعْبُدُ ءَابَآؤُنَآ أَوْ أَنْ نَّفْعَلَ فِيْٓ أَمْوَالِنَا مَا نَشٰؤُا ۚ إِنَّكَ لَأَنْتَ الْحَلِيْمُ الرَّشِيْدُ ۞

قَالَ يَا قَوْمِ أَرَءَيْتُمْ إِنْ كُنْتُ عَلٰى بَيِّنَةٍ مِّنْ رَّبِّيْ وَرَزَقَنِيْ مِنْهُ رِزْقًا حَسَنًا ۚ وَمَآ أُرِيْدُ أَنْ أُخَالِفَكُمْ إِلٰى مَآ أَنْهٰىكُمْ عَنْهُ ۚ إِنْ أُرِيْدُ إِلَّا الْإِصْلَاحَ مَا اسْتَطَعْتُ ۚ وَمَا تَوْفِيْقِيْٓ إِلَّا بِاللّٰهِ ۚ عَلَيْهِ تَوَكَّلْتُ وَإِلَيْهِ أُنِيْبُ ۞

وَيَا قَوْمِ لَا يَجْرِمَنَّكُمْ شِقَاقِيْٓ أَنْ يُّصِيْبَكُمْ مِّثْلُ مَآ أَصَابَ قَوْمَ نُوْحٍ أَوْ قَوْمَ هُوْدٍ أَوْ قَوْمَ صَالِحٍ ۚ وَمَا قَوْمُ لُوْطٍ مِّنْكُمْ بِبَعِيْدٍ ۞

وَاسْتَغْفِرُوْا رَبَّكُمْ ثُمَّ تُوْبُوْٓا إِلَيْهِ ۚ إِنَّ رَبِّيْ رَحِيْمٌ وَّدُوْدٌ ۞

قَالُوْا يَا شُعَيْبُ مَا نَفْقَهُ كَثِيْرًا مِّمَّا تَقُوْلُ وَإِنَّا لَنَرٰىكَ فِيْنَا ضَعِيْفًا ۚ وَلَوْلَا رَهْطُكَ لَرَجَمْنٰكَ ۖ وَمَآ أَنْتَ عَلَيْنَا بِعَزِيْزٍ ۞

قَالَ يَا قَوْمِ أَرَهْطِيْٓ أَعَزُّ عَلَيْكُمْ مِّنَ اللّٰهِ ۚ وَاتَّخَذْتُمُوْهُ وَرَآءَكُمْ ظِهْرِيًّا ۚ إِنَّ رَبِّيْ بِمَا تَعْمَلُوْنَ مُحِيْطٌ ۞

وَيَا قَوْمِ اعْمَلُوْا عَلٰى مَكَانَتِكُمْ إِنِّيْ عَامِلٌ ۖ سَوْفَ تَعْلَمُوْنَ مَنْ يَّأْتِيْهِ عَذَابٌ يُّخْزِيْهِ وَمَنْ هُوَ كَاذِبٌ ۖ وَارْتَقِبُوْٓا إِنِّيْ مَعَكُمْ رَقِيْبٌ ۞

94. And when Our commandment came to pass we saved Shu'ayb and those who believed with Him by a mercy from Us; and the (Awful) Cry seized those who did injustice, and morning found them prostrate in their dwellings.

95. As though they had not dwelt there. A far removal for Madian, even as Thamūd had been removed afar!

96. And truly We sent Moses with Our revelations and a clear warrant.

97. Unto Pharaoh and his chiefs, but they did follow the command of Pharaoh, and the command of Pharaoh was no right guide.

98. He will go before his people on the Day of Resurrection and will lead them to the Fire for watering place. Ah, unlucky is the watering place (whither they are) led.

99. A curse is made to follow them in the world and on the Day of Resurrection. Unlucky is the gift (that will be) given (them).

100. That is (something) of the tidings of the townships[134](which were destroyed of old). We relate it unto you (Muhammad). Some of them are standing and some (already) reaped.

101. We wronged them not, but they did wrong themselves; and their gods on whom they call beside Allah availed them nothing when came your Lords command; they added to them nothing save ruin.

102. Even thus is the grasp of your Lord when he grasps the townships while they are doing wrong. Lo! His grasp is painful, very strong.

103. Lo! herein surely there is a portent for those who fear the doom of the Hereafter. That is a day unto which man-kind will be gathered, and that is a day that will be witnessed.

104. And We defer it only as a term already reckoned.

﴿٩٤﴾ وَلَمَّا جَآءَ أَمْرُنَا نَجَّيْنَا شُعَيْبًا وَالَّذِينَ ءَامَنُوا مَعَهُ بِرَحْمَةٍ مِّنَّا وَأَخَذَتِ الَّذِينَ ظَلَمُوا الصَّيْحَةُ فَأَصْبَحُوا فِي دِيَارِهِمْ جَٰثِمِينَ

﴿٩٥﴾ كَأَن لَّمْ يَغْنَوْا فِيهَآ أَلَا بُعْدًا لِّمَدْيَنَ كَمَا بَعِدَتْ ثَمُودُ

﴿٩٦﴾ وَلَقَدْ أَرْسَلْنَا مُوسَىٰ بِـَٔايَٰتِنَا وَسُلْطَٰنٍ مُّبِينٍ

﴿٩٧﴾ إِلَىٰ فِرْعَوْنَ وَمَلَإِيْهِ فَٱتَّبَعُوا أَمْرَ فِرْعَوْنَ وَمَآ أَمْرُ فِرْعَوْنَ بِرَشِيدٍ

﴿٩٨﴾ يَقْدُمُ قَوْمَهُ يَوْمَ الْقِيَٰمَةِ فَأَوْرَدَهُمُ النَّارَ وَبِئْسَ الْوِرْدُ الْمَوْرُودُ

﴿٩٩﴾ وَأُتْبِعُوا فِي هَٰذِهِ لَعْنَةً وَيَوْمَ الْقِيَٰمَةِ بِئْسَ الرِّفْدُ الْمَرْفُودُ

﴿١٠٠﴾ ذَٰلِكَ مِنْ أَنۢبَآءِ الْقُرَىٰ نَقُصُّهُ عَلَيْكَ مِنْهَا قَآئِمٌ وَحَصِيدٌ

﴿١٠١﴾ وَمَا ظَلَمْنَٰهُمْ وَلَٰكِن ظَلَمُوا أَنفُسَهُمْ فَمَآ أَغْنَتْ عَنْهُمْ ءَالِهَتُهُمُ الَّتِي يَدْعُونَ مِن دُونِ اللَّهِ مِن شَيْءٍ لَّمَّا جَآءَ أَمْرُ رَبِّكَ وَمَا زَادُوهُمْ غَيْرَ تَتْبِيبٍ

﴿١٠٢﴾ وَكَذَٰلِكَ أَخْذُ رَبِّكَ إِذَآ أَخَذَ الْقُرَىٰ وَهِيَ ظَٰلِمَةٌ إِنَّ أَخْذَهُ أَلِيمٌ شَدِيدٌ

﴿١٠٣﴾ إِنَّ فِي ذَٰلِكَ لَـَٔايَةً لِّمَنْ خَافَ عَذَابَ الْءَاخِرَةِ ذَٰلِكَ يَوْمٌ مَّجْمُوعٌ لَّهُ النَّاسُ وَذَٰلِكَ يَوْمٌ مَّشْهُودٌ

﴿١٠٤﴾ وَمَا نُؤَخِّرُهُ إِلَّا لِأَجَلٍ مَّعْدُودٍ

---

[134]Or communities.

105. On the day when it comes no soul will speak except by His permission; some among them will be wretched, (others) glad.

۞ يَوْمَ يَأْتِ لَا تَكَلَّمُ نَفْسٌ إِلَّا بِإِذْنِهِ فَمِنْهُمْ شَقِيٌّ وَسَعِيدٌ

106. As for those who will be wretched (on that day) they will be in the Fire; sighing and wailing will be their portion therein.

۞ فَأَمَّا الَّذِينَ شَقُوا فَفِي النَّارِ لَهُمْ فِيهَا زَفِيرٌ وَشَهِيقٌ

107. Abiding there so long as the heavens and the earth endure save for that which your Lord wills. Lo! your Lord is Doer of what He will.

۞ خَالِدِينَ فِيهَا مَا دَامَتِ السَّمَوَاتُ وَالْأَرْضُ إِلَّا مَا شَاءَ رَبُّكَ إِنَّ رَبَّكَ فَعَّالٌ لِمَا يُرِيدُ

108. And as for those who will be glad (that day) they will be in the Garden, abiding there so long as the heavens and the earth endure save for that which your Lord wills: a gift unfailing.

۞ ۞ وَأَمَّا الَّذِينَ سُعِدُوا فَفِي الْجَنَّةِ خَالِدِينَ فِيهَا مَا دَامَتِ السَّمَوَاتُ وَالْأَرْضُ إِلَّا مَا شَاءَ رَبُّكَ عَطَاءً غَيْرَ مَجْذُوذٍ

109. So be not you in doubt concerning that which these (folk) worship. They worship only as their fathers worshiped before. Lo! We shall pay them their whole due un-abated.

۞ فَلَا تَكُ فِي مِرْيَةٍ مِمَّا يَعْبُدُ هَؤُلَاءِ مَا يَعْبُدُونَ إِلَّا كَمَا يَعْبُدُ آبَاؤُهُم مِّن قَبْلُ وَإِنَّا لَمُوَفُّوهُمْ نَصِيبَهُمْ غَيْرَ مَنقُوصٍ

110. And We truly gave unto Moses the Scripture, and there was strife thereupon; and had it not been for a Word that had already gone forth from your Lord, the case would have been judged between them, and Lo! they are in grave doubt concerning it.

۞ وَلَقَدْ آتَيْنَا مُوسَى الْكِتَابَ فَاخْتُلِفَ فِيهِ وَلَوْلَا كَلِمَةٌ سَبَقَتْ مِن رَّبِّكَ لَقُضِيَ بَيْنَهُمْ وَإِنَّهُمْ لَفِي شَكٍّ مِّنْهُ مُرِيبٍ

111. And lo! unto each your Lord will surely repay his works in full. Lo! He is Informed of what they do.

۞ وَإِنَّ كُلًّا لَّمَّا لَيُوَفِّيَنَّهُمْ رَبُّكَ أَعْمَالَهُمْ إِنَّهُ بِمَا يَعْمَلُونَ خَبِيرٌ

112. So tread you the straight path as you are commanded, and those who turn (unto Allah) with you, and transgress not. Lo! He is Seer of what you do.

۞ فَاسْتَقِمْ كَمَا أُمِرْتَ وَمَن تَابَ مَعَكَ وَلَا تَطْغَوْا إِنَّهُ بِمَا تَعْمَلُونَ بَصِيرٌ

113. And incline not toward those who do wrong lest the Fire touch you, and you have no protecting friends against Allah, and afterward you would not be helped.

۞ وَلَا تَرْكَنُوا إِلَى الَّذِينَ ظَلَمُوا فَتَمَسَّكُمُ النَّارُ وَمَا لَكُم مِّن دُونِ اللَّهِ مِنْ أَوْلِيَاءَ ثُمَّ لَا تُنصَرُونَ

114. Establish prayer at the two ends of the day and in some watches of the night. Lo! good deeds annul ill deeds. This is a reminder for the mindful.

115. And have patience, (O Muhammad), for lo! Allah loses not the wages of the good.

116. If only there had been among the generations before you men possessing a remnant (of good sense) to warn (their people) from corruption in the earth, as did a few of those whom We saved from them! The wrongdoers followed that by which they were made sapless, and were criminals.

117. In truth your Lord destroyed not the townships tyrannously while their folk were doing right.

118. And if your Lord had willed, He surely would have made mankind one nation, yet they cease not differing,

119. Save them on whom your Lord has mercy; and for that He did create them. And the Word of your Lord has been fulfilled: Surely I shall fill Hell with the jinn and mankind together.

120. And all that We relate unto you of the stories of the messengers is in order that thereby We may make firm your heart. And herein has come unto you the Truth and an exhortation and a reminder for believers.

121. And say unto those who believe not: Act according to your power. Lo! We (too) are acting.

122. And wait! Lo! We (too) are waiting.

123. And Allah's is the Invisible of the heavens and the earth, and unto Him the whole matter will be returned. So worship Him and put your trust in Him. Lo! your Lord is not unaware of what you (mortals) do.

١١٤ وَأَقِمِ الصَّلَوٰةَ طَرَفِيِ النَّهَارِ وَزُلَفًا مِّنَ الَّيْلِ إِنَّ الْحَسَنَاتِ يُذْهِبْنَ السَّيِّئَاتِ ذَٰلِكَ ذِكْرَىٰ لِلذَّاكِرِينَ

١١٥ وَاصْبِرْ فَإِنَّ اللَّهَ لَا يُضِيعُ أَجْرَ الْمُحْسِنِينَ

١١٦ فَلَوْلَا كَانَ مِنَ الْقُرُونِ مِن قَبْلِكُمْ أُوْلُوا بَقِيَّةٍ يَنْهَوْنَ عَنِ الْفَسَادِ فِي الْأَرْضِ إِلَّا قَلِيلًا مِّمَّنْ أَنجَيْنَا مِنْهُمْ وَاتَّبَعَ الَّذِينَ ظَلَمُوا مَا أُتْرِفُوا فِيهِ وَكَانُوا مُجْرِمِينَ

١١٧ وَمَا كَانَ رَبُّكَ لِيُهْلِكَ الْقُرَىٰ بِظُلْمٍ وَأَهْلُهَا مُصْلِحُونَ

١١٨ وَلَوْ شَاءَ رَبُّكَ لَجَعَلَ النَّاسَ أُمَّةً وَاحِدَةً وَلَا يَزَالُونَ مُخْتَلِفِينَ

١١٩ إِلَّا مَن رَّحِمَ رَبُّكَ وَلِذَٰلِكَ خَلَقَهُمْ وَتَمَّتْ كَلِمَةُ رَبِّكَ لَأَمْلَأَنَّ جَهَنَّمَ مِنَ الْجِنَّةِ وَالنَّاسِ أَجْمَعِينَ

١٢٠ وَكُلًّا نَّقُصُّ عَلَيْكَ مِنْ أَنبَاءِ الرُّسُلِ مَا نُثَبِّتُ بِهِ فُؤَادَكَ وَجَاءَكَ فِي هَٰذِهِ الْحَقُّ وَمَوْعِظَةٌ وَذِكْرَىٰ لِلْمُؤْمِنِينَ

١٢١ وَقُل لِّلَّذِينَ لَا يُؤْمِنُونَ اعْمَلُوا عَلَىٰ مَكَانَتِكُمْ إِنَّا عَامِلُونَ

١٢٢ وَانتَظِرُوا إِنَّا مُنتَظِرُونَ

١٢٣ وَلِلَّهِ غَيْبُ السَّمَوَاتِ وَالْأَرْضِ وَإِلَيْهِ يُرْجَعُ الْأَمْرُ كُلُّهُ فَاعْبُدْهُ وَتَوَكَّلْ عَلَيْهِ وَمَا رَبُّكَ بِغَافِلٍ عَمَّا تَعْمَلُونَ

Joseph

Surat Yūsuf takes its name from its subject: the life-story of Joseph. It differs from all other surahs in having only one subject. The differences from the Bible narrative are striking. Here, Jacob is a prophet who is not deceived by the story of his son's death. Rather, he is is distressed because, due to the suspension of his clairvoyance, he cannot see what has become of Joseph. The real importance of the narrative, its psychic burden, is emphasized throughout, and the manner of narration, though astonishing to western readers, is vivid.

Tradition says that it was recited by the Prophet at Makkah to the first converts from Yathrib (the pre-Islamic name of al Madinah), in the year 2 AH. However, as Noldeke points out, this does not mean that it was not revealed till then, but that it had been revealed by then.

A late Makkan surah.

Joseph

Revealed at Makkah

*In the name of Allah,
the Beneficent, the Merciful*

بِسْمِ اللّٰهِ الرَّحْمٰنِ الرَّحِيْمِ

1. **A**lif. Lām. Rā'.[135] These are verses of the Scripture that makes plain.

الٓرٰ تِلْكَ اٰيٰتُ الْكِتٰبِ الْمُبِيْنِ ۝

2. Lo! We have revealed it, a Lecture[136] in Arabic, that you may understand.

اِنَّآ اَنْزَلْنٰهُ قُرْءٰنًا عَرَبِيًّا لَّعَلَّكُمْ تَعْقِلُوْنَ ۝

3. We narrate unto you (Muhammad) the best of narratives in that We have inspired in you this Qur'an, though before it you were of the heedless.

نَحْنُ نَقُصُّ عَلَيْكَ اَحْسَنَ الْقَصَصِ بِمَآ اَوْحَيْنَآ اِلَيْكَ هٰذَا الْقُرْءٰانَ وَاِنْ كُنْتَ مِنْ قَبْلِهٖ لَمِنَ الْغٰفِلِيْنَ ۝

4. When Joseph said unto his father: O my father! Lo! I saw in a dream eleven planets and the sun and the moon, I saw them prostrating themselves unto me.

اِذْ قَالَ يُوْسُفُ لِاَبِيْهِ يٰٓاَبَتِ اِنِّيْ رَاَيْتُ اَحَدَ عَشَرَ كَوْكَبًا وَّالشَّمْسَ وَالْقَمَرَ رَاَيْتُهُمْ لِيْ سٰجِدِيْنَ ۝

5. He said: O my son! Tell not your brothers of your vision, lest they plot a plot against you. Lo! the Devil is for man an open foe.

قَالَ يٰبُنَيَّ لَا تَقْصُصْ رُءْيَاكَ عَلٰٓى اِخْوَتِكَ فَيَكِيْدُوْا لَكَ كَيْدًا اِنَّ الشَّيْطٰنَ لِلْاِنْسَانِ عَدُوٌّ مُّبِيْنٌ ۝

6. Thus your Lord will prefer you and will teach you the interpretation of events, and will perfect his grace upon you and upon the family of Jacob as he perfected it upon your forefathers, Abraham and Isaac. Lo! your Lord is Knower, Wise.

وَكَذٰلِكَ يَجْتَبِيْكَ رَبُّكَ وَيُعَلِّمُكَ مِنْ تَأْوِيْلِ الْاَحَادِيْثِ وَيُتِمُّ نِعْمَتَهٗ عَلَيْكَ وَعَلٰٓى اٰلِ يَعْقُوْبَ كَمَآ اَتَمَّهَا عَلٰٓى اَبَوَيْكَ مِنْ قَبْلُ اِبْرٰهِيْمَ وَاِسْحٰقَ اِنَّ رَبَّكَ عَلِيْمٌ حَكِيْمٌ ۝

7. Verily in Joseph and his brothers are signs (of Allah's Sovereignty) for the inquiring.

لَقَدْ كَانَ فِيْ يُوْسُفَ وَاِخْوَتِهٖٓ اٰيٰتٌ لِّلسَّآئِلِيْنَ ۝

8. When they said: Verily Joseph and his brother are dearer to our father than we are, many though we be. Lo! our father is in plain aberration.

اِذْ قَالُوْا لَيُوْسُفُ وَاَخُوْهُ اَحَبُّ اِلٰٓى اَبِيْنَا مِنَّا وَنَحْنُ عُصْبَةٌ اِنَّ اَبَانَا لَفِيْ ضَلٰلٍ مُّبِيْنٍ ۝

9. (One said): Kill Joseph or cast him to some (other) land, so that your father's favor may be all for you, and (that) you may afterward be righteous folk.

اُقْتُلُوْا يُوْسُفَ اَوِ اطْرَحُوْهُ اَرْضًا يَّخْلُ لَكُمْ وَجْهُ اَبِيْكُمْ وَتَكُوْنُوْا مِنْ بَعْدِهٖ قَوْمًا صٰلِحِيْنَ ۝

---

[135]See Surah 2:1, footnote.
[136]Arabic: Qur'an.

10. One among them said: Kill not Joseph but, if you must be doing, fling him into the depth of the pit; some caravan will find him.

11. They said: O our father! Why will you not trust us with Joseph, when lo! we are good friends to him?

12. Send him with us tomorrow that he may enjoy himself and play. And lo! we shall take good care of him.

13. He said: Lo! in truth it saddens me that you should take him with you, and I fear lest the wolf devour him while you are heedless of him.

14. They said: If the wolf should devour him when we are (so strong) a band, then surely we should be losers.

15. Then, when they led him off, and were of one mind that they should place him in the depth of the pit, We inspired in him: You will tell them of this deed of theirs when they know (you) not.

16. And they came weeping to their father in the evening.

17. Saying: O our father! We went racing one with another, and left Joseph by our things, and the wolf devoured him, and you will not believe our sayings even if we speak the truth.

18. And they came with false blood on his shirt. He said: Nay, but your minds have beguiled you into something. (My course is) comely patience. And Allah it is whose help is to be sought in that (predicament) which you describe.

19. And there came a caravan, and they sent their water-drawer. He let down his pail (into the pit). He said: Good luck! Here is a youth. And they hid him as goods, and Allah was Aware of what they did.

١٠ قَالَ قَائِلٌ مِّنْهُمْ لَا تَقْتُلُوا يُوسُفَ وَأَلْقُوهُ فِى غَيَبَتِ الْجُبِّ يَلْتَقِطْهُ بَعْضُ السَّيَّارَةِ إِن كُنتُمْ فَاعِلِينَ

١١ قَالُوا يَا أَبَانَا مَا لَكَ لَا تَأْمَنَّا عَلَىٰ يُوسُفَ وَإِنَّا لَهُ لَنَاصِحُونَ

١٢ أَرْسِلْهُ مَعَنَا غَدًا يَرْتَعْ وَيَلْعَبْ وَإِنَّا لَهُ لَحَافِظُونَ

١٣ قَالَ إِنِّى لَيَحْزُنُنِى أَن تَذْهَبُوا بِهِ وَأَخَافُ أَن يَأْكُلَهُ الذِّئْبُ وَأَنتُمْ عَنْهُ غَافِلُونَ

١٤ قَالُوا لَئِنْ أَكَلَهُ الذِّئْبُ وَنَحْنُ عُصْبَةٌ إِنَّا إِذًا لَّخَاسِرُونَ

١٥ فَلَمَّا ذَهَبُوا بِهِ وَأَجْمَعُوا أَن يَجْعَلُوهُ فِى غَيَبَتِ الْجُبِّ وَأَوْحَيْنَا إِلَيْهِ لَتُنَبِّئَنَّهُم بِأَمْرِهِمْ هَٰذَا وَهُمْ لَا يَشْعُرُونَ

١٦ وَجَاءُوا أَبَاهُمْ عِشَاءً يَبْكُونَ

١٧ قَالُوا يَا أَبَانَا إِنَّا ذَهَبْنَا نَسْتَبِقُ وَتَرَكْنَا يُوسُفَ عِندَ مَتَاعِنَا فَأَكَلَهُ الذِّئْبُ وَمَا أَنتَ بِمُؤْمِنٍ لَّنَا وَلَوْ كُنَّا صَادِقِينَ

١٨ وَجَاءُوا عَلَىٰ قَمِيصِهِ بِدَمٍ كَذِبٍ قَالَ بَلْ سَوَّلَتْ لَكُمْ أَنفُسُكُمْ أَمْرًا فَصَبْرٌ جَمِيلٌ وَاللَّهُ الْمُسْتَعَانُ عَلَىٰ مَا تَصِفُونَ

١٩ وَجَاءَتْ سَيَّارَةٌ فَأَرْسَلُوا وَارِدَهُمْ فَأَدْلَىٰ دَلْوَهُ قَالَ يَا بُشْرَىٰ هَٰذَا غُلَامٌ وَأَسَرُّوهُ بِضَاعَةً وَاللَّهُ عَلِيمٌ بِمَا يَعْمَلُونَ

20. And they sold him for a low price, a number of silver coins; and they attached no value to him.

٢٠ وَشَرَوْهُ بِثَمَنٍ بَخْسٍ دَرَاهِمَ مَعْدُودَةٍ وَكَانُوا فِيهِ مِنَ الزَّاهِدِينَ

21. And he of Egypt who purchased him said unto his wife: Receive him honorably. Perchance he may prove useful to us or we may adopt him as a son. Thus We established Joseph in the land that We might teach him the interpretation of events. And Allah was predominant in his career, but most of mankind know not.

٢١ وَقَالَ الَّذِي اشْتَرَاهُ مِن مِّصْرَ لِامْرَأَتِهِ أَكْرِمِي مَثْوَاهُ عَسَى أَن يَنفَعَنَا أَوْ نَتَّخِذَهُ وَلَدًا وَكَذَلِكَ مَكَّنَّا لِيُوسُفَ فِي الْأَرْضِ وَلِنُعَلِّمَهُ مِن تَأْوِيلِ الْأَحَادِيثِ وَاللَّهُ غَالِبٌ عَلَى أَمْرِهِ وَلَكِنَّ أَكْثَرَ النَّاسِ لَا يَعْلَمُونَ

22. And when he reached his prime We gave him wisdom and knowledge. Thus We reward the good.

٢٢ وَلَمَّا بَلَغَ أَشُدَّهُ آتَيْنَاهُ حُكْمًا وَعِلْمًا وَكَذَلِكَ نَجْزِي الْمُحْسِنِينَ

23. And she, in whose house he was, asked of him an evil act. She bolted the doors and said: I am ready (for you)! He said: I seek refuge in Allah! Lo! He* is my lord, who has treated me honorably. Wrongdoers never prosper.

٢٣ وَرَاوَدَتْهُ الَّتِي هُوَ فِي بَيْتِهَا عَن نَّفْسِهِ وَغَلَّقَتِ الْأَبْوَابَ وَقَالَتْ هَيْتَ لَكَ قَالَ مَعَاذَ اللَّهِ إِنَّهُ رَبِّي أَحْسَنَ مَثْوَايَ إِنَّهُ لَا يُفْلِحُ الظَّالِمُونَ

24. She verily desired him, and he would have desired her if it had not been that he saw the Divine proof of his Lord. Thus it was, that We might ward off from him evil and lewdness. Lo! he was of Our chosen slaves.

٢٤ وَلَقَدْ هَمَّتْ بِهِ وَهَمَّ بِهَا لَوْلَا أَن رَّأَى بُرْهَانَ رَبِّهِ كَذَلِكَ لِنَصْرِفَ عَنْهُ السُّوءَ وَالْفَحْشَاءَ إِنَّهُ مِنْ عِبَادِنَا الْمُخْلَصِينَ

25. And they raced with one another to the door, and she tore his shirt from behind, and they met her master at the door. She said: What shall be his reward, who wishes evil to your folk, save prison or a painful doom?

٢٥ وَاسْتَبَقَا الْبَابَ وَقَدَّتْ قَمِيصَهُ مِن دُبُرٍ وَأَلْفَيَا سَيِّدَهَا لَدَى الْبَابِ قَالَتْ مَا جَزَاءُ مَنْ أَرَادَ بِأَهْلِكَ سُوءًا إِلَّا أَن يُسْجَنَ أَوْ عَذَابٌ أَلِيمٌ

26. (Joseph) said: She it was who asked of me an evil act. And a witness of her own folk testified: If his shirt is torn from before, then she speaks truth and he is of the liars.

٢٦ قَالَ هِيَ رَاوَدَتْنِي عَن نَّفْسِي وَشَهِدَ شَاهِدٌ مِّنْ أَهْلِهَا إِن كَانَ قَمِيصُهُ قُدَّ مِن قُبُلٍ فَصَدَقَتْ وَهُوَ مِنَ الْكَاذِبِينَ

27. And if his shirt is torn from behind, then she has lied and he is of the truthful.

28. So when he saw his shirt torn from behind, he said: Lo! this is of the guile of you women. Lo! the guile of you is very great.

29. O Joseph! Turn away from this, and you, (O woman), ask forgiveness for your sin. Lo! you are of the sinful.

30. And women in the city said: The chief's wife is asking of her slave boy an ill deed. Indeed he has smitten her to the heart with love. We behold her in plain aberration.

31. And when she heard of their sly talk, she sent to them and prepared for them a cushioned couch (to lie on at the feast) and gave to every one of them a knife and said (to Joseph): Come out unto them! And when they saw him they exalted him and cut their hands, exclaiming: Allah Blameless! This is not a human being. This is no other than some gracious angel.

32. She said: This is he on whose account you blamed me. I asked of him an evil act, but he proved continent, but if he does not do my behest he verily shall be imprisoned, and verily shall he be of those brought low.

33. He said: O my Lord! Prison is more dear than that unto which they urge me, and if You fend not off their wiles from me I shall incline unto them and become of the foolish.

34. So his Lord answered his prayer and fended off their wiles from him. Lo! He is Hearer, Knower.

٢٧) وَإِن كَانَ قَمِيصُهُ قُدَّ مِن دُبُرٍ فَكَذَبَتْ وَهُوَ مِنَ ٱلصَّٰدِقِينَ

٢٨) فَلَمَّا رَءَا قَمِيصَهُ قُدَّ مِن دُبُرٍ قَالَ إِنَّهُ مِن كَيْدِكُنَّ إِنَّ كَيْدَكُنَّ عَظِيمٌ

٢٩) يُوسُفُ أَعْرِضْ عَنْ هَٰذَا وَٱسْتَغْفِرِي لِذَنۢبِكِ إِنَّكِ كُنتِ مِنَ ٱلْخَاطِئِينَ

٣٠) وَقَالَ نِسْوَةٌ فِي ٱلْمَدِينَةِ ٱمْرَأَتُ ٱلْعَزِيزِ تُرَٰوِدُ فَتَىٰهَا عَن نَّفْسِهِ قَدْ شَغَفَهَا حُبًّا إِنَّا لَنَرَىٰهَا فِي ضَلَٰلٍ مُّبِينٍ

٣١) فَلَمَّا سَمِعَتْ بِمَكْرِهِنَّ أَرْسَلَتْ إِلَيْهِنَّ وَأَعْتَدَتْ لَهُنَّ مُتَّكَـًٔا وَءَاتَتْ كُلَّ وَٰحِدَةٍ مِّنْهُنَّ سِكِّينًا وَقَالَتِ ٱخْرُجْ عَلَيْهِنَّ فَلَمَّا رَأَيْنَهُۥ أَكْبَرْنَهُۥ وَقَطَّعْنَ أَيْدِيَهُنَّ وَقُلْنَ حَٰشَ لِلَّهِ مَا هَٰذَا بَشَرًا إِنْ هَٰذَا إِلَّا مَلَكٌ كَرِيمٌ

٣٢) قَالَتْ فَذَٰلِكُنَّ ٱلَّذِي لُمْتُنَّنِي فِيهِ وَلَقَدْ رَٰوَدتُّهُۥ عَن نَّفْسِهِ فَٱسْتَعْصَمَ وَلَئِن لَّمْ يَفْعَلْ مَا ءَامُرُهُۥ لَيُسْجَنَنَّ وَلَيَكُونًا مِّنَ ٱلصَّٰغِرِينَ

٣٣) قَالَ رَبِّ ٱلسِّجْنُ أَحَبُّ إِلَيَّ مِمَّا يَدْعُونَنِي إِلَيْهِ وَإِلَّا تَصْرِفْ عَنِّي كَيْدَهُنَّ أَصْبُ إِلَيْهِنَّ وَأَكُن مِّنَ ٱلْجَٰهِلِينَ

٣٤) فَٱسْتَجَابَ لَهُۥ رَبُّهُۥ فَصَرَفَ عَنْهُ كَيْدَهُنَّ إِنَّهُۥ هُوَ ٱلسَّمِيعُ ٱلْعَلِيمُ

35. And it seemed good to them (the men folk) after they had seen the signs (of his innocence) to imprison him for a time.

٣٥ ثُمَّ بَدَا لَهُمْ مِنْ بَعْدِ مَا رَأَوُا الْآيَاتِ لَيَسْجُنُنَّهُ حَتَّى حِينٍ

36. And two young men went to prison with him. One of them said: I dreamed that I was pressing wine. The other said I dreamed that I was carrying upon my head bread whereof the birds were eating. Announce unto us the interpretation, for we see you of those good (at interpretation).

٣٦ وَدَخَلَ مَعَهُ السِّجْنَ فَتَيَانِ قَالَ أَحَدُهُمَا إِنِّي أَرَانِي أَعْصِرُ خَمْرًا وَقَالَ الْآخَرُ إِنِّي أَرَانِي أَحْمِلُ فَوْقَ رَأْسِي خُبْزًا تَأْكُلُ الطَّيْرُ مِنْهُ نَبِّئْنَا بِتَأْوِيلِهِ إِنَّا نَرَاكَ مِنَ الْمُحْسِنِينَ

37. He said: The food which you are given (daily) shall not come unto you but I shall tell you the interpretation before it comes unto you. This is of that which my Lord has taught me. Lo! I have forsaken the religion of folk who believe not in Allah and are disbelievers in the Hereafter.

٣٧ قَالَ لَا يَأْتِيكُمَا طَعَامٌ تُرْزَقَانِهِ إِلَّا نَبَّأْتُكُمَا بِتَأْوِيلِهِ قَبْلَ أَنْ يَأْتِيَكُمَا ذَلِكُمَا مِمَّا عَلَّمَنِي رَبِّي إِنِّي تَرَكْتُ مِلَّةَ قَوْمٍ لَا يُؤْمِنُونَ بِاللَّهِ وَهُمْ بِالْآخِرَةِ هُمْ كَافِرُونَ

38. And I have followed the religion of my fathers, Abraham and Isaac and Jacob. It never was for us to attribute anything as partner to Allah. This is of the bounty of Allah unto us (the seed of Abraham) and unto mankind; but most men give not thanks.

٣٨ وَاتَّبَعْتُ مِلَّةَ آبَائِي إِبْرَاهِيمَ وَإِسْحَاقَ وَيَعْقُوبَ مَا كَانَ لَنَا أَنْ نُشْرِكَ بِاللَّهِ مِنْ شَيْءٍ ذَلِكَ مِنْ فَضْلِ اللَّهِ عَلَيْنَا وَعَلَى النَّاسِ وَلَكِنَّ أَكْثَرَ النَّاسِ لَا يَشْكُرُونَ

39. O my two fellow prisoners! Are divers lords better, or Allah the One, the Almighty?

٣٩ يَا صَاحِبَيِ السِّجْنِ أَأَرْبَابٌ مُتَفَرِّقُونَ خَيْرٌ أَمِ اللَّهُ الْوَاحِدُ الْقَهَّارُ

40. Those whom you worship beside Him are but names which you have named, you and your fathers. Allah has revealed no sanction for them. The decision rests with Allah only, Who has commanded you that you worship none save Him. This is the right religion, but most men know not.

٤٠ مَا تَعْبُدُونَ مِنْ دُونِهِ إِلَّا أَسْمَاءً سَمَّيْتُمُوهَا أَنْتُمْ وَآبَاؤُكُمْ مَا أَنْزَلَ اللَّهُ بِهَا مِنْ سُلْطَانٍ إِنِ الْحُكْمُ إِلَّا لِلَّهِ أَمَرَ أَلَّا تَعْبُدُوا إِلَّا إِيَّاهُ ذَلِكَ الدِّينُ الْقَيِّمُ وَلَكِنَّ أَكْثَرَ النَّاسِ لَا يَعْلَمُونَ

41. O my two fellow prisoners! As for one of you, he will pour out wine for his lord to drink; and as for the other, he will be crucified so that the birds will eat from his head. Thus is the case judged concerning which you did inquire.

٤١ يَا صَاحِبَيِ السِّجْنِ أَمَّا أَحَدُكُمَا فَيَسْقِي رَبَّهُ خَمْرًا وَأَمَّا الْآخَرُ فَيُصْلَبُ فَتَأْكُلُ الطَّيْرُ مِنْ رَأْسِهِ قُضِيَ الْأَمْرُ الَّذِي فِيهِ تَسْتَفْتِيَانِ

42. And he said unto him of the two whom he guessed would be saved: Mention me in the presence of your lord. But the Devil caused him to forget to mention it to his lord, so he (Joseph) stayed in prison for some years.

43. And the king said: Lo! I saw in a dream seven fat kine which seven lean ones were eating, and seven green ears of corn and other (seven) dry. O notables! Expound for me my vision, if you can interpret dreams.

44. They answered: Jumbled dreams! And we are not knowing in the interpretation of dreams.

45. And he of the two who was saved, and (now) at length remembered, said: I am going to announce unto you the interpretation, therefore send me forth.

46. (And when he came to Joseph in the prison, he exclaimed): Joseph! O you truthful one! Expound for us the seven fat kine which seven lean ones were eating and the seven green ears of corn and other (seven) dry, that I may return unto the people, so that they may know.

47. He said: You shall sow seven years as usual, but that which you reap, leave it in the ear, all save a little which you eat.

48. Then after that will come seven hard years which will devour all that you have prepared for them, save a little of that which you have stored.

49. Then, after that, will come a year when the people will have plenteous crops and when they will press (wine and oil).

50. And the King said: Bring him unto me. And when the messenger came unto him, he (Joseph) said: Return unto your lord and ask him what was the case of the women who cut their. hands. Lo! my Lord surely knows their guile.

وَقَالَ لِلَّذِى ظَنَّ أَنَّهُ نَاجٍ مِّنْهُمَا اذْكُرْنِى عِندَ رَبِّكَ فَأَنسَاهُ الشَّيْطَانُ ذِكْرَ رَبِّهِ فَلَبِثَ فِى السِّجْنِ بِضْعَ سِنِينَ ۝

وَقَالَ الْمَلِكُ إِنِّى أَرَى سَبْعَ بَقَرَاتٍ سِمَانٍ يَأْكُلُهُنَّ سَبْعٌ عِجَافٌ وَسَبْعَ سُنْبُلَاتٍ خُضْرٍ وَأُخَرَ يَابِسَاتٍ يَا أَيُّهَا الْمَلَأُ أَفْتُونِى فِى رُؤْيَايَ إِن كُنتُمْ لِلرُّؤْيَا تَعْبُرُونَ ۝

قَالُوا أَضْغَاثُ أَحْلَامٍ وَمَا نَحْنُ بِتَأْوِيلِ الْأَحْلَامِ بِعَالِمِينَ ۝

وَقَالَ الَّذِى نَجَا مِنْهُمَا وَادَّكَرَ بَعْدَ أُمَّةٍ أَنَا أُنَبِّئُكُم بِتَأْوِيلِهِ فَأَرْسِلُونِ ۝

يُوسُفُ أَيُّهَا الصِّدِّيقُ أَفْتِنَا فِى سَبْعِ بَقَرَاتٍ سِمَانٍ يَأْكُلُهُنَّ سَبْعٌ عِجَافٌ وَسَبْعِ سُنْبُلَاتٍ خُضْرٍ وَأُخَرَ يَابِسَاتٍ لَّعَلِّى أَرْجِعُ إِلَى النَّاسِ لَعَلَّهُمْ يَعْلَمُونَ ۝

قَالَ تَزْرَعُونَ سَبْعَ سِنِينَ دَأَبًا فَمَا حَصَدتُّمْ فَذَرُوهُ فِى سُنْبُلِهِ إِلَّا قَلِيلًا مِّمَّا تَأْكُلُونَ ۝

ثُمَّ يَأْتِى مِن بَعْدِ ذَلِكَ سَبْعٌ شِدَادٌ يَأْكُلْنَ مَا قَدَّمْتُمْ لَهُنَّ إِلَّا قَلِيلًا مِّمَّا تُحْصِنُونَ ۝

ثُمَّ يَأْتِى مِن بَعْدِ ذَلِكَ عَامٌ فِيهِ يُغَاثُ النَّاسُ وَفِيهِ يَعْصِرُونَ ۝

وَقَالَ الْمَلِكُ ائْتُونِى بِهِ فَلَمَّا جَاءَهُ الرَّسُولُ قَالَ ارْجِعْ إِلَى رَبِّكَ فَسْأَلْهُ مَا بَالُ النِّسْوَةِ اللَّاتِى قَطَّعْنَ أَيْدِيَهُنَّ إِنَّ رَبِّى بِكَيْدِهِنَّ عَلِيمٌ ۝

51. He (the king) (then sent for those women and) said: What happened when you asked an evil act of Joseph? They answered: Allah Blameless! We know no evil of him. Said the wife of the chief: Now the truth is out. I asked of him an evil act, and he is surely of the truthful.

٥١ قَالَ مَا خَطْبُكُنَّ إِذْ رَاوَدْتُنَّ يُوسُفَ عَن نَّفْسِهِ قُلْنَ حَاشَ لِلَّهِ مَا عَلِمْنَا عَلَيْهِ مِن سُوءٍ قَالَتِ امْرَأَتُ الْعَزِيزِ الْآنَ حَصْحَصَ الْحَقُّ أَنَا رَاوَدتُّهُ عَن نَّفْسِهِ وَإِنَّهُ لَمِنَ الصَّادِقِينَ

52. This (testimony), that he* (my lord) may know that I betrayed him not in secret, and that surely Allah guides not the snare of the betrayers.

٥٢ ذَٰلِكَ لِيَعْلَمَ أَنِّي لَمْ أَخُنْهُ بِالْغَيْبِ وَأَنَّ اللَّهَ لَا يَهْدِي كَيْدَ الْخَائِنِينَ

53. I do not exculpate myself. Lo! the (human) soul enjoins unto evil, save that whereon my Lord has mercy. Lo! my Lord is Forgiving, Merciful.

٥٣ وَمَا أُبَرِّئُ نَفْسِي إِنَّ النَّفْسَ لَأَمَّارَةٌ بِالسُّوءِ إِلَّا مَا رَحِمَ رَبِّي إِنَّ رَبِّي غَفُورٌ رَّحِيمٌ

54. And the king said: Bring him unto me that I may attach him to my person. And when he had talked with him he said: Lo! you are today in our presence established and trusted.

٥٤ وَقَالَ الْمَلِكُ ائْتُونِي بِهِ أَسْتَخْلِصْهُ لِنَفْسِي فَلَمَّا كَلَّمَهُ قَالَ إِنَّكَ الْيَوْمَ لَدَيْنَا مَكِينٌ أَمِينٌ

55. He said: Set me over the storehouses of the land. Lo! I am a skilled custodian.

٥٥ قَالَ اجْعَلْنِي عَلَى خَزَائِنِ الْأَرْضِ إِنِّي حَفِيظٌ عَلِيمٌ

56. Thus gave We power to Joseph in the land. He was the owner of it where he pleased. We reach with our mercy whom We will. We lose not the reward of the good.

٥٦ وَكَذَٰلِكَ مَكَّنَّا لِيُوسُفَ فِي الْأَرْضِ يَتَبَوَّأُ مِنْهَا حَيْثُ يَشَاءُ نُصِيبُ بِرَحْمَتِنَا مَن نَّشَاءُ وَلَا نُضِيعُ أَجْرَ الْمُحْسِنِينَ

57. And the reward of the Hereafter is better, for those who believe and ward off (evil).

٥٧ وَلَأَجْرُ الْآخِرَةِ خَيْرٌ لِّلَّذِينَ آمَنُوا وَكَانُوا يَتَّقُونَ

58. And Joseph's brothers came and presented themselves before him, and he knew them but they knew him not.

٥٨ وَجَاءَ إِخْوَةُ يُوسُفَ فَدَخَلُوا عَلَيْهِ فَعَرَفَهُمْ وَهُمْ لَهُ مُنكِرُونَ

59. And when he provided them with their provision he said: Bring unto me a brother of yours from your father. See you not that I fill up the measure and I am the best of hosts?

٥٩ وَلَمَّا جَهَّزَهُم بِجَهَازِهِمْ قَالَ ائْتُونِي بِأَخٍ لَّكُم مِّنْ أَبِيكُمْ أَلَا تَرَوْنَ أَنِّي أُوفِي الْكَيْلَ وَأَنَا خَيْرُ الْمُنزِلِينَ

60. And if you bring him not unto me, then there shall be no measure for you with me, nor shall you draw near.

٦٠ فَإِن لَّمْ تَأْتُونِي بِهِ فَلَا كَيْلَ لَكُمْ عِندِي وَلَا تَقْرَبُونِ

61. They said: We will try to win him from his father: that we will surely do.

62. He said unto his young men: Place their merchandise in their saddlebags, so that they may know it when they go back to their folk, and so they will come again.

63. Thus when they went back to their father they said: O our father! The measure is denied us, so send with us our brother that we may obtain the measure, surely we will guard him well.

64. He said: Can I entrust him to you save as I entrusted his brother to you before? Allah is better at guarding, and He is the Most Merciful of those who show mercy.

65. And when they opened their belongings they discovered that their merchandise had been returned to them. They said: O our father! What (more) can we ask? Here is our merchandise returned to us. We shall get provision for our folk and guard our brother, and we shall have the extra measure of a camel (load). This (that we bring now) is a light measure.

66. He said: I will not send him with you till you give me a covenant in the name of Allah that you will bring him back to me, unless you are surrounded. And when they gave him their oath he said: Allah is the Warden over what we say.

67. And he said: O my sons! Go not in by one gate; go in by different gates. I can not avail you as against Allah. Lo! the decision rests with Allah only. In Him do I put my trust, and in Him let all the trusting put their trust.

68. And when they entered in the manner which their father had enjoined, it would have not availed them as against Allah; it was but a need of Jacob's soul which he thus satisfied;[137] and lo! he was a lord of knowledge because We had taught him; but most of mankind know not.

---

[137] As a prophet of Allah, Jacob had been informed by Allah of what was going on.

69. And when they went in before Joseph, he took his brother unto himself, saying: Lo; I, even I, am your brother, therefore sorrow not for what they did.

70. And when he provided them with their provision, he put the drinking cup in his brother's saddlebag, and then a crier cried: O camel riders! You are surely thieves!

71. They cried, coming toward them: What is it you have lost?

72. They said: We have lost the king's cup, and he who brings it shall have a camel load, and I (said Joseph) am answerable for it.

73. They said: By Allah, well you know we came not to do evil in the land, and are no thieves.

74. They said: And what shall be the penalty for it if you prove liars?

75. They said: The penalty for it! He in whose bag (the cup) is found, he is the penalty for it. Thus we requite wrongdoers.

76. Then he (Joseph) began the search with their bags before his brother's bag, then he produced it from his brother's bag. Thus did We contrive for Joseph. He could not have taken his brother according to the king's law unless Allah willed. We raise by grades (of mercy) whom We will, and over every lord of knowledge there is one more knowing.

77. They said: If he steals, a brother of his stole before. But Joseph kept it secret in his soul and revealed it not unto them. He said: You are in worse case and Allah knows best (the truth of) that which you allege.

78. They said: O Chief! Lo! he has an aged father, so take one of us instead of him. Lo! we behold you of those who do kindness.

79. He said: Allah forbid that we should seize save him with whom we found our property; then truly we should be wrongdoers.

80. So, when they despaired of (moving) him, they conferred together apart. The eldest of them said: Know you not how your father took an oath from you in Allah's name and how you failed in the case of Joseph before? Therefore I shall not go forth from the land until my father gives me leave or Allah judges for me. He is the Best of Judges.

81. Return unto your father and say: O our father! Lo! your son has stolen. We testify only to that which we know; we are not guardians of the unseen.

82. Ask the township wherein we were, and the caravan with which we travelled hither. Lo! we speak the truth.

83. (And when they came unto their father and had spoken thus to him) he said: Nay, but your minds have beguiled you into something. (My course is) comely patience! It may be that Allah will bring them all unto me. Lo! He, only He, is the Knower, the Wise.

84. And he turned away from them and said: Alas, my grief for Joseph! And his eyes were whitened with the sorrow that he was suppressing.

85. They said: By Allah, you will never cease remembering Joseph till your health is ruined or you are of those who perish!

86. He said: I expose my distress and anguish only unto Allah, and I know from Allah that which you know not.

87. Go, O my sons, and ascertain concerning Joseph and his brother, and despair not of the Spirit of Allah. Lo! none despairs of the Spirit of Allah save disbelieving folk.

88. And when they came (again) before him (Joseph) they said: O chief! Misfortune has touched us and our folk, and we bring but poor merchandise, so fill for us the measure and be charitable unto us. Lo! Allah will requite the charitable.

89. He said: Know you what you did unto Joseph and his brother in your ignorance?

90. They said: Is it indeed you who are Joseph? He said: I am Joseph and this is my brother. Allah has shown us favor. Lo! he who wards off (evil) and endures (finds favor); for surely Allah loses not the wages of the kindly.

91. They said: By Allah, surely Allah has preferred you above us, and we were indeed sinful.

92. He said: Have no fear this day! May Allah forgive you, and He is the Most Merciful of those who show mercy.

93. Go with this shirt of mine and lay it on my father's face, he will become (again) a seer; and come to me with all your folk.

94. When the caravan departed their father had said: Truly I am conscious of the breath of Joseph, though you call me dotard.

95. (Those around him) said: By Allah, Lo! you are in your old aberration.

96. Then, when the bearer of glad tidings came, he laid it on his face and he became a seer once more. He said: Said I not unto you that I know from Allah that which you know not?

97. They said: O our father! Ask forgiveness of our sins for us, for lo! we were sinful.

٨٨ فَلَمَّا دَخَلُوا عَلَيْهِ قَالُوا يَا أَيُّهَا الْعَزِيزُ مَسَّنَا وَأَهْلَنَا الضُّرُّ وَجِئْنَا بِبِضَاعَةٍ مُّزْجَاةٍ فَأَوْفِ لَنَا الْكَيْلَ وَتَصَدَّقْ عَلَيْنَا إِنَّ اللَّهَ يَجْزِي الْمُتَصَدِّقِينَ

٨٩ قَالَ هَلْ عَلِمْتُم مَّا فَعَلْتُم بِيُوسُفَ وَأَخِيهِ إِذْ أَنتُمْ جَاهِلُونَ

٩٠ قَالُوا أَإِنَّكَ لَأَنتَ يُوسُفُ قَالَ أَنَا يُوسُفُ وَهَذَا أَخِي قَدْ مَنَّ اللَّهُ عَلَيْنَا إِنَّهُ مَن يَتَّقِ وَيَصْبِرْ فَإِنَّ اللَّهَ لَا يُضِيعُ أَجْرَ الْمُحْسِنِينَ

٩١ قَالُوا تَاللَّهِ لَقَدْ آثَرَكَ اللَّهُ عَلَيْنَا وَإِن كُنَّا لَخَاطِئِينَ

٩٢ قَالَ لَا تَثْرِيبَ عَلَيْكُمُ الْيَوْمَ يَغْفِرُ اللَّهُ لَكُمْ وَهُوَ أَرْحَمُ الرَّاحِمِينَ

٩٣ اذْهَبُوا بِقَمِيصِي هَذَا فَأَلْقُوهُ عَلَى وَجْهِ أَبِي يَأْتِ بَصِيرًا وَأْتُونِي بِأَهْلِكُمْ أَجْمَعِينَ

٩٤ وَلَمَّا فَصَلَتِ الْعِيرُ قَالَ أَبُوهُمْ إِنِّي لَأَجِدُ رِيحَ يُوسُفَ لَوْلَا أَن تُفَنِّدُونِ

٩٥ قَالُوا تَاللَّهِ إِنَّكَ لَفِي ضَلَالِكَ الْقَدِيمِ

٩٦ فَلَمَّا أَن جَاءَ الْبَشِيرُ أَلْقَاهُ عَلَى وَجْهِهِ فَارْتَدَّ بَصِيرًا قَالَ أَلَمْ أَقُل لَّكُمْ إِنِّي أَعْلَمُ مِنَ اللَّهِ مَا لَا تَعْلَمُونَ

٩٧ قَالُوا يَا أَبَانَا اسْتَغْفِرْ لَنَا ذُنُوبَنَا إِنَّا كُنَّا خَاطِئِينَ

98. He said: I shall ask forgiveness for you of my Lord. He is the Forgiving, the Merciful.

99. And when they came in before Joseph, he took his parents unto him, and said: Come into Egypt safe, if Allah will!

100. And he placed his parents on the dais and they fell down before him prostrate, and he said: O my father! This is the interpretation of my dream of old. My Lord has made it true, and He has shown me kindness, since He took me out of the prison and has brought you from the desert after the Devil had made strife between me and my brothers. Lo! my Lord is tender unto whom He will. He is the Knower, the Wise.

101. O my Lord! You have given me (something) of sovereignty and have taught me (something) of the interpretation of events, Creator of the heavens and the earth! You are my Protecting Friend in the world and the Hereafter. Make me to die submissive (unto You), and join me to the righteous.

102. This is of the tidings of the Unseen which We inspire in you (Muhammad). You were not present with them when they fixed their plan and they were scheming.

103. And though you try much, most men will not believe.

104. You ask them no fee for it. It is nothing else than a reminder unto the worlds.

105. How many a portent is there in the heavens and the earth which they pass by with face averted!

106. And most of them believe not in Allah except that they attribute partners (unto Him).

۹۸ قَالَ سَوْفَ أَسْتَغْفِرُ لَكُمْ رَبِّيَ إِنَّهُ هُوَ الْغَفُورُ الرَّحِيمُ

۹۹ فَلَمَّا دَخَلُوا عَلَى يُوسُفَ ءَاوَى إِلَيْهِ أَبَوَيْهِ وَقَالَ ادْخُلُوا مِصْرَ إِن شَاءَ اللَّهُ ءَامِنِينَ

۱۰۰ وَرَفَعَ أَبَوَيْهِ عَلَى الْعَرْشِ وَخَرُّوا لَهُ سُجَّدًا وَقَالَ يَاأَبَتِ هَذَا تَأْوِيلُ رُءْيَايَ مِن قَبْلُ قَدْ جَعَلَهَا رَبِّي حَقًّا وَقَدْ أَحْسَنَ بِي إِذْ أَخْرَجَنِي مِنَ السِّجْنِ وَجَاءَ بِكُم مِّنَ الْبَدْوِ مِنۢ بَعْدِ أَن نَّزَغَ الشَّيْطَانُ بَيْنِي وَبَيْنَ إِخْوَتِي إِنَّ رَبِّي لَطِيفٌ لِّمَا يَشَاءُ إِنَّهُ هُوَ الْعَلِيمُ الْحَكِيمُ

۱۰۱ رَبِّ قَدْ ءَاتَيْتَنِي مِنَ الْمُلْكِ وَعَلَّمْتَنِي مِن تَأْوِيلِ الْأَحَادِيثِ فَاطِرَ السَّمَوَاتِ وَالْأَرْضِ أَنتَ وَلِيِّي فِي الدُّنْيَا وَالْآخِرَةِ تَوَفَّنِي مُسْلِمًا وَأَلْحِقْنِي بِالصَّالِحِينَ

۱۰۲ ذَلِكَ مِنْ أَنۢبَاءِ الْغَيْبِ نُوحِيهِ إِلَيْكَ وَمَا كُنتَ لَدَيْهِمْ إِذْ أَجْمَعُوا أَمْرَهُمْ وَهُمْ يَمْكُرُونَ

۱۰۳ وَمَا أَكْثَرُ النَّاسِ وَلَوْ حَرَصْتَ بِمُؤْمِنِينَ

۱۰٤ وَمَا تَسْـَٔلُهُمْ عَلَيْهِ مِنْ أَجْرٍ إِنْ هُوَ إِلَّا ذِكْرٌ لِّلْعَالَمِينَ

۱۰٥ وَكَأَيِّن مِّنْ ءَايَةٍ فِي السَّمَوَاتِ وَالْأَرْضِ يَمُرُّونَ عَلَيْهَا وَهُمْ عَنْهَا مُعْرِضُونَ

۱۰٦ وَمَا يُؤْمِنُ أَكْثَرُهُم بِاللَّهِ إِلَّا وَهُم مُّشْرِكُونَ

107. Deem they themselves secure from the coming on them of a pall of Allah's punishment, or the coming of the Hour suddenly while they are unaware?

١٠٧ أَفَأَمِنُوٓاْ أَن تَأْتِيَهُمْ غَـٰشِيَةٌ مِّنْ عَذَابِ ٱللَّهِ أَوْ تَأْتِيَهُمُ ٱلسَّاعَةُ بَغْتَةً وَهُمْ لَا يَشْعُرُونَ

108. Say: This is my Way: I call to Allah with sure knowledge, I and whosoever follows me—Glory be to Allah!— and I am not of the idolaters.

١٠٨ قُلْ هَـٰذِهِۦ سَبِيلِيٓ أَدْعُوٓاْ إِلَى ٱللَّهِ عَلَىٰ بَصِيرَةٍ أَنَا۠ وَمَنِ ٱتَّبَعَنِى وَسُبْحَـٰنَ ٱللَّهِ وَمَآ أَنَا۠ مِنَ ٱلْمُشْرِكِينَ

109. We sent not before you (any messengers) save men whom We inspired from among the folk of the townships— Have they not travelled in the land and seen the nature of the consequence for those who were before them? And surely the abode of the Hereafter, for those who ward off (evil), is best. Have you then no sense?—

١٠٩ وَمَآ أَرْسَلْنَا مِن قَبْلِكَ إِلَّا رِجَالًا نُّوحِىٓ إِلَيْهِم مِّنْ أَهْلِ ٱلْقُرَىٰٓ أَفَلَمْ يَسِيرُواْ فِى ٱلْأَرْضِ فَيَنظُرُواْ كَيْفَ كَانَ عَـٰقِبَةُ ٱلَّذِينَ مِن قَبْلِهِمْ وَلَدَارُ ٱلْأَخِرَةِ خَيْرٌ لِّلَّذِينَ ٱتَّقَوْاْ أَفَلَا تَعْقِلُونَ

110. Till, when the messengers despaired and thought that they were denied, then came unto them Our help, and whom We would was saved. And our wrath cannot be warded from the guilty people.

١١٠ حَتَّىٰٓ إِذَا ٱسْتَيْـَٔسَ ٱلرُّسُلُ وَظَنُّوٓاْ أَنَّهُمْ قَدْ كُذِبُواْ جَآءَهُمْ نَصْرُنَا فَنُجِّىَ مَن نَّشَآءُ وَلَا يُرَدُّ بَأْسُنَا عَنِ ٱلْقَوْمِ ٱلْمُجْرِمِينَ

111. In their history verily there is a lesson for men of understanding. It is no invented story but a confirmation of the existing (Scripture) and a detailed explanation of everything, and a guidance and a mercy for folk who believe.

١١١ لَقَدْ كَانَ فِى قَصَصِهِمْ عِبْرَةٌ لِّأُوْلِى ٱلْأَلْبَـٰبِ مَا كَانَ حَدِيثًا يُفْتَرَىٰ وَلَـٰكِن تَصْدِيقَ ٱلَّذِى بَيْنَ يَدَيْهِ وَتَفْصِيلَ كُلِّ شَىْءٍ وَهُدًى وَرَحْمَةً لِّقَوْمٍ يُؤْمِنُونَ

The Thunder

Al Ra'd, "The Thunder," takes its name from a word in verse 13. The subject is divine guidance in relation to the law of consequences: there is no partiality or aversion on the part of God, and reward and punishment are the result of obeying or rejecting natural (or divine) laws. According to some ancient authorities, it is a Makkan surah (with the exception of two verses revealed at al Madinah). According to others, it is a Madinan surah (with the exception of two verses revealed at Makkah). The very fact of such wholesale difference of opinion favors the Makkan attribution, because there could be no doubt about a complete Madinan surah due to the large number of witnesses. The Madinan ascription may have arisen from the recognition of some verses by those witnesses as having been revealed at al Madinah on a certain occasion.

A late Makkan surah for the most part.

The Thunder

Revealed at Makkah

In the name of Allah,
the Beneficent, the Merciful

1. **A**lif. Lām. Mīm. Rā'.[138] These are verses of the Scrip-ture. That which is revealed unto you from your Lord is the Truth, but most of mankind believe not.

2. Allah it is who raised up the heavens without visible supports, then mounted the Throne, and compelled the sun and the moon to be of service, each runs unto an appointed term; He orders the course; He details the revelations, that haply you may be certain of the meeting with your Lord.

3. And He it is who spread out the earth and placed therein firm hills and flowing streams, and of all fruits He placed therein two spouses (male and female). He covers the night with the day. Lo! herein verily are portents for people who take thought.

4. And in the Earth are neighboring tracts, vineyards and ploughed lands, and date palms, like and unlike,[139] which are watered with one water. And We have made some of them to excel others in fruit. Lo! herein verily are portents for people who have sense.

5. And if you wonder, then wondrous is their saying: When we are dust, are we then in truth (to be raised) in a new cre-ation? Such are they who disbelieve in their Lord; such have carcans on their necks; such are rightful owners of the Fire, they will abide therein.

6. And they bid you hasten on the evil rather than the good, when exemplary pun-ishments have indeed occurred before them. But lo! your Lord is rich in pardon for mankind despite their wrong, and lo! your Lord is strong in punishment!

---

[138]See Surah 2:12, footnote.
[139]Or it may be, "growing thickly or alone."

7. Those who disbelieve say: If only some portent were sent down upon him from his Lord! You are a warner only, and for every folk a guide.

٧ وَيَقُولُ الَّذِينَ كَفَرُوا لَوْلَا أُنزِلَ عَلَيْهِ ءَايَةٌ مِّن رَّبِّهِۦٓ إِنَّمَآ أَنتَ مُنذِرٌ وَلِكُلِّ قَوْمٍ هَادٍ

8. Allah knows that which every female bears and that which the wombs absorb and that which they grow. And everything with Him is measured.

٨ اللَّهُ يَعْلَمُ مَا تَحْمِلُ كُلُّ أُنثَىٰ وَمَا تَغِيضُ الْأَرْحَامُ وَمَا تَزْدَادُ وَكُلُّ شَيْءٍ عِندَهُۥ بِمِقْدَارٍ

9. He is the Knower of the invisible and the visible, the Great, the High Exalted.

٩ عَٰلِمُ الْغَيْبِ وَالشَّهَٰدَةِ الْكَبِيرُ الْمُتَعَالِ

10. Alike of you is he who hides the saying and he who noises it abroad, he who lurks in the night and he who goes freely in the daytime.

١٠ سَوَآءٌ مِّنكُم مَّنْ أَسَرَّ الْقَوْلَ وَمَن جَهَرَ بِهِۦ وَمَنْ هُوَ مُسْتَخْفٍ بِالَّيْلِ وَسَارِبٌ بِالنَّهَارِ

11. For him are angels ranged before him and behind him who guard him by Allah's command.[140] Lo! Allah changes not the condition of a folk until they (first) change that which is in their hearts; and if Allah wills misfortune for a folk there is none that can repel it, nor have they a defender beside Him.

١١ لَهُۥ مُعَقِّبَٰتٌ مِّنۢ بَيْنِ يَدَيْهِ وَمِنْ خَلْفِهِۦ يَحْفَظُونَهُۥ مِنْ أَمْرِ اللَّهِ إِنَّ اللَّهَ لَا يُغَيِّرُ مَا بِقَوْمٍ حَتَّىٰ يُغَيِّرُوا مَا بِأَنفُسِهِمْ وَإِذَآ أَرَادَ اللَّهُ بِقَوْمٍ سُوٓءًا فَلَا مَرَدَّ لَهُۥ وَمَا لَهُم مِّن دُونِهِۦ مِن وَالٍ

12. He it is Who shows you the lightning, a fear and a hope,[141] and raises the heavy clouds.

١٢ هُوَ الَّذِي يُرِيكُمُ الْبَرْقَ خَوْفًا وَطَمَعًا وَيُنشِئُ السَّحَابَ الثِّقَالَ

13. The thunder hymns His praise and (so do) the angels for awe of Him. He launches the thunder bolts and smites with them whom He will while they dispute (in doubt) concerning Allah, and He is mighty in wrath.

١٣ وَيُسَبِّحُ الرَّعْدُ بِحَمْدِهِۦ وَالْمَلَٰٓئِكَةُ مِنْ خِيفَتِهِۦ وَيُرْسِلُ الصَّوَٰعِقَ فَيُصِيبُ بِهَا مَن يَشَآءُ وَهُمْ يُجَٰدِلُونَ فِي اللَّهِ وَهُوَ شَدِيدُ الْمِحَالِ

14. Unto Him is the real prayer. Those unto whom they pray beside Allah respond to them not at all, save as (if the response to) one who stretches forth his hands toward water (asking) that it may come unto his mouth, and it will never reach it. The prayer of disbelievers goes (far) astray.

١٤ لَهُۥ دَعْوَةُ الْحَقِّ وَالَّذِينَ يَدْعُونَ مِن دُونِهِۦ لَا يَسْتَجِيبُونَ لَهُم بِشَيْءٍ إِلَّا كَبَٰسِطِ كَفَّيْهِ إِلَى الْمَآءِ لِيَبْلُغَ فَاهُ وَمَا هُوَ بِبَٰلِغِهِۦ وَمَا دُعَآءُ الْكَٰفِرِينَ إِلَّا فِي ضَلَٰلٍ

15. And unto Allah falls prostrate whoever is in the heavens and the earth, willingly or unwillingly, as do their shadows in the morning and the evening hours.

١٥ وَلِلَّهِ يَسْجُدُ مَن فِي السَّمَٰوَٰتِ وَالْأَرْضِ طَوْعًا وَكَرْهًا وَظِلَٰلُهُم بِالْغُدُوِّ وَالْءَاصَالِ ۩

---

[140]This is taken by some commentators to refer to "him who goes freely in the daytime" in the previous verse. In that case it would read: "for whom are guards before him and behind him as if to guard against Allah's commandment."

[141]The fear is of the lightning, and the hope is of the rain.

16. Say (O Muhammad): Who is Lord of the heaven and the earth? Say: Allah! Say: Take you then (others) beside Him for protectors which, even for themselves, have neither benefit nor hurt? Say: Is the blind man equal to the seer, or is darkness equal to light? Or assign they unto Allah partners Who created the like of His creation so that the creation (which they made and His creation) seemed alike to them? Say: Allah is the Creator of all things, and He is the One, the Almighty.

17. He sends down water from the sky, so that valleys flow according to their measure, and the flood bears (on its surface) swelling foam—from that which they smelt in the fire in order to make ornaments and tools rises a foam like unto it—thus Allah coins (the similitude of) the true and the false. Then, as for the foam, it passes away as scum upon the banks, while, as for that which is of use to mankind, it re-mains in the earth. Thus Allah coins the similitudes.

18. For those who answered Allah's call is bliss; and for those who answered not His call, if they had all that is in the earth, and therewith the like thereof, they would proffer it as ransom. Such will have a woeful reckoning, and their habitation will be hell, a dire abode.

19. Is he who knows that what is revealed unto you from your Lord is the truth like him who is blind? But only men of understanding heed;

20. Such as keep the pact of Allah, and break not the covenant;

21. Such as unite that which Allah has commanded should be joined, and fear their Lord, and dread a woeful reckoning:

١٦ قُل مَّن رَّبُّ ٱلسَّمَٰوَٰتِ وَٱلأَرْضِ قُلِ ٱللَّهُ قُلْ أَفَٱتَّخَذْتُم مِّن دُونِهِۦ أَوْلِيَآءَ لَا يَمْلِكُونَ لِأَنفُسِهِمْ نَفْعًا وَلَا ضَرًّا قُلْ هَلْ يَسْتَوِى ٱلأَعْمَىٰ وَٱلْبَصِيرُ أَمْ هَلْ تَسْتَوِى ٱلظُّلُمَٰتُ وَٱلنُّورُ أَمْ جَعَلُوا۟ لِلَّهِ شُرَكَآءَ خَلَقُوا۟ كَخَلْقِهِۦ فَتَشَٰبَهَ ٱلْخَلْقُ عَلَيْهِمْ قُلِ ٱللَّهُ خَٰلِقُ كُلِّ شَىْءٍ وَهُوَ ٱلْوَٰحِدُ ٱلْقَهَّٰرُ

١٧ أَنزَلَ مِنَ ٱلسَّمَآءِ مَآءً فَسَالَتْ أَوْدِيَةٌۢ بِقَدَرِهَا فَٱحْتَمَلَ ٱلسَّيْلُ زَبَدًا رَّابِيًا وَمِمَّا يُوقِدُونَ عَلَيْهِ فِى ٱلنَّارِ ٱبْتِغَآءَ حِلْيَةٍ أَوْ مَتَٰعٍ زَبَدٌ مِّثْلُهُۥ كَذَٰلِكَ يَضْرِبُ ٱللَّهُ ٱلْحَقَّ وَٱلْبَٰطِلَ فَأَمَّا ٱلزَّبَدُ فَيَذْهَبُ جُفَآءً وَأَمَّا مَا يَنفَعُ ٱلنَّاسَ فَيَمْكُثُ فِى ٱلأَرْضِ كَذَٰلِكَ يَضْرِبُ ٱللَّهُ ٱلأَمْثَالَ

١٨ لِلَّذِينَ ٱسْتَجَابُوا۟ لِرَبِّهِمُ ٱلْحُسْنَىٰ وَٱلَّذِينَ لَمْ يَسْتَجِيبُوا۟ لَهُۥ لَوْ أَنَّ لَهُم مَّا فِى ٱلأَرْضِ جَمِيعًا وَمِثْلَهُۥ مَعَهُۥ لَٱفْتَدَوْا۟ بِهِۦٓ أُو۟لَٰٓئِكَ لَهُمْ سُوٓءُ ٱلْحِسَابِ وَمَأْوَىٰهُمْ جَهَنَّمُ وَبِئْسَ ٱلْمِهَادُ

١٩ ۞ أَفَمَن يَعْلَمُ أَنَّمَآ أُنزِلَ إِلَيْكَ مِن رَّبِّكَ ٱلْحَقُّ كَمَنْ هُوَ أَعْمَىٰٓ إِنَّمَا يَتَذَكَّرُ أُو۟لُوا۟ ٱلأَلْبَٰبِ

٢٠ ٱلَّذِينَ يُوفُونَ بِعَهْدِ ٱللَّهِ وَلَا يَنقُضُونَ ٱلْمِيثَٰقَ

٢١ وَٱلَّذِينَ يَصِلُونَ مَآ أَمَرَ ٱللَّهُ بِهِۦٓ أَن يُوصَلَ وَيَخْشَوْنَ رَبَّهُمْ وَيَخَافُونَ سُوٓءَ ٱلْحِسَابِ

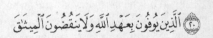

22. Such as persevere in seeking their Lord's countenance and are regular in prayer and spend of that which We bestow upon them secretly and openly, and overcome evil with good. Theirs will be the sequel of the (heavenly) Home,

٢٢ وَالَّذِينَ صَبَرُوا ابْتِغَاءَ وَجْهِ رَبِّهِمْ وَأَقَامُوا الصَّلَوٰةَ وَأَنْفَقُوا مِمَّا رَزَقْنَاهُمْ سِرًّا وَعَلَانِيَةً وَيَدْرَءُونَ بِالْحَسَنَةِ السَّيِّئَةَ أُولَئِكَ لَهُمْ عُقْبَى الدَّارِ

23. Gardens of Eden which they enter, along with all who do right of their fathers and their spouses and their offspring. The angels enter unto them from every gate,

٢٣ جَنَّاتُ عَدْنٍ يَدْخُلُونَهَا وَمَنْ صَلَحَ مِنْ ءَابَائِهِمْ وَأَزْوَاجِهِمْ وَذُرِّيَّاتِهِمْ وَالْمَلَائِكَةُ يَدْخُلُونَ عَلَيْهِمْ مِنْ كُلِّ بَابٍ

24. (Saying): Peace be unto you because you persevered. Ah, passing sweet will be the sequel of the (heavenly) Home.

٢٤ سَلَامٌ عَلَيْكُمْ بِمَا صَبَرْتُمْ فَنِعْمَ عُقْبَى الدَّارِ

25. And those who break the covenant of Allah after ratifying it, and sever that which Allah has commanded should be joined, and make mischief in the earth: theirs is the curse and theirs is the ill abode.

٢٥ وَالَّذِينَ يَنْقُضُونَ عَهْدَ اللَّهِ مِنْ بَعْدِ مِيثَاقِهِ وَيَقْطَعُونَ مَا أَمَرَ اللَّهُ بِهِ أَنْ يُوصَلَ وَيُفْسِدُونَ فِي الْأَرْضِ أُولَئِكَ لَهُمُ اللَّعْنَةُ وَلَهُمْ سُوءُ الدَّارِ

26. Allah enlarges livelihood for whom He will, and straitens (it for whom He will); and they rejoice in the life of the world, whereas the life of the world is but brief comfort as compared with the Hereafter.

٢٦ اللَّهُ يَبْسُطُ الرِّزْقَ لِمَنْ يَشَاءُ وَيَقْدِرُ وَفَرِحُوا بِالْحَيَوٰةِ الدُّنْيَا وَمَا الْحَيَوٰةُ الدُّنْيَا فِي الْآخِرَةِ إِلَّا مَتَاعٌ

27. Those who disbelieve say: If only a portent were sent down upon him from his Lord! Say: Lo! Allah sends whom He will astray, and guides unto Himself all who turn (unto Him),

٢٧ وَيَقُولُ الَّذِينَ كَفَرُوا لَوْلَا أُنْزِلَ عَلَيْهِ ءَايَةٌ مِنْ رَبِّهِ قُلْ إِنَّ اللَّهَ يُضِلُّ مَنْ يَشَاءُ وَيَهْدِي إِلَيْهِ مَنْ أَنَابَ

28. Who have believed and whose hearts have rest in the remembrance of Allah. Surely in the remembrance of Allah do hearts find rest!

٢٨ الَّذِينَ ءَامَنُوا وَتَطْمَئِنُّ قُلُوبُهُمْ بِذِكْرِ اللَّهِ أَلَا بِذِكْرِ اللَّهِ تَطْمَئِنُّ الْقُلُوبُ

29. Those who believe and do right: Joy is for them, and bliss (their) journey's end.

٢٩ الَّذِينَ ءَامَنُوا وَعَمِلُوا الصَّالِحَاتِ طُوبَى لَهُمْ وَحُسْنُ مَآبٍ

30. Thus We send you (O Muhammad) unto a nation, before whom other nations have passed away, that you may recite unto them that which We have inspired in you, while they are disbelievers in the Beneficent. Say: He is my Lord; there is no God save Him. In Him do I put my trust and unto Him is my recourse.

31. Had it been possible for a Qur'an to cause the mountains to move, or the earth to be torn asunder, or the dead to speak, (this Qur'an would have done so). Nay, but Allah's is the whole command. Do not those who believe know that, had Allah willed, He could have guided all mankind? As for those who disbelieve, disaster ceases not to strike them because of what they do, or it dwells near their home until the threat of Allah come to pass. Lo! Allah fails not to keep the appointed time.

32. And verily messengers (of Allah) were mocked before you, but long I bore with those who disbelieved. At length I seized them, and how (awful) was My punishment!

33. Is He Who is aware of the deserts of every soul (as he who is aware of nothing)? Yet they ascribe unto Allah partners. Say: Name them. Is it that you would inform Him of something which He knows not in the earth? Or is it but a way of speaking? Nay, but their contrivance is made seeming fair for those who disbelieve and they are kept from the right road. He whom Allah sends astray, for him there is no guide.

34. For them is torment in the life of the world, and surely the doom of the Hereafter is more painful, and they have no defender from Allah.

35. A similitude of the Garden which is promised unto those who keep their duty (to Allah): Underneath it rivers flow; its food is everlasting, and its shade; this is the reward of those who keep their duty, while the reward of disbelievers is the Fire.

٣٠ كَذَٰلِكَ أَرْسَلْنَاكَ فِىٓ أُمَّةٍ قَدْ خَلَتْ مِن قَبْلِهَآ أُمَمٌ لِّتَتْلُوَا۟ عَلَيْهِمُ ٱلَّذِىٓ أَوْحَيْنَآ إِلَيْكَ وَهُمْ يَكْفُرُونَ بِٱلرَّحْمَٰنِ قُلْ هُوَ رَبِّى لَآ إِلَٰهَ إِلَّا هُوَ عَلَيْهِ تَوَكَّلْتُ وَإِلَيْهِ مَتَابِ

٣١ وَلَوْ أَنَّ قُرْءَانًا سُيِّرَتْ بِهِ ٱلْجِبَالُ أَوْ قُطِّعَتْ بِهِ ٱلْأَرْضُ أَوْ كُلِّمَ بِهِ ٱلْمَوْتَىٰ بَل لِّلَّهِ ٱلْأَمْرُ جَمِيعًا أَفَلَمْ يَا۟يْـَٔسِ ٱلَّذِينَ ءَامَنُوٓا۟ أَن لَّوْ يَشَآءُ ٱللَّهُ لَهَدَى ٱلنَّاسَ جَمِيعًا وَلَا يَزَالُ ٱلَّذِينَ كَفَرُوا۟ تُصِيبُهُم بِمَا صَنَعُوا۟ قَارِعَةٌ أَوْ تَحُلُّ قَرِيبًا مِّن دَارِهِمْ حَتَّىٰ يَأْتِىَ وَعْدُ ٱللَّهِ إِنَّ ٱللَّهَ لَا يُخْلِفُ ٱلْمِيعَادَ

٣٢ وَلَقَدِ ٱسْتُهْزِئَ بِرُسُلٍ مِّن قَبْلِكَ فَأَمْلَيْتُ لِلَّذِينَ كَفَرُوا۟ ثُمَّ أَخَذْتُهُمْ فَكَيْفَ كَانَ عِقَابِ

٣٣ أَفَمَنْ هُوَ قَآئِمٌ عَلَىٰ كُلِّ نَفْسٍۭ بِمَا كَسَبَتْ وَجَعَلُوا۟ لِلَّهِ شُرَكَآءَ قُلْ سَمُّوهُمْ أَمْ تُنَبِّئُونَهُۥ بِمَا لَا يَعْلَمُ فِى ٱلْأَرْضِ أَم بِظَٰهِرٍ مِّنَ ٱلْقَوْلِ بَلْ زُيِّنَ لِلَّذِينَ كَفَرُوا۟ مَكْرُهُمْ وَصُدُّوا۟ عَنِ ٱلسَّبِيلِ وَمَن يُضْلِلِ ٱللَّهُ فَمَا لَهُۥ مِنْ هَادٍ

٣٤ لَّهُمْ عَذَابٌ فِى ٱلْحَيَوٰةِ ٱلدُّنْيَا وَلَعَذَابُ ٱلْءَاخِرَةِ أَشَقُّ وَمَا لَهُم مِّنَ ٱللَّهِ مِن وَاقٍ

٣٥ مَّثَلُ ٱلْجَنَّةِ ٱلَّتِى وُعِدَ ٱلْمُتَّقُونَ تَجْرِى مِن تَحْتِهَا ٱلْأَنْهَٰرُ أُكُلُهَا دَآئِمٌ وَظِلُّهَا تِلْكَ عُقْبَى ٱلَّذِينَ ٱتَّقَوا۟ وَّعُقْبَى ٱلْكَٰفِرِينَ ٱلنَّارُ

36. Those unto whom We gave the Scripture rejoice in that which is revealed unto you. And of the clans there are who deny some of it. Say: I am commanded only that I worship Allah and ascribe unto Him no partner. Unto Him do I call, and unto Him is my return.

37. Thus have We revealed it, a decisive utterance in Arabic; and if you should follow their desires after that which has come unto you of knowledge, then truly would you have from Allah no protecting friend nor defender.

38. And verily We sent messengers (to mankind) before you, and We appointed for them wives and offspring, and it was not (given) to any messenger that he should bring a portent save by Allah's leave. For everything there is a time prescribed.

39. Allah effaces what He will, and establishes (what He will), and with Him is the source of ordinance.

40. Whether We let you see something of that which We have promised them, or make you die (before its happening), yours is but conveyance (of the message), Ours the reckoning.

41. See they not how We visit the land, reducing it of its outlying parts?[142] (When) Allah dooms there is none that can postpone His doom, and He is swift at reckoning.

42. Those who were before them plotted; but all plotting is Allah's. He knows that which each soul earns. The disbelievers will come to know for whom will be the sequel of the (heavenly) Home.

43. They who disbelieve say: You are no messenger (of Allah). Say: Allah, and whoever has true knowledge of the Scripture, is sufficient witness between me and you.

---

[142]If this is a Madinan verse, the reference would be to the spread of Islam, if a Makkan verse, it would be to the Persian and Eastern Roman empires encroaching on Arabia.

Abraham

    Surat Ibrāhīm (the Arabic name of Abraham) takes its name from the prayer made by Abraham (verses 35-41) when he was establishing his son Ishmael, the ancestor of the Arabs, in the "uncultivable valley" of Makkah. Other than that, the subject of the surah is the same as that of other Makkan surahs revealed during the last three years before the Hijrah. The reference in verse 46 to the plot of the idolaters makes it probable that it is among the last of the Makkan revelations.

    A late Makkan surah, except for verses 28-30, which were revealed at al Madinah.

Abraham

Revealed at Makkah

In the name of Allah,
the Beneficent, the Merciful

1. **A**lif. Lām. Rā'.[143] (This is) a Scripture which We have revealed unto you (Muhammad) that thereby you may bring forth mankind from darkness unto light, by the permission of their Lord, unto the path of the Mighty, the Owner of Praise.

2. Allah, unto Whom belongs whatsoever is in the heavens and whatsoever is in the earth. And woe unto the disbelievers from an awful doom.

3. Those who love the life of the world more than the Hereafter, and debar (men) from the way of Allah and would have it crooked: such are far astray.

4. And We never sent a messenger save with the language of his folk, that he might make (the message) clear for them. Then Allah sends whom He will astray, and guides whom He will. He is the Mighty, the Wise.

5. We verily sent Moses with Our revelations, saying: Bring your people forth from darkness unto light. And remind them of the days of Allah. Lo! therein are revelations for each steadfast, thankful (heart).

6. And (remind them) how Moses said unto his people: Remember Allah's favor unto you when He delivered you from Pharaoh's folk who were afflicting you with dreadful torment, and were slaying your sons and sparing your women; that was a tremendous trial from your Lord.

---

[143]See Surah 2:1, footnote.

7. And when your Lord proclaimed: If you give thanks, I will give you more; but if you are thankless, lo! my punishment is dire.

8. And Moses said: Though you and all who are in the earth prove thankless, lo! Allah verily is Absolute, Owner of Praise.

9. Has not the history of those before you reached you: the folk of Noah. and (the tribes of) 'Ād and Thamūd, and those after them? None save Allah knows them. Their messengers came unto them with clear proofs, but they thrust their hands into their mouths, and said: Lo! we disbelieve in that with which you have been sent, and lo! we are in grave doubt concerning that to which you call us.

10. Their messengers said: Can there be doubt concerning Allah, the Creator of the heavens and the earth? He calls you that He may forgive you your sins and reprieve you unto an appointed term. They said: You are but mortals like us, who would turn us away from what our fathers used to worship. Then bring some clear warrant.

11. Their messengers said unto them: We are but mortals like you, but Allah gives grace unto whom He will of His slaves. It is not ours to bring you a warrant unless by the permission of Allah. In Allah let believers put their trust!

12. How should we not put our trust in Allah when He has shown us our ways? We surely will endure that hurt you do us. In Allah let the trusting put their trust!

٧ وَإِذْ تَأَذَّنَ رَبُّكُمْ لَئِن شَكَرْتُمْ لَأَزِيدَنَّكُمْ وَلَئِن كَفَرْتُمْ إِنَّ عَذَابِي لَشَدِيدٌ

٨ وَقَالَ مُوسَىٰ إِن تَكْفُرُوا أَنتُمْ وَمَن فِي الْأَرْضِ جَمِيعًا فَإِنَّ اللَّهَ لَغَنِيٌّ حَمِيدٌ

٩ أَلَمْ يَأْتِكُمْ نَبَؤُا الَّذِينَ مِن قَبْلِكُمْ قَوْمِ نُوحٍ وَعَادٍ وَثَمُودَ وَالَّذِينَ مِنْ بَعْدِهِمْ لَا يَعْلَمُهُمْ إِلَّا اللَّهُ جَاءَتْهُمْ رُسُلُهُم بِالْبَيِّنَاتِ فَرَدُّوا أَيْدِيَهُمْ فِي أَفْوَاهِهِمْ وَقَالُوا إِنَّا كَفَرْنَا بِمَا أُرْسِلْتُم بِهِ وَإِنَّا لَفِي شَكٍّ مِّمَّا تَدْعُونَنَا إِلَيْهِ مُرِيبٍ

١٠ قَالَتْ رُسُلُهُمْ أَفِي اللَّهِ شَكٌّ فَاطِرِ السَّمَاوَاتِ وَالْأَرْضِ يَدْعُوكُمْ لِيَغْفِرَ لَكُم مِّن ذُنُوبِكُمْ وَيُؤَخِّرَكُمْ إِلَىٰ أَجَلٍ مُّسَمًّى قَالُوا إِنْ أَنتُمْ إِلَّا بَشَرٌ مِّثْلُنَا تُرِيدُونَ أَن تَصُدُّونَا عَمَّا كَانَ يَعْبُدُ ءَابَاؤُنَا فَأْتُونَا بِسُلْطَانٍ مُّبِينٍ

١١ قَالَتْ لَهُمْ رُسُلُهُمْ إِن نَّحْنُ إِلَّا بَشَرٌ مِّثْلُكُمْ وَلَٰكِنَّ اللَّهَ يَمُنُّ عَلَىٰ مَن يَشَاءُ مِنْ عِبَادِهِ وَمَا كَانَ لَنَا أَن نَّأْتِيَكُم بِسُلْطَانٍ إِلَّا بِإِذْنِ اللَّهِ وَعَلَى اللَّهِ فَلْيَتَوَكَّلِ الْمُؤْمِنُونَ

١٢ وَمَا لَنَا أَلَّا نَتَوَكَّلَ عَلَى اللَّهِ وَقَدْ هَدَانَا سُبُلَنَا وَلَنَصْبِرَنَّ عَلَىٰ مَا ءَاذَيْتُمُونَا وَعَلَى اللَّهِ فَلْيَتَوَكَّلِ الْمُتَوَكِّلُونَ

13. And those who disbelieved said unto their messengers: Verily we will drive you out from our land, unless you return to our religion. Then their Lord inspired them, (saying): Surely We shall destroy the wrongdoers,

١٣ وَقَالَ الَّذِينَ كَفَرُوا لِرُسُلِهِمْ لَنُخْرِجَنَّكُمْ مِّنْ أَرْضِنَا أَوْ لَتَعُودُنَّ فِي مِلَّتِنَا فَأَوْحَى إِلَيْهِمْ رَبُّهُمْ لَنُهْلِكَنَّ الظَّالِمِينَ

14. And surely We shall make you to dwell in the land after them. This is for him who fears My Majesty and fears My threats.

١٤ وَلَنُسْكِنَنَّكُمُ الْأَرْضَ مِنْ بَعْدِهِمْ ذَلِكَ لِمَنْ خَافَ مَقَامِي وَخَافَ وَعِيدِ

15. And they sought help (from their Lord) and every froward potentate was brought to nothing;

١٥ وَاسْتَفْتَحُوا وَخَابَ كُلُّ جَبَّارٍ عَنِيدٍ

16. Hell is before him, and he is made to drink a festering water,

١٦ مِّنْ وَرَائِهِ جَهَنَّمُ وَيُسْقَى مِنْ مَّاءٍ صَدِيدٍ

17. Which he sips but can hardly swallow, and death comes unto him from every side while yet he cannot die, and before him is a harsh doom.

١٧ يَتَجَرَّعُهُ وَلَا يَكَادُ يُسِيغُهُ وَيَأْتِيهِ الْمَوْتُ مِنْ كُلِّ مَكَانٍ وَمَا هُوَ بِمَيِّتٍ وَمِنْ وَرَائِهِ عَذَابٌ غَلِيظٌ

18. A similitude of those who disbelieve in their Lord: Their works are as ashes which the wind blows hard upon a stormy day. They have no control of anything that they have earned. That is the extreme failure.

١٨ مَثَلُ الَّذِينَ كَفَرُوا بِرَبِّهِمْ أَعْمَالُهُمْ كَرَمَادٍ اشْتَدَّتْ بِهِ الرِّيحُ فِي يَوْمٍ عَاصِفٍ لَا يَقْدِرُونَ مِمَّا كَسَبُوا عَلَى شَيْءٍ ذَلِكَ هُوَ الضَّلَالُ الْبَعِيدُ

19. Have you not seen that Allah has created the heavens and the earth with truth? If He will, He can remove you and bring (in) some new creation.

١٩ أَلَمْ تَرَ أَنَّ اللَّهَ خَلَقَ السَّمَاوَاتِ وَالْأَرْضَ بِالْحَقِّ إِنْ يَشَأْ يُذْهِبْكُمْ وَيَأْتِ بِخَلْقٍ جَدِيدٍ

20. And that is no great matter for Allah.

٢٠ وَمَا ذَلِكَ عَلَى اللَّهِ بِعَزِيزٍ

21. They all come forth unto their Lord. Then those who were despised say unto those who were scornful: We were unto you a following, can you then avert from us anything of Allah's doom? They say: Had Allah guided us, we should have guided you. Whether we rage or patiently endure is (now) all one for us: we have no place of refuge.

٢١ وَبَرَزُوا لِلَّهِ جَمِيعًا فَقَالَ الضُّعَفَاءُ لِلَّذِينَ اسْتَكْبَرُوا إِنَّا كُنَّا لَكُمْ تَبَعًا فَهَلْ أَنْتُمْ مُغْنُونَ عَنَّا مِنْ عَذَابِ اللَّهِ مِنْ شَيْءٍ قَالُوا لَوْ هَدَانَا اللَّهُ لَهَدَيْنَاكُمْ سَوَاءٌ عَلَيْنَا أَجَزِعْنَا أَمْ صَبَرْنَا مَا لَنَا مِنْ مَحِيصٍ

22. And Satan says, when the matter has been decided: Lo! Allah promised you a promise of truth; and I promised you, then failed you. And I had no power over you save that I called unto you and you obeyed me. So blame me not, but blame yourselves. I cannot help you, nor can you help me. Lo! I disbelieved in that which you before ascribed to me. Lo! for wrongdoers is a painful doom.

23. And those who believed and did good works are made to enter Gardens underneath which rivers flow, therein abiding by permission of their Lord, their greeting therein: Peace!

24. Do you not see how Allah coins a similitude: A goodly saying, as a goodly tree, its root set firm, its branches reaching into heaven,

25. Giving its fruit at every season by permission of its Lord? Allah coins the similitudes for mankind in order that they may reflect.

26. And the similitude of a bad saying is as a bad tree, uprooted from upon the earth, possessing no stability.

27. Allah confirms those who believe by a firm saying in the life of the world and in the Hereafter, and Allah sends wrongdoers astray. And Allah does what He will.

28. Have you not seen those who gave the grace of Allah in exchange for thanklessness and led their people down to the Abode of Loss,

29. (Even to) hell? They are exposed thereto. An unlucky end!

وَقَالَ ٱلشَّيْطَنُ لَمَّا قُضِيَ ٱلْأَمْرُ إِنَّ ٱللَّهَ وَعَدَكُمْ وَعْدَ ٱلْحَقِّ وَوَعَدتُّكُمْ فَأَخْلَفْتُكُمْ ۖ وَمَا كَانَ لِيَ عَلَيْكُم مِّن سُلْطَٰنٍ إِلَّآ أَن دَعَوْتُكُمْ فَٱسْتَجَبْتُمْ لِى ۖ فَلَا تَلُومُونِى وَلُومُوٓا۟ أَنفُسَكُم ۖ مَّآ أَنَا۠ بِمُصْرِخِكُمْ وَمَآ أَنتُم بِمُصْرِخِىَّ ۖ إِنِّى كَفَرْتُ بِمَآ أَشْرَكْتُمُونِ مِن قَبْلُ ۗ إِنَّ ٱلظَّٰلِمِينَ لَهُمْ عَذَابٌ أَلِيمٌ ۝

وَأُدْخِلَ ٱلَّذِينَ ءَامَنُوا۟ وَعَمِلُوا۟ ٱلصَّٰلِحَٰتِ جَنَّٰتٍ تَجْرِى مِن تَحْتِهَا ٱلْأَنْهَٰرُ خَٰلِدِينَ فِيهَا بِإِذْنِ رَبِّهِمْ ۖ تَحِيَّتُهُمْ فِيهَا سَلَٰمٌ ۝

أَلَمْ تَرَ كَيْفَ ضَرَبَ ٱللَّهُ مَثَلًا كَلِمَةً طَيِّبَةً كَشَجَرَةٍ طَيِّبَةٍ أَصْلُهَا ثَابِتٌ وَفَرْعُهَا فِى ٱلسَّمَآءِ ۝

تُؤْتِىٓ أُكُلَهَا كُلَّ حِينٍۭ بِإِذْنِ رَبِّهَا ۗ وَيَضْرِبُ ٱللَّهُ ٱلْأَمْثَالَ لِلنَّاسِ لَعَلَّهُمْ يَتَذَكَّرُونَ ۝

وَمَثَلُ كَلِمَةٍ خَبِيثَةٍ كَشَجَرَةٍ خَبِيثَةٍ ٱجْتُثَّتْ مِن فَوْقِ ٱلْأَرْضِ مَا لَهَا مِن قَرَارٍ ۝

يُثَبِّتُ ٱللَّهُ ٱلَّذِينَ ءَامَنُوا۟ بِٱلْقَوْلِ ٱلثَّابِتِ فِى ٱلْحَيَوٰةِ ٱلدُّنْيَا وَفِى ٱلْءَاخِرَةِ ۖ وَيُضِلُّ ٱللَّهُ ٱلظَّٰلِمِينَ ۚ وَيَفْعَلُ ٱللَّهُ مَا يَشَآءُ ۝

أَلَمْ تَرَ إِلَى ٱلَّذِينَ بَدَّلُوا۟ نِعْمَتَ ٱللَّهِ كُفْرًا وَأَحَلُّوا۟ قَوْمَهُمْ دَارَ ٱلْبَوَارِ ۝

جَهَنَّمَ يَصْلَوْنَهَا ۖ وَبِئْسَ ٱلْقَرَارُ ۝

30. And they set up rivals to Allah that they may mislead (men) from His way. Say: Enjoy life (while you may) for lo! your journey's end will be the Fire.

31. Tell My bondmen who believe to establish worship and spend of that which We have given them, secretly and publicly, before a day comes wherein there will be neither bargaining nor befriending.

32. Allah is He Who created the heavens and the earth, and causes water to descend from the sky, thereby producing fruits as food for you, and makes the ships to be of service unto you, that they may run upon the sea at His command, and has made of service unto you the rivers;

33. And makes the sun and the moon, constant in their courses, to be of service unto you, and has made of service unto you the night and the day.

34. And He gives you of all you ask of Him, and if you would count the bounty of Allah you cannot reckon it. Lo! man is verily a wrongdoer, an ingrate.

35. And when Abraham said: My Lord! Make safe this territory, and preserve me and my sons from serving idols.

36. My Lord! Lo! they have led many of mankind astray. But who follows me, he verily is of me. And who disobeys me, still You are Forgiving, Merciful.

37. Our Lord! Lo! I have settled some of my posterity in an uncultivable valley near unto Your holy House,[144] our Lord! that they may establish proper worship; so incline some hearts of men that they may yearn toward them, and provide You them with fruits in order that they may be thankful.

---

[144]The valley of Makkah.

38. Our Lord! Lo! You know that which we hide and that which we proclaim. Nothing in the earth or in the heaven is hidden from Allah.

٣٨ رَبَّنَا إِنَّكَ تَعْلَمُ مَا نُخْفِى وَمَا نُعْلِنُ وَمَا يَخْفَى عَلَى اللَّهِ مِن شَىْءٍ فِى الأَرْضِ وَلَا فِى السَّمَاءِ

39. Praise be to Allah Who has given me, in my old age, Ishmael and Isaac! Lo! my Lord is indeed the Hearer of Prayer.

٣٩ الْحَمْدُ لِلَّهِ الَّذِى وَهَبَ لِى عَلَى الْكِبَرِ إِسْمَاعِيلَ وَإِسْحَاقَ إِنَّ رَبِّى لَسَمِيعُ الدُّعَاءِ

40. My Lord! Make me to establish proper worship, and some of my posterity (also); our Lord! and accept my prayer.

٤٠ رَبِّ اجْعَلْنِى مُقِيمَ الصَّلَوةِ وَمِن ذُرِّيَّتِى رَبَّنَا وَتَقَبَّلْ دُعَاءِ

41. Our Lord! Forgive me and my parents and believers on the day when the account is cast.

٤١ رَبَّنَا اغْفِرْ لِى وَلِوَالِدَىَّ وَلِلْمُؤْمِنِينَ يَوْمَ يَقُومُ الْحِسَابُ

42. Deem not that Allah is unaware of what the wicked do. He but gives them a respite till a day when eyes will stare (in terror).

٤٢ وَلَا تَحْسَبَنَّ اللَّهَ غَافِلًا عَمَّا يَعْمَلُ الظَّالِمُونَ إِنَّمَا يُؤَخِّرُهُمْ لِيَوْمٍ تَشْخَصُ فِيهِ الأَبْصَارُ

43. As they come hurrying on in fear, their heads upraised, their gaze returning not to them, and their hearts as air.

٤٣ مُهْطِعِينَ مُقْنِعِى رُءُوسِهِمْ لَا يَرْتَدُّ إِلَيْهِمْ طَرْفُهُمْ وَأَفْئِدَتُهُمْ هَوَاءٌ

44. And warn mankind of a day when the doom will come upon them, and those who did wrong will say: Our Lord! Reprieve us for a little while. We will obey Your call and will follow the messengers. (It will be answered): Did you not swear before that there would be no end for you?

٤٤ وَأَنذِرِ النَّاسَ يَوْمَ يَأْتِيهِمُ الْعَذَابُ فَيَقُولُ الَّذِينَ ظَلَمُوا رَبَّنَا أَخِّرْنَا إِلَى أَجَلٍ قَرِيبٍ نُّجِبْ دَعْوَتَكَ وَنَتَّبِعِ الرُّسُلَ أَوَلَمْ تَكُونُوا أَقْسَمْتُم مِّن قَبْلُ مَا لَكُم مِّن زَوَالٍ

45. And (have you not) dwelt in the dwellings of those who wronged themselves (of old) and (has it not) become plain to you how We dealt with them, and made examples for you?

٤٥ وَسَكَنتُمْ فِى مَسَاكِنِ الَّذِينَ ظَلَمُوا أَنفُسَهُمْ وَتَبَيَّنَ لَكُمْ كَيْفَ فَعَلْنَا بِهِمْ وَضَرَبْنَا لَكُمُ الأَمْثَالَ

46. Verily they have plotted their plot, and their plot is with Allah, though their plot were one whereby the mountains should be moved.

٤٦ وَقَدْ مَكَرُوا مَكْرَهُمْ وَعِندَ اللَّهِ مَكْرُهُمْ وَإِن كَانَ مَكْرُهُمْ لِتَزُولَ مِنْهُ الْجِبَالُ

47. So think not that Allah will fail to keep His promise to His messengers. Lo! Allah is Mighty, Able to Requite (the wrong).

٤٧ فَلَا تَحْسَبَنَّ اللَّهَ مُخْلِفَ وَعْدِهِ رُسُلَهُ إِنَّ اللَّهَ عَزِيزٌ ذُو انتِقَامٍ

48. On the day when the earth will be changed to other than the earth, and the heavens (also will be changed) and they will come forth unto Allah, the One, the Almighty.

49. You will see the guilty on that day linked together in chains.

50. Their raiment of pitch, and the Fire covering their faces.

51. That Allah may repay each soul what it has earned. Lo! Allah is swift at reckoning.

52. This is a clear message for mankind in order that they may be warned thereby, and that they may know that He is only One God, and that men of understanding may take heed.

﴿٤٨﴾ يَوْمَ تُبَدَّلُ الْأَرْضُ غَيْرَ الْأَرْضِ وَالسَّمَوَاتُ وَبَرَزُوا لِلَّهِ الْوَاحِدِ الْقَهَّارِ

﴿٤٩﴾ وَتَرَى الْمُجْرِمِينَ يَوْمَئِذٍ مُّقَرَّنِينَ فِي الْأَصْفَادِ

﴿٥٠﴾ سَرَابِيلُهُم مِّن قَطِرَانٍ وَتَغْشَى وُجُوهَهُمُ النَّارُ

﴿٥١﴾ لِيَجْزِيَ اللَّهُ كُلَّ نَفْسٍ مَّا كَسَبَتْ إِنَّ اللَّهَ سَرِيعُ الْحِسَابِ

﴿٥٢﴾ هَذَا بَلَاغٌ لِّلنَّاسِ وَلِيُنذَرُوا بِهِ وَلِيَعْلَمُوا أَنَّمَا هُوَ إِلَهٌ وَاحِدٌ وَلِيَذَّكَّرَ أُولُوا الْأَلْبَابِ

Al Ḥijr

Al Ḥijr, which I take to be a place-name, is mentioned for the first time in verses 80-84, where the fate of its dwellers is described. It was revealed earlier than those Makkan surahs that precede it in the Qur'anic arrangement, although the subject and the tone are similar, which accounts for its position. Noldeke places it in his middle group of Makkan surahs, that is—as far as one can judge from the inclusions—those revealed after the eighth year and before the third year before the Hijrah. He thus confirms the judgment of the best Muslim authorities, although some of the latter would place it among the earliest revelations.

It belongs to the middle group of Makkan surahs.

Al Ḥijr

Revealed at Makkah

*In the name of Allah,
the Beneficent, the Merciful*

1. **A**lif. Lām. Rā'.145 These are verses of the Scripture and a plain Reading.146

2. It may be that those who disbelieve wish ardently that they were Muslims.147

3. Let them eat and enjoy life, and let (false) hope beguile them. They will come to know!

4. And We destroyed no township but there was a known decree for it.

5. No nation can outstrip its term nor can they lag behind.

6. And they say: O you unto whom the Reminder is revealed, lo! you are indeed a madman!

7. Why bring you not angels unto Us, if you are of the truthful?

8. We send not down the angels save with the Truth, and in that case (the disbelievers) would not be tolerated.

9. Lo! We even We, reveal the Reminder, and lo! We surely are its Guardian.

10. We surely sent (messengers) before you among the factions of the men of old.

11. And never came there unto them a messenger but they did mock him.

12. Thus do We make it traverse the hearts of criminals:

13. They believe not therein, though the example of the men of old has gone before.

14. And even if We opened unto them a Gate of Heaven and they kept mounting through it.

15. They would say: Our sight is intoxicated (dazzled)—nay, but we are folk bewitched.

16. And surely in the heaven We have set mansions of the stars, and We have beautified it for beholders.

17. And We have guarded it from every outcast devil,

145See Surah 2:1, footnote.-146Arabic: Qur'an.-147Or "those who have surrendered."

18. Save him who steals the hearing, and them does a clear flame pursue.

١٨ إِلَّا مَنِ اسْتَرَقَ السَّمْعَ فَأَتْبَعَهُ شِهَابٌ مُّبِينٌ

19. And the earth have We spread out, and placed therein firm hills, and caused each seemly thing to grow therein.

١٩ وَالْأَرْضَ مَدَدْنَاهَا وَأَلْقَيْنَا فِيهَا رَوَاسِيَ وَأَنْبَتْنَا فِيهَا مِن كُلِّ شَيْءٍ مَّوْزُونٍ

20. And We have given unto you livelihoods therein, and unto those for whom you provide not.

٢٠ وَجَعَلْنَا لَكُمْ فِيهَا مَعَايِشَ وَمَن لَّسْتُمْ لَهُ بِرَازِقِينَ

21. And there is not a thing but with Us are the stores thereof. And We send it not down save in appointed measure.

٢١ وَإِن مِّن شَيْءٍ إِلَّا عِندَنَا خَزَائِنُهُ وَمَا نُنَزِّلُهُ إِلَّا بِقَدَرٍ مَّعْلُومٍ

22. And We send the winds fertilizing, and cause water to descend from the sky, and give it you to drink. It is not you who are the holders of the store thereof.

٢٢ وَأَرْسَلْنَا الرِّيَاحَ لَوَاقِحَ فَأَنزَلْنَا مِنَ السَّمَاءِ مَاءً فَأَسْقَيْنَاكُمُوهُ وَمَا أَنتُمْ لَهُ بِخَازِنِينَ

23. Lo! and it is We, even We, Who quicken and give death, and We are the Inheritors.

٢٣ وَإِنَّا لَنَحْنُ نُحْيِي وَنُمِيتُ وَنَحْنُ الْوَارِثُونَ

24. And surely We know the eager among you and surely We know the laggards.

٢٤ وَلَقَدْ عَلِمْنَا الْمُسْتَقْدِمِينَ مِنكُمْ وَلَقَدْ عَلِمْنَا الْمُسْتَأْخِرِينَ

25. Lo! your Lord will gather them together. Lo! He is Wise, Aware.

٢٥ وَإِنَّ رَبَّكَ هُوَ يَحْشُرُهُمْ إِنَّهُ حَكِيمٌ عَلِيمٌ

26. Surely We created man of potter's clay of black mud altered,

٢٦ وَلَقَدْ خَلَقْنَا الْإِنسَانَ مِن صَلْصَالٍ مِّنْ حَمَإٍ مَّسْنُونٍ

27. And the jinn did We create aforetime of essential fire.

٢٧ وَالْجَانَّ خَلَقْنَاهُ مِن قَبْلُ مِن نَّارِ السَّمُومِ

28. And (remember) when your Lord said unto the angels: Lo! I am creating a mortal out of potter's clay of black mud altered.

٢٨ وَإِذْ قَالَ رَبُّكَ لِلْمَلَائِكَةِ إِنِّي خَالِقٌ بَشَرًا مِّن صَلْصَالٍ مِّنْ حَمَإٍ مَّسْنُونٍ

29. So, when I have made him and have breathed into him of My spirit, do you fall down, prostrating yourselves unto him.

٢٩ فَإِذَا سَوَّيْتُهُ وَنَفَخْتُ فِيهِ مِن رُّوحِي فَقَعُوا لَهُ سَاجِدِينَ

30. So the angels fell prostrate, all of them together

٣٠ فَسَجَدَ الْمَلَائِكَةُ كُلُّهُمْ أَجْمَعُونَ

31. Save Iblīs. He refused to be among the prostrate.

٣١ إِلَّا إِبْلِيسَ أَبَى أَن يَكُونَ مَعَ السَّاجِدِينَ

32. He said: O Iblīs! What ails you that you are not among the prostrate?

٣٢ قَالَ يَـٰٓإِبْلِيسُ مَالَكَ أَلَّا تَكُونَ مَعَ السَّٰجِدِينَ

33. He said: I am not going to prostrate myself unto a mortal whom You have created out of potter's clay of black mud altered.

٣٣ قَالَ لَمْ أَكُن لِّأَسْجُدَ لِبَشَرٍ خَلَقْتَهُ مِن صَلْصَٰلٍ مِّنْ حَمَإٍ مَّسْنُونٍ

34. He said: Then go you forth from hence, for surely you are outcast.

٣٤ قَالَ فَٱخْرُجْ مِنْهَا فَإِنَّكَ رَجِيمٌ

35. And lo! The curse shall be upon you till the Day of Judgment.

٣٥ وَإِنَّ عَلَيْكَ ٱللَّعْنَةَ إِلَىٰ يَوْمِ ٱلدِّينِ

36. He said: My Lord! Reprieve me till the day when they are raised.

٣٦ قَالَ رَبِّ فَأَنظِرْنِى إِلَىٰ يَوْمِ يُبْعَثُونَ

37. He said: Then lo! You are of those reprieved

٣٧ قَالَ فَإِنَّكَ مِنَ ٱلْمُنظَرِينَ

38. Till an appointed time.

٣٨ إِلَىٰ يَوْمِ ٱلْوَقْتِ ٱلْمَعْلُومِ

39. He said: My Lord, Because You have sent me astray, I verily shall adorn the path of error for them in the earth, and shall mislead them every one.

٣٩ قَالَ رَبِّ بِمَآ أَغْوَيْتَنِى لَأُزَيِّنَنَّ لَهُمْ فِى ٱلْأَرْضِ وَلَأُغْوِيَنَّهُمْ أَجْمَعِينَ

40. Save such of them as are Your perfectly devoted slaves.

٤٠ إِلَّا عِبَادَكَ مِنْهُمُ ٱلْمُخْلَصِينَ

41. He said: This is a right course incumbent upon Me:

٤١ قَالَ هَٰذَا صِرَٰطٌ عَلَىَّ مُسْتَقِيمٌ

42. Lo! as for My slaves, you have no power over any of them save such of the froward as follow you,

٤٢ إِنَّ عِبَادِى لَيْسَ لَكَ عَلَيْهِمْ سُلْطَٰنٌ إِلَّا مَنِ ٱتَّبَعَكَ مِنَ ٱلْغَاوِينَ

43. And lo! for all such, hell will be the promised place.

٤٣ وَإِنَّ جَهَنَّمَ لَمَوْعِدُهُمْ أَجْمَعِينَ

44. It has seven gates, and each gate has an appointed portion.

٤٤ لَهَا سَبْعَةُ أَبْوَٰبٍ لِّكُلِّ بَابٍ مِّنْهُمْ جُزْءٌ مَّقْسُومٌ

45. Lo! those who ward off (evil) are among gardens and watersprings.

٤٥ إِنَّ ٱلْمُتَّقِينَ فِى جَنَّٰتٍ وَعُيُونٍ

46. (And it is said unto them): Enter them in peace, secure.

٤٦ ٱدْخُلُوهَا بِسَلَٰمٍ ءَامِنِينَ

47. And We remove whatever rancor may be in their breasts. As brothers, face to face, (they rest) on couches raised.

٤٧ وَنَزَعْنَا مَا فِى صُدُورِهِم مِّنْ غِلٍّ إِخْوَٰنًا عَلَىٰ سُرُرٍ مُّتَقَٰبِلِينَ

48. Toil comes not unto them there, nor will they be expelled from thence.

٤٨ لَا يَمَسُّهُمْ فِيهَا نَصَبٌ وَمَا هُم مِّنْهَا بِمُخْرَجِينَ

49. Announce, (O Muhammad) unto My slaves that surely I am the Forgiving, the Merciful.

٤٩ نَبِّئْ عِبَادِى أَنِّى أَنَا ٱلْغَفُورُ ٱلرَّحِيمُ

50. And that My doom is the dolorous doom.

51. And tell them of Abraham's guests,

52. (How) when they came in unto him, and said: Peace. He said: Lo! we are afraid of you.

53. They said: Be not afraid! Lo! we bring you good tidings of a boy possessing wisdom.

54. He said: Bring you me good tidings (of a son) when old age has overtaken me? Of what then can you bring good tidings?

55. They said: We bring you good tidings in truth. So be not you of the despairing.

56. He said: And who else despairs the mercy of his Lord save those who are astray?

57. He said: And afterward what is your business, O you messengers (of Allah)?

58. They said: We have been sent unto a criminal folk.

59. (All) save the family of Lot. Them we shall deliver everyone,

60. Except his wife, of whom We had decreed that she should be of those who stay behind.

61. And when the messengers came unto the family of Lot,

62. He said: Lo! you are folk unknown (to me).

63. They said: Nay, but we bring you that concerning which they keep disputing,

64. And bring you the Truth, and lo! we are truth tellers.

65. So travel with your household in a portion of the night, and follow you their backs. Let none of you turn round, but go whither you are commanded.

66. And We made plain the case to him, that the root of them (who did wrong) was to be cut at early morn.

67. And the people of the city came, rejoicing at the news (of new arrivals).

68. He said: Lo! they are my guests. Affront me not!

69. And keep your duty to Allah, and shame me not!

٥٠ وَأَنَّ عَذَابِي هُوَ الْعَذَابُ الْأَلِيمُ

٥١ وَنَبِّئْهُمْ عَن ضَيْفِ إِبْرَٰهِيمَ

٥٢ إِذْ دَخَلُوا عَلَيْهِ فَقَالُوا سَلَٰمًا قَالَ إِنَّا مِنكُمْ وَجِلُونَ

٥٣ قَالُوا لَا تَوْجَلْ إِنَّا نُبَشِّرُكَ بِغُلَٰمٍ عَلِيمٍ

٥٤ قَالَ أَبَشَّرْتُمُونِي عَلَىٰ أَن مَّسَّنِيَ الْكِبَرُ فَبِمَ تُبَشِّرُونَ

٥٥ قَالُوا بَشَّرْنَٰكَ بِالْحَقِّ فَلَا تَكُن مِّنَ الْقَٰنِطِينَ

٥٦ قَالَ وَمَن يَقْنَطُ مِن رَّحْمَةِ رَبِّهِ إِلَّا الضَّآلُّونَ

٥٧ قَالَ فَمَا خَطْبُكُمْ أَيُّهَا الْمُرْسَلُونَ

٥٨ قَالُوا إِنَّا أُرْسِلْنَا إِلَىٰ قَوْمٍ مُّجْرِمِينَ

٥٩ إِلَّا آلَ لُوطٍ إِنَّا لَمُنَجُّوهُمْ أَجْمَعِينَ

٦٠ إِلَّا امْرَأَتَهُ قَدَّرْنَا إِنَّهَا لَمِنَ الْغَٰبِرِينَ

٦١ فَلَمَّا جَآءَ آلَ لُوطٍ الْمُرْسَلُونَ

٦٢ قَالَ إِنَّكُمْ قَوْمٌ مُّنكَرُونَ

٦٣ قَالُوا بَلْ جِئْنَٰكَ بِمَا كَانُوا فِيهِ يَمْتَرُونَ

٦٤ وَأَتَيْنَٰكَ بِالْحَقِّ وَإِنَّا لَصَٰدِقُونَ

٦٥ فَأَسْرِ بِأَهْلِكَ بِقِطْعٍ مِّنَ الَّيْلِ وَاتَّبِعْ أَدْبَٰرَهُمْ وَلَا يَلْتَفِتْ مِنكُمْ أَحَدٌ وَامْضُوا حَيْثُ تُؤْمَرُونَ

٦٦ وَقَضَيْنَا إِلَيْهِ ذَٰلِكَ الْأَمْرَ أَنَّ دَابِرَ هَٰؤُلَآءِ مَقْطُوعٌ مُّصْبِحِينَ

٦٧ وَجَآءَ أَهْلُ الْمَدِينَةِ يَسْتَبْشِرُونَ

٦٨ قَالَ إِنَّ هَٰؤُلَآءِ ضَيْفِي فَلَا تَفْضَحُونِ

٦٩ وَاتَّقُوا اللَّهَ وَلَا تُخْزُونِ

70. They said: Have we not forbidden you from (entertaining) anyone?

71. He said: Here are my daughters, if you must be doing (so).

72. By your life (O Muhammad) they moved blindly in the frenzy of approaching death.

73. Then the (Awful) Cry overtook them at the sunrise.

74. And We utterly confounded them, and We rained upon them stones of heated clay.

75. Lo! therein verily are portents for those who read the signs.

76. And lo! it is upon a road still uneffaced.

77. Lo! therein is indeed a portent for believers.

78. And the dwellers in the wood[148] indeed were evildoers.

79. So. We took vengeance on them; and lo! they both are on a high road plain to see.

80. And the dwellers in al Ḥijr indeed denied (Our) messengers.

81. And We gave them Our revelations, but they were averse to them.

82. And they used to hew out dwellings from the mountains, (wherein they dwelt) secure.

83. But the (Awful) Cry overtook them at the morning hour,

84. And that which they were wont to count as gain availed them not.

85. We created not the heavens and the earth and all that is between them save with truth, and lo! the Hour is surely coming. So forgive, O Muhammad, with a gracious forgiveness.

86. Lo! your Lord! He is the Creator, the Knower.

87. We have given you seven of the oft repeated (verses)[149] and the great Qur'an.

﴿٧٠﴾ قَالُوٓا أَوَلَمْ نَنْهَكَ عَنِ ٱلْعَٰلَمِينَ

﴿٧١﴾ قَالَ هَٰٓؤُلَآءِ بَنَاتِىٓ إِن كُنتُمْ فَٰعِلِينَ

﴿٧٢﴾ لَعَمْرُكَ إِنَّهُمْ لَفِى سَكْرَتِهِمْ يَعْمَهُونَ

﴿٧٣﴾ فَأَخَذَتْهُمُ ٱلصَّيْحَةُ مُشْرِقِينَ

﴿٧٤﴾ فَجَعَلْنَا عَٰلِيَهَا سَافِلَهَا وَأَمْطَرْنَا عَلَيْهِمْ حِجَارَةً مِّن سِجِّيلٍ

﴿٧٥﴾ إِنَّ فِى ذَٰلِكَ لَأَيَٰتٍ لِّلْمُتَوَسِّمِينَ

﴿٧٦﴾ وَإِنَّهَا لَبِسَبِيلٍ مُّقِيمٍ

﴿٧٧﴾ إِنَّ فِى ذَٰلِكَ لَأَيَةً لِّلْمُؤْمِنِينَ

﴿٧٨﴾ وَإِن كَانَ أَصْحَٰبُ ٱلْأَيْكَةِ لَظَٰلِمِينَ

﴿٧٩﴾ فَٱنتَقَمْنَا مِنْهُمْ وَإِنَّهُمَا لَبِإِمَامٍ مُّبِينٍ

﴿٨٠﴾ وَلَقَدْ كَذَّبَ أَصْحَٰبُ ٱلْحِجْرِ ٱلْمُرْسَلِينَ

﴿٨١﴾ وَءَاتَيْنَٰهُمْ ءَايَٰتِنَا فَكَانُوا۟ عَنْهَا مُعْرِضِينَ

﴿٨٢﴾ وَكَانُوا۟ يَنْحِتُونَ مِنَ ٱلْجِبَالِ بُيُوتًا ءَامِنِينَ

﴿٨٣﴾ فَأَخَذَتْهُمُ ٱلصَّيْحَةُ مُصْبِحِينَ

﴿٨٤﴾ فَمَآ أَغْنَىٰ عَنْهُم مَّا كَانُوا۟ يَكْسِبُونَ

﴿٨٥﴾ وَمَا خَلَقْنَا ٱلسَّمَٰوَٰتِ وَٱلْأَرْضَ وَمَا بَيْنَهُمَآ إِلَّا بِٱلْحَقِّ وَإِنَّ ٱلسَّاعَةَ لَأَتِيَةٌ فَٱصْفَحِ ٱلصَّفْحَ ٱلْجَمِيلَ

﴿٨٦﴾ إِنَّ رَبَّكَ هُوَ ٱلْخَلَّٰقُ ٱلْعَلِيمُ

﴿٨٧﴾ وَلَقَدْ ءَاتَيْنَٰكَ سَبْعًا مِّنَ ٱلْمَثَانِى وَٱلْقُرْءَانَ ٱلْعَظِيمَ

---

[148] Another name for Madian.

[149] According to a strong tradition, the reference is to Surah 1, which consists of seven verses and forms a part of every Muslim prayer.

88. Strain not your eyes toward that which We cause some pairs among them to enjoy, and be not grieved on their account, and lower your wing (in tenderness) for the believers.

89. And say: Lo! I, even I, am a plain warner,

90. Such as We send down for those who make division,

91. Those who break the Qur'an into parts.

92. Them, by your Lord, We shall question, every one,

93. Of what they used to do.

94. So proclaim that which you are commanded, and withdraw from the idolaters.

95. Lo! We defend you from the scoffers,

96. Who set some other god along with Allah. But they will come to know.

97. Well know We that your bosom is at times oppressed by what they say,

98. But hymn the praise of your Lord, and be of those who make prostration (unto Him).

99. And worship your Lord till the inevitable[150] comes unto you.

٨٨ لَا تَمُدَّنَّ عَيْنَيْكَ إِلَى مَا مَتَّعْنَا بِهِ أَزْوَاجًا مِّنْهُمْ وَلَا تَحْزَنْ عَلَيْهِمْ وَاخْفِضْ جَنَاحَكَ لِلْمُؤْمِنِينَ

٨٩ وَقُلْ إِنِّي أَنَا النَّذِيرُ الْمُبِينُ

٩٠ كَمَا أَنْزَلْنَا عَلَى الْمُقْتَسِمِينَ

٩١ الَّذِينَ جَعَلُوا الْقُرْآنَ عِضِينَ

٩٢ فَوَرَبِّكَ لَنَسْأَلَنَّهُمْ أَجْمَعِينَ

٩٣ عَمَّا كَانُوا يَعْمَلُونَ

٩٤ فَاصْدَعْ بِمَا تُؤْمَرُ وَأَعْرِضْ عَنِ الْمُشْرِكِينَ

٩٥ إِنَّا كَفَيْنَاكَ الْمُسْتَهْزِئِينَ

٩٦ الَّذِينَ يَجْعَلُونَ مَعَ اللَّهِ إِلَهًا آخَرَ فَسَوْفَ يَعْلَمُونَ

٩٧ وَلَقَدْ نَعْلَمُ أَنَّكَ يَضِيقُ صَدْرُكَ بِمَا يَقُولُونَ

٩٨ فَسَبِّحْ بِحَمْدِ رَبِّكَ وَكُنْ مِنَ السَّاجِدِينَ

٩٩ وَاعْبُدْ رَبَّكَ حَتَّى يَأْتِيَكَ الْيَقِينُ

---

[150]i.e., death.

The Bee

Al Naḥl, "The Bee," takes its name from verse 68, where its activities are mentioned as a type of duty and of usefulness. It calls attention to God's providence for creation, and to His guidance to mankind as a necessary part of it, and warns disbelievers that the folly of rejecting is as great as rejecting food and drink. The surah is ascribed to the last Makkan group, though some ancient authorities regard that ascription as valid only for verses 1-40 and consider the entire latter portion as revealed at al Madinah. The only verse that is self-evidently of Madinan revelation is verse 110, where the fugitives from persecution are said to have fought (in the Makkan period fighting was unlawful for the Muslims, with the result that many fled to Abyssinia to escape persecution).

A late Makkan surah, with the exception of verse 110, which must have been revealed at al Madinah not earlier than the year 2 AH, and possibly many other verses toward the end.

The Bee

Revealed at Makkah

*In the name of Allah,
the Beneficent, the Merciful*

1. The commandment of Allah will come to pass, so seek not you to hasten it. Glorified and Exalted be He above all that they associate (with Him).

2. He sends down the angels with the Spirit of His command unto whom He will of His bondmen, (saying): Warn mankind that there is no god save Me, so keep your duty unto Me.

3. He has created the heavens and the earth with truth. High be He exalted above all that they associate (with Him).

4. He has created man from a drop of fluid, yet behold! he is an open opponent.

5. And the cattle has He created, whence you have warm clothing and uses, and whereof you eat.

6. And wherein is beauty for you, when you bring them home, and when you take them out to pasture.

7. And they bear your loads for you unto a land you could not reach save with great trouble to yourselves. Lo! your Lord is Full of Pity, Merciful.

8. And horses and mules and asses (has He created) that you may ride them, and for ornament. And He creates that which you know not.

9. And Allah's is the direction of the way, and some (roads) go not straight. And had He willed He would have led you all aright.

10. He it is Who sends down water from the sky, whence you have drink, and whence are trees on which you send your beasts to pasture.[151]

---

[151]As there is hardly any heritage in Arabia, the cattle eat the leaves of trees and shrubs..

11. Therewith He causes crops to grow for you, and the olive and the date palm and grapes and all kinds of fruit. Lo! herein is indeed a portent for people who reflect.

12. And he has constrained the night and the day and the sun and the moon to be of service unto you, and the stars are made subservient by His command. Lo! herein indeed are portents for people who have sense.

13. And whatsoever He has created for you in the earth of divers hues, lo! therein is indeed a portent for people who take heed.

14. And He it is Who has constrained the sea to be of service that you eat fresh meat from thence, and bring forth from thence ornaments which you wear. And you see the ships plowing it that you (mankind) may seek of His bounty, and that you may give thanks.

15. And He has cast into the earth firm hills that it quake not with you, and streams and roads that you may find a way.

16. And landmarks (too), and by the star they find a way.

17. Is He then Who creates as him who creates not? Will you not then remember?

18. And if you would count the favor of Allah you cannot reckon it. Lo! Allah is indeed Forgiving, Merciful.

19. And Allah knows that which you keep hidden and that which you proclaim.

20. Those unto whom they cry beside Allah created nothing, but are themselves created.

21. (They are) dead, not living. And they know not when they will be raised.

١١ يُنۢبِتُ لَكُم بِهِ ٱلزَّرۡعَ وَٱلزَّيۡتُونَ وَٱلنَّخِيلَ وَٱلۡأَعۡنَٰبَ وَمِن كُلِّ ٱلثَّمَرَٰتِۚ إِنَّ فِى ذَٰلِكَ لَءَايَةً لِّقَوۡمٍ يَتَفَكَّرُونَ

١٢ وَسَخَّرَ لَكُمُ ٱلَّيۡلَ وَٱلنَّهَارَ وَٱلشَّمۡسَ وَٱلۡقَمَرَۖ وَٱلنُّجُومُ مُسَخَّرَٰتُۢ بِأَمۡرِهِۦٓۚ إِنَّ فِى ذَٰلِكَ لَءَايَٰتٍ لِّقَوۡمٍ يَعۡقِلُونَ

١٣ وَمَا ذَرَأَ لَكُمۡ فِى ٱلۡأَرۡضِ مُخۡتَلِفًا أَلۡوَٰنُهُۥٓۚ إِنَّ فِى ذَٰلِكَ لَءَايَةً لِّقَوۡمٍ يَذَّكَّرُونَ

١٤ وَهُوَ ٱلَّذِى سَخَّرَ ٱلۡبَحۡرَ لِتَأۡكُلُواْ مِنۡهُ لَحۡمًا طَرِيًّا وَتَسۡتَخۡرِجُواْ مِنۡهُ حِلۡيَةً تَلۡبَسُونَهَاۖ وَتَرَى ٱلۡفُلۡكَ مَوَاخِرَ فِيهِ وَلِتَبۡتَغُواْ مِن فَضۡلِهِۦ وَلَعَلَّكُمۡ تَشۡكُرُونَ

١٥ وَأَلۡقَىٰ فِى ٱلۡأَرۡضِ رَوَٰسِىَ أَن تَمِيدَ بِكُمۡ وَأَنۡهَٰرًا وَسُبُلًا لَّعَلَّكُمۡ تَهۡتَدُونَ

١٦ وَعَلَٰمَٰتٍۚ وَبِٱلنَّجۡمِ هُمۡ يَهۡتَدُونَ

١٧ أَفَمَن يَخۡلُقُ كَمَن لَّا يَخۡلُقُۚ أَفَلَا تَذَكَّرُونَ

١٨ وَإِن تَعُدُّواْ نِعۡمَةَ ٱللَّهِ لَا تُحۡصُوهَآۗ إِنَّ ٱللَّهَ لَغَفُورٌ رَّحِيمٌ

١٩ وَٱللَّهُ يَعۡلَمُ مَا تُسِرُّونَ وَمَا تُعۡلِنُونَ

٢٠ وَٱلَّذِينَ يَدۡعُونَ مِن دُونِ ٱللَّهِ لَا يَخۡلُقُونَ شَيۡـًٔا وَهُمۡ يُخۡلَقُونَ

٢١ أَمۡوَٰتٌ غَيۡرُ أَحۡيَآءٍۖ وَمَا يَشۡعُرُونَ أَيَّانَ يُبۡعَثُونَ

22. Your God is One God. But as for those who believe not in the Hereafter their hearts refuse to know, for they are proud.

23. Assuredly Allah knows that which they keep hidden and that which they proclaim. Lo! He loves not the proud.

24. And when it is said unto them: What has your Lord revealed? they say: (Mere) fables of the men of old.

25. That they may bear their burdens undiminished on the Day of Resurrection, with somewhat of the burdens of those whom they mislead without knowledge. Ah! evil is that which they bear!

26. Those before them plotted, so Allah struck at the foundations of their building, and then the roof fell down upon them from above them, and the doom came on them whence they knew not;

27. Then on the Day of Resurrection He will disgrace them and will say: Where are My partners, for whose sake you opposed (My Guidance)? Those who have been given knowledge will say: Disgrace this day and evil are upon the disbelievers,

28. Whom the angels cause to die while they are wronging themselves. Then will they make full submission (saying): We used not to do any wrong. Nay! Surely Allah is Knower of what you used to do.

29. So enter the gates of Hell, to dwell therein for ever. Woeful indeed will be the lodging of the arrogant.

30. And it is said unto those who ward off (evil): What has your Lord revealed? They say Good: For those who do good in this world there is a good (reward) and the home of the Hereafter will be better. Pleasant indeed will be the home of those who ward off (evil)—

٢٢ اِلٰهُكُمْ اِلٰهٌ وَّاحِدٌ فَالَّذِيْنَ لَا يُؤْمِنُوْنَ بِالْاٰخِرَةِ قُلُوْبُهُمْ مُّنْكِرَةٌ وَّهُمْ مُّسْتَكْبِرُوْنَ

٢٣ لَا جَرَمَ اَنَّ اللّٰهَ يَعْلَمُ مَا يُسِرُّوْنَ وَمَا يُعْلِنُوْنَ اِنَّهُ لَا يُحِبُّ الْمُسْتَكْبِرِيْنَ

٢٤ وَاِذَا قِيْلَ لَهُمْ مَّاذَا اَنْزَلَ رَبُّكُمْ قَالُوْا اَسَاطِيْرُ الْاَوَّلِيْنَ

٢٥ لِيَحْمِلُوْا اَوْزَارَهُمْ كَامِلَةً يَّوْمَ الْقِيٰمَةِ وَمِنْ اَوْزَارِ الَّذِيْنَ يُضِلُّوْنَهُمْ بِغَيْرِ عِلْمٍ اَلَا سَاءَ مَا يَزِرُوْنَ

٢٦ قَدْ مَكَرَ الَّذِيْنَ مِنْ قَبْلِهِمْ فَاَتَى اللّٰهُ بُنْيَانَهُمْ مِّنَ الْقَوَاعِدِ فَخَرَّ عَلَيْهِمُ السَّقْفُ مِنْ فَوْقِهِمْ وَاَتٰهُمُ الْعَذَابُ مِنْ حَيْثُ لَا يَشْعُرُوْنَ

٢٧ ثُمَّ يَوْمَ الْقِيٰمَةِ يُخْزِيْهِمْ وَيَقُوْلُ اَيْنَ شُرَكَآئِيَ الَّذِيْنَ كُنْتُمْ تُشَاقُّوْنَ فِيْهِمْ قَالَ الَّذِيْنَ اُوْتُوا الْعِلْمَ اِنَّ الْخِزْيَ الْيَوْمَ وَالسُّوْٓءَ عَلَى الْكٰفِرِيْنَ

٢٨ الَّذِيْنَ تَتَوَفّٰهُمُ الْمَلٰئِكَةُ ظَالِمِيْ اَنْفُسِهِمْ فَاَلْقَوُا السَّلَمَ مَا كُنَّا نَعْمَلُ مِنْ سُوْٓءٍ بَلٰى اِنَّ اللّٰهَ عَلِيْمٌ بِمَا كُنْتُمْ تَعْمَلُوْنَ

٢٩ فَادْخُلُوْا اَبْوَابَ جَهَنَّمَ خٰلِدِيْنَ فِيْهَا فَلَبِئْسَ مَثْوَى الْمُتَكَبِّرِيْنَ

٣٠ وَقِيْلَ لِلَّذِيْنَ اتَّقَوْا مَاذَا اَنْزَلَ رَبُّكُمْ قَالُوْا خَيْرًا لِّلَّذِيْنَ اَحْسَنُوْا فِيْ هٰذِهِ الدُّنْيَا حَسَنَةٌ وَلَدَارُ الْاٰخِرَةِ خَيْرٌ وَلَنِعْمَ دَارُ الْمُتَّقِيْنَ

31. Gardens of Eden which they enter, underneath which rivers flow, wherein they have what they will. Thus Allah repays those who ward off (evil),

٣١ جَنَّتُ عَدْنٍ يَدْخُلُونَهَا تَجْرِى مِن تَحْتِهَا الْأَنْهَٰرُ لَهُمْ فِيهَا مَا يَشَاءُونَ كَذَٰلِكَ يَجْزِى اللَّهُ الْمُتَّقِينَ

32. Those whom the angels cause to die (when they are) good. They say: Peace be unto you! Enter the Garden because of what you used to do.

٣٢ الَّذِينَ تَتَوَفَّاهُمُ الْمَلَٰئِكَةُ طَيِّبِينَ يَقُولُونَ سَلَٰمٌ عَلَيْكُمُ ادْخُلُوا الْجَنَّةَ بِمَا كُنتُمْ تَعْمَلُونَ

33. Await they anything save that the angels should come unto them or your Lord's command should come to pass? Even so did those before them. Allah wronged them not, but they did wrong themselves,

٣٣ هَلْ يَنظُرُونَ إِلَّا أَن تَأْتِيَهُمُ الْمَلَٰئِكَةُ أَوْ يَأْتِىَ أَمْرُ رَبِّكَ كَذَٰلِكَ فَعَلَ الَّذِينَ مِن قَبْلِهِمْ وَمَا ظَلَمَهُمُ اللَّهُ وَلَٰكِن كَانُوا أَنفُسَهُمْ يَظْلِمُونَ

34. So that the evil of what they did smote them, and that which they used to mock surrounded them.

٣٤ فَأَصَابَهُمْ سَيِّئَاتُ مَا عَمِلُوا وَحَاقَ بِهِم مَّا كَانُوا بِهِ يَسْتَهْزِءُونَ

35. And the idolaters say: Had Allah willed, we had not worshiped anything beside Him, we and our fathers, nor had we forbidden anything without (command from) Him. Even so did those before them. Are the messengers charged with anything save plain conveyance (of the message)?

٣٥ وَقَالَ الَّذِينَ أَشْرَكُوا لَوْ شَاءَ اللَّهُ مَا عَبَدْنَا مِن دُونِهِ مِن شَىْءٍ نَّحْنُ وَلَا ءَابَاؤُنَا وَلَا حَرَّمْنَا مِن دُونِهِ مِن شَىْءٍ كَذَٰلِكَ فَعَلَ الَّذِينَ مِن قَبْلِهِمْ فَهَلْ عَلَى الرُّسُلِ إِلَّا الْبَلَٰغُ الْمُبِينُ

36. And verily We have raised in every nation a messenger, (proclaiming): Worship Allah and shun false gods. Then some of them (there were) whom Allah guided, and some of them (there were) upon whom error became inevitably established. Do but travel in the land and see the nature of the consequence for the deniers!

٣٦ وَلَقَدْ بَعَثْنَا فِى كُلِّ أُمَّةٍ رَّسُولًا أَنِ اعْبُدُوا اللَّهَ وَاجْتَنِبُوا الطَّٰغُوتَ فَمِنْهُم مَّنْ هَدَى اللَّهُ وَمِنْهُم مَّنْ حَقَّتْ عَلَيْهِ الضَّلَٰلَةُ فَسِيرُوا فِى الْأَرْضِ فَانظُرُوا كَيْفَ كَانَ عَٰقِبَةُ الْمُكَذِّبِينَ

37. Even if you (O Muhammad) desire their right guidance, still Allah assuredly will not guide him who misleads. Such have no helpers.

٣٧ إِن تَحْرِصْ عَلَىٰ هُدَٰهُمْ فَإِنَّ اللَّهَ لَا يَهْدِى مَن يُضِلُّ وَمَا لَهُم مِّن نَّٰصِرِينَ

38. And they swear by Allah their most binding oaths (that) Allah will not raise up him who dies. Nay, but it is a promise (binding) upon Him in truth, but most of mankind know not,

٣٨ وَأَقْسَمُوا بِاللَّهِ جَهْدَ أَيْمَٰنِهِمْ لَا يَبْعَثُ اللَّهُ مَن يَمُوتُ بَلَىٰ وَعْدًا عَلَيْهِ حَقًّا وَلَٰكِنَّ أَكْثَرَ النَّاسِ لَا يَعْلَمُونَ

39. That he may explain unto them that wherein they differ, and that those who disbelieved may know that they were liars.

٣٩ لِيُبَيِّنَ لَهُمُ الَّذِى يَخْتَلِفُونَ فِيهِ وَلِيَعْلَمَ الَّذِينَ كَفَرُوۤا أَنَّهُمْ كَانُوا كَاذِبِينَ

40. And Our word unto a thing, when We intend it, is only that We say unto it: Be! and it is.

٤٠ إِنَّمَا قَوْلُنَا لِشَىْءٍ إِذَاۤ أَرَدْنَاهُ أَنْ نَّقُولَ لَهُ كُنْ فَيَكُونُ

41. And those who became fugitives for the cause of Allah after they had been oppressed, We surely shall give them goodly lodging in the world, and surely the reward of the Hereafter is greater, if they but knew;

٤١ وَالَّذِينَ هَاجَرُوا فِى اللهِ مِنْ بَعْدِ مَا ظُلِمُوا لَنُبَوِّئَنَّهُمْ فِى الدُّنْيَا حَسَنَةً وَلَأَجْرُ الْآخِرَةِ أَكْبَرُ لَوْ كَانُوا يَعْلَمُونَ

42. Such as are steadfast and put their trust in Allah.

٤٢ الَّذِينَ صَبَرُوا وَعَلَى رَبِّهِمْ يَتَوَكَّلُونَ

43. And We sent not (as Our messengers) before you other than men whom We inspired—Ask the followers of the Remembrance if you know not!—

٤٣ وَمَاۤ أَرْسَلْنَا مِنْ قَبْلِكَ إِلَّا رِجَالًا نُّوحِى إِلَيْهِمْ فَسْئَلُوۤا أَهْلَ الذِّكْرِ إِنْ كُنْتُمْ لَا تَعْلَمُونَ

44. With clear proofs and writings; and We have revealed unto you the Remembrance that you may explain to mankind that which has been revealed for them, and that they may reflect.

٤٤ بِالْبَيِّنَاتِ وَالزُّبُرِ وَأَنْزَلْنَاۤ إِلَيْكَ الذِّكْرَ لِتُبَيِّنَ لِلنَّاسِ مَا نُزِّلَ إِلَيْهِمْ وَلَعَلَّهُمْ يَتَفَكَّرُونَ

45. Are they who plan ill deeds then secure that Allah will not cause the earth to swallow them, or that the doom will not come on them whence they know not?

٤٥ أَفَأَمِنَ الَّذِينَ مَكَرُوا السَّيِّئَاتِ أَنْ يَّخْسِفَ اللهُ بِهِمُ الْأَرْضَ أَوْ يَأْتِيَهُمُ الْعَذَابُ مِنْ حَيْثُ لَا يَشْعُرُونَ

46. Or that He will not seize them in their going to and fro so that there is no escape for them?

٤٦ أَوْ يَأْخُذَهُمْ فِى تَقَلُّبِهِمْ فَمَا هُمْ بِمُعْجِزِينَ

47. Or that He will seize them striking terror (in them)? Lo! your Lord is indeed Full of Pity, Merciful!

٤٧ أَوْ يَأْخُذَهُمْ عَلَى تَخَوُّفٍ فَإِنَّ رَبَّكُمْ لَرَءُوفٌ رَّحِيمٌ

48. Have they not observed all things that Allah has created, how their shadows incline to the right and to the left, making prostration unto Allah, and they are lowly?

٤٨ أَوَلَمْ يَرَوْا إِلَى مَا خَلَقَ اللهُ مِنْ شَىْءٍ يَتَفَيَّؤُا ظِلَالُهُ عَنِ الْيَمِينِ وَالشَّمَآئِلِ سُجَّدًا لِّلهِ وَهُمْ دَاخِرُونَ

49. And unto Allah makes prostration whatsoever is in the heavens and whatsoever is in the earth of living creatures, and the angels (also), and they are not proud.

٤٩ وَلِلهِ يَسْجُدُ مَا فِى السَّمَوَاتِ وَمَا فِى الْأَرْضِ مِنْ دَآبَّةٍ وَالْمَلَآئِكَةُ وَهُمْ لَا يَسْتَكْبِرُونَ

50. They fear their Lord above them, and do what they are bidden.

٥٠ يَخَافُونَ رَبَّهُمْ مِّنْ فَوْقِهِمْ وَيَفْعَلُونَ مَا يُؤْمَرُونَ

51. And Allah has said: Choose not two gods. There is only One God. So of Me, Me only, be in awe.

52. Unto Him belongs whatsoever is in the heavens and the earth, and religion is His for ever. Will you then fear any other than Allah?

53. And whatever fortune you enjoy, it is from Allah. Then, when misfortune reaches you, unto Him you cry for help.

54. And afterward, when He has rid you of the misfortune, behold! a set of you attribute partners to their Lord,

55. So as to deny that which We have given them. Then enjoy life (while you may), for you will come to know.

56. And they assign a portion of that which We have given them unto what they know not. By Allah! but you will indeed be asked concerning (all) that you used to invent.

57. And they assign unto Allah daughters. Be He glorified! and unto themselves what they desire;

58. When if one of them receives tidings of the birth of a female, his face remains darkened, and he is filled with inward anger.

59. He hides himself from the folk because of the evil of that whereof he has bad tidings, (asking himself): Shall he keep it in contempt, or bury it beneath the dust. Surely evil is their judgment.

60. For those who believe not in the Hereafter is an evil similitude, and Allah's is the Sublime Similitude. He is the Mighty, the Wise.

61. If Allah were to take mankind to task for their wrong-doing, he would not leave on it a living creature, but He reprieves them to an appointed term, and when their term comes they cannot put (it) off an hour nor (yet) advance (it).

62. And they assign unto Allah that which they (themselves) dislike, and their tongues expound the lie that the better portion will be theirs. Assuredly theirs will be the Fire, and they will be abandoned.

63. By Allah, We verily sent messengers unto the nations before you, but the Devil made their deeds fair seeming unto them. So he is their patron this day, and theirs will be a painful doom.

64. And we have revealed the Scripture unto you only that you may explain unto them that wherein they differ, and (as) a guidance and a mercy for a people who believe.

65. Allah sends down water from the sky and therewith revives the earth after her death! Lo! herein is indeed a portent for a folk who hear.

66. And lo! in the cattle there is a lesson for you. We give you to drink of that which is in their bellies, from between the digested food and the blood, pure milk palatable to the drinkers.

67. And of the fruits of the date palm, and grapes, whence you derive strong drink and (also) good nourishment. Lo! therein, is indeed a portent for people who have sense.

68. And your Lord inspired the bee, saying: Choose you habitations in the hills and in the trees and in that which they thatch;

69. Then eat of all fruits, and follow the ways of your Lord, made smooth (for you). There comes forth from their bellies a drink diverse of hues, wherein is healing for mankind. Lo! herein is indeed a portent for people who reflect.

70. And Allah creates you, then causes you to die, and among you is he who is brought back to the most abject stage of life, so that he knows nothing after (having had) knowledge. Lo! Allah is Knower, Powerful.

﴿٦٢﴾ وَيَجْعَلُونَ لِلَّهِ مَا يَكْرَهُونَ وَتَصِفُ أَلْسِنَتُهُمُ الْكَذِبَ أَنَّ لَهُمُ الْحُسْنَىٰ لَا جَرَمَ أَنَّ لَهُمُ النَّارَ وَأَنَّهُم مُّفْرَطُونَ

﴿٦٣﴾ تَاللَّهِ لَقَدْ أَرْسَلْنَا إِلَىٰ أُمَمٍ مِّن قَبْلِكَ فَزَيَّنَ لَهُمُ الشَّيْطَانُ أَعْمَالَهُمْ فَهُوَ وَلِيُّهُمُ الْيَوْمَ وَلَهُمْ عَذَابٌ أَلِيمٌ

﴿٦٤﴾ وَمَا أَنزَلْنَا عَلَيْكَ الْكِتَابَ إِلَّا لِتُبَيِّنَ لَهُمُ الَّذِي اخْتَلَفُوا فِيهِ وَهُدًى وَرَحْمَةً لِّقَوْمٍ يُؤْمِنُونَ

﴿٦٥﴾ وَاللَّهُ أَنزَلَ مِنَ السَّمَاءِ مَاءً فَأَحْيَا بِهِ الْأَرْضَ بَعْدَ مَوْتِهَا إِنَّ فِي ذَٰلِكَ لَآيَةً لِّقَوْمٍ يَسْمَعُونَ

﴿٦٦﴾ وَإِنَّ لَكُمْ فِي الْأَنْعَامِ لَعِبْرَةً نُّسْقِيكُم مِّمَّا فِي بُطُونِهِ مِن بَيْنِ فَرْثٍ وَدَمٍ لَّبَنًا خَالِصًا سَائِغًا لِّلشَّارِبِينَ

﴿٦٧﴾ وَمِن ثَمَرَاتِ النَّخِيلِ وَالْأَعْنَابِ تَتَّخِذُونَ مِنْهُ سَكَرًا وَرِزْقًا حَسَنًا إِنَّ فِي ذَٰلِكَ لَآيَةً لِّقَوْمٍ يَعْقِلُونَ

﴿٦٨﴾ وَأَوْحَىٰ رَبُّكَ إِلَى النَّحْلِ أَنِ اتَّخِذِي مِنَ الْجِبَالِ بُيُوتًا وَمِنَ الشَّجَرِ وَمِمَّا يَعْرِشُونَ

﴿٦٩﴾ ثُمَّ كُلِي مِن كُلِّ الثَّمَرَاتِ فَاسْلُكِي سُبُلَ رَبِّكِ ذُلُلًا يَخْرُجُ مِن بُطُونِهَا شَرَابٌ مُّخْتَلِفٌ أَلْوَانُهُ فِيهِ شِفَاءٌ لِّلنَّاسِ إِنَّ فِي ذَٰلِكَ لَآيَةً لِّقَوْمٍ يَتَفَكَّرُونَ

﴿٧٠﴾ وَاللَّهُ خَلَقَكُمْ ثُمَّ يَتَوَفَّاكُمْ وَمِنكُم مَّن يُرَدُّ إِلَىٰ أَرْذَلِ الْعُمُرِ لِكَيْ لَا يَعْلَمَ بَعْدَ عِلْمٍ شَيْئًا إِنَّ اللَّهَ عَلِيمٌ قَدِيرٌ

71. And Allah has favored some of you above others in provision. Now those who are more favored will by no means hand over their provision to those (slaves) whom their right hands possess, so that they may be equal with them in respect thereof. Is it then the grace of Allah that they deny?

72. And Allah has given you wives of your own kind, and has given you, from your wives, sons and grandsons, and has made provision of good things for you. Is it then in vanity that they believe and in the grace of Allah that they disbelieve?

73. And they worship beside Allah that which owns no provision whatsoever for them from the heavens or the earth, nor have they (whom they worship) any power.

74. So coin not similitudes for Allah. Lo! Allah knows; you know not.

75. Allah coins a similitude: (on the one hand) a (mere) chattel slave, who has control of nothing, and (on the other hand) one on whom We have bestowed a fair provision from Us, and he spends thereof secretly and openly. Are they equal? Praise be to Allah! But most of them know not.

76. And Allah coins a similitude Two men, one of them dumb, having control of nothing, and he is a burden on his owner; whichever way he directs him to go, he brings no good. Is he equal with one who enjoins justice and follows a straight path (of conduct)?

77. And unto Allah belongs the Unseen of the heavens and the earth, and the matter of the Hour (of Doom) is but as a twinkling of the eye, or it is nearer still. Lo! Allah is Able to do all things.

﴿٧١﴾ وَاللّٰهُ فَضَّلَ بَعْضَكُمْ عَلَىٰ بَعْضٍ فِي الرِّزْقِ فَمَا الَّذِينَ فُضِّلُوا بِرَآدِّي رِزْقِهِمْ عَلَىٰ مَا مَلَكَتْ أَيْمَانُهُمْ فَهُمْ فِيهِ سَوَآءٌ أَفَبِنِعْمَةِ اللّٰهِ يَجْحَدُونَ

﴿٧٢﴾ وَاللّٰهُ جَعَلَ لَكُمْ مِنْ أَنفُسِكُمْ أَزْوَاجًا وَجَعَلَ لَكُمْ مِنْ أَزْوَاجِكُمْ بَنِينَ وَحَفَدَةً وَرَزَقَكُمْ مِنَ الطَّيِّبَاتِ أَفَبِالْبَاطِلِ يُؤْمِنُونَ وَبِنِعْمَتِ اللّٰهِ هُمْ يَكْفُرُونَ

﴿٧٣﴾ وَيَعْبُدُونَ مِن دُونِ اللّٰهِ مَا لَا يَمْلِكُ لَهُمْ رِزْقًا مِنَ السَّمَاوَاتِ وَالْأَرْضِ شَيْئًا وَلَا يَسْتَطِيعُونَ

﴿٧٤﴾ فَلَا تَضْرِبُوا لِلّٰهِ الْأَمْثَالَ إِنَّ اللّٰهَ يَعْلَمُ وَأَنتُمْ لَا تَعْلَمُونَ

﴿٧٥﴾ ضَرَبَ اللّٰهُ مَثَلًا عَبْدًا مَّمْلُوكًا لَّا يَقْدِرُ عَلَىٰ شَيْءٍ وَمَن رَّزَقْنَاهُ مِنَّا رِزْقًا حَسَنًا فَهُوَ يُنفِقُ مِنْهُ سِرًّا وَجَهْرًا هَلْ يَسْتَوُونَ الْحَمْدُ لِلّٰهِ بَلْ أَكْثَرُهُمْ لَا يَعْلَمُونَ

﴿٧٦﴾ وَضَرَبَ اللّٰهُ مَثَلًا رَّجُلَيْنِ أَحَدُهُمَا أَبْكَمُ لَا يَقْدِرُ عَلَىٰ شَيْءٍ وَهُوَ كَلٌّ عَلَىٰ مَوْلَاهُ أَيْنَمَا يُوَجِّههُّ لَا يَأْتِ بِخَيْرٍ هَلْ يَسْتَوِي هُوَ وَمَن يَأْمُرُ بِالْعَدْلِ وَهُوَ عَلَىٰ صِرَاطٍ مُّسْتَقِيمٍ

﴿٧٧﴾ وَلِلّٰهِ غَيْبُ السَّمَاوَاتِ وَالْأَرْضِ وَمَا أَمْرُ السَّاعَةِ إِلَّا كَلَمْحِ الْبَصَرِ أَوْ هُوَ أَقْرَبُ إِنَّ اللّٰهَ عَلَىٰ كُلِّ شَيْءٍ قَدِيرٌ

78. And Allah brought you forth from the wombs of your mothers knowing nothing, and gave you hearing and sight and hearts that haply you might give thanks.

79. Have they not seen the birds obedient[152] in mid-air? None holds them save Allah. Lo! herein, verily, are portents for a people who believe.

80. And Allah has given you in your houses an abode, and has given you (also), of the hides of cattle, houses[153] which you find light (to carry) on the day of migration and on the day of pitching camp; and of their wool and their fur and their hair, furniture and articles of convenience for a while.

81. And Allah has given you, of that which He has created, shelter from the sun; and has given you places of refuge in the mountains, and has given you coats to ward off the heat from you, and coats (of armor) to save you from your own mutual violence. Thus does He perfect His favor unto you, in order that you may surrender (unto Him).

82. Then, if they turn away, your duty (O Muhammad) is but plain conveyance (of the message).

83. They know the favor of Allah and then deny it. Most of them are ingrates.

84. And (bethink you of) the day when We raise up of every nation a witness, then there is no leave for disbelievers, nor are they allowed to make amends.

85. And when those who did wrong behold the doom, it will not be made light for them, nor will they be reprieved.

86. And when those who ascribed partners to Allah behold those partners of theirs, they will say: Our Lord! these are our partners unto whom we used to cry instead of You. But they will fling to them the saying: Lo! you verily are liars!

---

[152]Lit: made subservient to the Law of Allah.
[153]i.e., tents.

87. And they proffer unto Allah submission on that day, and all that they used to invent has failed them.

٨٧ وَأَلْقَوْا إِلَى اللَّهِ يَوْمَئِذٍ السَّلَمَ وَضَلَّ عَنْهُم مَّا كَانُوا يَفْتَرُونَ

88. For those who disbelieve and debar (men) from the way of Allah, We add doom to doom because they wrought corruption.

٨٨ الَّذِينَ كَفَرُوا وَصَدُّوا عَن سَبِيلِ اللَّهِ زِدْنَاهُمْ عَذَابًا فَوْقَ الْعَذَابِ بِمَا كَانُوا يُفْسِدُونَ

89. And (bethink you of) the day when We raise in every nation a witness against them of their own folk, and We bring you (Muhammad) as a witness against these. And We reveal the Scripture unto you as an exposition of all things, and a guidance and a mercy and good tidings for those who have surrendered (to Allah).

٨٩ وَيَوْمَ نَبْعَثُ فِي كُلِّ أُمَّةٍ شَهِيدًا عَلَيْهِم مِّنْ أَنفُسِهِمْ وَجِئْنَا بِكَ شَهِيدًا عَلَىٰ هَـٰؤُلَاءِ وَنَزَّلْنَا عَلَيْكَ الْكِتَبَ تِبْيَانًا لِّكُلِّ شَيْءٍ وَهُدًى وَرَحْمَةً وَبُشْرَىٰ لِلْمُسْلِمِينَ

90. Lo! Allah enjoins justice and kindness, and giving to kinsfolk, and forbids lewdness and abomination and wickedness. He exhorts you in order that you may take heed.[154]

٩٠ ۞ إِنَّ اللَّهَ يَأْمُرُ بِالْعَدْلِ وَالْإِحْسَـٰنِ وَإِيتَآيِ ذِي الْقُرْبَىٰ وَيَنْهَىٰ عَنِ الْفَحْشَآءِ وَالْمُنكَرِ وَالْبَغْيِ يَعِظُكُمْ لَعَلَّكُمْ تَذَكَّرُونَ

91. Fulfill the covenant of Allah whenever you make a covenant, and break not your oaths after asserting them, and after you have made Allah surety over you. Lo! Allah knows what you do.

٩١ وَأَوْفُوا بِعَهْدِ اللَّهِ إِذَا عَـٰهَدتُّمْ وَلَا تَنقُضُوا الْأَيْمَـٰنَ بَعْدَ تَوْكِيدِهَا وَقَدْ جَعَلْتُمُ اللَّهَ عَلَيْكُمْ كَفِيلًا إِنَّ اللَّهَ يَعْلَمُ مَا تَفْعَلُونَ

92. And be not like unto her who unravels the thread, after she has made it strong, to thin filaments, making your oaths a deceit between you because of a nation being more numerous than (another) nation. Allah only tries you thereby, and He verily will explain to you on the Day of Resurrection that wherein you differed.

٩٢ وَلَا تَكُونُوا كَالَّتِي نَقَضَتْ غَزْلَهَا مِنْ بَعْدِ قُوَّةٍ أَنكَـٰثًا تَتَّخِذُونَ أَيْمَـٰنَكُمْ دَخَلًا بَيْنَكُمْ أَن تَكُونَ أُمَّةٌ هِيَ أَرْبَىٰ مِنْ أُمَّةٍ إِنَّمَا يَبْلُوكُمُ اللَّهُ بِهِ وَلَيُبَيِّنَنَّ لَكُمْ يَوْمَ الْقِيَـٰمَةِ مَا كُنتُمْ فِيهِ تَخْتَلِفُونَ

93. Had Allah willed He could have made you (all) one nation, but He sends whom He will astray and guides whom He will, and you will indeed be asked of what you used to do.

٩٣ وَلَوْ شَآءَ اللَّهُ لَجَعَلَكُمْ أُمَّةً وَٰحِدَةً وَلَـٰكِن يُضِلُّ مَن يَشَآءُ وَيَهْدِي مَن يَشَآءُ وَلَتُسْـَٔلُنَّ عَمَّا كُنتُمْ تَعْمَلُونَ

---

[154] Since the time of 'Umar ibn 'Abd al 'Azīz (the 'Umayyad), this verse has been recited at the end of almost every Friday sermon in all Sunni congregations.

94. Make not your oaths a deceit between you, lest a foot should slip after being firmly planted and you should taste evil forasmuch as you debarred (men) from the way of Allah, and yours should be an awful doom.

٩٤ وَلَا تَتَّخِذُوٓاْ أَيۡمَٰنَكُمۡ دَخَلَۢا بَيۡنَكُمۡ فَتَزِلَّ قَدَمُۢ بَعۡدَ ثُبُوتِهَا وَتَذُوقُواْ السُّوٓءَ بِمَا صَدَدتُّمۡ عَن سَبِيلِ ٱللَّهِ وَلَكُمۡ عَذَابٌ عَظِيمٌ

95. And purchase not a small gain at the price of Allah's covenant. Lo! that which Allah has is better for you, if you did but know.

٩٥ وَلَا تَشۡتَرُواْ بِعَهۡدِ ٱللَّهِ ثَمَنًا قَلِيلًا إِنَّمَا عِندَ ٱللَّهِ هُوَ خَيۡرٌ لَّكُمۡ إِن كُنتُمۡ تَعۡلَمُونَ

96. That which you have wastes away, and that which Allah has remains. And surely We shall pay those who are steadfast a recompense in proportion to the best of what they used to do.

٩٦ مَا عِندَكُمۡ يَنفَدُ وَمَا عِندَ ٱللَّهِ بَاقٍ وَلَنَجۡزِيَنَّ ٱلَّذِينَ صَبَرُوٓاْ أَجۡرَهُم بِأَحۡسَنِ مَا كَانُواْ يَعۡمَلُونَ

97. Whosoever does right, whether male or female, and is a believer, him surely We shall quicken with good life, and We shall pay them a recompense in proportion to the best of what they used to do.

٩٧ مَنۡ عَمِلَ صَٰلِحًا مِّن ذَكَرٍ أَوۡ أُنثَىٰ وَهُوَ مُؤۡمِنٌ فَلَنُحۡيِيَنَّهُۥ حَيَوٰةً طَيِّبَةً وَلَنَجۡزِيَنَّهُمۡ أَجۡرَهُم بِأَحۡسَنِ مَا كَانُواْ يَعۡمَلُونَ

98. And when you recite the Qur'an, seek refuge in Allah from the Devil the outcast.

٩٨ فَإِذَا قَرَأۡتَ ٱلۡقُرۡءَانَ فَٱسۡتَعِذۡ بِٱللَّهِ مِنَ ٱلشَّيۡطَٰنِ ٱلرَّجِيمِ

99. Lo! he has no power over those who believe and put trust in their Lord.

٩٩ إِنَّهُۥ لَيۡسَ لَهُۥ سُلۡطَٰنٌ عَلَى ٱلَّذِينَ ءَامَنُواْ وَعَلَىٰ رَبِّهِمۡ يَتَوَكَّلُونَ

100. His power is only over those who make a friend of him, and those who ascribe partners unto Him (Allah).

١٠٠ إِنَّمَا سُلۡطَٰنُهُۥ عَلَى ٱلَّذِينَ يَتَوَلَّوۡنَهُۥ وَٱلَّذِينَ هُم بِهِۦ مُشۡرِكُونَ

101. And when We put a revelation in place of (another) revelation—and Allah knows best what He reveals—they say: Lo! you are but inventing. Most of them know not.

١٠١ وَإِذَا بَدَّلۡنَآ ءَايَةً مَّكَانَ ءَايَةٍ وَٱللَّهُ أَعۡلَمُ بِمَا يُنَزِّلُ قَالُوٓاْ إِنَّمَآ أَنتَ مُفۡتَرِۭ بَلۡ أَكۡثَرُهُمۡ لَا يَعۡلَمُونَ

102. Say: The holy Spirit[155] has revealed it from your Lord with truth, that it may confirm (the faith of) those who believe, and as guidance and good tidings for Muslims.[156]

١٠٢ قُلۡ نَزَّلَهُۥ رُوحُ ٱلۡقُدُسِ مِن رَّبِّكَ بِٱلۡحَقِّ لِيُثَبِّتَ ٱلَّذِينَ ءَامَنُواْ وَهُدًى وَبُشۡرَىٰ لِلۡمُسۡلِمِينَ

---

[155]i.e., Gabriel.
[156]Those who surrender and submit to Allah.

103. And We know well that they say:
Only a mortal teaches him. The speech of
him at whom they falsely hint is out-
landish, and this is clear Arabic speech.[157]

104. Lo! those who disbelieve the revelations of Allah, Allah guides them not
and theirs will be a painful doom.

105. Only they invent falsehood who
believe not Allah's revelations, and
(only) they are the liars.

106. Who disbelieves in Allah after his
belief—save him who is forced thereto
and whose heart is still content with
Faith—but who finds ease in disbelief:
On them is wrath from Allah. Theirs will
be an awful doom.

107. That is because they have chosen
the life of the world rather than the
Hereafter, and because Allah guides not
the disbelieving folk.

108. Such are they whose hearts and
ears and eyes Allah has sealed. And such
are the heedless.

109. Doubtless in the Hereafter they
are the losers.

110. Then lo! your Lord—for those
who become fugitives after they had
been persecuted, and then fought and
were steadfast—lo! your Lord afterward
is (for them) indeed For-giving,
Merciful,

111. On the Day when every soul will
come pleading for itself, and every soul
will be repaid what it did, and they will
not be wronged.

---

[157]Among the various attempts of the idolaters to deride the Qur'an was the charge that a Christian
slave among the earliest converts taught it to the Pro-phet. The same slave suffered cruel
persecution for his belief in the divine inspiration of the Qur'an.

112. Allah coins a similitude: a township that dwelt secure and well content, its provision coming to it in abundance from every place, but it disbelieved in Allah's favors, so Allah made it experience the garb of dearth and fear because of what they used to do.

١١٢ وَضَرَبَ اللّٰهُ مَثَلًا قَرْيَةً كَانَتْ ءَامِنَةً مُّطْمَئِنَّةً يَأْتِيهَا رِزْقُهَا رَغَدًا مِّنْ كُلِّ مَكَانٍ فَكَفَرَتْ بِأَنْعُمِ اللّٰهِ فَأَذَاقَهَا اللّٰهُ لِبَاسَ الْجُوعِ وَالْخَوْفِ بِمَا كَانُوا يَصْنَعُونَ

113. And surely there had come unto them a messenger from among them, but they had denied him, and so the torment seized them while they were wrongdoers.

١١٣ وَلَقَدْ جَآءَهُمْ رَسُولٌ مِّنْهُمْ فَكَذَّبُوهُ فَأَخَذَهُمُ الْعَذَابُ وَهُمْ ظَالِمُونَ

114. So eat of the lawful and good food which Allah has provided for you, and thank the bounty of your Lord if it is Him you worship.

١١٤ فَكُلُوا مِمَّا رَزَقَكُمُ اللّٰهُ حَلَالًا طَيِّبًا وَاشْكُرُوا نِعْمَتَ اللّٰهِ إِنْ كُنْتُمْ إِيَّاهُ تَعْبُدُونَ

115. He has forbidden for you only carrion and blood and swine flesh and that which has been immolated in the name of any other than Allah; but he who is driven thereto, neither craving nor transgressing, lo! then Allah is Forgiving, Mer-ciful.

١١٥ إِنَّمَا حَرَّمَ عَلَيْكُمُ الْمَيْتَةَ وَالدَّمَ وَلَحْمَ الْخِنْزِيرِ وَمَآ أُهِلَّ لِغَيْرِ اللّٰهِ بِهِ فَمَنِ اضْطُرَّ غَيْرَ بَاغٍ وَلَا عَادٍ فَإِنَّ اللّٰهَ غَفُورٌ رَّحِيمٌ

116. And speak not, concerning that which your own tongues qualify (as clean or unclean), the falsehood: "This is lawful, and this is forbidden," so that you invent a lie against Allah. Lo! those who invent a lie against Allah will not succeed.

١١٦ وَلَا تَقُولُوا لِمَا تَصِفُ أَلْسِنَتُكُمُ الْكَذِبَ هٰذَا حَلَالٌ وَهٰذَا حَرَامٌ لِّتَفْتَرُوا عَلَى اللّٰهِ الْكَذِبَ إِنَّ الَّذِينَ يَفْتَرُونَ عَلَى اللّٰهِ الْكَذِبَ لَا يُفْلِحُونَ

117. A brief enjoyment (will be theirs); and theirs will be a painful doom.

١١٧ مَتَاعٌ قَلِيلٌ وَلَهُمْ عَذَابٌ أَلِيمٌ

118. And unto those who are Jews We have forbidden that which We have already related unto you. And We wronged them not, but they were wont to wrong themselves.

١١٨ وَعَلَى الَّذِينَ هَادُوا حَرَّمْنَا مَا قَصَصْنَا عَلَيْكَ مِنْ قَبْلُ وَمَا ظَلَمْنَاهُمْ وَلَٰكِنْ كَانُوا أَنْفُسَهُمْ يَظْلِمُونَ

119. Then lo! your Lord—for those who do evil in ignorance and afterward repent and amend—lo! (for them) your Lord is afterward indeed Forgiving, Merciful.

١١٩ ثُمَّ إِنَّ رَبَّكَ لِلَّذِينَ عَمِلُوا السُّوءَ بِجَهَالَةٍ ثُمَّ تَابُوا مِنْ بَعْدِ ذَٰلِكَ وَأَصْلَحُوا إِنَّ رَبَّكَ مِنْ بَعْدِهَا لَغَفُورٌ رَّحِيمٌ

120. Lo! Abraham was a nation obedient to Allah, by nature upright, and he was not of the idolaters;

١٢٠ إِنَّ إِبْرَاهِيمَ كَانَ أُمَّةً قَانِتًا لِّلّٰهِ حَنِيفًا وَلَمْ يَكُ مِنَ الْمُشْرِكِينَ

121. Thankful for His bounties; He chose him and He guided him unto a straight path.

١٢١ شَاكِرًا لِّأَنْعُمِهِ اجْتَبَاهُ وَهَدَاهُ إِلَى صِرَاطٍ مُّسْتَقِيمٍ

122. And We gave him good in the world, and in the Here-after he is among the righteous.

١٢٢ وَءَاتَيْنَاهُ فِى الدُّنْيَا حَسَنَةً وَإِنَّهُ فِى الْأَخِرَةِ لَمِنَ الصَّالِحِينَ

123. And afterward We inspired you (Muhammad, saying): Follow the religion of Abraham, as one by nature upright. He was not of the idolaters.

١٢٣ ثُمَّ أَوْحَيْنَا إِلَيْكَ أَنِ اتَّبِعْ مِلَّةَ إِبْرَاهِيمَ حَنِيفًا وَمَا كَانَ مِنَ الْمُشْرِكِينَ

124. The Sabbath was appointed only for those who differed concerning it, and lo! your Lord will judge between them on the Day of Resurrection concerning that wherein they used to differ.

١٢٤ إِنَّمَا جُعِلَ السَّبْتُ عَلَى الَّذِينَ اخْتَلَفُوا فِيهِ وَإِنَّ رَبَّكَ لَيَحْكُمُ بَيْنَهُمْ يَوْمَ الْقِيَمَةِ فِيمَا كَانُوا فِيهِ يَخْتَلِفُونَ

125. Call unto the way of your Lord with wisdom and fair exhortation, and reason with them in the better way. Lo! your Lord is best aware of him who strays from His way, and He is Best Aware of those who go aright.

١٢٥ ادْعُ إِلَى سَبِيلِ رَبِّكَ بِالْحِكْمَةِ وَالْمَوْعِظَةِ الْحَسَنَةِ وَجَادِلْهُم بِالَّتِى هِىَ أَحْسَنُ إِنَّ رَبَّكَ هُوَ أَعْلَمُ بِمَن ضَلَّ عَن سَبِيلِهِ وَهُوَ أَعْلَمُ بِالْمُهْتَدِينَ

126. If you punish, then punish with the like of that with which you were afflicted. But if you endure patiently, verily it is better for the patient.

١٢٦ وَإِنْ عَاقَبْتُمْ فَعَاقِبُوا بِمِثْلِ مَا عُوقِبْتُم بِهِ وَلَئِن صَبَرْتُمْ لَهُوَ خَيْرٌ لِّلصَّابِرِينَ

127. Endure you patiently (O Muhammad). Your endur-ance is only by (the help of) Allah. Grieve not for them, and be not in distress because of that which they devise.

١٢٧ وَاصْبِرْ وَمَا صَبْرُكَ إِلَّا بِاللَّهِ وَلَا تَحْزَنْ عَلَيْهِمْ وَلَا تَكُ فِى ضَيْقٍ مِّمَّا يَمْكُرُونَ

128. Lo! Allah is with those who keep their duty unto Him and those who are doers of good.

١٢٨ إِنَّ اللَّهَ مَعَ الَّذِينَ اتَّقَوا وَّالَّذِينَ هُم مُّحْسِنُونَ

The Night Journey

or

The Children of Israel

Surat al Isrā', "The Night Journey" or *Banī Isrā'īl*, "The Children of Israel," begins and ends with references to the Israelites. Verse 1 relates to the Prophet's journey, in which he was carried by a heavenly steed to the Temple of Jerusalem during one night and from there he was taken through the seven heavens to the very presence of God. The surah may be taken as belonging to the middle group of Makkan surahs, except for verse 81 or, according to other commentators verses 76-82, which was revealed at al Madinah.

The Night Journey
or
The Children of Israel

Revealed at Makkah
In the name of Allah,
the Beneficent, the Merciful

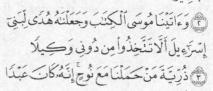

1. Glorified be He Who carried His servant by night from the Inviolable Place of Worship[158] to the Far Distant Mosque[159] the neighborhood whereof We have blessed, that We might show him of Our tokens! Lo! He, only He, is the Hearer, the Seer.

2. We gave unto Moses the Scripture, and We appointed it a guidance for the Children of Israel, saying: Choose no guardian beside Me.

3. (They were) the seed of those whom We carried (in the ship) along with Noah. Lo! he was a grateful slave.

4. And We decreed for the Children of Israel in the scripture: You verily will work corruption in the earth twice, and you will become great tyrants.

5. So when the time for the first of the two came, We roused against you slaves of Ours of great might who ravaged (the) country, and it was a threat performed.

6. Then we gave you once again your turn against them, and We aided you with wealth and children and made you more in soldiery,

7. (Saying): If you do good, you do good for your own souls, and if you do evil, it is for them (in like manner). So, when the time for the second (of the judgments) came (We roused against you others of Our slaves) to ravage you, and to enter the Mosque even as they entered it the first time, and to lay waste all that they conquered with an utter wasting.

8. It may be that your Lord will have mercy on you, but if you repeat (the crime) We shall repeat (the punishment), and We have appointed Hell a dungeon for disbelievers.

---

[158] The Sacred Mosque in Makkah.—[159] In Jerusalem.

9. Lo! this Qur'an guides unto that which is straightest, and gives tidings unto the believers who do good works that theirs will be a great reward.

10. And that those who believe not in the Hereafter, for them We have prepared a painful doom.

11. Man prays for evil as he prays for good; for man was ever hasty.

12. And we appoint the night and the day two portents. Then We make dark the portent of the night, and We make the portent of the day sight giving, that you may seek bounty from your Lord, and that you may know the computation of the years, and the reckoning; and everything have We expounded with a clear expounding.

13. And every man's augury have We fastened to his own neck, and We shall bring forth for him on the Day of Resurrection a book which he will find wide open.

14. (And it will be said unto him): Read your book. Your soul suffices as reckoner against you this day.

15. Whoever goes right, it is only for (the good of) his own soul that he goes right, and whoever errs, errs only to its hurt. No laden soul can bear another's load. We never punish until We have sent a messenger.

16. And when We would destroy a township We send commandment to its folk who live at ease, and afterward they commit abomination therein, and so the Word (of doom) has effect for it, and We annihilate it with complete annihilation.

17. How many generations have we destroyed after Noah! And Allah suffices as Knower and Beholder of the sins of His slaves.

﴿٩﴾ إِنَّ هَٰذَا الْقُرْآنَ يَهْدِي لِلَّتِي هِيَ أَقْوَمُ وَيُبَشِّرُ الْمُؤْمِنِينَ الَّذِينَ يَعْمَلُونَ الصَّالِحَاتِ أَنَّ لَهُمْ أَجْرًا كَبِيرًا

﴿١٠﴾ وَأَنَّ الَّذِينَ لَا يُؤْمِنُونَ بِالْآخِرَةِ أَعْتَدْنَا لَهُمْ عَذَابًا أَلِيمًا

﴿١١﴾ وَيَدْعُ الْإِنْسَانُ بِالشَّرِّ دُعَاءَهُ بِالْخَيْرِ وَكَانَ الْإِنْسَانُ عَجُولًا

﴿١٢﴾ وَجَعَلْنَا اللَّيْلَ وَالنَّهَارَ آيَتَيْنِ فَمَحَوْنَا آيَةَ اللَّيْلِ وَجَعَلْنَا آيَةَ النَّهَارِ مُبْصِرَةً لِتَبْتَغُوا فَضْلًا مِّن رَّبِّكُمْ وَلِتَعْلَمُوا عَدَدَ السِّنِينَ وَالْحِسَابَ وَكُلَّ شَيْءٍ فَصَّلْنَاهُ تَفْصِيلًا

﴿١٣﴾ وَكُلَّ إِنْسَانٍ أَلْزَمْنَاهُ طَائِرَهُ فِي عُنُقِهِ وَنُخْرِجُ لَهُ يَوْمَ الْقِيَامَةِ كِتَابًا يَلْقَاهُ مَنْشُورًا

﴿١٤﴾ اقْرَأْ كِتَابَكَ كَفَىٰ بِنَفْسِكَ الْيَوْمَ عَلَيْكَ حَسِيبًا

﴿١٥﴾ مَّنِ اهْتَدَىٰ فَإِنَّمَا يَهْتَدِي لِنَفْسِهِ وَمَن ضَلَّ فَإِنَّمَا يَضِلُّ عَلَيْهَا وَلَا تَزِرُ وَازِرَةٌ وِزْرَ أُخْرَىٰ وَمَا كُنَّا مُعَذِّبِينَ حَتَّىٰ نَبْعَثَ رَسُولًا

﴿١٦﴾ وَإِذَا أَرَدْنَا أَن نُّهْلِكَ قَرْيَةً أَمَرْنَا مُتْرَفِيهَا فَفَسَقُوا فِيهَا فَحَقَّ عَلَيْهَا الْقَوْلُ فَدَمَّرْنَاهَا تَدْمِيرًا

﴿١٧﴾ وَكَمْ أَهْلَكْنَا مِنَ الْقُرُونِ مِن بَعْدِ نُوحٍ وَكَفَىٰ بِرَبِّكَ بِذُنُوبِ عِبَادِهِ خَبِيرًا بَصِيرًا

18. Who desires the (worldly life) that hastens away, We hasten for him therein that We will for whom We please. And afterward We have appointed for him Hell; he will endure the heat thereof, condemned, rejected.

١٨ مَنْ كَانَ يُرِيدُ الْعَاجِلَةَ عَجَّلْنَا لَهُ فِيهَا مَا نَشَاءُ لِمَنْ نُرِيدُ ثُمَّ جَعَلْنَا لَهُ جَهَنَّمَ يَصْلَاهَا مَذْمُومًا مَّدْحُورًا

19. And who desires the Hereafter and strives for it with the effort necessary, being a believer; for such, their effort finds favor (with their Lord).

١٩ وَمَنْ أَرَادَ الْآخِرَةَ وَسَعَى لَهَا سَعْيَهَا وَهُوَ مُؤْمِنٌ فَأُولَٰئِكَ كَانَ سَعْيُهُمْ مَّشْكُورًا

20. Each do We supply, both these and those, from the bounty of your Lord. And the bounty of your Lord can never be walled up.

٢٠ كُلًّا نُّمِدُّ هَٰؤُلَاءِ وَهَٰؤُلَاءِ مِنْ عَطَاءِ رَبِّكَ وَمَا كَانَ عَطَاءُ رَبِّكَ مَحْظُورًا

21. See how We prefer one above another, and surely the Hereafter will be greater in degrees and greater in preferment.

٢١ انْظُرْ كَيْفَ فَضَّلْنَا بَعْضَهُمْ عَلَىٰ بَعْضٍ وَلَلْآخِرَةُ أَكْبَرُ دَرَجَاتٍ وَأَكْبَرُ تَفْضِيلًا

22. Set not up with Allah any other god (O man) lest you sit down reproved, forsaken.

٢٢ لَا تَجْعَلْ مَعَ اللَّهِ إِلَٰهًا آخَرَ فَتَقْعُدَ مَذْمُومًا مَّخْذُولًا

23. Your Lord has decreed, that you worship none save Him, and (that you show) kindness to parents. If one of them or both of them attain to old age with you, say not "Fie" unto them nor repulse them, but speak unto them a gracious word.

٢٣ وَقَضَىٰ رَبُّكَ أَلَّا تَعْبُدُوا إِلَّا إِيَّاهُ وَبِالْوَالِدَيْنِ إِحْسَانًا إِمَّا يَبْلُغَنَّ عِنْدَكَ الْكِبَرَ أَحَدُهُمَا أَوْ كِلَاهُمَا فَلَا تَقُلْ لَهُمَا أُفٍّ وَلَا تَنْهَرْهُمَا وَقُلْ لَهُمَا قَوْلًا كَرِيمًا

24. And lower unto them the wing of submission through mercy, and say: My Lord! Have mercy on them both as they did care for me when I was little.

٢٤ وَاخْفِضْ لَهُمَا جَنَاحَ الذُّلِّ مِنَ الرَّحْمَةِ وَقُلْ رَبِّ ارْحَمْهُمَا كَمَا رَبَّيَانِي صَغِيرًا

25. Your Lord is best aware of what is in your minds. If you are righteous, then lo! He was ever Forgiving unto those who turn (unto Him).

٢٥ رَبُّكُمْ أَعْلَمُ بِمَا فِي نُفُوسِكُمْ إِنْ تَكُونُوا صَالِحِينَ فَإِنَّهُ كَانَ لِلْأَوَّابِينَ غَفُورًا

26. Give the kinsman his due, and the needy, and the wayfarer, and squander not (your wealth) in wantonness.

٢٦ وَآتِ ذَا الْقُرْبَىٰ حَقَّهُ وَالْمِسْكِينَ وَابْنَ السَّبِيلِ وَلَا تُبَذِّرْ تَبْذِيرًا

27. Lo! the squanderers were ever brothers of the devils, and the Devil was ever an ingrate to his Lord.

٢٧ إِنَّ الْمُبَذِّرِينَ كَانُوا إِخْوَانَ الشَّيَاطِينِ وَكَانَ الشَّيْطَانُ لِرَبِّهِ كَفُورًا

28. But if you turn away from them, seeking mercy from your Lord, for which you hope, then speak unto them a reasonable word.

29. And let not your hand be chained to your neck nor open it with a complete opening, lest you sit down rebuked, denuded.

30. Lo! your Lord enlarges the provision for whom He will, and straitens (it for whom He will). Lo, He was ever Knower, Seer of His slaves.

31. Slay not your children, fearing a fall to poverty, We shall provide for them and for you. Lo! the slaying of them is great sin.

32. And come not near unto adultery. Lo! it is an abomination and an evil way.

33. And slay not the life which Allah has forbidden save with right. Who is slain wrongfully, We have given power unto his heir, but let him not commit excess in slaying. Lo! he will be helped.

34. Come not near the wealth of the orphan save with that which is better till he come to strength; and keep the covenant. Lo! of the covenant it will be asked.

35. Fill the measure when you measure, and weigh with a right balance; that is meet, and better in the end.

36. (O man), follow not that whereof you have no knowledge. Lo! the hearing and the sight and the heart—of each of these it will be asked.

37. And walk not in the earth exultant. Lo! you can not rend the earth, nor can you stretch to the height of the mountains.

38. The evil of all that is hateful in the sight of your Lord.

﴿٢٨﴾ وَإِمَّا تُعْرِضَنَّ عَنْهُمُ ابْتِغَاءَ رَحْمَةٍ مِّن رَّبِّكَ تَرْجُوهَا فَقُل لَّهُمْ قَوْلًا مَّيْسُورًا

﴿٢٩﴾ وَلَا تَجْعَلْ يَدَكَ مَغْلُولَةً إِلَىٰ عُنُقِكَ وَلَا تَبْسُطْهَا كُلَّ الْبَسْطِ فَتَقْعُدَ مَلُومًا مَّحْسُورًا

﴿٣٠﴾ إِنَّ رَبَّكَ يَبْسُطُ الرِّزْقَ لِمَن يَشَاءُ وَيَقْدِرُ إِنَّهُ كَانَ بِعِبَادِهِ خَبِيرًا بَصِيرًا

﴿٣١﴾ وَلَا تَقْتُلُوا أَوْلَادَكُمْ خَشْيَةَ إِمْلَاقٍ نَّحْنُ نَرْزُقُهُمْ وَإِيَّاكُمْ إِنَّ قَتْلَهُمْ كَانَ خِطْئًا كَبِيرًا

﴿٣٢﴾ وَلَا تَقْرَبُوا الزِّنَىٰ إِنَّهُ كَانَ فَاحِشَةً وَسَاءَ سَبِيلًا

﴿٣٣﴾ وَلَا تَقْتُلُوا النَّفْسَ الَّتِي حَرَّمَ اللَّهُ إِلَّا بِالْحَقِّ وَمَن قُتِلَ مَظْلُومًا فَقَدْ جَعَلْنَا لِوَلِيِّهِ سُلْطَانًا فَلَا يُسْرِف فِّي الْقَتْلِ إِنَّهُ كَانَ مَنصُورًا

﴿٣٤﴾ وَلَا تَقْرَبُوا مَالَ الْيَتِيمِ إِلَّا بِالَّتِي هِيَ أَحْسَنُ حَتَّىٰ يَبْلُغَ أَشُدَّهُ وَأَوْفُوا بِالْعَهْدِ إِنَّ الْعَهْدَ كَانَ مَسْئُولًا

﴿٣٥﴾ وَأَوْفُوا الْكَيْلَ إِذَا كِلْتُمْ وَزِنُوا بِالْقِسْطَاسِ الْمُسْتَقِيمِ ذَٰلِكَ خَيْرٌ وَأَحْسَنُ تَأْوِيلًا

﴿٣٦﴾ وَلَا تَقْفُ مَا لَيْسَ لَكَ بِهِ عِلْمٌ إِنَّ السَّمْعَ وَالْبَصَرَ وَالْفُؤَادَ كُلُّ أُولَٰئِكَ كَانَ عَنْهُ مَسْئُولًا

﴿٣٧﴾ وَلَا تَمْشِ فِي الْأَرْضِ مَرَحًا إِنَّكَ لَن تَخْرِقَ الْأَرْضَ وَلَن تَبْلُغَ الْجِبَالَ طُولًا

﴿٣٨﴾ كُلُّ ذَٰلِكَ كَانَ سَيِّئُهُ عِندَ رَبِّكَ مَكْرُوهًا

39. This is (part) of that wisdom with which your Lord has inspired you (O Muhammad). And set not up with Allah any other god, lest you be cast into Hell, reproved, abandoned.

40. Has your Lord then distinguished you (O men of Makkah) by giving you sons, and has chosen for Himself females from among the angels? Lo! surely you speak an awful word!

41. We verily have displayed (Our warnings) in this Qur'an that they may take heed, but it increases them in nothing save aversion.

42. Say (O Muhammad, to the disbelievers): If there were other gods along with Him, as they say, then had they sought a way against the Lord of the Throne.

43. Glorified is He, and High Exalted above what they say!

44. The seven heavens and the earth and all that is therein praise Him, and there is not a thing but hymns his praise; but you understand not their praise. Lo! He is ever Clement, Forgiving.

45. And when you recite the Qur'an We place between you and those who believe not in the Hereafter a hidden barrier;

46. And We place upon their hearts veils lest they should understand it, and in their ears a deafness; and when you make mention of your Lord alone in the Qur'an, they turn their backs in aversion.

47. We are best aware of what they wish to hear when they give ear to you and when they take secret counsel, when the evildoers say: You follow but a man bewitched.

48. See what similitudes they coin for you, and thus are all astray, and cannot find a road!

٣٩ ذَٰلِكَ مِمَّآ أَوْحَىٰٓ إِلَيْكَ رَبُّكَ مِنَ ٱلْحِكْمَةِ وَلَا تَجْعَلْ مَعَ ٱللَّهِ إِلَٰهًا ءَاخَرَ فَتُلْقَىٰ فِى جَهَنَّمَ مَلُومًا مَّدْحُورًا

٤٠ أَفَأَصْفَىٰكُمْ رَبُّكُم بِٱلْبَنِينَ وَٱتَّخَذَ مِنَ ٱلْمَلَٰٓئِكَةِ إِنَٰثًا إِنَّكُمْ لَتَقُولُونَ قَوْلًا عَظِيمًا

٤١ وَلَقَدْ صَرَّفْنَا فِى هَٰذَا ٱلْقُرْءَانِ لِيَذَّكَّرُوا۟ وَمَا يَزِيدُهُمْ إِلَّا نُفُورًا

٤٢ قُل لَّوْ كَانَ مَعَهُۥٓ ءَالِهَةٌ كَمَا يَقُولُونَ إِذًا لَّٱبْتَغَوْا۟ إِلَىٰ ذِى ٱلْعَرْشِ سَبِيلًا

٤٣ سُبْحَٰنَهُۥ وَتَعَٰلَىٰ عَمَّا يَقُولُونَ عُلُوًّا كَبِيرًا

٤٤ تُسَبِّحُ لَهُ ٱلسَّمَٰوَٰتُ ٱلسَّبْعُ وَٱلْأَرْضُ وَمَن فِيهِنَّ وَإِن مِّن شَىْءٍ إِلَّا يُسَبِّحُ بِحَمْدِهِۦ وَلَٰكِن لَّا تَفْقَهُونَ تَسْبِيحَهُمْ إِنَّهُۥ كَانَ حَلِيمًا غَفُورًا

٤٥ وَإِذَا قَرَأْتَ ٱلْقُرْءَانَ جَعَلْنَا بَيْنَكَ وَبَيْنَ ٱلَّذِينَ لَا يُؤْمِنُونَ بِٱلْأَخِرَةِ حِجَابًا مَّسْتُورًا

٤٦ وَجَعَلْنَا عَلَىٰ قُلُوبِهِمْ أَكِنَّةً أَن يَفْقَهُوهُ وَفِىٓ ءَاذَانِهِمْ وَقْرًا وَإِذَا ذَكَرْتَ رَبَّكَ فِى ٱلْقُرْءَانِ وَحْدَهُۥ وَلَّوْا۟ عَلَىٰٓ أَدْبَٰرِهِمْ نُفُورًا

٤٧ نَّحْنُ أَعْلَمُ بِمَا يَسْتَمِعُونَ بِهِۦٓ إِذْ يَسْتَمِعُونَ إِلَيْكَ وَإِذْ هُمْ نَجْوَىٰٓ إِذْ يَقُولُ ٱلظَّٰلِمُونَ إِن تَتَّبِعُونَ إِلَّا رَجُلًا مَّسْحُورًا

٤٨ ٱنظُرْ كَيْفَ ضَرَبُوا۟ لَكَ ٱلْأَمْثَٰلَ فَضَلُّوا۟ فَلَا يَسْتَطِيعُونَ سَبِيلًا

49. And they say: When we are bones and fragments, shall we, really, be raised up as a new creation?

50. Say: Be you stones or iron

51. Or some created thing that is yet greater in your thoughts! Then they will say: Who shall bring us back (to life). Say: He who created you at the first. Then will they shake their heads at you, and say: When will it be? Say: It will perhaps be soon;

52. A day when He will call you and you will answer with His praise, and you will think that you have tarried but a little while.

53. Tell My bondmen to speak that which is kindlier. Lo! the Devil sows discord among them. Lo! the Devil is for man an open foe.

54. Your Lord is best aware of you. If He will, He will have mercy on you, or if He will, He will punish you. We have not sent you (O Muhammad) as a warden over them.

55. And your Lord is best aware of all who are in the heavens and the earth. And we preferred some of the Prophets above others, and unto David We gave the Psalms.

56. Say: Cry unto those (saints and angels) whom you assume (to be gods) beside Him, yet they have no power to rid you of misfortune nor to change.

57. Those unto whom they cry seek the way of approach to their Lord, which of them shall be the nearest; they hope for His mercy and they fear His doom. Lo! the doom of your Lord is to be shunned.

58. There is not a township[160] but We shall destroy it ere the Day of Resurrection, or punish it with dire punishment. That is set forth in the Book (of Our decrees).

59. Nothing hinders Us from sending portents save that the folk of old denied them. And We gave Thamūd the she-camel—a clear portent—but they did wrong in respect of her. We send not portents save to warn.

60. And (it was a warning) when We told you: Lo! your Lord encompasses mankind, and We appointed the vision[161] which We showed you as an ordeal for mankind, and (likewise) the Accursed Tree in the Qur'an.[162] We warn them, but it increases them in nothing save gross impiety.

61. And when We said unto the angels: Fall down prostrate before Adam and they fell prostrate all save Iblīs, he said: Shall I fall prostrate before that which You have created of clay?

62. He said: Do You see this (creature) whom You have honored above me, if You give me grace until the Day of Resurrection I surely will seize his seed, save but a few.

63. He said: Go, and whoever of them follows you—lo! Hell will be your payment, ample payment.

64. And excite any of them whom you can with your voice, and urge your horse and foot against them, and be a partner in their wealth and children, and promise them. What the Devil promises is but deceit.

65. Lo! My (faithful) bondmen—over them you have no power, and your Lord suffices as (their) guardian.

66. (O mankind), your Lord is He Who drives for you ships upon the sea that you may seek of His bounty. Lo! He was ever Merciful toward you.

---

[160]Or community.
[161]The Prophet's vision of his ascent through the seven heavens.
[162]See Surah 44:43-49.

67. And when harm touches you upon the sea, all unto whom you cry (for succor) fail save Him (alone), but when He brings you safe to land, you turn away, for man was ever thankless.

68. Feel you then secure that He will not cause a slope of the land to engulf you, or send a sandstorm upon you, and then you will find that you have no protector?

69. Or feel you secure that He will not return you to that (plight) a second time, and send against you a hurricane of wind and drown you for your thanklessness, and then you will not find therein that you have any avenger against Us?

70. Truly We have honored the children of Adam. We carry them on the land and the sea, and have made provision of good things for them, and have preferred them above many of those whom We created with a marked preferment.

71. On the day when We shall summon all men with their record, whoever is given his book in his right hand—such will read their book and they will not be wronged a shred.

72. Who is blind here will be blind in the Hereafter, and yet further from the road.

73. And they indeed strove hard to beguile you (Muhammad) away from that with which We have inspired you, that you should invent other than it against Us; and then would they have accepted you as a friend.[163]

74. And if We had not made you wholly firm you might almost have inclined unto them a little.

75. Then had We made you taste a double (punishment) of living and a double (punishment) of dying, then had you found no helper against Us.

٦٧ وَإِذَا مَسَّكُمُ الضُّرُّ فِي الْبَحْرِ ضَلَّ مَنْ تَدْعُونَ إِلَّا إِيَّاهُ فَلَمَّا نَجَّاكُمْ إِلَى الْبَرِّ أَعْرَضْتُمْ وَكَانَ الْإِنْسَانُ كَفُورًا

٦٨ أَفَأَمِنْتُمْ أَنْ يَخْسِفَ بِكُمْ جَانِبَ الْبَرِّ أَوْ يُرْسِلَ عَلَيْكُمْ حَاصِبًا ثُمَّ لَا تَجِدُوا لَكُمْ وَكِيلًا

٦٩ أَمْ أَمِنْتُمْ أَنْ يُعِيدَكُمْ فِيهِ تَارَةً أُخْرَى فَيُرْسِلَ عَلَيْكُمْ قَاصِفًا مِنَ الرِّيحِ فَيُغْرِقَكُمْ بِمَا كَفَرْتُمْ ثُمَّ لَا تَجِدُوا لَكُمْ عَلَيْنَا بِهِ تَبِيعًا

٧٠ وَلَقَدْ كَرَّمْنَا بَنِي آدَمَ وَحَمَلْنَاهُمْ فِي الْبَرِّ وَالْبَحْرِ وَرَزَقْنَاهُمْ مِنَ الطَّيِّبَاتِ وَفَضَّلْنَاهُمْ عَلَى كَثِيرٍ مِمَّنْ خَلَقْنَا تَفْضِيلًا

٧١ يَوْمَ نَدْعُوا كُلَّ أُنَاسٍ بِإِمَامِهِمْ فَمَنْ أُوتِيَ كِتَابَهُ بِيَمِينِهِ فَأُولَئِكَ يَقْرَؤُونَ كِتَابَهُمْ وَلَا يُظْلَمُونَ فَتِيلًا

٧٢ وَمَنْ كَانَ فِي هَذِهِ أَعْمَى فَهُوَ فِي الْآخِرَةِ أَعْمَى وَأَضَلُّ سَبِيلًا

٧٣ وَإِنْ كَادُوا لَيَفْتِنُونَكَ عَنِ الَّذِي أَوْحَيْنَا إِلَيْكَ لِتَفْتَرِيَ عَلَيْنَا غَيْرَهُ وَإِذًا لَاتَّخَذُوكَ خَلِيلًا

٧٤ وَلَوْلَا أَنْ ثَبَّتْنَاكَ لَقَدْ كِدْتَ تَرْكَنُ إِلَيْهِمْ شَيْئًا قَلِيلًا

٧٥ إِذًا لَأَذَقْنَاكَ ضِعْفَ الْحَيَاةِ وَضِعْفَ الْمَمَاتِ ثُمَّ لَا تَجِدُ لَكَ عَلَيْنَا نَصِيرًا

---

[163]More than once, the idolaters offered to compromise with the Prophet.

76. And they indeed wished to scare you from the land that they might drive you forth from thence, and then they would have stayed (there) but a little after you.[164]

77. (Such was Our) method in the case of those whom We sent before you (to mankind), and you will not find for Our method any to change.

78. Establish prayer at the inclining of the sun (after midday) until the dark of night, and (the recital of) the Qur'an at dawn. Lo! (the recital of) the Qur'an at dawn is ever witnessed.

79. And some part of the night awake for it, a spiritual profit for you. It may be that your Lord will raise you to a praised estate.

80. And say: My Lord! Cause me to come in with a firm incoming and to go out with a firm outgoing. And give me from Your presence a sustaining Power.

81. And say: Truth has come and falsehood has vanished away. Lo! falsehood is ever bound to vanish.[165]

82. And We reveal of the Qur'an that which is a healing and a mercy for believers though it increase the evildoers in nothing save ruin.

83. And when We make life pleasant unto man, he turns away and is averse; and when ill touches him he is in des-pair.

84. Say: Each one does according to his rule of conduct, and your Lord is best aware of him whose way is right.

85. They will ask you concerning the Soul. Say: The Soul is by command of my Lord, and of knowledge you have been granted but little.

86. And if We willed We could withdraw that which We have revealed unto you (Muhammad), then would you find no guardian for you against Us in respect thereof.

﷾ وَإِن كَادُوا۟ لَيَسْتَفِزُّونَكَ مِنَ ٱلْأَرْضِ لِيُخْرِجُوكَ مِنْهَا ۖ وَإِذًا لَّا يَلْبَثُونَ خِلَٰفَكَ إِلَّا قَلِيلًا

﷾ سُنَّةَ مَن قَدْ أَرْسَلْنَا قَبْلَكَ مِن رُّسُلِنَا ۖ وَلَا تَجِدُ لِسُنَّتِنَا تَحْوِيلًا

﷾ أَقِمِ ٱلصَّلَوٰةَ لِدُلُوكِ ٱلشَّمْسِ إِلَىٰ غَسَقِ ٱلَّيْلِ وَقُرْءَانَ ٱلْفَجْرِ ۖ إِنَّ قُرْءَانَ ٱلْفَجْرِ كَانَ مَشْهُودًا

﷾ وَمِنَ ٱلَّيْلِ فَتَهَجَّدْ بِهِۦ نَافِلَةً لَّكَ عَسَىٰٓ أَن يَبْعَثَكَ رَبُّكَ مَقَامًا مَّحْمُودًا

﷾ وَقُل رَّبِّ أَدْخِلْنِي مُدْخَلَ صِدْقٍ وَأَخْرِجْنِي مُخْرَجَ صِدْقٍ وَٱجْعَل لِّي مِن لَّدُنكَ سُلْطَٰنًا نَّصِيرًا

﷾ وَقُلْ جَاءَ ٱلْحَقُّ وَزَهَقَ ٱلْبَٰطِلُ ۚ إِنَّ ٱلْبَٰطِلَ كَانَ زَهُوقًا

﷾ وَنُنَزِّلُ مِنَ ٱلْقُرْءَانِ مَا هُوَ شِفَاءٌ وَرَحْمَةٌ لِّلْمُؤْمِنِينَ ۙ وَلَا يَزِيدُ ٱلظَّٰلِمِينَ إِلَّا خَسَارًا

﷾ وَإِذَآ أَنْعَمْنَا عَلَى ٱلْإِنسَٰنِ أَعْرَضَ وَنَـَٔا بِجَانِبِهِۦ ۖ وَإِذَا مَسَّهُ ٱلشَّرُّ كَانَ يَـُٔوسًا

﷾ قُلْ كُلٌّ يَعْمَلُ عَلَىٰ شَاكِلَتِهِۦ فَرَبُّكُمْ أَعْلَمُ بِمَنْ هُوَ أَهْدَىٰ سَبِيلًا

﷾ وَيَسْـَٔلُونَكَ عَنِ ٱلرُّوحِ ۖ قُلِ ٱلرُّوحُ مِنْ أَمْرِ رَبِّي وَمَآ أُوتِيتُم مِّنَ ٱلْعِلْمِ إِلَّا قَلِيلًا

﷾ وَلَئِن شِئْنَا لَنَذْهَبَنَّ بِٱلَّذِىٓ أَوْحَيْنَآ إِلَيْكَ ثُمَّ لَا تَجِدُ لَكَ بِهِۦ عَلَيْنَا وَكِيلًا

---

[164]If, as the *Jalālayn* declare, verses. 76-82 were revealed at al Madinah, the reference here is to the plotting of the Jews and Hypocrites.

[165]These words were recited by the Prophet when he witnessed the destruction of the idols around the Ka'bah after the conquest of Makkah.

87. (It is nothing) but mercy from your Lord. Lo! His kindness unto you was ever great.[166]

٨٧ إِلَّا رَحْمَةً مِّن رَّبِّكَ إِنَّ فَضْلَهُ كَانَ عَلَيْكَ كَبِيرًا

88. Say: Verily, though mankind and the jinn should assemble to produce the like of this Qur'an, they could not produce the like thereof though they were helpers one of another.

٨٨ قُل لَّئِنِ ٱجْتَمَعَتِ ٱلْإِنسُ وَٱلْجِنُّ عَلَىٰٓ أَن يَأْتُوا۟ بِمِثْلِ هَٰذَا ٱلْقُرْءَانِ لَا يَأْتُونَ بِمِثْلِهِ وَلَوْ كَانَ بَعْضُهُمْ لِبَعْضٍ ظَهِيرًا

89. And verily We have displayed for mankind in this Qur'an all kinds of similitudes, but most of mankind refuse anything save disbelief.

٨٩ وَلَقَدْ صَرَّفْنَا لِلنَّاسِ فِى هَٰذَا ٱلْقُرْءَانِ مِن كُلِّ مَثَلٍ فَأَبَىٰٓ أَكْثَرُ ٱلنَّاسِ إِلَّا كُفُورًا

90. And they say: We will not put faith in you till you cause a spring to gush forth from the earth for us;

٩٠ وَقَالُوا۟ لَن نُّؤْمِنَ لَكَ حَتَّىٰ تَفْجُرَ لَنَا مِنَ ٱلْأَرْضِ يَنۢبُوعًا

91. Or you have a garden of date palms and grapes, and cause rivers to gush forth therein abundantly;

٩١ أَوْ تَكُونَ لَكَ جَنَّةٌ مِّن نَّخِيلٍ وَعِنَبٍ فَتُفَجِّرَ ٱلْأَنْهَٰرَ خِلَٰلَهَا تَفْجِيرًا

92. Or you cause the heaven to fall upon us piecemeal, as you have pretended, or bring Allah and the angels as a warrant;

٩٢ أَوْ تُسْقِطَ ٱلسَّمَآءَ كَمَا زَعَمْتَ عَلَيْنَا كِسَفًا أَوْ تَأْتِىَ بِٱللَّهِ وَٱلْمَلَٰٓئِكَةِ قَبِيلًا

93. Or that you have a house of gold; or you ascend up into heaven, and even then we will put no faith in your ascension till you bring down for us a book that we can read. Say (O Muhammad): My Lord be glorified! Am I nothing save a mortal messenger?

٩٣ أَوْ يَكُونَ لَكَ بَيْتٌ مِّن زُخْرُفٍ أَوْ تَرْقَىٰ فِى ٱلسَّمَآءِ وَلَن نُّؤْمِنَ لِرُقِيِّكَ حَتَّىٰ تُنَزِّلَ عَلَيْنَا كِتَٰبًا نَّقْرَؤُهُ قُلْ سُبْحَانَ رَبِّى هَلْ كُنتُ إِلَّا بَشَرًا رَّسُولًا

94. And nothing prevented mankind from believing when the guidance came unto them save that they said: Has Allah sent a mortal as (His) messenger?

٩٤ وَمَا مَنَعَ ٱلنَّاسَ أَن يُؤْمِنُوٓا۟ إِذْ جَآءَهُمُ ٱلْهُدَىٰٓ إِلَّآ أَن قَالُوٓا۟ أَبَعَثَ ٱللَّهُ بَشَرًا رَّسُولًا

95. Say: If there were in the earth angels walking secure, We had sent down for them from heaven an angel as messenger.

٩٥ قُل لَّوْ كَانَ فِى ٱلْأَرْضِ مَلَٰٓئِكَةٌ يَمْشُونَ مُطْمَئِنِّينَ لَنَزَّلْنَا عَلَيْهِم مِّنَ ٱلسَّمَآءِ مَلَكًا رَّسُولًا

96. Say: Allah suffices for a witness between me and you Lo! He is Knower, Seer of His slaves.

٩٦ قُلْ كَفَىٰ بِٱللَّهِ شَهِيدًۢا بَيْنِى وَبَيْنَكُمْ إِنَّهُ كَانَ بِعِبَادِهِ خَبِيرًۢا بَصِيرًا

---

[166]Verses 85-87 are said to have been revealed as the third answer to the third question which some Jewish rabbis prompted the idolaters to ask (the first two questions are answered in the following surah).

97. And he whom Allah guides, he is led aright; while, as for him whom He sends astray, for them you will find no protecting friends beside Him, and We shall assemble them on the Day of Resurrection on their faces, blind, dumb and deaf; their habitation will be Hell; whenever it abates, We increase the flame for them.

98. That is their reward because they disbelieved Our revelations and said: When we are bones and fragments shall we, really, be raised up as a new creation?

99. Have they not seen that Allah Who created the heavens and the earth is Able to create the like of them, and has appointed for them a term whereof there is no doubt? But the wrongdoers refuse anything save disbelief.

100. Say (unto them): If you possessed the treasures of the mercy of my Lord, you would surely hold them back for fear of spending, for man was ever grudging.

101. And verily We gave unto Moses nine tokens, clear proofs (of Allah's Sovereignty). Do but ask the Children of Israel how he came unto them, then Pharaoh said unto him: Lo! I deem you one bewitched, O Moses.

102. He said: In truth you know that none sent down these (portents) save the Lord of the heavens and the earth as proofs, and lo! (for my part) I deem you lost, O Phar-aoh.

103. And he wished to scare them from the land, but We drowned him and those with him, all together.

104. And We said unto the Children of Israel after him: Dwell in the land; but when the promise of the Hereafter comes to pass we shall bring you as a crowd gathered out of various nations.[167]

105. With truth have We sent it down, and with truth has it descended. And We have sent you as nothing else save a bearer of good tidings and a warner.

---

[167] A reference to the dispersal of the Jews as the consequence of their own deeds after God had established them in the land.

106. And (it is) a Qur'an that We have divided, that you may recite it unto mankind at intervals, and We have revealed it by (successive) revelation.

١٠٦ وَقُرْآنًا فَرَقْنَاهُ لِتَقْرَأَهُ عَلَى النَّاسِ عَلَى مُكْثٍ وَنَزَّلْنَاهُ تَنْزِيلًا

107. Say: Believe therein or believe not, lo! those who were given knowledge before it, when it is read unto them, fall down prostrate on their faces, adoring,

١٠٧ قُلْ آمِنُوا بِهِ أَوْ لَا تُؤْمِنُوا إِنَّ الَّذِينَ أُوتُوا الْعِلْمَ مِن قَبْلِهِ إِذَا يُتْلَى عَلَيْهِمْ يَخِرُّونَ لِلْأَذْقَانِ سُجَّدًا

108. Saying: Glory to our Lord! Surely the promise of our Lord must be fulfilled.

١٠٨ وَيَقُولُونَ سُبْحَانَ رَبِّنَا إِنْ كَانَ وَعْدُ رَبِّنَا لَمَفْعُولًا

109. They fall down on their faces, weeping, and it increases humility in them.

١٠٩ وَيَخِرُّونَ لِلْأَذْقَانِ يَبْكُونَ وَيَزِيدُهُمْ خُشُوعًا

110. Say (unto mankind): Cry unto Allah, or cry unto the Beneficent,[168] unto whichever you cry (it is the same). His are the most beautiful names. And you (Muhammad), be not loud voiced in your prayer nor yet silent therein, but follow a way between.

١١٠ قُلِ ادْعُوا اللَّهَ أَوِ ادْعُوا الرَّحْمَٰنَ أَيًّا مَّا تَدْعُوا فَلَهُ الْأَسْمَاءُ الْحُسْنَىٰ وَلَا تَجْهَرْ بِصَلَاتِكَ وَلَا تُخَافِتْ بِهَا وَابْتَغِ بَيْنَ ذَٰلِكَ سَبِيلًا

111. And say: Praise be to Allah, Who has not taken unto Himself a son, and Who has no partner in the Sovereignty, nor has He any protecting friend through dependence. And magnify Him with all magnificence.

١١١ وَقُلِ الْحَمْدُ لِلَّهِ الَّذِي لَمْ يَتَّخِذْ وَلَدًا وَلَمْ يَكُنْ لَّهُ شَرِيكٌ فِي الْمُلْكِ وَلَمْ يَكُنْ لَّهُ وَلِيٌّ مِّنَ الذُّلِّ وَكَبِّرْهُ تَكْبِيرًا

---

[168]The idolaters had a peculiar objection to the name of al Raḥmān, "The Beneficent," in the Qur'an. They said: "We do not know this Raḥmān." Some of them claimed that al Raḥmān was a man living in Yamamah!

The Cave

Al Kahf, "The Cave," takes its name from the story of the youths who took refuge from persecution in a cave (verses 10-27) and were preserved there as if asleep for a long time. Such western writers as Gibbon generally identify the account with the legend of the Seven Sleepers of Ephesus. But a strong tradition in the Muslim world asserts that this story and that of Dhū al Qarnayn ("The Two-Horned One"), in verses 83-98, and possibly also that of Moses and the holy man of God in verses 60-82, were revealed to the Prophet to enable him to answer questions that the Jewish rabbis of Yathrib had instructed the idolaters to ask him to test his prophethood.

The questions were three: "Ask him," said the rabbis," of some youth who were of old, what was their fate, for they have a strange story; and ask him of a much-travelled man who reached the sunrise regions of the earth and the sunset regions thereof, what was his history; and ask him of the Soul, what it is."

The tormentors of the Prophet, who had been to Yathrib to get hints from the Jews, returned to Makkah and asked the Prophet these questions after having told the people that it was to be a crucial test. The Prophet said that he would surely answer them the following day, without adding "if God will," as though he could command God's revelation. As a reproof for that omission, the wished-for revelation was withheld from him for some days. When it came, it included the rebuke contained in verse 24.[169]

There is no reason to doubt the truth of the tradition that connects this surah with the three questions set by Jewish rabbis. The answers must have been considered satisfying, or at least silencing, or else the Jews would certainly have made fun of them when they were taunting the Prophet daily after his flight to Yathrib (al Madinah). That being so, it would seem rash to identify the story with that of the Christian Seven Sleepers. It must belong, as the story of the "Two-Horned One" actually does, to rabbinical lore. The third question is answered in Surah 17:85 ff.

It belongs to the middle group of Makkan surahs.

---

[169]Ibn Hishām, 1:102-103.

The Cave

Revealed at Makkah

*In the name of Allah,
the Beneficent, the Merciful*

1. **P**raise be to Allah Who has revealed the Scripture unto His slave, and has not placed therein any crookedness,

2. (But has made it) straight, to give warning of stern punishment from Him, and to bring unto the believers who do good works the news that theirs will be a fair reward.

3. Wherein they will abide for ever;

4. And to warn those who say: Allah has chosen a son,

5. (A thing) whereof they have no knowledge, nor (had) their fathers. Dreadful is the word that comes out of their mouths. They speak nothing but a lie.

6. Yet it may be, if they believe not in this statement, that you (Muhammad) will torment your soul with grief over their footsteps.

7. Lo! We have placed all that is in the earth as an ornament thereof that we may try them: which of them is best in conduct.

8. And lo! We shall make all that is therein a barren mound.

9. Or deem you that the People of the Cave and the Inscrip-tion are a wonder among Our portents?

10. When the young men fled for refuge to the Cave and said: Our Lord! Give us mercy from Your presence and shape for us right conduct in our plight.

11. Then We sealed up their hearing in the Cave for a number of years.

١١ فَضَرَبْنَا عَلَىٰٓ ءَاذَانِهِمْ فِى ٱلْكَهْفِ سِنِينَ عَدَدًا

12. And afterward We raised them up that We might know which of the two parties would best calculate the time that they had tarried.

١٢ ثُمَّ بَعَثْنَٰهُمْ لِنَعْلَمَ أَىُّ ٱلْحِزْبَيْنِ أَحْصَىٰ لِمَا لَبِثُوٓا۟ أَمَدًا

13. We narrate unto you their story with truth. Lo! they were young men who believed in their Lord, and We increased them in guidance.

١٣ نَحْنُ نَقُصُّ عَلَيْكَ نَبَأَهُم بِٱلْحَقِّ إِنَّهُمْ فِتْيَةٌ ءَامَنُوا۟ بِرَبِّهِمْ وَزِدْنَٰهُمْ هُدًى

14. And We made firm their hearts when they stood forth and said: Our Lord is the Lord of the heavens and the earth. We cry unto no god beside Him, for then should we utter an enormity.

١٤ وَرَبَطْنَا عَلَىٰ قُلُوبِهِمْ إِذْ قَامُوا۟ فَقَالُوا۟ رَبُّنَا رَبُّ ٱلسَّمَٰوَٰتِ وَٱلْأَرْضِ لَن نَّدْعُوَا۟ مِن دُونِهِۦٓ إِلَٰهًا لَّقَدْ قُلْنَآ إِذًا شَطَطًا

15. These, our people, have chosen (other) gods beside Him though they bring no clear warrant (vouchsafed) to them. And who does greater wrong than he who invents a lie concerning Allah?

١٥ هَٰٓؤُلَآءِ قَوْمُنَا ٱتَّخَذُوا۟ مِن دُونِهِۦٓ ءَالِهَةً لَّوْلَا يَأْتُونَ عَلَيْهِم بِسُلْطَٰنٍ بَيِّنٍ فَمَنْ أَظْلَمُ مِمَّنِ ٱفْتَرَىٰ عَلَى ٱللَّهِ كَذِبًا

16. And when you withdraw from them and that which they worship except Allah, then seek refuge in the Cave; your Lord will spread for you of His mercy and will prepare for you a solace in your plight.

١٦ وَإِذِ ٱعْتَزَلْتُمُوهُمْ وَمَا يَعْبُدُونَ إِلَّا ٱللَّهَ فَأْوُۥٓا۟ إِلَى ٱلْكَهْفِ يَنشُرْ لَكُمْ رَبُّكُم مِّن رَّحْمَتِهِۦ وَيُهَيِّئْ لَكُم مِّنْ أَمْرِكُم مِّرْفَقًا

17. And you might have seen the sun when it rose move away from their cave to the right, and when it set go past them on the left, and they were in the cleft thereof. That was (one) of the portents of Allah. He whom Allah guides, he indeed is led aright, and he whom He sends astray, for him you will not find a guiding friend.

١٧ ۞ وَتَرَى ٱلشَّمْسَ إِذَا طَلَعَت تَّزَٰوَرُ عَن كَهْفِهِمْ ذَاتَ ٱلْيَمِينِ وَإِذَا غَرَبَت تَّقْرِضُهُمْ ذَاتَ ٱلشِّمَالِ وَهُمْ فِى فَجْوَةٍ مِّنْهُ ذَٰلِكَ مِنْ ءَايَٰتِ ٱللَّهِ مَن يَهْدِ ٱللَّهُ فَهُوَ ٱلْمُهْتَدِ وَمَن يُضْلِلْ فَلَن تَجِدَ لَهُۥ وَلِيًّا مُّرْشِدًا

18. And you would have deemed them waking though they were asleep, and we caused them to turn over to the right and the left, and their dog stretching out his paws on the threshold. If you had observed them closely you had assuredly turned away from them in flight, and had been filled with awe of them.

١٨ وَتَحْسَبُهُمْ أَيْقَاظًا وَهُمْ رُقُودٌ وَنُقَلِّبُهُمْ ذَاتَ ٱلْيَمِينِ وَذَاتَ ٱلشِّمَالِ وَكَلْبُهُم بَٰسِطٌ ذِرَاعَيْهِ بِٱلْوَصِيدِ لَوِ ٱطَّلَعْتَ عَلَيْهِمْ لَوَلَّيْتَ مِنْهُمْ فِرَارًا وَلَمُلِئْتَ مِنْهُمْ رُعْبًا

19. And in like manner We awakened them that they might question one another. A speaker from among them said: How long have you tarried? They said: We have tarried a day or some part of a day. (Others) said: Your Lord best knows what you have tarried. Now send one of you with this your silver coin unto the city, and let him see what food is purest there and bring you a supply thereof. Let him be courteous and let him not make anyone know of you.

20. For they, if they should come to know of you, will stone you or turn you back to their religion; then you will never prosper.

21. And in like manner We disclosed them (to the people of the city) that they might know that the promise of Allah is true, and that, as for the Hour, there is no doubt concerning it. When (the people of the city) disputed of their case among themselves, they said: Build over them a building; their Lord knows best concerning them. Those who won their point said: We verily shall build a mosque over them.

22. (Some) will say: They were three, their dog the fourth, and (some) say: Five, their dog the sixth, guessing at random; and (some) say: Seven, and their dog the eighth. Say (O Muhammad): My Lord is best aware of their number. None knows them save a few. So contend not concerning them except with an outward contending, and ask not any of them to pronounce concerning them.

23. And say not of anything: Lo! I shall do that tomorrow,

24. Except if Allah will. And remember your Lord when you forget, and say: It may be that my Lord guides me unto a nearer way of truth than this.

١٩ وَكَذَٰلِكَ بَعَثْنَاهُمْ لِيَتَسَاءَلُوا بَيْنَهُمْ قَالَ قَائِلٌ مِّنْهُمْ كَمْ لَبِثْتُمْ قَالُوا لَبِثْنَا يَوْمًا أَوْ بَعْضَ يَوْمٍ قَالُوا رَبُّكُمْ أَعْلَمُ بِمَا لَبِثْتُمْ فَابْعَثُوا أَحَدَكُمْ بِوَرِقِكُمْ هَٰذِهِ إِلَى الْمَدِينَةِ فَلْيَنْظُرْ أَيُّهَا أَزْكَىٰ طَعَامًا فَلْيَأْتِكُمْ بِرِزْقٍ مِّنْهُ وَلْيَتَلَطَّفْ وَلَا يُشْعِرَنَّ بِكُمْ أَحَدًا

٢٠ إِنَّهُمْ إِن يَظْهَرُوا عَلَيْكُمْ يَرْجُمُوكُمْ أَوْ يُعِيدُوكُمْ فِي مِلَّتِهِمْ وَلَن تُفْلِحُوا إِذًا أَبَدًا

٢١ وَكَذَٰلِكَ أَعْثَرْنَا عَلَيْهِمْ لِيَعْلَمُوا أَنَّ وَعْدَ اللَّهِ حَقٌّ وَأَنَّ السَّاعَةَ لَا رَيْبَ فِيهَا إِذْ يَتَنَازَعُونَ بَيْنَهُمْ أَمْرَهُمْ فَقَالُوا ابْنُوا عَلَيْهِم بُنْيَانًا رَّبُّهُمْ أَعْلَمُ بِهِمْ قَالَ الَّذِينَ غَلَبُوا عَلَىٰ أَمْرِهِمْ لَنَتَّخِذَنَّ عَلَيْهِم مَّسْجِدًا

٢٢ سَيَقُولُونَ ثَلَاثَةٌ رَّابِعُهُمْ كَلْبُهُمْ وَيَقُولُونَ خَمْسَةٌ سَادِسُهُمْ كَلْبُهُمْ رَجْمًا بِالْغَيْبِ وَيَقُولُونَ سَبْعَةٌ وَثَامِنُهُمْ كَلْبُهُمْ قُل رَّبِّي أَعْلَمُ بِعِدَّتِهِم مَّا يَعْلَمُهُمْ إِلَّا قَلِيلٌ فَلَا تُمَارِ فِيهِمْ إِلَّا مِرَاءً ظَاهِرًا وَلَا تَسْتَفْتِ فِيهِم مِّنْهُمْ أَحَدًا

٢٣ وَلَا تَقُولَنَّ لِشَيْءٍ إِنِّي فَاعِلٌ ذَٰلِكَ غَدًا

٢٤ إِلَّا أَن يَشَاءَ اللَّهُ وَاذْكُر رَّبَّكَ إِذَا نَسِيتَ وَقُلْ عَسَىٰ أَن يَهْدِيَنِ رَبِّي لِأَقْرَبَ مِنْ هَٰذَا رَشَدًا

25. So they tarried in their Cave three hundred years and some add nine more.

26. Say: Allah is best aware how long they tarried. His is the Invisible of the heavens and the earth. How clear of sight is He and keen of hearing! They have no protecting friend beside Him, and He makes none to share in His government.

27. And recite that which has been revealed unto you of the scripture of your Lord. There is none who can change His words, and you will find no refuge beside Him.

28. Restrain yourself along with those who cry unto their Lord at morn and evening, seeking His countenance; and let not your eyes overlook them, desiring the pomp of the life of the world; and obey not him whose heart We have made heedless of Our remembrance, who follows his own lust and whose case has been abandoned.

29. Say: (It is) the truth from the Lord of you (all). Then whoever will, let him believe, and whoever will, let him disbelieve. Lo! We have prepared for disbelievers Fire. Its tent encloses them. If they ask for showers, they will be showered with water like to molten lead which burns the faces. Calamitous the drink and ill the resting place!

30. Lo! as for those who believe and do good works—Lo! We suffer not the reward of one whose work is goodly to be lost.

31. As for such, theirs will be Gardens of Eden, wherein rivers flow beneath them; therein they will be given armlets of gold and will wear green robes of finest silk and gold embroidery, reclining upon thrones therein. Blest the reward, and fair the resting place!

٢٥ وَلَبِثُوا فِي كَهْفِهِمْ ثَلَاثَ مِائَةٍ سِنِينَ وَازْدَادُوا تِسْعًا

٢٦ قُلِ اللَّهُ أَعْلَمُ بِمَا لَبِثُوا لَهُ غَيْبُ السَّمَوَاتِ وَالْأَرْضِ أَبْصِرْ بِهِ وَأَسْمِعْ مَا لَهُمْ مِنْ دُونِهِ مِنْ وَلِيٍّ وَلَا يُشْرِكُ فِي حُكْمِهِ أَحَدًا

٢٧ وَاتْلُ مَا أُوحِيَ إِلَيْكَ مِنْ كِتَابِ رَبِّكَ لَا مُبَدِّلَ لِكَلِمَاتِهِ وَلَنْ تَجِدَ مِنْ دُونِهِ مُلْتَحَدًا

٢٨ وَاصْبِرْ نَفْسَكَ مَعَ الَّذِينَ يَدْعُونَ رَبَّهُمْ بِالْغَدَاةِ وَالْعَشِيِّ يُرِيدُونَ وَجْهَهُ وَلَا تَعْدُ عَيْنَاكَ عَنْهُمْ تُرِيدُ زِينَةَ الْحَيَوةِ الدُّنْيَا وَلَا تُطِعْ مَنْ أَغْفَلْنَا قَلْبَهُ عَنْ ذِكْرِنَا وَاتَّبَعَ هَوَاهُ وَكَانَ أَمْرُهُ فُرُطًا

٢٩ وَقُلِ الْحَقُّ مِنْ رَبِّكُمْ فَمَنْ شَاءَ فَلْيُؤْمِنْ وَمَنْ شَاءَ فَلْيَكْفُرْ إِنَّا أَعْتَدْنَا لِلظَّالِمِينَ نَارًا أَحَاطَ بِهِمْ سُرَادِقُهَا وَإِنْ يَسْتَغِيثُوا يُغَاثُوا بِمَاءٍ كَالْمُهْلِ يَشْوِي الْوُجُوهَ بِئْسَ الشَّرَابُ وَسَاءَتْ مُرْتَفَقًا

٣٠ إِنَّ الَّذِينَ آمَنُوا وَعَمِلُوا الصَّالِحَاتِ إِنَّا لَا نُضِيعُ أَجْرَ مَنْ أَحْسَنَ عَمَلًا

٣١ أُولَئِكَ لَهُمْ جَنَّاتُ عَدْنٍ تَجْرِي مِنْ تَحْتِهِمُ الْأَنْهَارُ يُحَلَّوْنَ فِيهَا مِنْ أَسَاوِرَ مِنْ ذَهَبٍ وَيَلْبَسُونَ ثِيَابًا خُضْرًا مِنْ سُنْدُسٍ وَإِسْتَبْرَقٍ مُتَّكِئِينَ فِيهَا عَلَى الْأَرَائِكِ نِعْمَ الثَّوَابُ وَحَسُنَتْ مُرْتَفَقًا

32. Coin for them a similitude: Two men, unto one of whom We had assigned two gardens of grapes, and We had surrounded both with date palms and had put between them tillage.

33. Each of the gardens gave its fruit and withheld nothing thereof. And We caused a river to gush forth therein.

34. And he had fruit. And he said unto his comrade, when he spoke with him: I am more than you in wealth, and stronger in respect of men.

35. And he went into his garden, while he (thus) wronged himself. He said: I think not that all this will ever perish.

36. I think not that the Hour will ever come, and if indeed I am brought back unto my Lord I surely shall find better than this as a resort.

37. And his comrade, while he disputed with him, exclaimed: Do you disbelieve in Him Who created you of dust, then of a drop (of seed), and then fashioned you a man?

38. But as for me He is Allah, my Lord, and I ascribe unto my Lord no partner.

39. If only, when you entered your garden, you had said: That which Allah wills (will come to pass)! There is no strength save in Allah! Though you see me as less than you in wealth and children.

40. Yet it may be that my Lord will give me better than your garden, and will send on it a bolt from heaven, and some morning it will be a smooth hillside,

41. Or some morning the water thereof will be lost in the earth so that you can not make search for it.

42. And his fruit was beset (with destruction). Then began he to wring his hands for all that he had spent upon it, when (now) it was all ruined on its trellises, and to say: Would that I had ascribed no partner to my Lord!

43. And he had no troop of men to help him as against Allah, nor could he save himself.

44. In this case is protection only from Allah, the True. He is best for reward, and best for consequence.

45. And coin for them the similitude of the life of the world as water which We send down from the sky, and the vegetation of the earth mingles with it and then becomes dry twigs that the winds scatter. Allah is Able to do all things.

46. Wealth and children are an ornament of the life of the world. But the good deeds which endure are better in your Lord's sight for reward, and better in respect of hope.

47. And (bethink you of) the Day when We remove the hills and you see the earth emerging, and We gather them together so as to leave not one of them behind.

48. And they are set before your Lord in ranks (and it is said unto them): Now verily have you come unto Us as We created you at the first. But you thought that We had set no appointed time for you.

49. And the Book is placed, and you see criminals fearful of that which is therein, and they say: What Kind of a book is this that leaves not a small thing nor a great thing but has counted it! And they find all that they did confronting them, and your Lord wrongs no one.

﴿٤١﴾ أَوْ يُصْبِحَ مَاؤُهَا غَوْرًا فَلَن تَسْتَطِيعَ لَهُ طَلَبًا

﴿٤٢﴾ وَأُحِيطَ بِثَمَرِهِ فَأَصْبَحَ يُقَلِّبُ كَفَّيْهِ عَلَى مَا أَنفَقَ فِيهَا وَهِيَ خَاوِيَةٌ عَلَى عُرُوشِهَا وَيَقُولُ يَالَيْتَنِى لَمْ أُشْرِكْ بِرَبِّى أَحَدًا

﴿٤٣﴾ وَلَمْ تَكُن لَّهُ فِئَةٌ يَنصُرُونَهُ مِن دُونِ اللّهِ وَمَا كَانَ مُنتَصِرًا

﴿٤٤﴾ هُنَالِكَ الْوَلَايَةُ لِلّهِ الْحَقِّ هُوَ خَيْرٌ ثَوَابًا وَخَيْرٌ عُقْبًا

﴿٤٥﴾ وَاضْرِبْ لَهُم مَّثَلَ الْحَيَوةِ الدُّنْيَا كَمَاءٍ أَنزَلْنَهُ مِنَ السَّمَاءِ فَاخْتَلَطَ بِهِ نَبَاتُ الْأَرْضِ فَأَصْبَحَ هَشِيمًا تَذْرُوهُ الرِّيَحُ وَكَانَ اللّهُ عَلَى كُلِّ شَيْءٍ مُّقْتَدِرًا

﴿٤٦﴾ الْمَالُ وَالْبَنُونَ زِينَةُ الْحَيَوةِ الدُّنْيَا وَالْبَقِيَتُ الصَّلِحَتُ خَيْرٌ عِندَ رَبِّكَ ثَوَابًا وَخَيْرٌ أَمَلًا

﴿٤٧﴾ وَيَوْمَ نُسَيِّرُ الْجِبَالَ وَتَرَى الْأَرْضَ بَارِزَةً وَحَشَرْنَهُمْ فَلَمْ نُغَادِرْ مِنْهُمْ أَحَدًا

﴿٤٨﴾ وَعُرِضُوا عَلَى رَبِّكَ صَفًّا لَّقَدْ جِئْتُمُونَا كَمَا خَلَقْنَكُمْ أَوَّلَ مَرَّةٍ بَلْ زَعَمْتُمْ أَلَّن نَّجْعَلَ لَكُم مَّوْعِدًا

﴿٤٩﴾ وَوُضِعَ الْكِتَبُ فَتَرَى الْمُجْرِمِينَ مُشْفِقِينَ مِمَّا فِيهِ وَيَقُولُونَ يَاوَيْلَتَنَا مَالِ هَذَا الْكِتَبِ لَا يُغَادِرُ صَغِيرَةً وَلَا كَبِيرَةً إِلَّا أَحْصَهَا وَوَجَدُوا مَا عَمِلُوا حَاضِرًا وَلَا يَظْلِمُ رَبُّكَ أَحَدًا

50. And (remember) when We said unto the angels: Fall prostrate before Adam, and they fell prostrate, all save Iblīs. He was of the Jinn,[170] so he rebelled against his Lord's command. Will you choose him and his seed for your protecting friends instead of Me, when they are an enemy unto you? Calamitous is the exchange for evildoers!

51. I made them not to witness the creation of the heavens and the earth, nor their own creation; nor choose I misleaders for (My) helpers.

52. And (be mindful of) the Day when He will say: Call those partners of Mine whom you pretended. Then they will cry unto them, but they will not hear their prayer, and We shall set a gulf of doom between them.

53. And the criminals beheld the Fire and knew that they were about to fall therein, and they found no way of escape thence:

54. And surely We have displayed for mankind in this Qur'an all manner of similitudes, but man is more than anything contentious.

55. And nothing hinders mankind from believing when the guidance comes unto them, and from asking for forgiveness of their Lord, unless (it be that they wish) that the judgment of the men of old should come upon them or (that) they should be confronted with the Doom.

56. We send not the messengers save as bearers of good news and warners. Those who disbelieve contend with falsehood in order to refute the Truth thereby. And they take Our revelations and that with which they are threatened as a jest.

57. And who does greater wrong than he who has been reminded of the revelations of his Lord, yet turns away from them and forgets what his hands send forward (to the Judgment)? Lo! on their hearts We have placed coverings so that they understand not, and in their ears a deafness. And though you call them to guidance, in that case they can never be led aright.

---

[170]The fact that Iblīs (Satan) is one of the Jinn and not of the angels, though he was among the latter, explains his disobedience, for Jinn can choose their path of conduct (like man, they have free will).

58. Your Lord is the Forgiver, Full of Mercy. If He took them to task (now) for what they earn, He would hasten on the doom for them; but theirs is an appointed term from which they will find no escape.

59. And (all) those townships! We destroyed them when they did wrong, and We appointed a fixed time for their destruction.

60. And when Moses said unto his servant: I will not give up until I reach the point where the two seas meet, though I march on for ages.

61. And when they reached the point where the two met, they forgot their fish, and it took its way into the waters, being free.

62. And when they had gone further, he said unto his servant: Bring us our breakfast. Surely we have found fatigue in this our journey.

63. He said: Did you see, when we took refuge on the rock, and I forgot the fish and none but Satan caused me to forget to mention it, it took its way into the waters by a marvel.

64. He said: This is that which we have been seeking. They retraced their steps again.

65. Then found they one of Our slaves, unto whom We had given mercy from Us, and had taught him knowledge from Our presence.

66. Moses said unto him: May I follow you, to the end that you may teach me right conduct of that which you have been taught?

67. He said: Lo! you can not bear with me.

68. How can you bear with that whereof you can not compass any knowledge?

٥٨ وَرَبُّكَ الْغَفُورُ ذُو الرَّحْمَةِ لَوْ يُؤَاخِذُهُم بِمَا كَسَبُوا لَعَجَّلَ لَهُمُ الْعَذَابَ بَل لَّهُم مَّوْعِدٌ لَّن يَجِدُوا مِن دُونِهِ مَوْئِلًا

٥٩ وَتِلْكَ الْقُرَىٰ أَهْلَكْنَاهُمْ لَمَّا ظَلَمُوا وَجَعَلْنَا لِمَهْلِكِهِم مَّوْعِدًا

٦٠ وَإِذْ قَالَ مُوسَىٰ لِفَتَاهُ لَا أَبْرَحُ حَتَّىٰ أَبْلُغَ مَجْمَعَ الْبَحْرَيْنِ أَوْ أَمْضِيَ حُقُبًا

٦١ فَلَمَّا بَلَغَا مَجْمَعَ بَيْنِهِمَا نَسِيَا حُوتَهُمَا فَاتَّخَذَ سَبِيلَهُ فِي الْبَحْرِ سَرَبًا

٦٢ فَلَمَّا جَاوَزَا قَالَ لِفَتَاهُ آتِنَا غَدَاءَنَا لَقَدْ لَقِينَا مِن سَفَرِنَا هَٰذَا نَصَبًا

٦٣ قَالَ أَرَأَيْتَ إِذْ أَوَيْنَا إِلَى الصَّخْرَةِ فَإِنِّي نَسِيتُ الْحُوتَ وَمَا أَنسَانِيهُ إِلَّا الشَّيْطَانُ أَنْ أَذْكُرَهُ وَاتَّخَذَ سَبِيلَهُ فِي الْبَحْرِ عَجَبًا

٦٤ قَالَ ذَٰلِكَ مَا كُنَّا نَبْغِ فَارْتَدَّا عَلَىٰ آثَارِهِمَا قَصَصًا

٦٥ فَوَجَدَا عَبْدًا مِّنْ عِبَادِنَا آتَيْنَاهُ رَحْمَةً مِّنْ عِندِنَا وَعَلَّمْنَاهُ مِن لَّدُنَّا عِلْمًا

٦٦ قَالَ لَهُ مُوسَىٰ هَلْ أَتَّبِعُكَ عَلَىٰ أَن تُعَلِّمَنِ مِمَّا عُلِّمْتَ رُشْدًا

٦٧ قَالَ إِنَّكَ لَن تَسْتَطِيعَ مَعِيَ صَبْرًا

٦٨ وَكَيْفَ تَصْبِرُ عَلَىٰ مَا لَمْ تُحِطْ بِهِ خُبْرًا

69. He said: Allah willing, you shall find me patient and I shall not in anything gainsay you.

70. He said: Well, if you go with me, ask me not concerning anything till I myself mention of it unto you.

71. So the two set out till, when they were in the ship, he made a hole therein. (Moses) said: Have you made a hole therein to drown the folk thereof? You surely have done a dreadful thing.

72. He said: Did I not tell you you could not bear with me?

73. (Moses) said: Be not angry with me that I forgot, and be not hard upon me for my fault.

74. So the two journeyed on till, when they met a lad, he slew him. (Moses) said: What! Have you slain an innocent soul who has slain no man? Surely you have done a horrid thing.

75. He said: Did I not tell you that you could not bear with me?

76. (Moses) said: If I ask you after this concerning anything, keep not company with me. You have received an excuse from me.

77. So the two journeyed on till, when they came unto the folk of a certain township, they asked its folk for food, but they refused to make them guests. And they found therein a wall upon the point of falling into ruin, and he repaired it. (Moses) said: If you had wished, you could have taken payment for it.

78. He said: This is the parting between you and me! I will announce unto you the interpretation of that you could not bear with patience.

٦٩ قَالَ سَتَجِدُنِيَ إِن شَآءَ ٱللَّهُ صَابِرًا وَلَآ أَعْصِى لَكَ أَمْرًا

٧٠ قَالَ فَإِنِ ٱتَّبَعْتَنِى فَلَا تَسْـَٔلْنِى عَن شَىْءٍ حَتَّىٰ أُحْدِثَ لَكَ مِنْهُ ذِكْرًا

٧١ فَٱنطَلَقَا حَتَّىٰ إِذَا رَكِبَا فِى ٱلسَّفِينَةِ خَرَقَهَا قَالَ أَخَرَقْتَهَا لِتُغْرِقَ أَهْلَهَا لَقَدْ جِئْتَ شَيْئًا إِمْرًا

٧٢ قَالَ أَلَمْ أَقُلْ إِنَّكَ لَن تَسْتَطِيعَ مَعِىَ صَبْرًا

٧٣ قَالَ لَا تُؤَاخِذْنِى بِمَا نَسِيتُ وَلَا تُرْهِقْنِى مِنْ أَمْرِى عُسْرًا

٧٤ فَٱنطَلَقَا حَتَّىٰ إِذَا لَقِيَا غُلَٰمًا فَقَتَلَهُۥ قَالَ أَقَتَلْتَ نَفْسًا زَكِيَّةًۢ بِغَيْرِ نَفْسٍ لَّقَدْ جِئْتَ شَيْئًا نُّكْرًا

٧٥ ۞ قَالَ أَلَمْ أَقُل لَّكَ إِنَّكَ لَن تَسْتَطِيعَ مَعِىَ صَبْرًا

٧٦ قَالَ إِن سَأَلْتُكَ عَن شَىْءٍۭ بَعْدَهَا فَلَا تُصَٰحِبْنِى قَدْ بَلَغْتَ مِن لَّدُنِّى عُذْرًا

٧٧ فَٱنطَلَقَا حَتَّىٰ إِذَآ أَتَيَآ أَهْلَ قَرْيَةٍ ٱسْتَطْعَمَآ أَهْلَهَا فَأَبَوْا۟ أَن يُضَيِّفُوهُمَا فَوَجَدَا فِيهَا جِدَارًا يُرِيدُ أَن يَنقَضَّ فَأَقَامَهُۥ قَالَ لَوْ شِئْتَ لَتَّخَذْتَ عَلَيْهِ أَجْرًا

٧٨ قَالَ هَٰذَا فِرَاقُ بَيْنِى وَبَيْنِكَ سَأُنَبِّئُكَ بِتَأْوِيلِ مَا لَمْ تَسْتَطِع عَّلَيْهِ صَبْرًا

79. As for the ship, it belonged to some poor people working on the water,[171] and I wished to mar it, for there was a king behind them who is taking every ship by force.

80. And as for the lad, his parents were believers and We feared lest he should oppress them by rebellion and disbelief.

81. And We intended that their Lord should change him for them for one better in purity and nearer to mercy.

82. And as for the wall, it belonged to two orphan boys in the city, and there was beneath it a treasure belonging to them and their father had been righteous, and your Lord intended that they should come to their full strength and should bring forth their treasure as a mercy from your Lord; and I did it not upon my own command. Such is the interpretation of that with which you could not bear.

83. They will ask you of Dhū al Qarnayn. Say: I shall recite unto you a (true) account of him.

84. Lo! We made him strong in the land and gave him unto everything a road.

85. And he followed a road

86. Till, when he reached the setting place of the sun, he found it setting in a muddy spring, and found a people thereabout: We said: O Dhū al Qarnayn! Either punish or show them kindness.

---

[171] It could be "sea" or "river."

87. He said: As for him who does wrong, we shall punish him, and then he will be brought back unto his Lord, who will punish him with awful punishment!

٨٧ قَالَ أَمَّا مَن ظَلَمَ فَسَوْفَ نُعَذِّبُهُ ثُمَّ يُرَدُّ إِلَى رَبِّهِ فَيُعَذِّبُهُ عَذَابًا نُّكْرًا

88. But as for him who believes and does right, good will be his reward, and We shall speak unto him a mild command.

٨٨ وَأَمَّا مَنْ ءَامَنَ وَعَمِلَ صَٰلِحًا فَلَهُ جَزَآءً الْحُسْنَىٰ وَسَنَقُولُ لَهُ مِنْ أَمْرِنَا يُسْرًا

89. Then he followed a road

٨٩ ثُمَّ أَتْبَعَ سَبَبًا

90. Till, when he reached the rising place of the sun, he found it rising on a people for whom We had appointed no shelter therefrom.

٩٠ حَتَّىٰ إِذَا بَلَغَ مَطْلِعَ الشَّمْسِ وَجَدَهَا تَطْلُعُ عَلَىٰ قَوْمٍ لَّمْ نَجْعَل لَّهُم مِّن دُونِهَا سِتْرًا

91. So (it was). And We knew all concerning him.

٩١ كَذَٰلِكَ وَقَدْ أَحَطْنَا بِمَا لَدَيْهِ خُبْرًا

92. Then he followed a road

٩٢ ثُمَّ أَتْبَعَ سَبَبًا

93. Till, when he came between the two mountains, he found upon their hither side a folk that scarce could understand a saying.

٩٣ حَتَّىٰ إِذَا بَلَغَ بَيْنَ السَّدَّيْنِ وَجَدَ مِن دُونِهِمَا قَوْمًا لَّا يَكَادُونَ يَفْقَهُونَ قَوْلًا

94. They said: O Dhū al Qarnayn! Lo! Gog and Magog are spoiling the land. So may we pay you tribute on condition that you set a barrier between us and them?

٩٤ قَالُوا يَٰذَا الْقَرْنَيْنِ إِنَّ يَأْجُوجَ وَمَأْجُوجَ مُفْسِدُونَ فِي الْأَرْضِ فَهَلْ نَجْعَلُ لَكَ خَرْجًا عَلَىٰ أَن تَجْعَلَ بَيْنَنَا وَبَيْنَهُمْ سَدًّا

95. He said: That wherein my Lord has established me is better (than your tribute). Do but help me with strength (of men), I will set between you and them a bank.

٩٥ قَالَ مَا مَكَّنِّي فِيهِ رَبِّي خَيْرٌ فَأَعِينُونِي بِقُوَّةٍ أَجْعَلْ بَيْنَكُمْ وَبَيْنَهُمْ رَدْمًا

96. Give me chains of iron till, when he had levelled up (the gap) between the cliffs, he said: Blow! till, when he had made it a fire, he said: Bring me molten copper to pour thereon.

٩٦ ءَاتُونِي زُبَرَ الْحَدِيدِ حَتَّىٰ إِذَا سَاوَىٰ بَيْنَ الصَّدَفَيْنِ قَالَ انفُخُوا حَتَّىٰ إِذَا جَعَلَهُ نَارًا قَالَ ءَاتُونِي أُفْرِغْ عَلَيْهِ قِطْرًا

97. And (Gog and Magog) were not able to surmount, nor could they pierce (it).

٩٧ فَمَا اسْطَٰعُوا أَن يَظْهَرُوهُ وَمَا اسْتَطَٰعُوا لَهُ نَقْبًا

98. He said: This is a mercy from my Lord; but when the promise of my Lord comes to pass, He will crush it, for the promise of my Lord is true.

٩٨ قَالَ هَذَا رَحْمَةٌ مِّن رَّبِّى فَإِذَا جَآءَ وَعْدُ رَبِّى جَعَلَهُ دَكَّآءَ وَكَانَ وَعْدُ رَبِّى حَقًّا

99. And on that day We shall let some of them surge against others, and the Trumpet will be blown. Then We shall gather them together in one gathering.

٩٩ ۞ وَتَرَكْنَا بَعْضَهُمْ يَوْمَئِذٍ يَمُوجُ فِى بَعْضٍ وَنُفِخَ فِى الصُّورِ فَجَمَعْنَاهُمْ جَمْعًا

100. On that day We shall present Hell to disbelievers, plain to view,

١٠٠ وَعَرَضْنَا جَهَنَّمَ يَوْمَئِذٍ لِّلْكَافِرِينَ عَرْضًا

101. Those whose eyes were hoodwinked from My reminder, and who could not bear to hear.

١٠١ الَّذِينَ كَانَتْ أَعْيُنُهُمْ فِى غِطَآءٍ عَن ذِكْرِى وَكَانُوا لَا يَسْتَطِيعُونَ سَمْعًا

102. Do disbelievers reckon that they can choose My bondmen as protecting friends beside Me? Lo! We have prepared Hell as a welcome for the disbelievers.

١٠٢ أَفَحَسِبَ الَّذِينَ كَفَرُوا أَن يَتَّخِذُوا عِبَادِى مِن دُونِى أَوْلِيَآءَ إِنَّا أَعْتَدْنَا جَهَنَّمَ لِلْكَافِرِينَ نُزُلًا

103. Say: Shall We inform you who will be the greatest losers by their works?

١٠٣ قُلْ هَلْ نُنَبِّئُكُم بِالْأَخْسَرِينَ أَعْمَالًا

104. Those whose effort goes astray in the life of the world, and yet they reckon that they do good work.

١٠٤ الَّذِينَ ضَلَّ سَعْيُهُمْ فِى الْحَيَوةِ الدُّنْيَا وَهُمْ يَحْسَبُونَ أَنَّهُمْ يُحْسِنُونَ صُنْعًا

105. Those are they who disbelieve in the revelations of their Lord and in the meeting with Him. Therefor their works are vain, and on the Day of Resurrection We assign no weight to them.

١٠٥ أُوْلَئِكَ الَّذِينَ كَفَرُوا بِآيَاتِ رَبِّهِمْ وَلِقَآئِهِ فَحَبِطَتْ أَعْمَالُهُمْ فَلَا نُقِيمُ لَهُمْ يَوْمَ الْقِيَامَةِ وَزْنًا

106. That is their reward: Hell, because they disbelieved, and made a jest of Our revelations and Our messengers.

١٠٦ ذَلِكَ جَزَآؤُهُمْ جَهَنَّمُ بِمَا كَفَرُوا وَاتَّخَذُوا آيَاتِى وَرُسُلِى هُزُوًا

107. Lo! those who believe and do good works, theirs are the Gardens of Paradise, for welcome,

١٠٧ إِنَّ الَّذِينَ آمَنُوا وَعَمِلُوا الصَّالِحَاتِ كَانَتْ لَهُمْ جَنَّاتُ الْفِرْدَوْسِ نُزُلًا

108. Wherein they will abide, with no desire to be removed from thence.

١٠٨ خَالِدِينَ فِيهَا لَا يَبْغُونَ عَنْهَا حِوَلًا

109. Say: Though the sea became ink for the Words of my Lord, surely the sea would be used up before the Words of my Lord were exhausted, even though We brought the like thereof to help.

قُل لَّوْ كَانَ ٱلْبَحْرُ مِدَادًا لِّكَلِمَٰتِ رَبِّى لَنَفِدَ ٱلْبَحْرُ قَبْلَ أَن تَنفَدَ كَلِمَٰتُ رَبِّى وَلَوْ جِئْنَا بِمِثْلِهِۦ مَدَدًا ١٠٩

110. Say: I am only a mortal like you. My Lord inspires in me that your God is only One God. And whoever hopes for the meeting with his Lord, let him do righteous work, and make none sharer of the worship due unto his Lord.

قُلْ إِنَّمَآ أَنَا۠ بَشَرٌ مِّثْلُكُمْ يُوحَىٰٓ إِلَىَّ أَنَّمَآ إِلَٰهُكُمْ إِلَٰهٌ وَٰحِدٌ فَمَن كَانَ يَرْجُوا۟ لِقَآءَ رَبِّهِۦ فَلْيَعْمَلْ عَمَلًا صَٰلِحًا وَلَا يُشْرِكْ بِعِبَادَةِ رَبِّهِۦٓ أَحَدًا ١١٠

Mary

Maryam takes its name from verses 16 ff. That it is a quite early Makkan revelation is established by the following tradition: In the fifth year of the Prophet's mission (the ninth year before the Prophet's emigration to al Madinah), the Prophet allowed a number of the poorer converts to emigrate to Abyssinia, a Christian country, where they would not be persecuted for worshipping the One God. This is known as the first Hijrah. The rulers of Makkah sent ambassadors to ask the Negus (the local ruler) for their extradition. They were accused of having left the religion of their own people without entering the Christian religion and of having done wrong in their own country.

The Negus sent for the refugee's spokesmen, against the wish of the envoys, and in the presence of the bishops of his realm questioned them about their religion. Ja'far ibn Abī Ṭālib, the Prophet's cousin, answered (I translate from the account given by Ibn Isḥāq.):

"We were folk immersed in ignorance, worshipping idols, eating carrion, given to lewdness, severing the ties of kinship, bad neighbors, and the strong among us preyed upon the weak. Thus were we till Allah sent to us a messenger of our own, whose lineage, honesty, trustworthiness, and chastity we knew. He called us to Allah, that we should acknowledge His unity, worship Him, and eschew all the stones and idols that we and our fathers used to worship beside Him. He ordered us to be truthful, to restore the pledge, to observe the ties of kinship, to be good neighbors, to abstain from what is forbidden and from blood. He forbade us from lewdness and false speech, to prey upon the wealth of orphans, to accuse good women, and commanded us to worship Allah only, ascribing nothing unto Him as partner. He enjoined upon us prayer and legal alms and fasting. (And he enumerated for him the teachings of Islam.)" So we trusted him, believed in him, and followed that which he had brought from Allah. We worshiped Allah only and ascribed no partner to Him. We refrained from that which was forbidden to us and indulged in that which was made lawful for us. Our people became hostile to us and tormented us. They sought to turn us from our religion that they might bring us back to the worship of idols from the worship of Allah Most High, and that we might indulge in those iniquities that before we had deemed lawful.

"And when they persecuted and oppressed us, hemmed us in, and kept us from the practice of our religion, we came to your land. We chose you above all others, sought your protection, and hoped that we should not be troubled in your land, O King!"

Then the Negus asked: Do you have with you anything of that which he brought from Allah? Ja'far answered: Yes. Then the Negus said: Relate it to me. Ja'far recited the beginning of *Kāf, Hā', Yā', 'Ayn, Ṣād*—the Arabic letters with which this surah begins (such letters were generally used by the early Muslims instead of titles). Therefore this surah must have been revealed and well known before the departure of the emigrants for Abyssinia.

An early Makkan surah, with the possible exception of verses 59-60, which, according to some authorities, were revealed at al Madinah.

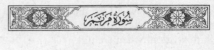

Mary

Revealed at Makkah
In the name of Allah,
the Beneficent, the Merciful

1. Kāf. Hā'. Yā'. 'Ayn. Ṣād.[172]

2. A mention of the mercy of your Lord unto His servant Zachariah.

3. When he cried unto his Lord a cry in secret,

4. Saying: My Lord! Lo! the bones of me wax feeble and my head is shining with grey hair, and I have never been unblessed in prayer to You, my Lord.

5. Lo! I fear my kinsfolk after me, since my wife is barren. Oh, give me from Your presence a successor

6. Who shall inherit of me and inherit (also) of the house of Jacob. And make him, my Lord, acceptable (unto You).

7. (It was said unto him): O Zachariah! Lo! We bring you tidings of a son whose name is John[173]; We have given the same name to none before (him).

8. He said: My Lord! How can I have a son when my wife is barren and I have reached infirm old age?

9. He said: So (it will be). Your Lord says: It is easy for Me, even as I created you before, when you were nothing.

10. He said: My Lord! Appoint for me some token. He said: Your token is that you shall not speak unto mankind three nights with no bodily defect.

11. Then he came forth unto his people from the sanctuary, and signified to them: Glorify your Lord at break of day and fall of night.

---

[172]See Surah 2:1, footnote. -[173]Arabic: Yaḥyā.

12. (And it was said unto his son): O John! Hold the Scrip-ture. And We gave him wisdom when a child.

١٢ يَـٰيَحۡيَىٰ خُذِ ٱلۡكِتَـٰبَ بِقُوَّةٍ وَءَاتَيۡنَـٰهُ ٱلۡحُكۡمَ صَبِيًّا

13. And compassion from Our presence, and purity; and he was devout,

١٣ وَحَنَانًا مِّن لَّدُنَّا وَزَكَوٰةً وَكَانَ تَقِيًّا

14. And dutiful toward his parents. And he was not arrogant, rebellious.

١٤ وَبَرًّۢا بِوَٰلِدَيۡهِ وَلَمۡ يَكُن جَبَّارًا عَصِيًّا

15. Peace on him the day he was born, the day he dies and the day he shall be raised alive!

١٥ وَسَلَـٰمٌ عَلَيۡهِ يَوۡمَ وُلِدَ وَيَوۡمَ يَمُوتُ وَيَوۡمَ يُبۡعَثُ حَيًّا

16. And make mention of Mary in the Scripture, when she had withdrawn from her people to a chamber looking East,

١٦ وَٱذۡكُرۡ فِى ٱلۡكِتَـٰبِ مَرۡيَمَ إِذِ ٱنتَبَذَتۡ مِنۡ أَهۡلِهَا مَكَانًا شَرۡقِيًّا

17. And had chosen seclusion from them. Then We sent unto her Our spirit and it assumed for her the likeness of a perfect man.

١٧ فَٱتَّخَذَتۡ مِن دُونِهِمۡ حِجَابًا فَأَرۡسَلۡنَآ إِلَيۡهَا رُوحَنَا فَتَمَثَّلَ لَهَا بَشَرًا سَوِيًّا

18. She said: Lo! I seek refuge in the Beneficent One from you, if you are God fearing.

١٨ قَالَتۡ إِنِّىٓ أَعُوذُ بِٱلرَّحۡمَـٰنِ مِنكَ إِن كُنتَ تَقِيًّا

19. He said: I am only a messenger of your Lord, that I may bestow on you a faultless son.

١٩ قَالَ إِنَّمَآ أَنَا۠ رَسُولُ رَبِّكِ لِأَهَبَ لَكِ غُلَـٰمًا زَكِيًّا

20. She said: How can I have a son when no mortal has touched me, neither have I been unchaste!

٢٠ قَالَتۡ أَنَّىٰ يَكُونُ لِى غُلَـٰمٌ وَلَمۡ يَمۡسَسۡنِى بَشَرٌ وَلَمۡ أَكُ بَغِيًّا

21. He said: So (it will be). Your Lord says: It is easy for Me. And (it will be) that We may make of him a miracle for mankind and a mercy from Us, and it is a thing ordained.

٢١ قَالَ كَذَٰلِكِ قَالَ رَبُّكِ هُوَ عَلَىَّ هَيِّنٌ وَلِنَجۡعَلَهُۥٓ ءَايَةً لِّلنَّاسِ وَرَحۡمَةً مِّنَّا وَكَانَ أَمۡرًا مَّقۡضِيًّا

22. She conceived him, and she withdrew with him to a far place.

٢٢ فَحَمَلَتۡهُ فَٱنتَبَذَتۡ بِهِۦ مَكَانًا قَصِيًّا

23. The pangs of childbirth drove her unto the trunk of the palm tree. She said: Oh, would that I had died before this and had become a thing forgotten and out of sight.

٢٣ فَأَجَآءَهَا ٱلۡمَخَاضُ إِلَىٰ جِذۡعِ ٱلنَّخۡلَةِ قَالَتۡ يَـٰلَيۡتَنِى مِتُّ قَبۡلَ هَـٰذَا وَكُنتُ نَسۡيًا مَّنسِيًّا

24. Then (one) cried unto her from below her, saying: Grieve not! Your Lord has placed a rivulet beneath you,

٢٤ فَنَادَىٰهَا مِن تَحۡتِهَآ أَلَّا تَحۡزَنِى قَدۡ جَعَلَ رَبُّكِ تَحۡتَكِ سَرِيًّا

25. And shake the trunk of the palm tree toward you, it will cause ripe dates to fall upon you.

26. So eat and drink and be consoled. And if you meet any human, say: Lo! I have vowed a fast unto the Beneficent, so I shall not speak this day to any mortal.

27. Then she brought him to her own folk, carrying him. They said: O Mary! You have come with an amazing (unprecedented) thing.

28. Oh sister of Aaron![174] Your father was not a wicked man nor was your mother a harlot.

29. Then she pointed to him. They said How can we talk to one who is in the cradle, a little child?

30. He spoke: Lo! I am the slave of Allah. He has given me the Scripture and has appointed me a Prophet,

31. And has made me blessed wheresoever I may be, and has enjoined upon me prayer and almsgiving so long as I remain alive,

32. And (has made me) dutiful toward my mother, and has not made me arrogant, unblessed.

33. Peace on me the day I was born, the day I die, and the day I shall be raised alive!

34. Such was Jesus, son of Mary: (this is) a statement of the truth concerning which they doubt.

35. It befits not (the Majesty of) Allah that He should take unto Himself a son. Glory be to Him! When He decrees a thing, He says unto it only: Be! and it is.

٢٥ وَهُزِّي إِلَيْكِ بِجِذْعِ النَّخْلَةِ تُسَاقِطْ عَلَيْكِ رُطَبًا جَنِيًّا

٢٦ فَكُلِي وَاشْرَبِي وَقَرِّي عَيْنًا فَإِمَّا تَرَيِنَّ مِنَ الْبَشَرِ أَحَدًا فَقُولِي إِنِّي نَذَرْتُ لِلرَّحْمَٰنِ صَوْمًا فَلَنْ أُكَلِّمَ الْيَوْمَ إِنْسِيًّا

٢٧ فَأَتَتْ بِهِ قَوْمَهَا تَحْمِلُهُ قَالُوا يَا مَرْيَمُ لَقَدْ جِئْتِ شَيْئًا فَرِيًّا

٢٨ يَا أُخْتَ هَارُونَ مَا كَانَ أَبُوكِ امْرَأَ سَوْءٍ وَمَا كَانَتْ أُمُّكِ بَغِيًّا

٢٩ فَأَشَارَتْ إِلَيْهِ قَالُوا كَيْفَ نُكَلِّمُ مَنْ كَانَ فِي الْمَهْدِ صَبِيًّا

٣٠ قَالَ إِنِّي عَبْدُ اللَّهِ آتَانِيَ الْكِتَابَ وَجَعَلَنِي نَبِيًّا

٣١ وَجَعَلَنِي مُبَارَكًا أَيْنَ مَا كُنْتُ وَأَوْصَانِي بِالصَّلَاةِ وَالزَّكَاةِ مَا دُمْتُ حَيًّا

٣٢ وَبَرًّا بِوَالِدَتِي وَلَمْ يَجْعَلْنِي جَبَّارًا شَقِيًّا

٣٣ وَالسَّلَامُ عَلَيَّ يَوْمَ وُلِدْتُ وَيَوْمَ أَمُوتُ وَيَوْمَ أُبْعَثُ حَيًّا

٣٤ ذَٰلِكَ عِيسَى ابْنُ مَرْيَمَ قَوْلَ الْحَقِّ الَّذِي فِيهِ يَمْتَرُونَ

٣٥ مَا كَانَ لِلَّهِ أَنْ يَتَّخِذَ مِنْ وَلَدٍ سُبْحَانَهُ إِذَا قَضَى أَمْرًا فَإِنَّمَا يَقُولُ لَهُ كُنْ فَيَكُونُ

---

[174]See Surah 3, introduction.

36. And lo! Allah is my Lord and your Lord. So worship Him. That is a straight path.

37. But the sects among them differed: woe unto the disbelievers from the meeting of an awful Day.

38. How much they will see and hear on the Day they come unto Us! Yet the evildoers are today in error manifest.

39. And warn them of the Day of anguish when the case has been decided. Now they are in a state of carelessness, and they believe not.

40. Lo! We inherit the earth and all who are thereon, and unto Us they are returned.

41. And make mention (O Muhammad) in the Scripture of Abraham. Lo! he was a saint, a Prophet.

42. When he said unto his father: O my father! Why worship you that which hears not nor sees, nor can in anything avail you?

43. O my father! Lo! there has come unto me of knowledge that which came not unto you. So follow me, and I will lead you on a straight path.

44. O my father! Worship not the Devil. Lo! the Devil is a rebel unto the Beneficent.

45. O my father! Lo! I fear lest a punishment from the Beneficent overtake you so that you become a comrade of the Devil.

46. He said: Will you reject my gods, O Abraham? If you cease not, I shall surely stone you. Depart from me a long while!

47. He said: Peace be unto you! I shall ask forgiveness of my Lord for you. Lo! He was ever gracious unto me.

٤٧ قَالَ سَلَمٌ عَلَيْكَ سَأَسْتَغْفِرُ لَكَ رَبِّي إِنَّهُ كَانَ بِي حَفِيًّا

48. I shall withdraw from you and that unto which you pray beside Allah, and I shall pray unto my Lord. Perchance, in prayer unto my Lord, I shall not be unblessed.

٤٨ وَأَعْتَزِلُكُمْ وَمَا تَدْعُونَ مِن دُونِ اللّٰهِ وَأَدْعُوا رَبِّي عَسَىٰ أَلَّا أَكُونَ بِدُعَاءِ رَبِّي شَقِيًّا

49. So, when he had withdrawn from them and that which they were worshipping beside Allah, We gave him Isaac and Jacob. Each of them We made a Prophet.

٤٩ فَلَمَّا اعْتَزَلَهُمْ وَمَا يَعْبُدُونَ مِن دُونِ اللّٰهِ وَهَبْنَا لَهُ إِسْحَٰقَ وَيَعْقُوبَ وَكُلًّا جَعَلْنَا نَبِيًّا

50. And We gave them of Our mercy, and assigned to them a high and true renown.

٥٠ وَوَهَبْنَا لَهُم مِّن رَّحْمَتِنَا وَجَعَلْنَا لَهُمْ لِسَانَ صِدْقٍ عَلِيًّا

51. And make mention in the Scripture of Moses. Lo! he was chosen, and he was a messenger (of Allah), a Prophet.

٥١ وَاذْكُرْ فِي الْكِتَٰبِ مُوسَىٰ إِنَّهُ كَانَ مُخْلَصًا وَكَانَ رَسُولًا نَبِيًّا

52. We called him from the right slope of the Mount, and brought him near in communion.

٥٢ وَنَٰدَيْنَٰهُ مِن جَانِبِ الطُّورِ الْأَيْمَنِ وَقَرَّبْنَٰهُ نَجِيًّا

53. And We bestowed upon him of Our mercy his brother Aaron, a Prophet (likewise).

٥٣ وَوَهَبْنَا لَهُ مِن رَّحْمَتِنَا أَخَاهُ هَٰرُونَ نَبِيًّا

54. And make mention in the Scripture of Ishmael. Lo! he was a keeper of his promise, and he was a messenger (of Allah) a Prophet.

٥٤ وَاذْكُرْ فِي الْكِتَٰبِ إِسْمَٰعِيلَ إِنَّهُ كَانَ صَادِقَ الْوَعْدِ وَكَانَ رَسُولًا نَبِيًّا

55. He used to enjoin prayer upon his people and alms giving, and was acceptable in the sight of his Lord.

٥٥ وَكَانَ يَأْمُرُ أَهْلَهُ بِالصَّلَوٰةِ وَالزَّكَوٰةِ وَكَانَ عِندَ رَبِّهِ مَرْضِيًّا

56. And make mention in the Scripture of Idrīs.[175] Lo! he was a saint, a Prophet;

٥٦ وَاذْكُرْ فِي الْكِتَٰبِ إِدْرِيسَ إِنَّهُ كَانَ صِدِّيقًا نَبِيًّا

57. And We raised him to high station.

٥٧ وَرَفَعْنَٰهُ مَكَانًا عَلِيًّا

---

[175]Identified with Enoch.

58. These are they unto whom Allah showed favor from among the Prophets, of the seed of Adam and of those whom We carried (in the ship) with Noah, and of the seed of Abraham and Israel, and from among those whom We guided and chose. When the revelations of the Beneficent were recited unto them, they fell down, adoring and weeping.

٥٨ أُوْلَٰئِكَ ٱلَّذِينَ أَنْعَمَ ٱللَّهُ عَلَيْهِم مِّنَ ٱلنَّبِيِّـۧنَ مِن ذُرِّيَّةِ ءَادَمَ وَمِمَّنْ حَمَلْنَا مَعَ نُوحٍ وَمِن ذُرِّيَّةِ إِبْرَٰهِيمَ وَإِسْرَٰٓءِيلَ وَمِمَّنْ هَدَيْنَا وَٱجْتَبَيْنَا ۚ إِذَا تُتْلَىٰ عَلَيْهِمْ ءَايَٰتُ ٱلرَّحْمَٰنِ خَرُّوا۟ سُجَّدًا وَبُكِيًّا ۩

59. Now there has succeeded them a later generation who have missed Prayer and have followed lusts. But they will meet deception,

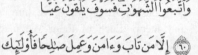

٥٩ ۞ فَخَلَفَ مِنۢ بَعْدِهِمْ خَلْفٌ أَضَاعُوا۟ ٱلصَّلَوٰةَ وَٱتَّبَعُوا۟ ٱلشَّهَوَٰتِ ۖ فَسَوْفَ يَلْقَوْنَ غَيًّا

60. Save him who shall repent and believe and do right. Such will enter the Garden and they will not be wronged in anything—

٦٠ إِلَّا مَن تَابَ وَءَامَنَ وَعَمِلَ صَٰلِحًا فَأُو۟لَٰٓئِكَ يَدْخُلُونَ ٱلْجَنَّةَ وَلَا يُظْلَمُونَ شَيْـًٔا

61. Gardens of Eden, which the Beneficent has promised to His slaves in the Unseen. Lo! His promise is ever sure of fulfillment—

٦١ جَنَّٰتِ عَدْنٍ ٱلَّتِي وَعَدَ ٱلرَّحْمَٰنُ عِبَادَهُۥ بِٱلْغَيْبِ ۚ إِنَّهُۥ كَانَ وَعْدُهُۥ مَأْتِيًّا

62. They hear therein no idle talk, but only Peace; and therein they have food for morn and evening.

٦٢ لَّا يَسْمَعُونَ فِيهَا لَغْوًا إِلَّا سَلَٰمًا ۖ وَلَهُمْ رِزْقُهُمْ فِيهَا بُكْرَةً وَعَشِيًّا

63. Such is the Garden which We cause the devout among Our bondmen to inherit.

٦٣ تِلْكَ ٱلْجَنَّةُ ٱلَّتِي نُورِثُ مِنْ عِبَادِنَا مَن كَانَ تَقِيًّا

64. We (angels) come not down save by commandment of your Lord. Unto Him belongs all that is before us and all that is behind us and all that is between those two, and your Lord was never forgetful—

٦٤ وَمَا نَتَنَزَّلُ إِلَّا بِأَمْرِ رَبِّكَ ۖ لَهُۥ مَا بَيْنَ أَيْدِينَا وَمَا خَلْفَنَا وَمَا بَيْنَ ذَٰلِكَ ۚ وَمَا كَانَ رَبُّكَ نَسِيًّا

65. Lord of the heavens and the earth and all that is between them! Therefore, worship you Him and be you steadfast in His worship. Do you know one that can be named along with Him?

٦٥ رَّبُّ ٱلسَّمَٰوَٰتِ وَٱلْأَرْضِ وَمَا بَيْنَهُمَا فَٱعْبُدْهُ وَٱصْطَبِرْ لِعِبَٰدَتِهِۦ ۚ هَلْ تَعْلَمُ لَهُۥ سَمِيًّا

66. And man says: When I am dead, shall I really be brought forth alive?

٦٦ وَيَقُولُ ٱلْإِنسَٰنُ أَءِذَا مَا مِتُّ لَسَوْفَ أُخْرَجُ حَيًّا

67. Does not man remember that We created him before, when he was nothing?

٦٧ أَوَلَا يَذْكُرُ ٱلْإِنسَٰنُ أَنَّا خَلَقْنَٰهُ مِن قَبْلُ وَلَمْ يَكُ شَيْـًٔا

68. And, by your Lord, surely We shall assemble them and the devils, then We shall bring them, crouching, around Hell.

٦٨ فَوَرَبِّكَ لَنَحْشُرَنَّهُمْ وَالشَّيَاطِينَ ثُمَّ لَنُحْضِرَنَّهُمْ حَوْلَ جَهَنَّمَ جِثِيًّا

69. Then We shall pluck out from every sect whichever of them was most stern in rebellion to the Beneficent.

٦٩ ثُمَّ لَنَنْزِعَنَّ مِن كُلِّ شِيعَةٍ أَيُّهُمْ أَشَدُّ عَلَى الرَّحْمَٰنِ عِتِيًّا

70. And surely We are best aware of those most worthy to be burned therein.

٧٠ ثُمَّ لَنَحْنُ أَعْلَمُ بِالَّذِينَ هُمْ أَوْلَىٰ بِهَا صِلِيًّا

71. There is not one of you but shall approach it. That is a fixed ordinance of your Lord.

٧١ وَإِن مِّنكُمْ إِلَّا وَارِدُهَا كَانَ عَلَىٰ رَبِّكَ حَتْمًا مَّقْضِيًّا

72. Then We shall rescue those who kept from evil, and leave the evildoers crouching there.

٧٢ ثُمَّ نُنَجِّي الَّذِينَ اتَّقَوا وَّنَذَرُ الظَّالِمِينَ فِيهَا جِثِيًّا

73. And when Our clear revelations are recited unto them those who disbelieve say unto those who believe: Which of the two parties (yours or ours) is better in position, and more imposing as an army?

٧٣ وَإِذَا تُتْلَىٰ عَلَيْهِمْ ءَايَٰتُنَا بَيِّنَٰتٍ قَالَ الَّذِينَ كَفَرُوا لِلَّذِينَ ءَامَنُوا أَيُّ الْفَرِيقَيْنِ خَيْرٌ مَّقَامًا وَأَحْسَنُ نَدِيًّا

74. How many a generation have We destroyed before them, who were more imposing in respect of gear and outward seeming!

٧٤ وَكَمْ أَهْلَكْنَا قَبْلَهُم مِّن قَرْنٍ هُمْ أَحْسَنُ أَثَٰثًا وَرِئْيًا

75. Say: As for him who is in error, the Beneficent will surely prolong his span of life until, when they behold that which they were promised, whether it be punishment (in the world), or Hour (of Doom), they will know who is worse in position and who is weaker as an army.

٧٥ قُلْ مَن كَانَ فِي الضَّلَٰلَةِ فَلْيَمْدُدْ لَهُ الرَّحْمَٰنُ مَدًّا حَتَّىٰ إِذَا رَأَوْا مَا يُوعَدُونَ إِمَّا الْعَذَابَ وَإِمَّا السَّاعَةَ فَسَيَعْلَمُونَ مَنْ هُوَ شَرٌّ مَّكَانًا وَأَضْعَفُ جُندًا

76. Allah increases in right guidance those who walk aright, and the good deeds which endure are better in your Lord's sight for reward, and better for resort.

٧٦ وَيَزِيدُ اللَّهُ الَّذِينَ اهْتَدَوْا هُدًى وَالْبَٰقِيَٰتُ الصَّٰلِحَٰتُ خَيْرٌ عِندَ رَبِّكَ ثَوَابًا وَخَيْرٌ مَّرَدًّا

77. Have you seen him who disbelieves in Our revelations and says: Assuredly I shall be given wealth and children!

٧٧ أَفَرَءَيْتَ الَّذِي كَفَرَ بِـَٔايَٰتِنَا وَقَالَ لَأُوتَيَنَّ مَالًا وَوَلَدًا

78. Has he perused the Unseen, or has he made a pact with the Beneficent?

٧٨ أَطَّلَعَ الْغَيْبَ أَمِ اتَّخَذَ عِندَالرَّحْمَٰنِ عَهْدًا

79. Nay, but We shall record that which he says and prolong for him a span of torment.

٧٩ كَلَّا سَنَكْتُبُ مَايَقُولُ وَنَمُدُّ لَهُۥ مِنَ الْعَذَابِ مَدًّا

80. And We shall inherit from him that whereof he spoke, and he will come unto Us, alone (without his wealth and children).

٨٠ وَنَرِثُهُۥ مَايَقُولُ وَيَأْتِينَا فَرْدًا

81. And they have chosen (other) gods beside Allah that they may be a power for them.

٨١ وَاتَّخَذُوا مِن دُونِ اللَّهِ ءَالِهَةً لِّيَكُونُوا لَهُمْ عِزًّا

82. Nay, but they will deny their worship of them, and become opponents unto them.

٨٢ كَلَّا سَيَكْفُرُونَ بِعِبَادَتِهِمْ وَيَكُونُونَ عَلَيْهِمْ ضِدًّا

83. Do you not see that We have set the devils on the disbelievers to confound them with confusion?

٨٣ أَلَمْ تَرَ أَنَّا أَرْسَلْنَا الشَّيَٰطِينَ عَلَى الْكَٰفِرِينَ تَؤُزُّهُمْ أَزًّا

84. So make no haste against them (O Muhammad). We do but count to them a (limited) number (of days).

٨٤ فَلَا تَعْجَلْ عَلَيْهِمْ إِنَّمَا نَعُدُّ لَهُمْ عَدًّا

85. On the Day when We shall gather the righteous unto the Beneficent, a goodly company.

٨٥ يَوْمَ نَحْشُرُ الْمُتَّقِينَ إِلَى الرَّحْمَٰنِ وَفْدًا

86. And drive the criminals unto Hell, a weary herd,

٨٦ وَنَسُوقُ الْمُجْرِمِينَ إِلَىٰ جَهَنَّمَ وِرْدًا

87. They will have no power of intercession, save him who has made a covenant with the Beneficent.

٨٧ لَا يَمْلِكُونَ الشَّفَٰعَةَ إِلَّا مَنِ اتَّخَذَ عِندَ الرَّحْمَٰنِ عَهْدًا

88. And they say: The Beneficent has taken unto Himself a son.

٨٨ وَقَالُوا اتَّخَذَ الرَّحْمَٰنُ وَلَدًا

89. Assuredly you utter a disastrous thing,

٨٩ لَقَدْ جِئْتُمْ شَيْئًا إِدًّا

90. Whereby the heavens are almost torn, and the earth is split asunder and the mountains fall in ruins,

٩٠ تَكَادُ السَّمَٰوَٰتُ يَتَفَطَّرْنَ مِنْهُ وَتَنشَقُّ الْأَرْضُ وَتَخِرُّ الْجِبَالُ هَدًّا

91. That you ascribe unto the Beneficent a son,

٩١ أَن دَعَوْا لِلرَّحْمَٰنِ وَلَدًا

92. When it is not consonant with (the Majesty of) the Beneficent that He should choose a son.

٩٢ وَمَا يَنۢبَغِي لِلرَّحْمَٰنِ أَن يَتَّخِذَ وَلَدًا

93. There is none in the heavens and the earth but comes unto the Beneficent as a slave.

٩٣ إِن كُلُّ مَن فِي السَّمَٰوَٰتِ وَالْأَرْضِ إِلَّا ءَاتِي الرَّحْمَٰنِ عَبْدًا

94. Surely He knows them and numbers them with (right) numbering.

٩٥ لَقَدْ أَحْصَاهُمْ وَعَدَّهُمْ عَدًّا

95. And each one of them will come unto Him on the Day of Resurrection, alone.

٩٤ وَكُلُّهُمْ ءَاتِيهِ يَوْمَ الْقِيَامَةِ فَرْدًا

96. Lo! those who believe and do good works, the Bene-ficent will appoint for them love.

٩٦ إِنَّ الَّذِينَ ءَامَنُوا وَعَمِلُوا الصَّالِحَاتِ سَيَجْعَلُ لَهُمُ الرَّحْمَٰنُ وُدًّا

97. And We make (this Scripture) easy in your tongue, (O Muhammad) only that you may bear good tidings therewith unto those who ward off (evil), and warn therewith the froward folk.

٩٧ فَإِنَّمَا يَسَّرْنَٰهُ بِلِسَانِكَ لِتُبَشِّرَ بِهِ الْمُتَّقِينَ وَتُنذِرَ بِهِ قَوْمًا لُّدًّا

98. And how many a generation before them have We destroyed! Can you (Muhammad) see a single man of them, or hear from them the slightest sound?

٩٨ وَكَمْ أَهْلَكْنَا قَبْلَهُم مِّن قَرْنٍ هَلْ تُحِسُّ مِنْهُم مِّنْ أَحَدٍ أَوْ تَسْمَعُ لَهُمْ رِكْزًا

Ṭā Hā

Ṭā Hā takes its name from the Arabic letters that form the first verse. As in the case of Surah 19, the early date of revelation is established by a strong tradition.

'Umar ibn al Khaṭṭāb, the second political successor of the Prophet, was one of the bitterest opponents of Islam in early days. One day, he went out with his sword intending to kill the Prophet, whom he referred to as "this Sabaean who has split the unity of Quraysh, calls their ideals foolish and their religion shameful, and blasphemes their gods." On the way, he met a friend who dissuaded him by reminding him that if he carried out his plan, he would have to reckon with the vengeance of a powerful clan—"Do you think that the Banū 'Abd Manāf would let you walk on the earth if you slew Muhammad?"—for tribal pride survived religious difference. He continued: "Is it not better for you to return to the folk of your own house and keep them straight?" 'Umar asked: "Which of the folk of my house?" "Your brother-in-law and cousin, Sa'īd ibn Zayd, and your sister, Fāṭimah bint al Khaṭṭāb. By Allah, they have become Muslims and followers of Muhammad in his religion. Look after them."

'Umar, enraged against his sister and brother-in-law, returned home and found with them Khabbāb ibn al 'Aratt. This man had a leaf on which was written *Ṭā Hā* (this *surah*) and was reading it aloud to them. When they heard 'Umar coming, Khabbāb hid in a closet and Fāṭimah hid the leaf under her thigh. But 'Umar had heard Khabbāb reading as he drew near the house. When he entered, he said: "What was that mumbling that I heard?" They said: "You heard nothing." 'Umar said: "By Allah! I have already been informed that you have become followers of Muhammad in his religion." Then he attacked his brother-in-law. Fāṭimah sprang to keep him off her husband, and he struck and wounded her. When he had done that, his sister and his brother-in-law said to him: "Yes, we are Muslims and we believe in Allah and His messenger, so do what you will!" But when 'Umar saw the blood upon his sister, he was sorry for what he had done and said to his sister: "Give me that leaf from which I heard you reading just now, that I may see what Muhammad has brought." 'Umar was a scribe. When he said that, his sister said: "We fear to trust you with it." He said: "Fear not!" and swore by his gods that he would return it to her after he had read it. When he said that, she hoped for his conversion to Islam, but said: "O my brother, you are unclean on account of your idolatry and none may touch it save the purified." Then 'Umar went out and washed himself, and she gave him the leaf.

After he had read it, he said: "How excellent are these words!" and praised it highly. When he heard that, Khabbāb came out to him and said: "O 'Umar, I hope that Allah has brought you in answer to the prayer of the Prophet, for only yesterday I heard him saying: O Allah! Strengthen Islam with Abū al Ḥakam ibn Hishām or 'Umar ibn al Khaṭṭāb; and Allah is Allah, O 'Umar!" At that he said: "O Khabbāb, direct me to Muhammad that I may go to him and become a Muslim."[176]

The conversion of 'Umar took place in the fifth year of the Prophet's mission (the ninth year before the Hijrah), soon after the departure of the emigrants to Abyssinia. At that time, this surah was already written down and in circulation.

An early Makkan surah.

---

[176]Ibn Hishām, 1:119-120.

Ṭā Hā

Revealed at Makkah

*In the name of Allah,
the Beneficent, the Merciful*

1. Ṭā. Hā.

2. We have not revealed unto you (Muhammad) this Qur'an that you should be distressed,

3. But as a reminder unto him who fears,

4. A revelation from Him Who created the earth and the high heavens,

5. The Beneficent One, Who is established on the Throne.

6. Unto Him belongs whatsoever is in the heavens and whatsoever is in the earth, and whatsoever is between them, and whatsoever is beneath the sod.

7. And if you speak aloud, then Lo! He knows the secret (thought) and (that which is yet) more hidden.

8. Allah! There is no God save Him. His are the most beautiful names.

9. Has there come unto you the story of Moses?

10. When he saw a fire and said unto his folk: Wait! I see a fire afar off. Peradventure I may bring you a brand therefrom or may find guidance at the fire.

11. And when he reached it, he was called by name: O Moses!

12. Lo! I, even I, am your Lord. So take off your shoes, for Lo! you are in the holy valley of Ṭuwā.

13. And I have chosen you, so hearken unto that which is inspired.

14. Lo! I, even I, am Allah. There is no God save Me. So worship Me and establish prayer for My remembrance.

15. Lo! the Hour is surely coming. But I almost keep it hidden, that every soul may be rewarded for that which it strives (to achieve).

١٥ إِنَّ السَّاعَةَ ءَاتِيَةٌ أَكَادُ أُخْفِيهَا لِتُجْزَى كُلُّ نَفْسٍ بِمَا تَسْعَى

16. Therefore, let not him turn you aside from (the thought of) it who believes not therein but follows his own desire, lest you perish.

١٦ فَلَا يَصُدَّنَّكَ عَنْهَا مَن لَّا يُؤْمِنُ بِهَا وَٱتَّبَعَ هَوَىٰهُ فَتَرْدَىٰ

17. And what is that in your right hand, O Moses?

١٧ وَمَا تِلْكَ بِيَمِينِكَ يَٰمُوسَىٰ

18. He said: This is my staff whereon I lean, and with which I beat down branches for my sheep, and wherein I find other uses.

١٨ قَالَ هِيَ عَصَايَ أَتَوَكَّؤُا عَلَيْهَا وَأَهُشُّ بِهَا عَلَىٰ غَنَمِي وَلِيَ فِيهَا مَآرِبُ أُخْرَىٰ

19. He said: Cast it down, O Moses!

١٩ قَالَ أَلْقِهَا يَٰمُوسَىٰ

20. So he cast it down, and Lo! it was a serpent, gliding.

٢٠ فَأَلْقَىٰهَا فَإِذَا هِيَ حَيَّةٌ تَسْعَىٰ

21. He said: Grasp it and fear not. We shall return it to its former state.

٢١ قَالَ خُذْهَا وَلَا تَخَفْ سَنُعِيدُهَا سِيرَتَهَا ٱلْأُولَىٰ

22. And thrust your hand within your armpit, it will come forth white without hurt. (That will be) another token.

٢٢ وَٱضْمُمْ يَدَكَ إِلَىٰ جَنَاحِكَ تَخْرُجْ بَيْضَآءَ مِنْ غَيْرِ سُوءٍ ءَايَةً أُخْرَىٰ

23. That We may show you (some) of Our greater portents,

٢٣ لِنُرِيَكَ مِنْ ءَايَٰتِنَا ٱلْكُبْرَى

24. Go you unto Pharaoh! Lo! he has transgressed (the bounds).

٢٤ ٱذْهَبْ إِلَىٰ فِرْعَوْنَ إِنَّهُ طَغَىٰ

25. (Moses) said: My Lord! Expand my breast

٢٥ قَالَ رَبِّ ٱشْرَحْ لِي صَدْرِي

26. And ease my task for me;

٢٦ وَيَسِّرْ لِي أَمْرِي

27. And loose a knot from my tongue,

٢٧ وَٱحْلُلْ عُقْدَةً مِّن لِّسَانِي

28. That they may understand my saying.

٢٨ يَفْقَهُوا قَوْلِي

29. Appoint for me a faithful supporter from my folk,

٢٩ وَٱجْعَل لِّي وَزِيرًا مِّنْ أَهْلِي

30. Aaron, my brother.

٣٠ هَٰرُونَ أَخِي

31. Confirm my strength with him.

٣١ ٱشْدُدْ بِهِ أَزْرِي

32. And let him share my task,

33. That we may glorify You much.

34. And much remember You.

35. Lo! You are ever Seeing us.

36. He said: You are granted your request, O Moses.

37. And indeed, another time, already We have shown you favor,

38. When We inspired in your mother that which is inspired,

39. Saying: Throw him into the chest, and throw it into the river, then the river shall throw it on to the bank, and there an enemy to Me and an enemy to him shall take him. And I endued you with love from Me that you might be trained according to My will,

40. When your sister went and said: Shall I show you one who will nurse him? and We restored you to your mother that her eyes might be refreshed and might not sorrow. And you did kill a man and We delivered you from great distress, and tried you with a heavy trial. And you did tarry years among the folk of Madian. Then came you (hither) by (My) providence, O Moses,

41. And I have attached you to Myself.

42. Go, you and your brother, with My tokens, and be not faint in remembrance of Me.

43. Go, both of you, unto Pharaoh. Lo! he has transgressed (the bounds).

44. And speak unto him a gentle word, that peradventure he may heed or fear.

45. They said: Our Lord! Lo! we fear that he may hasten with insolence against us or that he may play the tyrant.

46. He said: Fear not. Lo! I am with you two, Hearing and Seeing.

47. So go you unto him and say: Lo! we are two messengers of your Lord. So let the Children of Israel go with us, and torment them not. We bring you a token from your Lord And peace will be for him who follows right guidance.

48. Lo! it has been revealed unto us that the doom will be for him who denies and turns away.

49. (Pharaoh) said: Who then is the Lord of you two, O Moses?

50. He said: Our Lord is He Who gave unto everything its nature, then guided it aright.

51. He said: What then is the state of the generations of old?

52. He said: The knowledge thereof is with my Lord in a Record. My Lord neither errs nor forgets,

53. Who has appointed the earth as a bed and has threaded roads for you therein and has sent down water from the sky and thereby We have brought forth divers kinds of vegetation,

54. (Saying): Eat you and feed your cattle. Lo! herein surely are portents for men of thought.

55. Thereof We created you, and thereunto we return you and thence We bring you forth a second time.

56. And We surely did show him all Our tokens, but he denied them and refused.

57. He said: Have you come to drive us out from our land by your magic, O Moses?

58. But we surely can produce magic the like thereof; so appoint an appointed time between us and you, which neither we nor you shall fail to keep, at a place convenient (to us both).

59. (Moses) said: Your appointed time shall be the day of the feast, and let the people assemble when the sun has risen high.

٤٧ فَأْتِيَاهُ فَقُولَا إِنَّا رَسُولَا رَبِّكَ فَأَرْسِلْ مَعَنَا بَنِي إِسْرَآءِيلَ وَلَا تُعَذِّبْهُمْ قَدْ جِئْنَاكَ بِآيَةٍ مِّنْ رَّبِّكَ وَالسَّلَامُ عَلَى مَنِ اتَّبَعَ الْهُدَى

٤٨ إِنَّا قَدْ أُوحِيَ إِلَيْنَا أَنَّ الْعَذَابَ عَلَى مَن كَذَّبَ وَتَوَلَّى

٤٩ قَالَ فَمَن رَّبُّكُمَا يَا مُوسَى

٥٠ قَالَ رَبُّنَا الَّذِي أَعْطَى كُلَّ شَيْءٍ خَلْقَهُ ثُمَّ هَدَى

٥١ قَالَ فَمَا بَالُ الْقُرُونِ الْأُولَى

٥٢ قَالَ عِلْمُهَا عِندَ رَبِّي فِي كِتَابٍ لَّا يَضِلُّ رَبِّي وَلَا يَنسَى

٥٣ الَّذِي جَعَلَ لَكُمُ الْأَرْضَ مَهْدًا وَسَلَكَ لَكُمْ فِيهَا سُبُلًا وَأَنزَلَ مِنَ السَّمَآءِ مَآءً فَأَخْرَجْنَا بِهِ أَزْوَاجًا مِّن نَّبَاتٍ شَتَّى

٥٤ كُلُوا وَارْعَوْا أَنْعَامَكُمْ إِنَّ فِي ذَلِكَ لَآيَاتٍ لِّأُولِي النُّهَى

٥٥ مِنْهَا خَلَقْنَاكُمْ وَفِيهَا نُعِيدُكُمْ وَمِنْهَا نُخْرِجُكُمْ تَارَةً أُخْرَى

٥٦ وَلَقَدْ أَرَيْنَاهُ آيَاتِنَا كُلَّهَا فَكَذَّبَ وَأَبَى

٥٧ قَالَ أَجِئْتَنَا لِتُخْرِجَنَا مِنْ أَرْضِنَا بِسِحْرِكَ يَا مُوسَى

٥٨ فَلَنَأْتِيَنَّكَ بِسِحْرٍ مِّثْلِهِ فَاجْعَلْ بَيْنَنَا وَبَيْنَكَ مَوْعِدًا لَّا نُخْلِفُهُ نَحْنُ وَلَا أَنتَ مَكَانًا سُوًى

٥٩ قَالَ مَوْعِدُكُمْ يَوْمُ الزِّينَةِ وَأَن يُحْشَرَ النَّاسُ ضُحًى

60. Then Pharaoh went and gathered his strength and came (to the appointed tryst).

61. Moses said unto them: Woe unto you! Invent not a lie against Allah, lest He extirpate you by some punishment. He who lies fails miserably.

62. Then they debated one with another what they must do, and they kept their counsel secret.

63. They said: Lo! these are two wizards who would drive you out from your country by their magic, and destroy your best traditions;

64. So arrange your plan, and come in battle line. Who is uppermost this day will be indeed successful.

65. They said: O Moses! Either you throw first, or let us be the first to throw?

66. He said: Nay, do you throw! Then Lo! their cords and their staves, by their magic, appeared to him as though they ran.

67. Thus Moses conceived a fear in his mind.

68. We said: Fear not! Lo! you are the higher.

69. Throw that which is in your right hand! It will eat up that which they have made. Lo! that which they have made is but a wizard's artifice, and a wizard shall not be successful to whatever point (of skill) he may attain.

70. Then the wizards were (all) flung down prostrate, crying: We believe in the Lord of Aaron and Moses.

71. (Pharaoh) said: You put faith in him before I give you leave. Lo! he is your chief who taught you magic. Now surely I shall cut off your hands and your feet alternately, and I shall crucify you on the trunks of palm trees, and you shall know for certain which of us has sterner and more lasting punishment.

﴿٦٠﴾ فَتَوَلّٰى فِرْعَوْنُ فَجَمَعَ كَيْدَهُ ثُمَّ أَتٰى

﴿٦١﴾ قَالَ لَهُمْ مُّوسٰى وَيْلَكُمْ لَا تَفْتَرُوْا عَلَى اللّٰهِ كَذِبًا فَيُسْحِتَكُمْ بِعَذَابٍ وَقَدْ خَابَ مَنِ افْتَرٰى

﴿٦٢﴾ فَتَنَازَعُوْا أَمْرَهُمْ بَيْنَهُمْ وَأَسَرُّوا النَّجْوٰى

﴿٦٣﴾ قَالُوْا إِنْ هٰذٰنِ لَسَاحِرٰنِ يُرِيْدٰنِ أَنْ يُّخْرِجٰكُمْ مِّنْ أَرْضِكُمْ بِسِحْرِهِمَا وَيَذْهَبَا بِطَرِيْقَتِكُمُ الْمُثْلٰى

﴿٦٤﴾ فَأَجْمِعُوْا كَيْدَكُمْ ثُمَّ ائْتُوْا صَفًّا وَقَدْ أَفْلَحَ الْيَوْمَ مَنِ اسْتَعْلٰى

﴿٦٥﴾ قَالُوْا يٰمُوْسٰى إِمَّا أَنْ تُلْقِيَ وَإِمَّا أَنْ نَّكُوْنَ أَوَّلَ مَنْ أَلْقٰى

﴿٦٦﴾ قَالَ بَلْ أَلْقُوْا فَإِذَا حِبَالُهُمْ وَعِصِيُّهُمْ يُخَيَّلُ إِلَيْهِ مِنْ سِحْرِهِمْ أَنَّهَا تَسْعٰى

﴿٦٧﴾ فَأَوْجَسَ فِيْ نَفْسِهِ خِيْفَةً مُّوْسٰى

﴿٦٨﴾ قُلْنَا لَا تَخَفْ إِنَّكَ أَنْتَ الْأَعْلٰى

﴿٦٩﴾ وَأَلْقِ مَا فِيْ يَمِيْنِكَ تَلْقَفْ مَا صَنَعُوْا إِنَّمَا صَنَعُوْا كَيْدُ سَاحِرٍ وَلَا يُفْلِحُ السَّاحِرُ حَيْثُ أَتٰى

﴿٧٠﴾ فَأُلْقِيَ السَّحَرَةُ سُجَّدًا قَالُوْا آمَنَّا بِرَبِّ هٰرُوْنَ وَمُوْسٰى

﴿٧١﴾ قَالَ آمَنْتُمْ لَهُ قَبْلَ أَنْ آذَنَ لَكُمْ إِنَّهُ لَكَبِيْرُكُمُ الَّذِيْ عَلَّمَكُمُ السِّحْرَ فَلَأُقَطِّعَنَّ أَيْدِيَكُمْ وَأَرْجُلَكُمْ مِّنْ خِلَافٍ وَلَأُصَلِّبَنَّكُمْ فِيْ جُذُوْعِ النَّخْلِ وَلَتَعْلَمُنَّ أَيُّنَا أَشَدُّ عَذَابًا وَأَبْقٰى

72. They said: We choose you not above the clear proofs that have come unto us, by Him Who created us. So decree what you will decree. You will end for us only the life of the world.

٧٢ قَالُوا لَن نُّؤْثِرَكَ عَلَىٰ مَا جَاءَنَا مِنَ ٱلْبَيِّنَٰتِ وَٱلَّذِى فَطَرَنَا ۖ فَٱقْضِ مَا أَنتَ قَاضٍ ۖ إِنَّمَا تَقْضِى هَٰذِهِ ٱلْحَيَوٰةَ ٱلدُّنْيَا

73. Lo! we believe in our Lord, that He may forgive us our sins and the magic unto which you did force us. Allah is better and more lasting.

٧٣ إِنَّا آمَنَّا بِرَبِّنَا لِيَغْفِرَ لَنَا خَطَٰيَٰنَا وَمَا أَكْرَهْتَنَا عَلَيْهِ مِنَ ٱلسِّحْرِ ۗ وَٱللَّهُ خَيْرٌ وَأَبْقَىٰ

74. Lo! who comes guilty unto his Lord, surely for him is Hell. There he will neither die nor live.

٧٤ إِنَّهُ مَن يَأْتِ رَبَّهُ مُجْرِمًا فَإِنَّ لَهُ جَهَنَّمَ لَا يَمُوتُ فِيهَا وَلَا يَحْيَىٰ

75. But who comes unto Him a believer, having done good works, for such are the high stations;

٧٥ وَمَن يَأْتِهِ مُؤْمِنًا قَدْ عَمِلَ ٱلصَّٰلِحَٰتِ فَأُولَٰئِكَ لَهُمُ ٱلدَّرَجَٰتُ ٱلْعُلَىٰ

76. Gardens of Eden underneath which rivers flow, wherein they will abide for ever. That is the reward of him who is pure (from sins).

٧٦ جَنَّٰتُ عَدْنٍ تَجْرِى مِن تَحْتِهَا ٱلْأَنْهَٰرُ خَٰلِدِينَ فِيهَا ۚ وَذَٰلِكَ جَزَاءُ مَن تَزَكَّىٰ

77. And surely We inspired Moses, saying: Take away My slaves by night and strike for them a dry path in the sea, fearing not to be overtaken, neither being afraid (of the sea).

٧٧ وَلَقَدْ أَوْحَيْنَا إِلَىٰ مُوسَىٰ أَنْ أَسْرِ بِعِبَادِى فَٱضْرِبْ لَهُمْ طَرِيقًا فِى ٱلْبَحْرِ يَبَسًا لَّا تَخَٰفُ دَرَكًا وَلَا تَخْشَىٰ

78. Then Pharaoh followed them with his hosts and there covered them that which did cover them of the sea.

٧٨ فَأَتْبَعَهُمْ فِرْعَوْنُ بِجُنُودِهِ فَغَشِيَهُم مِّنَ ٱلْيَمِّ مَا غَشِيَهُمْ

79. And Pharaoh led his folk astray, he did not guide them.

٧٩ وَأَضَلَّ فِرْعَوْنُ قَوْمَهُ وَمَا هَدَىٰ

80. O Children of Israel! We delivered you from your enemy, and We made a covenant with you on the holy mountain's side, and sent down on you the honey and the quails,

٨٠ يَٰبَنِى إِسْرَٰئِيلَ قَدْ أَنجَيْنَٰكُم مِّنْ عَدُوِّكُمْ وَوَٰعَدْنَٰكُمْ جَانِبَ ٱلطُّورِ ٱلْأَيْمَنَ وَنَزَّلْنَا عَلَيْكُمُ ٱلْمَنَّ وَٱلسَّلْوَىٰ

81. (Saying): Eat of the good things with which We have provided you, and transgress not in respect thereof lest My wrath come upon you; and he on whom My wrath comes, he is lost indeed.

٨١ كُلُوا مِن طَيِّبَٰتِ مَا رَزَقْنَٰكُمْ وَلَا تَطْغَوْا فِيهِ فَيَحِلَّ عَلَيْكُمْ غَضَبِى ۖ وَمَن يَحْلِلْ عَلَيْهِ غَضَبِى فَقَدْ هَوَىٰ

82. And lo! surely I am Forgiving toward him who repents and believes and does good, and afterward walks aright.

﴿٨٢﴾ وَإِنِّي لَغَفَّارٌ لِّمَن تَابَ وَءَامَنَ وَعَمِلَ صَـٰلِحًا ثُمَّ اهْتَدَىٰ

83. And (it was said): What has made you hasten from your folk, O Moses?

﴿٨٣﴾ ۞ وَمَآ أَعْجَلَكَ عَن قَوْمِكَ يَـٰمُوسَىٰ

84. He said: They are close upon my track. I hastened unto You My Lord that You might be well pleased.

﴿٨٤﴾ قَالَ هُمْ أُوْلَآءِ عَلَىٰٓ أَثَرِى وَعَجِلْتُ إِلَيْكَ رَبِّ لِتَرْضَىٰ

85. He said: Lo! We have tried your folk in your absence, and al Sāmirī has misled them.

﴿٨٥﴾ قَالَ فَإِنَّا قَدْ فَتَنَّا قَوْمَكَ مِنۢ بَعْدِكَ وَأَضَلَّهُمُ ٱلسَّامِرِىُّ

86. Then Moses went back unto his folk, angry and sad. He said: O my people! Has not your Lord promised you a fair promise? Did the time appointed then appear too long for you, or did you wish that wrath from your Lord should come upon you, that you broke appointed time with me?

﴿٨٦﴾ فَرَجَعَ مُوسَىٰٓ إِلَىٰ قَوْمِهِۦ غَضْبَـٰنَ أَسِفًا قَالَ يَـٰقَوْمِ أَلَمْ يَعِدْكُمْ رَبُّكُمْ وَعْدًا حَسَنًا أَفَطَالَ عَلَيْكُمُ ٱلْعَهْدُ أَمْ أَرَدتُّمْ أَن يَحِلَّ عَلَيْكُمْ غَضَبٌ مِّن رَّبِّكُمْ فَأَخْلَفْتُم مَّوْعِدِى

87. They said: We broke not appointed time with you of our own will, but we were laden with burdens of ornaments of the folk, then cast them (in the fire), for thus al Sāmirī proposed.

﴿٨٧﴾ قَالُوا مَآ أَخْلَفْنَا مَوْعِدَكَ بِمَلْكِنَا وَلَـٰكِنَّا حُمِّلْنَآ أَوْزَارًا مِّن زِينَةِ ٱلْقَوْمِ فَقَذَفْنَـٰهَا فَكَذَٰلِكَ أَلْقَى ٱلسَّامِرِىُّ

88. Then he produced for them a calf, of saffron hue,[177] which gave forth a lowing sound. And they cried: This is your God and the God of Moses, but he has forgotten.

﴿٨٨﴾ فَأَخْرَجَ لَهُمْ عِجْلًا جَسَدًا لَّهُۥ خُوَارٌ فَقَالُوا هَـٰذَآ إِلَـٰهُكُمْ وَإِلَـٰهُ مُوسَىٰ فَنَسِىَ

89. See they not, then, that it returns no saying unto them and possesses for them neither hurt nor use?

﴿٨٩﴾ أَفَلَا يَرَوْنَ أَلَّا يَرْجِعُ إِلَيْهِمْ قَوْلًا وَلَا يَمْلِكُ لَهُمْ ضَرًّا وَلَا نَفْعًا

90. And Aaron indeed had told them beforehand: O my people! You are but being seduced therewith, for lo! your Lord is the Beneficent, so follow me and obey my order.

﴿٩٠﴾ وَلَقَدْ قَالَ لَهُمْ هَـٰرُونُ مِن قَبْلُ يَـٰقَوْمِ إِنَّمَا فُتِنتُم بِهِۦ وَإِنَّ رَبَّكُمُ ٱلرَّحْمَـٰنُ فَٱتَّبِعُونِى وَأَطِيعُوٓا أَمْرِى

91. They said: We shall by no means cease to be its votaries till Moses return unto us.

﴿٩١﴾ قَالُوا لَن نَّبْرَحَ عَلَيْهِ عَـٰكِفِينَ حَتَّىٰ يَرْجِعَ إِلَيْنَا مُوسَىٰ

---

[177]Or "a body." See Surah 7:148, footnote.

92. He (Moses) said: O Aaron! What held you back when you did see them gone astray,

قَالَ يَـٰهَرُونُ مَامَنَعَكَ إِذْ رَأَيْتَهُمْ ضَلُّوٓا ۝

93. That you followed me not? Have you then disobeyed my order?

أَلَّا تَتَّبِعَنِّ أَفَعَصَيْتَ أَمْرِى ۝

94. He said: O son of my mother! Clutch not my beard nor my head! I feared lest you should say: You have caused division among the Children of Israel, and you have not complied with my word.

قَالَ يَبْنَؤُمَّ لَا تَأْخُذْ بِلِحْيَتِى وَلَا بِرَأْسِىٓ إِنِّى خَشِيتُ أَن تَقُولَ فَرَّقْتَ بَيْنَ بَنِىٓ إِسْرَ ٰٓءِيلَ وَلَمْ تَرْقُبْ قَوْلِى ۝

95. (Moses) said: And what have you to say, O Sāmirī?

قَالَ فَمَا خَطْبُكَ يَسَٰمِرِىُّ ۝

96. He said: I perceived what they perceived not, so I seized a handful from the footsteps of the messenger, and then threw it in. Thus my soul commended to me.178

قَالَ بَصُرْتُ بِمَا لَمْ يَبْصُرُوا بِهِۦ فَقَبَضْتُ قَبْضَةً مِّنْ أَثَرِ الرَّسُولِ فَنَبَذْتُهَا وَكَذَٰلِكَ سَوَّلَتْ لِى نَفْسِى ۝

97. (Moses) said: Then go! And lo! in this life it is for you to say: Touch me not! and lo! there is for you an appointed time you can not break. Now look upon your god of which you have remained a votary. Surely we will burn it and will scatter its dust over the sea.

قَالَ فَاذْهَبْ فَإِنَّ لَكَ فِى الْحَيَوٰةِ أَن تَقُولَ لَا مِسَاسَ وَإِنَّ لَكَ مَوْعِدًا لَّن تُخْلَفَهُۥ وَانظُرْ إِلَىٰٓ إِلَٰهِكَ الَّذِى ظَلْتَ عَلَيْهِ عَاكِفًا لَّنُحَرِّقَنَّهُۥ ثُمَّ لَنَنسِفَنَّهُۥ فِى الْيَمِّ نَسْفًا ۝

98. Your God is only Allah, than Whom there is no other God. He embraces all things in His knowledge.

إِنَّمَآ إِلَٰهُكُمُ اللَّهُ الَّذِى لَآ إِلَٰهَ إِلَّا هُوَ وَسِعَ كُلَّ شَىْءٍ عِلْمًا ۝

99. Thus do We relate unto you (Muhammad) some tidings of that which happened of old, and We have given you from Our presence a Reminder.

كَذَٰلِكَ نَقُصُّ عَلَيْكَ مِنْ أَنْبَآءِ مَا قَدْ سَبَقَ وَقَدْ ءَاتَيْنَٰكَ مِن لَّدُنَّا ذِكْرًا ۝

100. Who turns away from it, he surely will bear a burden on the Day of Resurrection,

مَّنْ أَعْرَضَ عَنْهُ فَإِنَّهُۥ يَحْمِلُ يَوْمَ الْقِيَٰمَةِ وِزْرًا ۝

101. Abiding under it—an evil burden for them on the Day of Resurrection,

خَٰلِدِينَ فِيهِ وَسَآءَ لَهُمْ يَوْمَ الْقِيَٰمَةِ حِمْلًا ۝

102. The day when the Trumpet is blown. On that day we assemble the guilty white-eyed (with terror),

يَوْمَ يُنفَخُ فِى الصُّورِ وَنَحْشُرُ الْمُجْرِمِينَ يَوْمَئِذٍ زُرْقًا ۝

103. Murmuring among themselves: You have tarried but ten (days).

يَتَخَافَتُونَ بَيْنَهُمْ إِن لَّبِثْتُمْ إِلَّا عَشْرًا ۝

178The explanation usually given is that al Sāmirī had seen the angel Gabriel pass by, and had taken some of the dust which he had hallowed, and thrown it into the image of the calf, thus giving it a semblance of life. Others say al Sāmirī was an adept of Egyptian idolatry who had believed for a little while and half-heartedly in the God of Moses.

104. We are best aware of what they utter when their best in conduct say: You have tarried but a day.

105. They will ask you of the mountains (on that day). Say: My Lord will break them into scattered dust.

106. And leave it (the earth) as an empty plain,

107. Wherein you see neither curve nor ruggedness.

108. On that day they follow the summoner who deceives not, and voices are hushed for the Beneficent, and you hear but a faint murmur.

109. On that Day no intercession avails save (that of) him unto whom the Beneficent has given leave and whose word He accepts:

110. He knows (all) that is before them and (all) that is behind them, while they cannot compass Him in knowledge.

111. And faces humble themselves before the Living, the Eternal. And he who bears (a burden of) wrongdoing is indeed a failure (on that Day).

112. And he who has done some good works, being a believer, he fears not injustice nor begrudging (of his wage).

113. Thus We have revealed it as the Qur'an in Arabic, and have displayed therein certain threats, that peradventure they may keep from evil or that it may cause them to take heed.

114. Then exalted be Allah, the True King! And hasten not (O Muhammad) with the Qur'an before its revelation has been perfected unto you, and say: My Lord! Increase me in knowledge.

115. And surely We made a covenant of old with Adam, but he forgot, and We found no constancy in him.

١٠٤ نَحْنُ أَعْلَمُ بِمَا يَقُولُونَ إِذْ يَقُولُ أَمْثَلُهُمْ طَرِيقَةً إِن لَّبِثْتُمْ إِلَّا يَوْمًا

١٠٥ وَيَسْأَلُونَكَ عَنِ الْجِبَالِ فَقُلْ يَنسِفُهَا رَبِّي نَسْفًا

١٠٦ فَيَذَرُهَا قَاعًا صَفْصَفًا

١٠٧ لَّا تَرَى فِيهَا عِوَجًا وَلَا أَمْتًا

١٠٨ يَوْمَئِذٍ يَتَّبِعُونَ الدَّاعِيَ لَا عِوَجَ لَهُ وَخَشَعَتِ الْأَصْوَاتُ لِلرَّحْمَٰنِ فَلَا تَسْمَعُ إِلَّا هَمْسًا

١٠٩ يَوْمَئِذٍ لَّا تَنفَعُ الشَّفَاعَةُ إِلَّا مَنْ أَذِنَ لَهُ الرَّحْمَٰنُ وَرَضِيَ لَهُ قَوْلًا

١١٠ يَعْلَمُ مَا بَيْنَ أَيْدِيهِمْ وَمَا خَلْفَهُمْ وَلَا يُحِيطُونَ بِهِ عِلْمًا

١١١ وَعَنَتِ الْوُجُوهُ لِلْحَيِّ الْقَيُّومِ وَقَدْ خَابَ مَنْ حَمَلَ ظُلْمًا

١١٢ وَمَن يَعْمَلْ مِنَ الصَّالِحَاتِ وَهُوَ مُؤْمِنٌ فَلَا يَخَافُ ظُلْمًا وَلَا هَضْمًا

١١٣ وَكَذَٰلِكَ أَنزَلْنَاهُ قُرْءَانًا عَرَبِيًّا وَصَرَّفْنَا فِيهِ مِنَ الْوَعِيدِ لَعَلَّهُمْ يَتَّقُونَ أَوْ يُحْدِثُ لَهُمْ ذِكْرًا

١١٤ فَتَعَالَى اللَّهُ الْمَلِكُ الْحَقُّ وَلَا تَعْجَلْ بِالْقُرْءَانِ مِن قَبْلِ أَن يُقْضَى إِلَيْكَ وَحْيُهُ وَقُل رَّبِّ زِدْنِي عِلْمًا

١١٥ وَلَقَدْ عَهِدْنَا إِلَىٰ آدَمَ مِن قَبْلُ فَنَسِيَ وَلَمْ نَجِدْ لَهُ عَزْمًا

116. And when We said unto the angels: Fall prostrate before Adam, they fell prostrate (all) save Iblīs; he re-fused.

117. Therefore We said: O Adam! This is an enemy unto you and unto your wife, so let him not drive you both out of the Garden thus you come to toil.

118. It is (vouchsafed) unto you that you hunger not therein nor are naked,

119. And you thirst not therein nor are exposed to the sun's heat.

120. But the Devil whispered to him, saying: O Adam! Shall I show you the tree of immortality and a Kingdom that wastes not away?

121. Then they two ate thereof, so that their shame became apparent unto them, and they began to hide by heaping on themselves some of the leaves of the Garden. And Adam disobeyed his Lord, so went astray.[179]

122. Then his Lord chose him, and relented toward him, and guided him.

123. He said: Go down hence, both of you, one of you a foe unto the other. But if there come unto you from Me a guid-ance, then who follows My guidance, he will not go astray nor will be unhappy.[180]

124. But he who turns away from remembrance of Me, his will be a narrow life, and I shall bring him blind to the assembly on the Day of Resurrection.

125. He will say: My Lord! Wherefore have You gathered me (hither) blind, when I was wont to see?

126. He will say: So (it must be). Our revelations came unto you but you did forget them. In like manner you are forgotten this Day.

127. Thus do We reward him who is prodigal and believes not the revelations of his Lord; and surely the doom of the Hereafter will be sterner and more lasting.

١١٦ وَإِذْ قُلْنَا لِلْمَلَٰٓئِكَةِ اسْجُدُوا لِآدَمَ فَسَجَدُوٓا إِلَّآ إِبْلِيسَ أَبَىٰ

١١٧ فَقُلْنَا يَٰٓـَٔادَمُ إِنَّ هَٰذَا عَدُوٌّ لَّكَ وَلِزَوْجِكَ فَلَا يُخْرِجَنَّكُمَا مِنَ ٱلْجَنَّةِ فَتَشْقَىٰٓ

١١٨ إِنَّ لَكَ أَلَّا تَجُوعَ فِيهَا وَلَا تَعْرَىٰ

١١٩ وَأَنَّكَ لَا تَظْمَؤُا۟ فِيهَا وَلَا تَضْحَىٰ

١٢٠ فَوَسْوَسَ إِلَيْهِ ٱلشَّيْطَٰنُ قَالَ يَٰٓـَٔادَمُ هَلْ أَدُلُّكَ عَلَىٰ شَجَرَةِ ٱلْخُلْدِ وَمُلْكٍ لَّا يَبْلَىٰ

١٢١ فَأَكَلَا مِنْهَا فَبَدَتْ لَهُمَا سَوْءَٰتُهُمَا وَطَفِقَا يَخْصِفَانِ عَلَيْهِمَا مِن وَرَقِ ٱلْجَنَّةِ وَعَصَىٰٓ ءَادَمُ رَبَّهُۥ فَغَوَىٰ

١٢٢ ثُمَّ ٱجْتَبَٰهُ رَبُّهُۥ فَتَابَ عَلَيْهِ وَهَدَىٰ

١٢٣ قَالَ ٱهْبِطَا مِنْهَا جَمِيعًۢا بَعْضُكُمْ لِبَعْضٍ عَدُوٌّ فَإِمَّا يَأْتِيَنَّكُم مِّنِّى هُدًى فَمَنِ ٱتَّبَعَ هُدَاىَ فَلَا يَضِلُّ وَلَا يَشْقَىٰ

١٢٤ وَمَنْ أَعْرَضَ عَن ذِكْرِى فَإِنَّ لَهُۥ مَعِيشَةً ضَنكًا وَنَحْشُرُهُۥ يَوْمَ ٱلْقِيَٰمَةِ أَعْمَىٰ

١٢٥ قَالَ رَبِّ لِمَ حَشَرْتَنِىٓ أَعْمَىٰ وَقَدْ كُنتُ بَصِيرًا

١٢٦ قَالَ كَذَٰلِكَ أَتَتْكَ ءَايَٰتُنَا فَنَسِيتَهَا وَكَذَٰلِكَ ٱلْيَوْمَ تُنسَىٰ

١٢٧ وَكَذَٰلِكَ نَجْزِى مَنْ أَسْرَفَ وَلَمْ يُؤْمِنۢ بِـَٔايَٰتِ رَبِّهِۦ وَلَعَذَابُ ٱلْءَاخِرَةِ أَشَدُّ وَأَبْقَىٰ

---

[179]Cf. Surah 7:20 ff.
[180]Cf. Surah 2, and the passage leading up to it.

128. Is it not a guidance for them (to know) how many a generation We destroyed before them, amid whose dwellings they walk? Lo! therein surely are signs for men of thought.

﴿١٢٨﴾ أَفَلَمْ يَهْدِ لَهُمْ كَمْ أَهْلَكْنَا قَبْلَهُم مِّنَ ٱلْقُرُونِ يَمْشُونَ فِى مَسَـٰكِنِهِمْ إِنَّ فِى ذَٰلِكَ لَـَٔايَـٰتٍ لِّأُوْلِى ٱلنُّهَىٰ

129. And but for a decree that had already gone forth from your Lord, and a term already fixed, (the punishment) would (have) been inevitable (in this world).

﴿١٢٩﴾ وَلَوْلَا كَلِمَةٌ سَبَقَتْ مِن رَّبِّكَ لَكَانَ لِزَامًا وَأَجَلٌ مُّسَمًّى

130. Therefore (O Muhammad), bear with what they say, and celebrate the praises of your Lord before the rising of the sun and before the setting thereof. And glorify Him some hours of the night and at the two ends of the day, that you may find acceptance.

﴿١٣٠﴾ فَٱصْبِرْ عَلَىٰ مَا يَقُولُونَ وَسَبِّحْ بِحَمْدِ رَبِّكَ قَبْلَ طُلُوعِ ٱلشَّمْسِ وَقَبْلَ غُرُوبِهَا وَمِنْ ءَانَآئِ ٱلَّيْلِ فَسَبِّحْ وَأَطْرَافَ ٱلنَّهَارِ لَعَلَّكَ تَرْضَىٰ

131. And strain not your eyes toward that which We cause some wedded pairs among them to enjoy, the flower of the life of the world, that We may try them thereby. The provision of your Lord is better and more lasting.

﴿١٣١﴾ وَلَا تَمُدَّنَّ عَيْنَيْكَ إِلَىٰ مَا مَتَّعْنَا بِهِۦٓ أَزْوَٰجًا مِّنْهُمْ زَهْرَةَ ٱلْحَيَوٰةِ ٱلدُّنْيَا لِنَفْتِنَهُمْ فِيهِ وَرِزْقُ رَبِّكَ خَيْرٌ وَأَبْقَىٰ

132. And enjoin upon your people Prayer, and be constant therein. We ask not of you a provision: We provide for you. And the sequel is for righteousness.

﴿١٣٢﴾ وَأْمُرْ أَهْلَكَ بِٱلصَّلَوٰةِ وَٱصْطَبِرْ عَلَيْهَا لَا نَسْـَٔلُكَ رِزْقًا نَّحْنُ نَرْزُقُكَ وَٱلْعَـٰقِبَةُ لِلتَّقْوَىٰ

133. And they say: If only he would bring us a miracle from his Lord! Has there not come unto them the proof of what is in the former Scriptures?

﴿١٣٣﴾ وَقَالُوا لَوْلَا يَأْتِينَا بِـَٔايَةٍ مِّن رَّبِّهِۦٓ أَوَلَمْ تَأْتِهِم بَيِّنَةُ مَا فِى ٱلصُّحُفِ ٱلْأُولَىٰ

134. And if We had destroyed them with some punishment before it, they would assuredly have said: Our Lord! If only You had sent unto us a messenger, so that we might have followed Your revelations before we were (thus) humbled and disgraced!

﴿١٣٤﴾ وَلَوْ أَنَّآ أَهْلَكْنَـٰهُم بِعَذَابٍ مِّن قَبْلِهِۦ لَقَالُوا رَبَّنَا لَوْلَآ أَرْسَلْتَ إِلَيْنَا رَسُولًا فَنَتَّبِعَ ءَايَـٰتِكَ مِن قَبْلِ أَن نَّذِلَّ وَنَخْزَىٰ

135. Say: Each is awaiting; so await you! You will come to know who are the owners of the straight path, and who have received guidance.

﴿١٣٥﴾ قُلْ كُلٌّ مُّتَرَبِّصٌ فَتَرَبَّصُوا فَسَتَعْلَمُونَ مَنْ أَصْحَـٰبُ ٱلصِّرَٰطِ ٱلسَّوِيِّ وَمَنِ ٱهْتَدَىٰ

The Prophets

Al Anbiyā', "The Prophets," is named for its subject: the history of the former prophets. The speaker in verses 4 and 112 is every prophet. There is no historical reference or tradition that makes it possible for us to fix the date of its revelation. It is undoubtedly of Makkan revelation, but lacks the characteristics of the latest and earliest Makkan surahs. It may, therefore, be taken as belonging to the middle group of Makkan surahs.

The Prophets

Revealed at Makkah

*In the name of Allah,
the Beneficent, the Merciful*

1. Their reckoning draws near for mankind, while they turn away in heedlessness.

2. Never comes there unto them a new reminder from their Lord but they listen to it while they play.

3. With hearts preoccupied. And they confer in secret. The wrongdoers say: Is this other than a mortal like you? Will you then succumb to magic when you see (it)?

4. He said: My Lord knows what is spoken in the heaven and the earth. He is the Hearer, the Knower.

5. Nay, say they, (these are but) muddled dreams; nay, he has but invented it; nay, he is but a poet. Let him bring us a portent even as those of old (who were God's messengers) were sent (with portents).

6. Not a township believed of those which We destroyed before them (though We sent them portents): would they then believe?

7. And We sent not (as Our messengers) before you other than men whom We inspired. Ask the owners of the Reminder[181] if you know not?

8. We gave them not bodies that would not eat food, nor were they immortals.

9. Then We fulfilled the promise unto them. So We delivered them and whom We would, and We destroyed the prodigals.

10. Now We have revealed unto you a Scripture wherein is your Reminder. Have you then no sense?

---

[181]i.e., the Jewish Scripture.

11. How many a community that dealt unjustly have We shattered, and raised up after them another folk!

12. And, when they felt Our might, behold them fleeing from it!

13. (But it was said unto them): Flee not, but return to that (existence) which emasculated you and to your dwellings, that you may be questioned.

14. They cried: Alas for us! Lo! we were wrongdoers.

15. And this their crying ceased not till We made them as reaped corn, extinct.

16. We created not the heaven and the earth and all that is between them in play.

17. If We had wished to find a pastime, We could have found it in Our presence if We ever did.

18. Nay, but We hurl the true against the false, and it does break its head and lo! it vanishes. And yours will be woe for that which you ascribe (unto Him).

19. Unto Him belongs whoever is in the heavens and the earth. And those who dwell in His presence are not too proud to worship Him nor do they weary;

20. They glorify (Him) night and day; they flag not.

21. Or have they chosen Gods from the earth who raise the dead?

22. If there were therein Gods beside Allah, then surely both (the heavens and the earth) had been disordered. Glorified be Allah, the Lord of the Throne, from all that they ascribe (unto Him).

23. He will not be questioned as to that which He does, but they will be questioned.

24. Or have they chosen other gods beside Him? Say: Bring your proof (of their godhead). This is the Reminder of those with me and those before me, but most of them know not the Truth and so they are averse.

﴿١١﴾ وَكَمْ قَصَمْنَا مِن قَرْيَةٍ كَانَتْ ظَالِمَةً وَأَنشَأْنَا بَعْدَهَا قَوْمًا ءَاخَرِينَ

﴿١٢﴾ فَلَمَّا أَحَسُّوا بَأْسَنَا إِذَا هُم مِّنْهَا يَرْكُضُونَ

﴿١٣﴾ لَا تَرْكُضُوا وَارْجِعُوا إِلَىٰ مَا أُتْرِفْتُمْ فِيهِ وَمَسَاكِنِكُمْ لَعَلَّكُمْ تُسْأَلُونَ

﴿١٤﴾ قَالُوا يَا وَيْلَنَا إِنَّا كُنَّا ظَالِمِينَ

﴿١٥﴾ فَمَا زَالَت تِّلْكَ دَعْوَاهُمْ حَتَّىٰ جَعَلْنَاهُمْ حَصِيدًا خَامِدِينَ

﴿١٦﴾ وَمَا خَلَقْنَا السَّمَاءَ وَالْأَرْضَ وَمَا بَيْنَهُمَا لَاعِبِينَ

﴿١٧﴾ لَوْ أَرَدْنَا أَن نَّتَّخِذَ لَهْوًا لَّاتَّخَذْنَاهُ مِن لَّدُنَّا إِن كُنَّا فَاعِلِينَ

﴿١٨﴾ بَلْ نَقْذِفُ بِالْحَقِّ عَلَى الْبَاطِلِ فَيَدْمَغُهُ فَإِذَا هُوَ زَاهِقٌ وَلَكُمُ الْوَيْلُ مِمَّا تَصِفُونَ

﴿١٩﴾ وَلَهُ مَن فِي السَّمَاوَاتِ وَالْأَرْضِ وَمَنْ عِندَهُ لَا يَسْتَكْبِرُونَ عَنْ عِبَادَتِهِ وَلَا يَسْتَحْسِرُونَ

﴿٢٠﴾ يُسَبِّحُونَ الَّيْلَ وَالنَّهَارَ لَا يَفْتُرُونَ

﴿٢١﴾ أَمِ اتَّخَذُوا ءَالِهَةً مِّنَ الْأَرْضِ هُمْ يُنشِرُونَ

﴿٢٢﴾ لَوْ كَانَ فِيهِمَا ءَالِهَةٌ إِلَّا اللَّهُ لَفَسَدَتَا فَسُبْحَانَ اللَّهِ رَبِّ الْعَرْشِ عَمَّا يَصِفُونَ

﴿٢٣﴾ لَا يُسْأَلُ عَمَّا يَفْعَلُ وَهُمْ يُسْأَلُونَ

﴿٢٤﴾ أَمِ اتَّخَذُوا مِن دُونِهِ ءَالِهَةً قُلْ هَاتُوا بُرْهَانَكُمْ هَٰذَا ذِكْرُ مَن مَّعِيَ وَذِكْرُ مَن قَبْلِي بَلْ أَكْثَرُهُمْ لَا يَعْلَمُونَ الْحَقَّ فَهُم مُّعْرِضُونَ

25. And We sent no messenger before you but We inspired him, (saying): There is no God save Me (Allah), so worship Me.

26. And they say: The Beneficent has taken unto Himself a son. Be He glorified! Nay, but (those whom they call sons) are honored slaves;

27. They precede Him not in speech, and they act by His command.

28. He knows what is before them and what is behind them, and they cannot intercede except for him whom He accepts, and they quake for awe of Him.

29. And one of them who should say: Lo! I am a God beside Him, that one We should repay with Hell. Thus We repay wrongdoers.

30. Have not those who disbelieve known that the heavens and the earth were of one piece, then We parted them, and We made every living thing of water? Will they not then believe?

31. And We have placed in the earth firm hills lest it quake with them, and We have placed therein ravines as roads that they may find their way.

32. And We have made the sky a roof withheld (from them). Yet they turn away from its portents.

33. And He it is Who created the night and the day, and the sun and the moon. They float, each in an orbit.

34. We appointed immortality for no mortal before you. What! if you die, can they be immortal?

35. Every soul must taste of death, and We try you with evil and with good, for ordeal. And unto Us you will be returned.

٢٥ وَمَا أَرْسَلْنَا مِن قَبْلِكَ مِن رَّسُولٍ إِلَّا نُوحِى إِلَيْهِ أَنَّهُ لَا إِلَهَ إِلَّا أَنَا فَاعْبُدُونِ

٢٦ وَقَالُوا اتَّخَذَ الرَّحْمَنُ وَلَدًا سُبْحَانَهُ بَلْ عِبَادٌ مُّكْرَمُونَ

٢٧ لَا يَسْبِقُونَهُ بِالْقَوْلِ وَهُم بِأَمْرِهِ يَعْمَلُونَ

٢٨ يَعْلَمُ مَا بَيْنَ أَيْدِيهِمْ وَمَا خَلْفَهُمْ وَلَا يَشْفَعُونَ إِلَّا لِمَنِ ارْتَضَى وَهُم مِّنْ خَشْيَتِهِ مُشْفِقُونَ

٢٩ وَمَن يَقُلْ مِنْهُمْ إِنِّي إِلَهٌ مِّن دُونِهِ فَذَلِكَ نَجْزِيهِ جَهَنَّمَ كَذَلِكَ نَجْزِي الظَّالِمِينَ

٣٠ أَوَلَمْ يَرَ الَّذِينَ كَفَرُوا أَنَّ السَّمَوَاتِ وَالْأَرْضَ كَانَتَا رَتْقًا فَفَتَقْنَاهُمَا وَجَعَلْنَا مِنَ الْمَاءِ كُلَّ شَيْءٍ حَيٍّ أَفَلَا يُؤْمِنُونَ

٣١ وَجَعَلْنَا فِي الْأَرْضِ رَوَاسِيَ أَن تَمِيدَ بِهِمْ وَجَعَلْنَا فِيهَا فِجَاجًا سُبُلًا لَّعَلَّهُمْ يَهْتَدُونَ

٣٢ وَجَعَلْنَا السَّمَاءَ سَقْفًا مَّحْفُوظًا وَهُمْ عَنْ ءَايَاتِهَا مُعْرِضُونَ

٣٣ وَهُوَ الَّذِي خَلَقَ الَّيْلَ وَالنَّهَارَ وَالشَّمْسَ وَالْقَمَرَ كُلٌّ فِي فَلَكٍ يَسْبَحُونَ

٣٤ وَمَا جَعَلْنَا لِبَشَرٍ مِّن قَبْلِكَ الْخُلْدَ أَفَإِن مِّتَّ فَهُمُ الْخَالِدُونَ

٣٥ كُلُّ نَفْسٍ ذَائِقَةُ الْمَوْتِ وَنَبْلُوكُم بِالشَّرِّ وَالْخَيْرِ فِتْنَةً وَإِلَيْنَا تُرْجَعُونَ

36. And when those who disbelieve behold you, they but choose you out for mockery, (saying): Is this he who makes mention of your gods? And they would deny all mention of the Beneficent.

٣٦ وَإِذَا رَآكَ الَّذِينَ كَفَرُوا إِن يَتَّخِذُونَكَ إِلَّا هُزُوًا أَهَٰذَا الَّذِى يَذْكُرُ ءَالِهَتَكُمْ وَهُم بِذِكْرِ الرَّحْمَٰنِ هُمْ كَٰفِرُونَ

37. Man is made of haste. I shall show you My portents, but ask Me not to hasten.

٣٧ خُلِقَ الْإِنسَٰنُ مِنْ عَجَلٍ سَأُورِيكُمْ ءَايَٰتِى فَلَا تَسْتَعْجِلُونِ

38. And they say: When will this promise (be fulfilled), if you are truthful?

٣٨ وَيَقُولُونَ مَتَىٰ هَٰذَا الْوَعْدُ إِن كُنتُمْ صَٰدِقِينَ

39. If those who disbelieved but knew the time when they will not be able to drive off the fire from their faces and from their backs, and they will not be helped!

٣٩ لَوْ يَعْلَمُ الَّذِينَ كَفَرُوا حِينَ لَا يَكُفُّونَ عَن وُجُوهِهِمُ النَّارَ وَلَا عَن ظُهُورِهِمْ وَلَا هُمْ يُنصَرُونَ

40. Nay, but it will come upon them unawares so that it will stupefy them, and they will be unable to repel it, neither will they be reprieved.

٤٠ بَلْ تَأْتِيهِم بَغْتَةً فَتَبْهَتُهُمْ فَلَا يَسْتَطِيعُونَ رَدَّهَا وَلَا هُمْ يُنظَرُونَ

41. Messengers before you, indeed, were mocked, but that whereat they mocked surrounded those who scoffed at them.

٤١ وَلَقَدِ اسْتُهْزِئَ بِرُسُلٍ مِّن قَبْلِكَ فَحَاقَ بِالَّذِينَ سَخِرُوا مِنْهُم مَّا كَانُوا بِهِ يَسْتَهْزِءُونَ

42. Say: Who guards you in the night or in the day from the Beneficent? Nay, but they turn away from the mention of their Lord!

٤٢ قُلْ مَن يَكْلَؤُكُم بِالَّيْلِ وَالنَّهَارِ مِنَ الرَّحْمَٰنِ بَلْ هُمْ عَن ذِكْرِ رَبِّهِم مُّعْرِضُونَ

43. Or have they gods who can shield them from Us? They cannot help themselves nor can they be defended from Us.

٤٣ أَمْ لَهُمْ ءَالِهَةٌ تَمْنَعُهُم مِّن دُونِنَا لَا يَسْتَطِيعُونَ نَصْرَ أَنفُسِهِمْ وَلَا هُم مِّنَّا يُصْحَبُونَ

44. Nay, but We gave these and their fathers ease until life grew long for them. See they not how we visit the land, reducing it of its outlying parts?[182] Can they then be the conquerors?

٤٤ بَلْ مَتَّعْنَا هَٰؤُلَاءِ وَءَابَاءَهُمْ حَتَّىٰ طَالَ عَلَيْهِمُ الْعُمُرُ أَفَلَا يَرَوْنَ أَنَّا نَأْتِى الْأَرْضَ نَنقُصُهَا مِنْ أَطْرَافِهَا أَفَهُمُ الْغَٰلِبُونَ

45. Say (O Muhammad, unto mankind): I warn you only by the Inspiration. But the deaf hear not the call when they are warned.

٤٥ قُلْ إِنَّمَا أُنذِرُكُم بِالْوَحْىِ وَلَا يَسْمَعُ الصُّمُّ الدُّعَاءَ إِذَا مَا يُنذَرُونَ

---

[182]See Surah 13:41, footnote.

46. And if a breath of your Lord's punishment were to touch them, they assuredly would say: Alas for us! Lo! we were wrongdoers.

47. And We set a just balance for the Day of Resurrection so that no soul is wronged in anything. Though it be of the weight of a grain of mustard seed, We bring it. And We suffice for reckoners.

48. And We verily gave Moses and Aaron the Criterion (of right and wrong) and a light and a Reminder for those who keep from evil,

49. Those who fear their Lord in secret and who dread the Hour (of doom).

50. And this is a blessed Reminder that We have revealed: Will you then reject it?

51. And We verily gave Abraham of old his proper course, and We were Aware of him,

52. When he said unto his father and his folk: What are these images unto which you pay devotion?

53. They said: We found our fathers worshippers of them.

54. He said: Surely you and your fathers were in plain error.

55. They said: Do you bring unto us the truth, or are you some jester?

56. He said: Nay, but your Lord is the Lord of the heavens and the earth, Who created them; and I am of those who testify unto that.

57. And, by Allah, I shall circumvent your idols after you have gone away and turned your backs.

٤٦ وَلَئِن مَّسَّتْهُمْ نَفْحَةٌ مِّنْ عَذَابِ رَبِّكَ لَيَقُولُنَّ يَٰوَيْلَنَآ إِنَّا كُنَّا ظَٰلِمِينَ

٤٧ وَنَضَعُ ٱلْمَوَٰزِينَ ٱلْقِسْطَ لِيَوْمِ ٱلْقِيَٰمَةِ فَلَا تُظْلَمُ نَفْسٌ شَيْـًٔا وَإِن كَانَ مِثْقَالَ حَبَّةٍ مِّنْ خَرْدَلٍ أَتَيْنَا بِهَا وَكَفَىٰ بِنَا حَٰسِبِينَ

٤٨ وَلَقَدْ ءَاتَيْنَا مُوسَىٰ وَهَٰرُونَ ٱلْفُرْقَانَ وَضِيَآءً وَذِكْرًا لِّلْمُتَّقِينَ

٤٩ ٱلَّذِينَ يَخْشَوْنَ رَبَّهُم بِٱلْغَيْبِ وَهُم مِّنَ ٱلسَّاعَةِ مُشْفِقُونَ

٥٠ وَهَٰذَا ذِكْرٌ مُّبَارَكٌ أَنزَلْنَٰهُ أَفَأَنتُمْ لَهُۥ مُنكِرُونَ

٥١ وَلَقَدْ ءَاتَيْنَآ إِبْرَٰهِيمَ رُشْدَهُۥ مِن قَبْلُ وَكُنَّا بِهِۦ عَٰلِمِينَ

٥٢ إِذْ قَالَ لِأَبِيهِ وَقَوْمِهِۦ مَا هَٰذِهِ ٱلتَّمَاثِيلُ ٱلَّتِىٓ أَنتُمْ لَهَا عَٰكِفُونَ

٥٣ قَالُوا۟ وَجَدْنَآ ءَابَآءَنَا لَهَا عَٰبِدِينَ

٥٤ قَالَ لَقَدْ كُنتُمْ أَنتُمْ وَءَابَآؤُكُمْ فِى ضَلَٰلٍ مُّبِينٍ

٥٥ قَالُوٓا۟ أَجِئْتَنَا بِٱلْحَقِّ أَمْ أَنتَ مِنَ ٱللَّٰعِبِينَ

٥٦ قَالَ بَل رَّبُّكُمْ رَبُّ ٱلسَّمَٰوَٰتِ وَٱلْأَرْضِ ٱلَّذِى فَطَرَهُنَّ وَأَنَا۠ عَلَىٰ ذَٰلِكُم مِّنَ ٱلشَّٰهِدِينَ

٥٧ وَتَٱللَّٰهِ لَأَكِيدَنَّ أَصْنَٰمَكُم بَعْدَ أَن تُوَلُّوا۟ مُدْبِرِينَ

58. Then he reduced them to fragments, all save the chief of them, that haply they might have recourse to it.

59. They said: Who has done this to our gods? Surely it must be some evildoer.

60. They said: We heard a youth make mention of them, who is called Abraham.

61. They said: Then bring him (hither) before the people's eyes that they may testify.

62. They said: Is it you who have done this to our gods, O Abraham?

63. He said: But this, their chief has done it. So question them, if they can speak.

64. Then gathered they apart and said: Lo! you yourselves are the wrongdoers.

65. And they were utterly confounded, and they said (unto Abraham): Well you know that these speak not.

66. He said: Worship you then instead of Allah that which cannot profit you at all, nor harm you?

67. Fie on you and all that you worship instead of Allah! Have you then no sense?

68. They cried: Burn him and stand by your gods, if you will be doing.

69. We said: O fire, be coolness and peace for Abraham.

70. And they wished to set a snare for him, but We made them the greater losers.

71. And We rescued him and Lot (and brought them) to the land which We have blessed for (all) mankind.

72. And We bestowed upon him Isaac, and Jacob as a grandson. Each of them We made righteous.

٥٨ فَجَعَلَهُمْ جُذَاذًا إِلَّا كَبِيرًا لَّهُمْ لَعَلَّهُمْ إِلَيْهِ يَرْجِعُونَ

٥٩ قَالُوا مَن فَعَلَ هَٰذَا بِآلِهَتِنَا إِنَّهُ لَمِنَ الظَّالِمِينَ

٦٠ قَالُوا سَمِعْنَا فَتًى يَذْكُرُهُمْ يُقَالُ لَهُ إِبْرَاهِيمُ

٦١ قَالُوا فَأْتُوا بِهِ عَلَىٰ أَعْيُنِ النَّاسِ لَعَلَّهُمْ يَشْهَدُونَ

٦٢ قَالُوا أَأَنتَ فَعَلْتَ هَٰذَا بِآلِهَتِنَا يَا إِبْرَاهِيمُ

٦٣ قَالَ بَلْ فَعَلَهُ كَبِيرُهُمْ هَٰذَا فَاسْأَلُوهُمْ إِن كَانُوا يَنطِقُونَ

٦٤ فَرَجَعُوا إِلَىٰ أَنفُسِهِمْ فَقَالُوا إِنَّكُمْ أَنتُمُ الظَّالِمُونَ

٦٥ ثُمَّ نُكِسُوا عَلَىٰ رُءُوسِهِمْ لَقَدْ عَلِمْتَ مَا هَٰؤُلَاءِ يَنطِقُونَ

٦٦ قَالَ أَفَتَعْبُدُونَ مِن دُونِ اللَّهِ مَا لَا يَنفَعُكُمْ شَيْئًا وَلَا يَضُرُّكُمْ

٦٧ أُفٍّ لَّكُمْ وَلِمَا تَعْبُدُونَ مِن دُونِ اللَّهِ أَفَلَا تَعْقِلُونَ

٦٨ قَالُوا حَرِّقُوهُ وَانصُرُوا آلِهَتَكُمْ إِن كُنتُمْ فَاعِلِينَ

٦٩ قُلْنَا يَا نَارُ كُونِي بَرْدًا وَسَلَامًا عَلَىٰ إِبْرَاهِيمَ

٧٠ وَأَرَادُوا بِهِ كَيْدًا فَجَعَلْنَاهُمُ الْأَخْسَرِينَ

٧١ وَنَجَّيْنَاهُ وَلُوطًا إِلَى الْأَرْضِ الَّتِي بَارَكْنَا فِيهَا لِلْعَالَمِينَ

٧٢ وَوَهَبْنَا لَهُ إِسْحَاقَ وَيَعْقُوبَ نَافِلَةً وَكُلًّا جَعَلْنَا صَالِحِينَ

73. And We made them chiefs who guide by Our command, and We inspired in them the doing of good deeds and the right establishment of prayer and the giving of alms and they were worshippers of Us (alone).

74. And unto Lot We gave judgment and knowledge, and We delivered him from the community that did abominations. Lo! they were folk of evil, lewd.

75. And We brought him in unto Our mercy. Lo! he was of the righteous.

76. And Noah, when he cried of old, We heard his prayer and saved him and his household from the great affliction.

77. And delivered him from the people who denied Our revelations. Lo! they were folk of evil, therefore did We drown them all.

78. And David and Solomon, when they gave judgment concerning the field, when people's sheep had strayed and browsed therein by night; and We were witnesses to their judgment.

79. And We made Solomon to understand (the case); and unto each of them We gave judgment and knowledge. And We subdued the mountains and the birds to hymn (His) praise along with David. We were the doers (thereof).

80. And We taught him the art of making garments (of mail) to protect you in your daring. Are you then thankful?

81. And unto Solomon (We subdued) the wind in its raging. It set by His command toward the land which We had blessed. And of everything We are aware.

82. And of the devils[183] (subdued We unto him) some who dived (for pearls) for him and did other work, and We were warders unto them.

---

[183] Arabic: Shayāṭīn, literally "devils."

83. And Job, when he cried unto his Lord, (saying): Lo! adversity afflicts me, and You are Most Merciful of all who show mercy.

84. Then We heard his prayer and removed that adversity from which he suffered, and We gave him his household (that he had lost) and the like thereof along with them, a mercy from Our store, and a remembrance for the worshippers;

85. And (mention) Ishmael, and Idrīs, and Dhū al Kifl.[184] All were of the steadfast.

86. And We brought them in unto Our mercy. Lo! they are among the righteous.

87. And (mention) Dhū al Nūn,[185] when he went off in anger and deemed that We were not going to test him further, he cried out in the darkness, saying: There is no God save You. Be You glorified! I have been a wrongdoer.

88. Then We heard his prayer and saved him from the anguish. Thus We save believers.

89. And Zachariah, when he cried unto his Lord: My Lord! Leave me not childless, though You are the best of inheritors.

90. Then We heard his prayer, and bestowed upon him John, and adjusted his wife (to bear a child) for him. Lo! they used to vie one with the other in good deeds, and they cried unto Us in longing and in fear, and were submissive unto Us.

91. And she who was chaste,[186] therefore We breathed into her (something) of Our spirit and made her and her son a token for (all) the worlds.

92. Lo! this, your religion, is one religion, and I am your Lord, so worship Me.

---

[184]A prophet famous among the Arabs, whose story resembles that of Ezekiel.
[185]Lit: "Lord of the Fish," or Jonah.
[186]The reference here is to the Virgin Mary.

93. And they have broken their religion (into fragments) among them, (yet) all are returning unto Us.

٩٣ وَتَقَطَّعُوٓا أَمْرَهُم بَيْنَهُمْ كُلٌّ إِلَيْنَا رَٰجِعُونَ

94. Then who does good works and is a believer, there will be no rejection of his effort. Lo! We record (it) for him.

٩٤ فَمَن يَعْمَلْ مِنَ ٱلصَّٰلِحَٰتِ وَهُوَ مُؤْمِنٌ فَلَا كُفْرَانَ لِسَعْيِهِ وَإِنَّا لَهُۥ كَٰتِبُونَ

95. And there is a ban upon any community which We have destroyed: that they shall not return,

٩٥ وَحَرَٰمٌ عَلَىٰ قَرْيَةٍ أَهْلَكْنَٰهَآ أَنَّهُمْ لَا يَرْجِعُونَ

96. Until, when Gog and Magog are let loose, and they hasten out of every mound.

٩٦ حَتَّىٰٓ إِذَا فُتِحَتْ يَأْجُوجُ وَمَأْجُوجُ وَهُم مِّن كُلِّ حَدَبٍ يَنسِلُونَ

97. And the True Promise draws near; then behold them, starring wide (in terror), the eyes of those who disbelieve! (They say): Alas for us! We (lived) in forgetfulness of this. Ah, but we were wrongdoers!

٩٧ وَٱقْتَرَبَ ٱلْوَعْدُ ٱلْحَقُّ فَإِذَا هِىَ شَٰخِصَةٌ أَبْصَٰرُ ٱلَّذِينَ كَفَرُوا۟ يَٰوَيْلَنَا قَدْ كُنَّا فِى غَفْلَةٍ مِّنْ هَٰذَا بَلْ كُنَّا ظَٰلِمِينَ

98. Lo! you (idolaters) and that which you worship beside Allah are fuel of Hell. Thereunto you will come.

٩٨ إِنَّكُمْ وَمَا تَعْبُدُونَ مِن دُونِ ٱللَّهِ حَصَبُ جَهَنَّمَ أَنتُمْ لَهَا وَٰرِدُونَ

99. If these had been Gods they would not have come thither, but all will abide therein.

٩٩ لَوْ كَانَ هَٰٓؤُلَآءِ ءَالِهَةً مَّا وَرَدُوهَا وَكُلٌّ فِيهَا خَٰلِدُونَ

100. Therein wailing is their portion, and therein they hear not.

١٠٠ لَهُمْ فِيهَا زَفِيرٌ وَهُمْ فِيهَا لَا يَسْمَعُونَ

101. Lo! those unto whom kindness has gone forth before from Us, they will be far removed from there.

١٠١ إِنَّ ٱلَّذِينَ سَبَقَتْ لَهُم مِّنَّا ٱلْحُسْنَىٰٓ أُو۟لَٰٓئِكَ عَنْهَا مُبْعَدُونَ

102. They will not hear the slightest sound thereof, while they abide in that which their souls desire.

١٠٢ لَا يَسْمَعُونَ حَسِيسَهَا وَهُمْ فِى مَا ٱشْتَهَتْ أَنفُسُهُمْ خَٰلِدُونَ

103. The Supreme Horror will not grieve them, and the angels will welcome them, (saying): This is your Day which you were promised;

١٠٣ لَا يَحْزُنُهُمُ ٱلْفَزَعُ ٱلْأَكْبَرُ وَتَتَلَقَّىٰهُمُ ٱلْمَلَٰٓئِكَةُ هَٰذَا يَوْمُكُمُ ٱلَّذِى كُنتُمْ تُوعَدُونَ

104. The Day when We shall roll up the heavens as a recorder rolls up a written scroll. As We began the first creation, We shall repeat it. (It is) a promise (binding) upon Us. Lo! We are to perform it.

١٠٤ يَوْمَ نَطْوِى ٱلسَّمَآءَ كَطَىِّ ٱلسِّجِلِّ لِلْكُتُبِ كَمَا بَدَأْنَآ أَوَّلَ خَلْقٍ نُّعِيدُهُۥ وَعْدًا عَلَيْنَآ إِنَّا كُنَّا فَٰعِلِينَ

105. And indeed We have written in the Scripture, after the Reminder: My righteous slaves will inherit the earth:

106. Verily in this (Qur'an) is a message for folk who are devout.

107. We sent you not (O Muhammad) save as a mercy for the worlds.

108. Say: It is only inspired in me that your God is One God. Will you then surrender (unto Him)!

109. But if they are averse, then say: I have warned you all alike, although I know not whether near or far is that which you are promised.

110. Lo! He knows that which is said openly, and that which you conceal.

111. And I know not but that this may be a trial for you, and enjoyment for a while.

112. He says: My Lord! Judge You with truth. Our Lord is the Beneficent, whose help is to be implored against that which you ascribe (unto Him).

١٠٥ وَلَقَدْ كَتَبْنَا فِي الزَّبُورِ مِنْ بَعْدِ الذِّكْرِ أَنَّ الْأَرْضَ يَرِثُهَا عِبَادِيَ الصَّالِحُونَ

١٠٦ إِنَّ فِي هَذَا لَبَلَاغًا لِقَوْمٍ عَابِدِينَ

١٠٧ وَمَا أَرْسَلْنَاكَ إِلَّا رَحْمَةً لِلْعَالَمِينَ

١٠٨ قُلْ إِنَّمَا يُوحَى إِلَيَّ أَنَّمَا إِلَهُكُمْ إِلَهٌ وَاحِدٌ فَهَلْ أَنْتُمْ مُسْلِمُونَ

١٠٩ فَإِنْ تَوَلَّوْا فَقُلْ آذَنْتُكُمْ عَلَى سَوَاءٍ وَإِنْ أَدْرِي أَقَرِيبٌ أَمْ بَعِيدٌ مَا تُوعَدُونَ

١١٠ إِنَّهُ يَعْلَمُ الْجَهْرَ مِنَ الْقَوْلِ وَيَعْلَمُ مَا تَكْتُمُونَ

١١١ وَإِنْ أَدْرِي لَعَلَّهُ فِتْنَةٌ لَكُمْ وَمَتَاعٌ إِلَى حِينٍ

١١٢ قَالَ رَبِّ احْكُمْ بِالْحَقِّ وَرَبُّنَا الرَّحْمَنُ الْمُسْتَعَانُ عَلَى مَا تَصِفُونَ

The Pilgrimage

Al Ḥajj, "The Pilgrimage," takes its name from verses 26-38, which relate to the pilgrimage to Makkah. This surah is ascribed by some authorities to the Makkan, by others to the Madinah period. The copy of the Qur'an which I have followed throughout has the Madinah ascription, and, as it was copied long before the days of "higher" criticism and was authorized for use throughout the Ottoman Empire, I retain that ascription. Verses 11-13, 25-30, 39-41, and 58-60 were, according to all authorities, revealed at al Madinah. Nol-deke, greatest of the "higher" critics, says that the ascription is justified on account of the importance of the verses which must, from the nature of their contents, have been revealed at al Madinah. He holds that much of the surah belongs to the last Makkan period.

The Pilgrimage

Revealed at al Madinah
In the name of Allah,
the Beneficent, the Merciful

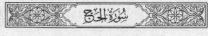

1. mankind! Fear your Lord. Lo! the earthquake of the Hour (of Doom) is a tremendous thing.

2. On the day when you behold it, every nursing mother will forget her nursling and every pregnant one will be delivered of her burden, and you (Muhammad) will see mankind as drunken, yet they will not be drunken, but the Punishment of Allah will be severe (upon them).

3. Among mankind is he who disputes concerning Allah without knowledge, and follows each perverse devil;

4. For him it is decreed that who takes him for friend, he surely will mislead him and will guide him to the punishment of the Flame.

5. O mankind! if you are in doubt concerning the Resurrec-tion, then lo! We have created you from dust, then from a drop of seed, then from a clot, then from a little lump of flesh shapely and shapeless, that We may make (it) clear for you. And We cause what We will to remain in the wombs for an appointed time, and afterward We bring you forth as infants, then (give you growth) that you attain your full strength. And among you there is he who dies (young), and among you there is he who is brought back to the most abject time of life, so that, after knowledge, he knows nothing. And you (Muhammad) see the earth barren, but when We send down water thereon, it does shake and swell and put forth every lovely kind[187] (of growth).

---

[187]Or "every lovely pair." Prof. Ghamrawi, who helped me in the revision of the text, kept exclaiming on the subtlety and wealth of meaning of every expression used in the Qur'an concerning natural phenomena. Thus the word "pair" occurs often in the sense of "species," commemorating the fact that the word "pair" of the earth exists as male and female. See, in particular, Surah 36:35.

6. That is because Allah, He is the Truth. Lo! He quickens the dead, and lo! He is Able to do all things;

٦ ذٰلِكَ بِأَنَّ اللَّهَ هُوَ الْحَقُّ وَأَنَّهُ يُحْيِ الْمَوْتَىٰ وَأَنَّهُ عَلَىٰ كُلِّ شَيْءٍ قَدِيرٌ

7. And because the Hour will come, there is no doubt thereof; and because Allah will raise those who are in the graves.

٧ وَأَنَّ السَّاعَةَ ءَاتِيَةٌ لَّا رَيْبَ فِيهَا وَأَنَّ اللَّهَ يَبْعَثُ مَن فِي الْقُبُورِ

8. And among mankind is he who disputes concerning Allah without knowledge or guidance or a Scripture giving light.

٨ وَمِنَ النَّاسِ مَن يُجَٰدِلُ فِي اللَّهِ بِغَيْرِ عِلْمٍ وَلَا هُدًى وَلَا كِتَٰبٍ مُّنِيرٍ

9. Turning away in pride to beguile (men) from the way of Allah. For him in this world is ignominy, and on the Day of Resurrection We make him taste the doom of burning.

٩ ثَانِيَ عِطْفِهِ لِيُضِلَّ عَن سَبِيلِ اللَّهِ لَهُ فِي الدُّنْيَا خِزْيٌ وَنُذِيقُهُ يَوْمَ الْقِيَٰمَةِ عَذَابَ الْحَرِيقِ

10. (And unto him it will be said): This is for that which your two hands have sent before, and because Allah is no oppressor of His slaves.

١٠ ذٰلِكَ بِمَا قَدَّمَتْ يَدَاكَ وَأَنَّ اللَّهَ لَيْسَ بِظَلَّٰمٍ لِّلْعَبِيدِ

11. And among mankind is he who worships Allah upon a narrow marge so that if good befalls him he is content therewith, but if a trial befalls him, he falls away utterly. He loses both the world and the Hereafter. That is the sheer loss.[188]

١١ وَمِنَ النَّاسِ مَن يَعْبُدُ اللَّهَ عَلَىٰ حَرْفٍ فَإِنْ أَصَابَهُ خَيْرٌ اطْمَأَنَّ بِهِ وَإِنْ أَصَابَتْهُ فِتْنَةٌ انقَلَبَ عَلَىٰ وَجْهِهِ خَسِرَ الدُّنْيَا وَالْءَاخِرَةَ ذٰلِكَ هُوَ الْخُسْرَانُ الْمُبِينُ

12. He calls, beside Allah, unto that which hurts him not nor benefits him. That is the far error.

١٢ يَدْعُواْ مِن دُونِ اللَّهِ مَا لَا يَضُرُّهُ وَمَا لَا يَنفَعُهُ ذٰلِكَ هُوَ الضَّلَٰلُ الْبَعِيدُ

13. He calls unto him whose harm is nearer than his benefit; verily an evil patron and verily an evil friend!

١٣ يَدْعُواْ لَمَن ضَرُّهُ أَقْرَبُ مِن نَّفْعِهِ لَبِئْسَ الْمَوْلَىٰ وَلَبِئْسَ الْعَشِيرُ

14. Lo! Allah causes those who believe and do good works to enter the Gardens underneath which rivers flow. Lo! Allah does what He intends.

١٤ إِنَّ اللَّهَ يُدْخِلُ الَّذِينَ ءَامَنُواْ وَعَمِلُواْ الصَّٰلِحَٰتِ جَنَّٰتٍ تَجْرِي مِن تَحْتِهَا الْأَنْهَٰرُ إِنَّ اللَّهَ يَفْعَلُ مَا يُرِيدُ

---

[188]Tradition says that the reference is to certain Arabs who came to the Pro-phet at al Madinah and professed Islam. When times were good, they prospered in a worldly sense and were content, but if they had to suffer at all they returned to idolatry.

15. Who is wont to think (through envy) that Allah will not give him (Muhammad) victory in the world and the Hereafter (and is enraged at the thought of his victory), let him stretch a rope up to the roof (of his dwelling), and let him hang himself. Then let him see whether his strategy dispels that whereat he rages![189]

١٥ مَن كَانَ يَظُنُّ أَن لَّن يَنصُرَهُ اللَّهُ فِي الدُّنْيَا وَالْآخِرَةِ فَلْيَمْدُدْ بِسَبَبٍ إِلَى السَّمَاءِ ثُمَّ لْيَقْطَعْ فَلْيَنظُرْ هَلْ يُذْهِبَنَّ كَيْدُهُ مَا يَغِيظُ

16. Thus We reveal it as plain revelations, and surely Allah guides whom He will.

١٦ وَكَذَلِكَ أَنزَلْنَاهُ ءَايَتٍ بَيِّنَتٍ وَأَنَّ اللَّهَ يَهْدِي مَن يُرِيدُ

17. Lo! those who believe (this Revelation), and those who are Jews, and the Sabaeans and the Christians and the Magians and the idolaters. Lo! Allah will decide between them on the Day of Resurrection. Lo! Allah is Witness over all things.

١٧ إِنَّ الَّذِينَ ءَامَنُوا وَالَّذِينَ هَادُوا وَالصَّابِئِينَ وَالنَّصَارَىٰ وَالْمَجُوسَ وَالَّذِينَ أَشْرَكُوا إِنَّ اللَّهَ يَفْصِلُ بَيْنَهُمْ يَوْمَ الْقِيَامَةِ إِنَّ اللَّهَ عَلَىٰ كُلِّ شَيْءٍ شَهِيدٌ

18. Have you not seen that unto Allah pays adoration whoever is in the heavens and whoever is in the earth, and the sun, and the moon, and the stars, and the mountains, and the trees, and the beasts, and many of mankind, while there are many unto whom the doom is justly due. He whom Allah scorns, there is none to give him honor. Lo! Allah does what He will.

١٨ أَلَمْ تَرَ أَنَّ اللَّهَ يَسْجُدُ لَهُ مَن فِي السَّمَوَاتِ وَمَن فِي الْأَرْضِ وَالشَّمْسُ وَالْقَمَرُ وَالنُّجُومُ وَالْجِبَالُ وَالشَّجَرُ وَالدَّوَابُّ وَكَثِيرٌ مِّنَ النَّاسِ وَكَثِيرٌ حَقَّ عَلَيْهِ الْعَذَابُ وَمَن يُهِنِ اللَّهُ فَمَا لَهُ مِن مُّكْرِمٍ إِنَّ اللَّهَ يَفْعَلُ مَا يَشَاءُ ۩

19. These two (the believers and the disbelievers) are two opponents who contend concerning their Lord. But as for those who disbelieve, garments of fire will be cut out for them; boiling fluid will be poured down on their heads.

١٩ هَذَانِ خَصْمَانِ اخْتَصَمُوا فِي رَبِّهِمْ فَالَّذِينَ كَفَرُوا قُطِّعَتْ لَهُمْ ثِيَابٌ مِّن نَّارٍ يُصَبُّ مِن فَوْقِ رُءُوسِهِمُ الْحَمِيمُ

20. Whereby that which is in their bellies, and their skins too, will be melted;

٢٠ يُصْهَرُ بِهِ مَا فِي بُطُونِهِمْ وَالْجُلُودُ

21. And for them are hooked rods of iron.

٢١ وَلَهُم مَّقَامِعُ مِنْ حَدِيدٍ

22. Whenever, in their anguish, they would go forth from thence they are driven back therein and (it is said unto them): Taste the doom of burning.

٢٢ كُلَّمَا أَرَادُوا أَن يَخْرُجُوا مِنْهَا مِنْ غَمٍّ أُعِيدُوا فِيهَا وَذُوقُوا عَذَابَ الْحَرِيقِ

---

[189]The meaning is that Allah will undoubtedly cause the Prophet to triumph in both worlds, and thus his opponents have no strategy save that of despair.

23. Lo! Allah will cause those who believe and do good works to enter Gardens underneath which rivers flow, wherein they will be allowed armlets of gold, and pearls, and their raiment therein will be silk.

24. They are guided unto gentle speech; they are guided unto the path of the Glorious One.

25. Lo! those who disbelieve and bar (men) from the way of Allah and from the Sacred Mosque, which We have appointed for mankind together, the dweller therein and the nomad; whoever seeks wrongful partiality therein, him We shall cause to taste a painful doom.

26. And (remember) when We prepared for Abraham the place of the (holy) House, saying: Ascribe you no thing as partner unto Me, and purify My House for those who make the round (thereof) and those who stand and those who bow and make prostration.

27. And proclaim unto mankind the Pilgrimage.[190] They will come unto you on foot and on every lean camel; they will come from every deep ravine.

28. That they may witness things that are of benefit to them, and mention the name of Allah on appointed days over the beast of cattle that He has bestowed upon them. Then eat thereof and feed therewith the poor unfortunate.

29. Then let them make an end of their unkemptness and pay their vows and go around the ancient House.

30. That (is the command). And whoso magnifies the sacred things of Allah, it will be well for him in the sight of his Lord. The cattle are lawful unto you save that which has been told you. So shun the filth of idols, and shun lying speech.

---

[190]See Surah 2:196 ff.

31. Turning unto Allah (only), not ascribing partners unto Him; for whoso ascribes partners unto Allah, it is as if he had fallen from the sky and the birds had snatched him or the wind had blown him to a far off place.

32. That (is the command). And who magnifies the offerings consecrated to Allah, it surely is from devotion of the hearts.

33. Therein are benefits for you for an appointed term; and afterward they are brought for sacrifice[191] unto the ancient House.

34. And for every nation have We appointed a ritual, that they may mention the name of Allah over the beast of cattle that He has given them for food[192]; and your God is One God, therefore surrender unto Him. And give good tidings (O Mu-hammad) to the humble,

35. Whose hearts fear when Allah is mentioned, and the patient of whatever may befall them, and those who establish prayer and who spend of that We have bestowed on them.

36. And the camels! We have appointed them among the ceremonies of Allah. Therein you have much good. So mention the name of Allah over them when they are drawn up in lines. Then when their flanks fall (dead), eat thereof and feed the beggar and the suppliant. Thus have We made them subject unto you, that you may give thanks.

37. Their flesh and their blood reach not Allah, but the devotion from you reaches Him. Thus have We made them subject unto you that you may magnify Allah that He has guided you. And give good tidings (O Muhammad) to the good.

38. Lo! Allah defends those who believe. Lo! Allah loves not each treacherous ingrate.

---

[191]The slaughter of animals for food for the poor, which is one of the ceremonies of the Muslim pilgrimage, is not a propitiatory sacrifice, but is in commemoration of the sacrifice of Abraham which marked the end of human sacrifices for the Semitic race, and which made it clear that the only sacrifice which Allah requires of man is the surrender of his will and purpose—i.e., al-Islam.
[192]In order that they may realize the awfulness of taking life and the solemn nature of the trusts that Allah has imposed on them by giving them His permission to eat animal food.

39. Sanction (to fight) is given unto those who are fought against because they have been wronged; and Allah is indeed Able to give them victory;

٣٩ أُذِنَ لِلَّذِينَ يُقَٰتَلُونَ بِأَنَّهُمْ ظُلِمُوا ۚ وَإِنَّ اللَّهَ عَلَىٰ نَصْرِهِمْ لَقَدِيرٌ

40. Those who have been driven from their homes unjustly only because they said: Our Lord is Allah. For had it not been for Allah's repelling some men by means of others, cloisters and churches and oratories and mosques, wherein the name of Allah is oft mentioned, would assuredly have been pulled down. Truly Allah helps one who helps His cause. Lo! Allah is Strong, Almighty.

٤٠ الَّذِينَ أُخْرِجُوا مِن دِيَٰرِهِم بِغَيْرِ حَقٍّ إِلَّا أَن يَقُولُوا رَبُّنَا اللَّهُ ۗ وَلَوْلَا دَفْعُ اللَّهِ النَّاسَ بَعْضَهُم بِبَعْضٍ لَّهُدِّمَتْ صَوَٰمِعُ وَبِيَعٌ وَصَلَوَٰتٌ وَمَسَٰجِدُ يُذْكَرُ فِيهَا اسْمُ اللَّهِ كَثِيرًا ۗ وَلَيَنصُرَنَّ اللَّهُ مَن يَنصُرُهُ ۗ إِنَّ اللَّهَ لَقَوِيٌّ عَزِيزٌ

41. Those who, if We give them power in the land, establish prayer and pay the poor due and enjoin kindness and forbid iniquity. And Allah's is the sequel of events.

٤١ الَّذِينَ إِن مَّكَّنَّٰهُمْ فِي الْأَرْضِ أَقَامُوا الصَّلَوٰةَ وَءَاتَوُا الزَّكَوٰةَ وَأَمَرُوا بِالْمَعْرُوفِ وَنَهَوْا عَنِ الْمُنكَرِ ۗ وَلِلَّهِ عَٰقِبَةُ الْأُمُورِ

42. If they deny you (Muhammad), even so the folk of Noah, and (the tribes of) 'Ād and Thamūd, before you, denied (Our messengers);

٤٢ وَإِن يُكَذِّبُوكَ فَقَدْ كَذَّبَتْ قَبْلَهُمْ قَوْمُ نُوحٍ وَعَادٌ وَثَمُودُ

43. And the folk of Abraham and the folk of Lot;

٤٣ وَقَوْمُ إِبْرَٰهِيمَ وَقَوْمُ لُوطٍ

44. (And) the dwellers in Madian. And Moses was denied; but I indulged the disbelievers a long while, then I seized them, and how (terrible) was My abhorrence!

٤٤ وَأَصْحَٰبُ مَدْيَنَ ۖ وَكُذِّبَ مُوسَىٰ فَأَمْلَيْتُ لِلْكَٰفِرِينَ ثُمَّ أَخَذْتُهُمْ ۖ فَكَيْفَ كَانَ نَكِيرِ

45. How many a township have We destroyed while it was sinful, so that it lies (to this day) in ruins, and (how many) a deserted well and lofty tower!

٤٥ فَكَأَيِّن مِّن قَرْيَةٍ أَهْلَكْنَٰهَا وَهِيَ ظَالِمَةٌ فَهِيَ خَاوِيَةٌ عَلَىٰ عُرُوشِهَا وَبِئْرٍ مُّعَطَّلَةٍ وَقَصْرٍ مَّشِيدٍ

46. Have they not travelled in the land, and have they hearts with which to feel and ears with which to hear? For indeed it is not the eyes that grow blind, but it is the hearts, which are within the bosoms, that grow blind.

٤٦ أَفَلَمْ يَسِيرُوا فِي الْأَرْضِ فَتَكُونَ لَهُمْ قُلُوبٌ يَعْقِلُونَ بِهَا أَوْ ءَاذَانٌ يَسْمَعُونَ بِهَا ۖ فَإِنَّهَا لَا تَعْمَى الْأَبْصَٰرُ وَلَٰكِن تَعْمَى الْقُلُوبُ الَّتِي فِي الصُّدُورِ

47. And they will bid you hasten on the Doom, and Allah fails not His promise, but lo! a Day with Allah is as a thousand years of what you reckon.

48. And how many a township did I suffer long though it was sinful! Then I grasped it. Unto Me is the return.

49. Say: O mankind! I am only a plain warner unto you.

50. Those who believe and do good works, for them pardon and a rich provision;

51. While those who strive to thwart Our revelations, such are rightful owners of the Fire.

52. Never sent We a messenger or a Prophet before you but when He recited (the message) Satan proposed (opposition) in respect of that which he recited thereof. But Allah abolishes that which Satan proposes. Then Allah establishes His revelations. Allah is Knower, Wise;

53. That He may make that which the Devil proposes a temptation for those in whose hearts is a disease, and those whose hearts are hardened—Lo! the evil-doers are in open schism—

54. And that those who have been given knowledge may know that it is the truth from your Lord, so that they may believe therein and their hearts may submit humbly unto Him. Lo! Allah truly is guiding those who believe unto a right path.

55. And those who disbelieve will not cease to be in doubt thereof until the Hour come upon them unawares, or there come unto them the doom of a disastrous day.

وَيَسْتَعْجِلُونَكَ بِالْعَذَابِ وَلَن يُخْلِفَ اللَّهُ ﴿٤٧﴾ وَعْدَهُ وَإِنَّ يَوْمًا عِندَ رَبِّكَ كَأَلْفِ سَنَةٍ مِّمَّا تَعُدُّونَ

وَكَأَيِّن مِّن قَرْيَةٍ أَمْلَيْتُ لَهَا وَهِيَ ظَالِمَةٌ ﴿٤٨﴾ ثُمَّ أَخَذْتُهَا وَإِلَيَّ الْمَصِيرُ

قُلْ يَا أَيُّهَا النَّاسُ إِنَّمَا أَنَا لَكُمْ نَذِيرٌ مُّبِينٌ ﴿٤٩﴾

فَالَّذِينَ آمَنُوا وَعَمِلُوا الصَّالِحَاتِ لَهُم ﴿٥٠﴾ مَّغْفِرَةٌ وَرِزْقٌ كَرِيمٌ

وَالَّذِينَ سَعَوْا فِي آيَاتِنَا مُعَاجِزِينَ أُولَٰئِكَ ﴿٥١﴾ أَصْحَابُ الْجَحِيمِ

وَمَا أَرْسَلْنَا مِن قَبْلِكَ مِن رَّسُولٍ وَلَا نَبِيٍّ ﴿٥٢﴾ إِلَّا إِذَا تَمَنَّىٰ أَلْقَى الشَّيْطَانُ فِي أُمْنِيَّتِهِ فَيَنسَخُ اللَّهُ مَا يُلْقِي الشَّيْطَانُ ثُمَّ يُحْكِمُ اللَّهُ آيَاتِهِ وَاللَّهُ عَلِيمٌ حَكِيمٌ

لِّيَجْعَلَ مَا يُلْقِي الشَّيْطَانُ فِتْنَةً لِّلَّذِينَ فِي ﴿٥٣﴾ قُلُوبِهِم مَّرَضٌ وَالْقَاسِيَةِ قُلُوبُهُمْ وَإِنَّ الظَّالِمِينَ لَفِي شِقَاقٍ بَعِيدٍ

وَلِيَعْلَمَ الَّذِينَ أُوتُوا الْعِلْمَ أَنَّهُ الْحَقُّ مِن ﴿٥٤﴾ رَّبِّكَ فَيُؤْمِنُوا بِهِ فَتُخْبِتَ لَهُ قُلُوبُهُمْ وَإِنَّ اللَّهَ لَهَادِ الَّذِينَ آمَنُوا إِلَىٰ صِرَاطٍ مُّسْتَقِيمٍ

وَلَا يَزَالُ الَّذِينَ كَفَرُوا فِي مِرْيَةٍ مِّنْهُ حَتَّىٰ ﴿٥٥﴾ تَأْتِيَهُمُ السَّاعَةُ بَغْتَةً أَوْ يَأْتِيَهُمْ عَذَابُ يَوْمٍ عَقِيمٍ

56. The Sovereignty on that day will be Allah's. He will judge between them. Then those who believed and did good works will be in Gardens of Delight,

57. While those who disbelieved and denied Our revelations, for them will be a shameful doom.

58. Those who fled their homes for the cause of Allah and then were slain or died, Allah surely will provide for them a good provision. Lo! Allah, He surely is Best of all who make provision.

59. Assuredly He will cause them to enter by an entry that they will love. Lo! Allah surely is Knower, Indulgent.

60. That (is so). And who has retaliated with the like of that which he was made to suffer and then has (again) been wronged, Allah will succor him. Lo! Allah surely is, Mild, Forgiving.

61. That is because Allah makes the night to pass into the day and makes the day to pass into the night, and because Allah is Hearer, Seer.

62. That is because Allah, He is the True, and that whereon they call instead of Him, it is the False, and because Allah, He is the High, the Great.

63. Do you not see how Allah sends down water from the sky and then the earth becomes green upon the morrow? Lo! Allah is Subtle, Aware.

64. Unto Him belongs all that is in the heavens and all that is in the earth. Lo! Allah, He surely is the Absolute, the Owner of Praise.

١٥٦ اَلْمُلْكُ يَوْمَئِذٍ لِلَّهِ يَحْكُمُ بَيْنَهُمْ فَالَّذِيْنَ اٰمَنُوْا وَعَمِلُوا الصّٰلِحٰتِ فِيْ جَنّٰتِ النَّعِيْمِ

١٥٧ وَالَّذِيْنَ كَفَرُوْا وَكَذَّبُوْا بِاٰيٰتِنَا فَاُولٰٓئِكَ لَهُمْ عَذَابٌ مُّهِيْنٌ

١٥٨ وَالَّذِيْنَ هَاجَرُوْا فِيْ سَبِيْلِ اللّٰهِ ثُمَّ قُتِلُوْا اَوْ مَاتُوْا لَيَرْزُقَنَّهُمُ اللّٰهُ رِزْقًا حَسَنًا وَاِنَّ اللّٰهَ لَهُوَ خَيْرُ الرّٰزِقِيْنَ

١٥٩ لَيُدْخِلَنَّهُمْ مُّدْخَلًا يَّرْضَوْنَهٗ وَاِنَّ اللّٰهَ لَعَلِيْمٌ حَلِيْمٌ

٦٠ ذٰلِكَ وَمَنْ عَاقَبَ بِمِثْلِ مَا عُوْقِبَ بِهٖ ثُمَّ بُغِيَ عَلَيْهِ لَيَنْصُرَنَّهُ اللّٰهُ اِنَّ اللّٰهَ لَعَفُوٌّ غَفُوْرٌ

٦١ ذٰلِكَ بِاَنَّ اللّٰهَ يُوْلِجُ الَّيْلَ فِي النَّهَارِ وَيُوْلِجُ النَّهَارَ فِي الَّيْلِ وَاَنَّ اللّٰهَ سَمِيْعٌ بَصِيْرٌ

٦٢ ذٰلِكَ بِاَنَّ اللّٰهَ هُوَ الْحَقُّ وَاَنَّ مَا يَدْعُوْنَ مِنْ دُوْنِهٖ هُوَ الْبَاطِلُ وَاَنَّ اللّٰهَ هُوَ الْعَلِيُّ الْكَبِيْرُ

٦٣ اَلَمْ تَرَ اَنَّ اللّٰهَ اَنْزَلَ مِنَ السَّمَآءِ مَآءً فَتُصْبِحُ الْاَرْضُ مُخْضَرَّةً اِنَّ اللّٰهَ لَطِيْفٌ خَبِيْرٌ

٦٤ لَهٗ مَا فِي السَّمٰوٰتِ وَمَا فِي الْاَرْضِ وَاِنَّ اللّٰهَ لَهُوَ الْغَنِيُّ الْحَمِيْدُ

65. Have you not seen how Allah has made all that is in the earth subservient unto you? And ships run upon the sea by His command, and He holds back the heaven from falling on the earth unless by His leave. Lo! Allah is, for mankind, Full of Pity, Merciful.

66. And He it is Who gave you life, then He will cause you to die, and then will give you life (again). Lo! man is surely an ingrate.

67. Unto each nation have We given sacred rites which they are to perform; so let them not dispute with you of the matter, but summon you unto your Lord. Lo! you indeed follow right guidance.

68. And if they wrangle with you, say: Allah is best aware of what you do.

69. Allah will judge between you on the Day of Resurrec-tion concerning that wherein you used to differ.

70. Have you not known that Allah knows all that is in the heaven and the earth? Lo! that is in a record. Lo! that is easy for Allah.

71. And they worship instead of Allah that for which no warrant has been revealed unto them, and that whereof they have no knowledge. For evildoers there is no helper.

72. And when Our revelations are clearly recited unto them, you know the denial in the faces of those who disbelieve; they all but attack those who recite Our revelations unto them. Say: Shall I proclaim unto you worse than that? The Fire! Allah has promised it for those who disbelieve. An unlucky journey's end!

٦٥ أَلَمْ تَرَ أَنَّ ٱللَّهَ سَخَّرَ لَكُم مَّا فِي ٱلْأَرْضِ وَٱلْفُلْكَ تَجْرِي فِي ٱلْبَحْرِ بِأَمْرِهِۦ وَيُمْسِكُ ٱلسَّمَآءَ أَن تَقَعَ عَلَى ٱلْأَرْضِ إِلَّا بِإِذْنِهِۦٓ إِنَّ ٱللَّهَ بِٱلنَّاسِ لَرَءُوفٌ رَّحِيمٌ

٦٦ وَهُوَ ٱلَّذِيٓ أَحْيَاكُمْ ثُمَّ يُمِيتُكُمْ ثُمَّ يُحْيِيكُمْ إِنَّ ٱلْإِنسَـٰنَ لَكَفُورٌ

٦٧ لِكُلِّ أُمَّةٍ جَعَلْنَا مَنسَكًا هُمْ نَاسِكُوهُ فَلَا يُنَـٰزِعُنَّكَ فِي ٱلْأَمْرِ وَٱدْعُ إِلَىٰ رَبِّكَ إِنَّكَ لَعَلَىٰ هُدًى مُّسْتَقِيمٍ

٦٨ وَإِن جَـٰدَلُوكَ فَقُلِ ٱللَّهُ أَعْلَمُ بِمَا تَعْمَلُونَ

٦٩ ٱللَّهُ يَحْكُمُ بَيْنَكُمْ يَوْمَ ٱلْقِيَـٰمَةِ فِيمَا كُنتُمْ فِيهِ تَخْتَلِفُونَ

٧٠ أَلَمْ تَعْلَمْ أَنَّ ٱللَّهَ يَعْلَمُ مَا فِي ٱلسَّمَآءِ وَٱلْأَرْضِ إِنَّ ذَٰلِكَ فِي كِتَـٰبٍ إِنَّ ذَٰلِكَ عَلَى ٱللَّهِ يَسِيرٌ

٧١ وَيَعْبُدُونَ مِن دُونِ ٱللَّهِ مَا لَمْ يُنَزِّلْ بِهِۦ سُلْطَـٰنًا وَمَا لَيْسَ لَهُم بِهِۦ عِلْمٌ وَمَا لِلظَّـٰلِمِينَ مِن نَّصِيرٍ

٧٢ وَإِذَا تُتْلَىٰ عَلَيْهِمْ ءَايَـٰتُنَا بَيِّنَـٰتٍ تَعْرِفُ فِي وُجُوهِ ٱلَّذِينَ كَفَرُوا ٱلْمُنكَرَ يَكَادُونَ يَسْطُونَ بِٱلَّذِينَ يَتْلُونَ عَلَيْهِمْ ءَايَـٰتِنَا قُلْ أَفَأُنَبِّئُكُم بِشَرٍّ مِّن ذَٰلِكُمُ ٱلنَّارُ وَعَدَهَا ٱللَّهُ ٱلَّذِينَ كَفَرُوا وَبِئْسَ ٱلْمَصِيرُ

73. O mankind! A similitude is coined, so pay you heed to it: Lo! those on whom you call beside Allah will never create a fly though they combine together for the purpose. And if the fly took something from them, they could not rescue it from him. So weak are (both) the seeker and the sought!

74. They measure not Allah His rightful measure. Lo! Allah is Strong, Almighty.

75. Allah chooses from the angels messengers, and (also) from mankind. Lo! Allah is Hearer, Seer.

76. He knows all that is before them and all that is behind them, and unto Allah all things are returned.

77. O, you who believe! Bow down and prostrate yourselves, and worship your Lord, and do good, that you may prosper.

78. And strive for Allah with the endeavor which is His right. He has chosen you and has not laid upon you in religion any hardship; the faith of your father Abraham (is yours). He has named you Muslims[193] of old time and in this (Scripture), that the messenger may be a witness over you, and that you may be witnesses over mankind. So establish prayer, pay the poor-due, and hold fast to Allah. He is your Protecting Friend. A blessed Patron and a blessed Helper!

[193]"Those who have surrendered."

Believers

Al Mu'minūn, "Believers," derives its name from a word occurring in the first verse or, it may be said, from its subject: the triumph of believers. It is considered to be the last Makkan surah and as being revealed immediately before the Prophet's emigration to Yathrib (al Madinah).

A late Makkan surah.

Believers

Revealed at Makkah

*In the name of Allah,
the Beneficent, the Merciful*

1. Successful indeed are believers

2. Who are humble in their prayers,

3. And who shun vain conversation,

4. And who are payers of the poor-due;

5. And who guard their modesty

6. Save from their wives or the (slaves) that their right hands possess, for then they are not blameworthy,

7. But who craves beyond that, such are transgressors,

8. And who are shepherds of their pledge and their covenant,

9. And who pay heed to their prayers.

10. These are the heirs

11. Who will inherit Paradise: There they will abide forever.

12. Verily We created man from a product of wet earth;

13. Then placed him as a drop (of seed) in a safe lodging;

14. Then fashioned We the drop a clot, then fashioned We the clot a little lump, then fashioned We the little lump bones, then clothed the bones with flesh, and then produced it another creation. So blessed be Allah, the Best of Creators!

15. Then lo! after that you surely die.

16. Then lo! on the Day of Resurrection you are raised (again).

17. And We have created above you seven paths, and We are never unmindful of creation.

18. And We send down from the sky water in measure, and We give it lodging in the earth, and lo! We are able to withdraw it.

19. Then We produce for you therewith gardens of date palms and grapes, wherein is much fruit for you and whereof you eat;

20. And a tree that springs forth from Mount Sinai that grows oil and relish for the eaters.

21. And lo! in the cattle there is surely a lesson for you. We give you to drink of that which is in their bellies, and many uses have you in them, and of them do you eat;

22. And on them and on ships you are carried.

23. And We verily sent Noah unto his folk, and he said: O my people! Worship Allah. You have no other god save Him. Will you not ward off (evil)?

24. But the chieftains of his folk, who disbelieved, said: This is only a mortal like you who would make himself superior to you. Had Allah willed, He surely could have sent down angels. We heard not of this in the case of our fathers of old.

25. He is only a man in whom is a madness, so watch him for a while.

26. He said: My Lord! Help me because they deny me.

27. Then We inspired in him, saying: Make the ship under Our eyes and Our inspiration. Then, when Our command comes and the oven gushes water, introduce therein of every (kind) two spouses, and your household save him thereof against whom the Word has already gone forth. And plead not with Me on behalf of those who have done wrong: Lo! they will be drowned.

١٧ وَلَقَدْ خَلَقْنَا فَوْقَكُمْ سَبْعَ طَرَآئِقَ وَمَا كُنَّا عَنِ الْخَلْقِ غَافِلِينَ

١٨ وَأَنزَلْنَا مِنَ السَّمَآءِ مَآءً بِقَدَرٍ فَأَسْكَنَّهُ فِي الْأَرْضِ وَإِنَّا عَلَى ذَهَابٍ بِهِ لَقَادِرُونَ

١٩ فَأَنشَأْنَا لَكُمْ بِهِ جَنَّاتٍ مِّن نَّخِيلٍ وَأَعْنَابٍ لَّكُمْ فِيهَا فَوَاكِهُ كَثِيرَةٌ وَمِنْهَا تَأْكُلُونَ

٢٠ وَشَجَرَةً تَخْرُجُ مِن طُورِ سَيْنَآءَ تَنبُتُ بِالدُّهْنِ وَصِبْغٍ لِّلْآكِلِينَ

٢١ وَإِنَّ لَكُمْ فِي الْأَنْعَامِ لَعِبْرَةً نُّسْقِيكُم مِّمَّا فِي بُطُونِهَا وَلَكُمْ فِيهَا مَنَافِعُ كَثِيرَةٌ وَمِنْهَا تَأْكُلُونَ

٢٢ وَعَلَيْهَا وَعَلَى الْفُلْكِ تُحْمَلُونَ

٢٣ وَلَقَدْ أَرْسَلْنَا نُوحًا إِلَى قَوْمِهِ فَقَالَ يَاقَوْمِ اعْبُدُوا اللَّهَ مَا لَكُم مِّنْ إِلَهٍ غَيْرُهُ أَفَلَا تَتَّقُونَ

٢٤ فَقَالَ الْمَلَأُ الَّذِينَ كَفَرُوا مِن قَوْمِهِ مَا هَذَا إِلَّا بَشَرٌ مِّثْلُكُمْ يُرِيدُ أَن يَتَفَضَّلَ عَلَيْكُمْ وَلَوْ شَآءَ اللَّهُ لَأَنزَلَ مَلَائِكَةً مَّا سَمِعْنَا بِهَذَا فِي ءَابَآئِنَا الْأَوَّلِينَ

٢٥ إِنْ هُوَ إِلَّا رَجُلٌ بِهِ جِنَّةٌ فَتَرَبَّصُوا بِهِ حَتَّى حِينٍ

٢٦ قَالَ رَبِّ انصُرْنِي بِمَا كَذَّبُونِ

٢٧ فَأَوْحَيْنَا إِلَيْهِ أَنِ اصْنَعِ الْفُلْكَ بِأَعْيُنِنَا وَوَحْيِنَا فَإِذَا جَآءَ أَمْرُنَا وَفَارَ التَّنُّورُ فَاسْلُكْ فِيهَا مِن كُلٍّ زَوْجَيْنِ اثْنَيْنِ وَأَهْلَكَ إِلَّا مَن سَبَقَ عَلَيْهِ الْقَوْلُ مِنْهُمْ وَلَا تُخَاطِبْنِي فِي الَّذِينَ ظَلَمُوا إِنَّهُم مُّغْرَقُونَ

28. And when you are on board the ship, you and those with you, then say: Praise be to Allah Who has saved us from the wrongdoing folk!

29. And say: My Lord! Cause me to land at a blessed landing place, for You are best of all who bring to land.

30. Lo! herein surely are portents, for lo! We are ever putting (mankind) to the test.

31. Then, after them, We brought forth another generation;

32. And We sent among them a messenger of their own saying: Worship Allah. You have no other god save Him. Will you not ward off (evil)?

33. And the chieftains of his folk, who disbelieved and de-nied the meeting of the Hereafter, and whom We had made soft in the life of the world, said: This is only a mortal like you, who eats of that whereof you eat and drinks of that you drink.

34. If you were to obey a mortal like yourselves, you surely would be losers.

35. Does he promise you that you, when you are dead and have become dust and bones, will (again) be brought forth?

36. Begone, begone, with that which you are promised!

37. There is nothing but our life of the world; we die and we live, and we shall not be raised (again).

38. He is only a man who has invented a lie about Allah. We are not going to put faith in him.

39. He said: My Lord! Help me because they deny me,

40. He said: In a little while they surely will become repentant.

﴿٢٨﴾ فَإِذَا اسْتَوَيْتَ أَنْتَ وَمَنْ مَعَكَ عَلَى الْفُلْكِ فَقُلِ الْحَمْدُ لِلّٰهِ الَّذِي نَجّٰنَا مِنَ الْقَوْمِ الظّٰلِمِينَ

﴿٢٩﴾ وَقُلْ رَبِّ أَنْزِلْنِي مُنْزَلًا مُبَارَكًا وَأَنْتَ خَيْرُ الْمُنْزِلِينَ

﴿٣٠﴾ إِنَّ فِي ذٰلِكَ لَآيَاتٍ وَإِنْ كُنَّا لَمُبْتَلِينَ

﴿٣١﴾ ثُمَّ أَنْشَأْنَا مِنْ بَعْدِهِمْ قَرْنًا آخَرِينَ

﴿٣٢﴾ فَأَرْسَلْنَا فِيهِمْ رَسُولًا مِنْهُمْ أَنِ اعْبُدُوا اللّٰهَ مَا لَكُمْ مِنْ إِلٰهٍ غَيْرُهُ أَفَلَا تَتَّقُونَ

﴿٣٣﴾ وَقَالَ الْمَلَأُ مِنْ قَوْمِهِ الَّذِينَ كَفَرُوا وَكَذَّبُوا بِلِقَاءِ الْآخِرَةِ وَأَتْرَفْنَاهُمْ فِي الْحَيَاةِ الدُّنْيَا مَا هٰذَا إِلَّا بَشَرٌ مِثْلُكُمْ يَأْكُلُ مِمَّا تَأْكُلُونَ مِنْهُ وَيَشْرَبُ مِمَّا تَشْرَبُونَ

﴿٣٤﴾ وَلَئِنْ أَطَعْتُمْ بَشَرًا مِثْلَكُمْ إِنَّكُمْ إِذًا لَخَاسِرُونَ

﴿٣٥﴾ أَيَعِدُكُمْ أَنَّكُمْ إِذَا مِتُّمْ وَكُنْتُمْ تُرَابًا وَعِظَامًا أَنَّكُمْ مُخْرَجُونَ

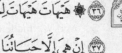

﴿٣٦﴾ هَيْهَاتَ هَيْهَاتَ لِمَا تُوعَدُونَ

﴿٣٧﴾ إِنْ هِيَ إِلَّا حَيَاتُنَا الدُّنْيَا نَمُوتُ وَنَحْيَا وَمَا نَحْنُ بِمَبْعُوثِينَ

﴿٣٨﴾ إِنْ هُوَ إِلَّا رَجُلٌ افْتَرَىٰ عَلَى اللّٰهِ كَذِبًا وَمَا نَحْنُ لَهُ بِمُؤْمِنِينَ

﴿٣٩﴾ قَالَ رَبِّ انْصُرْنِي بِمَا كَذَّبُونِ

﴿٤٠﴾ قَالَ عَمَّا قَلِيلٍ لَيُصْبِحُنَّ نَادِمِينَ

41. So the (Awful) Cry overtook them rightfully, and We made them like as wreckage (that a torrent hurls). A far removal for wrongdoing folk!

42. Then after them We brought forth other generations.

43. No nation can outstrip its term, nor yet postpone it.

44. Then We sent our messengers one after another. Whenever its messenger came unto a nation they denied him; so We caused them to follow one another (to disaster) and We made them bywords. A far removal for folk who believe not!

45. Then We sent Moses and his brother Aaron with Our tokens and a clear warrant

46. Unto Pharaoh and his chiefs, but they scorned (them) and they were despotic folk.

47. And they said: Shall we put faith in two mortals like ourselves, and whose folk are servile unto us?

48. So they denied them, and became of those who were destroyed.

49. And we surely gave Moses the Scripture, that they might go aright.

50. And We made the son of Mary and his mother a portent, and We gave them refuge on a height, a place of flocks and water springs.

51. O you messengers! Eat of the good things and do right. Lo! I am Aware of what you do.

52. And lo! this your religion is one religion and I am your Lord, so keep your duty unto Me.

53. But they (mankind) have broken their religion among them into sects, each sect rejoicing in its tenets.

٤١ فَأَخَذَتْهُمُ الصَّيْحَةُ بِالْحَقِّ فَجَعَلْنَاهُمْ غُثَاءً فَبُعْدًا لِلْقَوْمِ الظَّالِمِينَ

٤٢ ثُمَّ أَنْشَأْنَا مِنْ بَعْدِهِمْ قُرُونًا آخَرِينَ

٤٣ مَا تَسْبِقُ مِنْ أُمَّةٍ أَجَلَهَا وَمَا يَسْتَأْخِرُونَ

٤٤ ثُمَّ أَرْسَلْنَا رُسُلَنَا تَتْرَا كُلَّ مَا جَاءَ أُمَّةً رَسُولُهَا كَذَّبُوهُ فَأَتْبَعْنَا بَعْضَهُمْ بَعْضًا وَجَعَلْنَاهُمْ أَحَادِيثَ فَبُعْدًا لِقَوْمٍ لَا يُؤْمِنُونَ

٤٥ ثُمَّ أَرْسَلْنَا مُوسَى وَأَخَاهُ هَارُونَ بِآيَاتِنَا وَسُلْطَانٍ مُبِينٍ

٤٦ إِلَى فِرْعَوْنَ وَمَلَإِيهِ فَاسْتَكْبَرُوا وَكَانُوا قَوْمًا عَالِينَ

٤٧ فَقَالُوا أَنُؤْمِنُ لِبَشَرَيْنِ مِثْلِنَا وَقَوْمُهُمَا لَنَا عَابِدُونَ

٤٨ فَكَذَّبُوهُمَا فَكَانُوا مِنَ الْمُهْلَكِينَ

٤٩ وَلَقَدْ آتَيْنَا مُوسَى الْكِتَابَ لَعَلَّهُمْ يَهْتَدُونَ

٥٠ وَجَعَلْنَا ابْنَ مَرْيَمَ وَأُمَّهُ آيَةً وَآوَيْنَاهُمَا إِلَى رَبْوَةٍ ذَاتِ قَرَارٍ وَمَعِينٍ

٥١ يَا أَيُّهَا الرُّسُلُ كُلُوا مِنَ الطَّيِّبَاتِ وَاعْمَلُوا صَالِحًا إِنِّي بِمَا تَعْمَلُونَ عَلِيمٌ

٥٢ وَإِنَّ هَذِهِ أُمَّتُكُمْ أُمَّةً وَاحِدَةً وَأَنَا رَبُّكُمْ فَاتَّقُونِ

٥٣ فَتَقَطَّعُوا أَمْرَهُمْ بَيْنَهُمْ زُبُرًا كُلُّ حِزْبٍ بِمَا لَدَيْهِمْ فَرِحُونَ

54. So leave them in their error till a time.

55. Think they that in the wealth and sons with which We provide them

56. We hasten unto them with good things? Nay, but they perceive not.

57. Lo! those who go in awe for fear of their Lord,

58. And those who believe in the revelations of their Lord,

59. And those who ascribe not partners unto their Lord,

60. And those who give that which they give with hearts afraid because they are about to return unto their Lord,

61. These race for the good things, and they shall win them in the race.

62. And We task not any soul beyond its scope, and with Us is a Record which speaks the truth, and they will not be wronged.

63. Nay, but their hearts are in ignorance of this (Qur'an), and they have other works, besides, which they are doing;

64. Till when We grasp their luxurious ones with the punishment, behold! they supplicate.

65. Supplicate not this day! Assuredly you will not be helped by Us.

66. My revelations were recited unto you, but you used to turn back on your heels,

67. In scorn thereof. Nightly did you rave together.

68. Have they not pondered the Word, or has that come unto them which came not unto their fathers of old?

٥٤ فَذَرْهُمْ فِي غَمْرَتِهِمْ حَتَّىٰ حِينٍ

٥٥ أَيَحْسَبُونَ أَنَّمَا نُمِدُّهُم بِهِ مِن مَّالٍ وَبَنِينَ

٥٦ نُسَارِعُ لَهُمْ فِي الْخَيْرَاتِ بَل لَّا يَشْعُرُونَ

٥٧ إِنَّ الَّذِينَ هُم مِّنْ خَشْيَةِ رَبِّهِم مُّشْفِقُونَ

٥٨ وَالَّذِينَ هُم بِآيَاتِ رَبِّهِمْ يُؤْمِنُونَ

٥٩ وَالَّذِينَ هُم بِرَبِّهِمْ لَا يُشْرِكُونَ

٦٠ وَالَّذِينَ يُؤْتُونَ مَا آتَوا وَّقُلُوبُهُمْ وَجِلَةٌ أَنَّهُمْ إِلَىٰ رَبِّهِمْ رَاجِعُونَ

٦١ أُولَٰئِكَ يُسَارِعُونَ فِي الْخَيْرَاتِ وَهُمْ لَهَا سَابِقُونَ

٦٢ وَلَا نُكَلِّفُ نَفْسًا إِلَّا وُسْعَهَا وَلَدَيْنَا كِتَابٌ يَنطِقُ بِالْحَقِّ وَهُمْ لَا يُظْلَمُونَ

٦٣ بَلْ قُلُوبُهُمْ فِي غَمْرَةٍ مِّنْ هَٰذَا وَلَهُمْ أَعْمَالٌ مِّن دُونِ ذَٰلِكَ هُمْ لَهَا عَامِلُونَ

٦٤ حَتَّىٰ إِذَا أَخَذْنَا مُتْرَفِيهِم بِالْعَذَابِ إِذَا هُمْ يَجْأَرُونَ

٦٥ لَا تَجْأَرُوا الْيَوْمَ إِنَّكُم مِّنَّا لَا تُنصَرُونَ

٦٦ قَدْ كَانَتْ آيَاتِي تُتْلَىٰ عَلَيْكُمْ فَكُنتُمْ عَلَىٰ أَعْقَابِكُمْ تَنكِصُونَ

٦٧ مُسْتَكْبِرِينَ بِهِ سَامِرًا تَهْجُرُونَ

٦٨ أَفَلَمْ يَدَّبَّرُوا الْقَوْلَ أَمْ جَاءَهُم مَّا لَمْ يَأْتِ آبَاءَهُمُ الْأَوَّلِينَ

69. Or know they not their messenger, and so reject him?

٦٩ اَمْ لَمْ يَعْرِفُوْا رَسُوْلَهُمْ فَهُمْ لَهُ مُنْكِرُوْنَ

70. Or say they: There is a madness in him? Nay, but he brings them the Truth; and most of them are haters of the Truth.

٧٠ اَمْ يَقُوْلُوْنَ بِهِ جِنَّةٌ بَلْ جَآءَهُمْ بِالْحَقِّ وَاَكْثَرُهُمْ لِلْحَقِّ كَارِهُوْنَ

71. And if the Truth had followed their desires, surely the heavens and the earth and whoever is therein had been corrupted. Nay, We have brought them their Reminder, but from their Reminder they now turn away.

٧١ وَلَوِ اتَّبَعَ الْحَقُّ اَهْوَآءَهُمْ لَفَسَدَتِ السَّمٰوٰتُ وَالْاَرْضُ وَمَنْ فِيْهِنَّ بَلْ اَتَيْنٰهُمْ بِذِكْرِهِمْ فَهُمْ عَنْ ذِكْرِهِمْ مُّعْرِضُوْنَ

72. Or do you ask of them (O Muhammad) any tribute? But! the bounty of your Lord is better, for He is best of all who make provision.

٧٢ اَمْ تَسْئَلُهُمْ خَرْجًا فَخَرَاجُ رَبِّكَ خَيْرٌ وَّهُوَ خَيْرُ الرّٰزِقِيْنَ

73. And lo! you summon them indeed unto a right path.

٧٣ وَاِنَّكَ لَتَدْعُوْهُمْ اِلٰى صِرَاطٍ مُّسْتَقِيْمٍ

74. And lo! those who believe not in the Hereafter are indeed astray from the path.

٧٤ وَاِنَّ الَّذِيْنَ لَا يُؤْمِنُوْنَ بِالْاٰخِرَةِ عَنِ الصِّرَاطِ لَنَاكِبُوْنَ

75. Though We had mercy on them and relieved them of the harm afflicting them, they still would wander blindly on in their contumacy.

٧٥ وَلَوْ رَحِمْنٰهُمْ وَكَشَفْنَا مَا بِهِمْ مِّنْ ضُرٍّ لَّلَجُّوْا فِيْ طُغْيَانِهِمْ يَعْمَهُوْنَ

76. Already have We grasped them with punishment, but they humble not themselves unto their Lord, nor do they pray,

٧٦ وَلَقَدْ اَخَذْنٰهُمْ بِالْعَذَابِ فَمَا اسْتَكَانُوْا لِرَبِّهِمْ وَمَا يَتَضَرَّعُوْنَ

77. Until, when We open for them the gate of extreme punishment, behold! they are aghast thereat.

٧٧ حَتّٰى اِذَا فَتَحْنَا عَلَيْهِمْ بَابًا ذَا عَذَابٍ شَدِيْدٍ اِذَاهُمْ فِيْهِ مُبْلِسُوْنَ

78. He it is Who has created for you ears and eyes and hearts. Small thanks give you!

٧٨ وَهُوَ الَّذِيْ اَنْشَاَ لَكُمُ السَّمْعَ وَالْاَبْصَارَ وَالْاَفْئِدَةَ قَلِيْلًا مَّا تَشْكُرُوْنَ

79. And He it is Who has sown you broadcast in the earth, and unto Him you will be gathered.

٧٩ وَهُوَ الَّذِيْ ذَرَاَكُمْ فِي الْاَرْضِ وَاِلَيْهِ تُحْشَرُوْنَ

80. And He it is Who gives life and causes death, and His is the difference of night and day. Have you then no sense?

٨٠ وَهُوَ الَّذِيْ يُحْيٖ وَيُمِيْتُ وَلَهُ اخْتِلَافُ الَّيْلِ وَالنَّهَارِ اَفَلَا تَعْقِلُوْنَ

81. Nay, but they say the like of that which said the men of old;

٨١ بَلْ قَالُوا مِثْلَ مَا قَالَ الْأَوَّلُونَ

82. They say: When we are dead and have become (mere dust and bones, shall we then, really, be raised again?

٨٢ قَالُوا أَءِذَا مِتْنَا وَكُنَّا تُرَابًا وَعِظَامًا أَءِنَّا لَمَبْعُوثُونَ

83. We were already promised this, we and our forefathers. Lo! this is nothing but fables of the men of old.

٨٣ لَقَدْ وُعِدْنَا نَحْنُ وَءَابَاؤُنَا هَٰذَا مِنْ قَبْلُ إِنْ هَٰذَا إِلَّا أَسَاطِيرُ الْأَوَّلِينَ

84. Say: Unto Whom (belongs) the earth and whoever is therein, if you have knowledge?

٨٤ قُلْ لِمَنِ الْأَرْضُ وَمَنْ فِيهَا إِنْ كُنْتُمْ تَعْلَمُونَ

85. They will say: Unto Allah. Say: Will you not then remember?

٨٥ سَيَقُولُونَ لِلَّهِ قُلْ أَفَلَا تَذَكَّرُونَ

86. Say: Who is Lord of the seven heavens, and Lord of the Tremendous Throne?

٨٦ قُلْ مَنْ رَبُّ السَّمَاوَاتِ السَّبْعِ وَرَبُّ الْعَرْشِ الْعَظِيمِ

87. They will say: Unto Allah (all that belongs). Say: Will you not then keep duty (unto Him)?

٨٧ سَيَقُولُونَ لِلَّهِ قُلْ أَفَلَا تَتَّقُونَ

88. Say: In Whose hand is the dominion over all things and He protects, while against Him there is no protection, if you have knowledge?

٨٨ قُلْ مَنْ بِيَدِهِ مَلَكُوتُ كُلِّ شَيْءٍ وَهُوَ يُجِيرُ وَلَا يُجَارُ عَلَيْهِ إِنْ كُنْتُمْ تَعْلَمُونَ

89. They will say: Unto Allah (all that belongs). Say: How then are you bewitched?

٨٩ سَيَقُولُونَ لِلَّهِ قُلْ فَأَنَّىٰ تُسْحَرُونَ

90. Nay, but We have brought them the Truth, and lo! they are liars.

٩٠ بَلْ أَتَيْنَاهُمْ بِالْحَقِّ وَإِنَّهُمْ لَكَاذِبُونَ

91. Allah has not chosen any son, nor is there any God along with Him; else would each God have assuredly championed that which he created, and some of them would assuredly have overcome others. Glorified be Allah above all that they allege.

٩١ مَا اتَّخَذَ اللَّهُ مِنْ وَلَدٍ وَمَا كَانَ مَعَهُ مِنْ إِلَٰهٍ إِذًا لَذَهَبَ كُلُّ إِلَٰهٍ بِمَا خَلَقَ وَلَعَلَا بَعْضُهُمْ عَلَىٰ بَعْضٍ سُبْحَانَ اللَّهِ عَمَّا يَصِفُونَ

92. Knower of the invisible and the visible! And exalted be He over all that they ascribe as partners (unto Him)!

٩٢ عَالِمِ الْغَيْبِ وَالشَّهَادَةِ فَتَعَالَىٰ عَمَّا يُشْرِكُونَ

93. Say: My Lord! If you should show me that which they are promised,

٩٣ قُلْ رَبِّ إِمَّا تُرِيَنِّي مَا يُوعَدُونَ

94. My Lord! then set me not among the wrongdoing folk.

٩٤ رَبِّ فَلَا تَجْعَلْنِي فِي الْقَوْمِ الظَّالِمِينَ

95. And surely We are Able to show you that which We have promised them.

٩٥ وَإِنَّا عَلَىٰ أَنْ نُرِيَكَ مَا نَعِدُهُمْ لَقَادِرُونَ

96. Repel evil with that which is better. We are best Aware of that which they allege.

97. And say: My Lord! I seek refuge in You from suggestions of the evil ones,

98. And I seek refuge in You, my Lord, lest they be present with me,

99. Until, when death comes unto one of them, he says: My Lord! Send me back,

100. That I may do right in that which I have left behind! But nay! It is but a word that he speaks; and behind them is a barrier until the day when they are raised.

101. And when the trumpet is blown there will be no kinship among them that day, nor will they ask of one another.

102. Then those whose scales are heavy, they are the successful.

103. And those whose scales are light are those who lose their souls, in Hell abiding.

104. The fire burns their faces, and they are glum therein.

105. (It will be said): Were not My revelations recited unto you, and then you used to deny them?

106. They will say: Our Lord! Our evil fortune conquered us, and we were erring folk.

107. Our Lord! Oh, bring us forth from hence! If we return (to evil) then indeed we shall be wrongdoers.

108. He says: Begone therein, and speak not unto Me.

109. Lo! there was a party of My slaves who said: Our Lord! We believe, therefore forgive us and have mercy on us for You are best of all who show mercy;

٩٦ اُدْفَعْ بِالَّتِيْ هِيَ اَحْسَنُ السَّيِّئَةَ نَحْنُ اَعْلَمُ بِمَا يَصِفُوْنَ

٩٧ وَقُلْ رَّبِّ اَعُوْذُ بِكَ مِنْ هَمَزٰتِ الشَّيٰطِيْنِ

٩٨ وَاَعُوْذُ بِكَ رَبِّ اَنْ يَّحْضُرُوْنِ

٩٩ حَتّٰۤى اِذَا جَآءَ اَحَدَهُمُ الْمَوْتُ قَالَ رَبِّ ارْجِعُوْنِ

١٠٠ لَعَلِّيْۤ اَعْمَلُ صَالِحًا فِيْمَا تَرَكْتُ كَلَّا اِنَّهَا كَلِمَةٌ هُوَ قَآئِلُهَا وَمِنْ وَّرَآئِهِمْ بَرْزَخٌ اِلٰى يَوْمِ يُبْعَثُوْنَ

١٠١ فَاِذَا نُفِخَ فِى الصُّوْرِ فَلَاۤ اَنْسَابَ بَيْنَهُمْ يَوْمَئِذٍ وَّلَا يَتَسَآءَلُوْنَ

١٠٢ فَمَنْ ثَقُلَتْ مَوَازِيْنُهُ فَاُولٰٓئِكَ هُمُ الْمُفْلِحُوْنَ

١٠٣ وَمَنْ خَفَّتْ مَوَازِيْنُهُ فَاُولٰٓئِكَ الَّذِيْنَ خَسِرُوْۤا اَنْفُسَهُمْ فِيْ جَهَنَّمَ خٰلِدُوْنَ

١٠٤ تَلْفَحُ وُجُوْهَهُمُ النَّارُ وَهُمْ فِيْهَا كٰلِحُوْنَ

١٠٥ اَلَمْ تَكُنْ اٰيٰتِيْ تُتْلٰى عَلَيْكُمْ فَكُنْتُمْ بِهَا تُكَذِّبُوْنَ

١٠٦ قَالُوْا رَبَّنَا غَلَبَتْ عَلَيْنَا شِقْوَتُنَا وَكُنَّا قَوْمًا ضَآلِّيْنَ

١٠٧ رَبَّنَاۤ اَخْرِجْنَا مِنْهَا فَاِنْ عُدْنَا فَاِنَّا ظٰلِمُوْنَ

١٠٨ قَالَ اخْسَؤُا فِيْهَا وَلَا تُكَلِّمُوْنِ

١٠٩ اِنَّهُ كَانَ فَرِيْقٌ مِّنْ عِبَادِيْ يَقُوْلُوْنَ رَبَّنَاۤ اٰمَنَّا فَاغْفِرْ لَنَا وَارْحَمْنَا وَاَنْتَ خَيْرُ الرّٰحِمِيْنَ

110. But you chose them from a laughing stock until they caused you to forget remembrance of Me, while you laughed at them.

111. Lo! I have rewarded them this day forasmuch as they were steadfast; and they surely are the triumphant.

112. He will say: How long tarried you in the earth, counting by years?

113. They will say: We tarried but a day or part of a day. Ask of those who keep count!

114. He will say: You tarried but a little if you only knew.

115. Deemed you then that We had created you in vain, and that you would not be returned unto Us?

116. Now Allah be exalted, the True King! There is no God save Him, the Lord of the Throne of Grace.

117. He who cries unto any other god along with Allah has no proof thereof. His reckoning is only with his Lord. Lo! disbelievers will not be successful.

118. And (O Muhammad) say: My Lord! Forgive and have mercy, for You are best of all who show mercy.

١١٠) فَاتَّخَذْتُمُوهُمْ سِخْرِيًّا حَتَّىٰ أَنسَوْكُمْ ذِكْرِى وَكُنتُم مِّنْهُمْ تَضْحَكُونَ

١١١) إِنِّى جَزَيْتُهُمُ الْيَوْمَ بِمَا صَبَرُوٓا أَنَّهُمْ هُمُ الْفَآئِزُونَ

١١٢) قَالَ كَمْ لَبِثْتُمْ فِى الْأَرْضِ عَدَدَ سِنِينَ

١١٣) قَالُوا لَبِثْنَا يَوْمًا أَوْ بَعْضَ يَوْمٍ فَسْـَٔلِ الْعَآدِّينَ

١١٤) قَالَ إِن لَّبِثْتُمْ إِلَّا قَلِيلًا لَّوْ أَنَّكُمْ كُنتُمْ تَعْلَمُونَ

١١٥) أَفَحَسِبْتُمْ أَنَّمَا خَلَقْنَاكُمْ عَبَثًا وَأَنَّكُمْ إِلَيْنَا لَا تُرْجَعُونَ

١١٦) فَتَعَالَى اللَّهُ الْمَلِكُ الْحَقُّ لَآ إِلَٰهَ إِلَّا هُوَ رَبُّ الْعَرْشِ الْكَرِيمِ

١١٧) وَمَن يَدْعُ مَعَ اللَّهِ إِلَٰهًا ءَاخَرَ لَا بُرْهَانَ لَهُۥ بِهِۦ فَإِنَّمَا حِسَابُهُۥ عِندَ رَبِّهِۦٓ إِنَّهُۥ لَا يُفْلِحُ الْكَافِرُونَ

١١٨) وَقُل رَّبِّ اغْفِرْ وَارْحَمْ وَأَنتَ خَيْرُ الرَّاحِمِينَ

Light

Al Nūr, "Light," takes its name from verses 35-40, which describe the Light of God as it should shine in the homes of believers. The greater part of this surah consists of legislation for purifying one's home life. All of its verses were revealed at al Madinah. Tradition says that verses 11-20 relate to the slanderers of 'Ā'ishah in connection with an incident that occurred in the year 5 AH. When the Prophet was returning from the campaign against the Banī al Mustaliq, 'Ā'ishah was left behind on a march. She was found and brought back by a young soldier, who let her mount his camel and then led it himself. A weaker tradition places the revelation of verses 1-10 as late as the year 9 AH.

The period of revelation is the fifth and sixth years of the Hijrah.

Light

Revealed at al Madinah

*In the name of Allah,
the Beneficent, the Merciful*

1. (Here is) a Surah which We have revealed and en-joined, and wherein We have revealed plain tokens, that you may take heed.

2. The adulteress and the adulterer, scourge you each one of them (with) a hundred stripes. And let not pity for the two withhold you from obedience to Allah, if you believe in Allah and the Last Day. And let a party of believers witness their punishment.

3. The adulterer shall not marry save an adulteress or an idolatress, and the adulteress none shall marry save an adulterer or an idolater. All that is forbidden unto believers.

4. And those who accuse honorable women but bring not four witnesses, scourge them (with) eighty stripes and never (afterward) accept their testimony—They indeed are evil-doers—

5. Save those who afterward repent and make amends. (For such) lo! Allah is Forgiving, Merciful.

6. As for those who accuse their wives but have no witnesses except themselves; let the testimony of one of them be four testimonies, (swearing) by Allah that he is of those who speak the truth;

7. And yet a fifth, invoking the curse of Allah on him if he is of those who lie.

٧ وَالْخَامِسَةَ أَنَّ لَعْنَتَ اللَّهِ عَلَيْهِ إِن كَانَ مِنَ الْكَاذِبِينَ

8. And it shall avert the punishment from her if she bear witness before Allah four times that the thing he says is indeed false,

٨ وَيَدْرَؤُا عَنْهَا الْعَذَابَ أَن تَشْهَدَ أَرْبَعَ شَهَادَاتٍ بِاللَّهِ إِنَّهُ لَمِنَ الْكَاذِبِينَ

9. And a fifth (time) that the wrath of Allah be upon her if he speaks truth.

٩ وَالْخَامِسَةَ أَنَّ غَضَبَ اللَّهِ عَلَيْهَا إِن كَانَ مِنَ الصَّادِقِينَ

10. And had it not been for the grace of Allah and His mercy unto you, and that Allah is Clement, Wise, (you had been undone).

١٠ وَلَوْلَا فَضْلُ اللَّهِ عَلَيْكُمْ وَرَحْمَتُهُ وَأَنَّ اللَّهَ تَوَّابٌ حَكِيمٌ

11. Lo! they who spread the slander are a gang among you. Deem it not a bad thing for you; nay, it is good for you. Unto every man of them (will be paid that which he has earned of the sin; and as for him among them who had the greater share therein, his will be an awful doom.

١١ إِنَّ الَّذِينَ جَاءُوا بِالْإِفْكِ عُصْبَةٌ مِّنكُمْ لَا تَحْسَبُوهُ شَرًّا لَّكُم بَلْ هُوَ خَيْرٌ لَّكُمْ لِكُلِّ امْرِئٍ مِّنْهُم مَّا اكْتَسَبَ مِنَ الْإِثْمِ وَالَّذِي تَوَلَّى كِبْرَهُ مِنْهُمْ لَهُ عَذَابٌ عَظِيمٌ

12. Why did not the believers, men and women, when you heard it, think good of their own folk; and say: It is a manifest untruth?

١٢ لَّوْلَا إِذْ سَمِعْتُمُوهُ ظَنَّ الْمُؤْمِنُونَ وَالْمُؤْمِنَاتُ بِأَنفُسِهِمْ خَيْرًا وَقَالُوا هَٰذَا إِفْكٌ مُّبِينٌ

13. Why did they not produce four witnesses? Since they produce not witnesses, they surely are liars in the sight of Allah.

١٣ لَّوْلَا جَاءُوا عَلَيْهِ بِأَرْبَعَةِ شُهَدَاءَ فَإِذْ لَمْ يَأْتُوا بِالشُّهَدَاءِ فَأُولَٰئِكَ عِندَ اللَّهِ هُمُ الْكَاذِبُونَ

14. Had it not been for the grace of Allah and His mercy unto you in the world and the Hereafter an awful doom had overtaken you for that whereof you murmured.

١٤ وَلَوْلَا فَضْلُ اللَّهِ عَلَيْكُمْ وَرَحْمَتُهُ فِي الدُّنْيَا وَالْآخِرَةِ لَمَسَّكُمْ فِي مَا أَفَضْتُمْ فِيهِ عَذَابٌ عَظِيمٌ

15. When you welcomed it with your tongues, and uttered with your mouths that whereof you had no knowledge, you counted it a trifle. In the sight of Allah it is very great.

١٥ إِذْ تَلَقَّوْنَهُ بِأَلْسِنَتِكُمْ وَتَقُولُونَ بِأَفْوَاهِكُم مَّا لَيْسَ لَكُم بِهِ عِلْمٌ وَتَحْسَبُونَهُ هَيِّنًا وَهُوَ عِندَ اللَّهِ عَظِيمٌ

16. Wherefor, when you heard it, said you not: It is not for us to speak of this. Glory be to You (O Allah); This is awful calumny.

17. Allah admonishes you that you repeat not the like thereof ever, if you are (in truth) believers.

18. And He expounds unto you His revelations. Allah is Knower, Wise.

19. Lo! those who love that slander should be spread concerning those who believe, theirs will be a painful punishment in the world and the Hereafter. Allah knows. You know not.

20. Had it not been for the grace of Allah and His mercy unto you, and that Allah is Clement, Merciful, (you had been undone).

21. O you who believe! Follow not the footsteps of the Devil. Unto whom follows the footsteps of the Devil, lo! he commands filthiness and wrong. Had it not been for the grace of Allah and His mercy unto you, not one of you would ever have grown pure. But Allah causes whom He will to be pure. And Allah is Hearer, Knower.

22. And let not those who possess dignity and ease among you swear not to give to the near of kin and to the needy, and to fugitives for the cause of Allah.[194] Let them forgive and show indulgence. Yearn you not that Allah may forgive you? Allah is Forgiving, Merciful.

23. Lo! as for those who traduce virtuous, believing women (who are) careless, cursed are they in the world and the Hereafter. Theirs will be an awful doom

١٦ وَلَوْلَا إِذْ سَمِعْتُمُوهُ قُلْتُم مَّا يَكُونُ لَنَا أَن نَّتَكَلَّمَ بِهَٰذَا سُبْحَانَكَ هَٰذَا بُهْتَانٌ عَظِيمٌ

١٧ يَعِظُكُمُ اللَّهُ أَن تَعُودُوا لِمِثْلِهِ أَبَدًا إِن كُنتُم مُّؤْمِنِينَ

١٨ وَيُبَيِّنُ اللَّهُ لَكُمُ الْآيَاتِ وَاللَّهُ عَلِيمٌ حَكِيمٌ

١٩ إِنَّ الَّذِينَ يُحِبُّونَ أَن تَشِيعَ الْفَاحِشَةُ فِي الَّذِينَ آمَنُوا لَهُمْ عَذَابٌ أَلِيمٌ فِي الدُّنْيَا وَالْآخِرَةِ وَاللَّهُ يَعْلَمُ وَأَنتُمْ لَا تَعْلَمُونَ

٢٠ وَلَوْلَا فَضْلُ اللَّهِ عَلَيْكُمْ وَرَحْمَتُهُ وَأَنَّ اللَّهَ رَءُوفٌ رَّحِيمٌ

٢١ يَا أَيُّهَا الَّذِينَ آمَنُوا لَا تَتَّبِعُوا خُطُوَاتِ الشَّيْطَانِ وَمَن يَتَّبِعْ خُطُوَاتِ الشَّيْطَانِ فَإِنَّهُ يَأْمُرُ بِالْفَحْشَاءِ وَالْمُنكَرِ وَلَوْلَا فَضْلُ اللَّهِ عَلَيْكُمْ وَرَحْمَتُهُ مَا زَكَىٰ مِنكُم مِّنْ أَحَدٍ أَبَدًا وَلَٰكِنَّ اللَّهَ يُزَكِّي مَن يَشَاءُ وَاللَّهُ سَمِيعٌ عَلِيمٌ

٢٢ وَلَا يَأْتَلِ أُولُو الْفَضْلِ مِنكُمْ وَالسَّعَةِ أَن يُؤْتُوا أُولِي الْقُرْبَىٰ وَالْمَسَاكِينَ وَالْمُهَاجِرِينَ فِي سَبِيلِ اللَّهِ وَلْيَعْفُوا وَلْيَصْفَحُوا أَلَا تُحِبُّونَ أَن يَغْفِرَ اللَّهُ لَكُمْ وَاللَّهُ غَفُورٌ رَّحِيمٌ

٢٣ إِنَّ الَّذِينَ يَرْمُونَ الْمُحْصَنَاتِ الْغَافِلَاتِ الْمُؤْمِنَاتِ لُعِنُوا فِي الدُّنْيَا وَالْآخِرَةِ وَلَهُمْ عَذَابٌ عَظِيمٌ

---

[194]Tradition says that when Abū Bakr heard that one of his relatives, whom he was supporting, was one of those who had slandered his daughter ʿĀ'ishah, swore that he would no longer support him, and that this verse was revealed on that occasion.

24. On the day when their tongues and their hands and their feet testify against them as to what they used to do,

﴿٢٤﴾ يَوْمَ تَشْهَدُ عَلَيْهِمْ أَلْسِنَتُهُمْ وَأَيْدِيهِمْ وَأَرْجُلُهُم بِمَا كَانُوا يَعْمَلُونَ

25. On that day Allah will pay them their just due, and they will know that Allah, He is the Manifest Truth.

﴿٢٥﴾ يَوْمَئِذٍ يُوَفِّيهِمُ اللّهُ دِينَهُمُ الْحَقَّ وَيَعْلَمُونَ أَنَّ اللّهَ هُوَ الْحَقُّ الْمُبِينُ

26. Vile women are for vile men, and vile men for vile women. Good women are for good men, and good men for good women; such are innocent of that which people say: For them is pardon and a bountiful provision.

﴿٢٦﴾ الْخَبِيثَاتُ لِلْخَبِيثِينَ وَالْخَبِيثُونَ لِلْخَبِيثَاتِ وَالطَّيِّبَاتُ لِلطَّيِّبِينَ وَالطَّيِّبُونَ لِلطَّيِّبَاتِ أُوْلَئِكَ مُبَرَّؤُونَ مِمَّا يَقُولُونَ لَهُم مَّغْفِرَةٌ وَرِزْقٌ كَرِيمٌ

27. O you who believe! Enter not houses other than your own without first announcing your presence and invoking peace upon the folk thereof. That is better for you, that you may be heedful.

﴿٢٧﴾ يَا أَيُّهَا الَّذِينَ آمَنُوا لَا تَدْخُلُوا بُيُوتًا غَيْرَ بُيُوتِكُمْ حَتَّى تَسْتَأْنِسُوا وَتُسَلِّمُوا عَلَى أَهْلِهَا ذَلِكُمْ خَيْرٌ لَّكُمْ لَعَلَّكُمْ تَذَكَّرُونَ

28. And if you find no one therein, still enter not until permission has been given. And if it be said unto you: Go away again, then go away, for it is purer for you. Allah knows what you do.

﴿٢٨﴾ فَإِن لَّمْ تَجِدُوا فِيهَا أَحَدًا فَلَا تَدْخُلُوهَا حَتَّى يُؤْذَنَ لَكُمْ وَإِن قِيلَ لَكُمُ ارْجِعُوا فَارْجِعُوا هُوَ أَزْكَى لَكُمْ وَاللّهُ بِمَا تَعْمَلُونَ عَلِيمٌ

29. (It is) no sin for you to enter uninhabited houses wherein is comfort for you. Allah knows what you proclaim and what you hide.

﴿٢٩﴾ لَّيْسَ عَلَيْكُمْ جُنَاحٌ أَن تَدْخُلُوا بُيُوتًا غَيْرَ مَسْكُونَةٍ فِيهَا مَتَاعٌ لَّكُمْ وَاللّهُ يَعْلَمُ مَا تُبْدُونَ وَمَا تَكْتُمُونَ

30. Tell the believing men to lower their gaze and be modest. That is purer for them. Lo! Allah is Aware of what they do.

﴿٣٠﴾ قُل لِّلْمُؤْمِنِينَ يَغُضُّوا مِنْ أَبْصَارِهِمْ وَيَحْفَظُوا فُرُوجَهُمْ ذَلِكَ أَزْكَى لَهُمْ إِنَّ اللّهَ خَبِيرٌ بِمَا يَصْنَعُونَ

31. And tell the believing women to lower their gaze and be modest, and to display of their adornment only that which is apparent, and to draw their veils over their bosoms, and not to reveal their adornment save to their own husbands or fathers or husbands' fathers, or their sons or their husbands' sons, or their brothers or their brothers' sons or their sisters' sons, or their women, or their slaves, or male attendants who lack vigor, or children who know nothing of women's nakedness. And let them not stamp their feet so as to reveal what they hide of their adornment. And turn unto Allah together, O believers, in order that you may succeed.

32. And marry such of you as are solitary and the pious of your slaves and maidservants. If they be poor; Allah will enrich them of His bounty. Allah is of ample means, Aware.

33. And let those who cannot find a match keep chaste till Allah give them independence by His grace. And such of your slaves as seek a writing (of emancipation), write it for them if you are aware of anything of good in them, and bestow upon them of the wealth of Allah which He has bestowed upon you. Force not your slave girls to whoredom that you may seek enjoyment of the life of the world, if they would preserve their chastity. And if one force them, then (unto them), after their compulsion, Lo! Allah will be For-giving, Merciful.

34. And verily We have sent down for you revelations that make plain, and the example of those who passed away before you. An admonition unto those who ward off (evil).

٣١ وَقُل لِّلْمُؤْمِنَاتِ يَغْضُضْنَ مِنْ أَبْصَارِهِنَّ وَيَحْفَظْنَ فُرُوجَهُنَّ وَلَا يُبْدِينَ زِينَتَهُنَّ إِلَّا مَا ظَهَرَ مِنْهَا وَلْيَضْرِبْنَ بِخُمُرِهِنَّ عَلَىٰ جُيُوبِهِنَّ وَلَا يُبْدِينَ زِينَتَهُنَّ إِلَّا لِبُعُولَتِهِنَّ أَوْ ءَابَائِهِنَّ أَوْ ءَابَاءِ بُعُولَتِهِنَّ أَوْ أَبْنَائِهِنَّ أَوْ أَبْنَاءِ بُعُولَتِهِنَّ أَوْ إِخْوَانِهِنَّ أَوْ بَنِي إِخْوَانِهِنَّ أَوْ بَنِي أَخَوَاتِهِنَّ أَوْ نِسَائِهِنَّ أَوْ مَا مَلَكَتْ أَيْمَانُهُنَّ أَوِ التَّابِعِينَ غَيْرِ أُولِي الْإِرْبَةِ مِنَ الرِّجَالِ أَوِ الطِّفْلِ الَّذِينَ لَمْ يَظْهَرُوا عَلَىٰ عَوْرَاتِ النِّسَاءِ وَلَا يَضْرِبْنَ بِأَرْجُلِهِنَّ لِيُعْلَمَ مَا يُخْفِينَ مِن زِينَتِهِنَّ وَتُوبُوا إِلَى اللَّهِ جَمِيعًا أَيُّهَ الْمُؤْمِنُونَ لَعَلَّكُمْ تُفْلِحُونَ

٣٢ وَأَنكِحُوا الْأَيَامَىٰ مِنكُمْ وَالصَّالِحِينَ مِنْ عِبَادِكُمْ وَإِمَائِكُمْ إِن يَكُونُوا فُقَرَاءَ يُغْنِهِمُ اللَّهُ مِن فَضْلِهِ وَاللَّهُ وَاسِعٌ عَلِيمٌ

٣٣ وَلْيَسْتَعْفِفِ الَّذِينَ لَا يَجِدُونَ نِكَاحًا حَتَّىٰ يُغْنِيَهُمُ اللَّهُ مِن فَضْلِهِ وَالَّذِينَ يَبْتَغُونَ الْكِتَابَ مِمَّا مَلَكَتْ أَيْمَانُكُمْ فَكَاتِبُوهُمْ إِنْ عَلِمْتُمْ فِيهِمْ خَيْرًا وَءَاتُوهُم مِّن مَّالِ اللَّهِ الَّذِي ءَاتَاكُمْ وَلَا تُكْرِهُوا فَتَيَاتِكُمْ عَلَى الْبِغَاءِ إِنْ أَرَدْنَ تَحَصُّنًا لِّتَبْتَغُوا عَرَضَ الْحَيَاةِ الدُّنْيَا وَمَن يُكْرِههُّنَّ فَإِنَّ اللَّهَ مِن بَعْدِ إِكْرَاهِهِنَّ غَفُورٌ رَّحِيمٌ

٣٤ وَلَقَدْ أَنزَلْنَا إِلَيْكُمْ ءَايَاتٍ مُّبَيِّنَاتٍ وَمَثَلًا مِّنَ الَّذِينَ خَلَوْا مِن قَبْلِكُمْ وَمَوْعِظَةً لِّلْمُتَّقِينَ

35. Allah is the Light of the heavens and the earth. The similitude of His light is as a niche wherein is a lamp. The lamp is in a glass. The glass is as it were a shining star. (This lamp is) kindled from a blessed tree, an olive neither of the East nor of the West, whose oil would almost glow forth (of itself) though no fire touched it. Light upon light, Allah guides unto His light whom He will. And Allah speaks to mankind in allegories, for Allah is Knower of all things.

٣٥ ۞ اللَّهُ نُورُ السَّمَوَاتِ وَالْأَرْضِ مَثَلُ نُورِهِ كَمِشْكَوٰةٍ فِيهَا مِصْبَاحُ الْمِصْبَاحُ فِي زُجَاجَةٍ الزُّجَاجَةُ كَأَنَّهَا كَوْكَبٌ دُرِّيٌّ يُوقَدُ مِن شَجَرَةٍ مُّبَرَكَةٍ زَيْتُونَةٍ لَّا شَرْقِيَّةٍ وَلَا غَرْبِيَّةٍ يَكَادُ زَيْتُهَا يُضِيءُ وَلَوْ لَمْ تَمْسَسْهُ نَارٌ نُّورٌ عَلَى نُورٍ يَهْدِي اللَّهُ لِنُورِهِ مَن يَشَاءُ وَيَضْرِبُ اللَّهُ الْأَمْثَالَ لِلنَّاسِ وَاللَّهُ بِكُلِّ شَيْءٍ عَلِيمٌ

36. (This lamp is found) in houses which Allah has allowed to be exalted and that His name shall be remembered therein. Therein do offer praise to Him at morn and evening—

٣٦ فِي بُيُوتٍ أَذِنَ اللَّهُ أَن تُرْفَعَ وَيُذْكَرَ فِيهَا اسْمُهُ يُسَبِّحُ لَهُ فِيهَا بِالْغُدُوِّ وَالْآصَالِ

37. Men whom neither merchandise nor sale beguiles from remembrance of Allah and constancy in prayer and paying to the poor their due; who fear a day when hearts and eyeballs will be overturned;

٣٧ رِجَالٌ لَّا تُلْهِيهِمْ تِجَارَةٌ وَلَا بَيْعٌ عَن ذِكْرِ اللَّهِ وَإِقَامِ الصَّلَوٰةِ وَإِيتَاءِ الزَّكَوٰةِ يَخَافُونَ يَوْمًا تَتَقَلَّبُ فِيهِ الْقُلُوبُ وَالْأَبْصَارُ

38. That Allah may reward them with the best of what they did, and increase reward for them of His bounty. Allah gives blessings without stint to whom He will.

٣٨ لِيَجْزِيَهُمُ اللَّهُ أَحْسَنَ مَا عَمِلُوا وَيَزِيدَهُم مِّن فَضْلِهِ وَاللَّهُ يَرْزُقُ مَن يَشَاءُ بِغَيْرِ حِسَابٍ

39. As for those who disbelieve, their deeds are as a mirage in a desert. The thirsty one supposes it to be water till he comes unto it and finds it nothing, and finds, in the place thereof, Allah, Who pays him his due; and Allah is swift at reckoning.

٣٩ وَالَّذِينَ كَفَرُوا أَعْمَالُهُمْ كَسَرَابٍ بِقِيعَةٍ يَحْسَبُهُ الظَّمْآنُ مَاءً حَتَّى إِذَا جَاءَهُ لَمْ يَجِدْهُ شَيْئًا وَوَجَدَ اللَّهَ عِندَهُ فَوَفَّاهُ حِسَابَهُ وَاللَّهُ سَرِيعُ الْحِسَابِ

40. Or as darkness on a vast, abysmal sea. There covers him a wave, above which is a wave, above which is a cloud. Layer upon layer of darkness. When he holds out his hand he scarce can see it. And he for whom Allah has not appointed light, for him there is no light.

٤٠ أَوْ كَظُلُمَاتٍ فِي بَحْرٍ لُّجِّيٍّ يَغْشَاهُ مَوْجٌ مِّن فَوْقِهِ مَوْجٌ مِّن فَوْقِهِ سَحَابٌ ظُلُمَاتٌ بَعْضُهَا فَوْقَ بَعْضٍ إِذَا أَخْرَجَ يَدَهُ لَمْ يَكَدْ يَرَاهَا وَمَن لَّمْ يَجْعَلِ اللَّهُ لَهُ نُورًا فَمَا لَهُ مِن نُّورٍ

41. Have you not seen that Allah, He it is Whom all who are in the heavens and the earth glorify; and the birds in their flight? Each one knows verily its worship and its glorification; and Allah is Aware of what they do.

﴿٤١﴾ أَلَمْ تَرَ أَنَّ اللَّهَ يُسَبِّحُ لَهُ مَن فِي السَّمَٰوَٰتِ وَالْأَرْضِ وَالطَّيْرُ صَـٰٓفَّـٰتٍ كُلٌّ قَدْ عَلِمَ صَلَاتَهُ وَتَسْبِيحَهُ وَاللَّهُ عَلِيمٌۢ بِمَا يَفْعَلُونَ

42. And unto Allah belongs the sovereignty of the heavens and the earth, and unto Allah is the journeying.

﴿٤٢﴾ وَلِلَّهِ مُلْكُ السَّمَٰوَٰتِ وَالْأَرْضِ وَإِلَى اللَّهِ الْمَصِيرُ

43. Have you not seen how Allah wafts the clouds, then gathers them, then makes them layers, and you see the rain come forth from between them; He sends down from the heaven mountains wherein is hail, and smites therewith whom He will, and averts it from whom He will. The flashing of His lightning all but snatches away the sight.

﴿٤٣﴾ أَلَمْ تَرَ أَنَّ اللَّهَ يُزْجِي سَحَابًا ثُمَّ يُؤَلِّفُ بَيْنَهُ ثُمَّ يَجْعَلُهُ رُكَامًا فَتَرَى الْوَدْقَ يَخْرُجُ مِنْ خِلَالِهِ وَيُنَزِّلُ مِنَ السَّمَاءِ مِن جِبَالٍ فِيهَا مِنۢ بَرَدٍ فَيُصِيبُ بِهِۦ مَن يَشَاءُ وَيَصْرِفُهُۥ عَن مَّن يَشَاءُ يَكَادُ سَنَا بَرْقِهِۦ يَذْهَبُ بِالْأَبْصَٰرِ

44. Allah causes the revolution of the day and the night. Lo! herein is indeed a lesson for those who see.

﴿٤٤﴾ يُقَلِّبُ اللَّهُ الَّيْلَ وَالنَّهَارَ إِنَّ فِي ذَٰلِكَ لَعِبْرَةً لِّأُولِي الْأَبْصَٰرِ

45. Allah has created every animal of water. Of them is (a kind) that goes upon its belly and (a kind) that goes upon two legs and (a kind) that goes upon four. Allah creates what He will. Lo! Allah is Able to do all things.

﴿٤٥﴾ وَاللَّهُ خَلَقَ كُلَّ دَابَّةٍ مِّن مَّاءٍ فَمِنْهُم مَّن يَمْشِي عَلَىٰ بَطْنِهِۦ وَمِنْهُم مَّن يَمْشِي عَلَىٰ رِجْلَيْنِ وَمِنْهُم مَّن يَمْشِي عَلَىٰٓ أَرْبَعٍ يَخْلُقُ اللَّهُ مَا يَشَاءُ إِنَّ اللَّهَ عَلَىٰ كُلِّ شَيْءٍ قَدِيرٌ

46. Verily We have sent down revelations and explained them. Allah guides whom He will unto a straight path.

﴿٤٦﴾ لَّقَدْ أَنزَلْنَآ ءَايَٰتٍ مُّبَيِّنَٰتٍ وَاللَّهُ يَهْدِي مَن يَشَاءُ إِلَىٰ صِرَٰطٍ مُّسْتَقِيمٍ

47. And they say: We believe in Allah and the Messenger, and we obey; then after that a faction of them turn away. Such are not believers.

﴿٤٧﴾ وَيَقُولُونَ ءَامَنَّا بِاللَّهِ وَبِالرَّسُولِ وَأَطَعْنَا ثُمَّ يَتَوَلَّىٰ فَرِيقٌ مِّنْهُم مِّنۢ بَعْدِ ذَٰلِكَ وَمَآ أُو۟لَٰٓئِكَ بِالْمُؤْمِنِينَ

48. And when they are called unto Allah and His Messenger to judge between them, lo! a faction of them are averse;

﴿٤٨﴾ وَإِذَا دُعُوٓا۟ إِلَى اللَّهِ وَرَسُولِهِۦ لِيَحْكُمَ بَيْنَهُمْ إِذَا فَرِيقٌ مِّنْهُم مُّعْرِضُونَ

49. But if right had been with them they would have come unto it willingly.

﴿٤٩﴾ وَإِن يَكُن لَّهُمُ الْحَقُّ يَأْتُوٓا۟ إِلَيْهِ مُذْعِنِينَ

50. Is there in their hearts a disease, or have they doubts, or fear they lest Allah and His Messenger should wrong them in judgment? Nay, but such are evil-doers.

51. The saying of (all true) believers when they are called unto Allah and His Messenger to judge between them is only that they say: We hear and we obey. And such are the successful.

52. He who obeys Allah and His Messenger, and fears Allah, and keeps duty (unto Him): such indeed are the victorious.

53. They swear by Allah solemnly that, if you order them, they will go forth. Say: Swear not; known obedience (is better). Lo! Allah is Informed of what you do.

54. Say: Obey Allah and obey the Messenger. But if you turn away, then (it is) for him (to do) only that with which he has been charged, and for you (to do) only that with which you have been charged. If you obey him, you will go aright. But the Messenger has no other charge than to convey (the message), plainly.

55. Allah has promised such of you as believe and do good works that He will surely make them to succeed (the present rulers) in the earth even as He caused those who were before them to succeed others); and that He willsurely establish for them their religion which He has approved for them, and will give them in exchange safety after their fear. They worship Me. They ascribe no thing as partner unto Me. Those who disbelieve henceforth, they are the miscreants.

56. Establish prayer and pay the poor due and obey the Messenger, that you may find mercy.

57. Think not that disbelievers can escape in the land. Fire will be their home, an unlucky journey's end!

٥٠ أَفِى قُلُوبِهِم مَّرَضٌ أَمِ ارْتَابُوا أَمْ يَخَافُونَ أَن يَحِيفَ اللَّهُ عَلَيْهِمْ وَرَسُولُهُ بَلْ أُوْلَئِكَ هُمُ الظَّالِمُونَ

٥١ إِنَّمَا كَانَ قَوْلَ الْمُؤْمِنِينَ إِذَا دُعُوا إِلَى اللَّهِ وَرَسُولِهِ لِيَحْكُمَ بَيْنَهُمْ أَن يَقُولُوا سَمِعْنَا وَأَطَعْنَا وَأُوْلَئِكَ هُمُ الْمُفْلِحُونَ

٥٢ وَمَن يُطِعِ اللَّهَ وَرَسُولَهُ وَيَخْشَ اللَّهَ وَيَتَّقْهِ فَأُوْلَئِكَ هُمُ الْفَائِزُونَ

٥٣ وَأَقْسَمُوا بِاللَّهِ جَهْدَ أَيْمَانِهِمْ لَئِنْ أَمَرْتَهُمْ لَيَخْرُجُنَّ قُل لَّا تُقْسِمُوا طَاعَةٌ مَّعْرُوفَةٌ إِنَّ اللَّهَ خَبِيرٌ بِمَا تَعْمَلُونَ

٥٤ قُلْ أَطِيعُوا اللَّهَ وَأَطِيعُوا الرَّسُولَ فَإِن تَوَلَّوْا فَإِنَّمَا عَلَيْهِ مَا حُمِّلَ وَعَلَيْكُم مَّا حُمِّلْتُمْ وَإِن تُطِيعُوهُ تَهْتَدُوا وَمَا عَلَى الرَّسُولِ إِلَّا الْبَلَاغُ الْمُبِينُ

٥٥ وَعَدَ اللَّهُ الَّذِينَ آمَنُوا مِنكُمْ وَعَمِلُوا الصَّالِحَاتِ لَيَسْتَخْلِفَنَّهُمْ فِي الْأَرْضِ كَمَا اسْتَخْلَفَ الَّذِينَ مِن قَبْلِهِمْ وَلَيُمَكِّنَنَّ لَهُمْ دِينَهُمُ الَّذِي ارْتَضَى لَهُمْ وَلَيُبَدِّلَنَّهُم مِّن بَعْدِ خَوْفِهِمْ أَمْنًا يَعْبُدُونَنِي لَا يُشْرِكُونَ بِي شَيْئًا وَمَن كَفَرَ بَعْدَ ذَلِكَ فَأُوْلَئِكَ هُمُ الْفَاسِقُونَ

٥٦ وَأَقِيمُوا الصَّلَاةَ وَآتُوا الزَّكَاةَ وَأَطِيعُوا الرَّسُولَ لَعَلَّكُمْ تُرْحَمُونَ

٥٧ لَا تَحْسَبَنَّ الَّذِينَ كَفَرُوا مُعْجِزِينَ فِي الْأَرْضِ وَمَأْوَاهُمُ النَّارُ وَلَبِئْسَ الْمَصِيرُ

58. O you who believe! Let your slaves, and those of you who have not come to puberty, ask leave of you at three times (before they come into your presence): Before the prayer of dawn, and when you lay aside your raiment for the heat of noon, and after the prayer of night.[195] Three times of privacy for you. It is no sin for them or for you at other times, when some of you go round attendant upon others (if they come into your presence without leave). Thus Allah makes clear the revelations for you. Allah is Knower, Wise.

59. And when the children among you come to puberty then let them ask leave even as those before them used to ask leave. Thus Allah makes clear His revelations for you. Allah is Knower, Wise.

60. As for women past childbearing, who have no hope of marriage, it is no sin for them if they discard their (outer) clothing in such a way as not to show adornment. But to refrain is better for them. Allah is Hearer, Knower.

61. No blame is there upon the blind nor any blame upon the lame nor any blame upon the sick nor on yourselves if you eat from your houses, or the houses of your fathers, or the houses of your mothers, or the houses of your brothers, or the houses of your sisters, or the houses of your fathers' brothers, or the houses of your fathers' sisters, or the houses of your mothers' brothers, or the houses of your mothers' sisters, or (from that) whereof you hold the keys, or (from the house) of a friend. No sin shall it be for you whether you eat together or apart. But when you enter houses, salute one another with a greeting from Allah, blessed and sweet. Thus Allah makes clear His revelations for you, that you may understand.

---

[195]'Ishā', the prayer to be offered when the night has fully come.

62. They only are the true believers who believe in Allah and His Messenger and, when they are with him on some common errand, go not away until they have asked leave of him. Lo! those who ask leave of you (O Muhammad), those are they who believe in Allah and His Messenger. So, if they ask your leave for some affair of theirs, give leave to whom you will of them, and ask for them forgiveness of Allah. Lo! Allah is Forgiving, Merciful.

63. Make not the calling of the Messenger among you as your calling one of another. Allah knows those of you who steal away, hiding themselves. And let those who conspire to evade orders beware lest trial or painful punishment befall them.

64. Lo! verily unto Allah belongs whatsoever is in the heavens and the earth. He knows your condition. And (He knows) the Day when they are returned unto Him so that He may inform them of what they did. Allah is Knower of all things.

﴿٦٢﴾ إِنَّمَا الْمُؤْمِنُونَ الَّذِينَ ءَامَنُوا بِاللَّهِ وَرَسُولِهِ وَإِذَا كَانُوا مَعَهُ عَلَىٰ أَمْرٍ جَامِعٍ لَّمْ يَذْهَبُوا حَتَّىٰ يَسْتَأْذِنُوهُ إِنَّ الَّذِينَ يَسْتَأْذِنُونَكَ أُوْلَٰئِكَ الَّذِينَ يُؤْمِنُونَ بِاللَّهِ وَرَسُولِهِ فَإِذَا اسْتَأْذَنُوكَ لِبَعْضِ شَأْنِهِمْ فَأْذَن لِّمَن شِئْتَ مِنْهُمْ وَاسْتَغْفِرْ لَهُمُ اللَّهَ إِنَّ اللَّهَ غَفُورٌ رَّحِيمٌ

﴿٦٣﴾ لَّا تَجْعَلُوا دُعَاءَ الرَّسُولِ بَيْنَكُمْ كَدُعَاءِ بَعْضِكُم بَعْضًا قَدْ يَعْلَمُ اللَّهُ الَّذِينَ يَتَسَلَّلُونَ مِنكُمْ لِوَاذًا فَلْيَحْذَرِ الَّذِينَ يُخَالِفُونَ عَنْ أَمْرِهِ أَن تُصِيبَهُمْ فِتْنَةٌ أَوْ يُصِيبَهُمْ عَذَابٌ أَلِيمٌ

﴿٦٤﴾ أَلَا إِنَّ لِلَّهِ مَا فِي السَّمَاوَاتِ وَالْأَرْضِ قَدْ يَعْلَمُ مَا أَنتُمْ عَلَيْهِ وَيَوْمَ يُرْجَعُونَ إِلَيْهِ فَيُنَبِّئُهُم بِمَا عَمِلُوا وَاللَّهُ بِكُلِّ شَيْءٍ عَلِيمٌ

The Criterion

Al Furqān, "The Criterion," takes its name from a word occurring in verse 1. The subject is the folly of superstition and the craving for miraculous events in face of the wonders of God's creation.

It belongs to the middle group of Makkan surahs, except for verses 68-70, which were revealed at al Madinah.

The Criterion

Revealed at Makkah

In the name of Allah, the Beneficent, the Merciful

1. Blessed is He Who has revealed unto His slave the Criterion (of right and wrong), that he may be a warner to mankind.

2. He unto Whom belongs the sovereignty of the heavens and the earth. He has chosen no son nor has He any partner in the sovereignty. He has created everything and has meted out for it a measure.

3. Yet they choose beside Him other gods who create nothing but are themselves created, and possess not hurt nor profit for themselves, and possess not death nor life, nor power to raise the dead.

4. Those who disbelieve say: This is nothing but a lie that he has invented, and other folk have helped him with it, so that they have produced a slander and a lie.

5. And they say: Fables of the men of old which he has had written down so that they are dictated to him morn and evening.

6. Say (unto them, O Muhammad): He Who knows the secret in the heavens and the earth has revealed it. Lo! He ever is Forgiving, Merciful.

7. And they say: What ails this messenger (of Allah) that he eats food and walks in the markets? Why is not an angel sent down unto him, to be a warner with him.

8. Or (why is not) a treasure thrown down unto him, or why has he not a paradise from whence to eat? And the evildoers say: You are but following a man bewitched.

9. See how they coin similitudes for you, so that they are all astray and cannot find a road!

10. Blessed is He Who, if He will, will assign you better than (all) that—Gardens underneath which rivers flow—and will assign you mansions.

11. Nay, but they deny (the coming of) the Hour, and for those who deny (the coming of) the Hour We have prepared a flame.

12. When it sees them from afar, they hear the crackling and the roar thereof.

13. And when they are flung into a narrow place thereof, chained together, they pray for destruction there.

14. Pray not that day for one destruction, but pray for many destructions!

15. Say: Is that (doom) better or the Garden of Immortality which is promised unto those who ward off (evil)? It will be their reward and journey's end.

16. Therein abiding, they have all that they desire. It is for your Lord a promise that must be fulfilled.

17. And on the day when He will assemble them and that which they worship instead of Allah and will say: Was it you who misled these my slaves or did they (themselves) wander from the way?

٨ أَوَيُلْقَىٰ إِلَيْهِ كَنزٌ أَوْ تَكُونُ لَهُ جَنَّةٌ يَأْكُلُ مِنْهَا وَقَالَ الظَّالِمُونَ إِن تَتَّبِعُونَ إِلَّا رَجُلًا مَّسْحُورًا

٩ انظُرْ كَيْفَ ضَرَبُوا لَكَ الْأَمْثَالَ فَضَلُّوا فَلَا يَسْتَطِيعُونَ سَبِيلًا

١٠ تَبَارَكَ الَّذِي إِن شَاءَ جَعَلَ لَكَ خَيْرًا مِّن ذَٰلِكَ جَنَّاتٍ تَجْرِي مِن تَحْتِهَا الْأَنْهَارُ وَيَجْعَل لَّكَ قُصُورًا

١١ بَلْ كَذَّبُوا بِالسَّاعَةِ وَأَعْتَدْنَا لِمَن كَذَّبَ بِالسَّاعَةِ سَعِيرًا

١٢ إِذَا رَأَتْهُم مِّن مَّكَانٍ بَعِيدٍ سَمِعُوا لَهَا تَغَيُّظًا وَزَفِيرًا

١٣ وَإِذَا أُلْقُوا مِنْهَا مَكَانًا ضَيِّقًا مُّقَرَّنِينَ دَعَوْا هُنَالِكَ ثُبُورًا

١٤ لَّا تَدْعُوا الْيَوْمَ ثُبُورًا وَاحِدًا وَادْعُوا ثُبُورًا كَثِيرًا

١٥ قُلْ أَذَٰلِكَ خَيْرٌ أَمْ جَنَّةُ الْخُلْدِ الَّتِي وُعِدَ الْمُتَّقُونَ كَانَتْ لَهُمْ جَزَاءً وَمَصِيرًا

١٦ لَّهُمْ فِيهَا مَا يَشَاءُونَ خَالِدِينَ كَانَ عَلَىٰ رَبِّكَ وَعْدًا مَّسْئُولًا

١٧ وَيَوْمَ يَحْشُرُهُمْ وَمَا يَعْبُدُونَ مِن دُونِ اللَّهِ فَيَقُولُ أَأَنتُمْ أَضْلَلْتُمْ عِبَادِي هَٰؤُلَاءِ أَمْ هُمْ ضَلُّوا السَّبِيلَ

18. They will say: Be You glorified! It was not for us to choose any protecting friends beside You; but You did give them and their fathers ease till they forgot the remembrance and became useless folk.

19. Thus they will give you the lie regarding what you say, then you can neither avert (the doom) nor obtain help. And who among you does wrong, We shall make him taste great torment.

20. We never sent before you any messengers but lo! they ate food and walked in the markets. And We have appointed some of you a test for others: Will you be steadfast? And your Lord is ever Seer.

21. And those who look not for a meeting with Us say: Why are angels not sent down unto us and (why) do we not see our Lord? Assuredly they think too highly of themselves and are scornful with great pride.

22. On the day when they behold the angels, on that day there will be no good tidings for the criminals; and they will cry: A forbidding ban!

23. And We shall turn unto the work they did and make it scattered motes.

24. Those who have earned the Garden on that day will be better in their home and happier in their place of noonday rest;

25. A day when the heaven with the clouds will be rent asunder and the angels will be sent down, a grand descent.

26. The Sovereignty on that day will be the True (Sover-eignty) belonging to the Beneficent One, and it will be a hard day for disbelievers.

١٨ قَالُوا سُبْحَانَكَ مَا كَانَ يَنْبَغِي لَنَا أَن نَّتَّخِذَ مِن دُونِكَ مِنْ أَوْلِيَاءَ وَلَٰكِن مَّتَّعْتَهُمْ وَءَابَاءَهُمْ حَتَّىٰ نَسُوا الذِّكْرَ وَكَانُوا قَوْمًا بُورًا

١٩ فَقَدْ كَذَّبُوكُم بِمَا تَقُولُونَ فَمَا تَسْتَطِيعُونَ صَرْفًا وَلَا نَصْرًا وَمَن يَظْلِم مِّنكُمْ نُذِقْهُ عَذَابًا كَبِيرًا

٢٠ وَمَا أَرْسَلْنَا قَبْلَكَ مِنَ الْمُرْسَلِينَ إِلَّا إِنَّهُمْ لَيَأْكُلُونَ الطَّعَامَ وَيَمْشُونَ فِي الْأَسْوَاقِ وَجَعَلْنَا بَعْضَكُمْ لِبَعْضٍ فِتْنَةً أَتَصْبِرُونَ وَكَانَ رَبُّكَ بَصِيرًا

٢١ وَقَالَ الَّذِينَ لَا يَرْجُونَ لِقَاءَنَا لَوْلَا أُنزِلَ عَلَيْنَا الْمَلَائِكَةُ أَوْ نَرَىٰ رَبَّنَا لَقَدِ اسْتَكْبَرُوا فِي أَنفُسِهِمْ وَعَتَوْا عُتُوًّا كَبِيرًا

٢٢ يَوْمَ يَرَوْنَ الْمَلَائِكَةَ لَا بُشْرَىٰ يَوْمَئِذٍ لِّلْمُجْرِمِينَ وَيَقُولُونَ حِجْرًا مَّحْجُورًا

٢٣ وَقَدِمْنَا إِلَىٰ مَا عَمِلُوا مِنْ عَمَلٍ فَجَعَلْنَاهُ هَبَاءً مَّنثُورًا

٢٤ أَصْحَابُ الْجَنَّةِ يَوْمَئِذٍ خَيْرٌ مُّسْتَقَرًّا وَأَحْسَنُ مَقِيلًا

٢٥ وَيَوْمَ تَشَقَّقُ السَّمَاءُ بِالْغَمَامِ وَنُزِّلَ الْمَلَائِكَةُ تَنزِيلًا

٢٦ الْمُلْكُ يَوْمَئِذٍ الْحَقُّ لِلرَّحْمَٰنِ وَكَانَ يَوْمًا عَلَى الْكَافِرِينَ عَسِيرًا

27. On the day when the wrongdoer gnaws his hands, he will say: Ah, would that I had chosen a way together with the Messenger (of Allah)!

28. Alas for me! Ah, would that I had never taken such an one for friend!

29. He verily led me astray from the Reminder after it had reached me. The Devil was ever man's deserter (in the hour of need).

30. And the Messenger says: O my Lord! Lo! mine own folk make this Qur'an of no account.

31. Even so have We appointed unto every Prophet an opponent from among the criminals; but Allah suffices for a Guide and Helper.

32. And those who disbelieve say: Why is the Qur'an not revealed unto him all at once? (It is revealed) thus that We may strengthen your heart therewith; and We have arranged it in right order.

33. And they bring you no similitude but We bring you the Truth (as against it), and better (than their similitude) as argument.

34. Those who will be gathered on their faces unto Hell: such are worse in plight and further from the right road.

35. We verily gave Moses the Scripture and placed with him his brother Aaron as minister.

36. Then We said: Go together unto the folk who have denied Our revelations. Then We destroyed them, a complete destruction.

37. And Noah's folk, when they denied the messengers, We drowned them and made of them a portent for mankind. We have prepared a painful doom for evildoers.

٢٧ وَيَوْمَ يَعَضُّ الظَّالِمُ عَلَىٰ يَدَيْهِ يَقُولُ يَٰلَيْتَنِى اتَّخَذْتُ مَعَ الرَّسُولِ سَبِيلًا

٢٨ يَٰوَيْلَتَىٰ لَيْتَنِى لَمْ أَتَّخِذْ فُلَانًا خَلِيلًا

٢٩ لَقَدْ أَضَلَّنِى عَنِ الذِّكْرِ بَعْدَ إِذْ جَآءَنِى وَكَانَ الشَّيْطَٰنُ لِلْإِنسَٰنِ خَذُولًا

٣٠ وَقَالَ الرَّسُولُ يَٰرَبِّ إِنَّ قَوْمِى اتَّخَذُوا هَٰذَا الْقُرْءَانَ مَهْجُورًا

٣١ وَكَذَٰلِكَ جَعَلْنَا لِكُلِّ نَبِيٍّ عَدُوًّا مِّنَ الْمُجْرِمِينَ وَكَفَىٰ بِرَبِّكَ هَادِيًا وَنَصِيرًا

٣٢ وَقَالَ الَّذِينَ كَفَرُوا لَوْلَا نُزِّلَ عَلَيْهِ الْقُرْءَانُ جُمْلَةً وَٰحِدَةً كَذَٰلِكَ لِنُثَبِّتَ بِهِ فُؤَادَكَ وَرَتَّلْنَٰهُ تَرْتِيلًا

٣٣ وَلَا يَأْتُونَكَ بِمَثَلٍ إِلَّا جِئْنَٰكَ بِالْحَقِّ وَأَحْسَنَ تَفْسِيرًا

٣٤ الَّذِينَ يُحْشَرُونَ عَلَىٰ وُجُوهِهِمْ إِلَىٰ جَهَنَّمَ أُولَٰئِكَ شَرٌّ مَّكَانًا وَأَضَلُّ سَبِيلًا

٣٥ وَلَقَدْ ءَاتَيْنَا مُوسَى الْكِتَٰبَ وَجَعَلْنَا مَعَهُ أَخَاهُ هَٰرُونَ وَزِيرًا

٣٦ فَقُلْنَا اذْهَبَا إِلَى الْقَوْمِ الَّذِينَ كَذَّبُوا بِـَٔايَٰتِنَا فَدَمَّرْنَٰهُمْ تَدْمِيرًا

٣٧ وَقَوْمَ نُوحٍ لَّمَّا كَذَّبُوا الرُّسُلَ أَغْرَقْنَٰهُمْ وَجَعَلْنَٰهُمْ لِلنَّاسِ ءَايَةً وَأَعْتَدْنَا لِلظَّٰلِمِينَ عَذَابًا أَلِيمًا

38. And (the tribes of) 'Ād and Thamūd, and the dwellers in al Rass,[196] and many generations in between.

٣٨ وَعَادًا وَثَمُودَا۟ وَأَصْحَٰبَ الرَّسِّ وَقُرُونًۢا بَيْنَ ذَٰلِكَ كَثِيرًا

39. Each (of them) We warned by examples, and each (of them) We brought to utter ruin.

٣٩ وَكُلًّا ضَرَبْنَا لَهُ الْأَمْثَٰلَ وَكُلًّا تَبَّرْنَا تَتْبِيرًا

40. And indeed they have passed by the township whereon was rained the fatal rain.[197] Can it be that they have not seen it? Nay, but they hope for no resurrection.

٤٠ وَلَقَدْ أَتَوْا۟ عَلَى الْقَرْيَةِ الَّتِىٓ أُمْطِرَتْ مَطَرَ السَّوْءِ أَفَلَمْ يَكُونُوا۟ يَرَوْنَهَا ۚ بَلْ كَانُوا۟ لَا يَرْجُونَ نُشُورًا

41. And when they see you (O Muhammad) they treat you only as a jest (saying): Is this he whom Allah sends as a messenger?

٤١ وَإِذَا رَأَوْكَ إِن يَتَّخِذُونَكَ إِلَّا هُزُوًا أَهَٰذَا الَّذِى بَعَثَ اللَّهُ رَسُولًا

42. He would have led us far away from our gods if we had not been staunch to them. They will know, when they behold the doom, who is more astray as to the road.

٤٢ إِن كَادَ لَيُضِلُّنَا عَنْ ءَالِهَتِنَا لَوْلَآ أَن صَبَرْنَا عَلَيْهَا ۚ وَسَوْفَ يَعْلَمُونَ حِينَ يَرَوْنَ الْعَذَابَ مَنْ أَضَلُّ سَبِيلًا

43. Have you seen him who chooses for his god his own lust? Would you then be guardian over him?

٤٣ أَرَءَيْتَ مَنِ اتَّخَذَ إِلَٰهَهُۥ هَوَىٰهُ أَفَأَنتَ تَكُونُ عَلَيْهِ وَكِيلًا

44. Or do you deem that most of them hear or understand? They are but as the cattle—nay, but they are farther astray!

٤٤ أَمْ تَحْسَبُ أَنَّ أَكْثَرَهُمْ يَسْمَعُونَ أَوْ يَعْقِلُونَ ۚ إِنْ هُمْ إِلَّا كَالْأَنْعَٰمِ ۖ بَلْ هُمْ أَضَلُّ سَبِيلًا

45. Have you not seen how your Lord has spread the shade—And if He willed He could have made it still—then We have made the sun its pilot;

٤٥ أَلَمْ تَرَ إِلَىٰ رَبِّكَ كَيْفَ مَدَّ الظِّلَّ وَلَوْ شَآءَ لَجَعَلَهُۥ سَاكِنًا ثُمَّ جَعَلْنَا الشَّمْسَ عَلَيْهِ دَلِيلًا

46. Then We withdraw it unto Us, a gradual withdrawal?

٤٦ ثُمَّ قَبَضْنَٰهُ إِلَيْنَا قَبْضًا يَسِيرًا

47. And He it is Who makes night a garment for you, and sleep stillness, and makes day a resurrection.

٤٧ وَهُوَ الَّذِى جَعَلَ لَكُمُ الَّيْلَ لِبَاسًا وَالنَّوْمَ سُبَاتًا وَجَعَلَ النَّهَارَ نُشُورًا

48. And He it is Who sends the winds as glad tidings heralding His mercy, and We send down purifying water from the sky.

٤٨ وَهُوَ الَّذِىٓ أَرْسَلَ الرِّيَٰحَ بُشْرًۢا بَيْنَ يَدَىْ رَحْمَتِهِۦ ۚ وَأَنزَلْنَا مِنَ السَّمَآءِ مَآءً طَهُورًا

---

[196]Said to have been a town in Yamāmah.
[197]The great trade caravans from Makkah into Syria passed by the Dead Sea.

49. That We may give life thereby to a dead land, and We give many beasts and men that We have created to drink thereof.

50. And verily We have repeated it among them that they may remember, but most of mankind begrudge anything save ingratitude.

51. If We willed, We could raise up a warner in every village.

52. So obey not disbelievers, but strive against them herewith with a great endeavor.

53. And He it is Who has given independence to the two seas[198] (though they meet); one palatable, sweet, and the other saltish, bitter; and has set a bar and a forbidding ban between them.

54. And He it is Who has created man from water, and has appointed for him kindred by blood and kindred by marriage; for your Lord is ever Powerful.

55. Yet they worship instead of Allah that which can neither benefit them nor hurt them. The disbeliever was ever a partisan against his Lord.

56. And We have sent you (O Muhammad) only as a bearer of good tidings and a warner.

57. Say: I ask of you no reward for this, save that whoso will may choose a way unto his Lord.

58. And trust you in the Living One Who dies not, and hymn His praise. He suffices as the Knower of His bondmen's sins,

59. Who created the heavens and the earth and all that is between them in six Days,[199] then He mounted the Throne. The Beneficent! Ask any one informed concerning Him!

60. And when it is said unto them: Prostrate yourselves to the Beneficent! they say: And what is the Beneficent? Are we to prostrate to whatever you (Muhammad) bid us? And it increases aversion in them.

---

[198]i.e., the two kinds of water in the earth.
[199]See Surahs 22:47, 32:5, and 70:4.

61. Blessed be He Who has placed in the heaven mansions of stars, and has placed therein a great lamp and a moon giving light!

62. And He it is Who has appointed night and day in succession, for him who desires to remember, or desires thankfulness.

63. The (faithful) slaves of the Beneficent are they who walk upon the earth modestly, and when the foolish ones address them answer: Peace;

64. And who spend the night before their Lord, prostrate and standing,

65. And who say: Our Lord! Avert from us the doom of Hell; lo! the doom thereof is anguish;

66. Lo! it is wretched as abode and station;

67. And those who, when they spend, are neither prodigal nor grudging; and there is ever a firm station between the two;

68. And those who cry not unto any other god along with Allah, nor take the life which Allah has forbidden save in (course of) justice, nor commit adultery and who does this shall pay the penalty;

69. The doom will be doubled for him on the Day of Resurrection, and he will abide therein disdained forever;

70. Save him who repents and believes and does righteous work; as for such, Allah will change their evil deeds to good deeds. Allah is ever Forgiving, Merciful.

71. And who repents and does good, he verily repents toward Allah with true repentance.

٦١ تَبَارَكَ الَّذِى جَعَلَ فِى السَّمَاءِ بُرُوجًا وَجَعَلَ فِيهَا سِرَاجًا وَقَمَرًا مُّنِيرًا

٦٢ وَهُوَ الَّذِى جَعَلَ الَّيْلَ وَالنَّهَارَ خِلْفَةً لِّمَنْ أَرَادَ أَن يَذَّكَّرَ أَوْ أَرَادَ شُكُورًا

٦٣ وَعِبَادُ الرَّحْمَٰنِ الَّذِينَ يَمْشُونَ عَلَى الْأَرْضِ هَوْنًا وَإِذَا خَاطَبَهُمُ الْجَاهِلُونَ قَالُوا سَلَامًا

٦٤ وَالَّذِينَ يَبِيتُونَ لِرَبِّهِمْ سُجَّدًا وَقِيَامًا

٦٥ وَالَّذِينَ يَقُولُونَ رَبَّنَا اصْرِفْ عَنَّا عَذَابَ جَهَنَّمَ إِنَّ عَذَابَهَا كَانَ غَرَامًا

٦٦ إِنَّهَا سَاءَتْ مُسْتَقَرًّا وَمُقَامًا

٦٧ وَالَّذِينَ إِذَا أَنفَقُوا لَمْ يُسْرِفُوا وَلَمْ يَقْتُرُوا وَكَانَ بَيْنَ ذَٰلِكَ قَوَامًا

٦٨ وَالَّذِينَ لَا يَدْعُونَ مَعَ اللَّهِ إِلَٰهًا آخَرَ وَلَا يَقْتُلُونَ النَّفْسَ الَّتِى حَرَّمَ اللَّهُ إِلَّا بِالْحَقِّ وَلَا يَزْنُونَ وَمَن يَفْعَلْ ذَٰلِكَ يَلْقَ أَثَامًا

٦٩ يُضَاعَفْ لَهُ الْعَذَابُ يَوْمَ الْقِيَامَةِ وَيَخْلُدْ فِيهِ مُهَانًا

٧٠ إِلَّا مَن تَابَ وَآمَنَ وَعَمِلَ عَمَلًا صَالِحًا فَأُولَٰئِكَ يُبَدِّلُ اللَّهُ سَيِّئَاتِهِمْ حَسَنَاتٍ وَكَانَ اللَّهُ غَفُورًا رَّحِيمًا

٧١ وَمَن تَابَ وَعَمِلَ صَالِحًا فَإِنَّهُ يَتُوبُ إِلَى اللَّهِ مَتَابًا

72. And those who will not witness vanity, but when they pass near senseless play, pass by with dignity.

٧٢ وَالَّذِينَ لَا يَشْهَدُونَ الزُّورَ وَإِذَا مَرُّوا بِاللَّغْوِ مَرُّوا كِرَامًا

73. And those who, when they are reminded of the revelations of their Lord, fall not deaf and blind thereat.

٧٣ وَالَّذِينَ إِذَا ذُكِّرُوا بِآيَاتِ رَبِّهِمْ لَمْ يَخِرُّوا عَلَيْهَا صُمًّا وَعُمْيَانًا

74. And who say: Our Lord! Vouchsafe us comfort of our wives and of our offspring, and make us patterns for (all) those who ward off (evil).

٧٤ وَالَّذِينَ يَقُولُونَ رَبَّنَا هَبْ لَنَا مِنْ أَزْوَاجِنَا وَذُرِّيَّاتِنَا قُرَّةَ أَعْيُنٍ وَاجْعَلْنَا لِلْمُتَّقِينَ إِمَامًا

75. They will be awarded the high place forasmuch as they were steadfast, and they will be met therein with welcome peace,

٧٥ أُولَئِكَ يُجْزَوْنَ الْغُرْفَةَ بِمَا صَبَرُوا وَيُلَقَّوْنَ فِيهَا تَحِيَّةً وَسَلَامًا

76. Abiding there forever. Happy is it as abode and station!

٧٦ خَالِدِينَ فِيهَا حَسُنَتْ مُسْتَقَرًّا وَمُقَامًا

77. Say (O Muhammad, unto disbelievers): My Lord would not concern Himself with you but for your prayer. But now you have denied (the Truth), therefore there will be judgment.[200]

٧٧ قُلْ مَا يَعْبَأُ بِكُمْ رَبِّي لَوْلَا دُعَاؤُكُمْ فَقَدْ كَذَّبْتُمْ فَسَوْفَ يَكُونُ لِزَامًا

---

[200]Another interpretation is this: Say: My Lord would not concern Himself with you had it not been necessary to convey the message to you. Now that you have denied (it) therefore (punishment) will be inevitable. (Editor).

Poets

Al Shu'arā', "Poets," takes its title from verses 224 ff., where the difference between poets and a prophet is tersely pointed out: poets say what they do not mean, while a prophet always practices what he preaches. The pagan Arabs and their poets believed poetic inspiration to be the work of Jinn.

The story of a number of former prophets is given here to console believers at a time of persecution and to assure them that it is not a new thing for a messenger of God to be persecuted and that persecutors always suffer in the end. It also shows that all messengers of God came with the same message.

It belongs to the middle group of Makkan surahs, with the exception of verses 224-227, which were revealed at al Madinah.

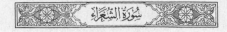

Poets

Revealed at Makkah

*In the name of Allah,
the Beneficent, the Merciful*

1. Tā’. Sīn. Mīm.[201]

2. These are revelations of the Scripture that makes plain.

3. It may be that you. torment yourself (O Muhammad) because they believe not.

4. If We will, We can send down on them from the sky a portent so that their necks would remain bowed before it.

5. Never comes there unto them a fresh reminder from the Beneficent One, but they turn away from it.

6. Now they have denied (the Truth); but there will come unto them tidings of that whereat they used to scoff.

7. Have they not seen the earth, how much of every fruitful kind We make to grow therein?

8. Lo! herein is indeed a portent; yet most of them are not believers.

9. And lo! your Lord! He is indeed the Mighty, the Merciful.

10. And when your Lord called Moses, saying: Go unto the wrongdoing folk,

11. The folk of Pharaoh. Will they not ward off (evil)?

12. He said: My Lord! Lo! I fear that they will deny me,

13. And I shall be embarrassed, and my tongue will not speak plainly, therefore send for Aaron (to help me).

14. And they have a crime against me, so I fear that they will kill me.

15. He said: Nay, surely. So go you two with Our tokens. Lo! We shall be with you, Hearing.

---

[201]See Surah 2:1, footnote.

16. And come together unto Pharaoh and say: Lo! we bear the message of the Lord of the Worlds,

17. (Saying): Let the Children of Israel go with Us.

18. (Pharaoh) said (unto Moses): Did we not rear you among us as a child? And you did dwell many years of your life among us,

19. And you did that your deed which you did, and you were one of the ingrates,

20. He said: I did it then, when I was of those who are astray.

21. Then I fled from you when I feared you, and my Lord vouchsafed me a command and appointed me (as one) of the messengers.

22. And this is the past favor with which you reproach me: that you have enslaved the Children of Israel.

23. Pharaoh said: And what is the Lord of the Worlds?

24. (Moses) said: Lord of the heavens and the earth and all that is between them, if you had but sure belief.

25. (Pharaoh) said unto those around him: Hear you not?

26. He said: Your Lord and the Lord of your fathers.

27. (Pharaoh) said: Lo! your messenger who has been sent unto you is indeed a madman!

28. He said: Lord of the East and the West and all that is between them, if you did but understand.

29. (Pharaoh) said: If you choose a god other than me, I assuredly shall place you among the prisoners.

30. He said: Even though I show you something plain?

31. (Pharaoh) said: Produce it then, if you are of the truthful!

32. Then he flung down his staff and it became a serpent manifest,

١٦ فَأْتِيَا فِرْعَوْنَ فَقُولَا إِنَّا رَسُولُ رَبِّ الْعَالَمِينَ

١٧ أَنْ أَرْسِلْ مَعَنَا بَنِي إِسْرَائِيلَ

١٨ قَالَ أَلَمْ نُرَبِّكَ فِينَا وَلِيدًا وَلَبِثْتَ فِينَا مِنْ عُمُرِكَ سِنِينَ

١٩ وَفَعَلْتَ فَعْلَتَكَ الَّتِي فَعَلْتَ وَأَنْتَ مِنَ الْكَافِرِينَ

٢٠ قَالَ فَعَلْتُهَا إِذًا وَأَنَا مِنَ الضَّالِّينَ

٢١ فَفَرَرْتُ مِنْكُمْ لَمَّا خِفْتُكُمْ فَوَهَبَ لِي رَبِّي حُكْمًا وَجَعَلَنِي مِنَ الْمُرْسَلِينَ

٢٢ وَتِلْكَ نِعْمَةٌ تَمُنُّهَا عَلَيَّ أَنْ عَبَّدْتَ بَنِي إِسْرَائِيلَ

٢٣ قَالَ فِرْعَوْنُ وَمَا رَبُّ الْعَالَمِينَ

٢٤ قَالَ رَبُّ السَّمَاوَاتِ وَالْأَرْضِ وَمَا بَيْنَهُمَا إِنْ كُنْتُمْ مُوقِنِينَ

٢٥ قَالَ لِمَنْ حَوْلَهُ أَلَا تَسْتَمِعُونَ

٢٦ قَالَ رَبُّكُمْ وَرَبُّ آبَائِكُمُ الْأَوَّلِينَ

٢٧ قَالَ إِنَّ رَسُولَكُمُ الَّذِي أُرْسِلَ إِلَيْكُمْ لَمَجْنُونٌ

٢٨ قَالَ رَبُّ الْمَشْرِقِ وَالْمَغْرِبِ وَمَا بَيْنَهُمَا إِنْ كُنْتُمْ تَعْقِلُونَ

٢٩ قَالَ لَئِنِ اتَّخَذْتَ إِلَٰهًا غَيْرِي لَأَجْعَلَنَّكَ مِنَ الْمَسْجُونِينَ

٣٠ قَالَ أَوَلَوْ جِئْتُكَ بِشَيْءٍ مُبِينٍ

٣١ قَالَ فَأْتِ بِهِ إِنْ كُنْتَ مِنَ الصَّادِقِينَ

٣٢ فَأَلْقَى عَصَاهُ فَإِذَا هِيَ ثُعْبَانٌ مُبِينٌ

33. And he drew forth his hand and lo! it was white to the beholders.

٣٣ وَنَزَعَ يَدَهُ فَإِذَا هِىَ بَيْضَاءُ لِلنَّاظِرِينَ

34. (Pharaoh) said unto the chiefs about him: Lo, this is surely a knowing wizard,

٣٤ قَالَ لِلْمَلَإِ حَوْلَهُ إِنَّ هَذَا لَسَاحِرٌ عَلِيمٌ

35. Who would drive you out of your land by his magic. Now what counsel you?

٣٥ يُرِيدُ أَنْ يُخْرِجَكُمْ مِنْ أَرْضِكُمْ بِسِحْرِهِ فَمَاذَا تَأْمُرُونَ

36. They said: Put him off, (him) and his brother, and send then into the cities summoners

٣٦ قَالُوا أَرْجِهْ وَأَخَاهُ وَابْعَثْ فِى الْمَدَائِنِ حَاشِرِينَ

37. Who shall bring unto you every knowing wizard.

٣٧ يَأْتُوكَ بِكُلِّ سَحَّارٍ عَلِيمٍ

38. So the wizards were gathered together at a set time on a day appointed.

٣٨ فَجُمِعَ السَّحَرَةُ لِمِيقَاتِ يَوْمٍ مَعْلُومٍ

39. And it was said unto the people: Are you (also) gathering?

٣٩ وَقِيلَ لِلنَّاسِ هَلْ أَنْتُمْ مُجْتَمِعُونَ

40. (They said): Aye, so that we may follow the wizards if they are the winners.

٤٠ لَعَلَّنَا نَتَّبِعُ السَّحَرَةَ إِنْ كَانُوا هُمُ الْغَالِبِينَ

41. And when the wizards came they said unto Pharaoh: Will there surely be a reward for us if we are the winners?

٤١ فَلَمَّا جَاءَ السَّحَرَةُ قَالُوا لِفِرْعَوْنَ أَئِنَّ لَنَا لَأَجْرًا إِنْ كُنَّا نَحْنُ الْغَالِبِينَ

42. He said: Aye, and you will then surely be of those brought near (to me).

٤٢ قَالَ نَعَمْ وَإِنَّكُمْ إِذًا لَمِنَ الْمُقَرَّبِينَ

43. Moses said unto them: Throw what you are going to throw!

٤٣ قَالَ لَهُمْ مُوسَى أَلْقُوا مَا أَنْتُمْ مُلْقُونَ

44. Then they threw down their cords and their staves and said: By Pharaoh's might, lo! we surely are the winners.

٤٤ فَأَلْقَوْا حِبَالَهُمْ وَعِصِيَّهُمْ وَقَالُوا بِعِزَّةِ فِرْعَوْنَ إِنَّا لَنَحْنُ الْغَالِبُونَ

45. Then Moses threw his staff and lo! it swallowed that which they did falsely show.

٤٥ فَأَلْقَى مُوسَى عَصَاهُ فَإِذَا هِىَ تَلْقَفُ مَا يَأْفِكُونَ

46. And the wizards were flung prostrate,

٤٦ فَأُلْقِىَ السَّحَرَةُ سَاجِدِينَ

47. Crying: We believe in the Lord of the Worlds,

٤٧ قَالُوا آمَنَّا بِرَبِّ الْعَالَمِينَ

48. The Lord of Moses and Aaron.

٤٨ رَبِّ مُوسَى وَهَارُونَ

49. (Pharaoh) said, You put your faith in him before I give you leave. Lo! he doubtless is your chief who taught you magic! But surely you shall come to know. Surely I will cut off your hands and your feet alternately, and surely I will crucify you every one.

٤٩ قَالَ آمَنْتُمْ لَهُ قَبْلَ أَنْ آذَنَ لَكُمْ إِنَّهُ لَكَبِيرُكُمُ الَّذِى عَلَّمَكُمُ السِّحْرَ فَلَسَوْفَ تَعْلَمُونَ لَأُقَطِّعَنَّ أَيْدِيَكُمْ وَأَرْجُلَكُمْ مِنْ خِلَافٍ وَلَأُصَلِّبَنَّكُمْ أَجْمَعِينَ

50. They said: It is no hurt, for lo! unto our Lord we shall return.

51. Lo! we ardently hope that our Lord will forgive us our sins because we are the first of the believers.

52. And We inspired Moses, saying: Take away My slaves by night, for you will be pursued.

53. Then Pharaoh sent into the cities summoners,

54. (Who said): Lo! these indeed are but a little troop,

55. And lo! they are offenders against us.

56. And lo! we are a ready host.

57. Thus did We take them away from gardens and water springs,

58. And treasures and a fair estate.

59. Thus (were those things taken from them) and We caused the Children of Israel to inherit them.

60. And they overtook them at sunrise.

61. And when the two hosts saw each other, those with Moses said: Lo! we are indeed caught.

62. He said: Nay, surely! for lo! my Lord is with me. He will guide me.

63. Then We inspired Moses, saying: Smite the sea with your staff. And it parted, and each part was as a mountain vast.

64. Then brought We near the others to that place.

65. And We saved Moses and those with him, every one;

66. Then We drowned the others.

67. Lo! herein is indeed a portent, yet most of them are not believers.

68. And lo, your Lord! He is indeed the Mighty, the Merciful.

٥٠ قَالُوا لَا ضَيْرَ إِنَّا إِلَى رَبِّنَا مُنقَلِبُونَ

٥١ إِنَّا نَطْمَعُ أَن يَغْفِرَ لَنَا رَبُّنَا خَطَايَانَا أَن كُنَّا أَوَّلَ الْمُؤْمِنِينَ

٥٢ ۞ وَأَوْحَيْنَا إِلَى مُوسَى أَنْ أَسْرِ بِعِبَادِي إِنَّكُم مُّتَّبَعُونَ

٥٣ فَأَرْسَلَ فِرْعَوْنُ فِي الْمَدَائِنِ حَاشِرِينَ

٥٤ إِنَّ هَٰؤُلَاءِ لَشِرْذِمَةٌ قَلِيلُونَ

٥٥ وَإِنَّهُمْ لَنَا لَغَائِظُونَ

٥٦ وَإِنَّا لَجَمِيعٌ حَاذِرُونَ

٥٧ فَأَخْرَجْنَاهُم مِّن جَنَّاتٍ وَعُيُونٍ

٥٨ وَكُنُوزٍ وَمَقَامٍ كَرِيمٍ

٥٩ كَذَٰلِكَ وَأَوْرَثْنَاهَا بَنِي إِسْرَائِيلَ

٦٠ فَأَتْبَعُوهُم مُّشْرِقِينَ

٦١ فَلَمَّا تَرَاءَا الْجَمْعَانِ قَالَ أَصْحَابُ مُوسَى إِنَّا لَمُدْرَكُونَ

٦٢ قَالَ كَلَّا إِنَّ مَعِيَ رَبِّي سَيَهْدِينِ

٦٣ فَأَوْحَيْنَا إِلَى مُوسَى أَنِ اضْرِب بِّعَصَاكَ الْبَحْرَ فَانفَلَقَ فَكَانَ كُلُّ فِرْقٍ كَالطَّوْدِ الْعَظِيمِ

٦٤ وَأَزْلَفْنَا ثَمَّ الْآخَرِينَ

٦٥ وَأَنجَيْنَا مُوسَى وَمَن مَّعَهُ أَجْمَعِينَ

٦٦ ثُمَّ أَغْرَقْنَا الْآخَرِينَ

٦٧ إِنَّ فِي ذَٰلِكَ لَآيَةً وَمَا كَانَ أَكْثَرُهُم مُّؤْمِنِينَ

٦٨ وَإِنَّ رَبَّكَ لَهُوَ الْعَزِيزُ الرَّحِيمُ

69. Recite unto them the story of Abraham:

70. When he said unto his father and his folk: What worship you?

71. They said: We worship idols, and are ever devoted unto them.

72. He said: Do they hear you when you cry?

73. Or do they benefit or harm you?

74. They said: Nay, but we found our fathers acting on this wise.

75. He said: See now that which you worship,

76. You and your forefathers!

77. Lo! they are (all) an enemy unto me, save the Lord of the Worlds.

78. Who created me, and He does guide me,

79. And Who feeds me and waters me.

80. And when I sicken, then He heals me,

81. And Who causes me to die, then gives me life (again),

82. And Who, I ardently hope, will forgive me my sin on the Day of Judgement.

83. My Lord! Vouchsafe me wisdom and unite me to the righteous.

84. And give unto me a good report in later generations.

85. And place me among the inheritors of the Garden of Delight,

86. And forgive my father. Lo! he is of those who err.

87. And abase me not on the day when they are raised,

88. The day when wealth and sons avail not (any man)

89. Save him who brings unto Allah a whole heart.

90. And the Garden will be brought near for those who ward off (evil).

٦٩ وَاتْلُ عَلَيْهِمْ نَبَأَ إِبْرَاهِيمَ

٧٠ إِذْ قَالَ لِأَبِيهِ وَقَوْمِهِ مَا تَعْبُدُونَ

٧١ قَالُوا نَعْبُدُ أَصْنَامًا فَنَظَلُّ لَهَا عَاكِفِينَ

٧٢ قَالَ هَلْ يَسْمَعُونَكُمْ إِذْ تَدْعُونَ

٧٣ أَوْ يَنْفَعُونَكُمْ أَوْ يَضُرُّونَ

٧٤ قَالُوا بَلْ وَجَدْنَا آبَاءَنَا كَذَلِكَ يَفْعَلُونَ

٧٥ قَالَ أَفَرَأَيْتُمْ مَا كُنْتُمْ تَعْبُدُونَ

٧٦ أَنْتُمْ وَآبَاؤُكُمُ الْأَقْدَمُونَ

٧٧ فَإِنَّهُمْ عَدُوٌّ لِي إِلَّا رَبَّ الْعَالَمِينَ

٧٨ الَّذِي خَلَقَنِي فَهُوَ يَهْدِينِ

٧٩ وَالَّذِي هُوَ يُطْعِمُنِي وَيَسْقِينِ

٨٠ وَإِذَا مَرِضْتُ فَهُوَ يَشْفِينِ

٨١ وَالَّذِي يُمِيتُنِي ثُمَّ يُحْيِينِ

٨٢ وَالَّذِي أَطْمَعُ أَنْ يَغْفِرَ لِي خَطِيئَتِي يَوْمَ الدِّينِ

٨٣ رَبِّ هَبْ لِي حُكْمًا وَأَلْحِقْنِي بِالصَّالِحِينَ

٨٤ وَاجْعَلْ لِي لِسَانَ صِدْقٍ فِي الْآخِرِينَ

٨٥ وَاجْعَلْنِي مِنْ وَرَثَةِ جَنَّةِ النَّعِيمِ

٨٦ وَاغْفِرْ لِأَبِي إِنَّهُ كَانَ مِنَ الضَّالِّينَ

٨٧ وَلَا تُخْزِنِي يَوْمَ يُبْعَثُونَ

٨٨ يَوْمَ لَا يَنْفَعُ مَالٌ وَلَا بَنُونَ

٨٩ إِلَّا مَنْ أَتَى اللَّهَ بِقَلْبٍ سَلِيمٍ

٩٠ وَأُزْلِفَتِ الْجَنَّةُ لِلْمُتَّقِينَ

91. And Hell will appear plainly to the erring.

92. And it will be said unto them: Where is (all) that you used to worship

93. Instead of Allah? Can they help you or help themselves?

94. Then they will be hurled therein, they and the seducers

95. And the hosts of Iblīs, together.

96. And they will say, when they are quarreling therein:

97. By Allah, of a truth we were in error manifest

98. When we made you equal with the Lord of the Worlds.

99. It was but the criminals who misled us.

100. Now we have no intercessors

101. Nor any loving friend.

102. Oh, that we had another turn (on earth), that we might be of the believers!

103. Lo! herein is indeed a portent, yet most of them are not believers!

104. And lo, your Lord! He is Indeed the Mighty, the Merciful.

105. Noah's folk denied the messengers (of Allah),

106. When their brother Noah said unto them: Will you not ward off (evil)?

107. Lo! I am a faithful messenger unto you,

108. So keep your duty to Allah, and obey me.

109. And I ask of you no wage therefor; my wage is the concern only of the Lord of the Worlds.

110. So keep your duty to Allah, and obey me.

111. They said: Shall we put faith in you, when the lowest (of the people) follow you?

٩١ وَبُرِّزَتِ الْجَحِيمُ لِلْغَاوِينَ

٩٢ وَقِيلَ لَهُمْ أَيْنَ مَا كُنتُمْ تَعْبُدُونَ

٩٣ مِن دُونِ اللَّهِ هَلْ يَنصُرُونَكُمْ أَوْ يَنتَصِرُونَ

٩٤ فَكُبْكِبُوا فِيهَا هُمْ وَالْغَاوُونَ

٩٥ وَجُنُودُ إِبْلِيسَ أَجْمَعُونَ

٩٦ قَالُوا وَهُمْ فِيهَا يَخْتَصِمُونَ

٩٧ تَاللَّهِ إِن كُنَّا لَفِي ضَلَالٍ مُّبِينٍ

٩٨ إِذْ نُسَوِّيكُم بِرَبِّ الْعَالَمِينَ

٩٩ وَمَا أَضَلَّنَا إِلَّا الْمُجْرِمُونَ

١٠٠ فَمَا لَنَا مِن شَافِعِينَ

١٠١ وَلَا صَدِيقٍ حَمِيمٍ

١٠٢ فَلَوْ أَنَّ لَنَا كَرَّةً فَنَكُونَ مِنَ الْمُؤْمِنِينَ

١٠٣ إِنَّ فِي ذَلِكَ لَآيَةً وَمَا كَانَ أَكْثَرُهُم مُّؤْمِنِينَ

١٠٤ وَإِنَّ رَبَّكَ لَهُوَ الْعَزِيزُ الرَّحِيمُ

١٠٥ كَذَّبَتْ قَوْمُ نُوحٍ الْمُرْسَلِينَ

١٠٦ إِذْ قَالَ لَهُمْ أَخُوهُمْ نُوحٌ أَلَا تَتَّقُونَ

١٠٧ إِنِّي لَكُمْ رَسُولٌ أَمِينٌ

١٠٨ فَاتَّقُوا اللَّهَ وَأَطِيعُونِ

١٠٩ وَمَا أَسْأَلُكُمْ عَلَيْهِ مِنْ أَجْرٍ إِنْ أَجْرِيَ إِلَّا عَلَى رَبِّ الْعَالَمِينَ

١١٠ فَاتَّقُوا اللَّهَ وَأَطِيعُونِ

١١١ قَالُوا أَنُؤْمِنُ لَكَ وَاتَّبَعَكَ الْأَرْذَلُونَ

112. He said: And what knowledge have I of what they may have been doing (in the past)?

113. Lo! their reckoning is my Lord's concern, if you but knew;

114. And I am not (here) to repulse believers.

115. I am only a plain warner.

116. They said: If you cease not, O Noah, you will surely be among those stoned (to death).

117. He said: My Lord! Lo! my own folk deny me.

118. Therefore judge You between us, a (conclusive) judgment, and save me and those believers who are with me.

119. So We saved him and those with him in the laden ship.

120. Then afterward We drowned the others.

121. Lo! herein is indeed a portent, yet most of them are not believers.

122. And lo, your Lord, He is indeed the Mighty, the Merciful.

123. (The tribe of) 'Ād denied the messengers (of Allah),

124. When their brother Hūd said unto them: Will you not ward off (evil)?

125. Lo! I am a faithful messenger unto you,

126. So keep your duty to Allah and obey me.

127. And I ask of you no wage therefor; my wage is the concern only of the Lord of the Worlds.

128. Build you on every high place a monument for vain delight?

129. And seek you out strongholds, that you may last forever?

130. And if you punish, you punish as tyrants?

131. Rather keep your duty to Allah, and obey me.

١١٢ قَالَ وَمَا عِلْمِي بِمَا كَانُوا يَعْمَلُونَ

١١٣ إِنْ حِسَابُهُمْ إِلَّا عَلَى رَبِّي لَوْ تَشْعُرُونَ

١١٤ وَمَا أَنَا بِطَارِدِ الْمُؤْمِنِينَ

١١٥ إِنْ أَنَا إِلَّا نَذِيرٌ مُبِينٌ

١١٦ قَالُوا لَئِن لَّمْ تَنتَهِ يَا نُوحُ لَتَكُونَنَّ مِنَ الْمَرْجُومِينَ

١١٧ قَالَ رَبِّ إِنَّ قَوْمِي كَذَّبُونِ

١١٨ فَافْتَحْ بَيْنِي وَبَيْنَهُمْ فَتْحًا وَنَجِّنِي وَمَن مَّعِيَ مِنَ الْمُؤْمِنِينَ

١١٩ فَأَنجَيْنَاهُ وَمَن مَّعَهُ فِي الْفُلْكِ الْمَشْحُونِ

١٢٠ ثُمَّ أَغْرَقْنَا بَعْدُ الْبَاقِينَ

١٢١ إِنَّ فِي ذَلِكَ لَآيَةً وَمَا كَانَ أَكْثَرُهُم مُّؤْمِنِينَ

١٢٢ وَإِنَّ رَبَّكَ لَهُوَ الْعَزِيزُ الرَّحِيمُ

١٢٣ كَذَّبَتْ عَادٌ الْمُرْسَلِينَ

١٢٤ إِذْ قَالَ لَهُمْ أَخُوهُمْ هُودٌ أَلَا تَتَّقُونَ

١٢٥ إِنِّي لَكُمْ رَسُولٌ أَمِينٌ

١٢٦ فَاتَّقُوا اللَّهَ وَأَطِيعُونِ

١٢٧ وَمَا أَسْأَلُكُمْ عَلَيْهِ مِنْ أَجْرٍ إِنْ أَجْرِيَ إِلَّا عَلَى رَبِّ الْعَالَمِينَ

١٢٨ أَتَبْنُونَ بِكُلِّ رِيعٍ آيَةً تَعْبَثُونَ

١٢٩ وَتَتَّخِذُونَ مَصَانِعَ لَعَلَّكُمْ تَخْلُدُونَ

١٣٠ وَإِذَا بَطَشْتُم بَطَشْتُمْ جَبَّارِينَ

١٣١ فَاتَّقُوا اللَّهَ وَأَطِيعُونِ

132. Keep your duty toward Him who has aided you with (the good things) that you know,

﴿١٣٢﴾ وَاتَّقُوا الَّذِىٓ أَمَدَّكُم بِمَا تَعْلَمُونَ

133. Has aided you with cattle and sons.

﴿١٣٣﴾ أَمَدَّكُم بِأَنْعَامٍ وَبَنِينَ

134. And gardens and watersprings.

﴿١٣٤﴾ وَجَنَّاتٍ وَعُيُونٍ

135. Lo! I fear for you the retribution of an awful day.

﴿١٣٥﴾ إِنِّىٓ أَخَافُ عَلَيْكُمْ عَذَابَ يَوْمٍ عَظِيمٍ

136. They said: It is all one to us whether you preach or are not of those who preach;

﴿١٣٦﴾ قَالُوا سَوَآءٌ عَلَيْنَآ أَوَعَظْتَ أَمْ لَمْ تَكُن مِّنَ الْوَاعِظِينَ

137. This is but a fable of the men of old,

﴿١٣٧﴾ إِنْ هَٰذَآ إِلَّا خُلُقُ الْأَوَّلِينَ

138. And we shall not be doomed.

﴿١٣٨﴾ وَمَا نَحْنُ بِمُعَذَّبِينَ

139. And they denied him; therefore We destroyed them. Lo! herein is indeed a portent, yet most of them are not believers.

﴿١٣٩﴾ فَكَذَّبُوهُ فَأَهْلَكْنَٰهُمْ إِنَّ فِى ذَٰلِكَ لَآيَةً وَمَا كَانَ أَكْثَرُهُم مُّؤْمِنِينَ

140. And lo! your Lord, He is indeed the Mighty, the Mer-ciful.

﴿١٤٠﴾ وَإِنَّ رَبَّكَ لَهُوَ الْعَزِيزُ الرَّحِيمُ

141. (The tribe of) Thamūd denied the messengers (of Allah)

﴿١٤١﴾ كَذَّبَتْ ثَمُودُ الْمُرْسَلِينَ

142. When their brother Ṣāliḥ said unto them: Will you not ward off (evil)?

﴿١٤٢﴾ إِذْ قَالَ لَهُمْ أَخُوهُمْ صَٰلِحٌ أَلَا تَتَّقُونَ

143. Lo! I am a faithful messenger unto you,

﴿١٤٣﴾ إِنِّى لَكُمْ رَسُولٌ أَمِينٌ

144. So keep your duty to Allah and obey me.

﴿١٤٤﴾ فَاتَّقُوا اللَّهَ وَأَطِيعُونِ

145. And I ask of you no wage there-for; my wage is the concern only of the Lord of the Worlds.

﴿١٤٥﴾ وَمَآ أَسْـَٔلُكُمْ عَلَيْهِ مِنْ أَجْرٍ إِنْ أَجْرِىَ إِلَّا عَلَىٰ رَبِّ الْعَٰلَمِينَ

146. Will you be left secure in that which is here before us,

﴿١٤٦﴾ أَتُتْرَكُونَ فِى مَا هَٰهُنَآ ءَامِنِينَ

147. In gardens and watersprings

﴿١٤٧﴾ فِى جَنَّاتٍ وَعُيُونٍ

148. And tilled fields and heavy sheathed palm trees,

﴿١٤٨﴾ وَزُرُوعٍ وَنَخْلٍ طَلْعُهَا هَضِيمٌ

149. Though you hew out dwellings in the mountains, being skilful?

﴿١٤٩﴾ وَتَنْحِتُونَ مِنَ الْجِبَالِ بُيُوتًا فَٰرِهِينَ

150. Therefore keep your duty to Allah and obey me,

﴿١٥٠﴾ فَاتَّقُوا اللَّهَ وَأَطِيعُونِ

151. And obey not the command of the prodigal,

﴿١٥١﴾ وَلَا تُطِيعُوٓا أَمْرَ الْمُسْرِفِينَ

152. Who spread corruption in the earth, and reform not.

153. They said: You are but one of the bewitched;

154. You are but a mortal like us. So bring some token if you are of the truthful.

155. He said: (Behold) this she-camel. She has the right to drink (at the well), and you have the right to drink, (each) on an appointed day.

156. And touch her not with ill lest there come on you the retribution of an awful day.

157. But they hamstrung her, and then were penitent.

158. So the retribution came on them. Lo! herein is indeed a portent, yet most of them are not believers.

159. And lo! your Lord! He is indeed the Mighty, the Merciful.

160. The folk of Lot denied the messengers (of Allah),

161. When their brother Lot said unto them: Will you not ward off (evil)?

162. Lo! I am a faithful messenger unto you,

163. So keep your duty to Allah and obey me.

164. And I ask of you no wage therefor; my wage is the concern only of the Lord of the Worlds.

165. What! Of all creatures do you come unto the males,

166. And leave the wives your Lord created for you? Nay, but you are froward folk.

167. They said: If you cease not, O Lot, you will soon be those expelled.

168. He said: I am in truth of those who hate your conduct.

١٥٢ الَّذِينَ يُفْسِدُونَ فِي الْأَرْضِ وَلَا يُصْلِحُونَ

١٥٣ قَالُوا إِنَّمَا أَنتَ مِنَ الْمُسَحَّرِينَ

١٥٤ مَا أَنتَ إِلَّا بَشَرٌ مِّثْلُنَا فَأْتِ بِآيَةٍ إِن كُنتَ مِنَ الصَّادِقِينَ

١٥٥ قَالَ هَٰذِهِ نَاقَةٌ لَّهَا شِرْبٌ وَلَكُمْ شِرْبُ يَوْمٍ مَّعْلُومٍ

١٥٦ وَلَا تَمَسُّوهَا بِسُوءٍ فَيَأْخُذَكُمْ عَذَابُ يَوْمٍ عَظِيمٍ

١٥٧ فَعَقَرُوهَا فَأَصْبَحُوا نَادِمِينَ

١٥٨ فَأَخَذَهُمُ الْعَذَابُ إِنَّ فِي ذَٰلِكَ لَآيَةً وَمَا كَانَ أَكْثَرُهُم مُّؤْمِنِينَ

١٥٩ وَإِنَّ رَبَّكَ لَهُوَ الْعَزِيزُ الرَّحِيمُ

١٦٠ كَذَّبَتْ قَوْمُ لُوطٍ الْمُرْسَلِينَ

١٦١ إِذْ قَالَ لَهُمْ أَخُوهُمْ لُوطٌ أَلَا تَتَّقُونَ

١٦٢ إِنِّي لَكُمْ رَسُولٌ أَمِينٌ

١٦٣ فَاتَّقُوا اللَّهَ وَأَطِيعُونِ

١٦٤ وَمَا أَسْأَلُكُمْ عَلَيْهِ مِنْ أَجْرٍ إِنْ أَجْرِيَ إِلَّا عَلَىٰ رَبِّ الْعَالَمِينَ

١٦٥ أَتَأْتُونَ الذُّكْرَانَ مِنَ الْعَالَمِينَ

١٦٦ وَتَذَرُونَ مَا خَلَقَ لَكُمْ رَبُّكُم مِّنْ أَزْوَاجِكُم بَلْ أَنتُمْ قَوْمٌ عَادُونَ

١٦٧ قَالُوا لَئِن لَّمْ تَنتَهِ يَا لُوطُ لَتَكُونَنَّ مِنَ الْمُخْرَجِينَ

١٦٨ قَالَ إِنِّي لِعَمَلِكُم مِّنَ الْقَالِينَ

169. My Lord! Save me and my household from what they do.

170. So We saved him and his household, every one,

171. Save an old woman among those who stayed behind.

172. Then afterward We destroyed the others.

173. And We rained on them a rain. And dreadful is the rain of those who have been warned.

174. Lo! herein is indeed a portent, yet most of them are not believers.

175. And lo! your Lord, He is indeed the Mighty, the Merciful.

176. The dwellers in the wood (of Madian) denied the messengers (of Allah),

177. When Shu'ayb said unto them: Will you not ward off (evil)?

178. Lo! I am a faithful messenger unto you,

179. So keep your duty to Allah and obey me.

180. And I ask of you no wage for it; my wage is the concern only of the Lord of the Worlds.

181. Give full measure, and be not of those who give less (than the due).

182. And weigh with the true balance.

183. Wrong not mankind in their goods, and do not evil, making mischief, in the earth.

184. And keep your duty unto Him Who created you and the generations of the men of old.

185. They said: You are but one of the bewitched;

186. You are but a mortal like us, and lo! we deem you of the liars.

187. Then make fragments of the heaven fall upon us, if you are of the truthful.

١٦٩ رَبِّ نَجِّنِي وَأَهْلِي مِمَّا يَعْمَلُونَ

١٧٠ فَنَجَّيْنَاهُ وَأَهْلَهُ أَجْمَعِينَ

١٧١ إِلَّا عَجُوزًا فِي الْغَابِرِينَ

١٧٢ ثُمَّ دَمَّرْنَا الْآخَرِينَ

١٧٣ وَأَمْطَرْنَا عَلَيْهِم مَّطَرًا فَسَاءَ مَطَرُ الْمُنذَرِينَ

١٧٤ إِنَّ فِي ذَلِكَ لَآيَةً وَمَا كَانَ أَكْثَرُهُم مُّؤْمِنِينَ

١٧٥ وَإِنَّ رَبَّكَ لَهُوَ الْعَزِيزُ الرَّحِيمُ

١٧٦ كَذَّبَ أَصْحَابُ لْئَيْكَةِ الْمُرْسَلِينَ

١٧٧ إِذْ قَالَ لَهُمْ شُعَيْبٌ أَلَا تَتَّقُونَ

١٧٨ إِنِّي لَكُمْ رَسُولٌ أَمِينٌ

١٧٩ فَاتَّقُوا اللَّهَ وَأَطِيعُونِ

١٨٠ وَمَا أَسْأَلُكُمْ عَلَيْهِ مِنْ أَجْرٍ إِنْ أَجْرِيَ إِلَّا عَلَى رَبِّ الْعَالَمِينَ

١٨١ أَوْفُوا الْكَيْلَ وَلَا تَكُونُوا مِنَ الْمُخْسِرِينَ

١٨٢ وَزِنُوا بِالْقِسْطَاسِ الْمُسْتَقِيمِ

١٨٣ وَلَا تَبْخَسُوا النَّاسَ أَشْيَاءَهُمْ وَلَا تَعْثَوْا فِي الْأَرْضِ مُفْسِدِينَ

١٨٤ وَاتَّقُوا الَّذِي خَلَقَكُمْ وَالْجِبِلَّةَ الْأَوَّلِينَ

١٨٥ قَالُوا إِنَّمَا أَنتَ مِنَ الْمُسَحَّرِينَ

١٨٦ وَمَا أَنتَ إِلَّا بَشَرٌ مِّثْلُنَا وَإِن نَّظُنُّكَ لَمِنَ الْكَاذِبِينَ

١٨٧ فَأَسْقِطْ عَلَيْنَا كِسَفًا مِّنَ السَّمَاءِ إِن كُنتَ مِنَ الصَّادِقِينَ

188. He said: My Lord is best aware of what you do.

189. But they denied him, so there came on them the retribution of the day of gloom. Lo! it was the retribution of an awful day.

190. Lo! herein is indeed a portent; yet most of them are not believers.

191. And lo! your Lord! He is indeed the Mighty, the Mer-ciful.

192. And lo! it is a revelation of the Lord of the Worlds,

193. Which the True Spirit has brought down

194. Upon your heart (O Muhammad), that you may be (one) of the warners,

195. In plain Arabic speech.

196. And lo, it is in the Scriptures of the men of old.

197. Is it not a token for them that the doctors of the Children of Israel[202] know it?

198. And if We had revealed it unto one of any of the non-Arabs,

199. And he had read it unto them, they would not have believed in it.

200. Thus do We make it traverse the hearts of criminals.

201. They will not believe in it till they behold the painful doom,

202. So that it will come upon them suddenly, when they perceive not.

203. Then they will say: Are we to be reprieved?

204. Would they (now) hasten on Our doom?

205. Have you then seen, We content them for (long) years,

206. And then comes that which they were promised,

207. That with which they were con-tented nothing avails them?

---

[202]The Jews knew, from their Scripture, that a prophet had been promised to the Arabs.

208. And We destroyed no township but it had its warners

209. For reminder, for We never were oppressors.

210. The devils did not bring it down.

211. It is not meet for them, nor is it in their power,

212. Lo! surely they are banished from the hearing.

213. Therefore invoke not with Allah another god, lest you be one of the doomed.

214. And warn your tribe of near kindred,

215. And lower your wing (in kindness) unto those believers who follow you.

216. And if they (your kinsfolk) disobey you, say: Lo! I am innocent of what you do.

217. And put your trust in the Mighty, the Merciful.

218. Who sees you when you stand up (to pray)

219. And (sees) your movements among those who fall prostrate (in worship).

220. Lo! He, only He, is the Hearer, the Knower.

221. Shall I inform you upon whom the devils descend?

222. They descend on every sinful, false one.

223. They listen eagerly, but most of them are liars.

224. As for poets, the erring follow them.

225. Have you not seen how they stray in every valley,

226. And how they say that which they do not?

227. Save those who believe and do good works, and remember Allah much, and vindicate themselves after they have been wronged. Those who do wrong will come to know by what a (great) reverse they will be overturned!

٢٠٨ وَمَا أَهْلَكْنَا مِن قَرْيَةٍ إِلَّا لَهَا مُنذِرُونَ

٢٠٩ ذِكْرَىٰ وَمَا كُنَّا ظَالِمِينَ

٢١٠ وَمَا تَنَزَّلَتْ بِهِ الشَّيَاطِينُ

٢١١ وَمَا يَنبَغِي لَهُمْ وَمَا يَسْتَطِيعُونَ

٢١٢ إِنَّهُمْ عَنِ السَّمْعِ لَمَعْزُولُونَ

٢١٣ فَلَا تَدْعُ مَعَ اللَّهِ إِلَٰهًا ءَاخَرَ فَتَكُونَ مِنَ الْمُعَذَّبِينَ

٢١٤ وَأَنذِرْ عَشِيرَتَكَ الْأَقْرَبِينَ

٢١٥ وَاخْفِضْ جَنَاحَكَ لِمَنِ اتَّبَعَكَ مِنَ الْمُؤْمِنِينَ

٢١٦ فَإِنْ عَصَوْكَ فَقُلْ إِنِّي بَرِيءٌ مِّمَّا تَعْمَلُونَ

٢١٧ وَتَوَكَّلْ عَلَى الْعَزِيزِ الرَّحِيمِ

٢١٨ الَّذِي يَرَاكَ حِينَ تَقُومُ

٢١٩ وَتَقَلُّبَكَ فِي السَّاجِدِينَ

٢٢٠ إِنَّهُ هُوَ السَّمِيعُ الْعَلِيمُ

٢٢١ هَلْ أُنَبِّئُكُمْ عَلَىٰ مَن تَنَزَّلُ الشَّيَاطِينُ

٢٢٢ تَنَزَّلُ عَلَىٰ كُلِّ أَفَّاكٍ أَثِيمٍ

٢٢٣ يُلْقُونَ السَّمْعَ وَأَكْثَرُهُمْ كَاذِبُونَ

٢٢٤ وَالشُّعَرَاءُ يَتَّبِعُهُمُ الْغَاوُونَ

٢٢٥ أَلَمْ تَرَ أَنَّهُمْ فِي كُلِّ وَادٍ يَهِيمُونَ

٢٢٦ وَأَنَّهُمْ يَقُولُونَ مَا لَا يَفْعَلُونَ

٢٢٧ إِلَّا الَّذِينَ ءَامَنُوا وَعَمِلُوا الصَّالِحَاتِ وَذَكَرُوا اللَّهَ كَثِيرًا وَانتَصَرُوا مِن بَعْدِ مَا ظُلِمُوا وَسَيَعْلَمُ الَّذِينَ ظَلَمُوا أَيَّ مُنقَلَبٍ يَنقَلِبُونَ

The Ants

Al Naml, "The Ants," takes its name from the ant mentioned in verse 18. It belongs to the middle group of Makkan surahs.

A number of surahs, like this one, are called after some insects and animals. They draw our attention to the miracles of Allah manifested in His creation, even in the most minute living beings. The Qur'an clearly shows, as in this surah, that Solomon could understand the language of ants, birds and others. Allah granted him a kingdom like unto which no one before or after could master. The miracles mentioned in the surah sould be taken literally. (The editor)

The Ants

Revealed at Makkah

*In the name of Allah,
the Beneficent, the Merciful*

1. Ṭā'. Sīn.203 These are revelations of the Qur'an and a Scripture that makes plain;

2. A guidance and good tidings for believers

3. Who establish prayer and pay the poor-due and are sure of the Hereafter.

4. Lo! as for those who believe not in the Hereafter, We have made their works fair-seeming unto them so that they are all astray.

5. Those are they for whom is the worst of punishment, and in the Hereafter they will be the greatest losers.

6. Lo! as for you (Muhammad), you surely receive the Qur'an from the presence of One Wise, Aware.

7. (Remember) when Moses said unto his household: Lo! I spy afar off a fire; I will bring you tidings thence, or bring to you a borrowed flame that you may warm yourselves.

8. But when he reached it, he was called, saying: Blessed is whosoever is in the fire and whosoever is round about it! And glorified be Allah, the Lord of the Worlds!

9. O Moses! Lo! it is I, Allah, the Mighty, the Wise.

10. And throw down your staff! But when he saw it writhing as it were a demon, he turned to flee headlong; (but it was said unto him): O Moses! Fear not! Lo! the emissaries fear not in My presence,

11. Save him who has done wrong and afterward has changed evil for good.204 And lo! I am Forgiving, Merciful.

203See Surah 2:2, footnote. - 204Moses had been guilty of a crime in Egypt.

12. And put your hand into the bosom of your robe, it will come forth white but unhurt. (This will be one) among nine tokens unto Pharaoh and his people. Lo! they were ever evil-living folk.

13. But when Our tokens came unto them, plain to see, they said: This is plain magic,

14. And they denied them, though their souls acknowledged them, for spite and arrogance. Then see the nature of the consequence for the wrongdoers!

15. And We surely gave knowledge unto David and Solo-mon, and they said: Praise be to Allah, Who has preferred us above many of His believing slaves!

16. And Solomon was David's heir. And he said: O people! Lo! we have been taught the language of birds, and have been given (abundance) of all things. This surely is evident favor.

17. And there were gathered together unto Solomon his armies of the jinn and humankind, and of the birds, and they were set in battle order;

18. Till, when they reached the Valley of the Ants, an ant exclaimed: O ants! Enter your dwellings lest Solomon and his armies crush you, unperceiving.

19. And (Solomon) smiled, laughing at her speech, and said: My Lord, arouse me to be thankful for Your favor wherewith You have favored me and my parents, and to do good that shall be pleasing unto You, and include me in (the number of) Your righteous slaves.

﴿١٢﴾ وَأَدْخِلْ يَدَكَ فِي جَيْبِكَ تَخْرُجْ بَيْضَاءَ مِنْ غَيْرِ سُوءٍ فِي تِسْعِ ءَايَاتٍ إِلَىٰ فِرْعَوْنَ وَقَوْمِهِ إِنَّهُمْ كَانُوا قَوْمًا فَاسِقِينَ

﴿١٣﴾ فَلَمَّا جَاءَتْهُمْ ءَايَاتُنَا مُبْصِرَةً قَالُوا هَٰذَا سِحْرٌ مُبِينٌ

﴿١٤﴾ وَجَحَدُوا بِهَا وَاسْتَيْقَنَتْهَا أَنفُسُهُمْ ظُلْمًا وَعُلُوًّا فَانظُرْ كَيْفَ كَانَ عَاقِبَةُ الْمُفْسِدِينَ

﴿١٥﴾ وَلَقَدْ ءَاتَيْنَا دَاوُدَ وَسُلَيْمَانَ عِلْمًا وَقَالَا الْحَمْدُ لِلَّهِ الَّذِي فَضَّلَنَا عَلَىٰ كَثِيرٍ مِّنْ عِبَادِهِ الْمُؤْمِنِينَ

﴿١٦﴾ وَوَرِثَ سُلَيْمَانُ دَاوُدَ وَقَالَ يَا أَيُّهَا النَّاسُ عُلِّمْنَا مَنطِقَ الطَّيْرِ وَأُوتِينَا مِن كُلِّ شَيْءٍ إِنَّ هَٰذَا لَهُوَ الْفَضْلُ الْمُبِينُ

﴿١٧﴾ وَحُشِرَ لِسُلَيْمَانَ جُنُودُهُ مِنَ الْجِنِّ وَالْإِنسِ وَالطَّيْرِ فَهُمْ يُوزَعُونَ

﴿١٨﴾ حَتَّىٰ إِذَا أَتَوْا عَلَىٰ وَادِ النَّمْلِ قَالَتْ نَمْلَةٌ يَا أَيُّهَا النَّمْلُ ادْخُلُوا مَسَاكِنَكُمْ لَا يَحْطِمَنَّكُمْ سُلَيْمَانُ وَجُنُودُهُ وَهُمْ لَا يَشْعُرُونَ

﴿١٩﴾ فَتَبَسَّمَ ضَاحِكًا مِّن قَوْلِهَا وَقَالَ رَبِّ أَوْزِعْنِي أَنْ أَشْكُرَ نِعْمَتَكَ الَّتِي أَنْعَمْتَ عَلَيَّ وَعَلَىٰ وَالِدَيَّ وَأَنْ أَعْمَلَ صَالِحًا تَرْضَاهُ وَأَدْخِلْنِي بِرَحْمَتِكَ فِي عِبَادِكَ الصَّالِحِينَ

20. And he sought among the birds and said: How is it that I see not the hoopoe, or is he among the absent?

21. I surely will punish him with hard punishment or I surely will slay him, or he surely shall bring me a plain excuse.

22. But he was not long in coming, and he said: I have found out (a thing) that you apprehend not, and I come unto you from Sheba with sure tidings.

23. Lo! I found a woman ruling over them, and she has been given (abundance) of all things, and hers is a mighty throne.

24. I found her and her people worshipping the sun instead of Allah; and the Devil makes their works fair-seeming unto them, and debarred them from the way (of Truth), so that they did not go aright:

25. So that they worshiped not Allah, Who brings forth the hidden in the heavens and the earth, and knows what you hide and what you proclaim,

26. Allah; there is no God save Him, the Lord of the tremendous Throne.

27. (Solomon) said: We shall see whether you speak truth or whether you are of the liars.

28. Go with this my letter and throw it down unto them; then turn away and see what (answer) they return,

29. (The Queen of Sheba) said (when she received the letter): O chieftains! Lo! there has been thrown unto me a noble letter.

30. Lo! it is from Solomon, and lo! it is: In the name of Allah the Beneficent, the Merciful;

31. Exalt not yourselves against me, but come unto me as Muslims.

32. She said: O chieftains! Pronounce for me in my case. I decide no case till you are present with me.

٢٠ وَتَفَقَّدَ الطَّيْرَ فَقَالَ مَا لِيَ لَا أَرَى الْهُدْهُدَ أَمْ كَانَ مِنَ الْغَائِبِينَ

٢١ لَأُعَذِّبَنَّهُ عَذَابًا شَدِيدًا أَوْ لَأَاذْبَحَنَّهُ أَوْ لَيَأْتِيَنِّي بِسُلْطَانٍ مُبِينٍ

٢٢ فَمَكَثَ غَيْرَ بَعِيدٍ فَقَالَ أَحَطتُ بِمَا لَمْ تُحِطْ بِهِ وَجِئْتُكَ مِن سَبَإٍ بِنَبَإٍ يَقِينٍ

٢٣ إِنِّي وَجَدتُّ امْرَأَةً تَمْلِكُهُمْ وَأُوتِيَتْ مِن كُلِّ شَيْءٍ وَلَهَا عَرْشٌ عَظِيمٌ

٢٤ وَجَدتُّهَا وَقَوْمَهَا يَسْجُدُونَ لِلشَّمْسِ مِن دُونِ اللَّهِ وَزَيَّنَ لَهُمُ الشَّيْطَانُ أَعْمَالَهُمْ فَصَدَّهُمْ عَنِ السَّبِيلِ فَهُمْ لَا يَهْتَدُونَ

٢٥ أَلَّا يَسْجُدُوا لِلَّهِ الَّذِي يُخْرِجُ الْخَبْءَ فِي السَّمَاوَاتِ وَالْأَرْضِ وَيَعْلَمُ مَا تُخْفُونَ وَمَا تُعْلِنُونَ

٢٦ اللَّهُ لَا إِلَهَ إِلَّا هُوَ رَبُّ الْعَرْشِ الْعَظِيمِ

٢٧ قَالَ سَنَنظُرُ أَصَدَقْتَ أَمْ كُنتَ مِنَ الْكَاذِبِينَ

٢٨ اذْهَب بِكِتَابِي هَذَا فَأَلْقِهْ إِلَيْهِمْ ثُمَّ تَوَلَّ عَنْهُمْ فَانظُرْ مَاذَا يَرْجِعُونَ

٢٩ قَالَتْ يَا أَيُّهَا الْمَلَأُ إِنِّي أُلْقِيَ إِلَيَّ كِتَابٌ كَرِيمٌ

٣٠ إِنَّهُ مِن سُلَيْمَانَ وَإِنَّهُ بِسْمِ اللَّهِ الرَّحْمَنِ الرَّحِيمِ

٣١ أَلَّا تَعْلُوا عَلَيَّ وَأْتُونِي مُسْلِمِينَ

٣٢ قَالَتْ يَا أَيُّهَا الْمَلَأُ أَفْتُونِي فِي أَمْرِي مَا كُنتُ قَاطِعَةً أَمْرًا حَتَّى تَشْهَدُونِ

33. They said: We are lords of might and lords of great prowess, but it is for you to command; so consider what you will command.

34. She said: Lo! kings, when they enter a township, ruin it and make the honor of its people shame. Thus will they do.

35. But lo! I am going to send a present unto them, and to see with what (answer) the messengers return.

36. So when (the envoy) came unto Solomon, (the King) said: What! Would you help me with wealth? But that which Allah has given me is better than that which He has given you. Nay it is you (and not I) who exult in your gift.

37. Return unto them. We surely shall come unto them with hosts that they cannot resist, and we shall drive them out from thence with shame, and they will be abased.

38. He said: O chiefs! Which of you will bring me her throne before they come unto me, surrendering?

39. A stalwart of the Jinn said: I will bring it you before you can rise from your place. Lo! I surely am strong and trusty for such work.

40. One with whom was knowledge of the Scripture said: I will bring it you before your gaze returns unto you. And when he saw it set in his presence, (Solomon) said: This is of the bounty of my Lord, that He may try me whether I give thanks or am ungrateful. Whosoever gives thanks he only gives thanks for (the good of) his own soul: and whosoever is ungrateful (is ungrateful only to his own soul's hurt). For lo! my Lord is Absolute in independence, Bountiful.

41. He said: Disguise her throne for her that we may see whether she will go aright or be of those not rightly guided.

۝ قَالُوا نَحْنُ أُولُوا قُوَّةٍ وَأُولُوا بَأْسٍ شَدِيدٍ وَالْأَمْرُ إِلَيْكِ فَانظُرِي مَاذَا تَأْمُرِينَ

۝ قَالَتْ إِنَّ الْمُلُوكَ إِذَا دَخَلُوا قَرْيَةً أَفْسَدُوهَا وَجَعَلُوا أَعِزَّةَ أَهْلِهَا أَذِلَّةً وَكَذَلِكَ يَفْعَلُونَ

۝ وَإِنِّي مُرْسِلَةٌ إِلَيْهِم بِهَدِيَّةٍ فَنَاظِرَةٌ بِمَ يَرْجِعُ الْمُرْسَلُونَ

۝ فَلَمَّا جَاءَ سُلَيْمَانَ قَالَ أَتُمِدُّونَنِ بِمَالٍ فَمَا آتَانِيَ اللَّهُ خَيْرٌ مِّمَّا آتَاكُم بَلْ أَنتُم بِهَدِيَّتِكُمْ تَفْرَحُونَ

۝ ارْجِعْ إِلَيْهِمْ فَلَنَأْتِيَنَّهُم بِجُنُودٍ لَّا قِبَلَ لَهُم بِهَا وَلَنُخْرِجَنَّهُم مِّنْهَا أَذِلَّةً وَهُمْ صَاغِرُونَ

۝ قَالَ يَا أَيُّهَا الْمَلَأُ أَيُّكُمْ يَأْتِينِي بِعَرْشِهَا قَبْلَ أَن يَأْتُونِي مُسْلِمِينَ

۝ قَالَ عِفْرِيتٌ مِّنَ الْجِنِّ أَنَا آتِيكَ بِهِ قَبْلَ أَن تَقُومَ مِن مَّقَامِكَ وَإِنِّي عَلَيْهِ لَقَوِيٌّ أَمِينٌ

۝ قَالَ الَّذِي عِندَهُ عِلْمٌ مِّنَ الْكِتَابِ أَنَا آتِيكَ بِهِ قَبْلَ أَن يَرْتَدَّ إِلَيْكَ طَرْفُكَ فَلَمَّا رَآهُ مُسْتَقِرًّا عِندَهُ قَالَ هَذَا مِن فَضْلِ رَبِّي لِيَبْلُوَنِي أَأَشْكُرُ أَمْ أَكْفُرُ وَمَن شَكَرَ فَإِنَّمَا يَشْكُرُ لِنَفْسِهِ وَمَن كَفَرَ فَإِنَّ رَبِّي غَنِيٌّ كَرِيمٌ

۝ قَالَ نَكِّرُوا لَهَا عَرْشَهَا نَنظُرْ أَتَهْتَدِي أَمْ تَكُونُ مِنَ الَّذِينَ لَا يَهْتَدُونَ

42. So, when she came, it was said (unto her): Is your throne like this? She said: (It is) as though it were the very one. And (Solomon said): We were given the knowledge before her and we had surrendered (to Allah).

43. And (all) that she was wont to worship instead of Allah hindered her, for she came of disbelieving folk.

44. It was said unto her: Enter the hall. And when she saw it she deemed it a pool and bared her legs. (Solomon) said: Lo! it is a hall, made smooth, of glass. She said: My Lord! Lo! I have wronged myself, and I surrender with Solomon unto Allah, the Lord of the Worlds.

45. And We surely sent unto Thamūd their brother Ṣāliḥ, saying: Worship Allah. And lo! they (then) became two parties quarreling.

46. He said: O my people! Why will you hasten on the evil rather than the good? Why will you not ask pardon of Allah, that you may receive mercy.

47. They said: We augur evil of you and those with you. He said: Your evil augury is with Allah. Nay, but you are folk that are being tested.

48. And there were in the city nine groups who made mischief in the land and reformed not.

49. They said: Swear one to another by Allah that we surely will attack him and his household by night, and afterward we will surely say unto his friend: We witnessed not the de-struction of his household. And lo! we are truthtellers.

50. So they plotted a plot: and We plotted a plot, while they perceived not.

51. Then see the nature of the consequence of their plotting, for lo! We destroyed them and their people, every one.

٤٢ فَلَمَّا جَاءَتْ قِيلَ أَهَكَذَا عَرْشُكِ قَالَتْ كَأَنَّهُ هُوَ وَأُوتِينَا الْعِلْمَ مِن قَبْلِهَا وَكُنَّا مُسْلِمِينَ

٤٣ وَصَدَّهَا مَا كَانَت تَّعْبُدُ مِن دُونِ اللَّهِ إِنَّهَا كَانَتْ مِن قَوْمٍ كَافِرِينَ

٤٤ قِيلَ لَهَا ادْخُلِي الصَّرْحَ فَلَمَّا رَأَتْهُ حَسِبَتْهُ لُجَّةً وَكَشَفَتْ عَن سَاقَيْهَا قَالَ إِنَّهُ صَرْحٌ مُّمَرَّدٌ مِّن قَوَارِيرَ قَالَتْ رَبِّ إِنِّي ظَلَمْتُ نَفْسِي وَأَسْلَمْتُ مَعَ سُلَيْمَانَ لِلَّهِ رَبِّ الْعَالَمِينَ

٤٥ وَلَقَدْ أَرْسَلْنَا إِلَى ثَمُودَ أَخَاهُمْ صَالِحًا أَنِ اعْبُدُوا اللَّهَ فَإِذَا هُمْ فَرِيقَانِ يَخْتَصِمُونَ

٤٦ قَالَ يَا قَوْمِ لِمَ تَسْتَعْجِلُونَ بِالسَّيِّئَةِ قَبْلَ الْحَسَنَةِ لَوْلَا تَسْتَغْفِرُونَ اللَّهَ لَعَلَّكُمْ تُرْحَمُونَ

٤٧ قَالُوا اطَّيَّرْنَا بِكَ وَبِمَن مَّعَكَ قَالَ طَائِرُكُمْ عِندَ اللَّهِ بَلْ أَنتُمْ قَوْمٌ تُفْتَنُونَ

٤٨ وَكَانَ فِي الْمَدِينَةِ تِسْعَةُ رَهْطٍ يُفْسِدُونَ فِي الْأَرْضِ وَلَا يُصْلِحُونَ

٤٩ قَالُوا تَقَاسَمُوا بِاللَّهِ لَنُبَيِّتَنَّهُ وَأَهْلَهُ ثُمَّ لَنَقُولَنَّ لِوَلِيِّهِ مَا شَهِدْنَا مَهْلِكَ أَهْلِهِ وَإِنَّا لَصَادِقُونَ

٥٠ وَمَكَرُوا مَكْرًا وَمَكَرْنَا مَكْرًا وَهُمْ لَا يَشْعُرُونَ

٥١ فَانظُرْ كَيْفَ كَانَ عَاقِبَةُ مَكْرِهِمْ أَنَّا دَمَّرْنَاهُمْ وَقَوْمَهُمْ أَجْمَعِينَ

52. See, these are their dwellings empty and in ruins because they did wrong. Lo! herein is indeed a portent for a people who have knowledge.

٥٢ فَتِلْكَ بُيُوتُهُمْ خَاوِيَةً بِمَا ظَلَمُوٓاْ إِنَّ فِي ذَٰلِكَ لَآيَةً لِّقَوْمٍ يَعْلَمُونَ

53. And we saved those who believed and used to ward off (evil).

٥٣ وَأَنجَيْنَا ٱلَّذِينَ ءَامَنُواْ وَكَانُواْ يَتَّقُونَ

54. And Lot! when he said unto his folk: will you commit abomination knowingly?

٥٤ وَلُوطًا إِذْ قَالَ لِقَوْمِهِۦٓ أَتَأْتُونَ ٱلْفَٰحِشَةَ وَأَنتُمْ تُبْصِرُونَ

55. Must you seek lust in men instead of women? Nay, but you are folk who act senselessly.

٥٥ أَئِنَّكُمْ لَتَأْتُونَ ٱلرِّجَالَ شَهْوَةً مِّن دُونِ ٱلنِّسَآءِ بَلْ أَنتُمْ قَوْمٌ تَجْهَلُونَ

56. But the answer of his folk was nothing but that they said: Expel the household of Lot from your township, for they (no doubt) are folk who would keep clean!

٥٦ ۞ فَمَا كَانَ جَوَابَ قَوْمِهِۦٓ إِلَّآ أَن قَالُوٓاْ أَخْرِجُوٓاْ ءَالَ لُوطٍ مِّن قَرْيَتِكُمْ إِنَّهُمْ أُنَاسٌ يَتَطَهَّرُونَ

57. Then we saved him and his household save his wife; We destined her to be of those who stayed behind.

٥٧ فَأَنجَيْنَٰهُ وَأَهْلَهُۥٓ إِلَّا ٱمْرَأَتَهُۥ قَدَّرْنَٰهَا مِنَ ٱلْغَٰبِرِينَ

58. And We rained a rain upon them. Dreadful is the rain of those who have been warned.

٥٨ وَأَمْطَرْنَا عَلَيْهِم مَّطَرًا فَسَآءَ مَطَرُ ٱلْمُنذَرِينَ

59. Say (O Muhammad): Praise be to Allah, and peace be on His slaves whom He has chosen! Is Allah best, or (all) that you ascribe as partners (unto Him)?

٥٩ قُلِ ٱلْحَمْدُ لِلَّهِ وَسَلَٰمٌ عَلَىٰ عِبَادِهِ ٱلَّذِينَ ٱصْطَفَىٰٓ ءَآللَّهُ خَيْرٌ أَمَّا يُشْرِكُونَ

60. Is not He (best) who created the heavens and the earth, and sends down for you water from the sky wherewith We cause to spring forth joyous orchards, whose trees it never has been yours to cause to grow. Is there any God beside Allah? Nay, but they are folk who ascribe equals (unto Him)!

٦٠ أَمَّنْ خَلَقَ ٱلسَّمَٰوَٰتِ وَٱلْأَرْضَ وَأَنزَلَ لَكُم مِّنَ ٱلسَّمَآءِ مَآءً فَأَنبَتْنَا بِهِۦ حَدَآئِقَ ذَاتَ بَهْجَةٍ مَّا كَانَ لَكُمْ أَن تُنۢبِتُواْ شَجَرَهَآ أَءِلَٰهٌ مَّعَ ٱللَّهِ بَلْ هُمْ قَوْمٌ يَعْدِلُونَ

61. Is not He (best) Who made the earth a fixed abode, and placed rivers in the folds thereof, and placed firm hills therein, and has set a barrier between the two seas? Is there any God beside Allah? Nay, but most of them know not!

٦١ أَمَّن جَعَلَ ٱلْأَرْضَ قَرَارًا وَجَعَلَ خِلَٰلَهَآ أَنْهَٰرًا وَجَعَلَ لَهَا رَوَٰسِيَ وَجَعَلَ بَيْنَ ٱلْبَحْرَيْنِ حَاجِزًا أَءِلَٰهٌ مَّعَ ٱللَّهِ بَلْ أَكْثَرُهُمْ لَا يَعْلَمُونَ

62. Is not He (best) who answers the wronged one when he cries unto Him and removes the evil, and has made you viceroys of the earth? Is there any God beside Allah? Little do they reflect!

٦٢ أَمَّن يُجِيبُ الْمُضْطَرَّ إِذَا دَعَاهُ وَيَكْشِفُ السُّوءَ وَيَجْعَلُكُمْ خُلَفَاءَ الْأَرْضِ أَءِلَهٌ مَّعَ اللَّهِ قَلِيلًا مَّا تَذَكَّرُونَ

63. Is not He (best) Who guides you in the darkness of the land and the sea, He Who sends the winds as heralds of His mercy? Is there any God beside Allah? High exalted be Allah from all that they ascribe as partner (unto Him)!

٦٣ أَمَّن يَهْدِيكُمْ فِي ظُلُمَاتِ الْبَرِّ وَالْبَحْرِ وَمَن يُرْسِلُ الرِّيَاحَ بُشْرًا بَيْنَ يَدَيْ رَحْمَتِهِ أَءِلَهٌ مَّعَ اللَّهِ تَعَالَى اللَّهُ عَمَّا يُشْرِكُونَ

64. Is not He (best), Who produces creation, then reproduces it, and Who provides for you from the heaven and the earth? Is there any God beside Allah? Say: Bring your proof, if you are truthful!

٦٤ أَمَّن يَبْدَؤُا الْخَلْقَ ثُمَّ يُعِيدُهُ وَمَن يَرْزُقُكُم مِّنَ السَّمَاءِ وَالْأَرْضِ أَءِلَهٌ مَّعَ اللَّهِ قُلْ هَاتُوا بُرْهَانَكُمْ إِن كُنتُمْ صَادِقِينَ

65. Say (O Muhammad): None in the heavens and the earth knows the Unseen save Allah; and they know not when they will be raised (again).

٦٥ قُل لَّا يَعْلَمُ مَن فِي السَّمَوَاتِ وَالْأَرْضِ الْغَيْبَ إِلَّا اللَّهُ وَمَا يَشْعُرُونَ أَيَّانَ يُبْعَثُونَ

66. Still less can their knowledge comprehend the Hereafter. Nay, for they are in doubt concerning it. Nay, for they cannot see it.

٦٦ بَلِ ادَّارَكَ عِلْمُهُمْ فِي الْآخِرَةِ بَلْ هُمْ فِي شَكٍّ مِّنْهَا بَلْ هُم مِّنْهَا عَمُونَ

67. Yet those who disbelieve say: when we have become dust like our fathers, shall we surely be brought forth (again)?

٦٧ وَقَالَ الَّذِينَ كَفَرُوا أَءِذَا كُنَّا تُرَابًا وَآبَاؤُنَا أَءِنَّا لَمُخْرَجُونَ

68. We were promised this, no doubt, we and our fathers. (All) this is nothing but fables of the men of old.

٦٨ لَقَدْ وُعِدْنَا هَذَا نَحْنُ وَآبَاؤُنَا مِن قَبْلُ إِنْ هَذَا إِلَّا أَسَاطِيرُ الْأَوَّلِينَ

69. Say (unto them, O Muhammad): Travel in the land and see the nature of the sequel for the criminals!

٦٩ قُلْ سِيرُوا فِي الْأَرْضِ فَانظُرُوا كَيْفَ كَانَ عَاقِبَةُ الْمُجْرِمِينَ

70. And grieve you not for them, nor be in distress because of what they plot (against you).

٧٠ وَلَا تَحْزَنْ عَلَيْهِمْ وَلَا تَكُن فِي ضَيْقٍ مِّمَّا يَمْكُرُونَ

71. And they say: When (will) this promise (be fulfilled), if you are truthful?

٧١ وَيَقُولُونَ مَتَى هَذَا الْوَعْدُ إِن كُنتُمْ صَادِقِينَ

72. Say: It may be that a part of that which you would hasten on is close behind you.

٧٢ قُلْ عَسَى أَن يَكُونَ رَدِفَ لَكُم بَعْضُ الَّذِي تَسْتَعْجِلُونَ

73. Lo! your Lord is full of bounty for mankind, but most of them do not give thanks.

74. Lo! your Lord knows surely all that their bosoms hide, and all that they proclaim.

75. And there is nothing hidden in the heaven or the earth but it is in a clear Record.

76. Lo! this Qur'an narrates unto the Children of Israel most of that concerning which they differ.

77. And lo! it is a guidance and a mercy for believers.

78. Lo! your Lord will judge between them His decision, and He is the Mighty, the Wise.

79. Therefore (O Muhammad) put your trust in Allah, for you (stand) on the plain Truth.

80. Lo! you can not make the dead to hear, nor can you make the deaf to hear the call when they have turned to flee;

81. Nor can you lead the blind out of their error. You can make none to hear, save those who believe Our revelations and who are Muslims.

82. And when the word is fulfilled concerning them, We shall bring forth a beast of the earth to speak unto them because mankind had not faith in Our revelations.

83. And (remind them of) the Day when We shall gather out of every nation a host of those who denied Our revelations, and they will be set in array;

84. Till, when they come (before their Lord), He will say: Did you deny My revelations when you could not compass them in knowledge, or what was it that you did?

٧٣ وَإِنَّ رَبَّكَ لَذُو فَضْلٍ عَلَى النَّاسِ وَلَكِنَّ أَكْثَرَهُمْ لَا يَشْكُرُونَ

٧٤ وَإِنَّ رَبَّكَ لَيَعْلَمُ مَا تُكِنُّ صُدُورُهُمْ وَمَا يُعْلِنُونَ

٧٥ وَمَا مِنْ غَائِبَةٍ فِي السَّمَاءِ وَالْأَرْضِ إِلَّا فِي كِتَابٍ مُبِينٍ

٧٦ إِنَّ هَذَا الْقُرْآنَ يَقُصُّ عَلَى بَنِي إِسْرَائِيلَ أَكْثَرَ الَّذِي هُمْ فِيهِ يَخْتَلِفُونَ

٧٧ وَإِنَّهُ لَهُدًى وَرَحْمَةٌ لِلْمُؤْمِنِينَ

٧٨ إِنَّ رَبَّكَ يَقْضِي بَيْنَهُمْ بِحُكْمِهِ وَهُوَ الْعَزِيزُ الْعَلِيمُ

٧٩ فَتَوَكَّلْ عَلَى اللَّهِ إِنَّكَ عَلَى الْحَقِّ الْمُبِينِ

٨٠ إِنَّكَ لَا تُسْمِعُ الْمَوْتَى وَلَا تُسْمِعُ الصُّمَّ الدُّعَاءَ إِذَا وَلَّوْا مُدْبِرِينَ

٨١ وَمَا أَنْتَ بِهَادِي الْعُمْيِ عَنْ ضَلَالَتِهِمْ إِنْ تُسْمِعُ إِلَّا مَنْ يُؤْمِنُ بِآيَاتِنَا فَهُمْ مُسْلِمُونَ

٨٢ وَإِذَا وَقَعَ الْقَوْلُ عَلَيْهِمْ أَخْرَجْنَا لَهُمْ دَابَّةً مِنَ الْأَرْضِ تُكَلِّمُهُمْ أَنَّ النَّاسَ كَانُوا بِآيَاتِنَا لَا يُوقِنُونَ

٨٣ وَيَوْمَ نَحْشُرُ مِنْ كُلِّ أُمَّةٍ فَوْجًا مِمَّنْ يُكَذِّبُ بِآيَاتِنَا فَهُمْ يُوزَعُونَ

٨٤ حَتَّى إِذَا جَاءُوا قَالَ أَكَذَّبْتُمْ بِآيَاتِي وَلَمْ تُحِيطُوا بِهَا عِلْمًا أَمَّاذَا كُنْتُمْ تَعْمَلُونَ

85. And the Word will be fulfilled concerning them because they have done wrong, and they will not utter.

٨٥ وَوَقَعَ الْقَوْلُ عَلَيْهِمْ بِمَا ظَلَمُوا فَهُمْ لَا يَنْطِقُونَ

86. Have they not seen how We have appointed the night that they may rest therein, and the day sight giving? Lo! therein surely are portents for a people who believe.

٨٦ أَلَمْ يَرَوْا أَنَّا جَعَلْنَا الَّيْلَ لِيَسْكُنُوا فِيهِ وَالنَّهَارَ مُبْصِرًا إِنَّ فِي ذَلِكَ لَآيَاتٍ لِقَوْمٍ يُؤْمِنُونَ

87. And (remind them of) the Day when the Trumpet will be blown, and all who are in the heavens and the earth will start in fear, save him whom Allah wills. And all come unto Him, humbled.

٨٧ وَيَوْمَ يُنْفَخُ فِي الصُّورِ فَفَزِعَ مَنْ فِي السَّمَوَاتِ وَمَنْ فِي الْأَرْضِ إِلَّا مَنْ شَاءَ اللَّهُ وَكُلٌّ أَتَوْهُ دَاخِرِينَ

88. And you see the hills you deem them solid while they are flying the flight of clouds: the doing of Allah Who perfects all things. Lo! He is Informed of what you do.

٨٨ وَتَرَى الْجِبَالَ تَحْسَبُهَا جَامِدَةً وَهِيَ تَمُرُّ مَرَّ السَّحَابِ صُنْعَ اللَّهِ الَّذِي أَتْقَنَ كُلَّ شَيْءٍ إِنَّهُ خَبِيرٌ بِمَا تَفْعَلُونَ

89. Who brings a good deed will have better than its worth; and such are safe from fear that Day.

٨٩ مَنْ جَاءَ بِالْحَسَنَةِ فَلَهُ خَيْرٌ مِنْهَا وَهُمْ مِنْ فَزَعٍ يَوْمَئِذٍ آمِنُونَ

90. And who brings an ill deed, such will be flung down on their faces in the Fire. Are you rewarded anything save what you did?

٩٠ وَمَنْ جَاءَ بِالسَّيِّئَةِ فَكُبَّتْ وُجُوهُهُمْ فِي النَّارِ هَلْ تُجْزَوْنَ إِلَّا مَا كُنْتُمْ تَعْمَلُونَ

91. (Say): I (Muhammad) am commanded only to worship the Lord of this city (Makkah) which He has hallowed, and unto Whom all things belong. And I am commanded to be of those who are Muslims,

٩١ إِنَّمَا أُمِرْتُ أَنْ أَعْبُدَ رَبَّ هَذِهِ الْبَلْدَةِ الَّذِي حَرَّمَهَا وَلَهُ كُلُّ شَيْءٍ وَأُمِرْتُ أَنْ أَكُونَ مِنَ الْمُسْلِمِينَ

92. And to recite the Qur'an. And who goes right, goes right only for (the good of) his own soul; and as for him who goes astray (Unto him) say: Lo! I am only a warner.

٩٢ وَأَنْ أَتْلُوَ الْقُرْآنَ فَمَنِ اهْتَدَى فَإِنَّمَا يَهْتَدِي لِنَفْسِهِ وَمَنْ ضَلَّ فَقُلْ إِنَّمَا أَنَا مِنَ الْمُنْذِرِينَ

93. And say: Praise be to Allah who will show you His portents so that you shall know them. And your Lord is not unaware of what you (mortals) do.

٩٣ وَقُلِ الْحَمْدُ لِلَّهِ سَيُرِيكُمْ آيَاتِهِ فَتَعْرِفُونَهَا وَمَا رَبُّكَ بِغَافِلٍ عَمَّا تَعْمَلُونَ

The Stories

Al Qaṣṣaṣ, "The Story," takes its name from a word in verse 25. The name is justified, moreover, by the nature of this surah, which consists mostly of the story of Moses, his early struggles, and ultimate triumph. It was revealed at a time when the Prophet's case seemed desperate and is one of the last Makkan surahs. Some Arab writers even say that it was revealed during the Hijrah, while others maintain that only verse 85 was revealed during the emigration.

A late Makkah surah, except for verse 85 (revealed during the Prophet's emigration from Makkah to al Madinah) and verses 52-55 (revealed at al Madinah).[205]

---

[205]*Tafsīr al Jalālayn.*

The Story

Revealed at Makkah

*In the name of Allah,
the Beneficent, the Merciful*

1. Ṭā'. Sīn. Mīm.206

2. These are revelations of the Scripture that makes plain.

3. We narrate unto you (somewhat) of the story of Moses and Pharaoh with truth, for folk who believe.

4. Lo! Pharaoh exalted himself in the earth and made its people castes. A tribe among them he suppressed, killing their sons and sparing their women. Lo! he was of those who work corruption.

5. And We desired to show favor unto those who were oppressed in the earth, and to make them examples and to make them the inheritors,

6. And to establish them in the earth, and to show Pharaoh and Hāmān and their hosts that which they feared from them.

7. And We inspired the mother of Moses, saying: Suckle him and, when you fear for him, then cast him into the river and fear not nor grieve. Lo! We shall bring him back unto you and shall make him (one) of the messengers.

8. And the family of Pharaoh picked him up, that he might become for them an enemy and a sorrow. Lo! Pharaoh and Hāmān and their hosts were ever sinning.

9. And the wife of Pharaoh said: (He will be) a consolation for me and for you. Kill him not. Peradventure he may be of use to us, or we may choose him for a son. And they perceived not.

206See Surah 2:1, footnote.

10. And the heart of the mother of Moses became void, and she would have betrayed him if We had not fortified her heart, that she might be of the believers.

11. And she said unto his sister: Trace him. So she observed him from afar, while they perceived not.

12. And We had before forbidden foster-mothers for him, so she said: Shall I show you a household who will rear him for you and take care of him?

13. So We restored him to his mother that she might be comforted and not grieve, and that she might know that the promise of Allah is true. But most of them know not.

14. And when he reached his full strength and was ripe, We gave him wisdom and knowledge. Thus do We reward the good.

15. And he entered the city when its inhabitants were heedless, and he found therein two men fighting, one of his own caste, and the other of his enemies; and he who was of his caste asked him for help against him who was of his enemies. So Moses struck him with his fist and killed him. He said: This is of the Devil's work. Lo! he is an enemy, a mere misleader.

16. He said: My Lord! Lo! I have wronged my soul, so forgive me. Thus He forgave him. Lo! He is the Forgiving, the Merciful.

17. He said: My Lord! Forasmuch as You have favored me, I will nevermore be a supporter of the criminals.

18. The next morning found him in the city, fearing, vigilant, when behold! he who had appealed to him the day before cried out to him for help. Moses said unto him: Lo! you are indeed a mere hothead.

١٠ وَأَصْبَحَ فُؤَادُ أُمِّ مُوسَىٰ فَارِغًا إِن كَادَتْ لَتُبْدِي بِهِ لَوْلَآ أَن رَّبَطْنَا عَلَىٰ قَلْبِهَا لِتَكُونَ مِنَ ٱلْمُؤْمِنِينَ

١١ وَقَالَتْ لِأُخْتِهِ قُصِّيهِ فَبَصُرَتْ بِهِ عَن جُنُبٍ وَهُمْ لَا يَشْعُرُونَ

١٢ وَحَرَّمْنَا عَلَيْهِ ٱلْمَرَاضِعَ مِن قَبْلُ فَقَالَتْ هَلْ أَدُلُّكُمْ عَلَىٰ أَهْلِ بَيْتٍ يَكْفُلُونَهُ لَكُمْ وَهُمْ لَهُ نَاصِحُونَ

١٣ فَرَدَدْنَاهُ إِلَىٰ أُمِّهِ كَيْ تَقَرَّ عَيْنُهَا وَلَا تَحْزَنَ وَلِتَعْلَمَ أَنَّ وَعْدَ ٱللَّهِ حَقٌّ وَلَٰكِنَّ أَكْثَرَهُمْ لَا يَعْلَمُونَ

١٤ وَلَمَّا بَلَغَ أَشُدَّهُ وَٱسْتَوَىٰ ءَاتَيْنَاهُ حُكْمًا وَعِلْمًا وَكَذَٰلِكَ نَجْزِي ٱلْمُحْسِنِينَ

١٥ وَدَخَلَ ٱلْمَدِينَةَ عَلَىٰ حِينِ غَفْلَةٍ مِّنْ أَهْلِهَا فَوَجَدَ فِيهَا رَجُلَيْنِ يَقْتَتِلَانِ هَٰذَا مِن شِيعَتِهِ وَهَٰذَا مِنْ عَدُوِّهِ فَٱسْتَغَاثَهُ ٱلَّذِي مِن شِيعَتِهِ عَلَى ٱلَّذِي مِنْ عَدُوِّهِ فَوَكَزَهُ مُوسَىٰ فَقَضَىٰ عَلَيْهِ قَالَ هَٰذَا مِنْ عَمَلِ ٱلشَّيْطَانِ إِنَّهُ عَدُوٌّ مُّضِلٌّ مُّبِينٌ

١٦ قَالَ رَبِّ إِنِّي ظَلَمْتُ نَفْسِي فَٱغْفِرْ لِي فَغَفَرَ لَهُ إِنَّهُ هُوَ ٱلْغَفُورُ ٱلرَّحِيمُ

١٧ قَالَ رَبِّ بِمَآ أَنْعَمْتَ عَلَيَّ فَلَنْ أَكُونَ ظَهِيرًا لِّلْمُجْرِمِينَ

١٨ فَأَصْبَحَ فِي ٱلْمَدِينَةِ خَائِفًا يَتَرَقَّبُ فَإِذَا ٱلَّذِي ٱسْتَنصَرَهُ بِٱلْأَمْسِ يَسْتَصْرِخُهُ قَالَ لَهُ مُوسَىٰ إِنَّكَ لَغَوِيٌّ مُّبِينٌ

19. And when he would have fallen upon the man who was an enemy unto them both, he said: O Moses! Would you kill me as you did kill a person yesterday. You would be nothing but a tyrant in the land, you would not be of the reformers.

20. And a man came from the farthest end of the city, running. He said: O Moses! Lo! the chiefs take counsel against you to slay you; therefore escape. Lo! I am of those who give you good advice.

21. So he escaped from thence, fearing, vigilant. He said: My Lord! Deliver me from the wrongdoing folk.

22. And when he turned his face toward Madian, he said: Peradventure my Lord will guide me in the right road.

23. And when he came unto the water of Madian he found there a whole tribe of men, watering. And he found apart from them two women keeping back (their flocks). He said: What ails you? The two said: We cannot give (our flocks) to drink till the shepherds return from the water; and our father is a very old man.

24. So he watered (their flock) for them. Then he turned aside into the shade, and said: My Lord! I am needy of whatever good you would send down for me.

25. Then there came unto him one of the two women, walking shyly. She said: Lo! my father bids you, that he may reward you with a payment for that you did water (the flock) for us. Then, when he came unto him and told him the (whole) story, he said: Fear not! You are saved from the wrongdoing folk.

۱۹ فَلَمَّآ أَنْ أَرَادَ أَن يَبْطِشَ بِالَّذِى هُوَ عَدُوٌّ لَّهُمَا قَالَ يَٰمُوسَىٰٓ أَتُرِيدُ أَن تَقْتُلَنِى كَمَا قَتَلْتَ نَفْسًۢا بِالْأَمْسِ إِن تُرِيدُ إِلَّآ أَن تَكُونَ جَبَّارًا فِى الْأَرْضِ وَمَا تُرِيدُ أَن تَكُونَ مِنَ الْمُصْلِحِينَ

۲۰ وَجَآءَ رَجُلٌ مِّنْ أَقْصَا الْمَدِينَةِ يَسْعَىٰ قَالَ يَٰمُوسَىٰٓ إِنَّ الْمَلَأَ يَأْتَمِرُونَ بِكَ لِيَقْتُلُوكَ فَٱخْرُجْ إِنِّى لَكَ مِنَ النَّٰصِحِينَ

۲۱ فَخَرَجَ مِنْهَا خَآئِفًا يَتَرَقَّبُ قَالَ رَبِّ نَجِّنِى مِنَ الْقَوْمِ الظَّٰلِمِينَ

۲۲ وَلَمَّا تَوَجَّهَ تِلْقَآءَ مَدْيَنَ قَالَ عَسَىٰ رَبِّىٓ أَن يَهْدِيَنِى سَوَآءَ السَّبِيلِ

۲۳ وَلَمَّا وَرَدَ مَآءَ مَدْيَنَ وَجَدَ عَلَيْهِ أُمَّةً مِّنَ النَّاسِ يَسْقُونَ وَوَجَدَ مِن دُونِهِمُ ٱمْرَأَتَيْنِ تَذُودَانِ قَالَ مَا خَطْبُكُمَا قَالَتَا لَا نَسْقِى حَتَّىٰ يُصْدِرَ الرِّعَآءُ وَأَبُونَا شَيْخٌ كَبِيرٌ

۲۴ فَسَقَىٰ لَهُمَا ثُمَّ تَوَلَّىٰ إِلَى الظِّلِّ فَقَالَ رَبِّ إِنِّى لِمَآ أَنزَلْتَ إِلَىَّ مِنْ خَيْرٍ فَقِيرٌ

۲۵ فَجَآءَتْهُ إِحْدَىٰهُمَا تَمْشِى عَلَى ٱسْتِحْيَآءٍ قَالَتْ إِنَّ أَبِى يَدْعُوكَ لِيَجْزِيَكَ أَجْرَ مَا سَقَيْتَ لَنَا فَلَمَّا جَآءَهُۥ وَقَصَّ عَلَيْهِ الْقَصَصَ قَالَ لَا تَخَفْ نَجَوْتَ مِنَ الْقَوْمِ الظَّٰلِمِينَ

26. One of the two women said: O my father! Hire him! For the best (man) that you can hire is the strong, the trust-worthy.

٢٦ قَالَتْ إِحْدَىٰهُمَا يَـٰٓأَبَتِ ٱسْتَـْٔجِرْهُ إِنَّ خَيْرَ مَنِ ٱسْتَـْٔجَرْتَ ٱلْقَوِىُّ ٱلْأَمِينُ

27. He said: Lo! I fain would marry you to one of these two daughters of mine on condition that you hire yourself to me for (the term of) eight years. But if you complete ten it will be of your own accord, for I would not make it hard for you. Allah willing, you will find me of the righteous.

٢٧ قَالَ إِنِّىٓ أُرِيدُ أَنْ أُنكِحَكَ إِحْدَى ٱبْنَتَىَّ هَـٰتَيْنِ عَلَىٰٓ أَن تَأْجُرَنِى ثَمَـٰنِىَ حِجَجٍ فَإِنْ أَتْمَمْتَ عَشْرًا فَمِنْ عِندِكَ وَمَآ أُرِيدُ أَنْ أَشُقَّ عَلَيْكَ سَتَجِدُنِىٓ إِن شَآءَ ٱللَّهُ مِنَ ٱلصَّـٰلِحِينَ

28. He said: That (is settled) between you and me. Which-ever of the two terms I fulfill, there will be no injustice to me, and Allah is Surety over what we say.

٢٨ قَالَ ذَٰلِكَ بَيْنِى وَبَيْنَكَ أَيَّمَا ٱلْأَجَلَيْنِ قَضَيْتُ فَلَا عُدْوَٰنَ عَلَىَّ وَٱللَّهُ عَلَىٰ مَا نَقُولُ وَكِيلٌ

29. Then, when Moses had fulfilled the term, and was travelling with his house-folk, he saw in the distance a fire; he said unto his housefolk: Bide you (here). Lo! I see in the distance a fire; peradventure I shall bring you tidings thence, or a brand from the fire that you may warm yourselves.

٢٩ فَلَمَّا قَضَىٰ مُوسَى ٱلْأَجَلَ وَسَارَ بِأَهْلِهِۦٓ ءَانَسَ مِن جَانِبِ ٱلطُّورِ نَارًا قَالَ لِأَهْلِهِ ٱمْكُثُوٓا۟ إِنِّىٓ ءَانَسْتُ نَارًا لَّعَلِّىٓ ءَاتِيكُم مِّنْهَا بِخَبَرٍ أَوْ جَذْوَةٍ مِّنَ ٱلنَّارِ لَعَلَّكُمْ تَصْطَلُونَ

30. And when he reached it, he was called from the right side of the valley in the blessed field, from the tree: O Moses! Lo! I, even I, am Allah, the Lord of the Worlds;

٣٠ فَلَمَّآ أَتَىٰهَا نُودِىَ مِن شَـٰطِئِ ٱلْوَادِ ٱلْأَيْمَنِ فِى ٱلْبُقْعَةِ ٱلْمُبَـٰرَكَةِ مِنَ ٱلشَّجَرَةِ أَن يَـٰمُوسَىٰٓ إِنِّىٓ أَنَا ٱللَّهُ رَبُّ ٱلْعَـٰلَمِينَ

31. Throw down your staff. And when he saw it writhing as it had been a demon, he turned to flee headlong, (and it was said unto him): O Moses! Draw nigh and fear not. Lo! you are of those who are secure.

٣١ وَأَنْ أَلْقِ عَصَاكَ فَلَمَّا رَءَاهَا تَهْتَزُّ كَأَنَّهَا جَآنٌّ وَلَّىٰ مُدْبِرًا وَلَمْ يُعَقِّبْ يَـٰمُوسَىٰٓ أَقْبِلْ وَلَا تَخَفْ إِنَّكَ مِنَ ٱلْءَامِنِينَ

32. Thrust your hand into the bosom of your robe, it will come forth white without hurt. And draw (your arm) close to your side (to guard) against fear. Then these shall be two proofs from your Lord unto Pharaoh and his chiefs: Lo! they are evil-living folk.

٣٢ ٱسْلُكْ يَدَكَ فِى جَيْبِكَ تَخْرُجْ بَيْضَآءَ مِنْ غَيْرِ سُوٓءٍ وَٱضْمُمْ إِلَيْكَ جَنَاحَكَ مِنَ ٱلرَّهْبِ فَذَٰنِكَ بُرْهَـٰنَانِ مِن رَّبِّكَ إِلَىٰ فِرْعَوْنَ وَمَلَإِي۟هِۦٓ إِنَّهُمْ كَانُوا۟ قَوْمًا فَـٰسِقِينَ

33. He said: My Lord! Lo! I killed a man among them and I fear that they will kill me.

34. My brother Aaron is more eloquent than me in speech. Therefore send him with me as a helper to confirm me. Lo! I fear that they will give the lie to me.

35. He said: We will strengthen your arm with your brother, and We will give unto you both power so that they cannot reach you. With Our signs you two, and those who follow you, will be the conquerors.

36. But when Moses came unto them with Our clear tokens, they said: This is nothing but invented magic. We never heard of this among our fathers of old.

37. And Moses said: My Lord is best aware of him who brings guidance from His presence, and whose will be the sequel of the Home (of bliss). Lo! wrongdoers will not be successful.

38. And Pharaoh said: O chiefs! I know not that you have a god other than me, so kindle for me (a fire), O Hāmān, to bake the mud; and set up for me a lofty tower in order that I may survey the god of Moses; and lo! I deem him of the liars.

39. And he and his hosts were haughty in the land without right, and deemed that they would never be brought back to Us.

40. Therefore We seized him and his hosts, and abandoned them unto the sea. Behold the nature of the consequence for evildoers!

41. And We made them patterns that invite unto the Fire, and on the Day of Resurrection they will not be helped.

42. And We made a curse to follow them in this world, and on the Day of Resurrection they will be among the hateful.

٤٢ وَأَتْبَعْنَاهُمْ فِى هَٰذِهِ الدُّنْيَا لَعْنَةً وَيَوْمَ الْقِيَٰمَةِ هُم مِّنَ الْمَقْبُوحِينَ

43. And We surely gave the Scripture unto Moses after We had destroyed the generations of old; clear testimonies for mankind, and a guidance and a mercy, that they might reflect.

٤٣ وَلَقَدْ ءَاتَيْنَا مُوسَى الْكِتَٰبَ مِنۢ بَعْدِ مَا أَهْلَكْنَا الْقُرُونَ الْأُولَىٰ بَصَآئِرَ لِلنَّاسِ وَهُدًى وَرَحْمَةً لَّعَلَّهُمْ يَتَذَكَّرُونَ

44. And you (Muhammad) were not on the western side (of the Mount) when We expounded unto Moses the commandment, and you were not among those present;

٤٤ وَمَا كُنتَ بِجَانِبِ الْغَرْبِىِّ إِذْ قَضَيْنَآ إِلَىٰ مُوسَى الْأَمْرَ وَمَا كُنتَ مِنَ الشَّٰهِدِينَ

45. But We brought forth generations, and their life spans dragged on for them. And you were not a dweller in Madian, reciting unto them Our revelations, but We kept sending (messengers to men).

٤٥ وَلَٰكِنَّآ أَنشَأْنَا قُرُونًا فَتَطَاوَلَ عَلَيْهِمُ الْعُمُرُ وَمَا كُنتَ ثَاوِيًا فِىٓ أَهْلِ مَدْيَنَ تَتْلُوا۟ عَلَيْهِمْ ءَايَٰتِنَا وَلَٰكِنَّا كُنَّا مُرْسِلِينَ

46. And you were not beside the Mount when We did call; but (the knowledge of it is) a mercy from your Lord that you may warn a folk unto whom no warner came before you, that they may give heed.

٤٦ وَمَا كُنتَ بِجَانِبِ الطُّورِ إِذْ نَادَيْنَا وَلَٰكِن رَّحْمَةً مِّن رَّبِّكَ لِتُنذِرَ قَوْمًا مَّآ أَتَىٰهُم مِّن نَّذِيرٍ مِّن قَبْلِكَ لَعَلَّهُمْ يَتَذَكَّرُونَ

47. Otherwise, if disaster should afflict them because of that which their own hands have sent before (them), they might say: Our Lord! Why sent You no messenger unto us, that we might have followed Your revelations and been of the believers?

٤٧ وَلَوْلَآ أَن تُصِيبَهُم مُّصِيبَةٌ بِمَا قَدَّمَتْ أَيْدِيهِمْ فَيَقُولُوا۟ رَبَّنَا لَوْلَآ أَرْسَلْتَ إِلَيْنَا رَسُولًا فَنَتَّبِعَ ءَايَٰتِكَ وَنَكُونَ مِنَ الْمُؤْمِنِينَ

48. But when there came unto them the Truth from Our presence, they said: Why is he not given the like of what was given unto Moses? Did they not disbelieve in that which was given unto Moses of old? They say: Two magics[207] that support each other; and they say: Lo! in both we are disbelievers.

٤٨ فَلَمَّا جَآءَهُمُ الْحَقُّ مِنْ عِندِنَا قَالُوا۟ لَوْلَآ أُوتِىَ مِثْلَ مَآ أُوتِىَ مُوسَىٰ أَوَلَمْ يَكْفُرُوا۟ بِمَآ أُوتِىَ مُوسَىٰ مِن قَبْلُ قَالُوا۟ سِحْرَانِ تَظَٰهَرَا وَقَالُوٓا۟ إِنَّا بِكُلٍّ كَٰفِرُونَ

49. Say (unto them, O Muhammad): Then bring a Scripture from the presence of Allah that gives clearer guidance than these two (that) I may follow it, if you are truthful.

٤٩ قُلْ فَأْتُوا۟ بِكِتَٰبٍ مِّنْ عِندِ اللَّهِ هُوَ أَهْدَىٰ مِنْهُمَآ أَتَّبِعْهُ إِن كُنتُمْ صَٰدِقِينَ

---

[207]I.e., the Scripture of Moses and the Qur'an.

50. And if they answer you not, then know that what they follow is their lusts. And who goes farther astray than he who follows his lust without guidance from Allah. Lo! Allah guides not wrongdoing folk.

51. And now verily We have caused the Word to reach them, that they may give heed.

52. Those unto whom We gave the Scripture before it, they believe in it,

53. And when it is recited unto them, they say: We believe in it. Lo! it is the Truth from our Lord. Lo! even before it we were Muslims.

54. These will be given their reward twice over, because they are steadfast and repel evil with good, and spend of that wherewith We have provided them,

55. And when they hear vanity they withdraw from it and say: Unto us our works and unto you your works. Peace be unto you! We desire not the ignorant.

56. Lo! you (O Muhammad) guide not whom you love, but Allah guides whom He will. And He is best aware of those who walk aright.

57. And they say: If we were to follow the Guidance with you we should be torn out of our land. Have We not established for them a sure sanctuary,[208] whereunto the produce of all things is brought (in trade), a provision from Our presence? But most of them know not.

58. And how many a community have We destroyed that was thankless for its means of livelihood! And yonder are their dwellings, which have not been inhabited after them save a little. And We, even We, were the inheritors.

59. And never did your Lord destroy the townships, till He had raised up in their mother(town) a messenger reciting unto them Our revelations. And never did We destroy the townships unless the folk thereof were evildoers.

---

[208]The sacred territory of Makkah.

60. And whatsoever you have been given is a comfort of the life of the world and an ornament thereof; and that which Allah has is better and more lasting. Have you then no sense?

٦٠ وَمَا أُوتِيتُم مِّن شَيْءٍ فَمَتَاعُ الْحَيَوٰةِ الدُّنْيَا وَزِينَتُهَا وَمَا عِندَ اللَّهِ خَيْرٌ وَأَبْقَىٰ أَفَلَا تَعْقِلُونَ

61. Is he whom We have promised a fair promise which he will find (true) like him whom We suffer to enjoy awhile the comfort of the life of the world, then on the Day of Resur-rection he will be of those arraigned?

٦١ أَفَمَن وَعَدْنَاهُ وَعْدًا حَسَنًا فَهُوَ لَاقِيهِ كَمَن مَّتَّعْنَاهُ مَتَاعَ الْحَيَوٰةِ الدُّنْيَا ثُمَّ هُوَ يَوْمَ الْقِيَامَةِ مِنَ الْمُحْضَرِينَ

62. On the Day when He will call unto them and say: Where are My partners whom you claimed?

٦٢ وَيَوْمَ يُنَادِيهِمْ فَيَقُولُ أَيْنَ شُرَكَاءِيَ الَّذِينَ كُنتُمْ تَزْعُمُونَ

63. Those concerning whom the Word will have come true will say: Our Lord! These are they whom we led astray. We led them astray even as we ourselves were astray. We de-clare our innocence before You: us they never worshiped.

٦٣ قَالَ الَّذِينَ حَقَّ عَلَيْهِمُ الْقَوْلُ رَبَّنَا هَٰؤُلَاءِ الَّذِينَ أَغْوَيْنَا أَغْوَيْنَاهُمْ كَمَا غَوَيْنَا تَبَرَّأْنَا إِلَيْكَ مَا كَانُوا إِيَّانَا يَعْبُدُونَ

64. And it will be said: Cry unto your (so called) partners (of Allah). And they will cry unto them, and they will give no answer unto them, and they will see the Doom. Ah, if they had but been guided!

٦٤ وَقِيلَ ادْعُوا شُرَكَاءَكُمْ فَدَعَوْهُمْ فَلَمْ يَسْتَجِيبُوا لَهُمْ وَرَأَوُا الْعَذَابَ لَوْ أَنَّهُمْ كَانُوا يَهْتَدُونَ

65. And on the Day when He will call unto them and say: What answer gave you to the messengers?

٦٥ وَيَوْمَ يُنَادِيهِمْ فَيَقُولُ مَاذَا أَجَبْتُمُ الْمُرْسَلِينَ

66. On that day (all) tidings will be barred for them, nor will they ask one of another,

٦٦ فَعَمِيَتْ عَلَيْهِمُ الْأَنبَاءُ يَوْمَئِذٍ فَهُمْ لَا يَتَسَاءَلُونَ

67. But as for him who shall repent and believe and do right, he may be one of the successful.

٦٧ فَأَمَّا مَن تَابَ وَآمَنَ وَعَمِلَ صَالِحًا فَعَسَىٰ أَن يَكُونَ مِنَ الْمُفْلِحِينَ

68. Your Lord brings to pass what He wills and chooses. They have never any choice. Glorified be Allah and exalted above all that they associate (with Him)!

٦٨ وَرَبُّكَ يَخْلُقُ مَا يَشَاءُ وَيَخْتَارُ مَا كَانَ لَهُمُ الْخِيَرَةُ سُبْحَانَ اللَّهِ وَتَعَالَىٰ عَمَّا يُشْرِكُونَ

69. And your Lord knows what their breasts conceal, and what they publish.

٦٩ وَرَبُّكَ يَعْلَمُ مَا تُكِنُّ صُدُورُهُمْ وَمَا يُعْلِنُونَ

70. And He is Allah; there is no God save Him. His is all praise in the former and the latter (state), and His is the command, and unto Him you will be brought back.

٧٠ وَهُوَ اللَّهُ لَا إِلَٰهَ إِلَّا هُوَ لَهُ الْحَمْدُ فِي الْأُولَىٰ وَالْآخِرَةِ وَلَهُ الْحُكْمُ وَإِلَيْهِ تُرْجَعُونَ

71. Say: Have you thought, if Allah made night everlasting for you till the Day of Resurrection, who is a God beside Allah who could bring you light? Will you not then hear?

72. Say: Have you thought, if Allah made day everlasting for you till the Day of Resurrection, who is a God beside Allah who could bring you night wherein you rest? Will you not then see?

73. Of His mercy has He appointed for you night and day that therein you may rest, and that you may seek His bounty, and that you may be thankful.

74. And on the Day when He shall call unto them and say: Where are My partners whom you pretended?

75. And We shall take out from every nation a witness and We shall say: Bring your proof. Then they will know that Truth belongs to Allah, and all that they invented will have failed them.

76. Now Qārūn[209] was of Moses' folk, but he oppressed them and We gave him so much treasure that the keys thereof would verily have been a burden for a troop of mighty men. When his own folk said unto him: Exult not; lo! Allah loves not the exultant;

77. But seek the abode of the Hereafter in that which Allah has given you and neglect not your portion of the world, and be you kind even as Allah has been kind to you, and seek not corruption in the earth; lo! Allah loves not corrupters,

﴿٧١﴾ قُلْ أَرَءَيْتُمْ إِن جَعَلَ اللَّهُ عَلَيْكُمُ الَّيْلَ سَرْمَدًا إِلَىٰ يَوْمِ الْقِيَامَةِ مَنْ إِلَٰهٌ غَيْرُ اللَّهِ يَأْتِيكُم بِضِيَاءٍ أَفَلَا تَسْمَعُونَ

﴿٧٢﴾ قُلْ أَرَءَيْتُمْ إِن جَعَلَ اللَّهُ عَلَيْكُمُ النَّهَارَ سَرْمَدًا إِلَىٰ يَوْمِ الْقِيَامَةِ مَنْ إِلَٰهٌ غَيْرُ اللَّهِ يَأْتِيكُم بِلَيْلٍ تَسْكُنُونَ فِيهِ أَفَلَا تُبْصِرُونَ

﴿٧٣﴾ وَمِن رَّحْمَتِهِ جَعَلَ لَكُمُ الَّيْلَ وَالنَّهَارَ لِتَسْكُنُوا فِيهِ وَلِتَبْتَغُوا مِن فَضْلِهِ وَلَعَلَّكُمْ تَشْكُرُونَ

﴿٧٤﴾ وَيَوْمَ يُنَادِيهِمْ فَيَقُولُ أَيْنَ شُرَكَائِيَ الَّذِينَ كُنتُمْ تَزْعُمُونَ

﴿٧٥﴾ وَنَزَعْنَا مِن كُلِّ أُمَّةٍ شَهِيدًا فَقُلْنَا هَاتُوا بُرْهَانَكُمْ فَعَلِمُوا أَنَّ الْحَقَّ لِلَّهِ وَضَلَّ عَنْهُم مَّا كَانُوا يَفْتَرُونَ

﴿٧٦﴾ إِنَّ قَارُونَ كَانَ مِن قَوْمِ مُوسَىٰ فَبَغَىٰ عَلَيْهِمْ وَآتَيْنَاهُ مِنَ الْكُنُوزِ مَا إِنَّ مَفَاتِحَهُ لَتَنُوأُ بِالْعُصْبَةِ أُولِي الْقُوَّةِ إِذْ قَالَ لَهُ قَوْمُهُ لَا تَفْرَحْ إِنَّ اللَّهَ لَا يُحِبُّ الْفَرِحِينَ

﴿٧٧﴾ وَابْتَغِ فِيمَا آتَاكَ اللَّهُ الدَّارَ الْآخِرَةَ وَلَا تَنسَ نَصِيبَكَ مِنَ الدُّنْيَا وَأَحْسِن كَمَا أَحْسَنَ اللَّهُ إِلَيْكَ وَلَا تَبْغِ الْفَسَادَ فِي الْأَرْضِ إِنَّ اللَّهَ لَا يُحِبُّ الْمُفْسِدِينَ

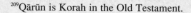

---

[209]Qārūn is Korah in the Old Testament.

78. He said: I have been given it only on account of knowledge I possess. Knew he not that Allah had destroyed already of the generations before him men who were mightier than Him in strength and greater in wealth and following? The criminals are not questioned of their sins.

79. Then went he forth before his people in his pomp. Those who were desirous of the life of the world said: Ah, would that unto us had been given the like of what has been given unto Qārūn! Lo! he is lord of rare good fortune.

80. But those who had been given knowledge said: Woe unto you! The reward of Allah for him who believes and does right is better, and only the steadfast will obtain it.

81. So We caused the earth to swallow him and his dwell-ing place. Then he had no host to help him against Allah, nor was he of those who could save themselves.

82. And morning found those who had coveted his place but yesterday crying: Ah! Allah enlarges the provision for whom He will of His slaves and straitens it (for whom He will). If Allah had not been gracious unto us He would have caused it to swallow us (also). Ah! the disbelievers can never attain prosperity.

83. As for that Abode of the Hereafter, We assign it unto those who seek not oppression in the earth, nor yet corruption. The sequel is for those who ward off (evil).

84. Who brings a good deed, he will have better than the same; while as for him who brings an ill deed, those who do ill deeds will be requited only what they did.

85. Lo! He Who has given you the Qur'an for a law will surely bring you to an appointment.[210] Say: My Lord is best aware of he who brings guidance and him who is in error manifest.

---

[210]A tradition says that this verse was revealed during the Prophet's emigration from Makkah to al Madinah.

86. You (O Muhammad) had no hope that the Scripture would be inspired in you; but it is a mercy from your Lord, so never be a helper to disbelievers.

87. And let them not divert you from the revelations of Allah after they have been sent down unto you; but call (mankind) unto your Lord, and be not of those who ascribe partners (unto Him).

88. And cry not unto any other god along with Allah. There is no God save him. Everything will perish save His countenance. His is the command, and unto Him you will be brought back.

٨٦ وَمَا كُنتَ تَرْجُوٓاْ أَن يُلْقَىٰٓ إِلَيْكَ ٱلْكِتَٰبُ إِلَّا رَحْمَةً مِّن رَّبِّكَ فَلَا تَكُونَنَّ ظَهِيرًا لِّلْكَٰفِرِينَ

٨٧ وَلَا يَصُدُّنَّكَ عَنْ ءَايَٰتِ ٱللَّهِ بَعْدَ إِذْ أُنزِلَتْ إِلَيْكَ وَٱدْعُ إِلَىٰ رَبِّكَ وَلَا تَكُونَنَّ مِنَ ٱلْمُشْرِكِينَ

٨٨ وَلَا تَدْعُ مَعَ ٱللَّهِ إِلَٰهًا ءَاخَرَ لَآ إِلَٰهَ إِلَّا هُوَ كُلُّ شَىْءٍ هَالِكٌ إِلَّا وَجْهَهُۥ لَهُ ٱلْحُكْمُ وَإِلَيْهِ تُرْجَعُونَ

The Spider

Al 'Ankabūt, "The Spider," takes its name from verse 41, where false beliefs are likened to the spider's frail web. Most of this surah belongs to the middle or last Makkan period. Some authorities consider verses 7-8, while others consider the whole latter portion,[211] to have been revealed at al Madi-nah. It gives comfort to the Muslims in a time of persecution.

A late Makkan surah.

---

[211]*Al Nāsikh wa al Mansūkh* by Ibn Salamā.

The Spider

Revealed at Makkah

*In the name of Allah,
the Beneficent, the Merciful*

1. **A**lif. Lām. Mīm.[212]

2. Do men imagine that they will be left (at ease) because they say, We believe, and will not be tested with affliction?

3. Lo! We tested those who were before them, for Allah will surely know those who are sincere, and will know those who feign.

4. Or do those who do ill deeds imagine that they can outstrip Us: Evil (for them) is that which they decide.

5. Who looks forward to the meeting with Allah (let him know that) Allah's term is surely coming, and He is the Hearer, the Knower.

6. And whosoever strives, strives only for himself, for lo! Allah is altogether Independent of all the worlds.

7. And as for those who believe and do good works, We shall remit from them their evil deeds and shall repay them the best that they did.

8. We have enjoined on people kindness to parents; but if they strive to make you join with Me that of which you have no knowledge, then obey them not. Unto Me is your return and I shall tell you what you used to do.

9. And as for those who believe and do good works, We surely shall make them enter in among the righteous.

---

[212]See Surah 2:1, footnote.

10. Of mankind is he who said: We believe in Allah, but, if he is made to suffer for the sake of Allah, he mistakes the persecution of mankind for Allah's punishment; and then, if victory comes from your Lord, will say: Lo! we were with you (all the while). Is not Allah best aware of what is in the bosoms of (His) creatures?

11. Surely Allah will know those who believe, and surely He will know the hypocrites.

12. Those who disbelieve say unto those who believe: Follow our way (of religion) and we surely will bear your sins (for you). They cannot bear anything of their sins. Lo! they surely are liars.

13. But they surely will bear their own loads and other loads beside their own, and they surely will be questioned on the Day of Resurrection concerning that which they invented.

14. And surely We sent Noah (as Our messenger) unto his folk, and he continued with them for a thousand years save fifty years; and the flood engulfed them, for they were wrongdoers.

15. And We rescued him and those with him in the ship, and made of it a portent for mankind.

16. And Abraham! (Remember) when he said unto his folk: worship Allah, and keep your duty unto Him; that is better for you if you did but know.

17. You worship instead of Allah only idols, and you only invent a lie. Lo! those whom you worship instead of Allah own no provision for you. So seek your provision from Allah, and worship Him, and give thanks unto Him, (for) unto Him you will be returned.

18. But if you deny, then nations have denied before you. The Messenger is only to convey (the Message) plainly.

١٠ وَمِنَ ٱلنَّاسِ مَن يَقُولُ ءَامَنَّا بِٱللَّهِ فَإِذَآ أُوذِيَ فِى ٱللَّهِ جَعَلَ فِتْنَةَ ٱلنَّاسِ كَعَذَابِ ٱللَّهِ وَلَئِن جَآءَ نَصْرٌ مِّن رَّبِّكَ لَيَقُولُنَّ إِنَّا كُنَّا مَعَكُمْ أَوَلَيْسَ ٱللَّهُ بِأَعْلَمَ بِمَا فِى صُدُورِ ٱلْعَٰلَمِينَ

١١ وَلَيَعْلَمَنَّ ٱللَّهُ ٱلَّذِينَ ءَامَنُوا۟ وَلَيَعْلَمَنَّ ٱلْمُنَٰفِقِينَ

١٢ وَقَالَ ٱلَّذِينَ كَفَرُوا۟ لِلَّذِينَ ءَامَنُوا۟ ٱتَّبِعُوا۟ سَبِيلَنَا وَلْنَحْمِلْ خَطَٰيَٰكُمْ وَمَا هُم بِحَٰمِلِينَ مِنْ خَطَٰيَٰهُم مِّن شَىْءٍ إِنَّهُمْ لَكَٰذِبُونَ

١٣ وَلَيَحْمِلُنَّ أَثْقَالَهُمْ وَأَثْقَالًا مَّعَ أَثْقَالِهِمْ وَلَيُسْـَٔلُنَّ يَوْمَ ٱلْقِيَٰمَةِ عَمَّا كَانُوا۟ يَفْتَرُونَ

١٤ وَلَقَدْ أَرْسَلْنَا نُوحًا إِلَىٰ قَوْمِهِ فَلَبِثَ فِيهِمْ أَلْفَ سَنَةٍ إِلَّا خَمْسِينَ عَامًا فَأَخَذَهُمُ ٱلطُّوفَانُ وَهُمْ ظَٰلِمُونَ

١٥ فَأَنجَيْنَٰهُ وَأَصْحَٰبَ ٱلسَّفِينَةِ وَجَعَلْنَٰهَآ ءَايَةً لِّلْعَٰلَمِينَ

١٦ وَإِبْرَٰهِيمَ إِذْ قَالَ لِقَوْمِهِ ٱعْبُدُوا۟ ٱللَّهَ وَٱتَّقُوهُ ذَٰلِكُمْ خَيْرٌ لَّكُمْ إِن كُنتُمْ تَعْلَمُونَ

١٧ إِنَّمَا تَعْبُدُونَ مِن دُونِ ٱللَّهِ أَوْثَٰنًا وَتَخْلُقُونَ إِفْكًا إِنَّ ٱلَّذِينَ تَعْبُدُونَ مِن دُونِ ٱللَّهِ لَا يَمْلِكُونَ لَكُمْ رِزْقًا فَٱبْتَغُوا۟ عِندَ ٱللَّهِ ٱلرِّزْقَ وَٱعْبُدُوهُ وَٱشْكُرُوا۟ لَهُۥٓ إِلَيْهِ تُرْجَعُونَ

١٨ وَإِن تُكَذِّبُوا۟ فَقَدْ كَذَّبَ أُمَمٌ مِّن قَبْلِكُمْ وَمَا عَلَى ٱلرَّسُولِ إِلَّا ٱلْبَلَٰغُ ٱلْمُبِينُ

19. See they not how Allah produces creation, then reproduces it? Lo! for Allah that is easy.

١٩ أَوَلَمْ يَرَوْا كَيْفَ يُبْدِئُ اللَّهُ الْخَلْقَ ثُمَّ يُعِيدُهُ إِنَّ ذَلِكَ عَلَى اللَّهِ يَسِيرٌ

20. Say (O Muhammad): Travel in the land and see how He originated creation, then Allah brings forth the later growth. Lo! Allah is Able to do all things.

٢٠ قُلْ سِيرُوا فِي الْأَرْضِ فَانْظُرُوا كَيْفَ بَدَأَ الْخَلْقَ ثُمَّ اللَّهُ يُنْشِئُ النَّشْأَةَ الْآخِرَةَ إِنَّ اللَّهَ عَلَى كُلِّ شَيْءٍ قَدِيرٌ

21. He punishes whom He will and shows mercy unto whom He will, and unto Him you will be turned.

٢١ يُعَذِّبُ مَنْ يَشَاءُ وَيَرْحَمُ مَنْ يَشَاءُ وَإِلَيْهِ تُقْلَبُونَ

22. You cannot escape (from Him) in the earth or in the sky, and beside Allah there is for you no friend nor helper.

٢٢ وَمَا أَنْتُمْ بِمُعْجِزِينَ فِي الْأَرْضِ وَلَا فِي السَّمَاءِ وَمَا لَكُمْ مِنْ دُونِ اللَّهِ مِنْ وَلِيٍّ وَلَا نَصِيرٍ

23. Those who disbelieve in the revelations of Allah and in (their) Meeting with Him, such are hopeless of My mercy. For such there is a painful doom.

٢٣ وَالَّذِينَ كَفَرُوا بِآيَاتِ اللَّهِ وَلِقَائِهِ أُولَئِكَ يَئِسُوا مِنْ رَحْمَتِي وَأُولَئِكَ لَهُمْ عَذَابٌ أَلِيمٌ

24. But the answer of his folk was only that they said: "Kill him" or "Burn him." Then Allah saved him from the fire. Lo! herein surely are portents for folk who believe.

٢٤ فَمَا كَانَ جَوَابَ قَوْمِهِ إِلَّا أَنْ قَالُوا اقْتُلُوهُ أَوْ حَرِّقُوهُ فَأَنْجَاهُ اللَّهُ مِنَ النَّارِ إِنَّ فِي ذَلِكَ لَآيَاتٍ لِقَوْمٍ يُؤْمِنُونَ

25. He said: You have chosen idols instead of Allah due to the love between you in the life of the world. Then on the Day of Resurrection you will deny each other and curse each other, and your abode will be the Fire, and you will have no helpers.

٢٥ وَقَالَ إِنَّمَا اتَّخَذْتُمْ مِنْ دُونِ اللَّهِ أَوْثَانًا مَوَدَّةَ بَيْنِكُمْ فِي الْحَيَاةِ الدُّنْيَا ثُمَّ يَوْمَ الْقِيَامَةِ يَكْفُرُ بَعْضُكُمْ بِبَعْضٍ وَيَلْعَنُ بَعْضُكُمْ بَعْضًا وَمَأْوَاكُمُ النَّارُ وَمَا لَكُمْ مِنْ نَاصِرِينَ

26. And Lot believed him, and he (Abraham) said: Lo! I am a fugitive unto my Lord. Lo! He, only He, is the Mighty, the Wise.

٢٦ فَآمَنَ لَهُ لُوطٌ وَقَالَ إِنِّي مُهَاجِرٌ إِلَى رَبِّي إِنَّهُ هُوَ الْعَزِيزُ الْحَكِيمُ

27. Thus We bestowed on him Isaac and Jacob, and We established the Prophethood and the Scripture among his seed, and We gave him his reward in the world, and lo! in the Hereafter he surely is among the righteous.

٢٧ وَوَهَبْنَا لَهُ إِسْحَاقَ وَيَعْقُوبَ وَجَعَلْنَا فِي ذُرِّيَّتِهِ النُّبُوَّةَ وَالْكِتَابَ وَآتَيْنَاهُ أَجْرَهُ فِي الدُّنْيَا وَإِنَّهُ فِي الْآخِرَةِ لَمِنَ الصَّالِحِينَ

28. And Lot! (Remember) when he said unto his folk: Lo! you commit lewdness such as no creature did before you.

29. For come you not in unto males, and cut you not the road (for travellers), and commit you not abomination in your meetings? But the answer of his folk was only that they said: Bring Allah's doom upon us if you are a truth teller!

30. He said: My Lord! Give me victory over folk who work corruption.

31. And when Our messengers brought Abraham the good news,[213] they said: Lo! we are about to destroy the people of this township, for its people are wrongdoers.

32. He said: Lo! Lot is there. They said: We are best aware of who is there. We are to deliver him and his household, all save his wife, who is of those who stay behind.

33. And when Our messengers came unto Lot, he was troubled upon their account, for he could not protect them; but they said: Fear not, nor grieve! Lo! we are to deliver you and your household, (all) save your wife, who is of those who stay behind.

34. Lo! we are about to bring down upon folk of this township a fury from the sky because they are evildoers.

35. And surely of that We have left a clear sign for people who have sense.

36. And unto Madian We sent Shu'ayb, their brother. He said O my people! Worship Allah, and look forward to the Last Day, and do not evil, making mischief, in the earth.

وَلُوطًا إِذْ قَالَ لِقَوْمِهِ إِنَّكُمْ لَتَأْتُونَ الْفَاحِشَةَ ﴿٢٨﴾ مَا سَبَقَكُم بِهَا مِنْ أَحَدٍ مِّنَ الْعَالَمِينَ ﴿٢٩﴾ أَئِنَّكُمْ لَتَأْتُونَ الرِّجَالَ وَتَقْطَعُونَ السَّبِيلَ وَتَأْتُونَ فِي نَادِيكُمُ الْمُنكَرَ فَمَا كَانَ جَوَابَ قَوْمِهِ إِلَّا أَن قَالُوا ائْتِنَا بِعَذَابِ اللَّهِ إِن كُنتَ مِنَ الصَّادِقِينَ ﴿٣٠﴾ قَالَ رَبِّ انصُرْنِي عَلَى الْقَوْمِ الْمُفْسِدِينَ ﴿٣١﴾ وَلَمَّا جَاءَتْ رُسُلُنَا إِبْرَاهِيمَ بِالْبُشْرَىٰ قَالُوا إِنَّا مُهْلِكُوا أَهْلِ هَٰذِهِ الْقَرْيَةِ إِنَّ أَهْلَهَا كَانُوا ظَالِمِينَ ﴿٣٢﴾ قَالَ إِنَّ فِيهَا لُوطًا قَالُوا نَحْنُ أَعْلَمُ بِمَن فِيهَا لَنُنَجِّيَنَّهُ وَأَهْلَهُ إِلَّا امْرَأَتَهُ كَانَتْ مِنَ الْغَابِرِينَ ﴿٣٣﴾ وَلَمَّا أَن جَاءَتْ رُسُلُنَا لُوطًا سِيءَ بِهِمْ وَضَاقَ بِهِمْ ذَرْعًا وَقَالُوا لَا تَخَفْ وَلَا تَحْزَنْ إِنَّا مُنَجُّوكَ وَأَهْلَكَ إِلَّا امْرَأَتَكَ كَانَتْ مِنَ الْغَابِرِينَ ﴿٣٤﴾ إِنَّا مُنزِلُونَ عَلَىٰ أَهْلِ هَٰذِهِ الْقَرْيَةِ رِجْزًا مِّنَ السَّمَاءِ بِمَا كَانُوا يَفْسُقُونَ ﴿٣٥﴾ وَلَقَد تَّرَكْنَا مِنْهَا آيَةً بَيِّنَةً لِّقَوْمٍ يَعْقِلُونَ ﴿٣٦﴾ وَإِلَىٰ مَدْيَنَ أَخَاهُمْ شُعَيْبًا فَقَالَ يَا قَوْمِ اعْبُدُوا اللَّهَ وَارْجُوا الْيَوْمَ الْآخِرَ وَلَا تَعْثَوْا فِي الْأَرْضِ مُفْسِدِينَ

213That he was to have a son.

37. But they denied him, and the dreadful earthquake took them, and morning found them prostrate in their dwelling place.

38. And (the tribes of) 'Ād and Thamūd! (Their fate) is manifest unto you from their (ruined and deserted) dwellings. The Devil made their deeds seem fair unto them and so debarred them from the Way, though they were keen observers.

39. And Qārūn, Pharaoh and Hāmān! Moses came unto them with clear proofs (of Allah's sovereignty), but they were boastful in the land. And they were not winners (in the race).

40. So We took each one in his sin; of them was he on whom We sent a hurricane, and of them was he who was overtaken by the (Awful) Cry, and of them was he whom We caused the earth to swallow, and of them was he whom We drowned. It was not for Allah to wrong them, but they wronged themselves.

41. The likeness of those who choose other patrons than Allah is as the likeness of the spider when she takes unto herself a house, and lo! the frailest of all houses is the spider's house, if they but knew.

42. Lo! Allah knows what thing they invoke instead of Him. He is the Mighty, the Wise.

43. As for these similitudes, We coin them for mankind, but none will grasp their meaning save the wise.

44. Allah created the heavens and the earth with truth. Lo! therein is indeed a portent for believers.

45. Recite that which has been inspired in you of the Scripture, and establish prayer. Lo! prayer preserves from lewdness and iniquity, but surely remembrance of Allah is more important. And Allah knows what you do.

٣٧ فَكَذَّبُوهُ فَأَخَذَتْهُمُ الرَّجْفَةُ فَأَصْبَحُوا فِى دَارِهِمْ جَاثِمِينَ

٣٨ وَعَادًا وَثَمُودَا وَقَد تَّبَيَّنَ لَكُم مِّن مَّسَاكِنِهِمْ وَزَيَّنَ لَهُمُ الشَّيْطَانُ أَعْمَالَهُمْ فَصَدَّهُمْ عَنِ السَّبِيلِ وَكَانُوا مُسْتَبْصِرِينَ

٣٩ وَقَارُونَ وَفِرْعَوْنَ وَهَامَانَ وَلَقَدْ جَاءَهُم مُّوسَى بِالْبَيِّنَاتِ فَاسْتَكْبَرُوا فِى الْأَرْضِ وَمَا كَانُوا سَابِقِينَ

٤٠ فَكُلًّا أَخَذْنَا بِذَنبِهِ فَمِنْهُم مَّنْ أَرْسَلْنَا عَلَيْهِ حَاصِبًا وَمِنْهُم مَّنْ أَخَذَتْهُ الصَّيْحَةُ وَمِنْهُم مَّنْ خَسَفْنَا بِهِ الْأَرْضَ وَمِنْهُم مَّنْ أَغْرَقْنَا وَمَا كَانَ اللَّهُ لِيَظْلِمَهُمْ وَلَكِن كَانُوا أَنفُسَهُمْ يَظْلِمُونَ

٤١ مَثَلُ الَّذِينَ اتَّخَذُوا مِن دُونِ اللَّهِ أَوْلِيَاءَ كَمَثَلِ الْعَنكَبُوتِ اتَّخَذَتْ بَيْتًا وَإِنَّ أَوْهَنَ الْبُيُوتِ لَبَيْتُ الْعَنكَبُوتِ لَوْ كَانُوا يَعْلَمُونَ

٤٢ إِنَّ اللَّهَ يَعْلَمُ مَا يَدْعُونَ مِن دُونِهِ مِن شَيْءٍ وَهُوَ الْعَزِيزُ الْحَكِيمُ

٤٣ وَتِلْكَ الْأَمْثَالُ نَضْرِبُهَا لِلنَّاسِ وَمَا يَعْقِلُهَا إِلَّا الْعَالِمُونَ

٤٤ خَلَقَ اللَّهُ السَّمَوَاتِ وَالْأَرْضَ بِالْحَقِّ إِنَّ فِى ذَلِكَ لَآيَةً لِّلْمُؤْمِنِينَ

٤٥ اتْلُ مَا أُوحِيَ إِلَيْكَ مِنَ الْكِتَابِ وَأَقِمِ الصَّلَاةَ إِنَّ الصَّلَاةَ تَنْهَى عَنِ الْفَحْشَاءِ وَالْمُنكَرِ وَلَذِكْرُ اللَّهِ أَكْبَرُ وَاللَّهُ يَعْلَمُ مَا تَصْنَعُونَ

46. And argue not with the People of the Scripture unless it be in (a way) that is better, save with such of them as do wrong; and say: We believe in that which has been revealed unto us and revealed unto you; our God and your God is One, and unto Him we surrender.

47. In like manner We have revealed unto you the Scripture, and those unto whom We gave the Scripture before will believe therein; and of these (also)[214] there are some who believe therein. And none deny our revelations save the disbelievers.

48. And you (O Muhammad) were not a reader of any scripture before it, nor did you write it with your right hand, for then might those have doubted who follow falsehood.

49. But it is clear revelations in the hearts of those who have been given knowledge, and none deny our revelations save wrongdoers.

50. And they say: Why are not portents sent down upon him from his Lord? Say: Portents are with Allah only, and I am but a plain warner.

51. Is it not enough for them that We have sent down unto you the Scripture which is read unto them? Lo! herein surely is mercy, and a reminder for folk who believe.

52. Say (unto them, O Muhammad): Allah suffices for witness between me and you. He knows whatsoever is in the heavens and the earth. And those who believe in vanity and disbelieve in Allah, they it is who are the losers.

53. They bid you hasten on the doom (of Allah). And if a term had not been appointed, the doom would assuredly have come unto them (before now). And surely it will come upon them suddenly when they perceive not.

54. They bid you hasten on the doom, when lo! Hell surely will encompass the disbelievers.

---

[214]i.e., the people of Makkah.

55. On the day when the doom will overwhelm them from above them and from underneath their feet, and He will say: Taste what you used to do!

٥٥ يَوْمَ يَغْشَاهُمُ الْعَذَابُ مِنْ فَوْقِهِمْ وَمِنْ تَحْتِ أَرْجُلِهِمْ وَيَقُولُ ذُوقُوا مَا كُنْتُمْ تَعْمَلُونَ

56. O my bondmen who believe! Lo! My earth is spacious. Therefore worship Me only.

٥٦ يَا عِبَادِيَ الَّذِينَ آمَنُوا إِنَّ أَرْضِي وَاسِعَةٌ فَإِيَّايَ فَاعْبُدُونِ

57. Every soul will taste of death. Then unto Us you will be returned.

٥٧ كُلُّ نَفْسٍ ذَائِقَةُ الْمَوْتِ ثُمَّ إِلَيْنَا تُرْجَعُونَ

58. Those who believe and do good works, them surely We shall house in lofty dwellings of the Garden underneath which rivers flow. There they will dwell secure. How sweet the reward of the toilers,

٥٨ وَالَّذِينَ آمَنُوا وَعَمِلُوا الصَّالِحَاتِ لَنُبَوِّئَنَّهُمْ مِنَ الْجَنَّةِ غُرَفًا تَجْرِي مِنْ تَحْتِهَا الْأَنْهَارُ خَالِدِينَ فِيهَا نِعْمَ أَجْرُ الْعَامِلِينَ

59. Who persevere, and put their trust in their Lord!

٥٩ الَّذِينَ صَبَرُوا وَعَلَى رَبِّهِمْ يَتَوَكَّلُونَ

60. And how many a living being there is that bears not its own provision! Allah provides for it and for you. He is the Hearer, the Knower.

٦٠ وَكَأَيِّنْ مِنْ دَابَّةٍ لَا تَحْمِلُ رِزْقَهَا اللَّهُ يَرْزُقُهَا وَإِيَّاكُمْ وَهُوَ السَّمِيعُ الْعَلِيمُ

61. And if you were to ask them: Who created the heavens and the earth, and constrained the sun and the moon (to their appointed work)? they would say: Allah. How then are they turned away?

٦١ وَلَئِنْ سَأَلْتَهُمْ مَنْ خَلَقَ السَّمَوَاتِ وَالْأَرْضَ وَسَخَّرَ الشَّمْسَ وَالْقَمَرَ لَيَقُولُنَّ اللَّهُ فَأَنَّى يُؤْفَكُونَ

62. Allah makes the provision wide for whom He will of His bondmen, and straitens it for whom (He will). Lo! Allah is Aware of all things.

٦٢ اللَّهُ يَبْسُطُ الرِّزْقَ لِمَنْ يَشَاءُ مِنْ عِبَادِهِ وَيَقْدِرُ لَهُ إِنَّ اللَّهَ بِكُلِّ شَيْءٍ عَلِيمٌ

63. And if you were to ask them: Who causes water to come down from the sky, and therewith revives the earth after its death? they surely would say: Allah. Say: Praise be to Allah! But most of them have no sense.

٦٣ وَلَئِنْ سَأَلْتَهُمْ مَنْ نَزَّلَ مِنَ السَّمَاءِ مَاءً فَأَحْيَا بِهِ الْأَرْضَ مِنْ بَعْدِ مَوْتِهَا لَيَقُولُنَّ اللَّهُ قُلِ الْحَمْدُ لِلَّهِ بَلْ أَكْثَرُهُمْ لَا يَعْقِلُونَ

64. This life of the world is but a pastime and a game. Lo! the home of the Hereafter that is Life, if they but knew.

٦٤ وَمَا هَذِهِ الْحَيَاةُ الدُّنْيَا إِلَّا لَهْوٌ وَلَعِبٌ وَإِنَّ الدَّارَ الْآخِرَةَ لَهِيَ الْحَيَوَانُ لَوْ كَانُوا يَعْلَمُونَ

65. And when they mount upon the ships they pray to Allah, making their faith pure for Him only, but when He brings them safe to land, behold! they ascribe partners (unto Him),

٦٥ فَإِذَا رَكِبُوا فِي الْفُلْكِ دَعَوُا اللَّهَ مُخْلِصِينَ لَهُ الدِّينَ فَلَمَّا نَجَّاهُمْ إِلَى الْبَرِّ إِذَا هُمْ يُشْرِكُونَ

66. That they may disbelieve in that which We have given them, and that they may take their ease. But they will come to know.

67. Have they not seen that We have appointed a sanctuary immune (from violence),[215] while people are ravaged all around them? Do they then believe in falsehood and disbelieve in the bounty of Allah?

68. Who does greater wrong than he who invents a lie concerning Allah, or denies the truth when it comes unto him? Is not there a home in Hell for disbelievers?

69. As for those who strive in Us, We surely will guide them to Our paths, and lo! Allah is with the good.

٦٦ لِيَكْفُرُوا بِمَآ ءَاتَيْنَهُمْ وَلِيَتَمَتَّعُوا فَسَوْفَ يَعْلَمُونَ

٦٧ أَوَلَمْ يَرَوْا أَنَّا جَعَلْنَا حَرَمًا ءَامِنًا وَيُتَخَطَّفُ ٱلنَّاسُ مِنْ حَوْلِهِمْ أَفَبِالْبَطِلِ يُؤْمِنُونَ وَبِنِعْمَةِ ٱللَّهِ يَكْفُرُونَ

٦٨ وَمَنْ أَظْلَمُ مِمَّنِ ٱفْتَرَىٰ عَلَى ٱللَّهِ كَذِبًا أَوْ كَذَّبَ بِٱلْحَقِّ لَمَّا جَاءَهُ أَلَيْسَ فِي جَهَنَّمَ مَثْوًى لِلْكَٰفِرِينَ

٦٩ وَٱلَّذِينَ جَهَدُوا فِينَا لَنَهْدِيَنَّهُمْ سُبُلَنَا وَإِنَّ ٱللَّهَ لَمَعَ ٱلْمُحْسِنِينَ

---

[215]The territory of Makkah.

The Romans

Al Rūm, "The Romans," takes its name from a word in the first verse.

The armies of the Eastern Roman Empire had been defeated by the Persians in all of the territories near Arabia. Jerusalem and Damascus fell in 613 CE, and Egypt fell the following year. A Persian army invaded Anatolia and was threatening Constantinople itself in 615 or 616 CE (the sixth or seventh year before the Hijrah). According to the best authorities, this surah was revealed at Makkah at this time. The pagan Arabs celebrated the news of Persian victories over the Prophet and his little band of followers, because the Christian Romans were believers in the One God, whereas the Persians were not. They argued that the power of Allah could not be supreme and absolute, as the Prophet kept proclaiming it to be, since the forces of a pagan empire had been able to defeat His worshippers.

The Prophet's answer was provided for him in this grand assertion of Theocracy, which shows the folly of all those who think that Allah is partisan. It opens with two prophecies: that the Romans would be victorious over the Persians, and that the little persecuted company of Muslims in Arabia would have reason to rejoice "in less than ten years."[216] In 624 CE, the Roman armies entered purely Persian territory and, in the same year, a little army of Muslims led by the Prophet overthrew the flower of Arab chivalry upon the field of Badr.

But the prophecies are only a prelude to a proclamation of God's universal kingdom, which is shown to be an actual sovereignty. The laws of nature are expounded as the laws of Allah in the physical sphere, and, in the moral and political spheres, mankind is informed that there are similar laws of life and death, good and evil, action and inaction, and their consequences—laws that no one can escape by wisdom or cunning. Allah's mercy, like His law, surrounds all things, and the standard of His judgment is the same for all. He is not remote or indifferent, partial or capricious. Those who do good earn His favor, and those who do ill earn His wrath, no matter what their creed or race. No one, through only a verbal profession of a creed, is able to escape His law of consequences.

It belongs to the middle group of Makkan surahs.

---

[216]The word in Arabic (*bid'a*) implies a space of not less than three years and not more than nine years.

The Romans

Revealed at Makkah

*In the name of Allah,
the Beneficent, the Merciful*

1. **A**lif. Lām. Mīm.[217]

2. The Romans have been defeated

3. In the nearer land, and they, after their defeat will be victorious

4. Within a few years—Allah's is the command in the former case and in the latter—and in that day believers will rejoice

5. In Allah's help to victory. He helps to victory whom He will. He is the Mighty, the Merciful.

6. It is a promise of Allah. Allah fails not His promise, but most of mankind know not.

7. They know only some appearance of the life of the world, and are heedless of the Hereafter.

8. Have they not pondered upon themselves? Allah created not the heavens and the earth, and that which is between them, save with truth and for a destined end. But truly many of mankind are disbelievers in the meeting with their Lord.

9. Have they not traveled in the land and seen the nature of the consequence for those who were before them?[218] They were stronger than these in power, and they dug the earth and built upon it more than these have built. Messengers of their own came unto them with clear proofs (of Allah's Sovereignty). Surely Allah wronged them not, but they did wrong themselves.

---

[217]See Surah 2:1, footnote.

[218]Those who journeyed from Makkah northward into Mesopotamia and Syria or southward to the Yaman and Ḥaḍramawt saw the ruins of old civilizations. According to tradition, these had been destroyed on account of their corruption and disobedience to the will of God.

10. Then evil was the consequence to those who dealt in evil, because they denied the revelations of Allah and made a mock of them.

11. Allah produces creation, then He reproduces it, then unto Him you will be returned.

12. And on the day when the Hour rises the criminals will despair.

13. There will be none to intercede for them of those whom they made equal with Allah. And they will reject their partners (whom they ascribed unto Him).

14. On the day when the Hour comes, that day they will be sundered.

15. As for those who believed and did good works, they will be made happy in a Garden.

16. But as for those who disbelieved and denied Our revelations, and denied the meeting of the Hereafter, such will be brought to doom.

17. So glory be to Allah when you enter the night and when you enter the morning

18. Unto Him be praise in the heavens and the earth! and at the sun's decline and in the noonday.

19. He brings forth the living from the dead, and He brings forth the dead from the living, and He revives the earth after her death. And even so will you be brought forth.

20. And of His signs is this: He created you of dust, and behold you are human beings, scattered widely!

21. And of His signs is this: He created for you spouses from yourselves that you might find rest in them, and He ordained between you love and mercy. Lo, herein indeed are portents for folk who reflect.

١٠ ثُمَّ كَانَ عَاقِبَةَ الَّذِينَ أَسَاءُوا السُّوأَى أَن كَذَّبُوا بِآيَاتِ اللَّهِ وَكَانُوا بِهَا يَسْتَهْزِءُونَ

١١ اللَّهُ يَبْدَؤُا الْخَلْقَ ثُمَّ يُعِيدُهُ ثُمَّ إِلَيْهِ تُرْجَعُونَ

١٢ وَيَوْمَ تَقُومُ السَّاعَةُ يُبْلِسُ الْمُجْرِمُونَ

١٣ وَلَمْ يَكُن لَّهُم مِّن شُرَكَائِهِمْ شُفَعَاءُ وَكَانُوا بِشُرَكَائِهِمْ كَافِرِينَ

١٤ وَيَوْمَ تَقُومُ السَّاعَةُ يَوْمَئِذٍ يَتَفَرَّقُونَ

١٥ فَأَمَّا الَّذِينَ آمَنُوا وَعَمِلُوا الصَّالِحَاتِ فَهُمْ فِي رَوْضَةٍ يُحْبَرُونَ

١٦ وَأَمَّا الَّذِينَ كَفَرُوا وَكَذَّبُوا بِآيَاتِنَا وَلِقَاءِ الْآخِرَةِ فَأُولَٰئِكَ فِي الْعَذَابِ مُحْضَرُونَ

١٧ فَسُبْحَانَ اللَّهِ حِينَ تُمْسُونَ وَحِينَ تُصْبِحُونَ

١٨ وَلَهُ الْحَمْدُ فِي السَّمَوَاتِ وَالْأَرْضِ وَعَشِيًّا وَحِينَ تُظْهِرُونَ

١٩ يُخْرِجُ الْحَيَّ مِنَ الْمَيِّتِ وَيُخْرِجُ الْمَيِّتَ مِنَ الْحَيِّ وَيُحْيِي الْأَرْضَ بَعْدَ مَوْتِهَا وَكَذَٰلِكَ تُخْرَجُونَ

٢٠ وَمِنْ آيَاتِهِ أَنْ خَلَقَكُم مِّن تُرَابٍ ثُمَّ إِذَا أَنتُم بَشَرٌ تَنتَشِرُونَ

٢١ وَمِنْ آيَاتِهِ أَنْ خَلَقَ لَكُم مِّنْ أَنفُسِكُمْ أَزْوَاجًا لِّتَسْكُنُوا إِلَيْهَا وَجَعَلَ بَيْنَكُم مَّوَدَّةً وَرَحْمَةً إِنَّ فِي ذَٰلِكَ لَآيَاتٍ لِّقَوْمٍ يَتَفَكَّرُونَ

22. And of His signs is the creation of the heavens and the earth, and the difference of your languages and colors. Lo! herein indeed are portents for men of knowledge.

٢٢ وَمِنْ ءَايَٰتِهِۦ خَلْقُ ٱلسَّمَٰوَٰتِ وَٱلْأَرْضِ وَٱخْتِلَٰفُ أَلْسِنَتِكُمْ وَأَلْوَٰنِكُمْ إِنَّ فِى ذَٰلِكَ لَأَيَٰتٍ لِّلْعَٰلِمِينَ

23. And of His signs is your slumber by night and by day, and your seeking of His bounty. Lo! herein indeed are portents for folk who heed.

٢٣ وَمِنْ ءَايَٰتِهِۦ مَنَامُكُم بِٱلَّيْلِ وَٱلنَّهَارِ وَٱبْتِغَآؤُكُم مِّن فَضْلِهِۦٓ إِنَّ فِى ذَٰلِكَ لَأَيَٰتٍ لِّقَوْمٍ يَسْمَعُونَ

24. And of His signs is this: He shows you the lightning for a fear and for a hope, and sends down water from the sky, and thereby quickens the earth after her death. Lo! herein indeed are portents for folk who understand.

٢٤ وَمِنْ ءَايَٰتِهِۦ يُرِيكُمُ ٱلْبَرْقَ خَوْفًا وَطَمَعًا وَيُنَزِّلُ مِنَ ٱلسَّمَآءِ مَآءً فَيُحْىِۦ بِهِ ٱلْأَرْضَ بَعْدَ مَوْتِهَآ إِنَّ فِى ذَٰلِكَ لَأَيَٰتٍ لِّقَوْمٍ يَعْقِلُونَ

25. And of His signs is this: The heavens and the earth stand fast by His command, and afterward, when He calls you, lo! from the earth you will emerge.

٢٥ وَمِنْ ءَايَٰتِهِۦٓ أَن تَقُومَ ٱلسَّمَآءُ وَٱلْأَرْضُ بِأَمْرِهِۦ ثُمَّ إِذَا دَعَاكُمْ دَعْوَةً مِّنَ ٱلْأَرْضِ إِذَآ أَنتُمْ تَخْرُجُونَ

26. Unto Him belongs whoever is in the heavens and in the earth. All are obedient unto Him.

٢٦ وَلَهُۥ مَن فِى ٱلسَّمَٰوَٰتِ وَٱلْأَرْضِ كُلٌّ لَّهُۥ قَٰنِتُونَ

27. He it is who produces creation, then reproduces it and it is easier for Him. His is the Sublime Similitude in the heavens and in the earth. He is the Mighty, the Wise.

٢٧ وَهُوَ ٱلَّذِى يَبْدَؤُا۟ ٱلْخَلْقَ ثُمَّ يُعِيدُهُۥ وَهُوَ أَهْوَنُ عَلَيْهِ وَلَهُ ٱلْمَثَلُ ٱلْأَعْلَىٰ فِى ٱلسَّمَٰوَٰتِ وَٱلْأَرْضِ وَهُوَ ٱلْعَزِيزُ ٱلْحَكِيمُ

28. He coins for you a similitude of yourselves. Have you, from among those whom your right hands possess,[219] partners in the wealth We have bestowed upon you, equal with you in respect thereof, so that you fear them as you fear each other (that you ascribe unto Us partners out of that which We created)? Thus We display the revelations for people who have sense.

٢٨ ضَرَبَ لَكُم مَّثَلًا مِّنْ أَنفُسِكُمْ هَل لَّكُم مِّن مَّا مَلَكَتْ أَيْمَٰنُكُم مِّن شُرَكَآءَ فِى مَا رَزَقْنَٰكُمْ فَأَنتُمْ فِيهِ سَوَآءٌ تَخَافُونَهُمْ كَخِيفَتِكُمْ أَنفُسَكُمْ كَذَٰلِكَ نُفَصِّلُ ٱلْأَيَٰتِ لِقَوْمٍ يَعْقِلُونَ

29. Nay, but those who do wrong follow their own lusts without knowledge. Who is able to guide him whom Allah has sent astray? For such there are no helpers.

٢٩ بَلِ ٱتَّبَعَ ٱلَّذِينَ ظَلَمُوٓا۟ أَهْوَآءَهُم بِغَيْرِ عِلْمٍ فَمَن يَهْدِى مَنْ أَضَلَّ ٱللَّهُ وَمَا لَهُم مِّن نَّٰصِرِينَ

---

[219] i.e., the slaves.

30. So set your purpose (O Muhammad) for religion as a man by nature upright—the nature (framed) of Allah, in which He has created man. There is no altering (the laws of) Allah's creation. That is the right religion, but most people know not—

31. Turning unto Him (only); and be careful of your duty unto Him, and establish prayer, and be not of those who ascribe partners (unto Him);

32. Of those who split up their religion and became schismatics, each sect exulting in what they have.

33. And when harm touches humans they cry unto their Lord, turning to Him in repentance; then, when they have tasted of His mercy, behold! some of them attribute partners to their Lord.

34. So as to disbelieve in that which We have given them (Unto such it is said): Enjoy yourselves awhile, but you will come to know.

35. Or have We revealed unto them any warrant which speaks of that which they associate with Him?

36. And when We cause mankind to taste of mercy they rejoice therein; but if an evil thing befall them as the consequence of their own deeds, lo! they are in despair!

37. See they not that Allah enlarges the provision for whom He will, and straitens (it for whom He will). Lo! herein indeed are portents for folk who believe.

38. So give to the kinsman his due, and to the needy, and to the wayfarer. That is best for those who seek Allah's countenance. And such are they who are successful.

39. That which you give in usury in order that it may increase on (other) people's property has no increase with Allah; but that which you give in charity, seeking Allah's countenance, has increase manifold.

٤٠. اللهُ الَّذِي خَلَقَكُمْ ثُمَّ رَزَقَكُمْ ثُمَّ يُمِيتُكُمْ ثُمَّ يُحْيِيكُمْ هَلْ مِن شُرَكَآئِكُم مَّن يَفْعَلُ مِن ذَلِكُم مِّن شَيْءٍ سُبْحَانَهُ وَتَعَالَى عَمَّا يُشْرِكُونَ

40. Allah is He Who created you and then sustained you, then causes you to die, then gives life to you again. Is there any of your (so called) partners (of Allah) that does anything of that? Praised and exalted be He above what they associate (with Him)!

٤١. ظَهَرَ الْفَسَادُ فِي الْبَرِّ وَالْبَحْرِ بِمَا كَسَبَتْ أَيْدِي النَّاسِ لِيُذِيقَهُم بَعْضَ الَّذِي عَمِلُوا لَعَلَّهُمْ يَرْجِعُونَ

41. Corruption does appear on land and sea because of (the evil) which men's hands have done, that He may make them taste a part of that which they have done, in order that they may return.

٤٢. قُلْ سِيرُوا فِي الْأَرْضِ فَانظُرُوا كَيْفَ كَانَ عَاقِبَةُ الَّذِينَ مِن قَبْلُ كَانَ أَكْثَرُهُم مُّشْرِكِينَ

42. Say (O Muhammad, to disbelievers): Travel in the land, and see the nature of the consequence for those who were before you! Most of them were idolaters.

٤٣. فَأَقِمْ وَجْهَكَ لِلدِّينِ الْقَيِّمِ مِن قَبْلِ أَن يَأْتِيَ يَوْمٌ لَّا مَرَدَّ لَهُ مِنَ اللهِ يَوْمَئِذٍ يَصَّدَّعُونَ

43. So set your purpose resolutely for the right religion, before the inevitable day comes from Allah. On that day mankind will be sundered—

٤٤. مَن كَفَرَ فَعَلَيْهِ كُفْرُهُ وَمَنْ عَمِلَ صَالِحًا فَلِأَنفُسِهِمْ يَمْهَدُونَ

44. Whoso disbelieves must (then) bear the consequences of his disbelief, while those who do right make provision for themselves—

٤٥. لِيَجْزِيَ الَّذِينَ ءَامَنُوا وَعَمِلُوا الصَّالِحَاتِ مِن فَضْلِهِ إِنَّهُ لَا يُحِبُّ الْكَافِرِينَ

45. That He may reward out of His bounty those who be-lieve and do good works. Lo! He loves not the disbelievers (in His guidance).

٤٦. وَمِنْ ءَايَاتِهِ أَن يُرْسِلَ الرِّيَاحَ مُبَشِّرَاتٍ وَلِيُذِيقَكُم مِّن رَّحْمَتِهِ وَلِتَجْرِيَ الْفُلْكُ بِأَمْرِهِ وَلِتَبْتَغُوا مِن فَضْلِهِ وَلَعَلَّكُمْ تَشْكُرُونَ

46. And of His signs is this: He sends herald winds to make you taste His mercy, and that the ships may sail at His command, and that you may seek His favor, and that haply you may be thankful.

٤٧. وَلَقَدْ أَرْسَلْنَا مِن قَبْلِكَ رُسُلًا إِلَى قَوْمِهِمْ فَجَآءُوهُم بِالْبَيِّنَاتِ فَانتَقَمْنَا مِنَ الَّذِينَ أَجْرَمُوا وَكَانَ حَقًّا عَلَيْنَا نَصْرُ الْمُؤْمِنِينَ

47. Surely We sent before you (Muhammad) messengers to their own folk. They brought them clear proofs (of Allah's Sovereignty). Then We took vengeance upon those who were guilty (in regard to them). To help believers is incumbent upon Us.

48. Allah is He who sends the winds so that they raise clouds, and spreads them along the sky as pleases Him, and causes them to break and you see the rain downpouring from within them. And when He makes it to fall on whom He will of His bondmen, lo! they rejoice;

﴿٤٨﴾ اللَّهُ الَّذِي يُرْسِلُ الرِّيَاحَ فَتُثِيرُ سَحَابًا فَيَبْسُطُهُ فِي السَّمَاءِ كَيْفَ يَشَاءُ وَيَجْعَلُهُ كِسَفًا فَتَرَى الْوَدْقَ يَخْرُجُ مِنْ خِلَالِهِ فَإِذَا أَصَابَ بِهِ مَنْ يَشَاءُ مِنْ عِبَادِهِ إِذَا هُمْ يَسْتَبْشِرُونَ

49. Though before that, even before it was sent down upon them, they were in despair.

﴿٤٩﴾ وَإِنْ كَانُوا مِنْ قَبْلِ أَنْ يُنَزَّلَ عَلَيْهِمْ مِنْ قَبْلِهِ لَمُبْلِسِينَ

50. Look, therefore, at the prints of Allah's mercy (in creation): how He quickens the earth after her death. Lo! He surely is the Quickener of the Dead, and He is Able to do all things.

﴿٥٠﴾ فَانْظُرْ إِلَى آثَارِ رَحْمَتِ اللَّهِ كَيْفَ يُحْيِي الْأَرْضَ بَعْدَ مَوْتِهَا إِنَّ ذَلِكَ لَمُحْيِي الْمَوْتَى وَهُوَ عَلَى كُلِّ شَيْءٍ قَدِيرٌ

51. And if We sent a wind and they beheld it yellow; they surely would still continue in their disbelief.

﴿٥١﴾ وَلَئِنْ أَرْسَلْنَا رِيحًا فَرَأَوْهُ مُصْفَرًّا لَظَلُّوا مِنْ بَعْدِهِ يَكْفُرُونَ

52. For surely you (Muhammad) can not make the dead to hear, nor can you make the deaf to hear the call when they have turned to flee.

﴿٥٢﴾ فَإِنَّكَ لَا تُسْمِعُ الْمَوْتَى وَلَا تُسْمِعُ الصُّمَّ الدُّعَاءَ إِذَا وَلَّوْا مُدْبِرِينَ

53. Nor can you guide the blind out of their error. You can make none to hear save those who believe in Our revelations so that they surrender (unto Him).

﴿٥٣﴾ وَمَا أَنْتَ بِهَادِ الْعُمْيِ عَنْ ضَلَالَتِهِمْ إِنْ تُسْمِعُ إِلَّا مَنْ يُؤْمِنُ بِآيَاتِنَا فَهُمْ مُسْلِمُونَ

54. Allah is He who shaped you out of weakness, then ap-pointed after weakness strength, then, after strength, ap-pointed weakness and grey hair. He creates what He will. He is the Knower, the Mighty.

﴿٥٤﴾ اللَّهُ الَّذِي خَلَقَكُمْ مِنْ ضَعْفٍ ثُمَّ جَعَلَ مِنْ بَعْدِ ضَعْفٍ قُوَّةً ثُمَّ جَعَلَ مِنْ بَعْدِ قُوَّةٍ ضَعْفًا وَشَيْبَةً يَخْلُقُ مَا يَشَاءُ وَهُوَ الْعَلِيمُ الْقَدِيرُ

55. And on the day when the Hour rises criminals will vow that they did tarry but an hour—thus were they ever deceived.

﴿٥٥﴾ وَيَوْمَ تَقُومُ السَّاعَةُ يُقْسِمُ الْمُجْرِمُونَ مَا لَبِثُوا غَيْرَ سَاعَةٍ كَذَلِكَ كَانُوا يُؤْفَكُونَ

56. But those to whom knowledge and faith are given will say: The truth is, you have tarried, by Allah's decree, until the Day of Resurrection. This is the Day of Resurrection, but you used not to know.

﴿٥٦﴾ وَقَالَ الَّذِينَ أُوتُوا الْعِلْمَ وَالْإِيمَانَ لَقَدْ لَبِثْتُمْ فِي كِتَابِ اللَّهِ إِلَى يَوْمِ الْبَعْثِ فَهَذَا يَوْمُ الْبَعْثِ وَلَكِنَّكُمْ كُنْتُمْ لَا تَعْلَمُونَ

57. In that day their excuses will not profit those who did injustice, nor will they be allowed to make amends.

58. Surely We have coined for mankind in the Qur'an all kinds of similitudes; and indeed if you came unto them with a miracle, those who disbelieve would surely exclaim: You are but tricksters!

59. Thus does Allah seal the hearts of those who know not.

60. So have patience (O Muhammad)! Allah's promise is the very truth, and let not those who have no certainty make you impatient.

٥٧ فَيَوْمَئِذٍ لَّا يَنفَعُ ٱلَّذِينَ ظَلَمُوا۟ مَعْذِرَتُهُمْ وَلَا هُمْ يُسْتَعْتَبُونَ

٥٨ وَلَقَدْ ضَرَبْنَا لِلنَّاسِ فِى هَٰذَا ٱلْقُرْءَانِ مِن كُلِّ مَثَلٍ وَلَئِن جِئْتَهُم بِـَٔايَةٍ لَّيَقُولَنَّ ٱلَّذِينَ كَفَرُوٓا۟ إِنْ أَنتُمْ إِلَّا مُبْطِلُونَ

٥٩ كَذَٰلِكَ يَطْبَعُ ٱللَّهُ عَلَىٰ قُلُوبِ ٱلَّذِينَ لَا يَعْلَمُونَ

٦٠ فَٱصْبِرْ إِنَّ وَعْدَ ٱللَّهِ حَقٌّ وَلَا يَسْتَخِفَّنَّكَ ٱلَّذِينَ لَا يُوقِنُونَ

Luqmān

Luqmān takes its name from verses 12 ff., which mention of the wisdom of Luqmān, a sage whose memory the Arabs reverenced but who is unknown to Jewish Scripture. He is said to have been a black slave, but he was a wise righteous man. The surah reveals precious pieces of advice from him to his son. It conveys an assurance of success to the Muslims at a time of persecution.

It belongs to the middle or last group of Makkan surahs, except for verses 27-28, which were revealed at al Madinah.

Luqmān

Revealed at Makkah

*In the name of Allah,
the Beneficent, the Merciful*

1. Alif. Lām. Mīm.[220]

2. These are revelations of the wise Scripture,

3. A guidance and a mercy for the good,

4. Those who establish prayer and pay the poor due and have sure faith in the Hereafter.

5. Such have guidance from their Lord. Such are the successful.

6. And of mankind is he who pays for mere pastime of discourse, that he may mislead from Allah's way without knowledge, and makes it the butt of mockery. For such there is a shameful doom.

7. And when Our revelations are recited unto him he turns away in his pride as if he heard them not, as if there were a deafness in his ears. So give him tidings of a painful doom.

8. Lo! those who believe and do good works, for them are gardens of delight,

9. Wherein they will abide. It is a promise of Allah in truth. He is the Mighty, the Wise.

10. He has created the heavens without supports that you can see, and has cast into the earth firm mountains, so that it quake not with you; and He has dispersed therein all kinds of beasts. And We send down water from the sky and We cause (plants) of every goodly kind to grow therein.

---

[220]See Surah 2:1, footnote.

11. This is the Creation of Allah. Now show me that which those (you worship) beside Him have created. Nay, but wrongdoers are in error manifest!

12. And surely We gave Luqmān wisdom, saying: Give thanks unto Allah; and whosoever gives thanks, he gives thanks for (the good of) his soul. And whosoever dis-believes—Lo! Allah is All Independent, Owner of Praise.

13. And (remember) when Luqmān said unto his son, when he was exhorting him: O my dear son! Ascribe no partners unto Allah. Lo! to ascribe partners (unto Him) is a tremendous wrong—

14. And We have enjoined upon man concerning his parents —His mother bears him in weakness upon weakness, and his weaning is in two years—Give thanks unto Me and unto your parents. Unto Me is the journeying.

15. But if they strive with you to make you ascribe unto Me as partner that of which you have no knowledge, then obey them not. Consort with them in the world kindly, and follow the path of him who repents unto Me. Then unto Me will be your return, and I shall tell you what you used to do—

16. O my dear son! Lo! though it be but the weight of a grain of mustard seed, and though it be in a rock, or in the heavens, or in the earth, Allah will bring it forth. Allah is Subtle, Aware.

17. O my dear son! Establish prayer and enjoin kindness and forbid iniquity, and persevere whatever may befall you. Lo! that is of the steadfast heart of things.

18. Turn not your cheek in scorn toward folk, nor walk with pertness in the land. Lo! Allah loves not each braggart boaster.

١١ هَـٰذَا خَلْقُ اللَّهِ فَأَرُونِي مَاذَا خَلَقَ الَّذِينَ مِن دُونِهِ ۚ بَلِ الظَّالِمُونَ فِي ضَلَالٍ مُّبِينٍ

١٢ وَلَقَدْ ءَاتَيْنَا لُقْمَـٰنَ الْحِكْمَةَ أَنِ اشْكُرْ لِلَّهِ ۚ وَمَن يَشْكُرْ فَإِنَّمَا يَشْكُرُ لِنَفْسِهِ ۖ وَمَن كَفَرَ فَإِنَّ اللَّهَ غَنِيٌّ حَمِيدٌ

١٣ وَإِذْ قَالَ لُقْمَـٰنُ لِابْنِهِ وَهُوَ يَعِظُهُ يَـٰبُنَيَّ لَا تُشْرِكْ بِاللَّهِ ۖ إِنَّ الشِّرْكَ لَظُلْمٌ عَظِيمٌ

١٤ وَوَصَّيْنَا الْإِنسَـٰنَ بِوَٰلِدَيْهِ حَمَلَتْهُ أُمُّهُ وَهْنًا عَلَىٰ وَهْنٍ وَفِصَـٰلُهُ فِي عَامَيْنِ أَنِ اشْكُرْ لِي وَلِوَٰلِدَيْكَ إِلَيَّ الْمَصِيرُ

١٥ وَإِن جَـٰهَدَاكَ عَلَىٰ أَن تُشْرِكَ بِي مَا لَيْسَ لَكَ بِهِ عِلْمٌ فَلَا تُطِعْهُمَا ۖ وَصَاحِبْهُمَا فِي الدُّنْيَا مَعْرُوفًا ۖ وَاتَّبِعْ سَبِيلَ مَنْ أَنَابَ إِلَيَّ ۚ ثُمَّ إِلَيَّ مَرْجِعُكُمْ فَأُنَبِّئُكُم بِمَا كُنتُمْ تَعْمَلُونَ

١٦ يَـٰبُنَيَّ إِنَّهَا إِن تَكُ مِثْقَالَ حَبَّةٍ مِّنْ خَرْدَلٍ فَتَكُن فِي صَخْرَةٍ أَوْ فِي السَّمَـٰوَٰتِ أَوْ فِي الْأَرْضِ يَأْتِ بِهَا اللَّهُ ۚ إِنَّ اللَّهَ لَطِيفٌ خَبِيرٌ

١٧ يَـٰبُنَيَّ أَقِمِ الصَّلَوٰةَ وَأْمُرْ بِالْمَعْرُوفِ وَانْهَ عَنِ الْمُنكَرِ وَاصْبِرْ عَلَىٰ مَا أَصَابَكَ ۖ إِنَّ ذَٰلِكَ مِنْ عَزْمِ الْأُمُورِ

١٨ وَلَا تُصَعِّرْ خَدَّكَ لِلنَّاسِ وَلَا تَمْشِ فِي الْأَرْضِ مَرَحًا ۖ إِنَّ اللَّهَ لَا يُحِبُّ كُلَّ مُخْتَالٍ فَخُورٍ

19. Be modest in your bearing and subdue your voice. Lo! the harshest of all voices is the voice of the ass.

(١٩) وَاقْصِدْ فِى مَشْيِكَ وَاغْضُضْ مِن صَوْتِكَ إِنَّ أَنكَرَ الْأَصْوَاتِ لَصَوْتُ الْحَمِيرِ

20. See you not how Allah has made serviceable unto you whatsoever is in the skies and whatsoever is in the earth and has loaded you with His favors both without and within? Yet of mankind is he who disputes concerning Allah, without knowledge or guidance or a Scripture giving light.

(٢٠) أَلَمْ تَرَوْا أَنَّ اللَّهَ سَخَّرَ لَكُم مَّا فِى السَّمَوَاتِ وَمَا فِى الْأَرْضِ وَأَسْبَغَ عَلَيْكُمْ نِعَمَهُ ظَاهِرَةً وَبَاطِنَةً وَمِنَ النَّاسِ مَن يُجَادِلُ فِى اللَّهِ بِغَيْرِ عِلْمٍ وَلَا هُدًى وَلَا كِتَبٍ مُّنِيرٍ

21. And if it be said unto them: Follow that which Allah has revealed, they say: Nay, but we follow that wherein we found our fathers. What! Even though the Devil were inviting them unto the doom of flame?

(٢١) وَإِذَا قِيلَ لَهُمُ اتَّبِعُوا مَا أَنزَلَ اللَّهُ قَالُوا بَلْ نَتَّبِعُ مَا وَجَدْنَا عَلَيْهِ ءَابَاءَنَا أَوَلَوْ كَانَ الشَّيْطَنُ يَدْعُوهُمْ إِلَى عَذَابِ السَّعِيرِ

22. Whoever surrenders his purpose to Allah while doing good, he surely has grasped the firm handhold. Unto Allah belongs the sequel of all things.

(٢٢) ۞ وَمَن يُسْلِمْ وَجْهَهُ إِلَى اللَّهِ وَهُوَ مُحْسِنٌ فَقَدِ اسْتَمْسَكَ بِالْعُرْوَةِ الْوُثْقَى وَإِلَى اللَّهِ عَقِبَةُ الْأُمُورِ

23. And whoever disbelieve, let not his disbelief afflict you (O Muhammad). Unto Us is their return, and We shall tell them what they did. Lo! Allah is Aware of what is in the breasts (of men).

(٢٣) وَمَن كَفَرَ فَلَا يَحْزُنكَ كُفْرُهُ إِلَيْنَا مَرْجِعُهُمْ فَنُنَبِّئُهُم بِمَا عَمِلُوا إِنَّ اللَّهَ عَلِيمٌ بِذَاتِ الصُّدُورِ

24. We give them comfort for a little, and then We drive them to a heavy doom.

(٢٤) نُمَتِّعُهُمْ قَلِيلًا ثُمَّ نَضْطَرُّهُمْ إِلَى عَذَابٍ غَلِيظٍ

25. If you should ask them: Who created the heavens and the earth? they would answer: Allah. Say: Praise be to Allah! But most of them know not.

(٢٥) وَلَئِن سَأَلْتَهُم مَّنْ خَلَقَ السَّمَوَاتِ وَالْأَرْضَ لَيَقُولُنَّ اللَّهُ قُلِ الْحَمْدُ لِلَّهِ بَلْ أَكْثَرُهُمْ لَا يَعْلَمُونَ

26. Unto Allah belongs whatsoever is in the heavens and the earth. Allah, He is the Absolute, the Owner of Praise.

(٢٦) لِلَّهِ مَا فِى السَّمَوَاتِ وَالْأَرْضِ إِنَّ اللَّهَ هُوَ الْغَنِىُّ الْحَمِيدُ

27. And if all the trees in the earth were pens, and the sea, with seven more seas to support it, (were ink), the words of Allah could not be exhausted. Allah is Mighty, Wise.

(٢٧) وَلَوْ أَنَّمَا فِى الْأَرْضِ مِن شَجَرَةٍ أَقْلَمٌ وَالْبَحْرُ يَمُدُّهُ مِنْ بَعْدِهِ سَبْعَةُ أَبْحُرٍ مَّا نَفِدَتْ كَلِمَتُ اللَّهِ إِنَّ اللَّهَ عَزِيزٌ حَكِيمٌ

28. Your creation and your raising (from the dead) are only as (the creation and the raising of) a single soul. Lo! Allah is Hearer, Seer.

29. Have you not seen how Allah causes the night to pass into the day and causes the day to pass into the night, and has subdued the sun and the moon (to do their work), each running unto an appointed term; and that Allah is Informed of what you do?

30. That (is so) because Allah, He is the True, and that which they invoke beside Him is the False, and because Allah, He is the Sublime, the Great.

31. Have you not seen how the ships glide on the sea by Allah's grace, that He may show you of His wonders? Lo! therein indeed are portents for every steadfast, grateful (heart).

32. And if a wave enshrouds them like mountains, they cry unto Allah, making their faith pure for Him only. But when He brings them safe to land, some of them compromise. None denies Our signs save every traitor ingrate.

33. O mankind! Keep your duty to your Lord and fear a Day when the parent will not be able to avail the child in anything, nor the child to avail the parent. Lo! Allah's promise is the very truth. Let not the life of the world beguile you, nor let the deceiver (the Devil) beguile you, in regard to Allah.

34. Lo! Allah! With Him is knowledge of the Hour. He sends down the rain, and knows that which is in the wombs. No soul knows what it will earn tomorrow, and no soul knows in what land it will die. Lo! Allah is Knower, Aware.

٢٨ مَا خَلْقُكُمْ وَلَا بَعْثُكُمْ إِلَّا كَنَفْسٍ وَاحِدَةٍ إِنَّ ٱللَّهَ سَمِيعٌ بَصِيرٌ

٢٩ أَلَمْ تَرَ أَنَّ ٱللَّهَ يُولِجُ ٱلَّيْلَ فِى ٱلنَّهَارِ وَيُولِجُ ٱلنَّهَارَ فِى ٱلَّيْلِ وَسَخَّرَ ٱلشَّمْسَ وَٱلْقَمَرَ كُلٌّ يَجْرِى إِلَىٰ أَجَلٍ مُّسَمًّى وَأَنَّ ٱللَّهَ بِمَا تَعْمَلُونَ خَبِيرٌ

٣٠ ذَٰلِكَ بِأَنَّ ٱللَّهَ هُوَ ٱلْحَقُّ وَأَنَّ مَا يَدْعُونَ مِن دُونِهِ ٱلْبَاطِلُ وَأَنَّ ٱللَّهَ هُوَ ٱلْعَلِىُّ ٱلْكَبِيرُ

٣١ أَلَمْ تَرَ أَنَّ ٱلْفُلْكَ تَجْرِى فِى ٱلْبَحْرِ بِنِعْمَتِ ٱللَّهِ لِيُرِيَكُم مِّنْ ءَايَـٰتِهِ إِنَّ فِى ذَٰلِكَ لَأَيَـٰتٍ لِّكُلِّ صَبَّارٍ شَكُورٍ

٣٢ وَإِذَا غَشِيَهُم مَّوْجٌ كَٱلظُّلَلِ دَعَوُا ٱللَّهَ مُخْلِصِينَ لَهُ ٱلدِّينَ فَلَمَّا نَجَّاهُمْ إِلَى ٱلْبَرِّ فَمِنْهُم مُّقْتَصِدٌ وَمَا يَجْحَدُ بِـَٔايَـٰتِنَا إِلَّا كُلُّ خَتَّارٍ كَفُورٍ

٣٣ يَـٰٓأَيُّهَا ٱلنَّاسُ ٱتَّقُوا رَبَّكُمْ وَٱخْشَوْا يَوْمًا لَّا يَجْزِى وَالِدٌ عَن وَلَدِهِ وَلَا مَوْلُودٌ هُوَ جَازٍ عَن وَالِدِهِ شَيْـًٔا إِنَّ وَعْدَ ٱللَّهِ حَقٌّ فَلَا تَغُرَّنَّكُمُ ٱلْحَيَوٰةُ ٱلدُّنْيَا وَلَا يَغُرَّنَّكُم بِٱللَّهِ ٱلْغَرُورُ

٣٤ إِنَّ ٱللَّهَ عِندَهُ عِلْمُ ٱلسَّاعَةِ وَيُنَزِّلُ ٱلْغَيْثَ وَيَعْلَمُ مَا فِى ٱلْأَرْحَامِ وَمَا تَدْرِى نَفْسٌ مَّاذَا تَكْسِبُ غَدًا وَمَا تَدْرِى نَفْسٌ بِأَىِّ أَرْضٍ تَمُوتُ إِنَّ ٱللَّهَ عَلِيمٌ خَبِيرٌ

Prostration

Al Sajdah, "Prostration," takes its name from a word in verse 15. It belongs in the middle group of Makkan surahs. The Prophet used to recite this surah during every Friday morning prayer.

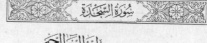

Prostration

Revealed at Makkah

In the name of Allah,
the Beneficent, the Merciful

1. Alif. Lām. Mīm.[221]

2. The revelation of the Scripture whereof there is no doubt is from the Lord of the Worlds.

3. Or say they: He has invented it? Nay, but it is the Truth from your Lord, that you may warn a folk to whom no warner came before you, that they may walk aright.

4. Allah it is Who created the heavens and the earth, and that which is between them, in six Days. Then He mounted the throne. You have not beside Him a protecting friend or mediator. Will you not then remember?

5. He directs the ordinance from the heaven unto the earth; then it ascends unto Him in a Day whereof the measure is a thousand years of that you reckon.

6. Such is the Knower of the invisible and the manifest, the Mighty, the Merciful,

7. Who made all things good which He created, and He began the creation of man from clay;

8. Then He made his seed from a draught of despised fluid;

9. Then He fashioned him and breathed into him of His spirit; and appointed for you hearing and sight and hearts. Small thanks give you!

10. And they say: When we are lost in the earth, shall we be recreated? Nay but they are disbelievers in the meeting with their Lord.

---

[221]See Surah 2:1, footnote.

11. Say: The angel of death, who has charge concerning you, will gather you, and afterward unto your Lord you will be returned.

12. Could you but see when the criminals hang their heads before their Lord, (and say): Our Lord! We have now seen and heard, so send us back; we will do right, now we are sure.

13. And if We had so willed, We could have given every soul its guidance, but the word from Me concerning evil-doers took effect: that I will fill Hell with the jinn and man-kind together.

14. So taste (the evil of your deeds). Forasmuch as you forgot the meeting of this your day, lo! We forget you. Taste the doom of immortality because of what you used to do.

15. Only those believe in Our revelations who, when they are reminded of them, fall down prostrate and hymn the praise of their Lord, and they are not scornful,

16. Who forsake their beds to cry unto their Lord in fear and hope, and spend of what we have bestowed on them.

17. No soul knows what is kept hidden for them of joy, as a reward for what they used to do.

18. Is he who is a believer like unto him who is an evil-liver? They are not alike.

19. For those who believe and do good works, for them are the Gardens of Retreat—a welcome (in reward) for what they used to do.

20. And as for those who do evil, their retreat is the Fire. Whenever they desire to issue forth from thence, they are brought back thither. Unto them it is said: Taste the torment of the Fire which you used to deny.

١١ ۞ قُلْ يَتَوَفَّىٰكُم مَّلَكُ ٱلْمَوْتِ ٱلَّذِى وُكِّلَ بِكُمْ ثُمَّ إِلَىٰ رَبِّكُمْ تُرْجَعُونَ

١٢ وَلَوْ تَرَىٰ إِذِ ٱلْمُجْرِمُونَ نَاكِسُوا۟ رُءُوسِهِمْ عِندَ رَبِّهِمْ رَبَّنَآ أَبْصَرْنَا وَسَمِعْنَا فَٱرْجِعْنَا نَعْمَلْ صَٰلِحًا إِنَّا مُوقِنُونَ

١٣ وَلَوْ شِئْنَا لَءَاتَيْنَا كُلَّ نَفْسٍ هُدَىٰهَا وَلَٰكِنْ حَقَّ ٱلْقَوْلُ مِنِّى لَأَمْلَأَنَّ جَهَنَّمَ مِنَ ٱلْجِنَّةِ وَٱلنَّاسِ أَجْمَعِينَ

١٤ فَذُوقُوا۟ بِمَا نَسِيتُمْ لِقَآءَ يَوْمِكُمْ هَٰذَآ إِنَّا نَسِينَٰكُمْ وَذُوقُوا۟ عَذَابَ ٱلْخُلْدِ بِمَا كُنتُمْ تَعْمَلُونَ

١٥ إِنَّمَا يُؤْمِنُ بِـَٔايَٰتِنَا ٱلَّذِينَ إِذَا ذُكِّرُوا۟ بِهَا خَرُّوا۟ سُجَّدًا وَسَبَّحُوا۟ بِحَمْدِ رَبِّهِمْ وَهُمْ لَا يَسْتَكْبِرُونَ ۩

١٦ تَتَجَافَىٰ جُنُوبُهُمْ عَنِ ٱلْمَضَاجِعِ يَدْعُونَ رَبَّهُمْ خَوْفًا وَطَمَعًا وَمِمَّا رَزَقْنَٰهُمْ يُنفِقُونَ

١٧ فَلَا تَعْلَمُ نَفْسٌ مَّآ أُخْفِىَ لَهُم مِّن قُرَّةِ أَعْيُنٍ جَزَآءً بِمَا كَانُوا۟ يَعْمَلُونَ

١٨ أَفَمَن كَانَ مُؤْمِنًا كَمَن كَانَ فَاسِقًا لَّا يَسْتَوُۥنَ

١٩ أَمَّا ٱلَّذِينَ ءَامَنُوا۟ وَعَمِلُوا۟ ٱلصَّٰلِحَٰتِ فَلَهُمْ جَنَّٰتُ ٱلْمَأْوَىٰ نُزُلًا بِمَا كَانُوا۟ يَعْمَلُونَ

٢٠ وَأَمَّا ٱلَّذِينَ فَسَقُوا۟ فَمَأْوَىٰهُمُ ٱلنَّارُ كُلَّمَآ أَرَادُوٓا۟ أَن يَخْرُجُوا۟ مِنْهَآ أُعِيدُوا۟ فِيهَا وَقِيلَ لَهُمْ ذُوقُوا۟ عَذَابَ ٱلنَّارِ ٱلَّذِى كُنتُم بِهِۦ تُكَذِّبُونَ

21. And surely We will make them taste the lower punishment[222] before the greater, that they may return.

22. And who does greater wrong than he who is reminded of the revelations of his Lord, then turns from them. Lo! We shall requite the criminals.

23. We surely gave Moses the Scripture; so be not you in doubt of his receiving it with satisfaction and readiness; and We appointed it a guidance for the Children of Israel.

24. And when they became steadfast and believed firmly in Our revelations, We appointed from among them leaders who guided by Our command.

25. Lo! your Lord will judge between them on the Day of Resurrection concerning that wherein they used to differ.

26. Is it not a guidance for them (to observe) how many generations We destroyed before them, amid whose dwelling places they do walk? Lo, therein surely are portents! Will they not then heed?

27. Have they not seen how We lead the water to the barren land and therewith bring forth crops whereof their cattle eat, and they themselves? Will they not then see?

28. And they say: When comes this victory (of yours) if you are truthful?

29. Say (unto them): On the day of the victory the faith of those who disbelieve (and who then will believe) will not avail them, neither will they be granted a respite.

30. So withdraw from them (O Muhammad), and await (the event). Lo! they also are awaiting (it).

---

[222]i.e., punishment in this world.

The Clans

Al Aḥzāb, "The Clans," takes its name from the army of the allied clans that came against Yathrib (pre-Islamic al Madinah) in the year 5AH (verses 9-25). Certain members of the Banī Naḍīr, a Jewish tribe whom the Prophet had expelled from Yathrib on the grounds of treason (see Surah 59), went to the leaders of Quraysh in Makkah and then to the chiefs of the great desert tribe of Ghatafān and urged them to extirpate the Muslims. They promised help from the Jewish population of Yathrib. As a result of their efforts, all of the Qurayshī and the Ghatafānī clans marched towards Yathrib to destroy it.

When news of their design reached the Prophet, he ordered a trench to be dug before the city and then himself led the project. The trench was finished when the clans arrived—10,000 strong. The Prophet took the field with his army of 3000, keeping the trench between the two armies. For nearly a month, the Muslims were exposed to showers of arrows and were in constant expectation of an attack by the far superior enemy forces. To make matters worse, news came that the Jewish tribe of Banī Qurayẓah in their rear had broken their alliance with the Muslims and joined the Quraysh. The women and children had been put in strongholds—towers like the peel-towers of northern England (every family of note had one for refuge in time of raids). These were practically unguarded, and some of the Muslims asked the Pro-phet's permission to leave the battlefront in order to guard them. These towers were not then in danger, because the Banī Qurayẓah were not likely to show their treachery until the clans' victory was certain.

The case of the Muslims seemed hopeless. However, a secret sympathizer in the enemy camp managed to sow distrust between the Banī Qurayẓah and the chiefs of the clans, making both feel uneasy. The obstacle of the trench was unexpected and seemed formidable. In addition, when a fierce and bitter wind from the sea blew for three days and nights so furiously that they could not keep a shelter up, light a fire, or boil a pot of liquid, Abū Sufyān, the leader of Quraysh, raised the siege in disgust. When the Ghatafān learned that the Quraysh had gone, they also departed for their homes.

On the very day when the Muslims returned from the trench, they besieged the traitorous Banī Qurayzah in their towers of refuge for twenty-five days. After they surrendered, some members of the 'Aws tribe, of which they were members, asked the Prophet to show them the same grace that he had shown to the tribe of Khazraj, in the case of Banī Naḍīr, by allowing them to intercede for their dependents.

The Prophet said: "Would you like one of your own to decide their fate?" They said: "Yes," and he appointed Sa'd ibn Mu'ādh, a great chief of the 'Aws who had been wounded and was being cared for in the mosque. This man was sent for and, after hearing the case, ordered their men to be put to death, their women and children to be made captive, and their property to be divided among the Muslims as the Pro-phet directed.

I have taken this account from the narrative of Ibn Khal-dūn, which is concise, rather than from Ibn Hishām, which is exceedingly diffuse. The two accounts are, however, in absolute agreement. Verses 26-27 refer to the punishment of the Banī Qurayẓah.

In verse 37, the unhappy marriage of Zayd (the Prophet's freedman and adopted son) with Zaynab (the Prophet's cousin and a proud Qurayshī lady) is mentioned. The Prophet had arranged the marriage with the idea of breaking down the old barrier of caste pride and had shown little consideration for Zaynab's feelings. Tradition says that both she and her brother were averse to the match and that she had always wished to marry the Prophet. For Zayd, the marriage was a source of embarrassment and humiliation. When the Pro-phet's attention was first called to their unhappiness, he urged Zayd to not to divorce her, for he was apprehensive of the talk that would arise if it became known that a marriage arranged by him had turned out to be unhappy. Eventually Zayd did divorce Zaynab, and the Prophet was commanded to marry her in order, by his example, to disown the superstitious custom of the pagan Arabs of treating their adopted sons as their real sons. This was against the laws of God (i.e., the laws of nature), for in arranging a marriage the woman's inclinations ought to be considered. Unhappy marriage was no part of Allah's ordinance and was not to be held sacred in Islam.

The surah contains further references to the Prophet's wives. In connection with this, it may be mentioned that from the age of twenty-five till the age of fifty, the Prophet had only one wife, Khadījah, who was fifteen years his senior, to whom he was devotedly attached, and whose memory he cherished till his dying day. With the exception of 'Ā'ishah, the daughter of his closest friend Abū Bakr and whom he married at her father's request when she was still a child, all of his later marriages were with widows who were facing difficult circumstances. Some were widows of men killed in war. One was a captive, whom he married in order to emancipate the conquered tribe and restore its property. Two were daughters of his enemies, and his alliance with them was a cause of peace. It is noteworthy that the period of these marriages was also the period of his greatest activity, when he had little rest from campaigning and was always busy with the problems of a growing empire.

The period of revelation is between the end of the fifth and the end of the seventh years of the Hijrah.

The Clans

Revealed at al Madinah

*In the name of Allah,
the Beneficent, the Merciful*

1. ⓞ Prophet! Keep your duty to Allah and obey not the disbelievers and the hypocrites. Lo! Allah is Knower, Wise.

2. And follow that which is inspired in you from your Lord. Lo! Allah is informed of what you do.

3. And put your trust in Allah, for Allah is sufficient as Trustee.

4. Allah has not assigned unto any man two hearts within his body, nor has he made your wives whom you declare (to be your mothers) your mothers,[223] nor has he made those whom you claim (to be your sons) your sons. This is but a saying of your mouths. But Allah says the truth and He shows the way.

5. Proclaim their real parentage. That will be more equitable in the sight of Allah. And if you know not their fathers, then (they are) your brethren in the faith, and your clients. And there is no sin for you in the mistakes that you make unintentionally, but what your hearts purpose (that will be a sin for you). Allah is Forgiving, Merciful.

6. The Prophet is closer to the believers than their selves, and his wives are (as) their mothers. And the owners of kinship are closer one to another in the ordinance of Allah than (other) believers and the emigrants (who fled from Makkah) except that you should do kindness to your friends.[224] This is written in the Book (of nature).

بِسْمِ اللَّهِ الرَّحْمَٰنِ الرَّحِيمِ

١ يَٰٓأَيُّهَا ٱلنَّبِيُّ ٱتَّقِ ٱللَّهَ وَلَا تُطِعِ ٱلْكَٰفِرِينَ وَٱلْمُنَٰفِقِينَ إِنَّ ٱللَّهَ كَانَ عَلِيمًا حَكِيمًا

٢ وَٱتَّبِعْ مَا يُوحَىٰٓ إِلَيْكَ مِن رَّبِّكَ إِنَّ ٱللَّهَ كَانَ بِمَا تَعْمَلُونَ خَبِيرًا

٣ وَتَوَكَّلْ عَلَى ٱللَّهِ وَكَفَىٰ بِٱللَّهِ وَكِيلًا

٤ مَّا جَعَلَ ٱللَّهُ لِرَجُلٍ مِّن قَلْبَيْنِ فِي جَوْفِهِ وَمَا جَعَلَ أَزْوَٰجَكُمُ ٱلَّٰٓـِٔى تُظَٰهِرُونَ مِنْهُنَّ أُمَّهَٰتِكُمْ وَمَا جَعَلَ أَدْعِيَآءَكُمْ أَبْنَآءَكُمْ ذَٰلِكُمْ قَوْلُكُم بِأَفْوَٰهِكُمْ وَٱللَّهُ يَقُولُ ٱلْحَقَّ وَهُوَ يَهْدِى ٱلسَّبِيلَ

٥ ٱدْعُوهُمْ لِءَابَآئِهِمْ هُوَ أَقْسَطُ عِندَ ٱللَّهِ فَإِن لَّمْ تَعْلَمُوٓا۟ ءَابَآءَهُمْ فَإِخْوَٰنُكُمْ فِي ٱلدِّينِ وَمَوَٰلِيكُمْ وَلَيْسَ عَلَيْكُمْ جُنَاحٌ فِيمَآ أَخْطَأْتُم بِهِۦ وَلَٰكِن مَّا تَعَمَّدَتْ قُلُوبُكُمْ وَكَانَ ٱللَّهُ غَفُورًا رَّحِيمًا

٦ ٱلنَّبِيُّ أَوْلَىٰ بِٱلْمُؤْمِنِينَ مِنْ أَنفُسِهِمْ وَأَزْوَٰجُهُۥٓ أُمَّهَٰتُهُمْ وَأُو۟لُوا۟ ٱلْأَرْحَامِ بَعْضُهُمْ أَوْلَىٰ بِبَعْضٍ فِي كِتَٰبِ ٱللَّهِ مِنَ ٱلْمُؤْمِنِينَ وَٱلْمُهَٰجِرِينَ إِلَّآ أَن تَفْعَلُوٓا۟ إِلَىٰٓ أَوْلِيَآئِكُم مَّعْرُوفًا كَانَ ذَٰلِكَ فِي ٱلْكِتَٰبِ مَسْطُورًا

---

[223]This refers to pagan Arab custom by which a man could put away his wife by merely saying: "To me you are as my mother's back."

[224]The Prophet had ordained brotherhood between individuals of the Anṣār (the Muslims of al Madinah) and the Muhājirīn (fugitives from Makkah), a brotherhood which was closer than kinship by blood. This verse abolished such brotherhood insofar as inheritance was concerned.

7. And when We exacted a covenant from the Prophets, and from you (O Muhammad) and from Noah and Abraham and Moses and Jesus son of Mary. We took from them a solemn covenant;

8. That He may ask the loyal about their loyalty. And He has prepared a painful doom for the unfaithful.

9. O you who believe. Remember Allah's favor unto you when there came against you hosts, and We sent against them a great wind and hosts you could not see. And Allah is ever Seer of what you do.

10. When they came upon you from above you and from below you, and when eyes grew wild and hearts reached to the throats, and you were imagining vain thoughts concerning Allah.

11. There were the believers sorely tried, and shaken with a mighty shock.

12. And When the hypocrites, and those in whose hearts is a disease, were saying: Allah and His Messenger promised us nothing but delusion.

13. And when a party of them said: O folk of Yathrib! There is no stand (possible) for you, therefore turn back. And certain of them (even) sought permission of the Pro-phet, saying: Our homes lie open (to the enemy). And they lay not open. They but wished to flee.

14. If (the enemy) had entered upon them from all sides and they had been exhorted to treachery, they would have committed it, and would have hesitated thereupon but little.

15. And surely they had already sworn unto Allah that they would not turn their backs (to the foe). An oath to Allah must be answered for.

٧ وَإِذْ أَخَذْنَا مِنَ ٱلنَّبِيِّنَ مِيثَٰقَهُمْ وَمِنكَ وَمِن نُّوحٍ وَإِبْرَٰهِيمَ وَمُوسَىٰ وَعِيسَى ٱبْنِ مَرْيَمَ وَأَخَذْنَا مِنْهُم مِّيثَٰقًا غَلِيظًا

٨ لِّيَسْـَٔلَ ٱلصَّٰدِقِينَ عَن صِدْقِهِمْ وَأَعَدَّ لِلْكَٰفِرِينَ عَذَابًا أَلِيمًا

٩ يَٰٓأَيُّهَا ٱلَّذِينَ ءَامَنُوا ٱذْكُرُوا نِعْمَةَ ٱللَّهِ عَلَيْكُمْ إِذْ جَآءَتْكُمْ جُنُودٌ فَأَرْسَلْنَا عَلَيْهِمْ رِيحًا وَجُنُودًا لَّمْ تَرَوْهَا وَكَانَ ٱللَّهُ بِمَا تَعْمَلُونَ بَصِيرًا

١٠ إِذْ جَآءُوكُم مِّن فَوْقِكُمْ وَمِنْ أَسْفَلَ مِنكُمْ وَإِذْ زَاغَتِ ٱلْأَبْصَٰرُ وَبَلَغَتِ ٱلْقُلُوبُ ٱلْحَنَاجِرَ وَتَظُنُّونَ بِٱللَّهِ ٱلظُّنُونَا

١١ هُنَالِكَ ٱبْتُلِيَ ٱلْمُؤْمِنُونَ وَزُلْزِلُوا زِلْزَالًا شَدِيدًا

١٢ وَإِذْ يَقُولُ ٱلْمُنَٰفِقُونَ وَٱلَّذِينَ فِى قُلُوبِهِم مَّرَضٌ مَّا وَعَدَنَا ٱللَّهُ وَرَسُولُهُۥ إِلَّا غُرُورًا

١٣ وَإِذْ قَالَت طَّآئِفَةٌ مِّنْهُمْ يَٰٓأَهْلَ يَثْرِبَ لَا مُقَامَ لَكُمْ فَٱرْجِعُوا وَيَسْتَـْٔذِنُ فَرِيقٌ مِّنْهُمُ ٱلنَّبِيَّ يَقُولُونَ إِنَّ بُيُوتَنَا عَوْرَةٌ وَمَا هِىَ بِعَوْرَةٍ إِن يُرِيدُونَ إِلَّا فِرَارًا

١٤ وَلَوْ دُخِلَتْ عَلَيْهِم مِّنْ أَقْطَارِهَا ثُمَّ سُئِلُوا ٱلْفِتْنَةَ لَأَتَوْهَا وَمَا تَلَبَّثُوا بِهَآ إِلَّا يَسِيرًا

١٥ وَلَقَدْ كَانُوا عَٰهَدُوا ٱللَّهَ مِن قَبْلُ لَا يُوَلُّونَ ٱلْأَدْبَٰرَ وَكَانَ عَهْدُ ٱللَّهِ مَسْـُٔولًا

16. Say: Flight will not avail you if you flee from death or killing, and then you dwell in comfort but a little while.

17. Say: Who is he who can preserve you from Allah if He intends harm for you, or intends mercy for you. They will not find that they have any friend or helper other than Allah.

18. Allah already knows those of you who hinder, and those who say unto their brothers: "Come you here unto us!" and they come not to the stress of battle save a little,

19. Being sparing of their help to you (believers). But when fear comes, then you (Muhammad) see them regarding you with rolling eyes like one who faints unto death. Then, when fear departs, they scald you with sharp tongues in their greed for wealth (from the spoil). Such have not believed. Therefore Allah makes their deeds fruitless. And that is easy for Allah.

20. They hold that the clans have not retired (for good); and if the clans should advance (again), they would fain be in the desert with the wandering Arabs, asking for the news of you and if they were among you, they would not give battle, save a little.

21. Surely in the Messenger of Allah you have a good example for him who looks unto Allah and the last Day, and remembers Allah much.

22. And when true believers saw the clans, they said: This is that which Allah and His Messenger promised us. Allah and His Messenger are true. This did but confirm them in their faith and resignation.

١٦ ﴿ قُل لَّن يَنفَعَكُمُ ٱلْفِرَارُ إِن فَرَرْتُم مِّنَ ٱلْمَوْتِ أَوِ ٱلْقَتْلِ وَإِذًا لَّا تُمَتَّعُونَ إِلَّا قَلِيلًا ﴾

١٧ ﴿ قُلْ مَن ذَا ٱلَّذِى يَعْصِمُكُم مِّنَ ٱللَّهِ إِنْ أَرَادَ بِكُمْ سُوٓءًا أَوْ أَرَادَ بِكُمْ رَحْمَةً وَلَا يَجِدُونَ لَهُم مِّن دُونِ ٱللَّهِ وَلِيًّا وَلَا نَصِيرًا ﴾

١٨ ﴿ قَدْ يَعْلَمُ ٱللَّهُ ٱلْمُعَوِّقِينَ مِنكُمْ وَٱلْقَآئِلِينَ لِإِخْوَٰنِهِمْ هَلُمَّ إِلَيْنَا وَلَا يَأْتُونَ ٱلْبَأْسَ إِلَّا قَلِيلًا ﴾

١٩ ﴿ أَشِحَّةً عَلَيْكُمْ فَإِذَا جَآءَ ٱلْخَوْفُ رَأَيْتَهُمْ يَنظُرُونَ إِلَيْكَ تَدُورُ أَعْيُنُهُمْ كَٱلَّذِى يُغْشَىٰ عَلَيْهِ مِنَ ٱلْمَوْتِ فَإِذَا ذَهَبَ ٱلْخَوْفُ سَلَقُوكُم بِأَلْسِنَةٍ حِدَادٍ أَشِحَّةً عَلَى ٱلْخَيْرِ أُوْلَٰٓئِكَ لَمْ يُؤْمِنُوا فَأَحْبَطَ ٱللَّهُ أَعْمَٰلَهُمْ وَكَانَ ذَٰلِكَ عَلَى ٱللَّهِ يَسِيرًا ﴾

٢٠ ﴿ يَحْسَبُونَ ٱلْأَحْزَابَ لَمْ يَذْهَبُوا وَإِن يَأْتِ ٱلْأَحْزَابُ يَوَدُّوا لَوْ أَنَّهُم بَادُونَ فِى ٱلْأَعْرَابِ يَسْـَٔلُونَ عَنْ أَنۢبَآئِكُمْ وَلَوْ كَانُوا فِيكُم مَّا قَٰتَلُوٓا إِلَّا قَلِيلًا ﴾

٢١ ﴿ لَّقَدْ كَانَ لَكُمْ فِى رَسُولِ ٱللَّهِ أُسْوَةٌ حَسَنَةٌ لِّمَن كَانَ يَرْجُوا ٱللَّهَ وَٱلْيَوْمَ ٱلْأَخِرَ وَذَكَرَ ٱللَّهَ كَثِيرًا ﴾

٢٢ ﴿ وَلَمَّا رَءَا ٱلْمُؤْمِنُونَ ٱلْأَحْزَابَ قَالُوا هَٰذَا مَا وَعَدَنَا ٱللَّهُ وَرَسُولُهُ وَصَدَقَ ٱللَّهُ وَرَسُولُهُ وَمَا زَادَهُمْ إِلَّا إِيمَٰنًا وَتَسْلِيمًا ﴾

23. Of the believers are men who are true to that which they covenanted with Allah. Some of them have paid their vow by death (in battle), and some of them still are waiting; and they have not altered in the least;

﴿٢٣﴾ مِنَ ٱلْمُؤْمِنِينَ رِجَالٌ صَدَقُوا۟ مَا عَـٰهَدُوا۟ ٱللَّهَ عَلَيْهِ فَمِنْهُم مَّن قَضَىٰ نَحْبَهُۥ وَمِنْهُم مَّن يَنتَظِرُ وَمَا بَدَّلُوا۟ تَبْدِيلًا

24. That Allah may reward the true men for their truth, and punish the hypocrites if He will, or relent toward them (if He will). Lo! Allah is Forgiving, Merciful.

﴿٢٤﴾ لِّيَجْزِيَ ٱللَّهُ ٱلصَّـٰدِقِينَ بِصِدْقِهِمْ وَيُعَذِّبَ ٱلْمُنَـٰفِقِينَ إِن شَآءَ أَوْ يَتُوبَ عَلَيْهِمْ إِنَّ ٱللَّهَ كَانَ غَفُورًا رَّحِيمًا

25. And Allah repulsed the disbelievers in their wrath; they gained no good. Allah averted their attack from the believers. Allah is Strong, Mighty.

﴿٢٥﴾ وَرَدَّ ٱللَّهُ ٱلَّذِينَ كَفَرُوا۟ بِغَيْظِهِمْ لَمْ يَنَالُوا۟ خَيْرًا وَكَفَى ٱللَّهُ ٱلْمُؤْمِنِينَ ٱلْقِتَالَ وَكَانَ ٱللَّهُ قَوِيًّا عَزِيزًا

26. And He brought those of the People of the Scripture who supported them down from their strongholds, and cast panic into their hearts. Some you slew, and some you made captive.

﴿٢٦﴾ وَأَنزَلَ ٱلَّذِينَ ظَـٰهَرُوهُم مِّنْ أَهْلِ ٱلْكِتَـٰبِ مِن صَيَاصِيهِمْ وَقَذَفَ فِى قُلُوبِهِمُ ٱلرُّعْبَ فَرِيقًا تَقْتُلُونَ وَتَأْسِرُونَ فَرِيقًا

27. And He caused you to inherit their land and their houses and their wealth, and land you have not trodden. Allah is Able to do all things.

﴿٢٧﴾ وَأَوْرَثَكُمْ أَرْضَهُمْ وَدِيَـٰرَهُمْ وَأَمْوَٰلَهُمْ وَأَرْضًا لَّمْ تَطَـُٔوهَا وَكَانَ ٱللَّهُ عَلَىٰ كُلِّ شَىْءٍ قَدِيرًا

28. O Prophet! Say unto your wives: If you desire the world's life and its adornment, come! I will content you and will release you with a fair release.

﴿٢٨﴾ يَـٰٓأَيُّهَا ٱلنَّبِىُّ قُل لِّأَزْوَٰجِكَ إِن كُنتُنَّ تُرِدْنَ ٱلْحَيَوٰةَ ٱلدُّنْيَا وَزِينَتَهَا فَتَعَالَيْنَ أُمَتِّعْكُنَّ وَأُسَرِّحْكُنَّ سَرَاحًا جَمِيلًا

29. But if you desire Allah and His Messenger and the abode of the Hereafter, then lo! Allah has prepared for the good among you an immense reward.

﴿٢٩﴾ وَإِن كُنتُنَّ تُرِدْنَ ٱللَّهَ وَرَسُولَهُۥ وَٱلدَّارَ ٱلْءَاخِرَةَ فَإِنَّ ٱللَّهَ أَعَدَّ لِلْمُحْسِنَـٰتِ مِنكُنَّ أَجْرًا عَظِيمًا

30. O you wives of the Prophet! Whosoever of you commits manifest lewdness, the punishment for her will be doubled, and that is easy for Allah.

﴿٣٠﴾ يَـٰنِسَآءَ ٱلنَّبِىِّ مَن يَأْتِ مِنكُنَّ بِفَـٰحِشَةٍ مُّبَيِّنَةٍ يُضَـٰعَفْ لَهَا ٱلْعَذَابُ ضِعْفَيْنِ وَكَانَ ذَٰلِكَ عَلَى ٱللَّهِ يَسِيرًا

31. And whoever of you is submissive unto Allah and His Messenger and does right, We shall give her reward twice over, and We have prepared for her a rich provision.

32. O you wives of the Prophet! You are not like any other women. If you keep your duty (to Allah), then be not soft of speech, lest he in whose heart is a disease aspire (to you), but utter customary speech.

33. And stay in your houses. Display not yourselves like that of the Time of Ignorance. Be regular in prayer, and pay the poor-due, and obey Allah and His Messenger. Allah's wish is but to remove uncleanness far from you, O Folk of the Household, and cleanse you with a thorough cleansing.

34. And bear in mind that which is recited in your houses of the revelations of Allah and wisdom. Lo! Allah is Subtile, Aware.

35. Lo! men who surrender unto Allah and women who surrender, and men who believe and women who believe, and men who obey and women who obey, and men who speak the truth and women who speak the truth, and men who persevere (in righteousness) and women who persevere, and men who are humble and women who are humble, and men who give alms and women who give alms, and men who fast and women who fast, and men who guard their modesty and women who guard (their modesty), and men who remember Allah much and women who remember, Allah has prepared for them forgiveness and a vast reward.

36. And it becomes not a believing man or a believing woman, when Allah and His Messenger have decided an affair (for them), that they should (after that) claim any say in their affair; and who is rebellious to Allah and His Mes-senger, he surely goes astray in error manifest.

٣١ ۞ وَمَن يَقْنُتْ مِنكُنَّ لِلَّهِ وَرَسُولِهِ وَتَعْمَلْ صَلِحًا نُّؤْتِهَا أَجْرَهَا مَرَّتَيْنِ وَأَعْتَدْنَا لَهَا رِزْقًا كَرِيمًا

٣٢ يَنِسَاءَ ٱلنَّبِيِّ لَسْتُنَّ كَأَحَدٍ مِّنَ ٱلنِّسَاءِ إِنِ ٱتَّقَيْتُنَّ فَلَا تَخْضَعْنَ بِٱلْقَوْلِ فَيَطْمَعَ ٱلَّذِي فِي قَلْبِهِ مَرَضٌ وَقُلْنَ قَوْلًا مَّعْرُوفًا

٣٣ وَقَرْنَ فِي بُيُوتِكُنَّ وَلَا تَبَرَّجْنَ تَبَرُّجَ ٱلْجَاهِلِيَّةِ ٱلْأُولَىٰ وَأَقِمْنَ ٱلصَّلَوٰةَ وَءَاتِينَ ٱلزَّكَوٰةَ وَأَطِعْنَ ٱللَّهَ وَرَسُولَهُ إِنَّمَا يُرِيدُ ٱللَّهُ لِيُذْهِبَ عَنكُمُ ٱلرِّجْسَ أَهْلَ ٱلْبَيْتِ وَيُطَهِّرَكُمْ تَطْهِيرًا

٣٤ وَٱذْكُرْنَ مَا يُتْلَىٰ فِي بُيُوتِكُنَّ مِنْ ءَايَتِ ٱللَّهِ وَٱلْحِكْمَةِ إِنَّ ٱللَّهَ كَانَ لَطِيفًا خَبِيرًا

٣٥ إِنَّ ٱلْمُسْلِمِينَ وَٱلْمُسْلِمَتِ وَٱلْمُؤْمِنِينَ وَٱلْمُؤْمِنَتِ وَٱلْقَنِتِينَ وَٱلْقَنِتَتِ وَٱلصَّدِقِينَ وَٱلصَّدِقَتِ وَٱلصَّبِرِينَ وَٱلصَّبِرَتِ وَٱلْخَشِعِينَ وَٱلْخَشِعَتِ وَٱلْمُتَصَدِّقِينَ وَٱلْمُتَصَدِّقَتِ وَٱلصَّئِمِينَ وَٱلصَّئِمَتِ وَٱلْحَفِظِينَ فُرُوجَهُمْ وَٱلْحَفِظَتِ وَٱلذَّكِرِينَ ٱللَّهَ كَثِيرًا وَٱلذَّكِرَتِ أَعَدَّ ٱللَّهُ لَهُم مَّغْفِرَةً وَأَجْرًا عَظِيمًا

٣٦ وَمَا كَانَ لِمُؤْمِنٍ وَلَا مُؤْمِنَةٍ إِذَا قَضَى ٱللَّهُ وَرَسُولُهُ أَمْرًا أَن يَكُونَ لَهُمُ ٱلْخِيَرَةُ مِنْ أَمْرِهِمْ وَمَن يَعْصِ ٱللَّهَ وَرَسُولَهُ فَقَدْ ضَلَّ ضَلَلًا مُّبِينًا

37. And when you said unto him on whom Allah has conferred favor and you have conferred favor: Keep your wife to yourself, and fear Allah. And you did hide in your mind that which Allah was to bring to light, and you did fear mankind whereas Allah had a better right that you should fear Him. So when Zayd had performed the necessary formality (of divorce) from her, We gave her unto you in marriage, so that (henceforth) there may be no sin for believers in respect of wives of their adopted sons, when the latter have performed the necessary formality (of release) from them. The commandment of Allah must be fulfilled.

38. There is no reproach for the Prophet in that which Allah makes his due. That was Allah's way with those who passed away of old and the commandment of Allah is certain destiny.

39. Who delivered the messages of Allah and feared Him, and feared none save Allah. Allah keeps good account.

40. Muhammad is not the father of any man among you, but he is the Messenger of Allah and the Seal of the Prophets; and Allah is Aware of all things.

41. O you who believe! Remember Allah with much re-membrance.

42. And glorify Him early and late.

43. He it is who blesses you, and His angels (bless you), that He may bring you forth from darkness unto light; and He is Merciful to the believers.

44. Their salutation on the day when they shall meet Him will be: Peace. And He has prepared for them a goodly recompense.

45. O Prophet! Lo! We have sent you as a witness and a bringer of good tidings and a warner,

46. And as a summoner unto Allah by His permission, and as a lamp that gives light.

٣٧ وَإِذْ تَقُولُ لِلَّذِىٓ أَنْعَمَ اللَّهُ عَلَيْهِ وَأَنْعَمْتَ عَلَيْهِ أَمْسِكْ عَلَيْكَ زَوْجَكَ وَاتَّقِ اللَّهَ وَتُخْفِى فِى نَفْسِكَ مَا اللَّهُ مُبْدِيهِ وَتَخْشَى النَّاسَ وَاللَّهُ أَحَقُّ أَن تَخْشَٰهُ فَلَمَّا قَضَىٰ زَيْدٌ مِّنْهَا وَطَرًا زَوَّجْنَٰكَهَا لِكَىْ لَا يَكُونَ عَلَى الْمُؤْمِنِينَ حَرَجٌ فِىٓ أَزْوَٰجِ أَدْعِيَآئِهِمْ إِذَا قَضَوْا مِنْهُنَّ وَطَرًا وَكَانَ أَمْرُ اللَّهِ مَفْعُولًا

٣٨ مَّا كَانَ عَلَى النَّبِىِّ مِنْ حَرَجٍ فِيمَا فَرَضَ اللَّهُ لَهُ سُنَّةَ اللَّهِ فِى الَّذِينَ خَلَوْا مِن قَبْلُ وَكَانَ أَمْرُ اللَّهِ قَدَرًا مَّقْدُورًا

٣٩ الَّذِينَ يُبَلِّغُونَ رِسَٰلَٰتِ اللَّهِ وَيَخْشَوْنَهُ وَلَا يَخْشَوْنَ أَحَدًا إِلَّا اللَّهَ وَكَفَىٰ بِاللَّهِ حَسِيبًا

٤٠ مَّا كَانَ مُحَمَّدٌ أَبَآ أَحَدٍ مِّن رِّجَالِكُمْ وَلَٰكِن رَّسُولَ اللَّهِ وَخَاتَمَ النَّبِيِّـۧنَ وَكَانَ اللَّهُ بِكُلِّ شَىْءٍ عَلِيمًا

٤١ يَٰٓأَيُّهَا الَّذِينَ ءَامَنُوا اذْكُرُوا اللَّهَ ذِكْرًا كَثِيرًا

٤٢ وَسَبِّحُوهُ بُكْرَةً وَأَصِيلًا

٤٣ هُوَ الَّذِى يُصَلِّى عَلَيْكُمْ وَمَلَٰٓئِكَتُهُ لِيُخْرِجَكُم مِّنَ الظُّلُمَٰتِ إِلَى النُّورِ وَكَانَ بِالْمُؤْمِنِينَ رَحِيمًا

٤٤ تَحِيَّتُهُمْ يَوْمَ يَلْقَوْنَهُ سَلَٰمٌ وَأَعَدَّ لَهُمْ أَجْرًا كَرِيمًا

٤٥ يَٰٓأَيُّهَا النَّبِىُّ إِنَّآ أَرْسَلْنَٰكَ شَٰهِدًا وَمُبَشِّرًا وَنَذِيرًا

٤٦ وَدَاعِيًا إِلَى اللَّهِ بِإِذْنِهِ وَسِرَاجًا مُّنِيرًا

47. And announce unto the believers the good tidings that they will have great bounty from Allah.

٤٧ وَبَشِّرِ ٱلْمُؤْمِنِينَ بِأَنَّ لَهُم مِّنَ ٱللَّهِ فَضْلًا كَبِيرًا

48. And incline not to the disbelievers and the hypocrites. Disregard their noxious talk, and put your trust in Allah. Allah is sufficient as Trustee.

٤٨ وَلَا تُطِعِ ٱلْكَٰفِرِينَ وَٱلْمُنَٰفِقِينَ وَدَعْ أَذَىٰهُمْ وَتَوَكَّلْ عَلَى ٱللَّهِ وَكَفَىٰ بِٱللَّهِ وَكِيلًا

49. O you who believe! If you wed believing women and divorce them before you have touched them, then there is no period that you should reckon. But content them and release them handsomely.

٤٩ يَٰٓأَيُّهَا ٱلَّذِينَ ءَامَنُوٓا إِذَا نَكَحْتُمُ ٱلْمُؤْمِنَٰتِ ثُمَّ طَلَّقْتُمُوهُنَّ مِن قَبْلِ أَن تَمَسُّوهُنَّ فَمَا لَكُمْ عَلَيْهِنَّ مِنْ عِدَّةٍ تَعْتَدُّونَهَا فَمَتِّعُوهُنَّ وَسَرِّحُوهُنَّ سَرَاحًا جَمِيلًا

50. O Prophet! Lo! We have made lawful unto you your wives unto whom you have paid their dowries, and those whom your right hand possesses of those whom Allah has given you as spoils of war, and the daughters of your uncle on the father's side and the daughters of your aunts on the father's side, and the daughters of your uncles on the mother's side who emigrated with you, and a believing woman if she give herself unto the Prophet if the Prophet desire to ask her in marriage—a privilege for you only, not for the (rest of) believers—We are aware of that which We enjoined upon them concerning their wives and those whom their right hands possess— that you may be free from blame, for Allah is For-giving, Merciful.

٥٠ يَٰٓأَيُّهَا ٱلنَّبِيُّ إِنَّآ أَحْلَلْنَا لَكَ أَزْوَٰجَكَ ٱلَّٰتِىٓ ءَاتَيْتَ أُجُورَهُنَّ وَمَا مَلَكَتْ يَمِينُكَ مِمَّآ أَفَآءَ ٱللَّهُ عَلَيْكَ وَبَنَاتِ عَمِّكَ وَبَنَاتِ عَمَّٰتِكَ وَبَنَاتِ خَالِكَ وَبَنَاتِ خَٰلَٰتِكَ ٱلَّٰتِى هَاجَرْنَ مَعَكَ وَٱمْرَأَةً مُّؤْمِنَةً إِن وَهَبَتْ نَفْسَهَا لِلنَّبِيِّ إِنْ أَرَادَ ٱلنَّبِيُّ أَن يَسْتَنكِحَهَا خَالِصَةً لَّكَ مِن دُونِ ٱلْمُؤْمِنِينَ قَدْ عَلِمْنَا مَا فَرَضْنَا عَلَيْهِمْ فِىٓ أَزْوَٰجِهِمْ وَمَا مَلَكَتْ أَيْمَٰنُهُمْ لِكَيْلَا يَكُونَ عَلَيْكَ حَرَجٌ وَكَانَ ٱللَّهُ غَفُورًا رَّحِيمًا

51. You can defer whom you will of them and receive unto you whom you will, and whomsoever you desire of those whom you have set aside (temporarily), it is no sin for you (to receive her again); that is better; that they may be comforted and not grieve, and may all be pleased with what you give them. Allah knows what is in your hearts (O men) and Allah is Forgiving, Clement.

٥١ تُرْجِى مَن تَشَآءُ مِنْهُنَّ وَتُـْٔوِىٓ إِلَيْكَ مَن تَشَآءُ وَمَنِ ٱبْتَغَيْتَ مِمَّنْ عَزَلْتَ فَلَا جُنَاحَ عَلَيْكَ ذَٰلِكَ أَدْنَىٰٓ أَن تَقَرَّ أَعْيُنُهُنَّ وَلَا يَحْزَنَّ وَيَرْضَيْنَ بِمَآ ءَاتَيْتَهُنَّ كُلُّهُنَّ وَٱللَّهُ يَعْلَمُ مَا فِى قُلُوبِكُمْ وَكَانَ ٱللَّهُ عَلِيمًا حَلِيمًا

52. It is not allowed for you (O Muhammad) to take (other) women henceforth nor that you should change them for other wives even though their beauty pleased you, save those whom your right hand possess. And Allah is Watcher over all things.

٥٢ لَّا يَحِلُّ لَكَ ٱلنِّسَآءُ مِنۢ بَعْدُ وَلَآ أَن تَبَدَّلَ بِهِنَّ مِنْ أَزْوَٰجٍ وَلَوْ أَعْجَبَكَ حُسْنُهُنَّ إِلَّا مَا مَلَكَتْ يَمِينُكَ وَكَانَ ٱللَّهُ عَلَىٰ كُلِّ شَىْءٍ رَّقِيبًا

53. O you who believe! Enter not the dwellings of the Pro-phet until leave is given to you for a meal and then not so early as to wait for its preparation. But if you are invited, enter, and, when your meal is over, then disperse. Linger not for conversation. Lo! that would cause annoyance to the Prophet, and he would be shy of (asking) you (to go); but Allah is not shy of the truth. And when you ask of them (the wives of the Prophet) anything, ask it of them from behind a curtain. That is purer for your hearts and for their hearts. And it is not for you to cause annoyance to the Messenger of Allah, nor that you should ever marry his wives after him. Lo! that in Allah's sight would be an enormity.

54. Whether you divulge a thing or keep it hidden, lo! Allah is ever Knower of all things.

55. It is no sin for them (your wives) (to converse freely) with their fathers, or their sons: or their brothers, or their brothers sons, or the sons of their sisters or of their own women, or their slaves. O women! Keep your duty to Allah. Lo! Allah is Witness over all things.

56. Lo! Allah and His angels shower blessings on the Pro-phet. O you who believe! Ask blessings on him and salute him with a worthy salutation.

57. Lo! those who malign Allah and His Messenger, Allah has cursed them in the world and the Hereafter, and has prepared for them the doom of the disdained.

58. And those who malign believing men and believing women unde servedly, they bear the guilt of slander and manifest sin.

﴿٥٣﴾ يَـٰٓأَيُّهَا ٱلَّذِينَ ءَامَنُوا لَا تَدۡخُلُوا بُيُوتَ ٱلنَّبِيِّ إِلَّآ أَن يُؤۡذَنَ لَكُمۡ إِلَىٰ طَعَامٍ غَيۡرَ نَـٰظِرِينَ إِنَىٰهُ وَلَـٰكِنۡ إِذَا دُعِيتُمۡ فَٱدۡخُلُوا فَإِذَا طَعِمۡتُمۡ فَٱنتَشِرُوا وَلَا مُسۡتَـٔۡنِسِينَ لِحَدِيثٍ إِنَّ ذَٰلِكُمۡ كَانَ يُؤۡذِى ٱلنَّبِيَّ فَيَسۡتَحۡىِۦ مِنكُمۡ وَٱللَّهُ لَا يَسۡتَحۡىِۦ مِنَ ٱلۡحَقِّ وَإِذَا سَأَلۡتُمُوهُنَّ مَتَـٰعًا فَسۡـَٔلُوهُنَّ مِن وَرَآءِ حِجَابٍ ذَٰلِكُمۡ أَطۡهَرُ لِقُلُوبِكُمۡ وَقُلُوبِهِنَّ وَمَا كَانَ لَكُمۡ أَن تُؤۡذُوا رَسُولَ ٱللَّهِ وَلَآ أَن تَنكِحُوٓا أَزۡوَٰجَهُۥ مِنۢ بَعۡدِهِۦٓ أَبَدًا إِنَّ ذَٰلِكُمۡ كَانَ عِندَ ٱللَّهِ عَظِيمًا

﴿٥٤﴾ إِن تُبۡدُوا شَيۡـًٔا أَوۡ تُخۡفُوهُ فَإِنَّ ٱللَّهَ كَانَ بِكُلِّ شَىۡءٍ عَلِيمًا

﴿٥٥﴾ لَّا جُنَاحَ عَلَيۡهِنَّ فِىٓ ءَابَآئِهِنَّ وَلَآ أَبۡنَآئِهِنَّ وَلَآ إِخۡوَٰنِهِنَّ وَلَآ أَبۡنَآءِ إِخۡوَٰنِهِنَّ وَلَآ أَبۡنَآءِ أَخَوَٰتِهِنَّ وَلَا نِسَآئِهِنَّ وَلَا مَا مَلَكَتۡ أَيۡمَـٰنُهُنَّ وَٱتَّقِينَ ٱللَّهَ إِنَّ ٱللَّهَ كَانَ عَلَىٰ كُلِّ شَىۡءٍ شَهِيدًا

﴿٥٦﴾ إِنَّ ٱللَّهَ وَمَلَـٰٓئِكَتَهُۥ يُصَلُّونَ عَلَى ٱلنَّبِيِّ يَـٰٓأَيُّهَا ٱلَّذِينَ ءَامَنُوا صَلُّوا عَلَيۡهِ وَسَلِّمُوا تَسۡلِيمًا

﴿٥٧﴾ إِنَّ ٱلَّذِينَ يُؤۡذُونَ ٱللَّهَ وَرَسُولَهُۥ لَعَنَهُمُ ٱللَّهُ فِى ٱلدُّنۡيَا وَٱلۡأَخِرَةِ وَأَعَدَّ لَهُمۡ عَذَابًا مُّهِينًا

﴿٥٨﴾ وَٱلَّذِينَ يُؤۡذُونَ ٱلۡمُؤۡمِنِينَ وَٱلۡمُؤۡمِنَـٰتِ بِغَيۡرِ مَا ٱكۡتَسَبُوا فَقَدِ ٱحۡتَمَلُوا بُهۡتَـٰنًا وَإِثۡمًا مُّبِينًا

59. O Prophet! Tell your wives and your daughters and the women of the believers to draw their cloaks close round them (when they go abroad). That will be better, so that they may be recognized and not annoyed. Allah is ever Forgiving, Merciful.

60. If the hypocrites, and those in whose hearts is a disease, and the alarmists in the city do not cease, We verily shall urge you on against them, then they will be your neighbors in it but a little while.

61. Accursed, they will be seized wherever found and slain with a (fierce) slaughter.

62. That was the way of Allah in the case of those who passed away of old; you will not find for the way of Allah anything of power to change.

63. Men ask you of the Hour. Say: The knowledge of it is with Allah only. What can convey (the knowledge) unto you? It may be that the Hour is near.

64. Lo! Allah has cursed disbelievers, and has prepared for them a flaming fire,

65. Wherein they will abide forever. They will find (then) no protecting friend nor helper.

66. On the day when their faces are turned over in the fire, they say: Oh, would that we had obeyed Allah and had obeyed His Messenger!

67. And they say: Our Lord! Lo! we obeyed our masters and great men, and they misled us from the Way.

68. Our Lord! Oh, give them double torment and curse them with a mighty curse.

69. O you who believe! Be not as those who slandered Moses, but Allah proved his innocence of that which they alleged, and he was well esteemed in Allah's sight.

70. O you who believe! Guard your duty to Allah, and speak words straight to the point;

71. He will adjust your works for you and will forgive you your sins. Who obeys Allah and His Messenger, he surely has gained a signal victory.

72. Lo! We offered the trust unto the heavens and the earth and the mountains, but they shrank from bearing it and were afraid of it. And man assumed it. Lo! he has proved a tyrant and a fool.

73. Allah punishes hypocritical men and hypocritical women, and idolatrous men and idolatrous women. But Allah pardons believing men and believing women, and Allah is Forgiving, Merciful.

٧١ يُصْلِحْ لَكُمْ أَعْمَالَكُمْ وَيَغْفِرْ لَكُمْ ذُنُوبَكُمْ وَمَن يُطِعِ اللَّهَ وَرَسُولَهُ فَقَدْ فَازَ فَوْزًا عَظِيمًا

٧٢ إِنَّا عَرَضْنَا الْأَمَانَةَ عَلَى السَّمَوَاتِ وَالْأَرْضِ وَالْجِبَالِ فَأَبَيْنَ أَن يَحْمِلْنَهَا وَأَشْفَقْنَ مِنْهَا وَحَمَلَهَا الْإِنسَانُ إِنَّهُ كَانَ ظَلُومًا جَهُولًا

٧٣ لِيُعَذِّبَ اللَّهُ الْمُنَافِقِينَ وَالْمُنَافِقَاتِ وَالْمُشْرِكِينَ وَالْمُشْرِكَاتِ وَيَتُوبَ اللَّهُ عَلَى الْمُؤْمِنِينَ وَالْمُؤْمِنَاتِ وَكَانَ اللَّهُ غَفُورًا رَّحِيمًا

Sheba

Saba', "Sheba," takes its name from verses 15 ff., where Sheba (Saba'), a region in the Yemen, is mentioned as having been devastated by a flood. It warns of the effects of luxury.

An early Makkan surah.

Sheba

Revealed at Makkah

*In the name of Allah,
the Beneficent, the Merciful*

1. Praise be to Allah, unto Whom belongs whatsoever is in the heavens and whatsoever is in the earth. His is the praise in the Hereafter, and He is the Wise, the Informed.

2. He knows that which goes down into the earth and that which comes forth from it, and that which descends from the heaven and that which ascends into it. He is the Merciful, the Forgiving.

3. Those who disbelieve say: The Hour will never come unto us. Say: Nay, by my Lord, but it is coming unto you surely. (He is) the Knower of the Unseen. Not an atom's weight, or less than that or greater, escapes Him in the heavens or in the earth, but it is in a clear Record,

4. That He may reward those who believe and do good works. For them is pardon and a rich provision.

5. But those who strive against Our revelations, challenging (Us), theirs will be a painful doom of wrath.

6. Those who have been given knowledge see that what is revealed unto you from your Lord is the truth and leads unto the path of the Mighty, the Owner of Praise.

7. Those who disbelieve say: Shall we show you a man who will tell you (that) when you have become dispersed in dust with most complete dispersal, still, even then, you will be created anew?

8. Has he invented a lie concerning Allah, or is there in him a madness? Nay, but those who disbelieve in the Here-after are in torment and far error.

9. Have they not observed what is before them and what is behind them of the sky and the earth? If We will, We can make the earth swallow them, or cause obliteration from the sky to fall on them. Lo! herein surely is a portent for every slave who turns (to Allah) repentant.

10. And assuredly We gave David grace from Us, (saying): O you mountains and birds, echo his psalms of praise! And we made iron supple unto him,

11. Saying: Make you long coats of mail and measure the links (thereof). And do you right. Lo! I am Seer of what you do.

12. And unto Solomon (We gave) the wind, whereof the morning course was a month's journey and the evening course a month's journey, and We caused the fount of copper to gush forth for him, and (We gave him) certain of the jinn who worked before him by permission of his Lord. And such of them as deviated from Our command, them We caused to taste the punishment of flaming fire.

13. They made for him what he willed: synagogues and statues, basins like wells and boilers built into the ground. Give thanks, O House of David! Few of My bondmen are thankful.

14. And when We decreed death for him, nothing showed his death to them save the woodworm which gnawed away his staff. And when he fell the jinn saw clearly how, if they had known the unseen, they would not have continued in despised toil.

﴿٨﴾ أَفْتَرَىٰ عَلَى ٱللَّهِ كَذِبًا أَم بِهِۦ جِنَّةٌ ۗ بَلِ ٱلَّذِينَ لَا يُؤْمِنُونَ بِٱلْآخِرَةِ فِى ٱلْعَذَابِ وَٱلضَّلَٰلِ ٱلْبَعِيدِ

﴿٩﴾ أَفَلَمْ يَرَوْا۟ إِلَىٰ مَا بَيْنَ أَيْدِيهِمْ وَمَا خَلْفَهُم مِّنَ ٱلسَّمَآءِ وَٱلْأَرْضِ ۚ إِن نَّشَأْ نَخْسِفْ بِهِمُ ٱلْأَرْضَ أَوْ نُسْقِطْ عَلَيْهِمْ كِسَفًا مِّنَ ٱلسَّمَآءِ ۚ إِنَّ فِى ذَٰلِكَ لَآيَةً لِّكُلِّ عَبْدٍ مُّنِيبٍ

﴿١٠﴾ ۞ وَلَقَدْ ءَاتَيْنَا دَاوُۥدَ مِنَّا فَضْلًا ۖ يَٰجِبَالُ أَوِّبِى مَعَهُۥ وَٱلطَّيْرَ ۖ وَأَلَنَّا لَهُ ٱلْحَدِيدَ

﴿١١﴾ أَنِ ٱعْمَلْ سَٰبِغَٰتٍ وَقَدِّرْ فِى ٱلسَّرْدِ ۖ وَٱعْمَلُوا۟ صَٰلِحًا ۖ إِنِّى بِمَا تَعْمَلُونَ بَصِيرٌ

﴿١٢﴾ وَلِسُلَيْمَٰنَ ٱلرِّيحَ غُدُوُّهَا شَهْرٌ وَرَوَاحُهَا شَهْرٌ ۖ وَأَسَلْنَا لَهُ عَيْنَ ٱلْقِطْرِ ۖ وَمِنَ ٱلْجِنِّ مَن يَعْمَلُ بَيْنَ يَدَيْهِ بِإِذْنِ رَبِّهِۦ ۖ وَمَن يَزِغْ مِنْهُمْ عَنْ أَمْرِنَا نُذِقْهُ مِنْ عَذَابِ ٱلسَّعِيرِ

﴿١٣﴾ يَعْمَلُونَ لَهُۥ مَا يَشَآءُ مِن مَّحَٰرِيبَ وَتَمَٰثِيلَ وَجِفَانٍ كَٱلْجَوَابِ وَقُدُورٍ رَّاسِيَٰتٍ ۚ ٱعْمَلُوٓا۟ ءَالَ دَاوُۥدَ شُكْرًا ۚ وَقَلِيلٌ مِّنْ عِبَادِىَ ٱلشَّكُورُ

﴿١٤﴾ فَلَمَّا قَضَيْنَا عَلَيْهِ ٱلْمَوْتَ مَا دَلَّهُمْ عَلَىٰ مَوْتِهِۦٓ إِلَّا دَآبَّةُ ٱلْأَرْضِ تَأْكُلُ مِنسَأَتَهُۥ ۖ فَلَمَّا خَرَّ تَبَيَّنَتِ ٱلْجِنُّ أَن لَّوْ كَانُوا۟ يَعْلَمُونَ ٱلْغَيْبَ مَا لَبِثُوا۟ فِى ٱلْعَذَابِ ٱلْمُهِينِ

15. There was indeed a sign for Sheba in their dwelling place: Two gardens on the right hand and the left (saying): Eat of the provision of your Lord and render thanks to Him. A fair land and an indulgent Lord!

١٥ لَقَدْ كَانَ لِسَبَإٍ فِى مَسْكَنِهِمْ ءَايَةٌ جَنَّتَانِ عَن يَمِينٍ وَشِمَالٍ كُلُوا مِن رِّزْقِ رَبِّكُمْ وَاشْكُرُوا لَهُ بَلْدَةٌ طَيِّبَةٌ وَرَبٌّ غَفُورٌ

16. But they were froward, and so We sent on them the flood of Arim, and in exchange for their two gardens gave them two gardens bearing bitter fruit, the tamarisk and here and there a lote-tree.

١٦ فَأَعْرَضُوا فَأَرْسَلْنَا عَلَيْهِمْ سَيْلَ الْعَرِمِ وَبَدَّلْنَهُم بِجَنَّتَيْهِمْ جَنَّتَيْنِ ذَوَاتَىْ أُكُلٍ خَمْطٍ وَأَثْلٍ وَشَىْءٍ مِّن سِدْرٍ قَلِيلٍ

17. This We awarded them because of their ingratitude. Punish We ever any save the ingrates?

١٧ ذَلِكَ جَزَيْنَهُم بِمَا كَفَرُوا وَهَلْ نُجَزِى إِلَّا الْكَفُورَ

18. And We set, between them and the towns which We had blessed, towns easy to be seen, and We made the stage between them easy, (saying): Travel in them safely both by night and day.

١٨ وَجَعَلْنَا بَيْنَهُمْ وَبَيْنَ الْقُرَى الَّتِى بَرَكْنَا فِيهَا قُرًى ظَهِرَةً وَقَدَّرْنَا فِيهَا السَّيْرَ سِيرُوا فِيهَا لَيَالِىَ وَأَيَّامًا ءَامِنِينَ

19. But they said: Our Lord! Make the stage between our journeys longer. And they wronged themselves, therefore We made them bywords (in the land) and scattered them abroad, a total scattering. Lo! Herein surely are portents for each steadfast, grateful (heart).

١٩ فَقَالُوا رَبَّنَا بَعِدْ بَيْنَ أَسْفَارِنَا وَظَلَمُوا أَنفُسَهُمْ فَجَعَلْنَهُمْ أَحَادِيثَ وَمَزَّقْنَهُمْ كُلَّ مُمَزَّقٍ إِنَّ فِى ذَلِكَ لَءَايَتٍ لِّكُلِّ صَبَّارٍ شَكُورٍ

20. And Satan indeed found his calculation true concerning them, for they followed him, all save a group of true believers.

٢٠ وَلَقَدْ صَدَّقَ عَلَيْهِمْ إِبْلِيسُ ظَنَّهُ فَاتَّبَعُوهُ إِلَّا فَرِيقًا مِّنَ الْمُؤْمِنِينَ

21. And he had no warrant whatsoever against them, save that We would know him who believes in the Hereafter from him who is in doubt thereof; and your Lord (O Muhammad) takes note of all things.

٢١ وَمَا كَانَ لَهُ عَلَيْهِم مِّن سُلْطَنٍ إِلَّا لِنَعْلَمَ مَن يُؤْمِنُ بِالْءَاخِرَةِ مِمَّنْ هُوَ مِنْهَا فِى شَكٍّ وَرَبُّكَ عَلَى كُلِّ شَىْءٍ حَفِيظٌ

22. Say (O Muhammad): Call upon those whom you set up beside Allah! They possess not an atom's weight either in the heavens or the earth, nor have they any share either, nor has He an auxiliary among them.

٢٢ قُلِ ادْعُوا الَّذِينَ زَعَمْتُم مِّن دُونِ اللَّهِ لَا يَمْلِكُونَ مِثْقَالَ ذَرَّةٍ فِى السَّمَوَتِ وَلَا فِى الْأَرْضِ وَمَا لَهُمْ فِيهِمَا مِن شِرْكٍ وَمَا لَهُ مِنْهُم مِّن ظَهِيرٍ

23. No intercession avails with Him save for him whom He permits. Yet, when fear is banished from their hearts, (on the Day of Judgement) they would say: What was it that your Lord commanded? They will say: The Truth. And He is the Sublime, the Great.

24. Say: Who gives you provision from the sky and the earth? Say: Allah. Lo! we or you assuredly are rightly guided or in error manifest.

25. Say: You will not be asked of what we committed, nor shall we be asked of what you do.

26. Say: Our Lord will bring us all together, then He will judge between us with truth. He is the All-knowing Judge.

27. Say: Show me those whom you have joined unto Him as partners. Nay (you dare not)! For He is Allah, the Mighty, the Wise.

28. And We have not sent you (O Muhammad) save as a bringer of good tidings and a warner unto all mankind; but most of mankind know it not.

29. And they say: When is this promise (to be fulfilled) if you are truthful?

30. Say (O Muhammad): Yours is the promise of a Day which you cannot postpone nor hasten by an hour.

31. And those who disbelieve say: We believe not in this Qur'an nor in that which was before it; but oh, if you could see, when the wrongdoers are brought up before their Lord, how they cast the blame one to another, how those who were despised (in the earth) say unto those who were proud: But for you, we should have been believers.

32. And those who were proud say unto those who were despised: Did we drive you away from the guidance after it had come unto you? Nay, but you were criminals.

٢٣ وَلَا تَنفَعُ ٱلشَّفَٰعَةُ عِندَهُۥٓ إِلَّا لِمَنۡ أَذِنَ لَهُۥ ۚ حَتَّىٰٓ إِذَا فُزِّعَ عَن قُلُوبِهِمۡ قَالُواْ مَاذَا قَالَ رَبُّكُمۡ ۖ قَالُواْ ٱلۡحَقَّ ۖ وَهُوَ ٱلۡعَلِيُّ ٱلۡكَبِيرُ

٢٤ ۞ قُلۡ مَن يَرۡزُقُكُم مِّنَ ٱلسَّمَٰوَٰتِ وَٱلۡأَرۡضِ ۖ قُلِ ٱللَّهُ ۖ وَإِنَّآ أَوۡ إِيَّاكُمۡ لَعَلَىٰ هُدًى أَوۡ فِي ضَلَٰلٍ مُّبِينٍ

٢٥ قُل لَّا تُسۡـَٔلُونَ عَمَّآ أَجۡرَمۡنَا وَلَا نُسۡـَٔلُ عَمَّا تَعۡمَلُونَ

٢٦ قُلۡ يَجۡمَعُ بَيۡنَنَا رَبُّنَا ثُمَّ يَفۡتَحُ بَيۡنَنَا بِٱلۡحَقِّ وَهُوَ ٱلۡفَتَّاحُ ٱلۡعَلِيمُ

٢٧ قُلۡ أَرُونِيَ ٱلَّذِينَ أَلۡحَقۡتُم بِهِۦ شُرَكَآءَ ۖ كَلَّا ۚ بَلۡ هُوَ ٱللَّهُ ٱلۡعَزِيزُ ٱلۡحَكِيمُ

٢٨ وَمَآ أَرۡسَلۡنَٰكَ إِلَّا كَآفَّةً لِّلنَّاسِ بَشِيرًا وَنَذِيرًا وَلَٰكِنَّ أَكۡثَرَ ٱلنَّاسِ لَا يَعۡلَمُونَ

٢٩ وَيَقُولُونَ مَتَىٰ هَٰذَا ٱلۡوَعۡدُ إِن كُنتُمۡ صَٰدِقِينَ

٣٠ قُل لَّكُم مِّيعَادُ يَوۡمٍ لَّا تَسۡتَـٔۡخِرُونَ عَنۡهُ سَاعَةً وَلَا تَسۡتَقۡدِمُونَ

٣١ وَقَالَ ٱلَّذِينَ كَفَرُواْ لَن نُّؤۡمِنَ بِهَٰذَا ٱلۡقُرۡءَانِ وَلَا بِٱلَّذِي بَيۡنَ يَدَيۡهِ ۗ وَلَوۡ تَرَىٰٓ إِذِ ٱلظَّٰلِمُونَ مَوۡقُوفُونَ عِندَ رَبِّهِمۡ يَرۡجِعُ بَعۡضُهُمۡ إِلَىٰ بَعۡضٍ ٱلۡقَوۡلَ يَقُولُ ٱلَّذِينَ ٱسۡتُضۡعِفُواْ لِلَّذِينَ ٱسۡتَكۡبَرُواْ لَوۡلَآ أَنتُمۡ لَكُنَّا مُؤۡمِنِينَ

٣٢ قَالَ ٱلَّذِينَ ٱسۡتَكۡبَرُواْ لِلَّذِينَ ٱسۡتُضۡعِفُوٓاْ أَنَحۡنُ صَدَدۡنَٰكُمۡ عَنِ ٱلۡهُدَىٰ بَعۡدَ إِذۡ جَآءَكُم ۖ بَلۡ كُنتُم مُّجۡرِمِينَ

33. Those who were despised say unto those who were proud: Nay but (it was your) scheming night and day, when you commanded us to disbelieve in Allah and set up rivals unto Him. And they are filled with remorse when they behold the doom; and We place yokes on the necks of those who disbelieved. Are they requited anything save what they used to do?

34. And We sent not unto any township a warner, but its pampered ones declared: Lo! we are disbelievers in that which you bring unto Us.

35. And they say: We are more (than you) in wealth and children. We are not to be punished!

36. Say (O Muhammad): Lo! my Lord enlarges the provision for whom He will and narrows it (for whom He will). But most of mankind know not.

37. And it is not your wealth nor your children that will bring you near unto us, but he who believes and does good (he draws near). As for such, theirs will be twofold reward for what they did, and they will dwell secure in lofty chambers.

38. And as for those who strive against Our revelations, challenging, they will be brought to the doom.

39. Say: Lo! my Lord enlarges the provision for whom He will of His bondmen, and narrows (it) for him. And whatsoever you spend (for good) He replaces it. And He is the Best of Providers.

40. And on the day when He will gather them all together, He will say unto the angels: Did these worship you?

٣٣ وَقَالَ الَّذِينَ اسْتُضْعِفُوا لِلَّذِينَ اسْتَكْبَرُوا بَلْ مَكْرُ الَّيْلِ وَالنَّهَارِ إِذْ تَأْمُرُونَنَا أَن نَّكْفُرَ بِاللَّهِ وَنَجْعَلَ لَهُ أَندَادًا وَأَسَرُّوا النَّدَامَةَ لَمَّا رَأَوُا الْعَذَابَ وَجَعَلْنَا الْأَغْلَالَ فِي أَعْنَاقِ الَّذِينَ كَفَرُوا هَلْ يُجْزَوْنَ إِلَّا مَا كَانُوا يَعْمَلُونَ

٣٤ وَمَا أَرْسَلْنَا فِي قَرْيَةٍ مِّن نَّذِيرٍ إِلَّا قَالَ مُتْرَفُوهَا إِنَّا بِمَا أُرْسِلْتُم بِهِ كَافِرُونَ

٣٥ وَقَالُوا نَحْنُ أَكْثَرُ أَمْوَالًا وَأَوْلَادًا وَمَا نَحْنُ بِمُعَذَّبِينَ

٣٦ قُلْ إِنَّ رَبِّي يَبْسُطُ الرِّزْقَ لِمَن يَشَاءُ وَيَقْدِرُ وَلَكِنَّ أَكْثَرَ النَّاسِ لَا يَعْلَمُونَ

٣٧ وَمَا أَمْوَالُكُمْ وَلَا أَوْلَادُكُم بِالَّتِي تُقَرِّبُكُمْ عِندَنَا زُلْفَى إِلَّا مَنْ ءَامَنَ وَعَمِلَ صَالِحًا فَأُوْلَئِكَ لَهُمْ جَزَاءُ الضِّعْفِ بِمَا عَمِلُوا وَهُمْ فِي الْغُرُفَاتِ ءَامِنُونَ

٣٨ وَالَّذِينَ يَسْعَوْنَ فِي ءَايَاتِنَا مُعَاجِزِينَ أُوْلَئِكَ فِي الْعَذَابِ مُحْضَرُونَ

٣٩ قُلْ إِنَّ رَبِّي يَبْسُطُ الرِّزْقَ لِمَن يَشَاءُ مِنْ عِبَادِهِ وَيَقْدِرُ لَهُ وَمَا أَنفَقْتُم مِّن شَيْءٍ فَهُوَ يُخْلِفُهُ وَهُوَ خَيْرُ الرَّازِقِينَ

٤٠ وَيَوْمَ يَحْشُرُهُمْ جَمِيعًا ثُمَّ يَقُولُ لِلْمَلَائِكَةِ أَهَؤُلَاءِ إِيَّاكُمْ كَانُوا يَعْبُدُونَ

41. They will say: Be You glorified. You are our Protector from them! Nay, but they worshiped the jinn; most of them were believers in them.

42. This day you will possess no Use nor hurt for one another. And we shall say unto those who did wrong: Taste the doom of the Fire which you used to deny.

43. And if Our revelations are recited unto them in plain terms, they say: This is nothing else than a man who would turn you away from what your fathers used to worship; and they say: This is nothing else than an invented lie. Those who disbelieve say of the truth when it reaches them: This is nothing else than clear magic.

44. And We have given them no Scriptures which they study, nor sent We unto them, before you, any warner.

45. Those before them denied, and these have not attained a title of that which We bestowed on them (of old); yet they denied My messengers. How intense then was My abhorrence (of them)!

46. Say (unto them, O Muhammad): I exhort you unto one thing only: that you stand up, for Allah's sake, by twos and singly, and then reflect: There is no madness in your comrade. He is nothing else than a warner unto you in face of a terrific doom.

47. Say: Whatever reward I might have asked of you is yours. My reward is the affair of Allah only. He is Witness over all things.

48. Say: Lo! my Lord hurls the truth. (He is) the Knower of Things Hidden.

49. Say: The Truth has come, and falsehood shows not its face and will not return.

50. Say: If I err, I err only to my own loss, and if I am rightly guided it is because of that which my Lord has revealed unto me. Lo! He is Hearer, Near.

51. Could you but see when they are terrified with no escape, and are seized from near at hand.

٥١) وَلَوْ تَرَىٰ إِذْ فَزِعُوا فَلَا فَوْتَ وَأُخِذُوا مِن مَّكَانٍ قَرِيبٍ

52. And they say: We (now) believe therein. But never can they reach (faith) from afar off,

٥٢) وَقَالُوٓا ءَامَنَّا بِهِۦ وَأَنَّىٰ لَهُمُ ٱلتَّنَاوُشُ مِن مَّكَانٍ بَعِيدٍ

53. When they disbelieved in it before. They aim at the unseen from afar off.

٥٣) وَقَدْ كَفَرُوا بِهِۦ مِن قَبْلُ وَيَقْذِفُونَ بِٱلْغَيْبِ مِن مَّكَانٍ بَعِيدٍ

54. And a gulf is set between them and that which they desire, as was done for people of their kind of old. Lo! they were in hopeless doubt.

٥٤) وَحِيلَ بَيْنَهُمْ وَبَيْنَ مَا يَشْتَهُونَ كَمَا فُعِلَ بِأَشْيَاعِهِم مِّن قَبْلُ إِنَّهُمْ كَانُوا فِي شَكٍّ مُّرِيبٍ

The Creator or Angels

This surah, called *Fāṭir*, "The Creator," takes its name from a word in the first verse. It is also called *al Malā'ikah* (angels), who are mentioned in the same verse. An early Makkan surah.

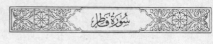

The Creator or Angels

Revealed at Makkah

In the name of Allah,
the Beneficent, the Merciful

1. Praise be to Allah, the Creator of the heavens and the earth, who appoints the angels messengers having wings: two, three and four. He multiplies in creation what He will. Lo! Allah is Able to do all things.

2. That which Allah opens unto mankind of mercy none can withhold it; and that which He withholds none can release it after Him. He is the Mighty, the Wise.

3. O mankind! Remember Allah's grace toward you! Is there any creator other than Allah who provides for you from the sky and the earth? There is no God save Him. Whither then are you turned?

4. And if they deny you, (O Muhammad), messengers (of Allah) were denied before you. Unto Allah all things are brought back.

5. O mankind! Lo! the promise of Allah is true. So let not the life of the world beguile you, and let not the (avowed) beguiler (Satan) beguile you with regard to Allah.

6. Lo! the Devil is an enemy for you, so treat him as an enemy. He only summons his faction to be owners of the Flaming Fire.

7. Those who disbelieve, theirs will be an awful doom; and those who believe and do good works, theirs will be forgiveness and a great reward.

8. Is he, the evil of whose deeds is made fair seeming unto him so that he deems it good, (other than Satan's dupe)? Allah verily sends whom He will astray, and guides whom He will, so let not your soul, (O Muhammad) expire in sighings for them. Lo! Allah is Aware of what they do!

9. And Allah it is who sends the winds and they raise clouds; then We lead it (rain) unto a dead land and revive therewith the earth after its death. Such is the Resurrection.

10. Who desires power (should know that) all power belongs to Allah. Unto Him good words ascend, and the pious deed does He exalt; but those who plot iniquities, theirs will be an awful doom; and the plotting of such (folk) will come to nothing.

11. Allah created you from dust, then from a little fluid, then He made you pairs (the male and female). No female bears or brings forth save with His knowledge. And no man long-lived is granted length of days, nor is anything lessened of his life, but it is recorded in a Book. Lo! that is easy for Allah.

12. And the two seas[225] are not alike: this, fresh, sweet, good to drink, this (other) bitter, salt. And from them both you eat fresh meat and derive the ornament that you wear. And you see ships cleaving them with prows that you may seek of His bounty, and that you may give thanks.

13. He makes the night to pass into the day and He makes the day to pass into the night. He has subdued the sun and moon to service. Each runs unto an appointed term. Such is Allah, your Lord; His is the Sovereignty; and those unto whom you pray instead of Him own not so much as the white spot on a date stone.

---

[225]i.e., the two kinds of water in the earth.

14. If you pray unto them they hear not your prayer, and if they heard they could not grant it you. On the Day of Resur-rection they will disown association with you. None can inform you like Him Who is Informed.

15. O mankind! You are the poor in your relation to Allah. And Allah! He is the Absolute, the Owner of Praise.

16. If He will, He can be rid of you and bring (instead of you) some new creation.

17. That is not a hard thing for Allah.

18. And no burdened soul can bear another's burden, and if one heavy laden cries for (help with) his load, nothing of it will be lifted even though he (unto whom he cries) be of kin. You warn only those who fear their Lord in secret, and have established prayer. He who grows (in goodness), grows only for himself, (he cannot by his merit redeem others). Unto Allah is the journeying.

19. The blind man is not equal with the seer;

20. Nor is darkness (tantamount to) light;

21. Nor is the shadow equal with the sun's full heat;

22. Nor are the living equal with the dead. Lo! Allah makes whom He will to hear. You can not reach those who are in the graves.

23. You are but a warner.

24. Lo! We have sent you with the Truth, a bearer of glad tidings and a warner; and there is not a nation but a warner has passed among them.

25. And if they deny you: those before them also denied. Their messengers came unto them with clear proofs (of Allah's sovereignty), and with the Psalms and the Scripture giving light.

١٤ إِنْ تَدْعُوهُمْ لَا يَسْمَعُوا دُعَاءَكُمْ وَلَوْ سَمِعُوا مَا اسْتَجَابُوا لَكُمْ وَيَوْمَ الْقِيَامَةِ يَكْفُرُونَ بِشِرْكِكُمْ وَلَا يُنَبِّئُكَ مِثْلُ خَبِيرٍ

١٥ ۞ يَا أَيُّهَا النَّاسُ أَنْتُمُ الْفُقَرَاءُ إِلَى اللَّهِ وَاللَّهُ هُوَ الْغَنِيُّ الْحَمِيدُ

١٦ إِنْ يَشَأْ يُذْهِبْكُمْ وَيَأْتِ بِخَلْقٍ جَدِيدٍ

١٧ وَمَا ذَلِكَ عَلَى اللَّهِ بِعَزِيزٍ

١٨ وَلَا تَزِرُ وَازِرَةٌ وِزْرَ أُخْرَى وَإِنْ تَدْعُ مُثْقَلَةٌ إِلَى حِمْلِهَا لَا يُحْمَلْ مِنْهُ شَيْءٌ وَلَوْ كَانَ ذَا قُرْبَى إِنَّمَا تُنْذِرُ الَّذِينَ يَخْشَوْنَ رَبَّهُمْ بِالْغَيْبِ وَأَقَامُوا الصَّلَاةَ وَمَنْ تَزَكَّى فَإِنَّمَا يَتَزَكَّى لِنَفْسِهِ وَإِلَى اللَّهِ الْمَصِيرُ

١٩ وَمَا يَسْتَوِي الْأَعْمَى وَالْبَصِيرُ

٢٠ وَلَا الظُّلُمَاتُ وَلَا النُّورُ

٢١ وَلَا الظِّلُّ وَلَا الْحَرُورُ

٢٢ وَمَا يَسْتَوِي الْأَحْيَاءُ وَلَا الْأَمْوَاتُ إِنَّ اللَّهَ يُسْمِعُ مَنْ يَشَاءُ وَمَا أَنْتَ بِمُسْمِعٍ مَنْ فِي الْقُبُورِ

٢٣ إِنْ أَنْتَ إِلَّا نَذِيرٌ

٢٤ إِنَّا أَرْسَلْنَاكَ بِالْحَقِّ بَشِيرًا وَنَذِيرًا وَإِنْ مِنْ أُمَّةٍ إِلَّا خَلَا فِيهَا نَذِيرٌ

٢٥ وَإِنْ يُكَذِّبُوكَ فَقَدْ كَذَّبَ الَّذِينَ مِنْ قَبْلِهِمْ جَاءَتْهُمْ رُسُلُهُمْ بِالْبَيِّنَاتِ وَبِالزُّبُرِ وَبِالْكِتَابِ الْمُنِيرِ

26. Then seized I those who disbelieved, and how intense was My abhorrence!

27. Have you not seen that Allah causes water to fall from the sky, and We produce therewith fruit of divers hues; and among the mountains are streaks white and red, of divers hues, and (others) raven black;

28. And of men and beasts and cattle, in like manner, divers hues? The erudite among His bondsmen fear Allah alone. Lo! Allah is Mighty, Forgiving.

29. Lo! those who read the Scripture of Allah, and establish prayer, and spend of that which We have bestowed on them secretly and openly, they look forward to imperishable gain,

30. That He will pay them their wages and increase them of His grace. Lo! He is Forgiving, Responsive.

31. As for that which We inspire in you of the Scripture, it is the Truth confirming that which was (revealed) before it. Lo! Allah is indeed Observer, Seer of his slaves.

32. Then We gave the Scripture as inheritance unto those whom We elected of our bondmen. But of them are some who wrong themselves and of them are some who are lukewarm and of them are some who outstrip (others) through good deeds, by Allah's leave. That is the great favor!

33. Gardens of Eden! They enter them wearing armlets of gold and pearl and their raiment therein is silk.

34. And they say: Praise be to Allah who has put grief away from us. Lo! Our Lord is Forgiving, Bountiful,

35. Who, of His grace, has installed us in the mansion of eternity, where toil touches us not nor can weariness affect us.

36. But as for those who disbelieve, for them is fire of Hell; it takes not complete effect upon them so that they can die, nor is its torment lightened for them. Thus We punish every ingrate.

37. And they cry therein for help, (saying): Our Lord! Release us; we will do right, not (the wrong) that we used to do. Did not We grant you a life long enough for who re-flected to reflect therein? And the warner came unto you. Now taste (the flavor of your deeds), for evildoers have no helper.

38. Lo! Allah is the Knower of the Unseen of the heavens and the earth. Lo! He is Aware of the secret of (men's) breasts.

39. He it is who has made you regents in the earth; so he who disbelieves, his disbelief be on his own head. Their disbelief increases for the disbelievers, in their Lord's sight, nothing save abhorrence. Their disbelief increases for the disbelievers nothing save loss.

40. Say: Have you seen your partner gods to whom you pray beside Allah? Show me what they created of the earth! Or have they any portion in the heavens? Or have We given them a Scripture so that they act on clear proof therefrom? Nay, the evildoers promise one another only to deceive.

41. Lo! Allah grasps the heavens and the earth that they disappear not, and if they were to disappear there is not one that could grasp them after Him. Lo! He is ever Clement, Forgiving.

42. And they swore by Allah, their most binding oath, that if a warner came unto them they would be more tractable than any of the nations; yet, when a warner came unto them it aroused in them nothing save repugnance,

43. (Shown in their) behaving arrogantly in the land and plotting evil; and the evil plot encloses but the men who make it. Then, can they expect anything but the treatment of the folk of old? You will not find for Allah's way of treatment any substitute, nor will you find for Allah's way of treatment anything of power to change.

44. Have they not travelled in the land and seen the nature of the consequence for those who were before them, and they were mightier than these in power? Allah is not such that anything in the heavens or in the earth escapes Him. Lo! He is the Knower, the Mighty.

45. If Allah took mankind to task by that which they de-serve, He would not leave a living creature on the surface of the earth; but He reprieves them until an appointed term, and when their term comes then surely (they will know that) Allah is ever Seer of His slaves.

Yā Sīn

Yā Sīn takes its name from the two letters of the Arabic alphabet, which stand as the first verse and are generally held to signify *Yā Insān* ("O Man"). This surah is regarded with special reverence and is recited in times of adversity, illness, fasting, and on the approach of death.

It belongs to the middle group of Makkan surahs.

Yā Sīn

Revealed at Makkah

*In the name of Allah,
the Beneficent, the Merciful*

1. Yā Sīn.

2. By the wise Qur'an,

3. Lo! you are of those sent

4. On a straight path,

5. A revelation of the Mighty, the Merciful,

6. That you may warn a folk whose fathers were not warned, so they are heedless.

7. Already has the word proved true of most of them, for they believe not.

8. Lo! we have put on their necks yokes reaching unto the chins, so that they are made stiff necked.

9. And We have set a bar before them and a bar behind them, and (thus) have covered them so that they see not.

10. Whether you warn them or you warn them not, it is alike for them, for they believe not.

11. You warn only him who follows the Reminder and fears the Beneficent in secret. To him bear tidings of forgiveness and a rich reward.

12. Lo! We it is Who bring the dead to life. We record that which they send before (them), and their footprints. And all things We have kept in a clear register.

13. Coin for them a similitude: The people of the city when those sent (from Allah) came unto them;

١٣ وَٱضْرِبْ لَهُم مَّثَلًا أَصْحَبَ ٱلْقَرْيَةِ إِذْ جَاءَهَا ٱلْمُرْسَلُونَ

14. When We sent unto them two, and they denied them both, so We reinforced them with a third, and they said; Lo! we have been sent unto you.

١٤ إِذْ أَرْسَلْنَا إِلَيْهِمُ ٱثْنَيْنِ فَكَذَّبُوهُمَا فَعَزَّزْنَا بِثَالِثٍ فَقَالُوٓاْ إِنَّآ إِلَيْكُم مُّرْسَلُونَ

15. They said: You are but mortals like unto us. The Beneficent has nothing revealed. You do but lie!

١٥ قَالُوٓاْ مَآ أَنتُمْ إِلَّا بَشَرٌ مِّثْلُنَا وَمَآ أَنزَلَ ٱلرَّحْمَٰنُ مِن شَىْءٍ إِنْ أَنتُمْ إِلَّا تَكْذِبُونَ

16. They answered: Our lord knows that we are indeed sent unto you,

١٦ قَالُوا رَبُّنَا يَعْلَمُ إِنَّآ إِلَيْكُمْ لَمُرْسَلُونَ

17. And our duty is but plain conveyance (of the message).

١٧ وَمَا عَلَيْنَآ إِلَّا ٱلْبَلَٰغُ ٱلْمُبِينُ

18. (The people of the city) said: We augur ill of you. If you desist not, we shall surely stone you, and grievous torture will befall you from us.

١٨ قَالُوٓاْ إِنَّا تَطَيَّرْنَا بِكُمْ لَئِن لَّمْ تَنتَهُواْ لَنَرْجُمَنَّكُمْ وَلَيَمَسَّنَّكُم مِّنَّا عَذَابٌ أَلِيمٌ

19. They said: Your evil augury be with you! Is it because you are reminded (of the truth)? Nay, but you are froward folk?

١٩ قَالُواْ طَٰٓئِرُكُم مَّعَكُمْ أَئِن ذُكِّرْتُم بَلْ أَنتُمْ قَوْمٌ مُّسْرِفُونَ

20. And there came from the uttermost part of the city a man running. He cried: O my people! Follow those who have been sent!

٢٠ وَجَآءَ مِنْ أَقْصَا ٱلْمَدِينَةِ رَجُلٌ يَسْعَىٰ قَالَ يَٰقَوْمِ ٱتَّبِعُواْ ٱلْمُرْسَلِينَ

21. Follow those who ask of you no fee, and who are rightly guided.

٢١ ٱتَّبِعُواْ مَن لَّا يَسْـَٔلُكُمْ أَجْرًا وَهُم مُّهْتَدُونَ

22. For what cause should I not worship Him Who has created me, and unto Whom you will be brought back?

٢٢ وَمَا لِىَ لَآ أَعْبُدُ ٱلَّذِى فَطَرَنِى وَإِلَيْهِ تُرْجَعُونَ

23. Shall I take (other) gods in place of Him when, if the Beneficent should wish me any harm, their intercession will avail me nothing, nor can they save me?

٢٣ ءَأَتَّخِذُ مِن دُونِهِۦٓ ءَالِهَةً إِن يُرِدْنِ ٱلرَّحْمَٰنُ بِضُرٍّ لَّا تُغْنِ عَنِّى شَفَٰعَتُهُمْ شَيْـًٔا وَلَا يُنقِذُونِ

24. Then truly I should be in error manifest.

٢٤ إِنِّىٓ إِذًا لَّفِى ضَلَٰلٍ مُّبِينٍ

25. Lo! I have believed in your Lord, so hear me!

٢٥ إِنِّىٓ ءَامَنتُ بِرَبِّكُمْ فَٱسْمَعُونِ

26. It was said (unto him): Enter Paradise. He said: Would that my people knew

27. With what my Lord has pardoned me and made me of the honored ones!

28. We sent not down against his people after him a host from heaven, nor do We ever send.

29. It was but one Shout, and lo! they were extinct.

30. Ah, the anguish for the bondmen! Never came there unto them a messenger but they did mock him!

31. Have they not seen how many generations We de-stroyed before them, which indeed return not unto them;

32. But all, without exception, will be brought before Us.

33. A token unto them is the dead earth. We revive it, and We bring forth from it grain so that they eat thereof;

34. And We have placed therein gardens of the date palm and grapes, and We have caused springs of water to gush forth therein,

35. That they may eat of the fruit there-of, although their hands made it not.* Will they not, then, give thanks?

36. Glory be to Him Who created all the sexual pairs, of that which the earth grows, and of themselves, and of that which they know not!

37. A token unto them is night. We strip it of the day, and lo! they are in darkness.

38. And the sun runs on unto a resting place for him. That is the measuring of the Mighty, the Wise.

---

٢٦ قِيلَ ادْخُلِ الْجَنَّةَ قَالَ يٰلَيْتَ قَوْمِي يَعْلَمُونَ

٢٧ بِمَا غَفَرَ لِي رَبِّي وَجَعَلَنِي مِنَ الْمُكْرَمِينَ

٢٨ وَمَا أَنزَلْنَا عَلَى قَوْمِهِ مِنْ بَعْدِهِ مِنْ جُنْدٍ مِّنَ السَّمَاءِ وَمَا كُنَّا مُنزِلِينَ

٢٩ إِن كَانَتْ إِلَّا صَيْحَةً وَاحِدَةً فَإِذَا هُمْ خَامِدُونَ

٣٠ يٰحَسْرَةً عَلَى الْعِبَادِ مَا يَأْتِيهِم مِّن رَّسُولٍ إِلَّا كَانُوا بِهِ يَسْتَهْزِءُونَ

٣١ أَلَمْ يَرَوْا كَمْ أَهْلَكْنَا قَبْلَهُم مِّنَ الْقُرُونِ أَنَّهُمْ إِلَيْهِمْ لَا يَرْجِعُونَ

٣٢ وَإِن كُلٌّ لَّمَّا جَمِيعٌ لَّدَيْنَا مُحْضَرُونَ

٣٣ وَآيَةٌ لَّهُمُ الْأَرْضُ الْمَيْتَةُ أَحْيَيْنَاهَا وَأَخْرَجْنَا مِنْهَا حَبًّا فَمِنْهُ يَأْكُلُونَ

٣٤ وَجَعَلْنَا فِيهَا جَنَّاتٍ مِّن نَّخِيلٍ وَأَعْنَابٍ وَفَجَّرْنَا فِيهَا مِنَ الْعُيُونِ

٣٥ لِيَأْكُلُوا مِن ثَمَرِهِ وَمَا عَمِلَتْهُ أَيْدِيهِمْ أَفَلَا يَشْكُرُونَ

٣٦ سُبْحَانَ الَّذِي خَلَقَ الْأَزْوَاجَ كُلَّهَا مِمَّا تُنبِتُ الْأَرْضُ وَمِنْ أَنفُسِهِمْ وَمِمَّا لَا يَعْلَمُونَ

٣٧ وَآيَةٌ لَّهُمُ اللَّيْلُ نَسْلَخُ مِنْهُ النَّهَارَ فَإِذَا هُم مُّظْلِمُونَ

٣٨ وَالشَّمْسُ تَجْرِي لِمُسْتَقَرٍّ لَّهَا ذَٰلِكَ تَقْدِيرُ الْعَزِيزِ الْعَلِيمِ

---

* It may also mean: and of what their hands made (the editor).

39. And for the moon We have appointed mansions till she return like an old shrivelled palm leaf.

٣٩ وَالْقَمَرَ قَدَّرْنَاهُ مَنَازِلَ حَتَّى عَادَ كَالْعُرْجُونِ الْقَدِيمِ

40. It is not for the sun to overtake the moon, nor does the night outstrip the day. They float each in an orbit.

٤٠ لَا الشَّمْسُ يَنبَغِي لَهَا أَن تُدْرِكَ الْقَمَرَ وَلَا الَّيْلُ سَابِقُ النَّهَارِ وَكُلٌّ فِي فَلَكٍ يَسْبَحُونَ

41. And a token unto them is that We bore their offspring in the laden ships,

٤١ وَءَايَةٌ لَّهُمْ أَنَّا حَمَلْنَا ذُرِّيَّتَهُمْ فِي الْفُلْكِ الْمَشْحُونِ

42. And have created for them of the like thereof whereon they ride.

٤٢ وَخَلَقْنَا لَهُم مِّن مِّثْلِهِ مَا يَرْكَبُونَ

43. And if We will, We drown them, and there is no help for them, neither can they be saved;

٤٣ وَإِن نَّشَأْ نُغْرِقْهُمْ فَلَا صَرِيخَ لَهُمْ وَلَاهُمْ يُنقَذُونَ

44. Unless by mercy from Us and as comfort for a while.

٤٤ إِلَّا رَحْمَةً مِّنَّا وَمَتَاعًا إِلَى حِينٍ

45. When it is said unto them: Beware of that which is before you and that which is behind you, that you may find mercy (they are heedless).

٤٥ وَإِذَا قِيلَ لَهُمُ اتَّقُوا مَا بَيْنَ أَيْدِيكُمْ وَمَا خَلْفَكُمْ لَعَلَّكُمْ تُرْحَمُونَ

46. Never came a token of the tokens of their Lord to them, but they did turn away from it!

٤٦ وَمَا تَأْتِيهِم مِّنْ ءَايَةٍ مِّنْ ءَايَتِ رَبِّهِمْ إِلَّا كَانُوا عَنْهَا مُعْرِضِينَ

47. And when it is said unto them: Spend of that wherewith Allah has provided you. those who disbelieve say unto those who believe: Shall we feed those whom Allah, if He willed, would feed? You are in nothing else than error manifest.

٤٧ وَإِذَا قِيلَ لَهُمْ أَنفِقُوا مِمَّا رَزَقَكُمُ اللَّهُ قَالَ الَّذِينَ كَفَرُوا لِلَّذِينَ ءَامَنُوا أَنُطْعِمُ مَن لَّوْ يَشَاءُ اللَّهُ أَطْعَمَهُ إِنْ أَنتُمْ إِلَّا فِي ضَلَالٍ مُّبِينٍ

48. And they say: When will this promise be fulfilled, if you are truthful?

٤٨ وَيَقُولُونَ مَتَى هَذَا الْوَعْدُ إِن كُنتُمْ صَدِقِينَ

49. They await but one Blast, which will surprise them while they are disputing.

٤٩ مَا يَنظُرُونَ إِلَّا صَيْحَةً وَحِدَةً تَأْخُذُهُمْ وَهُمْ يَخِصِّمُونَ

50. Then they cannot make bequest, nor can they return to their own folk.

٥٠ فَلَا يَسْتَطِيعُونَ تَوْصِيَةً وَلَا إِلَى أَهْلِهِمْ يَرْجِعُونَ

51. And the trumpet is blown and lo! from the graves they hie unto their Lord,

٥١ وَنُفِخَ فِي الصُّورِ فَإِذَا هُم مِّنَ الْأَجْدَاثِ إِلَى رَبِّهِمْ يَنسِلُونَ

52. Crying: Woe upon us! Who has raised us from our place of sleep? This is that which the Beneficent did promise, and the messengers spoke truth,

٥٢ قَالُوا يَا وَيْلَنَا مَنْ بَعَثَنَا مِنْ مَّرْقَدِنَا هَٰذَا مَا وَعَدَ الرَّحْمَٰنُ وَصَدَقَ الْمُرْسَلُونَ

53. It is but one Blast, and behold them brought together before Us!

٥٣ إِنْ كَانَتْ إِلَّا صَيْحَةً وَاحِدَةً فَإِذَا هُمْ جَمِيعٌ لَّدَيْنَا مُحْضَرُونَ

54. This day no soul is wronged in anything; nor are you requited anything save that which you used to do.

٥٤ فَالْيَوْمَ لَا تُظْلَمُ نَفْسٌ شَيْئًا وَلَا تُجْزَوْنَ إِلَّا مَا كُنْتُمْ تَعْمَلُونَ

55. Lo! those who merit Paradise this day are happily employed,

٥٥ إِنَّ أَصْحَابَ الْجَنَّةِ الْيَوْمَ فِي شُغُلٍ فَاكِهُونَ

56. They and their wives, are in pleasant shade, on thrones reclining;

٥٦ هُمْ وَأَزْوَاجُهُمْ فِي ظِلَالٍ عَلَى الْأَرَائِكِ مُتَّكِئُونَ

57. Theirs in it will be fruits and theirs in it will be (all) that they ask;

٥٧ لَهُمْ فِيهَا فَاكِهَةٌ وَلَهُمْ مَا يَدَّعُونَ

58. Peace is the word (to them) from a Merciful Lord.

٥٨ سَلَامٌ قَوْلًا مِنْ رَّبٍّ رَّحِيمٍ

59. But begone you, O you criminals, this day!

٥٩ وَامْتَازُوا الْيَوْمَ أَيُّهَا الْمُجْرِمُونَ

60. Did I not charge you, O you sons of Adam, that you worship not the Devil Lo! he is your open foe!

٦٠ أَلَمْ أَعْهَدْ إِلَيْكُمْ يَا بَنِي آدَمَ أَنْ لَّا تَعْبُدُوا الشَّيْطَانَ إِنَّهُ لَكُمْ عَدُوٌّ مُّبِينٌ

61. But that you worship Me? That was the right path.

٦١ وَأَنِ اعْبُدُونِي هَٰذَا صِرَاطٌ مُّسْتَقِيمٌ

62. Yet he has led astray of you a great multitude. Had you then no sense?

٦٢ وَلَقَدْ أَضَلَّ مِنْكُمْ جِبِلًّا كَثِيرًا أَفَلَمْ تَكُونُوا تَعْقِلُونَ

63. This is Hell which you were promised.

٦٣ هَٰذِهِ جَهَنَّمُ الَّتِي كُنْتُمْ تُوعَدُونَ

64. Burn therein this day for that you disbelieved.

٦٤ اصْلَوْهَا الْيَوْمَ بِمَا كُنْتُمْ تَكْفُرُونَ

65. This day We seal up their mouths, and their hands speak out and their legs bear witness as to what they used to earn.

٦٥ الْيَوْمَ نَخْتِمُ عَلَى أَفْوَاهِهِمْ وَتُكَلِّمُنَا أَيْدِيهِمْ وَتَشْهَدُ أَرْجُلُهُمْ بِمَا كَانُوا يَكْسِبُونَ

66. And had We willed, We surely could have quenched their eyesight so that they should struggle for the way. Then they would never see.

67. And had We willed, We surely could have fixed them in their place, making them powerless to go forward nor turn back.[226]

68. He whom We bring unto old age, We reverse him in creation. Have you then no sense?

69. And we have not taught him (Muhammad) poetry, nor is it meet for him. This is nothing else than a Reminder and a Lecture[227] making plain,

70. To warn whoever lives, and that the word may be fulfilled against the disbelievers.

71. Have they not seen how We have created for them of Our handiwork the cattle, so that they are their owners,

72. And have subdued them unto them, so that some of them they have for riding, some for food?

73. Benefits and (divers) drinks have they from them. Will they not then give thanks?

74. And they have taken (other) gods beside Allah, in order that they may be helped.

75. It is not in their power to help them; although they are unto them a host in arms.

76. So let not their speech grieve you (O Muhammad). Lo! We know what they conceal and what they proclaim.

77. Has not man seen that We have created him from a drop of seed? Yet lo! he is an open opponent.

78. And he has coined for Us a similitude, and has forgotten the fact of his creation, He said: Who will revive these bones when they have rotted away?

---

[226] But they have sight and power of motion, so they can choose their way.
[227] Arabic: Qur'an.

79. Say: He will revive them Who produced them at the first, for He is Knower of every creation,

﴿٧٩﴾ قُلْ يُحْيِيهَا الَّذِى أَنْشَأَهَا أَوَّلَ مَرَّةٍ وَهُوَ بِكُلِّ خَلْقٍ عَلِيمٌ

80. Who has appointed for you fire from the green trees, and behold! you kindle from them.

﴿٨٠﴾ الَّذِى جَعَلَ لَكُمْ مِنَ الشَّجَرِ الْأَخْضَرِ نَارًا فَإِذَا أَنْتُمْ مِنْهُ تُوقِدُونَ

81. Is not He Who created the heavens and the earth Able to create the like of them? Aye, that He is! for He is the Creator, the Knower.

﴿٨١﴾ أَوَلَيْسَ الَّذِى خَلَقَ السَّمَوَاتِ وَالْأَرْضَ بِقَادِرٍ عَلَى أَنْ يَخْلُقَ مِثْلَهُمْ بَلَى وَهُوَ الْخَلَّاقُ الْعَلِيمُ

82. His command, when He intends a thing, is only that he says unto it: Be! and it is.

﴿٨٢﴾ إِنَّمَا أَمْرُهُ إِذَا أَرَادَ شَيْئًا أَنْ يَقُولَ لَهُ كُنْ فَيَكُونُ

83. Therefore glory be to Him in Whose hand is the dominion over all things! Unto Him you will be brought back.

﴿٨٣﴾ فَسُبْحَانَ الَّذِى بِيَدِهِ مَلَكُوتُ كُلِّ شَيْءٍ وَإِلَيْهِ تُرْجَعُونَ

Those Who Set the Ranks

Al Ṣāffāt takes its name from a word in the first verse. The reference in the first three verses is to the angels, which is made clear by verses 164-166, where the revealing angel speaks in person. Tradition says that soothsayers and astrologers throughout the East were bewildered at the time of the Prophet's coming by the appearance in the heavens of a comet and many meteors that baffled their scientists and made them afraid to sit at nights on high peaks to watch the stars, as was their general custom. They told enquirers that their familiars could no longer guide them, as they themselves were completely at a loss and terrified. This is the explanation usually given of verses 7-9 and of a passage of similar import in Surah 72:8-10.

It stands early in the middle group of Makkan surahs.

Those Who Set the Ranks

Revealed at Makkah

*In the name of Allah,
the Beneficent, the Merciful*

1. By those who set the ranks in battle order

2. And those who drive away (the wicked) with reproof

3. And those who read (the Word) for a reminder,

4. Lo! your Lord is surely One.

5. Lord of the heavens and of the earth and all that is between them, and Lord of the sun's risings.

6. Lo! We have adorned the lowest heaven with an ornament, the planets:

7. With security from every froward devil.

8. They cannot listen to the Highest Chiefs for they are pelted from every side,

9. Outcast, and theirs is a perpetual torment;

10. Save him who snatches a fragment, and there pursues him a piercing flame.[228]

11. Then ask them (O Muhammad): Are they stronger as a creation, or those (others) whom We have created? Lo! We created them of plastic clay.

12. Nay, but you do marvel when they mock

13. And they heed not when they are reminded,

14. And seek to scoff when they behold a portent

15. And they say: lo! this is mere magic;

---

16. When we are dead and have become dust and bones, shall we then, really, be raised (again)?

١٦ أَءِذَا مِتْنَا وَكُنَّا تُرَابًا وَعِظَامًا أَءِنَّا لَمَبْعُوثُونَ

17. And our forefathers?

١٧ أَوَءَابَاؤُنَا الْأَوَّلُونَ

18. Say (O Muhammad): Yea, in truth; and you will be brought low.

١٨ قُلْ نَعَمْ وَأَنتُمْ دَاخِرُونَ

19. There is but one Blast, and lo! they behold,

١٩ فَإِنَّمَا هِيَ زَجْرَةٌ وَاحِدَةٌ فَإِذَا هُمْ يَنظُرُونَ

20. And say: Ah, woe for us! This is the Day of Judgment.

٢٠ وَقَالُوا يَا وَيْلَنَا هَذَا يَوْمُ الدِّينِ

21. This is the Day of Separation, which you used to deny.

٢١ هَذَا يَوْمُ الْفَصْلِ الَّذِي كُنتُم بِهِ تُكَذِّبُونَ

22. Assemble those who did wrong, together with their wives and what they used to worship

٢٢ اُحْشُرُوا الَّذِينَ ظَلَمُوا وَأَزْوَاجَهُمْ وَمَا كَانُوا يَعْبُدُونَ

23. Instead of Allah, and lead them to the path to Hell;

٢٣ مِن دُونِ اللَّهِ فَاهْدُوهُمْ إِلَى صِرَاطِ الْجَحِيمِ

24. And stop them, for they must be questioned.

٢٤ وَقِفُوهُمْ إِنَّهُم مَّسْئُولُونَ

25. What ails you that you help not one another?

٢٥ مَا لَكُمْ لَا تَنَاصَرُونَ

26. Nay, but this day they make full submission.

٢٦ بَلْ هُمُ الْيَوْمَ مُسْتَسْلِمُونَ

27. And some of them draw near unto others, mutually questioning.

٢٧ وَأَقْبَلَ بَعْضُهُمْ عَلَى بَعْضٍ يَتَسَاءَلُونَ

28. They say: Lo! you used to come unto us, imposing, (swearing that you spoke the truth).

٢٨ قَالُوا إِنَّكُمْ كُنتُمْ تَأْتُونَنَا عَنِ الْيَمِينِ

29. They answer: Nay, but you (yourselves) were not believers.

٢٩ قَالُوا بَل لَّمْ تَكُونُوا مُؤْمِنِينَ

30. We had no power over you, but you were wayward folk.

٣٠ وَمَا كَانَ لَنَا عَلَيْكُم مِّن سُلْطَانٍ بَلْ كُنتُمْ قَوْمًا طَاغِينَ

31. Now the Word of our Lord has been fulfilled concerning us. Lo! we are about to taste (the doom).

٣١ فَحَقَّ عَلَيْنَا قَوْلُ رَبِّنَا إِنَّا لَذَائِقُونَ

32. Thus we misled you. Lo! we were (ourselves) astray.

٣٢ فَأَغْوَيْنَاكُمْ إِنَّا كُنَّا غَاوِينَ

33. Then lo! this day they (both) are sharers in the doom.

٣٣ فَإِنَّهُمْ يَوْمَئِذٍ فِي الْعَذَابِ مُشْتَرِكُونَ

34. Lo! thus deal We with the criminals.

٣٤ إِنَّا كَذَلِكَ نَفْعَلُ بِالْمُجْرِمِينَ

35. For when it was said unto them, There is no god save Allah, they were scornful

٣٥ إِنَّهُمْ كَانُوا إِذَا قِيلَ لَهُمْ لَا إِلَهَ إِلَّا اللَّهُ يَسْتَكْبِرُونَ

36. And said: Shall we forsake our gods for a mad poet?

37. Nay, but he brought the Truth, and he confirmed the messengers.

38. Lo! surely you will taste the painful doom—

39. You are requited nothing save what you did—

40. Save single minded slaves of Allah;

41. For them there is a known provision,

42. Fruits. And they will be honored

43. In the Gardens of delight,

44. On couches facing one another;

45. A cup from a gushing spring is brought round for them,

46. White, delicious to the drinkers,

47. Wherein there is no headache nor are they made mad thereby.

48. And with them are those of modest gaze, with lovely eyes,

49. (Pure) as they were hidden eggs.

50. And some of them draw near unto others, mutually questioning.

51. A speaker of them said: Lo! I had a comrade

52. Who used to say: are you in truth of those who put faith (in his words)?

53. Can we, when we are dead and have become mere dust and bones—can we (then) truly be brought to book?

54. He said: Will you look?

55. Then looks he and sees him in the depth of Hell.

56. He said: (By Allah, you) verily did all but cause my ruin,

٣٦ وَيَقُولُونَ أَئِنَّا لَتَارِكُوا آلِهَتِنَا لِشَاعِرٍ مَّجْنُونٍ

٣٧ بَلْ جَاءَ بِالْحَقِّ وَصَدَّقَ الْمُرْسَلِينَ

٣٨ إِنَّكُمْ لَذَائِقُوا الْعَذَابِ الْأَلِيمِ

٣٩ وَمَا تُجْزَوْنَ إِلَّا مَا كُنتُمْ تَعْمَلُونَ

٤٠ إِلَّا عِبَادَ اللَّهِ الْمُخْلَصِينَ

٤١ أُولَٰئِكَ لَهُمْ رِزْقٌ مَّعْلُومٌ

٤٢ فَوَاكِهُ وَهُم مُّكْرَمُونَ

٤٣ فِي جَنَّاتِ النَّعِيمِ

٤٤ عَلَىٰ سُرُرٍ مُّتَقَابِلِينَ

٤٥ يُطَافُ عَلَيْهِم بِكَأْسٍ مِّن مَّعِينٍ

٤٦ بَيْضَاءَ لَذَّةٍ لِّلشَّارِبِينَ

٤٧ لَا فِيهَا غَوْلٌ وَلَا هُمْ عَنْهَا يُنزَفُونَ

٤٨ وَعِندَهُمْ قَاصِرَاتُ الطَّرْفِ عِينٌ

٤٩ كَأَنَّهُنَّ بَيْضٌ مَّكْنُونٌ

٥٠ فَأَقْبَلَ بَعْضُهُمْ عَلَىٰ بَعْضٍ يَتَسَاءَلُونَ

٥١ قَالَ قَائِلٌ مِّنْهُمْ إِنِّي كَانَ لِي قَرِينٌ

٥٢ يَقُولُ أَئِنَّكَ لَمِنَ الْمُصَدِّقِينَ

٥٣ أَئِذَا مِتْنَا وَكُنَّا تُرَابًا وَعِظَامًا أَئِنَّا لَمَدِينُونَ

٥٤ قَالَ هَلْ أَنتُم مُّطَّلِعُونَ

٥٥ فَاطَّلَعَ فَرَآهُ فِي سَوَاءِ الْجَحِيمِ

٥٦ قَالَ تَاللَّهِ إِن كِدتَّ لَتُرْدِينِ

57. And had it not been for the favor of my Lord, I too had been of those haled forth (to doom).

٥٧ وَلَوْلَا نِعْمَةُ رَبِّي لَكُنْتُ مِنَ الْمُحْضَرِينَ

58. Are we then not to die

٥٨ أَفَمَا نَحْنُ بِمَيِّتِينَ

59. Saving our former death, and are we not to be punished?

٥٩ إِلَّا مَوْتَتَنَا الْأُولَى وَمَا نَحْنُ بِمُعَذَّبِينَ

60. Lo! this is the supreme triumph.

٦٠ إِنَّ هَذَا لَهُوَ الْفَوْزُ الْعَظِيمُ

61. For the like of this, then, let the workers work.

٦١ لِمِثْلِ هَذَا فَلْيَعْمَلِ الْعَامِلُونَ

62. Is this better as a welcome, or the tree of Zaqqūm?[229]

٦٢ أَذَلِكَ خَيْرٌ نُزُلًا أَمْ شَجَرَةُ الزَّقُّومِ

63. Lo! We have appointed it a torment for wrongdoers.

٦٣ إِنَّا جَعَلْنَاهَا فِتْنَةً لِلظَّالِمِينَ

64. Lo! it is a tree that springs in the heart of Hell.

٦٤ إِنَّهَا شَجَرَةٌ تَخْرُجُ فِي أَصْلِ الْجَحِيمِ

65. Its crop is as it were the heads of devils,

٦٥ طَلْعُهَا كَأَنَّهُ رُءُوسُ الشَّيَاطِينِ

66. And lo! they surely must eat thereof, and fill (their) bellies therewith.

٦٦ فَإِنَّهُمْ لَآكِلُونَ مِنْهَا فَمَالِئُونَ مِنْهَا الْبُطُونَ

67. And afterward, lo! thereupon they have a drink of boiling water,

٦٧ ثُمَّ إِنَّ لَهُمْ عَلَيْهَا لَشَوْبًا مِنْ حَمِيمٍ

68. And then, lo! their return is surely unto Hell.

٦٨ ثُمَّ إِنَّ مَرْجِعَهُمْ لَإِلَى الْجَحِيمِ

69. They indeed found their fathers astray,

٦٩ إِنَّهُمْ أَلْفَوْا آبَاءَهُمْ ضَالِّينَ

70. So they make haste (to follow) in their footsteps.

٧٠ فَهُمْ عَلَى آثَارِهِمْ يُهْرَعُونَ

71. And surely most of the men of old went astray before them,

٧١ وَلَقَدْ ضَلَّ قَبْلَهُمْ أَكْثَرُ الْأَوَّلِينَ

72. And surely We sent among them warners.

٧٢ وَلَقَدْ أَرْسَلْنَا فِيهِمْ مُنْذِرِينَ

73. Then see the nature of the consequence for those warned,

٧٣ فَانْظُرْ كَيْفَ كَانَ عَاقِبَةُ الْمُنْذَرِينَ

74. Save single minded slaves of Allah.

٧٤ إِلَّا عِبَادَ اللَّهِ الْمُخْلَصِينَ

75. And Noah surely prayed unto Us, and gracious was the Hearer of his prayer.

٧٥ وَلَقَدْ نَادَانَا نُوحٌ فَلَنِعْمَ الْمُجِيبُونَ

76. And We saved him and his household from the great distress,

٧٦ وَنَجَّيْنَاهُ وَأَهْلَهُ مِنَ الْكَرْبِ الْعَظِيمِ

77. And We made his seed the survivors,

٧٧ وَجَعَلْنَا ذُرِّيَّتَهُ هُمُ الْبَاقِينَ

78. And We left for him among the later folk (the salutation):

٧٨ وَتَرَكْنَا عَلَيْهِ فِي الْآخِرِينَ

---

[229]See Surahs 44:43 and 56:52.

79. Peace be unto Noah among the worlds!

80. Lo! thus do We reward the good.

81. Lo! he is one of Our believing slaves.

82. Then We did drown the others.

83. And lo! of his persuasion verily was Abraham

84. When he came unto his Lord with a whole heart;

85. When he said unto his father and his folk: What is it that you worship?

86. Is it a falsehood—gods beside Allah—that you de-sire?

87. What then is your opinion of the Lord of the Worlds?

88. And he glanced a glance at the stars,

89. Then said: Lo! I feel sick!

90. So they turned their backs and went away from him.

91. Then he turned to their gods and said: Will you not eat?

92. What ails you that you speak not?

93. Then he attacked them, striking with his right hand.

94. And (his people) came toward him, hastening.

95. He said: Worship you that which you yourselves do carve

96. When Allah has created you and what you make?

97. They said: Build for him a building and fling him in the red hot fire.

98. And they designed a snare for him, but We made them the undermost.

99. And he said: Lo! I am going unto my Lord Who will guide me;

100. My Lord! Vouchsafe me of the righteous.

﴿٧٩﴾ سَلَامٌ عَلَىٰ نُوحٍ فِي ٱلْعَالَمِينَ

﴿٨٠﴾ إِنَّا كَذَٰلِكَ نَجْزِي ٱلْمُحْسِنِينَ

﴿٨١﴾ إِنَّهُ مِنْ عِبَادِنَا ٱلْمُؤْمِنِينَ

﴿٨٢﴾ ثُمَّ أَغْرَقْنَا ٱلْآخَرِينَ

﴿٨٣﴾ ۞ وَإِنَّ مِن شِيعَتِهِ لَإِبْرَٰهِيمَ

﴿٨٤﴾ إِذْ جَآءَ رَبَّهُ بِقَلْبٍ سَلِيمٍ

﴿٨٥﴾ إِذْ قَالَ لِأَبِيهِ وَقَوْمِهِ مَاذَا تَعْبُدُونَ

﴿٨٦﴾ أَئِفْكًا ءَالِهَةً دُونَ ٱللَّهِ تُرِيدُونَ

﴿٨٧﴾ فَمَا ظَنُّكُم بِرَبِّ ٱلْعَالَمِينَ

﴿٨٨﴾ فَنَظَرَ نَظْرَةً فِي ٱلنُّجُومِ

﴿٨٩﴾ فَقَالَ إِنِّي سَقِيمٌ

﴿٩٠﴾ فَتَوَلَّوْا عَنْهُ مُدْبِرِينَ

﴿٩١﴾ فَرَاغَ إِلَىٰ ءَالِهَتِهِمْ فَقَالَ أَلَا تَأْكُلُونَ

﴿٩٢﴾ مَا لَكُمْ لَا تَنطِقُونَ

﴿٩٣﴾ فَرَاغَ عَلَيْهِمْ ضَرْبًا بِٱلْيَمِينِ

﴿٩٤﴾ فَأَقْبَلُوا إِلَيْهِ يَزِفُّونَ

﴿٩٥﴾ قَالَ أَتَعْبُدُونَ مَا تَنْحِتُونَ

﴿٩٦﴾ وَٱللَّهُ خَلَقَكُمْ وَمَا تَعْمَلُونَ

﴿٩٧﴾ قَالُوا ٱبْنُوا لَهُ بُنْيَٰنًا فَأَلْقُوهُ فِي ٱلْجَحِيمِ

﴿٩٨﴾ فَأَرَادُوا بِهِ كَيْدًا فَجَعَلْنَٰهُمُ ٱلْأَسْفَلِينَ

﴿٩٩﴾ وَقَالَ إِنِّي ذَاهِبٌ إِلَىٰ رَبِّي سَيَهْدِينِ

﴿١٠٠﴾ رَبِّ هَبْ لِي مِنَ ٱلصَّٰلِحِينَ

101. So We gave him tidings of a gentle son.

102. And when (his son) was old enough to walk with him, (Abraham) said: O my dear son, I have seen in a dream that I must sacrifice you. So look, what think you? He said: O my father! Do that which you are commanded. Allah willing, you shall find me of the steadfast.

103. Then, when they had both surrendered (to Allah), and he had flung him down upon his face,

104. We called unto him: O Abraham:

105. You have already fulfilled the vision. Lo! thus do We reward the good.

106. Lo! that surely was a clear test.

107. Then We ransomed him with a tremendous victim.

108. And We left for him among the later folk (the salutation):

109. Peace be unto Abraham!

110. Thus do We reward the good.

111. Lo! he is one of Our believing slaves.

112. And We gave him tidings of the birth of Isaac, a Pro-phet of the righteous.

113. And We blessed him and Isaac. And of their seed are some who do good, and some who plainly wrong themselves.

114. And We surely gave grace unto Moses and Aaron,

115. And saved them and their people from the great distress,

116. And helped them so that they became the victors.

117. And We gave them the clear Scripture

118. And showed them the right path.

١٠١ فَبَشَّرْنَاهُ بِغُلَامٍ حَلِيمٍ

١٠٢ فَلَمَّا بَلَغَ مَعَهُ السَّعْىَ قَالَ يَا بُنَىَّ إِنِّى أَرَى فِى الْمَنَامِ أَنِّى أَذْبَحُكَ فَانْظُرْ مَاذَا تَرَى قَالَ يَا أَبَتِ افْعَلْ مَا تُؤْمَرُ سَتَجِدُنِى إِنْ شَاءَ اللَّهُ مِنَ الصَّابِرِينَ

١٠٣ فَلَمَّا أَسْلَمَا وَتَلَّهُ لِلْجَبِينِ

١٠٤ وَنَادَيْنَاهُ أَنْ يَا إِبْرَاهِيمُ

١٠٥ قَدْ صَدَّقْتَ الرُّؤْيَا إِنَّا كَذَلِكَ نَجْزِى الْمُحْسِنِينَ

١٠٦ إِنَّ هَذَا لَهُوَ الْبَلَاءُ الْمُبِينُ

١٠٧ وَفَدَيْنَاهُ بِذِبْحٍ عَظِيمٍ

١٠٨ وَتَرَكْنَا عَلَيْهِ فِى الْآخِرِينَ

١٠٩ سَلَامٌ عَلَى إِبْرَاهِيمَ

١١٠ كَذَلِكَ نَجْزِى الْمُحْسِنِينَ

١١١ إِنَّهُ مِنْ عِبَادِنَا الْمُؤْمِنِينَ

١١٢ وَبَشَّرْنَاهُ بِإِسْحَقَ نَبِيًّا مِنَ الصَّالِحِينَ

١١٣ وَبَارَكْنَا عَلَيْهِ وَعَلَى إِسْحَقَ وَمِنْ ذُرِّيَّتِهِمَا مُحْسِنٌ وَظَالِمٌ لِنَفْسِهِ مُبِينٌ

١١٤ وَلَقَدْ مَنَنَّا عَلَى مُوسَى وَهَارُونَ

١١٥ وَنَجَّيْنَاهُمَا وَقَوْمَهُمَا مِنَ الْكَرْبِ الْعَظِيمِ

١١٦ وَنَصَرْنَاهُمْ فَكَانُوا هُمُ الْغَالِبِينَ

١١٧ وَآتَيْنَاهُمَا الْكِتَابَ الْمُسْتَبِينَ

١١٨ وَهَدَيْنَاهُمَا الصِّرَاطَ الْمُسْتَقِيمَ

119. And We left for them, among the later folk (the salutation):

وَتَرَكْنَا عَلَيْهِمَا فِى الْآخِرِينَ ۞

120. Peace be unto Moses and Aaron!

سَلَامٌ عَلَىٰ مُوسَىٰ وَهَارُونَ ۞

121. Lo! thus do We reward the good.

إِنَّا كَذَٰلِكَ نَجْزِى الْمُحْسِنِينَ ۞

122. Lo! they are two of our believing slaves.

إِنَّهُمَا مِنْ عِبَادِنَا الْمُؤْمِنِينَ ۞

123. And lo! Elias was of those sent (to warn),

وَإِنَّ إِلْيَاسَ لَمِنَ الْمُرْسَلِينَ ۞

124. When he said unto his folk: Will you not ward off (evil)?

إِذْ قَالَ لِقَوْمِهِ أَلَا تَتَّقُونَ ۞

125. Will you cry unto Baal and forsake the best of Creators,

أَتَدْعُونَ بَعْلًا وَتَذَرُونَ أَحْسَنَ الْخَالِقِينَ ۞

126. Allah, your Lord and the Lord of your forefathers?

اللَّهَ رَبَّكُمْ وَرَبَّ آبَائِكُمُ الْأَوَّلِينَ ۞

127. But they denied him, so they surely will be haled forth (to the doom)

فَكَذَّبُوهُ فَإِنَّهُمْ لَمُحْضَرُونَ ۞

128. Save single-minded slaves of Allah.

إِلَّا عِبَادَ اللَّهِ الْمُخْلَصِينَ ۞

129. And we left for him among the later folk (the salutation):

وَتَرَكْنَا عَلَيْهِ فِى الْآخِرِينَ ۞

130. Peace be unto Elias!

سَلَامٌ عَلَىٰ إِلْ يَاسِينَ ۞

131. Lo! thus do We reward the good.

إِنَّا كَذَٰلِكَ نَجْزِى الْمُحْسِنِينَ ۞

132. Lo! he is one of our believing slaves.

إِنَّهُ مِنْ عِبَادِنَا الْمُؤْمِنِينَ ۞

133. And Lot surely was of the messengers,

وَإِنَّ لُوطًا لَمِنَ الْمُرْسَلِينَ ۞

134. When We saved him and his household, every one,

إِذْ نَجَّيْنَاهُ وَأَهْلَهُ أَجْمَعِينَ ۞

135. Save an old woman among those who stayed be-hind;

إِلَّا عَجُوزًا فِى الْغَابِرِينَ ۞

136. Then We destroyed the others.

ثُمَّ دَمَّرْنَا الْآخَرِينَ ۞

137. And Lo! you surely pass by (the ruin of) them in the morning

وَإِنَّكُمْ لَتَمُرُّونَ عَلَيْهِمْ مُصْبِحِينَ ۞

138. And at night time; have you then no sense?

وَبِاللَّيْلِ أَفَلَا تَعْقِلُونَ ۞

139. And lo! Jonah surely was of the messengers

وَإِنَّ يُونُسَ لَمِنَ الْمُرْسَلِينَ ۞

140. When he fled unto the laden ship,

إِذْ أَبَقَ إِلَى الْفُلْكِ الْمَشْحُونِ ۞

141. And then drew lots and was of those subdued;

﴿١٤١﴾ فَسَاهَمَ فَكَانَ مِنَ ٱلْمُدْحَضِينَ

142. And the fish swallowed him while he was blameworthy;

﴿١٤٢﴾ فَٱلْتَقَمَهُ ٱلْحُوتُ وَهُوَ مُلِيمٌ

143. And had he not been one of those who glorify (Allah)

﴿١٤٣﴾ فَلَوْلَا أَنَّهُ كَانَ مِنَ ٱلْمُسَبِّحِينَ

144. He would have tarried in its belly till the day when they are raised;

﴿١٤٤﴾ لَلَبِثَ فِى بَطْنِهِ إِلَىٰ يَوْمِ يُبْعَثُونَ

145. Then We cast him on a desert shore while he was sick;

﴿١٤٥﴾ ۞ فَنَبَذْنَٰهُ بِٱلْعَرَآءِ وَهُوَ سَقِيمٌ

146. And We caused a tree of gourd to grow above him;

﴿١٤٦﴾ وَأَنۢبَتْنَا عَلَيْهِ شَجَرَةً مِّن يَقْطِينٍ

147. And We sent him to a hundred thousand (folk) or more,

﴿١٤٧﴾ وَأَرْسَلْنَٰهُ إِلَىٰ مِائَةِ أَلْفٍ أَوْ يَزِيدُونَ

148. And they believed in him, therefore We gave them comfort for a while.

﴿١٤٨﴾ فَـَٔامَنُوا فَمَتَّعْنَٰهُمْ إِلَىٰ حِينٍ

149. Now ask them (O Muhammad): Have your Lord daughters whereas they have sons?

﴿١٤٩﴾ فَٱسْتَفْتِهِمْ أَلِرَبِّكَ ٱلْبَنَاتُ وَلَهُمُ ٱلْبَنُونَ

150. Or created We the angels females while they were present?

﴿١٥٠﴾ أَمْ خَلَقْنَا ٱلْمَلَٰٓئِكَةَ إِنَٰثًا وَهُمْ شَٰهِدُونَ

151. Lo! it is of their falsehood that they say:

﴿١٥١﴾ أَلَآ إِنَّهُم مِّنْ إِفْكِهِمْ لَيَقُولُونَ

152. Allah has begotten. And lo! surely they tell a lie.

﴿١٥٢﴾ وَلَدَ ٱللَّهُ وَإِنَّهُمْ لَكَٰذِبُونَ

153. Has he preferred daughters to sons?

﴿١٥٣﴾ أَصْطَفَى ٱلْبَنَاتِ عَلَى ٱلْبَنِينَ

154. What ails you? How judge you?

﴿١٥٤﴾ مَا لَكُمْ كَيْفَ تَحْكُمُونَ

155. Will you not then reflect?

﴿١٥٥﴾ أَفَلَا تَذَكَّرُونَ

156. Or have you a clear warrant?

﴿١٥٦﴾ أَمْ لَكُمْ سُلْطَٰنٌ مُّبِينٌ

157. Then produce your writ, if you are truthful.

﴿١٥٧﴾ فَأْتُوا بِكِتَٰبِكُمْ إِن كُنتُمْ صَٰدِقِينَ

158. And they imagine kinship between Him and the jinn, whereas the jinn know well that they will be brought before (Him).

﴿١٥٨﴾ وَجَعَلُوا بَيْنَهُ وَبَيْنَ ٱلْجِنَّةِ نَسَبًا وَلَقَدْ عَلِمَتِ ٱلْجِنَّةُ إِنَّهُمْ لَمُحْضَرُونَ

159. Glorified be Allah from that which they attribute (unto Him),

﴿١٥٩﴾ سُبْحَٰنَ ٱللَّهِ عَمَّا يَصِفُونَ

160. Save single minded slaves of Allah.

﴿١٦٠﴾ إِلَّا عِبَادَ ٱللَّهِ ٱلْمُخْلَصِينَ

161. Lo! surely, you and that which you worship,

﴿١٦١﴾ فَإِنَّكُمْ وَمَا تَعْبُدُونَ

162. You cannot excite (anyone) against Him

﴿١٦٢﴾ مَآ أَنتُمْ عَلَيْهِ بِفَٰتِنِينَ

163. Save him who is to burn in Hell.

﴿١٦٣﴾ إِلَّا مَنْ هُوَ صَالِ الْجَحِيمِ

164. There is not one of Us[230] but has his known position.

﴿١٦٤﴾ وَمَا مِنَّآ إِلَّا لَهُۥ مَقَامٌ مَّعْلُومٌ

165. Lo! We, even We are they who set the ranks.

﴿١٦٥﴾ وَإِنَّا لَنَحْنُ الصَّآفُّونَ

166. Lo! We, even We are they who hymn His praise.

﴿١٦٦﴾ وَإِنَّا لَنَحْنُ الْمُسَبِّحُونَ

167. And indeed they used to say:

﴿١٦٧﴾ وَإِن كَانُوا لَيَقُولُونَ

168. If we had but a reminder from the men of old

﴿١٦٨﴾ لَوْ أَنَّ عِندَنَا ذِكْرًا مِّنَ الْأَوَّلِينَ

169. We would be single-minded slaves of Allah.

﴿١٦٩﴾ لَكُنَّا عِبَادَ اللَّهِ الْمُخْلَصِينَ

170. Yet (now that it is come) they disbelieved therein: but they will come to know.

﴿١٧٠﴾ فَكَفَرُوا بِهِ ۖ فَسَوْفَ يَعْلَمُونَ

171. And surely Our word went forth of old unto Our bondmen sent (to warn)

﴿١٧١﴾ وَلَقَدْ سَبَقَتْ كَلِمَتُنَا لِعِبَادِنَا الْمُرْسَلِينَ

172. That they surely would be helped,

﴿١٧٢﴾ إِنَّهُمْ لَهُمُ الْمَنصُورُونَ

173. And that Our host, they surely would be the victors.

﴿١٧٣﴾ وَإِنَّ جُندَنَا لَهُمُ الْغَٰلِبُونَ

174. So withdraw from them (O Muhammad) awhile,

﴿١٧٤﴾ فَتَوَلَّ عَنْهُمْ حَتَّىٰ حِينٍ

175. And watch them, for they will (soon) see.

﴿١٧٥﴾ وَأَبْصِرْهُمْ فَسَوْفَ يُبْصِرُونَ

176. Would they hasten on Our doom?

﴿١٧٦﴾ أَفَبِعَذَابِنَا يَسْتَعْجِلُونَ

177. But when it comes home to them, then it will be an unlucky morn for those who have been warned.

﴿١٧٧﴾ فَإِذَا نَزَلَ بِسَاحَتِهِمْ فَسَآءَ صَبَاحُ الْمُنذَرِينَ

178. Withdraw from them awhile

﴿١٧٨﴾ وَتَوَلَّ عَنْهُمْ حَتَّىٰ حِينٍ

179. And watch them, for they will (soon) see.

﴿١٧٩﴾ وَأَبْصِرْ فَسَوْفَ يُبْصِرُونَ

180. Glorified be your Lord, the Lord of Majesty, from that which they attribute (unto Him)

﴿١٨٠﴾ سُبْحَٰنَ رَبِّكَ رَبِّ الْعِزَّةِ عَمَّا يَصِفُونَ

181. And peace be unto the messengers.

﴿١٨١﴾ وَسَلَٰمٌ عَلَى الْمُرْسَلِينَ

182. And praise be to Allah, Lord of the Worlds!

﴿١٨٢﴾ وَالْحَمْدُ لِلَّهِ رَبِّ الْعَٰلَمِينَ

---

[230]Here the revealing angel speaks in person.

Ṣād

Ṣād. This surah takes its name from the Arabic letter that stands alone as the first verse. Tradition says that the first ten verses were revealed either when the leaders of Quraysh tried to persuade Abū Ṭālib to withdraw his protection from the Prophet or when Abū Ṭālib died. The former is the more probable.

Its place is in the middle group of Makkan surahs.

Ṣād

Revealed at Makkah

*In the name of Allah,
the Beneficent, the Merciful*

1. **S**ād.
By the renowned Qur'an,

2. Nay, but those who disbelieve are in false pride and schism.

3. How many a generation We destroyed before them, and they cried out when it was no longer the time for escape!

4. And they marvel that a warner from among themselves has come unto them, and the disbelievers say: This is a wizard, a charlatan.

5. Makes he the gods One God? Lo! this is an astounding thing.

6. The chiefs among them go about, exhorting: Go and be staunch to your gods! Lo! this is a thing designed.

7. We have not heard of this in later religion. This is nothing but an invention.

8. Has the reminder been revealed unto him (alone) among us? Nay, but they are in doubt concerning My reminder; nay but they have not yet tasted My doom.

9. Or are theirs the treasures of the mercy of your Lord, the Mighty, the Bestower?

10. Or is the kingdom of the heavens and the earth and all that is between them theirs? Then let them ascend by ropes!

11. A defeated host are (all) the factions that are there.

12. The folk of Noah before them denied (their messenger) and (so did the tribe of) ʿĀd, and Pharaoh firmly planted,

١٢ كَذَّبَتْ قَبْلَهُمْ قَوْمُ نُوحٍ وَعَادٌ وَفِرْعَوْنُ ذُو الْأَوْتَادِ

13. And (the tribe of) Thamūd; and the folk of Lot, and the dwellers in the wood:[231] these were the factions.

١٣ وَثَمُودُ وَقَوْمُ لُوطٍ وَأَصْحَابُ لْئَيْكَةِ أُولَٰئِكَ الْأَحْزَابُ

14. Not one of them but did deny the messengers, therefore My doom was justified,

١٤ إِنْ كُلٌّ إِلَّا كَذَّبَ الرُّسُلَ فَحَقَّ عِقَابِ

15. These wait for but one Blast, there will be no second thereto.

١٥ وَمَا يَنْظُرُ هَٰؤُلَاءِ إِلَّا صَيْحَةً وَاحِدَةً مَا لَهَا مِنْ فَوَاقٍ

16. They say: Our Lord! Hasten on for us our fate before the Day of Reckoning.

١٦ وَقَالُوا رَبَّنَا عَجِّلْ لَنَا قِطَّنَا قَبْلَ يَوْمِ الْحِسَابِ

17. Bear with what they say, and remember Our bondman David, lord of might. Lo! he was ever turning in repentance (toward Allah).

١٧ اصْبِرْ عَلَىٰ مَا يَقُولُونَ وَاذْكُرْ عَبْدَنَا دَاوُودَ ذَا الْأَيْدِ إِنَّهُ أَوَّابٌ

18. Lo! We subdued the mountains to hymn the praises (of their Lord) with him at nightfall and sunrise,

١٨ إِنَّا سَخَّرْنَا الْجِبَالَ مَعَهُ يُسَبِّحْنَ بِالْعَشِيِّ وَالْإِشْرَاقِ

19. And the birds assembled; all were turning unto Him.

١٩ وَالطَّيْرَ مَحْشُورَةً كُلٌّ لَهُ أَوَّابٌ

20. We made his kingdom strong and gave him wisdom and decisive speech.

٢٠ وَشَدَدْنَا مُلْكَهُ وَآتَيْنَاهُ الْحِكْمَةَ وَفَصْلَ الْخِطَابِ

21. And has the story of the litigants come unto you? How they climbed the wall into the royal chamber;

٢١ وَهَلْ أَتَاكَ نَبَأُ الْخَصْمِ إِذْ تَسَوَّرُوا الْمِحْرَابَ

22. How they burst in upon David, and he was afraid of them. They said be not afraid (We are) two litigants, one of whom has wronged the other, therefore judge aright between us; be not unjust; and show us the fair way.

٢٢ إِذْ دَخَلُوا عَلَىٰ دَاوُودَ فَفَزِعَ مِنْهُمْ قَالُوا لَا تَخَفْ خَصْمَانِ بَغَىٰ بَعْضُنَا عَلَىٰ بَعْضٍ فَاحْكُمْ بَيْنَنَا بِالْحَقِّ وَلَا تُشْطِطْ وَاهْدِنَا إِلَىٰ سَوَاءِ الصِّرَاطِ

23. Lo! this my brother has ninety-nine ewes while I had one ewe; and he said: Entrust it to me, and he conquered me in speech.

٢٣ إِنَّ هَٰذَا أَخِي لَهُ تِسْعٌ وَتِسْعُونَ نَعْجَةً وَلِيَ نَعْجَةٌ وَاحِدَةٌ فَقَالَ أَكْفِلْنِيهَا وَعَزَّنِي فِي الْخِطَابِ

---

 [231]Madian.

24. (David) said: He has wronged you in demanding your ewe in addition to his ewes, and lo! many partners oppress one another, save such as believe and do good works, and they are few. And David guessed that We had tried him, and he sought forgiveness of his Lord, and he bowed himself and fell down prostrate and repented.

25. So We forgave him that; and lo! he had access to Our presence and a happy journey's end.

26. O David! Lo! We have set you as a viceroy in the earth; therefore judge aright between mankind, and follow not desire that it beguile you from the way of Allah. Lo! those who wander from the way of Allah have an awful doom, forasmuch as they forgot the Day of Reckoning.

27. So We created not the heaven and the earth and all that is between them in vain. That is the opinion of those who disbelieve. And woe unto those who disbelieve, from the Fire!

28. Shall We treat those who believe and do good works as those who spread corruption in the earth; or shall We treat the pious as the wicked?

29. (This is) a Scripture that We have revealed unto you, full of blessing, that they may ponder its revelations, and that men of understanding may reflect.

30. And We bestowed on David, Solomon. How excellent a slave! Lo! he was ever turning in repentance (toward Allah).

31. When there were shown to him at eventide light footed coursers

32. And he said: Lo! I have preferred the good things (of the world) to the remembrance of my Lord; till they were taken out of sight behind the curtain.

33. (Then he said): Bring them back to me, and fell to slashing (with his sword their) legs and necks.

34. And surely We tried Solomon, and set upon his throne a (mere) body. Then did he repent.

35. He said: My Lord! Forgive me and bestow on me sovereignty such shall not belong to any after me. Lo! You are indeed the Bestower.

36. So We made the wind subservient unto him, setting fair by his command whithersoever he intended.

37. And the devils, every builder and diver (made We subservient),

38. And others linked together in chains,

39. (Saying): This is Our gift, so bestow you, or withhold, without reckoning.

40. And lo! he has favor with Us, and a happy journey's end.

41. And make mention (O Muhammad) of Our bondman Job, when he cried unto his Lord (saying): Lo! the Devil does afflict me with distress and torment.

42. (And it was said unto him): Strike the ground with your foot. This (spring) is a cool bath and a refreshing drink.

43. And We bestowed on him (again) his household and therewith the like thereof, a mercy from Us, and a memorial for men of understanding.

44. And (it was said unto him): Take in your hand a bunch and smite therewith, and break not your oath. Lo! We found him steadfast, how excellent a slave! Lo! he was ever turning in repentance (to his Lord).

45. And make mention of our bondmen, Abraham, Isaac and Jacob, men of hands and sights.

46. Lo! We purified them with a pure thought, remembrance of the Home (of the Hereafter).

47. Lo! in Our sight they are surely of the elect, the excellent.

٣٣ رُدُّوهَا عَلَيَّ فَطَفِقَ مَسْحًا بِالسُّوقِ وَالْأَعْنَاقِ

٣٤ وَلَقَدْ فَتَنَّا سُلَيْمَنَ وَأَلْقَيْنَا عَلَى كُرْسِيِّهِ جَسَدًا ثُمَّ أَنَابَ

٣٥ قَالَ رَبِّ اغْفِرْ لِي وَهَبْ لِي مُلْكًا لَّا يَنْبَغِي لِأَحَدٍ مِّنْ بَعْدِيٓ إِنَّكَ أَنتَ الْوَهَّابُ

٣٦ فَسَخَّرْنَا لَهُ الرِّيحَ تَجْرِي بِأَمْرِهِ رُخَاءً حَيْثُ أَصَابَ

٣٧ وَالشَّيَٰطِينَ كُلَّ بَنَّاءٍ وَغَوَّاصٍ

٣٨ وَءَاخَرِينَ مُقَرَّنِينَ فِي الْأَصْفَادِ

٣٩ هَذَا عَطَاؤُنَا فَامْنُنْ أَوْ أَمْسِكْ بِغَيْرِ حِسَابٍ

٤٠ وَإِنَّ لَهُ عِندَنَا لَزُلْفَىٰ وَحُسْنَ مَئَابٍ

٤١ وَاذْكُرْ عَبْدَنَآ أَيُّوبَ إِذْ نَادَىٰ رَبَّهُ أَنِّي مَسَّنِيَ الشَّيْطَنُ بِنُصْبٍ وَعَذَابٍ

٤٢ ارْكُضْ بِرِجْلِكَ هَذَا مُغْتَسَلٌ بَارِدٌ وَشَرَابٌ

٤٣ وَوَهَبْنَا لَهُ أَهْلَهُ وَمِثْلَهُم مَّعَهُمْ رَحْمَةً مِّنَّا وَذِكْرَىٰ لِأُولِي الْأَلْبَٰبِ

٤٤ وَخُذْ بِيَدِكَ ضِغْثًا فَاضْرِب بِّهِ وَلَا تَحْنَثْ إِنَّا وَجَدْنَٰهُ صَابِرًا نِّعْمَ الْعَبْدُ إِنَّهُ أَوَّابٌ

٤٥ وَاذْكُرْ عِبَٰدَنَآ إِبْرَٰهِيمَ وَإِسْحَٰقَ وَيَعْقُوبَ أُوْلِي الْأَيْدِي وَالْأَبْصَٰرِ

٤٦ إِنَّآ أَخْلَصْنَٰهُم بِخَالِصَةٍ ذِكْرَى الدَّارِ

٤٧ وَإِنَّهُمْ عِندَنَا لَمِنَ الْمُصْطَفَيْنَ الْأَخْيَارِ

48. And make mention of Ishmael and Elisha and Dhū al Kifl.232 All are of the chosen.

49. This is a reminder. And lo! for those who ward off (evil) is a happy journey's end,

50. Gardens of Eden, whereof the gates are opened for them.

51. Wherein, reclining, they call for plenteous fruit and cool drink (that is) therein.

52. And with them are those of modest gaze, companions.

53. This it is that you are promised for the Day of Reckoning.

54. Lo! this in truth is Our provision, which will never waste away.

55. This (is for the righteous). And lo! for the transgressors there will be an evil journey's end,

56. Hell, where they will burn, an evil resting place.

57. Here is a boiling and an ice cold draught, so let them taste it,

58. And other (torment) of the kind in pairs (the two extremes)!

59. Here is an army rushing blindly with you. (Those who are already in the fire say): No word of welcome for them. Lo! they will roast at the Fire.

60. They say: Nay, but you (misleaders), for you there is no word of welcome. You prepared this for us (by your misleading). Now unlucky is the plight.

61. They say: Our Lord! Whoever did prepare this for Us, oh, give him double portion of the Fire!

62. And they say: What ails us that we behold not men whom we were wont to count among the wicked?

63. Did we take them (wrongly) for a laughing stock, or have our eyes missed them?

232A prophet of the Arabs whose story is like that of Ezekiel.

64. Lo! that is the truth indeed: the wrangling of the dwellers in the Fire.

٦٤ إِنَّ ذَٰلِكَ لَحَقٌّ تَخَاصُمُ أَهْلِ النَّارِ

65. Say (unto them, O Muhammad): I am only a warner, and there is no God save Allah, the One, the Overcoming,

٦٥ قُلْ إِنَّمَا أَنَا مُنذِرٌ وَمَا مِنْ إِلَٰهٍ إِلَّا اللَّهُ الْوَاحِدُ الْقَهَّارُ

66. Lord of the heavens and the earth and all that is between them, the Mighty, the Pardoning.

٦٦ رَبُّ السَّمَاوَاتِ وَالْأَرْضِ وَمَا بَيْنَهُمَا الْعَزِيزُ الْغَفَّارُ

67. Say: It is a tremendous tidings

٦٧ قُلْ هُوَ نَبَأٌ عَظِيمٌ

68. Whereof you turn away!

٦٨ أَنتُمْ عَنْهُ مُعْرِضُونَ

69. I had no knowledge of the Highest Chiefs (the arch-angels) when they disputed;

٦٩ مَا كَانَ لِيَ مِنْ عِلْمٍ بِالْمَلَإِ الْأَعْلَىٰ إِذْ يَخْتَصِمُونَ

70. It is revealed unto me only that I may be a plain warner.

٧٠ إِن يُوحَىٰ إِلَيَّ إِلَّا أَنَّمَا أَنَا نَذِيرٌ مُّبِينٌ

71. When your Lord said unto the angels: lo! I am about to create a mortal out of mire,

٧١ إِذْ قَالَ رَبُّكَ لِلْمَلَائِكَةِ إِنِّي خَالِقٌ بَشَرًا مِّن طِينٍ

72. And when I have fashioned him and breathed into him of My spirit, then fall down before him prostrate,

٧٢ فَإِذَا سَوَّيْتُهُ وَنَفَخْتُ فِيهِ مِن رُّوحِي فَقَعُوا لَهُ سَاجِدِينَ

73. The angels fell down prostrate, every one.

٧٣ فَسَجَدَ الْمَلَائِكَةُ كُلُّهُمْ أَجْمَعُونَ

74. Saving Iblīs, he was arrogant and became one of the disbelievers.

٧٤ إِلَّا إِبْلِيسَ اسْتَكْبَرَ وَكَانَ مِنَ الْكَافِرِينَ

75. He said: O Iblīs! What hinders you from falling prostrate before that which I have created with both My hands?[233] Are you too proud or are you of the high exalted?

٧٥ قَالَ يَا إِبْلِيسُ مَا مَنَعَكَ أَن تَسْجُدَ لِمَا خَلَقْتُ بِيَدَيَّ أَسْتَكْبَرْتَ أَمْ كُنتَ مِنَ الْعَالِينَ

76. He said: I am better than him. You created me of fire, whilst him You did create of clay.

٧٦ قَالَ أَنَا خَيْرٌ مِّنْهُ خَلَقْتَنِي مِن نَّارٍ وَخَلَقْتَهُ مِن طِينٍ

77. He said: Go forth from hence, for lo! you are outcast,

٧٧ قَالَ فَاخْرُجْ مِنْهَا فَإِنَّكَ رَجِيمٌ

78. And lo! My curse is on you till the Day of Judgment.

٧٨ وَإِنَّ عَلَيْكَ لَعْنَتِي إِلَىٰ يَوْمِ الدِّينِ

---

[233]Man, as typified by Adam, is in himself nothing but frail clay. But as fashioned by Allah's creative power into something with Allah's spirit breathed into him, his dignity is raised above that of the highest creatures (the editor).

79. He said: My Lord! Reprieve me till the day when they are raised.

٧٩) قَالَ رَبِّ فَأَنظِرْنِيٓ إِلَىٰ يَوْمِ يُبْعَثُونَ

80. He said: Lo! you are of those reprieved

٨٠) قَالَ فَإِنَّكَ مِنَ ٱلْمُنظَرِينَ

81. Until the day of the time appointed.

٨١) إِلَىٰ يَوْمِ ٱلْوَقْتِ ٱلْمَعْلُومِ

82. He said: Then, by Your might, I surely will beguile them every one,

٨٢) قَالَ فَبِعِزَّتِكَ لَأُغْوِيَنَّهُمْ أَجْمَعِينَ

83. Save Your single-minded slaves among them.

٨٣) إِلَّا عِبَادَكَ مِنْهُمُ ٱلْمُخْلَصِينَ

84. He said: The Truth is, and the Truth I speak,

٨٤) قَالَ فَٱلْحَقُّ وَٱلْحَقَّ أَقُولُ

85. That I shall fill Hell with you and with such of them as follow you, together.

٨٥) لَأَمْلَأَنَّ جَهَنَّمَ مِنكَ وَمِمَّن تَبِعَكَ مِنْهُمْ أَجْمَعِينَ

86. Say (O Muhammad, unto mankind): I ask of you no fee for this, and I am no impostor.

٨٦) قُلْ مَآ أَسْـَٔلُكُمْ عَلَيْهِ مِنْ أَجْرٍ وَمَآ أَنَا۠ مِنَ ٱلْمُتَكَلِّفِينَ

87. Lo! it is nothing else than a reminder for all mankind

٨٧) إِنْ هُوَ إِلَّا ذِكْرٌ لِّلْعَٰلَمِينَ

88. And you will come in time to know the truth thereof.

٨٨) وَلَتَعْلَمُنَّ نَبَأَهُ بَعْدَ حِينٍ

The Troops

Al Zumar, "The Troops," takes its name from a peculiar word, which appears in verses 71 and 73, that means "troops or companies." Some authorities think that verses 53-54 were revealed at al Madinah.

It seems manifestly to belong to the middle group of Makkan surahs, though Noldeke places it in his last group.

The Troops

Revealed at Makkah

*In the name of Allah,
the Beneficent, the Merciful*

1. The revelation of the Scripture is from Allah, the Mighty, the Wise.

2. Lo! We have revealed the Scripture unto you (Muham-mad) with truth; so worship Allah, making religion pure for Him (only).

3. Surely pure religion is for Allah only. And those who choose protecting friends beside Him (say): We worship them only that they may bring us near unto Allah. Lo! Allah will judge between them concerning that wherein they differ. Lo! Allah guides not him who is a liar, an ingrate.

4. If Allah had willed to choose a son, he could have chosen what he would of that which He has created. Be He glorified! He is Allah, the One, the Absolute.

5. He has created the heavens and the earth with truth. He makes night to encircle day, and He makes day to encircle night, and He constrains the sun and the moon to give service, each running on for an appointed term. Indeed He is the Mighty, the Forgiver?

6. He created you from one being, then from that (being) He made its mate; and He has provided for you of cattle eight kinds. He created you in the wombs of your mothers, creation after creation, in a threefold gloom. Such is Allah, your Lord. His is the Sovereignty. There is no God save Him. How then are you turned away?,

7. If you are thankless, yet Allah is Independent of you, though He is not pleased with thanklessness for His bondmen; and if you are thankful He is pleased therewith for you. No laden soul will bear another's load. Then unto your Lord is your return; and He will tell you what you used to do. Lo! He knows what is in the breasts (of men).

٧ إِن تَكْفُرُوا فَإِنَّ اللَّهَ غَنِيٌّ عَنكُمْ وَلَا يَرْضَىٰ لِعِبَادِهِ الْكُفْرَ وَإِن تَشْكُرُوا يَرْضَهُ لَكُمْ وَلَا تَزِرُ وَازِرَةٌ وِزْرَ أُخْرَىٰ ثُمَّ إِلَىٰ رَبِّكُم مَّرْجِعُكُمْ فَيُنَبِّئُكُم بِمَا كُنتُمْ تَعْمَلُونَ إِنَّهُ عَلِيمٌ بِذَاتِ الصُّدُورِ

8. And when some hurt touches man, he cries unto his Lord, turning unto Him (repentant). Then, when He grants him a boon from Him he forgets that for which he cried unto Him before, and sets up rivals to Allah that he may beguile (men) from His way. Say (O Muhammad, unto such one): Take pleasure in your disbelief a while. Lo! you are of the owners of the Fire.

٨ وَإِذَا مَسَّ الْإِنسَانَ ضُرٌّ دَعَا رَبَّهُ مُنِيبًا إِلَيْهِ ثُمَّ إِذَا خَوَّلَهُ نِعْمَةً مِّنْهُ نَسِيَ مَا كَانَ يَدْعُوا إِلَيْهِ مِن قَبْلُ وَجَعَلَ لِلَّهِ أَندَادًا لِّيُضِلَّ عَن سَبِيلِهِ قُلْ تَمَتَّعْ بِكُفْرِكَ قَلِيلًا إِنَّكَ مِنْ أَصْحَابِ النَّارِ

9. Is he who pays adoration in the watches of the night, prostrate and standing, bewaring of the Hereafter and hoping for the mercy of his Lord, (to be accounted equal with a disbeliever)? Say (unto them, O Muhammad): Are those who know equal with those who know not? But only men of understanding will pay heed.

٩ أَمَّنْ هُوَ قَانِتٌ آنَاءَ اللَّيْلِ سَاجِدًا وَقَائِمًا يَحْذَرُ الْآخِرَةَ وَيَرْجُوا رَحْمَةَ رَبِّهِ قُلْ هَلْ يَسْتَوِي الَّذِينَ يَعْلَمُونَ وَالَّذِينَ لَا يَعْلَمُونَ إِنَّمَا يَتَذَكَّرُ أُولُوا الْأَلْبَابِ

10. Say: O My bondmen who believe! Observe your duty to your Lord. For those who do good in this world there is good, and Allah's earth is spacious. Verily the steadfast will be paid their wages without stint.

١٠ قُلْ يَا عِبَادِ الَّذِينَ آمَنُوا اتَّقُوا رَبَّكُمْ لِلَّذِينَ أَحْسَنُوا فِي هَٰذِهِ الدُّنْيَا حَسَنَةٌ وَأَرْضُ اللَّهِ وَاسِعَةٌ إِنَّمَا يُوَفَّى الصَّابِرُونَ أَجْرَهُم بِغَيْرِ حِسَابٍ

11. Say (O Muhammad): Lo! I am commanded to worship Allah, making religion pure for Him (only).

١١ قُلْ إِنِّي أُمِرْتُ أَنْ أَعْبُدَ اللَّهَ مُخْلِصًا لَّهُ الدِّينَ

12. And I am commanded to be the first of Muslims.[234]

١٢ وَأُمِرْتُ لِأَنْ أَكُونَ أَوَّلَ الْمُسْلِمِينَ

13. Say: Lo! if I should disobey my Lord, I fear the doom of a tremendous Day.

١٣ قُلْ إِنِّي أَخَافُ إِنْ عَصَيْتُ رَبِّي عَذَابَ يَوْمٍ عَظِيمٍ

14. Say: Allah I worship, making my religion pure for Him (only).

١٤ قُلِ اللَّهَ أَعْبُدُ مُخْلِصًا لَّهُ دِينِي

---

[234]Those who surrender to Allah.

15. Then worship what you will beside Him. Say: The losers will be those who lose themselves and their housefolk on the Day of Resurrection. Ah, that will be the manifest loss!

16. They have an awning of fire above them and beneath them a dais (of fire). With this does Allah appall His bond-men. O My bondmen, therefore fear Me!

17. And those who put away false gods lest they should worship them and turn to Allah in repentance, for them there are glad tidings. Therefore give good tidings (O Muham-mad) to my bondmen

18. Who hear advice and follow the best thereof. Such are those whom Allah guides, and such are men of under-standing.

19. Is he on whom the word of doom is fulfilled (to be helped), and can you (O Muhammad) rescue him who is in the Fire?

20. But those who keep their duty to their Lord, for them are lofty chambers with lofty chambers above them, built (for them), beneath which rivers flow. (It is) a promise of Allah. Allah fails not His promise.

21. Have you not seen how Allah has sent down water from the sky and has caused it to penetrate the earth as water springs, and afterward thereby produces crops of divers hues; and afterward they wither and you see them turn yellow; then He makes them chaff. Lo! herein truly is a reminder for men of understanding.

22. Is he whose bosom Allah has expanded for the Surrender,[235] so that he follows a light from His Lord, (as he who disbelieves)? Then woe unto those whose hearts are hardened against remembrance of Allah. Such are in plain error.

﴿١٥﴾ فَاعْبُدُوا مَا شِئْتُم مِّن دُونِهِ قُلْ إِنَّ الْخَاسِرِينَ الَّذِينَ خَسِرُوا أَنفُسَهُمْ وَأَهْلِيهِمْ يَوْمَ الْقِيَامَةِ أَلَا ذَٰلِكَ هُوَ الْخُسْرَانُ الْمُبِينُ

﴿١٦﴾ لَهُم مِّن فَوْقِهِمْ ظُلَلٌ مِّنَ النَّارِ وَمِن تَحْتِهِمْ ظُلَلٌ ذَٰلِكَ يُخَوِّفُ اللَّهُ بِهِ عِبَادَهُ يَا عِبَادِ فَاتَّقُونِ

﴿١٧﴾ وَالَّذِينَ اجْتَنَبُوا الطَّاغُوتَ أَن يَعْبُدُوهَا وَأَنَابُوا إِلَى اللَّهِ لَهُمُ الْبُشْرَىٰ فَبَشِّرْ عِبَادِ

﴿١٨﴾ الَّذِينَ يَسْتَمِعُونَ الْقَوْلَ فَيَتَّبِعُونَ أَحْسَنَهُ أُولَٰئِكَ الَّذِينَ هَدَاهُمُ اللَّهُ وَأُولَٰئِكَ هُمْ أُولُو الْأَلْبَابِ

﴿١٩﴾ أَفَمَنْ حَقَّ عَلَيْهِ كَلِمَةُ الْعَذَابِ أَفَأَنتَ تُنقِذُ مَن فِي النَّارِ

﴿٢٠﴾ لَٰكِنِ الَّذِينَ اتَّقَوْا رَبَّهُمْ لَهُمْ غُرَفٌ مِّن فَوْقِهَا غُرَفٌ مَّبْنِيَّةٌ تَجْرِي مِن تَحْتِهَا الْأَنْهَارُ وَعْدَ اللَّهِ لَا يُخْلِفُ اللَّهُ الْمِيعَادَ

﴿٢١﴾ أَلَمْ تَرَ أَنَّ اللَّهَ أَنزَلَ مِنَ السَّمَاءِ مَاءً فَسَلَكَهُ يَنَابِيعَ فِي الْأَرْضِ ثُمَّ يُخْرِجُ بِهِ زَرْعًا مُّخْتَلِفًا أَلْوَانُهُ ثُمَّ يَهِيجُ فَتَرَاهُ مُصْفَرًّا ثُمَّ يَجْعَلُهُ حُطَامًا إِنَّ فِي ذَٰلِكَ لَذِكْرَىٰ لِأُولِي الْأَلْبَابِ

﴿٢٢﴾ أَفَمَن شَرَحَ اللَّهُ صَدْرَهُ لِلْإِسْلَامِ فَهُوَ عَلَىٰ نُورٍ مِّن رَّبِّهِ فَوَيْلٌ لِّلْقَاسِيَةِ قُلُوبُهُم مِّن ذِكْرِ اللَّهِ أُولَٰئِكَ فِي ضَلَالٍ مُّبِينٍ

---

[235]Arabic: Islām.

23. Allah has (now) revealed the fairest of statements, a Scripture consistent, (wherein promises of reward are) paired (with threats of punishment), whereat does tremble the skins of those who fear their Lord, then their skins and their hearts soften to Allah's reminder. Such is Allah's guidance, wherewith He guides whom He will. And him whom Allah sends astray, for him there is no guide.

24. Is he then, who will strike his face against the awful doom upon the Day of Resurrection (as he who does right)? And it will be said unto the wrongdoers: Taste what you used to earn.

25. Those before them denied, and so the doom came on them whence they knew not.

26. Thus Allah made them taste humiliation in the life of the world, and surely the doom of the Hereafter will be greater if they did but know.

27. And surely We have coined for mankind in this Qur'an all kinds of similitudes, that they may reflect;

28. A Lecture236 in Arabic, containing no crookedness, that they may ward off (evil).

29. Allah coins a similitude: A man in relation to whom are several part-owners, quarreling, and a man belonging wholly to one man. Are the two equal in similitude? Praise be to Allah! But most of them know not.

30. Lo! you will die, and lo! they will die;

31. Then lo! on the Day of Resurrection, before your Lord you will dispute.

32. And who does greater wrong than he who tells a lie against Allah, and denies the truth when it reaches him? Will not the home of disbelievers be in Hell?

236Arabic: Qur'ān.

٢٣ اللَّهُ نَزَّلَ أَحْسَنَ الْحَدِيثِ كِتَابًا مُّتَشَابِهًا مَّثَانِيَ تَقْشَعِرُّ مِنْهُ جُلُودُ الَّذِينَ يَخْشَوْنَ رَبَّهُمْ ثُمَّ تَلِينُ جُلُودُهُمْ وَقُلُوبُهُمْ إِلَى ذِكْرِ اللَّهِ ذَلِكَ هُدَى اللَّهِ يَهْدِي بِهِ مَن يَشَاءُ وَمَن يُضْلِلِ اللَّهُ فَمَا لَهُ مِنْ هَادٍ

٢٤ أَفَمَن يَتَّقِي بِوَجْهِهِ سُوءَ الْعَذَابِ يَوْمَ الْقِيَامَةِ وَقِيلَ لِلظَّالِمِينَ ذُوقُوا مَا كُنتُمْ تَكْسِبُونَ

٢٥ كَذَّبَ الَّذِينَ مِن قَبْلِهِمْ فَأَتَاهُمُ الْعَذَابُ مِنْ حَيْثُ لَا يَشْعُرُونَ

٢٦ فَأَذَاقَهُمُ اللَّهُ الْخِزْيَ فِي الْحَيَاةِ الدُّنْيَا وَلَعَذَابُ الْآخِرَةِ أَكْبَرُ لَوْ كَانُوا يَعْلَمُونَ

٢٧ وَلَقَدْ ضَرَبْنَا لِلنَّاسِ فِي هَذَا الْقُرْآنِ مِن كُلِّ مَثَلٍ لَّعَلَّهُمْ يَتَذَكَّرُونَ

٢٨ قُرْآنًا عَرَبِيًّا غَيْرَ ذِي عِوَجٍ لَّعَلَّهُمْ يَتَّقُونَ

٢٩ ضَرَبَ اللَّهُ مَثَلًا رَّجُلًا فِيهِ شُرَكَاءُ مُتَشَاكِسُونَ وَرَجُلًا سَلَمًا لِّرَجُلٍ هَلْ يَسْتَوِيَانِ مَثَلًا الْحَمْدُ لِلَّهِ بَلْ أَكْثَرُهُمْ لَا يَعْلَمُونَ

٣٠ إِنَّكَ مَيِّتٌ وَإِنَّهُم مَّيِّتُونَ

٣١ ثُمَّ إِنَّكُمْ يَوْمَ الْقِيَامَةِ عِندَ رَبِّكُمْ تَخْتَصِمُونَ

٣٢ فَمَنْ أَظْلَمُ مِمَّن كَذَبَ عَلَى اللَّهِ وَكَذَّبَ بِالصِّدْقِ إِذْ جَاءَهُ أَلَيْسَ فِي جَهَنَّمَ مَثْوًى لِّلْكَافِرِينَ

33. And who brings the truth and believes therein—such are the dutiful.

34. They shall have what they will of their Lord's bounty. That is the reward of the good:

35. That Allah will remit from them the worst of what they did, and will pay them for reward the best they used to do.

36. Will not Allah defend His slave? Yet they would frighten you with those beside Him. He whom Allah sends astray, for him there is no guide.

37. And he whom Allah guides, for him there can be no misleader. Is not Allah Mighty, Able to Requite (the wrong)?

38. And surely, if you should ask them: Who created the heavens and the earth? they will say: Allah. Say: Think you then of those you worship beside Allah, if Allah willed some hurt for me, could they remove from me His hurt; or if He willed some mercy for me, could they restrain His mercy? Say: Allah is my all. In Him do (all) the trusting put their trust.

39. Say: O my people! Act in your manner. I too am acting. Thus you will come to know

40. Who it is unto whom comes a doom that will abase him, and on whom there falls everlasting doom.

41. Lo! We have revealed unto you (Muhammad) the Scrip-ture for mankind with truth. Then whosoever goes right it is for his soul, and whoever strays, strays only to its hurt. And you are not a warder over them.

٣٣ وَالَّذِى جَآءَ بِالصِّدْقِ وَصَدَّقَ بِهِۦٓ أُوْلَٰٓئِكَ هُمُ الْمُتَّقُونَ

٣٤ لَهُم مَّا يَشَآءُونَ عِندَ رَبِّهِمْ ذَٰلِكَ جَزَآءُ الْمُحْسِنِينَ

٣٥ لِيُكَفِّرَ اللَّهُ عَنْهُمْ أَسْوَأَ الَّذِى عَمِلُواْ وَيَجْزِيَهُمْ أَجْرَهُم بِأَحْسَنِ الَّذِى كَانُواْ يَعْمَلُونَ

٣٦ أَلَيْسَ اللَّهُ بِكَافٍ عَبْدَهُۥ وَيُخَوِّفُونَكَ بِالَّذِينَ مِن دُونِهِۦ وَمَن يُضْلِلِ اللَّهُ فَمَا لَهُۥ مِنْ هَادٍ

٣٧ وَمَن يَهْدِ اللَّهُ فَمَا لَهُۥ مِن مُّضِلٍّ أَلَيْسَ اللَّهُ بِعَزِيزٍ ذِى انتِقَامٍ

٣٨ وَلَئِن سَأَلْتَهُم مَّنْ خَلَقَ السَّمَٰوَٰتِ وَالْأَرْضَ لَيَقُولُنَّ اللَّهُ قُلْ أَفَرَءَيْتُم مَّا تَدْعُونَ مِن دُونِ اللَّهِ إِنْ أَرَادَنِىَ اللَّهُ بِضُرٍّ هَلْ هُنَّ كَٰشِفَٰتُ ضُرِّهِۦٓ أَوْ أَرَادَنِى بِرَحْمَةٍ هَلْ هُنَّ مُمْسِكَٰتُ رَحْمَتِهِۦ قُلْ حَسْبِىَ اللَّهُ عَلَيْهِ يَتَوَكَّلُ الْمُتَوَكِّلُونَ

٣٩ قُلْ يَٰقَوْمِ اعْمَلُواْ عَلَىٰ مَكَانَتِكُمْ إِنِّى عَٰمِلٌ فَسَوْفَ تَعْلَمُونَ

٤٠ مَن يَأْتِيهِ عَذَابٌ يُخْزِيهِ وَيَحِلُّ عَلَيْهِ عَذَابٌ مُّقِيمٌ

٤١ إِنَّآ أَنزَلْنَا عَلَيْكَ الْكِتَٰبَ لِلنَّاسِ بِالْحَقِّ فَمَنِ اهْتَدَىٰ فَلِنَفْسِهِۦ وَمَن ضَلَّ فَإِنَّمَا يَضِلُّ عَلَيْهَا وَمَآ أَنتَ عَلَيْهِم بِوَكِيلٍ

42. Allah receives (men's) souls at the time of their death, and that (soul) which dies not (yet) in its sleep. He keeps that (soul) for which He has ordained death and dismisses the rest till an appointed term. Lo! herein verily are portents for people who take thought.

43. Or choose they intercessors other than Allah? Say: What! Even though they have power over nothing and have no intelligence?

44. Say: Unto Allah belongs all intercession. His is the Sovereignty of the heavens and the earth. And afterward unto Him you will be brought back.

45. And when Allah alone is mentioned, the hearts of those who believe not in the Hereafter are repelled, and when those (whom they worship) beside Him are mentioned, behold! they are glad.

46. Say: O Allah! Creator of the heavens and the earth! Knower of the invisible and the visible! You will judge between Your slaves concerning that wherein they used to differ.

47. Had those who do wrong the possession of all that is in the earth, and therewith as much again, they surely will seek to ransom themselves therewith on the Day of Resurrection from the awful doom; and there will appear unto them, from their Lord, that wherewith they never reckoned.

48. And the evils that they earned will appear unto them, and that whereat they used to scoff will surround them.

49. Now when hurt touches a man he cries unto Us, and afterward when We have granted him a boon from Us, he said: Only by force of knowledge I obtained it. Nay, but it is a test. But most of them know not.

٤٢ اللهُ يَتَوَفَّى الْأَنْفُسَ حِينَ مَوْتِهَا وَالَّتِي لَمْ تَمُتْ فِي مَنَامِهَا فَيُمْسِكُ الَّتِي قَضَى عَلَيْهَا الْمَوْتَ وَيُرْسِلُ الْأُخْرَى إِلَى أَجَلٍ مُسَمًّى إِنَّ فِي ذَلِكَ لَآيَاتٍ لِقَوْمٍ يَتَفَكَّرُونَ

٤٣ أَمِ اتَّخَذُوا مِن دُونِ اللهِ شُفَعَاءَ قُلْ أَوَلَوْ كَانُوا لَا يَمْلِكُونَ شَيْئًا وَلَا يَعْقِلُونَ

٤٤ قُل لِّلَّهِ الشَّفَاعَةُ جَمِيعًا لَّهُ مُلْكُ السَّمَوَاتِ وَالْأَرْضِ ثُمَّ إِلَيْهِ تُرْجَعُونَ

٤٥ وَإِذَا ذُكِرَ اللهُ وَحْدَهُ اشْمَأَزَّتْ قُلُوبُ الَّذِينَ لَا يُؤْمِنُونَ بِالْآخِرَةِ وَإِذَا ذُكِرَ الَّذِينَ مِن دُونِهِ إِذَا هُمْ يَسْتَبْشِرُونَ

٤٦ قُلِ اللَّهُمَّ فَاطِرَ السَّمَوَاتِ وَالْأَرْضِ عَالِمَ الْغَيْبِ وَالشَّهَادَةِ أَنتَ تَحْكُمُ بَيْنَ عِبَادِكَ فِي مَا كَانُوا فِيهِ يَخْتَلِفُونَ

٤٧ وَلَوْ أَنَّ لِلَّذِينَ ظَلَمُوا مَا فِي الْأَرْضِ جَمِيعًا وَمِثْلَهُ مَعَهُ لَافْتَدَوْا بِهِ مِن سُوءِ الْعَذَابِ يَوْمَ الْقِيَامَةِ وَبَدَا لَهُم مِّنَ اللهِ مَا لَمْ يَكُونُوا يَحْتَسِبُونَ

٤٨ وَبَدَا لَهُمْ سَيِّئَاتُ مَا كَسَبُوا وَحَاقَ بِهِم مَّا كَانُوا بِهِ يَسْتَهْزِئُونَ

٤٩ فَإِذَا مَسَّ الْإِنسَانَ ضُرٌّ دَعَانَا ثُمَّ إِذَا خَوَّلْنَاهُ نِعْمَةً مِّنَّا قَالَ إِنَّمَا أُوتِيتُهُ عَلَى عِلْمٍ بَلْ هِيَ فِتْنَةٌ وَلَكِنَّ أَكْثَرَهُمْ لَا يَعْلَمُونَ

50. Those before them said it, yet (all) that they had earned availed them not;

51. But the evils that they earned smote them; and such of these as do wrong, the evils that they earn will smite them; they cannot escape.

52. Know they not that Allah enlarges providence for whom He will, and straitens it (for whom He will). Lo! herein surely are portents for people who believe.

53. Say: My slaves who have been prodigal against their own souls! Despair not of the mercy of Allah, For Allah indeed forgives all sins. Lo! He is the Forgiving, the Merciful.

54. Turn unto your Lord repentant, and surrender unto Him, before there come unto you the doom, when you cannot be helped.

55. And follow the best (the Qur'an) of that which is revealed unto you from your Lord, before the doom comes on you suddenly when you feel not,

56. Lest any soul should say Alas, my grief that I was unmindful of Allah, and I was indeed among the scoffers!

57. Or should say: if Allah had but guided me I should have been among the dutiful!

58. Or should say, when it sees the doom: Oh, that I had but a second chance that I might be among the righteous!

59. (But now the answer will be): Nay, for My revelations came unto you, but you did deny them and were scornful and were among the disbelievers.

﴿٥٠﴾ قَدْ قَالَهَا الَّذِينَ مِن قَبْلِهِمْ فَمَا أَغْنَىٰ عَنْهُم مَّا كَانُوا يَكْسِبُونَ

﴿٥١﴾ فَأَصَابَهُمْ سَيِّئَاتُ مَا كَسَبُوا وَالَّذِينَ ظَلَمُوا مِنْ هَٰؤُلَاءِ سَيُصِيبُهُمْ سَيِّئَاتُ مَا كَسَبُوا وَمَا هُم بِمُعْجِزِينَ

﴿٥٢﴾ أَوَلَمْ يَعْلَمُوا أَنَّ اللَّهَ يَبْسُطُ الرِّزْقَ لِمَن يَشَاءُ وَيَقْدِرُ إِنَّ فِي ذَٰلِكَ لَآيَاتٍ لِّقَوْمٍ يُؤْمِنُونَ

﴿٥٣﴾ ۞ قُلْ يَا عِبَادِيَ الَّذِينَ أَسْرَفُوا عَلَىٰ أَنفُسِهِمْ لَا تَقْنَطُوا مِن رَّحْمَةِ اللَّهِ إِنَّ اللَّهَ يَغْفِرُ الذُّنُوبَ جَمِيعًا إِنَّهُ هُوَ الْغَفُورُ الرَّحِيمُ

﴿٥٤﴾ وَأَنِيبُوا إِلَىٰ رَبِّكُمْ وَأَسْلِمُوا لَهُ مِن قَبْلِ أَن يَأْتِيَكُمُ الْعَذَابُ ثُمَّ لَا تُنصَرُونَ

﴿٥٥﴾ وَاتَّبِعُوا أَحْسَنَ مَا أُنزِلَ إِلَيْكُم مِّن رَّبِّكُم مِّن قَبْلِ أَن يَأْتِيَكُمُ الْعَذَابُ بَغْتَةً وَأَنتُمْ لَا تَشْعُرُونَ

﴿٥٦﴾ أَن تَقُولَ نَفْسٌ يَا حَسْرَتَىٰ عَلَىٰ مَا فَرَّطتُ فِي جَنبِ اللَّهِ وَإِن كُنتُ لَمِنَ السَّاخِرِينَ

﴿٥٧﴾ أَوْ تَقُولَ لَوْ أَنَّ اللَّهَ هَدَانِي لَكُنتُ مِنَ الْمُتَّقِينَ

﴿٥٨﴾ أَوْ تَقُولَ حِينَ تَرَى الْعَذَابَ لَوْ أَنَّ لِي كَرَّةً فَأَكُونَ مِنَ الْمُحْسِنِينَ

﴿٥٩﴾ بَلَىٰ قَدْ جَاءَتْكَ آيَاتِي فَكَذَّبْتَ بِهَا وَاسْتَكْبَرْتَ وَكُنتَ مِنَ الْكَافِرِينَ

60. And on the Day of Resurrection you (Muhammad) see those who lied concerning Allah with their faces blackened. Is not the home of the arrogant in Hell?

61. And Allah delivers those who ward off (evil) because of their deserts. Evil touches them not, nor do they grieve.

62. Allah is Creator of all things, and He is Guardian over all things.

63. His are the keys of the heavens and the earth, and they who disbelieve the revelations of Allah—such are they who are the losers.

64. Say (O Muhammad, to the disbelievers): Do you bid me worship other than Allah? O you fools!

65. And surely it has been revealed unto you (Muhammad) as unto those before you (saying): If you ascribe a partner to Allah your work will fail and you indeed will be among the losers.

66. Nay, but Allah must you worship, and be among the thankful!

67. And they esteem not Allah as He has the right to be esteemed, when the whole earth is His handful on the Day of Resurrection, and the heavens are rolled in His right hand. Glorified is He and High Exalted from all that they ascribe as partner (unto Him).

68. And the trumpet is blown, and all who are in the heavens and the earth swoon away, save him whom Allah wills. Then it is blown a second time, and behold them standing looking!

69. And the earth shines with the light of her Lord, and the Book is set up, and the Prophets and the witnesses are brought, and it is judged between them with truth, and they are not wronged.

70. And each soul is paid in full for what it did. And He is best aware of what they do.

٦٠ وَيَوْمَ الْقِيَامَةِ تَرَى الَّذِينَ كَذَبُوا عَلَى اللَّهِ وُجُوهُهُم مُّسْوَدَّةٌ أَلَيْسَ فِي جَهَنَّمَ مَثْوًى لِّلْمُتَكَبِّرِينَ

٦١ وَيُنَجِّي اللَّهُ الَّذِينَ اتَّقَوْا بِمَفَازَتِهِمْ لَا يَمَسُّهُمُ السُّوءُ وَلَا هُمْ يَحْزَنُونَ

٦٢ اللَّهُ خَالِقُ كُلِّ شَيْءٍ وَهُوَ عَلَى كُلِّ شَيْءٍ وَكِيلٌ

٦٣ لَّهُ مَقَالِيدُ السَّمَاوَاتِ وَالْأَرْضِ وَالَّذِينَ كَفَرُوا بِآيَاتِ اللَّهِ أُولَٰئِكَ هُمُ الْخَاسِرُونَ

٦٤ قُلْ أَفَغَيْرَ اللَّهِ تَأْمُرُونِّي أَعْبُدُ أَيُّهَا الْجَاهِلُونَ

٦٥ وَلَقَدْ أُوحِيَ إِلَيْكَ وَإِلَى الَّذِينَ مِن قَبْلِكَ لَئِنْ أَشْرَكْتَ لَيَحْبَطَنَّ عَمَلُكَ وَلَتَكُونَنَّ مِنَ الْخَاسِرِينَ

٦٦ بَلِ اللَّهَ فَاعْبُدْ وَكُن مِّنَ الشَّاكِرِينَ

٦٧ وَمَا قَدَرُوا اللَّهَ حَقَّ قَدْرِهِ وَالْأَرْضُ جَمِيعًا قَبْضَتُهُ يَوْمَ الْقِيَامَةِ وَالسَّمَاوَاتُ مَطْوِيَّاتٌ بِيَمِينِهِ سُبْحَانَهُ وَتَعَالَى عَمَّا يُشْرِكُونَ

٦٨ وَنُفِخَ فِي الصُّورِ فَصَعِقَ مَن فِي السَّمَاوَاتِ وَمَن فِي الْأَرْضِ إِلَّا مَن شَاءَ اللَّهُ ثُمَّ نُفِخَ فِيهِ أُخْرَىٰ فَإِذَا هُمْ قِيَامٌ يَنظُرُونَ

٦٩ وَأَشْرَقَتِ الْأَرْضُ بِنُورِ رَبِّهَا وَوُضِعَ الْكِتَابُ وَجِيءَ بِالنَّبِيِّينَ وَالشُّهَدَاءِ وَقُضِيَ بَيْنَهُم بِالْحَقِّ وَهُمْ لَا يُظْلَمُونَ

٧٠ وَوُفِّيَتْ كُلُّ نَفْسٍ مَّا عَمِلَتْ وَهُوَ أَعْلَمُ بِمَا يَفْعَلُونَ

71. And those who disbelieve are driven unto Hell in troops till, when they reach it and the gates thereof are opened, and the warders thereof say unto them: Came there not unto you messengers of your own, reciting unto you the revelations of your Lord and warning you of the meeting of this your Day? they say Yea, surely. But the word of doom for disbelievers is fulfilled.

72. It is said (unto them): Enter you the gates of Hell to dwell therein. Thus unlucky is the journey's end of the scorners.

73. And those who keep their duty to their Lord are driven unto the Garden in troops till, when they reach it, and the gates thereof are opened, and the warders thereof say unto them: Peace be unto you! You are good, so enter you (the Garden of delight), to dwell therein;

74. They say: Praise be to Allah, Who has fulfilled His promise unto us and has made us inherit the land, sojourning in the Garden where we will! So bounteous is the wage of workers.

75. And you (O Muhammad) see the angels thronging round the Throne, hymning the praises of their Lord. And they are judged aright. And it is said: Praise be to Allah, the Lord of the Worlds!

٧١ وَسِيقَ الَّذِينَ كَفَرُوٓا إِلَىٰ جَهَنَّمَ زُمَرًا ۖ حَتَّىٰٓ إِذَا جَآءُوهَا فُتِحَتْ أَبْوَٰبُهَا وَقَالَ لَهُمْ خَزَنَتُهَآ أَلَمْ يَأْتِكُمْ رُسُلٌ مِّنكُمْ يَتْلُونَ عَلَيْكُمْ ءَايَٰتِ رَبِّكُمْ وَيُنذِرُونَكُمْ لِقَآءَ يَوْمِكُمْ هَٰذَا ۚ قَالُوا بَلَىٰ وَلَٰكِنْ حَقَّتْ كَلِمَةُ الْعَذَابِ عَلَى الْكَٰفِرِينَ

٧٢ قِيلَ ادْخُلُوٓا أَبْوَٰبَ جَهَنَّمَ خَٰلِدِينَ فِيهَا ۖ فَبِئْسَ مَثْوَى الْمُتَكَبِّرِينَ

٧٣ وَسِيقَ الَّذِينَ اتَّقَوْا رَبَّهُمْ إِلَى الْجَنَّةِ زُمَرًا ۖ حَتَّىٰٓ إِذَا جَآءُوهَا وَفُتِحَتْ أَبْوَٰبُهَا وَقَالَ لَهُمْ خَزَنَتُهَا سَلَٰمٌ عَلَيْكُمْ طِبْتُمْ فَادْخُلُوهَا خَٰلِدِينَ

٧٤ وَقَالُوا الْحَمْدُ لِلَّهِ الَّذِي صَدَقَنَا وَعْدَهُ وَأَوْرَثَنَا الْأَرْضَ نَتَبَوَّأُ مِنَ الْجَنَّةِ حَيْثُ نَشَآءُ ۖ فَنِعْمَ أَجْرُ الْعَٰمِلِينَ

٧٥ وَتَرَى الْمَلَٰٓئِكَةَ حَآفِّينَ مِنْ حَوْلِ الْعَرْشِ يُسَبِّحُونَ بِحَمْدِ رَبِّهِمْ ۖ وَقُضِيَ بَيْنَهُم بِالْحَقِّ وَقِيلَ الْحَمْدُ لِلَّهِ رَبِّ الْعَٰلَمِينَ

The Believer

Al Mu'min, "The Believer," takes its name from verses 28- 45, which describe the attempt of a believer, in the house of Pharaoh, to dissuade his people from opposing Moses and Aaron. It is also called *Ghāfir* i.e., the Forgiver, which occurs in verse 3. It is the first of seven surahs beginning with the Arabic letters *Ḥā Mīm*, all of which are sometimes referred to as *Ḥā Mīm*.

It belongs to the middle group of Makkan surahs. Some authorities hold verses 56-57 to have been revealed at al Madinah.

The Believer

Revealed at Makkah

*In the name of Allah,
the Beneficent, the Merciful*

1. **H**ā. Mīm.[237]

2. The revelation of the Scripture is from Allah, the Mighty, the Knower,

3. The Forgiver of sin, the Acceptor of repentance, the Stern in punishment, the Bountiful. There is no God save Him. Unto Him is the journeying.

4. None argue concerning the revelations of Allah save those who disbelieve, so let not their turn of fortune in the land deceive you (O Muhammad).

5. The folk of Noah and the factions after them denied (their messengers) before these, and every nation purposed to seize their messenger and argued falsely, (thinking) thereby to refute the Truth. Then I seized them, and how (awful) was My punishment.

6. Thus was the word of your Lord concerning those who disbelieve fulfilled: that they are owners of the Fire.

7. Those who bear the Throne, and all who are round about it, hymn the praises of their Lord and believe in Him and ask forgiveness for those who believe (saying): Our Lord! You comprehend all things in mercy and knowledge, therefore forgive those who repent and follow Your way. And ward off from them the punishment of Hell.

8. Our Lord! And make them enter the Gardens of Eden which you have promised them, with such of their fathers and their wives and their descendants as do right. Lo! You, only You, are the Mighty, the Wise.

بِسْمِ اللهِ الرَّحْمٰنِ الرَّحِيمِ

① حٰمٓ

② تَنْزِيلُ الْكِتٰبِ مِنَ اللهِ الْعَزِيزِ الْعَلِيمِ

③ غَافِرِ الذَّنْبِ وَقَابِلِ التَّوْبِ شَدِيدِ الْعِقَابِ ذِى الطَّوْلِ لَآ إِلٰهَ إِلَّا هُوَ إِلَيْهِ الْمَصِيرُ

④ مَا يُجَادِلُ فِىٓ ءَايٰتِ اللهِ إِلَّا الَّذِينَ كَفَرُوا فَلَا يَغْرُرْكَ تَقَلُّبُهُمْ فِى الْبِلٰدِ

⑤ كَذَّبَتْ قَبْلَهُمْ قَوْمُ نُوحٍ وَالْأَحْزَابُ مِنْ بَعْدِهِمْ وَهَمَّتْ كُلُّ أُمَّةٍ بِرَسُولِهِمْ لِيَأْخُذُوهُ وَجٰدَلُوا بِالْبَاطِلِ لِيُدْحِضُوا بِهِ الْحَقَّ فَأَخَذْتُهُمْ فَكَيْفَ كَانَ عِقَابِ

⑥ وَكَذٰلِكَ حَقَّتْ كَلِمَتُ رَبِّكَ عَلَى الَّذِينَ كَفَرُوٓا أَنَّهُمْ أَصْحٰبُ النَّارِ

⑦ الَّذِينَ يَحْمِلُونَ الْعَرْشَ وَمَنْ حَوْلَهُ يُسَبِّحُونَ بِحَمْدِ رَبِّهِمْ وَيُؤْمِنُونَ بِهِ وَيَسْتَغْفِرُونَ لِلَّذِينَ ءَامَنُوا رَبَّنَا وَسِعْتَ كُلَّ شَىْءٍ رَّحْمَةً وَعِلْمًا فَاغْفِرْ لِلَّذِينَ تَابُوا وَاتَّبَعُوا سَبِيلَكَ وَقِهِمْ عَذَابَ الْجَحِيمِ

⑧ رَبَّنَا وَأَدْخِلْهُمْ جَنّٰتِ عَدْنٍ الَّتِى وَعَدْتَّهُمْ وَمَنْ صَلَحَ مِنْ ءَابَآئِهِمْ وَأَزْوٰجِهِمْ وَذُرِّيّٰتِهِمْ إِنَّكَ أَنْتَ الْعَزِيزُ الْحَكِيمُ

9. And ward off from them ill deeds; and he from whom You ward off ill deeds that day, him surely have You taken into mercy. That is the supreme triumph.

10. Lo! (on that day) those who disbelieve are informed by proclamation: Surely Allah's abhorrence is more terrible than your abhorrence of yourselves, when you were called unto the faith but did refuse.

11. They said: Our Lord! Twice have You made us die, and twice have You made us live. Now we confess our sins. Is there any way to go out?

12. (It is said unto them): This is (your plight) because, when Allah only was invoked, you disbelieved, but when some partner was ascribed to Him you were believing. But the judgment belongs only to Allah, the Sublime, the Majestic.

13. He it is who shows you His portents, and sends down for you provision from the sky. None pays heed save him who turns (unto Him) repentant.

14. Therefore (O believers) pray unto Allah, making religion pure for Him (only), however much the disbelievers be averse—

15. The Exalted in Ranks, the Lord of the Throne. He casts the Spirit of His command upon whom He will of His slaves, that He may warn of the Day of Meeting,

16. The day when they are exposed, nothing of them being hidden from Allah. Whose is the sovereignty this day? It is Allah's, the One, the Almighty.

17. This day is each soul requited that which it has earned; no wrong (is done) this day. Lo! Allah is swift at reckoning.

18. Warn them (O Muhammad) of the Day of the approaching (doom), when the hearts will be choking the throats, (when) there will be no friend for the wrongdoers, nor any intercessor who will be obeyed.

19. He knows the traitor of the eyes, and that which the bosoms hide.

20. Allah judges with truth, while those to whom they cry instead of Him judge not at all. Lo! Allah, He is the Hearer, the Seer.

21. Have they not travelled in the land to see the nature of the consequence for those who were before them? They were mightier than these in power and (in the) traces (which they left behind them) in the earth. Yet Allah seized them for their sins, and they had no protector from Allah.

22. That was because their messengers kept bringing them clear proofs (of Allah's sovereignty) but they disbelieved; so Allah seized them. Lo! He is Strong, Severe in punishment.

23. And surely We sent Moses with Our revelations and a clear warrant

24. Unto Pharaoh and Hāmān and Qārūn, but they said: A lying sorcerer!

25. And when he brought them the Truth from Our presence, they said: Slay the sons of those who believe with him, and spare their women. But the plot of disbelievers is in nothing but error.

26. And Pharaoh said: Suffer me to kill Moses, and let him cry unto his Lord. Lo! I fear that he will alter your religion or that he will cause mischief in the land.

١٨ وَأَنذِرْهُمْ يَوْمَ الْآزِفَةِ إِذِ الْقُلُوبُ لَدَى الْحَنَاجِرِ كَاظِمِينَ مَا لِلظَّالِمِينَ مِنْ حَمِيمٍ وَلَا شَفِيعٍ يُطَاعُ

١٩ يَعْلَمُ خَائِنَةَ الْأَعْيُنِ وَمَا تُخْفِي الصُّدُورُ

٢٠ وَاللَّهُ يَقْضِي بِالْحَقِّ وَالَّذِينَ يَدْعُونَ مِن دُونِهِ لَا يَقْضُونَ بِشَيْءٍ إِنَّ اللَّهَ هُوَ السَّمِيعُ الْبَصِيرُ

٢١ أَوَلَمْ يَسِيرُوا فِي الْأَرْضِ فَيَنظُرُوا كَيْفَ كَانَ عَاقِبَةُ الَّذِينَ كَانُوا مِن قَبْلِهِمْ كَانُوا هُمْ أَشَدَّ مِنْهُمْ قُوَّةً وَءَاثَارًا فِي الْأَرْضِ فَأَخَذَهُمُ اللَّهُ بِذُنُوبِهِمْ وَمَا كَانَ لَهُم مِّنَ اللَّهِ مِن وَاقٍ

٢٢ ذَلِكَ بِأَنَّهُمْ كَانَت تَّأْتِيهِمْ رُسُلُهُم بِالْبَيِّنَاتِ فَكَفَرُوا فَأَخَذَهُمُ اللَّهُ إِنَّهُ قَوِيٌّ شَدِيدُ الْعِقَابِ

٢٣ وَلَقَدْ أَرْسَلْنَا مُوسَى بِآيَاتِنَا وَسُلْطَانٍ مُّبِينٍ

٢٤ إِلَى فِرْعَوْنَ وَهَامَانَ وَقَارُونَ فَقَالُوا سَاحِرٌ كَذَّابٌ

٢٥ فَلَمَّا جَاءَهُم بِالْحَقِّ مِنْ عِندِنَا قَالُوا اقْتُلُوا أَبْنَاءَ الَّذِينَ ءَامَنُوا مَعَهُ وَاسْتَحْيُوا نِسَاءَهُمْ وَمَا كَيْدُ الْكَافِرِينَ إِلَّا فِي ضَلَالٍ

٢٦ وَقَالَ فِرْعَوْنُ ذَرُونِي أَقْتُلْ مُوسَى وَلْيَدْعُ رَبَّهُ إِنِّي أَخَافُ أَن يُبَدِّلَ دِينَكُمْ أَوْ أَن يُظْهِرَ فِي الْأَرْضِ الْفَسَادَ

27. Moses said: Lo! I seek refuge in my Lord and your Lord from every arrogant one who believes not in the Day of Reckoning.

28. And a believing man of Pharaoh's family, who hid his faith, said: Would you kill a man because he said: My Lord is Allah, and has brought you clear proofs from your Lord? If he is lying, then his lie is upon himself; and if he is truthful then some of that wherewith he threatens you will strike you. Lo! Allah guides not one who is a prodigal, a liar.

29. O my people! Yours is the kingdom today, you be-ing uppermost in the land. But who would save us from the wrath of Allah should it reach us? Pharaoh said: I do but show you what I think, and I do but guide you to wise policy.

30. And he who believed said: O my people! Lo! I fear for you a fate like that of the factions (of old);

31. A plight like that of Noah's folk, and 'Ād and Thamūd, and those after them, and Allah wills no injustice for (His) slaves.

32. And, O my people! Lo! I fear for you a Day of Sum-moning,

33. A day when you will turn to flee, having no preserver from Allah: and he whom Allah sends astray, for him there is no guide.

34. And surely Joseph brought you of old clear proofs, yet you ceased not to be in doubt concerning what he brought you till, when he died, you said: Allah will not send any messenger after him. Thus Allah leads astray him who is a prodigal, a doubter.

٢٧ وَقَالَ مُوسَىٰ إِنِّي عُذْتُ بِرَبِّي وَرَبِّكُم مِّن كُلِّ مُتَكَبِّرٍ لَّا يُؤْمِنُ بِيَوْمِ الْحِسَابِ

٢٨ وَقَالَ رَجُلٌ مُّؤْمِنٌ مِّنْ ءَالِ فِرْعَوْنَ يَكْتُمُ إِيمَٰنَهُۥٓ أَتَقْتُلُونَ رَجُلًا أَن يَقُولَ رَبِّيَ اللَّهُ وَقَدْ جَآءَكُم بِالْبَيِّنَٰتِ مِن رَّبِّكُمْ ۖ وَإِن يَكُ كَٰذِبًا فَعَلَيْهِ كَذِبُهُۥ ۖ وَإِن يَكُ صَادِقًا يُصِبْكُم بَعْضُ الَّذِي يَعِدُكُمْ ۖ إِنَّ اللَّهَ لَا يَهْدِي مَنْ هُوَ مُسْرِفٌ كَذَّابٌ

٢٩ يَٰقَوْمِ لَكُمُ الْمُلْكُ الْيَوْمَ ظَٰهِرِينَ فِي الْأَرْضِ فَمَن يَنصُرُنَا مِنۢ بَأْسِ اللَّهِ إِن جَآءَنَا ۚ قَالَ فِرْعَوْنُ مَآ أُرِيكُمْ إِلَّا مَآ أَرَىٰ وَمَآ أَهْدِيكُمْ إِلَّا سَبِيلَ الرَّشَادِ

٣٠ وَقَالَ الَّذِيٓ ءَامَنَ يَٰقَوْمِ إِنِّيٓ أَخَافُ عَلَيْكُم مِّثْلَ يَوْمِ الْأَحْزَابِ

٣١ مِثْلَ دَأْبِ قَوْمِ نُوحٍ وَعَادٍ وَثَمُودَ وَالَّذِينَ مِنۢ بَعْدِهِمْ ۚ وَمَا اللَّهُ يُرِيدُ ظُلْمًا لِّلْعِبَادِ

٣٢ وَيَٰقَوْمِ إِنِّيٓ أَخَافُ عَلَيْكُمْ يَوْمَ التَّنَادِ

٣٣ يَوْمَ تُوَلُّونَ مُدْبِرِينَ مَا لَكُم مِّنَ اللَّهِ مِنْ عَاصِمٍ ۗ وَمَن يُضْلِلِ اللَّهُ فَمَا لَهُۥ مِنْ هَادٍ

٣٤ وَلَقَدْ جَآءَكُمْ يُوسُفُ مِن قَبْلُ بِالْبَيِّنَٰتِ فَمَا زِلْتُمْ فِي شَكٍّ مِّمَّا جَآءَكُم بِهِۦ ۖ حَتَّىٰٓ إِذَا هَلَكَ قُلْتُمْ لَن يَبْعَثَ اللَّهُ مِنۢ بَعْدِهِ رَسُولًا ۚ كَذَٰلِكَ يُضِلُّ اللَّهُ مَنْ هُوَ مُسْرِفٌ مُّرْتَابٌ

35. Those who wrangle concerning the revelations of Allah without any warrant that has come unto them, it is greatly hateful in the sight of Allah and in the sight of those who believe. Thus does Allah print on every arrogant, disdainful heart.

36. And Pharaoh said: O Hāmān! Build for me a tower that I may reach the roads,

37. The roads of the heavens, and may look upon the God of Moses, though surely I think him a liar. Thus was the evil that he did make fair-seeming unto Pharaoh, and he was debarred from the (right) way. The plot of Pharaoh ended but in ruin.

38. And he who believed said: O my people! Follow me. I will show you the way of right conduct.

39. O my people! Lo! this life of the world is but a passing comfort, and lo! the Hereafter, that is the enduring home.

40. Who does an ill deed, he will be repaid the like thereof, while who does right, whether male or female, and is a believer, (all) such will enter the Garden, where they will be nourished without measure.

41. And, O my people! What ails me that I call you unto deliverance when you call me unto the Fire?

42. You call me to disbelieve in Allah and ascribe unto Him as partners that whereof I have no knowledge, while I call you unto the Mighty, the Forgiver.

٣٥ اَلَّذِينَ يُجَادِلُونَ فِىٓ ءَايَٰتِ ٱللَّهِ بِغَيْرِ سُلْطَٰنٍ أَتَىٰهُمْ كَبُرَ مَقْتًا عِندَ ٱللَّهِ وَعِندَ ٱلَّذِينَ ءَامَنُوا۟ كَذَٰلِكَ يَطْبَعُ ٱللَّهُ عَلَىٰ كُلِّ قَلْبِ مُتَكَبِّرٍ جَبَّارٍ

٣٦ وَقَالَ فِرْعَوْنُ يَٰهَٰمَٰنُ ٱبْنِ لِى صَرْحًا لَّعَلِّىٓ أَبْلُغُ ٱلْأَسْبَٰبَ

٣٧ أَسْبَٰبَ ٱلسَّمَٰوَٰتِ فَأَطَّلِعَ إِلَىٰٓ إِلَٰهِ مُوسَىٰ وَإِنِّى لَأَظُنُّهُۥ كَٰذِبًا وَكَذَٰلِكَ زُيِّنَ لِفِرْعَوْنَ سُوٓءُ عَمَلِهِۦ وَصُدَّ عَنِ ٱلسَّبِيلِ وَمَا كَيْدُ فِرْعَوْنَ إِلَّا فِى تَبَابٍ

٣٨ وَقَالَ ٱلَّذِىٓ ءَامَنَ يَٰقَوْمِ ٱتَّبِعُونِ أَهْدِكُمْ سَبِيلَ ٱلرَّشَادِ

٣٩ يَٰقَوْمِ إِنَّمَا هَٰذِهِ ٱلْحَيَوٰةُ ٱلدُّنْيَا مَتَٰعٌ وَإِنَّ ٱلْءَاخِرَةَ هِىَ دَارُ ٱلْقَرَارِ

٤٠ مَنْ عَمِلَ سَيِّئَةً فَلَا يُجْزَىٰٓ إِلَّا مِثْلَهَا وَمَنْ عَمِلَ صَٰلِحًا مِّن ذَكَرٍ أَوْ أُنثَىٰ وَهُوَ مُؤْمِنٌ فَأُو۟لَٰٓئِكَ يَدْخُلُونَ ٱلْجَنَّةَ يُرْزَقُونَ فِيهَا بِغَيْرِ حِسَابٍ

٤١ وَيَٰقَوْمِ مَا لِىٓ أَدْعُوكُمْ إِلَى ٱلنَّجَوٰةِ وَتَدْعُونَنِىٓ إِلَى ٱلنَّارِ

٤٢ تَدْعُونَنِى لِأَكْفُرَ بِٱللَّهِ وَأُشْرِكَ بِهِۦ مَا لَيْسَ لِى بِهِۦ عِلْمٌ وَأَنَا۠ أَدْعُوكُمْ إِلَى ٱلْعَزِيزِ ٱلْغَفَّٰرِ

43. Assuredly that whereunto you call me has no claim in the world or in the Hereafter, and our return will be unto Allah, and the prodigals will be owners of the fire.

٤٣ لَاجَرَمَ أَنَّمَا تَدْعُونَنِيَ إِلَيْهِ لَيْسَ لَهُ دَعْوَةٌ فِى الدُّنْيَا وَلَا فِى الْأَخِرَةِ وَأَنَّ مَرَدَّنَا إِلَى اللّٰهِ وَأَنَّ الْمُسْرِفِينَ هُمْ أَصْحَابُ النَّارِ

44. And you will remember what I say unto you. I confide my cause unto Allah. Lo! Allah is Seer of (His) slaves.

٤٤ فَسَتَذْكُرُونَ مَا أَقُولُ لَكُمْ وَأُفَوِّضُ أَمْرِىَ إِلَى اللّٰهِ إِنَّ اللّٰهَ بَصِيرٌ بِالْعِبَادِ

45. So Allah warded off from him the evils which they plotted, while a dreadful doom encompassed Pharaoh's folk.

٤٥ فَوَقَاهُ اللّٰهُ سَيِّئَاتِ مَا مَكَرُواْ وَحَاقَ بِالِ فِرْعَوْنَ سُوءُ الْعَذَابِ

46. The Fire; they are exposed to it morning and evening; and on the day when the Hour uprises (it is said): Cause Pharaoh's folk to enter the most awful doom.

٤٦ النَّارُ يُعْرَضُونَ عَلَيْهَا غُدُوًّا وَعَشِيًّا وَيَوْمَ تَقُومُ السَّاعَةُ أَدْخِلُواْ ءَالَ فِرْعَوْنَ أَشَدَّ الْعَذَابِ

47. And when they wrangle in the fire, the weak say unto those who were proud: Lo! we were a following unto you: will you therefore rid us of a portion of the Fire?

٤٧ وَإِذْ يَتَحَاجُّونَ فِى النَّارِ فَيَقُولُ الضُّعَفَاؤُاْ لِلَّذِينَ اسْتَكْبَرُواْ إِنَّا كُنَّا لَكُمْ تَبَعًا فَهَلْ أَنتُم مُّغْنُونَ عَنَّا نَصِيبًا مِّنَ النَّارِ

48. Those who were proud say: Lo! we are all (together) herein. Lo! Allah has judged between (His) slaves.

٤٨ قَالَ الَّذِينَ اسْتَكْبَرُواْ إِنَّا كُلٌّ فِيهَا إِنَّ اللّٰهَ قَدْ حَكَمَ بَيْنَ الْعِبَادِ

49. And those in the Fire say unto the guards of Hell: Entreat your Lord that He relieve us of a day of the torment.

٤٩ وَقَالَ الَّذِينَ فِى النَّارِ لِخَزَنَةِ جَهَنَّمَ ادْعُواْ رَبَّكُمْ يُخَفِّفْ عَنَّا يَوْمًا مِّنَ الْعَذَابِ

50. They say: Came not your messengers unto you with clear proofs? They say: Yea, surely. They say: Then do you pray, although the prayer of disbelievers is in vain.

٥٠ قَالُواْ أَوَلَمْ تَكُ تَأْتِيكُمْ رُسُلُكُم بِالْبَيِّنَتِ قَالُواْ بَلَىٰ قَالُواْ فَادْعُواْ وَمَا دُعَاؤُاْ الْكَافِرِينَ إِلَّا فِى ضَلَلٍ

51. Lo! We surely do help Our messengers, and those who believe, in the life of the world and on the day when the witnesses arise,

٥١ إِنَّا لَنَنصُرُ رُسُلَنَا وَالَّذِينَ ءَامَنُواْ فِى الْحَيَوٰةِ الدُّنْيَا وَيَوْمَ يَقُومُ الْأَشْهَدُ

52. The day when their excuse avails not the evildoers, and theirs is the curse, and theirs is the ill abode.

53. And we surely gave Moses the guidance, and We caused the Children of Israel to inherit the Scripture,

54. A guide and a reminder for men of understanding.

55. Then have patience (O Muhammad). Lo! the promise of Allah is true. And ask forgiveness of your sin, and hymn the praise of your Lord at fall of night and in the early hours.

56. Lo! those who wrangle concerning the revelations of Allah without a warrant having come unto them, there is nothing else in their breasts save pride which they will never attain. So take you refuge in Allah. Lo! He, only He, is the Hearer, the Seer.

57. Assuredly the creation of the heavens and the earth is greater than the creation of mankind; but most of mankind know not.

58. And the blind man and the seer are not equal, neither are those who believe and do good works (equal with) the evildoer. Little do you reflect!

59. Lo! the Hour is surely coming, there is no doubt thereof; yet most of mankind believe not.

60. And your Lord has said: Pray unto me and I will hear your prayer. Lo! those who scorn My worship, they will enter Hell, disgraced.

61. Allah it is Who has appointed for you night that you may rest therein, and day for seeing. Lo! Allah is a Lord of bounty for mankind, yet most of mankind give not thanks.

١٥٢ يَوْمَ لَا يَنفَعُ ٱلظَّٰلِمِينَ مَعْذِرَتُهُمْ وَلَهُمُ ٱللَّعْنَةُ وَلَهُمْ سُوءُ ٱلدَّارِ

٥٣ وَلَقَدْ ءَاتَيْنَا مُوسَى ٱلْهُدَىٰ وَأَوْرَثْنَا بَنِىٓ إِسْرَٰٓءِيلَ ٱلْكِتَٰبَ

٥٤ هُدًى وَذِكْرَىٰ لِأُو۟لِى ٱلْأَلْبَٰبِ

٥٥ فَٱصْبِرْ إِنَّ وَعْدَ ٱللَّهِ حَقٌّ وَٱسْتَغْفِرْ لِذَنۢبِكَ وَسَبِّحْ بِحَمْدِ رَبِّكَ بِٱلْعَشِىِّ وَٱلْإِبْكَٰرِ

٥٦ إِنَّ ٱلَّذِينَ يُجَٰدِلُونَ فِىٓ ءَايَٰتِ ٱللَّهِ بِغَيْرِ سُلْطَٰنٍ أَتَىٰهُمْ إِن فِى صُدُورِهِمْ إِلَّا كِبْرٌ مَّا هُم بِبَٰلِغِيهِ فَٱسْتَعِذْ بِٱللَّهِ إِنَّهُۥ هُوَ ٱلسَّمِيعُ ٱلْبَصِيرُ

٥٧ لَخَلْقُ ٱلسَّمَٰوَٰتِ وَٱلْأَرْضِ أَكْبَرُ مِنْ خَلْقِ ٱلنَّاسِ وَلَٰكِنَّ أَكْثَرَ ٱلنَّاسِ لَا يَعْلَمُونَ

٥٨ وَمَا يَسْتَوِى ٱلْأَعْمَىٰ وَٱلْبَصِيرُ وَٱلَّذِينَ ءَامَنُوا۟ وَعَمِلُوا۟ ٱلصَّٰلِحَٰتِ وَلَا ٱلْمُسِىٓءُ قَلِيلًا مَّا تَتَذَكَّرُونَ

٥٩ إِنَّ ٱلسَّاعَةَ لَءَاتِيَةٌ لَّا رَيْبَ فِيهَا وَلَٰكِنَّ أَكْثَرَ ٱلنَّاسِ لَا يُؤْمِنُونَ

٦٠ وَقَالَ رَبُّكُمُ ٱدْعُونِىٓ أَسْتَجِبْ لَكُمْ إِنَّ ٱلَّذِينَ يَسْتَكْبِرُونَ عَنْ عِبَادَتِى سَيَدْخُلُونَ جَهَنَّمَ دَاخِرِينَ

٦١ ٱللَّهُ ٱلَّذِى جَعَلَ لَكُمُ ٱلَّيْلَ لِتَسْكُنُوا۟ فِيهِ وَٱلنَّهَارَ مُبْصِرًا إِنَّ ٱللَّهَ لَذُو فَضْلٍ عَلَى ٱلنَّاسِ وَلَٰكِنَّ أَكْثَرَ ٱلنَّاسِ لَا يَشْكُرُونَ

62. Such is Allah, your Lord, the Creator of all things. There is no God save Him. How then are you perverted?

٦٢ ذَلِكُمُ اللَّهُ رَبُّكُمْ خَالِقُ كُلِّ شَيْءٍ لَآ إِلَهَ إِلَّا هُوَ فَأَنَّى تُؤْفَكُونَ

63. Thus are they perverted who deny the revelations of Allah.

٦٣ كَذَلِكَ يُؤْفَكُ الَّذِينَ كَانُوا بِئَايَتِ اللَّهِ يَجْحَدُونَ

64. Allah it is Who appointed for you the earth for a dwelling place and the sky for a canopy, and fashioned you and perfected your shapes, and has provided you with good things. Such is Allah, your Lord. Then blessed be Allah, the Lord of the Worlds!

٦٤ اللَّهُ الَّذِى جَعَلَ لَكُمُ الْأَرْضَ قَرَارًا وَالسَّمَآءَ بِنَآءً وَصَوَّرَكُمْ فَأَحْسَنَ صُوَرَكُمْ وَرَزَقَكُمْ مِنَ الطَّيِّبَتِ ذَلِكُمُ اللَّهُ رَبُّكُمْ فَتَبَارَكَ اللَّهُ رَبُّ الْعَلَمِينَ

65. He is the Living One. There is no God save Him. So pray unto Him, making religion pure for Him (only). Praise be to Allah, the Lord of the Worlds!

٦٥ هُوَ الْحَىُّ لَآ إِلَهَ إِلَّا هُوَ فَادْعُوهُ مُخْلِصِينَ لَهُ الدِّينَ الْحَمْدُ لِلَّهِ رَبِّ الْعَلَمِينَ

66. Say (O Muhammad): I am forbidden to worship those unto whom you cry beside Allah since there have come unto me clear proofs from my Lord, and I am commanded to surrender to the Lord of the Worlds.

٦٦ قُلْ إِنِّى نُهِيتُ أَنْ أَعْبُدَ الَّذِينَ تَدْعُونَ مِن دُونِ اللَّهِ لَمَّا جَآءَنِى الْبَيِّنَتُ مِن رَّبِّى وَأُمِرْتُ أَنْ أُسْلِمَ لِرَبِّ الْعَلَمِينَ

67. He it is Who created you from dust, then from a drop (of seed) then from a clot, then brings you forth as a child, then (ordains) that you attain full strength and afterward that you become old men—though some among you die before—and that you reach an appointed term, that you may understand.

٦٧ هُوَ الَّذِى خَلَقَكُم مِّن تُرَابٍ ثُمَّ مِن نُّطْفَةٍ ثُمَّ مِنْ عَلَقَةٍ ثُمَّ يُخْرِجُكُمْ طِفْلًا ثُمَّ لِتَبْلُغُوا أَشُدَّكُمْ ثُمَّ لِتَكُونُوا شُيُوخًا وَمِنكُم مَّن يُتَوَفَّى مِن قَبْلُ وَلِتَبْلُغُوا أَجَلًا مُّسَمًّى وَلَعَلَّكُمْ تَعْقِلُونَ

68. He it is who quickens and gives death. When He ordains a thing, He says unto it only: Be! and it is.

٦٨ هُوَ الَّذِى يُحْىِ وَيُمِيتُ فَإِذَا قَضَى أَمْرًا فَإِنَّمَا يَقُولُ لَهُ كُن فَيَكُونُ

69. Have you not seen those who wrangle concerning the revelations of Allah, how they are turned away?—

٦٩ أَلَمْ تَرَ إِلَى الَّذِينَ يُجَدِلُونَ فِى ءَايَتِ اللَّهِ أَنَّى يُصْرَفُونَ

70. Those who deny the Scripture and that wherewith we send Our messengers. But they will come to know,

٧٠ الَّذِينَ كَذَّبُوا بِالْكِتَبِ وَبِمَا أَرْسَلْنَا بِهِ رُسُلَنَا فَسَوْفَ يَعْلَمُونَ

71. When yokes are about their necks and chains. They are dragged

72. Through boiling waters; then they are thrust into the Fire.

73. Then it is said unto them: Where are (all) that you used to make partners (in the Sovereignty)

74. Beside Allah? They say: They have failed us: but we used not to pray to anything before. Thus does Allah send astray the disbelievers (in His guidance).

75. (And it is said unto them): This is because you exulted in the earth without right, and because you were petulant.

76. Enter you the gates of Hell, to dwell therein. Evil is the habitation of the arrogant.

77. Then have patience (O Muhammad). Lo! the promise of Allah is true. And whether we let you see a part of that which We promise them, or (whether) We cause you to die, still unto us they will be brought back.

78. Surely We sent messengers before you, among them those of whom We have told you, and some of whom We have not told you; and it was not given to any messenger that he should bring a portent save by Allah's leave, but when Allah's commandment comes (the cause) is judged aright, and the followers of vanity will then be lost.

79. Allah it is Who has appointed for you cattle, that you may ride on some of them, and eat of some—

80. (Many) benefits you have from them—and that you may satisfy by their means a need that is in your breasts, and may be borne upon them as upon ships.

81. And He shows you His tokens. Which, then, of the tokens of Allah do you deny?

82. Have they not travelled in the land to see the nature of the consequence for those before them? They were more numerous than these, and mightier in power and (in the) traces (which they left behind them) in the earth. But all that they used to earn availed them not.

83. And when their messengers brought them clear proofs (of Allah's Sovereignty) they exulted in the knowledge they (themselves) possessed. And that which they were wont to mock befell them.

84. Then, when they saw Our doom, they said: We believe in Allah only and reject (all) that we used to associate (with Him).

85. But their faith could not avail them when they saw Our doom. This is Allah's law which has ever taken course for his Bondsmen. And then the disbelievers will be ruined.

٨٢ أَفَلَمْ يَسِيرُوا فِي الْأَرْضِ فَيَنظُرُوا كَيْفَ كَانَ عَاقِبَةُ الَّذِينَ مِن قَبْلِهِمْ كَانُوا أَكْثَرَ مِنْهُمْ وَأَشَدَّ قُوَّةً وَءَاثَارًا فِي الْأَرْضِ فَمَا أَغْنَىٰ عَنْهُم مَّا كَانُوا يَكْسِبُونَ

٨٣ فَلَمَّا جَاءَتْهُمْ رُسُلُهُم بِالْبَيِّنَاتِ فَرِحُوا بِمَا عِندَهُم مِّنَ الْعِلْمِ وَحَاقَ بِهِم مَّا كَانُوا بِهِ يَسْتَهْزِءُونَ

٨٤ فَلَمَّا رَأَوْا بَأْسَنَا قَالُوا ءَامَنَّا بِاللَّهِ وَحْدَهُ وَكَفَرْنَا بِمَا كُنَّا بِهِ مُشْرِكِينَ

٨٥ فَلَمْ يَكُ يَنفَعُهُمْ إِيمَانُهُمْ لَمَّا رَأَوْا بَأْسَنَا سُنَّتَ اللَّهِ الَّتِي قَدْ خَلَتْ فِي عِبَادِهِ وَخَسِرَ هُنَالِكَ الْكَافِرُونَ

They Are Expounded

Fuṣṣilat, "They Are Expounded," derives its title from a word in verse 2. It is also often called *Ḥā Mīm al Sajdah*, from a word in verse 37. The qualifier *Ḥā Mīm* is added to distinguish it from Surah 32, which is called *al Sajdah*.

It belongs to the middle group of Makkan surahs.

They Are Expounded

Revealed at Makkah

*In the name of Allah,
the Beneficent, the Merciful*

1. **H**ā. Mim.[238]

2. A revelation from the Beneficent, the Merciful,

3. A scripture whereof the verses are expounded, a Qur'an in Arabic for people who have knowledge.

4. Good tidings and a warning. But most of them turn away so that they hear not.

5. And they say: Our hearts are protected from that unto which you (O Muhammad) call us, and in our ears there is a deafness, and between us and you there is a veil. Act, then. Lo! we also shall be acting.

6. Say (unto them O Muhammad): I am only a mortal like you. It is inspired in me that your God is One God, therefore take the straight path unto Him and seek forgiveness of Him. And woe unto the idolaters,

7. Who give not the poor due, and who are disbelievers in the Hereafter.

8. Lo! as for those who believe and do good works, for them is a reward enduring.

9. Say (O Muhammad, unto the idolaters): Disbelieve you surely in Him Who created the earth in two Days,[239] and ascribe you unto Him rivals? He (and none else) is the Lord of the Worlds.

10. He placed therein firm mountains rising above it, and blessed it and measured therein its sustenance in four Days, alike for (all) who ask;

238See Surah 2:1, footnote.
239Surahs 22:47, 32:5, and 70:4.

11. Then turned He to the heaven when it was smoke, and said unto it and unto the earth: Come both of you, willingly or loth. They said: We come, obedient.

١١ ثُمَّ ٱسْتَوَىٰٓ إِلَى ٱلسَّمَآءِ وَهِىَ دُخَانٌ فَقَالَ لَهَا وَلِلْأَرْضِ ٱئْتِيَا طَوْعًا أَوْ كَرْهًا قَالَتَآ أَتَيْنَا طَآئِعِينَ

12. Then He ordained them seven heavens in two Days[240] and inspired in each heaven its mandate; and we decked the nether heaven with lamps, and rendered it inviolable.[241] That is the measuring of the Mighty, the Knower.

١٢ فَقَضَىٰهُنَّ سَبْعَ سَمَٰوَاتٍ فِى يَوْمَيْنِ وَأَوْحَىٰ فِى كُلِّ سَمَآءٍ أَمْرَهَا وَزَيَّنَّا ٱلسَّمَآءَ ٱلدُّنْيَا بِمَصَٰبِيحَ وَحِفْظًا ذَٰلِكَ تَقْدِيرُ ٱلْعَزِيزِ ٱلْعَلِيمِ

13. But if they turn away, then say: I warn you of a thunderbolt like the thunderbolt (which fell of old upon the tribes) of 'Ād and Thamūd;

١٣ فَإِنْ أَعْرَضُوا فَقُلْ أَنذَرْتُكُمْ صَٰعِقَةً مِّثْلَ صَٰعِقَةِ عَادٍ وَثَمُودَ

14. When their messengers came unto them from before them and behind them, saying: Worship none but Allah! they said: If our Lord had willed, He surely would have sent down angels (unto us), so lo! we are disbelievers in that wherewith you have been sent.

١٤ إِذْ جَآءَتْهُمُ ٱلرُّسُلُ مِنۢ بَيْنِ أَيْدِيهِمْ وَمِنْ خَلْفِهِمْ أَلَّا تَعْبُدُوٓا إِلَّا ٱللَّهَ قَالُوا لَوْ شَآءَ رَبُّنَا لَأَنزَلَ مَلَٰٓئِكَةً فَإِنَّا بِمَآ أُرْسِلْتُم بِهِۦ كَٰفِرُونَ

15. As for 'Ād, they were arrogant in the land without right, and they said: Who is mightier than us in power? Could they not see that Allah Who created them, He was mightier than them in power? And they denied Our revelations.

١٥ فَأَمَّا عَادٌ فَٱسْتَكْبَرُوا فِى ٱلْأَرْضِ بِغَيْرِ ٱلْحَقِّ وَقَالُوا مَنْ أَشَدُّ مِنَّا قُوَّةً أَوَلَمْ يَرَوْا أَنَّ ٱللَّهَ ٱلَّذِى خَلَقَهُمْ هُوَ أَشَدُّ مِنْهُمْ قُوَّةً وَكَانُوا بِـَٔايَٰتِنَا يَجْحَدُونَ

16. Therefore We let loose on them a raging wind in evil days, that We might make them taste the torment of disgrace in the life of the world. And surely the doom of the Hereafter will be more shameful, and they will not be helped.

١٦ فَأَرْسَلْنَا عَلَيْهِمْ رِيحًا صَرْصَرًا فِىٓ أَيَّامٍ نَّحِسَاتٍ لِّنُذِيقَهُمْ عَذَابَ ٱلْخِزْىِ فِى ٱلْحَيَوٰةِ ٱلدُّنْيَا وَلَعَذَابُ ٱلْءَاخِرَةِ أَخْزَىٰ وَهُمْ لَا يُنصَرُونَ

17. And as for Thamūd, We gave them guidance, but they preferred blindness to guidance, so the bolt of the doom of humiliation overtook them because of what they used to earn.

١٧ وَأَمَّا ثَمُودُ فَهَدَيْنَٰهُمْ فَٱسْتَحَبُّوا ٱلْعَمَىٰ عَلَى ٱلْهُدَىٰ فَأَخَذَتْهُمْ صَٰعِقَةُ ٱلْعَذَابِ ٱلْهُونِ بِمَا كَانُوا يَكْسِبُونَ

---

[240]Surahs 22:47, 32:5, and 70:4. - [241]Surahs 27:6-10, 72:8-10.

18. And We delivered those who believed and used to keep their duty to Allah.

۱۸ وَنَجَّيْنَا الَّذِينَ ءَامَنُوا وَكَانُوا يَتَّقُونَ

19. And (make mention of) the day when the enemies of Allah are gathered unto the Fire, they are driven on

۱۹ وَيَوْمَ يُحْشَرُ أَعْدَاءُ اللَّهِ إِلَى النَّارِ فَهُمْ يُوزَعُونَ

20. Till, when they reach it, their ears and their eyes and their skins testify against them as to what they used to do.

۲۰ حَتَّىٰ إِذَا مَا جَاءُوهَا شَهِدَ عَلَيْهِمْ سَمْعُهُمْ وَأَبْصَارُهُمْ وَجُلُودُهُم بِمَا كَانُوا يَعْمَلُونَ

21. And they said unto their skins: Why testify you against us? They said: Allah has given us speech Who gives speech to all things, and Who created you at the first, and unto Whom you are returned.

۲۱ وَقَالُوا لِجُلُودِهِمْ لِمَ شَهِدتُّمْ عَلَيْنَا قَالُوا أَنطَقَنَا اللَّهُ الَّذِي أَنطَقَ كُلَّ شَيْءٍ وَهُوَ خَلَقَكُمْ أَوَّلَ مَرَّةٍ وَإِلَيْهِ تُرْجَعُونَ

22. You did not hide yourselves lest your ears and your eyes and your skins should testify against you, but you deemed that Allah knew not much of what you did.

۲۲ وَمَا كُنتُمْ تَسْتَتِرُونَ أَن يَشْهَدَ عَلَيْكُمْ سَمْعُكُمْ وَلَا أَبْصَارُكُمْ وَلَا جُلُودُكُمْ وَلَٰكِن ظَنَنتُمْ أَنَّ اللَّهَ لَا يَعْلَمُ كَثِيرًا مِّمَّا تَعْمَلُونَ

23. That, your thought which you did think about your Lord, has ruined you; and you find yourselves (this day) among the lost.

۲۳ وَذَٰلِكُمْ ظَنُّكُمُ الَّذِي ظَنَنتُم بِرَبِّكُمْ أَرْدَاكُمْ فَأَصْبَحْتُم مِّنَ الْخَاسِرِينَ

24. And though they are resigned, yet the Fire is still their home; and if they ask for favor, yet they are not of those unto whom favor can be shown.

۲۴ فَإِن يَصْبِرُوا فَالنَّارُ مَثْوًى لَّهُمْ وَإِن يَسْتَعْتِبُوا فَمَا هُم مِّنَ الْمُعْتَبِينَ

25. And We assigned them comrades (in the world), who made their present and their past fair seeming unto them. And the Word concerning nations of the jinn and humankind who passed away before them has effect for them. Verily they are the losers.

۲۵ وَقَيَّضْنَا لَهُمْ قُرَنَاءَ فَزَيَّنُوا لَهُم مَّا بَيْنَ أَيْدِيهِمْ وَمَا خَلْفَهُمْ وَحَقَّ عَلَيْهِمُ الْقَوْلُ فِي أُمَمٍ قَدْ خَلَتْ مِن قَبْلِهِم مِّنَ الْجِنِّ وَالْإِنسِ إِنَّهُمْ كَانُوا خَاسِرِينَ

26. Those who disbelieve say: Heed not this Qur'an, and drown the hearing of it; so that you may conquer.

۲۶ وَقَالَ الَّذِينَ كَفَرُوا لَا تَسْمَعُوا لِهَٰذَا الْقُرْآنِ وَالْغَوْا فِيهِ لَعَلَّكُمْ تَغْلِبُونَ

27. But surely We shall cause those who disbelieve to taste an awful doom, and surely We shall requite them the worst of what they used to do.

﴿٢٧﴾ فَلَنُذِيقَنَّ الَّذِينَ كَفَرُوا عَذَابًا شَدِيدًا وَلَنَجْزِيَنَّهُمْ أَسْوَأَ الَّذِي كَانُوا يَعْمَلُونَ

28. That is the reward of Allah's enemies: the Fire. Therein is their immortal home; payment forasmuch as they denied Our revelations.

﴿٢٨﴾ ذَلِكَ جَزَاءُ أَعْدَاءِ اللَّهِ النَّارُ لَهُمْ فِيهَا دَارُ الْخُلْدِ جَزَاءً بِمَا كَانُوا بِآيَاتِنَا يَجْحَدُونَ

29. And those who disbelieve will say: Our Lord! Show us these who beguiled us of the jinn and humankind. We will place them underneath our feet that they may be among the nethermost.

﴿٢٩﴾ وَقَالَ الَّذِينَ كَفَرُوا رَبَّنَا أَرِنَا الَّذَيْنِ أَضَلَّانَا مِنَ الْجِنِّ وَالْإِنْسِ نَجْعَلْهُمَا تَحْتَ أَقْدَامِنَا لِيَكُونَا مِنَ الْأَسْفَلِينَ

30. Lo! those who say: Our Lord is Allah, and afterward are upright, the angels descend upon them, saying: Fear not nor grieve, but bear good tidings of the paradise which you are promised.

﴿٣٠﴾ إِنَّ الَّذِينَ قَالُوا رَبُّنَا اللَّهُ ثُمَّ اسْتَقَامُوا تَتَنَزَّلُ عَلَيْهِمُ الْمَلَائِكَةُ أَلَّا تَخَافُوا وَلَا تَحْزَنُوا وَأَبْشِرُوا بِالْجَنَّةِ الَّتِي كُنْتُمْ تُوعَدُونَ

31. We are your protecting friends in the life of the world and in the Hereafter. There you will have (all) that your souls desire, and there you will have (all) for which you pray.

﴿٣١﴾ نَحْنُ أَوْلِيَاؤُكُمْ فِي الْحَيَاةِ الدُّنْيَا وَفِي الْآخِرَةِ وَلَكُمْ فِيهَا مَا تَشْتَهِي أَنْفُسُكُمْ وَلَكُمْ فِيهَا مَا تَدَّعُونَ

32. A gift of welcome from the Forgiving, the Merciful.

﴿٣٢﴾ نُزُلًا مِنْ غَفُورٍ رَحِيمٍ

33. And who is better in speech than him who calls unto Allah and does right, and said: Lo! I am one of the Muslims.[242]

﴿٣٣﴾ وَمَنْ أَحْسَنُ قَوْلًا مِمَّنْ دَعَا إِلَى اللَّهِ وَعَمِلَ صَالِحًا وَقَالَ إِنَّنِي مِنَ الْمُسْلِمِينَ

34. The good deed and the evil deed are not alike. Repel the evil deed with what is best, then he, between whom and you there was enmity (will become) as though he was a bosom friend.

﴿٣٤﴾ وَلَا تَسْتَوِي الْحَسَنَةُ وَلَا السَّيِّئَةُ ادْفَعْ بِالَّتِي هِيَ أَحْسَنُ فَإِذَا الَّذِي بَيْنَكَ وَبَيْنَهُ عَدَاوَةٌ كَأَنَّهُ وَلِيٌّ حَمِيمٌ

35. But none are granted this save those who are steadfast, and none is granted save him who has a great share (of righteousness).[243]

﴿٣٥﴾ وَمَا يُلَقَّاهَا إِلَّا الَّذِينَ صَبَرُوا وَمَا يُلَقَّاهَا إِلَّا ذُو حَظٍّ عَظِيمٍ

---

[242]Those who surrender unto Allah.

[243]I.e., not everyone is able to practise such forgiveness.

36. And if a whisper from the Devil reach you (O Muham-mad) then seek refuge in Allah. Lo! He is the Hearer, the Knower.

٣٦ وَإِمَّا يَنزَغَنَّكَ مِنَ ٱلشَّيْطَٰنِ نَزْغٌ فَٱسْتَعِذْ بِٱللَّهِ إِنَّهُۥ هُوَ ٱلسَّمِيعُ ٱلْعَلِيمُ

37. And of His portents are the night and the day and the sun and the moon. Prostrate not to the sun nor to the moon; but prostrate to Allah Who created them, if it is in truth Him whom you worship.

٣٧ وَمِنْ ءَايَٰتِهِ ٱلَّيْلُ وَٱلنَّهَارُ وَٱلشَّمْسُ وَٱلْقَمَرُ لَا تَسْجُدُوا۟ لِلشَّمْسِ وَلَا لِلْقَمَرِ وَٱسْجُدُوا۟ لِلَّهِ ٱلَّذِى خَلَقَهُنَّ إِن كُنتُمْ إِيَّاهُ تَعْبُدُونَ

38. But if they are too proud—still those who are with your Lord glorify Him night and day, and tire not.

٣٨ فَإِنِ ٱسْتَكْبَرُوا۟ فَٱلَّذِينَ عِندَ رَبِّكَ يُسَبِّحُونَ لَهُۥ بِٱلَّيْلِ وَٱلنَّهَارِ وَهُمْ لَا يَسْـَٔمُونَ ۩

39. And of His portents (is this): that you see the earth lowly, but when We send down water thereon it thrills and grows. Lo! He who quickens it is surely the Quickener of the dead. Lo! He is Able to do all things.

٣٩ وَمِنْ ءَايَٰتِهِۦٓ أَنَّكَ تَرَى ٱلْأَرْضَ خَٰشِعَةً فَإِذَآ أَنزَلْنَا عَلَيْهَا ٱلْمَآءَ ٱهْتَزَّتْ وَرَبَتْ إِنَّ ٱلَّذِىٓ أَحْيَاهَا لَمُحْىِ ٱلْمَوْتَىٰٓ إِنَّهُۥ عَلَىٰ كُلِّ شَىْءٍ قَدِيرٌ

40. Lo! those who distort Our revelations are not hid from Us. Is he who is hurled into the Fire better, or he who comes secure on the Day of Resurrection? Do what you will. Lo! He is Seer of what you do.

٤٠ إِنَّ ٱلَّذِينَ يُلْحِدُونَ فِىٓ ءَايَٰتِنَا لَا يَخْفَوْنَ عَلَيْنَآ أَفَمَن يُلْقَىٰ فِى ٱلنَّارِ خَيْرٌ أَم مَّن يَأْتِىٓ ءَامِنًا يَوْمَ ٱلْقِيَٰمَةِ ٱعْمَلُوا۟ مَا شِئْتُمْ إِنَّهُۥ بِمَا تَعْمَلُونَ بَصِيرٌ

41. Lo! those who disbelieve in the Reminder when it comes unto them (are guilty), for lo! it is an unassailable Scripture.

٤١ إِنَّ ٱلَّذِينَ كَفَرُوا۟ بِٱلذِّكْرِ لَمَّا جَآءَهُمْ وَإِنَّهُۥ لَكِتَٰبٌ عَزِيزٌ

42. Falsehood cannot come at it from before it or behind it. (It is) a revelation from the Wise, the Owner of Praise.

٤٢ لَا يَأْتِيهِ ٱلْبَٰطِلُ مِنۢ بَيْنِ يَدَيْهِ وَلَا مِنْ خَلْفِهِۦ تَنزِيلٌ مِّنْ حَكِيمٍ حَمِيدٍ

43. Nothing is said unto you (Muhammad) save what was said unto the messengers before you. Lo! your Lord is owner of forgiveness, and owner (also) of dire punishment.

٤٣ مَّا يُقَالُ لَكَ إِلَّا مَا قَدْ قِيلَ لِلرُّسُلِ مِن قَبْلِكَ إِنَّ رَبَّكَ لَذُو مَغْفِرَةٍ وَذُو عِقَابٍ أَلِيمٍ

44. And if We had appointed it a Qur'an in a foreign tongue they would assuredly have said: If only its verses were expounded (so that we might understand)? What! A foreign tongue and an Arab?—Say unto them (O Muhammad): For those who believe it is a guidance and a healing; and as for those who disbelieve, there is a deafness in their ears, and it is blindness for them. Such are called to from afar.

45. And We verily gave Moses the Scripture, but there has been dispute concerning it; and but for a Word that had already gone forth from your Lord, it would before now have been judged between them; but lo! they are in hopeless doubt concerning it.

46. Who does right it is for his soul, and who does wrong it is against it. And your Lord is not at all a tyrant to His slaves.

47. Unto Him is referred (all) knowledge of the Hour. And no fruits burst forth from their sheaths, and no female carries or brings forth but with His knowledge. And on the day when He calls unto them: Where are now My partners? they will say: We confess unto You, not one of us is a witness (for them).

48. And those to whom they used to cry of old have failed them, and they perceive they have no place of refuge.

49. Man tires not of praying for good, and if evil touches him, then he is disheartened, desperate.

50. And verily, if We cause him to taste mercy from Us after some hurt that has touched him, he will say: This is my own; and I deem not that the Hour will ever rise, and if I am brought back to my Lord, I surely shall be better off with Him—But We surely shall tell those who disbelieve (all) that they did, and We surely shall make them taste hard punishment.

51. When We show favor unto man, he withdraws and turns aside, but when ill touches him then he abounds in prayer.

٥١ وَإِذَآ أَنْعَمْنَا عَلَى الْإِنسَانِ أَعْرَضَ وَنَـَٔا بِجَانِبِهِ وَإِذَا مَسَّهُ الشَّرُّ فَذُو دُعَآءٍ عَرِيضٍ

52. Say you: If you see that it is from Allah and you reject it—Who is further astray than one who is at open feud (with Allah)?

٥٢ قُلْ أَرَءَيْتُمْ إِن كَانَ مِنْ عِندِ اللَّهِ ثُمَّ كَفَرْتُم بِهِ مَنْ أَضَلُّ مِمَّنْ هُوَ فِي شِقَاقٍ بَعِيدٍ

53. We shall show them Our portents on the horizons and within themselves until it will be manifest unto them that it is the Truth. Does not your Lord suffice, since He is Witness over all things?

٥٣ سَنُرِيهِمْ ءَايَـٰتِنَا فِي الْءَافَاقِ وَفِي أَنفُسِهِمْ حَتَّىٰ يَتَبَيَّنَ لَهُمْ أَنَّهُ الْحَقُّ أَوَلَمْ يَكْفِ بِرَبِّكَ أَنَّهُ عَلَىٰ كُلِّ شَيْءٍ شَهِيدٌ

54. Indeed, they are in doubt about the meeting with their Lord! Indeed He is encompassing all things.

٥٤ أَلَا إِنَّهُمْ فِي مِرْيَةٍ مِّن لِّقَآءِ رَبِّهِمْ أَلَا إِنَّهُ بِكُلِّ شَيْءٍ مُّحِيطٌ

Counsel

Al Shūrā, "Counsel," takes its name from a word in verse 38. It belongs to the middle group of Makkan surahs.

Counsel

Revealed at Makkah

*In the name of Allah,
the Beneficent, the Merciful*

1. **H**ā. Mīm.[244]

2. 'Ayn. Sīn. Qāf.

3. Thus Allah the Mighty, the Wise inspires you (Muham-mad) as (He inspired) those before you.

4. Unto Him belongs all that is in the heavens and all that is in the earth, and He is the Sublime, the Tremendous.

5. Almost the heavens above might be rent asunder while the angels hymn the praise of their Lord and ask forgiveness for those on the earth. Lo! Allah is the Forgiver, the Merciful.

6. And as for those who choose protecting friends beside Him, Allah is Warden over them, and you are in no wise a guardian over them.

7. And thus we have inspired in you a Qur'an in Arabic, that you may warn the mother-town[245] and those around it, and may warn of a day of assembling whereof there is no doubt. A host will be in the Garden, and a host (will be) in the Flame.

8. Had Allah willed, He could have made them one community, but He brings whom He will into His mercy. And the wrongdoers have no friend nor helper.

9. Or have they chosen protecting friends besides Him? But Allah, He (alone) is the Protecting Friend. He quickens the dead, and He is Able to do all things.

---

[244]See Surah 2:1, footnote.
[245]i.e., Makkah.

10. And in whatsoever you differ, the verdict therein belongs to Allah. Such is Allah my Lord, in Whom I put my trust, and unto Whom I turn.

﴿١٠﴾ وَمَا اخْتَلَفْتُمْ فِيهِ مِن شَىْءٍ فَحُكْمُهُ إِلَى اللَّهِ ذَلِكُمُ اللَّهُ رَبِّى عَلَيْهِ تَوَكَّلْتُ وَإِلَيْهِ أُنِيبُ

11. The Creator of the heavens and the earth. He has made for you pairs of yourselves, and of the cattle also pairs, whereby He multiplies you. Nothing is as His likeness; and He is the Hearer, the Seer.

﴿١١﴾ فَاطِرُ السَّمَوَاتِ وَالْأَرْضِ جَعَلَ لَكُم مِّنْ أَنفُسِكُمْ أَزْوَاجًا وَمِنَ الْأَنْعَامِ أَزْوَاجًا يَذْرَؤُكُمْ فِيهِ لَيْسَ كَمِثْلِهِ شَىْءٌ وَهُوَ السَّمِيعُ الْبَصِيرُ

12. His are the keys of the heavens and the earth. He enlarges providence for whom He will and straitens (it for whom He will). Lo! He is Knower of all things.

﴿١٢﴾ لَهُ مَقَالِيدُ السَّمَوَاتِ وَالْأَرْضِ يَبْسُطُ الرِّزْقَ لِمَن يَشَاءُ وَيَقْدِرُ إِنَّهُ بِكُلِّ شَىْءٍ عَلِيمٌ

13. He has ordained for you that religion which He commended unto Noah, and that which We inspire in you (Muhammad), and that which We commended unto Abra-ham and Moses and Jesus, saying: Establish the religion, and be not divided therein. Dreadful for the idolaters is that unto which you call them. Allah chooses for Himself whom He will, and guides unto Himself him who turns (toward Him).

﴿١٣﴾ شَرَعَ لَكُم مِّنَ الدِّينِ مَا وَصَّى بِهِ نُوحًا وَالَّذِى أَوْحَيْنَا إِلَيْكَ وَمَا وَصَّيْنَا بِهِ إِبْرَاهِيمَ وَمُوسَى وَعِيسَى أَنْ أَقِيمُوا الدِّينَ وَلَا تَتَفَرَّقُوا فِيهِ كَبُرَ عَلَى الْمُشْرِكِينَ مَا تَدْعُوهُمْ إِلَيْهِ اللَّهُ يَجْتَبِى إِلَيْهِ مَن يَشَاءُ وَيَهْدِى إِلَيْهِ مَن يُنِيبُ

14. And they were not divided until after the knowledge came unto them, through oppression among themselves; and had it not been for a Word that had already gone forth from your Lord for an appointed term, it surely had been judged between them. And those who were made to inherit the Scripture after them are surely in hopeless doubt concerning it.

﴿١٤﴾ وَمَا تَفَرَّقُوا إِلَّا مِنْ بَعْدِ مَا جَاءَهُمُ الْعِلْمُ بَغْيًا بَيْنَهُمْ وَلَوْلَا كَلِمَةٌ سَبَقَتْ مِن رَّبِّكَ إِلَى أَجَلٍ مُّسَمًّى لَقُضِىَ بَيْنَهُمْ وَإِنَّ الَّذِينَ أُورِثُوا الْكِتَابَ مِن بَعْدِهِمْ لَفِى شَكٍّ مِّنْهُ مُرِيبٍ

15. Unto this, then, summon (O Muhammad). And be you upright as you are commanded, and follow not their lusts, but say: I believe in whatever Scripture Allah has sent down, and I am commanded to be just among you. Allah is our Lord and your Lord. Unto us our works and unto you your works; no argument between us and you. Allah will bring us together, and unto Him is the journeying.

﴿١٥﴾ فَلِذَلِكَ فَادْعُ وَاسْتَقِمْ كَمَا أُمِرْتَ وَلَا تَتَّبِعْ أَهْوَاءَهُمْ وَقُلْ ءَامَنتُ بِمَا أَنزَلَ اللَّهُ مِن كِتَابٍ وَأُمِرْتُ لِأَعْدِلَ بَيْنَكُمُ اللَّهُ رَبُّنَا وَرَبُّكُمْ لَنَا أَعْمَالُنَا وَلَكُمْ أَعْمَالُكُمْ لَا حُجَّةَ بَيْنَنَا وَبَيْنَكُمُ اللَّهُ يَجْمَعُ بَيْنَنَا وَإِلَيْهِ الْمَصِيرُ

16. And those who argue concerning Allah after He has been acknowledged, their argument has no weight with their Lord, and wrath is upon them and theirs will be an awful doom.

17. Allah it is who has revealed the Scripture with truth, and the Balance. How can you know? It may be that the Hour is near.

18. Those who believe not therein seek to hasten it, while those who believe are fearful of it and know that it is the Truth. Indeed they who dispute (and are in doubt) concerning the Hour, are far astray.

19. Allah is gracious unto His slaves. He provides for whom He will. And He is the Strong, the Mighty.

20. Who desires the harvest of the Hereafter, We give him increase in its harvest. And Who desires the harvest of the world, We give him thereof, and he has no portion in the Hereafter.

21. Or have they partners (of Allah) who have made lawful for them in religion that which Allah allowed not? And but for a decisive word (gone forth already), it would have been judged between them. Lo! for wrongdoers is a painful doom.

22. You see the wrongdoers fearful of that which they have earned, and it will surely befall them; while those who believe and do good works (will be) in flowering meadows of the Gardens, having what they wish from their Lord. This is the great preferment.

١٦ وَالَّذِينَ يُحَاجُّونَ فِى اللَّهِ مِنْ بَعْدِ مَا اسْتُجِيبَ لَهُ حُجَّتُهُمْ دَاحِضَةٌ عِنْدَ رَبِّهِمْ وَعَلَيْهِمْ غَضَبٌ وَلَهُمْ عَذَابٌ شَدِيدٌ

١٧ اللَّهُ الَّذِى أَنْزَلَ الْكِتَابَ بِالْحَقِّ وَالْمِيزَانَ وَمَا يُدْرِيكَ لَعَلَّ السَّاعَةَ قَرِيبٌ

١٨ يَسْتَعْجِلُ بِهَا الَّذِينَ لَا يُؤْمِنُونَ بِهَا وَالَّذِينَ ءَامَنُوا مُشْفِقُونَ مِنْهَا وَيَعْلَمُونَ أَنَّهَا الْحَقُّ أَلَا إِنَّ الَّذِينَ يُمَارُونَ فِى السَّاعَةِ لَفِى ضَلَالٍ بَعِيدٍ

١٩ اللَّهُ لَطِيفٌ بِعِبَادِهِ يَرْزُقُ مَنْ يَشَاءُ وَهُوَ الْقَوِىُّ الْعَزِيزُ

٢٠ مَنْ كَانَ يُرِيدُ حَرْثَ الْآخِرَةِ نَزِدْ لَهُ فِى حَرْثِهِ وَمَنْ كَانَ يُرِيدُ حَرْثَ الدُّنْيَا نُؤْتِهِ مِنْهَا وَمَالَهُ فِى الْآخِرَةِ مِنْ نَصِيبٍ

٢١ أَمْ لَهُمْ شُرَكَاءُ شَرَعُوا لَهُمْ مِنَ الدِّينِ مَا لَمْ يَأْذَنْ بِهِ اللَّهُ وَلَوْلَا كَلِمَةُ الْفَصْلِ لَقُضِىَ بَيْنَهُمْ وَإِنَّ الظَّالِمِينَ لَهُمْ عَذَابٌ أَلِيمٌ

٢٢ تَرَى الظَّالِمِينَ مُشْفِقِينَ مِمَّا كَسَبُوا وَهُوَ وَاقِعٌ بِهِمْ وَالَّذِينَ ءَامَنُوا وَعَمِلُوا الصَّالِحَاتِ فِى رَوْضَاتِ الْجَنَّاتِ لَهُمْ مَا يَشَاءُونَ عِنْدَ رَبِّهِمْ ذَلِكَ هُوَ الْفَضْلُ الْكَبِيرُ

23. This it is which Allah announces unto His bondmen who believe and do good works. Say (O Muhammad, unto mankind): I ask of you no fee therefor, but loving kindness among kinsfolk. And who scores a good deed we add unto its good for him. Lo! Allah is Forgiving, Responsive.

24. Or say they: He has invented a lie concerning Allah? If Allah willed, He could have sealed your heart (against them). And Allah will wipe out the lie and will vindicate the truth by His words. Lo! He is aware of what is hidden in the breasts (of men).

25. And He it is Who accepts repentance from his bondmen, and pardons the evil deeds, and knows what you do.

26. And accepts those who believe and do good works, and gives in-crease unto them of His bounty. And as for disbelievers, theirs will be an awful doom.

27. And if Allah were to enlarge the provision for His slaves they would surely rebel in the earth, but He sends down by measure as He wills. Lo! He is Informed, a Seer of His bondmen.

28. And He it is Who sends down the saving rain after they have despaired, and spreads out His mercy. He is the Pro-tecting Friend, the Praiseworthy.

29. And of His portents is the creation of the heaven and the earth, and of whatever beasts He has dispersed there-in. And He is Able to gather them when He will.

30. Whatever of misfortune strikes you, it is what your right hands have earned. And He forgives much.

31. You cannot escape in the earth, for beside Allah you have no protecting friend nor any helper.

32. And of His portents are the ships, like mountains on the sea;

33. If He will He calms the wind so that they keep still upon its surface— Lo! herein surely are signs for every steadfast, grateful (heart)—

34. Or he causes them to perish on account of that which they have earned—And He forgives much—

35. And that those who argue concerning Our revelations may know they have no refuge.

36. Now whatever you have been given is but a passing comfort for the life of the world, and that which Allah has is better and more lasting for those who believe and put their trust in their Lord.

37. And those who shun the worst of sins and indecencies and, when they are wroth, forgive,

38. And those who answer the call of their Lord and establish prayer, and whose affairs are a matter of counsel, and who spend of what We have bestowed on them,

39. And those who, when great wrong is done to them, defend themselves,

40. The recompense of an ill deed is an ill the like thereof. But whosoever pardons and amends, his wage is the affair of Allah. Lo! He loves not wrongdoers.

41. And who defends himself after he has suffered wrong— for such, there is no way (of blame) against them.

42. The way (of blame) is only against those who oppress mankind, and wrongfully rebel in the earth. For such there is a painful doom.

(٣١) وَمَآ أَنتُم بِمُعۡجِزِينَ فِى ٱلۡأَرۡضِ وَمَا لَكُم مِّن دُونِ ٱللَّهِ مِن وَلِىٍّ وَلَا نَصِيرٍ

(٣٢) وَمِنۡ ءَايَٰتِهِ ٱلۡجَوَارِ فِى ٱلۡبَحۡرِ كَٱلۡأَعۡلَٰمِ

(٣٣) إِن يَشَأۡ يُسۡكِنِ ٱلرِّيحَ فَيَظۡلَلۡنَ رَوَاكِدَ عَلَىٰ ظَهۡرِهِۦٓ إِنَّ فِى ذَٰلِكَ لَأٓيَٰتٍ لِّكُلِّ صَبَّارٍ شَكُورٍ

(٣٤) أَوۡ يُوبِقۡهُنَّ بِمَا كَسَبُوا۟ وَيَعۡفُ عَن كَثِيرٍ

(٣٥) وَيَعۡلَمَ ٱلَّذِينَ يُجَٰدِلُونَ فِىٓ ءَايَٰتِنَا مَا لَهُم مِّن مَّحِيصٍ

(٣٦) فَمَآ أُوتِيتُم مِّن شَىۡءٍ فَمَتَٰعُ ٱلۡحَيَوٰةِ ٱلدُّنۡيَا وَمَا عِندَ ٱللَّهِ خَيۡرٌ وَأَبۡقَىٰ لِلَّذِينَ ءَامَنُوا۟ وَعَلَىٰ رَبِّهِمۡ يَتَوَكَّلُونَ

(٣٧) وَٱلَّذِينَ يَجۡتَنِبُونَ كَبَٰٓئِرَ ٱلۡإِثۡمِ وَٱلۡفَوَٰحِشَ وَإِذَا مَا غَضِبُوا۟ هُمۡ يَغۡفِرُونَ

(٣٨) وَٱلَّذِينَ ٱسۡتَجَابُوا۟ لِرَبِّهِمۡ وَأَقَامُوا۟ ٱلصَّلَوٰةَ وَأَمۡرُهُمۡ شُورَىٰ بَيۡنَهُمۡ وَمِمَّا رَزَقۡنَٰهُمۡ يُنفِقُونَ

(٣٩) وَٱلَّذِينَ إِذَآ أَصَابَهُمُ ٱلۡبَغۡىُ هُمۡ يَنتَصِرُونَ

(٤٠) وَجَزَٰٓؤُا۟ سَيِّئَةٍ سَيِّئَةٌ مِّثۡلُهَا فَمَنۡ عَفَا وَأَصۡلَحَ فَأَجۡرُهُۥ عَلَى ٱللَّهِ إِنَّهُۥ لَا يُحِبُّ ٱلظَّٰلِمِينَ

(٤١) وَلَمَنِ ٱنتَصَرَ بَعۡدَ ظُلۡمِهِۦ فَأُو۟لَٰٓئِكَ مَا عَلَيۡهِم مِّن سَبِيلٍ

(٤٢) إِنَّمَا ٱلسَّبِيلُ عَلَى ٱلَّذِينَ يَظۡلِمُونَ ٱلنَّاسَ وَيَبۡغُونَ فِى ٱلۡأَرۡضِ بِغَيۡرِ ٱلۡحَقِّ أُو۟لَٰٓئِكَ لَهُمۡ عَذَابٌ أَلِيمٌ

43. And surely who is patient and forgives, lo! that, surely, is (of) the steadfast heart of things.

44. He whom Allah sends astray, for him there is no protecting friend after Him. And you (Muhammad) will see the evildoers when they see the doom, (how) they say: Is there any way of return?

45. And you will see them exposed to (the Fire), made humble by disgrace, and looking with veiled eyes. And those who believe will say: Lo! the (eternal) losers are they who lose themselves and their housefolk on the Day of Resur-rection. Lo! Wrongdoers are indeed in perpetual torment

46. And they will have no protecting friends to help them instead of Allah. He whom Allah sends astray, for him there is no road.

47. Answer the call of your Lord before there comes unto you from Allah a Day for which there is no averting. You have no refuge on that Day, nor have you any (power of) refusal.

48. But if they are averse, We have not sent you (Muhammad) as a warder over them. Yours is only to convey (the message). And lo! when We cause man to taste of mercy from Us he exults therefor. And if some evil strikes them because of that which their own hands have sent before, then lo! man is an ingrate.

49. Unto Allah belongs the sovereignty of the heavens and the earth. He creates what He will. He bestows female (offspring) upon whom He will, and bestows male (offspring) upon whom He will;

50. Or He mingles them, males and females, and He makes barren whom He will. Lo! He is Knower, Powerful.

﴿٤٣﴾ وَلَمَن صَبَرَ وَغَفَرَ إِنَّ ذَٰلِكَ لَمِنْ عَزْمِ الْأُمُورِ

﴿٤٤﴾ وَمَن يُضْلِلِ اللَّهُ فَمَا لَهُ مِن وَلِيٍّ مِّنْ بَعْدِهِ ۗ وَتَرَى الظَّالِمِينَ لَمَّا رَأَوُا الْعَذَابَ يَقُولُونَ هَلْ إِلَىٰ مَرَدٍّ مِّن سَبِيلٍ

﴿٤٥﴾ وَتَرَاهُمْ يُعْرَضُونَ عَلَيْهَا خَاشِعِينَ مِنَ الذُّلِّ يَنظُرُونَ مِن طَرْفٍ خَفِيٍّ ۗ وَقَالَ الَّذِينَ آمَنُوا إِنَّ الْخَاسِرِينَ الَّذِينَ خَسِرُوا أَنفُسَهُمْ وَأَهْلِيهِمْ يَوْمَ الْقِيَامَةِ ۗ أَلَا إِنَّ الظَّالِمِينَ فِي عَذَابٍ مُّقِيمٍ

﴿٤٦﴾ وَمَا كَانَ لَهُم مِّنْ أَوْلِيَاءَ يَنصُرُونَهُم مِّن دُونِ اللَّهِ ۗ وَمَن يُضْلِلِ اللَّهُ فَمَا لَهُ مِن سَبِيلٍ

﴿٤٧﴾ اسْتَجِيبُوا لِرَبِّكُم مِّن قَبْلِ أَن يَأْتِيَ يَوْمٌ لَّا مَرَدَّ لَهُ مِنَ اللَّهِ ۚ مَا لَكُم مِّن مَّلْجَإٍ يَوْمَئِذٍ وَمَا لَكُم مِّن نَّكِيرٍ

﴿٤٨﴾ فَإِنْ أَعْرَضُوا فَمَا أَرْسَلْنَاكَ عَلَيْهِمْ حَفِيظًا ۖ إِنْ عَلَيْكَ إِلَّا الْبَلَاغُ ۗ وَإِنَّا إِذَا أَذَقْنَا الْإِنسَانَ مِنَّا رَحْمَةً فَرِحَ بِهَا ۖ وَإِن تُصِبْهُمْ سَيِّئَةٌ بِمَا قَدَّمَتْ أَيْدِيهِمْ فَإِنَّ الْإِنسَانَ كَفُورٌ

﴿٤٩﴾ لِّلَّهِ مُلْكُ السَّمَاوَاتِ وَالْأَرْضِ ۚ يَخْلُقُ مَا يَشَاءُ ۚ يَهَبُ لِمَن يَشَاءُ إِنَاثًا وَيَهَبُ لِمَن يَشَاءُ الذُّكُورَ

﴿٥٠﴾ أَوْ يُزَوِّجُهُمْ ذُكْرَانًا وَإِنَاثًا ۖ وَيَجْعَلُ مَن يَشَاءُ عَقِيمًا ۚ إِنَّهُ عَلِيمٌ قَدِيرٌ

51. And it was not (vouchsafed) to any mortal that Allah should speak to him unless (it be) by revelation or from behind a veil, or (that) He sends a messenger to reveal what He will by His leave. Lo! He is Exalted, Wise.

52. And thus have We inspired in you (Muhammad) a Spirit of Our command. You knew not what the Scripture was, nor what the Faith. But We have made it a light whereby We guide whom We will of Our bondmen. And lo! you surely do guide unto a right path.

53. The path of Allah, unto Whom belongs whatsoever is in the heavens and whatsoever is in the earth. Behold all things do indeed tend towards Allah.

﴿٥١﴾ ۞ وَمَا كَانَ لِبَشَرٍ أَن يُكَلِّمَهُ اللَّهُ إِلَّا وَحْيًا أَوْ مِن وَرَآىِٕ حِجَابٍ أَوْ يُرْسِلَ رَسُولًا فَيُوحِيَ بِإِذْنِهِ مَا يَشَآءُ إِنَّهُ عَلِيٌّ حَكِيمٌ

﴿٥٢﴾ وَكَذَٰلِكَ أَوْحَيْنَا إِلَيْكَ رُوحًا مِّنْ أَمْرِنَا مَا كُنتَ تَدْرِي مَا ٱلْكِتَابُ وَلَا ٱلْإِيمَانُ وَلَٰكِن جَعَلْنَاهُ نُورًا نَّهْدِي بِهِ مَن نَّشَآءُ مِنْ عِبَادِنَا وَإِنَّكَ لَتَهْدِي إِلَىٰ صِرَاطٍ مُّسْتَقِيمٍ

﴿٥٣﴾ صِرَاطِ ٱللَّهِ ٱلَّذِي لَهُ مَا فِي ٱلسَّمَاوَاتِ وَمَا فِي ٱلْأَرْضِ أَلَا إِلَى ٱللَّهِ تَصِيرُ ٱلْأُمُورُ

Ornaments of Gold

Al Zukhruf, "Ornaments of Gold," is the fourth of the *Ḥā Mīm* surahs. It takes its name from a word meaning "golden ornaments," which occurs in verse 35.

It belongs to the middle group of Makkan surahs.

Ornaments of Gold

Revealed at Makkah

*In the name of Allah,
the Beneficent, the Merciful*

1. *H*ā. Mīm.[246]

2. By the Scripture which makes plain,

3. Lo! We have appointed it a Qur'an in Arabic that you may understand.

4. And lo! in the Source of Decrees, which We possess, it is indeed sublime, decisive,

5. Shall We utterly ignore you because you are a wanton people?

6. How many a Prophet did We send among the men of old!

7. And never came there unto them a Prophet but they used to mock him.

8. Then we destroyed men mightier than these in prowess; and the example of the men of old has gone (before them).

9. And if you (Muhammad) ask them: Who created the heavens and the earth, they will surely answer: The Mighty, the Knower created them;

10. Who made the earth a resting place for you, and placed roads for you therein, that you may find your way;

11. And who sends down water from the sky in (due) measure, and We revive a dead land therewith. Even so will you be brought forth;

12. He who created all the pairs, and appointed for you ships and cattle whereupon you ride.

13. That you may mount upon their backs, and may remember your Lord's favor when you mount thereon, and may say: Glorified be He Who has subdued these unto us, and we were not capable (of subduing them);

---

[246]See Surah 2:1, footnote.

14. And lo! unto our Lord we are returning.

١٤ وَإِنَّا إِلَى رَبِّنَا لَمُنقَلِبُونَ

15. And they allot to Him a portion of His bondmen! Lo! man is surely a mere ingrate.

١٥ وَجَعَلُوا لَهُ مِنْ عِبَادِهِ جُزْءًا إِنَّ الْإِنسَانَ لَكَفُورٌ مُّبِينٌ

16. Or chooses He daughters of all that He has created, and honors He you with sons?

١٦ أَمِ اتَّخَذَ مِمَّا يَخْلُقُ بَنَاتٍ وَأَصْفَاكُم بِالْبَنِينَ

17. And if one of them has tidings of that which he likens to the Beneficent One,247 his countenance becomes black and he is full of inward rage.

١٧ وَإِذَا بُشِّرَ أَحَدُهُم بِمَا ضَرَبَ لِلرَّحْمَٰنِ مَثَلًا ظَلَّ وَجْهُهُ مُسْوَدًّا وَهُوَ كَظِيمٌ

18. (Liken they then to Allah) that which is bred up in outward show, and in dispute cannot make itself plain?

١٨ أَوَمَن يُنَشَّأُ فِي الْحِلْيَةِ وَهُوَ فِي الْخِصَامِ غَيْرُ مُبِينٍ

19. And they make the angels, who are the slaves of the Beneficent, females. Did they witness their creation? Their testimony will be recorded and they will be questioned.

١٩ وَجَعَلُوا الْمَلَائِكَةَ الَّذِينَ هُمْ عِبَادُ الرَّحْمَٰنِ إِنَاثًا أَشَهِدُوا خَلْقَهُمْ سَتُكْتَبُ شَهَادَتُهُمْ وَيُسْأَلُونَ

20. And they say: If the Beneficent One had (so) willed, we should not have worshiped them. They have no knowledge whatsoever of that. They do but guess.

٢٠ وَقَالُوا لَوْ شَاءَ الرَّحْمَٰنُ مَا عَبَدْنَاهُمْ مَّا لَهُم بِذَٰلِكَ مِنْ عِلْمٍ إِنْ هُمْ إِلَّا يَخْرُصُونَ

21. Or have We given them any Scripture before (this Qur'an) so that they are holding fast thereto?

٢١ أَمْ آتَيْنَاهُمْ كِتَابًا مِّن قَبْلِهِ فَهُم بِهِ مُسْتَمْسِكُونَ

22. Nay, for they say only: Lo! we found our fathers following a religion, and we are guided by their footprints.

٢٢ بَلْ قَالُوا إِنَّا وَجَدْنَا آبَاءَنَا عَلَىٰ أُمَّةٍ وَإِنَّا عَلَىٰ آثَارِهِم مُّهْتَدُونَ

23. And even so We sent not a warner before you (Muhammad) into any township but its luxurious ones said: Lo! we found our fathers following a religion, and we are following their footprints.

٢٣ وَكَذَٰلِكَ مَا أَرْسَلْنَا مِن قَبْلِكَ فِي قَرْيَةٍ مِّن نَّذِيرٍ إِلَّا قَالَ مُتْرَفُوهَا إِنَّا وَجَدْنَا آبَاءَنَا عَلَىٰ أُمَّةٍ وَإِنَّا عَلَىٰ آثَارِهِم مُّقْتَدُونَ

24. (And the warner) said: What! Even though I bring you better guidance than that you found your fathers following? They answered: Lo! in what you bring we are disbelievers.

٢٤ ۞ قَالَ أَوَلَوْ جِئْتُكُم بِأَهْدَىٰ مِمَّا وَجَدتُّمْ عَلَيْهِ آبَاءَكُمْ قَالُوا إِنَّا بِمَا أُرْسِلْتُم بِهِ كَافِرُونَ

25. So We requited them. Then see the nature of the consequence for the rejecters!

٢٥ فَانتَقَمْنَا مِنْهُمْ فَانظُرْ كَيْفَ كَانَ عَاقِبَةُ الْمُكَذِّبِينَ

247i.e., tidings of the birth of a daughter.

26. And when Abraham said unto his father and his folk: Lo! I am innocent of what you worship

27. Save Him Who did create me, for He will surely guide me.

28. And he made it a word enduring among his seed, that they might return.

29. Nay, but I let these and their fathers enjoy life (only) till there should come unto them the Truth and a messenger making plain.

30. And now that the Truth has come unto them they say: This is mere magic, and lo! we are disbelievers therein.

31. And they say: If only this Qur'an had been revealed to some great man of the two towns[248]!

32. Is it they who apportion your Lord's mercy? We have apportioned among them their livelihood in the life of the world, and raised some of them above others in rank that some of them may take labor from others; and the mercy of your Lord is better than (the wealth) that they amass.

33. And were it not that mankind would have become one community,[249] We might well have appointed, for those who disbelieve in the Beneficent, roofs of silver for their houses and lifts (of silver) whereby to mount,

34. And for their houses doors (of silver) and couches of silver whereon to recline,

35. And ornaments of gold. Yet all that would have been but a provision of the life of the world. And the Hereafter with your Lord would have been for those who keep from evil.

36. And he whose sight is dim to the remembrance of the Beneficent, We assign unto him a devil who becomes his comrade;

﴿٢٦﴾ وَإِذْ قَالَ إِبْرَاهِيمُ لِأَبِيهِ وَقَوْمِهِ إِنَّنِي بَرَاءٌ مِّمَّا تَعْبُدُونَ

﴿٢٧﴾ إِلَّا الَّذِي فَطَرَنِي فَإِنَّهُ سَيَهْدِينِ

﴿٢٨﴾ وَجَعَلَهَا كَلِمَةً بَاقِيَةً فِي عَقِبِهِ لَعَلَّهُمْ يَرْجِعُونَ

﴿٢٩﴾ بَلْ مَتَّعْتُ هَٰؤُلَاءِ وَآبَاءَهُمْ حَتَّى جَاءَهُمُ الْحَقُّ وَرَسُولٌ مُّبِينٌ

﴿٣٠﴾ وَلَمَّا جَاءَهُمُ الْحَقُّ قَالُوا هَٰذَا سِحْرٌ وَإِنَّا بِهِ كَافِرُونَ

﴿٣١﴾ وَقَالُوا لَوْلَا نُزِّلَ هَٰذَا الْقُرْآنُ عَلَى رَجُلٍ مِّنَ الْقَرْيَتَيْنِ عَظِيمٍ

﴿٣٢﴾ أَهُمْ يَقْسِمُونَ رَحْمَتَ رَبِّكَ نَحْنُ قَسَمْنَا بَيْنَهُم مَّعِيشَتَهُمْ فِي الْحَيَاةِ الدُّنْيَا وَرَفَعْنَا بَعْضَهُمْ فَوْقَ بَعْضٍ دَرَجَاتٍ لِّيَتَّخِذَ بَعْضُهُم بَعْضًا سُخْرِيًّا وَرَحْمَتُ رَبِّكَ خَيْرٌ مِّمَّا يَجْمَعُونَ

﴿٣٣﴾ وَلَوْلَا أَن يَكُونَ النَّاسُ أُمَّةً وَاحِدَةً لَّجَعَلْنَا لِمَن يَكْفُرُ بِالرَّحْمَٰنِ لِبُيُوتِهِمْ سُقُفًا مِّن فِضَّةٍ وَمَعَارِجَ عَلَيْهَا يَظْهَرُونَ

﴿٣٤﴾ وَلِبُيُوتِهِمْ أَبْوَابًا وَسُرُرًا عَلَيْهَا يَتَّكِئُونَ

﴿٣٥﴾ وَزُخْرُفًا وَإِن كُلُّ ذَٰلِكَ لَمَّا مَتَاعُ الْحَيَاةِ الدُّنْيَا وَالْآخِرَةُ عِندَ رَبِّكَ لِلْمُتَّقِينَ

﴿٣٦﴾ وَمَن يَعْشُ عَن ذِكْرِ الرَّحْمَٰنِ نُقَيِّضْ لَهُ شَيْطَانًا فَهُوَ لَهُ قَرِينٌ

---

[248]The towns of Makkah and Ṭā'if.
[249]Through love of riches.

37. And lo! they surely turn them from the way of Allah, and yet they deem that they are rightly guided;

38. Till, when he comes unto Us, he said (unto his comrade): Ah, would that between me and you there were the distance of the two horizons—an evil comrade![250]

39. And it profits you not this day, that you did wrong, that you will be sharers in the doom.

40. Can you (Muhammad) make the deaf to hear, or can you guide the blind or him who is in error manifest?

41. And if We take you away, We surely shall take ven-geance on them,

42. Or (if) We show you that wherewith We threaten them; for lo! We have complete command of them.

43. So hold you fast to that which is inspired in you. Lo! you are on a right path.

44. And lo! it is in truth a Reminder for you and for your folk; and you will be questioned.

45. And ask those of Our messengers whom We sent before you: Did We ever appoint gods to be worshiped beside the Beneficent?

46. And surely We sent Moses with Our revelations unto Pharaoh and his chiefs, and he said: I am a messenger of the Lord of the Worlds.

47. But when he brought them Our tokens, behold! they laughed at them.

48. And every token that We showed them was greater than its sister (token), and we grasped them with the torment, that they might turn again.

49. And they said: O wizard; Entreat your Lord for us by the pact that He has made with you. Lo! we surely will walk aright.

---

[250]The two horizons: lit. the two Easts.

50. But when We eased them of the torment, behold! they broke their word.

٥٠ فَلَمَّا كَشَفْنَا عَنْهُمُ الْعَذَابَ إِذَا هُمْ يَنكُثُونَ

51. And Pharaoh caused a proclamation to be made among his people. He said: O my people! Is not mine the sovereignty of Egypt and these rivers flowing under me? Can you not then discern?

٥١ وَنَادَىٰ فِرْعَوْنُ فِى قَوْمِهِ قَالَ يَٰقَوْمِ أَلَيْسَ لِى مُلْكُ مِصْرَ وَهَٰذِهِ الْأَنْهَٰرُ تَجْرِى مِن تَحْتِى أَفَلَا تُبْصِرُونَ

52. Am I not surely better than this fellow, who is despicable, and can hardly make (his meaning) plain?

٥٢ أَمْ أَنَا خَيْرٌ مِّنْ هَٰذَا الَّذِى هُوَ مَهِينٌ وَلَا يَكَادُ يُبِينُ

53. Why, then, have armlets of gold not been set upon him, or angels sent along with him?

٥٣ فَلَوْلَا أُلْقِىَ عَلَيْهِ أَسْوِرَةٌ مِّن ذَهَبٍ أَوْ جَاءَ مَعَهُ الْمَلَٰئِكَةُ مُقْتَرِنِينَ

54. Thus he persuaded his people to make light (of Moses), and they obeyed him. Lo! they were a wanton folk.

٥٤ فَاسْتَخَفَّ قَوْمَهُ فَأَطَاعُوهُ إِنَّهُمْ كَانُوا قَوْمًا فَٰسِقِينَ

55. So, when they angered Us, We punished them and drowned them every one.

٥٥ فَلَمَّا آسَفُونَا انتَقَمْنَا مِنْهُمْ فَأَغْرَقْنَٰهُمْ أَجْمَعِينَ

56. And We made them a thing past, and an example for those after (them).

٥٦ فَجَعَلْنَٰهُمْ سَلَفًا وَمَثَلًا لِّلْآخِرِينَ

57. And when the son of Mary is quoted as an example, behold! your folk laugh out,

٥٧ وَلَمَّا ضُرِبَ ابْنُ مَرْيَمَ مَثَلًا إِذَا قَوْمُكَ مِنْهُ يَصِدُّونَ

58. And they say: Are our gods better, or is he? They raise not the objection save for argument. Nay! but they are a contentious folk.

٥٨ وَقَالُوا أَآلِهَتُنَا خَيْرٌ أَمْ هُوَ مَا ضَرَبُوهُ لَكَ إِلَّا جَدَلًا بَلْ هُمْ قَوْمٌ خَصِمُونَ

59. He is nothing but a slave[251] on whom We bestowed favor, and We made him a pattern for the Children of Israel.

٥٩ إِنْ هُوَ إِلَّا عَبْدٌ أَنْعَمْنَا عَلَيْهِ وَجَعَلْنَٰهُ مَثَلًا لِّبَنِى إِسْرَٰئِيلَ

60. And had We willed We could have set among you angels to be viceroys in the earth.

٦٠ وَلَوْ نَشَاءُ لَجَعَلْنَا مِنكُم مَّلَٰئِكَةً فِى الْأَرْضِ يَخْلُفُونَ

61. And In (Jesus) shall be a sign of the Hour. So doubt you not concerning it, but follow Me. This is the right path.

٦١ وَإِنَّهُ لَعِلْمٌ لِّلسَّاعَةِ فَلَا تَمْتَرُنَّ بِهَا وَاتَّبِعُونِ هَٰذَا صِرَٰطٌ مُّسْتَقِيمٌ

62. And let not the Devil turn you aside. Lo! he is an open enemy for you.

٦٢ وَلَا يَصُدَّنَّكُمُ الشَّيْطَانُ إِنَّهُ لَكُمْ عَدُوٌّ مُّبِينٌ

---

[251] 'Abd Allāh, "servant or slave of God," is a proud designation for the Muslims, for bondage to Allah implies liberation from all earthly servitudes.

63. When Jesus came with clear proofs (of Allah's sovereignty), he said: I have come unto you with wisdom, and to make plain some of that concerning which you differ. So keep your duty to Allah, and obey me.

64. Lo! Allah, He is my Lord and your Lord. So worship Him. This is a right path.

65. But the factions among them differed. Then woe unto those who do wrong from the doom of a painful day.

66. Await they anything save the Hour, that it shall come upon them suddenly, when they know not?

67. Friends on that day will be foes one to another, save those who kept their duty (to Allah).

68. O My slaves! For you there is no fear this day, nor is it you who grieve;

69. (You) who believed Our revelations and were Muslims,

70. Enter the Garden, you and your wives, to be made glad.

71. Therein are brought round for them trays of gold and goblets, and therein is all that souls desire and eyes find sweet. And you are immortal therein.

72. This is the Garden which you are made to inherit be-cause of what you used to do.

73. Therein for you is fruit in plenty whence to eat.

74. Lo! the criminals are immortal in Hell's torment.

75. It is not relaxed for them, and they despair therein.

76. We wronged them not, but they it was who did the wrong.

٦٣ وَلَمَّا جَاءَ عِيسَى بِالْبَيِّنَاتِ قَالَ قَدْ جِئْتُكُمْ بِالْحِكْمَةِ وَلِأُبَيِّنَ لَكُمْ بَعْضَ الَّذِي تَخْتَلِفُونَ فِيهِ فَاتَّقُوا اللَّهَ وَأَطِيعُونِ

٦٤ إِنَّ اللَّهَ هُوَ رَبِّي وَرَبُّكُمْ فَاعْبُدُوهُ هَذَا صِرَاطٌ مُسْتَقِيمٌ

٦٥ فَاخْتَلَفَ الْأَحْزَابُ مِنْ بَيْنِهِمْ فَوَيْلٌ لِلَّذِينَ ظَلَمُوا مِنْ عَذَابِ يَوْمٍ أَلِيمٍ

٦٦ هَلْ يَنْظُرُونَ إِلَّا السَّاعَةَ أَنْ تَأْتِيَهُمْ بَغْتَةً وَهُمْ لَا يَشْعُرُونَ

٦٧ الْأَخِلَّاءُ يَوْمَئِذٍ بَعْضُهُمْ لِبَعْضٍ عَدُوٌّ إِلَّا الْمُتَّقِينَ

٦٨ يَا عِبَادِ لَا خَوْفٌ عَلَيْكُمُ الْيَوْمَ وَلَا أَنْتُمْ تَحْزَنُونَ

٦٩ الَّذِينَ آمَنُوا بِآيَاتِنَا وَكَانُوا مُسْلِمِينَ

٧٠ ادْخُلُوا الْجَنَّةَ أَنْتُمْ وَأَزْوَاجُكُمْ تُحْبَرُونَ

٧١ يُطَافُ عَلَيْهِمْ بِصِحَافٍ مِنْ ذَهَبٍ وَأَكْوَابٍ وَفِيهَا مَا تَشْتَهِيهِ الْأَنْفُسُ وَتَلَذُّ الْأَعْيُنُ وَأَنْتُمْ فِيهَا خَالِدُونَ

٧٢ وَتِلْكَ الْجَنَّةُ الَّتِي أُورِثْتُمُوهَا بِمَا كُنْتُمْ تَعْمَلُونَ

٧٣ لَكُمْ فِيهَا فَاكِهَةٌ كَثِيرَةٌ مِنْهَا تَأْكُلُونَ

٧٤ إِنَّ الْمُجْرِمِينَ فِي عَذَابِ جَهَنَّمَ خَالِدُونَ

٧٥ لَا يُفَتَّرُ عَنْهُمْ وَهُمْ فِيهِ مُبْلِسُونَ

٧٦ وَمَا ظَلَمْنَاهُمْ وَلَكِنْ كَانُوا هُمُ الظَّالِمِينَ

77. And they cry: O Mālik![252] Let your Lord make an end of us. He said: Lo! here you must remain.

78. We surely brought the Truth unto you, but you were, most of you, averse to the Truth.

79. Or do they determine any thing (against the Prophet)? Lo! We (also) are determining.

80. Or deem they that We cannot hear their secret thoughts and private conferences? Nay, but Our envoys, present with them, do record.

81. Say (O Muhammad): If the Beneficent had a son. I would be first among the worshippers.

82. Glorified be the Lord of the heavens and the earth, the Lord of the Throne, from that which they ascribe (unto Him)!

83. So let them flounder (in their talk) and play until they meet the Day which they are promised.

84. And He it is Who in heaven is God, and in the earth God. He is the Wise, the Knower.

85. And blessed be He unto Whom belongs the Sovereignty of the heavens and the earth and all that is between them, and with Whom is knowledge of the Hour, and unto Whom you will be returned.

86. And those unto whom they cry instead of Him possess no power of intercession, saving him who bears witness unto the Truth knowingly.

87. And if you ask them who created them, they will surely say: Allah. How then are they turned away?

88. And he said: O my Lord! Lo! those are a folk who believe not.

89. Then bear with them (O Muhammad) and say: Peace. But they will come to know.

[252]Mālik is the name of the angel who is the custodian of Hell (Editor).

Smoke

Al Dukhān, "Smoke," takes its name from a word in verse 10. Tradition says that it refers prophetically to the haze of dust that surrounded Makkah at the time of the great drought and famine that preceded the Muslim conquest of Makkah and facilitated it.

It belongs to the middle group of Makkan surahs.

Smoke

Revealed at Makkah

*In the name of Allah,
the Beneficent, the Merciful*

1. Hā. Mīm.[253]

2. By the Scripture that makes plain

3. Lo! We revealed it on a blessed night. Lo! We are ever warning—

4. Whereupon every wise command is made clear

5. As a command from Our presence— Lo! We are ever sending—

6. A mercy from your Lord. Lo! He is the Hearer, the Knower,

7. Lord of the heavens and the earth and all that is between them, if you would be sure.

8. There is no God save Him. He quickens and gives death; your Lord and Lord of your forefathers.

9. Nay, but they play in doubt.

10. But watch you (O Muhammad) for the day when the sky will produce visible smoke

11. That will envelop the people.[254] This will be a painful torment.

12. (Then they will say): Our Lord relieve us of the torment. Lo! we are believers:

13. How can there be remembrance for them, when a messenger making plain (the truth) had already come unto them,

14. And they had turned away from him and said: One taught (by others), a madman?

15. Lo! We shall withdraw the torment for a while. You will but truly return (to disbelief).

16. On the day when We shall seize them with the greater seizure (then), in truth We shall punish.

17. And surely We tried before them Pharaoh's folk, when there came unto them a noble messenger,

---

[253]See Surah 2:1, footnote. - [254]Of Makkah.

18. Saying: Give up to me the slaves of Allah. Lo! I am a faithful messenger unto you.

١٨ أَنْ أَدُّوا إِلَيَّ عِبَادَ اللَّهِ إِنِّي لَكُمْ رَسُولٌ أَمِينٌ

19. And saying: Be not proud against Allah. Lo! I bring you a clear warrant.

١٩ وَأَن لَّا تَعْلُوا عَلَى اللَّهِ إِنِّي ءَاتِيكُم بِسُلْطَانٍ مُّبِينٍ

20. And lo! I have sought refuge in my Lord and your Lord lest you stone me to death.

٢٠ وَإِنِّي عُذْتُ بِرَبِّي وَرَبِّكُمْ أَن تَرْجُمُونِ

21. And if you put no faith in me, then let me go.

٢١ وَإِن لَّمْ تُؤْمِنُوا لِي فَاعْتَزِلُونِ

22. And he cried unto his Lord (saying): These are a criminal folk.

٢٢ فَدَعَا رَبَّهُ أَنَّ هَٰؤُلَاءِ قَوْمٌ مُّجْرِمُونَ

23. Then (his Lord commanded) Take away my slaves by night. Lo! you will be followed,

٢٣ فَأَسْرِ بِعِبَادِي لَيْلًا إِنَّكُم مُّتَّبَعُونَ

24. And leave the sea behind at rest, for lo! they are a drowned host.

٢٤ وَاتْرُكِ الْبَحْرَ رَهْوًا إِنَّهُمْ جُندٌ مُّغْرَقُونَ

25. How many were the gardens and the water springs that they left behind,

٢٥ كَمْ تَرَكُوا مِن جَنَّاتٍ وَعُيُونٍ

26. And the cornlands and the goodly sites

٢٦ وَزُرُوعٍ وَمَقَامٍ كَرِيمٍ

27. And pleasant things wherein they took delight!

٢٧ وَنَعْمَةٍ كَانُوا فِيهَا فَاكِهِينَ

28. Even so (it was), and We made it an inheritance for other folk;

٢٨ كَذَٰلِكَ وَأَوْرَثْنَاهَا قَوْمًا ءَاخَرِينَ

29. And the heaven and the earth wept not for them, nor were they reprieved.

٢٩ فَمَا بَكَتْ عَلَيْهِمُ السَّمَاءُ وَالْأَرْضُ وَمَا كَانُوا مُنظَرِينَ

30. And We delivered the Children of Israel from the shameful doom

٣٠ وَلَقَدْ نَجَّيْنَا بَنِي إِسْرَائِيلَ مِنَ الْعَذَابِ الْمُهِينِ

31. (We delivered them) from Pharaoh. Lo! he was a tyrant of the wanton ones.

٣١ مِن فِرْعَوْنَ إِنَّهُ كَانَ عَالِيًا مِّنَ الْمُسْرِفِينَ

32. And We chose them, knowingly, above (all) creatures.

٣٢ وَلَقَدِ اخْتَرْنَاهُمْ عَلَىٰ عِلْمٍ عَلَى الْعَالَمِينَ

33. And We gave them portents wherein was a clear trial.

٣٣ وَءَاتَيْنَاهُم مِّنَ الْآيَاتِ مَا فِيهِ بَلَاءٌ مُّبِينٌ

34. Lo! these, no doubt, are saying:

٣٤ إِنَّ هَٰؤُلَاءِ لَيَقُولُونَ

35. There is nothing but our first death, and we shall not be raised again.

٣٥ إِنْ هِيَ إِلَّا مَوْتَتُنَا الْأُولَىٰ وَمَا نَحْنُ بِمُنشَرِينَ

36. Bring back our fathers, if you speak the truth!

٣٦ فَأْتُوا بِآبَائِنَا إِن كُنتُمْ صَادِقِينَ

37. Are they better, or the folk of Tubba'[255] and those before them? We destroyed them, for surely they were criminals.

٣٧ أَهُمْ خَيْرٌ أَمْ قَوْمُ تُبَّعٍ وَالَّذِينَ مِن قَبْلِهِمْ أَهْلَكْنَاهُمْ إِنَّهُمْ كَانُوا مُجْرِمِينَ

38. And We created not the heavens and the earth, and all that is between them, in play.

٣٨ وَمَا خَلَقْنَا السَّمَاوَاتِ وَالْأَرْضَ وَمَا بَيْنَهُمَا لَاعِبِينَ

---

[255] A name for many kings of Himyar (the South Arabians), each of whom was called Tubba', just as every king of Egypt was called Pharaoh.

39. We created them not save with truth; but most of them know not.

40. Assuredly the Day of Decision is the term of all of them,

41. A day when friend can in nothing avail friend, nor can they be helped,

42. Save him on whom Allah has mercy. Lo! He is the Mighty, the Merciful.

43. Lo! the tree of Zaqqūm[256] is

44. The food of the sinner!

45. Like molten brass, it seethes in their bellies

46. As the seething of boiling water.

47. (And it will be said): Take him and drag him to the midst of Hell,

48. Then pour upon his head the torment of boiling water.

49. (Saying): Taste! Lo! you were no doubt the mighty, the noble!

50. Lo! this is that whereof you used to doubt.

51. Lo! those who kept their duty will be in a place secure

52. Amid gardens and water springs,

53. Attired in silk and silk embroidery, facing one another.

54. Even so (it will be). And We shall wed them unto fair ones with wide, lovely eyes.

55. They call therein for every fruit in safety.

56. They taste not death therein, save the first death. And He has saved them from the doom of Hell,

57. A bounty from your Lord. That is the supreme triumph.

58. And We have made (this Scripture) easy in your language only that they may heed.

59. Wait then (O Muhammad). Lo! they (too) are waiting.

---

[256]See Surahs 37:62, 56:52.

Crouching

Al Jāthīyah, "Crouching," takes its name from a word in verse 28. It belongs to the middle group of Makkan surahs.

Crouching

Revealed at Makkah

*In the name of Allah,
the Beneficent, the Merciful*

1. **H**ā. Mīm.[257]

2. The revelation of the Scripture is from Allah, the Mighty, the Wise.

3. Lo! in the heavens and the earth are portents for believers.

4. And in your creation, and all the beasts that He scattered in the earth, are portents for a folk whose faith is sure.

5. And the difference of night and day and the provision that Allah sends down from the sky and thereby quickens the earth after her death, and the ordering of the winds, are portents for a people who have sense.

6. These are the portents of Allah which We recite unto you (Muhammad) with truth. Then in what fact, after Allah and His portents, will they believe?

7. Woe unto each sinful liar,

8. Who hears the revelations of Allah recited unto him, and then continues in pride as though he heard them not. Then give him tidings of a painful doom.

9. And when he knows anything of Our revelations he makes it a jest. For such there is a shameful doom.

10. Beyond them there is Hell, and that which they have earned will nothing avail them, nor those whom they have chosen for protecting friends beside Allah. Theirs will be an awful doom.

11. This is guidance. And those who disbelieve the revelations of their Lord, for them there is a painful doom of wrath.

---

12. Allah it is Who has made the sea of service unto you that the ships may run thereon by His command, and that you may seek of His bounty, and that you may be thankful;

13. And has made of service unto you whatsoever is in the heavens and whatsoever is in the earth; it is all from Him. Lo! herein surely are portents for people who reflect.

14. Tell those who believe to forgive those who hope not for the days of Allah; in order that He may requite folk what they used to earn.

15. Who does right, it is for his soul, and who does wrong, it is against it. And afterward unto your Lord you will be brought back.

16. And surely We gave the Children of Israel the Scrip-ture and the Command and the Prophethood, and provided them with good things and favored them above (all) peoples;

17. And gave them plain command-ments. And they differed not until after the knowledge came unto them, through oppression among themselves. Lo! your Lord will judge between them on the Day of Resurrection concerning that wherein they used to differ.

18. And now have We set you (O Muhammad) on a clear road of (Our) commandment; so follow it, and follow not the whims of those who know not.

19. Lo! they can avail you nothing against Allah. And lo! as for the wrong-doers, some of them are friends of others; and Allah is the Friend of those who ward off (evil).

20. This is clear indication for mankind, and a guidance and a mercy for a folk whose faith is sure.

21. Or do those who commit ill deeds suppose that We shall make them as those who believe and do good, the same life and death? Bad is their judgment!

22. And Allah has created the heavens and the earth with truth, and that every soul may be repaid what it has earned. And they will not be wronged.

٢٢ وَخَلَقَ اللَّهُ السَّمَوَاتِ وَالْأَرْضَ بِالْحَقِّ وَلِتُجْزَى كُلُّ نَفْسٍ بِمَا كَسَبَتْ وَهُمْ لَا يُظْلَمُونَ

23. Have you seen him who makes his desire his god, and Allah sends him astray despite his knowledge, and seals up his hearing and his heart, and sets on his sight a covering? Then who will lead him after Allah? Will you not then heed?

٢٣ أَفَرَأَيْتَ مَنِ اتَّخَذَ إِلَهَهُ هَوَاهُ وَأَضَلَّهُ اللَّهُ عَلَى عِلْمٍ وَخَتَمَ عَلَى سَمْعِهِ وَقَلْبِهِ وَجَعَلَ عَلَى بَصَرِهِ غِشَاوَةً فَمَنْ يَهْدِيهِ مِنْ بَعْدِ اللَّهِ أَفَلَا تَذَكَّرُونَ

24. And they say: There is nothing but our life of the world; we die and we live, and nothing destroys us save time; when they have no knowledge whatsoever of (all) that; they do but guess.

٢٤ وَقَالُوا مَا هِيَ إِلَّا حَيَاتُنَا الدُّنْيَا نَمُوتُ وَنَحْيَا وَمَا يُهْلِكُنَا إِلَّا الدَّهْرُ وَمَا لَهُمْ بِذَلِكَ مِنْ عِلْمٍ إِنْ هُمْ إِلَّا يَظُنُّونَ

25. And when Our clear revelations are recited unto them their only argument is that they say: Bring (back) our fathers then, if you are truthful.

٢٥ وَإِذَا تُتْلَى عَلَيْهِمْ آيَاتُنَا بَيِّنَاتٍ مَا كَانَ حُجَّتَهُمْ إِلَّا أَنْ قَالُوا ائْتُوا بِآبَائِنَا إِنْ كُنْتُمْ صَادِقِينَ

26. Say (unto them, O Muhammad): Allah gives life to you, then causes you to die, then gathers you unto the Day of Resurrection whereof there is no doubt. But most of mankind know not.

٢٦ قُلِ اللَّهُ يُحْيِيكُمْ ثُمَّ يُمِيتُكُمْ ثُمَّ يَجْمَعُكُمْ إِلَى يَوْمِ الْقِيَامَةِ لَا رَيْبَ فِيهِ وَلَكِنَّ أَكْثَرَ النَّاسِ لَا يَعْلَمُونَ

27. And unto Allah belongs the Sovereignty of the heavens and the earth; and on the day when the Hour rises, on that day those who follow falsehood will be the losers.

٢٧ وَلِلَّهِ مُلْكُ السَّمَوَاتِ وَالْأَرْضِ وَيَوْمَ تَقُومُ السَّاعَةُ يَوْمَئِذٍ يَخْسَرُ الْمُبْطِلُونَ

28. And you will see each nation crouching, each nation will be summoned to its record. (And it will be said unto them): This day you are requited what you used to do.

٢٨ وَتَرَى كُلَّ أُمَّةٍ جَاثِيَةً كُلُّ أُمَّةٍ تُدْعَى إِلَى كِتَابِهَا الْيَوْمَ تُجْزَوْنَ مَا كُنْتُمْ تَعْمَلُونَ

29. This Our Book pronounces against you with truth. Lo! We have caused (all) that you did to be recorded.

٢٩ هَذَا كِتَابُنَا يَنْطِقُ عَلَيْكُمْ بِالْحَقِّ إِنَّا كُنَّا نَسْتَنْسِخُ مَا كُنْتُمْ تَعْمَلُونَ

30. Then, as for those who believed and did good works, their Lord will bring them in unto His mercy. That is the evident triumph.

٣٠ فَأَمَّا الَّذِينَ آمَنُوا وَعَمِلُوا الصَّالِحَاتِ فَيُدْخِلُهُمْ رَبُّهُمْ فِي رَحْمَتِهِ ذَلِكَ هُوَ الْفَوْزُ الْمُبِينُ

31. And as for those who disbelieved (it will be said unto them): Were not Our revelations recited unto you? But you were scornful and became a criminal folk.

32. And when it was said: Lo! Allah's promise is the truth, and there is no doubt of the Hour's coming, you said: We know not what the Hour is. We deem it nothing but a conjecture, and we are by no means convinced.

33. And the evils of what they did will appear unto them, and that which they used to deride will befall them.

34. And it will be said: This day We forget you, even as you forgot the meeting of this your day; and your habitation is the Fire, and there is none to help you.

35. This, forasmuch as you made the revelations of Allah a jest, and the life of the world beguiled you. Therefore this day they come not forth from thence, nor will they be allowed to make amends.

36. Then praise be to Allah, Lord of the heavens and Lord of the earth, the Lord of the Worlds.

37. And unto Him (alone) belongs majesty in the heavens and the earth, and He is the Mighty, the Wise.

وَأَمَّا الَّذِينَ كَفَرُوٓا أَفَلَمْ تَكُنْ ءَايَٰتِى تُتْلَىٰ عَلَيْكُمْ فَٱسْتَكْبَرْتُمْ وَكُنتُمْ قَوْمًا مُّجْرِمِينَ ﴿٣١﴾

وَإِذَا قِيلَ إِنَّ وَعْدَ ٱللَّهِ حَقٌّ وَٱلسَّاعَةُ لَا رَيْبَ فِيهَا قُلْتُم مَّا نَدْرِى مَا ٱلسَّاعَةُ إِن نَّظُنُّ إِلَّا ظَنًّا وَمَا نَحْنُ بِمُسْتَيْقِنِينَ ﴿٣٢﴾

وَبَدَا لَهُمْ سَيِّئَاتُ مَا عَمِلُوا وَحَاقَ بِهِم مَّا كَانُوا بِهِۦ يَسْتَهْزِءُونَ ﴿٣٣﴾

وَقِيلَ ٱلْيَوْمَ نَنسَاكُمْ كَمَا نَسِيتُمْ لِقَآءَ يَوْمِكُمْ هَٰذَا وَمَأْوَىٰكُمُ ٱلنَّارُ وَمَا لَكُم مِّن نَّٰصِرِينَ ﴿٣٤﴾

ذَٰلِكُم بِأَنَّكُمُ ٱتَّخَذْتُمْ ءَايَٰتِ ٱللَّهِ هُزُوًا وَغَرَّتْكُمُ ٱلْحَيَوٰةُ ٱلدُّنْيَا فَٱلْيَوْمَ لَا يُخْرَجُونَ مِنْهَا وَلَا هُمْ يُسْتَعْتَبُونَ ﴿٣٥﴾

فَلِلَّهِ ٱلْحَمْدُ رَبِّ ٱلسَّمَٰوَٰتِ وَرَبِّ ٱلْأَرْضِ رَبِّ ٱلْعَٰلَمِينَ ﴿٣٦﴾

وَلَهُ ٱلْكِبْرِيَآءُ فِى ٱلسَّمَٰوَٰتِ وَٱلْأَرْضِ وَهُوَ ٱلْعَزِيزُ ٱلْحَكِيمُ ﴿٣٧﴾

The Wind-Curved Sandhills

Al Aḥqāf, "The Wind-Curved Sandhills" (a formation familiar to all desert travellers and which characterized the region in which the tribe of 'Ād were said originally to have lived), takes its name from a word in verse 21. It is the last surah of the *Ḥā Mīm* group.

It belongs to the middle group of Makkan surahs, with the exceptions of verses 10, 15-18, and 35, which were revealed at al Madinah.

The Wind-Curved Sandhills

Revealed at Makkah

*In the name of Allah,
the Beneficent, the Merciful*

1. Ḥā. Mīm.[258]

2. The revelation of the Scripture is from Allah, the Mighty, the Wise.

3. We created not the heavens and the earth and all that is between them save with truth, and for a term appointed. But those who disbelieve turn away from that whereof they are warned.

4. Say (unto them, O Muhammad): Have you thought on all that you invoke beside Allah? Show me what they have created of the earth. Or have they any portion in the heavens? Bring me a Scripture before this (Scripture), or some vestige of knowledge (in support of what you say), if you are truthful.

5. And who is further astray than those who, instead of Allah, pray unto such as hear not their prayer until the Day of Resurrection, and they are unconscious of their prayer,

6. And when mankind are gathered (to the Judgment) will become enemies for them, and will become deniers of having been worshiped.

7. And when Our clear revelations are recited unto them, those who disbelieve say of the Truth when it reaches them: This is mere magic.

8. Or say they: He has invented it? Say (O Muhammad): If I have invented it, still you have no power to support me against Allah. He is best aware of what you say among yourselves concerning it. He suffices for a witness between me and you. And He is the Forgiving, the Merciful.

---

[258]See Surah 2:1, footnote.

9. Say: I am no new thing among the messengers (of Allah), nor know I what will be done with me or with you. I do but follow that which is inspired in me, and I am but a plain warner.

10. Say: Bethink you: If it is from Allah and you disbelieve therein, and a witness of the Children of Israel[259] has already testified to the like thereof and has believed, and you are too proud (what plight is yours)? Lo! Allah, guides not wrong- doing folk.

11. And those who disbelieve say of those who believe: If it had been (any) good, they would not have been before us in attaining it. And since they will not be guided by it, they say: This is an ancient lie;

12. When before it there was the Scripture of Moses, an example and a mercy; and this is a confirming Scripture in the Arabic language, that it may warn those who do wrong and bring good tidings for the righteous.

13. Lo! those who say: our Lord is Allah, and thereafter walk aright, there shall no fear come upon them neither shall they grieve.

14. Such are rightful owners of the Garden, immortal therein as a reward for what they used to do.

15. And We have commended unto man kindness toward parents. His mother bears him with reluctance, and brings him forth with reluctance, and the bearing of him and the weaning of him is thirty months, till, when he attains full strength and reaches forty years, he says: My Lord! Arouse me that I may give thanks for the favor wherewith You have favored me and my parents, and that I may do right acceptable unto You. And be gracious unto me in the matter of my seed. Lo! I have turned unto You repentant, and lo! I am of the Muslims.[260]

---

[259] 'Abd Allāh ibn Salām, a learned Jew of al Madīnah who became a devout Muslim. This is the usual explanation, though the verse is still considered to be of Makkan revelation.
[260] Those who surrender to Allah.

16. Those are they from whom We accept the best of what they do, and We overlook their evil deeds. (They are) among the owners of the Garden. This is the true promise which they were promised (in the world).

17. And who said unto his parents: Fie upon you both! Do you threaten me that I shall be brought forth (again) when generations before me have passed away? And they two cry unto Allah for help (and say): Woe unto you! Believe! Lo! the promise of Allah is true. But he said: This is nothing save fables of the men of old:

18. Such are those on whom the Word concerning nations of the Jinn and mankind which have passed away before them has effect. Lo! they are the losers.

19. And for all there will be ranks from what they do, that He may pay them for their deeds! and they will not be wronged.

20. And on the day when those who disbelieve are exposed to the Fire (it will be said): You squandered your good things in the life of the world and you sought comfort therein. Now this day you are rewarded with the doom of ignominy because you were disdainful in the land without a right and because you used to transgress.

21. And make mention (O Muhammad) of the brother of 'Ād[261] when he warned his folk among the wind-curved sand-hills—and verily warners came and went before and after him—He said: Worship none but Allah. Lo! I fear for you the doom of a tremendous Day.

22. They said: Have you come to turn us away from our gods? Then bring upon us that wherewith you threaten us, if you are of the truthful.

---

[261]The prophet Hūd.

١٦ أُولَٰئِكَ الَّذِينَ نَتَقَبَّلُ عَنْهُمْ أَحْسَنَ مَا عَمِلُوا وَنَتَجَاوَزُ عَن سَيِّئَاتِهِمْ فِي أَصْحَابِ الْجَنَّةِ وَعْدَ الصِّدْقِ الَّذِي كَانُوا يُوعَدُونَ

١٧ وَالَّذِي قَالَ لِوَالِدَيْهِ أُفٍّ لَّكُمَا أَتَعِدَانِنِي أَنْ أُخْرَجَ وَقَدْ خَلَتِ الْقُرُونُ مِن قَبْلِي وَهُمَا يَسْتَغِيثَانِ اللَّهَ وَيْلَكَ ءَامِنْ إِنَّ وَعْدَ اللَّهِ حَقٌّ فَيَقُولُ مَا هَٰذَا إِلَّا أَسَاطِيرُ الْأَوَّلِينَ

١٨ أُولَٰئِكَ الَّذِينَ حَقَّ عَلَيْهِمُ الْقَوْلُ فِي أُمَمٍ قَدْ خَلَتْ مِن قَبْلِهِم مِّنَ الْجِنِّ وَالْإِنسِ إِنَّهُمْ كَانُوا خَاسِرِينَ

١٩ وَلِكُلٍّ دَرَجَاتٌ مِّمَّا عَمِلُوا وَلِيُوَفِّيَهُمْ أَعْمَالَهُمْ وَهُمْ لَا يُظْلَمُونَ

٢٠ وَيَوْمَ يُعْرَضُ الَّذِينَ كَفَرُوا عَلَى النَّارِ أَذْهَبْتُمْ طَيِّبَاتِكُمْ فِي حَيَاتِكُمُ الدُّنْيَا وَاسْتَمْتَعْتُم بِهَا فَالْيَوْمَ تُجْزَوْنَ عَذَابَ الْهُونِ بِمَا كُنتُمْ تَسْتَكْبِرُونَ فِي الْأَرْضِ بِغَيْرِ الْحَقِّ وَبِمَا كُنتُمْ تَفْسُقُونَ

٢١ وَاذْكُرْ أَخَا عَادٍ إِذْ أَنذَرَ قَوْمَهُ بِالْأَحْقَافِ وَقَدْ خَلَتِ النُّذُرُ مِن بَيْنِ يَدَيْهِ وَمِنْ خَلْفِهِ أَلَّا تَعْبُدُوا إِلَّا اللَّهَ إِنِّي أَخَافُ عَلَيْكُمْ عَذَابَ يَوْمٍ عَظِيمٍ

٢٢ قَالُوا أَجِئْتَنَا لِتَأْفِكَنَا عَنْ ءَالِهَتِنَا فَأْتِنَا بِمَا تَعِدُنَا إِن كُنتَ مِنَ الصَّادِقِينَ

23. He said: The knowledge is with Allah only. I convey unto you that wherewith I have been sent, but I see you are a folk that know not.

٢٣ قَالَ إِنَّمَا الْعِلْمُ عِندَ اللّهِ وَأُبَلِّغُكُم مَّا أُرْسِلْتُ بِهِ وَلَـٰكِنِّيٓ أَرَىٰكُمْ قَوْمًا تَجْهَلُونَ

24. Then when they beheld it a dense cloud coming toward their valleys, they said; Here is a cloud bringing us rain. Nay, but it is that which you did seek to hasten, a wind wherein is painful torment,

٢٤ فَلَمَّا رَأَوْهُ عَارِضًا مُّسْتَقْبِلَ أَوْدِيَتِهِمْ قَالُوا هَـٰذَا عَارِضٌ مُّمْطِرُنَا بَلْ هُوَ مَا اسْتَعْجَلْتُم بِهِ رِيحٌ فِيهَا عَذَابٌ أَلِيمٌ

25. Destroying all things by command-ment of its Lord. Morning found them so that nothing could be seen save their dwellings. Thus do We reward the criminal people.

٢٥ تُدَمِّرُ كُلَّ شَيْءٍ بِأَمْرِ رَبِّهَا فَأَصْبَحُوا لَا يُرَىٰ إِلَّا مَسَاكِنُهُمْ كَذَٰلِكَ نَجْزِي الْقَوْمَ الْمُجْرِمِينَ

26. And surely We had empowered them with that where- with We have not empowered you, and had assigned them ears and eyes and hearts; but their ears and eyes and hearts availed them nothing since they denied the revelations of Allah; and what they used to mock befell them.

٢٦ وَلَقَدْ مَكَّنَّاهُمْ فِيمَا إِن مَّكَّنَّاكُمْ فِيهِ وَجَعَلْنَا لَهُمْ سَمْعًا وَأَبْصَارًا وَأَفْئِدَةً فَمَا أَغْنَىٰ عَنْهُمْ سَمْعُهُمْ وَلَا أَبْصَارُهُمْ وَلَا أَفْئِدَتُهُم مِّن شَيْءٍ إِذْ كَانُوا يَجْحَدُونَ بِآيَاتِ اللّهِ وَحَاقَ بِهِم مَّا كَانُوا بِهِ يَسْتَهْزِئُونَ

27. And surely We have destroyed townships round about you, and dis-played (for them) Our revelation, that they might return.

٢٧ وَلَقَدْ أَهْلَكْنَا مَا حَوْلَكُم مِّنَ الْقُرَىٰ وَصَرَّفْنَا الْآيَاتِ لَعَلَّهُمْ يَرْجِعُونَ

28. Then why did those whom they had chosen for gods as a way of approach (unto Allah) not help them? Nay, but they did fail them utterly. And (all) that was their lie, and what they used to invent

٢٨ فَلَوْلَا نَصَرَهُمُ الَّذِينَ اتَّخَذُوا مِن دُونِ اللّهِ قُرْبَانًا آلِهَةً بَلْ ضَلُّوا عَنْهُمْ وَذَٰلِكَ إِفْكُهُمْ وَمَا كَانُوا يَفْتَرُونَ

29. And when We inclined toward you (Muhammad) certain of the Jinn, who wished to hear the Qur'an and, when they were in its presence, said: Give ear! and, when it was finished, turned back to their people, warning.

٢٩ وَإِذْ صَرَفْنَا إِلَيْكَ نَفَرًا مِّنَ الْجِنِّ يَسْتَمِعُونَ الْقُرْآنَ فَلَمَّا حَضَرُوهُ قَالُوا أَنصِتُوا فَلَمَّا قُضِيَ وَلَّوْا إِلَىٰ قَوْمِهِم مُّنذِرِينَ

30. They said: O our people! Lo! we have heard a Scripture which has been revealed after Moses,[262] confirming that which was before it, guiding unto the truth and unto a right path.

31. O our people! respond to Allah's summoner and believe in Him. He will forgive you some of your sins and guard you from a painful doom.

32. And whoso responds not to Allah's summoner he can nowise escape in the earth, and he (can find) no protecting friends instead of Him. Such are in error manifest.

33. Have they not seen that Allah, Who created the heavens and the earth and was not wearied by their creation, is Able to give life to the dead? Aye, He verily is Able to do all things.

34. And on the day when those who disbelieve are exposed to the Fire (they will be asked): Is not this real? They will say: Yea, by our Lord. He will say: Then taste the doom for that you disbelieved.

35. Then have patience (O Muhammad) even as the stout of heart among the messengers (of old) had patience, and seek not to hasten on the doom for them. On the day when they see that which they are promised (it will seem to them) as though they had tarried but an hour of daylight. A clear message. Shall any be destroyed save evil-living folk?

﴿٣٠﴾ قَالُوا يَٰقَوْمَنَا إِنَّا سَمِعْنَا كِتَٰبًا أُنزِلَ مِنۢ بَعْدِ مُوسَىٰ مُصَدِّقًا لِّمَا بَيْنَ يَدَيْهِ يَهْدِىٓ إِلَى ٱلْحَقِّ وَإِلَىٰ طَرِيقٍ مُّسْتَقِيمٍ

﴿٣١﴾ يَٰقَوْمَنَآ أَجِيبُوا دَاعِىَ ٱللَّهِ وَءَامِنُوا بِهِۦ يَغْفِرْ لَكُم مِّن ذُنُوبِكُمْ وَيُجِرْكُم مِّنْ عَذَابٍ أَلِيمٍ

﴿٣٢﴾ وَمَن لَّا يُجِبْ دَاعِىَ ٱللَّهِ فَلَيْسَ بِمُعْجِزٍ فِى ٱلْأَرْضِ وَلَيْسَ لَهُۥ مِن دُونِهِۦٓ أَوْلِيَآءُ أُوْلَٰٓئِكَ فِى ضَلَٰلٍ مُّبِينٍ

﴿٣٣﴾ أَوَلَمْ يَرَوْا أَنَّ ٱللَّهَ ٱلَّذِى خَلَقَ ٱلسَّمَٰوَٰتِ وَٱلْأَرْضَ وَلَمْ يَعْىَ بِخَلْقِهِنَّ بِقَٰدِرٍ عَلَىٰٓ أَن يُحْىِۦَ ٱلْمَوْتَىٰ بَلَىٰٓ إِنَّهُۥ عَلَىٰ كُلِّ شَىْءٍ قَدِيرٌ

﴿٣٤﴾ وَيَوْمَ يُعْرَضُ ٱلَّذِينَ كَفَرُوا عَلَى ٱلنَّارِ أَلَيْسَ هَٰذَا بِٱلْحَقِّ قَالُوا بَلَىٰ وَرَبِّنَا قَالَ فَذُوقُوا ٱلْعَذَابَ بِمَا كُنتُمْ تَكْفُرُونَ

﴿٣٥﴾ فَٱصْبِرْ كَمَا صَبَرَ أُوْلُوا ٱلْعَزْمِ مِنَ ٱلرُّسُلِ وَلَا تَسْتَعْجِل لَّهُمْ كَأَنَّهُمْ يَوْمَ يَرَوْنَ مَا يُوعَدُونَ لَمْ يَلْبَثُوا إِلَّا سَاعَةً مِّن نَّهَارٍ بَلَٰغٌ فَهَلْ يُهْلَكُ إِلَّا ٱلْقَوْمُ ٱلْفَٰسِقُونَ

---

[262]From the mention of Moses, it has been conjectured by some commentators that these Jinn were foreign (i.e., non-Arabian) Jews, for in old Arabic the word "Jinn" was applied to clever foreigners.

Muḥammad

Muhammad. This surah takes its name from the mention of the Prophet's name in verse 2. Most commentators agree that verse 18 was revealed when the Prophet, forced to flee from Makkah, looked back for a last sight of his native city and wept. Some have considered the whole surah to be a Makkan revelation, but without good reason.

It belongs to the first and second years after the Hijrah, with the exception of verse 18, which was revealed during the Hijrah.

Muhammad

Revealed at al Madinah

In the name of Allah,
the Beneficent, the Merciful

1. Those who disbelieve and turn (men) from the way of Allah, He renders their actions vain.

2. And those who believe and do good works and believe in that which is revealed unto Muhammad—and it is the truth from their Lord—He rids them of their ill deeds and improves their state.

3. That is because those who disbelieve follow falsehood and because those who believe follow the truth from their Lord. Thus Allah coins their similitudes for mankind.

4. Now when you meet in battle those who disbelieve, then it is smiting of the necks until, when you have routed them, then making fast of bonds; and afterward either grace or ransom till the war lay down its burdens. That (is the ordinance). And if Allah willed He could have punished them (without you) but (thus it is ordained) that He may try some of you by means of others. And those who are slain in the way of Allah, He renders not their actions vain.

5. He will guide them and improve their state,

6. And bring them in unto the Garden which He has made known to them.

7. O you who believe! If you help Allah, He will help you and will make your foothold firm.

8. And those who disbelieve, perdition is for them, and He will make their actions vain.

9. That is because they are averse to that which Allah has revealed, therefore He makes their actions fruitless.

10. Have they not travelled in the land to see the nature of the consequence for those who were before them? Allah wiped them out. And for the disbelievers there will be the like thereof.

١٠ ۞ أَفَلَمْ يَسِيرُوا فِي الْأَرْضِ فَيَنظُرُوا كَيْفَ كَانَ عَاقِبَةُ الَّذِينَ مِن قَبْلِهِمْ دَمَّرَ اللَّهُ عَلَيْهِمْ وَلِلْكَافِرِينَ أَمْثَالُهَا

11. That is because Allah is patron of those who believe, and because the disbelievers have no patron.

١١ ذَلِكَ بِأَنَّ اللَّهَ مَوْلَى الَّذِينَ ءَامَنُوا وَأَنَّ الْكَافِرِينَ لَا مَوْلَى لَهُمْ

12. Lo! Allah will cause those who believe and do good works to enter Gardens underneath which rivers flow; while those who disbelieve take their comfort in this life and eat even as the cattle eat, and the Fire is their habitation.

١٢ إِنَّ اللَّهَ يُدْخِلُ الَّذِينَ ءَامَنُوا وَعَمِلُوا الصَّالِحَاتِ جَنَّاتٍ تَجْرِي مِن تَحْتِهَا الْأَنْهَارُ وَالَّذِينَ كَفَرُوا يَتَمَتَّعُونَ وَيَأْكُلُونَ كَمَا تَأْكُلُ الْأَنْعَامُ وَالنَّارُ مَثْوًى لَهُمْ

13. And how many a township stronger than your township (O Muhammad) which has cast you out, have We destroyed, and they had no helper!

١٣ وَكَأَيِّن مِّن قَرْيَةٍ هِيَ أَشَدُّ قُوَّةً مِّن قَرْيَتِكَ الَّتِي أَخْرَجَتْكَ أَهْلَكْنَاهُمْ فَلَا نَاصِرَ لَهُمْ

14. Is he who relies on a clear proof from his Lord like those for whom the evil that they do is beautified while they follow their own lusts?

١٤ أَفَمَن كَانَ عَلَى بَيِّنَةٍ مِّن رَّبِّهِ كَمَن زُيِّنَ لَهُ سُوءُ عَمَلِهِ وَاتَّبَعُوا أَهْوَاءَهُم

15. The similitude of the Garden which those who keep their duty (to Allah) are promised: Therein are rivers of water unpolluted, and rivers of milk whereof the flavor changes not, and rivers of wine delicious to the drinkers, and rivers of clear run honey; therein for them is every kind of fruit, with pardon from their Lord. (Are those who enjoy all this) like those who are immortal in the Fire and are given boiling water to drink so that it tears their bowels?

١٥ مَثَلُ الْجَنَّةِ الَّتِي وُعِدَ الْمُتَّقُونَ فِيهَا أَنْهَارٌ مِّن مَّاءٍ غَيْرِ ءَاسِنٍ وَأَنْهَارٌ مِّن لَّبَنٍ لَّمْ يَتَغَيَّرْ طَعْمُهُ وَأَنْهَارٌ مِّنْ خَمْرٍ لَّذَّةٍ لِّلشَّارِبِينَ وَأَنْهَارٌ مِّنْ عَسَلٍ مُّصَفًّى وَلَهُمْ فِيهَا مِن كُلِّ الثَّمَرَاتِ وَمَغْفِرَةٌ مِّن رَّبِّهِمْ كَمَنْ هُوَ خَالِدٌ فِي النَّارِ وَسُقُوا مَاءً حَمِيمًا فَقَطَّعَ أَمْعَاءَهُمْ

16. Among them are some who give ear unto you (Muhammad) till, when they go forth from your presence, they say unto those who have been given knowledge: What was that he said just now? Those are they whose hearts Allah has sealed, and they follow their own lusts.

١٦ وَمِنْهُم مَّن يَسْتَمِعُ إِلَيْكَ حَتَّى إِذَا خَرَجُوا مِنْ عِندِكَ قَالُوا لِلَّذِينَ أُوتُوا الْعِلْمَ مَاذَا قَالَ ءَانِفًا أُوْلَئِكَ الَّذِينَ طَبَعَ اللَّهُ عَلَى قُلُوبِهِمْ وَاتَّبَعُوا أَهْوَاءَهُمْ

17. While as for those who walk aright, He adds to their guidance, and gives them their protection (against evil).

١٧ وَالَّذِينَ اهْتَدَوْا زَادَهُمْ هُدًى وَءَاتَاهُمْ تَقْوَاهُمْ

18. Await they anything save the Hour, that it should come upon them unawares? And the beginnings thereof have already come. But how, when it has come upon them, can they take their warning?

19. So know (O Muhammad) that there is no God save Allah, and ask forgiveness for your sin and for believing men and believing women. Allah knows (both) your place of turmoil and your place of rest.

20. And those who believe say: If only a surah were revealed! But when a decisive surah is revealed and war is mentioned therein, you see those in whose hearts is a disease looking at you with the look of men fainting unto death. But it is more fitting for them!

21. Obedience and a civil word. Then, when the matter is determined, if they are loyal to Allah it will be well for them.

22. Would you then, if you were given the command, work corruption in the land and sever your ties of kinship?

23. Such are they whom Allah curses so that he deafens them and makes blind their eyes.

24. Will they then not meditate on the Qur'an, or are there locks on the hearts?

25. Lo! those who turn back after the guidance has been manifested unto them, the Devil has seduced them, and has given them the rein.

26. That is because they say unto those who hate what Allah has revealed: We will obey you in some matters; and Allah knows their secret talk.

27. Then how (will it be with them) when the angels gather them, smiting their faces and their backs!

28. That will be because they followed that which angers Allah, and hated that which pleases Him. Therefore He has made their actions vain.

١٨ فَهَلْ يَنْظُرُونَ إِلَّا السَّاعَةَ أَنْ تَأْتِيَهُمْ بَغْتَةً فَقَدْ جَاءَ أَشْرَاطُهَا فَأَنَّى لَهُمْ إِذَا جَاءَتْهُمْ ذِكْرَاهُمْ

١٩ فَاعْلَمْ أَنَّهُ لَا إِلَهَ إِلَّا اللَّهُ وَاسْتَغْفِرْ لِذَنْبِكَ وَلِلْمُؤْمِنِينَ وَالْمُؤْمِنَاتِ وَاللَّهُ يَعْلَمُ مُتَقَلَّبَكُمْ وَمَثْوَاكُمْ

٢٠ وَيَقُولُ الَّذِينَ آمَنُوا لَوْلَا نُزِّلَتْ سُورَةٌ فَإِذَا أُنْزِلَتْ سُورَةٌ مُحْكَمَةٌ وَذُكِرَ فِيهَا الْقِتَالُ رَأَيْتَ الَّذِينَ فِي قُلُوبِهِمْ مَرَضٌ يَنْظُرُونَ إِلَيْكَ نَظَرَ الْمَغْشِيِّ عَلَيْهِ مِنَ الْمَوْتِ فَأَوْلَى لَهُمْ

٢١ طَاعَةٌ وَقَوْلٌ مَعْرُوفٌ فَإِذَا عَزَمَ الْأَمْرُ فَلَوْ صَدَقُوا اللَّهَ لَكَانَ خَيْرًا لَهُمْ

٢٢ فَهَلْ عَسَيْتُمْ إِنْ تَوَلَّيْتُمْ أَنْ تُفْسِدُوا فِي الْأَرْضِ وَتُقَطِّعُوا أَرْحَامَكُمْ

٢٣ أُولَئِكَ الَّذِينَ لَعَنَهُمُ اللَّهُ فَأَصَمَّهُمْ وَأَعْمَى أَبْصَارَهُمْ

٢٤ أَفَلَا يَتَدَبَّرُونَ الْقُرْآنَ أَمْ عَلَى قُلُوبٍ أَقْفَالُهَا

٢٥ إِنَّ الَّذِينَ ارْتَدُّوا عَلَى أَدْبَارِهِمْ مِنْ بَعْدِ مَا تَبَيَّنَ لَهُمُ الْهُدَى الشَّيْطَانُ سَوَّلَ لَهُمْ وَأَمْلَى لَهُمْ

٢٦ ذَلِكَ بِأَنَّهُمْ قَالُوا لِلَّذِينَ كَرِهُوا مَا نَزَّلَ اللَّهُ سَنُطِيعُكُمْ فِي بَعْضِ الْأَمْرِ وَاللَّهُ يَعْلَمُ إِسْرَارَهُمْ

٢٧ فَكَيْفَ إِذَا تَوَفَّتْهُمُ الْمَلَائِكَةُ يَضْرِبُونَ وُجُوهَهُمْ وَأَدْبَارَهُمْ

٢٨ ذَلِكَ بِأَنَّهُمُ اتَّبَعُوا مَا أَسْخَطَ اللَّهَ وَكَرِهُوا رِضْوَانَهُ فَأَحْبَطَ أَعْمَالَهُمْ

29. Or do those in whose hearts is a disease deem that Allah will not bring to light their (secret) hates?

30. And if We would, We could show them unto you (Muhammad) so that you should know them surely by their marks. And you shall know them by the tone of their speech. And Allah knows your deeds.

31. And surely We shall try you till We know those of you who strive hard (for the cause of Allah) and the steadfast, and till We test your record.

32. Lo! those who disbelieve and turn from the way of Allah and oppose the Messenger after the guidance has been manifested unto them, they hurt Allah not a jot, and He will make their actions fruitless.

33. O you who believe! Obey Allah and obey the Messenger, and render not your actions vain.

34. Lo! those who disbelieve and turn from the way of Allah and then die disbelievers, Allah surely will not pardon them.

35. So falter not and cry out for peace when you (will be) the uppermost, and Allah is with you, and He will not grudge (the reward of) your actions.

36. The life of the world is but a sport and a pastime. And if you believe and ward off (evil), He will give you your wages, and will not ask of you your worldly wealth.

37. If He should ask it of you and importune you, you would hoard it, and He would bring to light your (secret) hates.

38. Lo! you are those who are called to spend in the way of Allah, yet among you there are some who withhold. And as for him who withholds, he withholds only from his soul. And Allah is the Rich, and you are the poor. And if you turn away He will exchange you for some other folk, and they will not be the likes of you.

٢٩ أَمْ حَسِبَ الَّذِينَ فِى قُلُوبِهِم مَّرَضٌ أَن لَّن يُخْرِجَ اللَّهُ أَضْغَانَهُمْ

٣٠ وَلَوْ نَشَاءُ لَأَرَيْنَاكَهُمْ فَلَعَرَفْتَهُم بِسِيمَاهُمْ وَلَتَعْرِفَنَّهُمْ فِى لَحْنِ الْقَوْلِ وَاللَّهُ يَعْلَمُ أَعْمَالَكُمْ

٣١ وَلَنَبْلُوَنَّكُمْ حَتَّى نَعْلَمَ الْمُجَاهِدِينَ مِنكُمْ وَالصَّابِرِينَ وَنَبْلُوَا أَخْبَارَكُمْ

٣٢ إِنَّ الَّذِينَ كَفَرُوا وَصَدُّوا عَن سَبِيلِ اللَّهِ وَشَاقُّوا الرَّسُولَ مِن بَعْدِ مَا تَبَيَّنَ لَهُمُ الْهُدَى لَن يَضُرُّوا اللَّهَ شَيْئًا وَسَيُحْبِطُ أَعْمَالَهُمْ

٣٣ ۞ يَا أَيُّهَا الَّذِينَ ءَامَنُوا أَطِيعُوا اللَّهَ وَأَطِيعُوا الرَّسُولَ وَلَا تُبْطِلُوا أَعْمَالَكُمْ

٣٤ إِنَّ الَّذِينَ كَفَرُوا وَصَدُّوا عَن سَبِيلِ اللَّهِ ثُمَّ مَاتُوا وَهُمْ كُفَّارٌ فَلَن يَغْفِرَ اللَّهُ لَهُمْ

٣٥ فَلَا تَهِنُوا وَتَدْعُوا إِلَى السَّلْمِ وَأَنتُمُ الْأَعْلَوْنَ وَاللَّهُ مَعَكُمْ وَلَن يَتِرَكُمْ أَعْمَالَكُمْ

٣٦ إِنَّمَا الْحَيَاةُ الدُّنْيَا لَعِبٌ وَلَهْوٌ وَإِن تُؤْمِنُوا وَتَتَّقُوا يُؤْتِكُمْ أُجُورَكُمْ وَلَا يَسْأَلْكُمْ أَمْوَالَكُمْ

٣٧ إِن يَسْأَلْكُمُوهَا فَيُحْفِكُمْ تَبْخَلُوا وَيُخْرِجْ أَضْغَانَكُمْ

٣٨ هَا أَنتُمْ هَؤُلَاءِ تُدْعَوْنَ لِتُنفِقُوا فِى سَبِيلِ اللَّهِ فَمِنكُم مَّن يَبْخَلُ وَمَن يَبْخَلْ فَإِنَّمَا يَبْخَلُ عَن نَّفْسِهِ وَاللَّهُ الْغَنِيُّ وَأَنتُمُ الْفُقَرَاءُ وَإِن تَتَوَلَّوْا يَسْتَبْدِلْ قَوْمًا غَيْرَكُمْ ثُمَّ لَا يَكُونُوا أَمْثَالَكُم

Victory

Al Fatḥ takes its name from the word *fatḥ*, which means "victory." It occurs several times in the surah and refers not to the conquest of Makkah but to the truce of al Ḥudaybīyah. Although thought at the time a setback to the Muslims, it proved in fact to be the greatest victory for Islam.

In the year 6 AH, the Prophet set out with some 1,400 Muslims from al Madinah and the surrounding countryside. They were dressed for pilgrimage, not war, and wanted to visit the Ka'bah. When they drew close to Makkah, they were warned that the Quraysh had gathered their allies and that their cavalry, led by Khālid ibn al Walīd, was on the road before them. Making a detour through gullies of the hills, the Muslims eluded the cavalry and, coming into the valley of Makkah, they encamped at al Ḥudaybīyah (below the city). The Prophet resolutely refused to fight and persisted in attempts to talk with the Quraysh, who had sworn not to let him reach the Ka'bah. The Muslims were in a position of some danger. Finally 'Uthmān ibn 'Affān was sent into the city, for it was thought that he was the most likely to be well received on account of his relationships. 'Uthmān was detained by the Makkans, and news that he had been murdered reached the Muslim camp.[263]

It was then that the Prophet, sitting under a tree, took from his comrades the oath (referred to in verse 18) that they would hold together and fight to the death.[264] It then became known that the rumor of 'Uthmān's death was false. Finally, the Quraysh agreed to a truce whose terms were favorable to themselves. The Prophet and his followers were to give up the project of visiting the sanctuary for that year, but could make the pilgrimage the following year when the idolaters would evacuate Makkah for three days. People who ran away from the Quraysh to the Muslim camp would be returned, but people who ran away from the Muslims to the Quraysh would not be returned. In addition, there was to be no hostility between the parties for ten years.

"And there was never a victory," says Ibn Khaldūn, "greater than this victory, for as al Zuhrī says, when it was war the peoples did not meet, but when the truce came and war laid down its burdens, the people felt safe one with another and so they met and talked with each other. No man spoke of Islam to another but the latter embraced it, so that in the intervening two years (i.e., between al Ḥudaybīyah and the breaking of the truce by Quraysh), the number of people who became Muslim was equal to or more than the number of those who had already become Muslim."[265]

The date of revelation is the year 6 AH.

---

[263]Ibn Hishām, 2:176-178.
[264]Ibn Hishām, 2:179.
[265]Ibn Khaldūn, *Tārīkh*, Supplement to Part II, Būlāq 1284 A.H. He follows Ibn Hishām.

Victory

Revealed at al Madinah

*In the name of Allah,
the Beneficent, the Merciful*

1. Lo! We have given you (O Muhammad) a signal victory,

2. That Allah may forgive you of your sin that which is past and that which is to come, and may perfect His favor unto you, and may guide you on a right path,

3. And that Allah may help you with strong help—

4. He it is Who sent down tranquillity into the hearts of the believers that they might add faith unto their faith. And Allah's are the hosts of the heavens and the earth, and Allah is ever Knower, Wise—

5. That He may bring the believing men and the believing women into Gardens underneath which rivers flow, wherein they will abide, and may remit from them their evil deeds— That, in the sight of Allah, is the supreme triumph—

6. And may punish the hypocritical men and the hypocritical women, and the idolatrous men and the idolatrous women, who think an evil thought concerning Allah. For them is the evil turn of fortune, and Allah is wroth against them and has cursed them, and has made ready for them Hell, an unlucky journey's end.

7. Allah's are the hosts of the heavens and the earth, and Allah is ever Mighty, Wise.

8. Lo! We have sent you (O Muhammad) as a witness and a bearer of good tidings and a warner,

9. That you may believe in Allah and His Messenger, and may honor Him, and may revere Him, and may glorify Him at early dawn and at the close of the day.

﴿٩﴾ لِّتُؤْمِنُوا بِاللَّهِ وَرَسُولِهِ وَتُعَزِّرُوهُ وَتُوَقِّرُوهُ وَتُسَبِّحُوهُ بُكْرَةً وَأَصِيلًا

10. Lo! those who swear allegiance unto you (Muhammad), swear allegiance only unto Allah. The Hand of Allah is above their hands. So whosoever breaks his oath, breaks it only to his soul's hurt; while whosoever keeps his covenant with Allah, on him will He bestow immense reward.

﴿١٠﴾ إِنَّ الَّذِينَ يُبَايِعُونَكَ إِنَّمَا يُبَايِعُونَ اللَّهَ يَدُ اللَّهِ فَوْقَ أَيْدِيهِمْ فَمَن نَّكَثَ فَإِنَّمَا يَنكُثُ عَلَى نَفْسِهِ وَمَنْ أَوْفَى بِمَا عَاهَدَ عَلَيْهُ اللَّهَ فَسَيُؤْتِيهِ أَجْرًا عَظِيمًا

11. Those of the wandering Arabs who were left behind will tell you: Our possessions and our households occupied us, so ask forgiveness for us! They speak with their tongues that which is not in their hearts. Say: Who can avail you anything against Allah, if He intends you hurt or intends you profit? Nay, but Allah is ever Aware of what you do.

﴿١١﴾ سَيَقُولُ لَكَ الْمُخَلَّفُونَ مِنَ الْأَعْرَابِ شَغَلَتْنَا أَمْوَالُنَا وَأَهْلُونَا فَاسْتَغْفِرْ لَنَا يَقُولُونَ بِأَلْسِنَتِهِم مَّا لَيْسَ فِي قُلُوبِهِمْ قُلْ فَمَن يَمْلِكُ لَكُم مِّنَ اللَّهِ شَيْئًا إِنْ أَرَادَ بِكُمْ ضَرًّا أَوْ أَرَادَ بِكُمْ نَفْعًا بَلْ كَانَ اللَّهُ بِمَا تَعْمَلُونَ خَبِيرًا

12. Nay, but you deemed that the Messenger and the believers would never return to their own folk, and that was made fair-seeming in your hearts, and you did think an evil thought, and you were worthless folk.

﴿١٢﴾ بَلْ ظَنَنتُمْ أَن لَّن يَنقَلِبَ الرَّسُولُ وَالْمُؤْمِنُونَ إِلَى أَهْلِيهِمْ أَبَدًا وَزُيِّنَ ذَلِكَ فِي قُلُوبِكُمْ وَظَنَنتُمْ ظَنَّ السَّوْءِ وَكُنتُمْ قَوْمًا بُورًا

13. And as for him who believes not in Allah and His Mes-senger—Lo! We have prepared a flame for disbelievers.

﴿١٣﴾ وَمَن لَّمْ يُؤْمِن بِاللَّهِ وَرَسُولِهِ فَإِنَّا أَعْتَدْنَا لِلْكَافِرِينَ سَعِيرًا

14. And Allah's is the Sovereignty of the heavens and the earth. He forgives whom He will, and punishes whom He will. And Allah is ever Forgiving, Merciful.

﴿١٤﴾ وَلِلَّهِ مُلْكُ السَّمَاوَاتِ وَالْأَرْضِ يَغْفِرُ لِمَن يَشَاءُ وَيُعَذِّبُ مَن يَشَاءُ وَكَانَ اللَّهُ غَفُورًا رَّحِيمًا

15. Those who were left behind will say, when you set forth to capture booty: Let us go with you. They fain would change the verdict of Allah. Say (unto them, O Muhammad): You shall not go with us. Thus has Allah said beforehand. Then they will say: You are envious of us. Nay, but they understand not, save a little.

16. Say unto those of the wandering Arabs who were left behind: You will be called against a folk of mighty prowess,[266] to fight them until they surrender; and if you obey, Allah will give you a fair reward; but if you turn away as you did turn away before, He will punish you with a painful doom.

17. There is no blame for the blind, nor is there blame for the lame, nor is there blame for the sick. And who obeys Allah and His Messenger, He will make him enter Gardens underneath which rivers flow; and who turns back, him will He punish with a painful doom.

18. Allah was well pleased with the believers when they swore allegiance unto you beneath the tree, and He knew what was in their hearts, and He sent down tranquillity on them, and has rewarded them with a near victory;

19. And much booty that they will capture. Allah is ever Mighty, Wise.

20. Allah promises you much booty that you will capture, and has given you this in advance, and has withheld men's hands from you, that it may be a token for the believers, and that He may guide you on a right way.

﴿١٥﴾ سَيَقُولُ الْمُخَلَّفُونَ إِذَا انْطَلَقْتُمْ إِلَىٰ مَغَانِمَ لِتَأْخُذُوهَا ذَرُونَا نَتَّبِعْكُمْ يُرِيدُونَ أَن يُبَدِّلُوا كَلَامَ اللَّهِ قُل لَّن تَتَّبِعُونَا كَذَٰلِكُمْ قَالَ اللَّهُ مِن قَبْلُ فَسَيَقُولُونَ بَلْ تَحْسُدُونَنَا بَلْ كَانُوا لَا يَفْقَهُونَ إِلَّا قَلِيلًا

﴿١٦﴾ قُل لِّلْمُخَلَّفِينَ مِنَ الْأَعْرَابِ سَتُدْعَوْنَ إِلَىٰ قَوْمٍ أُولِي بَأْسٍ شَدِيدٍ تُقَاتِلُونَهُمْ أَوْ يُسْلِمُونَ فَإِن تُطِيعُوا يُؤْتِكُمُ اللَّهُ أَجْرًا حَسَنًا وَإِن تَتَوَلَّوْا كَمَا تَوَلَّيْتُم مِّن قَبْلُ يُعَذِّبْكُمْ عَذَابًا أَلِيمًا

﴿١٧﴾ لَّيْسَ عَلَى الْأَعْمَىٰ حَرَجٌ وَلَا عَلَى الْأَعْرَجِ حَرَجٌ وَلَا عَلَى الْمَرِيضِ حَرَجٌ وَمَن يُطِعِ اللَّهَ وَرَسُولَهُ يُدْخِلْهُ جَنَّاتٍ تَجْرِي مِن تَحْتِهَا الْأَنْهَارُ وَمَن يَتَوَلَّ يُعَذِّبْهُ عَذَابًا أَلِيمًا

﴿١٨﴾ لَّقَدْ رَضِيَ اللَّهُ عَنِ الْمُؤْمِنِينَ إِذْ يُبَايِعُونَكَ تَحْتَ الشَّجَرَةِ فَعَلِمَ مَا فِي قُلُوبِهِمْ فَأَنزَلَ السَّكِينَةَ عَلَيْهِمْ وَأَثَابَهُمْ فَتْحًا قَرِيبًا

﴿١٩﴾ وَمَغَانِمَ كَثِيرَةً يَأْخُذُونَهَا وَكَانَ اللَّهُ عَزِيزًا حَكِيمًا

﴿٢٠﴾ وَعَدَكُمُ اللَّهُ مَغَانِمَ كَثِيرَةً تَأْخُذُونَهَا فَعَجَّلَ لَكُمْ هَٰذِهِ وَكَفَّ أَيْدِيَ النَّاسِ عَنكُمْ وَلِتَكُونَ آيَةً لِّلْمُؤْمِنِينَ وَيَهْدِيَكُمْ صِرَاطًا مُّسْتَقِيمًا

---

[266]This prophecy is taken to refer to the war with the Persian or the Byzantine empires.

21. And other (gain), which you have not been able to achieve, Allah will compass it. Allah is Able to do all things.

22. And if those who disbelieve join battle with you they will take to flight, and afterward they will find no protecting friend nor helper.

23. It is the law of Allah which has taken course before. You will not find for the law of Allah anything of power to change.

24. And He it is Who has withheld men's hands from you, and has withheld your hands from them, in the valley of Makkah, after He had made you victors over them. Allah is Seer of what you do.

25. These it was who disbelieved and debarred you from the Sacred Mosque, and debarred the offering from reaching its goal. And if it had not been for believing men and believing women, whom you know not—lest you should tread them under foot and thus incur guilt for them unknowingly; that Allah might bring into His mercy whom He will— If (believers and disbelievers) had been clearly separated We surely had punished those of them who disbelieved with painful punishment.

26. When those who disbelieve had set up in their hearts zealotry, the zealotry of the Age of Ignorance, then Allah sent down His tranquillity upon His Messenger and upon the believers and imposed on them the word of self-restraint, for they were worthy of it and meet for it. And Allah is Aware of all things.

﴿٢١﴾ وَأُخْرَىٰ لَمْ تَقْدِرُوا عَلَيْهَا قَدْ أَحَاطَ ٱللَّهُ بِهَا ۚ وَكَانَ ٱللَّهُ عَلَىٰ كُلِّ شَىْءٍ قَدِيرًا

﴿٢٢﴾ وَلَوْ قَاتَلَكُمُ ٱلَّذِينَ كَفَرُوا لَوَلَّوُا ٱلْأَدْبَٰرَ ثُمَّ لَا يَجِدُونَ وَلِيًّا وَلَا نَصِيرًا

﴿٢٣﴾ سُنَّةَ ٱللَّهِ ٱلَّتِي قَدْ خَلَتْ مِن قَبْلُ ۖ وَلَن تَجِدَ لِسُنَّةِ ٱللَّهِ تَبْدِيلًا

﴿٢٤﴾ وَهُوَ ٱلَّذِي كَفَّ أَيْدِيَهُمْ عَنكُمْ وَأَيْدِيَكُمْ عَنْهُم بِبَطْنِ مَكَّةَ مِنۢ بَعْدِ أَنْ أَظْفَرَكُمْ عَلَيْهِمْ ۚ وَكَانَ ٱللَّهُ بِمَا تَعْمَلُونَ بَصِيرًا

﴿٢٥﴾ هُمُ ٱلَّذِينَ كَفَرُوا وَصَدُّوكُمْ عَنِ ٱلْمَسْجِدِ ٱلْحَرَامِ وَٱلْهَدْيَ مَعْكُوفًا أَن يَبْلُغَ مَحِلَّهُ ۚ وَلَوْلَا رِجَالٌ مُّؤْمِنُونَ وَنِسَاءٌ مُّؤْمِنَٰتٌ لَّمْ تَعْلَمُوهُمْ أَن تَطَـُٔوهُمْ فَتُصِيبَكُم مِّنْهُم مَّعَرَّةٌ بِغَيْرِ عِلْمٍ ۖ لِّيُدْخِلَ ٱللَّهُ فِي رَحْمَتِهِ مَن يَشَاءُ ۚ لَوْ تَزَيَّلُوا لَعَذَّبْنَا ٱلَّذِينَ كَفَرُوا مِنْهُمْ عَذَابًا أَلِيمًا

﴿٢٦﴾ إِذْ جَعَلَ ٱلَّذِينَ كَفَرُوا فِي قُلُوبِهِمُ ٱلْحَمِيَّةَ حَمِيَّةَ ٱلْجَٰهِلِيَّةِ فَأَنزَلَ ٱللَّهُ سَكِينَتَهُ عَلَىٰ رَسُولِهِ وَعَلَى ٱلْمُؤْمِنِينَ وَأَلْزَمَهُمْ كَلِمَةَ ٱلتَّقْوَىٰ وَكَانُوا أَحَقَّ بِهَا وَأَهْلَهَا ۚ وَكَانَ ٱللَّهُ بِكُلِّ شَىْءٍ عَلِيمًا

27. Allah has fulfilled the vision[267] for His Messenger in very truth. You shall indeed enter the Sacred Mosque, if Allah will, secure, (having your hair) shaven and cut, not fearing. But He knows that which you know not, and has given you a near victory beforehand.

28. He it is Who has sent His Messenger with the guidance and the religion of truth, that He may cause it to prevail over all religion. And Allah suffices as a witness.

29. Muhammad is the Messenger of Allah. And those with him are hard against disbelievers and merciful among themselves. You (O Muhammad) see them bowing and falling prostrate (in worship), seeking bounty from Allah and (His) acceptance. The mark of them is on their faces from the traces of prostration. Such is their likeness in the Torah and their likeness in the Gospel—like as sown corn that sends forth its shoot and strengthens it and rises firm upon its stalk, delighting the sowers—that He may enrage the disbelievers with (the sight of) them. Allah has promised, unto such of them as believe and do good works, forgiveness and immense reward.

﴿٢٧﴾ لَقَدْ صَدَقَ اللَّهُ رَسُولَهُ الرُّؤْيَا بِالْحَقِّ لَتَدْخُلُنَّ الْمَسْجِدَ الْحَرَامَ إِن شَاءَ اللَّهُ ءَامِنِينَ مُحَلِّقِينَ رُءُوسَكُمْ وَمُقَصِّرِينَ لَا تَخَافُونَ فَعَلِمَ مَا لَمْ تَعْلَمُوا فَجَعَلَ مِن دُونِ ذَلِكَ فَتْحًا قَرِيبًا

﴿٢٨﴾ هُوَ الَّذِي أَرْسَلَ رَسُولَهُ بِالْهُدَى وَدِينِ الْحَقِّ لِيُظْهِرَهُ عَلَى الدِّينِ كُلِّهِ وَكَفَى بِاللَّهِ شَهِيدًا

﴿٢٩﴾ مُحَمَّدٌ رَسُولُ اللَّهِ وَالَّذِينَ مَعَهُ أَشِدَّاءُ عَلَى الْكُفَّارِ رُحَمَاءُ بَيْنَهُمْ تَرَاهُمْ رُكَّعًا سُجَّدًا يَبْتَغُونَ فَضْلًا مِنَ اللَّهِ وَرِضْوَانًا سِيمَاهُمْ فِي وُجُوهِهِم مِنْ أَثَرِ السُّجُودِ ذَلِكَ مَثَلُهُمْ فِي التَّوْرَاةِ وَمَثَلُهُمْ فِي الْإِنجِيلِ كَزَرْعٍ أَخْرَجَ شَطْأَهُ فَآزَرَهُ فَاسْتَغْلَظَ فَاسْتَوَى عَلَى سُوقِهِ يُعْجِبُ الزُّرَّاعَ لِيَغِيظَ بِهِمُ الْكُفَّارَ وَعَدَ اللَّهُ الَّذِينَ ءَامَنُوا وَعَمِلُوا الصَّالِحَاتِ مِنْهُم مَغْفِرَةً وَأَجْرًا عَظِيمًا

The Private Apartments

Al Ḥujurāt takes its name from verse 4, which, with the following verse, is said to refer to the behavior of one of the deputations at a time when deputations from all parts of Arabia were coming to al Madinah to profess allegiance to the Pro-phet. The whole surah, dealing as it does with manners and particularly with behavior toward the Prophet, evidently belongs to a period when there were many people seeking an audience, many of whom were quite uncivilized.

The date of revelation is the year 9 AH, "the year of deputations," as it is called.

The Private Apartments

Revealed at al Madinah

In the name of Allah,
the Beneficent, the Merciful

1. ⊙ you who believe! Be not forward in the presence of Allah and His Messenger, and keep your duty to Allah. Lo! Allah is Hearer, Knower.

2. O you who believe! Lift not up your voices above the voice of the Prophet, nor shout when speaking to him as you shout one to another, lest your works be rendered vain while you perceive not.

3. Lo! they who subdue their voices in the presence of the Messenger of Allah, those are they whose hearts Allah has proven unto righteousness. Theirs will be forgiveness and immense reward.

4. Those who call you from behind the private apartments, most of them have no sense.

5. And if they had patience till you came forth unto them, it had been better for them. And Allah is Forgiving, Mer-ciful.

6. O you who believe! If an evildoer bring you tidings,[268] verify it, lest you smite some folk in ignorance and afterward repent of what you did.

7. And know that the Messenger of Allah is among you. If he were to obey you in much of the government, you would surely be in trouble; but Allah has endeared the faith to you and has beautified it in your hearts, and has made disbelief and lewdness and rebellion hateful unto you. Such are they who are rightly guided.

---

[268]The reference is to a man who brought false news of a revolt of the tribe of Banī al Muṣṭaliq, whom he claimed had apostasized.

8. (It is) a bounty and a grace from Allah; and Allah is Knower, Wise.

٨ فَضْلًا مِّنَ اللَّهِ وَنِعْمَةً وَاللَّهُ عَلِيمٌ حَكِيمٌ

9. And if two parties of believers fall to fighting, then make peace between them. And if one party of them does wrong to the other, fight you that which does wrong till it return unto the ordinance of Allah; then, if it return, make peace between them justly, and act equitably. Lo! Allah loves the equitable.

٩ وَإِن طَائِفَتَانِ مِنَ الْمُؤْمِنِينَ اقْتَتَلُوا فَأَصْلِحُوا بَيْنَهُمَا فَإِن بَغَتْ إِحْدَاهُمَا عَلَى الْأُخْرَى فَقَاتِلُوا الَّتِي تَبْغِي حَتَّى تَفِيءَ إِلَى أَمْرِ اللَّهِ فَإِن فَاءَتْ فَأَصْلِحُوا بَيْنَهُمَا بِالْعَدْلِ وَأَقْسِطُوا إِنَّ اللَّهَ يُحِبُّ الْمُقْسِطِينَ

10. The believers are nothing else than brothers. Therefore make peace between your brethren and observe your duty to Allah that you may obtain mercy.

١٠ إِنَّمَا الْمُؤْمِنُونَ إِخْوَةٌ فَأَصْلِحُوا بَيْنَ أَخَوَيْكُمْ وَاتَّقُوا اللَّهَ لَعَلَّكُمْ تُرْحَمُونَ

11. O you who believe! Let not a folk deride a folk who may be better than they (are), nor let women (deride) women who may be better than they are; neither defame one another, nor insult one another by nicknames. Bad is the name of lewdness after faith. And who turns not in repentance, such are evildoers.

١١ يَا أَيُّهَا الَّذِينَ آمَنُوا لَا يَسْخَرْ قَوْمٌ مِّن قَوْمٍ عَسَى أَن يَكُونُوا خَيْرًا مِّنْهُمْ وَلَا نِسَاءٌ مِّن نِّسَاءٍ عَسَى أَن يَكُنَّ خَيْرًا مِّنْهُنَّ وَلَا تَلْمِزُوا أَنفُسَكُمْ وَلَا تَنَابَزُوا بِالْأَلْقَابِ بِئْسَ الِاسْمُ الْفُسُوقُ بَعْدَ الْإِيمَانِ وَمَن لَّمْ يَتُبْ فَأُولَٰئِكَ هُمُ الظَّالِمُونَ

12. O you who believe! Shun much suspicion; for lo! some suspicion is evil. And spy not, neither backbite one another. Would one of you love to eat the flesh of his dead brother? You abhor that! And keep your duty (to Allah). Lo! Allah is Relenting, Merciful.

١٢ يَا أَيُّهَا الَّذِينَ آمَنُوا اجْتَنِبُوا كَثِيرًا مِّنَ الظَّنِّ إِنَّ بَعْضَ الظَّنِّ إِثْمٌ وَلَا تَجَسَّسُوا وَلَا يَغْتَب بَّعْضُكُم بَعْضًا أَيُحِبُّ أَحَدُكُمْ أَن يَأْكُلَ لَحْمَ أَخِيهِ مَيْتًا فَكَرِهْتُمُوهُ وَاتَّقُوا اللَّهَ إِنَّ اللَّهَ تَوَّابٌ رَّحِيمٌ

13. O mankind! Lo! We have created you from a single male and female, and have made you nations and tribes that you may know one another. Lo! the noblest of you, in the sight of Allah, is the best in conduct. Lo! Allah is Knower, Aware.

١٣ يَا أَيُّهَا النَّاسُ إِنَّا خَلَقْنَاكُم مِّن ذَكَرٍ وَأُنثَى وَجَعَلْنَاكُمْ شُعُوبًا وَقَبَائِلَ لِتَعَارَفُوا إِنَّ أَكْرَمَكُمْ عِندَ اللَّهِ أَتْقَاكُمْ إِنَّ اللَّهَ عَلِيمٌ خَبِيرٌ

14. The wandering Arabs say: We believe. Say (unto them): You believe not, but rather say, 'We submit,' for the faith has not yet entered into your hearts. Yet, if you obey Allah and His Messenger, He will not withhold from you anything of (the reward of) your deeds. Lo! Allah is Forgiving, Merciful.

﴿١٤﴾ ۞ قَالَتِ ٱلۡأَعۡرَابُ ءَامَنَّاۖ قُل لَّمۡ تُؤۡمِنُواْ وَلَٰكِن قُولُوٓاْ أَسۡلَمۡنَا وَلَمَّا يَدۡخُلِ ٱلۡإِيمَٰنُ فِى قُلُوبِكُمۡۖ وَإِن تُطِيعُواْ ٱللَّهَ وَرَسُولَهُۥ لَا يَلِتۡكُم مِّنۡ أَعۡمَٰلِكُمۡ شَيۡـًٔاۚ إِنَّ ٱللَّهَ غَفُورٞ رَّحِيمٌ

15. (True) believers are those only who believe in Allah and His Messenger and afterward doubt not, but strive with their wealth and their lives for the cause of Allah. Such are the sincere ones.

﴿١٥﴾ إِنَّمَا ٱلۡمُؤۡمِنُونَ ٱلَّذِينَ ءَامَنُواْ بِٱللَّهِ وَرَسُولِهِۦ ثُمَّ لَمۡ يَرۡتَابُواْ وَجَٰهَدُواْ بِأَمۡوَٰلِهِمۡ وَأَنفُسِهِمۡ فِى سَبِيلِ ٱللَّهِۚ أُوْلَٰٓئِكَ هُمُ ٱلصَّٰدِقُونَ

16. Say (unto them): Would you teach Allah your religion, when Allah knows all that is in the heavens and all that is in the earth, and Allah is Aware of all things?

﴿١٦﴾ قُلۡ أَتُعَلِّمُونَ ٱللَّهَ بِدِينِكُمۡ وَٱللَّهُ يَعۡلَمُ مَا فِى ٱلسَّمَٰوَٰتِ وَمَا فِى ٱلۡأَرۡضِۚ وَٱللَّهُ بِكُلِّ شَىۡءٍ عَلِيمٌ

17. They make it favor unto you that they have surrendered (unto Him). Say: Deem not your Surrender a favor unto me; nay, but Allah does confer a favor on you, inasmuch as He has led you to the Faith, if you are earnest.

﴿١٧﴾ يَمُنُّونَ عَلَيۡكَ أَنۡ أَسۡلَمُواْۖ قُل لَّا تَمُنُّواْ عَلَىَّ إِسۡلَٰمَكُمۖ بَلِ ٱللَّهُ يَمُنُّ عَلَيۡكُمۡ أَنۡ هَدَىٰكُمۡ لِلۡإِيمَٰنِ إِن كُنتُمۡ صَٰدِقِينَ

18. Lo! Allah knows the Unseen of the heavens and the earth. And Allah is Seer of what you do.

﴿١٨﴾ إِنَّ ٱللَّهَ يَعۡلَمُ غَيۡبَ ٱلسَّمَٰوَٰتِ وَٱلۡأَرۡضِۚ وَٱللَّهُ بَصِيرٌۢ بِمَا تَعۡمَلُونَ

Qāf

This surah takes its name from the Arabic letter that stands alone at the beginning of the first verse. It belongs to the middle group of Makkan surahs.

Qāf

Revealed at Makkah

*In the name of Allah,
the Beneficent, the Merciful*

1. **Q**āf. By the glorious Qur'an,

2. Nay, but they marvel that a warner of their own has come unto them; and disbelievers say: This is a strange thing:

3. When we are dead and have become dust? That would be a far return!

4. We know that which the earth takes of them,[269] and with Us is a recording Book.

5. Nay, but they have denied the truth when it came unto them, therefore they are now in troubled case.

6. Have they not then observed the sky above them, how We have constructed it and beautified it, and how there are no rifts therein?

7. And the earth have We spread out, and have flung firm mountains therein, and have caused of every lovely kind to grow thereon,

8. A vision and a reminder for every penitent slave.

9. And We send down from the sky blessed water whereby We give growth unto gardens and the grain of crops,

10. And lofty date palms with ranged clusters,

11. A provision (made) for men; and therewith We quicken a dead land. Even so will be the resurrection of the dead.

12. The folk of Noah denied (the truth) before them, and (so did) the dwellers at Al Rass and (the tribe of) Tha-mūd,

13. And (the tribe of) 'Ād, and Pharaoh, and the brothers of Lot.

---

[269]i.e., those of them who die and are buried in the earth.

14. And the owners of the wood,[270] and the folk of Tubba':[271] every one denied the messengers, therefore My threat took effect.

١٤ وَأَصْحَابُ الْأَيْكَةِ وَقَوْمُ تُبَّعٍ كُلٌّ كَذَّبَ الرُّسُلَ فَحَقَّ وَعِيدِ

15. Were We then worn out by the first creation? Yet they are in doubt about a new creation.

١٥ أَفَعَيِينَا بِالْخَلْقِ الْأَوَّلِ بَلْ هُمْ فِي لَبْسٍ مِنْ خَلْقٍ جَدِيدٍ

16. We surely created man and We know what his soul whispers to him, and We are nearer to him than his jugular vein.

١٦ وَلَقَدْ خَلَقْنَا الْإِنْسَانَ وَنَعْلَمُ مَا تُوَسْوِسُ بِهِ نَفْسُهُ وَنَحْنُ أَقْرَبُ إِلَيْهِ مِنْ حَبْلِ الْوَرِيدِ

17. When the two Receivers receive (him), seated on the right hand and on the left,

١٧ إِذْ يَتَلَقَّى الْمُتَلَقِّيَانِ عَنِ الْيَمِينِ وَعَنِ الشِّمَالِ قَعِيدٌ

18. He utters no word but there is with him an observer ready.

١٨ مَا يَلْفِظُ مِنْ قَوْلٍ إِلَّا لَدَيْهِ رَقِيبٌ عَتِيدٌ

19. And the agony of death comes in truth. This is that which you were wont to shun.

١٩ وَجَاءَتْ سَكْرَةُ الْمَوْتِ بِالْحَقِّ ذَلِكَ مَا كُنْتَ مِنْهُ تَحِيدُ

20. And the trumpet is blown. This is the threatened Day.

٢٠ وَنُفِخَ فِي الصُّورِ ذَلِكَ يَوْمُ الْوَعِيدِ

21. And every soul comes, along with it a driver and a witness

٢١ وَجَاءَتْ كُلُّ نَفْسٍ مَعَهَا سَائِقٌ وَشَهِيدٌ

22. (And unto the evildoer it is said): You were in heedlessness of this. Now We have removed from you your covering, and piercing is your sight this day.

٢٢ لَقَدْ كُنْتَ فِي غَفْلَةٍ مِنْ هَذَا فَكَشَفْنَا عَنْكَ غِطَاءَكَ فَبَصَرُكَ الْيَوْمَ حَدِيدٌ

23. And (unto the evildoer) his comrade said: This is that which I have ready (as testimony).

٢٣ وَقَالَ قَرِينُهُ هَذَا مَا لَدَيَّ عَتِيدٌ

24. Do you two[272] hurl to Hell each rebel ingrate,

٢٤ أَلْقِيَا فِي جَهَنَّمَ كُلَّ كَفَّارٍ عَنِيدٍ

25. Hinderer of good, transgressor, doubter,

٢٥ مَنَّاعٍ لِلْخَيْرِ مُعْتَدٍ مُرِيبٍ

26. Who sets up another god along with Allah. Do you two hurl him to the dreadful doom.

٢٦ الَّذِي جَعَلَ مَعَ اللَّهِ إِلَهًا آخَرَ فَأَلْقِيَاهُ فِي الْعَذَابِ الشَّدِيدِ

27. His comrade said: Our Lord! I did not cause him to rebel, but he was (himself) far gone in error.

٢٧ قَالَ قَرِينُهُ رَبَّنَا مَا أَطْغَيْتُهُ وَلَكِنْ كَانَ فِي ضَلَالٍ بَعِيدٍ

28. He said: Contend not in My presence, when I had already proffered unto you the warning.

٢٨ قَالَ لَا تَخْتَصِمُوا لَدَيَّ وَقَدْ قَدَّمْتُ إِلَيْكُمْ بِالْوَعِيدِ

29. The sentence that comes from Me cannot be changed, and I am in no wise a tyrant unto the slaves.

٢٩ مَا يُبَدَّلُ الْقَوْلُ لَدَيَّ وَمَا أَنَا بِظَلَّامٍ لِلْعَبِيدِ

---

[270]Madian.

[271]The name of a famous dynasty in al Yaman.

[272]The driver and the witness (verse 21) or the two receivers (verse 17).

30. On the day when We say unto Hell: are you filled? and it says: Can there be more to come?

٣٠ يَوْمَ نَقُوْلُ لِجَهَنَّمَ هَلِ امْتَلَأْتِ وَتَقُوْلُ هَلْ مِنْ مَّزِيْدٍ

31. And the Garden is brought nigh for those who kept from evil, no longer distant.

٣١ وَأُزْلِفَتِ الْجَنَّةُ لِلْمُتَّقِيْنَ غَيْرَ بَعِيْدٍ

32. That is that which you were promised. (It is) for every penitent and heedful one,

٣٢ هٰذَا مَا تُوْعَدُوْنَ لِكُلِّ أَوَّابٍ حَفِيْظٍ

33. Who fears the Beneficent in secret and comes with a contrite heart.

٣٣ مَنْ خَشِيَ الرَّحْمٰنَ بِالْغَيْبِ وَجَآءَ بِقَلْبٍ مُّنِيْبٍ

34. Enter it in peace. This is the day of immortality.

٣٤ ادْخُلُوْهَا بِسَلٰمٍ ذٰلِكَ يَوْمُ الْخُلُوْدِ

35. There they have all that they desire, and there is more with Us.

٣٥ لَهُمْ مَا يَشَآءُوْنَ فِيْهَا وَلَدَيْنَا مَزِيْدٌ

36. And how many a generation We destroyed before them, who were mightier than these in prowess so that they overran the lands! Had they any place of refuge (when the judgment came)?

٣٦ وَكَمْ أَهْلَكْنَا قَبْلَهُمْ مِنْ قَرْنٍ هُمْ أَشَدُّ مِنْهُمْ بَطْشًا فَنَقَّبُوْا فِي الْبِلَادِ هَلْ مِنْ مَّحِيْصٍ

37. Lo! therein verily is a reminder for him who has a heart, or gives ear with full intelligence.

٣٧ إِنَّ فِيْ ذٰلِكَ لَذِكْرٰى لِمَنْ كَانَ لَهُ قَلْبٌ أَوْ أَلْقَى السَّمْعَ وَهُوَ شَهِيْدٌ

38. And surely We created the heavens and the earth, and all that is between them, in six days,[273] and nothing of weariness touched Us.

٣٨ وَلَقَدْ خَلَقْنَا السَّمٰوٰتِ وَالْأَرْضَ وَمَا بَيْنَهُمَا فِيْ سِتَّةِ أَيَّامٍ وَمَا مَسَّنَا مِنْ لُّغُوْبٍ

39. Therefore (O Muhammad) bear with what they say: and hymn the praise of your Lord before the rising and before the setting of the sun;

٣٩ فَاصْبِرْ عَلٰى مَا يَقُوْلُوْنَ وَسَبِّحْ بِحَمْدِ رَبِّكَ قَبْلَ طُلُوْعِ الشَّمْسِ وَقَبْلَ الْغُرُوْبِ

40. And in the night time hymn His praise: And after the (prescribed) prostrations.

٤٠ وَمِنَ اللَّيْلِ فَسَبِّحْهُ وَأَدْبَارَ السُّجُوْدِ

41. And listen on the day when the crier cries from a near place,

٤١ وَاسْتَمِعْ يَوْمَ يُنَادِ الْمُنَادِ مِنْ مَّكَانٍ قَرِيْبٍ

42. The day when they will hear the (Awful) Cry in truth That is the day of coming forth (from the graves).

٤٢ يَوْمَ يَسْمَعُوْنَ الصَّيْحَةَ بِالْحَقِّ ذٰلِكَ يَوْمُ الْخُرُوْجِ

43. Lo! We it is Who quicken and give death, and unto Us is the journeying.

٤٣ إِنَّا نَحْنُ نُحْيِ وَنُمِيْتُ وَإِلَيْنَا الْمَصِيْرُ

44. On the day when the earth splits asunder from them, hastening forth (they come). That is a gathering easy for Us (to make).

٤٤ يَوْمَ تَشَقَّقُ الْأَرْضُ عَنْهُمْ سِرَاعًا ذٰلِكَ حَشْرٌ عَلَيْنَا يَسِيْرٌ

45. We are best aware of what they say, and you (O Mu-hammad) are in no wise a compeller over them. So warn by the Qur'an him who fears My threat.

٤٥ نَحْنُ أَعْلَمُ بِمَا يَقُوْلُوْنَ وَمَا أَنْتَ عَلَيْهِمْ بِجَبَّارٍ فَذَكِّرْ بِالْقُرْآنِ مَنْ يَخَافُ وَعِيْدِ

---

[273]Surahs 22:47, 32:5, and 70:4.

The Winnowing Winds

Al Dhāriyāt, "The Winnowing Winds," takes its name from a word in verse 1. I have followed the usual interpretation of the first four verses, but they may also be taken as referring to winds or to angels.

An early Makkan surah.

The Winnowing Winds

Revealed at Makkah

*In the Name of Allah,
the Beneficent, the Merciful*

1. By those that winnow with a winnowing

2. And those that bear the burden (of the rain)

3. And those that glide with ease (upon the sea)

4. And those who distribute (blessings) by command,

5. Lo! that wherewith you are threatened is indeed true,

6. And lo! the judgment will indeed befall.

7. By the heaven full of paths,

8. Lo! you, no doubt, are of various opinion (concerning the truth).

9. He is made to turn away from it who is (himself) averse.

10. Accursed be the conjecturers

11. Who are careless in an abyss!

12. They ask: When is the Day of Judgment?

13. (It is) the day when they will be tormented at the Fire,

14. Taste your torment. This is what you sought to hasten.

15. Lo! those who keep from evil will dwell amid gardens and watersprings.

16. Taking that which their Lord gives them; for lo! before they were doers of good;

17. They used to sleep but little of the night,

18. And before the dawning of each day would seek forgiveness,

19. And in their wealth the beggar and the outcast had due share.

٩) وَفِىٓ أَمۡوَٰلِهِمۡ حَقٌّ لِّلسَّآئِلِ وَٱلۡمَحۡرُومِ

20. And in the earth are portents for those whose faith is sure,

٢٠) وَفِى ٱلۡأَرۡضِ ءَايَٰتٌ لِّلۡمُوقِنِينَ

21. And (also) in yourselves. Can you then not see?

٢١) وَفِىٓ أَنفُسِكُمۡ أَفَلَا تُبۡصِرُونَ

22. And in the heaven is your providence and that which you are promised;

٢٢) وَفِى ٱلسَّمَآءِ رِزۡقُكُمۡ وَمَا تُوعَدُونَ

23. And by the Lord of the heavens and the earth, it is the truth, even as (it is true) that you speak.

٢٣) فَوَرَبِّ ٱلسَّمَآءِ وَٱلۡأَرۡضِ إِنَّهُۥ لَحَقٌّ مِّثۡلَ مَآ أَنَّكُمۡ تَنطِقُونَ

24. Has the story of Abraham's honored guests reached you (O Muhammad)?

٢٤) هَلۡ أَتَىٰكَ حَدِيثُ ضَيۡفِ إِبۡرَٰهِيمَ ٱلۡمُكۡرَمِينَ

25. When they came in unto him and said: Peace! he answered, Peace! (and thought): Folk unknown (to me).

٢٥) إِذۡ دَخَلُواْ عَلَيۡهِ فَقَالُواْ سَلَٰمًا قَالَ سَلَٰمٌ قَوۡمٌ مُّنكَرُونَ

26. Then he went apart unto his housefolk and brought a fatted calf;

٢٦) فَرَاغَ إِلَىٰٓ أَهۡلِهِۦ فَجَآءَ بِعِجۡلٍ سَمِينٍ

27. And he set it before them, saying: Will you not eat?

٢٧) فَقَرَّبَهُۥٓ إِلَيۡهِمۡ قَالَ أَلَا تَأۡكُلُونَ

28. Then he conceived a fear of them. They said: Fear not! and gave him tidings of (the birth of) a knowledgeable son.

٢٨) فَأَوۡجَسَ مِنۡهُمۡ خِيفَةً قَالُواْ لَا تَخَفۡ وَبَشَّرُوهُ بِغُلَٰمٍ عَلِيمٍ

29. Then his wife came forward, making moan, and smote her face, she cried: A barren old woman!

٢٩) فَأَقۡبَلَتِ ٱمۡرَأَتُهُۥ فِى صَرَّةٍ فَصَكَّتۡ وَجۡهَهَا وَقَالَتۡ عَجُوزٌ عَقِيمٌ

30. They said: Even so said your Lord. Lo! He is the Wise, the Knower.

٣٠) قَالُواْ كَذَٰلِكِ قَالَ رَبُّكِ إِنَّهُۥ هُوَ ٱلۡحَكِيمُ ٱلۡعَلِيمُ

31. (Abraham) said: And (afterward) what is your errand, O you sent (from Allah)?

٣١) ۞ قَالَ فَمَا خَطۡبُكُمۡ أَيُّهَا ٱلۡمُرۡسَلُونَ

32. They said: Lo! we are sent unto a guilty folk,

٣٢) قَالُوٓاْ إِنَّآ أُرۡسِلۡنَآ إِلَىٰ قَوۡمٍ مُّجۡرِمِينَ

33. That we may send upon them stones of clay,

٣٣) لِنُرۡسِلَ عَلَيۡهِمۡ حِجَارَةً مِّن طِينٍ

34. Marked by your Lord for (the destruction of) the wanton.

٣٤) مُّسَوَّمَةً عِندَ رَبِّكَ لِلۡمُسۡرِفِينَ

35. Then We brought forth such believers as were there.

٣٥) فَأَخۡرَجۡنَا مَن كَانَ فِيهَا مِنَ ٱلۡمُؤۡمِنِينَ

36. But We found there but one house of Muslims.[274]

٣٦ فَمَا وَجَدْنَا فِيهَا غَيْرَ بَيْتٍ مِّنَ الْمُسْلِمِينَ

37. And We left behind therein a portent for those who fear a painful doom.

٣٧ وَتَرَكْنَا فِيهَآ ءَايَةً لِّلَّذِينَ يَخَافُونَ الْعَذَابَ الْأَلِيمَ

38. And in Moses (too, there is a portent) when We sent him unto Pharaoh with clear warrant,

٣٨ وَفِي مُوسَىٰ إِذْ أَرْسَلْنَٰهُ إِلَىٰ فِرْعَوْنَ بِسُلْطَٰنٍ مُّبِينٍ

39. But he withdrew (confiding) in his might, and said: A wizard or a madman.

٣٩ فَتَوَلَّىٰ بِرُكْنِهِۦ وَقَالَ سَٰحِرٌ أَوْ مَجْنُونٌ

40. So We seized him and his hosts and flung them in the sea, for he was reprobate.

٤٠ فَأَخَذْنَٰهُ وَجُنُودَهُۥ فَنَبَذْنَٰهُمْ فِي الْيَمِّ وَهُوَ مُلِيمٌ

41. And in (the tribe of) 'Ād (there is a portent) when We sent the fatal wind against them.

٤١ وَفِي عَادٍ إِذْ أَرْسَلْنَا عَلَيْهِمُ الرِّيحَ الْعَقِيمَ

42. It spared nothing that it reached, but made it (all) as ashes.

٤٢ مَا تَذَرُ مِن شَىْءٍ أَتَتْ عَلَيْهِ إِلَّا جَعَلَتْهُ كَالرَّمِيمِ

43. And in (the tribe of) Thamūd (there is a portent) when it was told them: Take your ease awhile.

٤٣ وَفِي ثَمُودَ إِذْ قِيلَ لَهُمْ تَمَتَّعُوا حَتَّىٰ حِينٍ

44. But they rebelled against their Lord's decree, and so the thunderbolt overtook them even while they gazed;

٤٤ فَعَتَوْا عَنْ أَمْرِ رَبِّهِمْ فَأَخَذَتْهُمُ الصَّٰعِقَةُ وَهُمْ يَنظُرُونَ

45. And they were unable to rise up, nor could they help themselves.

٤٥ فَمَا اسْتَطَٰعُوا مِن قِيَامٍ وَمَا كَانُوا مُنتَصِرِينَ

46. And the folk of Noah before. Lo! they were licentious folk.

٤٦ وَقَوْمَ نُوحٍ مِّن قَبْلُ إِنَّهُمْ كَانُوا قَوْمًا فَٰسِقِينَ

47. We have built the heaven with might, and We it is who make the vast extent (thereof).

٤٧ وَالسَّمَآءَ بَنَيْنَٰهَا بِأَيْيْدٍ وَإِنَّا لَمُوسِعُونَ

48. And the earth have We laid out, how gracious was the Spreader (thereof)!

٤٨ وَالْأَرْضَ فَرَشْنَٰهَا فَنِعْمَ الْمَٰهِدُونَ

49. And all things We have created by pairs, that you may reflect.

٤٩ وَمِن كُلِّ شَىْءٍ خَلَقْنَا زَوْجَيْنِ لَعَلَّكُمْ تَذَكَّرُونَ

---

[274]Arabic: *Muslimūn*.

50. Therefore flee unto Allah; lo! I[275] am a plain warner unto you from Him;

٥٠ فَفِرُّوٓا إِلَى اللَّهِ إِنِّى لَكُمْ مِنْهُ نَذِيرٌ مُّبِينٌ

51. And set not any other god along with Allah; lo! I am a plain warner unto you from Him;

٥١ وَلَا تَجْعَلُوا مَعَ اللَّهِ إِلَٰهًا ءَاخَرَ إِنِّى لَكُمْ مِنْهُ نَذِيرٌ مُّبِينٌ

52. Even so there came no messenger unto those before them but they said: A wizard or a madman!

٥٢ كَذَٰلِكَ مَآ أَتَى الَّذِينَ مِن قَبْلِهِم مِّن رَّسُولٍ إِلَّا قَالُوا سَاحِرٌ أَوْ مَجْنُونٌ

53. Have they handed down (the saying) as an heirloom one unto another? Nay, but they are froward folk.

٥٣ أَتَوَاصَوْا بِهِ بَلْ هُمْ قَوْمٌ طَاغُونَ

54. So withdraw from them (O Muhammad), for you are in no wise blameworthy,

٥٤ فَتَوَلَّ عَنْهُمْ فَمَآ أَنتَ بِمَلُومٍ

55. And warn, for warning profits believers.

٥٥ وَذَكِّرْ فَإِنَّ الذِّكْرَىٰ تَنفَعُ الْمُؤْمِنِينَ

56. I created the jinn and humankind only that they might worship Me.

٥٦ وَمَا خَلَقْتُ الْجِنَّ وَالْإِنسَ إِلَّا لِيَعْبُدُونِ

57. I seek no livelihood from them, nor do I ask that they should feed Me.

٥٧ مَآ أُرِيدُ مِنْهُم مِّن رِّزْقٍ وَمَآ أُرِيدُ أَن يُطْعِمُونِ

58. Lo! Allah! He it is that gives livelihood, the Lord of unbreakable might.

٥٨ إِنَّ اللَّهَ هُوَ الرَّزَّاقُ ذُو الْقُوَّةِ الْمَتِينُ

59. And lo! for those who (now) do wrong there is an evil day like unto the evil day (which came for) their likes (of old); so let them not ask Me to hasten on (that day).

٥٩ فَإِنَّ لِلَّذِينَ ظَلَمُوا ذَنُوبًا مِّثْلَ ذَنُوبِ أَصْحَٰبِهِمْ فَلَا يَسْتَعْجِلُونِ

60. And woe unto those who disbelieve, from (that) their day which they are promised.

٦٠ فَوَيْلٌ لِّلَّذِينَ كَفَرُوا مِن يَوْمِهِمُ الَّذِى يُوعَدُونَ

---

[275]A reference to Prophet Muhammad.

The Mount

Al Ṭūr, "The Mount," takes its name from the opening verse. It refers to the mountain in Sinai on which Moses received divine revelation. An early Makkan surah.

The Mount

Revealed at Makkah

*In the Name of Allah,
the Beneficent, the Merciful*

سورة الطور

بِسْمِ اللّٰهِ الرَّحْمٰنِ الرَّحِيْمِ

1. By the Mount (Ṭūr of Revelation),

وَالطُّوْرِ ۞

2. And a Scripture inscribed

وَكِتَابٍ مَّسْطُوْرٍ ۞

3. In a scroll unfolded,

فِيْ رَقٍّ مَّنْشُوْرٍ ۞

4. And the House frequented,

وَالْبَيْتِ الْمَعْمُوْرِ ۞

5. And the canopy raised high (Heaven),

وَالسَّقْفِ الْمَرْفُوْعِ ۞

6. And the burning sea,

وَالْبَحْرِ الْمَسْجُوْرِ ۞

7. Lo! the doom of your Lord will surely come to pass;

إِنَّ عَذَابَ رَبِّكَ لَوَاقِعٌ ۞

8. There is none that can ward it off.

مَا لَهُ مِنْ دَافِعٍ ۞

9. On the day when the heaven will be in dreadful commotion,

يَوْمَ تَمُوْرُ السَّمَاءُ مَوْرًا ۞

10. And the mountains move away with (awful) movement,

وَتَسِيْرُ الْجِبَالُ سَيْرًا ۞

11. Then woe that day unto the deniers

فَوَيْلٌ يَوْمَئِذٍ لِّلْمُكَذِّبِيْنَ ۞

12. Who play in talk of grave matters;

الَّذِيْنَ هُمْ فِيْ خَوْضٍ يَلْعَبُوْنَ ۞

13. The day when they are thrust with a (disdainful) thrust, into the fire of Hell.

يَوْمَ يُدَعُّوْنَ إِلَى نَارِ جَهَنَّمَ دَعًّا ۞

14. This is the Fire which you were wont to deny.

هٰذِهِ النَّارُ الَّتِيْ كُنْتُمْ بِهَا تُكَذِّبُوْنَ ۞

15. Is this magic, or do you not see?

أَفَسِحْرٌ هٰذَا أَمْ أَنْتُمْ لَا تُبْصِرُوْنَ ۞

16. Endure the heat thereof, and whether you are patient of it or impatient of it is all one for you. You are only being paid for what you used to do.

اِصْلَوْهَا فَاصْبِرُوْا أَوْ لَا تَصْبِرُوْا سَوَاءٌ عَلَيْكُمْ اِنَّمَا تُجْزَوْنَ مَا كُنْتُمْ تَعْمَلُوْنَ ۞

17. Lo! the pious ones will dwell in gardens and delight,

إِنَّ الْمُتَّقِيْنَ فِيْ جَنَّاتٍ وَنَعِيْمٍ ۞

18. Happy because of what their Lord has given them, and (because) their Lord has warded off from them the torment of hellfire.

فَكِهِيْنَ بِمَا آتَاهُمْ رَبُّهُمْ وَوَقَاهُمْ رَبُّهُمْ عَذَابَ الْجَحِيْمِ ۞

19. Eat and drink in health (as reward) for what you used to do,

٢٩ كُلُوا وَاشْرَبُوا هَنِيئًا بِمَا كُنْتُمْ تَعْمَلُونَ

20. Reclining on ranged couches. And We wed them unto fair ones with wide, lovely eyes.

٢٠ مُتَّكِئِينَ عَلَى سُرُرٍ مَّصْفُوفَةٍ وَزَوَّجْنَاهُمْ بِحُورٍ عِينٍ

21. And they who believe and whose seed follow them in faith, We cause their seed to join them (there), and We deprive them of nothing of their (life's) work. Every man is a pledge for that which he has earned.

٢١ وَالَّذِينَ ءَامَنُوا وَاتَّبَعَتْهُمْ ذُرِّيَّتُهُمْ بِإِيمَانٍ أَلْحَقْنَا بِهِمْ ذُرِّيَّتَهُمْ وَمَا أَلَتْنَاهُمْ مِنْ عَمَلِهِمْ مِنْ شَيْءٍ كُلُّ امْرِئٍ بِمَا كَسَبَ رَهِينٌ

22. And We provide them with fruit and meat such as they desire.

٢٢ وَأَمْدَدْنَاهُمْ بِفَاكِهَةٍ وَلَحْمٍ مِّمَّا يَشْتَهُونَ

23. There they pass from hand to hand a cup wherein is neither vanity nor cause of sin.

٢٣ يَتَنَازَعُونَ فِيهَا كَأْسًا لَّا لَغْوٌ فِيهَا وَلَا تَأْثِيمٌ

24. And there go round, waiting on them handsome youth of their own, as if they were hidden pearls.

٢٤ وَيَطُوفُ عَلَيْهِمْ غِلْمَانٌ لَّهُمْ كَأَنَّهُمْ لُؤْلُؤٌ مَكْنُونٌ

25. And some of them draw near unto others, questioning,

٢٥ وَأَقْبَلَ بَعْضُهُمْ عَلَى بَعْضٍ يَتَسَاءَلُونَ

26. Saying: Lo! of old, when we were with our families, we were ever anxious and afraid;

٢٦ قَالُوا إِنَّا كُنَّا قَبْلُ فِي أَهْلِنَا مُشْفِقِينَ

27. So Allah has been gracious unto us and has protected us from the torment of the breath of Fire.

٢٧ فَمَنَّ اللَّهُ عَلَيْنَا وَوَقَانَا عَذَابَ السَّمُومِ

28. Lo! we used to pray unto Him of old. Lo! He is the Benign, the Merciful.

٢٨ إِنَّا كُنَّا مِنْ قَبْلُ نَدْعُوهُ إِنَّهُ هُوَ الْبَرُّ الرَّحِيمُ

29. Therefore warn (men, O Muhammad). By the grace of Allah you are neither soothsayer nor madman.

٢٩ فَذَكِّرْ فَمَا أَنْتَ بِنِعْمَتِ رَبِّكَ بِكَاهِنٍ وَلَا مَجْنُونٍ

30. Or say they: (he is) a poet, (one) for whom we may expect the accident of time?

٣٠ أَمْ يَقُولُونَ شَاعِرٌ نَّتَرَبَّصُ بِهِ رَيْبَ الْمَنُونِ

31. Say (unto them): Expect (your fill)! Lo! I am with you among the expectant.

٣١ قُلْ تَرَبَّصُوا فَإِنِّي مَعَكُمْ مِنَ الْمُتَرَبِّصِينَ

32. Do their minds command them to do this, or are they an outrageous folk?

٣٢ أَمْ تَأْمُرُهُمْ أَحْلَامُهُمْ بِهَذَا أَمْ هُمْ قَوْمٌ طَاغُونَ

33. Or say they: He has concocted it? Nay, but they will not believe!

٣٣ أَمْ يَقُولُونَ تَقَوَّلَهُ بَلْ لَّا يُؤْمِنُونَ

34. Then let them produce speech the like thereof, if they are truthful:

٣٤ فَلْيَأْتُوا بِحَدِيثٍ مِّثْلِهِ إِنْ كَانُوا صَادِقِينَ

35. Or were they created out of nothing? Or are they the creators?

٣٥ أَمْ خُلِقُوا مِنْ غَيْرِ شَيْءٍ أَمْ هُمُ الْخَالِقُونَ

36. Or did they create the heavens and the earth? Nay, but they are sure of nothing!

٣٦) أَمْ خَلَقُوا السَّمَوَاتِ وَالْأَرْضَ بَل لَّا يُوقِنُونَ

37. Or do they have the treasures of your Lord? Or have they been given charge (thereof)?

٣٧) أَمْ عِندَهُمْ خَزَائِنُ رَبِّكَ أَمْ هُمُ الْمُصَيْطِرُونَ

38. Or have they any stairway (unto heaven) by means of which they over-hear (decrees). Then let their listener produce warrant manifest!

٣٨) أَمْ لَهُمْ سُلَّمٌ يَسْتَمِعُونَ فِيهِ فَلْيَأْتِ مُسْتَمِعُهُم بِسُلْطَانٍ مُّبِينٍ

39. Or has He daughters whereas you have sons?

٣٩) أَمْ لَهُ الْبَنَاتُ وَلَكُمُ الْبَنُونَ

40. Or ask you (Muhammad) a fee from them so that they are plunged in debt?

٤٠) أَمْ تَسْأَلُهُمْ أَجْرًا فَهُم مِّن مَّغْرَمٍ مُّثْقَلُونَ

41. Or possess they the Unseen so that they can write (it) down?

٤١) أَمْ عِندَهُمُ الْغَيْبُ فَهُمْ يَكْتُبُونَ

42. Or seek they to ensnare (the Messenger)? But those who disbelieve, they are the ensnared!

٤٢) أَمْ يُرِيدُونَ كَيْدًا فَالَّذِينَ كَفَرُوا هُمُ الْمَكِيدُونَ

43. Or have they any god beside Allah? Glorified be Allah from all that they ascribe as partner (unto Him)!

٤٣) أَمْ لَهُمْ إِلَهٌ غَيْرُ اللَّهِ سُبْحَانَ اللَّهِ عَمَّا يُشْرِكُونَ

44. And if they were to see a fragment of the heaven falling, they would say: A heap of clouds.

٤٤) وَإِن يَرَوْا كِسْفًا مِّنَ السَّمَاءِ سَاقِطًا يَقُولُوا سَحَابٌ مَّرْكُومٌ

45. Then let them be (O Muhammad), till they meet their day, in which they will be thunder stricken,

٤٥) فَذَرْهُمْ حَتَّى يُلَاقُوا يَوْمَهُمُ الَّذِي فِيهِ يُصْعَقُونَ

46. A day in which their guile will nothing avail them, nor will they be helped.

٤٦) يَوْمَ لَا يُغْنِي عَنْهُمْ كَيْدُهُمْ شَيْئًا وَلَا هُمْ يُنصَرُونَ

47. And surely, for those who do wrong, there is a punishment beyond that. But most of them know not.

٤٧) وَإِنَّ لِلَّذِينَ ظَلَمُوا عَذَابًا دُونَ ذَلِكَ وَلَكِنَّ أَكْثَرَهُمْ لَا يَعْلَمُونَ

48. So wait patiently (O Muhammad) for your Lord's de-cree, for surely you are in Our sight; and hymn the praise of your Lord when you stand forth.

٤٨) وَاصْبِرْ لِحُكْمِ رَبِّكَ فَإِنَّكَ بِأَعْيُنِنَا وَسَبِّحْ بِحَمْدِ رَبِّكَ حِينَ تَقُومُ

49. And in the night time also glorify Him, and at the setting of the stars.

٤٩) وَمِنَ اللَّيْلِ فَسَبِّحْهُ وَإِدْبَارَ النُّجُومِ

The Star

Al Najm, "The Star," takes its name from a word in the first verse. An early Makkan surah.

The Star

Revealed at Makkah

*In the Name of Allah,
the Beneficent, the Merciful*

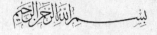

1. By the Star when it sets,

2. Your comrade errs not, nor is deceived;

3. Nor does he speak of (his own) desire.

4. It is nothing save an inspiration that is inspired,

5. Which one of mighty powers has taught him,

6. One vigorous; and he grew clear to view[276]

7. When he was on the uppermost horizon.

8. Then he drew near and came down

9. Till he was (distant) two bows' length or even nearer,

10. And He revealed unto His slave that which He revealed.

11. The heart lied not (in seeing) what it saw.

12. Will you then dispute with him concerning what he sees?

13. And surely he saw him, yet another time[277]

14. By the lote-tree of the utmost boundary,

15. Near unto which is the Garden of Abode.

16. When that which shrouds did enshroud the lote-tree,

17. The eye turned not aside nor yet was overbold.

18. Verily he saw one of the Signs of his Lord the Greatest!

19. Have you thought upon al Lāt and Al 'Uzzā[278]

---

[276]This and the five following verses are generally accepted as referring to the Prophet's vision on Mt. Ḥirā'.

[277]This is generally accepted as a reference to the Prophet's vision in which he ascended through the seven heavens.

[278]An idol of the pagan Arabs.

20. And Manāt,[279] the third, the other?

٢٠ وَمَنَوٰةَ الثَّالِثَةَ الْأُخْرَىٰ

21. Are yours the males and His the females?

٢١ أَلَكُمُ الذَّكَرُ وَلَهُ الْأُنثَىٰ

22. That indeed were an unfair division!

٢٢ تِلْكَ إِذًا قِسْمَةٌ ضِيزَىٰ

23. They are but names which you have named, you and your fathers, for which Allah has revealed no warrant. They follow but a guess and that which (they) themselves desire. And now the guidance from their Lord has come unto them.

٢٣ إِنْ هِيَ إِلَّا أَسْمَآءٌ سَمَّيْتُمُوهَآ أَنتُمْ وَءَابَآؤُكُم مَّآ أَنزَلَ اللَّهُ بِهَا مِن سُلْطَٰنٍ إِن يَتَّبِعُونَ إِلَّا الظَّنَّ وَمَا تَهْوَى الْأَنفُسُ وَلَقَدْ جَآءَهُم مِّن رَّبِّهِمُ الْهُدَىٰ

24. Or shall man have what he covets?

٢٤ أَمْ لِلْإِنسَٰنِ مَا تَمَنَّىٰ

25. But unto Allah belongs the after (life), and the former.

٢٥ فَلِلَّهِ الْآخِرَةُ وَالْأُولَىٰ

26. And how many angels are in the heavens whose intercession avails nothing save after Allah gives leave to whom He chooses and accepts!

٢٦ وَكَم مِّن مَّلَكٍ فِى السَّمَٰوَٰتِ لَا تُغْنِى شَفَٰعَتُهُمْ شَيْئًا إِلَّا مِنۢ بَعْدِ أَن يَأْذَنَ اللَّهُ لِمَن يَشَآءُ وَيَرْضَىٰ

27. Lo! it is those who disbelieve in the Hereafter who name the angels with the names of females.

٢٧ إِنَّ الَّذِينَ لَا يُؤْمِنُونَ بِالْآخِرَةِ لَيُسَمُّونَ الْمَلَٰئِكَةَ تَسْمِيَةَ الْأُنثَىٰ

28. And they have no knowledge thereof. They follow but a guess, and lo! a guess can never take the place of the truth.

٢٨ وَمَا لَهُم بِهِۦ مِنْ عِلْمٍ إِن يَتَّبِعُونَ إِلَّا الظَّنَّ وَإِنَّ الظَّنَّ لَا يُغْنِى مِنَ الْحَقِّ شَيْئًا

29. Then withdraw (O Muhammad) from him who flees from Our remembrance and desires but the life of the world.

٢٩ فَأَعْرِضْ عَن مَّن تَوَلَّىٰ عَن ذِكْرِنَا وَلَمْ يُرِدْ إِلَّا الْحَيَوٰةَ الدُّنْيَا

30. Such is their sum of knowledge. Lo! your Lord is best aware of him who strays, and He is best aware of him who goes right.

٣٠ ذَٰلِكَ مَبْلَغُهُم مِّنَ الْعِلْمِ إِنَّ رَبَّكَ هُوَ أَعْلَمُ بِمَن ضَلَّ عَن سَبِيلِهِۦ وَهُوَ أَعْلَمُ بِمَنِ اهْتَدَىٰ

31. And unto Allah belongs whatsoever is in the heavens and whatsoever is in the earth, that He may reward those who do evil with that which they have done, and reward those who do good with goodness.

٣١ وَلِلَّهِ مَا فِى السَّمَٰوَٰتِ وَمَا فِى الْأَرْضِ لِيَجْزِىَ الَّذِينَ أَسَٰٓـُٔوا بِمَا عَمِلُوا وَيَجْزِىَ الَّذِينَ أَحْسَنُوا بِالْحُسْنَى

[279]The pagan Arabs pretended that their idols were daughters of Allah.

32. Those who avoid enormities of sin and abominations, save the unwilled offences—(for them) lo! your Lord is of vast mercy. He is best aware of you (from the time) when He created you from the earth, and when you were hidden in the bellies of your mothers. Therefore ascribe not purity unto yourselves. He is best aware of him who wards off (evil).

33. Did you (O Muhammad) observe him who turned away,

34. And gave a little, then was grudging?

35. Has he knowledge of the Unseen so that he sees?

36. Or has he not had news of what is in the books of Moses

37. And Abraham who paid his debt:

38. That no laden one shall bear another's load,

39. And that man has only that for which he makes effort,

40. And that his effort will be seen,

41. And afterward he will be repaid for it with fullest payment;

42. And that your Lord, He is the goal;

43. And that He it is Who makes laugh, and makes weep,

44. And that He it is Who gives death and gives life;

45. And that He creates the two spouses, the male and the female,

46. From a drop (of seed) when it is poured forth;

47. And that He has ordained the second bringing forth;

48. And that He it is Who enriches and decides poverty:

49. And that He it is Who is the Lord of Sirius;

٣٢ اَلَّذِيْنَ يَجْتَنِبُوْنَ كَبَائِرَ الْاِثْمِ وَالْفَوَاحِشَ اِلَّا اللَّمَمَ ۚ اِنَّ رَبَّكَ وَاسِعُ الْمَغْفِرَةِ ۚ هُوَ اَعْلَمُ بِكُمْ اِذْ اَنْشَاَكُمْ مِّنَ الْاَرْضِ وَاِذْ اَنْتُمْ اَجِنَّةٌ فِيْ بُطُوْنِ اُمَّهٰتِكُمْ ۚ فَلَا تُزَكُّوْٓا اَنْفُسَكُمْ ۚ هُوَ اَعْلَمُ بِمَنِ اتَّقٰى ۟

٣٣ اَفَرَءَيْتَ الَّذِيْ تَوَلّٰى ۟

٣٤ وَاَعْطٰى قَلِيْلًا وَّاَكْدٰى ۟

٣٥ اَعِنْدَهٗ عِلْمُ الْغَيْبِ فَهُوَ يَرٰى ۟

٣٦ اَمْ لَمْ يُنَبَّاْ بِمَا فِيْ صُحُفِ مُوْسٰى ۟

٣٧ وَاِبْرٰهِيْمَ الَّذِيْ وَفّٰٓى ۟

٣٨ اَلَّا تَزِرُ وَازِرَةٌ وِّزْرَ اُخْرٰى ۟

٣٩ وَاَنْ لَّيْسَ لِلْاِنْسَانِ اِلَّا مَا سَعٰى ۟

٤٠ وَاَنَّ سَعْيَهٗ سَوْفَ يُرٰى ۟

٤١ ثُمَّ يُجْزٰىهُ الْجَزَاءَ الْاَوْفٰى ۟

٤٢ وَاَنَّ اِلٰى رَبِّكَ الْمُنْتَهٰى ۟

٤٣ وَاَنَّهٗ هُوَ اَضْحَكَ وَاَبْكٰى ۟

٤٤ وَاَنَّهٗ هُوَ اَمَاتَ وَاَحْيَا ۟

٤٥ وَاَنَّهٗ خَلَقَ الزَّوْجَيْنِ الذَّكَرَ وَالْاُنْثٰى ۟

٤٦ مِنْ نُّطْفَةٍ اِذَا تُمْنٰى ۟

٤٧ وَاَنَّ عَلَيْهِ النَّشْاَةَ الْاُخْرٰى ۟

٤٨ وَاَنَّهٗ هُوَ اَغْنٰى وَاَقْنٰى ۟

٤٩ وَاَنَّهٗ هُوَ رَبُّ الشِّعْرٰى ۟

50. And that He destroyed the former (tribe of) 'Ād,[280]

وَأَنَّهُۥ أَهْلَكَ عَادًا ٱلْأُولَىٰ ۝

51. And (the tribe of) Thamūd He spared not;

وَثَمُودَا۟ فَمَآ أَبْقَىٰ ۝

52. And the folk of Noah before, lo! they were more unjust and more rebellious;

وَقَوْمَ نُوحٍ مِّن قَبْلُ إِنَّهُمْ كَانُوا۟ هُمْ أَظْلَمَ وَأَطْغَىٰ ۝

53. And al Mutafikah[281] He destroyed

وَٱلْمُؤْتَفِكَةَ أَهْوَىٰ ۝

54. So that there covered them that which did cover.

فَغَشَّىٰهَا مَا غَشَّىٰ ۝

55. Concerning which then, of the bounties of your Lord, can you dispute?

فَبِأَيِّ ءَالَآءِ رَبِّكَ تَتَمَارَىٰ ۝

56. This is a warner of the warners of old.

هَٰذَا نَذِيرٌ مِّنَ ٱلنُّذُرِ ٱلْأُولَىٰ ۝

57. The threatened Hour is near.

أَزِفَتِ ٱلْأَزِفَةُ ۝

58. None beside Allah can disclose it.

لَيْسَ لَهَا مِن دُونِ ٱللَّهِ كَاشِفَةٌ ۝

59. Marvel you then at this statement,

أَفَمِنْ هَٰذَا ٱلْحَدِيثِ تَعْجَبُونَ ۝

60. And laugh and not weep,

وَتَضْحَكُونَ وَلَا تَبْكُونَ ۝

61. While you amuse yourselves?

وَأَنتُمْ سَٰمِدُونَ ۝

62. Rather prostrate yourselves before Allah and worship Him.

فَٱسْجُدُوا۟ لِلَّهِ وَٱعْبُدُوا۟ ۩ ۝

---

[280]There was still in existence a tribe of that name.
[281]Generally supposed to be a name for the villages of the people of Lot.

The Moon

Al Qamar, "The Moon," takes its name from the first verse: "The hour drew nigh and the moon was rent in two." A strange appearance of the moon in the sky, as if it had been torn asunder, is recorded in the traditions of several Companions of the Prophet as having astonished the people of Makkah about the time when the idolaters were beginning to persecute the Muslims.

An early Makkan surah.

The Moon

Revealed at Makkah

*In the Name of Allah,
the Beneficent, the Merciful*

1. The hour drew near and the moon was rent in two.

2. And if they behold a portent they turn away and say: Prolonged illusion.

3. They denied (the Truth) and followed their own lusts. Yet everything will come to a decision.

4. And surely there has come unto them news whereof the purport should deter,

5. Effective wisdom; but warnings avail not.

6. So withdraw from them (O Muhammad). On the day when the Summoner summons unto a painful thing,

7. With downcast eyes, they come forth from the graves as they were locusts spread abroad,

8. Hastening toward the Summoner; the disbelievers say: This is a hard day.

9. The folk of Noah denied before them, yea, they denied Our slave[282] and said: A madman; and he was repulsed.

10. So he cried unto his Lord, saying: I am vanquished, so give help.

11. Then opened We the gates of heaven with pouring water

12. And caused the earth to gush forth springs, so that the waters met for a pre-destined purpose.

13. And We carried him upon a thing of planks and nails,

14. That ran (upon the waters) in Our sight, as a reward for him who was rejected.

15. And surely We left it as a token; but is there any that remembers?

---

[282]To be 'Abd Allāh, "a slave or a servant of God," is the proudest rank a Muslim can claim, for bondage to Allah implies liberation from all other servitudes. All men who are especially devoted to Allah, all of the chosen ones, are called 'Ibād Allāh (slaves or servants of Allah) in the Qur'an.

16. Then see how (dreadful) was My punishment after My warnings!

17. And in truth We have made the Qur'an easy to remember[283]; but is there any that remembered?

18. (The tribe of) 'Ād rejected warnings. Then how dreadful) was My punishment after My warnings.

19. Lo! We let loose on them a raging wind on a day of constant calamity,

20. Sweeping men away as though they were uprooted trunks of palm trees.

21. Then see how (dreadful) was My punishment after My warnings!

22. And in truth We have made the Qur'an easy to remember; but is there any that remembers?

23. (The tribe of) Thamūd rejected warnings

24. For they said: Is it a mortal man, alone among us, that we are to follow? Then indeed we should fall into error and madness.

25. Has the remembrance been given unto him alone among us? Nay, but he is a rash liar.

26. Tomorrow they will know who is the rash liar.

27. Lo! We are sending the she-camel as a test for them; so watch them and have patience;

28. And inform them that the water is to be shared between (her and) them. Every drinking will be witnessed.

29. But they called their comrade and he took and hamstrung (her).

30. Then see how (dreadful) was My punishment after My warnings!

31. Lo! We sent upon them one Shout, and they became as the dry twigs (rejected by) the builder of a cattle fold.

32. And in truth We have made the Qur'an easy to remember; but is there any that remembers?

33. The folk of Lot rejected warnings.

34. Lo! We sent a storm of stones upon them (all) save the family of Lot, whom We rescued in the last watch of the night,

---

[283] It is very easy for the believers to memorize the entire Qur'an, and many many thousands, if not millions, of Muslims around the world can testify to this fact. The translator, who has great difficulty remembering well-known English quotations accurately, can remember page after page of the Qur'an in Arabic with perfect accuracy.

35. As grace from Us. Thus We reward him who gives thanks.

36. And he indeed had warned them of Our blow, but they did doubt the warnings.

37. They even asked of him his guests for an ill purpose. Then We blinded their eyes (and said): Taste now My punishment after My warnings!

38. And in truth the punishment decreed befell them early in the morning.

39. Now taste My punishment after My warnings!

40. And in truth We have made the Qur'an easy to remember; but is there any that remembers?

41. And warnings came in truth unto the house of Pharaoh

42. Who denied Our revelations, every one. Therefore We grasped them with the grasp of the Mighty, the Powerful.

43. Are your disbelievers better than those, or have you some immunity in the Scriptures?

44. Or say they: We are a host victorious?

45. The hosts will all be routed and will then turn and flee.

46. Nay, but the Hour (of doom) is their appointed time, and the Hour will be more wretched and more bitter (than their earthly failure).

47. Lo! the criminals are in error and madness.

48. On the day when they are dragged into the Fire upon their faces (it is said unto them): Feel the touch of Hell.

49. Lo! We have created every thing by measure.

50. And Our commandment is but one (commandment), as the twinkling of an eye.

51. And surely We have destroyed your fellows; but is there any that remembers?

52. And every thing they did is in the Scriptures,

53. And every small and great thing is recorded.

54. Lo! the righteous will dwell among gardens and rivers,

55. Firmly established in the favor of a Mighty King.

The Beneficent

Al Raḥmān takes its name from the first verse. In the refrain: "Which is it, of the favors of your Lord, that you deny?" the word "you" and the verb are in the dual form, and the question is generally believed to be addressed to man-kind and the Jinn. When this chapter was revealed, Prophet Muhammad said to his Companions: "The Jinn are more alert than you are. When the verse 'which is it, of the favors of your Lord, that you deny?,' the Jinn said: 'Nothing of your favors, our Lord, do we deny!'" (the editor)

An early Makkan surah.

The Beneficent

Revealed at Makkah

In the Name of Allah,
the Beneficent, the Merciful

1. The Beneficent

2. Has made known the Qur'an.

3. He has created man.

4. He has taught him expression.

5. The sun and the moon are made punctual.

6. The stars and the trees prostrate.

7. And the sky He has uplifted; and He has set the measure,

8. That you exceed not the measure,

9. But observe the measure strictly, nor fall short the measure.

10. And the earth has He appointed for (His) creatures,

11. Wherein are fruit and sheathed palm trees

12. Husked grain and scented herb.

13. Which is it, of the favors of your Lord, that you deny?

14. He created man of clay like the potter's,

15. And the jinn did He create of smokeless fire.

16. Which is it, of the favors of your Lord, that you deny?

17. Lord of the two Easts,[284] and Lord of the two Wests![285]

18. Which is it, of the favors of your Lord, that you deny?

19. He has loosed the two seas[286]; They meet.

۱ الرَّحْمَٰنُ ۝

۲ عَلَّمَ الْقُرْءَانَ ۝

۳ خَلَقَ الْإِنسَٰنَ ۝

۴ عَلَّمَهُ الْبَيَانَ ۝

۵ الشَّمْسُ وَالْقَمَرُ بِحُسْبَانٍ ۝

۶ وَالنَّجْمُ وَالشَّجَرُ يَسْجُدَانِ ۝

۷ وَالسَّمَآءَ رَفَعَهَا وَوَضَعَ الْمِيزَانَ ۝

۸ أَلَّا تَطْغَوْا فِي الْمِيزَانِ ۝

۹ وَأَقِيمُوا الْوَزْنَ بِالْقِسْطِ وَلَا تُخْسِرُوا الْمِيزَانَ ۝

۱۰ وَالْأَرْضَ وَضَعَهَا لِلْأَنَامِ ۝

۱۱ فِيهَا فَٰكِهَةٌ وَالنَّخْلُ ذَاتُ الْأَكْمَامِ ۝

۱۲ وَالْحَبُّ ذُو الْعَصْفِ وَالرَّيْحَانُ ۝

۱۳ فَبِأَيِّ ءَالَآءِ رَبِّكُمَا تُكَذِّبَانِ ۝

۱۴ خَلَقَ الْإِنسَٰنَ مِن صَلْصَٰلٍ كَالْفَخَّارِ ۝

۱۵ وَخَلَقَ الْجَآنَّ مِن مَّارِجٍ مِّن نَّارٍ ۝

۱۶ فَبِأَيِّ ءَالَآءِ رَبِّكُمَا تُكَذِّبَانِ ۝

۱۷ رَبُّ الْمَشْرِقَيْنِ وَرَبُّ الْمَغْرِبَيْنِ ۝

۱۸ فَبِأَيِّ ءَالَآءِ رَبِّكُمَا تُكَذِّبَانِ ۝

۱۹ مَرَجَ الْبَحْرَيْنِ يَلْتَقِيَانِ ۝

---

[284]The two points where the sun rises in winter and in summer.

[285]The two points where the sun sets in winter and in summer.

[286]i.e., the salt water and the sweet

20. There is a barrier between them. They encroach not (one upon the other).

٢٠ بَيْنَهُمَا بَرْزَخٌ لَّا يَبْغِيَانِ

21. Which is it, of the favors of your Lord, that you deny?

٢١ فَبِأَيِّ ءَالَاءِ رَبِّكُمَا تُكَذِّبَانِ

22. There comes forth from both of them the pearl and coral stone.

٢٢ يَخْرُجُ مِنْهُمَا اللُّؤْلُؤُ وَالْمَرْجَانُ

23. Which is it, of the favors of your Lord, that you deny?

٢٣ فَبِأَيِّ ءَالَاءِ رَبِّكُمَا تُكَذِّبَانِ

24. His are the running ships displayed upon the sea, like mountains.[287]

٢٤ وَلَهُ الْجَوَارِ الْمُنْشَآتُ فِي الْبَحْرِ كَالْأَعْلَامِ

25. Which is it, of the favors of your Lord, that you deny?

٢٥ فَبِأَيِّ ءَالَاءِ رَبِّكُمَا تُكَذِّبَانِ

26. Everyone that is thereon will pass away;

٢٦ كُلُّ مَنْ عَلَيْهَا فَانٍ

27. There remains but the countenance of your Lord of Might and Glory.

٢٧ وَيَبْقَىٰ وَجْهُ رَبِّكَ ذُو الْجَلَالِ وَالْإِكْرَامِ

28. Which is it, of the favors of your Lord, that you deny?

٢٨ فَبِأَيِّ ءَالَاءِ رَبِّكُمَا تُكَذِّبَانِ

29. All that are in the heavens and the earth entreat Him. Every day He exercises (universal) power.

٢٩ يَسْأَلُهُ مَنْ فِي السَّمَوَاتِ وَالْأَرْضِ كُلَّ يَوْمٍ هُوَ فِي شَأْنٍ

30. Which is it, of the favors of your Lord, that you deny?

٣٠ فَبِأَيِّ ءَالَاءِ رَبِّكُمَا تُكَذِّبَانِ

31. We shall dispose of you, O you two dependents (man and jinn).

٣١ سَنَفْرُغُ لَكُمْ أَيُّهَ الثَّقَلَانِ

32. Which is it, of the favors of your Lord, that you deny?

٣٢ فَبِأَيِّ ءَالَاءِ رَبِّكُمَا تُكَذِّبَانِ

33. O company of jinn and men, if you have power to penetrate (all) regions of the heavens and the earth; then penetrate (them)! You will never penetrate them save with (Our) sanction.

٣٣ يَمَعْشَرَ الْجِنِّ وَالْإِنْسِ إِنِ اسْتَطَعْتُمْ أَنْ تَنْفُذُوا مِنْ أَقْطَارِ السَّمَوَاتِ وَالْأَرْضِ فَانْفُذُوا لَا تَنْفُذُونَ إِلَّا بِسُلْطَانٍ

34. Which is it, of the favors of your Lord, that you deny?

٣٤ فَبِأَيِّ ءَالَاءِ رَبِّكُمَا تُكَذِّبَانِ

35. There will be sent, against you both, heat of fire and flash of brass, and you will not escape.

٣٥ يُرْسَلُ عَلَيْكُمَا شُوَاظٌ مِنْ نَارٍ وَنُحَاسٌ فَلَا تَنْتَصِرَانِ

36. Which is it, of the favors of your Lord, that you deny?

٣٦ فَبِأَيِّ ءَالَاءِ رَبِّكُمَا تُكَذِّبَانِ

37. And when the heaven splits asunder and becomes rosy like red hide—

٣٧ فَإِذَا انْشَقَّتِ السَّمَاءُ فَكَانَتْ وَرْدَةً كَالدِّهَانِ

---

[287]The usual explanation of the commentators is "built into the sea like mountains."

38. Which is it, of the favors of your Lord, that you deny?—

٣٨ فَبِأَيِّ ءَالَاءِ رَبِّكُمَا تُكَذِّبَانِ

39. On that day neither man nor jinn will be questioned of his sin.

٣٩ فَيَوْمَئِذٍ لَّا يُسْئَلُ عَن ذَنۢبِهِ إِنسٌ وَلَا جَآنٌّ

40. Which is it, of the favors of your Lord, that you deny?

٤٠ فَبِأَيِّ ءَالَاءِ رَبِّكُمَا تُكَذِّبَانِ

41. The criminals will be known by their marks, and will be taken by the forelocks and the feet.

٤١ يُعْرَفُ الْمُجْرِمُونَ بِسِيمَاهُمْ فَيُؤْخَذُ بِالنَّوَاصِى وَالْأَقْدَامِ

42. Which is it, of the favors of your Lord, that you deny?

٤٢ فَبِأَيِّ ءَالَاءِ رَبِّكُمَا تُكَذِّبَانِ

43. This is Hell which the criminals deny.

٤٣ هَٰذِهِ جَهَنَّمُ الَّتِى يُكَذِّبُ بِهَا الْمُجْرِمُونَ

44. They go circling round between it and fierce, boiling water.

٤٤ يَطُوفُونَ بَيْنَهَا وَبَيْنَ حَمِيمٍ ءَانٍ

45. Which is it, of the favors of your Lord, that you deny?

٤٥ فَبِأَيِّ ءَالَاءِ رَبِّكُمَا تُكَذِّبَانِ

46. But for him who fears the standing before his Lord there are two gardens.

٤٦ وَلِمَنْ خَافَ مَقَامَ رَبِّهِ جَنَّتَانِ

47. Which is it, of the favors of your Lord, that you deny?

٤٧ فَبِأَيِّ ءَالَاءِ رَبِّكُمَا تُكَذِّبَانِ

48. Of spreading branches.

٤٨ ذَوَاتَآ أَفْنَانٍ

49. Which is it, of the favors of your Lord, that you deny?

٤٩ فَبِأَيِّ ءَالَاءِ رَبِّكُمَا تُكَذِّبَانِ

50. Wherein are two fountains flowing.

٥٠ فِيهِمَا عَيْنَانِ تَجْرِيَانِ

51. Which is it, of the favors of your Lord, that you deny?

٥١ فَبِأَيِّ ءَالَاءِ رَبِّكُمَا تُكَذِّبَانِ

52. Wherein is every kind of fruit in pairs.

٥٢ فِيهِمَا مِن كُلِّ فَاكِهَةٍ زَوْجَانِ

53. Which is it, of the favors of your Lord, that you deny?

٥٣ فَبِأَيِّ ءَالَاءِ رَبِّكُمَا تُكَذِّبَانِ

54. Reclining upon couches lined with silk brocade, the fruit of both gardens near to hand.

٥٤ مُتَّكِئِينَ عَلَىٰ فُرُشٍ بَطَآئِنُهَا مِنْ إِسْتَبْرَقٍ وَجَنَى الْجَنَّتَيْنِ دَانٍ

55. Which is it, of the favors of your Lord, that you deny?

٥٥ فَبِأَيِّ ءَالَاءِ رَبِّكُمَا تُكَذِّبَانِ

56. Therein are damsels of modest gaze, whom neither man nor jinn will have touched before them,

٥٦ فِيهِنَّ قَاصِرَاتُ الطَّرْفِ لَمْ يَطْمِثْهُنَّ إِنسٌ قَبْلَهُمْ وَلَا جَآنٌّ

57. Which is it, of the favors of your Lord, that you deny?

٥٧ فَبِأَيِّ آلَاءِ رَبِّكُمَا تُكَذِّبَانِ

58. (In beauty) like the jacynth and the coral stone.

٥٨ كَأَنَّهُنَّ الْيَاقُوتُ وَالْمَرْجَانُ

59. Which is it, of the favors of your Lord, that you deny?

٥٩ فَبِأَيِّ آلَاءِ رَبِّكُمَا تُكَذِّبَانِ

60. Is the reward of goodness anything but goodness?

٦٠ هَلْ جَزَاءُ الْإِحْسَانِ إِلَّا الْإِحْسَانُ

61. Which is it, of the favors of your Lord, that you deny?

٦١ فَبِأَيِّ آلَاءِ رَبِّكُمَا تُكَذِّبَانِ

62. And beside them are two other gardens,

٦٢ وَمِن دُونِهِمَا جَنَّتَانِ

63. Which is it, of the favors of your Lord, that you deny?

٦٣ فَبِأَيِّ آلَاءِ رَبِّكُمَا تُكَذِّبَانِ

64. Dark green with foliage.

٦٤ مُدْهَامَّتَانِ

65. Which is it, of the favors of your Lord, that you deny?

٦٥ فَبِأَيِّ آلَاءِ رَبِّكُمَا تُكَذِّبَانِ

66. Wherein are two abundant springs.

٦٦ فِيهِمَا عَيْنَانِ نَضَّاخَتَانِ

67. Which is it, of the favors of your Lord, that you deny?

٦٧ فَبِأَيِّ آلَاءِ رَبِّكُمَا تُكَذِّبَانِ

68. Wherein is fruit, date palms and pomegranate.

٦٨ فِيهِمَا فَاكِهَةٌ وَنَخْلٌ وَرُمَّانٌ

69. Which is it, of the favors of your Lord, that you deny?

٦٩ فَبِأَيِّ آلَاءِ رَبِّكُمَا تُكَذِّبَانِ

70. Wherein (are found) good and beautiful companions—

٧٠ فِيهِنَّ خَيْرَاتٌ حِسَانٌ

71. Which is it, of the favors of your Lord, that you deny?—

٧١ فَبِأَيِّ آلَاءِ رَبِّكُمَا تُكَذِّبَانِ

72. Fair ones, close guarded in pavilions—

٧٢ حُورٌ مَقْصُورَاتٌ فِي الْخِيَامِ

73. Which is it, of the favors of your Lord, that you deny?—

٧٣ فَبِأَيِّ آلَاءِ رَبِّكُمَا تُكَذِّبَانِ

74. Whom neither man nor jinn will have touched before them—

٧٤ لَمْ يَطْمِثْهُنَّ إِنسٌ قَبْلَهُمْ وَلَا جَانٌّ

75. Which is it, of the favors of your Lord, that you deny?

٧٥ فَبِأَيِّ آلَاءِ رَبِّكُمَا تُكَذِّبَانِ

76. Reclining on green cushions and fair carpets.

٧٦ مُتَّكِئِينَ عَلَى رَفْرَفٍ خُضْرٍ وَعَبْقَرِيٍّ حِسَانٍ

77. Which is it, of the favors of your Lord, that you deny?

٧٧ فَبِأَيِّ آلَاءِ رَبِّكُمَا تُكَذِّبَانِ

78. Blessed be the name of your Lord, Mighty and Glorious!

٧٨ تَبَارَكَ اسْمُ رَبِّكَ ذِي الْجَلَالِ وَالْإِكْرَامِ

The Event

Al Wāqi'ah, "The Event," takes its name from a word in the first verse. An early Makkan surah.

The Event

Revealed at Makkah

*In the Name of Allah,
the Beneficent, the Merciful*

1. When the event befalls—

2. There is no denying that it will befall—

3. Abasing (some), exalting (others);

4. When the earth is shaken with a shock

5. And the mountains are ground to powder

6. So that they become a scattered dust,

7. And you will be three kinds:

8. (First) those on the right hand; what of those on the right hand?

9. And (then) those on the left hand; what of those on the left hand?

10. And the foremost in the race, the foremost in the race:

11. Those are they who will be brought near

12. In gardens of delight;

13. A multitude of those of old

14. And a few of those of later time,

15. On lined couches,

16. Reclining therein face to face.

17. There wait on them immortal youths

18. With bowls and ewers and a cup from a pure spring

19. Wherefrom they get no aching of the head nor any madness,

20. And fruit that they prefer

وَفَاكِهَةٍ مِّمَّا يَتَخَيَّرُونَ ۲۰

21. And flesh of fowls that they desire.

وَلَحْمِ طَيْرٍ مِّمَّا يَشْتَهُونَ ۲۱

22. And (there are) fair ones with wide, lovely eyes,

وَحُورٌ عِينٌ ۲۲

23. Like unto hidden pearls,

كَأَمْثَالِ اللُّؤْلُؤِ الْمَكْنُونِ ۲۳

24. Reward for what they used to do.

جَزَاءً بِمَا كَانُوا يَعْمَلُونَ ۲٤

25. There hear they no vain speaking nor recrimination,

لَا يَسْمَعُونَ فِيهَا لَغْوًا وَلَا تَأْثِيمًا ۲٥

26. Nothing but the saying: Peace, (and again) Peace.

إِلَّا قِيلًا سَلَامًا سَلَامًا ۲٦

27. And those on the right hand; what of those on the right hand?

وَأَصْحَابُ الْيَمِينِ مَا أَصْحَابُ الْيَمِينِ ۲۷

28. Among thornless lote-trees.

فِي سِدْرٍ مَّخْضُودٍ ۲۸

29. And clustered plantains,

وَطَلْحٍ مَّنْضُودٍ ۲۹

30. And spreading shade,

وَظِلٍّ مَّمْدُودٍ ۳۰

31. And water gushing,

وَمَاءٍ مَّسْكُوبٍ ۳۱

32. And fruit in plenty

وَفَاكِهَةٍ كَثِيرَةٍ ۳۲

33. Neither out of reach nor yet forbidden,

لَا مَقْطُوعَةٍ وَلَا مَمْنُوعَةٍ ۳۳

34. And raised couches,

وَفُرُشٍ مَّرْفُوعَةٍ ۳٤

35. Lo! We have created them a (new) creation

إِنَّا أَنْشَأْنَاهُنَّ إِنْشَاءً ۳٥

36. And made them virgins

فَجَعَلْنَاهُنَّ أَبْكَارًا ۳٦

37. Lovers, friends,

عُرُبًا أَتْرَابًا ۳۷

38. For those on the right hand;

لِأَصْحَابِ الْيَمِينِ ۳۸

39. A multitude of those of old

ثُلَّةٌ مِّنَ الْأَوَّلِينَ ۳۹

40. And a multitude of those of later time.[288]

وَثُلَّةٌ مِّنَ الْآخِرِينَ ٤۰

41. And those on the left hand: What of those on the left hand?

وَأَصْحَابُ الشِّمَالِ مَا أَصْحَابُ الشِّمَالِ ٤۱

---

[288]This verse is said to have been revealed at al Madinah.

42. In scorching wind and scalding water

٤٢ فِى سَمُومٍ وَحَمِيمٍ

43. And shadow of black smoke,

٤٣ وَظِلٍّ مِّن يَحْمُومٍ

44. Neither cool nor refreshing.

٤٤ لَّا بَارِدٍ وَلَا كَرِيمٍ

45. Lo! heretofore they were effete with luxury

٤٥ إِنَّهُمْ كَانُوا قَبْلَ ذَلِكَ مُتْرَفِينَ

46. And used to persist in the awful sin.

٤٦ وَكَانُوا يُصِرُّونَ عَلَى الْحِنْثِ الْعَظِيمِ

47. And they used to say: When we are dead and have be-come dust and bones, shall we then, no doubt, be raised again,

٤٧ وَكَانُوا يَقُولُونَ أَئِذَا مِتْنَا وَكُنَّا تُرَابًا وَعِظَامًا أَئِنَّا لَمَبْعُوثُونَ

48. And also our forefathers?

49. Say (unto them, O Muhammad): Lo! those of old and those of later time

٤٨ أَوَءَابَاؤُنَا الْأَوَّلُونَ

50. Will all be brought together at an appointed time on a day known (only to Allah).

٤٩ قُلْ إِنَّ الْأَوَّلِينَ وَالْآخِرِينَ

51. Then lo! you, the erring, the deniers,

٥٠ لَمَجْمُوعُونَ إِلَى مِيقَاتِ يَوْمٍ مَّعْلُومٍ

52. You surely will eat of a tree called Zaqqūm

٥١ ثُمَّ إِنَّكُمْ أَيُّهَا الضَّالُّونَ الْمُكَذِّبُونَ

53. And will fill your bellies therewith;

٥٢ لَآكِلُونَ مِن شَجَرٍ مِّن زَقُّومٍ

54. And thereon you will drink of boiling water,

٥٣ فَمَالِئُونَ مِنْهَا الْبُطُونَ

55. Drinking even as the camel drinks.

٥٤ فَشَارِبُونَ عَلَيْهِ مِنَ الْحَمِيمِ

56. This will be their welcome on the Day of Judgment.

٥٥ فَشَارِبُونَ شُرْبَ الْهِيمِ

57. We created you. If only you would believe.

٥٦ هَذَا نُزُلُهُمْ يَوْمَ الدِّينِ

58. Have you seen that which you emit?

٥٧ نَحْنُ خَلَقْنَاكُمْ فَلَوْلَا تُصَدِّقُونَ

59. Do you create it or are We the Creator?

٥٨ أَفَرَأَيْتُم مَّا تُمْنُونَ

60. We mete out death among you, and We are not to be outrun,

٥٩ أَأَنتُمْ تَخْلُقُونَهُ أَمْ نَحْنُ الْخَالِقُونَ

61. That We may transfigure you and make you what you know not.

٦٠ نَحْنُ قَدَّرْنَا بَيْنَكُمُ الْمَوْتَ وَمَا نَحْنُ بِمَسْبُوقِينَ

٦١ عَلَى أَن نُّبَدِّلَ أَمْثَالَكُمْ وَنُنشِئَكُمْ فِي مَا لَا تَعْلَمُونَ

62. And surely you know the first creation. Why, then, do you not reflect?

٦٢ وَلَقَدْ عَلِمْتُمُ النَّشْأَةَ الْأُولَى فَلَوْلَا تَذَكَّرُونَ

63. Have you seen that which you cultivate?

٦٣ أَفَرَءَيْتُمْ مَا تَحْرُثُونَ

64. Is it you who foster it, or are We the Fosterer?

٦٤ ءَأَنْتُمْ تَزْرَعُونَهُ أَمْ نَحْنُ الزَّارِعُونَ

65. If We willed, We surely could make it chaff, then would you cease not to exclaim:

٦٥ لَوْ نَشَاءُ لَجَعَلْنَاهُ حُطَامًا فَظَلْتُمْ تَفَكَّهُونَ

66. Lo! we are laden with debt!

٦٦ إِنَّا لَمُغْرَمُونَ

67. Nay, but we are deprived!

٦٧ بَلْ نَحْنُ مَحْرُومُونَ

68. Have you observed the water which you drink?

٦٨ أَفَرَءَيْتُمُ الْمَاءَ الَّذِى تَشْرَبُونَ

69. Is it you who shed it from the rain cloud, or are We the Shedder?

٦٩ ءَأَنْتُمْ أَنْزَلْتُمُوهُ مِنَ الْمُزْنِ أَمْ نَحْنُ الْمُنْزِلُونَ

70. If We willed We surely could make it bitter. Why, then, give you not thanks?

٧٠ لَوْ نَشَاءُ جَعَلْنَاهُ أُجَاجًا فَلَوْلَا تَشْكُرُونَ

71. Have you observed the fire which you strike out;

٧١ أَفَرَءَيْتُمُ النَّارَ الَّتِى تُورُونَ

72. Was it you who made the tree thereof to grow, or were We the Grower?

٧٢ ءَأَنْتُمْ أَنْشَأْتُمْ شَجَرَتَهَا أَمْ نَحْنُ الْمُنْشِئُونَ

73. We, even We, appointed it a memorial and a comfort for the dwellers in the wilderness.

٧٣ نَحْنُ جَعَلْنَاهَا تَذْكِرَةً وَمَتَاعًا لِلْمُقْوِينَ

74. Therefore (O Muhammad), praise the name of your Lord, the Tremendous.

٧٤ فَسَبِّحْ بِاسْمِ رَبِّكَ الْعَظِيمِ

75. Nay, I swear by the positions of the stars—

٧٥ فَلَا أُقْسِمُ بِمَوَاقِعِ النُّجُومِ

76. And lo! that truly is a tremendous oath, if you but knew—

٧٦ وَإِنَّهُ لَقَسَمٌ لَوْ تَعْلَمُونَ عَظِيمٌ

77. That (this) is indeed a noble Qur'an

٧٧ إِنَّهُ لَقُرْءَانٌ كَرِيمٌ

78. In a Book preserved

٧٨ فِى كِتَابٍ مَكْنُونٍ

79. Which none touches save the purified,

٧٩ لَا يَمَسُّهُ إِلَّا الْمُطَهَّرُونَ

80. A revelation from the Lord of the Worlds.

٨٠ تَنْزِيلٌ مِنْ رَبِّ الْعَالَمِينَ

81. Is it this Statement that you scorn,

٨١ أَفَبِهَذَا الْحَدِيثِ أَنْتُمْ مُدْهِنُونَ

82. And make denial thereof your livelihood?

﴿٨٢﴾ وَتَجْعَلُونَ رِزْقَكُمْ أَنَّكُمْ تُكَذِّبُونَ

83. Why, then, when (the soul) comes up to the throat (of the dying)

﴿٨٣﴾ فَلَوْلَا إِذَا بَلَغَتِ الْحُلْقُومَ

84. And you are at that moment looking—

﴿٨٤﴾ وَأَنتُمْ حِينَئِذٍ تَنظُرُونَ

85. And We are nearer unto him than you are, but you see not—

﴿٨٥﴾ وَنَحْنُ أَقْرَبُ إِلَيْهِ مِنكُمْ وَلَٰكِن لَّا تُبْصِرُونَ

86. Why then, if you are not in bondage (unto Us),

﴿٨٦﴾ فَلَوْلَا إِن كُنتُمْ غَيْرَ مَدِينِينَ

87. Do you not force it back, if you are truthful?

﴿٨٧﴾ تَرْجِعُونَهَا إِن كُنتُمْ صَادِقِينَ

88. Thus if he is of those brought near,

﴿٨٨﴾ فَأَمَّا إِن كَانَ مِنَ الْمُقَرَّبِينَ

89. Then breath of life, and plenty, and a Garden of delight.

﴿٨٩﴾ فَرَوْحٌ وَرَيْحَانٌ وَجَنَّتُ نَعِيمٍ

90. And if he is of those on the right hand,

﴿٩٠﴾ وَأَمَّا إِن كَانَ مِنْ أَصْحَابِ الْيَمِينِ

91. Then (the greeting) "Peace be unto you" from those on the right hand.

﴿٩١﴾ فَسَلَامٌ لَّكَ مِنْ أَصْحَابِ الْيَمِينِ

92. But if he is of the rejecters, the erring,

﴿٩٢﴾ وَأَمَّا إِن كَانَ مِنَ الْمُكَذِّبِينَ الضَّالِّينَ

93. Then the welcome will be boiling water

﴿٩٣﴾ فَنُزُلٌ مِّنْ حَمِيمٍ

94. And roasting at Hell fire.

﴿٩٤﴾ وَتَصْلِيَةُ جَحِيمٍ

95. Lo! this is certain truth.

﴿٩٥﴾ إِنَّ هَٰذَا لَهُوَ حَقُّ الْيَقِينِ

96. Therefore (O Muhammad) glorify the name of your Lord, the Tremendous.

﴿٩٦﴾ فَسَبِّحْ بِاسْمِ رَبِّكَ الْعَظِيمِ

Iron

Al Ḥadīd, "Iron," takes its name from a word in verse 25. The word "victory" (verse 10) undoubtedly refers to the conquest of Makkah, though Noldeke[289] takes it to refer to the battle of Badr. He therefore places the surah's revelation as during the fourth or fifth year of the Hijrah. The words of the verse are against such an assumption, for no Muslims "spent and fought" before the battle at Badr (this event represented the beginning of their fighting).

The date of revelation must be the eighth or ninth year of the Hijrah.

---

[289]Th. Noldeke, *Geschichte des Qorans,* 2nd ed., Leipzeg, 1909, 1:195.

Iron

Revealed at al-Madinah

*In the Name of Allah,
the Beneficent, the Merciful*

1. **A**ll that is in the heavens and the earth glorifies Allah and He is the Mighty, the Wise.

2. His is the Sovereignty of the heavens and the earth; He quickens and He gives death; and He is Able to do all things.

3. He is the First and the Last, and the Outward and the Inward; and He is Knower of all things.

4. He it is Who created the heavens and the earth in six Days[290]; then He mounted the Throne. He knows all that enters the earth and all that emerges therefrom and all that comes down from the sky and all that ascends therein; and He is with you wheresoever you may be. And Allah is Seer of what you do.

5. His is the Sovereignty of the heavens and the earth and, unto Allah (all) things are brought back.

6. He causes the night to pass into the day, and He causes the day to pass into the night, and He is Knower of all that is in the breasts.

7. Believe in Allah and His Messenger, and spend of that whereof He has made you trustees; and such of you as be-lieve and spend (aright), theirs will be a great reward

---

[290]Surahs 22:47, 32:5, and 70:4.

8. What ails you that you believe not in Allah, when the Messenger calls you to believe in your Lord, and He has already made a covenant with you, if you are believers?

9. He it is Who sends down clear revelations unto His slave, that He may bring you forth from darkness unto light; and lo! for you, Allah is Full of Pity, Merciful.

10. And what ails you that you spend not in the way of Allah, when unto Allah belongs the inheritance of the heavens and the earth? Those who spent and fought before the victory are not upon a level (with the rest of you). Such are greater in rank than those who spent and fought afterwards. Unto each has Allah promised good. And Allah is Informed of what you do.

11. Who is he that will lend unto Allah a goodly loan,[291] that He may double it for him and his may be a rich reward?

12. On the day when you (Muhammad) will see the believers, men and women, their light shining forth before them and on their right hands, (and will hear it said unto them): Glad news for you this day: Gardens underneath which rivers flow, wherein you are immortal. That is the supreme triumph.

13. On the day when the hypocritical men and the hypocritical women will say unto those who believe: Look on us that we may borrow from your light! it will be said: Go back and seek for light! Then there will separate them a wall wherein is a gate, the inner side whereof contains mercy, while the outer side thereof is toward the doom.

﴿٨﴾ وَمَا لَكُمْ لَا تُؤْمِنُونَ بِاللَّهِ وَالرَّسُولُ يَدْعُوكُمْ لِتُؤْمِنُوا بِرَبِّكُمْ وَقَدْ أَخَذَ مِيثَاقَكُمْ إِن كُنتُم مُّؤْمِنِينَ

﴿٩﴾ هُوَ الَّذِي يُنَزِّلُ عَلَىٰ عَبْدِهِ آيَاتٍ بَيِّنَاتٍ لِّيُخْرِجَكُم مِّنَ الظُّلُمَاتِ إِلَى النُّورِ وَإِنَّ اللَّهَ بِكُمْ لَرَءُوفٌ رَّحِيمٌ

﴿١٠﴾ وَمَا لَكُمْ أَلَّا تُنفِقُوا فِي سَبِيلِ اللَّهِ وَلِلَّهِ مِيرَاثُ السَّمَاوَاتِ وَالْأَرْضِ لَا يَسْتَوِي مِنكُم مَّنْ أَنفَقَ مِن قَبْلِ الْفَتْحِ وَقَاتَلَ أُولَٰئِكَ أَعْظَمُ دَرَجَةً مِّنَ الَّذِينَ أَنفَقُوا مِن بَعْدُ وَقَاتَلُوا وَكُلًّا وَعَدَ اللَّهُ الْحُسْنَىٰ وَاللَّهُ بِمَا تَعْمَلُونَ خَبِيرٌ

﴿١١﴾ مَّن ذَا الَّذِي يُقْرِضُ اللَّهَ قَرْضًا حَسَنًا فَيُضَاعِفَهُ لَهُ وَلَهُ أَجْرٌ كَرِيمٌ

﴿١٢﴾ يَوْمَ تَرَى الْمُؤْمِنِينَ وَالْمُؤْمِنَاتِ يَسْعَىٰ نُورُهُم بَيْنَ أَيْدِيهِمْ وَبِأَيْمَانِهِم بُشْرَاكُمُ الْيَوْمَ جَنَّاتٌ تَجْرِي مِن تَحْتِهَا الْأَنْهَارُ خَالِدِينَ فِيهَا ذَٰلِكَ هُوَ الْفَوْزُ الْعَظِيمُ

﴿١٣﴾ يَوْمَ يَقُولُ الْمُنَافِقُونَ وَالْمُنَافِقَاتُ لِلَّذِينَ آمَنُوا انظُرُونَا نَقْتَبِسْ مِن نُّورِكُمْ قِيلَ ارْجِعُوا وَرَاءَكُمْ فَالْتَمِسُوا نُورًا فَضُرِبَ بَيْنَهُم بِسُورٍ لَّهُ بَابٌ بَاطِنُهُ فِيهِ الرَّحْمَةُ وَظَاهِرُهُ مِن قِبَلِهِ

---

[291] A loan without interest or any thought of gain or loss.

14. They will cry unto them (saying): Were we not with you? They will say: Yea, indeed; but you tempted one another, and hesitated, and doubted, and vain desires beguiled you till the ordinance of Allah came to pass; and the deceiver deceived you concerning Allah;

15. So this day no ransom can be taken from you nor from those who disbelieved. Your home is the Fire; that is your patron, and an unlucky journey's end.

16. Is not the time ripe for the hearts of those who believe to submit to Allah's reminder and to the truth which is revealed, that they become not as those who received the Scripture of old but the term was prolonged for them and so their hearts were hardened, and many of them are evil doers.

17. Know that Allah quickens the earth after its death. We have made clear Our revelations for you, that haply you may understand.

18. Lo! those who give alms, both men and women, and lend unto Allah a goodly loan, it will be doubled for them, and theirs will be a rich reward.

19. And those who believe in Allah and His Messengers, they are the loyal; and the martyrs are with their Lord; they have their reward and their light; while as for those who disbelieve and deny Our revelations, they are owners of hellfire.

20. Know that the life of this world is only play, and idle talk, and pageantry, and boasting among you, and rivalry in respect of wealth and children; as the likeness of vegetation after rain, whereof the growth is pleasing to the husband-men, but afterward it dries up and you see it turning yellow then it becomes straw. And in the Hereafter there is grievous punishment, and (also) forgiveness from Allah and His good pleasure, whereas the life of the world is but a matter of illusion.

١٤ يُنَادُونَهُمْ أَلَمْ نَكُن مَّعَكُمْ قَالُوا بَلَى وَلَكِنَّكُمْ فَتَنتُمْ أَنفُسَكُمْ وَتَرَبَّصْتُمْ وَارْتَبْتُمْ وَغَرَّتْكُمُ الْأَمَانِيُّ حَتَّى جَاءَ أَمْرُ اللَّهِ وَغَرَّكُم بِاللَّهِ الْغَرُورُ

١٥ فَالْيَوْمَ لَا يُؤْخَذُ مِنكُمْ فِدْيَةٌ وَلَا مِنَ الَّذِينَ كَفَرُوا مَأْوَاكُمُ النَّارُ هِيَ مَوْلَاكُمْ وَبِئْسَ الْمَصِيرُ

١٦ ۞ أَلَمْ يَأْنِ لِلَّذِينَ آمَنُوا أَن تَخْشَعَ قُلُوبُهُمْ لِذِكْرِ اللَّهِ وَمَا نَزَلَ مِنَ الْحَقِّ وَلَا يَكُونُوا كَالَّذِينَ أُوتُوا الْكِتَابَ مِن قَبْلُ فَطَالَ عَلَيْهِمُ الْأَمَدُ فَقَسَتْ قُلُوبُهُمْ وَكَثِيرٌ مِّنْهُمْ فَاسِقُونَ

١٧ اعْلَمُوا أَنَّ اللَّهَ يُحْيِ الْأَرْضَ بَعْدَ مَوْتِهَا قَدْ بَيَّنَّا لَكُمُ الْآيَاتِ لَعَلَّكُمْ تَعْقِلُونَ

١٨ إِنَّ الْمُصَّدِّقِينَ وَالْمُصَّدِّقَاتِ وَأَقْرَضُوا اللَّهَ قَرْضًا حَسَنًا يُضَاعَفُ لَهُمْ وَلَهُمْ أَجْرٌ كَرِيمٌ

١٩ وَالَّذِينَ آمَنُوا بِاللَّهِ وَرُسُلِهِ أُولَئِكَ هُمُ الصِّدِّيقُونَ وَالشُّهَدَاءُ عِندَ رَبِّهِمْ لَهُمْ أَجْرُهُمْ وَنُورُهُمْ وَالَّذِينَ كَفَرُوا وَكَذَّبُوا بِآيَاتِنَا أُولَئِكَ أَصْحَابُ الْجَحِيمِ

٢٠ اعْلَمُوا أَنَّمَا الْحَيَاةُ الدُّنْيَا لَعِبٌ وَلَهْوٌ وَزِينَةٌ وَتَفَاخُرٌ بَيْنَكُمْ وَتَكَاثُرٌ فِي الْأَمْوَالِ وَالْأَوْلَادِ كَمَثَلِ غَيْثٍ أَعْجَبَ الْكُفَّارَ نَبَاتُهُ ثُمَّ يَهِيجُ فَتَرَاهُ مُصْفَرًّا ثُمَّ يَكُونُ حُطَامًا وَفِي الْآخِرَةِ عَذَابٌ شَدِيدٌ وَمَغْفِرَةٌ مِّنَ اللَّهِ وَرِضْوَانٌ وَمَا الْحَيَاةُ الدُّنْيَا إِلَّا مَتَاعُ الْغُرُورِ

21. Race one with another for forgiveness from your Lord and a Garden whereof the breadth is as the breadth of the heavens and the earth, which is in store for those who believe in Allah and His messengers. Such is the bounty of Allah, which He bestows upon whom He will, and Allah is of infinite bounty.

٢١ سَابِقُوٓاْ إِلَىٰ مَغْفِرَةٍ مِّن رَّبِّكُمْ وَجَنَّةٍ عَرْضُهَا كَعَرْضِ ٱلسَّمَآءِ وَٱلْأَرْضِ أُعِدَّتْ لِلَّذِينَ ءَامَنُواْ بِٱللَّهِ وَرُسُلِهِۦ ذَٰلِكَ فَضْلُ ٱللَّهِ يُؤْتِيهِ مَن يَشَآءُ وَٱللَّهُ ذُو ٱلْفَضْلِ ٱلْعَظِيمِ

22. No disaster befalls in the earth or in yourselves but it is in a Book before We bring it into being—Lo! that is easy for Allah—

٢٢ مَآ أَصَابَ مِن مُّصِيبَةٍ فِى ٱلْأَرْضِ وَلَا فِىٓ أَنفُسِكُمْ إِلَّا فِى كِتَٰبٍ مِّن قَبْلِ أَن نَّبْرَأَهَآ إِنَّ ذَٰلِكَ عَلَى ٱللَّهِ يَسِيرٌ

23. That you grieve not for the sake of that which has escaped you, nor yet exult because of that which has been given. Allah loves not all prideful boasters,

٢٣ لِّكَيْلَا تَأْسَوْاْ عَلَىٰ مَا فَاتَكُمْ وَلَا تَفْرَحُواْ بِمَآ ءَاتَىٰكُمْ وَٱللَّهُ لَا يُحِبُّ كُلَّ مُخْتَالٍ فَخُورٍ

24. Who hoard and who enjoin upon the people avarice. And whosoever turns away, still Allah is the Absolute, the Owner of Praise.

٢٤ ٱلَّذِينَ يَبْخَلُونَ وَيَأْمُرُونَ ٱلنَّاسَ بِٱلْبُخْلِ وَمَن يَتَوَلَّ فَإِنَّ ٱللَّهَ هُوَ ٱلْغَنِىُّ ٱلْحَمِيدُ

25. We surely sent Our messengers with clear proofs, and revealed with them the Scripture and the Balance, that mankind may observe right measure; and sent down iron, wherein is mighty power and (many) uses for mankind, and that Allah may know him who helps Him and His messengers, though unseen. Lo! Allah is Strong, Almighty.

٢٥ لَقَدْ أَرْسَلْنَا رُسُلَنَا بِٱلْبَيِّنَٰتِ وَأَنزَلْنَا مَعَهُمُ ٱلْكِتَٰبَ وَٱلْمِيزَانَ لِيَقُومَ ٱلنَّاسُ بِٱلْقِسْطِ وَأَنزَلْنَا ٱلْحَدِيدَ فِيهِ بَأْسٌ شَدِيدٌ وَمَنَٰفِعُ لِلنَّاسِ وَلِيَعْلَمَ ٱللَّهُ مَن يَنصُرُهُۥ وَرُسُلَهُۥ بِٱلْغَيْبِ إِنَّ ٱللَّهَ قَوِىٌّ عَزِيزٌ

26. And We surely sent Noah and Abraham and placed the Prophethood and the Scripture among their seed, and among them there is he who goes right, but many of them are evil livers.

٢٦ وَلَقَدْ أَرْسَلْنَا نُوحًا وَإِبْرَٰهِيمَ وَجَعَلْنَا فِى ذُرِّيَّتِهِمَا ٱلنُّبُوَّةَ وَٱلْكِتَٰبَ فَمِنْهُم مُّهْتَدٍ وَكَثِيرٌ مِّنْهُمْ فَٰسِقُونَ

27. Then We caused Our messengers to follow in their footsteps; and We caused Jesus son of Mary to follow, and gave him the Gospel, and placed compassion and mercy in the hearts of those who followed him. But monasticism they invented. We ordained it not for them. Only seeking Allah's pleasure, and they observed it not with right observance. So We give those of them who believe their reward, but many of them are evil-livers.

28. O you who believe! Be mindful of your duty to Allah and put faith in His Messenger. He will give you twofold of His mercy and will appoint for you a light wherein you shall walk, and will forgive you. Allah is Forgiving, Merciful;

29. That the People of the Scripture[292] may know that they control nothing of the bounty of Allah, but that the bounty is in Allah's hand to give to whom He will. And Allah is of abounding Grace.

ثُمَّ قَفَّيْنَا عَلَىٰٓ ءَاثَـٰرِهِم بِرُسُلِنَا وَقَفَّيْنَا بِعِيسَى ٱبْنِ مَرْيَمَ وَءَاتَيْنَـٰهُ ٱلْإِنجِيلَ وَجَعَلْنَا فِى قُلُوبِ ٱلَّذِينَ ٱتَّبَعُوهُ رَأْفَةً وَرَحْمَةً وَرَهْبَانِيَّةً ٱبْتَدَعُوهَا مَا كَتَبْنَـٰهَا عَلَيْهِمْ إِلَّا ٱبْتِغَآءَ رِضْوَٰنِ ٱللَّهِ فَمَا رَعَوْهَا حَقَّ رِعَايَتِهَا فَـَٔاتَيْنَا ٱلَّذِينَ ءَامَنُوا۟ مِنْهُمْ أَجْرَهُمْ وَكَثِيرٌ مِّنْهُمْ فَـٰسِقُونَ ۝

يَـٰٓأَيُّهَا ٱلَّذِينَ ءَامَنُوا۟ ٱتَّقُوا۟ ٱللَّهَ وَءَامِنُوا۟ بِرَسُولِهِۦ يُؤْتِكُمْ كِفْلَيْنِ مِن رَّحْمَتِهِۦ وَيَجْعَل لَّكُمْ نُورًا تَمْشُونَ بِهِۦ وَيَغْفِرْ لَكُمْ وَٱللَّهُ غَفُورٌ رَّحِيمٌ ۝

لِّئَلَّا يَعْلَمَ أَهْلُ ٱلْكِتَـٰبِ أَلَّا يَقْدِرُونَ عَلَىٰ شَىْءٍ مِّن فَضْلِ ٱللَّهِ وَأَنَّ ٱلْفَضْلَ بِيَدِ ٱللَّهِ يُؤْتِيهِ مَن يَشَآءُ وَٱللَّهُ ذُو ٱلْفَضْلِ ٱلْعَظِيمِ ۝

---

[292]i.e., Jews and Christians.

Dispute

Al Mujādilah, "Dispute," takes its name from a word in the first verse. A woman complained to the Prophet that her husband had put her away for no good reason by employing an old formula of the pagan Arabs: saying that her back was for him as the back of his mother. She "disputed" this with the Prophet, because he would not find a satisfactory solution for her problem in favor of her husband (whom she loved). Then this revelation came to him. There is a brief reference to the same method of getting rid of wives in Surah 33:4. This surah must therefore have been revealed before Surah 33.

The date of revelation is the fourth or fifth year of the Hijrah.

Dispute

Revealed at al Madinah

*In the Name of Allah,
the Beneficent, the Merciful*

1. Allah has heard the saying of her that disputes with you (Muhammad) concerning her husband, and complains unto Allah. And Allah hears your colloquy. Lo! Allah is Hearer, Knower.

2. Such of you as put away their wives (by saying they are as their mothers)—They are not their mothers[293]; none are their mothers except those who gave them birth—they indeed utter an ill word and a lie. And lo! Allah is Forgiving, Merciful.

3. Those who put away their wives (by saying they are as their mothers) and afterward would go back on that which they have said; (the penalty) in that case (is) the freeing of a slave before they touch one another. Unto this you are exhorted; and Allah is informed of what you do.

4. And he who finds not (the wherewithal), let him fast for two successive months before they touch one another; and for him who is unable to do so (the penance is) the feeding of sixty needy ones. This, that you may believe in Allah and His Messenger. Such are the limits (imposed by Allah); and for disbelievers is a painful doom.

5. Those who oppose Allah and His Messenger will be abased even as those before them were abased; and We have sent down clear tokens, and for disbelievers is a shameful doom

6. On the day when Allah will raise them all together and inform them of what they did. Allah has kept account of it while they forgot it. And Allah is Witness over all things.

---

[293]Surah 33:4.

7. Have you not seen that Allah knows all that is in the heavens and all that is in the earth? There is no secret conference of three but He is their fourth, nor of five but He is their sixth, nor of less than that or more but He is with them wheresoever they may be; and afterward, on the Day of Resurrection, He will inform them of what they did Lo! Allah is Knower of all things.

8. Have you not observed those who were forbidden secret counsels and afterward returned to that which they had been forbidden, and (now) conspire together for crime and wrongdoing and disobedience toward the Messenger? And when they come unto you they greet you with a greeting wherewith Allah greets you not, and say within themselves: Why does not Allah punish us for what we say? Hell will suffice them; they will feel the heat thereof—an unlucky journey's end!

9. O you who believe! when you hold secret counsel, do it not together for crime and wrongdoing and disobedience toward the Messenger, but conspire together for righteousness and piety, and keep your duty, toward Allah, unto whom you will be gathered.

10. Lo! Conspiracy is only of the Devil, that he may cause grief to those who believe; but he can harm them not at all unless by Allah's leave. In Allah let believers put their trust.

11. O you who believe! When it is said to you: Make room! in assemblies, then make room; Allah will make a way for you (hereafter). And when it is said: Rise, Allah will exalt those who believe among you, and those who have knowledge, to high ranks. Allah is informed of what you do.

٧ اَلَمْ تَرَ اَنَّ اللهَ يَعْلَمُ مَا فِي السَّمَوَاتِ وَمَا فِي الْاَرْضِ مَا يَكُونُ مِنْ نَجْوَى ثَلَثَةٍ اِلَّا هُوَ رَابِعُهُمْ وَلَا خَمْسَةٍ اِلَّا هُوَ سَادِسُهُمْ وَلَا اَدْنَى مِنْ ذَلِكَ وَلَا اَكْثَرَ اِلَّا هُوَ مَعَهُمْ اَيْنَ مَا كَانُوا ثُمَّ يُنَبِّئُهُمْ بِمَا عَمِلُوا يَوْمَ الْقِيَمَةِ اِنَّ اللهَ بِكُلِّ شَيْءٍ عَلِيمٌ

٨ اَلَمْ تَرَ اِلَى الَّذِينَ نُهُوا عَنِ النَّجْوَى ثُمَّ يَعُودُونَ لِمَا نُهُوا عَنْهُ وَيَتَنَاجَوْنَ بِالْاِثْمِ وَالْعُدْوَانِ وَمَعْصِيَتِ الرَّسُولِ وَاِذَا جَاءُوكَ حَيَّوْكَ بِمَا لَمْ يُحَيِّكَ بِهِ اللهُ وَيَقُولُونَ فِي اَنْفُسِهِمْ لَوْلَا يُعَذِّبُنَا اللهُ بِمَا نَقُولُ حَسْبُهُمْ جَهَنَّمُ يَصْلَوْنَهَا فَبِئْسَ الْمَصِيرُ

٩ يَا اَيُّهَا الَّذِينَ اَمَنُوا اِذَا تَنَاجَيْتُمْ فَلَا تَتَنَاجَوْا بِالْاِثْمِ وَالْعُدْوَانِ وَمَعْصِيَتِ الرَّسُولِ وَتَنَاجَوْا بِالْبِرِّ وَالتَّقْوَى وَاتَّقُوا اللهَ الَّذِي اِلَيْهِ تُحْشَرُونَ

١٠ اِنَّمَا النَّجْوَى مِنَ الشَّيْطَانِ لِيَحْزُنَ الَّذِينَ اَمَنُوا وَلَيْسَ بِضَارِّهِمْ شَيْئًا اِلَّا بِاِذْنِ اللهِ وَعَلَى اللهِ فَلْيَتَوَكَّلِ الْمُؤْمِنُونَ

١١ يَا اَيُّهَا الَّذِينَ اَمَنُوا اِذَا قِيلَ لَكُمْ تَفَسَّحُوا فِي الْمَجَالِسِ فَافْسَحُوا يَفْسَحِ اللهُ لَكُمْ وَاِذَا قِيلَ انْشُزُوا فَانْشُزُوا يَرْفَعِ اللهُ الَّذِينَ اَمَنُوا مِنْكُمْ وَالَّذِينَ اُوتُوا الْعِلْمَ دَرَجَاتٍ وَاللهُ بِمَا تَعْمَلُونَ خَبِيرٌ

12. O you who believe! When you hold conference with the Messenger, offer an alms before your conference. That is better and purer for you. But if you cannot find then Allah is Forgiving, Merciful.

13. Fear you to offer alms before your conference? Then, when you do it not and Allah has forgiven you, establish prayer and pay the poor due and obey Allah and His Mes-senger. And Allah is Aware of what you do.

14. Have you not seen those who take for friends a folk with whom Allah is wroth? They are neither of you nor of them, and they swear a false oath knowingly.

15. Allah has prepared for them a dreadful doom. Evil indeed is that which they are wont to do.

16. They make a shelter of their oaths and turn (men) from the way of Allah; so theirs will be a humiliating doom.

17. Their wealth and their children will avail them nothing against Allah. Such are rightful owners of the Fire; they will abide therein forever.

18. On the day when Allah will raise them all together, then will they swear unto Him as they (now) swear unto you, and they will fancy that they have some standing. Lo! indeed it is they who are the liars!

19. The Devil has engrossed them and so has caused them to forget remem-brance of Allah. They are the Devil's party. Truly the Devil's party will be the losers!

١٢ يَـٰٓأَيُّهَا ٱلَّذِينَ ءَامَنُوٓا۟ إِذَا نَـٰجَيْتُمُ ٱلرَّسُولَ فَقَدِّمُوا۟ بَيْنَ يَدَىْ نَجْوَىٰكُمْ صَدَقَةً ذَٰلِكَ خَيْرٌ لَّكُمْ وَأَطْهَرُ فَإِن لَّمْ تَجِدُوا۟ فَإِنَّ ٱللَّهَ غَفُورٌ رَّحِيمٌ

١٣ ءَأَشْفَقْتُمْ أَن تُقَدِّمُوا۟ بَيْنَ يَدَىْ نَجْوَىٰكُمْ صَدَقَـٰتٍ فَإِذْ لَمْ تَفْعَلُوا۟ وَتَابَ ٱللَّهُ عَلَيْكُمْ فَأَقِيمُوا۟ ٱلصَّلَوٰةَ وَءَاتُوا۟ ٱلزَّكَوٰةَ وَأَطِيعُوا۟ ٱللَّهَ وَرَسُولَهُۥ وَٱللَّهُ خَبِيرٌۢ بِمَا تَعْمَلُونَ

١٤ ۞ أَلَمْ تَرَ إِلَى ٱلَّذِينَ تَوَلَّوْا۟ قَوْمًا غَضِبَ ٱللَّهُ عَلَيْهِم مَّا هُم مِّنكُمْ وَلَا مِنْهُمْ وَيَحْلِفُونَ عَلَى ٱلْكَذِبِ وَهُمْ يَعْلَمُونَ

١٥ أَعَدَّ ٱللَّهُ لَهُمْ عَذَابًا شَدِيدًا إِنَّهُمْ سَآءَ مَا كَانُوا۟ يَعْمَلُونَ

١٦ ٱتَّخَذُوٓا۟ أَيْمَـٰنَهُمْ جُنَّةً فَصَدُّوا۟ عَن سَبِيلِ ٱللَّهِ فَلَهُمْ عَذَابٌ مُّهِينٌ

١٧ لَّن تُغْنِىَ عَنْهُمْ أَمْوَٰلُهُمْ وَلَآ أَوْلَـٰدُهُم مِّنَ ٱللَّهِ شَيْـًٔا أُو۟لَـٰٓئِكَ أَصْحَـٰبُ ٱلنَّارِ هُمْ فِيهَا خَـٰلِدُونَ

١٨ يَوْمَ يَبْعَثُهُمُ ٱللَّهُ جَمِيعًا فَيَحْلِفُونَ لَهُۥ كَمَا يَحْلِفُونَ لَكُمْ وَيَحْسَبُونَ أَنَّهُمْ عَلَىٰ شَىْءٍ أَلَآ إِنَّهُمْ هُمُ ٱلْكَـٰذِبُونَ

١٩ ٱسْتَحْوَذَ عَلَيْهِمُ ٱلشَّيْطَـٰنُ فَأَنسَىٰهُمْ ذِكْرَ ٱللَّهِ أُو۟لَـٰٓئِكَ حِزْبُ ٱلشَّيْطَـٰنِ أَلَآ إِنَّ حِزْبَ ٱلشَّيْطَـٰنِ هُمُ ٱلْخَـٰسِرُونَ

20. Lo! those who oppose Allah and His Messenger, they will be among the lowest.

٢٠ إِنَّ ٱلَّذِينَ يُحَآدُّونَ ٱللَّهَ وَرَسُولَهُۥٓ أُوْلَٰٓئِكَ فِى ٱلۡأَذَلِّينَ

21. Allah has decreed: Lo! I surely shall conquer, I and My messengers. Lo! Allah is Strong, Almighty.

٢١ كَتَبَ ٱللَّهُ لَأَغۡلِبَنَّ أَنَا۠ وَرُسُلِىٓ إِنَّ ٱللَّهَ قَوِىٌّ عَزِيزٌ

22. You will not find folk who believe in Allah and the Last Day loving those who oppose Allah and His Messenger, even though they be their fathers or their sons or their brothers or their clan. As for such, He has written faith upon their hearts and has strengthened them with a Spirit from Him, and He will bring them into Gardens underneath which rivers flow, wherein they will abide. Allah is well pleased with them, and they are well pleased with Him. They are Allah's party. Truly! it is Allah's party who are the successful!

٢٢ لَّا تَجِدُ قَوۡمًا يُؤۡمِنُونَ بِٱللَّهِ وَٱلۡيَوۡمِ ٱلۡأَخِرِ يُوَآدُّونَ مَنۡ حَآدَّ ٱللَّهَ وَرَسُولَهُۥ وَلَوۡ كَانُوٓاْ ءَابَآءَهُمۡ أَوۡ أَبۡنَآءَهُمۡ أَوۡ إِخۡوَٰنَهُمۡ أَوۡ عَشِيرَتَهُمۡ أُوْلَٰٓئِكَ كَتَبَ فِى قُلُوبِهِمُ ٱلۡإِيمَٰنَ وَأَيَّدَهُم بِرُوحٍ مِّنۡهُ وَيُدۡخِلُهُمۡ جَنَّٰتٍ تَجۡرِى مِن تَحۡتِهَا ٱلۡأَنۡهَٰرُ خَٰلِدِينَ فِيهَا رَضِىَ ٱللَّهُ عَنۡهُمۡ وَرَضُواْ عَنۡهُ أُوْلَٰٓئِكَ حِزۡبُ ٱللَّهِ أَلَآ إِنَّ حِزۡبَ ٱللَّهِ هُمُ ٱلۡمُفۡلِحُونَ

Exile

Al Ḥashr, "Exile," takes its name from verses 2-17, which refer to the exile of Banī al Naḍīr, a Jewish tribe of al Madi-nah (for treason and attempted murder of the Prophet) and the confiscation of their property. The "Hypocrites," as the lukewarm Muslims were called, had secretly sympathized with these Jews, whose opposition had grown strong since the Muslim reverse at Mt. Uhud. The hypocrites had also promised to side with them in the event of armed hostilities with the Muslims and to emigrate with them if they were forced to emigrate. But when the Muslims marched against Banī al Naḍīr, and the latter took refuge in their strong towers, the hypocrites did nothing. When they were finally de-feated and exiled, the hypocrites did not go with them.

The date of revelation is the fourth year of the Hijrah.

Exile

Revealed at al Madinah

*In the Name of Allah,
the Beneficent, the Merciful*

1. All that is in the heavens and all that is in the earth glorifies Allah, and He is the Mighty, the Wise.

2. He it is Who has caused those of the People of the Scripture[294] who disbelieved to go forth from their homes unto the first mustering. You deemed not that they would go forth, while they deemed that their strongholds would protect them from Allah. But Allah reached them from a place whereof they reckoned not, and cast terror in their hearts, they ruin their houses with their own hands and the hands of believers. So learn a lesson, O you who have eyes!

3. And if Allah had not decreed banishment for them, He surely would have punished them in this world, and theirs in the Hereafter is the punishment of the Fire.

4. That is because they were opposed to Allah and His messenger; and who is opposed to Allah, (for him) surely Allah is stern in reprisal.

5. Whatsoever palm trees you cut down or left standing on their roots, it was by Allah's leave, in order that He might confound the evildoers.

6. And that which Allah gave as spoil unto His Messenger from them, you urged not any horse or riding camel for the Messenger's sake thereof, but Allah gives His messengers lordship over whom He will and Allah is Able to do all things.

---

[294]The term for Jews and Christians. In this case it refers to Jews.

7. That which Allah gives as spoil unto His Messenger from the people of the townships, it is for Allah and His Messenger[295] and for the near of kin and the orphans and the needy and the wayfarer, that it become not a commodity between the rich among you. And whatsoever the Messenger gives you, take it. And whatsoever he forbids, abstain (from it). And keep your duty to Allah. Lo! Allah is stern in reprisal.

8. And (it is) for the poor migrants who have been driven out from their homes and their belongings, who seek bounty and pleasure from Allah and support Allah and His Mes-senger. These are the truthful.

9. Those who were established in the city and in the faith before them love these who flee unto them for refuge, and find in their breasts no need for that which has been given them, but prefer (the migrants) above themselves though poverty become their lot. And who is saved from his own avarice—such are they who are successful.

10. And those who came (into the faith) after them say: Our Lord! Forgive us and our brothers who were before us in the faith, and place not in our hearts any rancor toward those who believe. Our Lord! You are Full of Pity, Merciful.

11. Have you not observed those who are hypocrites, (how) they tell their brothers · who disbelieve among the People of the Scripture: If you are driven out, we surely will go out with you, and we will never obey anyone against you, and if you are attacked we surely will help you. And Allah bears witness that they surely are liars.

---

[295] i.e., for the State.

12. (For) indeed if they are driven out they go not out with them, and indeed if they are attacked they help them not, and indeed if they had helped them they would have turned and fled, and then they would not have been victorious.

١٢ لَئِنْ أُخْرِجُوا لَا يَخْرُجُونَ مَعَهُمْ وَلَئِن قُوتِلُوا لَا يَنصُرُونَهُمْ وَلَئِن نَّصَرُوهُمْ لَيُوَلُّنَّ الْأَدْبَارَ ثُمَّ لَا يُنصَرُونَ

13. You are more awful as a fear in their bosoms than Allah. That is because they are a folk who understand not.

١٣ لَأَنتُمْ أَشَدُّ رَهْبَةً فِي صُدُورِهِم مِّنَ اللَّهِ ذَلِكَ بِأَنَّهُمْ قَوْمٌ لَّا يَفْقَهُونَ

14. They will not fight against you in a body save in fortified villages or from behind walls. Their adversity among themselves is very great. You think of them as a whole whereas their hearts are divers. That is because they are a folk who have no sense.

١٤ لَا يُقَاتِلُونَكُمْ جَمِيعًا إِلَّا فِي قُرًى مُّحَصَّنَةٍ أَوْ مِن وَرَاءِ جُدُرٍ بَأْسُهُم بَيْنَهُمْ شَدِيدٌ تَحْسَبُهُمْ جَمِيعًا وَقُلُوبُهُمْ شَتَّى ذَلِكَ بِأَنَّهُمْ قَوْمٌ لَّا يَعْقِلُونَ

15. On the likeness of those (who suffered) a short time before them, they taste the ill effects of their conduct, and theirs is painful punishment.

١٥ كَمَثَلِ الَّذِينَ مِن قَبْلِهِمْ قَرِيبًا ذَاقُوا وَبَالَ أَمْرِهِمْ وَلَهُمْ عَذَابٌ أَلِيمٌ

16. As is the Devil when he tells man to disbelieve, then, when he disbelieves said: Lo! I am quit of you. Lo! I fear Allah, the Lord of the Worlds.

١٦ كَمَثَلِ الشَّيْطَانِ إِذْ قَالَ لِلْإِنسَانِ اكْفُرْ فَلَمَّا كَفَرَ قَالَ إِنِّي بَرِيءٌ مِّنكَ إِنِّي أَخَافُ اللَّهَ رَبَّ الْعَالَمِينَ

17. And the consequence for both will be that they are in the Fire, therein abiding forever. Such is the reward of evildoers.

١٧ فَكَانَ عَاقِبَتَهُمَا أَنَّهُمَا فِي النَّارِ خَالِدَيْنِ فِيهَا وَذَلِكَ جَزَاءُ الظَّالِمِينَ

18. O you who believe! Observe your duty to Allah. And let every soul look to that which it sends on before for the morrow. And observe your duty to Allah! Lo! Allah is informed of what you do.

١٨ يَا أَيُّهَا الَّذِينَ آمَنُوا اتَّقُوا اللَّهَ وَلْتَنظُرْ نَفْسٌ مَّا قَدَّمَتْ لِغَدٍ وَاتَّقُوا اللَّهَ إِنَّ اللَّهَ خَبِيرٌ بِمَا تَعْمَلُونَ

19. And be not you as those who forgot Allah, therefore He caused them to forget their souls. Such are the evildoers.

١٩ وَلَا تَكُونُوا كَالَّذِينَ نَسُوا اللَّهَ فَأَنسَاهُمْ أَنفُسَهُمْ أُولَئِكَ هُمُ الْفَاسِقُونَ

20. Not equal are the owners of the Fire and the owners of the Garden. The owners of the Garden, they are the victorious.

٢٠ لَا يَسْتَوِي أَصْحَابُ النَّارِ وَأَصْحَابُ الْجَنَّةِ أَصْحَابُ الْجَنَّةِ هُمُ الْفَائِزُونَ

21. If We had caused this Qur'an to descend upon a mountain, you (O Muhammad) surely had seen it humbled, rent asunder by the fear of Allah. Such similitudes coin We for mankind that they may reflect.

22. He is Allah, than whom there is no other God, the Knower of the invisible and the visible. He is the Beneficent, the Merciful.

23. He is Allah, than whom there is no other God, the Sovereign Lord, the Holy One, the Peace, the Keeper of Faith, the Ovewhelming, the Majestic, the Compeller, the Superb. Glorified be Allah from all that they ascribe as partner (unto Him).

24. He is Allah, the Creator, the Shaper out of nothing, the Fashioner. His are the most beautiful names. All that is in the heavens and the earth glorifies Him, and He is the Mighty, the Wise.

٢١ لَوْ أَنزَلْنَا هَـٰذَا ٱلْقُرْءَانَ عَلَىٰ جَبَلٍ لَّرَأَيْتَهُۥ خَـٰشِعًا مُّتَصَدِّعًا مِّنْ خَشْيَةِ ٱللَّهِ وَتِلْكَ ٱلْأَمْثَـٰلُ نَضْرِبُهَا لِلنَّاسِ لَعَلَّهُمْ يَتَفَكَّرُونَ

٢٢ هُوَ ٱللَّهُ ٱلَّذِى لَآ إِلَـٰهَ إِلَّا هُوَ عَـٰلِمُ ٱلْغَيْبِ وَٱلشَّهَـٰدَةِ هُوَ ٱلرَّحْمَـٰنُ ٱلرَّحِيمُ

٢٣ هُوَ ٱللَّهُ ٱلَّذِى لَآ إِلَـٰهَ إِلَّا هُوَ ٱلْمَلِكُ ٱلْقُدُّوسُ ٱلسَّلَـٰمُ ٱلْمُؤْمِنُ ٱلْمُهَيْمِنُ ٱلْعَزِيزُ ٱلْجَبَّارُ ٱلْمُتَكَبِّرُ سُبْحَـٰنَ ٱللَّهِ عَمَّا يُشْرِكُونَ

٢٤ هُوَ ٱللَّهُ ٱلْخَـٰلِقُ ٱلْبَارِئُ ٱلْمُصَوِّرُ لَهُ ٱلْأَسْمَآءُ ٱلْحُسْنَىٰ يُسَبِّحُ لَهُۥ مَا فِى ٱلسَّمَـٰوَٰتِ وَٱلْأَرْضِ وَهُوَ ٱلْعَزِيزُ ٱلْحَكِيمُ

She That is to be Examined

Al Mumtaḥanah, "She that is to be Examined," takes its name from verse 10, where the believers are told to examine women who come to them as fugitives from the idolaters and, if they find them sincere converts to Islam, not to send them back. This marked a modification in the terms of the Truce of Ḥudaybīyah, which obligated the Muslims to return all fugitives, whether male or female, while the idolaters did not have to reciprocate with those who left the Muslim camp. The more terrible persecution that women had to undergo, if extradited, and their helpless social condition were the causes of the change. Instead of giving up female refugees who were sincere, as opposed to those who were fugitives on account of crime or some family quarrel, the Muslims were to pay an indemnity for them. If the wife of a Muslim husband was to flee to the Quraysh, no indemnity was to be paid by the latter. However, when some turn of fortune brought wealth to the Islamic state, they were to be repaid by the state what their wives had taken of their property. In verse 12 is the pledge that was to be taken from female refugees after their examination.

The date of revelation is the eighth year of the Hijrah.

She That is to be Examined

Revealed at al Madinah

In the Name of Allah,
the Beneficent, the Merciful

1.  you who believe! Choose not My enemy and your enemy for friends. You give them friendship when they disbelieve in that truth which has come unto you, driving out the Messenger and you because you believe in Allah, your Lord? If you have come forth to strive in My way and seeking My good pleasure, (show them not friendship). Do you show friendship unto them in secret, when I am best Aware of what you hide and what you proclaim? And whoever does it among you, he surely has strayed from the right way.

2. If they have the upper hand of you, they will be your foes, and will stretch out their hands and their tongues toward you with evil (intent), and they long for you to disbelieve.

3. Your ties of kindred and your children will avail you nothing upon the Day of Resurrection. He will judge between you. Allah is Seer of what you do.

4. There is a goodly pattern for you in Abraham and those with him, when they told their folk: Lo! we are guiltless of you and all that you worship beside Allah. We have done with you. And there has arisen between us and you hostility and hate forever until you believe in Allah only— save that which Abraham promised his father (when he said): I will ask forgiveness for you, though I own nothing for you from Allah—Our Lord! In You we put our trust, and unto You we turn repentant, and unto You is the journeying.

5. Our Lord! Make us not a prey for those who disbelieve, and forgive us, our Lord! Lo! You, only You, are the Mighty, the Wise.

6. Surely you have in them a goodly pattern for everyone who looks to Allah and the Last Day. And whoever may turn away, lo! still Allah, He is the Absolute, the Owner of Praise.

7. It may be that Allah will ordain love between you and those of them with whom you are at enmity. Allah is Mighty, and Allah is Forgiving, Merciful.

8. Allah forbids you not those who warred not against you on account of religion and drove you not out from your homes, that you should show them kindness and deal justly with them. Lo! Allah loves the just dealers.

9. Allah forbids you only those who warred against you on account of religion and have driven you out from your homes and helped to drive you out, that you make friends of them. Whoever makes friends of them—(All) such are wrong-doers.

10. O you who believe! When believing women come unto you as refugees, examine them. Allah is best aware of their faith. Then, if you know them for true believers, send them not back unto the disbelievers. They are not lawful for them (disbelievers), nor are they (disbelievers) lawful for them. And give the disbelievers that which they have spent (upon them). And it is no sin for you to marry such women when you have given them their dues. And hold not to the ties of disbelieving women; and ask for (the return of) that which you have spent; and let them ask for that which they have spent. That is the judgment of Allah. He judges between you. And Allah is Knower, Wise.

11. And if any of your wives have gone from you unto the disbelievers and afterward you have your turn (of triumph), then give unto those whose wives have gone the like of that which they have spent, and keep your duty to Allah in whom you are believers.

﴿١١﴾ وَإِن فَاتَكُمْ شَيْءٌ مِّنْ أَزْوَٰجِكُمْ إِلَى ٱلْكُفَّارِ فَعَاقَبْتُمْ فَـَٔاتُوا۟ ٱلَّذِينَ ذَهَبَتْ أَزْوَٰجُهُم مِّثْلَ مَآ أَنفَقُوا۟ وَٱتَّقُوا۟ ٱللَّهَ ٱلَّذِىٓ أَنتُم بِهِۦ مُؤْمِنُونَ

12. O Prophet! If believing women come unto you, taking oath of allegiance unto you that they will ascribe nothing as partner unto Allah, and will neither steal nor commit adultery nor kill their children, nor produce any lie that they have devised between their hands and their legs, nor disobey you in what is right,[296] then accept their allegiance and ask Allah to forgive them. Lo! Allah is Forgiving, Merciful.

﴿١٢﴾ يَٰٓأَيُّهَا ٱلنَّبِىُّ إِذَا جَآءَكَ ٱلْمُؤْمِنَٰتُ يُبَايِعْنَكَ عَلَىٰٓ أَن لَّا يُشْرِكْنَ بِٱللَّهِ شَيْـًٔا وَلَا يَسْرِقْنَ وَلَا يَزْنِينَ وَلَا يَقْتُلْنَ أَوْلَٰدَهُنَّ وَلَا يَأْتِينَ بِبُهْتَٰنٍ يَفْتَرِينَهُۥ بَيْنَ أَيْدِيهِنَّ وَأَرْجُلِهِنَّ وَلَا يَعْصِينَكَ فِى مَعْرُوفٍ فَبَايِعْهُنَّ وَٱسْتَغْفِرْ لَهُنَّ ٱللَّهَ إِنَّ ٱللَّهَ غَفُورٌ رَّحِيمٌ

13. O you who believe! Be not friendly with a folk with whom Allah is angry, (a folk) who have despaired of the Hereafter as the disbelievers despair of those who are in the graves.

﴿١٣﴾ يَٰٓأَيُّهَا ٱلَّذِينَ ءَامَنُوا۟ لَا تَتَوَلَّوْا۟ قَوْمًا غَضِبَ ٱللَّهُ عَلَيْهِمْ قَدْ يَئِسُوا۟ مِنَ ٱلْءَاخِرَةِ كَمَا يَئِسَ ٱلْكُفَّارُ مِنْ أَصْحَٰبِ ٱلْقُبُورِ

---

[296]This is called the women's oath of allegiance. It was also taken by the men until the second pact of al 'Aqabah when the duty of defense was added.

The Ranks

Al Ṣaff, "The Ranks," takes its name from a word in verse 4. In the copy of the Qur'an that I have followed, it is stated to have been revealed at Makkah, although its contents evidently refer to the Madinan period. It may have been revealed while the Prophet and his companions were encamped in the valley of Makkah during the negotiations of the Truce of Ḥudaybīyah, with which some of its verses are associated by tradition.

In that case, the date of revelation would be the sixth year of the Hijrah.

The Ranks

Revealed at al Madinah

*In the Name of Allah,
the Beneficent, the Merciful*

1. **A**ll that is in the heavens and all that is in the earth glorifies Allah, and He is the Mighty, the Wise.

2. O you who believe! Why say you that which you do not?

3. It is most hateful in the sight of Allah that you say that which you do not.

4. Lo! Allah loves those who battle for His cause in ranks, as if they were a solid structure.

5. And (remember) when Moses said unto his people: O my people! Why hurt you me, when you well know that I am Allah's messenger unto you? So when they went astray Allah sent their hearts astray. And Allah guides not the evil-living folk.

6. And when Jesus son of Mary said: O Children of Israel! Lo! I am the messenger of Allah unto you, confirming that which was (revealed) before me in the Torah,[297] and bringing good tidings of a messenger who comes after me, whose name is the Praised One.[298] Yet when he has come unto them with clear proofs, they say: This is mere magic.

7. And who does greater wrong than he who invents a lie against Allah when he is summoned unto Islam?[299] And Allah guides not wrongdoing folk.

8. Fain would they put out the light of Allah with their mouths, but Allah will perfect His light however much disbelievers are averse.

---

[297]The Book of Moses.

[298]Arabic: Aḥmad. A name of the Prophet Muhammad. The promised "Com-forter" was believed by many Christian communities of the East to be a prophet yet to come, and most of them accepted Muhammad as that pro-phet.

[299]Lit.": "The Surrender."

9. He it is who has sent His Messenger with guidance and the religion of truth, that He may make it conqueror of all religion however much idolaters may be averse.

﴿٩﴾ هُوَ الَّذِىٓ أَرْسَلَ رَسُولَهُ بِالْهُدَىٰ وَدِينِ الْحَقِّ لِيُظْهِرَهُ عَلَى الدِّينِ كُلِّهِ وَلَوْ كَرِهَ الْمُشْرِكُونَ

10. O you who believe! Shall I show you a commerce that will save you from a painful doom?

﴿١٠﴾ يَٰٓأَيُّهَا الَّذِينَ ءَامَنُوا هَلْ أَدُلُّكُمْ عَلَىٰ تِجَٰرَةٍ تُنجِيكُم مِّنْ عَذَابٍ أَلِيمٍ

11. You should believe in Allah and His Messenger, and should strive for the cause of Allah with your wealth and your lives. That is better for you, if you did but know.

﴿١١﴾ تُؤْمِنُونَ بِاللَّهِ وَرَسُولِهِ وَتُجَٰهِدُونَ فِى سَبِيلِ اللَّهِ بِأَمْوَٰلِكُمْ وَأَنفُسِكُمْ ذَٰلِكُمْ خَيْرٌ لَّكُمْ إِن كُنتُمْ تَعْلَمُونَ

12. He will forgive you your sins and bring you into Gardens underneath which rivers flow, and pleasant dwellings in Gardens of Eden. That is the supreme triumph.

﴿١٢﴾ يَغْفِرْ لَكُمْ ذُنُوبَكُمْ وَيُدْخِلْكُمْ جَنَّٰتٍ تَجْرِى مِن تَحْتِهَا الْأَنْهَٰرُ وَمَسَٰكِنَ طَيِّبَةً فِى جَنَّٰتِ عَدْنٍ ذَٰلِكَ الْفَوْزُ الْعَظِيمُ

13. And (He will give you) another blessing which you love: help from Allah and an imminent conquest. Give good tidings (O Muhammad) to believers.

﴿١٣﴾ وَأُخْرَىٰ تُحِبُّونَهَا نَصْرٌ مِّنَ اللَّهِ وَفَتْحٌ قَرِيبٌ وَبَشِّرِ الْمُؤْمِنِينَ

14. O you who believe! Be Allah's helpers, even as Jesus son of Mary said unto the disciples: Who are my helpers for Allah? The disciples said: We are Allah's helpers. Thus a party of the Children of Israel believed, while a party disbelieved. Then We strengthened those who believed against their foe, and they became the uppermost.

﴿١٤﴾ يَٰٓأَيُّهَا الَّذِينَ ءَامَنُوا كُونُوٓا أَنصَارَ اللَّهِ كَمَا قَالَ عِيسَى ابْنُ مَرْيَمَ لِلْحَوَارِيِّنَ مَنْ أَنصَارِىٓ إِلَى اللَّهِ قَالَ الْحَوَارِيُّونَ نَحْنُ أَنصَارُ اللَّهِ فَـَٔامَنَت طَّآئِفَةٌ مِّنۢ بَنِىٓ إِسْرَٰٓءِيلَ وَكَفَرَت طَّآئِفَةٌ فَأَيَّدْنَا الَّذِينَ ءَامَنُوا عَلَىٰ عَدُوِّهِمْ فَأَصْبَحُوا ظَٰهِرِينَ

Friday

Al Jumu'ah, "Friday," takes its name from a word in verse 9, where obedience to the call to congregational prayer on Friday is enjoined. Tradition says that verses 9-11 refer to an occasion when a caravan entered al Madinah and announced its presence by beating its drums. Although the Prophet was delivering the Friday sermon, all but twelve men went out to look at the caravan. If, as one version of the tradition says, the caravan was that of Daḥyah al Kalbī, the incident must have occurred before the year 5 AH, by which time he was already a Muslim.

The date of revelation is between the second and fourth years after the Hijrah.

Friday

Revealed at al Madinah

In the Name of Allah,
the Beneficent, the Merciful

1. **A**ll that is in the heavens and all that is in the earth glorifies Allah, the Sovereign Lord, the Holy One, the Mighty, the Wise.

2. He it is Who has sent among the unlettered ones a messenger of their own, to recite unto them His revelations and to purify them, and to teach them the Scripture and Wisdom, though heretofore they were indeed in error manifest,

3. Along with others of them who have not yet joined them. He is the Mighty, the Wise.

4. That is the favor of Allah; which he gives unto whom he will. And Allah is of infinite bounty.

5. The likeness of those who are entrusted with the Law of Moses, yet apply it not, is as the likeness of the ass carrying books. Wretched is the likeness of folk who deny the revelations of Allah. And Allah guides not wrongdoing folk.

6. Say (O Muhammad): O you who are Jews! If you claim that you are friends of Allah apart from (all) mankind, then long for death if you are truthful.

7. But they will never long for it because of all that their own hands have sent before, and Allah is Knower of wrongdoers.

8. Say (unto them, O Muhammad): Lo! the death from which you shrink will surely meet you, and afterward you will be returned unto the Knower of the invisible and the visible, and He will tell you what you used to do.

9. O you who believe! When the call is sounded for Friday prayer, hasten to remembrance of Allah and leave your trading. That is better for you if you did but know.

10. Then when the prayer is ended, disperse in the land and seek of Allah's bounty, and remember Allah much, that you may be successful.

11. But when they spy some merchandise or pastime they break away to it and leave you standing. Say: That which Allah has is better than pastime and than merchandise, and Allah is the best of providers.

٨ قُلْ إِنَّ الْمَوْتَ الَّذِي تَفِرُّونَ مِنْهُ فَإِنَّهُ مُلَاقِيكُمْ ثُمَّ تُرَدُّونَ إِلَى عَالِمِ الْغَيْبِ وَالشَّهَادَةِ فَيُنَبِّئُكُم بِمَا كُنتُمْ تَعْمَلُونَ

٩ يَا أَيُّهَا الَّذِينَ آمَنُوا إِذَا نُودِيَ لِلصَّلَاةِ مِن يَوْمِ الْجُمُعَةِ فَاسْعَوْا إِلَى ذِكْرِ اللَّهِ وَذَرُوا الْبَيْعَ ذَلِكُمْ خَيْرٌ لَّكُمْ إِن كُنتُمْ تَعْلَمُونَ

١٠ فَإِذَا قُضِيَتِ الصَّلَاةُ فَانتَشِرُوا فِي الْأَرْضِ وَابْتَغُوا مِن فَضْلِ اللَّهِ وَاذْكُرُوا اللَّهَ كَثِيرًا لَّعَلَّكُمْ تُفْلِحُونَ

١١ وَإِذَا رَأَوْا تِجَارَةً أَوْ لَهْوًا انفَضُّوا إِلَيْهَا وَتَرَكُوكَ قَائِمًا قُلْ مَا عِندَ اللَّهِ خَيْرٌ مِّنَ اللَّهْوِ وَمِنَ التِّجَارَةِ وَاللَّهُ خَيْرُ الرَّازِقِينَ

The Hypocrites

Al Munāfiqūn, "The Hypocrites," takes its name from a word occurring in the first verse. Verse 8 refers to a remark made by 'Abd Allāh ibn Ubayy, their leader, expressing the desire that the old aristocracy of Yathrib, of which he had been the acknowledged chief, might regain the ascendancy and drive the Muslim refugees out of Madinah, whom he regarded as intruders. His own son, however, disgraced him and offered to kill him if needed.

The date of the revelation is the fourth year of the Hijrah.

The Hypocrites

Revealed at al Madinah

*In the Name of Allah,
the Beneficent, the Merciful*

1. When the hypocrites come unto you (O Muhammad), they say: We bear witness that you are indeed Allah's Messenger. And Allah knows that you are indeed His Messenger, and Allah bears witness that the Hypocrites are the liars.

2. They make their faith a pretext that they may turn (men) from the way of Allah. Surely evil is that which they are wont to do;

3. That is because they believed, then disbelieved, therefore their hearts are sealed so that they understand not.

4. And when you see them their figures please you; and if they speak you give ear unto their speech. (They are) as though they were blocks of wood in striped cloaks.[300] They deem every shout to be against them. They are the enemy, so beware of them. Allah confound them! How they are perverted!

5. And when it is said unto them: Come! The Messenger of Allah will ask forgiveness for you! they avert their faces and you see them turning away, disdainful.

6. Whether you ask forgiveness for them or ask not forgiveness for them, Allah will not forgive them. Lo! Allah guides not the evil-living folk.

7. They it is who say: Spend not on behalf of those (who dwell) with Allah's Messenger that they may disperse (and go away from you); when Allah's are the treasures of the heavens and the earth; but the hypocrites comprehend not.

---

[300]Or propped-up blocks of wood.

8. They say: Surely, if we return to al Madinah the more honorable will soon drive out the meaner; when honor belongs to Allah and to His Messenger and the believers; but the hypocrites know not.

9. O you who believe! Let not your wealth nor your children distract you from remembrance of Allah. Those who do so, they are the losers.

10. And spend of that wherewith We have provided you before death comes unto one of you and he said: My Lord! If only you would reprieve me for a little while, then I would give alms and be among the righteous.

11. But Allah reprieves no soul when its term comes, and Allah is Aware of what you do.

٨ يَقُولُونَ لَئِن رَّجَعْنَا إِلَى ٱلْمَدِينَةِ لَيُخْرِجَنَّ ٱلْأَعَزُّ مِنْهَا ٱلْأَذَلَّ وَلِلَّهِ ٱلْعِزَّةُ وَلِرَسُولِهِ وَلِلْمُؤْمِنِينَ وَلَٰكِنَّ ٱلْمُنَٰفِقِينَ لَا يَعْلَمُونَ

٩ يَٰٓأَيُّهَا ٱلَّذِينَ ءَامَنُوا لَا تُلْهِكُمْ أَمْوَٰلُكُمْ وَلَآ أَوْلَٰدُكُمْ عَن ذِكْرِ ٱللَّهِ وَمَن يَفْعَلْ ذَٰلِكَ فَأُو۟لَٰٓئِكَ هُمُ ٱلْخَٰسِرُونَ

١٠ وَأَنفِقُوا مِن مَّا رَزَقْنَٰكُم مِّن قَبْلِ أَن يَأْتِيَ أَحَدَكُمُ ٱلْمَوْتُ فَيَقُولَ رَبِّ لَوْلَآ أَخَّرْتَنِي إِلَىٰٓ أَجَلٍ قَرِيبٍ فَأَصَّدَّقَ وَأَكُن مِّنَ ٱلصَّٰلِحِينَ

١١ وَلَن يُؤَخِّرَ ٱللَّهُ نَفْسًا إِذَا جَآءَ أَجَلُهَا وَٱللَّهُ خَبِيرٌۢ بِمَا تَعْمَلُونَ

Mutual Disillusion

Al Taghābun, "Mutual Disillusion," takes its name from a word in verse 9.

The date of revelation is possibly the year 1 AH, though it is generally regarded as a late Makkan surah, for verses 14 ff. are considered as referring to the pressure brought to bear by wives and families to prevent the Muslims' departure from Makkah at the time of the Hijrah.

Mutual Disillusion

Revealed at Madinah

*In the Name of Allah,
the Beneficent, the Merciful*

1. All that is in the heavens and all that is in the earth glorifies Allah; unto Him belongs sovereignty and unto Him belongs praise, and He is Able to do all things.

2. He it is Who created you, some of you are disbelievers and some of you are believers, and Allah is Seer of what you do.

3. He created the heavens and the earth with truth, and He shaped you and made good your shapes, and unto Him is the journeying.

4. He knows all that is in the heavens and all that is in the earth, and He knows what you conceal and what you publish. and Allah is Aware of what is in the breasts (of men).

5. Has not the story reached you of those who disbelieved of old and so did taste the ill-effects of their conduct, and theirs will be a painful doom.

6. That was because their messengers (from Allah) kept coming unto them with clear proofs (of Allah's sovereignty), but they said: Shall mere mortals guide us? So they disbelieved and turned away, and Allah was independent (of them). Allah is Absolute, Owner of Praise.

7. Those who disbelieve assert that they will not be raised again. Say (unto them, O Muhammad): Yea, surely, by my Lord! you will be raised again and then you will be informed of what you did; and that is easy for Allah.

8. So believe in Allah and His Messenger and the light which We have revealed. And Allah is Aware of what you do.

9. The day when He shall gather you unto the Day of Assembling, that will be a day of mutual disillusion. And who believes in Allah and does right, He will remit from him his evil deeds and will bring him into Gardens underneath which rivers flow, therein to abide forever. That is the supreme triumph.

10. But those who disbelieve and deny Our revelations, such are owners of the Fire; they will abide therein—a hapless journey's end!

11. No calamity befalls save by Allah's leave. And whoever believes in Allah, He guides his heart. And Allah is Knower of all things.

12. Obey Allah and obey His Messenger; but if you turn away, then the duty of Our Messenger is only to convey (the message) plainly.

13. Allah! There is no God save Him. In Allah, therefore, let believers put their trust.

14. O you who believe! Lo! among your wives and your children there are enemies for you, therefore beware of them. And if you efface and overlook and forgive, then lo! Allah is Forgiving, Merciful.

15. Your wealth and your children are only a temptation, whereas Allah! with Him is an immense reward.

16. So keep your duty to Allah as best as you can, and listen, and obey, and spend; that is better for your souls. And who is saved from his own greed, such are the successful.

17. If you lend unto Allah a goodly loan,[301] He will double it for you and will forgive you, for Allah is Responsive, Clement,

18. Knower of the invisible and the visible, the Mighty, the Wise.

---

[301] i.e., a loan without interest or any thought of gain or loss.

Divorce

Al Ṭalāq, "Divorce," takes its name from verses 1-7, which contain an amendment to the laws of divorce set forth in Surah 2. Traditionally, this is understood to refer to a mistake made by Ibn 'Umar in divorcing his wife, which is said to have happened in 6 AH. Others relate that the Prophet only quoted this verse, which had already been revealed, on that occasion.

The date of revelation is the sixth year of the Hijrah or a little earlier.

Divorce

Revealed at al Madinah

In the Name of Allah,
the Beneficent, the Merciful

1. Prophet! When you (men) divorce women, divorce them for their (legal) period and reckon the period, and keep your duty to Allah, your Lord. Expel them not from their houses nor let them go forth unless they commit open immorality. Such are the limits (imposed by) Allah; and who transgresses Allah's limits, he surely wrongs his soul. You know not: it may be that Allah will afterward bring some new thing to pass.

2. Then, when they have reached their term, take them back in kindness or part from them in kindness, and call to witness two just men among you, and keep your testimony upright for Allah. Who believes in Allah and the Last Day is exhorted to act thus. And whoever keeps his duty to Allah, Allah will appoint a way out for him,

3. And will provide for him from (a quarter) whence he has no expectation. And whoever puts his trust in Allah, He will suffice him. Lo! Allah brings His command to pass. Allah has set a measure for all things.

4. And for such of your women as despair of menstruation, if you doubt, their period (of waiting) shall be three months along with those who have it not. And for those with child, their period shall be till they bring forth their burden. And whoever keeps his duty to Allah, He makes his course easy for him.

5. That is the commandment of Allah which He reveals unto you. And who keeps his duty to Allah, He will remit from him his evil deeds and magnify reward for him.

6. Lodge them where you dwell, according to your wealth, and harass them not so as to straiten life for them. And if they are with child, then spend for them till they bring forth their burden. Then, if they give suck for you, give them their due payment and consult together in kindness; but if you make difficulties for one another, then let some other woman give suck for him (the father of the child).

٦ اَسْكِنُوهُنَّ مِنْ حَيْثُ سَكَنْتُمْ مِنْ وُجْدِكُمْ وَلَا تُضَآرُّوهُنَّ لِتُضَيِّقُوا عَلَيْهِنَّ وَإِنْ كُنَّ أُولَاتِ حَمْلٍ فَأَنْفِقُوا عَلَيْهِنَّ حَتَّى يَضَعْنَ حَمْلَهُنَّ فَإِنْ أَرْضَعْنَ لَكُمْ فَاٰتُوهُنَّ أُجُورَهُنَّ وَأْتَمِرُوا بَيْنَكُمْ بِمَعْرُوفٍ وَإِنْ تَعَاسَرْتُمْ فَسَتُرْضِعُ لَهُ أُخْرَى

7. Let him who has abundance spend of his abundance, and he whose provision is straitened, let him spend of that which Allah has given him. Allah asks nothing of any soul save that which He has given it. Allah will vouchsafe, after hardship, ease.

٧ لِيُنْفِقْ ذُو سَعَةٍ مِنْ سَعَتِهِ وَمَنْ قُدِرَ عَلَيْهِ رِزْقُهُ فَلْيُنْفِقْ مِمَّا اٰتَاهُ اللّٰهُ لَا يُكَلِّفُ اللّٰهُ نَفْسًا إِلَّا مَا اٰتَاهَا سَيَجْعَلُ اللّٰهُ بَعْدَ عُسْرٍ يُسْرًا

8. And how many a community revolted against the ordinance of its Lord and His messengers, and we called it to a stern account and punished it with dire punishment,

٨ وَكَأَيِّنْ مِنْ قَرْيَةٍ عَتَتْ عَنْ أَمْرِ رَبِّهَا وَرُسُلِهِ فَحَاسَبْنَاهَا حِسَابًا شَدِيدًا وَعَذَّبْنَاهَا عَذَابًا نُكْرًا

9. So that it tasted the ill effects of its conduct, and the consequence of its conduct was loss.

٩ فَذَاقَتْ وَبَالَ أَمْرِهَا وَكَانَ عَاقِبَةُ أَمْرِهَا خُسْرًا

10. Allah has prepared for them stern punishment; so keep your duty to Allah, O men of understanding! O you who believe! Now Allah has sent down unto you a reminder,

١٠ أَعَدَّ اللّٰهُ لَهُمْ عَذَابًا شَدِيدًا فَاتَّقُوا اللّٰهَ يَا أُولِي الْأَلْبَابِ الَّذِينَ اٰمَنُوا قَدْ أَنْزَلَ اللّٰهُ إِلَيْكُمْ ذِكْرًا

11. A messenger reciting unto you the revelations of Allah made plain, that He may bring forth those who believe and do good works from darkness unto light. And whoever believes in Allah and does right, He will bring him into Gardens underneath which rivers flow, therein to abide forever. Allah has made good provision for him.

١١ رَسُولًا يَتْلُو عَلَيْكُمْ اٰيَاتِ اللّٰهِ مُبَيِّنَاتٍ لِيُخْرِجَ الَّذِينَ اٰمَنُوا وَعَمِلُوا الصَّالِحَاتِ مِنَ الظُّلُمَاتِ إِلَى النُّورِ وَمَنْ يُؤْمِنْ بِاللّٰهِ وَيَعْمَلْ صَالِحًا يُدْخِلْهُ جَنَّاتٍ تَجْرِي مِنْ تَحْتِهَا الْأَنْهَارُ خَالِدِينَ فِيهَا أَبَدًا قَدْ أَحْسَنَ اللّٰهُ لَهُ رِزْقًا

12. Allah it is who has created seven heavens, and of the earth the like thereof. The commandment comes down among them slowly, that you may know that Allah is Able to do all things, and that Allah surrounds all things in knowledge.

١٢ اللّٰهُ الَّذِي خَلَقَ سَبْعَ سَمٰوَاتٍ وَمِنَ الْأَرْضِ مِثْلَهُنَّ يَتَنَزَّلُ الْأَمْرُ بَيْنَهُنَّ لِتَعْلَمُوا أَنَّ اللّٰهَ عَلَى كُلِّ شَيْءٍ قَدِيرٌ وَأَنَّ اللّٰهَ قَدْ أَحَاطَ بِكُلِّ شَيْءٍ عِلْمًا

Banning

Al Taḥrīm, "Banning," takes its name from a word in the first verse.

There are three traditions dealing with the revelation of verses 1–4. They are:

(1) The Prophet was very fond of honey. One of his wives received some honey from a relative and used it to persuade the Prophet to stay with her longer than was customary. The others felt aggrieved, and 'Ā'ishah devised a plot. Knowing the Prophet's horror of unpleasant smells, she arranged with Ḥafṣah, another wife of the Prophet, to hold their noses when he came to them after eating the honey and say that he had eaten the produce of a very rank-smelling tree. When they accused him of having eaten maghāfir the Prophet said he had eaten only honey. They said: "The bees had fed on Maghāfir." The Prophet was dismayed and vowed to eat no more honey.

(2) Ḥafṣah found the Prophet in her room with Marya—the Coptic girl who had been presented to him by the ruler of Egypt and who had given birth to his son Ibrāhīm—on a day that his custom was to spend with 'Ā'ishah. Moved by Ḥafṣah's distress, the Prophet vowed he would have no more to do with Marya and asked her not to tell 'Ā'ishah. But Ḥafṣah's distress had been largely feigned, and no sooner had the Prophet left than she told 'Ā'ishah with glee how easily she had gotten rid of Marya.

(3) Before Islam, women had had no standing in Arabia. The Qur'an gave them legal rights and an assured position, which some of them were inclined to exaggerate. The Prophet was extremely kind to his wives. One day 'Umar rebuked his wife for replying to him in a tone which he considered disrespectful. She assured him it was the tone in which (his own daughter) Ḥafṣah, 'Ā'ishah, and other wives of the Prophet answered the Prophet. 'Umar went at once and remonstrated with Hafsah and with another of the Prophet's wives to whom he was related. He was told to mind his own business, which increased his horror and dismay. Soon afterwards the Prophet separated from his wives for a time, and it was thought that he was going to divorce them. 'Umar then told him the story of his own vain effort to reform them, and the Prophet laughed heartily.

Traditions (1) and (3) are considered more authentic and are alone adduced by the great traditionists. However, the commentators generally prefer (2) and view it as being more explanatory of the text. All allude to a tendency on the part of some of the Prophet's wives to presume on their new status and the Prophet's well-known kindness: a tendency so marked that, if allowed to continue, it would have been a bad example to the whole community. The Qur'an first rebukes the Prophet for yielding to their desires by undertaking to forgo a thing which Allah had made lawful for him in the case of (2), the fulfillment of his vow concerning Marya represented a wrong to Marya. It then reproves the two women for their double-dealing and intrigue.

Some non-Muslims writers have used the above traditions for strictures that appear irrelevant, because their ideology is altogether un-Islamic. The Prophet has never been regarded by Muslims as something more than a human messenger of God, and sanctity has never been identified with celibacy. For Christendom, the strictest religious ideal has been celibacy and monogamy is seen as a concession to human nature. For Muslims monogamy is the ideal and polygamy is the concession to human nature. Polygamy is considered to be the nature of men, to varying degrees, all over the world. Having set a great example of monogamous marriage, the Prophet set a great example of polygamous marriage by showing how a polygamous man could live a righteous life. He encountered all of the difficulties inherent in such a situation, and when he made mistakes he was corrected. Islam did not institute polygamy; rather it restricted an existing institution by limiting the number of a man's legal wives, by giving to every woman a legal personality and legal rights that had to be respected, and by making every man legally responsible for his conduct towards every woman. Whether monogamy or polygamy should prevail in a particular country or period is a matter of social and economic convenience. The Prophet was permitted to have more wives than others because, as the head of state, he was responsible for the support of women who had no other protector. With the one exception of 'Ā'ishah, all of his wives were widows or divorced when he married them.

Banning

Revealed at Madinah

In the Name of Allah,
the Beneficent, the Merciful

1. Prophet! Why prohibit you that which Allah has made lawful for you, seeking to please your wives? And Allah is Forgiving, Merciful.

2. Allah has made lawful for you (Muslims) absolution from your oaths (of such a kind), and Allah is your Protector. He is the Knower, the Wise.

3. When the Prophet confided a fact unto one of his wives and when she afterward divulged it and Allah apprised him thereof, he made known (to her) part thereof and passed over part. And when he told it her she said: Who has told you this? He said: The Knower, the Aware has told me.

4. If you two turn unto Allah repentant, (you have cause to do so) for your hearts desired (the ban); and if you aid one another against him (Muhammad) then lo! Allah, even He, is his protecting Friend, and Gabriel and the righteous among the believers; and furthermore the angels are his helpers.

5. It may happen that his Lord, if he divorce you, will give him in your stead wives better than you, submissive (to Allah), believing, pious, penitent, inclined to fasting, widows and virgins.

6. O you who believe! Ward off from yourselves and your families a Fire whereof the fuel is men and stones, over which are set angels strong, severe, who resist not Allah in that which He commands them, but do that which they are commanded.

7. (Then it will be said): O you who disbelieve! Make no excuses for yourselves this day. You are only being paid for what you used to do.

8. O you who believe! Turn unto Allah in sincere repentance! It may be that your Lord will remit from you your evil deeds and bring you into Gardens underneath which rivers flow, on the day when Allah will not abase the Prophet and those who believe with him. Their light will gush before them and on their right hands: they will say: Our Lord! Perfect our light for us, and forgive us! Lo! You are Able to do all things.

9. O Prophet! Strive against the disbelievers and the hypocrites, and be stern with them. Hell will be their home, an unfortunate journey's end.

10. Allah cites an example for those who disbelieve: the wife of Noah and the wife of Lot, who were under two of our righteous slaves yet betrayed them so that they (the husbands) availed them nothing against Allah and it was said (unto them): Enter the Fire along with those who enter.

11. And Allah cites an example for those who believe: the wife of Pharaoh when she said: My Lord! Build for me a home with you in the Garden, and deliver me from Pharaoh and his work, and deliver me from evildoing folk;

12. And Mary, daughter of 'Imrān, who guarded her chastity, therefore We breathed into (her body) something of Our Spirit. And she believed in the words of her Lord and His Scriptures, and was of the obedient.

Sovereignty

Al Mulk takes its name from a word in the first verse. The Prophet encouraged Muslims to recite it every day before going to bed. It reminds them of the sovereignty of Allah. It belongs to the middle group of Makkan surahs.

Sovereignty

Revealed at Makkah

In the Name of Allah,
the Beneficent, the Merciful

1. Blessed is He in Whose hand is the Sovereignty, and He is Able to do all things.

2. Who has created death and life that He may try you, which of you is best in conduct; and He is the Mighty, the Forgiving,

3. Who has created seven heavens in harmony. You (Muhammad) can see no fault in the Beneficent One's creation; then look again: Can you see any rifts?

4. Then look again and yet again, your sight will return unto you weakened and made dim.

5. And verily We have beautified the world's heaven with lamps, and We have made them missiles for the devils,[302] and for them We have prepared the doom of flame.

6. And for those who disbelieve in their Lord there is the doom of Hell, an unfortunate journey's end!

7. When they are flung therein they hear its roaring as it boils up,

8. As it would burst with rage. Whenever a (fresh) host flung therein the wardens thereof ask them: Came there unto you no warner?

9. They say: Yea, surely, a warner came unto us; but we denied and said: Allah has revealed nothing; you are in nothing but a great error.

---

[302]On the authority of a tradition of Ibn 'Abbās, this alludes to soothsayers and astrologers who saw the source of good and evil in the stars. See Surah 72:9, footnote.

10. And they say: Had we been wont to listen or have sense, we had not been among the dwellers in the flames.

11. So they acknowledge their sins; but far removed (from mercy) are the dwellers in the flames.

12. Lo! those who fear their Lord in secret, theirs will be forgiveness and a great reward.

13. And keep your opinion secret or proclaim it, lo! He is Knower of all that is in the breasts (of men).

14. Should He not know what He created? And He is the Subtile, the Aware.

15. He it is Who has made the earth subservient unto you, so walk in the paths thereof and eat of His providence. And unto Him will be the resurrection (of the dead).

16. Have you taken security from Him Who is in the heaven that He will not cause the earth to swallow you when lo! it is convulsed?

17. Or have you taken security from Him Who is in the heaven that He will not let loose on you a hurricane? But you shall know the manner of My warning.

18. And surely those before them denied, then (see) the manner of My wrath (with them)!

19. Have they not seen the birds above them spreading out their wings and closing them? Nothing upholds them save the Beneficent. Lo! He is Seer of all things.

20. Or who is he that will be an army unto you to help you instead of the Beneficent? Disbelievers are in manifest illusion.

21. Or who is he that will provide for you if He should withhold His providence? Nay, but they are set in pride and frowardness.

١٠ وَقَالُوا لَوْ كُنَّا نَسْمَعُ أَوْ نَعْقِلُ مَا كُنَّا فِي أَصْحَابِ السَّعِيرِ

١١ فَاعْتَرَفُوا بِذَنبِهِمْ فَسُحْقًا لِّأَصْحَابِ السَّعِيرِ

١٢ إِنَّ الَّذِينَ يَخْشَوْنَ رَبَّهُم بِالْغَيْبِ لَهُم مَّغْفِرَةٌ وَأَجْرٌ كَبِيرٌ

١٣ وَأَسِرُّوا قَوْلَكُمْ أَوِ اجْهَرُوا بِهِ إِنَّهُ عَلِيمٌ بِذَاتِ الصُّدُورِ

١٤ أَلَا يَعْلَمُ مَنْ خَلَقَ وَهُوَ اللَّطِيفُ الْخَبِيرُ

١٥ هُوَ الَّذِي جَعَلَ لَكُمُ الْأَرْضَ ذَلُولًا فَامْشُوا فِي مَنَاكِبِهَا وَكُلُوا مِن رِّزْقِهِ وَإِلَيْهِ النُّشُورُ

١٦ أَأَمِنتُم مَّن فِي السَّمَاءِ أَن يَخْسِفَ بِكُمُ الْأَرْضَ فَإِذَا هِيَ تَمُورُ

١٧ أَمْ أَمِنتُم مَّن فِي السَّمَاءِ أَن يُرْسِلَ عَلَيْكُمْ حَاصِبًا فَسَتَعْلَمُونَ كَيْفَ نَذِيرِ

١٨ وَلَقَدْ كَذَّبَ الَّذِينَ مِن قَبْلِهِمْ فَكَيْفَ كَانَ نَكِيرِ

١٩ أَوَلَمْ يَرَوْا إِلَى الطَّيْرِ فَوْقَهُمْ صَافَّاتٍ وَيَقْبِضْنَ مَا يُمْسِكُهُنَّ إِلَّا الرَّحْمَنُ إِنَّهُ بِكُلِّ شَيْءٍ بَصِيرٌ

٢٠ أَمَّنْ هَذَا الَّذِي هُوَ جُندٌ لَّكُمْ يَنصُرُكُم مِّن دُونِ الرَّحْمَنِ إِنِ الْكَافِرُونَ إِلَّا فِي غُرُورٍ

٢١ أَمَّنْ هَذَا الَّذِي يَرْزُقُكُمْ إِنْ أَمْسَكَ رِزْقَهُ بَل لَّجُّوا فِي عُتُوٍّ وَنُفُورٍ

22. Is he who goes groping on his face more rightly guided, or he who walks upright on a beaten road?

23. Say (unto them, O Muhammad): He it is Who gave you being, and has assigned unto you ears and eyes and hearts. Small thanks give you!

24. Say, He it is Who multiplies you in the earth, and unto Him you will be gathered.

25. And they say: When (will) this promise (be fulfilled), if you are truthful?

26. Say: The knowledge is with Allah only, and I am but a plain warner;

27. But when they see it nigh, the faces of those who disbelieve will be awry, and it will be said (unto them): This is that for which you used to call.

28. Say (O Muhammad): Have you observed: Whether Allah causes me (Muhammad) and those with me to perish or has mercy on us, still, who will protect disbelievers from a painful doom?

29. Say: He is the Beneficent. In Him we believe and in Him we put our trust. And you will soon know who it is that is in error manifest.

30. Say: Have you observed: If (all) your water were to disappear into the earth, who then could bring you gushing water?

٢٢ أَفَمَن يَمْشِي مُكِبًّا عَلَىٰ وَجْهِهِ أَهْدَىٰ أَمَّن يَمْشِي سَوِيًّا عَلَىٰ صِرَاطٍ مُّسْتَقِيمٍ

٢٣ قُلْ هُوَ الَّذِي أَنشَأَكُمْ وَجَعَلَ لَكُمُ السَّمْعَ وَالْأَبْصَارَ وَالْأَفْئِدَةَ قَلِيلًا مَّا تَشْكُرُونَ

٢٤ قُلْ هُوَ الَّذِي ذَرَأَكُمْ فِي الْأَرْضِ وَإِلَيْهِ تُحْشَرُونَ

٢٥ وَيَقُولُونَ مَتَىٰ هَٰذَا الْوَعْدُ إِن كُنتُمْ صَادِقِينَ

٢٦ قُلْ إِنَّمَا الْعِلْمُ عِندَ اللَّهِ وَإِنَّمَا أَنَا نَذِيرٌ مُّبِينٌ

٢٧ فَلَمَّا رَأَوْهُ زُلْفَةً سِيئَتْ وُجُوهُ الَّذِينَ كَفَرُوا وَقِيلَ هَٰذَا الَّذِي كُنتُم بِهِ تَدَّعُونَ

٢٨ قُلْ أَرَأَيْتُمْ إِنْ أَهْلَكَنِيَ اللَّهُ وَمَن مَّعِيَ أَوْ رَحِمَنَا فَمَن يُجِيرُ الْكَافِرِينَ مِنْ عَذَابٍ أَلِيمٍ

٢٩ قُلْ هُوَ الرَّحْمَٰنُ آمَنَّا بِهِ وَعَلَيْهِ تَوَكَّلْنَا فَسَتَعْلَمُونَ مَنْ هُوَ فِي ضَلَالٍ مُّبِينٍ

٣٠ قُلْ أَرَأَيْتُمْ إِنْ أَصْبَحَ مَاؤُكُمْ غَوْرًا فَمَن يَأْتِيكُم بِمَاءٍ مَّعِينٍ

The Pen

Al Qalam, "The Pen," takes its name from a word in the first verse. A very early Makkan surah.

The Pen

Revealed at Makkah

In the Name of Allah,

the Beneficent, the Merciful

1. **N**ūn.[303] By the pen and that which they write (therewith),

2. You are not (O Muhammad), for your Lord's favor unto you, a madman.

3. And lo! yours surely will he a reward unfailing.

4. And lo! you are of an exalted character.

5. And you will see and they will see

6. Which of you is the demented.

7. Lo! your Lord is best aware of him who strays from his way, and He is best aware of those who walk aright.

8. Therefore obey not you the rejecters

9. Who would have had you compromise, that they may compromise.

10. Neither obey you each feeble oath monger,

11. Detractor, spreader abroad of slanders?

12. Hinderer of the good, transgressor, malefactor

13. Greedy therewithal, intrusive.

14. It is because he is possessed of wealth and children

15. That, when Our revelations are recited unto him, he says: Mere fables of the men of old.

16. We shall brand him on the nose.

17. Lo! we have tried them as We tried the owners of the garden when they vowed they would pluck its fruit next morning.

---

[303]See Surah 2:1, footnote. "*Nūn*" is the equivalent of the letter "N" in English.

18. And made no exception (for the will of Allah)[304];

﴾١٨﴿ وَلَا يَسْتَثْنُوْنَ

19. Then a visitation came upon it from your Lord while they slept

﴾١٩﴿ فَطَافَ عَلَيْهَا طَآئِفٌ مِّنْ رَّبِّكَ وَهُمْ نَآئِمُوْنَ

20. Thus it became as if plucked (or black as if burnt).

﴾٢٠﴿ فَأَصْبَحَتْ كَالصَّرِيْمِ

21. And they cried out one unto another in the morning,

﴾٢١﴿ فَتَنَادَوْا مُصْبِحِيْنَ

22. Saying: Run unto your field if you would pluck (the fruit).

﴾٢٢﴿ أَنِ اغْدُوْا عَلَى حَرْثِكُمْ إِنْ كُنْتُمْ صَارِمِيْنَ

23. So they went off, saying one unto another in low tones:

﴾٢٣﴿ فَانْطَلَقُوْا وَهُمْ يَتَخَافَتُوْنَ

24. No needy man shall enter it today against you.[305]

﴾٢٤﴿ أَنْ لَّا يَدْخُلَنَّهَا الْيَوْمَ عَلَيْكُمْ مِّسْكِيْنٌ

25. They went betimes, strong in (this) purpose.

﴾٢٥﴿ وَغَدَوْا عَلَى حَرْدٍ قَادِرِيْنَ

26. But when they saw it, they said: Lo! we are in error!

﴾٢٦﴿ فَلَمَّا رَأَوْهَا قَالُوْا إِنَّا لَضَآلُّوْنَ

27. Nay, but we are deprived!

﴾٢٧﴿ بَلْ نَحْنُ مَحْرُوْمُوْنَ

28. The best among them said: Said I not unto you: Why glorify you not (Allah)?

﴾٢٨﴿ قَالَ أَوْسَطُهُمْ أَلَمْ أَقُلْ لَّكُمْ لَوْلَا تُسَبِّحُوْنَ

29. They said: Glorified be our Lord! Lo! we have been wrongdoers.

﴾٢٩﴿ قَالُوْا سُبْحَانَ رَبِّنَا إِنَّا كُنَّا ظَالِمِيْنَ

30. Then some of them drew near unto others, self reproaching.

﴾٣٠﴿ فَأَقْبَلَ بَعْضُهُمْ عَلَى بَعْضٍ يَتَلَاوَمُوْنَ

31. They said: Alas for us! In truth we were outrageous.

﴾٣١﴿ قَالُوْا يَا وَيْلَنَا إِنَّا كُنَّا طَاغِيْنَ

32. It may be that our Lord will give us better than this in place thereof. Lo! we beseech our Lord.

﴾٣٢﴿ عَسَى رَبُّنَا أَنْ يُّبْدِلَنَا خَيْرًا مِّنْهَا إِنَّا إِلَى رَبِّنَا رَاغِبُوْنَ

33. Such was the punishment. And surely the punishment of the Hereafter is greater if they did but know.

﴾٣٣﴿ كَذَلِكَ الْعَذَابُ وَلَعَذَابُ الْآخِرَةِ أَكْبَرُ لَوْ كَانُوْا يَعْلَمُوْنَ

34. Lo! for those who keep from evil are gardens of bliss with their Lord.

﴾٣٤﴿ إِنَّ لِلْمُتَّقِيْنَ عِنْدَ رَبِّهِمْ جَنَّاتِ النَّعِيْمِ

35. Shall We then treat those who are Muslims[306] as We treat the criminals?

﴾٣٥﴿ أَفَنَجْعَلُ الْمُسْلِمِيْنَ كَالْمُجْرِمِيْنَ

36. What ails you? How foolishly you judge!

﴾٣٦﴿ مَا لَكُمْ كَيْفَ تَحْكُمُوْنَ

37. Or have you a Scripture wherein you learn

﴾٣٧﴿ أَمْ لَكُمْ كِتَابٌ فِيْهِ تَدْرُسُوْنَ

---

[304] i.e., they forgot to say: "If God wills." Another interpretation is that they swore to leave nothing for the poor (the editor).

[305] It was the custom of their fathers to allow the poor to glean the harvests and to give them part of it.

[306] Those who have surrendered to Allah.

38. That you shall indeed have all that you choose?

٣٨ إِنَّ لَكُمْ فِيهِ لَمَا تَخَيَّرُونَ

39. Or have you a covenant on oath from Us that reaches to the Day of Judgment, that yours shall be all that you ordain?

٣٩ أَمْ لَكُمْ أَيْمَانٌ عَلَيْنَا بَالِغَةٌ إِلَى يَوْمِ الْقِيَامَةِ إِنَّ لَكُمْ لَمَا تَحْكُمُونَ

40. Ask them (O Muhammad) which of them will vouch for that!

٤٠ سَلْهُمْ أَيُّهُم بِذَلِكَ زَعِيمٌ

41. Or have they other gods? Then let them bring their other gods if they are truthful,

٤١ أَمْ لَهُمْ شُرَكَاءُ فَلْيَأْتُوا بِشُرَكَائِهِمْ إِن كَانُوا صَادِقِينَ

42. On the day when it befalls in earnest, and they are ordered to prostrate themselves but are not able,

٤٢ يَوْمَ يُكْشَفُ عَن سَاقٍ وَيُدْعَوْنَ إِلَى السُّجُودِ فَلَا يَسْتَطِيعُونَ

43. With eyes downcast, abasement stupefying them. And they had been summoned to prostrate themselves while they were yet unhurt.

٤٣ خَاشِعَةً أَبْصَارُهُمْ تَرْهَقُهُمْ ذِلَّةٌ وَقَدْ كَانُوا يُدْعَوْنَ إِلَى السُّجُودِ وَهُمْ سَالِمُونَ

44. Leave Me (to deal) with those who give the lie to this pronouncement. We shall lead them on by steps from whence they know not.

٤٤ فَذَرْنِي وَمَن يُكَذِّبُ بِهَذَا الْحَدِيثِ سَنَسْتَدْرِجُهُم مِّنْ حَيْثُ لَا يَعْلَمُونَ

45. Yet I bear with them, for lo! My scheme is firm.

٤٥ وَأُمْلِي لَهُمْ إِنَّ كَيْدِي مَتِينٌ

46. Or do you (Muhammad) ask a fee from them so that they are heavily taxed?

٤٦ أَمْ تَسْأَلُهُمْ أَجْرًا فَهُم مِّن مَّغْرَمٍ مُّثْقَلُونَ

47. Or is the Unseen theirs that they can write (thereof)?

٤٧ أَمْ عِندَهُمُ الْغَيْبُ فَهُمْ يَكْتُبُونَ

48. But wait you for your Lord's decree, and be not like him of the fish,307 who cried out in despair.

٤٨ فَاصْبِرْ لِحُكْمِ رَبِّكَ وَلَا تَكُن كَصَاحِبِ الْحُوتِ إِذْ نَادَى وَهُوَ مَكْظُومٌ

49. Had it not been that favor from his Lord had reached him he surely had been cast into the wilderness while he was reprobate.

٤٩ لَّوْلَا أَن تَدَارَكَهُ نِعْمَةٌ مِّن رَّبِّهِ لَنُبِذَ بِالْعَرَاءِ وَهُوَ مَذْمُومٌ

50. But his Lord chose him and made him one of the righteous.

٥٠ فَاجْتَبَاهُ رَبُّهُ فَجَعَلَهُ مِنَ الصَّالِحِينَ

51. And lo! those who disbelieve would disconcert you with their eyes when they hear the Reminder, and they say: Lo! he is indeed mad;

٥١ وَإِن يَكَادُ الَّذِينَ كَفَرُوا لَيُزْلِقُونَكَ بِأَبْصَارِهِمْ لَمَّا سَمِعُوا الذِّكْرَ وَيَقُولُونَ إِنَّهُ لَمَجْنُونٌ

52. When it is nothing else than a Reminder to creation.

٥٢ وَمَا هُوَ إِلَّا ذِكْرٌ لِّلْعَالَمِينَ

308i.e., Jonah.

Reality

Al Ḥāqqah takes its name from a word that occurs several itmes in the first three verses. It belongs to the middle group of Makkan surahs.

Reality

Revealed at Makkah

*In the Name of Allah,
the Beneficent, the Merciful*

1. Reality!

2. What is Reality?

3. Ah, what will convey unto you what reality is!

4. (The tribes of) Thamūd and ʿĀd disbelieved in the judgment to come.

5. As for Thamūd, they were destroyed by the lightning.

6. And as for ʿĀd, they were destroyed by a fierce roaring wind,

7. Which He imposed on them for seven long nights and eight long days so that you might have seen men lying overthrown, as if they were hollow trunks of palm trees.

8. Can you (O Muhammad) see any remnant of them?

9. And Pharaoh and those before him, and the communities that were destroyed, brought error,

10. And they disobeyed the messenger of their Lord, therefor did He grip them with a tightening grip.

11. Lo! when the waters rose, We carried you upon the running (ship)

12. That We might make it a memorial for you, and that remembering ears (that heard the story) might remember.

13. And when the trumpet shall sound one blast

14. And the earth with the mountains shall be lifted up and crushed with one crash,

15. Then, on that day will the Event befall.

16. And the heaven will split asunder, for that day it will be frail;

① الْحَاقَّةُ

② مَا الْحَاقَّةُ

③ وَمَا أَدْرَاكَ مَا الْحَاقَّةُ

④ كَذَّبَتْ ثَمُودُ وَعَادٌ بِالْقَارِعَةِ

⑤ فَأَمَّا ثَمُودُ فَأُهْلِكُوا بِالطَّاغِيَةِ

⑥ وَأَمَّا عَادٌ فَأُهْلِكُوا بِرِيحٍ صَرْصَرٍ عَاتِيَةٍ

⑦ سَخَّرَهَا عَلَيْهِمْ سَبْعَ لَيَالٍ وَثَمَانِيَةَ أَيَّامٍ حُسُومًا فَتَرَى الْقَوْمَ فِيهَا صَرْعَى كَأَنَّهُمْ أَعْجَازُ نَخْلٍ خَاوِيَةٍ

⑧ فَهَلْ تَرَى لَهُمْ مِنْ بَاقِيَةٍ

⑨ وَجَاءَ فِرْعَوْنُ وَمَنْ قَبْلَهُ وَالْمُؤْتَفِكَاتُ بِالْخَاطِئَةِ

⑩ فَعَصَوْا رَسُولَ رَبِّهِمْ فَأَخَذَهُمْ أَخْذَةً رَابِيَةً

⑪ إِنَّا لَمَّا طَغَى الْمَاءُ حَمَلْنَاكُمْ فِي الْجَارِيَةِ

⑫ لِنَجْعَلَهَا لَكُمْ تَذْكِرَةً وَتَعِيَهَا أُذُنٌ وَاعِيَةٌ

⑬ فَإِذَا نُفِخَ فِي الصُّورِ نَفْخَةٌ وَاحِدَةٌ

⑭ وَحُمِلَتِ الْأَرْضُ وَالْجِبَالُ فَدُكَّتَا دَكَّةً وَاحِدَةً

⑮ فَيَوْمَئِذٍ وَقَعَتِ الْوَاقِعَةُ

⑯ وَانْشَقَّتِ السَّمَاءُ فَهِيَ يَوْمَئِذٍ وَاهِيَةٌ

17. And the angels will be on the sides thereof, and eight will uphold the Throne of your Lord that day, above them.

١٧ وَالْمَلَكُ عَلَى أَرْجَائِهَا وَيَحْمِلُ عَرْشَ رَبِّكَ فَوْقَهُمْ يَوْمَئِذٍ ثَمَانِيَةٌ

18. On that day you will be exposed; not a secret of you will be hidden.

١٨ يَوْمَئِذٍ تُعْرَضُونَ لَا تَخْفَى مِنكُمْ خَافِيَةٌ

19. Then, as for him who is given his record in his right hand, he will say: Take, read my book!

١٩ فَأَمَّا مَنْ أُوتِيَ كِتَابَهُ بِيَمِينِهِ فَيَقُولُ هَاؤُمُ اقْرَؤُوا كِتَابِيَهْ

20. Surely I knew that I should have to meet my reckoning.

٢٠ إِنِّي ظَنَنتُ أَنِّي مُلَاقٍ حِسَابِيَهْ

21. Then he will be in blissful state

٢١ فَهُوَ فِي عِيشَةٍ رَّاضِيَةٍ

22. In a high Garden

٢٢ فِي جَنَّةٍ عَالِيَةٍ

23. Whereof the clusters are in easy reach.

٢٣ قُطُوفُهَا دَانِيَةٌ

24. (And it will be said unto those therein): Eat and drink at ease for that which you sent on before you in past days.

٢٤ كُلُوا وَاشْرَبُوا هَنِيئًا بِمَا أَسْلَفْتُمْ فِي الْأَيَّامِ الْخَالِيَةِ

25. But as for him who is given his record in his left hand, he will say: Oh, would that I had not been given my book

٢٥ وَأَمَّا مَنْ أُوتِيَ كِتَابَهُ بِشِمَالِهِ فَيَقُولُ يَا لَيْتَنِي لَمْ أُوتَ كِتَابِيَهْ

26. And knew not what my reckoning is!

٢٦ وَلَمْ أَدْرِ مَا حِسَابِيَهْ

27. Oh, would that it had been death!

٢٧ يَا لَيْتَهَا كَانَتِ الْقَاضِيَةَ

28. My wealth has not availed me,

٢٨ مَا أَغْنَى عَنِّي مَالِيَهْ

29. My power has gone from me.

٢٩ هَلَكَ عَنِّي سُلْطَانِيَهْ

30. (It will be said): Take him and fetter him

٣٠ خُذُوهُ فَغُلُّوهُ

31. And then expose him to hellfire

٣١ ثُمَّ الْجَحِيمَ صَلُّوهُ

32. And then insert him in a chain whereof the length is seventy cubits.

٣٢ ثُمَّ فِي سِلْسِلَةٍ ذَرْعُهَا سَبْعُونَ ذِرَاعًا فَاسْلُكُوهُ

33. Lo! he used not to believe in Allah the Tremendous,

٣٣ إِنَّهُ كَانَ لَا يُؤْمِنُ بِاللَّهِ الْعَظِيمِ

34. And urged not on the feeding of the wretched,

٣٤ وَلَا يَحُضُّ عَلَى طَعَامِ الْمِسْكِينِ

35. Therefore has he no lover here this day,

٣٥ فَلَيْسَ لَهُ الْيَوْمَ هَهُنَا حَمِيمٌ

36. Nor any food save filth

٣٦ وَلَا طَعَامٌ إِلَّا مِنْ غِسْلِينٍ

37. Which none but sinners eat.

٣٧ لَا يَأْكُلُهُ إِلَّا الْخَاطِئُونَ

38. But nay! I swear by all that you see

٣٨ فَلَا أُقْسِمُ بِمَا تُبْصِرُونَ

39. And all that you see not

٣٩ وَمَا لَا تُبْصِرُونَ

40. That it is indeed the speech of an illustrious messenger.

٤٠ إِنَّهُ لَقَوْلُ رَسُولٍ كَرِيمٍ

41. It is not a poet's speech—little is it that you believe!

٤١ وَمَا هُوَ بِقَوْلِ شَاعِرٍ قَلِيلًا مَا تُؤْمِنُونَ

42. Nor a diviner's speech—little is it that you remember!

٤٢ وَلَا بِقَوْلِ كَاهِنٍ قَلِيلًا مَا تَذَكَّرُونَ

43. It is a revelation from the Lord of the Worlds.

٤٣ تَنْزِيلٌ مِّن رَّبِّ الْعَالَمِينَ

44. And if he had invented false sayings concerning Us,

٤٤ وَلَوْ تَقَوَّلَ عَلَيْنَا بَعْضَ الْأَقَاوِيلِ

45. We assuredly had taken him by the right hand

٤٥ لَأَخَذْنَا مِنْهُ بِالْيَمِينِ

46. And then severed his life artery,

٤٦ ثُمَّ لَقَطَعْنَا مِنْهُ الْوَتِينَ

47. And not one of you could have held Us off from him.

٤٧ فَمَا مِنكُم مِّنْ أَحَدٍ عَنْهُ حَاجِزِينَ

48. And lo! it is a warrant unto those who ward off (evil).

٤٨ وَإِنَّهُ لَتَذْكِرَةٌ لِّلْمُتَّقِينَ

49. And lo! We know that some among you will deny (it).

٤٩ وَإِنَّا لَنَعْلَمُ أَنَّ مِنكُم مُّكَذِّبِينَ

50. And lo! it is indeed an anguish for the disbelievers.

٥٠ وَإِنَّهُ لَحَسْرَةٌ عَلَى الْكَافِرِينَ

51. And lo! it is absolute truth.

٥١ وَإِنَّهُ لَحَقُّ الْيَقِينِ

52. So glorify the name of your Tremendous Lord.

٥٢ فَسَبِّحْ بِاسْمِ رَبِّكَ الْعَظِيمِ

The Ascending Stairways

Al Ma'ārij takes its name from a word in the third verse. An early Makkan surah.

The Ascending
Stairways

Revealed at Makkah

*In the name of Allah, the Beneficent,
the Merciful*

1. A questioner questioned concerning the doom about to fall

2. Upon the disbelievers, which none can repel,

3. From Allah, Lord of the Ascending Stairways

4. (Whereby) the angels and the Spirit ascend unto Him in a Day whereof the span is fifty thousand years.

5. But be patient (O Muhammad) with a patience fair to see.

6. Lo! they behold it afar off

7. While We behold it near:

8. The day when the sky will become as molten copper,

9. And the hills become as flakes of wool,

10. And no familiar friend will ask a question of his friend

11. Though they will be given sight of them. The guilty man will long to be able to ransom himself from the punishment of that day at the price of his children

12. And his spouse and his brother

13. And his kin that harbored him

14. And all that are in the earth, if then it might deliver him.

15. But nay! for lo! it is the fire of Hell

16. Plucking out his skull's skin;

17. It calls him who turned and fled (from truth),

18. And hoarded (wealth) and withheld it.

١٨ وَجَمَعَ فَأَوْعَىٰ

19. Lo! man was created anxious,

١٩ إِنَّ الْإِنسَانَ خُلِقَ هَلُوعًا

20. Fretful when evil befalls him

٢٠ إِذَا مَسَّهُ الشَّرُّ جَزُوعًا

21. And, when good befalls him, grudging;

٢١ وَإِذَا مَسَّهُ الْخَيْرُ مَنُوعًا

22. Save worshippers

٢٢ إِلَّا الْمُصَلِّينَ

23. Who are constant at their prayer

٢٣ الَّذِينَ هُمْ عَلَىٰ صَلَاتِهِمْ دَائِمُونَ

24. And in whose wealth there is a right acknowledged

٢٤ وَالَّذِينَ فِي أَمْوَالِهِمْ حَقٌّ مَعْلُومٌ

25. For the beggar and the destitute;

٢٥ لِّلسَّائِلِ وَالْمَحْرُومِ

26. And those who believe in the Day of Judgment,

٢٦ وَالَّذِينَ يُصَدِّقُونَ بِيَوْمِ الدِّينِ

27. And those who are fearful of their Lord's doom—

٢٧ وَالَّذِينَ هُم مِّنْ عَذَابِ رَبِّهِم مُّشْفِقُونَ

28. Lo! the doom of their Lord is that before which none can feel secure—

٢٨ إِنَّ عَذَابَ رَبِّهِمْ غَيْرُ مَأْمُونٍ

29. And those who preserve their chastity

٢٩ وَالَّذِينَ هُمْ لِفُرُوجِهِمْ حَافِظُونَ

30. Save with their wives and those whom their right hands possess, for thus they are not blameworthy;

٣٠ إِلَّا عَلَىٰ أَزْوَاجِهِمْ أَوْ مَا مَلَكَتْ أَيْمَانُهُمْ فَإِنَّهُمْ غَيْرُ مَلُومِينَ

31. But who seeks more than that, those are they who are transgressors;

٣١ فَمَنِ ابْتَغَىٰ وَرَاءَ ذَٰلِكَ فَأُولَٰئِكَ هُمُ الْعَادُونَ

32. And those who keep their pledges and their covenant.

٣٢ وَالَّذِينَ هُمْ لِأَمَانَاتِهِمْ وَعَهْدِهِمْ رَاعُونَ

33. And those who stand by their testimony

٣٣ وَالَّذِينَ هُم بِشَهَادَاتِهِمْ قَائِمُونَ

34. And those who are attentive at their prayer,

٣٤ وَالَّذِينَ هُمْ عَلَىٰ صَلَاتِهِمْ يُحَافِظُونَ

35. These will dwell in Gardens, honored.

٣٥ أُولَٰئِكَ فِي جَنَّاتٍ مُّكْرَمُونَ

36. What ails those who disbelieve, that they keep staring toward you (O Muhammad), open eyed,

٣٦ فَمَالِ الَّذِينَ كَفَرُوا قِبَلَكَ مُهْطِعِينَ

37. On the right and on the left, in groups?

٣٧ عَنِ الْيَمِينِ وَعَنِ الشِّمَالِ عِزِينَ

38. Does every man among them hope to enter the Garden of Delight?

﴾٣٨﴿ أَيَطْمَعُ كُلُّ امْرِئٍ مِّنْهُمْ أَن يُدْخَلَ جَنَّةَ نَعِيمٍ

39. Nay, surely. Lo! We created them from what they know.

﴾٣٩﴿ كَلَّا إِنَّا خَلَقْنَاهُم مِّمَّا يَعْلَمُونَ

40. But nay! I swear by the Lord of the rising places and the setting places (of the planets) that We are Able

﴾٤٠﴿ فَلَا أُقْسِمُ بِرَبِّ الْمَشَارِقِ وَالْمَغَارِبِ إِنَّا لَقَادِرُونَ

41. To replace them by (others) better than them. And We are not to be outrun.

﴾٤١﴿ عَلَىٰ أَن نُّبَدِّلَ خَيْرًا مِّنْهُمْ وَمَا نَحْنُ بِمَسْبُوقِينَ

42. So let them chat and play until they meet their Day which they are promised,

﴾٤٢﴿ فَذَرْهُمْ يَخُوضُوا وَيَلْعَبُوا حَتَّىٰ يُلَاقُوا يَوْمَهُمُ الَّذِي يُوعَدُونَ

43. The day when they come forth from the graves in haste, as racing to a goal,

﴾٤٣﴿ يَوْمَ يَخْرُجُونَ مِنَ الْأَجْدَاثِ سِرَاعًا كَأَنَّهُمْ إِلَىٰ نُصُبٍ يُوفِضُونَ

44. With eyes aghast, abasement stupefying them: Such is the Day which they are promised.

﴾٤٤﴿ خَاشِعَةً أَبْصَارُهُمْ تَرْهَقُهُمْ ذِلَّةٌ ذَٰلِكَ الْيَوْمُ الَّذِي كَانُوا يُوعَدُونَ

Noah

Nūḥ takes its name from its subject, which is the preaching of the prophet Noah. An early Makkan surah.

Noah

Revealed at Makkah

*In the name of Allah,
the Beneficent, the Merciful*

بِسْمِ اللهِ الرَّحْمٰنِ الرَّحِيمِ

1. Lo! We sent Noah unto his people (saying): Warn your people before the painful doom come unto them.

ٱ إِنَّا أَرْسَلْنَا نُوحًا إِلَىٰ قَوْمِهِ أَنْ أَنذِرْ قَوْمَكَ مِن قَبْلِ أَن يَأْتِيَهُمْ عَذَابٌ أَلِيمٌ

2. He said: O my people! Lo! I am a plain warner unto you

٢ قَالَ يَٰقَوْمِ إِنِّى لَكُمْ نَذِيرٌ مُّبِينٌ

3. (Bidding you): Worship Allah and keep your duty unto Him and obey me,

٣ أَنِ ٱعْبُدُوا۟ ٱللَّهَ وَٱتَّقُوهُ وَأَطِيعُونِ

4. That He may forgive you somewhat of your sins and respite you to an appointed term. Lo! the term of Allah, when it comes, cannot be delayed, if you but knew.

٤ يَغْفِرْ لَكُم مِّن ذُنُوبِكُمْ وَيُؤَخِّرْكُمْ إِلَىٰ أَجَلٍ مُّسَمًّى إِنَّ أَجَلَ ٱللَّهِ إِذَا جَآءَ لَا يُؤَخَّرُ لَوْ كُنتُمْ تَعْلَمُونَ

5. He said: My Lord! Lo! I have called unto my people night and day,

٥ قَالَ رَبِّ إِنِّى دَعَوْتُ قَوْمِى لَيْلًا وَنَهَارًا

6. But all my calling did but add to their repugnance;

٦ فَلَمْ يَزِدْهُمْ دُعَآءِى إِلَّا فِرَارًا

7. And lo! whenever I call unto them that You may pardon them they thrust their fingers in their ears and cover themselves with their garments and persist (in their refusal) and magnify themselves in pride.

٧ وَإِنِّى كُلَّمَا دَعَوْتُهُمْ لِتَغْفِرَ لَهُمْ جَعَلُوٓا۟ أَصَٰبِعَهُمْ فِىٓ ءَاذَانِهِمْ وَٱسْتَغْشَوْا۟ ثِيَابَهُمْ وَأَصَرُّوا۟ وَٱسْتَكْبَرُوا۟ ٱسْتِكْبَارًا

8. And lo! I have called unto them aloud,

٨ ثُمَّ إِنِّى دَعَوْتُهُمْ جِهَارًا

9. And lo! I have made public proclamation unto them, and I have appealed to them in private.

٩ ثُمَّ إِنِّىٓ أَعْلَنتُ لَهُمْ وَأَسْرَرْتُ لَهُمْ إِسْرَارًا

10. And I have said: Seek pardon of your Lord. Lo! He was ever Forgiving.

١٠ فَقُلْتُ ٱسْتَغْفِرُوا۟ رَبَّكُمْ إِنَّهُۥ كَانَ غَفَّارًا

11. He will let loose the sky for you in plenteous rain,

١١ يُرْسِلِ ٱلسَّمَآءَ عَلَيْكُم مِّدْرَارًا

12. And will help you with wealth and sons, and will assign unto you Gardens and will assign unto you rivers.

١٢ وَيُمْدِدْكُم بِأَمْوَٰلٍ وَبَنِينَ وَيَجْعَل لَّكُمْ جَنَّٰتٍ وَيَجْعَل لَّكُمْ أَنْهَٰرًا

13. What ails you that you hope not toward Allah for dignity

١٣ مَّا لَكُمْ لَا تَرْجُونَ لِلَّهِ وَقَارًا

14. When He created you by (divers) stages?

١٤ وَقَدْ خَلَقَكُمْ أَطْوَارًا

15. See you not how Allah has created seven heavens in harmony,

١٥ ‏ أَلَمْ تَرَوْا كَيْفَ خَلَقَ اللّٰهُ سَبْعَ سَمٰوٰتٍ طِبَاقًا

16. And has made the moon a light therein, and made the sun a lamp?

١٦ ‏ وَجَعَلَ الْقَمَرَ فِيهِنَّ نُورًا وَّجَعَلَ الشَّمْسَ سِرَاجًا

17. And Allah has caused you to grow as a growth from the earth,

١٧ ‏ وَاللّٰهُ أَنْبَتَكُمْ مِّنَ الْأَرْضِ نَبَاتًا

18. And afterward He makes you return thereto, and He will bring you forth again, a (new) forthbringing.

١٨ ‏ ثُمَّ يُعِيدُكُمْ فِيهَا وَيُخْرِجُكُمْ إِخْرَاجًا

19. And Allah has made the earth a wide expanse for you

١٩ ‏ وَاللّٰهُ جَعَلَ لَكُمُ الْأَرْضَ بِسَاطًا

20. That you may thread the valley ways thereof.

٢٠ ‏ لِتَسْلُكُوا مِنْهَا سُبُلًا فِجَاجًا

21. Noah said: My Lord! they have disobeyed me and followed one whose wealth and children increase him in nothing save ruin;

٢١ ‏ قَالَ نُوحٌ رَّبِّ إِنَّهُمْ عَصَوْنِي وَاتَّبَعُوا مَن لَّمْ يَزِدْهُ مَالُهُ وَوَلَدُهُ إِلَّا خَسَارًا

22. And they have plotted a mighty plot,

٢٢ ‏ وَمَكَرُوا مَكْرًا كُبَّارًا

23. And they have said: Forsake not your gods. Forsake not Wadd, nor Suwāʻ, nor Yaghūth and Yaʻūq and Nasr.[308]

٢٣ ‏ وَقَالُوا لَا تَذَرُنَّ آلِهَتَكُمْ وَلَا تَذَرُنَّ وَدًّا وَّلَا سُوَاعًا وَّلَا يَغُوثَ وَيَعُوقَ وَنَسْرًا

24. And they have led many astray, and you increase the wrongdoers in nothing save error.

٢٤ ‏ وَقَدْ أَضَلُّوا كَثِيرًا وَلَا تَزِدِ الظّٰلِمِينَ إِلَّا ضَلَالًا

25. Because of their sins they were drowned, then made to enter a Fire. And they found they had no helpers in place of Allah.

٢٥ ‏ مِّمَّا خَطِيئَاتِهِمْ أُغْرِقُوا فَأُدْخِلُوا نَارًا فَلَمْ يَجِدُوا لَهُم مِّن دُونِ اللّٰهِ أَنْصَارًا

26. And Noah said: My Lord! Leave not one of the disbelievers in the land.

٢٦ ‏ وَقَالَ نُوحٌ رَّبِّ لَا تَذَرْ عَلَى الْأَرْضِ مِنَ الْكَافِرِينَ دَيَّارًا

27. If You should leave them, they will mislead Your slaves and will beget none save lewd ingrates.

٢٧ ‏ إِنَّكَ إِن تَذَرْهُمْ يُضِلُّوا عِبَادَكَ وَلَا يَلِدُوا إِلَّا فَاجِرًا كَفَّارًا

28. My Lord! Forgive me and my parents and him who enters my house believing, and believing men and believing women, and increase not the wrongdoers in anything save ruin.

٢٨ ‏ رَّبِّ اغْفِرْ لِي وَلِوَالِدَيَّ وَلِمَن دَخَلَ بَيْتِيَ مُؤْمِنًا وَلِلْمُؤْمِنِينَ وَالْمُؤْمِنَاتِ وَلَا تَزِدِ الظّٰلِمِينَ إِلَّا تَبَارًا

---

[308]Idols of the pagan Arabs.

The Jinn

Al Jinn takes its name from a word in the first verse and from the subject of verses 1-18. The meaning of "jinn" in the Qur'an has exercised the minds of Muslim commentators for centuries. Undoubtedly the first and obvious meaning of jinn is "elemental spirits," to whom the Qur'an also came as a guidance. The incident is said to have occurred during the Prophet's return from his unsuccessful missionary journey to Ṭā'if. A late Makkan surah.

The Jinn

Revealed at Makkah

*In the name of Allah,
the Beneficent, the Merciful*

1. Say (O Muhammad): It is revealed unto me that a company of the Jinn gave ear, and they said: Lo! we have heard it is a marvelous Qur'an,

2. Which guides unto righteousness, so we believe in it and we ascribe unto our Lord no partner.

3. And (we believe) that He—exalted be the glory of our Lord!—has taken neither wife nor son,

4. And that the foolish one among us used to speak concerning Allah an atrocious lie.

5. And lo! we had supposed that humankind and jinn would not speak a lie concerning Allah—

6. And indeed (O Muhammad) individuals of humankind used to invoke the protection of individuals of the jinn so that they increased them in revolt (against Allah);

7. And indeed they supposed, even as you suppose, that Allah would not raise anyone (from the dead)—

8. And (the Jinn who had listened to the Qur'an said): We had sought the heaven but had found it filled with strong warders and meteors.

9. And we used to sit on places (high) therein to listen. But he who listened now finds a flame in wait for him[309];

10. And we know not whether harm is boded unto all who are in the earth, or whether their Lord intends guidance for them.

11. And among us there are righteous folk and among us there are far from that. We are sects having different rules.

12. And we know that we cannot escape from Allah in the earth, nor can we escape by flight.

13. And when we heard the guidance, we believed therein, and who believes in his Lord, he fears neither loss nor oppression.

---

[309]About the time of the Prophet's mission, there were many meteors and other strange events in the heavens. Tradition says that these frightened the astrol- ogers who used to sit in their high observatories and watch the sky at night. These strange events caused them to throw out their earlier calculations.

14. And there are among us some who have surrendered (to Allah) and there are among us some who are unjust. Those who have surrendered to Allah, such have taken the right path purposefully.

15. And as for those who are unjust, they are firewood for Hell.

16. If they (the idolaters) tread the right path, We shall give them to drink of water in abundance

17. That We may test them thereby; and who turns away from the remembrance of his Lord, He will thrust him into ever growing torment.

18. And the mosques are only for Allah, so pray not unto anyone along with Allah.

19. And when the slave of Allah[310] stood up in prayer to Him, they crowded on him, almost stifling.[311]

20. Say (unto them, O Muhammad): I pray unto Allah only, and ascribe unto Him no partner.

21. Say: Lo! I control not hurt nor benefit for you.

22. Say: Lo! none can protect me from Allah, nor can I find any refuge beside Him

23. (Mine is) but conveyance (of the truth) from Allah, and His messages; and who disobeys Allah and His Messenger, lo! his is fire of Hell, wherein such dwell forever.

24. Till (the day) when they shall behold that which they are promised (they may doubt); but then they will know for certain) who is weaker in allies and less in multitude.

25. Say (O Muhammad, unto the disbelievers): I know not whether that which you are promised is near, or if my Lord has set a distant term for it.

26. (He is) the Knower of the Unseen, so He reveals unto none His secret,

27. Save unto every messenger whom he has chosen, and then He makes a guard to go before him and a guard behind him

28. That He may know that they have indeed conveyed the messages of their Lord. He surrounds all their doings, and He keeps count of all things.

---

[310]i.e., the Prophet.

[311]Generally taken to allude to the rough treatment that the Prophet received at the hands of the people of Ṭā'if.

The Enshrouded One

Al Muzzammil takes its title from a word in the first verse. After his first trance and vision, the Prophet went to his wife Khadījah and told her to wrap him up in cloaks. This became his habit on such occasions, at any rate, in the early days at Makkah. This is a very early Makkan revelation, with the exception of the last verse, which all authorities assign to the Madinan period.

The Enshrouded One

Revealed at Makkah

*In the name of Allah,
the Beneficent, the Merciful*

بِسْمِ اللهِ الرَّحْمٰنِ الرَّحِيْمِ

1. O you wrapped up in your raiment!

٢ يٰٓأَيُّهَا الْمُزَّمِّلُ

2. Keep vigil the night long, save a little—

٢ قُمِ الَّيْلَ إِلَّا قَلِيْلًا

3. A half thereof, or abate a little thereof

٣ نِصْفَهُۥٓ أَوِ انْقُصْ مِنْهُ قَلِيْلًا

4. Or add (a little) thereto—and chant the Qur'an in measure,

٤ أَوْ زِدْ عَلَيْهِ وَرَتِّلِ الْقُرْءَانَ تَرْتِيْلًا

5. For We shall charge you with a word of weight.

٥ إِنَّا سَنُلْقِيْ عَلَيْكَ قَوْلًا ثَقِيْلًا

6. Lo! the vigil of the night is (a time) when impression is more keen and speech more certain.

٦ إِنَّ نَاشِئَةَ الَّيْلِ هِيَ أَشَدُّ وَطْئًا وَأَقْوَمُ قِيْلًا

7. Lo! you have by day a chain of business.

٧ إِنَّ لَكَ فِى النَّهَارِ سَبْحًا طَوِيْلًا

8. So remember the name of your Lord and devote yourself with a complete devotion—

٨ وَاذْكُرِ اسْمَ رَبِّكَ وَتَبَتَّلْ إِلَيْهِ تَبْتِيْلًا

9. Lord of the East and the West; there is no God save Him; so choose you Him alone for your defender—

٩ رَبُّ الْمَشْرِقِ وَالْمَغْرِبِ لَا إِلٰهَ إِلَّا هُوَ فَاتَّخِذْهُ وَكِيْلًا

10. And bear with patience what they utter, and part from them with a fair leave-taking.

١٠ وَاصْبِرْ عَلَىٰ مَا يَقُوْلُوْنَ وَاهْجُرْهُمْ هَجْرًا جَمِيْلًا

11. Leave Me to deal with the deniers, lords of ease and comfort (in this life); and do you respite them awhile.

١١ وَذَرْنِيْ وَالْمُكَذِّبِيْنَ أُولِى النَّعْمَةِ وَمَهِّلْهُمْ قَلِيْلًا

12. Lo! with Us are heavy fetters and a raging fire,

١٢ إِنَّ لَدَيْنَآ أَنْكَالًا وَجَحِيْمًا

13. And food which chokes (the partaker), and a painful doom

١٣ وَطَعَامًا ذَا غُصَّةٍ وَعَذَابًا أَلِيْمًا

14. On the day when the earth and the hills rock, and the hills become a heap of running sand.

١٤ يَوْمَ تَرْجُفُ الْأَرْضُ وَالْجِبَالُ وَكَانَتِ الْجِبَالُ كَثِيْبًا مَهِيْلًا

15. Lo! We have sent unto you a messenger as witness against you, even as We sent unto Pharaoh a messenger.

١٥ إِنَّا أَرْسَلْنَآ إِلَيْكُمْ رَسُوْلًا شَاهِدًا عَلَيْكُمْ كَمَآ أَرْسَلْنَآ إِلَىٰ فِرْعَوْنَ رَسُوْلًا

16. But Pharaoh rebelled against the messenger, whereupon We sealed him with no gentle grip.

١٦ فَعَصَىٰ فِرْعَوْنُ الرَّسُولَ فَأَخَذْنَٰهُ أَخْذًا وَبِيلًا

17. Then how, if you disbelieve, will you protect yourselves upon the day which will turn children grey,

١٧ فَكَيْفَ تَتَّقُونَ إِن كَفَرْتُمْ يَوْمًا يَجْعَلُ الْوِلْدَٰنَ شِيبًا

18. The very heaven being then rent asunder. His promise is to be fulfilled.

١٨ السَّمَآءُ مُنفَطِرٌ بِهِۦ كَانَ وَعْدُهُۥ مَفْعُولًا

19. Lo! This is a Reminder. Let him who will, then, choose a way unto his Lord.

١٩ إِنَّ هَٰذِهِۦ تَذْكِرَةٌ فَمَن شَآءَ اتَّخَذَ إِلَىٰ رَبِّهِۦ سَبِيلًا

20. Lo! your Lord knows how you keep vigil sometimes nearly two thirds of the night, or (sometimes) half or a third thereof, as do a party of those with you. Allah measures the night and the day. He knows that you count it not, so He turns unto you in mercy. Recite, then, of the Qur'an that which is easy for you. He knows that there are sick folk among you, while others travel in the land in search of Allah's bounty, and others (still) are fighting for the cause of Allah. So recite of it that which is easy (for you), and establish prayer and pay the poor due and (so) lend unto Allah a goodly loan.[312] Whatsoever good you send before you for your souls, you will surely find it with Allah, better and greater in the recompense. And seek forgiveness of Allah. Lo! Allah is Forgiving, Merciful.

٢٠ إِنَّ رَبَّكَ يَعْلَمُ أَنَّكَ تَقُومُ أَدْنَىٰ مِن ثُلُثَيِ الَّيْلِ وَنِصْفَهُۥ وَثُلُثَهُۥ وَطَآئِفَةٌ مِّنَ الَّذِينَ مَعَكَ وَاللَّهُ يُقَدِّرُ الَّيْلَ وَالنَّهَارَ عَلِمَ أَن لَّن تُحْصُوهُ فَتَابَ عَلَيْكُمْ فَاقْرَءُوا مَا تَيَسَّرَ مِنَ الْقُرْءَانِ عَلِمَ أَن سَيَكُونُ مِنكُم مَّرْضَىٰ وَءَاخَرُونَ يَضْرِبُونَ فِى الْأَرْضِ يَبْتَغُونَ مِن فَضْلِ اللَّهِ وَءَاخَرُونَ يُقَٰتِلُونَ فِى سَبِيلِ اللَّهِ فَاقْرَءُوا مَا تَيَسَّرَ مِنْهُ وَأَقِيمُوا الصَّلَوٰةَ وَءَاتُوا الزَّكَوٰةَ وَأَقْرِضُوا اللَّهَ قَرْضًا حَسَنًا وَمَا تُقَدِّمُوا لِأَنفُسِكُم مِّنْ خَيْرٍ تَجِدُوهُ عِندَ اللَّهِ هُوَ خَيْرًا وَأَعْظَمَ أَجْرًا وَاسْتَغْفِرُوا اللَّهَ إِنَّ اللَّهَ غَفُورٌ رَّحِيمٌ

---

[312]i.e., a loan without interest or any thought of gain or loss.

The Cloaked One

Al Muddaththir, takes its name from a word in the first verse. The Prophet used to wrap himself in his cloak at the time of the revelations. A tradition says that a period of about six months elapsed between the first revelation (Surah 96:1-5) and the second revelation in this surah. After this second incident, when the Prophet again beheld the angel who had appeared to him on Mt. Hirā', he wrapped himself in his cloak and then received the revelation of this surah. Another opinion is that by this time, the Prophet had already been ordered to begin the public (as opposed to private) preaching of Islam. He is said to have begun his public preaching three years after his call.

In either case, this is a very early Makkan surah.

The Cloaked One

Revealed at Makkah

*In the name of Allah,
the Beneficent, the Merciful*

1. you enveloped in your cloak,

2. Arise and warn!

3. Your Lord magnify,

4. Your raiment purify,

5. Pollution shun!

6. And show not favor, seeking worldly gain!

7. For the sake of your Lord, be patient!

8. For when the trumpet shall sound,

9. Surely that day will be a day of anguish,

10. Not of ease, for disbelievers.

11. Leave Me (to deal) with him whom I created lonely,

12. And then bestowed upon him ample means,

13. And sons abiding in his presence

14. And made (life) smooth for him.

15. Yet he desires that I should give more.

16. Nay! For lo! he has been stubborn to Our revelations.

17. On him I shall impose a fearful doom.

18. For lo! he did consider; then he planned

19. (Self) destroyed is he, how he planned!

20. Again (self) destroyed is he, how he planned!

٢٠ ثُمَّ قُتِلَ كَيْفَ قَدَّرَ

21. Then looked he,

٢١ ثُمَّ نَظَرَ

22. Then frowned he and showed displeasure.

٢٢ ثُمَّ عَبَسَ وَبَسَرَ

23. Then turned he away in pride

٢٣ ثُمَّ أَدْبَرَ وَاسْتَكْبَرَ

24. And said: This is nothing else than magic from of old;

٢٤ فَقَالَ إِنْ هَٰذَا إِلَّا سِحْرٌ يُؤْثَرُ

25. This is nothing else than speech of mortal man.

٢٥ إِنْ هَٰذَا إِلَّا قَوْلُ الْبَشَرِ

26. Him shall I fling unto the burning.

٢٦ سَأُصْلِيهِ سَقَرَ

27. —Ah, what will convey unto you what that burning is!—

٢٧ وَمَا أَدْرَاكَ مَا سَقَرُ

28. It leaves nothing; It spares nothing;

٢٨ لَا تُبْقِي وَلَا تَذَرُ

29. It shrivels the man.

٢٩ لَوَّاحَةٌ لِلْبَشَرِ

30. Above it are nineteen.

٣٠ عَلَيْهَا تِسْعَةَ عَشَرَ

31. We have appointed only angels to be wardens of the fire, and their number have We made to be a stumbling block for those who disbelieve; that those to whom the scripture has been given may have certainty, and that believers may increase in faith; and that those to whom the Scripture has been given and believers may not doubt; and that those in whose hearts there is disease, and disbelievers, may say: What means Allah by this similitude? Thus Allah sends astray whom He will, and whom He will He guides. None knows the hosts of your Lord save Him. This is nothing else than a Reminder unto mortals.

٣١ وَمَا جَعَلْنَا أَصْحَابَ النَّارِ إِلَّا مَلَائِكَةً وَمَا جَعَلْنَا عِدَّتَهُمْ إِلَّا فِتْنَةً لِلَّذِينَ كَفَرُوا لِيَسْتَيْقِنَ الَّذِينَ أُوتُوا الْكِتَابَ وَيَزْدَادَ الَّذِينَ آمَنُوا إِيمَانًا وَلَا يَرْتَابَ الَّذِينَ أُوتُوا الْكِتَابَ وَالْمُؤْمِنُونَ وَلِيَقُولَ الَّذِينَ فِي قُلُوبِهِمْ مَرَضٌ وَالْكَافِرُونَ مَاذَا أَرَادَ اللَّهُ بِهَٰذَا مَثَلًا كَذَٰلِكَ يُضِلُّ اللَّهُ مَنْ يَشَاءُ وَيَهْدِي مَنْ يَشَاءُ وَمَا يَعْلَمُ جُنُودَ رَبِّكَ إِلَّا هُوَ وَمَا هِيَ إِلَّا ذِكْرَى لِلْبَشَرِ

32. Nay, by the Moon

٣٢ كَلَّا وَالْقَمَرِ

33. And the night when it withdraws

٣٣ وَاللَّيْلِ إِذْ أَدْبَرَ

34. And the morning when it shines forth.

٣٤ وَالصُّبْحِ إِذَا أَسْفَرَ

35. Lo! this is one of the greatest (portents)

٣٥) إِنَّهَا لَإِحْدَى ٱلْكُبَرِ

36. As a warning unto men,

٣٦) نَذِيرًا لِّلْبَشَرِ

37. Unto him of you who will advance or hang back.

٣٧) لِمَن شَآءَ مِنكُمْ أَن يَتَقَدَّمَ أَوْ يَتَأَخَّرَ

38. Every soul is a pledge for its own deeds;

٣٨) كُلُّ نَفْسٍ بِمَا كَسَبَتْ رَهِينَةٌ

39. Save these who will stand on the right hand.

٣٩) إِلَّآ أَصْحَبَ ٱلْيَمِينِ

40. In gardens they will ask one another

٤٠) فِى جَنَّتٍ يَتَسَآءَلُونَ

41. Concerning the criminals:

٤١) عَنِ ٱلْمُجْرِمِينَ

42. What has brought you to Hell?

٤٢) مَا سَلَكَكُمْ فِى سَقَرَ

43. They will answer: We were not of those who prayed

٤٣) قَالُوا لَمْ نَكُ مِنَ ٱلْمُصَلِّينَ

44. Nor did we feed the wretched.

٤٤) وَلَمْ نَكُ نُطْعِمُ ٱلْمِسْكِينَ

45. We used to wade (in vain dispute) with (all) waders,

٤٥) وَكُنَّا نَخُوضُ مَعَ ٱلْخَآئِضِينَ

46. And we used to deny the Day of Judgment,

٤٦) وَكُنَّا نُكَذِّبُ بِيَوْمِ ٱلدِّينِ

47. Till the inevitable came unto us.

٤٧) حَتَّىٰ أَتَىٰنَا ٱلْيَقِينُ

48. The mediation of no mediators will avail them then.

٤٨) فَمَا تَنفَعُهُمْ شَفَعَةُ ٱلشَّفِعِينَ

49. Why now turn they away from the Admonishment

٤٩) فَمَا لَهُمْ عَنِ ٱلتَّذْكِرَةِ مُعْرِضِينَ

50. As if they were frightened asses

٥٠) كَأَنَّهُمْ حُمُرٌ مُّسْتَنفِرَةٌ

51. Fleeing from a lion?

٥١) فَرَّتْ مِن قَسْوَرَةٍ

52. Nay, but everyone of them desires that he should be given open pages (from Allah).

٥٢) بَلْ يُرِيدُ كُلُّ ٱمْرِئٍ مِّنْهُمْ أَن يُؤْتَىٰ صُحُفًا مُّنَشَّرَةً

53. Nay, surely. They fear not the Hereafter.

٥٣) كَلَّا بَل لَّا يَخَافُونَ ٱلْءَاخِرَةَ

54. Nay, surely. Lo! this is an Admonishment.

٥٤) كَلَّآ إِنَّهُ تَذْكِرَةٌ

55. So whoever will may heed.

٥٥) فَمَن شَآءَ ذَكَرَهُ

56. And they will not heed unless Allah wills (it). He is the Lord of righteousness, and the Lord of Forgiveness.

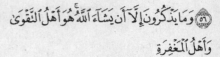

The Rising of the Dead

Al Qiyāmah takes its name from a word in the first verse. An early Makkan surah.

The Rising of the Dead

Revealed at Makkah

In the name of Allah,
the Beneficent, the Merciful

1. **N**ay, I swear by the Day of Resurrection;

2. Nay, I swear by the accusing soul (that this Scripture is true).

3. Does man think that We shall not assemble his bones?

4. Yea, surely. Yea, We are able to restore his very finger prints!

5. But man would deny what is before him.

6. He asks: When will be the Day of Resurrection?

7. But when sight is confounded

8. And the moon is eclipsed

9. And the sun and the moon are united,

10. On that day man will cry: Where to flee!

11. Alas! No refuge!

12. Unto your Lord is the recourse that day.

13. On that day man is told the tale of that which he has sent before and left behind.

14. Oh, but man is a telling witness against himself,

15. Although he tender his excuses.

16. (O Muhammad) Stir not your tongue herewith to hasten it (the Qur'an).[313]

17. Lo! upon Us (rests) the putting together thereof and the reading thereof.

18. So when We read it, follow you its reading;

19. Then lo! upon Us (rests) the explanation thereof.

---

[313]i.e., the Qur'an, which was revealed in sections over a period of twenty-three years.

20. Nay, but you do love the fleeting Now

21. And neglect the Hereafter.

22. That day will faces be resplendent,

23. Looking toward their Lord;

24. And that day will other faces be despondent,

25. They suspect that some great disaster is about to fall on them.

26. Nay, but when the life comes up to the throat

27. And men say: Sho is there to recite (to save it)?

28. And he thinks that it is the parting;

29. And agony is heaped on agony;

30. Unto your Lord that day will be the driving.

31. For he neither believed, nor prayed,

32. But he denied and flouted.

33. Then went he to his folk with glee.

34. Nearer unto you and nearer,

35. Again nearer unto you and nearer (is the doom).

36. Does man think that he is to be left aimless?

37. Was he not a drop of fluid which gushed forth?

38. Then he became a clot; then (Allah) shaped and fashioned

39. And made of him a pair, the male and female.

40. Is not He (who does so) able to bring the dead to life?

Time or Man

Both titles of this surah, *Al Dahr* or *Al Insān*, are derived from a word in the first verse. An early Makkan surah.

Time or Man

Revealed at Makkah

*In the name of Allah,
the Beneficent, the Merciful*

1. **H**as there come upon man (ever) any period of time in which he was a thing unremembered?

2. Lo! We created man from a drop of blended fluid to test him; so We made him hearing, knowing.

3. Lo! We have shown him the way, whether he be grateful or disbelieving.

4. Lo! We have prepared for disbelievers manacles and iron collars and a raging fire.

5. Lo! the righteous shall drink of a cup whereof the mixture is of water of Kāfūr,

6. A spring wherefrom the slaves of Allah drink, making it gush forth abundantly,

7. Because they perform the vow and fear a day whereof the evil is widespreading,

8. And they feed with food the needy wretch, the orphan and the prisoner, for love of Him,[314]

9. (Saying): We feed you, for the sake of Allah only. We wish for no reward nor thanks from you;

10. Lo! we fear from our Lord a day of frowning that is severe in frowning.

11. Therefore Allah has warded from them the evil of that day, and has made them find brightness and joy;

12. And has awarded them for all that they endured, a Garden and silk attire;

13. Reclining therein upon couches, they will find there neither (heat of) a sun nor bitter cold.

14. The shade thereof is close upon them and the clustered fruits thereof bow down.

15. Goblets of silver are brought round for them, and beakers (as) of glass

---

314Another meaning is that they feed the food despite their love to and need for it (the editor).

16. (Bright as) glass but (made) of silver, which they (themselves) have measured to the measure (of their deeds).

17. There are they watered with a cup whereof the mixture is of Zanjabīl,

18. The water of a spring therein, named Salsabīl.

19. There serve them youths of who perish not, whom, when you see, you would take for scattered pearls.

20. When you see, you will see there bliss and high estate.

21. Their raiment will be fine green silk and gold embroidery. Bracelets of silver will they wear. Their Lord will slake their thirst with a pure drink.

22. (And it will be said unto them): Lo! this is a reward for you. Your endeavor (upon earth) has found acceptance.

23. Lo! We, even We, have revealed unto you (O Muham-mad) the Qur'an, a revelation;

24. So submit patiently to your Lord's command, and obey not of them any guilty one or disbeliever.

25. Remember the name of your Lord at morn and evening.

26. And prostrate yourself unto Him (a portion) of the night. And glorify Him through the livelong night.

27. Lo! these love fleeting life, and put behind them (the remembrance of) a grievous day.

28. We, even We, created them, and strengthened their frame. And when We will, We can replace them, bringing others like them in their stead.

29. Lo! this is an Admonishment, that whoever will may choose a way unto his Lord.

30. Yet you will not, unless Allah wills. Lo! Allah is Knower, Wise.

31. He makes whom He will to enter His mercy, and for evildoers has prepared a painful doom.

١٦ قَوَارِيرَا۟ مِن فِضَّةٍ قَدَّرُوهَا تَقْدِيرًا

١٧ وَيُسْقَوْنَ فِيهَا كَأْسًا كَانَ مِزَاجُهَا زَنجَبِيلًا

١٨ عَيْنًا فِيهَا تُسَمَّىٰ سَلْسَبِيلًا

١٩ ۞ وَيَطُوفُ عَلَيْهِمْ وِلْدَانٌ مُّخَلَّدُونَ إِذَا رَأَيْتَهُمْ حَسِبْتَهُمْ لُؤْلُؤًا مَّنثُورًا

٢٠ وَإِذَا رَأَيْتَ ثَمَّ رَأَيْتَ نَعِيمًا وَمُلْكًا كَبِيرًا

٢١ عَٰلِيَهُمْ ثِيَابُ سُندُسٍ خُضْرٌ وَإِسْتَبْرَقٌ وَحُلُّوٓا۟ أَسَاوِرَ مِن فِضَّةٍ وَسَقَىٰهُمْ رَبُّهُمْ شَرَابًا طَهُورًا

٢٢ إِنَّ هَٰذَا كَانَ لَكُمْ جَزَآءً وَكَانَ سَعْيُكُم مَّشْكُورًا

٢٣ إِنَّا نَحْنُ نَزَّلْنَا عَلَيْكَ ٱلْقُرْءَانَ تَنزِيلًا

٢٤ فَٱصْبِرْ لِحُكْمِ رَبِّكَ وَلَا تُطِعْ مِنْهُمْ ءَاثِمًا أَوْ كَفُورًا

٢٥ وَٱذْكُرِ ٱسْمَ رَبِّكَ بُكْرَةً وَأَصِيلًا

٢٦ وَمِنَ ٱلَّيْلِ فَٱسْجُدْ لَهُ وَسَبِّحْهُ لَيْلًا طَوِيلًا

٢٧ إِنَّ هَٰٓؤُلَآءِ يُحِبُّونَ ٱلْعَاجِلَةَ وَيَذَرُونَ وَرَآءَهُمْ يَوْمًا ثَقِيلًا

٢٨ نَّحْنُ خَلَقْنَٰهُمْ وَشَدَدْنَآ أَسْرَهُمْ وَإِذَا شِئْنَا بَدَّلْنَآ أَمْثَٰلَهُمْ تَبْدِيلًا

٢٩ إِنَّ هَٰذِهِ تَذْكِرَةٌ فَمَن شَآءَ ٱتَّخَذَ إِلَىٰ رَبِّهِ سَبِيلًا

٣٠ وَمَا تَشَآءُونَ إِلَّآ أَن يَشَآءَ ٱللَّهُ إِنَّ ٱللَّهَ كَانَ عَلِيمًا حَكِيمًا

٣١ يُدْخِلُ مَن يَشَآءُ فِي رَحْمَتِهِ وَٱلظَّٰلِمِينَ أَعَدَّ لَهُمْ عَذَابًا أَلِيمًا

The Emissaries

Al Mursalāt takes its name from a word in the first verse. Verses 1-3 are taken to refer to winds, while verses 4 and 5 are said to refer to angels. An early Makkan surah.

The Emissaries

Revealed at Makkah

*In the name of Allah,
the Beneficent, the Merciful*

1. By the emissary winds, (sent) one after another

ٱ وَٱلْمُرْسَلَٰتِ عُرْفًا

2. By the raging hurricanes,

٢ فَٱلْعَٰصِفَٰتِ عَصْفًا

3. By those which cause earth's vegetation to revive;

٣ وَٱلنَّٰشِرَٰتِ نَشْرًا

4. By those who winnow with a winnowing,

٤ فَٱلْفَٰرِقَٰتِ فَرْقًا

5. By those who bring down the Reminder,

٥ فَٱلْمُلْقِيَٰتِ ذِكْرًا

6. To excuse or to warn,

٦ عُذْرًا أَوْ نُذْرًا

7. Surely that which you are promised will befall.

٧ إِنَّمَا تُوعَدُونَ لَوَٰقِعٌ

8. So when the stars are put out,

٨ فَإِذَا ٱلنُّجُومُ طُمِسَتْ

9. And when the sky is riven asunder,

٩ وَإِذَا ٱلسَّمَآءُ فُرِجَتْ

10. And when the mountains are blown away,

١٠ وَإِذَا ٱلْجِبَالُ نُسِفَتْ

11. And when the messengers are brought unto their time appointed—

١١ وَإِذَا ٱلرُّسُلُ أُقِّتَتْ

12. For what day is the time appointed?

١٢ لِأَيِّ يَوْمٍ أُجِّلَتْ

13. For the Day of Decision.

١٣ لِيَوْمِ ٱلْفَصْلِ

14. And what will convey unto you what the Day of Deci-sion is!—

١٤ وَمَآ أَدْرَىٰكَ مَا يَوْمُ ٱلْفَصْلِ

15. Woe unto the repudiators on that day!

١٥ وَيْلٌ يَوْمَئِذٍ لِّلْمُكَذِّبِينَ

16. Destroyed We not the former folk,

١٦ أَلَمْ نُهْلِكِ ٱلْأَوَّلِينَ

17. Then caused the latter folk to follow after?

١٧ ثُمَّ نُتْبِعُهُمُ ٱلْآخِرِينَ

18. Thus deal We ever with the criminals.

١٨ كَذَٰلِكَ نَفْعَلُ بِٱلْمُجْرِمِينَ

19. Woe unto the repudiators on that day!

١٩ وَيْلٌ يَوْمَئِذٍ لِّلْمُكَذِّبِينَ

20. Did We not create you from a base fluid

٢٠ أَلَمْ نَخْلُقْكُّم مِّن مَّآءٍ مَّهِينٍ

21. Which We laid up in a safe abode

٢١ فَجَعَلْنَهُ فِى قَرَارٍ مَّكِينٍ

22. For a known term?

٢٢ إِلَىٰ قَدَرٍ مَّعْلُومٍ

23. Thus We arranged. How excellent is Our arranging!

٢٣ فَقَدَرْنَا فَنِعْمَ ٱلْقَدِرُونَ

24. Woe unto the repudiators on that day!

٢٤ وَيْلٌ يَوْمَئِذٍ لِّلْمُكَذِّبِينَ

25. Have We not made the earth a receptacle

٢٥ أَلَمْ نَجْعَلِ ٱلْأَرْضَ كِفَاتًا

26. Both for the living and the dead,

٢٦ أَحْيَآءً وَأَمْوَٰتًا

27. And placed therein high mountains and given you to drink sweet water therein?

٢٧ وَجَعَلْنَا فِيهَا رَوَٰسِىَ شَٰمِخَٰتٍ وَأَسْقَيْنَٰكُم مَّآءً فُرَاتًا

28. Woe unto the repudiators on that day!

٢٨ وَيْلٌ يَوْمَئِذٍ لِّلْمُكَذِّبِينَ

29. (It will be said unto them:) Depart unto that (doom) which you used to deny;

٢٩ ٱنطَلِقُوٓا۟ إِلَىٰ مَا كُنتُم بِهِۦ تُكَذِّبُونَ

30. Depart unto the shadow falling threefold.

٣٠ ٱنطَلِقُوٓا۟ إِلَىٰ ظِلٍّ ذِى ثَلَٰثِ شُعَبٍ

31. (Which yet is) no relief nor shelter from the flame.

٣١ لَّا ظَلِيلٍ وَلَا يُغْنِى مِنَ ٱللَّهَبِ

32. Lo! it throws up sparks like castles,

٣٢ إِنَّهَا تَرْمِى بِشَرَرٍ كَٱلْقَصْرِ

33. (Or) as it might be camels of bright yellow hue.

٣٣ كَأَنَّهُۥ جِمَٰلَتٌ صُفْرٌ

34. Woe unto the repudiators on that day!

٣٤ وَيْلٌ يَوْمَئِذٍ لِّلْمُكَذِّبِينَ

35. This is a day wherein they speak not,

٣٥ هَٰذَا يَوْمُ لَا يَنطِقُونَ

36. Nor are they suffered to put forth excuses.

٣٦ وَلَا يُؤْذَنُ لَهُمْ فَيَعْتَذِرُونَ

37. Woe unto the repudiators on that day!

٣٧ وَيْلٌ يَوْمَئِذٍ لِّلْمُكَذِّبِينَ

38. This is the Day of Decision, We have brought you and the men of old together.

٣٨ هَٰذَا يَوْمُ ٱلْفَصْلِ جَمَعْنَٰكُمْ وَٱلْأَوَّلِينَ

39. If now you have any wit, outwit Me.

٣٩ فَإِن كَانَ لَكُمْ كَيْدٌ فَكِيدُونِ

40. Woe unto the repudiators on that day!

٤٠ وَيْلٌ يَوْمَئِذٍ لِّلْمُكَذِّبِينَ

41. Lo! those who kept their duty are amid shade and fountains,

٤١ إِنَّ الْمُتَّقِينَ فِي ظِلَالٍ وَعُيُونٍ

42. And fruits such as they desire.

٤٢ وَفَوَاكِهَ مِمَّا يَشْتَهُونَ

43. (Unto them it is said:) Eat, drink and welcome, O you blessed, in return for what you did.

٤٣ كُلُوا وَاشْرَبُوا هَنِيئًا بِمَا كُنْتُمْ تَعْمَلُونَ

44. Thus do We reward the good.

٤٤ إِنَّا كَذَلِكَ نَجْزِي الْمُحْسِنِينَ

45. Woe unto the repudiators on that day!

٤٥ وَيْلٌ يَوْمَئِذٍ لِلْمُكَذِّبِينَ

46. Eat and take your ease (on earth) a little. Lo! you are criminals.

٤٦ كُلُوا وَتَمَتَّعُوا قَلِيلًا إِنَّكُمْ مُجْرِمُونَ

47. Woe unto the repudiators on that day!

٤٧ وَيْلٌ يَوْمَئِذٍ لِلْمُكَذِّبِينَ

48. When it is said unto them: Bow down, they bow not down!

٤٨ وَإِذَا قِيلَ لَهُمُ ارْكَعُوا لَا يَرْكَعُونَ

49. Woe unto the repudiators on that day!

٤٩ وَيْلٌ يَوْمَئِذٍ لِلْمُكَذِّبِينَ

50. In what statement, after this, will they believe?

٥٠ فَبِأَيِّ حَدِيثٍ بَعْدَهُ يُؤْمِنُونَ

The Tidings

Al Naba' takes its name from a word in the second verse. An early Makkan surah.

The Tidings

Revealed at Makkah

*In the name of Allah,
the Beneficent, the Merciful*

1. Whereof do they question one another?

2. (It is) of the awful tidings,

3. Concerning which they are in disagreement.

4. Nay, but they will come to know!

5. Nay, again, but they will come to know!

6. Have We not made the earth an expanse,

7. And the high mountains bulwarks?

8. And We have created you in pairs,

9. And have appointed your sleep for repose,

10. And have appointed the night as a garment,

11. And have appointed the day for livelihood.

12. And We have built above you seven strong (heavens),

13. And have appointed a dazzling lamp,

14. And have sent down from the rainy clouds abundant water,

15. Thereby to produce grain and plant,

16. And gardens of thick foliage.

17. Lo! the Day of Decision is a fixed time,

18. A day when the trumpet is blown, and you come in multitudes,

19. And the heaven is opened and becomes as gates,

١ عَمَّ يَتَسَآءَلُونَ

٢ عَنِ ٱلنَّبَإِ ٱلْعَظِيمِ

٣ ٱلَّذِى هُمْ فِيهِ مُخْتَلِفُونَ

٤ كَلَّا سَيَعْلَمُونَ

٥ ثُمَّ كَلَّا سَيَعْلَمُونَ

٦ أَلَمْ نَجْعَلِ ٱلْأَرْضَ مِهَٰدًا

٧ وَٱلْجِبَالَ أَوْتَادًا

٨ وَخَلَقْنَٰكُمْ أَزْوَٰجًا

٩ وَجَعَلْنَا نَوْمَكُمْ سُبَاتًا

١٠ وَجَعَلْنَا ٱلَّيْلَ لِبَاسًا

١١ وَجَعَلْنَا ٱلنَّهَارَ مَعَاشًا

١٢ وَبَنَيْنَا فَوْقَكُمْ سَبْعًا شِدَادًا

١٣ وَجَعَلْنَا سِرَاجًا وَهَّاجًا

١٤ وَأَنزَلْنَا مِنَ ٱلْمُعْصِرَٰتِ مَآءً ثَجَّاجًا

١٥ لِنُخْرِجَ بِهِۦ حَبًّا وَنَبَاتًا

١٦ وَجَنَّٰتٍ أَلْفَافًا

١٧ إِنَّ يَوْمَ ٱلْفَصْلِ كَانَ مِيقَٰتًا

١٨ يَوْمَ يُنفَخُ فِى ٱلصُّورِ فَتَأْتُونَ أَفْوَاجًا

١٩ وَفُتِحَتِ ٱلسَّمَآءُ فَكَانَتْ أَبْوَابًا

20. And the hills are set in motion and become as a mirage.

21. Lo! Hell lurks in ambush,

22. A home for the rebellious.

23. They will abide therein for ages.

24. Therein taste they neither coolness nor (any) drink

25. Save boiling water and a paralyzing cold:

26. Reward proportioned (to their evil deeds).

27. For lo! they looked not for a reckoning;

28. They called Our revelations false with strong denial.

29. Everything have We recorded in a Book.

30. So taste (of that which you have earned). No increase do We give you save of torment.

31. Lo! for the duteous is achievement—

32. Gardens enclosed and vineyards,

33. And maidens for companions,

34. And a full cup.

35. There hear they neither vain discourse nor lying—

36. Requital from your Lord—a gift in payment—

37. Lord of the heavens and the earth, and (all) that is between them, the Beneficent; with Whom none can converse.

38. On the day when the angels and the Spirit stand arrayed, they speak not, saving him whom the Beneficent allows and who speaks right.

39. That is the True Day. So who will should seek recourse unto his Lord.

40. Lo! We warn you of a doom at hand, a day whereon a man will look on that which his own hands have sent before, and the disbeliever will cry: "Would that I were dust!"

٢٠ وَسُيِّرَتِ الْجِبَالُ فَكَانَتْ سَرَابًا

٢١ إِنَّ جَهَنَّمَ كَانَتْ مِرْصَادًا

٢٢ لِلطَّاغِينَ مَآبًا

٢٣ لَّابِثِينَ فِيهَا أَحْقَابًا

٢٤ لَّا يَذُوقُونَ فِيهَا بَرْدًا وَلَا شَرَابًا

٢٥ إِلَّا حَمِيمًا وَغَسَّاقًا

٢٦ جَزَآءً وِفَاقًا

٢٧ إِنَّهُمْ كَانُوا لَا يَرْجُونَ حِسَابًا

٢٨ وَكَذَّبُوا بِآيَاتِنَا كِذَّابًا

٢٩ وَكُلَّ شَيْءٍ أَحْصَيْنَاهُ كِتَابًا

٣٠ فَذُوقُوا فَلَن نَّزِيدَكُمْ إِلَّا عَذَابًا

٣١ إِنَّ لِلْمُتَّقِينَ مَفَازًا

٣٢ حَدَآئِقَ وَأَعْنَابًا

٣٣ وَكَوَاعِبَ أَتْرَابًا

٣٤ وَكَأْسًا دِهَاقًا

٣٥ لَّا يَسْمَعُونَ فِيهَا لَغْوًا وَلَا كِذَّابًا

٣٦ جَزَآءً مِّن رَّبِّكَ عَطَآءً حِسَابًا

٣٧ رَّبِّ السَّمَاوَاتِ وَالْأَرْضِ وَمَا بَيْنَهُمَا الرَّحْمَٰنِ لَا يَمْلِكُونَ مِنْهُ خِطَابًا

٣٨ يَوْمَ يَقُومُ الرُّوحُ وَالْمَلَائِكَةُ صَفًّا لَّا يَتَكَلَّمُونَ إِلَّا مَنْ أَذِنَ لَهُ الرَّحْمَٰنُ وَقَالَ صَوَابًا

٣٩ ذَٰلِكَ الْيَوْمُ الْحَقُّ فَمَن شَآءَ اتَّخَذَ إِلَىٰ رَبِّهِ مَآبًا

٤٠ إِنَّا أَنذَرْنَاكُمْ عَذَابًا قَرِيبًا يَوْمَ يَنظُرُ الْمَرْءُ مَا قَدَّمَتْ يَدَاهُ وَيَقُولُ الْكَافِرُ يَا لَيْتَنِي كُنتُ تُرَابًا

Those Who Drag Forth

Al Nāzi'āt takes its name from a word in the first verse. An early Makkan surah.

Those Who Drag Forth

Revealed at Makkah

*In the name of Allah,
the Beneficent, the Merciful*

1. By those who drag forth to destruction,

2. By the meteors rushing,

3. By the lone stars floating,[315]

4. By the angels hastening,

5. And those who govern the event,

6. On the day when the first trump resounds

7. And the second follows it,

8. On that day hearts beat painfully

9. While eyes are downcast

10. (Now) they are saying: Shall we really be restored to our first state

11. Even after we are crumbled bones?

12. They say: Then that would be a losing return.

13. Surely it will need but one shout,

14. And lo! they will be awakened.

15. Has there come unto you the history of Moses?

16. How his Lord called him in the holy vale of Ṭuwā,

17. (Saying:) Go you unto Pharaoh— Lo! he has rebelled—

18. And say (unto him): Have you (will) to grow (in grace)?

19. Then I will guide you to your Lord and you shall fear (Him).

---

[315]Some commentators say verses 2-3 refer to angels and explain them thus: "By those who console (the spirits of the righteous) tenderly" and "By those who come floating (down from heaven with their Lord's command)." The rendering given in the text above is the more obvious.

20. And he showed him the tremendous token.

21. But he denied and disobeyed,

22. Then turned he away in haste,

23. Then gathered he and summoned

24. And proclaimed: "I (Pharaoh) am your Lord the Highest."

25. So Allah seized him (and made him) an example for the after (life) and for the former.

26. Lo! herein is indeed a lesson for him who fears.

27. Are you the harder to create, or is the heaven that He built?

28. He raised the height thereof and ordered it;

29. And He made dark the night thereof, and He brought forth the morn thereof.

30. And after that He spread the earth,

31. And produced therefrom the water thereof and the pasture thereof,

32. And He made fast the mountains,

33. A provision for you and for your cattle.

34. But when the great disaster comes,

35. The day when man will call to mind his (whole) endeavor,

36. And Hell will stand forth visible to him who sees,

37. Then, as for him who rebelled

38. And preferred the life of the world,

39. Lo! Hell will be his home.

40. But as for him who feared to stand before his Lord and restrained his soul from lust,

41. Lo! the Garden will be his home.

42. They ask you of the Hour: when will it come to port?

٢٠ فَأَرَىٰهُ ٱلۡأٓيَةَ ٱلۡكُبۡرَىٰ

٢١ فَكَذَّبَ وَعَصَىٰ

٢٢ ثُمَّ أَدۡبَرَ يَسۡعَىٰ

٢٣ فَحَشَرَ فَنَادَىٰ

٢٤ فَقَالَ أَنَا۠ رَبُّكُمُ ٱلۡأَعۡلَىٰ

٢٥ فَأَخَذَهُ ٱللَّهُ نَكَالَ ٱلۡأٓخِرَةِ وَٱلۡأُولَىٰ

٢٦ إِنَّ فِى ذَٰلِكَ لَعِبۡرَةً لِّمَن يَخۡشَىٰ

٢٧ ءَأَنتُمۡ أَشَدُّ خَلۡقًا أَمِ ٱلسَّمَآءُ بَنَىٰهَا

٢٨ رَفَعَ سَمۡكَهَا فَسَوَّىٰهَا

٢٩ وَأَغۡطَشَ لَيۡلَهَا وَأَخۡرَجَ ضُحَىٰهَا

٣٠ وَٱلۡأَرۡضَ بَعۡدَ ذَٰلِكَ دَحَىٰهَا

٣١ أَخۡرَجَ مِنۡهَا مَآءَهَا وَمَرۡعَىٰهَا

٣٢ وَٱلۡجِبَالَ أَرۡسَىٰهَا

٣٣ مَتَٰعًا لَّكُمۡ وَلِأَنۡعَٰمِكُمۡ

٣٤ فَإِذَا جَآءَتِ ٱلطَّآمَّةُ ٱلۡكُبۡرَىٰ

٣٥ يَوۡمَ يَتَذَكَّرُ ٱلۡإِنسَٰنُ مَا سَعَىٰ

٣٦ وَبُرِّزَتِ ٱلۡجَحِيمُ لِمَن يَرَىٰ

٣٧ فَأَمَّا مَن طَغَىٰ

٣٨ وَءَاثَرَ ٱلۡحَيَوٰةَ ٱلدُّنۡيَا

٣٩ فَإِنَّ ٱلۡجَحِيمَ هِىَ ٱلۡمَأۡوَىٰ

٤٠ وَأَمَّا مَنۡ خَافَ مَقَامَ رَبِّهِ وَنَهَى ٱلنَّفۡسَ عَنِ ٱلۡهَوَىٰ

٤١ فَإِنَّ ٱلۡجَنَّةَ هِىَ ٱلۡمَأۡوَىٰ

٤٢ يَسۡـَٔلُونَكَ عَنِ ٱلسَّاعَةِ أَيَّانَ مُرۡسَىٰهَا

43. Why (ask they)? What have you
to tell thereof?

فِيْمَ اَنْتَ مِنْ ذِكْرَاهَا ﴿٤٣﴾

44. Unto your Lord belongs (knowledge of) the term thereof.

اِلٰى رَبِّكَ مُنْتَهَاهَا ﴿٤٤﴾

45. You are but a warner unto him
who fears it.

اِنَّمَاۤ اَنْتَ مُنْذِرُ مَنْ يَّخْشَاهَا ﴿٤٥﴾

46. On the day when they behold it,
it will be as if they had but tarried for
an evening or the morn thereof.

كَاَنَّهُمْ يَوْمَ يَرَوْنَهَا لَمْ يَلْبَثُوْۤا اِلَّا عَشِيَّةً اَوْ ضُحٰىهَا ﴿٤٦﴾

He Frowned

'Abasa, "He Frowned," takes its name from the first word. Once when the Prophet was talking with some of the great men of Quraysh (his tribe) in an attempt to persuade them of the truth of Islam, a blind man came and asked a question concerning the faith. The Prophet was annoyed at this interruption, and thus frowned and turned away from the blind man. Here, he is told that a man's importance is not to be derived from his appearance or worldly station.

An early Makkan surah.

He Frowned

Revealed at Makkah

*In the name of Allah,
the Beneficent, the Merciful*

1. He frowned and turned away

2. Because the blind man came unto him.

3. What could inform you but that he might grow (in grace)

4. Or take heed and so the reminder might avail him?

5. As for him who thinks himself independent,

6. Unto him you pay regard.

7. Yet it is not your concern if he grow not (in grace).

8. But as for him who comes unto you with earnest purpose

9. And has fear,

10. From him you are distracted.

11. Nay, but surely it is an Admonishment,

12. So let whosoever will pay heed to it,

13. (Written) in volumes honorable

14. Exalted, purified,

15. (Set down) by scribes (the angels)

16. Noble and righteous.

17. Man is (self) destroyed: how ungrateful!

18. From what thing does He create him?

19. From a drop of seed. He creates him and proportions him,

20. Then makes the way easy for him,

21. Then causes him to die, and buries him;

٢١ ثُمَّ أَمَاتَهُ فَأَقْبَرَهُ

22. Then, when He will, He brings him again to life.

٢٢ ثُمَّ إِذَا شَاءَ أَنْشَرَهُ

23. Nay, but (man) has not done what He commanded him.

٢٣ كَلَّا لَمَّا يَقْضِ مَا أَمَرَهُ

24. Let man consider his food:

٢٤ فَلْيَنْظُرِ الْإِنْسَنُ إِلَى طَعَامِهِ

25. How we pour water in showers

٢٥ أَنَّا صَبَبْنَا الْمَاءَ صَبًّا

26. Then split the earth in clefts

٢٦ ثُمَّ شَقَقْنَا الْأَرْضَ شَقًّا

27. And cause the grain to grow therein

٢٧ فَأَنْبَتْنَا فِيهَا حَبًّا

28. And grapes and green fodder

٢٨ وَعِنَبًا وَقَضْبًا

29. And olive trees and palm trees

٢٩ وَزَيْتُونًا وَنَخْلًا

30. And garden closes of thick foliage

٣٠ وَحَدَائِقَ غُلْبًا

31. And fruits and grasses:

٣١ وَفَكِهَةً وَأَبًّا

32. Provision for you and your cattle.

٣٢ مَتَاعًا لَكُمْ وَلِأَنْعَامِكُمْ

33. But when the Shout comes,

٣٣ فَإِذَا جَاءَتِ الصَّاخَّةُ

34. On the day when a man flees from his brother

٣٤ يَوْمَ يَفِرُّ الْمَرْءُ مِنْ أَخِيهِ

35. And his mother and his father

٣٥ وَأُمِّهِ وَأَبِيهِ

36. And his wife and his children,

٣٦ وَصَحِبَتِهِ وَبَنِيهِ

37. Every man that day will have concern enough to make him heedless (of others).

٣٧ لِكُلِّ امْرِئٍ مِنْهُمْ يَوْمَئِذٍ شَأْنٌ يُغْنِيهِ

38. On that day faces will be bright as dawn,

٣٨ وُجُوهٌ يَوْمَئِذٍ مُسْفِرَةٌ

39. Laughing, rejoicing at good news;

٣٩ ضَاحِكَةٌ مُسْتَبْشِرَةٌ

40. And other faces, on that day, with dust upon them,

٤٠ وَوُجُوهٌ يَوْمَئِذٍ عَلَيْهَا غَبَرَةٌ

41. Veiled in darkness,

٤١ تَرْهَقُهَا قَتَرَةٌ

42. Those are they who are the disbelievers, the wicked.

٤٢ أُولَئِكَ هُمُ الْكَفَرَةُ الْفَجَرَةُ

The Overthrowing

Al Takwīr takes its name from a word in the first verse. Verses 8 and 9 allude to the pagan Arabs' practice of burying newborn female infants, whom they deemed superfluous, alive. An early Makkan surah.

The Overthrowing

Revealed at Makkah

*In the name of Allah,
the Beneficent, the Merciful*

1. When the sun is overthrown,

2. And when the stars fall,

3. And when the mountains are moved,

4. And when the camels big with young are abandoned,

5. And when the wild beasts are herded together,

6. And when the seas boil over with a swell,

7. And when souls are reunited,

8. And when the girl child that was buried alive is asked

9. For what sin she was slain,

10. And when the pages are laid open,

11. And when the sky is torn away,

12. And when Hell is lighted

13. And when the garden is brought nigh

14. (Then) every soul will know what it has made ready.

15. Oh, but I call to witness the planets,

16. The stars which rise and set,

17. And the close of night,[316]

18. And the breath of morning[317]

19. That this is in truth the word of an honored messenger,

---

[316]Lit: "And the night when it closes."
[317] Lit: "And the morning when it breathes."

20. Mighty, established in the presence of the Lord of the Throne,

٢٠) ذِى قُوَّةٍ عِندَ ذِى الْعَرْشِ مَكِينٍ

21. (One) to be obeyed, and trust-worthy;

٢١) مُّطَاعٍ ثَمَّ أَمِينٍ

22. And your comrade is not mad.

٢٢) وَمَا صَاحِبُكُم بِمَجْنُونٍ

23. Surely he beheld him on the clear horizon.

٢٣) وَلَقَدْ رَءَاهُ بِالْأُفُقِ الْمُبِينِ

24. And he is not avid of the Unseen.

٢٤) وَمَا هُوَ عَلَى الْغَيْبِ بِضَنِينٍ

25. Nor is this the utterance of a devil worthy to be stoned

٢٥) وَمَا هُوَ بِقَوْلِ شَيْطَانٍ رَجِيمٍ

26. Whither then go you?

٢٦) فَأَيْنَ تَذْهَبُونَ

27. This is nothing else than a reminder unto the worlds,

٢٧) إِنْ هُوَ إِلَّا ذِكْرٌ لِّلْعَالَمِينَ

28. Unto whomsoever of you wills to walk straight.

٢٨) لِمَن شَآءَ مِنكُمْ أَن يَسْتَقِيمَ

29. And you will not, unless (it be) that Allah wills, the Lord of the worlds.

٢٩) وَمَا تَشَآءُونَ إِلَّا أَن يَشَآءَ اللَّهُ رَبُّ الْعَالَمِينَ

The Cleaving

Al Infiṭār takes its name from a word in the first verse. An early Makkan surah.

The Cleaving

Revealed at Makkah

*In the name of Allah,
the Beneficent, the Merciful*

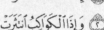

1. When the heaven is cleft asunder,

2. When the planets are dispersed,

3. When the seas are poured forth,

4. And the graves are overturned,

5. A soul will know what it has sent before (it) and what it left behind.

6. O man! What has made you careless concerning your Lord, the Bountiful,

7. Who created you, then fashioned you, then proportioned you?

8. Into whatsoever form He will, He casts you

9. Nay, but you deny the Judgment.

10. Lo! there are above you guardians,

11. Generous and recording,

12. Who know (all) that you do.

13. Lo! the righteous surely will be in delight

14. And lo! the wicked surely will be in Hell;

15. They will burn therein on the Day of Judgment,

16. And will not be absent thence.

17. Ah, what will convey unto you what the Day of Judg-ment is!

18. Again, what will convey unto you what the Day of Judgment is!

19. A day on which no soul has power at all for any (other) soul. The (absolute) command on that day is Allah's.

The Dealers in Fraud

Al Muṭaffifin "The Dealers in Fraud," takes its name from a word in the first verse. An early Makkan surah.

The Dealers in Fraud

Revealed at Makkah

*In the name of Allah,
the Beneficent, the Merciful*

1. Woe unto the defrauders:

2. Those who when they take the measure from mankind demand it full,

3. But if they measure unto them or weigh for them, they cause them loss.

4. Do such (men) not consider that they will be raised again

5. Unto an awful Day,

6. The day when (all) mankind stand before the Lord of the Worlds?

7. Nay, but the record of the vile is in Sijjīn—

8. Ah! what will convey unto you what Sijjīn is!—

9. A written record.

10. Woe unto the repudiators on that day!

11. Those who deny the Day of Judgment

12. Which none denies save each criminal transgressor,

13. Who, when you read unto him Our revelations, said: (Mere) fables of the men of old

14. Nay, but that which they have earned is rust upon their hearts.

15. Nay, but surely on that day they will be veiled from their Lord.

16. Then lo! they surely will burn in Hell,

17. And it will be said (unto them): This is that which you used to deny.

18. Nay, but the record of the righteous is in ʿIllīyīn—

19. Ah, what will convey unto you what ʿIllīyīn is!—

20. A written record,

٢٠. كِتَٰبٌ مَّرْقُومٌ

21. Attested by those who are brought near (unto their Lord).

٢١. يَشْهَدُهُ ٱلْمُقَرَّبُونَ

22. Lo! the righteous surely are in delight,

٢٢. إِنَّ ٱلْأَبْرَارَ لَفِى نَعِيمٍ

23. On couches, gazing,

٢٣. عَلَى ٱلْأَرَآئِكِ يَنظُرُونَ

24. You will know in their faces the radiance of delight.

٢٤. تَعْرِفُ فِى وُجُوهِهِمْ نَضْرَةَ ٱلنَّعِيمِ

25. They are given to drink of a pure wine, sealed,

٢٥. يُسْقَوْنَ مِن رَّحِيقٍ مَّخْتُومٍ

26. Whose seal is musk—For this let (all) those strive who strive for bliss—

٢٦. خِتَٰمُهُ مِسْكٌ وَفِى ذَٰلِكَ فَلْيَتَنَافَسِ ٱلْمُتَنَٰفِسُونَ

27. And mixed with water of Tasnīm,

٢٧. وَمِزَاجُهُ مِن تَسْنِيمٍ

28. A spring whence those brought near to Allah drink.

٢٨. عَيْنًا يَشْرَبُ بِهَا ٱلْمُقَرَّبُونَ

29. Lo! the criminals used to laugh at those who believed,

٢٩. إِنَّ ٱلَّذِينَ أَجْرَمُوا۟ كَانُوا۟ مِنَ ٱلَّذِينَ ءَامَنُوا۟ يَضْحَكُونَ

30. And wink one to another when they passed them;

٣٠. وَإِذَا مَرُّوا۟ بِهِمْ يَتَغَامَزُونَ

31. And when they returned to their own folk, they returned jesting;

٣١. وَإِذَا ٱنقَلَبُوٓا۟ إِلَىٰٓ أَهْلِهِمُ ٱنقَلَبُوا۟ فَكِهِينَ

32. And when they saw them they said: Lo! these have gone astray.

٣٢. وَإِذَا رَأَوْهُمْ قَالُوٓا۟ إِنَّ هَٰٓؤُلَآءِ لَضَآلُّونَ

33. Yet they were not sent as guardians over them.

٣٣. وَمَآ أُرْسِلُوا۟ عَلَيْهِمْ حَٰفِظِينَ

34. This day it is those who believe who have the laugh of disbelievers,

٣٤. فَٱلْيَوْمَ ٱلَّذِينَ ءَامَنُوا۟ مِنَ ٱلْكُفَّارِ يَضْحَكُونَ

35. On high couches, gazing.

٣٥. عَلَى ٱلْأَرَآئِكِ يَنظُرُونَ

36. Are not the disbelievers paid for what they used to do?

٣٦. هَلْ ثُوِّبَ ٱلْكُفَّارُ مَا كَانُوا۟ يَفْعَلُونَ

The Sundering

Al Inshiqāq,"The Sundering,"takes its name from a word in the first verse. An early Makkan surah.

The Sundering

Revealed at Makkah

In the name of Allah,
the Beneficent, the Merciful

سورة الانشقاق

بسم الله الرحمن الرحيم

1. When the heaven is split asunder

2. And it surrenders to her Lord and it has indeed (to do so).

3. And when the earth is spread out

4. And has cast out all that was in her, and is empty

5. And it surrenders to her Lord and it has indeed (to do so).

6. O man! surely, you are ever toiling on toward your Lord, painfully until you meet Him.

7. Then who is given his account in his right hand

8. He truly will receive an easy reckoning

9. And will return unto his folk in joy.

10. But who is given his account behind his back,

11. He surely will invoke destruction

12. And be thrown to scorching fire.

13. He verily lived joyous with his folk,

14. He verily deemed that he would never return (unto Allah).

15. Nay, but lo! his Lord is ever watchful of him!

16. Oh, I swear by the afterglow of sunset,

17. And by the night and all that it enshrouds,

18. And by the moon when she is at the full,

19. That you shall journey on from stage to stage.

٢ لَتَرْكَبُنَّ طَبَقًا عَن طَبَقٍ ١٩

20. What ails them, then, that they believe not

فَمَا لَهُمْ لَا يُؤْمِنُونَ ٢٠

21. And, when the Qur'an is recited unto them, prostrate not?

وَإِذَا قُرِئَ عَلَيْهِمُ الْقُرْءَانُ لَا يَسْجُدُونَ ۩ ٢١

22. Nay, but those who disbelieve will deny;

بَلِ الَّذِينَ كَفَرُوا يُكَذِّبُونَ ٢٢

23. And Allah knows best what they are hiding.

وَاللَّهُ أَعْلَمُ بِمَا يُوعُونَ ٢٣

24. So give them tidings of a painful doom,

فَبَشِّرْهُم بِعَذَابٍ أَلِيمٍ ٢٤

25. Save those who believe and do good works, for theirs is a reward unfailing.

إِلَّا الَّذِينَ ءَامَنُوا وَعَمِلُوا الصَّالِحَاتِ لَهُمْ أَجْرٌ ٢٥

غَيْرُ مَمْنُونٍ

Mansions of the Stars

Al Burūj takes its name from a word in the first verse. I have translated it as "mansions of the stars," for the word has the meaning of towers or mansions and is applied to the constellations. Verses 4–7 are generally taken to refer to the massacre of the Christians of Najrān (in al Yaman) by the Jewish king Dhū Nuwās. This was an event of great historical importance, for it caused the Negus of Abyssinia to intervene and establish his supremacy over the area until the War of the Elephant (Surah 105), the year in which the Prophet was born. Professor Horowitz thinks that the words "owners of the ditch, of the fuel-fed fire" do not refer to an actual historical event but rather to the condition of all persecutors in the hereafter.[318]

An early Makkan surah.

---

[318]See "Islamic Culture" (Hyderabad Deccan), April 1929.

Mansions of the Stars

Revealed at Makkah

*In the name of Allah,
the Beneficent, the Merciful*

1. By the heaven, holding mansions of the stars,

2. And by the Promised Day.

3. And by the witness and that whereunto he bears testimony,

4. (Self) destroyed were the owners of the ditch

5. Of the fuel-fed fire,

6. When they sat by it,

7. And were themselves the witnesses of what they did to the believers.[319]

8. They had nothing against them save that they believed in Allah, the Mighty, the Owner of Praise,

9. Him unto Whom belongs the Sovereignty of the heavens and the earth; and Allah is of all things the Witness.

10. Lo! they who persecuted believing men and believing women and repented not, theirs surely will be the doom of Hell, and theirs is the doom of burning.

11. Lo! those who believe and do good works, theirs will be Gardens underneath which rivers flow. That is the Great Success.

12. Lo! the punishment of your Lord is stern.

13. Lo! He it is Who produces, then reproduces,

---

[320]Or it might be: "(Self-)destroyed were the owners of the trench of fuel-fed fire (i.e., Hell) when they took their ease on earth and were themselves witnesses," etc.

14. And He is the Forgiving, the Loving,

١٤ ۝ وَهُوَ ٱلْغَفُورُ ٱلْوَدُودُ

15. Lord of the Throne of Glory,

١٥ ۝ ذُو ٱلْعَرْشِ ٱلْمَجِيدُ

16. Doer of what He will.

١٦ ۝ فَعَّالٌ لِمَا يُرِيدُ

17. Has there come unto you the story of the hosts

١٧ ۝ هَلْ أَتَىٰكَ حَدِيثُ ٱلْجُنُودِ

18. Of Pharaoh and (the tribe of) Thamūd?

١٨ ۝ فِرْعَوْنَ وَثَمُودَ

19. Nay, but those who disbelieve live in denial

١٩ ۝ بَلِ ٱلَّذِينَ كَفَرُوٓا۟ فِى تَكْذِيبٍ

20. And Allah, all unseen, surrounds them.

٢٠ ۝ وَٱللَّهُ مِن وَرَآئِهِم مُّحِيطٌۢ

21. Nay, but it is a glorious Qur'an

٢١ ۝ بَلْ هُوَ قُرْءَانٌ مَّجِيدٌ

22. On a guarded tablet.

٢٢ ۝ فِى لَوْحٍ مَّحْفُوظٍۭ

The Morning Star

Al Ṭāriq takes its name from a word in the first verse. Although it can have other meanings, I have chosen the one that has probably occurred to everyone who hears this surah, especially as in the third verse, where it is stated that a star is meant. Here, the Morning Star has a mystic sense and is taken to refer to the Prophet. Some have thought that it refers to a comet that alarmed people in the East at about the time of the Prophet's call. Others believe that this and other introductory verses, which are hard to elucidate, hide scientific facts that were unimagined at the period of revelation and are related to the verses following them. Ghamrawi Bey, my collaborator in the revision of this work, informed me that the late Dr. Sidqi, among others, considered that the reference here is to the fertilizing sperm penetrating the ovary, as the subject is the same as that found in verses 5-7.

An early Makkan surah.

The Morning Star

Revealed at Makkah

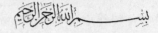

*In the name of Allah,
the Beneficent, the Merciful*

1. **B**y the heaven and the Morning Star[320]

2. —Ah, what will tell you what the Morning Star is!

3. —The piercing Star!

4. No human soul but has a guardian over it.

5. So let man consider from what he is created.

6. He is created from a gushing fluid

7. That issued from between the loins and the ribs.

8. Lo! He surely is Able to return him (unto life)

9. On the day when hidden thoughts shall be searched out.

10. Then will he have no might nor any helper.

11. By the heaven which gives the returning rain,

12. And the earth which splits (with the growth of trees and plants)

13. Lo! this (Qur'an) is a conclusive word,

14. It is no pleasantry.

15. Lo! they plot a plot (against you, O Muhammad)

16. And I plot a plot (against them).

17. So give a respite to disbelievers. Deal you gently with them for a while.

---

[320]The Arabic *al ṭāriq* word means originally "that which comes at night" or "one who knocks at the door."

The Most High

Al A'lā takes its name from a word in the first verse. An early Makkan surah.

The Most High

Revealed at Makkah

In the name of Allah,
the Beneficent, the Merciful

1. Praise the name of your Lord the Most High,

2. Who creates, then disposes;

3. Who measures, then guides;

4. Who brings forth the pasturage,

5. Then turns it to russet stubble.

6. We shall make you read (O Muhammad) so that you shall not forget

7. Save that which Allah wills. Lo! He knows the disclosed and that which still is hidden;

8. And We shall ease your way unto the state of ease.

9. Therefore remind (men), in case the reminder profits (the hearer).

10. He will heed who fears,

11. But the most unfortunate will flout it,

12. He who will be flung to the great fire

13. Wherein he will neither die nor live.

14. He is successful who grows,

15. And remembers the name of his Lord, so prays.

16. But you prefer the life of the world

17. Although the Hereafter is better and more lasting.

18. Lo! This is in the former scrolls,

19. The Books of Abraham and Moses.

The Overwhelming

Al Ghāshiyah takes its name from a word in the first verse. An early Makkan surah.

The Overwhelming

Revealed at Makkah

*In the name of Allah,
the Beneficent, the Merciful*

١ ﴾ هَلْ أَتَىٰكَ حَدِيثُ ٱلْغَاشِيَةِ

1. **H**as there come unto you tidings of the Overwhelming?

٢ ﴾ وُجُوهٌ يَوْمَئِذٍ خَاشِعَةٌ

2. On that day (many) faces will be downcast,

٣ ﴾ عَامِلَةٌ نَّاصِبَةٌ

3. Toiling, weary,

٤ ﴾ تَصْلَىٰ نَارًا حَامِيَةً

4. Scorched by burning fire,

٥ ﴾ تُسْقَىٰ مِنْ عَيْنٍ ءَانِيَةٍ

5. Drinking from a boiling spring,

٦ ﴾ لَّيْسَ لَهُمْ طَعَامٌ إِلَّا مِن ضَرِيعٍ

6. No food for them save bitter thorn fruit

٧ ﴾ لَّا يُسْمِنُ وَلَا يُغْنِي مِن جُوعٍ

7. Which does not nourish nor release from hunger.

٨ ﴾ وُجُوهٌ يَوْمَئِذٍ نَّاعِمَةٌ

8. In that day other faces will be calm,

٩ ﴾ لِّسَعْيِهَا رَاضِيَةٌ

9. Glad for their effort past,

١٠ ﴾ فِي جَنَّةٍ عَالِيَةٍ

10. In a high garden

١١ ﴾ لَّا تَسْمَعُ فِيهَا لَاغِيَةً

11. Where they hear no idle speech,

١٢ ﴾ فِيهَا عَيْنٌ جَارِيَةٌ

12. Wherein is a gushing spring,

١٣ ﴾ فِيهَا سُرُرٌ مَّرْفُوعَةٌ

13. Wherein are couches raised

١٤ ﴾ وَأَكْوَابٌ مَّوْضُوعَةٌ

14. And goblets set at hand

١٥ ﴾ وَنَمَارِقُ مَصْفُوفَةٌ

15. And cushions ranged

١٦ ﴾ وَزَرَابِيُّ مَبْثُوثَةٌ

16. And silken carts spread.

١٧ ﴾ أَفَلَا يَنظُرُونَ إِلَى ٱلْإِبِلِ كَيْفَ خُلِقَتْ

17. Will they not regard the camels, how they are created?

١٨ ﴾ وَإِلَى ٱلسَّمَاءِ كَيْفَ رُفِعَتْ

18. And the sky, how it is raised?

١٩ ﴾ وَإِلَى ٱلْجِبَالِ كَيْفَ نُصِبَتْ

19. And the mountains, how they are set up?

20. And the earth, how it is spread?

وَإِلَى ٱلْأَرْضِ كَيْفَ سُطِحَتْ ۝

21. Remind them, for you are but an admonisher,

فَذَكِّرْ إِنَّمَآ أَنتَ مُذَكِّرٌ ۝

22. You are not at all a warden over them.

لَّسْتَ عَلَيْهِم بِمُصَيْطِرٍ ۝

23. But who is averse and disbelieves,

إِلَّا مَن تَوَلَّىٰ وَكَفَرَ ۝

24. Allah will punish him with direst punishment.

فَيُعَذِّبُهُ ٱللَّهُ ٱلْعَذَابَ ٱلْأَكْبَرَ ۝

25. Lo! unto Us is their return

إِنَّ إِلَيْنَآ إِيَابَهُمْ ۝

26. And Ours is their reckoning.

ثُمَّ إِنَّ عَلَيْنَا حِسَابَهُم ۝

The Dawn

Al Fajr takes its name from the first verse. A very early Makkan surah.

The Dawn

Revealed at Makkah

In the name of Allah,
the Beneficent, the Merciful

1. By the Dawn

2. And ten nights,[321]

3. And the Even and the Odd,

4. And the night when it departs,

5. There surely is an oath for thinking man.

6. Do you not consider how your Lord dealt with (the tribe of) 'Ād,

7. With many-columned[322] Iram,

8. The like of which was not created in the lands;

9. And with (the tribe of) Thamūd, who clove the rocks in the valley;

10. And with Pharaoh, firm of right,

11. Who (all) were rebellious (to Allah) in the lands,

12. And multiplied iniquity therein?

13. Therefore your Lord poured on them the disaster of His punishment.

14. Lo! your Lord is ever watchful.

15. As for man, whenever his Lord tries him by honoring him, and is gracious unto him, he said: My Lord honors me.

16. But whenever He tries him by straitening his means of life, he said: My Lord despises me.

17. Nay, but you (for your part) honor not the orphan

---

[321]Of the month of pilgrimage.

[322]I had written "many-columned," following the custom of earlier commentators, who take the word *'imād* to mean columns or pillars, when I happened upon Ibn Khaldūn's diatribe against that rendering and all the legends to which it has given rise in the preface to the *Prolegomena*. Ibn Khaldūn points out that it meant "tent-poles" to the Arabs of the Prophet's day. In view of recent discoveries in the Yaman, however, I prefer the usual rendering.

18. And urge not on the feeding of the poor,

١٨ وَلَا تَحَاضُّونَ عَلَىٰ طَعَامِ الْمِسْكِينِ

19. And you devour heritages with devouring greed

١٩ وَتَأْكُلُونَ التُّرَاثَ أَكْلًا لَّمًّا

20. And love wealth with abounding love.

٢٠ وَتُحِبُّونَ الْمَالَ حُبًّا جَمًّا

21. Nay, but when the earth is ground to atoms, grinding, grinding,

٢١ كَلَّا إِذَا دُكَّتِ الْأَرْضُ دَكًّا دَكًّا

22. And your Lord shall come with angels, rank on rank,

٢٢ وَجَاءَ رَبُّكَ وَالْمَلَكُ صَفًّا صَفًّا

23. And Hell is brought near that day; on that day man will remember, but how will the remembrance (then avail him)?

٢٣ وَجِيءَ يَوْمَئِذٍ بِجَهَنَّمَ يَوْمَئِذٍ يَتَذَكَّرُ الْإِنسَانُ وَأَنَّىٰ لَهُ الذِّكْرَىٰ

24. He will say: Ah, would that I had sent before me (some provision) for my life!

٢٤ يَقُولُ يَا لَيْتَنِي قَدَّمْتُ لِحَيَاتِي

25. None punishes as He will punish on that day!

٢٥ فَيَوْمَئِذٍ لَّا يُعَذِّبُ عَذَابَهُ أَحَدٌ

26. None binds as He then will bind.

٢٦ وَلَا يُوثِقُ وَثَاقَهُ أَحَدٌ

27. But ah! you soul at peace!

٢٧ يَا أَيَّتُهَا النَّفْسُ الْمُطْمَئِنَّةُ

28. Return unto your Lord, content in His good pleasure!

٢٨ ارْجِعِي إِلَىٰ رَبِّكِ رَاضِيَةً مَّرْضِيَّةً

29. Enter you among My bondmen!

٢٩ فَادْخُلِي فِي عِبَادِي

30. Enter you My Garden!

٣٠ وَادْخُلِي جَنَّتِي

The City

Al Balad takes its a name from a word in the first verse. A very early Makkah surah.

The City

Revealed at Makkah

*In the name of Allah,
the Beneficent, the Merciful*

1. Nay, I swear by this city—

2. And you are an indweller of this city—[323]

3. And the begetter and that which he begat,

4. We surely have created man in toil and struggle[324]:

5. Thinks he that none has power over him?

6. And he said: I have destroyed vast wealth;

7. Thinks he that none beholds him?

8. Did We not assign unto him two eyes

9. And a tongue and two lips,

10. And guide him to the two highways?

11. But he has not attempted the Obstacle—

12. Ah, what will convey unto you what the Obstacle is!—

13. (It is) to free a slave,

14. And to feed in the day of hunger

15. An orphan near of kin,

16. Or some poor wretch in misery,

17. And to be of those who believe and exhort one another to perseverance and exhort one another to pity.

18. Their place will be on the right hand.

19. But those who disbelieve Our revelations, their place will be on the left hand.

20. On them will be Fire vaulted over (all around).

---

[323]Or "when you have control over this city" (prophetically).
[324]Or "in affliction."

The Sun

Al Shams takes its name from a word in the first verse. A very early Makkan surah.

The Sun

Revealed at Makkah

In the name of Allah,
the Beneficent, the Merciful

بِسْمِ اللهِ الرَّحْمٰنِ الرَّحِيْمِ

1. By the sun and his brightness,

١ وَالشَّمْسِ وَضُحٰهَا

2. And the moon when she follows him,

٢ وَالْقَمَرِ إِذَا تَلٰهَا

3. And the day when it reveals him,

٣ وَالنَّهَارِ إِذَا جَلّٰهَا

4. And the night when it enshrouds him,

٤ وَالَّيْلِ إِذَا يَغْشٰهَا

5. And the heaven and Him who built it,

٥ وَالسَّمَاءِ وَمَا بَنٰهَا

6. And the earth and Him who spread it,

٦ وَالْأَرْضِ وَمَا طَحٰهَا

7. And a soul and Him who perfected it

٧ وَنَفْسٍ وَمَا سَوّٰهَا

8. And inspired it (with conscience of) what is wrong for it and (what is) right for it.

٨ فَأَلْهَمَهَا فُجُورَهَا وَتَقْوٰهَا

9. He is indeed successful who causes it to grow,

٩ قَدْ أَفْلَحَ مَنْ زَكّٰهَا

10. And he is indeed a failure who stunts it.

١٠ وَقَدْ خَابَ مَنْ دَسّٰهَا

11. (The tribe of) Thamūd denied (the truth) in their rebellious pride.

١١ كَذَّبَتْ ثَمُودُ بِطَغْوٰهَا

12. When the basest of them broke forth

١٢ إِذِ انْبَعَثَ أَشْقٰهَا

13. And the messenger of Allah said: It is the she camel of Allah, so let her drink!

١٣ فَقَالَ لَهُمْ رَسُولُ اللهِ نَاقَةَ اللهِ وَسُقْيٰهَا

14. But they denied him, and they hamstrung her, so their Lord doomed them for their sin and razed (their dwellings).

١٤ فَكَذَّبُوهُ فَعَقَرُوهَا فَدَمْدَمَ عَلَيْهِمْ رَبُّهُمْ بِذَنْبِهِمْ فَسَوّٰهَا

15. He dreads not the sequel (of events).

١٥ وَلَا يَخَافُ عُقْبٰهَا

Night

Al Layl takes its name from a word in the first verse. A very early Makkan surah.

Night

Revealed at Makkah

In the name of Allah,
the Beneficent, the Merciful

سُورَةُ الليْلُ

بِسْمِ اللهِ الرَّحْمٰنِ الرَّحِيمِ

1. By the night enshrouding

2. And the day resplendent

3. And Him Who has created male and female,

4. Lo! your effort is dispersed (toward divers ends).

5. As for him who gives and is dutiful (toward Allah)

6. And believes in goodness;

7. Surely We will ease his way unto the state of ease.

8. But as for him who hoards and deems himself independent,

9. And disbelieves in goodness;

10. Surely We will ease his way unto adversity.

11. His riches will not save him when he perishes.

12. Lo! Ours it is (to give) the guidance

13. And lo! unto Us belong the latter portion and the former.

14. Therefore have I warned you of the flaming Fire

15. Which only the most wretched must endure,

16. He who denies and turns away.

17. Far removed from it will be the righteous

18. Who gives his wealth that he may grow (in goodness),

19. And none has with him any favor for reward,

20. Except as seeking (to fulfill) the purpose of his Lord Most High.

21. He surely will be content.

① وَالَّيْلِ إِذَا يَغْشَى

② وَالنَّهَارِ إِذَا تَجَلَّى

③ وَمَا خَلَقَ الذَّكَرَ وَالْأُنْثَى

④ إِنَّ سَعْيَكُمْ لَشَتَّى

⑤ فَأَمَّا مَنْ أَعْطَى وَاتَّقَى

⑥ وَصَدَّقَ بِالْحُسْنَى

⑦ فَسَنُيَسِّرُهُ لِلْيُسْرَى

⑧ وَأَمَّا مَنْ بَخِلَ وَاسْتَغْنَى

⑨ وَكَذَّبَ بِالْحُسْنَى

⑩ فَسَنُيَسِّرُهُ لِلْعُسْرَى

⑪ وَمَا يُغْنِي عَنْهُ مَالُهُ إِذَا تَرَدَّى

⑫ إِنَّ عَلَيْنَا لَلْهُدَى

⑬ وَإِنَّ لَنَا لَلْآخِرَةَ وَالْأُولَى

⑭ فَأَنْذَرْتُكُمْ نَارًا تَلَظَّى

⑮ لَا يَصْلَاهَا إِلَّا الْأَشْقَى

⑯ الَّذِي كَذَّبَ وَتَوَلَّى

⑰ وَسَيُجَنَّبُهَا الْأَتْقَى

⑱ الَّذِي يُؤْتِي مَالَهُ يَتَزَكَّى

⑲ وَمَا لِأَحَدٍ عِنْدَهُ مِنْ نِعْمَةٍ تُجْزَى

⑳ إِلَّا ابْتِغَاءَ وَجْهِ رَبِّهِ الْأَعْلَى

㉑ وَلَسَوْفَ يَرْضَى

The Morning Hours

Al Ḍuḥā, "The Morning Hours," takes its name from the first verse. There was an interval during which the Prophet received no revelation and the idolaters mocked him, saying: "Allah, of whom we used to hear so much, has forsaken poor Muhammad and now hates him." He then received this revelation. The Prophet, who had been a leading Makkan citizen until he received his call, was now regarded as a madman. He was almost fifty years old, and the prophecy here that "the latter portion would be better for him than the former" must have seemed absurd to those who heard it. Yet the latter portion (the last ten years) of the Prophet's life represents the most wonderful record of success in human history.

An early Makkan surah.

Solace

Al Inshirāḥ, "Solace," takes its name from a word in the first verse and, probably, from its subject: relief from anxiety. It was probably revealed on the same occasion as Surah 93, a time when the Prophet was being derided and shunned after having been respected and courted. Such a reversal of fortunes must have struck the disbelievers as ridiculous. It refers to the inward assurance that the Prophet had received by revelation and speaks of future events as accomplished. This latter style is usual in the Qur'an, for the revelation coming from a plane where time as understood by mankind does not exist. The fourth verse, which speaks of his fame as exalted, must have seemed particularly absurd during a time of humiliation and persecution. But today, from every mosque in the world, the Prophet is proclaimed five times a day as the Messenger of God, and every Muslim prays for blessings on him when his name is mentioned.

An early Makkan surah.

The Morning Hours

Revealed at Makkah
In the name of Allah, the Beneficent,
the Merciful

1. **B**y the morning hours

2. And by the night when it is stillest,

3. Your Lord has not forsaken you nor does He hate you (O Muhammad),

4. And surely the latter portion will be better for you than the former

5. And surely your Lord will give unto you so that you will be content.

6. Did He not find you an orphan and protect (you)?

7. Did He not find you wandering and direct (you)?

8. Did He not find you destitute and enrich (you)?

9. Therefore the orphan oppress not,

10. Therefore the beggar drive not away,

11. Therefore of the bounty of your Lord be your discourse.

Solace

Revealed at Makkah
In the name of Allah,
the Beneficent, the Merciful

1. **H**ave We not caused your bosom to dilate,

2. And eased you of your burden

3. Which weighed down your back;

4. And exalted your fame?

5. But lo! with hardship goes ease,

6. Lo! with hardship goes ease;

7. So when you are relieved, still toil

8. And strive to please your Lord.

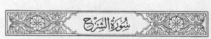

The Fig

Al Tīn, "The Fig," takes its name from a word in the first verse. The sense is symbolic: "fig" refers to the Book of Abraham, "olive" refers to Jerusalem (the Book of Jesus), "Mount Ṭūr" of Sinai refers to Moses' book, and "this land" is Makkah (the birthplace of Islam). A very early Makkan surah (the editor).

The Fig

Revealed at Makkah

In the name of Allah,
the Beneficent, the Merciful

بِسْمِ اللهِ الرَّحْمٰنِ الرَّحِيمِ

1. By the fig and the olive,

ٱ وَالتِّينِ وَالزَّيْتُونِ

2. By Mount Sinai,

٢ وَطُورِ سِينِينَ

3. And by this land made safe;

٣ وَهَٰذَا الْبَلَدِ الْأَمِينِ

4. Surely We created man of the best stature

٤ لَقَدْ خَلَقْنَا الْإِنسَٰنَ فِىٓ أَحْسَنِ تَقْوِيمٍ

5. Then We reduced him to the lowest of the low,

٥ ثُمَّ رَدَدْنَٰهُ أَسْفَلَ سَٰفِلِينَ

6. Save those who believe and do good works, and theirs is a reward unfailing.

٦ إِلَّا الَّذِينَ ءَامَنُوا وَعَمِلُوا الصَّٰلِحَٰتِ فَلَهُمْ أَجْرٌ غَيْرُ مَمْنُونٍ

7. So who henceforth will give the lie to you about the judgment?

٧ فَمَا يُكَذِّبُكَ بَعْدُ بِالدِّينِ

8. Is not Allah the most conclusive of all judges?

٨ أَلَيْسَ اللهُ بِأَحْكَمِ الْحَٰكِمِينَ

The Clot

Al 'Alaq takes its name from a word in the second verse. Verses 1-5 are the words that the Prophet received in the first experience of Divine Revelation at Hirā' and make up the first portion of the Qur'an to be revealed. A very early Makkan surah.

The Clot

Revealed at Makkah

*In the name of Allah,
the Beneficent, the Merciful*

1. **R**ead: In the name of your Lord who creates,

2. Creates man from a clot.

3. Read: And your Lord is the Most Bounteous,

4. Who teaches by the pen,

5. Teaches man that which he knew not.

6. Nay, but surely man is rebellious

7. That he thinks himself independent!

8. Lo! unto your Lord is the return.

9. Have you seen him who dissuades

10. A slave when he prays?

11. Have you seen if he (relies) on the guidance (of Allah)

12. Or enjoins piety?

13. Have you seen if he denies (Allah's guidance) and turns away?

14. Is he then unaware that Allah sees?

15. Nay, but if he cease not. We will seize him by the forelock—

16. The lying, sinful forelock—

17. Then let him call upon his henchmen!

18. We will call the guards of Hell.

19. Nay! Obey not you him. But prostrate yourself, and draw near (unto Allah).

Power

Al Qadr takes its name from a word in the first verse. It refers to the night (one of the last nights of Ramaḍān) on which the Prophet received his call and the first verses of the Qur'an were revealed in the vision of Mt. Hirā'. It is said to be the night on which God's decrees for the year are brought down to the earthly plane.

A very early Makkan surah.

The Clear Proof

Al Bayyinah takes its name from a word in the first verse. There is no certainty as to the period of revelation. Many regard it as a late Makkan surah. I follow the attribution in the *muṣḥaf* which I have followed throughout. The probable date of revelation is the year 1 AH.

Power
Revealed at Makkah
In the name of Allah,
the Beneficent, the Merciful

1. Lo! We revealed it on the Night of Power.

2. Ah, what will convey unto you what the Night of Power is!

3. The Night of Power is better than a thousand months.

4. The angels and the Spirit[325] descend therein, by the permission of their Lord, with all decrees.

5. (That night is) Peace until the rising of the dawn.

The Clear Proof
Revealed at Al Madinah

In the name of Allah,
the Beneficent, the Merciful

1. Those who disbelieve among the People of the Scrip-ture and the idolaters could not have left off (erring) till the clear proof came unto them,

2. A messenger from Allah, reading purified pages

3. Containing correct scriptures.

4. Nor were the People of the Scripture divided until after the clear proof came unto them.

5. And they are ordered nothing else than to worship Allah, keeping religion pure for Him, as men by nature upright, and to establish prayer and to pay the poor due. That is true religion.

6. Lo! those who disbelieve, among the People of the Scripture and the idolaters, will abide in fire of Hell. They are the worst of created beings.

7. (And) lo! those who believe and do good works are the best of created beings.

8. Their reward is with their Lord: Gardens of Eden underneath which rivers flow, wherein they dwell for ever. Allah has pleasure in them and they have pleasure in Him. This is (in store) for him who fears his Lord.

سُوْرَةُ الْقَدْرِ

بِسْمِ اللهِ الرَّحْمٰنِ الرَّحِيْمِ

١ اِنَّاۤ اَنْزَلْنٰهُ فِيْ لَيْلَةِ الْقَدْرِ

٢ وَمَاۤ اَدْرٰىكَ مَا لَيْلَةُ الْقَدْرِ

٣ لَيْلَةُ الْقَدْرِ خَيْرٌ مِّنْ اَلْفِ شَهْرٍ

٤ تَنَزَّلُ الْمَلٰٓئِكَةُ وَالرُّوْحُ فِيْهَا بِاِذْنِ رَبِّهِمْ مِّنْ كُلِّ اَمْرٍ

٥ سَلٰمٌ هِيَ حَتّٰى مَطْلَعِ الْفَجْرِ

سُوْرَةُ الْبَيِّنَةِ

بِسْمِ اللهِ الرَّحْمٰنِ الرَّحِيْمِ

١ لَمْ يَكُنِ الَّذِيْنَ كَفَرُوْا مِنْ اَهْلِ الْكِتٰبِ وَالْمُشْرِكِيْنَ مُنْفَكِّيْنَ حَتّٰى تَأْتِيَهُمُ الْبَيِّنَةُ

٢ رَسُوْلٌ مِّنَ اللهِ يَتْلُوْا صُحُفًا مُّطَهَّرَةً

٣ فِيْهَا كُتُبٌ قَيِّمَةٌ

٤ وَمَا تَفَرَّقَ الَّذِيْنَ اُوْتُوا الْكِتٰبَ اِلَّا مِنْۢ بَعْدِ مَا جَآءَتْهُمُ الْبَيِّنَةُ

٥ وَمَاۤ اُمِرُوْۤا اِلَّا لِيَعْبُدُوا اللهَ مُخْلِصِيْنَ لَهُ الدِّيْنَ حُنَفَآءَ وَيُقِيْمُوا الصَّلٰوةَ وَيُؤْتُوا الزَّكٰوةَ وَذٰلِكَ دِيْنُ الْقَيِّمَةِ

٦ اِنَّ الَّذِيْنَ كَفَرُوْا مِنْ اَهْلِ الْكِتٰبِ وَالْمُشْرِكِيْنَ فِيْ نَارِ جَهَنَّمَ خٰلِدِيْنَ فِيْهَا اُولٰٓئِكَ هُمْ شَرُّ الْبَرِيَّةِ

٧ اِنَّ الَّذِيْنَ اٰمَنُوْا وَعَمِلُوا الصّٰلِحٰتِ اُولٰٓئِكَ هُمْ خَيْرُ الْبَرِيَّةِ

٨ جَزَآؤُهُمْ عِنْدَ رَبِّهِمْ جَنّٰتُ عَدْنٍ تَجْرِيْ مِنْ تَحْتِهَا الْاَنْهٰرُ خٰلِدِيْنَ فِيْهَاۤ اَبَدًا رَضِيَ اللهُ عَنْهُمْ وَرَضُوْا عَنْهُ ذٰلِكَ لِمَنْ خَشِيَ رَبَّهُ

---

[325]i.e., Gabriel or, as some commentators think, a general term for angels of the highest rank.

The Earthquake

Al Zilzāl takes its name from a word in the first verse. A very early Makkan surah.

The Coursers

Al 'Ādiyāt takes its name from a word in the first verse. A very early Makkan surah.

The Earthquake

Revealed at Makkah

In the name of Allah,
the Beneficent, the Merciful

1. When Earth is shaken with her (final) earthquake

2. And Earth yields up her burdens,

3. And man said: What ails her?

4. That day she will relate her chronicles,

5. Because your Lord inspires her.

6. That day mankind will issue forth in scattered groups to be shown their deeds.

7. And who does good an atom's weight will see it then,

8. And who does ill an atom's weight will see it then.

The Coursers

Revealed at Makkah

In the name of Allah,
the Beneficent, the Merciful

1. By the snorting coursers,

2. Striking sparks of fire

3. And scouring to the raid at dawn,

4. Then, therewith, with their trail of dust,

5. Cleaving, as one, the center (of the foe),326

6. Lo! man is an ingrate unto his Lord

7. And lo! he is a witness unto that;

8. And lo! in the love of wealth he is violent.

9. Knows he not that, when the contents of the graves are poured forth

10. And the secrets of the breasts are made known.

11. On that day will their Lord be perfectly informed concerning them.

326The first five verses are eye-openers to one of the blessings of Allah, namely, horses that He made useful for us in wars; and yet man is ungrateful.

The Calamity

Al Qāri'ah takes its name from a word in the first verse that appears also in the next two verses.

Rivalry in Worldly Increase

Al Takāthur takes its name from a word in the first verse. A very early Makkan surah.

The Calamity

Revealed at Makkah

In the name of Allah,
the Beneficent, the Merciful

1. The Calamity!
2. What is the Calamity?
3. Ah, what will convey unto you what the Calamity is!
4. A day wherein mankind will be as thickly scattered moths
5. And the mountains will become as carded wool.
6. Then, as for him whose scales are heavy (with good works),
7. He will live a pleasant life.
8. But as for him whose scales are light,
9. The Bereft and Hungry One will be his mother (Hell).
10. Ah, what will convey unto you what she is!—
11. Raging fire.

Rivalry in Worldly Increase

Revealed at Makkah

In the name of Allah,
the Beneficent, the Merciful

1. Rivalry in worldly increase distracts you
2. Until you visit the graves.
3. Nay, but you will come to know!
4. Nay, but you will come to know!
5. Nay, would that you knew (now) with a sure knowledge!
6. For you will behold hellfire.
7. Then, you will behold it with sure vision.
8. Then, on that day, you will be asked concerning pleasure.

سُوۡرَةُ الۡقَارِعَةِ

بِسۡمِ اللهِ الرَّحۡمٰنِ الرَّحِيۡمِ

١ ٱلۡقَارِعَةُ

٢ مَا ٱلۡقَارِعَةُ

٣ وَمَآ أَدۡرَىٰكَ مَا ٱلۡقَارِعَةُ

٤ يَوۡمَ يَكُوۡنُ ٱلنَّاسُ كَٱلۡفَرَاشِ ٱلۡمَبۡثُوۡثِ

٥ وَتَكُوۡنُ ٱلۡجِبَالُ كَٱلۡعِهۡنِ ٱلۡمَنۡفُوۡشِ

٦ فَأَمَّا مَنۡ ثَقُلَتۡ مَوَازِيۡنُهُ

٧ فَهُوَ فِىۡ عِيۡشَةٍ رَّاضِيَةٍ

٨ وَأَمَّا مَنۡ خَفَّتۡ مَوَازِيۡنُهُ

٩ فَأُمُّهُ هَاوِيَةٌ

١٠ وَمَآ أَدۡرَىٰكَ مَا هِيَهۡ

١١ نَارٌ حَامِيَةٌ

سُوۡرَةُ التَّكَاثُرِ

بِسۡمِ اللهِ الرَّحۡمٰنِ الرَّحِيۡمِ

١ أَلۡهَىٰكُمُ ٱلتَّكَاثُرُ

٢ حَتّىٰ زُرۡتُمُ ٱلۡمَقَابِرَ

٣ كَلَّا سَوۡفَ تَعۡلَمُوۡنَ

٤ ثُمَّ كَلَّا سَوۡفَ تَعۡلَمُوۡنَ

٥ كَلَّا لَوۡ تَعۡلَمُوۡنَ عِلۡمَ ٱلۡيَقِيۡنِ

٦ لَتَرَوُنَّ ٱلۡجَحِيۡمَ

٧ ثُمَّ لَتَرَوُنَّهَا عَيۡنَ ٱلۡيَقِيۡنِ

٨ ثُمَّ لَتُسۡـَٔلُنَّ يَوۡمَئِذٍ عَنِ ٱلنَّعِيۡمِ

The Declining Day

Al 'Aṣr takes its name from a word in the first verse. A very early Makkan surah.

The Traducers

Al Humazah takes its name from a word in the first verse. The idolaters warned all newcomers to Makkah not to listen to the Prophet. An early Makkan surah.

The Declining Day

Revealed at Makkah

*In the name of Allah,
the Beneficent, the Merciful*

1. By the token of time (through the ages)

2. Lo! man is in a state of loss,

3. Save those who believe and do good works, and exhort one another to truth and exhort one another to endurance.

The Traducers

Revealed at Makkah

*In the name of Allah,
the Beneficent, the Merciful*

1. Woe unto every slandering traducer,

2. Who has gathered wealth (of this world) and arranged it.

3. Does he think that his wealth will render him immortal?

4. By no means, but surely he will be flung into the Con-suming One.

5. Ah, what will convey unto you what the Consuming One is?

6. (It is) the fire of Allah, kindled,

7. Which leaps up over the hearts (of men).

8. Lo! it is closed in on them

9. In outstretched columns.

The Elephant

Al Fīl, "The Elephant," takes its name from a word in the first verse. The allusion is to the campaign of Abrahā, the Abyssinian ruler of al Yaman, which he launched against Makkah in order to destroy the Kaʿbah (this was also the year of the Prophet's birth). Abrahā had an elephant that impressed the Arabs greatly. Tradition says that the elephant refused to advance on the last stage of the march and that swarms of flying creatures pelted the Abyssinians with stones. Another tradition says that they retired in disorder due to an outbreak of smallpox in the camp. At the time of this surah's revelation, many men in Makkah must have known what had happened. Dr. Krenkow, a sound Arabic scholar, is of opinion that the flying creatures may well have been swarms of insects carrying infection. In any case, the Kaʿbah was not destroyed and the campaign failed.

A very early Makkan surah.

Quraysh or Winter

Quraysh takes its name from a word in the first verse. It is also called *al Shitā'* (winter). A very early Makkan surah.

Small Kindnesses

Al Māʿūn takes its name from a word in the last verse. An early Makkan revelation.

The Elephant

Revealed at Makkah

In the name of Allah,
the Beneficent, the Merciful

1. **H**ave you not seen how your Lord dealt with the owners of the Elephant?
2. Did He not bring their stratagem to nothing,
3. And send against them swarms of flying creatures,
4. Which pelted them with stones of baked clay
5. And made them like green crops devoured (by cattle)?

Quraysh or Winter

Revealed at Makkah

In the name of Allah,
the Beneficent, the Merciful

1. **F**or the taming[327] of Quraysh
2. For their taming (We cause) the caravans to set forth in winter and summer.
3. So let them worship the Lord of this House,
4. Who has fed them against hunger and has made them safe from fear.

Small Kindnesses

Revealed at Makkah

In the name of Allah,
the Beneficent, the Merciful

1. **H**ave you observed him who belies religion?
2. That is he who repels the orphan,
3. And urges not the feeding of the needy.
4. Ah, woe unto worshippers
5. Who are heedless of their prayer;
6. Who would be seen (at worship)
7. Yet refuse small kindnesses!

---

[327]i.e., "civilizing."

Abundance

Al Kawthar takes its name from a word in the first verse. The disbelievers used to taunt the Prophet because his sons died young and, therefore, he had no one to uphold his religion after him.

Disbelievers

Al Kāfirūn takes its name from a word in the first verse. It was revealed at a time when the idolaters had asked the Prophet to compromise in matters of religion.

Succor

Al Naṣr takes its name from a word in the first verse. It is one of the very last revelations, having been revealed to the Prophet only a few weeks before his death. Though ascribed to the Madinan period, tradition says that it was actually revealed at Makkah during the days the Prophet spent there during his farewell pilgrimage. It is described in Ibn Hishām and elsewhere as the first announcement that the Prophet received of his approaching death.

The date of revelation is 10 AH.

Abundance
Revealed at Makkah
In the name of Allah,
the Beneficent, the Merciful

1. Lo! We have given you Abundance;

2. So pray unto your Lord, and sacrifice.

3. Lo! It is your insulter (and not you) who is without posterity.

Disbelievers
Revealed at Makkah
In the name of Allah,
the Beneficent, the Merciful

1. Say: O disbelievers!

2. I worship not that which you worship;

3. Nor worship you that which I worship.

4. And I shall not worship that which you worship.

5. Nor will you worship that which I worship.

6. Unto you your religion, and unto me my religion.

Succor
Revealed at al Madinah
In the name of Allah,
the Beneficent, the Merciful

1. When Allah's succor and the triumph comes

2. And you see mankind entering the religion of Allah in troops.

3. Then hymn the praises of your Lord, and seek forgiveness of Him. Lo! He is oft-returning (in Grace and Mercy).

Palm Fibre

Al Masad takes its name from a very homely Arab word that appears in the last verse. It is the only passage in the Qur'an that denounces an opponent of the Prophet by name. Abū Lahab (The Father of Flame), whose real name was 'Abd al 'Uzzā, was an uncle of the Prophet and the only member of his clan who bitterly opposed the Prophet. He tormented the Prophet, and his wife took pleasure in carrying thorn bushes and strewing them in the sand where she knew that the Prophet would walk barefooted. An early Makkan revelation.

Unity

Al Tawḥīd, "Unity," takes its name from its subject and has been called the essence of the Qur'an. Some authorities place it in the Madinah period and believe that it was revealed to answer a question asked by some Jewish rabbis on the nature of God. It is generally held to be an early Makkan surah.

Daybreak

Al Falaq, "Daybreak," takes its name from a word in the first verse and, along with the following surah, are prayers for protection from evil things. This one is for protection from the fear(s) of the unknown. Both surahs are known as al Mu'awwadhatayn—the two cries for refuge and protection.

An early Makkan surah.

Palm Fibre
Revealed at Makkah
In the name of Allah,
the Beneficent, the Merciful

1. The hands of Abū Lahab will perish, and he will perish.

2. His wealth and gains will not exempt him.

3. He will be plunged in flaming fire,

4. And his wife, the wood carrier,

5. Will have upon her neck a halter of palm fibre.

Unity
Revealed at Makkah
In the name of Allah,
the Beneficent, the Merciful

1. Say: He is Allah, the One!

2. Allah, the eternally Besought of all!

3. He begets not nor was begotten.

4. And there is none comparable unto Him.

Daybreak
Revealed at Makkah
In the name of Allah,
the Beneficent, the Merciful

1. Say: I seek refuge in the Lord of Daybreak

2. From the evil of that which He created;

3. From the evil of the darkness when it is intense,

4. And from the evil of malignant witchcraft,[328]

5. And from the evil of the envier when he envies.

سُورَةُ المَسَدِ

بِسْمِ اللهِ الرَّحْمَنِ الرَّحِيمِ

﴿١﴾ تَبَّتْ يَدَآ أَبِي لَهَبٍ وَتَبَّ

﴿٢﴾ مَآ أَغْنَىٰ عَنْهُ مَالُهُۥ وَمَا كَسَبَ

﴿٣﴾ سَيَصْلَىٰ نَارًا ذَاتَ لَهَبٍ

﴿٤﴾ وَامْرَأَتُهُۥ حَمَّالَةَ الْحَطَبِ

﴿٥﴾ فِي جِيدِهَا حَبْلٌ مِّن مَّسَدٍ

سُورَةُ الإِخْلَاصِ

بِسْمِ اللهِ الرَّحْمَنِ الرَّحِيمِ

﴿١﴾ قُلْ هُوَ اللهُ أَحَدٌ

﴿٢﴾ اللهُ الصَّمَدُ

﴿٣﴾ لَمْ يَلِدْ وَلَمْ يُولَدْ

﴿٤﴾ وَلَمْ يَكُن لَّهُۥ كُفُوًا أَحَدٌ

سُورَةُ الفَلَقِ

بِسْمِ اللهِ الرَّحْمَنِ الرَّحِيمِ

﴿١﴾ قُلْ أَعُوذُ بِرَبِّ الْفَلَقِ

﴿٢﴾ مِن شَرِّ مَا خَلَقَ

﴿٣﴾ وَمِن شَرِّ غَاسِقٍ إِذَا وَقَبَ

﴿٤﴾ وَمِن شَرِّ النَّفَّاثَاتِ فِي الْعُقَدِ

﴿٥﴾ وَمِن شَرِّ حَاسِدٍ إِذَا حَسَدَ

Mankind

Al Nās, the second of the two cries for refuge and protection, takes its name from a recurring word that marks the rhythm in Arabic. In this case, protection is sought especially from the evil in one's own heart and in the hearts of other men.

An early Makkan revelation.

Mankind

Revealed at Makkah

*In the name of Allah,
the Beneficent, the Merciful*

1. **S**ay: I seek refuge in the Lord of mankind,

2. The King of mankind,

3. The God of mankind,

4. From the evil of the sneaking whisperer,

5. Who whispers in the hearts of mankind,

6. Of the jinn and of mankind.

سورة الناس

بِسْمِ اللهِ الرَّحْمٰنِ الرَّحِيمِ

﴿١﴾ قُلْ أَعُوذُ بِرَبِّ النَّاسِ

﴿٢﴾ مَلِكِ النَّاسِ

﴿٣﴾ إِلٰهِ النَّاسِ

﴿٤﴾ مِن شَرِّ الْوَسْوَاسِ الْخَنَّاسِ

﴿٥﴾ الَّذِى يُوَسْوِسُ فِى صُدُورِ النَّاسِ

﴿٦﴾ مِنَ الْجِنَّةِ وَالنَّاسِ

Prayer

[To be recited after reading the Holy Qur'an]

O Allah! have mercy upon me through the Qur'an and make it my leader, a light, guidance and mercy.

O Allah! make me remember of it what I have forgotten, teach me of it what I know not, grant me reciting it by night and day and let it become my defence O Lord of the worlds.

O Allah! grant us good in this life and in the life hereafter and protect us from the torments of Hell Fire.

And peace be upon our Prophet Muhammed, his family and his noble companions.

دُعَاءُ خَتْمِ الْقُرْآنِ الْكَرِيمِ

اللَّهُمَّ ارْحَمْنِى بِالْقُرْآنِ وَاجْعَلْهُ لِى إِمَامًا

وَنُورًا وَهُدًى وَرَحْمَةً اللَّهُمَّ ذَكِّرْنِى مِنْهُ

مَا نَسِيتُ وَعَلِّمْنِى مِنْهُ مَا جَهِلْتُ وَارْزُقْنِى تِلَاوَتَهُ

آنَاءَ اللَّيْلِ وَأَطْرَافَ النَّهَارِ وَاجْعَلْهُ لِى حُجَّةً يَا رَبَّ الْعَالَمِينَ

رَبَّنَا آتِنَا فِى الدُّنْيَا حَسَنَةً وَفِى الْآخِرَةِ حَسَنَةً

وَقِنَا عَذَابَ النَّارِ وَصَلَّى اللهُ عَلَى نَبِيِّنَا مُحَمَّدٍ

وَعَلَى آلِهِ وَأَصْحَابِهِ الْأَخْيَارِ وَسَلَّمَ تَسْلِيمًا كَثِيرًا

- A -

'Ād (the tribe of), 7:651 ff.; 9:70; 11:50 ff.; 14:9; 22:42; 25:38; 26:123 ff.; 29:38. 41:13 ff.; 46:21 ff.; 41:41 f.; 54:18 ff.; 69:4 ff.; 89:6

Aaron, 2:248; 4:163; 6:85; 7:122; 10:76; 19:53, 20:90 ff.; 21:48; 23:45; 25:35 ff.; 26:13; 28:34 f.; 37:114 ff.

Abraham, 2:124 ff., 258, 260; 3:33, 55, 67 f., 84, 95, 97; 4:54, 125, 163; 21:51 ff.; 22:26, 43; 26:69 ff.; 29:16, 31; 37:83 ff.; 38:46 ff.; 42:13; 43:26 ff.; 51:24 ff.; 60:4 f.

   his conversion, 6: 75 ff., 162

   his prayer, 2:126 ff.; 9:114; 14:35 ff.; 11:69 ff.; 12:6, 38

   his guests, 15:51 ff.; 16:120 ff.

   his father, 19:41 ff.

   the Book of, 87:19

Abū Lahab, 111:1 ff.

Adam, 2:31 ff.; 3:33, 59; 7:11, 19 ff.; 20:115 ff.

Adoration, 41:37

Adultery, see Legislation.

Aḥmad, 41:6

Allah, 2:225 ff., 284 ff.; 3:26 ff., 26 f.; 5:17, 72 f.; 6:96 ff.; 24:35 ff.; 59:22 ff.; 64:1 ff.

Al Lāt, see Lāt (al).

Angels, 2:30 ff., 177, 210, 248, 285, 3:80.

   foretell birth of Jesus, 3:42, 125 f.; 4:97, 166; 7:11. 8:9, 12, 50; 13:11, 13, 23; 15:7 f., 17 f., 28 f.; 16:2, 32 f.; 17:61; 18:51; 20:116; 22:75; 34:40 f.; 35:1; 38:72 ff.; 39:75; 40:7; 41:30 f., 43:19; 66:6; 69:17; 70:4; 74:31; 69:38; 89:22; 97:4

   foretell birth of John, 3:39 ff.

Anṣār, 9:100, 117

Ant, 4:40; 27:18

Apostles (the Twelve), see Disciples.

Arabic, 12:2; 13.37; 16:103; 26:195; 39:28; 41:3; 42:7; 43:3; 46:12

Arabs (the Nomad), 9:90, 97 ff., 120; 33:20; 48:11, 16; 49:14

'Arafat, 2:198

Ark (the) 2:248; 7:64; 11:37 ff.; 23:27; 29:15; 54:9 ff.

Al Rass, see Rass (al).

Al Ṣafā, see Ṣafā (al).

Āzar, 6:74

- B -

Baal, 37:125

Babel, 2:102

Backbiting, 49:12

Badr, 3:13, 123, 140, 165; 8:5 ff., 42 ff.

Baḥīrah, 5:103

Bakkah, 3:96

Bee, 16:68

Birds, 16:79; 27:17; 67:19

Blood-money, see Legislation.

Book (the):

 of God's Decrees, 6:38; 7:37; 17:58; 57:22

 of Abraham, 53:36 f.

 of Moses, 6:92; 11:17; 53:36. 87:19

 Recording, 18:50; 36:11; 39:69; 45:29; 50:4; 78:29

- C -

Cain and Abel, 5:27 ff.

Calf (the Golden), 2:51 ff., 92; 4:153; 7:148 ff.; 20:88

 the roasted, 11.69; 51:26 f.

Camel, 7:73; 22:27

 the She-camel, 17:59; 26:155 ff.; 54:27 ff.; 91:13 f.

Cattle, 5:103; 6:137; 16:5

Cave (the People of the), 18:9 ff.

Children (killing of), 6:138, see also Legislation.

Children (the, of Adam), 7:26 ff., 172; 17:70

Children (the, of Israel):

 Admonitions to, 2:40 ff., 122

 Covenant with, 2:63, 83 ff.; 246; 3:93

 the Promised Land, 5:20 ff.

- D -

- E -

- F -

- N -

33:7; 37:75 ff.; 42:13

 the Deluge, 54:9 ff.; 71:1-28

 the wife of, 66:10

- O -

Oaths, see Legislation.

Offering, 5:2

Orphans, see Legislation.

- P -

Paradise, 2:25, 111; 7:40 ff.; 13:23; 15:45 ff.; 18:32, 108; 19:61 ff.; 22:23 f.; 25:15 f.; 36:54 ff.; 37:42 ff.; 38:5l ff.; 43:70 ff.; 44:51 ff.; 47:15; 52:17 ff.; 55:46 ff.; 56:12 ff.; 76:12 ff.

People of the Scriptures, see Scripture.

Pharaoh, 2:49 f.; 7:103-140; 10:76-93; 17:101 ff.; 20:43-79; 26:16-66; 28:3 ff., 38 ff.; 40:23-46; 43:46 ff.; 44:17-33; 51:38 ff.; 79:17 ff.

 his wife, 28:9; 66:11

Pilgrimage, see Legislation.

Plagues of Egypt, see Pharaoh.

Poor-due, see Zakah.

Prayer:

 Abraham's, 2:126 ff.; 9:84, 113; 26:83 ff.

 Joseph's, 12:101

 of disbelievers 13:14

 Zachariah's, 19:3 f.

 Solomon's, 27:19

 the call to, 62:9

 Noah's, 71:26 ff.

Priests, 5:44, 63, 82

Prophets, 2:61, 91, 136, 177, 213; 3:21, 80 ff.

 inspiration of, 4:163; 6:86 ff.

 an adversary to each, 6:113

 God's covenant with, 33:7